Strategies & Tactics® for the MBE

Sixth Edition

The late

Kimm Walton, J.D.

and

Steve Emanuel, J.D.

This revision prepared by

Steve Emanuel

Published by Wolters Kluwer in New York.

Wolters Kluwer Legal & Regulatory US serves customers worldwide with CCH, Aspen Publishers, and Kluwer Law International products. (www.WKLegaledu.com)

To contact Customer Service, e-mail customer.service@wolterskluwer.com, call 1-800-234-1660, fax 1-800-901-9075, or mail correspondence to:

Wolters Kluwer
Attn: Order Department
PO Box 990
Frederick, MD 21705

Printed in the United States of America.

4 5 6 7 8 9 0

ISBN 978-1-4548-7312-9

This book is intended as a general review of a legal subject. It is not intended as a source for advice for the solution of legal matters or problems. For advice on legal matters, the reader should consult an attorney.

About Wolters Kluwer Legal & Regulatory US

Wolters Kluwer Legal & Regulatory US delivers expert content and solutions in the areas of law, corporate compliance, health compliance, reimbursement, and legal education. Its practical solutions help customers successfully navigate the demands of a changing environment to drive their daily activities, enhance decision quality and inspire confident outcomes.

Serving customers worldwide, its legal and regulatory portfolio includes products under the Aspen Publishers, CCH Incorporated, Kluwer Law International, ftwilliam.com and MediRegs names. They are regarded as exceptional and trusted resources for general legal and practice-specific knowledge, compliance and risk management, dynamic workflow solutions, and expert commentary.

TABLE OF CONTENTS

PREFACE

Thanks for buying this book. I hope and believe that if you use it conscientiously, it will help you a lot on the MBE portion of your state's bar exam. In fact, there is some evidence that it helps students meaningfully improve their performance on bar-exam *essay questions* in the seven MBE subjects as well.

Newly-added to this edition are questions on Civil Procedure, a subject that became part of the MBE in February 2015. Unlike all the other questions in this book, the Civil Procedure questions here (both in the Civil Procedure section and in the Practice Exam) are not actual past MBE questions released by the examiners, but rather questions drafted by my editorial team and me that we hope will prove comparable to the ones you will encounter on the exam.

The first few editions of this book, dating to the 1990s, were written solely by the late Kimm Walton, J.D. Kimm and I then collaborated on several later editions in the early 2000s. Kimm was also the sole original author of the *Law in a Flash* series of legal flashcards published by Wolters Kluwer Law & Business. Kimm, who died tragically in 2013 at age 53, was a wonderful (and funny) legal writer whom my colleagues and I greatly miss.

For this 2016 edition, I did the substantial majority of the editorial revision work myself and take full responsibility for all errors. I would, however, like to express my thanks to several people who worked with me on this edition:

Helen Hershkoff, Herbert M. and Svetlana Wachtell Professor of Law, New York University Law School

Don Bushell, J.D., member of the California bar

Dana Wilson, J.D., editor

Good luck on the MBE and on the rest of the bar exam. If you'd like any other publication from Wolters Kluwer, you can find it at your bookstore or at www.WKlegaledu.com. If you'd like to contact me, you can email me at semanuel@westnet.com.

Steve Emanuel

Larchmont, NY

April 2016

ABOUT THE MBE

If you're like most students, there's quite a bit about the Multistate Bar Exam (MBE) that you don't know. Here are the answers to some of the questions we hear most frequently.

Is the MBE required in every state?

Almost. As of July 2016, only one state—Louisiana — ***doesn't*** administer the MBE. The District of Columbia, the Virgin Islands, Guam, the Northern Mariana Islands, and Palau also require the MBE.

When is the MBE given?

In most states, the MBE is given twice each year—on the last Wednesday in February and on the last Wednesday in July—but a few states offer the MBE only once a year. Most states also administer their own, state-specific exams on the day(s) immediately before or after the MBE; these state-specific exams usually consist of essays covering a variety of subjects. In addition, other multistate exams, such as the Multistate Essay Examination (MEE) and the Multistate Performance Test (MPT), take place on the day(s) immediately before or after the MBE.

What's the format of the MBE?

The Multistate Bar Examination is a six-hour examination consisting of 200 questions. The exam is divided into two parts: Part I is administered in the morning and Part II is administered in the afternoon. Each part takes three hours and contains 100 questions. ***Of the 200 questions, only 190 are scored, with the other 10 being evaluated for future use. You can't tell which 10 won't be scored, so you have to try hard on all 200.***

What subjects are covered on the Multistate Bar Exam?

Currently, there are seven subjects on the MBE: Civil Procedure, Constitutional Law, Contracts, Criminal Law, Evidence, Real Property, and Torts.

How many questions are there on each subject?

As of July 2016, the 190 questions that are scored are distributed as follows:

28 questions on Contracts and 27 questions each on Civil Procedure, Constitutional Law, Criminal Law (and Procedure), Evidence, Real Property, and Torts. In other words, ***all seven subjects on the MBE are given substantially equal weight, with a slight (one-question) overweighting to Contracts.***

What's the format of MBE questions?

The MBE is an "objective" exam; that is, it's ***multiple-choice from a given set of facts.*** Each question has four possible answer options, with one correct answer and three incorrect choices.

What order are the questions in?

Questions on the MBE are presented in a completely ***random*** manner. Both the level of difficulty and the subject matter may vary from one question to the next. This means that your first MBE question may be very difficult, but the following question may be relatively easy. Since MBE test questions are set up in a random order of difficulty, the MBE is different from many other standardized tests you've taken (such as the SAT), where the questions become progressively more difficult within each section of the test.

MBE questions are also random in subject matter, so a Property question may be followed by a Torts question, which may be followed by a Contracts question. Note also that you won't be told the subject matter of any question; you have to figure out what area is being tested by carefully reading the question itself.

Are all the questions on the MBE given the same weight?

Yes; difficult questions are worth no more than easy ones.

How is the MBE graded?

Each "scored" question is worth one point, making a total possible "raw" score of 190. Because the difficulty of the MBE may vary from one exam to another (for example, the July 2016 MBE may be somewhat more difficult than the February 2011 MBE), "raw" scores are not comparable from year to year. To handle this problem, the Bar Examiners use a statistical procedure, called "equating," to produce what are called "scaled" scores—raw scores that have been adjusted so that the performance of Bar Examinees can be compared from exam to exam (within the limitations of measurement and equating error). This scaling procedure helps to ensure that no applicant is unfairly penalized or rewarded for taking a particular version of the exam. I say more about the scaling process beginning on p. xi.

Keep in mind that no credit is given for any answer except the best one. Also, if you fill in more than one answer to a question, you'll get no credit for the question (even if one of your answers is the correct one).

Will I lose points for wrong answers?

No. The MBE isn't like the SAT or "Jeopardy"—you aren't penalized for wrong answers. (And you don't have to state your answer in the form of a question.) In other words, even if you don't have any idea what the right answer is to a particular question, it's best to guess! You've got nothing to lose, and, if you follow the advice in this book, you've got everything to gain.

Are the official answers to the MBE ever wrong?

Yes, but only very occasionally. Notice that we said that you are asked 200 questions, but only 190 are scored, with the rest being evaluated for future use. This "evaluation" process, coupled with the stringent pre- and post-exam review process used by the examiners, means that it's quite rare that the examiners conclude that a question has multiple correct answers or is otherwise flawed. In those rare cases, usually two rejected choices are clearly wrong, and the problem is that even high-scoring candidates have had trouble selecting accurately between the two remaining answer choices. In such cases, credit is given only to applicants who marked either of the two remaining answers.

What score do I need to pass?

The best source of information about what MBE score you need to be at a "passing level" for any given state is a publication issued by the NCBE, called "Comprehensive Guide to Bar Admission Requirements." The 2016 version of this Guide was, at the time we went to press, available by going to www.ncbex.org and selecting "Bar Admission Guide" and then "View Complete Guide." The information about what MBE score will put you on a passing track for your state is given in Chart 9 of the Guide, "Grading and Scoring."[1]

The score needed to pass the MBE varies according to ***where you're taking the exam,*** because the Bar Examiners of each jurisdiction use the MBE in different ways. In some states, if you score high enough on the

---

1. Much of the "score that's needed to be on track to pass" information from Chart 9 is reproduced in Table 1 beginning on p. xii below.

MBE, the Bar Examiners won't even look at your essays, since they assume that, if you did very well on the MBE, you're likely to score well on the essays, too, so there's really no need to grade your essays.

Most states, however, establish a specific score needed to "pass" their individual bar exams by combining MBE and essay scores. States use one of three formulas to combine the two scores: the standard deviation method, the comparative range method, and the equi-percentile method. All three methods are quite complex, and explaining them is beyond the scope of this book. What you need to know is that, even if the MBE isn't the sole determining factor in your passing the bar exam, it contributes significantly to the result—in most states, the MBE accounts for between 40% and 50% of your total score. (For July, 2016, California set a 35% MBE weighting and Ohio a 33% weighting, to pick a couple of populous states whose weighting was outside the usual 40%-50% range.)

So, what percentage of the questions do you have to answer correctly to be on track to pass your state's bar exam? That's a surprisingly difficult question to answer, for two main reasons:

1. As noted, each state gets to set its own passing score; and
2. The MBE varies in difficulty from one administration to another. Therefore, getting, say, 65% of the questions right on one test might put you on track to just barely pass in your state, while the same 65% might fall short of the on-track-to-pass threshold in that same state on a different administration of the test.

But we can make some *estimates* of the percentage-of-correct-answers you'll need to pass. First, we need to define two terms: "raw" score and "scaled" score:

Your raw score: Your ***"raw"*** score is ***the number of questions you answer correctly on the test.*** On your official score report, your "raw score" will be shown as the number you got correct out of the ***190 questions that counted (not*** the ones correct out of the 200 total that you saw and tried to answer, which includes the 10 non-counting questions). But for purposes of using this book (including the Practice Exam), I'll talk about your ***"S&T Raw Score,"*** which will be the number correct you get out of ***all 200 questions*** that appear (e.g., the full 200 on the Practice Exam at the back of this book)—that will help you then derive a computation of ***what percentage*** of questions you have to get right.

Your scaled score: Your ***"scaled"*** score is a number (between 1 and 200) that the NCBE computes separately for each administration of the exam, based on your raw score. The purpose of this scaling process is to ensure that differences in difficulty between one particular MBE and another don't affect your chances of passing. Here's how the MBE describes the scaling process (which they call the "equating" process in the explanation below):

> The statistical process of equating adjusts for variations in the difficulty of the questions, producing scaled scores that represent the same level of performance across all MBE administrations. For instance, if the questions appearing on the July MBE were more difficult than those appearing on the February MBE, then the scaled scores for the July MBE would be adjusted upward to account for this difference. These adjustments ensure that no examinee is unfairly penalized or rewarded for taking a more or less difficult exam.

Now that we've gotten our nomenclature defined—raw vs. scaled scores—let's look at what it typically takes to be "on track to pass." Notice that I don't refer to a "passing score," but instead talk about being "on track to pass." That's because, if you'll recall, each state gets to combine your scores on the MBE and non-MBE portions in whatever weights it wishes, and also gets to set its overall passing threshold however it wishes—so the concept of a single "passing score" on the MBE is meaningless. But, what I *can* talk meaningfully about is the minimum score needed to be "on track to pass"—that's the MBE score that, if you demonstrated the same proficiency (i.e., the same "percentile rank" relative to all fellow test-takers in your state on that administration) on the MBE as on the non-MBE part, would be just enough to let you pass the exam.

Scaled MBE Score Needed to Be On Track to Pass

So, then, let's first talk about what ***scaled*** MBE score you would typically need to be on track to pass (after which we'll talk about what raw score would typically correspond to that scaled score). The following table shows you, in the right-hand column, the lowest MBE Scaled Score that would put you on track to just barely pass, assuming your scores put you in the same "percentile rank" in your state's test-takers on the non-MBE parts as on the MBE itself.

Table 1

Lowest Scaled MBE Score Needed to Be on Track to Pass, By State

State	% Weight Given to MBE	Minimum Scaled MBE Score to Be on Track to Pass
Alabama	50	130
Alaska	50	140
Arizona	50	136.5
Arkansas	50	135
California	35	144
Colorado	50	138
Connecticut	50	132
Delaware	40	145
District of Columbia	50	133
Florida	50	136
Georgia	50	135
Hawaii	50	134
Idaho	50	140
Illinois	50	133
Indiana	50	132
Iowa	50	133
Kansas	50	133
Kentucky	—*	132
Louisiana	—	—
Maine	36	138
Maryland	33	135.3
Massachusetts	50	135
Michigan	50	135
Minnesota	50	130
Mississippi	40	132
Missouri	50	130
Montana	50	135
Nebraska	50	135
Nevada	33	140
New Hampshire	50	135
New Jersey	50	133
New Mexico	30	130
New York	50	133
North Carolina	40	138.4
North Dakota	50	130
Ohio	33	135
Oklahoma	50	132
Oregon	50	142

State	% Weight Given to MBE	Minimum Scaled MBE Score to Be on Track to Pass
Pennsylvania	45	136
Rhode Island	50	138
South Carolina	—**	125
South Dakota	—***	135
Tennessee	50	135
Texas	40	135
Utah	50	135
Vermont	50****	135
Virginia	40	140
Washington	50	135
West Virginia	50	135
Wisconsin	50	129
Wyoming	50	135

Source: Comprehensive Guide to Bar Admission Requirements 2016, Chart 9, by the National Conference of Bar Examiners, downloaded from www.ncbex.org on 4/7/16.

Notes:
* Kentucky: MBE and non-MBE are separate components, each with a minimum passing score; must have at least 132 on the MBE.
** South Carolina: To be "on track," you need 132 on the MBE (but a higher/lower written component can counterbalance a higher/lower MBE). However, a score of 110 or less on MBE "results in automatic failure."
*** South Dakota: MBE and non-MBE are separate components, each with a minimum passing score; you must have at least 135 on the MBE.
**** Vermont: Beginning with the July 2016 exam, uses Uniform Bar Exam as part (not whole) of exam; when that happens, an MBE score of 135 will be the minimum to be on track to pass.

As you can see from Table 1, the scaled MBE score to be barely on track to pass varies considerably across states. Putting aside the three states with separate per-component minimums, the minimum on track scaled score ranges from a low of 129 in Wisconsin (with the next lowest, 130, in effect in Alabama, Minnesota, Missouri, New Mexico, and North Dakota) to a high of 145 in Delaware (with the next highest, 144, in California).

For the five states with the largest number of bar-takers (accounting for about 51% of bar-takers nationally), here are the minimum on-track-to-pass MBE scores:

California: 144
Florida: 136
New Jersey: 133
New York: 133
Texas: 135

So if you've heard that "the California bar is the toughest," that's an almost-true statement; only Delaware, with a one-point higher threshold, is tougher. On the other hand, New York's reputation for being "almost as tough as California" is clearly NOT justified.

Well, then, what does it *mean*, in intuitive terms, to obtain a scaled MBE score of, say, 135 (which seems to be about the median minimum score on track to pass across all states)? One way to answer that question is to ask, *where would that score put you in a "national" competition against all recent law school graduates?*

Table 2 below shows, for all applicants nationally (both foreign- and US-trained, and both from ABA and non-ABA schools) who took the July 2015 bar, the distribution of scaled scores:

Table 2

July 2015 National Score Distribution, All Examinees

MBE Scaled Score	% of Examinees in this 5-pt range*	% of Examinees at this score or lower
85	0.0	0.0
90	0.1	0.1
95	0.3	0.4
100	0.6	1.0
105	1.4	2.4
110	1.7	4.1
115	3.0	7.1
120	5.5	12.6
125	7.0	19.6
130	9.1	28.7
135	10.9	39.6
140	10.3	49.9
145	12.5	62.4
150	10.4	72.8
155	9.6	82.4
160	7.7	90.1
165	5.4	95.5
170	3.2	98.7
175	1.2	99.9
180	0.5	100.4

Summary Statistics for July 2015:

Median Scaled Score	140.6
Standard Deviation	16.1

The data represent scaled scores in increments of 5. For example, the percentage reported in the "% of Examinees" column for a scaled score of 135 includes all examinees whose MBE scaled scores were between 130.5 and 135.4, and says that this group represented 10.9% of all July 2015 examinees nationwide. The right-hand column for that same scaled score of 135 says that examinees at the highest score in that group (135.4) had a score higher than or equal to 39.6% of all July 2015 examinees. The right-hand column value for a score of 180 is slightly higher than 100% because of rounding error.

Source: *The Bar Examiner*, March 2016, p. 40.

So if you had taken the California bar in July 2015 and you wanted to know what a 144 scaled MBE score (the minimum score to be on track to pass in California) would represent in terms of the distribution of all bar applicants nationally who took that same exam, Table 2 would let you get a close, though not exact, answer. There's no entry for "144," but there is one for "145." If you read the footnote to Table 2, you'll see that the highest score reported in the "145" entry was actually a score of 145.4. And the right-hand column for the 145 entry shows you that at that highest-in-the-category score of 145.4, you would have been ahead of or even with 62.4 percent of all takers nationally. If you "interpolate" to estimate the value for a score of 144, you'd need to have been at about the *60th percentile* nationally (since each full MBE scaled point seems to represent about 2% of the national test-taking population, according to Table 2).

But now, suppose you had taken the *New York* bar, on that same July 2015 session. Here, Table 1 tells you you'd need to get a scaled MBE of *just 133* to be on track to pass in New York. Again, you'd have to interpolate the values in Table 2 to see where this score would put you in the national population on that session: 133 would be about halfway between 130 (28.7% of national takers at or below this score) and 135 (39.6% takers at or below). Halfway between 28.7% and 39.6% is 34.1%. So you would have been on track (just barely) to pass New York in July 2015 by getting a score that would have put you above or even with just *34.1%* of all takers nationally on that session.

Notice what a very large portion of the national bar-taker population would have passed New York, but failed California, in July 2015: Rounding to the nearest percentile point, *everyone between the 35th percentile and the 59th percentile—almost one-quarter of the whole population—would have simultaneously passed New York and failed California!* So where you want to practice makes a large practical difference in how high you have to place in this hypothetical national competition.

By the way, law students seem to know—whether consciously or not—how much the minimum-score-to-pass varies from state to state. For instance, students in California seem to know that they have to score much higher than students in states of more average difficulty level, and they come into the exam hall better-prepared, on average, to meet this higher standard. You can see this by comparing the bar-passage statistics released by California to the nationwide set released by the NCBE. (I don't reproduce these statistics here, but I've obtained them and have reviewed them carefully.)

Raw MBE Score Needed to Pass

Now, then, you're probably wondering what kind of **raw** score you need in order to achieve the scaled score(s) we talked about previously for various jurisdictions. In other words, *what is the arithmetic transformation by which the examiners convert a raw score to a scaled score?*

If you've been following our technical discussion of how scaled scores "equate" exam administrations of differing difficulty (see p. xi), you'll know that there is no single answer—any given raw score will convert to a higher scaled score on an unusually difficult administration than on an unusually easy one.

Also, remember (see p. xi) that what the NCBE and state-bar officials report as your raw score is out of 190 questions, not 200. But to make this book easier to use, and to give you an idea of what sort of "batting average" you need on the MBE questions, we're going to use what I'll call an "S&T Raw Score"—this is the number of questions you get right ***out of 200,*** not 190. (So when you take the Practice Exam at the back of this book, your S&T Raw Score will be the number you get correct out of the full 200 questions in the Practice Exam.)

Unfortunately, neither the NCBE nor the individual state boards of bar examiners supply very much information to give us even an approximate sense of how many extra points would typically be added to one's raw score to produce the scaled score. But we do have one significant piece of historical information on this front: The California examiners released a chart for the February 2011 exam, showing the raw-to-scaled conversion for that particular administration.[2] The number of points that the examiners added varied that year (as it apparently always does) depending where on the "curve" of raw scores a score was. Far more points get added to a raw score of, say, 100 (which converted in Feb. 2011 to a scaled score of 121, an addition of 21 points) than get added to a raw score of, say, 160 (which converted for that same session to a scaled score of 171, an addition of just 11 points).

Therefore, rather than reproduce the whole conversion chart for California in February 2011, I'll just give you the conversions for scaled scores in the "meaty" part of the curve, the part running from about the 40th

---

2. This is the most recent raw-to-scaled chart I have been able to find for any state, let alone for the entire country, for any administration of the MBE. Note that the conversion from raw to scaled is done at a national level, by the NCBE, so on any given administration, a given raw score will be converted to the same scaled score no matter where you take the bar exam.

percentile in the national pool to the 60th percentile; that's the part of the curve that will cover the minimum on-track-to-pass scaled score for all but the easiest states. Here is that part of the conversion chart (rounded to the nearest point):

Table 3
Raw-to-Scaled Conversion, February 2011

Raw Score	Scaled Score
117	135
120	137
122	139
125	141
127	143
129	145
132	147
134	149
136	151

Source: California Bar Examiners

But remember, Table 3, which contains actual historical data, converts the raw score out of 190, not 200. What we want is to know how to convert a raw score on a *200-question* exam (with no non-counting questions), like the Practice Exam at the back of this book, to a scaled score. And that means we'll have to take the above 190-question-based raw scores and multiply them by 200/190, or 1.053 times, to determine how many points to add to a 200-question-based raw score to get a scaled score. And, remember, even that computation will be accurate only if we assume that the 200-question practice exam is of the same level of difficulty as the February 2011 exam—that may or may not be a good assumption, but since February 2011 is the only reasonably-recent session for which we have any raw-to-scaled conversion data, it's the best we can do.

So here, then, is how you should convert your practice scores on a 200-question exam (in which all questions count) like the Practice Exam at the back of this book into a projected scaled score, assuming that the exam you're scoring is the same difficulty as the Feb. 2011 MBE:

Table 4
200-Question Practice Exam,
Estimated Raw-to-Scaled Conversion

(1) Raw Score out of 200 Questions	(2) Scaled Score	(3)# of Points to Add to Raw to Get Scaled (Col 2 minus Col 1)	(4)% of Raw Answers Correct to Achieve This Scaled Score
123	135	12	62%
126	137	11	63%
128	139	11	64%
132	141	9	66%
134	143	9	67%
136	145	9	68%
139	147	8	69%
141	149	8	71%
143	151	8	72%

So in a state of average difficulty (one with a minimum on-track-to-pass scaled MBE score of 135), you'd need to get a raw score of 123 out of 200 questions, or a "batting average" of about *62% correct*. And for the two most difficult states (Delaware @ 145 scaled and California @ 144 scaled), you'd need raw scores of 136 (68% correct) for Delaware and 135 (67.5%) for California.

In sum, even in the second-most difficult state in the U.S., California, if you can get a hair more than ***two-thirds of the MBE questions correct, you will be on track to pass.*** Not a trivial task, to be sure, but eminently achievable if you prepare conscientiously. So as you practice, keep in mind that you'll pass nearly everywhere if you can get about two-thirds of the MBE questions correct, assuming you perform at the same relative level of competence (compared to others in your state) as between the MBE and non-MBE portions of your exam.

Who writes MBE questions?

As you may imagine, drafting MBE questions is an involved process that includes many people. Here's how the NCBE described the process in their most recent discussion of the topic, in 2012:

> MBE questions are developed by drafting committees composed of recognized experts in the various subject areas. Before a test question is selected for inclusion in the MBE, it undergoes a multistage review process over the course of several years. Besides intensive review by the drafting committee members and testing specialists, each test question is reviewed by other national and state experts. All test questions must successfully pass all reviews before they are included in the MBE. After an MBE is administered, the performance of each test question is reviewed and evaluated by content and testing experts. This final review is conducted to ensure that the exam is graded fairly, particularly with regard to any questions affected by recent changes in the law.

Source: ncbex.org/multistate-tests/mbe/development-of-the-mbe

HOW TO USE THIS BOOK

If you use this book correctly, it can have a dramatic impact on your MBE performance. In this introductory section, we'll discuss how you can get the most out of this book.

First, it's important to know what this book can do for you, and what it can't. Correctly preparing for the MBE involves developing two skills: a ***complete grasp of the substantive law***, and the ***ability to analyze MBE questions***. This book deals with the second skill: analysis. Substantive review, on the other hand, is the task of learning all the law you need to know in order to pass the MBE. You may think, "But I'm going to do every single question in this book! Shouldn't I know the law by then?"

Unfortunately, the answer is no. Many students every year try to learn the law simply by doing thousands of simulated MBE questions. This is not good enough. Studying by answering MBE questions, even actual ones from past exams, such as the ones in this book, can't substitute for a good review of substantive law; it can only ***supplement*** it. While answering MBE questions will help reinforce many of the principles you need to know, it will provide only a random review and the **techniques** for exam-taking; it's not guaranteed to teach you all the law you need to know. Studying just by answering questions would be like attempting to write a short story by writing random sentences that sound good, all the while hoping that, when you're done, you'll have put together enough sentences to make a whole story. This is a less-than-effective way to review ***every*** aspect of the law.

The most effective way to review all the substantive law you need for the MBE is to review substantive material, to the level of detail you need, in an organized fashion. We have two suggestions. First, the *Law in a Flash Multistate Bar Review Set* is an easy and effective way to review all the substantive detail you need to know for the MBE. Second, we've found that the Capsule Summary portions of the *Emanuel Law Outlines* or *CrunchTime* series of outlines in the eight MBE subjects (counting Criminal Procedure as a separate subject rather than as part of Criminal Law), even though these summaries don't explicitly focus on the MBE syllabus, can be quite useful in reviewing the substantive rules tested on the MBE. All of the study aids mentioned in this paragraph are likely to be available at your local law school bookstore or can be ordered from us directly at www.WKlegaledu.com.

HOW THIS BOOK IS ORGANIZED

Here are the major features in this book:

- First, we give you ***details about the MBE*** and advice on ***how you should attack it***.
- Next, we give you "***Strategies and Tactics***" for each of the six subjects on the MBE.
- These are followed immediately by **questions** on that particular MBE subject, so that you can practice the strategies. Except for Civil Procedure, these are ***actual past MBE questions***, which we are reprinting under special license from the MBE examiners. (Many are from exams given as recently as 2010.)
- We then give you an ***Answer Key*** (at the beginning of the answers for that subject) so you can quickly score yourself.
- Then, perhaps most important, we give you full ***explanatory answers*** for each question in that subject, with detailed explanations both of why the "correct" answer is the best one and why the other answer choices are not as good.

- As a last-minute addition before we went to press, we added **100 questions** (with the NCBE's own short-form "annotation"-style answers) that the examiners released as "OPE-4" in 2013.[3]
- Next, we give you a full-length, ***Practice MBE (again entirely from past actual MBE questions[4])***, with an Answer Key and full explanatory answers.
- Lastly, we give you ***answer sheets***, so you can practice doing questions under simulated exam conditions.

ATTACKING THE MBE

The first thing to read is our description of the MBE and our advice on attacking it. Those sections will give you pointers on studying and analyzing questions—in fact, on learning to think like the Bar Examiners.

STRATEGIES AND TACTICS FOR EVERY MAJOR SUBJECT: TIMING YOURSELF

After reading "How to Attack the MBE," you should choose the subject you want to review first and read the "Strategies and Tactics" section for that subject; then, complete the practice questions in that subject. While the MBE is a timed test, try to avoid timing yourself when you first begin to practice. When you actually sit for the MBE, you'll have about 1.8 minutes to answer each question (assuming you don't fall behind). Right now, though, you aren't sitting for the MBE; you're learning how to take it. The important things to learn are, first, the black-letter law, followed by the nuances of the language the Bar Examiners use, the nature of the details they test, and, in effect, how to think the way they do. Learning these things necessarily requires more than a minute or so per question. Take your time on each question, and you'll benefit in the long run. As you become more proficient at answering MBE questions and learn more black-letter law through your substantive review, your speed will naturally increase.

USING ANSWER SHEETS

When you answer the questions on each subject or take the practice exam, use the scoring sheets provided in the back of the book. If you need more sheets, make copies of the ones provided. These scoring sheets are replicas of those you will use on the actual MBE. As you answer each question, make a note on a separate sheet of paper about those answers that were only your best guesses and not based on a sure knowledge of the law; you should then check those answers more carefully against the full answers given in this book.

SCORING YOUR PERFORMANCE

At the beginning of each Answer section, we give you an Answer Key to let you quickly score yourself.

When you compute your raw score for a given subject (the number of correct responses), keep in mind that the subjects vary somewhat in the mean scores produced by applicants. The NCBE has not published mean-score information on a per-subject basis since the July 2004 exam. However, Illinois has published such information about its own applicants on the February 2013 exam, the most recent per-subject information I have been able to find for any state. Table 5 shows this information, which will give you some idea of the relative difficulty of the six subjects that were covered on that exam.[5]

---

3. The NCBE has released the OPE-4 set to end-users only in the form of an online interactive test module, for separate purchase.

4. The 28 Civil Procedure questions on the Practice Exam are not past actual MBE questions; they were written by us to simulate the topics covered in the actual MBE questions, based on the NCBE's syllabus and on the limited anecdotal reports of topic coverage we received from students who took the MBE beginning in February 2015, when Civil Procedure first appeared on the exam.

5. Civil Procedure is not included in these figures because it did not become part of the MBE until February 2015.

Table 5

Subject Difficulty on the February 2013 MBE, Based on Illinois' Published Results

Raw Scores	Con. Law	Contracts	Crim. Law	Evidence	Real Prop.	Torts
Median # correctly answered	18.5	20.5	20.6	18.9	19.45	22.05
# of Q's	31	33	31	31	31	33
Correct answers as % of total	59.7%	62.1%	66.5%	61.3%	62.7%	66.7%
Rank order of difficulty	1 (hardest)	3	5	2	4	6 (easiest)

So in Illinois for February 2013, Con Law was the hardest subject (applicants got, on average, only 59.7% of the questions correct), and Evidence was the second hardest (61.3%). Torts was the easiest (applicants got an average of 66.7% correct), and Criminal Law was the next easiest (66.5%). The other two subjects (Contracts and Real Property) were in the middle, clustered between 62.1% and 62.7%.

If we assume that the February 2013 exam was average in terms of the relative difficulty of the subjects, and that Illinois' applicants were representative of the whole country in terms of which subjects they found easiest/hardest (both reasonable though not empirically validated assumptions), here are a couple of conclusions that it seems sensible to draw:

1. The Criminal Law and Torts questions are on average the easiest, which means that you'd better "make hay while the sun shines" on these—these are probably the two subjects whose questions have the shortest average question-length, which is likely part of why they're easier. So if time runs short (or you think it may run short later on), your "yield per minute spent" is likely to be higher when spent on Crim Law and Torts questions than on the other subjects.
2. Conversely, since Con Law and Evidence are the two hardest, it may not be so profitable to spend quite as much time on these, on average—maybe taking an "either you know it or you don't" approach to these two subjects is a good strategy. In Evidence, particularly, the relevant principles (embodied in the Federal Rules of Evidence) are pretty hard to "guess" if you don't know them, so this isn't a good area in which to agonize in the hopes that you can "derive" or "intuit" the answer.
3. As of this writing (April 2016), no information has been officially published about the median student performance on the Civil Procedure questions, a subject first introduced in 2015. But anecdotal reports indicate that the Civ Pro questions are quite technical, are highly dependent on precise FRCP provisions, and are difficult to answer based on general principles. So I would expect them to be on average more difficult than the median MBE question, and probably not so worthy spending a lot of exam time on if you feel you can't narrow the answer down to, say, two choices.

When you score yourself using the Answer Key, compute the percentage you got correct, and compare: (1) how your own performance varies from subject to subject, to let you know where you need to spend the most time; and (2) how your performance in a subject compares with the above Illinois per-subject averages, again to get a clue about where you're relatively most deficient.

READ THE EXPLANATORY ANSWERS!

For every question you try, please ***read the explanatory answer***; if you do, you'll find that the answers in this book go far beyond telling you the basic principle involved in each question. We also analyze the specific error contained in every wrong answer; we even discuss what principles you may have been thinking about if you picked that answer. If your time is limited, you don't have to read every part of our explanatory answer to every question; you can choose to read only the discussion of the answer you chose, as well as the discussion of the correct choice (if you didn't pick the correct answer). If, however, you were unsure of one of the other answer choices (for example, if you originally marked choice A as the correct answer but then changed your mind), you may want to read the discussion of that answer as well. Remember, your goal in using this book is to become intimately familiar with MBE questions and how to answer them; reaching that goal requires that you feel comfortable with as many answer choices in this book as possible. In fact, you may even become frustrated sometimes, because you feel you're reading the same principles (for instance, the elements of strict product liability) over and over again, but that's intentional. We repeat those principles, in full, every time they're applicable, so that, by the time you take the MBE, those principles will be ***second nature*** to you. In our opinion, it's better to over-learn basic principles than have your knowledge be so tentative that you forget the principles when you take the MBE.

THE PRACTICE MBE

Some good advice: Complete the simulated, full-length MBE in our Practice MBE. By doing so, you may be able to save hundreds of dollars on Multistate seminars, which essentially give you a practice MBE and then tell you what your weak points are.

If you want to duplicate the "look and feel" of the real test, make sure the circumstances under which you take our Practice MBE are as similar as possible to those of the real MBE. First, time yourself! Second, sit in one room (perhaps a library) and work straight through, duplicating the two three-hour sessions of the actual MBE. Break only to use the bathroom, if necessary, but don't give yourself extra time for that (you won't get any on the MBE). Follow all the advice in our "Attacking the MBE" section when you take the practice MBE. Simulating the actual MBE in this way can significantly cut down on your anxiety when it's time for you to face the real thing. Taking the practice MBE under exam conditions gives you experience at actually sitting for the whole exam; you'll find that it's quite different from doing 25 or even 50 questions at a time. The experience of sitting for a practice MBE, both in simulating the environment and in practicing how your mind will organize, process, and function during the test (i.e., attacking the MBE), really is worth the six hours of time spent taking the Practice MBE.

WHAT TO DO WHEN YOUR STUDY TIME IS LIMITED

Ideally, you would have a month in which to use this book, so that you could cover an average of 20 pages a day. You may find, though, that you don't have the time to go through this entire process. If that's the case, you'll still find this book an invaluable study tool. You should prioritize your studies this way:

- Read "How to Attack the MBE."
- Read the Strategies and Tactics section for each subject, paying special attention to the coverage of each topic on the MBE.
- Do the practice questions for each subject, starting with Torts and Contracts.
- Do the Practice MBE.

In terms of your substantive review, if you don't have time to study every topic in every subject, pay special attention to the topics that are heavily tested by the MBE. For instance, in Torts, half the questions test only Negligence; thus, about 7.5 percent of the entire MBE is on Negligence, so you would be wise to learn the subject well. On the other hand, there are relatively few questions devoted to the subject of Future Interests within Real Property. So obviously you'll want to spend more time on Negligence than on Future Interests—especially since the latter not only represents fewer questions but is much more conceptually difficult and thus probably offers a lower yield per study hour.

In addition, keep in mind that some of the seven MBE subjects are easier than others, so, barring individual variables (e.g., you happen to be an expert on a difficult subject), you may want to concentrate your limited study time on questions in subjects that are likely to be easiest for you to answer. (See "Scoring Your Performance" above for more details.)

While the MBE requires a substantial amount of preparation, I believe that the time you spend in focused preparation really *will* in all likelihood be rewarded; your success will be proportionate to the amount of time you spend in reviewing the law and in understanding the techniques used by MBE examiners.

HOW TO ATTACK THE MBE

"How often have I said to you, that when you have eliminated the impossible, whatever remains, however impossible, must be the truth."

— Sherlock Holmes

UNDERSTANDING THE NATURE OF THE BEAST

Let's say that you had both a photographic memory and unlimited time in which to study for the MBE; in addition, assume you had time to read every textbook and every treatise concerning every subject on the MBE. Would you still need to know how to analyze MBE questions? The simple answer is—***no,*** provided of course, that you could read and understand exam fact patterns. Your substantive knowledge would always lead you to the correct answer.

For most of us, though, that's just not reality—we don't have photographic memories, and we don't have unlimited time to study. That's why using this book is so important. In this section, you'll learn ***how to analyze MBE questions***. This section gives you basic tips on how to study, advice on how to time yourself on the MBE, other general advice on taking the exam, how to analyze the facts in MBE questions, how to use the process of elimination to arrive at the correct answer, and how to guess at the best response when your reasoning fails you (as it does the best of us).

Learning how to attack the MBE requires, first, that you understand why it's such a difficult test. Not all objective tests are difficult, but this one is. Take a look at the following hypothetical question:

> Laurel and Hardy, who've never seen each other before, are guests at a party. Laurel is standing in a corner, minding his own business, holding a cream pie. Hardy walks over and snatches the cream pie out of Laurel's hands, for no apparent reason, and frightens him. If Laurel sues Hardy, the claim most likely to succeed will be:
>
> A. Battery
> B. Murder
> C. Conspiracy
> D. Breach of contract

It doesn't take a rocket scientist to figure out that A is the correct answer, does it? No. That's because none of the other answers are even close to being correct—so A ***must*** be the best answer.

Let's change the question a bit, though—same facts, different answer choices:

> A. Assault, because although Hardy intended to frighten Laurel, he didn't touch him.
> B. Battery, because it isn't necessary that the person himself be touched for the claim to succeed.
> C. Intentional infliction of emotional distress, because Hardy intended to frighten Laurel.
> D. There is no likely claim, because Hardy's conduct wasn't tortious.

We've taken a simple objective question and made it into one that's far more difficult. Why is it more difficult? Because even though the answer's the same—battery, you need a ***much more detailed knowledge*** of Tort law to answer the second version. In the second question, we've "masked" the correct answer with very similar answers, so it's harder to figure out what the correct answer is. That's why we call incorrect answers "distractors": They're designed to ***distract*** you by tempting you to pick a similar, but wrong, answer.

If you were the National Conference of Bar Examiners, and you wanted a test that would distinguish the examinees with the best grasp of the substantive law from those who didn't know the law as well, which question would you ask? The second one. And that's exactly what they do.

HOW TO STUDY FOR THE MULTISTATE BAR EXAM

In the "About the MBE" section of this book, we told you that each of the seven subjects on the MBE is treated with virtually equal weight. There are 27 scored questions on each subject, except for Contracts, which has 28. The Bar Examiners have decided that each subject should be treated equally on the bar exam, and you should divide your study time accordingly. As we've said before, however, this doesn't mean that all topics within a given subject are treated equally—e.g., negligence.

When planning your study for the MBE, take into consideration two aspects for your substantive review: the ***scope*** of what you need to study, and the ***depth*** to which you have to study. The scope of what you need to study about each subject is covered in the "Strategies and Tactics" sections in this book, which you'll find at the beginning of each subject area. As you'll see, the subject coverage is ***broad***; the MBE is likely to contain a couple of questions on each of a variety of topics, rather than many on any one topic. That's straightforward. The depth to which you must study each subject, on the other hand, is worth addressing.

First, and most importantly, keep in mind that the exam is given ***nationwide***. This means that, in general, you must learn the majority principles and ignore the vagaries of local law. You must know what the majority ***approach*** is on any given topic, since that's typically what you'll be asked. It doesn't do you any good on the MBE to know that there are two or more views on a topic; you have to know which is the prevailing view.[6]

The sample questions in this book will, first, give you a feel for the details you need to master in order to pass the MBE—make no mistake about it, ***the MBE tests details, not broad concepts of law***. The explanatory answers will then give you further understanding of the majority views on a wide variety of principles. Thus, when you study, make sure you're noting the not-so-obvious details and that you understand the aims and the rationales of rules. For instance, you probably already know that, in Contracts, third-party intended beneficiaries have rights under a contract, while incidental beneficiaries do not. On the MBE, though, if you're given a question on third-party beneficiaries, you're unlikely to be tested on something so basic. Instead, you may need to know, for instance, when an intended beneficiary's rights "vest." The Bar Examiners know that, if you have only a superficial knowledge of the subject, you'll see that a question deals with third-party beneficiaries, you'll likely decide that the beneficiary mentioned is an "intended" beneficiary, and you'll therefore deem him to have enforceable rights on that basis. This will probably not be correct. The Bar Examiners want to reward students with more thorough knowledge of beneficiaries, e.g., students who know that, before a beneficiary's rights have vested, his rights can be cancelled by action of the two original contracting parties.

Here's another example. If you remember the "Mercy Rule" from Evidence, you probably remember that it allows the defendant in a criminal case to introduce evidence of his good character. If you see an MBE question concerning the Mercy Rule, and that's all you remember about the Rule, you'll probably get the answer wrong. Why? Because there are ***two other important points*** to remember about the Mercy Rule. First, the character evidence must be ***pertinent*** (probative) in order to be admissible. Thus, in an MBE question, you may see evidence that a defendant charged with fraud was a "peaceful" man. You should realize, though, that his peacefulness is not pertinent to the crime with which he's charged, so the Mercy Rule wouldn't make the evidence admissible. Second, under the Mercy Rule, the character evidence can only be offered in the form of ***reputation or opinion***; it can't be evidence of specific instances of conduct. So, even if a criminal defendant charged with fraud introduced evidence of his honesty, if the evidence was in the form of a specific instance ("He was honest in his dealings with me when he sold me his car"), it wouldn't be admissible. Once again, the

---

6. This statement is at least true when one approach commands a strong majority. Where there are two approaches each of which commands at least a substantial minority, typically it *will* be enough for you to know that there are two approaches, without knowing which is the "majority" view. That's because where two approaches have significant support, and one approach would give victory to P and the other would give victory to D, the examiners are likely to ask you, "If P wins, what will be the most likely reason?," and you'll just have to supply the theory (without knowing whether it's a majority or minority theory) that would result in a victory for P.

Bar Examiners hope to catch those students with incomplete knowledge about the Rule. Even if you know the basics of the Rule, you could easily get the question wrong, because you don't know the Rule in enough depth to apply it to pertinent and specific facts!

As these examples indicate, your substantive review for the MBE must teach you to think about details; you simply cannot go into the MBE armed with only general superficial principles of law.

REMEMBER WHO WILL BE "TRIPPED UP" ON MBE QUESTIONS

Knowing what kind of person will be fooled by MBE questions can help you avoid becoming such a person. There are three general types of victims; they are those who

1. ***panic;***
2. ***operate by instinct***; and
3. are ***unprepared***.

If you analyze MBE questions, keeping in mind that these are the three kinds of people who will pick an incorrect answer, you can avoid the answers ***they'd*** pick and improve your chances of choosing the correct answers. Let's look at what each of these people might do on the MBE.

1. Panickers.

Unfortunately, there are many completely justifiable reasons to approach the MBE in a sweat. For instance, you may have a job riding on your passing the Bar Exam. You may feel you didn't prepare enough. You may face a couple of very tough questions early on that torpedo your confidence. Remember, though, that, no matter what causes it, panic can have disastrous effects on your performance.

What does panicking do? For one thing, severe anxiety actually inhibits your memory from functioning well. As you've probably experienced, the more anxious you are about remembering something, the less likely you are to remember it. The only real cure for this is ***adequate preparation***. If you've prepared sufficiently, both substantively and by practicing MBE questions (and keeping in mind you need nowhere near a perfect score to pass the MBE), you should be able to keep your nerves from undermining your performance. Remember, you're not shooting for an A+ here; law school is over. Many people carry over to the bar exam their law school mentality of "I have to get the best score in the class." That's a mistake! On the bar exam, there's no difference between a student who passes by 5 points and a student who passes by 55 points; ***both pass***, and that's all that matters.

What we're primarily concerned about ***here***, though, is not your attitude coming into the exam, but its impact on your ability to analyze questions. If you panic, you will not read questions carefully enough to pick the right response. Keep this in mind as you study the questions in this book. It's clear from past MBEs that the Bar Examiners know what people will overlook when they panic—some answers are clearly incorrect simply because they misapply some very basic fact in the question! Understanding what a panicker would do can help you avoid the same mistake.

2. People who operate by instinct.

You've probably heard the old saying a million times: "Your first instinct is generally correct." On the MBE, ***ignore this advice at all costs***. The Bar Examiners aren't looking for lawyers who fly by the seat of their pants; they want lawyers who can apply legal principles to factual situations in a rational, disciplined manner. You should, therefore, follow an instinct only if you can tie that instinct to a principle of law.

How can your instincts hurt you on the MBE? One, they may make you overlook stated facts. Suppose, for example, that, in a Criminal Law question, you're asked if the defendant will be found guilty under the facts. One of the elements of the crime described is intent, and the only evidence on this issue is the defendant's own testimony, in which he states that he didn't intend to commit the crime. The facts tell you to ***assume the jury believes the defendant***. Now, your instincts may tell you that the defendant is lying through his teeth and that no one over the age of five would believe him, so you leap for the answer that says the defendant will be found guilty. Watch out! If ***the facts*** tell you that the jury believes him, your instincts shouldn't matter. If you follow your instincts, you'll pick an incorrect response. The facts might tell you that the jury will find that the defendant lacked intent and so isn't guilty.

Here's another mistake you'll make if you follow your instincts. You probably remember from Evidence class that no piece of evidence is ever ***really*** inadmissible; virtually everything is admissible, somehow. If you let your instinct guide you on the MBE, therefore, you'd ***never*** pick the "inadmissible as hearsay not within any exception" response. And you'd be wrong fairly regularly. (For more on how to deal with this specific problem, see the "Strategies and Tactics" for Evidence.)

If you let your instincts guide you, you may also let your emotions control your reasoning. Look at this example from a past MBE:

> A father, disappointed by his eight-year-old son's failure to do well in school, began systematically depriving the child of food during summer vacation. Although his son became seriously ill from malnutrition, the father failed to call a doctor. He believed that, as a parent, he had the sole right to determine whether the child was fed or received medical treatment. Eventually the child died. An autopsy disclosed that the child had suffered agonizingly as a result of the starvation, that a physician's aid would have alleviated the suffering, and that, although the child would have died in a few months from malnutrition, the actual cause of death was an untreatable form of cancer, which did not happen any earlier because of the malnutrition. The father was prosecuted for murder, defined in the jurisdiction as "unlawful killing of a human being with malice aforethought." The father should be
>
> A. acquitted, because of the defendant's good-faith belief concerning parental rights in supervising children.
> B. acquitted, because summoning the physician or feeding the child would not have prevented the child's death from cancer.
> C. convicted, because the father's treatment of his son showed reckless indifference to the value of life.
> D. convicted, because the child would have died from malnutrition had he not been afflicted with cancer.

What's your gut reaction? The father is a slimeball, right? Sure he is. But the fact is that he ***didn't*** cause his child's death; the child died of cancer, so the father can't be liable for the child's death. If you let your instincts overwhelm you, you'll pick C—after all, the father ***was*** recklessly indifferent to his child's welfare and deserves to be punished. If you do this, you'll get this question wrong. Remember: In real life, being an emotional, caring person is an asset, but on the MBE, it's not—you have to be robot-like in applying the law to the facts you're given. The correct answer is B.

3. Those who are unprepared.

Obviously, the person the Bar Examiners most certainly intend to snare is the one who is unprepared for the MBE. Simply put, ***if you don't know the law, you shouldn't be a lawyer***. A person unprepared for the MBE will make mistakes, such as remembering only snippets of rules or forgetting how theories apply to facts. Of course, it's not possible to be completely prepared for every single legal issue on the MBE, so, to some extent, you're bound to be underprepared. If, though, you've recently completed law school when you take the MBE, you'll probably be able to answer as many as half of the MBE questions correctly simply on the basis of your classroom knowledge. If you review and understand the substantive law and learn from this book how to analyze questions, you should be able to answer enough of the remaining questions to pass.

HOW TO ANALYZE MBE QUESTIONS

The advice in this section addresses the MBE in general. The "Strategies and Tactics" section for each subject will give you specific tips on handling each particular subject, so you should always read the "Strategies and Tactics" before you attempt to answer any questions on a subject.

As you read further, you may find the process of analysis outlined here a bit overwhelming at first; you may even be tempted to skip over it. **Don't!** If you faithfully follow the procedure given below when you begin to practice answering questions, it will become second nature and you'll be able to apply it almost automatically. As a result, you'll be able to analyze MBE questions quickly and accurately, and you'll enter the MBE with a significant advantage.

A. Analyzing the facts of the question.

a. The composition of MBE questions.

Almost every MBE question will give you a factual setting and then a specific inquiry. Here's an example of a typical set of facts:

> The day after a seller completed the sale of his house and moved out, one of the slates flew off the roof during a windstorm. The slate struck a pedestrian, who was on the public sidewalk. The pedestrian was seriously injured. The roof is old and has lost several slates in ordinary windstorms on other occasions.

If the pedestrian sues the seller to recover damages for his injuries, will the pedestrian prevail?

A. Yes, because the roof was defective when the seller sold the house.
B. Yes, if the seller should have been aware of the condition of the roof and should have realized that it was dangerous to persons outside the premises.
C. No, because the seller was neither the owner nor the occupier of the house when the pedestrian was injured.
D. No, if the pedestrian knew that in the past slates had blown off the roof during windstorms.

The first paragraph is the factual setting. The final sentence, beginning with "If the pedestrian . . . " is the specific inquiry or "the call of the question."

b. Read carefully.

In general, because of the time constraints of the MBE, you'll only have time to read a factual setting in detail once, so make that reading count! You have to read carefully in order to answer correctly, because many wrong answers ("distractors") are aimed at people who skip over important facts. As you read a question, you may want to highlight important points (you're allowed to mark in the question book), but watch your time.

The following example from a past MBE illustrates the importance of careful reading.

> A landlord, the owner in fee simple of a small farm consisting of thirty acres of land improved with a house and several outbuildings, leased the same to a tenant for a ten-year period. After two years had expired, the government condemned twenty acres of the property and allocated the compensation award to the landlord and the tenant according to their respective interest so taken. It so happened, however, that the twenty acres taken embraced all of the farm's tillable land, leaving only the house, outbuildings, and a small woodlot. There is no applicable statute in the jurisdiction where the property is located, nor any provision in the lease relating to condemnation. The tenant quit possession, and the landlord brought suit against him to recover rent. The landlord will

A. lose, because there has been a frustration of purpose which excuses the tenant from further performance of his contract to pay rent.
B. lose, because there has been a breach of the implied covenant of quiet enjoyment by the landlord's inability to provide the tenant with possession of the whole of the property for the entire term.
C. win, because of the implied warranty on the part of the tenant to return the demised premises in the same condition at the end of the term as they were at the beginning.
D. win, because the relationship of landlord and tenant was unaffected by the condemnation, thus leaving the tenant still obligated to pay rent.

If you read that question quickly, you might have overlooked the fact that ***the tenant was already compensated for his loss by the condemnation award,*** and you might therefore have chosen A or B. Instead, if you read the question carefully, you could eliminate choices A and B, since under both of those choices the tenant prevails, and his prior recovery alone should suggest to you that he shouldn't. You could, therefore, narrow your choice down to C or D. (In fact, the correct response is D.) See how important it is to read the facts carefully?

c. Don't assume facts.

A corollary to the "read carefully" rule is that you should be careful not to read into the questions on the MBE facts that aren't there. The MBE is a meticulously crafted test; the facts you need in order to answer the question will be given to you, so you must rely only on those facts and on reasonable inferences from them. (This has important ramifications in choosing a correct response, which we'll discuss in detail a little later on.)

d. Choose the simple interpretation.

Don't make problems more complex than they really are. If there are multiple ways to interpret a question, one that makes the problem straightforward and others that make it very difficult, choose the straightforward interpretation.

e. "Trigger" factors to watch for in reading MBE questions.

While you should read every question carefully, there are a few "trigger" items that are extremely likely to determine the correct answer.

1. Statutes.

Some MBE questions contain statutes. A statute may be given for two reasons:

a. There are conflicting common law rules, but no one majority rule.

For instance, burglary is subject to several different rules: Some states limit burglary to a residence and to nighttime; others require neither or only one of these. The same conflict is evident in defining degrees of murder. If a question involves that kind of precise issue, you'll almost certainly be given a statute to guide you as to which rule applies.

b. The Examiners want to see if you can ignore your instincts.

Sometimes you'll be given a statute that doesn't comport with what you think ought to happen. For example, a criminal statute may require knowledge, but your gut reaction is that the conduct described need only constitute ***negligence*** to result in liability. Follow the statute, not your instinct.

As both (a) and (b) indicate, the most important things to do when you're faced with a statute are to read it carefully and to apply it ***mechanically***. If a question contains a statute, the statute almost certainly determines the central issue, and answering correctly almost certainly depends upon interpreting the statute as it was written.

Here's an example from a past MBE:

> A state statute requires any person licensed to sell prescription drugs to file with the State Board of Health a report listing the types and amounts of such drugs sold, if his sales of such drugs exceed $50,000 during a calendar year. The statute makes it a misdemeanor to "knowingly fail to file" such a report.
>
> A pharmacist, who is licensed to sell prescription drugs, sold $63,000 worth of prescription drugs during a particular year but did not file the report. Charged with committing the misdemeanor, the pharmacist testifies that he did a very poor job of keeping records and did not realize that his sales of prescription drugs had exceeded $50,000. If the jury believes the pharmacist, he should be found
>
> A. guilty, because this is a public welfare offense.
> B. guilty, because he cannot be excused on the basis of his own failure to keep proper records.
> C. not guilty, because the statute punishes omissions and he was not given fair warning of his duty to act.
> D. not guilty, because he was not aware of the value of the drugs he had sold.

Here, you're probably tempted to select choice B, because you figure that if the pharmacist is such a bonehead that he doesn't keep complete records, he should be liable—it's really not fair for him to rely on his sloppiness to avoid liability. Focus on the statute, though. The statute requires "knowing" behavior, so if the pharmacist's behavior wasn't "knowing," he can't be guilty. Since he didn't realize he'd sold more than $50,000 worth of prescription drugs, he didn't act knowingly when he failed to file the report, so he can't be guilty under the statute. Mechanically applying the statute to these facts will lead you straight to the correct response: D.

2. Pay special attention to seemingly meaningless details about people.

While the Bar Examiners do sometimes give you a ***deliberate*** red herring, you should always assume that ***every fact in every question is important.*** Even when the Examiners limit themselves to presenting only facts that are needed to make the question "airtight," the fact patterns and answer choices tend to become pretty lengthy. And the Examiners don't want the test to become a test of speed reading. So based on my review of many hundreds of past MBE questions, I can say this with confidence: *You should assume that if the examiners give you a fact, that fact is somehow needed to help make the right answer right, or at least one wrong answer choice wrong.*

For instance, normally, you won't be told any personal characteristics about people in the questions; you'll typically see only statements such as: "A man contracted with a woman" or "a farmer shot a rancher," and you can generally assume that all the people mentioned are sane, responsible adults. If, therefore, a question does tell you more about a person, such as that "A ten-year-old boy contracted with a man," the extra information given is likely to be important, so you should note it and use it. In Contract Law, what does including the boy's age suggest? An incapacity to contract.

The same kind of thing is true in the following examples. Say you're told that "A defense witness, who has been chronically unemployed since age 16, is testifying." Since the question has given you an additional fact about the witness, look at that fact. What does "chronically unemployed" tell you? It tells you, for one thing, that the witness probably isn't an expert witness, and so probably can't offer certain kinds of opinion testimony. Or, say you're told that "A novelist offered to sell his snow blower to his next-door neighbor." Ask yourself, what does the offeror's being a novelist suggest? For one thing, that he's not a merchant dealing in snow blowers, so his offer ***can't*** be irrevocable without consideration. See how it works? Here's another example, based on a past MBE question:

> A contractor, who had been in the painting and contracting business for ten years and had a fine reputation, contracted to paint a farmer's barn. The barn was a standard red barn with loft. The contract had no provision regarding assignment. The contractor recently assigned the contract to a commercial painter, whose experience and reputation with regard to commercial painting were comparable to those of the contractor. Which of the following statements is correct?
>
> A. The contractor is in breach of contract.
> B. The farmer may refuse to accept performance by the commercial painter.
> C. The farmer is required to accept performance by the commercial painter.
> D. There is a novation.

Focus specifically on the description after the commercial painter's identification in the question—"whose experience and reputation . . . are comparable. . . . " What does this suggest to you? If you remember the rules on assignment, you know that, to be valid, an assignment cannot *increase the risk* that the promisee (here, the farmer) will not receive the promised performance. What does the commercial painter's comparable experience and reputation suggest? That the farmer's *risk won't be increased*, and that the assignment is likely to be valid! Of course, assignments have other elements as well, but if you focused on the additional information given and ***applied*** it, you'd clearly eliminate choices A and B, and that would give you a 50-50 chance of choosing the correct answer. (In fact, the correct response is C. Choice D is wrong because a novation requires the consent of the promisee to performance by the assignee.)

f. Handling the specific inquiry in each question.

1. Reword the inquiry.

Most questions on the MBE are framed in the positive; that is, you're told to look, for example, for the "most likely outcome" or the "claim that is most likely to succeed" or the "best defense." You may find such questions difficult unless you reword them. This is how to do it:

Question: "What is the most likely outcome?"
Reword to: "What will the result be—and why?"

Question: "Which claim is most likely to succeed?
Reword to: "Which is the only claim that can succeed on these facts—and why?"

Question: "What is Defendant's best defense?"
Reword to: "Why won't the defendant be guilty on these facts?"

Question: "If party X loses, the most likely basis for the judgment is that . . . "
Reword to: "Party X loses because . . . "

What does this rewording do? It makes you look for one correct answer. Unless the Examiners have made a mistake in drafting the question, they're not going to ask you to choose the "better" answer as between two or more choices that each could be considered correct. Rather, the Examiners' mission is to design a question to which there is only one "correct" answer, and as to which each of the other three choices is indisputably wrong, because it misstates the facts, the law, or both. If you reword the specific inquiry and thus focus your mind on finding one correct answer, you're less likely to be seduced by distractors.

In a ***few*** MBE questions, the specific inquiry or "call" will be worded ***in the negative***; that is, you are asked to determine, for example, "which claim won't succeed," "which is the least sufficient basis for admitting the evidence," "of which crime is Defendant least likely to be guilty," etc. The primary difference between handling negative as opposed to positive inquiries is in ***how you apply a process of elimination*** to arrive at the correct response (this will be discussed in detail below). The process for ***rewording***, however, is the same. Here's an example from a past MBE:

> In a narcotics conspiracy prosecution against the defendant, the prosecutor offers in evidence a tape recording of a telephone call allegedly made by the defendant. A lay witness is called to testify that the voice on the recording is the defendant's. Her testimony to which of the following would be the LEAST sufficient basis for admitting the recording?
>
> A. She had heard the same voice on a similar tape recording, after which the voice was identified to her by the defendant's brother as being the defendant's voice.
> B. She had heard the defendant speak many times, but never over the telephone.
> C. She had, specifically for the purpose of preparing to testify, talked with the defendant over the telephone at a time after the recording was made.
> D. She had been present with the defendant when he engaged in the conversation in question but had heard only the defendant's side of the conversation.
>
> You should reword the question to read: "When ***won't*** the recording be admissible?" This forces you to look for the only insufficient basis for authentication and not to engage in drawing fine lines as to which type of authentication will be best. You'll find that rewording such questions makes it considerably easier to answer them. (In fact, the correct response is A, since it's the *only* one where the witness has no personal knowledge of the defendant's voice.)

2. Summon the applicable test immediately.

If you're asked whether a certain result should occur, ***immediately*** summon to your mind the ***appropriate test*** under the rules you've learned. For example, if you're asked whether Defendant will be guilty of murder, focus on what murder requires: an unlawful killing, neither justifiable nor excusable, with malice aforethought. If you're asked if a state statute is constitutional, think immediately of the three-prong standard for constitutionality of state statutes: within state's power, not violating any person's constitutional rights, not an undue burden on interstate commerce. Sometimes you won't know the nature of a claim or of an argument until you read each answer choice; strategies for dealing with that situation are discussed elsewhere. If, however, you're asked about a certain result in the question itself, immediately calling to mind the applicable rule or test will help prevent you from being seduced into choosing a distractor.

B. Analyzing responses—the process of elimination.

The MBE is like other standardized tests in one very important respect: The best, and sometimes only, way to arrive at the correct answer is to use a process of elimination. Basically, you should arrive at the correct answer by eliminating, one by one, any answer that clearly ***cannot*** be correct.

Think about it: In theory, for each MBE question, you should be able to eliminate three answers as definitely wrong and, by doing that, get a perfect score—without knowing that any answer was definitely correct! Of course, this would never happen in reality, but it does indicate the value of knowing how to eliminate incorrect responses.

On the MBE, knowing how to recognize a bad response is ***your most valuable analytical skill***, and we'll teach you how to do it in this section. First, we'll discuss the basic procedure for eliminating incorrect responses (issue spotting and modifiers), and then we'll discuss how answer choices can be wrong.

a. The basic concept.

First, let's take a look at a question and go over the basics of the process of elimination as applied to the MBE. Here's a question from a past MBE.

> Statutes in the jurisdiction define criminal assault as "an attempt to commit a criminal battery" and criminal battery as "causing an offensive touching."

> As a man was walking down the street, a gust of wind blew his hat off. The man reached out, trying to grab his hat, and narrowly missed striking a woman in the face with his hand. The woman, fearful of being struck by the man, pushed the man away.
>
> If charged with criminal assault, the man should be found
>
> A. guilty, because he caused the woman to be in apprehension of an offensive touching.
> B. guilty, because he should have realized he might strike someone by reaching out.
> C. not guilty, because he did not intend to hit the woman.
> D. not guilty, because he did not hit the woman.

In applying the process of elimination, you should analyze each answer choice separately, determining whether it's a possible correct answer or can instead be eliminated. Remember, in order for an answer to be correct, ***every aspect*** of it must be correct: It must correctly characterize the facts, it must state the correct law, its result must be consistent with its reasoning (if it's a "two part" answer), and it must address and resolve a central issue. If a response is ***potentially*** correct, mark a "Y" for "yes" next to the answer in the question booklet; if not, eliminate it with an "N" for "no."

Let's look at each of the responses for the question above.

As we discussed above, when you're told the nature of a claim in a specific question, you should ***immediately*** think of the test for that claim. The task is made easy for you in our grab-the-hat question, because the definition of criminal assault—"an attempt to commit a criminal battery"—is provided by the statute in the problem. Keeping this in mind, analyze each response. Choice A correctly characterizes the facts, but it understates the mens rea required for the crime: It suggests that merely causing apprehension is sufficient for guilt. Your knowledge of substantive law should, however, tell you that "attempt" requires ***intent***, but choice A suggests that causing an apprehension of imminent contact is a criminal act, without regard to the accused's mens rea; thus, choice A is definitely incorrect, and you should mark an "N" next to it.

Similarly, choice B is plausible on the facts, but it also misstates the law. The "should have realized" language in choice B suggests that ***negligence*** is the standard required by the statute. In fact, this understates the mental element required. By requiring attempt, the statute clearly requires intent, not mere negligence. Thus, choice B cannot be correct, and you should mark an "N" next to it, as well.

Choice C suggests that the man should not be guilty because he didn't intend to hit the woman. Choice C thus identifies the correct mental element, and it reflects one of the question's facts—that the man didn't intend to hit the woman but rather intended only to retrieve his hat. Furthermore, the man's lack of intent is a central issue, because the lack of this element of the crime would result in his acquittal. Finally, choice C's result agrees with its reasoning. Choice C is, therefore, a very strong likelihood, and you should mark a "Y" next to it.

Finally, choice D states that the man can't be guilty, because he didn't actually hit the woman. As discussed above, focus in on the language of the statute. The statute cited doesn't actually require a touching; a mere attempt to touch is enough to satisfy the statute. Choice D misstates the law, so it cannot be a correct response. Mark it with an "N."

Process of elimination on this question, then, leaves you with three "N's" and only one "Y." The "Y" response must be the correct one and, in fact, it is.

You may feel that this is a laborious way to go about answering MBE questions, especially since you'll be working under time constraints when you actually take the test. Actually, it's the best way to master the MBE process. In fact, on many questions, you'll go through this process very quickly, because you'll immediately spot the best response and quickly eliminate the other three. When that happens, ***great!*** Just mark the correct response on your answer sheet and keep moving. (When you begin practicing for the exam, though, use as much time as you need to master this process. You'll speed up as you practice.)

A few paragraphs back, we told you that process of elimination sometimes is the only way to arrive at a correct response to an MBE question. Just look at the following question, from a past MBE:

> A tenant occupied an apartment in a building owned by a landlord. She paid rent of $1250 in advance each month. During the second month of occupancy, the tenant organized the tenants in the building as a tenants' association and the association made demands of the landlord concerning certain repairs and improvements the tenants wanted. When the tenant tendered rent for the third month, the landlord notified her that rent for the fourth and subsequent months

would be $2000 per month. The tenant protested and pointed out that all other tenants paid rent of $1250 per month. Thereupon, the landlord gave the required statutory notice that the tenancy was being terminated at the end of the third month. By an appropriate proceeding, the tenant contests the landlord's right to terminate. If the tenant succeeds, it will be because

A. a periodic tenancy was created by implication.
B. the doctrine prohibiting retaliatory eviction is part of the law of the jurisdiction.
C. the $2000 rent demanded violates the agreement implied by the rate charged to other tenants.
D. the law implies a term of one year in the absence of any express agreement.

You can, if you like, go through a detailed "Y" and "N" elimination with each response here. We include this question here, though, to point out that there are times when a correct answer can only be deduced by a process of elimination. Here, with a basic knowledge of Property Law, you'd be able to eliminate choices A, C, and D conclusively. That would leave B, a response you'd be unlikely to choose as the correct answer under any other circumstances. For one thing, the MBE is a national exam, and choice B addresses local (perhaps minority) law;[7] furthermore, the doctrine of retaliatory eviction is a very minor point of Property Law, one you probably never covered in law school. If you've used the process of elimination, however, you know that the other three answers are unquestionably wrong under the rules that you've learned, so choice B must be the right response. And it is.

b. How to eliminate incorrect responses.

Now that you've got the basic concept down, let's address some specifics on how to eliminate incorrect responses.

1. Issue spotting on the MBE.

Your ability to identify and resolve the central issue in each question is crucial to your ability to answer MBE questions correctly. To do this, you must not only spot issues in the facts themselves, but also be sensitive to nuances in the answer choices. The "Strategies and Tactics" sections address this in detail for each subject, so we'll examine only some basic principles here.

If you're used to taking essay exams in school, you already know the importance of issue spotting. Since the MBE is an ***objective*** test, you may be tempted to believe you won't need to spot issues. That's only ***partially*** correct. The MBE requires only ***modified*** issue spotting, because you're working with a limited set of possibilities: One of the choices ***must*** identify and resolve a central issue. You don't have to ***supply*** the right answer—you only have to ***recognize*** it.

Don't get too excited, though; you aren't completely off the hook, because you also have to be able to (1) identify ***what issue each response is addressing***, and (2) identify ***the central issue in the problem***. If the central issue isn't obvious to you, based on your reading of the facts, you can sometimes use the answer choices to help identify what the central issue must be, if you work correctly and in a disciplined fashion.

Let's address the "central issue in the problem" aspect of issue spotting first. This requires you to ask yourself, "what, ***in theory***, is going on in this problem?" Say, for instance, that the question asks if the plaintiff's claim for negligence will succeed. You must know that, to prove negligence, the plaintiff will have to prove duty, breach, causation, and damages; you must also know that the plaintiff will only succeed if the defendant doesn't have a valid defense. An issue raising one of these elements must be present in the facts of the question; the correct response will be the one that addresses and resolves that issue.

Suppose, instead, that you're trying to solve a problem for which you must pick which plaintiff's claim is "most likely to succeed." To do this, you must find the answer choice that most closely addresses, and overcomes, the greatest obstacle to the plaintiff's success. You'll have to (1) think of what, theoretically, the plaintiff must prove; (2) identify which element of his position is weakest (or which defense is strongest); and (3) choose an answer that states a valid argument for overcoming that obstacle.

---

7. Notice that this question is of the form, "If [party X] wins, it will be because. . . ." As I said earlier, when the examiners want to test you on a doctrine that only a minority of jurisdictions follow, this is the way they'll typically construct the question, since even a very-rarely-applied doctrine can supply the correct answer if it's the only doctrine listed among the choices that would give a victory to the specified party.

To practice further, suppose you're faced with an Evidence question that asks you to identify the "most likely" basis on which a piece of evidence will be admissible. Ask yourself: What's the most likely reason the evidence **wouldn't** be admissible? Is it hearsay? Opinion? Character evidence? The correct response will have to address that central reason; by reading each of the choices, you'll find out, one way or another, what that issue is. Every answer choice, either explicitly or implicitly, addresses some issue. For example, in Torts questions, if an answer uses phrases such as "should have known," "reasonable care," and the like, the language used tells you that it must be addressing the issue of negligence.

Let's look at a fairly simple question from a past MBE.

> The plaintiff sued the defendant for damages for injuries that the plaintiff incurred when a badly rotted limb fell from a curbside tree in front of the defendant's home and hit the plaintiff. The defendant claimed that the tree was on city property and thus was the responsibility of the city. At trial, the plaintiff offered testimony that, a week ***after*** the accident, the defendant had cut the tree down with a chainsaw. The offered evidence is
>
> A. inadmissible, because there is a policy to encourage safety precautions.
> B. inadmissible, because it is irrelevant to the condition of the tree at the time of the accident.
> C. admissible to show the tree was on the defendant's property.
> D. admissible to show the tree was in a rotted condition.

What's going on here? The plaintiff is offering evidence of something the defendant did ***after*** an incident to fix a dangerous condition. What, in legal terms, is the plaintiff doing? He's offering evidence of a ***subsequent remedial measure***, and the fact that the defendant denied ownership of the property suggests that the plaintiff is offering the evidence to prove that the tree is on the defendant property. Remember that, while subsequent remedial measures are inadmissible to prove negligence or wrongdoing (due to the public policy concern of encouraging safety precautions), such evidence is admissible to prove *ownership and control*. Now look at the answer choices. Choice A states the general rationale of the subsequent remedial measure rule. Even if you didn't realize that the central issue in this problem was the admissibility of evidence of subsequent remedial measures, the language in A would suggest that you go back to the facts and see if you can't spot that issue. What does choice B do? It suggests that the evidence is inadmissible because it doesn't make any issue in the case any more or less likely—the choice raises the issue of relevancy. Choice C ***implicitly*** recognizes that the problem is one of admitting evidence of subsequent remedial measures ***by invoking an exception to the general rule: proving ownership***. Choice D implicitly states that the evidence should be admissible because it's relevant to the facts at issue—that is, the defendant's chopping the tree down a week after the accident indicates that it was, in fact, in a rotted condition.

Once you've broken down the answer choices into their theoretical bases, it becomes much simpler to spot both the central issue and the choice that correctly resolves it: C. The example also reinforces how important it is for you to be able to determine what ***exact issue*** a response is addressing, because that isn't always straightforward.

Generally, the central issue of each question is reasonably obvious in the fact pattern. Sometimes, though, the only way to spot the central issue is to determine the focus of the answer choices. Here's an example from a past MBE.

> The defendant is tried for armed bank robbery. The prosecution, in its case in chief, offers evidence that, when the defendant was arrested one day after the crime, he had a quantity of heroin and a hypodermic needle in his possession. This evidence should be
>
> A. admitted to prove the defendant's motive to commit the crime.
> B. admitted to prove the defendant's propensity to commit crimes.
> C. excluded, because its probative value is substantially outweighed by the danger of unfair prejudice.
> D. excluded, because such evidence may be offered only to rebut evidence of good character offered by defendant.

Let's focus on choice C. It suggests that the evidence is inadmissible because it's not legally relevant—that is, its probative value is substantially outweighed by the danger of unfair prejudice. To see if that's the correct response, you'd have to go back to the facts and, in essence, "spot" the issue. Is there a legal relevance problem in these facts? There ***is***, because the evidence is sufficiently "shocking" that a jury could give it undue weight and probably use it for purposes other than those that are proper under these facts (considering the choices here, the evidence offered could only be used to prove motive, i.e., that he needed money to purchase drugs). You can see that the MBE format can actually benefit you; with an objective test, issue spotting is simplified, because the central issue must be resolved by at least one of the answer choices. Note, though, that issue spotting is still a vital skill, a skill you must have in order to answer most MBE questions correctly.

2. Language specifics.

On the MBE, in order to distinguish correct from incorrect answer choices, you must meticulously read the alternatives.

a. Glance at the modifier quickly, then study the reasoning and, finally, the result.

Many MBE answers will have three distinct parts: the result, the reasoning to support that result, and a ***modifier*** linking the two. For instance, an answer might read, "admissible, because the statement is an admission of a party-opponent," or "liable, only if she was negligent," or "guilty, because they planned and conspired to steal the stamps." The portion ***before*** the comma is the "result"; the ***first word after*** the comma (because, if, unless, since) is the "modifier"; the portion ***after*** the modifier is the "reasoning."

When you first look at the alternative answers after reading a question, glance quickly at the modifier. Usually, the modifier is "because." If it's ***something else***, such as "if," "unless," "but," "only if," or the like, make special note of this. We'll discuss why in a moment.

After you've glanced at the modifier, you should analyze the reasoning to see if it's correct. (This may seem counterintuitive, since you're likely to want to look at the result next.) The reasoning can be incorrect due to misstating the facts, misstating the law, or both. (More on this below.) If the reasoning is incorrect, the answer cannot be correct; you can eliminate it and move on.

If the reasoning is correct, you have to take another look at the modifier. Here's how you should deal with the three most common modifiers: "because," "if," and "unless."

1. Where "because" is the modifier.

As we said earlier, "because" is by far the most common modifier on the MBE. If "***because***" is used as the modifier, the answer can be correct only if:

- The reasoning addresses and resolves a central issue (or at least a more central issue than any other response);
- The facts in the question ***completely satisfy*** the reasoning (that is, if the reasoning says, "because he was drunk," the facts must state or imply ***unequivocally*** that he was drunk); and
- The result is consistent with the reasoning (for instance, if the reasoning states, "because the statement was an admission by a party-opponent," the result ***must*** be "admissible" in order for the answer to be correct).

Keep in mind that there are synonyms for "because" that are used on the MBE; these include "***since***" and "***as***" (for example, "admissible ***as*** a prior identification" really means "admissible ***because it*** (the statement) is a prior identification").

Now, let's take a look at those modifiers we told you to watch for: "if" and "unless."

2. Where "if" is the modifier.

Where "if" is the modifier, in order to be correct, the reasoning need only be ***plausible*** under the facts (that is, there can't be anything in the facts to suggest the reasoning ***couldn't*** be true), the reasoning must address a central issue, and the result and the reasoning must agree.

As you can see, the big difference between "because" and "if" is that the "because" reasoning must flow unequivocally from the facts; the "if" reasoning must be ***only plausible***. Take a look at the following example.

> A husband and wife, walking on a country road, were frightened by a bull running loose on the road. They climbed over a fence to get onto the adjacent property, owned by a farmer. After climbing over the fence, the husband and wife damaged some of the

farmer's plants which were near the fence. The fence was posted with a large sign, "No Trespassing."

The farmer saw the husband and wife and came toward them with his large watchdog on a long leash. The dog rushed at the wife. The farmer had intended only to frighten the husband and wife, but the leash broke, and before the farmer could restrain the dog, the dog bit the wife. If the husband asserts a claim based on assault against the farmer, will the husband prevail?

A. Yes, because the farmer did not have a privilege to use excessive force.
B. Yes, if the husband reasonably believed that the dog might bite him.
C. No, if the dog did not come in contact with him.
D. No, if the farmer was trying to protect his property.

Let's look at choice B. Remember, before you even got to choice B, you should have thought of the elements for tortious assault: an act creating in plaintiff a reasonable apprehension of immediate harmful or offensive contact with plaintiff's person, intent to create this apprehension, and causation. You also should have noted that choices B, C, and D all use the modifier "if" (which is quite unusual, since "because" is the normal modifier). So much for preliminaries. Let's go through the "if" reasoning to see if choice B could be correct. First, is the reasoning plausible on the facts? Well, there's nothing to indicate that it ***couldn't*** be true, and since you could ***infer from the facts*** (remember, inferences are permissible) that the husband was physically close to ***the wife*** when the dog attacked her, it's plausible that ***the husband*** feared he'd be bitten, too. Second, does the choice resolve a central issue? Yes—it satisfies the apprehension element of assault, and that's the central issue on these facts, since it was the wife who was bitten, and so there would be some question as to whether the husband was put in apprehension of immediate contact. Finally, the reasoning and the result match: If the husband was put in fear, assuming the other elements of assault (which are not very much in question on these facts) were met, the husband would prevail. Of course, you'd have to eliminate the other possibilities to determine ***conclusively*** that B is correct, but it's clear from this analysis that B is the correct response.

Let's take a quick look at choice C to see how a response with an "if" modifier can be incorrect. First, is the reasoning plausible on the facts? Yes—it's possible that the dog didn't come into contact with the husband, because the facts don't state otherwise. Second, does this choice address and resolve a central issue? ***No***—this is where choice C falls apart. Assault doesn't require contact; battery does. Thus, the fact that the dog didn't come into contact with the husband would not determine if he'd prevail. Choice C can't, therefore, be the best response.

Keep in mind that "if" also has ***synonyms*** or ***equivalents*** ("as long as," for example); if you see such a synonym, your analysis should be the same.

3. Where "unless" is the modifier.

Now let's look at "unless" as a modifier. When this modifier is used, the reasoning must be the only circumstance under which the result cannot occur. If you can think of even ***one other way*** the result might come about, the response cannot be correct. Let's look at an example from a past MBE.

A chemical engineer knew of a particular small chemical company, but had no ownership interest in or connection with the company. The engineer noticed that the company's most recent, publicly issued financial statement listed, as part of the company's assets, a large inventory of a certain special chemical compound. This asset was listed at a cost of $100,000, but the engineer knew that the ingredients of the compound were in short supply and that the current market value of the inventory was in excess of $1,000,000. There was no current public quotation of the price of the company's stock. The book value of the company's stock, according to the financial statement, was $5 a share; its actual value was $30 a share.

Knowing these facts, the engineer offered to purchase from a stockholder of the company, at $6 a share, the 1,000 shares of company stock owned by the stockholder. The stockholder and the engineer had not previously met. The stockholder sold the stock to the engineer for $6 a share.

If the stockholder asserts a claim based on misrepresentation against the engineer, will the stockholder prevail?

A. Yes, because the engineer knew that the value of the stock was greater than the price she offered.
B. Yes, if the engineer did not inform the stockholder of the true value of the inventory.
C. No, unless the engineer told the stockholder that the stock was not worth more than $6 a share.
D. No, if the company's financial statement was available to the stockholder.

Let's focus on choice C, which uses "unless" as a modifier. Using our method, when you look at choice C, you should say to yourself: "Is there any way the stockholder could prevail if the engineer didn't tell her the stock was worth more than $6 a share?" Remember, as soon as you read the specific inquiry in this question, you should have summoned to your mind the elements of misrepresentation: defendant's misrepresentation of a material past or present fact, defendant's knowledge of falsity/reckless disregard for falsity, defendant's intent to induce plaintiff's reliance, plaintiff's actual and justifiable reliance, and damages. You should also remember other substantive law: that misrepresentation can take the form of non-disclosure only when there exists a *duty to disclose*, due to special circumstances (such as a fiduciary relationship between the two parties). Beyond that, you should recognize that the facts give you additional personal information—that the engineer and the stockholder had ***never met***—which should strongly suggest to you that there was no special circumstance (e.g., a fiduciary relationship) that imposed on the engineer a duty of disclosure as to the real value of the stock; without such a duty, the engineer's non-disclosure couldn't be actionable as misrepresentation. Thus, what choice C states is true: Without the engineer's representation to the stockholder that the stock was worth ***more*** than the engineer was proposing to pay for it, there is ***no way*** for the stockholder to prevail! C is the correct response.

Before we leave this question, let's look at choice B, which uses "if" as a modifier. Go through your analysis process. First, is the reasoning plausible on the facts? Yes. There's nothing to suggest that the engineer ***did*** inform the stockholder of the inventory's true value. Second, does this resolve a central issue? No. It doesn't resolve the engineer's liability, which must be based on the element of duty. The central issue here concerns the engineer's duty to disclose the value of the stock, so the result choice B reaches, that the stockholder will prevail, cannot be reached on its reasoning; it would ***have*** to provide a basis for liability. Since it doesn't, it can't be the best response.

Finally, look at choice A, which uses the "because" modifier. Remember, with "because," the reasoning must be unequivocally shown in the facts. Here, it is: You're expressly told that the engineer knew that the value of the company stock was far greater than what the engineer offered. But that fact doesn't resolve a central issue! Misrepresentation in the form of nondisclosure, as we discussed two paragraphs back, requires a duty to disclose. No such duty exists here. Thus, the engineer's knowledge of the true value of the stock ***doesn't*** make her liable, contrary to what choice A states. (Incidentally, if the representation here were "positive"—e.g., the engineer told the stockholder, "This stock isn't worth more than $6"—then the engineer's knowledge of its value ***would*** be one element supporting a misrepresentation claim.)

Remember that we told you to look at the reasoning before the result? After doing all this work with modifiers, you should see why. Modifiers like "if" and "unless" can ***change the result***—they're "catch words." If you only looked at the answer choices to find a specific result, you couldn't isolate and reject an incorrect answer.

c. How answer choices can be wrong.

Having discussed the threshold issues of issue spotting and modifiers, let's examine how answer choices can be wrong.

In the last section, we told you that your most important analysis skill on the MBE is the ability to identify when an answer choice is definitely wrong. In this section, we'll address the different ways in which choices can be wrong and the order in which you should analyze each choice.

There are three general ways in which an answer choice can be wrong: (1) it can mischaracterize the facts; (2) it can misstate the law; and/or (3) it can ignore a central issue in the question. This is the order in which you should address each of these possibilities. Remember, if a choice fails in ***any respect***, you can stop your analysis, eliminate it, and move on; in order to be correct, an answer choice must be correct ***in every respect***.

Let's look at each of these elements in detail.

1. The reasoning mischaracterizes the facts.

If the reasoning doesn't reflect either the facts as they appear in the question or reasonable inferences drawn from those facts, the answer choice cannot be correct. This can happen in several ways.

a. A blatant contradiction of the facts as stated.

Look at this example from a past MBE:

> The defendant watched a liquor store furtively for some time, planning to hold it up. He bought a realistic-looking toy gun for the job. One night, just before the store's closing time, the defendant drove to the store, opened the front door, and entered. He reached in his pocket for the toy gun, but he became frightened and began to move back toward the front door. However, the shopkeeper had seen the butt of the gun. Fearing a hold up, the shopkeeper produced a gun from under the counter, pointed it at the defendant, and yelled, "Stop!" The defendant ran to the door and the toy gun fell from his pocket. The shopkeeper fired. The shot missed the defendant but struck and killed a passerby outside the store.
>
> A statute in the jurisdiction defines burglary as "breaking and entering any building or structure with the intent to commit a felony or to steal therein." On a charge of burglary, the defendant's best defense would be that
>
> A. the intent required was not present.
> B. the liquor store was open to the public.
> C. he had a change of heart and withdrew before committing any crime inside the store.
> D. he was unsuccessful, and so at most could only be guilty of attempted burglary.

Look at choice A, which states that the defendant lacked the requisite intent. This is clearly wrong on the facts: The defendant planned a hold up and entered the store intending to hold it up. Thus, his best defense ***couldn't*** be that he lacked the requisite intent, because ***the facts indicate otherwise***. You don't have to spend any more time here; since choice A misstates the facts, it can't be correct—you can drop that choice without going further: You don't have to analyze the law or determine if the choice addresses a central issue more precisely than the other choices. (The correct choice is B, since there was no "breaking" given the fact that the store was open to the public.)

Look at another example dealing with misstating facts:

> A homeowner owned a house in City. On the lawn in front of his home and within five feet of the public sidewalk there was a large tree. The roots of the tree caused the sidewalk to buckle severely and become dangerous. An ordinance of City requires adjacent landowners to keep sidewalks in a safe condition. The homeowner engaged a contractor to repair the sidewalk, leaving it to the contractor to decide the details of how the repair should be made.
>
> The contractor dug up the sidewalk, cut back the roots of the tree, and laid a new sidewalk. Two days after the homeowner had paid the contractor the agreed price of the repair, the tree fell over onto the street and damaged a parked car belonging to a neighbor.
>
> The neighbor has asserted a claim against the contractor, who admits that cutting the roots caused the tree to fall.
>
> The best defense of the contractor is that
>
> A. the tree was on the property of the homeowner.
> B. he repaired the sidewalk in the manner directed by the homeowner.
> C. he could not reasonably foresee that the tree would fall.
> D. he was relieved of liability when the homeowner paid for the repair.

Look at choice B. You're told in the facts that the homeowner left "it to the contractor to decide the details of how the repair should be made." Choice B directly contradicts this by stating that the contractor repaired the sidewalk in the manner directed by the homeowner. You know, therefore, that choice B cannot be correct. (The correct answer is C, since *if* the contractor couldn't reasonably have foreseen that the tree would fall, he would not have been negligent, in a situation in which the plaintiff would have to prove negligence.)

You may already have guessed the reason you should eliminate factually incorrect choices; these choices often contain reasoning which is ***legally correct*** and would resolve a central issue in the question if it reflected the facts. As a result, you could easily be seduced (distracted) into choosing these choices if you didn't immediately check the facts and eliminate them from contention!

The examples we've looked at so far are examples of answer choices that directly contradict the facts. Be aware, however, that answer choices can be factually incorrect in ***other*** ways. Let's look at the other major ways an answer choice can misstate the facts.

b. The answer choice goes beyond the facts.

Look at this question, slightly modified from a past MBE:

> A salesman and a mechanic planned to hold up a bank. They drove to the bank in the salesman's car. The salesman entered while the mechanic remained as lookout in the car. After a few moments, the mechanic panicked and drove off.
>
> Soon after leaving the scene, the mechanic was stopped by two police officers for speeding. Noting his nervous condition, the police required the mechanic to exit the car, and one asked him if they might search the car. The mechanic agreed. The search turned up heroin concealed under the passenger seat. The heroin belonged to the salesman.
>
> In a prosecution of the salesman for heroin possession, the prosecution's best argument to sustain the validity of the search of the salesman's car would be that
>
> A. the search was reasonable under the circumstances, including the mechanic's nervous condition.
> B. the search was incident to a valid arrest.
> C. the mechanic had, under the circumstances, sufficient standing and authority to consent to the search.
> D. exigent circumstances, including the inherent mobility of the car, justified the search.

Look specifically at choice B, which presupposes there's been a valid arrest. The facts don't mention or imply an arrest; thus, choice B goes beyond the facts, and, as a result, it can't possibly be correct. This example illustrates how a careful reading of the factual assumptions embedded in each choice can be helpful: The legal reasoning stated in choice B might or might not be correct if the facts as stated in the choice were correct,[8] but the choice's misstatement of the facts makes it unquestionably incorrect.

c. The answer choice assumes a fact in dispute.

Sometimes, a choice will characterize a fact as settled when, in actuality, the facts don't show such a clear-cut resolution. Here's an example from a past MBE:

> A woman who owned a house and lot leased the same to a tenant for a term of five years. In addition to the house, there was also an unattached, two-car brick garage located on the lot. Although the tenant earned his living as an employee at the local grocery store, his hobby consisted of wood carving and the making of small furniture. The tenant installed a work bench, electric lights, and a radiator in the garage. He also laid pipes connecting the radiator with the heating plant inside the house. Thereafter the woman mortgaged the premises to a bank to secure a loan. The tenant was not given notice of the mortgage, but the mortgage was recorded. Still later, the woman defaulted on the mortgage payments, and the bank began foreclosure proceedings, as it was entitled to do under the terms of the mortgage. By this time the tenant's lease was almost ended. The tenant began the removal of the equipment he had installed in the garage. The bank brought an action to enjoin the removal of the equipment mentioned above. Both the woman and the tenant were named as defendants.
>
> If the court refuses the injunction, it will be because
>
> A. the tenant was without notice of the mortgage.
> B. the circumstances reveal that the equipment was installed for the tenant's exclusive benefit.
> C. in the absence of a contrary agreement, a residential tenant is entitled to remove any personal property he voluntarily brings upon the premises.
> D. the Statute of Frauds precludes the bank from claiming any interest in the equipment.

Look at choice C. Its reasoning characterizes the work bench, lights, and radiator ***conclusively*** as personal property. In fact, the central legal issue here is the characterization of those items—namely, whether they are personal property (and thus not subject to the mortgage) or "fixtures" (and thus subject to the mortgage). This is an issue because the items are of a type that ***could*** be subject to permanent annexation to the realty, depending on the intent of the annexor (here, the tenant) and other circumstances. They probably ***aren't*** fixtures here, though, because the tenant didn't intend to

---

8. There's no way to know whether the statement would be legally correct if the facts were correct; under *Arizona v. Gant*, the passenger-compartment search would be valid as incident to the arrest if and only if the mechanic posed a danger of interfering with the search; we're not told enough to know whether there was such a danger, given that one officer could have guarded the mechanic while the other did the search.

annex them permanently to the realty. Whatever the result, the point here is that choice C ***assumes an essential fact that is the very issue to be resolved***: whether or not the items are personalty. (The correct answer is B.)

2. The reasoning is legally wrong.

Once you've determined that the reasoning in an answer choice represents the facts, you should determine whether it's legally correct. This is where careful substantive preparation will pay off!

Just as an answer choice can be ***factually*** incorrect in several ways, it can contain a number of different kinds of ***legal*** errors, too:

- It may overstate the requirements of a crime, tort, or admissibility of evidence;
- It may state an antiquated or otherwise inapplicable rule;
- It may state a rule that has no application to the facts;
- It may make an overinclusive statement of the law, which will be wrong even if it happens to be correct on the facts; or
- It may overstate or understate the correct legal standard.

We'll look at each of these possibilities separately, but first, let's stress once again how important it is to determine what words a response is using in stating a legal ***theory***. Remember, we addressed this in the "issue spotting" section. Its real importance, however, is in determining the legal validity of each response. Simply put, you can't determine if a response is legally correct if you don't understand what legal principle it's addressing.

With that in mind, let's look, in detail, at the major ways in which an answer choice can be legally incorrect.

a. Reasoning that overstates the requirements of a crime, tort, or admissibility of evidence.

This is a common kind of legal inaccuracy. For instance, you may face a question in which someone is claiming negligence, but the answer choice states that the defendant can't be guilty because he didn't act intentionally. Or a choice may tell you that a piece of hearsay evidence is inadmissible as an "excited utterance," because the declarant is available to testify—but unavailability is not a requirement of the "excited utterance" hearsay exception. Or you may be told that a criminal defendant cannot be guilty of murder because he didn't intentionally kill his victim—but "depraved heart" murder does not require intent. As these examples indicate, the most common kind of legal misstatement is one that overstates the requirements of a crime, tort, or evidence-admissibility rule. If you don't have your legal principles memorized correctly, you can be fooled by these misstatements, because they sound as though they should be correct.

b. Reasoning that uses antiquated rules or rules from inapplicable bodies of law.

If a rule is not the modern one, or it doesn't reflect the body of law on which the MBE relies, it can't be the basis of a correct response. For example, a husband is no longer vicariously liable for his wife's torts simply because they're married, and the attractive nuisance doctrine no longer requires that a child be lured onto property by the attractive nuisance. If an answer choice states an outmoded rule like these, it cannot be correct.

Similarly, you need to keep in mind the bodies of law on which the MBE relies. For instance, in Evidence Law, the MBE applies the Federal Rules of Evidence, ***not the common law***. Usually, when the correct answer to a question involves a matter in which the FRE and the common law differ, one of the distractors will state the common-law rule. A frequently used distractor is res gestae; res gestae is a common-law concept not recognized by the FRE. Thus, ***an answer choice relying on res gestae as the source of admissibility for hearsay can't be correct***. Similarly, where transactions in goods are involved, the MBE relies on the UCC, Article 2. If you apply a contradictory common-law rule to questions in which a transaction in goods is involved, you'll get the wrong answer—you can be sure that there are distractors tailor-made for just such a mistake! And finally, in Civil Procedure, you are to assume the Federal Rules of Civil Procedure are in effect; so in an area where the FRCP supplies a different rule than the common law or statutory rules of many states, an answer based on the latter will be wrong.

c. Reasoning applying rules that do not apply to the facts.

A response can correctly characterize the facts but then state a rule of law that is inapplicable to those facts. Here's an example from a prior MBE.

> The defendant is tried for armed robbery of the First Bank of City. At the request of police, the teller who was robbed prepared a sketch bearing a strong likeness to the defendant, but the

> teller died in an automobile accident before the defendant was arrested. At trial the prosecution offers the sketch. The sketch is
>
> A. admissible as an identification of a person after perceiving him.
> B. admissible as past recollection recorded.
> C. inadmissible as hearsay not within any exception.
> D. inadmissible as an opinion of the teller.

Look at choice A. The teller's action concerning the defendant is an "identification" in the actual, physical sense, since she did "identify" him by making the sketch. While a prior identification can be admissible as an exclusion from the hearsay rule (and thus choice A may suggest the application of a correct rule) it doesn't apply to these facts; these identifications are admissible only if the one who made the identification is a *testifying witness*. Here, you're told that the teller died, and that does a fairly complete job of eliminating the possibility that she's a testifying witness. Thus, even though the exclusion of prior identifications from the hearsay rule is a valid principle of the Federal Rules of Evidence, it simply doesn't apply to these facts, so A can't be correct. (In fact, C is the best response.)

d. Answer choices that make overinclusive statements of the law; these choices are wrong even if they happen to apply to these facts.

An answer choice that misstates the law ***cannot*** be correct, even if there is a piece of truth in the statement, as it applies to the facts. Suppose, for example, that a factual setting involves testimony that is inadmissible hearsay. One of the choices states that the testimony is "inadmissible, because hearsay is inadmissible." Now, under these specific facts, it's true that the testimony is inadmissible hearsay, but that's ***not because hearsay in general is inadmissible***—as you know, there are lots of exceptions and exclusions to the hearsay rule. Thus, the choice cannot be correct, because it makes an overinclusive statement of the law of hearsay evidence.

e. Answer choices that overstate or understate the applicable legal standard.

Remember the "Three Bears," in which Goldilocks sought the porridge that was neither too hot nor too cold? Well, on some MBE questions, you'll undertake an analogous task: picking the appropriate legal standard from among others that are too strict or too lenient. Here's an example from a past MBE:

> During 2012 a series of arsons occurred in City. In early 2013 the City Council adopted this resolution:
>
> City will pay $10,000 for the arrest and conviction of anyone guilty of any of the 2012 arsons committed here.
>
> The foregoing was telecast by City's sole television station once daily for one week. Thereafter, in August 2013, the City Council by resolution repealed its reward offer and caused this resolution to be broadcast once daily for a week over two local radio stations, the local television station having meanwhile ceased operations.
>
> If the city's reward offer was revocable, revocation could be effectively accomplished only
>
> A. by publication in the legal notices of a local newspaper.
> B. in the same manner as made, i.e., by local telecast at least once daily for one week.
> C. in the same manner as made or by a comparable medium and frequency of publicity.
> D. by notice mailed to all residents of the city and all other reasonably identifiable, potential offerees.

Your job here is to choose the minimum that City must do to revoke its offer. The rule on revoking "general offers" is that the offer must be revoked by ***equivalent notice*** to the original offerees—typically via an ad in the same medium as the offer. Here, you have to face the additional obstacle that the original medium, the local TV station, is no longer available. (Note that this makes B an incorrect response—and one you might have chosen if you misread the facts.) Of the remaining three answer choices, D overstates the standard, and A, in a sense, understates it, because a newspaper ad wouldn't reach the same audience. That leaves choice C as "Baby Bear's porridge"—that is, the choice that states the correct legal standard.

f. CAVEAT: Answer choices stating only a snippet of a legal rule, which address a central issue.

Make a special note of one exception to our rule that says an under- or over-inclusive statement of the law cannot be correct. Be particularly careful about the following type of "under-inclusive" legal statement: MBE answer choices don't usually state ***every*** element of the crime or tort in the reasoning when the "call" asks if a particular crime or tort has been committed. Instead, the reasoning will most likely state only one essential piece of the principle; the answer can be correct only if that piece satisfies the central issue in the facts. (Remember our discussion about determining "central issues.") Look at this example from a past MBE:

A customer wanted to purchase a used motor vehicle from a car company. The used car lot of the company, in a remote section away from town, was enclosed by a ten-foot chain link fence. While the customer and a salesman for the company were in the used car lot looking at cars, a security guard locked the gate at 1:30 p.m., because it was Saturday and the lot was supposed to be closed after 1:00 p.m. Saturday until Monday morning. At 1:45 p.m., the customer and the salesman discovered they were locked in.

There was no traffic in the vicinity and no way in which help could be summoned. After two hours, the customer began to panic at the prospect of remaining undiscovered and without food and water until Monday morning. The salesman decided to wait in a car until help should come. The customer tried to climb over the fence and, in doing so, fell and was injured. The customer asserts a claim based on false imprisonment against the car company for damages for his injuries. Will the customer prevail?

A. Yes, because he was confined against his will.
B. Yes, because he was harmed as a result of his confinement.
C. No, unless the security guard was negligent in locking the gate.
D. No, unless the security guard knew that someone was in the lot at the time the guard locked the gate.

Look at choice D. False imprisonment requires: (1) a defendant's act or omission that confines or restraints plaintiff to a bounded area (such that plaintiff believes there's no reasonable means of escape); (2) defendant must have intended to confine or restrain the plaintiff; and (3) causation. Choice D doesn't mention anything about the customer's belief that there was no reasonable means of escape. The only element on which that choice focuses is the security guard's knowledge that someone was in the lot when he locked the gate. In spite of that, D is the correct response. Why? Because there's only one real issue here: the guard's intent. All the other elements are quite plainly satisfied by the facts or inferences drawn from them. Thus, choice D is correct; it focuses on the central issue here, ***even though it's an incomplete statement of a prima facie case of false imprisonment.***

3. An answer choice can be wrong even if it's factually and legally correct, if it's not as precise or effective as another answer choice.

Until now, we've addressed choices that cannot be correct because they include mistakes, either legal or factual. Here is something more subtle: an answer choice that, although correct, is less correct than one of the other choices and thus isn't the best response.

An answer choice can be incorrect simply because it doesn't meet the "call" as effectively as another choice. For instance, suppose that, under a given set of facts, there are two potential defenses available to a defendant; if one of those defenses meets an obstacle posed by the facts more effectively than the other, that will be the correct response. (Remember, we discussed this under "issue spotting.") Here are two rules to apply in determining which is the most "effective" of several potentially correct choices:

a. An answer choice that is easier to prove is more likely to be correct than an answer choice that is difficult to prove.

If you're asked for the plaintiff's best claim, and there are two potential claims, the better claim will generally be the one most easily proven on the facts. If you're asked the defendant's best defense, the same measure will apply: The easier, the better. Here's an example from a past MBE (one which we reviewed earlier):

A salesman and a mechanic planned to hold up a bank. They drove to the bank in the salesman's car. The salesman entered while the mechanic remained as lookout in the car. After a few moments, the mechanic panicked and drove off.

Soon after leaving the scene, the mechanic was stopped by two police officers for speeding. Noting his nervous condition, the police required the mechanic to exit the car, and c asked him if they might search the car. The mechanic agreed. The search turned up heroin concealed under the passenger seat. The heroin belonged to the salesman.

In a prosecution of the salesman for heroin possession, the prosecution's best argument to sustain the validity of the search of the salesman's car would be that

A. the search was reasonable under the circumstances, including the mechanic's nervous condition.
B. the search was incident to a valid arrest.
C. the mechanic had, under the circumstances, sufficient standing and authority to consent to the search.
D. exigent circumstances, including the inherent mobility of the car, justified the search.

You'll remember that we analyzed this question earlier in the "misstating the facts" section. Here we're faced with a more difficult task: choosing from among the three potential answers, A, C, and D (remember that we eliminated B). While it's certainly true that exigent circumstances can provide the basis for a valid search, this would require that the prosecution introduce all sorts of evidence bearing on the reasonableness of the officers' belief that a search was merited. Choice A would also raise issues of reasonableness. If, on the other hand, the prosecutor relies on the mechanic's consent, assuming the mechanic was in a position to offer his consent, the prosecutor's task will be straightforward: Prove that the mechanic consented, that he had the authority to consent, and that's it—the search is valid. Thus, of the three potential answers here, a "consent" search is the easiest to prove, making it the prosecutor's best argument, so choice C is correct.

b. A more precise answer is better than a less precise answer.

What do we mean by "precision?" Think of the question as a bull's-eye with many concentric circles. Precision means that one answer ***covers more of the bull's-eye than any other,*** i.e., ***it either addresses the factual situation in more respects*** than another, or it ***addresses more issues*** in the fact pattern than another. For instance, if you're asked whether a piece of evidence will be admissible, and you have two potential answers—"admissible even though it's hearsay" or "admissible under the 'present sense impression' exception to the hearsay rule"—the latter would be more precise and is more likely to be correct. Or, if there's a ***key legal issue*** in the problem, and one choice deals with that issue more head-on than another, the former is likely to be the best answer. Here's an example from a past MBE.

All lawyers practicing in a state must be members of the State Bar Association, by order of the state supreme court. Several state officials serve on the Bar Association's Board of Bar Governors. The Board of Bar Governors authorizes the payment of dues for two of its staff members to be members of the Cosmopolitan Club, a private dining club licensed to sell alcoholic beverages. The Cosmopolitan Club is frequented by affluent businessmen and professionals and by legislators. It is generally known that the purpose of the membership of the Bar Association staff is to enable them to go where members of the "elite" meet and to lobby for legislation in which the Bar Association is interested. The State Bar Association has numerous committees and subcommittees concerned with family law, real estate law, unauthorized practice, etc., and its recommendations often influence state policy. Some committee meetings are held at the Cosmopolitan Club. The club is known to have rules that restrict membership by race, religion, and sex.

Plaintiffs, husband and wife, who are members of the State Bar Association, petition the Board of Bar Governors to adopt a resolution prohibiting the payment of club dues to and the holding of meetings of the Bar Association or its committees at places that discriminate on the basis of race, religion, or sex. After substantial public discussion, the Board of Bar Governors, by a close vote, fails to pass such a resolution. These events receive extensive coverage in the local newspapers. Plaintiffs bring an action in federal court seeking an injunction against such payments and the holding of meetings in such places as the Cosmopolitan Club.

The strongest argument for plaintiffs is

A. private rights to discriminate and associate freely must defer to a public interest against discrimination on the basis at race, religion, or sex.
B. the failure of the State Bar Association to pass a resolution forbidding discrimination on the basis of race, religion, or sex constitutes a denial of equal protection.

C. the State Bar Association is an agency of the state and its payment of dues to such private clubs promotes discrimination on the basis of race, religion, and sex.
D. the State Bar Association's payment of dues to such private clubs promotes discrimination on the basis of race, religion, and sex.

Here, look at choices C and D. They are very similar, except that choice C has an element that D is missing: It characterizes the State Bar Association as an ***agency of the state***. This argument, if accepted by the court, would establish that there's ***state action*** involved here, and that's an important issue, since it enables plaintiffs to claim discrimination under the Fourteenth Amendment. (The Fourteenth Amendment doesn't bar purely private acts of discrimination.) If there were no choice C, choice D would be a reasonably good answer. But taking into account choice C's greater precision (it covers more of the bull's-eye, by dealing with the state-action issue head-on), C is a better argument than D. (Notice that it's not clear whether the State Bar Association really *is* an agency of the state—but you're asked for the plaintiffs' "best argument," and the best argument would have to be one that addresses the core issue of state action, which only C does.)

c. How to guess intelligently when your reasoning fails you.

No matter how well prepared you are for the MBE, there will be questions you simply can't figure out. ***Don't be lured into unthinking, unsophisticated guessing on those questions!*** Instead, keep in mind the tips outlined below. Remember, if there's one thing the Bar Examiners know how to do, it's how to write good "wrong" answers, and the reason those "wrong" answers are good is because they sound as though they should be correct!

1. Ignore some things you may already know about objective tests.

If you took objective tests in law school, this will be both a benefit ***and*** a detriment on the MBE. Obviously, you'll benefit from knowing how to take objective law exams, but this is a double-edged sword; many of the techniques of "gamesmanship" that may have helped you in law school ***won't*** help you on the MBE. There's a good reason for this: Your law school professors were experts on law, not test-making, and they most likely made mistakes that the Bar Examiners simply don't make. For instance, inexperienced test makers are more likely to make the correct answer be C or D. The Bar Examiners don't do this; they completely randomize the positioning of the correct answer as among A through D. Inexperienced test makers offer answers that are ***inadvertently*** overinclusive or underinclusive. Again, this is a mistake the Bar Examiners won't make. We could go on, but you get the point: Don't waste your time searching for lapses in test construction or reasoning.

2. Don't guess until you've eliminated all the definitely wrong responses.

Even if a question has you stumped, you'll almost certainly be able to eliminate at least one or two responses as definitely wrong. Don't try to guess until you've eliminated those responses. After all, if you can narrow your choice down to two potential answers, you've got a 50-50 chance of picking the best response, as opposed to the 1 in 4 chance you have if you choose at random.

3. Factors that should influence your guess.

Keep in mind that you should apply the following advice only **when your reasoning fails you**. You can undoubtedly think of exceptions to each one of these suggestions. Their only purpose is to state what's most likely to apply in the absence of other facts.

a. Look at the facts, and ask yourself, "So what?"

If you can't pick up what the central issue is from the four responses, go back and look at the fact pattern and see if there's an issue that you may have missed before and seems to predominate. If there is, then it's likely that the correct answer will address that issue.

b. Beware of "seducers."

We'll only touch on this issue here, since it's addressed in significant detail in each of the "Strategies and Tactics" sections at the beginning of each subject. In short, "seducers" exist in every subject. They're those terms that ***seem*** as though they ought to apply to a wide variety of facts, but that actually have no application to the particular fact situation.

For instance, take the "prior identifications" hearsay exception in Evidence. In lay terms, a prior identification would be defined as an identification made by one person of another at any time prior to a specified event. Wouldn't it be easy if that were all the hearsay exception required? In fact, the hearsay exception for prior identifications (actually, it's a hearsay "exclusion") is usually just a siren's song on the MBE, because it's very technical and won't make otherwise excludable evidence admissible in the vast majority of cases.

Another example? The choice "Privileges and Immunities Clause of the Fourteenth Amendment" in Constitutional Law questions. As a practical matter, there are very few laws that violate this clause, but the text of the clause sounds as though it ought to make a whole variety of laws unconstitutional. That's why it's an MBE favorite as a wrong choice. Make sure you pay close attention to these and similar seducers in every subject.

c. Beware of certainties.

As you know by now, there are few "definites" in law. So be careful when an answer choice uses the words "always," "never," "cannot," "must," and the like. If a choice states something as a certainty, and you can think of even one situation where it doesn't ***apply,*** it can't be the best response!

d. Beware of responses that rely on "people" relationships.

As a general rule, the fact that people are related doesn't change the rules of Contract Law or Criminal Law or Tort Law (with the most obvious exception being the fiduciary duty that parents owe to their children). Generally, if an answer choice implies that one's duties toward someone else are somehow different because of a familial relationship, barring other facts the answer is less likely to be correct than the others.

e. Beware of answers that focus only on results.

No one is liable in Torts or Criminal Law solely because of ***the results*** of his or another's acts or omissions. For instance, in Criminal Law, one can only be liable for a criminal act or omission; if those don't exist, the results of one's behavior won't make one guilty. In Negligence, if there's no duty and so no breach of a duty, there can't be liability, regardless of the results of one's actions. Here's an example from a past MBE.

> A thief was in the act of siphoning gasoline from his neighbor's car in the neighbor's garage and without his consent when the gasoline exploded and a fire followed. A rescuer, seeing the fire, grabbed a fire extinguisher from his car and put out the fire, saving the thief's life and the neighbor's car and garage. In doing so, the rescuer was badly burned. If the rescuer asserts a claim against the neighbor for personal injuries, the rescuer will
>
> A. prevail, because he saved the neighbor's property.
> B. prevail, because he acted reasonably in an emergency.
> C. not prevail, because the neighbor was not at fault.
> D. not prevail, because the rescuer knowingly assumed the risk.

Look at choice A. This states only ***the results*** of all the acts described. It doesn't deal with the other essential elements of negligence liability. The ***results*** of the rescuer's acts could be relevant only if there was a statement of how the defendant ***caused*** those results. Thus, as a general rule, a response finding liability only on the basis of results, without regard to the defendant's causation of those results, is unlikely to be correct. (In fact, the correct answer here is C, because it alone deals with the fact that aside from the strict-liability situation—not applicable here—a defendant can be liable only for fault or on a vicarious liability theory, neither of which was present here.)

f. Be wary of answer choices from unrelated subjects.

As we've noted elsewhere, what makes the MBE an excellent objective test is the fact that distractors are likely to resemble correct responses in some important respect. Thus, it stands to reason that a response that addresses a totally unrelated subject is ***less likely*** to be correct. Here's an example from a past MBE.

> A lawyer, an accountant, and a banker are charged in a common law jurisdiction with conspiracy to commit larceny. The state introduced evidence that they agreed to go to an investor's house to take stock certificates from a safe in the investor's bedroom, that they went to the house, and that they were arrested as they entered the investor's bedroom.
>
> The lawyer testified that he thought the stock certificates belonged to the banker, that the investor was improperly keeping them from the banker, and that he, the lawyer, went along to aid in retrieving the banker's property. The accountant testified that he suspected the lawyer and the banker of being thieves and joined up with them in order to catch them. He also testified that

he made an anonymous telephone call to the police alerting them to the crime and that the call caused the police to be waiting for them when they walked into the investor's bedroom.

The banker did not testify. If the jury believes both the lawyer and the accountant, it should find the banker

A. guilty, because there was an agreement and the entry into the bedroom is sufficient for the overt act.
B. guilty, because he intended to steal.
C. not guilty, because a conviction would penalize him for exercising his right not to be a witness.
D. not guilty, because the lawyer and the accountant did not intend to steal.

Look at choice C—it sticks out like a sore thumb. In every other respect, this question is a substantive Criminal Law question, but up pops choice C, stating a (bogus) principle of Constitutional Criminal Procedure. Now, questions of Constitutional Criminal Procedure certainly appear as "Criminal Law" questions—but almost invariably, a question is "about" *either* substantive Criminal Law *or* Constitutional Criminal Procedure, not both. So the mere fact that choice C is from "the other main branch" of the Criminal Law discipline compared with the other three choices makes it less likely to be the correct answer. (In fact, the correct response is D.)

g. If two answers are opposites, one is probably true.

This is a traditional rule of objective tests that holds true on the MBE. If there are two answers that are direct opposites, the test maker is probably testing your knowledge of the correct rule, so one of those two answers will likely be correct.

h. Remember minority rules.

Sometimes, if you're stuck when trying to find a party's best argument, it may help to think of minority rules. After all, if no other response makes sense to you, it could be that the case is taking place in a jurisdiction that recognizes a minority rule, and this makes an otherwise unattractive option the party's best argument. ***This doesn't mean that you should gear your studying to memorizing minority positions, because that is not a sensible use of your study time.*** If, however, you're reduced to guessing and you just happen to remember a rule that you know is followed by a minority of states, it might be worth applying it.

i. Choose the longest response.

If you've narrowed the responses down but simply cannot choose among the remaining answers, choose the longer one; since it probably contains more reasoning, it's more likely to be precise, and thus more likely to be the correct response (barring any clear facts indicating otherwise).

j. Most importantly, don't get bogged down on questions you don't know!

As you practice, learn to apply these guessing techniques quickly. When you're reduced to guessing, the most important thing is put down at least a ***tentative*** answer and move on to questions you're more likely to know. Remember, you're likely to answer about half the MBE questions fairly easily. If you waste time on questions you really don't know and can't reasonably guess, you run the risk of not having time to work on those you're capable of answering. Especially in Real Property and Civil Procedure, you'll find a number of questions that are technical, lengthy, and obviously difficult—so take care not to spend undue time on these.

What you might do is keep a list on a piece of scratch paper of the questions you want to come back to, if you have the time at the end of the session. Of course, as you answer each question, you should mark the responses you definitively eliminated as incorrect responses, so that, if you do have time to re-analyze the question, you won't waste time going over incorrect responses twice.

HOW TO TAKE THE MBE

So much for specifics on how to study and how to analyze questions. Let's focus on more general advice for taking the MBE.

1. How to prep physically for the test.

You've heard a million times that it's important to be sufficiently well-rested before you face an important exam, and that you shouldn't spend the evening before an exam popping stay-awake pills and cramming. That's true.

Watch out, though. You may be tempted to do the opposite, to get twelve hours of sleep. If you're not used to that, it will have just as soporific an effect on you as getting too little sleep! Instead, for a week or so before the exam, try getting up at the hour you'll have to get up on the day of the exam (including travel time, etc., in your wake-up time estimate). That way, you can be sure you'll be alert when you have to be.

As to advice about what to eat, what to wear, what to take to the exam—we're confident that you, as a law school graduate, know perfectly well without being told that you shouldn't wear clothing that cuts off circulation to your extremities or causes difficulty breathing, and that you shouldn't breakfast on Twinkies and Hershey bars when you have to spend the day thinking (not to mention sitting still).

2. When you take the exam itself.

a. Timing.

It's imperative that you stick to a schedule when you take the MBE. With a hundred questions to answer in each of the two, three-hour sessions, you should finish 17 questions every half hour. Whatever you do, don't get behind! Otherwise, you may chew up time on questions you don't know and run out of time for questions you do know. (Remember, the questions are distributed randomly with respect to difficulty, so there are just as likely to be easy questions at the end of the test as at the beginning!)

b. Remember that you can write in the question booklet.

You don't have to leave your question booklet in pristine condition. Take whatever notes help you, highlight whatever you feel needs highlighting, and mark correct and incorrect responses in the margins (given the time constraints). Of course, remember that this ***isn't*** true of the answer sheet—mark only one answer choice for each question on the sheet and make sure that you don't leave any stray marks.

c. Advice on "skipping around."

On some standardized tests, you have enough time to make a general pass through every question and then go back and answer them. You can't do this on the MBE—there just isn't time. The ***worst*** thing you can do is read every fact pattern, answer the questions you know, and go back to the ones you don't. You'll almost certainly find that you won't have time to go back.

However, if you find while practicing that answering a series of longer questions fatigues you, you may need to give your mind a rest and answer a few shorter questions. This is fine, so long as you ***check carefully to make sure you're marking the matching boxes on the answer sheet***. Note that this advice is not inconsistent with the advice in the last paragraph, because here we're saying that, if you ***must*** skip around, just glance at the sheer length of questions without reading them at all.

d. Answer questions in an episodic fashion.

Don't let your reaction to any one question influence how you face ensuing questions. For instance, there will frequently be questions you'll find very easy. If this happens, thank your lucky stars, fill in the answer sheet, and go on. By the same token, if you're stunned by a tough question, make your best guess and then ***start completely fresh*** on the next question—don't go on thinking about a question you had some doubt about. (Although, as we've discussed, you can answer tentatively and make a list of questions to return to, if you have the time.)

e. Maintain your concentration all the way through.

You'll probably find that it's difficult to concentrate in the last hour or so of each session. If you have to, get up and get a drink of water, bite the inside of your cheek, dig your fingernails into your palms—do anything you have to do to stay focused on your work. The questions are randomly organized, so, if you don't concentrate toward the end, you're likely to miss some questions you'd otherwise find simple.

A FINAL WORD OF ADVICE

When it comes time to take the MBE, and you've prepared as much as you can . . . ***relax!*** Tens of thousands of people every year pass their state's bar exam, and they aren't any smarter than you are. By working with this book, you've indicated your determination to succeed. We wish you the best of luck, both on the bar exam and in your legal career.

STRATEGIES AND TACTICS

CIVIL PROCEDURE

OUTLINE OF COVERAGE

The MBE Civil Procedure questions assume the application of: (1) the Federal Rules of Civil Procedure; and (2) the sections of Title 28 of the U.S. Code pertaining to jurisdiction, venue, and transfer.

The following Coverage Outline for the *Civil Procedure* portion of the MBE was adopted by the Bar Examiners for all exams to be given on or after February 2016. This is the most up-to-date outline of coverage released by the Examiners, and your substantive study for *Civil Procedure* should be focused on these topics.

Here's what you need to know:

I. Jurisdiction and venue
   - A. Federal subject matter jurisdiction (federal question, diversity, supplemental, and removal)
   - B. Personal jurisdiction
   - C. Service of process and notice
   - D. Venue, forum non conveniens, and transfer

II. Law applied by federal courts
   - A. State law in federal court
   - B. Federal common law

III. Pretrial procedures
   - A. Preliminary injunctions and temporary restraining orders
   - B. Pleadings and amended and supplemental pleadings
   - C. Rule 11
   - D. Joinder of parties and claims (including class actions)
   - E. Discovery (including e-discovery), disclosure, and sanctions
   - F. Adjudication without a trial
   - G. Pretrial conference and order

IV. Jury trials
   - A. Right to jury trial
   - B. Selection and composition of juries
   - C. Requests for and objections to jury instructions

V. Motions
   - A. Pretrial motions, including motions addressed to face of pleadings, motions to dismiss, and summary judgment motions
   - B. Motions for judgments as a matter of law (directed verdicts and judgments notwithstanding the verdict)
   - C. Posttrial motions, including motions for relief from judgment and for new trial

VI. Verdicts and judgments
   - A. Defaults and dismissals
   - B. Jury verdicts—types and challenges
   - C. Judicial findings and conclusions
   - D. Effect; claim and issue preclusion

VII. Appealability and review
   - A. Availability of interlocutory review
   - B. Final judgment rule
   - C. Scope of review for judge and jury

WHAT TO EXPECT

You'll face 27 Civil Procedure questions on the MBE. Of these, approximately two-thirds of them will be based on categories I, III, and V in the Coverage Outline above, and approximately one-third will be based on the remaining categories II, IV, VI, and VII.

Based on the few MBE sessions that have included Civil Procedure prior to this writing, here are some observations about what the examiners seem to be testing:

1. The questions tend to be far more focused on fine details embedded in the Federal Rules of Civil Procedure than questions you'd be asked on a typical law school *Civ Pro* exam. So you can pick up a lot of relatively easy points by mastering the FRCP's technical minutiae. As you review the "Study Strategies and Substantive Review" below or the sample questions themselves, you'll likely find it worthwhile to also read, as you go along, ***the full text of each Federal Rule sub-section we cite***—you'd be surprised how much useful detail you can pick up just by reading and re-reading the full text of the FRCP.
2. By way of illustrating point (1) above, you'll likely be handsomely rewarded for learning FRCP details like: the allowable means for ***serving process*** in a federal action, or the kinds of claims that can be asserted by or against a ***third-party defendant***, or the rules governing when an ***interlocutory appeal*** can be taken.
3. It follows from (1) and (2) above that, unlike many non-*Civ Pro* areas tested on the MBE, your general ***intuition*** about "what the law ought to be" will be of very little use in answering most questions. You'll be tested on many arbitrarily designed procedural rules, as to which even the world's best legal intuition won't much help you, because ***you just need to "know the rule."***
4. Pay special attention to the situations in which various rights will be ***deemed waived*** if not timely exercised. For instance, it's well worth memorizing the list of defenses (e.g., lack of personal jurisdiction, improper service, improper venue, etc.) that are waived if not asserted in the answer or in a pre-answer motion against the complaint.
5. Similarly, the examiners like to test key provisions of ***Title 28 of the U.S. Code*** relating to things like subject-matter jurisdiction, removal, and venue. As with the FRCP, the examiners tend to test pretty narrow black-letter provisions found in Title 28 (e.g., the bright-line rule that D cannot remove from state to federal court if he is a citizen of the state where the action is pending).
6. Conversely, there is relatively ***little*** premium placed on your handling of the kinds of ***abstract*** jurisprudential issues that professors emphasize in law school. You won't need to master, say, the subtleties of the minimum contacts test, or the intricacies of offensive use of collateral estoppel by strangers to the first action, or the federal/state balancing under *Erie v. Tompkins*. That's not to say that these abstract topics won't be tested—but they'll be tested at a relatively ***superficial*** level. And an hour spent preparing for these advanced conceptual topics is on average likely to pay you smaller dividends than an hour spent on the sort of FRCP minutia that you paid relatively little attention to in law school.

STUDY STRATEGIES AND SUBSTANTIVE REVIEW

We've carefully reviewed the above NCBE Coverage Outline and have tried to match the topics listed in the Outline with the particular substantive rules that seem to be tested most often. So this long section contains a pretty detailed review of those rules—together with examples of how the rules might be tested—organized in the same topic order as the Coverage Outline.

Because *Civil Procedure*'s presence on the MBE is so new (only since February 2015)—and because you may not yet have acquired narrative reviews covering the MBE approach to this subject that are as detailed as for the other six, traditional, MBE subjects—we've gone into much more detail here than in the "Study Strategies" sections for the other subjects. That's also why we've changed the title of this section to indicate that it includes not just "Study Strategies" but also a "Substantive Review."

1. Jurisdiction and venue.

You probably spent a huge amount of time in your law school *Civil Procedure* class on various aspects of jurisdiction. The good news is that this intense study won't be wasted on the MBE: The examiners seem to be using a significant percentage of their *Civ Pro* arsenal on the various sub-topics in this area, including (a) federal subject matter jurisdiction; (b) personal jurisdiction (both state and federal); (c) the mechanics of service of process and notice; and (d) venue. We estimate that these sub-topics will play a major role in between 15 percent and 20 percent of the *Civ Pro* questions.

A. Federal subject matter jurisdiction.

A majority of MBE *Civ Pro* questions seem to be set in ***federal*** court. Whenever the suit takes place in federal court (including when the defendant ***removes*** an action that the plaintiff brought in state court), you should check to be sure that the federal court has ***subject matter jurisdiction*** over the case. Here are some key points to keep in mind when you're assessing whether subject matter jurisdiction is present:

➡ **Diversity or federal question:** There has to be *either* (1) ***diversity of citizenship*** between the parties or (2) a ***federal question*** (which basically requires that the right P is suing on arises under a federal statute, federal regulation, or the U.S. Constitution).

So, for instance, let's imagine that in your question, the sole claim in the question is a tort or contracts claim by a single P against a single D. In that situation, the case cannot be heard in (or removed to) federal court unless P and D are ***"citizens" of different states***. (And the fact that D has raised, or is expected to raise, a *defense* based on, say, a federal statute doesn't create a "federal question"—such a question is deemed to exist only if the federal issue appears as part of P's "well-pleaded complaint," which generally means that P's claim has to be ***"based on" federal law***.)

➡ **"Complete" diversity:** For there to be "diversity," the diversity has to be ***"complete"—no P can be a citizen of the same state as any D.***

- **One claim:** More precisely, there has to be at least ***one "claim"*** as to which there is complete diversity—if such a claim is present, then additional claims might be added by "supplemental jurisdiction," in which case there would not have to be complete diversity as to these additional claims.
- **Typical fact patterns:** The examiners love to give you fact patterns in which the claim is based on state law, and there is either no diversity at all or incomplete diversity. And it may well be the case that neither the "stem" of the question nor any of the choices expressly mentions either "diversity" or "subject-matter jurisdiction" as being lacking. So it's up to you to always check, in any fact pattern involving a federal suit, whether the required subject-matter jurisdiction is present. Here are two examples to help you test your understanding of the requirement of complete diversity and also your understanding of how "supplemental jurisdiction" may repair what would otherwise be a fatal lack of diversity.

Example 1 (just one claim in case, but multiple Ds): P, a pedestrian who is a citizen of State A, brings an auto-negligence suit in State A federal court against two drivers, D1 (a citizen of State A) and D2 (a citizen of State B). Even though P and D2 are diverse, the required "complete diversity" is not present, since P and D1 are *both citizens of State A*. And there's no federal question present either (since P's claim is based on state law). Therefore, the federal court does not have subject matter jurisdiction over the case, and the case must be *dismissed* (even if all 3 litigants consent to have it heard in federal court).

Example 2 (multiple claims in case, with supplemental jurisdiction): P, a pedestrian who is a citizen of State A, is hit by a car driven by D (a citizen of State B) when the car fails to stop at a stop sign, apparently because of non-working brakes. P brings a negligence suit against D in State B federal court for $100,000, contending that D negligently failed to see that the brakes were kept in proper repair. D impleads X (a citizen of State B), a mechanic who worked on the brakes; D asserts that under state tort-law indemnity principles, if D is found liable for the bad brakes, X is required to indemnify D because X did the work negligently. Because impleader claims (brought under FRCP 14) by a Third Party Plaintiff against a Third Party Defendant are within the court's ***supplemental jurisdiction***, the federal court may hear the entire case (including D's claim against X), even though there is no diversity between D and X. (Furthermore, the D-X claim doesn't have to meet the amount in controversy requirement of $75,000 for diversity cases, again because supplemental jurisdiction obviates the need for that claim to meet the requirement.)

➡ **Supplemental jurisdiction:** Be on the lookout for situations in which there is an "anchor" or "main" claim, for which there is either complete diversity or a federal question, and then a second (or third) ***"additional"*** claim which, if viewed on a stand-alone basis, is not supported by either complete diversity or a federal question (or as to which there's diversity but less than $75,000 at stake). When you see such a multi-claim scenario, you MUST consider the possibility that ***supplemental jurisdiction (S.J.)*** applies to the additional claim—if so, the court ***can hear the whole case***, including the additional claim, even though the additional claim could not have been brought as a standalone claim in federal court due to the absence of subject matter jurisdiction. (Example 2 above is an illustration of how this can work.)

So whenever you've got this type of multi-claim scenario—and there wouldn't be subject matter jurisdiction for the additional claim on a standalone basis—you've got to be able to say whether S.J. does or doesn't apply to the additional claim. This means that you have to ***memorize two lists***: the situations in which the S.J. doctrine *applies* to the additional claim, and the ones in which S.J. *doesn't apply* to that additional claim.

- **Where S.J. applies to the additional claim:** Here are the most-likely-to-be-tested situations where S.J. ***applies*** to the extra (non-anchor) claim:
  - o ***Compulsory counterclaims***.

    Example 1: P (citizen of State A) brings a federal-question claim against D (citizen of State A). D asserts a state-law-based compulsory counterclaim (c.c.) against P (i.e., a claim based on the same transaction or occurrence) as the main P-vs.-D claim). The court can hear the c.c., even though there's no diversity between P and D, and even if less than $75,000 is at stake.

  - o ***Additional parties to a compulsory counterclaim***.

    Example 2: Same fact pattern as in Example 1. D can add P2 as a co-defendant to D's c.c. against P, even though P2 and D are non-diverse.

  - o ***Impleader of third-party defendants (TPDs)***, for purposes of claims ***by the third-party plaintiffs (TPPs) against the TPDs***, and claims ***by the TPDs against the TPPs***, but ***not*** claims by the ***original plaintiff*** against the TPDs.

    Example 3: P (citizen of State A) brings a state-law diversity claim against D (citizen of State B). D impleads X (a corporation that's a citizen of both State A and State B) on a state-law indemnity claim that will require X to reimburse D if D is found liable to P. The court can hear a $50,000 claim by D vs. X (even though D and X are not diverse, and the amount in controversy isn't met), and can hear a $50,000 state-law compulsory counterclaim by X vs. D (again, even though they're not diverse), as well as a $50,000 claim by X vs. P (even though *they're* not diverse). But the court *cannot* hear a state-law claim by P vs. X, because S.J. doesn't apply, and P is not diverse with X.

  - o ***Multiple plaintiffs joined under Rule 20***, but for ***amount-in-controversy purposes only.***

    Example 4: P1 (State A citizen) and P2 (State B citizen) join as Rule 20 co-plaintiffs to sue D (State C citizen) on state-law claims. P1's claim is for $100,000, and P2's for $50,000; both arise from the same transaction/occurrence. S.J. applies so that P2 doesn't have to meet the amount-in-controversy requirement. (But S.J. *can't* relieve a ***lack of complete diversity*** in the Rule 20 joinder situation. So if P3, State C citizen, wants to join the suit on a state-law claim arising from that same transaction/occurrence as the main claim, the court cannot hear the case while P3 is present, since the P3/D combo causes a lack of complete diversity that S.J. can't fix.)

- **Where S.J. doesn't apply to the additional claim:** Here are the most-likely-to-be-tested situations where S.J. ***doesn't*** apply:
  - o ***Impleader of third-party defendants***, for purposes of solving lack-of-diversity or lack-of-amount-in-controversy problems in ***claims by the original plaintiff against the third-party defendant(s).***

    Example 5: In Example 3 above, if P makes a state-law claim vs. X (the third-party defendant), S.J. doesn't apply to that claim. So if P and X aren't diverse (or if the claim is not for more than $75,000), the court can't hear that claim.

  - o ***Rule 20 joinder of co-plaintiffs and/or co-defendants***, for purposes of solving a lack of complete diversity.

    Example 6: P1 (citizen of State A) and P2 (citizen of State B) are injured in a single car crash involving cars driven by D1 (citizen of State A) and D2 (citizen of State B). P1 and P2 join as Rule 20 co-plaintiffs to bring state-law diversity claims, with each claiming against D1 and D2, who they join as Rule 20 co-defendants. Neither the P1-vs.-D1 claim nor the P2-vs.-D2 claim may be heard (because each lacks diversity). But the P1-vs.-D2 claim and the P2-vs.-D1 claims may go forward (even if only one of them is for more than $75,000—in the Rule 20 joinder situation S.J. can solve the amount-in-controversy problem, but not the lack-of-complete-diversity problem).

➡ ***"Moment of filing" rule:*** Remember that the time as of which the ***existence of diversity*** is calculated is the ***moment the claim is filed.*** Changes of citizenship post-filing ***can neither create nor destroy diversity*** (as long as the identity of the parties doesn't change).

Example 1: Partnership, a limited partnership, consists of three limited partners, X, Y, and Z, all individuals. At the moment of suit, X is a State A citizen, Y and Z are State B citizens, and the partnership operates solely in State A. Partnership brings a diversity suit against D, an individual who is a State B citizen. (Assume the suit does not say anything about who the individual limited partners in Partnership are or their citizenship; it merely asserts that Partnership is "a citizen of State A.") Three months after filing, Y and Z leave the partnership for reasons having nothing to do with the suit. After the trial is half-way over, D discovers for the first time that there is an issue of whether complete diversity now exists (or, indeed, *ever* existed).

The only moment that counts is the *moment of filing*. Since a partnership is deemed to be a citizen of every state in which any partner is a member, at the moment of filing the fact that Y, Z, and D were all State B citizens meant that there was not complete diversity. The fact that Y and Z later left the partnership (so that if Partnership brought a new suit today against D there *would* be complete diversity) is *irrelevant*. So the court ***must dismiss*** the action (even if neither side wants this result).

Example 2: Same facts, but the converse situation. That is, this time at the moment of filing no partner in Partnership is a citizen of the same state as defendant D. However, one month after filing, Y and Z (State B citizens) join as partners in Partnership, again for reasons having nothing to do with the suit, making Partnership now non-diverse with D (who's a citizen of State B). There *is* diversity (and the suit can continue) since there was complete diversity at the moment of filing. The fact that there wouldn't be diversity if the case was re-filed today is irrelevant.

- **If lineup of parties changes:** But where the ***lineup*** or roster of the actual parties (rather than the citizenship of an existing party) changes post-filing through joinder or dismissal, the "time of filing" rule ***doesn't*** apply.

  Example 3: Suppose P1 (State A) and P2 (State B) jointly sue D (State B), and D moves to dismiss for lack of complete diversity. If P2 *voluntarily dismisses* her claim, the P1 vs. D suit can *continue* (since the diversity analysis is re-done after P2's exit). And even if the statute of limitations as to P1's claim has passed before P2's exit, the "relation back" doctrine of Rule 25(c) will save the suit.

➡ **Citizenship of entities and representatives:** You must memorize the rules for determining the citizenship of ***artificial entities,*** as well as citizenship in cases involving ***representatives***. These are mainly specified in 28 U.S.C. § 1332(c).

- ***Corporations:*** A ***corporation*** is a citizen of *both*: (1) the state where it has its ***"principal place of business"*** (which is generally where it has its ***"headquarters"*** from which the executives direct the corporation's affairs); and (2) the state in which it was ***incorporated***. The corporation is *not* a citizen of the state in which it has the most employees or generates the most revenue. And even if the corporation's shares are owned by just one or a small number of individuals, the state of citizenship of the shareholders is irrelevant.

  Example: P1 (a citizen of State A) and P2 (a citizen of State B) bring a diversity suit against D, a manufacturing corporation. D is incorporated in State C, has a small executive office in the state A from which its CEO directs the company's affairs, and has the bulk of its employees at a manufacturing plant in State D at which nearly all the company's products are made. The required complete diversity does not exist, because D is deemed a citizen of both State A (its headquarters state) and State D (state of incorporation), and P1 is a citizen of State A as well. So the suit cannot go forward.

- ***Partnerships and associations: Partnerships*** (whether "general" or "limited"), ***associations,*** and other artificial entities that are not corporations, are deemed ***citizens of every state in which one of the members is a citizen.***

  Example: P is a limited partnership whose members are: a general partner who is a citizen of State A and four limited partners, citizens of States B, C, D, and E, respectively. P brings a diversity action against D, a corporation incorporated in State F and with principal place of business (i.e., headquarters) in State E. There is no diversity: P is deemed a citizen of States A, B, C, D, and E, so it's not diverse with D, which is a citizen of both States E and F. (But if E left the partnership *before* suit was filed, the suit could go forward.) The state in which P has its headquarters and/or in which most of its partners and employees perform their work for the partnership is *irrelevant* for purposes of determining P's citizenship.

- ***Administrators and other representatives:*** For purposes of a suit by or against an ***estate***, what counts is only the citizenship of the decedent, not the citizenship of the administrator or other representative of the state. Similarly, for a suit by or on behalf of an infant or incompetent, it's the citizenship of the infant or incompetent—not the citizenship of the guardian or other representative—that counts.

➡ **Amount in controversy:** Be on the lookout for three main sub-issues that relate to ***amount in controversy***:

- Amount in controversy ***only matters in diversity cases*** (where it means that the claim has to be for more than $75,000); there's no amount in controversy requirement for federal-question cases.
- The standard is ***"legal certainty"***: unless it can be said that there is a legal certainty that P's claim(s) as pled cannot result in a recovery of more than $75,000, the case cannot be dismissed for failure to meet the threshold. So if, say, P is seeking personal injury damages from a minor car accident, the fact that the trial judge believes it is ***highly unlikely*** that the jury would award more than $75,000 (or the fact that after trial, the jury ***has in fact awarded less*** than $75,000) ***won't*** trigger a dismissal.

- A ***single P*** can ***"aggregate"*** all of her claims against a single D for purposes of satisfying the $75,000 standard. And if one P meets the standard, Supplementary Jurisdiction may well let other parties with claims for less than $75,000 have their claims heard, too. But if ***no P has claim(s) of more than $75,000*** against any D, as a general rule the ***plaintiffs may not aggregate their claims*** to meet the amount.

  Example: Car accident. P1 and P2 (both passengers) join to sue D1 and D2 (drivers of two cars) in diversity. P1 has a claim of $40K vs. D1 and $50K vs. D2; P2 has a claim of $30K vs. D1 and $60K vs. D2. Since there is no instance in which a given plaintiff's claim against a given defendant exceeds $75K, the case does not meet the amount in controversy requirement for a diversity action. Therefore, the rule stated in the last sentence of the above paragraph means that the case may not go forward, even though the two plaintiffs' claims against D2, when added together, total $110K

➡ ***Removal*** from state to federal court is often tested. Here are the key rules:

- **Where removed to:** If a suit is filed in state court, the defendant may generally ***remove it to the federal court for the district in which the state action is pending***, if the case could originally have been brought in federal court.

  Example 1: P (citizen of State A) sues D (citizen of State B) in the state courts of state A, on a negligence claim worth $100,000. D may remove the case to federal court for the district of State A (and if there are multiple federal districts covering State A, D must remove it to the district that encompasses the state court where P filed), since the existence of complete diversity, and a claim for more than $75,000, mean that P could originally have filed the action in that State A federal court.

- **Special rule for diversity case:** Here's the most-often-tested rule about removal: If the only source of federal jurisdiction would be ***diversity***, D cannot remove ***unless no defendant is a citizen of the state in which the original state-court action is pending.*** (This "no removal allowed if any D is a citizen of the state where the action is pending" rule ***does not apply*** if the case raises a ***federal question***.)

  Example 2: Same facts as Example 1 above, except now, P brings her negligence claim in the state courts of State *B* (not State A as above). Since D is a citizen of State B, the state in which the action is pending, *D has no right to remove*. (And if there were two defendants, D1 who is a citizen of State B and D2 who is a citizen of State C, *neither* D could remove, since the requirement that *no* D be a citizen of State B, where the action is pending, is not satisfied.) However, if P's claim raises a federal question and could be heard either in state or federal court, then the fact that D (or one D of several) is a citizen of the state where the state-court action is pending would *not* prevent D from removing.

- **Remand to state court:** If the removal to federal court is not proper because some requirement for removal was not met, the plaintiff may ***request a remand to state court***, and the court will grant the request.

  - **Time limit:** For most defects in the removal process (e.g., the removal purports to be to a federal court that's in a district other than where the state action was filed), P must request the remand ***within 30 days*** after D filed the notice of removal, or the right to remand is waived. But the right to a remand for ***lack of subject matter jurisdiction*** is ***never waived***.

    Example 3: P sues D in State A court on a state-law claim. P is a citizen of State A. P believes that D is a citizen of State B. D removes to federal court for the district of State A. The trial starts.

Midway through trial, the federal judge discovers that D was really, at the moment of removal, a citizen of State A (though D moved to State B later in the case). The judge not only may but *must* remand the suit to State A state court, since (a) a defect in subject-matter jurisdiction is never waived prior to the entry of final judgment; and (b) in removal cases as in cases originally filed in federal court, the existence of diversity is determined solely based on the parties' citizenship as of the moment the case began (though in the case of removal actions there must be diversity both at the moment the state-court suit was filed and at the moment the notice-of-removal was filed).

B. Personal jurisdiction (state and federal actions).

Whether the fact pattern involves a federal-court or state-court suit, be on the lookout for whether the court has proper ***"personal jurisdiction,"*** a/k/a "jurisdiction over the parties." (We'll abbreviate personal jurisdiction as "P.J." to save space.)

➡ **When to Look:** Look for a P.J. issue ***whenever D is being sued in a federal or state court that is not located in D's "home state."*** (If D is an individual, her "home state" is typically where she resides. If D is a corporation, both the state in which it has its headquarters and the state in which it is incorporated will be deemed the "home states" for P.J. purposes.)

➡ **"Specific" vs. "general" jurisdiction:** Note whether the suit involves D's activities ***in the forum state***. If the suit arises in part out of D's in-forum-state activities, the suit is based on ***"specific jurisdiction"***; if not, the suit is based on ***"general jurisdiction."*** Most MBE *Civ Pro* questions seem to involve specific jurisdiction, and ***lesser contacts*** between D and the forum state will suffice in those cases. (In the discussion below, we'll assume that the suit is based on specific jurisdiction unless otherwise noted.)

➡ **Specific-jurisdiction rules:** In the **specific**-jurisdiction case (i.e., P's claim is based in significant part on D's in-forum-state activities), the court can constitutionally exercise P.J. over D if ***two requirements*** are satisfied (with the first being much more likely to be tested on the MBE):

- **Requirement 1 — "minimum contacts":** First, D must have such ***"minimum contacts"*** with the forum state that D should "reasonably anticipate being ***haled into court there***." Usually, this means that D must have ***"purposely availed itself"*** of the ***privilege of doing business*** in the forum state, and ***received that state's benefits and protections.*** And this in turn means that D must in some sense have ***"targeted"*** the forum state as a place from which to derive economic benefit.

  Example 1 (no minimum contacts present): D operates a sit-down restaurant in State A and advertises that restaurant only within a 10-mile radius (all of it in State A). X comes to the restaurant, orders a take-out pasta dish, and drives it 500 miles to the house of X's sister P in State B. P eats the pasta in State B, gets serious food poisoning, and sues D in State B court. Since D never "purposely availed herself" of the opportunity to do business in State B (and should not have "reasonably anticipated being haled into court" in State B), probably D lacks minimum contacts with State B, making it a violation of her federal constitutional 14th Amendment due process rights for the State B court to exercise P.J. over her, even for this claim that relates to in-forum-state harm (i.e., even though the claim invokes specific jurisdiction).

  Example 2 (minimum contacts present): D, a corporation, operates a factory in State A that manufactures packaged pasta. D makes most sales through a website and promotes the website nationally through advertising that includes ads on search engines designed to attract clicks regardless of where in the U.S. the user is located. Twenty percent of D's sales come from State B. P, an individual residing in State B, orders a pasta package from the website and enters a State B ship-to address; D ships the package to that address. P eats the pasta, gets food poisoning, and sues D in State B state court.

  A court would likely find that D "purposely availed itself" of the opportunity to solicit business from State B customers and should therefore have "reasonably anticipated being haled into court" in State B. If the court so finds, the court will hold that D had such minimum contacts with State B that it would not offend D's 14th Amendment due process rights to be required to defend the suit there, at least where the suit relates (as it does here) to a harm that occurred in the forum state.

- **Requirement 2 – "Not offensive to fair play":** Second, even if D *has* minimum contacts with the forum state, it must not be the case that it would be ***"unreasonable and unfair"*** or ***"offensive to fair play"*** to force D to defend in the forum state. But as a practical matter, on the MBE you will rarely see a fact pattern in which this second requirement makes a difference. (The only Supreme Court case where it has arguably made a difference was where D was a non-U.S. company brought in as a third-party impleader defendant, and the original parties had settled by the time the third-party claim against D was ready to go to trial.)

General-jurisdiction rules:

- **General-jurisdiction rules:** In the ***general***-jurisdiction case (i.e., P's claim is ***not*** based in any significant part on D's in-forum-state activities), D's contacts with the forum state must be ***much greater*** than in the specific-jurisdiction situation:
- **Individuals:** Where D is an ***individual***, the forum state may exercise general jurisdiction over D only if D is ***domiciled*** in that forum state.

  Corporations: Where D is a ***corporation***, the forum state may exercise general jurisdiction over D only if D is ***"essentially at home"*** in the forum state. Normally, a corporation will be deemed to be "at home" in the forum state ***only*** if D either:

  - Is ***incorporated*** in the forum state; or
  - Has its ***principal place of business*** in that state.

    Example: D is a corporation incorporated in State A, and with its principal place of business (i.e., its headquarters) in State B. D manufactures a product that it sells and delivers to a customer in France, where the product causes injury to P while P is travelling in France. P is a resident of State C, and sues D in a product liability action in the State C state courts. No matter how much business activity D does in State C (e.g., even if D derives 60 percent of its sales from deliveries made directly to customers located in State C), the State C courts cannot hear the suit. That's because: (1) the suit would have to be based on general jurisdiction (since the suit does not arise out of any conduct by D relating to State C); and (2) State C is neither the state in which D is incorporated (which is State A) nor the state in which D has its principal place of business (which is State B).

➡ **Federal service and P.J.:** Many MBE questions involving P.J. focus on federal suits and on: (1) the mechanics of ***serving process*** on D; and (2) the factors determining whether the federal court can exercise P.J. over D both as a constitutional matter and a matter of FRCP procedures. Key things to consider:

- **Service of process:** The examiners like to test you on whether the ***method used for serving process*** was adequate.

  Federally-authorized methods for serving individual: Read and master FRCP 4(e)(2), which lists the three "federally-authorized" service methods (i.e., the three methods that are approved in the Rule for all federal actions, regardless of what service procedures state law may allow). 4(e)(2) says that service on an ***individual*** can be accomplished by delivering the summons and complaint via ***any*** of the following three methods:

  - Delivering them ***"to the individual personally"*** (i.e., ***hand-delivery*** to D).
  - Leaving them at D's ***"dwelling or usual place of abode*** *with* ***someone of suitable age and discretion who resides there."***
  - Delivering them to "an ***agent*** authorized by appointment or law to receive service of process." (You won't see this method used very often on the MBE for service on an individual who is not operating a business, so you don't need to worry much about who is an "agent authorized by appointment or law.")

- **State-law methods:** Also, keep in mind that under Rule 4(e)(1), apart from the three "federally authorized" methods listed above, any service method may be used if it's authorized by ***state law*** (either the state in which the ***federal action is pending*** or the state in which the service takes place) for use in state-court suits.

  Example: P (a State A citizen) sues D (a State B citizen) in federal court for State A. P purports to make service by sending the summons and complaint by certified mail, return receipt requested, to D's last known address in State B. You have to decide whether this method was adequate. If you're told that neither State A nor State B law permits starting a state-court suit by this certified-mail procedure, the answer is "no," the procedure is not valid (because none of the three "federally authorized" service methods, the ones specifically listed in Rule 4(e)(2) as quoted above, includes service made by certified mail or indeed by any non-hand-delivery method).

  But now, suppose that State B allows any suit brought in that state's courts to be commenced by making certified-mail service, return receipt requested, on any defendant found within the state. The existence of this state-law provision means that the service here is valid. (And that's true even if the action is based solely on a federal question rather than on a state-law claim brought based on diversity.)

- **Federally-authorized methods for serving corporation, partnership, or association:** If D is a ***corporation***, ***partnership,*** or ***association***, there's only one broadly-available service method specifically authorized by the FRCP; Rule 4(h)(a)(B) says that the summons and complaint must be hand-delivered "to ***an officer [or] a managing or general agent"*** of D.

  Example: P wants to serve D, a State B corporation, in a federal suit brought in State A federal court. Putting aside any special State A federal statutes that may allow special service methods (e.g., service that under State A law may be made on a non-State-A corporation by serving the State A Secretary of State pursuant to a State A regulation requiring out-of-state corporations to register with the Secretary before doing business in-state), the only way P can make service is by arranging hand-delivery of the summons and complaint to an officer of D (e.g., the CEO or corporate secretary).

  Note: As with service on individuals, service on a corporation, partnership, or association may also be carried out by any method authorized by the law of either the state where the action is pending or the state where the service on the defendant entity is being made.

- **100-mile bulge for impleader claims:** If the case involves a third-party defendant (TPD), don't forget to check out the possibility that service on the TPD may be facilitated by the ***"100-mile bulge" provision*** of FRCP 4(k)1): The TPD may be served personally anywhere within 100 miles of the court where the action is filed, even if the TPD ***does not have minimum contacts*** with the state or district in which the case is pending.

  Example: P files suit against D, an individual, in a diversity action brought in federal district court for State A. P properly serves D at his home in State A. D wants to assert a third-party claim against an individual, X, under FRCP 14, alleging that if D is liable to P, X is required to indemnify D because of a contractual promise that X made to D. X lives in State B, at a home that is 90 miles from the State A federal courthouse where the main action is pending. X has no contacts whatsoever with State A.

  Because of the Rule 4(k)(1) bulge provision, D can serve the third-party complaint against X by personal service on X at his house in State B, and the State A federal court will thereby have personal jurisdiction over X. That's true even though D would not have been able to bring a standalone indemnity action against X in State A federal court due to X's lack of minimum contacts with State A.

- **Request for waiver of service:** Also, keep in mind that the FRCP authorize (and encourage) the ***"waiver of service"*** method of FRCP 4(d): P can send (by ***first-class mail*** or "other reliable means" like overnight-delivery) a copy of the summons and complaint, together with a request that D sign and return the enclosed "waiver of service" form. If D signs and returns the form within 30 days, P can file the signed waiver as a substitute for service. (But the method is ***voluntary*** on D's part—if D refuses to sign and return the form, P will have to make regular hand-delivered service, but in that situation P can recover from D the costs of making service, giving D a strong incentive to agree to the waiver request.)

2. Substantive law to be applied by federal courts.

A. State law in federal court.

If the plaintiff's claim is based ***solely on diversity*** (i.e., the claim arises from state law rather than from a federal-law source like a federal statute, regulation, or constitutional provision), remember that under ***Erie v. Tompkins***, the federal court ***must apply the substantive law of the state in which the federal court sits.***

➡ **Follow conflict-of-laws rule of forum state:** The examiners especially like to test one semi-tricky concept: In diversity cases, if there are ***multiple states*** each of which has some relation to the controversy, the federal court must identify *which* state's substantive law to apply by ***following the conflict-of-laws principles of the state in which the federal court hearing the action sits.*** (*Rationale:* That's the only way to assure that the same state's underlying substantive law applies regardless of whether the suit is pending in State X state court or State X federal court.)

Example 1: P, a property investor, lives in State A; D, an architect, lives in State B. With each working by phone and email from home, they negotiate a contract under which D is to design an office building that P plans to construct in State C. D delivers what P asserts is a non-conforming set of plans. P brings a diversity suit against D in State A federal court for breach of contract. The laws of States A, B, and C are all subtly different from each other in terms of how to compute damages for breach of a design contract such as this one. It's obvious that the State A federal court must apply "state law" (not "federal common law") in determining how to compute damages. But *which state's* law of damage-computation?

The answer is that the federal court must ask, "If P sued D on this contract in the State A state courts, then under State A's *conflict-of-laws rules*, which state's law of damages would the State A court apply?" If the federal court concludes, say, that under State A conflicts principles State A would apply the damages law of the state where the designed building is to be built (State C), then the federal court must similarly apply the damage-computation rules of State C.

➡ **Statute of limitations rules: *Statutes of limitations***, like conflict-of-laws rules, are deemed "substantive" for *Erie* purposes—so the federal court must ***follow the statute of limitations rule*** that would be applied by the state where the federal court sits if the action had been filed in that state.

Example 2: Same facts as Example 1 above. To figure out whether P's suit against D is time-barred, the federal court sitting in State A must ask, "Which state's statute of limitations rule would a State A court apply if this action were filed there?" If State A would apply State C's statute of limitations rule to this suit, and if the suit would be time-barred under that limitations rule, then the State A federal court may not hear the suit either.

➡ **Other types of rules:** If the state rule in question seems to reflect a ***strong state policy*** interest regarding the parties' conduct, and having the federal court follow that policy would not lead to an important loss of ***procedural uniformity*** across the federal system, then you should treat the state rule as being "substantive" and thus binding on the federal court. Here are some examples of state-law rules that are sufficiently reflective of strong state policy interests that the rule is probably binding on the federal court:

- A state's ***"remittitur"*** and ***"additur"*** rules, by which the trial judge is authorized to grant the party disappointed by a jury verdict the benefit of a conditional grant of a new trial on account of an unreasonably small or large verdict (i.e., new trial to occur unless the non-movant consents to a specified raising or lowering of the verdict), probably reflect strong state's substantive interests, and are thus binding on the federal court.
- A state's ***"notice-of-claim"*** requirements, by which a would-be plaintiff is required to give advance notice to the potential defendant before filing a particular type of suit, are likely to be binding, if there's evidence that the state legislature enacted the requirement in order to encourage settlements, to make cases harder to bring, or to fulfill some other underlying arguably substantive state policy.
- A state's ***"issue preclusion"*** rules—specifying the circumstances under which a factual finding made in one suit triggers "collateral estoppel" on that issue in a second suit—are generally binding on the federal court.

3. Pretrial procedures.

A. Pleadings.

Here are the aspects of pleadings that are most likely to be tested:

➡ **Amendments:** Know the rules for when a pleading may be ***amended***:

- **Of right:** Under Rule 15, a party (call that party "*A*," and the opposing party "*B*") may amend his pleading ***once as a matter of right*** in either of these two situations:
  - o (1) within ***21 days*** of when *A* ***served his original pleading*** (see Rule 15(a)(1)(A)) or,
  - o (2) if *A*'s pleading was one that required a ***responsive pleading*** by *B*, within ***21 days*** of when *B* either (i) ***served that responsive pleading*** or (ii) made a ***motion*** under Rule 12(b), (e), or (f) (with the 21 days starting on whichever of two events mentioned in (i) and (ii) happened *earlier*) (see Rule 15(a)(1)(B)).

    Example: P serves her complaint on D on April 1. Whether or not D has answered, P has until 21 days later (April 22) to amend of right. Now, suppose D makes no motion against the complaint and answers on May 1. P now has until 21 days later (May 22) to amend of right. Now, suppose that instead of answering on May 1, D does nothing until he makes a Rule 12(b), (e), or (f) motion against the complaint on May 5; then, P's time to amend of right will end 21 days after May 5 (i.e., May 26). And May 26 is the deadline regardless of whether (i) D hasn't yet answered by May 26 or (ii) D answers sometime between May 5 and 26 (since the *earlier* of D's answer and D's motion against the complaint triggers P's 21-period in which to amend).

- **Leave of court:** For any amendment after the above "amendment of right" deadlines have passed, P can amend *only* by getting either: (i) ***leave of court***; or (ii) the opposing party's ***consent***.

- **Allegations of fraud or mistake:** If the complaint alleges ***fraud or mistake***, the plaintiff must "***state with particularity the circumstances*** constituting [the] fraud or mistake." Rule 9(b).

- **Rule 11, and sanctions for violating it:** Remember that FRCP 11 establishes (i) what the party submitting a pleading or other document is deemed to represent, and (ii) what sanctions are available for violating the Rule. Here are the most important points about Rule 11:

  - **Signing required:** Every pleading and written motion must be ***signed*** by an attorney of record (or by the client, if the client is acting *pro se*).

  - **Representations:** By signing a pleading or motion, the attorney certifies that to the best of her knowledge and belief, ***"after an inquiry reasonable under the circumstances"***:

    - o The document "is not being presented for ***any improper purpose***, such as to ***harass***, ***cause unnecessary delay,*** or needlessly ***increase the cost*** of litigation";

    - o The ***"claims, defenses, and other legal contentions"*** in the document are "***warranted by existing law*** or by a ***nonfrivolous argument*** for ***extending***, ***modifying***, or reversing existing law or for establishing ***new law***";

    - o The ***"factual contentions"*** in the document either "have ***evidentiary support***" *or* (and this "or" applies only if the particular contention is "specifically so identified" in the document) "***will*** likely have evidentiary support after a reasonable opportunity for ***further investigation*** or ***discovery***"; and

    - o Any "***denials*** of ***factual contentions***" are "***warranted on the evidence*** or, if specifically so identified, are reasonably based on belief or a lack of information."

  - **Sanctions:** The court may award ***sanctions*** for violations of Rule 11. (But a party seeking to impose sanctions on the other must, before moving for sanctions, give the other ***21 days' advance written notice*** of the motion in which the other can ***withdraw*** or ***correct*** the document and thereby avoid sanctions.)

    The sanctions may be ***monetary*** (e.g., payment of the wronged party's attorney's fees resulting from the violation or payment of a fine to the court) or non-monetary. But any sanction must be "limited to what suffices to ***deter repetition*** of the conduct or comparable conduct by others similarly situated."

    - o **Against whom:** Most often, any sanction will be against the ***lawyer***, not the client; for instance, if the court concludes that the claims or defenses are not supported by existing law or by a nonfrivolous argument for extending the law, it is the lawyer, not the client, who must be sanctioned.

      But in some instances the ***client***, too, may be sanctioned. For instance, if the court concludes that the client has ***lied*** to the lawyer about the underlying ***factual circumstances*** (leading the lawyer to prepare a pleading or motion containing "factual contentions [lacking] evidentiary support"), monetary sanctions against the client may be appropriate.

B. Joinder of parties and claims (including class actions).

In the area of ***joinder*** of parties and claims, here are a couple of the points most likely to be tested:

- **Impleader:** The examiners like to test a couple of basics about Rule 14 "impleader," a/k/a "third party practice."

  - **Derivative liability:** If D impleads X (with X being the "third-party defendant" or "TPD"), to be valid, D's claim must be ***"derivative"*** – it must be the case that X will be liable to D only if D is found liable to P.

    Example: P, a pedestrian hurt by a hit-and-run driver, brings a diversity suit against D, claiming that D was the driver of the car that hit P. D purports to implead X, saying "It was a car driven by X, not the one driven by me, that hit P." That's not a valid impleader claim, since X's liability wouldn't be derivative of D's liability to P. Therefore, X is entitled to have the third-party claim against him dismissed.

- **TPD's defenses vs. main P:** As a general rule, the TPD may assert any defense to the underlying P-vs.-D claim that D could assert. That way, if D negligently fails to spot or assert an available defense, the TPD may do so, thus preventing D from being liable to P and consequently preventing TPD from having any derivative liability to P.

- o **Not "personal" defenses:** But TPD may ***not*** assert defenses that are deemed to be ***"personal"*** to D. Thus even if D could assert against P the defense of (i) lack of ***personal jurisdiction***; (ii) improper ***service of process***; or (iii) improper ***venue***, the TPD may not assert these defenses "on behalf of" D. (But the TPD may raise her *"own"* defenses of this type – so, for instance, the TPD may claim that D improperly made service on the TPD, or that the court lacks personal jurisdiction over the TPD because of the TPD's lack of minimum contacts with the state where the main action is pending.)

➡ **Class actions:** If the case involves a class action, the point most likely to be tested is the requirement—applicable to all types of class actions – that there be ***"questions of law or fact common to the class."*** Since 2011 (*Wal-Mart v. Duke*), the Supreme Court has interpreted this requirement to mean that each plaintiff's claim must depend on a ***"common contention,"*** such that that common contention can be resolved in one fell swoop on a ***"class-wide basis."***

- **Different harm suffered by each P:** Therefore, be on the lookout for any class action where each plaintiff's claim will be valid or invalid depending in part on ***the particular type of harm*** suffered by the plaintiff, or on the ***particular mental state*** in which the defendant or its agent had when dealing with the plaintiff – this type of class action probably flunks the "common question of law or fact" requirement. Mass ***employment-discrimination suits*** against large companies are especially likely to flunk this requirement.

  Example: 1,000 female employees of D, a large corporation, join together as a plaintiff class to assert that D violated their rights under a federal statute banning intentional discrimination based on gender. They contend that D violated the statute by giving local managers broad discretion on promotions and that each class member was injured when her particular manager exercised the discretion in a gender-discriminatory way towards that member.

  Since each class member's claim is valid only if her particular manager behaved in an intentionally-discriminatory way, there is no single "common question of law or fact" that can be resolved on a class-wide basis so as to resolve the overall suit. Therefore, the action cannot go forward as a class action. [*Wal-Mart v. Duke* 2011]

C. Discovery.

➡ **Discovery generally:** In the area of ***discovery***, here are a couple of points that are especially likely to pop up:

- **Impeachment-only items:** Normally, a party is entitled to discovery "regarding any nonprivileged matter that is ***relevant to any party's claim or defense*** and proportional to the needs of the case." Rule 26(b)(1). But one significant exception is that a party does not normally have to disclose the identity of a potential witness, or produce a document, where the disclosing party's use of that document or witness would be ***"solely for impeachment."***

- **Interrogatories only to parties:** Interrogatories (written questions requiring written answers) ***may only be addressed to parties***, not non-parties. (Instead, a combination of depositions and subpoenas *duces tecum* must be used to get discovery from non-parties.)

- **Work product immunity:** If a litigant is trying to get discovery of a document that seems to have been prepared by or for another party ***"in anticipation of litigation,"*** you've got to analyze whether ***work product immunity*** prevents the document from being discovered. Most likely scenario: one party gets a witness to write and/or sign a "witness statement," and the other party wants to get discovery of that statement.

  - o **Anticipation of litigation:** The work product immunity, stated in Rule 26(b)(3)(A), says that "Ordinarily, a party may not discover documents . . . that ***are prepared in anticipation of litigation or for trial*** by or for ***another party or its representative*** (including the other party's ***attorney***, consultant, surety, indemnitor, insurer, or ***agent***)." FRCP 26(b)(3)(A). There are two types of immunity: *qualified* and *absolute*.

  - o **Qualified immunity:** Start by assuming that any immunity is just "***qualified*** immunity" (we'll discuss the special case of "absolute" immunity below). The qualifiedly immune materials are presumed to be non-discoverable, but that presumption of immunity may be ***overcome*** if the discovering party shows that she:

    1. "has ***substantial need*** for the materials to prepare [her] case"; *and*
    2. "cannot, without undue hardship, obtain [the materials'] ***substantial equivalent by other means***."

Example 1: P, an African American male, goes to D's restaurant, where (P claims) he is insulted on racial grounds by a waiter. W, a customer sitting at another table, witnesses the encounter; there appear to be no other witnesses not affiliated with either party. P sues D for violating a federal statute barring racial discrimination in places of public accommodation. As part of D's preparation to defend the case, D's lawyer interviews W and induces W to write and sign a statement about the encounter. P's lawyer seeks discovery of a copy of the statement. Since the statement was "prepared in anticipation of litigation or for trial . . . for another party or its representative," the statement may not be discovered unless P can show that: (i) P has "substantial need" for the statement in order to prepare his case and (ii) he "cannot, without undue hardship," obtain the "substantial equivalent" of the statement by "other means."

If P's team has not even *tried* to conduct their own interview with X, the court will deny P's discovery request, on the grounds that P has not borne his burden of proving that his team cannot get the substantial equivalent of the statement by other means. But if the team tries to interview W and W refuses to meet with them, then the court probably will conclude that both of the required showings have now been met, in which case the court will order disclosure.

o **Absolute immunity:** But some materials get ***"absolute"*** immunity from discovery: Rule 26(b)(3)(B) says that if the court orders disclosure of qualifiedly immune materials (i.e., the court finds that the two conditions discussed above have been satisfied), the court "must ***protect against disclosure of the mental impressions, conclusions, opinions, or legal theories*** of a party's attorney or other representative concerning the litigation." In other words, the "mental impressions," "legal theories," etc. of the legal team representing the disclosing party receive ***an immunity that cannot be overcome.***

Example 2: Same facts as Example 1 above. Now, however, D's lawyer, who interviewed W and had W prepare and sign the statement, circles a sentence in the statement and hand-writes her own comment on the margin next to that sentence: "Let's be sure to have W emphasize this point when we call W at trial." Since the hand-written notation is a "mental impression" or "conclusion" by a party's attorney, that notation is absolutely immune from discovery, and any court order that the statement be released to P discovery must provide that the notation be redacted.

4. Jury trials.

A. Right to jury trial.

➡ **Right generally:** Remember that in federal civil trials, the ***Seventh Amendment*** guarantees either party the ***right to a jury trial*** on all claims that would have been deemed ***"legal"*** (rather than equitable) when the Seventh Amendment was adopted in 1789. The right belongs to both the plaintiff and the defendant, so either side may demand it, in which case there will be a jury even if the other side doesn't want one.

➡ **Mechanism and time for demanding:** You're most likely to be tested on ***when and how*** a party must demand a jury trial as to a claim for which the right exists. Review FRCP 38, which gives this information. In brief:

- **Service of demand:** The party that wants the jury trial must serve the other party or parties "with a ***written demand***—which may be included in a ***pleading***—no later than ***14 days after the last pleading*** directed to the issue is served." Rule 38(b)(1).
- **Filing of demand with court:** Then, the demanding party must ***file*** the demand with the court "within a reasonable time" after the demand was served on the other party or parties. See Rule 38(b)(2) and Rule 5(d)(1).
- **Waiver:** If a party doesn't meet the above deadlines, she is deemed to have ***waived*** the jury trial right. Rule 38(d). This waiver is "jurisdictional" – the court does not have discretion to ***excuse*** a late service or filing.

Example: P sues D in a diversity action seeking contract damages. Assume that although P has the right to include a demand for jury trial in the complaint, P does not do so. D then serves an answer (with no counterclaim) on P on May 1. Since the answer is the "last pleading directed to the issue," neither P nor D may serve a demand for jury trial later than May 14 (and the right is deemed waived once that deadline passes). If either P or D serves a demand for jury trial on the other on or before May 14, that party must then file the demand with the court "within a reasonable time" after the demand was served on the adversary.

B. Selection and composition of juries.

➡ **Size of jury:** A federal civil jury must begin with ***between 6 and 12 members***. Rule 48(a). (It is up to the judge, or to the rules of the district, to decide what number between 6 and 12 is to be used in a particular case.) Each of the seated jurors ***must participate*** in the verdict unless ***excused*** by the judge for "good cause." Rule 48(a) and Rule 47(c). In other words, in the federal system there are ***no "alternate" jurors*** (jurors who hear the case but don't deliberate unless a non-alternate juror is excused).

➡ **Unanimity and minimum size at time of verdict:** Unless the parties otherwise stipulate, the verdict must be ***unanimous***. Rule 48(b). Furthermore, unless the parties stipulate, the verdict must be ***returned by a jury of at least six members***. *Id*. (Otherwise, the jury is deemed "hung," and there must be a retrial.)

Example: Assume that P and D make no stipulations about unanimity or about the minimum number of jurors that must join in the verdict. Assume that in the particular case, the judge empanels a seven-member jury, and the case is tried. If the jurors split 6-1 in favor of P (and cannot resolve the dispute), the judge must declare a mistrial. Alternatively, suppose that in the middle of trial, two jurors are dismissed for illness. Even if the remaining jurors agree unanimously (5-0) for P, the judge must, similarly, declare a mistrial unless both P and D agree to accept this five-juror verdict.

➡ **Two types of challenges:** The two types of ***challenges*** to prospective jurors—"for cause" and "peremptory"—are often tested.

➡ **"For cause":** Each side may make an unlimited number of ***"for cause"*** objections to the seating of particular jurors.

- o **Impartial:** On the MBE, you are most likely to see a "for cause" issue based on a party's belief that the prospective juror cannot be relied upon to be ***impartial***.
- o **Financial interest:** If a prospective juror has a ***financial interest*** in one of the parties to the litigation, that interest will almost certainly cause the court to excuse the juror for cause, even though the juror may claim that his financial interest is too small to make a difference.

Example: P brings a product-liability action against D, a huge publicly traded automobile company. X, a prospective juror, owns 10 shares of D's stock, worth $100. The judge will almost certainly grant P's request to have X excused for cause, on the theory that even a juror's very small financial interest in a party raises the appearance of bias.

➡ **Peremptory challenges:** Each party in a federal trial is given ***three "peremptory challenges,"*** i.e., the right to dismiss three jurors without giving a reason. See 28 U.S.C. § 1870 and Rule 47(b). In a case involving ***multiple*** plaintiffs or multiple defendants, the judge has discretion to treat all those on a given side as a single party (but may instead grant each of the multiple parties on a side her own set of three challenges).

- **Not for race or gender reasons:** The most-often tested issue regarding peremptory challenges is that as a constitutional matter, a civil litigant may not exercise her peremptory challenges for the purpose of excluding jurors ***on account of their race or gender.***
  - o **Mechanics:** You might see a question involving the ***mechanics*** by which one party contends that the other is violating the "no race- or gender-based peremptory challenges" principle. The following Example shows how these mechanics work. The Example assumes that it's P, a woman, who is claiming that D, a man charged with gender discrimination in employment, is using his peremptory challenges to eliminate women from the jury.

Example: (1) After D has used peremptory challenges on at least two women (enough to arguably constitute a "pattern" of gender-based strikes), P can object to this pattern. (2) It's then up to D to state a "facially neutral" reason for the strikes (i.e., a reason based on something *other than* the fact that the jurors are women; a facially-neutral, though weak, explanation might be, "It wasn't because Juror X was a woman that I challenged her; it's that I didn't like the way she refused to look me in the eye"). (3) The burden then *shifts* to P to demonstrate that D's asserted reason is "pretextual," i.e., not the real reason (and that the real reason is indeed D's intent to make gender-based strikes). P's objection will be sustained if and only if P can make this showing of pretext by a preponderance of the evidence.

5. Motions.

A. Pretrial motions.

➡ **Summary judgment:** In the area of pretrial motions, you're most likely to be tested on motions for ***summary judgment***. Before trial has begun (but in most cases after discovery is completed), the way to resolve the case without trial is via a Rule 56 motion for summary judgment ("S.J."). Key testable points about S.J.:

- **"No genuine dispute":** The movant must show that there is ***"no genuine dispute as to any material fact"*** *and* that the movant is "entitled to judgment as a matter of law." These two aspects, taken together, essentially mean that the movant has to demonstrate that one of two Scenarios applies:
  - **Scenario 1:** that both sides ***agree as to all material facts***, and given those undisputed facts, as a matter of law (after giving the non-movant all reasonable inferences) no jury could properly find for the non-movant; *or*
  - **Scenario 2:** that although the parties disagree about the existence of at least one material fact, the non-movant has not been able to show that she possesses ***admissible evidence*** sufficient to allow the jury to properly find for her as to that fact, so that no jury could as a matter of law properly render a verdict for her.

    Example 1 (Scenario 2 applies): Diversity suit based on product liability, in which P claims to have been injured on Jan. 1, 2012, when a toaster made by D suddenly exploded while not even plugged in. P files suit on April 1, 2014. Both parties agree that the relevant statute of limitations for such product-defect suits is two years from the later of (i) the date of the injury, or (ii) the "defect discovery date," i.e., the date on which plaintiff first either actually learned, or *should* reasonably have learned, of the alleged product defect. D raises the statute of limitations as a defense. P claims that the "defect discovery date" did not come until May 1, 2012. Assume that after discovery, and in response to D's motion for S.J., P cannot point to any admissible evidence in her possession that would be sufficient for a jury to find that the defect discovery date occurred later than Jan. 1, 2012 (the explosion date).

    Even though P is claiming that there is a genuine issue of material fact about when the defect discovery date occurred, the fact that P cannot point to any admissible evidence available for trial that would justify a reasonable jury in finding a discovery date later than the explosion date means that the court should conclude that Possibility 2 above applies. Therefore, the court should grant S.J. to D and enter final judgment without the need for a trial.

  - **Negligence and credibility as issues:** Where the claim turns on certain types of issues, those issues will rarely be shown by the moving papers to satisfy either of the above two Scenarios, and the case will therefore generally be unsuitable for S.J. For instance, if the claim's validity depends on whether a party ***behaved negligently***, or on whether a party acted with a ***certain state of mind***, the issue of negligence or state or mind will rarely be sufficiently resolved prior to trial as to permit S.J.

    Example 2 (neither Scenario applies): P claims that D, her employer, fired her on account of her race. She quotes at length in the complaint certain racially-biased statements that, she says, D made to her in front of others before the firing. D in his answer claims that P is a pathological liar who has invented the alleged statements. D moves for S.J. on the grounds (and let's assume these grounds to be factually accurate) that during the course of discovery, P has not pointed to any evidence other than her own prospective trial testimony to demonstrate that D really made the remarks. Through P's lawyer's negligence, P fails to submit any opposition papers containing an affidavit or other evidence demonstrating that D really made the remarks.

    Despite P's lack of admissible evidence furnished in opposition to D's motion, the court should deny D's motion. That's because D's *own answer* suggests that P's credibility as a witness will be critical to a determination of whether D made the claimed remarks. (And as a purely legal matter, it's clear that if P's anticipated trial testimony were believed, a jury could properly find for her on the claim.) Since P's credibility is genuinely in issue on this material point, the case is not suitable for S.J., despite the absence of opposition papers from P.

  - **Pleadings don't count:** The non-movant's ***pleadings***, by themselves, are not admissible evidence, and thus not enough to establish the existence of a genuine issue of fact. For the non-movant to avoid S.J., she will normally have to point to the likely existence of ***admissible evidence*** (e.g., affidavits reciting expected trial testimony, or deposition testimony, or documents produced during discovery) that, if believed, would be enough to create a genuine issue.

    Example 3 (neither Scenario applies): Same basic facts as Example 2 above except that the race-based statements that P's complaint says D made purportedly took place outside of P's presence. Also, suppose that: (i) D's answer does not claim that P is a pathological liar and merely claims that D never made the statements attributed to him in the complaint; and (ii) when D deposes P, P admits that her only evidence of D's having made the remarks in question is that some fellow employee whose identity P can no longer remember told

P that D had made the statements (i.e., hearsay that would be inadmissible if recounted by P on the stand at trial). As in Example 1, suppose that P does not submit any papers (e.g., any affidavits, documents, or deposition testimony) in opposition to the motion. In this situation, the allegations of P's complaint about what D said are not admissible and are thus not sufficient to create a genuine issue about whether D acted with racial bias. Since P has not pointed to any *admissible* evidence that she could plausibly use at trial either to show that D made the statements or to otherwise demonstrate that D acted with bias, the judge *should* grant S.J. to D.

- o **Lack of opposing papers not fatal:** The fact that the non-movant has not submitted papers in opposition to the S.J. motion does not itself necessarily entitle the movant to S.J. As long as there is *anything* in the record—including statements in the movant's own papers—that establishes the existence of a genuine issue of material fact, the court should deny S.J. In other words, there is no such thing as "summary judgment ***by default***."

  Example 4: Example 2 above illustrates this principle. Recall that there, P did not submit opposition papers. But since D's own complaint and motion papers disclosed that the resolution of P's claim would turn on whether P's trial testimony about what D said (and/or D's testimony on the same issue) is found credible, the judge will deny S.J. to D even though D's motion was not opposed by any offer of admissible evidence from P.

B. Motions for judgments as a matter of law.

➡ **Motion for Judgment as a Matter of Law (JML) generally:** After one side has fully presented their case at trial, the other side may move for "Judgment as a Matter of Law" ("JML"), as authorized by Rule 50(a). Although the JML motion comes later (at least half-way through the trial) than a motion for summary judgment as described above, a similar test governs whether the court should grant it: The court should grant the movant's motion if and only if "the court finds that a reasonable jury ***would not have a legally sufficient evidentiary basis*** to ***find for the [non-moving] party*** on that issue." Rule 50(a)(1).

- **How granted:** The court grants the motion by taking two steps:
  - o Resolving the ***"issue"*** against the non-moving party; and
  - o Granting the judgment as a matter of law against the non-moving party as to any ***claim or defense*** "that, under the controlling law, can be maintained or defeated only with a ***favorable finding on that issue***." Rule 50(a)(1)(A) and (B).

  Example 5: Go back to Example 2 above, where P is claiming that D's firing of her was motivated by racial bias. Assume that the trial judge denies D's summary judgment motion, and P puts on her entire case. Let's also assume that during P's case, P is unable to get into evidence any proof that would justify a jury in finding that, more probably than not, D fired P for racially-biased reasons. (For instance, assume that P's testimony about what others told P about statements made by D is excluded as hearsay). Once P has rested, D will be entitled to move for JML. The court could then: (1) resolve the "mental state" issue by concluding that no jury could reasonably find that P has carried her burden of proving that D acted with racial bias when he fired her; and (2) order judgment as a matter of law against P on the claim, since under the relevant substantive employment law P cannot prevail on her claim without a finding of racial bias. The court would then order that judgment be immediately entered against P, without the court's even making D put on his case or submitting the case to the jury.

- **When moved for:** The JML motion may be made ***only "before the case is submitted to the jury."*** Rule 50(a)(2). In the more-common situation where it's the *defendant* who is the movant, the motion can be made either (i) after P's case but before D has put on his case or (ii) after both parties have put on their case. But either way, ***once the judge submits the case to the jury, no initial JML motion may then be made.***

➡ **Renewing the motion after verdict ("JNOV"):** You may also be tested on a type of "post-verdict" motion by the loser of the jury verdict, a motion that was traditionally called a motion for ***"JNOV"*** (or "judgment notwithstanding the verdict"). In federal practice, this post-verdict motion by the verdict-loser is now referred to as just another type of JML motion. Here's how the post-verdict variety of JML motion works:

- **After "provisional denial":** Assume that before the case goes to the jury, one side moves for JML, and the judge denies the motion. Under Rule 50(b), the judge "is considered to have submitted the action to the jury ***subject to the court's later deciding the legal questions*** raised by the motion." (In other words, the denial is treated as non-final, and subject to being reversed if the jury finds against the movant.)

- **"Renewed motion" post-verdict:** After the judge denies the JML motion, she submits the case to the jury. If the jury finds in favor of the movant, then the motion becomes moot. But if the jury finds *against* the movant, the movant may, if he acts ***within 28 days after the jury is discharged***, file a ***"renewed motion"*** for JML. The court may then do any of several things: (i) grant the motion (i.e., belatedly reverse the denial of the JML, and issue judgment for the movant despite the verdict in favor of the non-movant); (ii) order a new trial; or (iii) enter judgment on the jury's verdict.
  - **Biggest trap to avoid:** The biggest trap – and the one most likely to be tested – turns on the requirement that the JML ***motion must have initially been made before the case was submitted to the jury.*** If the movant misses that chance, he does not get another chance to move for JML after the jury finds against him.

    Example: P sues D for firing her based on her race. P puts on her case, D puts on his defense, and neither party makes any motion before the judge submits the case to the jury. The jury then finds for P. Now, D moves for JML, on the theory that P never put on sufficient proof (required for her type of discrimination claim) that D acted with racially-discriminatory intent. Even if the judge agrees with D—i.e., believes that no reasonable jury could have found that P carried her burden of proving racial bias—the judge must deny the motion, because D did not initially make the motion *before the case went to the jury*.

C. Motion for relief from judgment.

Keep in mind that even after a final judgment has been entered, the losing party may be able to get ***"relief"*** from the judgment. Such relief is governed by FRCP 60.

➡ **Grounds:** Rule 60(b) lists a number of grounds on which the court may grant the losing party relief from the adverse judgment or court order. Here are some of the more important ones:

1. ***Mistake***;
2. "Excusable ***neglect***";
3. ***Newly-discovered evidence*** (but only if the evidence could not, even with reasonable diligence, have been discovered in time for the losing party to move for a new trial, a motion that under Rule 59(b) must be made no later than 28 days after the entry of judgment);
4. The fact that the judgment is ***void*** (e.g., made without the court's having ***personal jurisdiction*** over the loser);
5. "***Any other reason*** that justifies relief."

➡ **Time limits:** Check to be sure that any Rule 60 motion for relief is made within the ***allowable time***. No matter what the grounds, the motion must be made ***"within a reasonable time."*** And for items (1), (2), and (3) in the list above (mistake, excusable neglect, and newly-discovered evidence) there is an ***absolute deadline*** of ***one year*** after the judgment or order was entered.

Example: P sues D in a diversity action. P wins at trial, and the judge enters a final judgment against D on July 1, 2016. D later discovers, based on an anonymous letter D receives on August 1, 2017, that P's "proof" at trial was based on documents that were forged by P. Even if it's clear that D could not have discovered the forgery any earlier no matter how diligent he had been, it's too late for D to get the judgment set aside or a new trial ordered—once the one-year anniversary of the entry of the judgment passed (something that happened on July 1, 2017), any motion by D to have the judgment set aside as obtained by fraud became time-barred.

➡ **Judgment entered without personal jurisdiction:** The relief-from-judgment scenario you're most likely to encounter is one in which the judgment was entered against D by default, and D is able to establish that the rendering court ***never had personal jurisdiction over him.*** Not only is D entitled to have the judgment set aside under Rule 60 as "void," but the one-year-after-judgment time limit does not apply to this "void judgment" scenario (though D must still make the motion "within a reasonable time" after becoming aware of the relevant facts).

Example: P brings a diversity action against D in State A federal court based on a car accident that occurred in State B, when a car owned by D and driven by X hit P, a pedestrian. Because State A service-of-process procedures allow service in state-court actions to be made by certified mail to the defendant's last-known out-of-state home address for any tort against a State A resident, P uses this state-law method (as allowed by Rule 4(e)(1)) to serve D. D has never even set foot in State A, and has never sought to do business in the state or otherwise engaged in any activities associated with the state. D does not receive the certified letter containing the summons (it is sent to a now-obsolete address and never forwarded to him). D therefore does not answer the complaint, and eventually P obtains a default judgment against him for $100,000, which is entered by the State A federal court on

Sept. 1, 2016. On Nov. 1, 2018, D happens to discover the judgment's existence when he applies for a mortgage, and a credit check by the bank discloses the judgment's existence. On Nov. 2, D makes a motion in State A federal court to have the judgment set aside as void for having been entered by a court that did not have personal jurisdiction over him (since he had absolutely no contacts, let alone "minimum contacts," with State A).

The State A federal court can and should *set aside the judgment* as void on the personal-jurisdiction ground asserted by D. A judgment entered by a court that does not have personal jurisdiction over the defendant is indeed void. Since D has sought relief under Rule 60 "within a reasonable time" of the earliest date on which he learned or reasonably could have learned of the judgment, his motion is timely. (But that's only because his claim for relief is that the judgment was *void*—had D's basis for relief been, say, fraud, mistake, excusable neglect, or newly-discovered evidence, his motion would have become time-barred on Sept. 1, 2017, the first anniversary of the entry of the default judgment.)

6. Verdicts and judgments.

A. Defaults and dismissals.

➡ **Default judgments:** You may see a question about the mechanism for obtaining a ***default judgment*** against the defendant. Issuance of default judgments is governed by Rule 55. Key points:

- **Entry by clerk:** If (and only if) P's claim is "for a ***sum certain*** or a sum that can be made certain by computation," the ***clerk*** may enter the default judgment based on an affidavit by P showing the amount due.

  Example: P sues D on a promissory note for the $100,000 principal balance. (The suit does not seek any interest, because interest was up-to-date at the moment of suit.) D never answers the complaint or appears. P submits an affidavit stating that the principal balance as shown in the note is $100,000, and that no part of the principal having been repaid, the entire $100,000 is now due. Since the suit is for a "sum certain" (no inferences or complex computations need to be made to determine how much is due), the clerk may enter a default judgment against D for the $100,000. No review by a judge is needed. Rule 55(b)(1).

- **Entry by judge:** But if the plaintiff's claim is ***not*** for "a sum certain" (and also not for a sum that can be *made* certain by computation), then ***only the judge***, not the clerk, may enter a default judgment on the claim. Rule 55(b)(2). If the judge feels that an ***evidentiary hearing*** is needed to compute the amount (e.g., it's a situation in which the proper amount is not apparent from the complaint), the judge is authorized to hold such a hearing. *Id*. If D appeared in the case before defaulting, D is entitled to 7 days ***advance written notice*** before any such hearing.

  Example: P sues D in diversity for breach of a contract under which D was to supply widgets to P for P to resell to various customers. The suit claims that D failed to deliver any widgets, and that D's breach has caused P not to make $200,000 in business profits that, P says, P would have made had D timely delivered conforming goods. D never appears and never answers. P, in support of a motion to have a default judgment for $200,000 entered against D, submits an affidavit asserting that, based on P's personal knowledge, P would have made $200,000 in profits from the deal, and that no other supplier of comparable goods was available.

  Since the $200,000 in claimed damages is not a "sum certain" (nor a sum that can be made certain by simple computation that isn't dependent on debatable assumptions), only the judge, not the court clerk, may enter the default judgment. If, as seems likely, the court concludes that some sort of evidentiary hearing is required in order to be sure that P is not overestimating the amount or certainty of the lost profits, the judge may order that such a hearing occur. The hearing might require P to give live testimony about the lost profits and/or to submit backup documentation showing the reasonableness of P's estimate that he would have made $200,000. Since D never appeared in the action either personally or by a lawyer, D is not entitled to advance written notice of the hearing.

➡ **Voluntary dismissals:** P may ***voluntarily dismiss*** the action, by filing a notice of dismissal before D has served either an answer or a motion for summary judgment.

- **2-dismissal rule:** The first voluntary dismissal is ***"without prejudice"*** (i.e., P ***can re-file*** or can file a different claim based on the same underlying facts). But under the ***"2-dismissal" rule***, a second voluntary dismissal is ***with prejudice***—so after 2 voluntary dismissals, P can no longer sue on the same claim or one arising out of the same circumstances. Rule 41(a)(1)(B).

  o **Multiple court systems:** Also, the 2-dismissal rule operates not only where both dismissals were in federal court, but also where the first was in state court in the second one was in federal court. (But not vice versa—so if Suit 1 is in federal court, P dismisses; Suit 2 is in state court, P dismisses; P is not prevented from suing on the same claim in federal court.)

B. Judicial findings.

➡ **Judicial findings generally:** If a federal case is tried as a ***"bench trial"*** (i.e., by the judge without a jury), the most important thing to remember is that the judge must make ***separate findings of fact*** (i.e., must express the factual findings separately from the court's "conclusions of law.") The judge may state the factual findings and conclusions of law ***orally*** (so they can be captured by the court reporter), or may instead put them in a written opinion or memorandum of law. Rule 52(a)(1).

C. Claim preclusion and issue preclusion.

In the area of "former adjudication," both ***"claim preclusion"*** (a/k/a "res judicata" or "merger" and "bar") and ***"issue preclusion"*** (a/k/a "collateral estoppel") are likely to be tested. These topics are too complex and technical to cover in detail now, but here are the key points to remember:

➡ **Same rules for state and federal suits:** Unlike many *Civ Pro* topics tested on the MBE, the rules for claim preclusion and issue preclusion apply pretty much ***the same way*** whether the actions are in ***state*** court or ***federal*** court. So whenever you see a fact pattern in which there are two or more successive suits and at least one of the litigants is present in each suit, you need to consider whether claim and/or issue preclusion may apply—and that's true whether both suits are brought in state court, both in federal court, or there's a federal/state split.

➡ **Distinguish claim from issue preclusion:** When you see a sequence of two or more suits, start by trying to figure out whether it's claim preclusion, issue preclusion, or both that might apply. Tactically, it's probably best to resolve the existence of ***claim preclusion first***.

➡ **Claim preclusion:** "Claim preclusion" is the doctrine that says that when P sues D in Suit 1 and then in Suite 2, the result in Suit 1 will prevent a new Suit 2 ***on any matter deemed to have been part of the "same claim"*** as was disposed of in Suit 1. Since the definition of a "claim" is relatively broad (and can thus include more than the particular relief P sought vs. D in Suit 1), claim preclusion can bind P much more extensively than issue preclusion.

- **How claim preclusion works ("merger" and "bar"):** Remember that claim preclusion works via the twin doctrines of "merger" and "bar."

  - **"Merger":** If P *wins* Suit 1 (i.e., gets a favorable judgment against D), ***"merger"*** prevents P from bringing Suit 2 on the "same claim" against D.

  - **"Bar":** If P *loses* Suit 1, ***"bar"*** prevents P from bringing Suit 2 on the "same claim" against D.

  - **"Claim" defined:** The guts of merger and bar turn on how ***"claim"*** is defined. P's "claim" in Suit 1 is deemed to include all rights of P to get any form of relief from D with respect to the ***transaction, or series of connected transactions***, that gave rise to P's Suit 1 complaint.

  - **Property damage and personal injury:** For instance, if P and D are involved in a ***single "accident"*** (e.g., car crash, plane crash, failure of a manufactured product), then P's claim vs. D in Suit 1 is deemed to include all relief that P either *actually* sough, or ***"might have sought"*** (taking into account procedural rules on joinder of claims), in Suit 1. This means that if in Suit 1 P seeks from D only, say, compensation for ***property damage*** suffered in an accident, Suit 1 will "use up" P's ability to obtain compensation for ***personal injuries*** or ***lost business profits*** caused by that same accident.

    Example: P, a business operator, buys a business machine made by D. The machine explodes, causing P to suffer (a) property damage (e.g., to nearby equipment and inventory); (b) physical injury to P's person; and (c) lost profits from the fact that P's business is shut down for 2 months. (Assume that under applicable joinder law, P could bring a single suit against D for all 3 types of loss; that would be an accurate assumption if the suit was a federal diversity action, since Rule 18 would permit P to join all claims he has against D in one suit, whether or not the claims all arose out of a single transaction or occurrence.) For unknown tactical reasons (or sheer neglect), in Suit 1 P decides to sue D for just damages falling into category (b) (his own physical injuries).

    Assume that Suit 1 proceeds to a verdict. Whether P wins or loses Suit 1, P *can no longer bring Suit 2* against D for any damages from the explosion. Thus P has "used up" not only his right to sue from the category (b) physical injuries actually litigated in Suit 1, but also the right to sue for either category (a) damages (property damage) or category (c) (lost profits). As a matter of nomenclature, if P *wins* Suit 1, P's property-damage and lost-profits claims are said to be "merged into" the Suit 1 judgment in P's favor. If P *loses* Suit 1, his property-damage and lost-profits claims are said to be "barred" by the Suit 1 judgment against P. Therefore, P made a bad error when he declined to bring in a single suit all of the claims he had against D arising out of this single explosion.

- **Stranger to Suit 1:** Normally, claim preclusion applies only where ***all litigants are the same*** in Suit 1 and Suit 2. Putting aside the special case of "privies" (see below), this general rule means that if you see that P has sued only *D1* in Suit 1, and has then sued *D2* in Suit 2 on a claim arising out of the same transaction as involved in Suit 1, you ***don't have to worry*** about the possibility that claim preclusion will affect P's ability to recover from D2 in Suit 2.

  Example 1: When cars driven by D1 and D2 collide, they both spin out of control and both hit a car driven by P. In Suit 1, P sues D1 (only) in State A state court, claiming that D1's negligent driving was the "but for" cause of P's injuries. P is awarded $50,000. Then, in Suit 2, P sues D2 (only) in that same State A court, claiming that D2's negligent driving was also a "but for" cause of P's injuries. D2 will not be able to use claim preclusion to prevent P's suit against D2 from going forward; since D2 was a stranger to Suit 1, P's claim against D2 is not "merged into" the Suit 1 judgment in favor of P. And that's true even though both claims by P arise out of the same underlying transaction (the three-way collision) and even though State A's joinder rules would have permitted P to sue both D1 and D2 in the same suit.

  - **Privies:** But in a few situations, two parties will be deemed to be so related to each other that they will be treated as ***"privies,"*** such that a judgment for or against one will cause a suit by or against the other to fall within the claim preclusion rules. In other words, if *A* and *B* are privies, and only *A* is a party to Suit 1, if *B* is a party to Suit 2, *B* will not be deemed to be a "stranger" to Suit 1, and will be eligible to get both the benefit and burden of claim preclusion in Suit 2.
  - **Vicarious liability:** The most likely-to-be-tested situation involving privies is the situation in which *A* is ***vicariously liable*** for the conduct of *B*; a suit by or against *A* will trigger claim preclusion to the benefit or burden of *B*, and vice versa. So, for instance, be on the lookout for claim preclusion when Suit 1 is a tort suit against *A*, and Suit 2 is against *B* (*A*'s ***employer***) for the same tortious conduct, based on a *respondeat superior* (vicarious liability) theory.

    Example: P, a pedestrian, is injured when she is hit by a truck owned by D1 and driven by D2, who is working as D1's employee at the time of the accident. P sues D2 (only) in Suit 1, for having driven negligently, and seeks $50,000 in damages for her medical expenses. The jury finds in favor of P and awards her $40,000, though P is unable to collect from D2, who is indigent. P now, in Suit 2, sues D1 for $10,000 representing the wages she lost when she was injured (a category of damages that does not overlap with those P sought from D2); P's theory is that D1 is vicariously liable for any negligence committed by D2 under *respondeat superior*.

    P's claim against D1 is "merged into" her claim against D2; therefore, she cannot recover for the lost profits. That's so because D1 and D2 are "privies" (since any liability on D1's part is based solely on D1's vicarious liability for D2's tortious conduct as employee), so that D1 will be treated as if he had been a party to Suit 1. Therefore, just as P's claim for lost profits would be forfeited if Suit 2 were against *D2* (i.e., the lost-profits claim would be deemed "merged into" the medical-expenses claim), so that lost-profits claim is forfeited as against *D1*. (But P could still seek to enforce the $40,000 medical-expenses judgment against D1—it's only the never-litigated lost-profits claim which, because it arose out of the same transaction as the medical-expenses claim, should have been litigated in the suit against D2, and is therefore forfeited by P for purposes of the suit against D1.)

➡ **Issue preclusion:** Once you've figured out that claim preclusion does not apply to your multiple-suit scenario, then analyze whether ***"issue preclusion"*** (a/k/a ***"collateral estoppel"***) applies.

- **Three requirements for issue to be covered:** Issue preclusion potentially applies in several contexts: to ***findings of "fact,"*** to ***conclusions of law***, and to conclusion about whether and how the ***law applies to the facts***. However, an "issue" will qualify for issue preclusion only if the resolution of the issue in Suit 1 satisfies ***all three*** of the following conditions:

  1. The issue must have been ***actually litigated*** in Suit 1;
  2. The issue must have been ***actually determined*** (decided) in Suit 1; and
  3. The determination of the issue must have been ***"essential to the judgment"*** in Suit 1.

Example ("essential to judgment" requirement not satisfied): P owns a particular patent for use in perfume dispensers. In 2014, D sells a perfume dispenser, the "Atomizer," that P contends violates P's patent. In 2015, in Suit 1, P sues D in federal court for patent infringement. D defends on 2 grounds: (1) that P's patent is invalid; and (2) that even if the patent were valid, the Atomizer doesn't infringe that patent. The judge (sitting without a jury), finds for D, saying in her opinion, "First, I find that P's patent is invalid. But second, I find that even if the patent were valid, the Atomizer doesn't infringe on the patent." In 2016, D starts to sell a new dispenser, the "Nebulizer." Later that year, in Suit 2, P sues D again, claiming that the Nebulizer violates the same patent.

D would of course like to invoke issue preclusion (collateral estoppel) to prevent P from claiming, in Suit 2, that the patent is valid, since the judge so held in Suit 1. But D won't be entitled to such a ruling. That's because the judgment in Suit 1 would have been exactly the same (D wins) whether the judge there found that the patent was valid or that it was *in*valid; in other words, the finding as to the patent's validity does not meet the requirement of having been "essential to the [first] judgment." And that's true even though the other two requirements for collateral estoppel—that the patent's validity was "actually litigated" and was "actually determined" in the prior suit – were satisfied.

- **Use by stranger to Suit 1:** If you're given an issue involving issue preclusion, there's a good chance that the fact pattern will require you to figure out whether a litigant in Suit 2 who was ***not a party*** (or even a privy to a party) in Suit 1 may use issue preclusion against her Suit 2 adversary as to an issue on which the adversary lost in Suit 1. There is a complex body of law—too complex to summarize here—on whether such a "stranger to Suit 1" may receive the benefits of collateral estoppel in Suit 2. But here's a good ***rule of thumb***:

  Unless the facts are such that you can perceive a ***clear unfairness*** in allowing the stranger to use c.e. against the Suit 1 party who lost on that issue, apply the "default rule" that the stranger ***may use*** c.e. (assuming that the issue is such that the Suit 1 winner on that issue would be permitted to use c.e. if both parties were the same in Suit 2 as in Suit 1).

  Example of rule of thumb: P1 and P2, both pedestrians walking alongside each other, are struck by a car driven by D. In 2015, in Suit 1, P1 sues D in state court for negligence, for P1's personal injuries. After a full trial, the jury finds for P1 and awards damages in the full amount sought by P1. (Assume that under the substantive law that applied to the case, such a verdict and judgment in P1's favor would be proper only if the jury concluded that D drove negligently.) In 2016, in Suit 2, P2 sues D in state court, also on a negligence theory, for P2's personal injuries. Assume that it's clear that in Suit 1, the issue of whether D drove negligently at the time of the accident was actually litigated, actually decided by the jury, and necessary to the judgment in that suit (so that if there were a second suit between P1 and D, it's clear that P1 would be entitled to use issue preclusion on the issue of negligence). The question, of course, is whether P2 (who was not a party to Suit 1, and was not a "privy" to P1, who *was* a party) should be allowed to benefit from issue preclusion as to negligence.

  On these facts, there is no particular reason to view it as unfair to D to apply collateral estoppel against him. (In other words, there's no obvious unfairness in denying D a chance to "re-litigate" the issue of whether she was driving negligently at the time of the accident.) Therefore, the "default" or "rule of thumb" solution – that P2 *may* use collateral estoppel – would apply, and the judge will instruct the jury that it must find that D drove negligently.

7. Appealability and review.

A. Availability of interlocutory review.

➡ **Interlocutory appeals generally:** As a general rule, in the federal system a party may take an appeal only where there has been a "final judgment" in the case. (For more about when a judgment is deemed "final," see B. below.) But there are scenarios in which an ***"interlocutory"*** appeal – i.e., an appeal when there has not yet been a final judgment in the case – is allowed. Here are the two situations you are most likely to encounter on the MBE in which an interlocutory appeal is allowed:

- **Injunctions:** First, an interlocutory appeal is allowed from most orders dealing with injunctions, whether the requested injunctive relief is granted or denied. (*Rationale:* Injunctions normally involve emergency situations that ***threaten immediate harm*** to the person seeking the injunction, so requiring litigants to wait until all non-injunction aspects of the case have been finally resolved risks making any post-final-judgment appeal too late to be of any use.) Therefore, under 28 U.S.C. § 1292(a)(1), an immediate appeal is permitted from orders:

  - ***granting***, continuing, or modifying ab injunction;
  - ***refusing to grant*** an injunction (or dissolving an already-issued injunction); or
  - ***refusing to dissolve or modify*** an already-issued injunction.

  This right of immediate appealability applies both to orders involving ***preliminary*** injunctions (i.e., injunctions that prevent a litigant from taking an action until the conclusion of a trial on the merits) and to those involving ***permanent*** injunctions.

Example: P owns a patent on a particular type of windshield-wiper blade. P brings a federal suit against D, an auto manufacturer, claiming that D's existing car models have been infringing this patent for years. P also seeks a preliminary injunction that would prevent D from putting the allegedly-infringing wipers on the new car models D will soon be introducing. Whether the district court grants or denies the requested injunction, the disappointed party (D, if the injunction is granted, and P, if the injunction is denied) may take an immediate appeal of the grant or denial—that is, the user does not have to wait until the district court enters a final judgment on the issue of whether D's past models were infringing, whether P's patent is valid, etc.

- **The "collateral order" doctrine:** Second, an immediate appeal is allowed in situations covered by the so-called ***"collateral order"*** doctrine. Strictly speaking, appeals allowed under this doctrine are not "interlocutory"—rather, the idea is that some orders are "offshoots" on the main litigation, but for practical reasons we allow an immediate appeal from that collateral order even though no final judgment has been rendered in the rest of the case.
  - o **Requirements:** For an order to be immediately appealable under the collateral order doctrine, the appellant has to show that:
    1. The court has made its ***final decision*** as to a ***particular matter*** on which immediate appeal is sought (even though there has been no final decision or judgment as to the rest of the case);
    2. The matter is ***separate from*** (i.e., "collateral to") the merits of the underlying claim;
    3. The matter is ***too important*** to be ***denied appellate review entirely***; and
    4. Deferring appeal until entry of a final judgment in the whole case would prevent the eventual review from being ***"effective"*** under the circumstances.
  - o **Grants and denials of immunity:** You're most likely to see a scenario calling for use of the collateral order doctrine where the defendant asserts a claim of ***immunity*** (and the claim is that D is not only immune from liability but immune from even having to ***stand trial***). If the claim of immunity is granted, there is no need for the collateral order doctrine, since an appealable final judgment ending the action will be entered anyway. But if the court denies the claim of immunity, that denial order is generally treated as the type of collateral order from which an immediate appeal is allowed—otherwise, D will have to stand trial, negating a major purpose of the immunity.

    Most commonly, you'll see the immunity issue where a government official asserts a claim of ***"governmental immunity,"*** and attempts to make an immediate appeal when the court rules that the immunity doesn't apply.

    Example: P is arrested by D, a police officer, but the arrest is eventually ruled invalid. P brings a federal suit against D for civil damages based on a federal statute allowing suit against one who violates another's constitutional rights "under color of law." D asserts that under the federal case law, she is entitled to qualified immunity for the arrest here; if the immunity applies, both parties agree that D would not have to stand trial, and the case will be dismissed on summary judgment. The court rules that under the particular circumstances here, D is not eligible for the qualified immunity. D may take an immediate appeal of this ruling, even though no final judgment has been rendered in the case.

B. Final judgment rule.

➡ **The rule generally:** Unless the case fits within one of the special "interlocutory appeal allowed" scenarios above, no appeal may be taken except from a *"final decision"* by the district court. This principle is known as the "final judgment rule."

- **Multi-claim or multi-party scenarios:** Usually it will be obvious from the fact pattern that the order or decision is or isn't final. But there is one special situation that can be confusing: that's the situation in which the case involves ***multiple parties and/or multiple claims***, and fewer than all of the claim/party combinations have been finally determined. Appealability in this type of situation is governed by FRCP 54(b), which provides more-or-less as follows:
  - o **"Default rule":** The "default rule" is that any order or decision by the court that adjudicates fewer than all of the claims by and against all of the parties ***is not deemed final.*** So if the judge disposes of fewer than all the claims as to fewer than all the parties, and makes no special determination about appealability, no part of the case may be appealed yet.
  - o **Judge's power to specify otherwise:** However, Rule 54(b) gives the trial court discretion to ***"direct entry of a final judgment"*** on fewer than all of the claims and/or parties in the case, so long as the court "***expressly determines*** that there is ***no reason for delay***." If the

court goes through this two-step process, then that partial judgment (i.e., the final judgment as to that particular combination of claims and/or parties) is ***immediately appealable*** even though the rest of the case remains pending before the trial court.

> *Example:* P joins two doctors who treated her, D1 and D2, as co-defendants in a federal diversity suit, making a separate malpractice claim against each. After discovery, D1 and D2 make separate motions for summary judgment. The trial judge grants summary judgment in favor of D1, but denies summary judgment as to the claim against D2. If the judge's order(s) and decision(s) are silent about appealability, the above "default rule" applies, so that as long as the P-vs.-D2 remains unresolved, P cannot appeal the grant of summary judgment in favor of D1, and D2 cannot appeal the denial of summary judgment as to the claim against him.
>
> But now, suppose that the trial judge concludes that there is no good reason to prevent P from taking an immediate appeal of the grant of summary judgment in favor of D1 while the claim against D2 awaits trial. If the judge not only directs the entry of "final judgment" in favor of D1, but "expressly determines" (e.g., in a written decision) that there is no reason to make P wait to appeal this final judgment, P may take an immediate appeal as to that judgment.

C. Scope of review on appeal.

➡ **Various standards of review:** If your fact pattern involves a procedurally proper appeal, you may be asked to specify what ***standard of review*** the appeals court should employ. For some types of alleged errors, the appeals court gives greater deference to the trial judge's ruling than for other types. Assuming that the case is a federal suit, here are some of the possible standards of review and the types of issues as to which that standard would be used:

- **The "de novo" standard for pure questions of law:** If the issue is an issue of ***law*** (including an issue of how to apply the law to particular facts), the appellate court will conduct a ***"de novo review."*** That is, the appeals court will analyze the issue from scratch, ***without giving any deference to the trial court's analysis.***

  > *Example:* In a medical malpractice case based on diversity, the trial judge grants D's motion for summary judgment after discovery; the judge so rules after concluding that P has failed to show, through affidavits, deposition transcripts, or documents, evidence that would be sufficient to allow a reasonable jury to find that D was negligent in treating P. P appeals the grant of summary judgment.
  >
  > The Court of Appeals will conduct a "de novo" review of all evidentiary items that the trial judge had before her when she granted the summary judgment and of the trial judge's reasoning regarding the legal sufficiency of that evidence. Because the availability of summary judgment is essentially a question of law—to be decided "on the papers," after making all reasonable inferences in favor of the non-movant—the appeals court is in as good a position to analyze that question as the trial court was, so there is no need for the appeals court to give meaningful deference to the trial court's analysis.

- **The "clearly erroneous" standard for judicial findings of fact:** If the case is tried by a judge ***sitting without a jury***, recall that FRCP 52(a) requires the judge to "find the facts specially." Then, Rule 52(a)(6) sets the standard that the appeals court is to use when reviewing these findings of fact: "Findings of fact, whether based on oral or other evidence (e.g., documentary evidence), must not be set aside ***unless clearly erroneous***, and the reviewing court must give due regard to the trial court's ***opportunity to judge the witnesses' credibility***."

  > *Example:* After a bench trial on P's diversity claim against D for medical malpractice, the trial judge makes various factual findings, including that D's treatment of P's condition conformed to reasonable medical standards. Based on these findings, the judge renders a verdict in favor of D. P appeals, asserting that the trial court's finding of no negligence is against the clear weight of the evidence.
  >
  > The appeals court will not reverse this no-negligence finding unless the court is convinced that the finding is "clearly erroneous." So even if the appeals judges believe that they would probably have decided the case differently had they tried the case, that fact will not be enough to cause them to reverse. As the concept is often put, the reviewing court will not reverse unless, after it reviews the entirety of the evidence, the court "is left with the definite and firm conclusion that a mistake has been committed."

- **The "abuse of discretion" standard for decisions entrusted to the trial court's discretion:** Certain decisions are committed to the trial court's ***"discretion."*** The appeals court will not reverse such discretionary decisions unless the court believes that the trial court has ***"abused"*** its discretion. Of the three standards of review that we're examining here, this "abuse of discretion" is ***the least favorable to the appellant***, and the one that gives the greatest deference to the trial court. Only if the reviewing court believes that the decision was essentially ***irrational*** will the court find an abuse of discretion. The abuse-of-discretion standard is generally used, for instance, for reviewing the trial court's decisions on whether to ***admit evidence***, in those situations in which the relevant rule of evidence puts the admissibility issue within the trial court's discretion.

> *Example:* In a federal case tried before a jury, W, a key witness testifying on behalf of D, gives testimony favorable to D's position. P's lawyer seeks to impeach W's credibility by asking W on cross, "Isn't it true that 10 years ago, you pled guilty to filing a false tax return?" (This is in fact true.) Assume that under the relevant Federal Rule of Evidence provision, the trial judge has discretion to exclude this type of impeachment evidence if the judge believes that the probative value of the evidence is substantially outweighed by the likelihood that it will cause unfair prejudice. The trial judge sustains D's lawyer's objection on this ground, so that P is unable to impeach W by use of the conviction. P loses, and claims on appeal that the evidentiary ruling was error. Since the relevant rule of evidence placed the decision on admissibility within the trial judge's discretion, the appeals court will review the ruling under the abuse-of-discretion standard. So unless the appeals court believes that the decision was irrational (a very unlikely conclusion, given the age of the evidence and its limited probative value here), the court will not find error.

- **The "harmless error" doctrine:** There's one more legal concept governing appeals you should be aware of; it's not a "standard of review," but rather a means of assessing the seriousness of any error(s) found by the appeals court. That concept is the ***"harmless error doctrine."*** Under this doctrine, even if the appellate court decides that a particular trial court ruling or set of rulings was incorrect, that court will not reverse (i.e., order a new trial or a judgment for the appellant) if the court believes that the error was ***unlikely to have changed the outcome of the trial***.

QUESTIONS
CIVIL PROCEDURE

QUESTIONS

CIVIL PROCEDURE

Question 1

A pedestrian was injured in State A when a taxicab hit her while she was crossing the street. The pedestrian, who is a citizen of State B, sued the cab-driver (a citizen of State A) for negligence in State A court. The pedestrian's lawyer then suggested that the pedestrian, as a State B citizen, might do better with a suit in federal rather than state court. Therefore, before the cab-driver filed an answer, the pedestrian voluntarily dismissed her state-court suit (as state law allowed), and filed a new suit in diversity in State A federal court against the cab-driver, alleging the same facts and theory of negligence as in the earliest state-court suit. The pedestrian then discovered that the cab-driver was judgment-proof and that the cab was owned by a small corporation, Cab Corp; the cab-driver was a minority shareholder of Cab Corp. and the cab-driver's wife owned the remaining majority interest. Therefore, acting before the cab-driver answered the federal suit, the pedestrian filed a notice with the federal court voluntarily dismissing that suit; the notice did not attempt to specify what effect the dismissal would have on future suits. Two weeks later, the pedestrian filed a new diversity action, still in State A federal court, against the cab-driver and Cab Corp., alleging that the cab-driver had negligently caused the accident and that Cab Corp., as owner of the cab, was vicariously liable for that negligence under State A tort principles. Prior to answering, both defendants have now moved to have the complaint dismissed on the grounds that the two prior dismissals compel this result. Should the court grant the dismissal motion?

(A) No, because the cab-driver had not answered or moved against either of the two prior complaints before they were dismissed.

(B) No, because the first dismissal was in state rather than federal court.

(C) No, because the third suit involves different parties than the first two suits.

(D) Yes, because the pedestrian previously voluntarily dismissed the same claim twice, causing the second dismissal to be with prejudice.

Question 2

A driver was badly injured when her car ran off the road for unknown reasons and hit a tree, and the car's airbags did not inflate. The driver sued the manufacturer in a federal diversity action for product liability, alleging that there was a defect in the airbags' inflating mechanism. At the jury trial, the plaintiff's lawyer offered testimony by two other consumers that the airbags in their cars, which were the same model and manufacturer as the driver's car, also failed to trigger during collisions. The manufacturer's lawyer objected to the evidence, arguing (without factual contradiction from the plaintiff) that the speed and other circumstances in the two witnesses' collisions had not been shown to be substantially similar to those of the present case, creating a large risk that these witnesses' testimony would mislead the jury and be unfairly prejudicial to the defense. The trial judge allowed the two witnesses to testify, and the jury returned a verdict in favor of the plaintiff. The manufacturer appealed; one of its arguments on appeal was that the two witnesses' testimony about their airbags' failure should have been excluded as irrelevant, misleading, and highly prejudicial.

What standard will the appeals court use in evaluating this argument?

(A) An "abuse of discretion" standard.

(B) A "clearly erroneous" standard, applied while giving due regard to the trial court's opportunity to judge the proposed witnesses' credibility.

(C) A "de novo" standard, giving no special deference to the trial court's decision to admit the evidence.

(D) A "harmless error" standard, requiring reversal unless the reviewing court believes that the evidence ruling was not only erroneous but probably changed the trial's outcome.

Question 3

Plaintiff, a State A citizen, worked in a plant in State A operated by Defendant, a company that manufactures radioactive materials used exclusively by the federal government. Defendant is incorporated in State B, but conducts all of its day-to-day operations (including all manufacturing, shipping, accounting, and sales-generation activities) at the State A plant. Defendant's corporate officers all work from a small office in State C, from which they direct, control, and coordinate the company's activities. Plaintiff was injured by radiation burns from radioactive materials he was handling at the State A plant, due to a fellow employee's negligent removal of a warning sign on the materials. Plaintiff sued Defendant for negligence in a State A state court (located in State A's capital city of Cap City) for $100,000. The complaint alleged that under *respondeat superior,* Defendant was liable to Plaintiff for his personal injuries caused by the fellow employee's negligence. Defendant timely removed the action to the federal district court located in Cap City. Defendant then filed an answer in the federal court denying liability, citing (correctly) a federal statute that gives any defense contractor an affirmative defense to any federal-law-based or state-law-based negligence claim by an employee if the claim is premised on the *respondeat superior* doctrine.

Now, in the State A federal court, Plaintiff opposes the removal and moves to have the case transferred back to the State A state court where it was originally filed. Should the federal court grant Plaintiff's transfer motion?

(A) Yes, because the fact that Defendant conducts its day-to-day operations in, and maintains its inventory in, State A causes it to be a citizen of that state, nullifying Defendant's right of removal.

(B) No, because Defendant is a citizen solely of States B and C and Plaintiff is a citizen of State A, thereby creating complete diversity and satisfying all requirements for Defendant to have a right to remove to the State A federal court.

(C) Yes, because Plaintiff is a citizen of State A and Defendant is a citizen of both State A and State C, preventing the required complete diversity from existing and nullifying Defendant's right of removal.

(D) No, because the case presents a federal question, thereby entitling Defendant to remove whether or not it is a citizen of State A, in whose state courts the action was originally filed.

Question 4

A doctor, a citizen of State A, went to shop at a factory outlet for computers located in that state. The outlet was operated by a corporation that makes computers and sells them throughout the U.S. While at the outlet, the doctor fell down the stairs in a poorly-lit stairwell, hit his head, and died instantly. The doctor died intestate, leaving only one relative and heir, his son, who is a citizen of State B. The son procured from the State B courts an order appointing him as the doctor's personal representative for purposes of bringing any wrongful-death action on behalf of the doctor's estate. The son then commenced a wrongful death action for negligence in the State B courts for $1 million against the corporation; the complaint listed the plaintiff as being the son suing "as personal representative of" the estate of the doctor and stated that the son was a citizen of State B. The corporation then removed the suit to the federal district court located in State B, and in its removal petition asserted that there was diversity of citizenship. The corporation's headquarters are located in a 2,000 square foot office in State A, from which all 3 officers of the corporation supervise the corporation's activities. Three-quarters of the corporation's employees work in a 200,000 square-foot plant located in State C, at which all of the computers made and sold by the corporation are manufactured. The corporation is incorporated in State D, where it has no employees or operations. All required pleadings were served several months ago, and the son has not opposed the removal.

You are the clerk for the federal judge sitting in State B who has been assigned the suit. The judge asks you for advice about how she should resolve any issue that may exist relating to the court's subject-matter jurisdiction over the case. You should tell her that her court

(A) has jurisdiction and may hear the case, because the son is a citizen of State B and the corporation is a citizen of States C and D only, thereby creating complete diversity.

(B) has jurisdiction and may hear the case, because the son is a citizen of State B and the corporation is a citizen of State D only, thereby creating complete diversity.

(C) does not have jurisdiction and may not hear the case, because the doctor was a citizen of State A at his death and the corporation is a citizen of States A and D, thereby preventing complete diversity from existing.

(D) may hear the case whether or not complete diversity exists, because the son has by now waived any objection based on lack of subject-matter jurisdiction.

Question 5

Plaintiff is a State A corporation that rents stage equipment for use in theatrical performances. Defendant is a small theater group that entered into a rental agreement with Plaintiff. Defendant is incorporated in State A and its main theater is in that state. Defendant's latest show was a box office failure. Defendant has been unable to pay Plaintiff the annual rental fee, and Plaintiff wanted to compel payment by means of a federal-court suit. Therefore, Plaintiff assigned its interest in the rental agreement for "one dollar" to Lawyer, an individual who lives and works in nearby State B. By separate agreement, Lawyer agreed that if he litigated or settled the assigned claim, he would pay Plaintiff two-thirds of any recovery he received, "solely as a bonus." Under State A law, an assignment is legal "when made for valid consideration, even if only for a nominal amount." After the assignment, Lawyer sued Defendant in diversity in federal district court for the District of State A, alleging breach of the rental agreement.

Defendant has moved to dismiss the action for lack of subject-matter jurisdiction. Assuming the amount-in-controversy is satisfied, the district court should

(A) grant the motion because diversity jurisdiction is not available if any defendant is a citizen of the state in which the federal court sits.

(B) deny the motion, because Lawyer and Defendant are citizens of different states, and the assignment was legal under state law.

(C) grant the motion, because the assignment was collusively made for the purpose of creating diversity of citizenship.

(D) deny the motion, because Defendant and Lawyer are citizens of different states, and Lawyer has a sufficiently large economic stake in the outcome to motivate him to vigorously litigate the suit.

Question 6

A consumer brought a diversity suit against a baker in State A federal district court, alleging that the baker made a defectively dangerous croissant that contained glass fragments that injured the consumer. The complaint asserted that the baker made the croissant at his sole proprietorship in State B, sold the croissant to a State B wholesaler, who sold it to a restaurant in State A, where the consumer bought it, ate it, badly cut his mouth, and had to be hospitalized for nearly a week. The suit sought $100,000 in damages.

The baker appeared in the action via his lawyer and filed an answer consisting solely of a general denial. The baker did not attend the trial and relied on his lawyer to conduct the trial without calling witnesses and relying solely on the lawyer's cross-examination of the consumer's witnesses. The trial evidence showed that the baker had never travelled to State A, sold all items he baked solely to wholesalers located in State B, and did no advertising outside of State B. On June 1, the jury awarded $55,000 to the consumer for various categories of damages. The baker made a post-trial motion to set aside the verdict on various grounds, including lack of jurisdiction; the motion was denied by the judge on July 1. On July 15, the judge had the court clerk file a judgment against the baker for $55,000, and notice of the entry of judgment was sent to the baker's lawyer. On Sept. 20, the baker via his lawyer filed a notice of appeal with the clerk of the district court. The notice of appeal correctly listed the parties and the judgment being appealed from, and the parties then timely submitted briefs to the federal Court of Appeals for the circuit encompassing State A. The baker based his appeal on two errors: that the district court had lacked subject-matter jurisdiction due to the award of less than $75,000, and that the court lacked personal jurisdiction over him because he did not have minimum contacts with State A.

How will the Court of Appeals likely rule in the appeal?

(A) The court will dismiss the appeal because it lacks jurisdiction, whether or not the district court had subject matter and personal jurisdiction over the action.

(B) The court will reverse the judgment, because the district court lacked personal jurisdiction over the baker.

(C) The court will reverse the judgment, because the district court lacked subject matter jurisdiction over the action.

(D) The court will affirm the judgment, because the baker waived both of the jurisdiction-related defenses at the district-court level.

Question 7

Company is a for-profit corporation that at the time of the relevant transactions was incorporated in and headquartered in State A. Company hired Partnership, a two-partner general partnership of the state where it was organized, to redesign its computer system so as to improve security. Partnership's two members were and are citizens of State B and State C respectively. After the contract work was done, the system was hacked by unknown persons, causing Company to sue Partnership for breach of contract in federal district court for State A. The suit sought damages in excess of $75,000. Partnership did not initially challenge subject-matter jurisdiction. During discovery, and after the time to make threshold objections had passed, Partnership learned that Company had reincorporated in State B during the course of the lawsuit.

Partnership now moves to dismiss the action for lack of subject-matter jurisdiction. How should the court resolve the motion?

(A) The court should deny the motion because it was made too late.

(B) The court should grant the motion, dismiss the action, and sanction Company for having withheld information pertinent to jurisdiction.

(C) The court should deny the motion because the court has subject-matter jurisdiction.

(D) The court should remand the matter to State A state court to be tried there.

Question 8

An animal-rights protester joined others in carrying a picket sign on the front steps of a U.S. Army facility in which, the protesters claimed, the Army was conducting experiments that abused monkeys. A military police officer employed by the Army arrested the protester for trespassing and forcibly handcuffed him. The protester brought a federal civil suit against the officer for violation of a federal statute making a person civilly liable for violating another person's constitutional rights under color of federal or state law (in this case, for violating the protester's Fourth Amendment rights). After discovery and before trial, the officer made two motions: (1) a motion for summary judgment on the grounds that his behavior was objectively reasonable and was therefore not a substantive violation of the protester's constitutional rights; and (2) a motion to dismiss the claim based on the judge-made doctrine of qualified immunity, under which a government official has civil immunity from trial if he reasonably though incorrectly believes that his conduct is lawful. The district court denied both motions on the grounds that it could not be said as a matter of law that the protester would not be able to establish the officer's civil liability at trial. The judge then ordered a trial. The officer immediately appealed the rulings denying each of his motions. The protester now argues in the Court of Appeals that neither ruling is properly appealable until after the case has been tried. How should the Court of Appeals rule as to the timeliness of the appeals of the two rulings?

(A) Neither the summary judgment ruling nor the immunity ruling is properly appealable now.

(B) Both of the rulings are properly appealable now.

(C) The immunity ruling is appealable now, but the summary judgment ruling is not.

(D) The summary judgment ruling is appealable now, but the immunity ruling is not.

Question 9

A teacher who was suffering from abdominal pain agreed to be operated on by a surgeon who practiced in State A. Immediately after the operation, the teacher developed a pelvic infection, which she suspected was the result of negligence by the surgeon during the operation. The teacher then consulted a tort lawyer, who urged that the teacher retain her to bring a federal diversity action in State A federal district court against the surgeon for medical malpractice.

The lawyer prepared a complaint that in its first count alleged malpractice. Without consulting the teacher, the lawyer added a second count alleging that the surgeon, in his advertising to the public, had made various false advertising claims (e.g., that he graduated from State A University Medical School), and that these false claims constituted a "pattern of racketeering activity" in violation of a State A anti-racketeering criminal statute. The teacher read the draft complaint, understood merely that it was a suit for "medical malpractice," did not know what was meant by "pattern of racketeering activity," and authorized the lawyer to file the complaint. The lawyer signed the complaint and brought the action. During discovery, it became clear that (1) the lawyer's only reason for believing the surgeon had made false advertising claims was hearsay passed on to the lawyer by a colleague (and the lawyer did not check with the Medical School, which would immediately have confirmed that the surgeon really *did* graduate from the School); (2) the claims of false advertising were in fact themselves all false; and (3) the lawyer had previously made virtually the same racketeering allegations in a state-court malpractice suit against the same surgeon on behalf of a different client, which allegations had been dismissed on summary judgment as being both legally and factually completely without merit. Defense counsel therefore drafted a motion reciting the above facts about the racketeering count and seeking as a Rule 11 sanction an award against both the teacher and her lawyer of the attorney's fees actually spent by the surgeon in defending against the count. Defense counsel followed proper procedures for filing and serving the motion.

Assume that the federal court has now concluded that the motion's allegation that there was no factual or legal basis for the racketeering count was correct. The court, in response to the defense motion for attorney's fees as a sanction under Rule 11

(A) may order that the surgeon be reimbursed for the defense attorney's fees, with the teacher to be vicariously liable for the reimbursement if the teacher's lawyer does not pay.

(B) may order that the teacher reimburse the surgeon for the defense attorney's fees, because the teacher should have known that she did not have actual knowledge about whether there was evidentiary support for the racketeering charge.

(C) may not order the teacher's lawyer to reimburse the surgeon for the defense attorney's fees, because Rule 11 sanctions, if monetary, must take the form of fines paid to the court.

(D) may order that the teacher's lawyer reimburse the surgeon for the defense attorney's fees even if the lawyer honestly believed the racketeering count was supported by evidence, if the court finds that the lawyer failed to make reasonable inquiries into whether there was factual support for the count.

Question 10

A broker, who was African American, worked for a brokerage company. The broker applied to be promoted to supervisor, but the company's sole owner awarded the promotion to a white male who worked in the same office. The broker quit and then sued the company in federal court for violating a federal statute prohibiting intentional racial discrimination in employment. The complaint quoted several detailed conversations that the broker claimed to have overheard in the office, in which the owner said he would never promote the plaintiff or any other African American as a supervisor because blacks rarely have managerial talent. The company filed a general denial. Shortly thereafter, the company moved for summary judgment on the grounds that there was no evidence that the owner's decision to pass over the broker for the promotion was caused by racial animus. In support of the motion, the company submitted an affidavit from the owner in which he stated, "I never made any of the statements imputed to me in the complaint; all of those supposed statements are lies the plaintiff is telling in order to coerce me into settling this suit." The broker's lawyer, who was out-of-state tending to a dying parent, failed to submit papers in opposition to the motion within the allowable time. The trial judge granted summary judgment in favor of the defendant. The full text of the judge's opinion was as follows: "Because the plaintiff failed to submit papers in opposition to the motion, I will treat all statements made by the defendant and its owner as undisputed. Therefore, I find that the plaintiff has come forward with no evidence which would be sufficient to allow a reasonable jury to find that the plaintiff has carried his burden of proving that he was passed over on account of his race."

The broker has appealed the grant of summary judgment. Will the Court of Appeals likely reverse the grant of summary judgment?

(A) Yes, because the owner's moving papers established that the broker's credibility was a central issue that must be resolved during a trial rather than as a matter of law.

(B) Yes, because the complaint contained detailed factual allegations that, if believed by a jury, would justify a finding that the defendant violated the plaintiff's federal rights.

(C) No, because the broker's failure to submit papers in opposition to the motion meant that there was no sworn affidavit as required to support the factual allegations of the complaint.

(D) No, because the broker's failure to submit papers in opposition to the motion constituted a default, entitling the judge to treat the defendant's uncontested allegations as true.

Question 11

Plaintiff, while a pedestrian, was struck by a truck owned by Defendant, a corporation in the business of making local deliveries. The truck was driven by Driver, a full-time employee of Defendant. Since Plaintiff and Defendant were citizens of different states, Plaintiff brought a diversity suit in Defendant's home state against Defendant for negligence, seeking more than $75,000 in damages. Plaintiff elected not to make Driver (who left Defendant's employ soon after the accident) a co-defendant. Defendant served an answer denying liability on the grounds that the accident occurred because Driver had a sudden epileptic seizure that neither Driver nor Defendant could have foreseen. Plaintiff then served on Defendant a motion under FRCP 35 to compel Defendant to produce Driver for a physical examination to be conducted by a physician identified in the motion papers. In support of the motion, Plaintiff asserted that the examination was necessary in order for Plaintiff's attorneys to assess the accuracy of Defendant's assertion that the accident was caused by a seizure. Defendant opposed the motion. The district court hearing the suit should rule on Plaintiff's motion by

(A) granting the discovery request because a physical examination is relevant to at least one claim or defense in the action.

(B) denying the discovery request because Driver no longer works for Defendant and is thus not under Defendant's legal control.

(C) denying the discovery request unless the court finds that Plaintiff has shown good cause for the examination.

(D) granting the request and, if Defendant does not produce Driver for the examination, treating Defendant's failure as a contempt of court.

Question 12

On January 1 three years ago, Defendant, a technology company, hired Plaintiff, a technology specialist, on a one-year contract terminable only for cause. The parties agreed that any dispute was to be governed by the substantive law of State A. Three months after the contract began, Defendant fired Plaintiff on April 1 for what Plaintiff believed was no cause at all. The statute of limitations on a contract action, according to State A's laws, is three years, and was therefore about to expire on April 1 of this year. Consequently, on March 15 of this year, Plaintiff filed a diversity action against Defendant in federal district court for State A alleging that the firing breached her contract. On June 1 of this year, Plaintiff remembered that on May 1 three years ago (i.e., 30 days after the firing), Defendant wrongfully interfered with Plaintiff's ability to take a new job (also in State A) that another potential employer had offered her by falsely telling the new employer that Defendant had recently fired Plaintiff for cheating on her expense account. Therefore, on June 2 of this year, Plaintiff amended her suit to add a new state-law claim: that by telling this lie, Defendant tortiously interfered with Plaintiff's new employment contract. The statute of limitations for tortious interference in State A is also three years; therefore, if the new tortious-interference claim had been a separate action, it would have become time-barred in the courts of State A on May 1 of this year.

Defendant has now moved in federal court to have the tortious-interference claim dismissed as time-barred. Under the procedural law of State A, when an existing complaint is amended, the doctrine of "relation back" applies for statute of limitations purposes if and only if any newly-added claims (1) arise out of the same conduct, transaction, or occurrence as set out in the original pleading *and* (2) are supported by the same or nearly-same legal theory as at least one claim set out in the original pleading.

If Defendant's motion succeeds, which of the following is the most likely legal explanation for that success? In evaluating each choice, assume that any *factual* allegation contained in that choice is correct (though do *not* necessarily assume that any *legal* conclusion the choice draws from that fact is correct).

(A) Under State A law, the relation-back rule does not permit relation back.

(B) The tort claim rests on a legal theory different from that of the original contract claim.

(C) The tort claim arose out of a different transaction or occurrence than the original contract claim.

(D) Plaintiff unduly delayed in amending her complaint.

Question 13

Plaintiff, a company that manufactures pencils, is organized under the laws of China and has its operating plant and management office in that country. It bought wood pulp from Defendant, a corporation incorporated and located in State A. The sales contract provided that "the laws of China will govern any dispute that might arise between the parties pertinent to this agreement." Defendant was late in delivering the wood pulp, and Plaintiff sued Defendant in State A federal district court. Plaintiff has no office or agents in the United States, and the contract was negotiated and executed through the Internet.

Defendant has moved to dismiss the action under the doctrine of *forum non conveniens* on the ground that the case should be heard in a court in China. How should the court resolve the motion?

(A) The court should grant the motion because the requirements of the federal "transfer of venue" statute are satisfied.

(B) The court should deny the motion if a court in China will apply law less favorable to Plaintiff than will the Delaware district court.

(C) The court should grant the motion if it determines that China is an appropriate alternative forum for the lawsuit.

(D) The court has a duty to first establish that it has jurisdiction before deciding the motion to dismiss.

Question 14

A musician, who lived in State A, was a member of a touring rock band. On a day the musician was away from State A, an envelope sent "first class, certified, return receipt requested" via the U.S. Postal Service mail arrived at his residence. The envelope contained a summons and complaint for an action being brought against the musician by an accountant. The summons and complaint stated on their face that the action was for breach of contract and was being brought in federal court for the district of State B, which was the accountant's state of residence. The suit was properly based on diversity and met the jurisdictional amount. The musician had authorized his fiancée to accept mailed letters and packages he might receive and to sign receipts for them. Therefore, the fiancée signed the delivery receipt for the envelope and handed the receipt to the mail carrier. The musician never answered or otherwise responded to the summons or complaint, and the court in due course entered a $1.7 million default judgment against him. Two years after the entry of judgment, the musician happened to discover on the Internet that the default judgment against him had been entered. He immediately moved under FRCP Rule 60 to have the judgment set aside as void because proper service had never been made on him. At a judicial hearing on his motion, the musician testified that he had seen the original sealed certified-mail envelope on his desk when he returned from his trip, but had never opened it because he thought it related to some other completed business transaction. The accountant's lawyer did not contest this factual testimony. At the time of the original mailing, neither the law of State A nor the law of State B authorized in-state service of process on an individual by means of certified mail (or, indeed, by any means other than personal service).

Should the federal judge set aside the default judgment as requested by the musician?

(A) Yes, but only if the judge finds that the musician was not negligent in failing to open the certified letter envelope.

(B) Yes, because the judgment was void due to lack of proper service on the musician.

(C) No, because the musician did not make his motion until more than one year had elapsed from the entry of the default judgment.

(D) No, because the musician had authorized his fiancée to sign for mail, causing her receipt of the envelope to constitute valid service on the musician.

Question 15

A consumer was driving a car late at night when the headlights went out, causing the consumer to run off the road and hit a tree, injuring him badly. The consumer brought a product liability suit in diversity against the car's manufacturer, a large publicly-traded corporation. The suit alleged that the headlight system failed on account of a defective design. The consumer demanded a jury trial. During voir dire, one prospective juror testified that he owned $100 of publicly-traded stock in the defendant manufacturer. Under questioning by the judge, the prospective juror said that she was confident that her stock ownership would not interfere with her ability to be impartial in the case. The consumer's lawyer has challenged the prospective juror for cause. Should the judge dismiss the juror for cause?

(A) No, because the juror's financial stake is sufficiently small that it would not affect the ability of an average juror to be impartial.

(B) Yes, because there is a presumption that any direct financial relationship between a juror and a party will impair the juror's ability to be impartial.

(C) Yes, so long as there is at least one other potential juror in the pool who would not be challengeable for cause.

(D) No, so long as the judge believes the juror's testimony that she can be impartial.

Question 16

Until she was fired, a cook worked in a restaurant owned by a corporation. The cook sued the corporation in federal court, alleging that her firing violated a federal statute forbidding intentional discrimination against employees on the basis of gender. In her suit, the cook asked for an order that she be reinstated to her job, plus money damages as compensation for the firing. The cook also timely asked for a jury trial on the issues of liability and damages, but conceded that under court rules the decision about reinstatement would have to be made by the judge. During jury selection, the two sides each used one peremptory challenge during the course of seating the first 10 members of a proposed 12-member jury of whom 6 were men and 4 were women. Then, as to the next prospective Jurors, XX and YY (who if accepted would fill the final two seats, and who were both women), the plaintiff approved these jurors, but the defendant's lawyer announced that she wanted to use her final two peremptory challenges on them, giving as her only explanation that, "I'm sure these two ladies would be fair, but I think that on average males will be more sympathetic to my client's position than women will be." The judge is now prepared to decide two motions before him:

Motion 1: The defendant corporation has moved to have the facts bearing on "Did the defendant discriminate against the plaintiff on gender grounds?" tried first. Then, it argues, the judge should immediately decide whether the defendant discriminated, and if so, whether the defendant should be ordered to reinstate the plaintiff. After that, the motion says, if the court found that discrimination occurred, the jury should be asked to decide on the amount of damages. The plaintiff opposes this motion, saying that the jury should first decide whether there was discrimination, and if so, decide what damages to award; only then should the judge decide on reinstatement.

Motion 2: The plaintiff has moved to have the defendant's peremptory challenges to potential jurors XX and YY disallowed, on the grounds that allowing these challenges would violate the excluded jurors' equal protection right not to be disqualified from a jury on account of their gender and that the plaintiff has standing to assert these jurors' rights.

The court will most likely rule on the two motions by

(A) denying Motion 1 and granting Motion 2.

(B) granting Motion 1 and denying Motion 2.

(C) granting both motions.

(D) denying both motions.

Question 17

A statute passed by the legislature of State A, the "Employee Check Act" or "ECA," provides that if five or more persons work in the state for a given employer, the employer may pay them by check only if the employer offers the employees a free method of cashing the check within one mile or less of the workplace. The statute also provides a flat damages award of $1,000 per employee for each check as to which the employer violates the ECA. A brokerage firm with many employees in State A failed to comply with the statute. Twenty employees of the firm, each of whom was given payroll five checks in violation of the ECA, joined as co-plaintiffs in a non-class-action suit against the brokerage firm filed in the State A state courts; each plaintiff asserted a claim for $5,000. The brokerage firm promptly filed a notice removing the action to the local federal court for State A. Ninety days after the firm filed the notice of removal, all plaintiffs jointly filed a motion to remand the case to the State A court from which it had been removed, on the grounds that the case did not satisfy the relevant amount-in-controversy requirement.

Should the court grant the plaintiffs' motion to remand the case?

(A) No, because the federal supplemental jurisdiction statute permits the court to aggregate all of the plaintiffs' claims since they all derive from a common series of transactions, and when aggregated the claims are collectively worth in excess of $75,000.

(B) No, because by case law the claims here may be aggregated for amount-in-controversy purposes since they arise from a common series of transactions, and when aggregated the claims are collectively worth in excess of $75,000.

(C) No, because the plaintiffs waived their right to request remand when more than 30 days passed following the brokerage firm's filing of its notice of removal.

(D) Yes, because by case law the fact that the claims are not for a single right in which all plaintiffs have a common interest prevents the claims from being aggregated for amount-in-controversy purposes.

Question 18

A construction company was incorporated and headquartered in State A. A distributor (a corporation that was a citizen of State B) was in the business of distributing asphalt used in the construction of residential driveways. The construction company placed a large order for asphalt with the distributor, and the distributor failed to deliver the product on time. The construction company sued the distributor in diversity in State A federal court for breach of contract, claiming losses of more than $3 million from the delay. The distributor then impleaded a trucker that it had hired to ship the products in question to the construction company. In the distributor's third-party complaint against the trucker, the distributor alleged that the trucker "is or may be liable" to the distributor if the distributor were found liable to the construction company.

Which of the following defenses, if supported by the facts, may the trucker properly assert?

(A) The construction company could not recover directly against the trucker.

(B) The distributor may seek to implead the trucker only after, not before, a judgment is entered in the construction company's suit against the distributor.

(C) The court lacks venue over the distributor.

(D) The statute of limitations has lapsed on the construction company's claim against the distributor.

Question 19

A messenger, who is a citizen of State A, drove his truck onto a construction site in State A in order to deliver a package. There were a number of other vehicles on the site. The messenger's truck was hit from the rear by one of these vehicles, injuring the messenger. He sued an electrician (a citizen of State B), alleging that the electrician had negligently driven the vehicle, a van, that hit the messenger's truck. The suit, seeking $100,000 in damages, was based on diversity and was filed in State A federal court. The electrician filed an answer denying that he had driven the vehicle that had hit the messenger's truck. Eleven days after the electrician served his answer, he also served a third-party impleader complaint against a plumber (a citizen of State B) who had been driving a truck on the same site; that complaint alleged that it was the plumber whose truck hit the messenger, and that if there was anyone whose negligence caused the accident, that person was the plumber. The electrician made personal service of the third-party complaint on the plumber by having the summons and complaint handed to the plumber while the plumber was doing a multi-week project at a job site in State C, at a location 80 miles from the State A federal courthouse where the messenger-electrician suit was pending. No provision of State A law would permit service of process on a defendant found at the State C job site for a complaint in the State A courts on facts analogous to the facts of the electrician-plumber complaint here.

The plumber would like to try to get the third-party ("TP") complaint against him dismissed by the federal court. Which of the following arguments offers the plumber the best chance of achieving that result?

(A) The court does not have subject-matter jurisdiction to adjudicate the TP complaint, because the electrician and the plumber are both citizens of State B.

(B) The court does not have personal jurisdiction over the plumber for purposes of adjudicating the TP complaint.

(C) The electrician did not serve the TP complaint within the "of right" time limit for such service and did not obtain leave of court as required for a TP complaint served after expiration of that "of right" time limit.

(D) The TP complaint fails to state a valid third-party claim.

Question 20

A novelist sued her accountant, an individual, in a federal-court diversity action based on breach of contract. The novelist, who is a citizen of State A, brought the suit in that state's federal court. After the novelist filed the complaint, she instructed a process server to serve the summons and complaint personally on the accountant at what a recent check of the accountant's business website check showed to be his business address, 123 Main Street, Suite 101, in City, State B. Unbeknownst to the novelist, the accountant had moved his office to a different location in City one month before and had neglected to update his website with the new address. The process server arrived at Suite 101 in the 123 Main Street office building and asked the receptionist there if the accountant was present to receive papers. The receptionist replied that the accountant had moved, but mentioned that she would be seeing him the next day; she therefore offered to take the papers and give them to the accountant. The process server agreed, leaving the papers with the receptionist, who as promised gave the papers to the accountant the next day. The accountant then immediately filed a timely answer, in which he raised the defense of improper service. The provisions of State A and State B regarding valid methods of service are identical to the ones set forth for federal courts in the Federal Rules of Civil Procedure.

Should the court dismiss the complaint for improper service?

(A) Yes, because although the papers were left with a person of suitable age and discretion, this was done at a location that was no longer the accountant's usual place of business.

(B) Yes, because no federal or relevant state statute allows service on an individual by leaving papers with a person of suitable age and discretion at that person's usual place of business.

(C) No, because the process server left the papers with a person of suitable age and discretion at what the accountant represented to the world to be his usual place of business.

(D) No, because the accountant waived any objection to improper service by asserting the defense in an answer instead of by a motion made before the answer.

Question 21

A skydiver was injured in a skydiving accident in State A when his parachute opened late. The skydiver brought a product liability suit, based on diversity, against the manufacturer of the parachute in State A federal court. At trial, one of the issues was the extent of the skydiver's injuries. The skydiver's lawyer offered into evidence that the hospital that treated the skydiver for his injuries billed him $200,000 for care, and that this amount was paid in full by the skydiver's health insurance carrier on his behalf. The manufacturer's lawyer did not contest the accuracy or reasonableness of the hospital's bill. Nor did the manufacturer offer evidence that any person other than itself was fully or partly at fault. The case was submitted to the jury without any motion having been made by either side. The jury returned a verdict of $100,000, and the judge entered judgment for this amount. Under the relevant law of State A, a state trial judge is encouraged to use the "additur" technique where appropriate, i.e., to conditionally grant a new trial in response to a verdict for an amount markedly lower than that shown by the clear weight of the evidence; the grant is conditional in the sense that the new trial will be canceled if the defendant agrees to pay an amount specified by the trial judge as being the minimum justified by the evidence. After the disappointing verdict in the federal action, the skydiver's lawyer asked the judge by motion either (1) to issue an additur under which the manufacturer would be given a choice between undergoing a new trial solely on the issue of damages (with liability deemed decided in the first trial) or agreeing to pay $200,000 in damages; or (2) alternatively, to issue judgment as a matter of law for $200,000.

Assume that the district judge believes that the weight of the evidence clearly shows that the skydiver has sustained at least $200,000 of damages—the amount of the hospital bill—for injuries that would be compensable under State A's case law on tort damages. Which of the following represents the ruling the judge is most clearly authorized to make on the skydiver's alternative motions?

(A) The court may award judgment as a matter of law (JML) for $200,000, so long as the skydiver made his JML motion for within 28 days after the entry of the judgment for $100,000.

(B) The court may award additur as proposed by the skydiver, because additur represents a substantive legal rule of State A that should be applied by the federal court sitting in diversity.

(C) The court may not award additur as proposed by the skydiver, because additur may be applied only in federal-question cases, not in cases based solely on diversity.

(D) The court may not apply additur as proposed by the skydiver, because to do so would violate the defendant's jury trial rights under the Seventh Amendment.

Question 22

A landscaper who was a citizen of State A bought a lawn mower produced in State B by a manufacturer incorporated and headquartered in State B. While the landscaper was doing a job in State C, he was badly injured when the mower rolled over his foot. The landscaper brought a $1 million strict product liability action in diversity against the manufacturer in State C federal court, based on the allegedly defective design of the mower. States A, B, and C all impose slightly different tests for determining whether a product's design should be deemed defective. Which of the three states' substantive test for determining whether a design is defective should the federal court apply?

(A) The design-defect test used by the State C courts in cases involving only State C's tort laws, because State C is where the federal court sits.

(B) The design-defect test developed by the federal courts for use in claims arising under federal statutes.

(C) The design-defect test of the state whose design-defect law the State C courts would apply if the suit had been filed in the State C court system.

(D) The design-defect test developed by whichever of the three states the federal court believes has the strongest interest in having its own substantive laws apply to this controversy.

Question 23

Plaintiff, an individual who is a citizen of State A, wanted to bring a diversity suit against Defendant, a corporation incorporated and with its headquarters in State B. The suit alleged that some years ago, Defendant committed fraud on Plaintiff. On July 1, Plaintiff filed the civil fraud complaint against Defendant with the federal district court located in State A. On July 5, Plaintiff sent, by first-class mail, a package containing the following documents to Defendant ("c/o President") at Defendant's headquarters address in State B: (1) a copy of the complaint; (2) two copies of a form (appended to a copy of FRCP 4) by which Defendant could by signing agree to waive service of a summons; and (3) a prepaid means for Defendant to return a signed copy of the waiver form. The mailing also included a notice to Defendant stating that the suit had been commenced and requesting that Defendant waive service of a summons by signing and returning a copy of the waiver form by no later than 30 days after the July 5 mailing date. The notice-and-request met all requirements set forth in Federal Rule 4(d)(1).

In order to determine whether Plaintiff satisfied the statute of limitations, it has become important to know *the earliest date* as of which all events needed for the complaint to be deemed served via the waiver method had occurred. The earliest date as of which service in the action will be treated as complete would be

(A) July 5, by virtue of Plaintiff's act of mailing the package to Defendant.

(B) August 10, if on that day Plaintiff, not having received from Defendant the signed waiver form or any communication, filed a sworn statement with the court stating that Defendant had not submitted the requested signed waiver within the 30 days specified in the waiver request.

(C) August 20, if on that day Plaintiff received from Defendant a return of the signed waiver form.

(D) August 22, if on that day Plaintiff filed the signed waiver form with the court, after having received it from Defendant on August 20.

Question 24

A husband got into a heated argument with his wife. During the course of the argument, he fired a hand gun, and the bullet ricocheted off the floor and hit her, causing her instant death. The man was charged with second degree murder but instead was permitted to plead guilty to voluntary manslaughter under a plea agreement with the county prosecutor. A State A statute provides that voluntary manslaughter is "an intentional or reckless killing committed under the effect of extreme emotional distress." The plea agreement stated that the husband "intentionally killed the wife while under the effect of extreme emotional distress," but contained no other details. The State A judge, in accepting the plea, required the husband to make an oral allocution before the court, whose purpose was to assure the court that there was a "factual basis" for the plea; the judge concluded that there was such a basis, though the husband in the allocution denied that he had intended for the bullet to strike his wife. Meanwhile, the husband was the named beneficiary of a life insurance policy bought by the wife on her own life. The policy contained a "homicide clause," which provided that the insurer would not be liable under the policy if the insured's death was the result of a voluntary act by the insured or her spouse committed with the intent of causing the insured's death. In reliance on this clause, the insurer refused to make payment on the policy. The husband, a State A resident, filed suit in a State A state court to establish his right to the policy proceeds. The insurance company, as a non-citizen of State A, properly removed to the federal district court for State A. The husband and the insurer have agreed to have the case decided by the federal judge rather than a jury.

The insurer has moved for summary judgment, based on the theory that the husband's guilty plea conclusively established the fact that he intentionally killed the wife, thereby making the policy's homicide clause applicable. State A follows the prevailing national approach to issue preclusion. The federal Court of Appeals for the circuit that includes State A, acting in cases where the court was free to make its own determination about whether issue preclusion applied, has issued opinions taking that same prevailing national approach to issue preclusion. How should the federal court rule on the insurer's motion?

(A) Because the State A courts would apply issue preclusion to prevent the husband from denying that he intentionally killed the wife, the federal court must follow the State A approach and apply such preclusion too.

(B) Because the State A courts would not apply issue preclusion to prevent the husband from denying that he intentionally killed the wife, the federal court must follow the State A approach and decline to apply such preclusion too.

(C) The federal court should follow federal case law from the circuit, and under that case law issue preclusion will not apply, because the issue of the husband's intent was never actually litigated in the criminal proceeding.

(D) The federal court should follow federal case law from the circuit, and under that case law issue preclusion will apply, because the husband's guilty plea constituted a final and conclusive determination that the killing was intentional.

Question 25

Plaintiff brought a diversity suit in federal court against Defendant. The suit claimed that several years previously, Defendant, an individual, had breached a contract to deliver certain food colorings to Plaintiff, also an individual, for use in Plaintiff's bakery. Plaintiff filed the complaint with the district court on March 1. On March 3, Plaintiff requested by mail that Defendant waive service, and Defendant did so by returning the waiver form on March 10. On March 15, Defendant served his answer, which consisted solely of a general denial. On April 20, Defendant first realized that he probably had a valid defense based on the statute of limitations. Defendant's lawyer decided not to ask Plaintiff to consent to Defendant's immediate filing of an amended answer that would include the limitations defense.

Which of the following statements best describes whether and how Defendant may, on April 20, assert the limitations defense?

(A) Defendant may assert the defense by amending his answer as of right, because due to his having signed the waiver his original time to answer has not yet run.

(B) Defendant may not assert the defense by amending his answer unless he receives leave of court to do so, because more than 21 days have passed since Defendant's service of his original answer, and that answer did not require a responsive pleading.

(C) Defendant may not assert the defense by amending his answer unless he receives leave of court, because his filing of an answer that did not contain an affirmative defense in his answer resulted in his automatic waiver of that defense and left him without the ability to amend as of right.

(D) Defendant may, as of right, make a motion asserting the defense.

Question 26

Defendant, a corporation that manufactures automobile tires, entered into a long-term sales contract with Plaintiff, company that distributes used cars. Plaintiff, dissatisfied with the quality of Defendant's tires, filed a diversity action in federal court against Defendant. The complaint alleged three claims: breach of warranty, strict liability, and breach of contract. On April 1, the district court granted Plaintiff's motion for partial summary judgment (judgment only as to the contract claim) and ordered a trial on the two remaining claims. The court's opinion granting the partial summary judgment said nothing about whether the judgment was deemed final or whether there was any reason to allow an immediate appeal from it. On April 15, Defendant filed a motion in the appropriate federal court of appeals, asking that court to hear an immediate appeal of the grant of partial summary judgment. On April 25, Plaintiff filed a written consent to this appeal—he did so in the hopes that if he won that appeal, Defendant would immediately settle the contract claim without a trial in return for Plaintiff's dropping the other two claims.

Assuming that the appeals court desires to hear the immediate appeal, does that court have jurisdiction to do so?

(A) Yes, because the grant of partial summary judgment is a final judgment.

(B) Yes, because the grant of partial summary judgment, although an interlocutory order, may be immediately appealed in the discretion of either the trial or appeals court.

(C) No, because the grant of partial summary judgment here was an interlocutory order from which no immediate appeal is possible.

(D) No, because the parties did not file their consent to the appeal within ten days of the court's entry of its order.

Question 27

An engineer worked for many years for a manufacturer of auto airbags. The engineer's job was both to design, and to evaluate the safety of, the manufacturer's airbag inflation systems. Three years ago, the engineer quit and began giving paid expert testimony against the manufacturer in civil suits brought by consumers who said they had been injured when airbags made by the manufacturer had detonated prematurely; the engineer testified that based on his own experience working for the manufacturer, the airbags in question were defectively designed. The manufacturer responded to this testimony by suing the engineer in State A state court, alleging that his testimony unfairly disclosed the manufacturer's trade secrets. The manufacturer and the engineer then settled this suit. As part of the settlement, both parties asked the State A judge to enter an injunction prohibiting the engineer from "giving testimony, by deposition or trial testimony, in any personal injury suit brought in any American state or federal court against [the manufacturer] concerning [the engineer's] knowledge of the design of manufacturer's airbag systems." The judge entered the requested injunction.

Shortly thereafter, a consumer was injured in a car crash in State B when an airbag system made by the manufacturer allegedly failed to inflate properly in the consumer's car. The consumer brought a diversity action based on product liability against the manufacturer in federal district court for State B. The consumer's lawyer issued a subpoena to compel the engineer to testify about his personal knowledge of the design of the airbag at issue in the consumer's case. The state courts of State B have said in past opinions that the state has a strong public interest in ensuring that potential witnesses with knowledge of pertinent matters not be barred from testifying to that knowledge on account of confidentiality agreements between the witness and another private party. The manufacturer has now asserted in the federal court action that under the relevant federal full faith and credit statute, the federal court has a duty to exclude any testimony by the engineer about matters covered by the injunction, including the engineer's knowledge about the manufacturer's airbag designs. Should the federal court grant the manufacturer's request to exclude the engineer's testimony?

(A) No, because the application of full faith and credit principles must yield to any strong countervailing public-policy interest on the part of State B, and admitting the engineer's testimony here would serve such a public-policy interest held by that state.

(B) No, because the admissibility of evidence is not governed by full faith and credit principles.

(C) Yes, because the principles of claim preclusion embodied in the federal full faith and credit statute require a State B federal court to enforce the injunction issued by the State A court even if a State B state court would not issue such an injunction on comparable facts if the suit were pending in that court.

(D) Yes, so long as the federal court believes that the State A judge who issued the injunction would on request modify it to allow the engineer to obey the subpoena and give the testimony sought here.

Question 28

Plaintiff is a widow whose husband was killed in an accident while working for Defendant, a construction company. Plaintiff is a citizen of State A. Defendant is incorporated in and has its principal place of business in State B. Plaintiff brought a diversity action against Defendant in federal district court for State A, alleging negligence and seeking $100,000 in damages. Defendant filed a third-party claim against Distributor, seeking $100,000 in damages and alleging that if Defendant were to be found liable to Plaintiff, Distributor would be liable to Defendant for having leased to Defendant the defective equipment that caused the accident. Distributor is incorporated in State A and has its principal place of business there. Plaintiff then amended her complaint to assert a defective-product claim directly against Distributor; the claim sought $100,000 in damages.

Defendant and Distributor have now moved to dismiss the claims against them based on lack of subject-matter jurisdiction. Defendant moves to dismiss Plaintiff's negligence claim, and Distributor moves to dismiss both claims against it, Defendant's third-party claim, and Plaintiff's direct claim. The court should dispose of these motions by

(A) granting all of the motions.

(B) granting only Distributor's motion as to both claims against it.

(C) granting only Distributor's motion, and only as to Plaintiff's claim against it.

(D) granting only Defendant's motion.

Question 29

A screenwriter wanted to bring a federal lawsuit for copyright infringement against a movie studio that he believed had copied elements of his unpublished screenplay. He consulted a lawyer, who agreed to bring the case. The lawyer drafted a complaint, signed it, and filed it with the court. At about the same time, the screenwriter and the lawyer agreed that a jury would probably be more sympathetic to the screenwriter's claim than would be a judge, so they tentatively decided to demand a jury trial on the infringement claim. However, the lawyer and the screenwriter also decided that it would be best to postpone making the jury-trial demand as long as possible, since later events in the case, including the attitude of whatever judge was assigned, might cause them to change their mind and prefer a bench trial instead of a jury trial.

The following times for the screenwriter to demand a jury trial are arranged in anticipated chronological order, with the earliest-to-occur listed first. Which choice represents the LATEST stage at which the screenwriter can serve a demand on the studio for a jury trial while being confident that his demand will not be deemed to have been waived?

(A) At the same time as the summons and complaint are served on the studio.

(B) Within 60 days after the studio serves its answer, if the answer does not contain a counterclaim.

(C) On or before the date on which the parties' lawyers conduct their initial case-planning conference required by FRCP 26(f).

(D) On or before the date on which the first pretrial conference in the case occurs.

Question 30

The plaintiff, while driving on April 2, was injured in a collision with a car driven by the defendant. The plaintiff believed that the defendant had gone through a stop sign. The police officer at the scene did not perform a sobriety test, but the plaintiff thought she smelled liquor on the defendant's breath. The plaintiff brought a negligence suit against the defendant in State A state court. The plaintiff's lawyer then engaged a private investigator to try to find out whether the defendant had been drinking prior to the accident. The investigator located a musician who had the status of "friend" of the defendant on a particular social media website. The investigator conducted an interview with the musician, at which she told the investigator that on April 3, the defendant had posted a message on the social media website in which he said "I had a few beers yesterday and then got into a car accident, but fortunately the dumb cop didn't make me walk a white line." The musician then at the investigator's request wrote a handwritten statement with these facts, signed it, and handed it to the investigator, who gave it to the plaintiff's lawyer. The plaintiff's lawyer plans to call the musician at trial to testify about the defendant's admission of drinking, and plans to use the statement either in its case in chief, or to rehabilitate that testimony if the defendant claims on cross-examination that the musician's testimony is a recent fabrication.

The defendant, during discovery, made a demand for the production of any written statements in the possession of the plaintiff or her attorney by any person with knowledge relevant to the accident. The plaintiff's lawyer submitted a "privilege log" to the defendant, mentioning the musician by name, and stating that the musician had given a written statement to the plaintiff's legal team about a matter relevant to the accident; but the plaintiff's lawyer refused to produce the statement itself on the grounds that it was protected by work-product immunity. The defendant has now moved for a court order compelling production of the statement on the grounds that any work-product immunity should not prevent production on these facts. State A follows the Federal Rules of Civil Procedure on all matters relevant to discovery.

Should the court grant the defendant's motion to compel the plaintiff to produce the statement?

(A) Yes, because the defendant is entitled to a copy of his own prior admissions regarding the action or its subject matter.

(B) Yes, because the statement contains only the musician's own words and does not reveal any mental impressions or legal theories of the plaintiff's legal team.

(C) No, because the defendant and his attorney have not demonstrated that they cannot obtain their own statement from the musician that would be substantially equivalent to the one being sought.

(D) No, because the use the plaintiff intends to make of the statement at trial, if it's used at all, will be solely to enhance the musician's credibility as a witness.

Question 31

Plaintiff lives in State A. He bought hiking equipment from Defendant, a catalog retailer that is incorporated in, and has its headquarters in, State B. Plaintiff, from his home in State A, selected his purchase from a copy of Defendant's hard-copy catalog; he then placed his order by telephone to a sales agent working out of Defendant's State B headquarters. 20% of Defendant's annual sales are made by mail-order and Internet-order to customers who live in State A. However, Defendant has no employees or agents physically located in State A. The hiking equipment turned out to be defective, and Plaintiff decided to sue Defendant in State A state court for a refund. Before filing the suit, Plaintiff looked on the Internet and located Defendant's published street address in State B. However, Plaintiff did not serve a copy of the summons and complaint on Defendant either by mail or hand-delivery to that State B address. Instead, Plaintiff discovered a State A statute providing that "Service for an action in this state may be made upon a nonresident company that is registered to do business in this state by means of hand-delivery of the summons and complaint to the State A Secretary of State at the Secretary's official address in Capital City, State A." Plaintiff therefore served Defendant by having his agent hand-deliver a copy of the summons and complaint to the State A Secretary of State as provided in the statute. It is unclear what additional actions, if any, were taken by either Plaintiff or the Secretary of State to attempt to give Defendant actual notice of the suit.

Defendant did not appear in the action, and a default judgment was entered against it by the State A court last year. Defendant now seeks to have the default judgment re-opened, and the suit dismissed for improper service; Defendant claims not to have received actual notice of the suit until this year. (The statute of limitations ran on Dec. 31 of last year, so if the court finds that Defendant was not validly served prior to Dec. 31, Plaintiff will not be able to re-serve Defendant.) Defendant does not dispute that it is registered to do business in State A, but claims that whatever service occurred did not comport with the Due Process Clause of the Fourteenth Amendment. The following choices list, in estimated ascending order of the likelihood that they would have given Defendant actual notice of the suit, various additional steps that might have been taken to notify Defendant of the suit. Which choice represents the additional step(s) beyond service on the Secretary of State that would be the LEAST likely-to-be-effective notice steps that would nonetheless have been sufficient to give Defendant constitutionally-sufficient notice of the suit?

(A) No other acts calculated to give notice to Defendant were required, because service was constitutionally sufficient as soon as Plaintiff hand-delivered the summons and complaint to the state official.

(B) Notice published in a newspaper of general circulation widely distributed through State B would have sufficed (if done in addition to the delivery of the summons and complaint to the state official).

(C) A mailing of the summons and complaint to Defendant at its last-known address, by either Plaintiff or the Secretary of State, would have sufficed (if done in addition to the delivery of the summons and complaint to the state official).

(D) Only hand delivery of the summons and complaint by Plaintiff or his agent to Defendant's published address in State B would have sufficed (even if there had been delivery of the summons and complaint to the state official), given that Plaintiff knew that published address.

Question 32

Plaintiff was born in State A and has lived there her entire life. For the last 20 years she worked as a data-entry operator for Employer, a corporation incorporated in, and with its principal place of business in, State B. Employer announced one day that it was outsourcing its data-entry operations and gave Plaintiff the choice between transferring to a lower-paying job and being fired. Plaintiff refused the transfer and was fired. Plaintiff believed that Employer had discriminated against her because of her age. She therefore brought a lawsuit against Employer and Manager, the controlling shareholder of Employer who, Plaintiff believed, made the decision to force her to choose between being fired or taking the lower-paying job. Manager, an individual, lives and works in State A. The complaint contained two claims. The first claim was against Employer alone and asserted that Employer had violated the federal Age Bias Act (ABA Act), which provides, "No employer shall discriminate on the basis of age." The second claim was against both Manager and Employer; it alleged that (1) Employer breached Plaintiff's employment contract, a clause of which said that Employee could only be fired for "repeated unwillingness or inability to perform the essential functions of the job"; and (2) Manager used his control of Employer to cause Employer to breach the contract, thereby himself committing the tort of interference with contract.

Plaintiff filed her lawsuit in a federal district court located in State A. Both claims seek more than $100,000 in damages against each party. Manager has moved to dismiss the claim against him for lack of subject-matter jurisdiction. How should the court resolve the motion?

(A) The court should deny the motion because the court can exercise federal-question jurisdiction over Manager since the ABA claim arises under a federal statute.

(B) The court should deny the motion because it can exercise federal diversity jurisdiction over Manager.

(C) The court has power to hear the claim against Manager since that claim is closely related to a federal-question claim in the case, and there is no reason for the court to exercise its discretion not to hear the claim against Manager.

(d) The court should grant the motion because Manager is a pendent party over whom the court cannot exercise jurisdiction on these facts.

Question 33

In State A, an accountant got into a taxi cab owned by a company that employed the driver as a full-time driver. During the trip, the cab collided with a truck whose driver sped away and was never located. The accountant brought a negligence suit in a State A court known as a "city court," whose jurisdiction was limited to claims not to exceed $250,000, but whose procedures were otherwise identical to those of the State A courts of general jurisdiction. The suit was solely against the cab driver, and the relief sought was $20,000 to compensate for property damage caused during the collision to a framed oil painting that the accountant owned and was carrying with her in the cab. After the resulting jury trial, the jury returned a verdict in favor of the cab driver, and the judge entered final judgment. The accountant then brought a $200,000 negligence suit in a State A court of general jurisdiction against the company that owned the cab, for personal injuries the accountant had sustained in the same collision. The company moved to dismiss the suit on account of the earlier judgment in favor of the cab driver. Will the court dismiss the suit on this ground?

(A) Yes, based on the doctrine of issue preclusion (or "collateral estoppel").

(B) Yes, based on the doctrine of claim preclusion (or "res judicata").

(C) No, because the cab company would not have been bound had the judgment in the earlier suit been in favor of the accountant.

(D) No, because the first suit was in a court of limited jurisdiction, making any form of preclusion unfair to the accountant.

Question 34

A plumber who lived in State A had surgery in a hospital, which was operated by a non-profit corporation incorporated and located in State A. A serious infection set in, which the plumber believed was negligently handled by the hospital. After partly recovering, the plumber moved permanently to State B. Then, shortly before expiration of State A's two-year statute of limitations on medical malpractice claims, the plumber brought a $300,000 diversity action for malpractice against the hospital in the federal district court located in State A. The legislature of State A has enacted a statute providing that before any medical malpractice suit may be filed in the State A courts against a hospital located in that state, the claimant must first send a "notice of claim" to the hospital stating the claimant's intent to sue and the nature of the claimed malpractice; only after waiting for 60 days following the giving of this notice is the claimant permitted to file the malpractice suit in the state A courts. The purpose of the notice-of-claim provision is to give the hospital the chance to investigate and negotiate a settlement before a malpractice suit is publicly filed, thereby reducing the cost of hospital malpractice insurance by encouraging lower-cost settlements. In the case of the plumber's federal suit, the hospital's lawyer noticed that the plumber had not given a notice of claim prior to filing that suit.

The hospital has now, in a timely manner, moved the State A federal court to dismiss the case. The motion makes two arguments for dismissal: (1) because diversity of citizenship is lacking; and (2) because the federal court must enforce the notice-of claim requirement, thus requiring it to dismiss for failure to state a claim for which relief may be granted. The federal judge should

(A) allow the suit to proceed, because there is diversity, and the notice-of-claim provision is a procedural rule that is therefore not binding on the federal court.

(B) dismiss the suit, because the plumber was a citizen of State A at the time the malpractice claim arose, preventing him from having diversity of citizenship as to the hospital.

(C) dismiss the suit, because the notice-of-claim requirement is sufficiently bound up with the substantive rights of the parties that the federal court must enforce that requirement since the State A courts would do so.

(D) dismiss the suit, because the court must apply the State A notice-of-claim rule as long as there is a non-trivial chance that the decision on whether to apply that rule will be outcome-determinative.

Question 35

A woman brought suit in State A federal district court against the company she worked for, claiming that it had failed to promote her on account of her gender, in violation of a federal employment-discrimination statute. The woman is a citizen of State A; the company is a corporation incorporated in State B, with its headquarters in State C and with most of its employees working at the office in State A where the woman works. The relief sought by the suit consisted solely of $46,000 in back pay. Two months after the company timely filed its answer, and while discovery was still pending, the company made a motion to dismiss the suit for lack of subject-matter jurisdiction. Will the federal court grant the motion?

(A) Yes, because the company is a citizen of several states, one of which is the same as the woman's state of citizenship.

(B) Yes, because although there is diversity of citizenship, the amount in controversy requirement is not met.

(C) No, because the woman's claim arises under federal law.

(D) No, because the company waived its objection by failing to assert it either in its answer or in a motion made before it served its answer.

Question 36

Plaintiff is a franchisor of brake-repair services for automobiles. Plaintiff's headquarters are in State A, a state located in the southwestern part of the U.S. Plaintiff issues franchises for the operation of local brake-repair stores to franchisees located in all 50 states, as well as in 20 foreign countries. Defendant, an individual with considerable business sophistication, was and is a citizen and resident of Canada. After meeting with Plaintiff's two-person Canadian sales office regarding his desire to buy a franchise from Plaintiff, Defendant negotiated for 6 months to complete the purchase. The franchise was to be located in eastern Canada, about 2,000 miles from Plaintiff's State A headquarters. Most negotiations occurred by telephone and email, with Defendant participating from his home in Canada and Plaintiff from its State A headquarters. During that period, Plaintiff's only connections with State A were that he travelled twice to Plaintiff's headquarters for face-to-face negotiating sessions, and on one of those trips also attended a three-day "prospective franchisee training session" there. Defendant then signed his copy of the final contract in Canada, and Plaintiff signed its copy in State A. The contract said that any disputes would be "resolved according to the laws of State A," and said nothing about in which court(s) a suit on the contract could be brought. The contract also required Plaintiff to support Defendant's efforts as to sales, marketing, finance, and operations, and indicated that most such support work by Plaintiff would be done by employees working from Plaintiff's headquarters. After signing the contract, Plaintiff never travelled to State A, and never did any business in the state, or with State A parties, other than having some dealings by telephone with Plaintiff's personnel located in the state.

After Defendant failed to make required payments of monthly franchise fees, Plaintiff brought a breach-of-contract action against Defendant based on diversity in federal district court for State A. The State A long-arm grants the State A courts personal jurisdiction to hear all disputes concerning contracts, if one party to the contract is an individual or business located in State A, and if such exercise of personal jurisdiction "would be consistent with the due process limits imposed by the U.S. Constitution." Before filing an answer to the suit, Defendant made a timely motion that the court lacked personal jurisdiction over him. The trial court denied the motion. Defendant tried the case on the merits, lost, and then appealed the adverse judgment to the appropriate federal Court of Appeal on the grounds that the trial court erred in concluding that it had personal jurisdiction over Defendant.

Should the federal Court of Appeals reverse the judgment and dismiss the case for lack of personal jurisdiction?

(A) No, because by raising and losing the jurisdiction question and then continuing to trial on the merits, Defendant waived the right to raise the jurisdiction issue on appeal.

(B) No, because Defendant should have anticipated being required to defend an action in State A, making it not unfair to require him to do so.

(C) Yes, because although Defendant had minimum contacts with State A, it would violate traditional notions of fair play and substantial justice to require him to defend this suit in State A.

(D) Yes, because Defendant did not voluntarily avail himself of the privilege of doing business in State A, thereby preventing him from having minimum contacts with that state.

Question 37

Company manufactures off-road recreational vehicles. Driver owns a vehicle manufactured by Company. Driver was injured while driving the vehicle on the highway. A state trooper was called and arrived at the scene of the accident. Driver has informed Company that he intends to file a federal action, based on diversity jurisdiction, for injuries caused by the car's alleged product-design defects; Driver claims that the vehicle accelerated when it was supposed to brake, and as a result it rolled into a ditch. Company now wants to find out whatever the state trooper knows about the accident. Company has filed a verified petition with the federal district court in the district in which the accident occurred, asking the court to issue an order granting Company permission to depose the state trooper. The petition does not specify any particular topics to be covered in the deposition.

Should the court issue the requested order?

(A) No, because in federal civil practice a party may not take discovery from a nonparty before the commencement of a lawsuit.

(B) No, because a party may take discovery before a suit is commenced only if the request is accompanied by a draft complaint against the party from whom discovery is sought.

(C) Yes, because a party to an anticipated federal civil suit may depose a non-party witness who is believed to be in possession of information that is relevant to a claim or defense that is expected to be raised in the suit.

(D) No, because a party may not take discovery before the commencement of a federal lawsuit absent a special need to preserve testimony.

Question 38

Plaintiff is an insurance company incorporated and headquartered in State A. It issued a liability insurance policy to Defendant, a company incorporated and headquartered in State B that operates an interstate bus line. A bus driver employed by Defendant crashed into a car on an interstate highway in State B. More than a dozen individuals, both drivers and passengers, were seriously injured. Under the policy, Plaintiff insured Defendant for claims aggregating up to $3 million arising from any accidents occurring during the one-year policy period where a single driver was at the wheel of a bus owned by the Defendant. Ten of the injured parties brought individual negligence suits against Defendant in various state courts. Two of the claimants are citizens of State A, three are citizens of State B, and the remaining five are citizens of States C, D, E, F, and G, respectively. The individual claims were for sums between $10,000 and $3 million. Plaintiff then filed a statutory interpleader action in federal court in State B. The interpleader action purported to join all ten state-court claimants (each of whom was individually personally served in his or her home state). As part of the interpleader action, Plaintiff requested that the federal court enjoin each claimant from trying to collect any amounts from Plaintiff under the policy in the separate state-court actions (though Plaintiff did not ask that the claimants be enjoined from seeking judgments against Defendant in those state-court actions). The ten claimants hired a lawyer to represent them jointly in the interpleader action. The lawyer sought to have the interpleader action dismissed on procedural grounds so that the 10 state-court suits could proceed unimpeded.

Which of the following statements best summarizes how the federal court should dispose of one or both requests of the parties (i.e., Plaintiff's request for injunctions and/or the claimants' joint request for dismissal of the interpleader action)?

(A) The court must dismiss the entire interpleader suit if complete diversity does not exist between Plaintiff and all of the claimants.

(B) The court must dismiss from the interpleader suit any claimant whose individual claims, when aggregated together, do not total at least $75,000 in value.

(C) The court must dismiss the interpleader suit if Plaintiff fails to either deposit the $3 million policy limit in cash with the court or to furnish a bond in that amount, after being ordered by the court to do so.

(D) Even if the court properly declines to dismiss the interpleader suit, the court may not issue the injunctions against continuation of the state-court actions.

Question 39

Three years ago, a limited partnership as plaintiff brought a suit, stated to be based on the alienage variety of diversity, against the defendant, a corporation, in federal court for the district of State A. The defendant corporation was and is a citizen of State A, since it was incorporated in that state and has its principal place of business there. The partnership was and still is organized under the law of Canada, with its principal place of business also in Canada. At the time the suit was filed, the partnership consisted of a general partner (a corporation that was solely a citizen of Canada) and ten limited partners, all individuals. Eight of the limited partners were citizens of Canada; two were citizens of State A. Last year, after discovery had been completed but the case not yet tried, the two limited partners who were citizens of State A left the partnership because they sold their interests to the other limited partners, and under the partnership agreement were thus required to leave the partnership. (This sale and exit happened for reasons unrelated to the lawsuit.) This year, after a one-month trial, the jury rendered a verdict in favor of the plaintiff partnership. The next day, before any judgment had been entered, the defendant corporation moved to have the action dismissed for lack of subject matter jurisdiction, in that there had not been complete diversity of citizenship between the parties at the time the suit was filed three years ago.

Should the district court grant the defense motion and dismiss the suit for lack of subject-matter jurisdiction?

(A) Yes, because at the time suit was commenced the partnership was a citizen of both Canada and State A, preventing the existence of complete alienage diversity between the partnership and the corporation.

(B) Yes, so long as the court does not believe that the defendant learned or should have learned of the two limited partners' State A citizenship prior to the start of the trial.

(C) No, because the two limited partners' exit from the partnership prior to the start of trial was a timely cure for any lack of subject-matter jurisdiction that might otherwise have existed.

(D) No, because a partnership is deemed to be a citizen of the place where it was formed, plus the place of its principal place of business, so there was complete alienage diversity jurisdiction at the time the suit was filed.

Question 40

Purchaser is an individual who lives in State A and operates a factory in State B. He entered into a contract with Seller, a company incorporated in State C. The contract provided that goods purchased under the contract were to be delivered from Seller's warehouse in State D to Purchaser's factory in State B. Seller failed to deliver the goods on time, and Purchaser brought a diversity suit against Seller in federal court for the District of State A. Soon after the case was filed (but after the statute of limitations for bringing such an action had expired), Purchaser moved for a change of venue to the Western District of State B, the district in which Purchaser's factory was located. Seller opposed the transfer. Assume that the court has concluded that litigating in the Western District of State B would be more convenient overall for the parties and the witnesses, considered as a group, than litigation in the District of State A.

How should the district court resolve the transfer motion?

(A) Grant the motion, so long as Purchaser could initially have brought the action in the Western District of State B.

(B) Deny the motion, because Purchaser, having chosen the action's original venue, waived the right to request a transfer of the action.

(C) Deny the motion, because changes of venue, even in the federal system, may not cross state boundaries if the suit is based solely on diversity of citizenship.

(D) Dismiss the action if the court concludes that the District of State A was not a district in which venue was ever proper.

ANSWERS

CIVIL PROCEDURE

Answer Key

Use this Answer Key to quickly identify the answer to each question.

(1) D	(11) B	(21) B	(31) C
(2) A	(12) C	(22) C	(32) C
(3) B	(13) C	(23) D	(33) B
(4) C	(14) B	(24) B	(34) C
(5) C	(15) B	(25) A	(35) C
(6) A	(16) A	(26) C	(36) B
(7) C	(17) D	(27) B	(37) D
(8) C	(18) D	(28) C	(38) C
(9) D	(19) D	(29) A	(39) A
(10) A	(20) B	(30) C	(40) A

ANSWERS

CIVIL PROCEDURE

Answer 1

(D) is the best response,

because the "two dismissal" rule means that the second voluntary dismissal of the claim acted as an adjudication on the merits, causing the third version of the claim to be barred by claim preclusion.

The FRCP implements the so-called ***"two dismissal rule,"*** by which when a party dismisses the same claim voluntarily twice, the second dismissal is ordinarily "with prejudice," preventing the bringing of that claim a third time against the same or related parties. The rule is implemented by two sub-sections of FRCP 41. First, Rule 41(a)(1)(A) says that subject to some exceptions not relevant here, "the plaintiff may ***dismiss an action without a court order*** by filing: (i) a ***notice of dismissal before the opposing party serves either an answer or a motion for summary judgment***[.]" This provision, viewed in isolation, gave the pedestrian the right to make a voluntary dismissal of her first federal-court suit without getting leave of the court. (The facts tell you that before that, the pedestrian had the right to voluntarily dismiss the state-court suit.) But then, the *effect* of this second dismissal was controlled by a later section of Rule 41; 41(a)(1)(B), entitled "Effect," says that:

"Unless the notice . . . states otherwise, ***the dismissal is without prejudice***. But if the plaintiff ***previously dismissed any federal- or state-court action based on or including the same claim***, a ***notice of dismissal operates as an adjudication on the merits.***"

So if the pedestrian had never brought the state-court suit, the effect of her dismissal of the federal-court suit would have been controlled by the first sentence of 41(a)(1)(B) quoted above, making the dismissal "without prejudice" (i.e., without impairment of her right to re-file). But because the pedestrian *did* bring, and then voluntarily dismiss, the state-court suit, her voluntary dismissal caused the second sentence of 41(a)(1)(B) to take effect; the pedestrian had indeed "***previously dismissed [a] federal- or state-court action based on or including the same claim***," so the second voluntary dismissal ***"operates as an adjudication on the merits"*** unless the notice of dismissal "state[d] otherwise." And the facts tell you that the notice of dismissal of the second suit "did not attempt to specify what effect the dismissal would have on future suits." So the second dismissal indeed operated as an "adjudication on the merits." (Note, by the way, how 41(a)(1)(B) refers to a previous dismissal of a "federal- or ***state-court*** action"—so the fact that the first action was in state rather than federal court did ***not*** prevent the federal two-dismissal rule from operating. On the other hand, had the sequence been ***reversed***, so that the first suit was in federal court and dismissed, and the second was a state action later dismissed, then 41(a)(1)(B) would ***not*** have applied, and the pedestrian ***would*** be allowed to bring a second federal action.)

If all three claims had involved only the ***same parties***—the pedestrian versus the cab-driver—the conclusion that the second dismissal took away the pedestrian's right to bring the third suit would be crystal clear. But what do we make of the fact that between the second and third suits, the pedestrian ***added a new co-defendant***, the corporation? If the third suit had involved a completely different party (as where the plaintiff learned that she had simply been suing the wrong party until now), probably the two-dismissal rule of FRCP 41 wouldn't apply. But where the defendant(s) to the third action are ***closely related*** to the original defendant(s), most courts have interpreted the change as not blocking application of the two-dismissal rule. This makes sense—the purpose of the rule is mainly to prevent harassment of the defendant(s). So in a situation like the one here, the fact that the corporation was controlled by the same person who was an individual defendant in the first two actions means that that individual defendant (the cab-driver) and his family-controlled corporation have indeed been harassed by having to devote resources to answering and preparing a defense to three separate actions, making the situation fall within the anti-harassment purpose of the rule. *See, e.g., Lake at Las Vegas Investors Group. v. Pacific Malibu Dev. Corp.*, 933 F.2d 724, 728 (9th Cir. 1991) (where two prior suits were against a parent corporation, and the third suit on the same claim was against both the parent's subsidiary and a partnership of which the subsidiary was the general partner, the subsidiary and partnership were so "closely related" to the parent that the anti-harassment purpose of Rule 41(a)(1) would be served by letting the subsidiary and partnership invoke the two-dismissal rule).

Given that the dismissal of the federal suit is deemed to be "with prejudice," the consequence is that that suit is equivalent to a disposal of the suit on the merits. Therefore, under the basic doctrine of claim preclusion (a/k/a "res judicata"), that same claim may not be brought against the same or closely-related parties in the future.

(A) is not the best response,

because the cab-driver's failure to answer the two prior complaints is irrelevant to whether the third claim is barred.

It's true that the fact that the defendant did not answer or move against a complaint *sometimes* plays a role in whether the plaintiff can dismiss without leave of court: Rule 41(a)(1)((A) says that as a general matter, "the plaintiff may dismiss an action without a court order by filing: (i) a notice of dismissal ***before the opposing party serves either an answer*** or a ***motion for summary judgment***[.]" But the two-dismissal rule—which makes a second voluntary dismissal of the same claim operate with prejudice—applies even where one or both of the dismissals is made prior to the defendant's service of an answer or motion. (Indeed, in the case of the second dismissal, a dismissal pre-answer/pre-motion is the *only* situation to which 41(a)(1)(A)'s formulation of the two-dismissal rule applies; once the defendant answers or moves, the plaintiff loses her right to dismiss without leave of court, so that any dismissal would have to be with leave of court, in which case it would be up to the judge to specify in the order whether the dismissal is to be with or without prejudice.)

(B) is not the best response,

because the two-dismissal rule applies even where the first dismissal is in state court.

The two-dismissal rule is set forth in FRCP 41(a)(1)(B), which says that ordinarily, a dismissal will operate as an adjudication on the merits (i.e., be "with prejudice"), if the plaintiff had previously dismissed "any federal- or ***state-court*** action based on or including the same claim[.]" In other words, the two-dismissal rule explicitly applies the same way where the first dismissal was on a state-court claim as where it was on a federal claim. (But note that the ***converse*** is ***not*** true: if the first suit is in federal court and the plaintiff voluntarily dismisses it, then does the same thing as to a second suit in state court, Rule 41(a)(1)(B)'s two-dismissal rule will not apply to bar a later, third, suit in federal court.)

(C) is not the best response,

because the two-dismissal rule applies even if the configuration of the parties changes, as long as the new parties are closely related to the old ones.

The purpose of the two-dismissal rule is to prevent the harassment of the defendant that would occur if he were forced to defend three actions on the same claim. Therefore, the courts interpreting the rule have held that even if the third claim involves a "new" defendant, the claim is barred if there is such a ***close relationship*** between the defendant(s) to the first two claims and the defendant(s) to the new claim that allowing the new claim would have the effect of forcing a single or small group to defend multiple actions. (For more about this, see the discussion of this point in the analysis of Choice (D) above, including the cite to the *Lake at Las Vegas Investors Group* case.) So here, where the cab-driver is a defendant to all three suits, and where the only new defendant is a corporation wholly owned by the cab-driver and his wife, a court would surely say that the fact that a "new" party has been added doesn't negate the need to interpret the two-dismissal rule as applicable, in order to prevent harassment of the cab-driver.

Answer 2

(A) is the best response,

because the evidence issue here required balancing various factors that are left to the discretion of the trial judge.

This is a Civil Procedure question, not an Evidence question, but the solution nonetheless depends on the technical rule of evidence that applies to this particular admissibility issue. The manufacturer's objection to the evidence would have to have been based on FRE Rule 403, which says that "The court may exclude relevant evidence if its ***probative value*** is ***substantially outweighed*** by a danger of one or more of the following: ***unfair prejudice***, confusing the issues, ***misleading the jury***, undue delay, wasting time, or needlessly presenting cumulative evidence." Since the rule requires the trial judge not only to estimate the "probative value" of the evidence (which in turn depends on an assessment of all other evidence in the case dealing with the same issue), but also to "weigh" that probative value against a whole range of hard-to-quantify dangers (like prejudice and juror confusion), the trial judge is in a much better position to make this complex assessment than is the reviewing court. Therefore, Rule 403 gives wide discretion to the trial judge about whether to admit or exclude the evidence, and the appellate court will reverse only if the judge has clearly "abused" that discretion, a very hard standard for the appellant to satisfy. *See, e.g., Rigby v. Beech Aircraft Co.*, 548 F.2d 288, 293 (10th Cir. 1977): "The [Rule 403] task of balancing the probative value of evidence against danger of confusion of the issues is one for which the trial judge, because of his familiarity with the full array of evidence in the case, is particularly suited."

(B) is not the best response,

because the standard to which it refers applies to a judge's findings of fact in a non-jury case, not to the ruling on evidence at issue here.

If the phrasing of this choice seemed familiar to you, you were not imagining things. FRCP 52 governs the procedures for bench trials; Rule 52(a)(1) says that the judge must "find the facts specially," and then put those findings into the record. Then, Rule 52(a)(6) goes on to say that these "[f]indings of fact, whether based on oral or other evidence, must not be set aside [on appeal] ***unless clearly erroneous***, and the ***reviewing court must give due regard to the trial court's opportunity to judge the witnesses' credibility***." So as you can see, this "clearly erroneous" standard applies only to appellate review of the "findings of fact" made by the judge sitting without a jury—it does not apply to review of the judge's decision on evidentiary matters.

(C) is not the best response,

because the standard to which it refers applies only to certain issues of pure law.

Appellate courts give greater or lesser deference to the trial judge's rulings depending on how fact-intensive the ruling under review is. A "de novo" review is a review taken from scratch, i.e., from the same position as the trial judge would have been in. De novo review tends to occur only when the main issue is how the law applies to a given set of facts. *See, e.g.,* F,K&M (5th Ed.), §13.4, p. 603: "The fullest scope of review, not surprisingly, is for errors of law; the appellate court will decide questions of law de novo." The issue here, which requires the court to consider how the jury is likely to react to a mass of factual evidence, is not considered the sort of purely-legal issue that is suitable for de novo review. (As you would guess, de novo review involves the appellate court's giving virtually no deference to the trial judge's familiarity with the case or her opportunity to see the demeanor of the witnesses; the issue here is at the other end of the spectrum in terms of the degree of deference which the appeals court should and will give to the trial court's initial decision.)

(D) is not the best response,

because this choice does not list a standard, but rather a method of judging whether one or more errors justify a reversal on appeal.

The question asks you to specify the "standard" for evaluating the manufacturer's argument that the judge committed error in allowing the testimony. That is, the question asks you to describe the test that the appellate court will use to determine whether the judge's ruling was an error at all. The concept of "harmless error" deals with a separate issue—whether, on the ***assumption that a ruling was erroneous***, the error was ***sufficiently grave*** that the judgment below cannot be affirmed. Even when the appellate court decides that a particular ruling or set of rulings was incorrect, that court will not reverse (i.e., order a new trial, or a judgment for the other party) if the court believes that the error was ***unlikely to have changed the outcome of the trial***. Here, given the large degree of deference given by the appellate court to a trial court's ruling on a Rule 403 "probative value" objection, the appellate court would probably not find error at all (i.e., would find that the trial judge did not "abuse his discretion"), so the court would never even *get to* the question of whether any error that may have occurred was harmless. So, in short, this choice is incorrect in saying that "harmless error" specifies a "standard" by which the appellate court will evaluate whether the trial judge's ruling was correct.

Answer 3

(B) is the best response,

because there is complete diversity of citizenship, and Defendant is not a citizen of the state where the action was filed.

In those cases where Congress has chosen to allow a defendant to remove a state-court action to federal court, the removal is "of right"—if the pre-conditions for removal are met, the court does not have discretion to send the case back to state court. Thus 28 U.S.C. § 1441(a) says that unless Congress has specifically said otherwise, "any civil action brought in a State court of which the district courts of the United States have original jurisdiction, may be removed by the defendant or the defendants, to the district court of the United States for the district and division embracing the place where such action is pending." Here, since Plaintiff brought suit in state court in Cap City, State A, Defendant had the right to remove the case to the federal district court in the district that includes Cap City, so long as (1) Congress didn't expressly impose a limitation on removal that would apply to these facts; and (2) the federal district court here would have had "original jurisdiction" had the case been initially filed in that federal court. Both of these requirements are satisfied here.

Because the claim asserted by Plaintiff is a state-law tort claim, any federal-court jurisdiction over the claim would have to be based on diversity of citizenship (not on the presence of a federal question). For the court to exercise diversity jurisdiction, both citizenship and amount-in-controversy requirements must be met. *See* 28 U.S.C. § 1332. In particular, the citizenship of *all* plaintiffs must be diverse from the citizenship of *all* defendants—a rule known as the requirement of ***complete diversity***. Since Plaintiff is a citizen of State A, the required complete diversity is present if and only if Defendant is *not* a citizen of State A. The fact that defendant not only operates a factory in State A but does all of its day-to-day manufacturing in State A might lead you to guess that defendant would be considered to be a citizen of that state. But such a guess would be incorrect. Under 28 U.S.C. § 1332(c), the citizenship of a corporation includes the state in which it is incorporated and the state in which it has its principal place of business. The Supreme Court has held that the principal place of business of a corporation is the state from which the company's high level officers, such as the chief executive officer, the treasurer, and the secretary, direct the corporation's decisions—the so-called "nerve center test." *See Hertz Corp. v. Friend*, 559 U.S. 77 (2010). Since all of Defendant's corporate officers direct the corporation's affairs from their office in State C, only State C, not State A, is the Defendant's principal place of business under *Hertz*, making the Defendant's State A-based factory operations irrelevant to the citizenship issue. Therefore, Defendant is a citizen of both State C and State B (its state of incorporation) but not of State A. That, in turn, means that there is complete diversity of citizenship—the sole plaintiff is not a citizen of any of the two states in which Defendant is a citizen.

As to the requirement that there not exist any provision by which Congress explicitly took away the removal right of a defendant in the position of Defendant, there is no such provision.

(A) is not the best response,

because Defendant is not in fact a citizen of State A.

As is more fully explained with respect to Choice (B), a corporation is deemed to be a citizen only of its state of incorporation and the state in which it has its principal place of business. "Principal place of business" has been defined by the Supreme Court as the place from which the corporations-level officers control business, which in this case is Texas. So the fact that day-to-day operations all took place in State A is not sufficient to make Defendant a citizen of State A, making Choice (A) factually incorrect. (If Defendant *were* a citizen of State A, however, the outcome predicted by this choice—removal not allowed—would be correct for two reasons: (1) there would not be the required complete diversity of citizenship between Plaintiff and Defendant, thereby depriving the federal court of original jurisdiction since there is no federal question present; and (2) even if there *were* diversity, under 28 U.S.C. § 1441(b)(2), a case based solely on diversity may not be removed if any defendant is a citizen of the state where the action was originally brought.)

(C) is not correct,

for the same reason (A) is not correct; the choice incorrectly asserts that Defendant is a citizen of State A.

See the more extensive discussion of why Defendant is not a citizen of State A in the treatment of choices (A) and (B) above. (If Defendant *were* a citizen of State A, this choice would be correct, though no more correct than Choice (A) would be as well.)

(D) is not correct,

because it is factually incorrect; the claim does not fall within the federal courts federal-question jurisdiction.

If Plaintiff's claim *did* present a federal question, this choice would be correct; Defendant would have the right to remove even if it *was* a citizen of State A, the state where the action was originally brought by plaintiff. But here, Plaintiff has alleged negligent infliction of harm, which is a state-law claim. It's true that Defendant has raised an *affirmative defense* that is based on federal law. But under *Louisville & Nashville R.R. Co. v. Mottley*, 211 U.S. 149 (1908), a claim will fall within the federal court's federal-question jurisdiction only if the claim "arises under" a federal constitutional provision or federal statute, and this fact must appear on the face of the (well-pleaded) complaint—it's not enough that the federal question is raised in the answer or raised by a defense that is certain to be litigated. Therefore, the fact that Defendant has already raised an appropriate affirmative defense based on a federal statute is not enough to convert the claim into one raising a federal question, and jurisdiction will have to be premised solely on diversity of citizenship.

Answer 4

(C) is the best response,

because the suit is deemed to be between the doctor and the corporation, who are both citizens of State A.

For jurisdiction to be based on diversity, the diversity must be ***"complete."*** That is, it must be the case that no plaintiff is a citizen of the same state as any defendant. Determining whether there is diversity here requires you to answer two different questions: (1) Whose citizenship counts when a ***personal representative*** sues on behalf of an ***estate,*** and (2) of what state(s) is a ***corporation*** deemed to be a citizen?

As to problem (1), the answer is given quite specifically in a federal statute. According to 28 U.S.C. § 1332(c)(2), "The ***legal representative*** of the ***estate of a decedent*** shall be deemed to be a citizen ***only of the same state as the decedent***[.]" So here, the fact that the son is domiciled in State B is irrelevant—given that the son is bringing suit here as the legal representative of the estate of his father the doctor, § 1332(c)(2) requires that the son be deemed to be a citizen of State A, since that was the state of citizenship of the doctor at the moment of his death. (For purposes of applying § 1332(c)(2), the "decedent" is deemed to be a citizen of whatever state he was domiciled in ***at the moment of his death***, which in the case of the doctor is State A.)

Now, as to problem (2), how to determine the citizenship of a corporation is specified in almost the same place as the citizenship of an estate. 28 U.S.C. § 1332(c)(1) says that a corporation is deemed to be a citizen of both of the following, if they are different: (a) the state in which the corporation was ***incorporated***; and (b) the state in which the corporation "has its ***principal place of business.***" Place (a) is easy; the facts tell you the corporation was incorporated in

State D. But what is the state in which the corporation here "has its principal place of business"?

The Supreme Court has given guidance on the meaning of this term in *Hertz Corp. v. Friend*, 559 U.S. 77 (2010), by applying the so-called ***"nerve center" test***. That is, a corporation's "principal place of business" is "best read as referring to the place where a ***corporation's officers direct, control, and coordinate the corporation's activities***." In practice, the Court said in *Hertz*, this will normally be "the place where the corporation ***maintains its headquarters***—provided that the headquarters is the actual center of direction, control, and coordination, i.e., the 'nerve center.'" Here, the nerve center is clearly State A, since the facts tell you that State A is not only the state in which the corporation's "headquarters" are located, but the state from which all the officers of the corporation supervise the corporation's activities. Because the "nerve center" test is used, the fact that three quarters of the corporation's employees work in State C, and all of the corporation's products are made in that state, is irrelevant. In sum, the corporation here is a citizen of both State D (its state of incorporation) and State A (its state of principal place of business, i.e., the state of its "headquarters," from which its executives supervise the business).

Since the plaintiff is deemed to be a citizen of State A (because that was the doctor's state of domicile at his death), and the defendant is a citizen of both State A and State D, the same state (State A) is represented on both sides of the suit. And that is enough to destroy the required complete diversity. Furthermore, as discussed more extensively in the treatment of Choice (D) below, the federal court must refuse to hear the case once it realizes that the required complete diversity is absent, even if no litigant has raised the subject-matter-jurisdiction issue.

(A) is not the best response,

because it misstates the relevant citizenship on both sides of the suit.

On the plaintiff side of the equation, the relevant citizenship is that of the decedent (the doctor), not that of the nominal plaintiff (the son as personal representative). See the discussion of Choice (C) above for why this is the case. And on the defendant side, the corporation, in addition to being a citizen of the state of incorporation (State D), is deemed a citizen of its headquarters location (State A), and not the state where most employees work and most production occurs (i.e., not State C). This, too, is discussed further in the treatment of Choice (C) above.

(B) is not the best choice,

because like choice (A), it misstates the relevant citizenship on both sides.

On the plaintiff side, it's the citizenship of the decedent, not the personal representative, that counts. On the defendant side, while it's true that the corporation is a citizen of State D (its state of incorporation), the choice incorrectly fails to list State A as the second state of which the corporation is deemed a citizen; it's a citizen of State A because that's the state in which the corporation's principal place of business (i.e., its headquarters) is located.

(D) is not the best choice,

because lack of federal subject matter jurisdiction is never waived.

Many defenses are deemed waived if not promptly asserted. That's true even of the defense that the court lacks *personal* jurisdiction over the defendant. (*See* Rule 12(h)(1), saying that the defense of lack of personal jurisdiction is among those waived if the defendant doesn't raise it by either making a timely motion under Rule 12(b) or asserting it as part of his answer.) But there is a different rule for the defense of lack of ***subject-matter*** jurisdiction: Rule 12(h)(3) says that ***"If the court determines at any time that it lacks subject-matter jurisdiction, the court must dismiss the action."*** So the son's failure to raise this defense prior to the completion of the pleadings is irrelevant—the judge has no choice but to dismiss the action for lack of subject-matter jurisdiction "sua sponte" (on her own). And that would be true even if, say, the trial was already complete, and even if the reason the lack of jurisdiction wasn't discovered before then was because, say, one of the parties fraudulently concealed the lack.

Answer 5

(C) is the best response,

because it recognizes that diversity jurisdiction cannot be created through the collusive assignment of a claim.

Had Plaintiff not assigned the claim to Lawyer, diversity jurisdiction would not be present in a lawsuit filed by Plaintiff against Defendant, because Plaintiff and Defendant are citizens of the same state, State A. *See* 28 U.S.C. § 1332(a). So the issue is whether Plaintiff's assignment of its claim to Lawyer, a citizen of State B, creates diversity jurisdiction (since if Lawyer is viewed as now being the true plaintiff, he is diverse with Defendant). The answer is "no," because of a statute enacted by Congress to deal with exactly this sort of scenario. 28 U.S.C. § 1359 provides that a "district court shall not have jurisdiction of a civil action in which any party, by ***assignment*** or otherwise, has been ***improperly or collusively made or joined to invoke the jurisdiction of such court***." One of the circumstances in which the courts are especially likely to find that an assignment was collusive is where "the assignee merely functions as a collection agent for the assignor[.]" F,K&M (5th Ed.), § 2.7, p. 42. Here, notice that Lawyer (1) has not paid any of his own money (beyond the token $1) as compensation for the assignment; (2) will do all the work of collecting the debt; and (3) holds as his only economic interest the possibility of receiving one-third of the amount collected (a fairly standard fee-split in contingent-fee debt-collections cases). So a court would almost certainly conclude that Lawyer is merely ***functioning as a collection agent*** for the assignor, bringing the case squarely within § 1359. *See, e.g., Kramer v. Caribbean Mills*, 394 U.S. 823, 824 (1969) (assignment held collusive where assignee paid $1 for the assignment and at the same time promised to pay back to the assignor 95% of any net recovery on the assigned claim).

(A) is not correct,

because the rule that it relies upon is not accurate. Diversity jurisdiction may be invoked by a plaintiff even in a suit against a defendant who is a citizen of the state in which the federal court sits. The exception to which this choice seems to pertain applies only in ***removal*** cases; a defendant who is sued in the state courts of his state of residence may not remove the suit to that state's federal court on the basis of diversity jurisdiction. *See* 28 U.S.C. § 1441(b)(2). Here, the action was filed in federal court as an original matter, so the ban on removal by an in-state defendant is irrelevant.

(B) is not the best response,

because the relevant test here for the purpose of determining federal diversity jurisdiction is whether the assignment is impermissibly collusive, not whether it is valid under state law.

As discussed in the context of Choice (C), 28 U.S.C. § 1359 prohibits a district court from exercising diversity jurisdiction if the requisite diversity is brought about (by assignment or otherwise) "improperly or collusively." The factual issue of whether the joinder here was collusive is a matter of federal, not state, law—so the fact that the assignment may have been effective or legal under State A law is irrelevant to whether § 1359 applies.

(D) is not the best response,

because the assignment is collusive under 28 U.S.C. § 1359 and therefore does not create diversity jurisdiction.

The likely vigor of Lawyer's representation will not cure the fact that the assignment here was collusive and done for the purpose of manufacturing diversity.

Answer 6

(A) is correct,

because the baker's notice of appeal was filed too late, and the lateness divested the Court of Appeals of jurisdiction.

Federal Rule of Appellate Proc. 4(a)(1)(A) says that as a general rule, in a civil case a "notice of appeal" must be "be filed with the district clerk ***within 30 days after entry of the judgment*** or order appealed from." The facts tell you that the judgment for $55,000 was filed on July 15. Therefore, once 30 days passed, it was too late for the baker to file his notice of appeal. There are a few exceptions to this strict 30-day filing period, but none applies here. For instance, an extension can be given by the trial judge if the party seeking to appeal makes a motion for the extension no more than 30 days after the end of the 30-day-of-right period; but even that 30 day period in which to move for an extension ended on September 15. So by Sept. 20, the baker's time to file a notice of appeal had passed, and the failure to timely file such a notice is "jurisdictional"—that is, neither the district court nor the Court of Appeals has the power to excuse the lateness even if it wants to (putting aside the special case where the would-be appellant shows that he never got notice of the entry of the judgment, not something that he can show here).

Therefore, the Court of Appeals will have no choice but to dismiss the late-filed appeal. And that's true even in situations where the would-be appellant would have had a good chance of demonstrating on appeal that the district court lacked subject matter jurisdiction (an objection that is never deemed waived as long as the case is alive). Once the time for filing a notice of appeal has passed, the case is over, even for purposes of determining that there was never valid subject-matter jurisdiction in the first place. (In any event, as is discussed in the treatment of Choice (C) below, the lower court *did* have subject-matter jurisdiction.)

(B) is not the best response,

both because the appeal was not timely filed, and because the baker had waived any objection to personal jurisdiction.

On the underlying facts, there is a relatively good chance that the baker would have been able to establish that his contacts with State A were so slight that he would not have been found to have "purposely availed himself" of the opportunity to do business in the state, making the State A federal court's exercise of personal jurisdiction over him a denial of due process. (The resolution of this issue would depend on just how the court applied the "stream of commerce" theory, under which a defendant who knowingly puts an article into interstate commerce may be found to have minimum contacts with the place where the article ends up causing injury; application of the test depends on subtleties of the particular facts, including how much of the defendant's product went into the forum state, what the defendant knew about the likelihood that an article would find its way to that state, etc.) But for this question, you don't have to decide how the minimum contacts issue would have been decided had it been properly raised; that's because the baker waived any lack of personal jurisdiction by neither making a pre-answer motion raising that defense nor including the defense in his answer. So even if the baker had timely filed his notice of appeal, he would still have been found to have waived the personal-jurisdiction objection, and would not be permitted to re-litigate the objection as part of his appeal.

(C) is not the best response,

in part because the district court had subject matter jurisdiction over the action.

The facts tell you that the baker's objection to lack of subject-matter jurisdiction is based on the fact that the jury's award was for less than $75,000, and $75,000 is the minimal amount-in-controversy requirement for diversity cases. But an action will not be dismissed based on failure to meet the amount-in-controversy requirement unless it is clear ***at the moment of filing*** that ***to a legal certainty***, more than $75,000 cannot be in issue. Here, where the claim is for personal injuries that led to a hospital stay, it certainly cannot be said as a legal certainty that no jury could reasonably award more than $75,000. So the fact that the ***ultimate judgment*** awarded by the jury was less than the jurisdictional amount does not mean that the case failed to satisfy the requirement. In any event, this choice is also wrong because the appeal was not timely filed (as discussed in Choice (A)), so no reversal would have been possible even if, in fact, the district court had lacked subject-matter jurisdiction.

(D) is not the best response,

both because there could not have been a waiver of the subject-matter jurisdiction defense and because the lack of a timely notice of appeal would prevent the appeals court from affirming the judgment.

Unlike an objection to lack of personal jurisdiction, an objection to lack of subject-matter jurisdiction is *never* waived—as long as the case is still alive (i.e., there has not been a final judgment entered from which any appeal is now time-barred), either party can raise the objection, and the district court or Court of Appeals must dismiss the case if it notices the lack of subject-matter jurisdiction on its own. So this choice, by saying that "both" of the jurisdiction-related defenses were waived at the district-court level, incorrectly describes how a subject-matter jurisdiction objection would be treated. Furthermore, the Court of Appeals can "affirm" the judgment of the lower court only if the appeal is properly before the appellate court; here, where the notice of appeal was not timely filed, the Court of Appeals never got jurisdiction over an appeal, and is not in a position to "affirm" the judgment. All the Court of Appeals can do is to dismiss the improperly-asserted appeal, leaving the judgment in place.

Answer 7

(C) is the best response,

because subject-matter jurisdiction is determined based on the facts regarding citizenship on the day that the lawsuit is commenced.

Changes in a party's citizenship post-commencement do not affect the court's jurisdiction unless they suggest that a party acted in bad faith. *See Grupo Dataflux v. Atlas Global Group, LP*, 541 U.S. 567 (2004). Thus, although a defect in subject-matter jurisdiction can be raised at any time during a lawsuit, and even for the first time on appeal, the federal court does not lose subject-matter jurisdiction over the action because of changes in the citizenship of an existing party that occurred after the commencement of the suit. Here, the court properly exercised diversity jurisdiction over the suit when it was filed. *See* 28 U.S.C. § 1332(a). Diversity jurisdiction requires a showing of complete diversity—meaning that no plaintiff may be a citizen of a state that is also the state of citizenship of any defendant. A corporation is a citizen of the state(s) in which it is incorporated and of the state in which it has its principal place of business; so in this problem, Company was a citizen of State A (and only State A) at the moment the action was filed. *See* 28 U.S.C. § 1332(c); *Hertz Corp. v. Friend,* 559 U.S. 77 (2010). A partnership is an unincorporated association and is deemed to be a citizen of every state in which any member of the partnership is a citizen. *See Carden v. Arkoma Associates,* 494 U.S. 185 (1990). Since neither of the partners on the date of the commencement of the suit was a citizen of State A (Company's sole state of citizenship on that date), the requirement of complete diversity was satisfied on that date. And the fact that Company's own state of citizenship changed after the date the suit was filed (so that Company then became a citizen of the same state as one partner of Partnership) did not trigger the need to re-evaluate the existence of diversity.

(A) is not the best response,

because objections to lack of subject-matter jurisdiction are never waived.

In the federal system, objections to lack of subject-matter jurisdiction are never waived and can thus be raised at any time during the lawsuit and even for the first time on appeal. *See* FRCP 12(h)(3): "If the court determines at any time that it lacks subject-matter jurisdiction, the court must dismiss the action." *See also Capron v. Van Noorden,* 6 U.S. 126 (1804). (So if the district court lacked jurisdiction as of the time of the commencement of the suit, the court would have an obligation to dismiss the lawsuit if it later discovered this lack.) However, as discussed in the treatment of Choice (C), diversity jurisdiction did exist at the time of the commencement of the suit, and no change in one party's citizenship post-commencement could divest the court of subject-matter jurisdiction. Therefore, the motion to dismiss should be denied not because it was made too late, but because it is incorrect on the merits.

(B) is not the best response,

because there is no subject-matter jurisdiction problem, and in any event sanctions would not be appropriate here.

As to the absence of a subject-matter jurisdiction problem, the existence of subject-matter jurisdiction is determined as of the moment the case is filed, and a post-filing change in the citizenship of a party cannot divest jurisdiction that existed at the time of filing, as is more fully explained in the discussion of Choice (C). As to sanctions, sanctions would be warranted, with appropriate notice, if the party in question had violated its obligations of pleading in good faith (see FRCP 11) or had violated its obligations to comply with the discovery rules (see FRCP 37). But the mere fact that Company changed its state of incorporation after the filing of the action does not indicate bad faith in pleading, and Company's failure to tell the court about the change after it occurred does not indicate bad faith either (especially given that the change didn't in fact affect the existence of jurisdiction).

(D) is not the best response,

because no remand was called for (or even authorized) on these facts.

Remand to a state court is a procedural step that would be appropriate only if plaintiff had originally filed the action in state court and defendant had improperly removed it. In this case, the action was filed as an original matter in federal court; therefore, remand would not be an option even if subject-matter jurisdiction did not exist. Rather, if subject-matter jurisdiction did not exist, the appropriate course of action would be for the district court to dismiss the suit, not to remand it to state court. (And in any event, as discussed in Choice (C), subject-matter jurisdiction does exist.)

Answer 8

(C) is the best response,

because only the decision on the immunity motion falls within an exception to the final-judgment rule.

As a general rule, only "final judgments" may be appealed from the federal district court to the federal Court of Appeals. Thus 28 U.S.C. § 1291 gives the Court of Appeals jurisdiction over "appeals from all final decisions of the district courts of the United States[.]" There are a few situations in which an "interlocutory" appeal—i.e., an appeal from a lower-court decision that has not yet been embodied in a final judgment—is allowed in the federal system. But unless the decision falls within one of this handful of exceptions (mostly, decisions granting or denying injunctions), the decision is not appealable if there has not yet been a final judgment in the case.

Here, the trial judge has denied both motions and has set the case for trial. So you should be able to infer that there has been no final judgment in the case. Therefore, the problem boils down to determining whether either of the two rulings here falls within one of the rare exceptions to the general principle that interlocutory appeals—appeals from decisions that have not led to a final judgment—are usually not allowed.

Let's look first at the denial of the officer's motion for summary judgment on the "objectively reasonable" contention. Motions for summary judgment—like motions for other dispositions that would end the case, like Rule 12(b)(6) motions for dismissal for failure to state a claim—are part of the category called "motions to dismiss." And the denial of a motion to dismiss is virtually *never* a final judgment. *See* W, M&C (2d Ed.), Vol. 15A, § 3914.6 ("Orders refusing to dismiss an action are almost always not final.") Since there is nothing about the present denial of summary judgment that would bring it within one of the rare situations allowing an interlocutory appeal, the court's refusal to grant summary judgment was not properly appealable. That being the case, the Court of Appeals has no choice—it *must*, as a jurisdictional matter, refuse to review the correctness of the denial, even if both parties would like the court to conduct the review now.

Now, let's look at the other ruling, the trial court's denial of immunity to the defendant officer. Denials of motions for governmental immunity are one of the rare situations in which an interlocutory appeal may be allowed.

Under the ***"collateral order"*** doctrine, certain orders are characterized as "final" for appeal purposes, even though they don't terminate any part of the action; where the collateral order doctrine is or may be applicable, the only "finality" required is that the lower court "have made its final determination of the ***matter in question***." W,M&C (2d Ed.), Vol. 15A, § 3911, p. 329. A collateral order that meets this definition of finality can be immediately appealed if: (1) the matter is separate from (i.e., "collateral to") the merits of the claim being pursued; (2) the matter is too important to be denied appellate review entirely; and (3) deferring appeal until entry of a final judgment in the whole case would prevent the eventual review from being "effective" in the circumstances. *Id.* at p. 330; *Cohen v. Beneficial Indus. Loan Corp.*, 337 U.S. 541 (1949). Trial-court decisions denying a defendant's claim of governmental immunity often satisfy the requirements of the collateral order doctrine, and that is the case here: (1) the issue of whether the officer is entitled to immunity for his official acts is quite distinct from the issue of whether he actually violated the protester's constitutional rights (since immunity at least sometimes applies to a situation in which, were there no immunity, the defendant would be liable for such a violation); (2) a grant of immunity here would be completely outcome-determinative (the case would end), so the issue is too important to deny the officer forever a right to appellate review; and (3) governmental immunity, where it applies, confers on the defendant not just freedom from ultimate liability, but also freedom from the burden of having to ***prepare for and go through a trial***, so forcing the defendant to wait until after trial to appeal the denial of immunity would make eventual review "ineffective," thereby denying him this core "avoidance of trial" benefit.

Note that the claim here is for "qualified immunity," i.e., immunity that applies unless the defendant's actions violated the plaintiff's rights under "clearly established law." So when the court denied the defendant's motion asserting that he had qualified immunity, this was a collateral order that met the above requirements for immediate appealability, at least as to "the purely legal [issue] of whether the facts alleged by the plaintiff . . . support a claim of violation of clearly established law." *Mitchell v. Forsyth*, 472 U.S. 511 (1985). (In other words, the appeals court will *avoid* reviewing the highly fact-intensive issue of whether the defendant actually and reasonably believed that his conduct was lawful; the court will review only the purely legal/pleadings-driven issue of whether the plaintiff has alleged facts that *if proven* at trial would constitute a violation of a clearly established legal right.)

Neither Choices (A), (B), or (D) is the best response,

because each resolves the appealability of one of the two rulings in a way that is inconsistent with the correct resolution described in the discussion of Choice (C).

Answer 9

(D) is the best response,

because Rule 11 sanctions are available against a lawyer who fails to make reasonable inquiries, even if the lawyer behaves in good faith.

FRCP 11 specifies the obligations imposed on a lawyer who submits a pleading to a court, as well as the sanctions that are available if the lawyer does not discharge these obligations. Rule 11(a) requires that where a party is represented, at least one lawyer of record must sign the pleading (which happened here). Then, 11(b) specifies that when a lawyer signs or files the pleading, that lawyer "certifies that to the best of the [lawyer's] knowledge, information, and belief, ***formed after an inquiry reasonable under the circumstances***," certain things are true. One of the propositions that the lawyer is deemed to certify is that "the ***factual contentions have evidentiary support*** or, if specifically so identified, will likely have evidentiary support after a reasonable opportunity for further investigation or discovery" (11(b)(3)). Since there's no indication in the facts here that the complaint identified the racketeering allegations as needing further investigation or discovery in the future in order to be supported by evidence, the lawyer's filing of the pleading containing those allegations constituted his certification that, to the best of the lawyer's present knowledge, information, and belief, those racketeering allegations (e.g., the allegation that the surgeon falsely advertised where he had gone to medical school) currently ***"have evidentiary support."*** Unverified hearsay based on a rumor passed to the lawyer by another lawyer (and without any attempt to perform an easily-done fact-check) would not be considered "evidentiary support" of those allegations. Therefore, the court can and should easily determine that by making the factually-false racketeering allegations, the lawyer violated the "evidentiary support" certification imposed by Rule 11(b)(3).

Furthermore, Rule 11(b)(2) says that the lawyer is also certifying a belief, again "formed after an inquiry reasonable under the circumstances," that "the ***claims***, defenses, and other legal contentions are ***warranted by existing law*** or by a nonfrivolous argument for extending, modifying, or reversing existing law or for establishing new law." Since the facts tell us that the lawyer had previously made these same racketeering allegations against the same surgeon on behalf of a different malpractice client in a state proceeding, and that that court had dismissed the allegations as meritless, the federal court seems justified in concluding that the lawyer's reusing the same allegations against the same defendant in a different court violates this "warranted by existing law" certification.

The next sub-issue is whether, even if the teacher's lawyer had an "honest" but erroneous belief that the racketeering count was "supported by evidence" and "warranted by existing law," that good-faith but unreasonable belief insulates the lawyer against sanctions. The answer is "no," at the least where the lawyer arrives at her honest belief without having performed the "***inquiry*** reasonable under the circumstances" that Rule 11(b) requires. As one court put it, "[W]e must inquire whether [the attorney] ***would have been aware*** that [the claim] was frivolous if she had conducted a reasonable inquiry. If an attorney has failed to conduct a reasonable inquiry into the matter, then the court is obligated to impose sanctions ***even if the attorney had a good faith belief that the claim was sound***." *In Re Mroz*, 65 F.3d 1567, 1573

(11th Cir. 1995). That's the situation here: The teacher's lawyer knew he was relying only on hearsay as to the racketeering matters and that he had made no independent attempt to check the underlying facts (a check that would have immediately disclosed that at least the medical school attendance allegation was false); therefore, even if the attorney had a "good faith belief that the claim was sound" (which is questionable), that belief would not insulate him from Rule 11 sanctions.

Finally, there is a sub-issue about whether, given that some sort of Rule 11 sanction was appropriate, requiring reimbursement of the defendant's attorney's fees spent in combating the frivolous count is an appropriate form of sanction. The answer is yes, in the circumstances. It's true that, in general, Rule 11 reflects a preference that a monetary sanction be paid to the court, not the movant, in most circumstances. Thus, the Advisory Committee Note to the 1993 Amendments to Rule 11 say that "[s]ince the purpose of Rule 11 sanctions is to deter rather than to compensate, the rule provides that, if a monetary sanction is imposed, it should ordinarily be paid into court as a penalty." But the Rule itself says, in 11(c)(4), that "The sanction may include . . . if imposed on motion and ***warranted for effective deterrence***, an order ***directing payment to the movant of part or all of the reasonable attorney's fees*** and other expenses ***directly resulting from the violation***." Here, the fact that the lawyer had already made the same false allegations in a different suit and has repeated them here suggests that an award of attorney's fees is indeed "warranted for effective deterrence"; also, the award that's being sought is limited to the attorney's fees spent by the surgeon on rebutting the wrongfully-asserted racketeering claim, not rebutting the plaintiff's entire case, so it's fair to say that the fees being sought are ones "directly resulting from the violation."

(A) is not the best response,

because nothing in Rule 11 allows the court to make the client vicariously liable for a sanction that is imposed on the lawyer without any wrongdoing by the client.

You have to read this choice carefully to see exactly what it's asserting. The choice does not assert that the judge should find the teacher herself in violation of any Rule 11 obligation; it merely asserts that sanctions should be awarded against the lawyer and that the client should be made vicariously liable as a "back-up" source of payment. But nothing in Rule 11 authorizes the court to make the client vicariously liable for a sanction imposed against the lawyer—and, indeed, vicarious liability would be inconsistent with Rule 11's general approach, which focuses mainly on *lawyer* misconduct rather than client misconduct.

(B) is not the best response,

because it relies on a factual assertion about the teacher's state of mind that, even if true, would not by itself justify the conclusion that the teacher violated Rule 11.

The scheme of Rule 11 generally favors sanctions against attorneys, not against the client when the client is represented by an attorney. There are exceptions, but none applies here. As is described in the analysis of Choice (D) above, the wrongdoing here has two components: (1) a lack of belief, formed after reasonable inquiry, that the "factual contentions" of the racketeering claim "have evidentiary support" (a violation of Rule 11(b)(3)); and (2) a lack of belief, again formed after reasonable inquiry, that the "claims [of racketeering] are warranted by existing law" (a violation of Rule 11(b)(2)). As to component (2), the violation of 11(b)(2), Rule 11 specifically prohibits the judge from imposing a sanction on the client (since 11(c)(5) says that "The court must not impose a monetary sanction: (A) against a represented party for violating Rule 11(b)(2)." (The idea is that it's up to the lawyer, not the client, to form a belief, after reasonable inquiry, that the claims are "warranted by existing law.") And here, where the facts tell you that the teacher did not even know what the complaint meant by "a pattern of racketeering activity," it would be especially inappropriate to sanction the teacher. As to component (1) (that the claim had "evidentiary support") the facts indicate that the racketeering claim was invented by the lawyer, not the client, and that the client did not supply any factual background at all relating to the supposed advertising falsehoods that were alleged to constitute racketeering. Therefore, any wrongdoing in connection with the frivolous racketeering claim was solely that of the lawyer, not the client, and nothing in Rule 11 authorizes sanctions against the client in this "innocent client" scenario.

To put it another way, it is simply not the case, as this choice says it is, that Rule 11 sanctions can be imposed on a client merely because the client "should have known that she did not have actual knowledge about whether there was evidentiary support" for the claim in question. *See, e.g., Byrne v. Nezhat,* 261 F.3d 1075, 1118 (11th Cir. 2001), a case on facts similar to those in this question; the court held that the client could not be sanctioned because there was no evidence that the client "knew the complaint filed on her behalf was factually or legally baseless," and no evidence that she had "provided false information to her attorneys, thereby facilitating a factually groundless complaint." That's equally the case in our question.

(C) is incorrect,

because it misstates what Rule 11 provides.

It's true that Rule 11, and the Advisory Committee Notes to it from the 1993 Amendments, say that *ordinarily*, if the sanctions are monetary, the payment should take the form of a fine paid to the court. But this is not a hard-and-fast rule; if the court believes that deterrence will be better accomplished by an award of attorney's fees payable to the movant who has incurred the expense of defending against the frivolous claim, such a fee award is permitted. For more about this, see the last paragraph in the explanation of Choice (D) above.

Answer 10

(A) is the best response,

because issues of credibility will almost never be suitable for summary judgment, and the defendant's papers establish that credibility is a key issue here.

The standards for granting summary judgment are set out in FRCP 56, which says that the court "shall grant summary judgment if the movant shows that there ***is no genuine dispute as to any material fact*** and the ***movant is entitled to judgment as a matter of law***." Since the defendant company is not disputing the fact that the company promoted someone else rather than the plaintiff, the only real issue in the case is whether the company's (i.e., its owner's) reason for doing so was racially discriminatory. The basis for the defendant's claim that it is entitled to judgment as a matter of law is that the only potential evidence cited by the plaintiff about the defendant's racially-discriminatory mental state—the quotations recited in the complaint—are "lies." In other words, the defendant's own affidavit in support of the summary judgment motion ***puts the plaintiff's credibility*** (as well as the owner's actual intent) ***in issue*** and suggests that the defendant will win at trial only if the plaintiff's expected admissible testimony is found not to be credible. In general, summary judgment is not a suitable vehicle for disposing of a case where a witness's credibility—especially as to matters of mental state (such as intent to lie or intent to discriminate)—is central. *See, e.g.,* W,M&K (3d Ed.), Vol. 10A, § 2727, p. 485: "[I]f the evidence contained in the moving party's affidavit raises ***subjective questions*** such as ***motive, intent, or conscience***, there may have to be a trial inasmuch as ***cross-examination is the best means of testing the credibility*** of this kind of evidence." *See also* the Advisory Committee Note to the 1963 amendment of Rule 56: "Where an issue as to a material fact ***cannot be resolved without observation of the demeanor of witnesses in order to evaluate their credibility***, summary judgment is not appropriate."

Furthermore, as is discussed more fully in the analysis of Choice (C) below, the plaintiff's failure to submit an affidavit or other sworn testimony in opposition to the motion does not entitle the court to treat the company's factual allegations in the motion papers as undisputed, if the motion papers *themselves* show that there is a disputed factual issue. Here, the reference in the owner's affidavit to the plaintiff's "lies" shows that the plaintiff's credibility, as well as the owner's state of mind, are genuinely disputed issues that will require trial.

(B) is not the best response,

because the factual allegations of the complaint, no matter how detailed, cannot themselves rebut the movant's claim that there is no available evidence that would permit the plaintiff to carry her burden of production at trial.

This choice essentially asserts that the detailed factual allegations in the complaint here are sufficient by themselves that if they are believed, they would rebut the defendant's claim that there is no "genuine dispute as to any material fact." But that assertion is unduly broad, and is contradicted by something in Rule 56(c). Rule 56(c)(2) says that "A party may object that the material cited to . . . dispute a fact cannot be ***presented in a form that would be admissible in evidence***." This means that if the papers in support of the motion (here, the defendant's submission) contain evidence that if uncontradicted would demonstrate that there is no genuine dispute of material fact, the nonmovant will lose on the motion unless he can point to ***"admissible evidence"*** that if believed would put some fact into dispute. The plaintiff's pleadings here are not themselves "admissible evidence," so factual allegations in the pleadings—unless they're specifically shown to be embodied in admissible evidence—can't create a genuine issue. The reason that the appeals court will reverse is *not* that the pleadings themselves can be enough to create a genuine dispute of material fact—the reason is that the *defendant's affidavit* demonstrates (by putting the plaintiff's credibility at issue) that there will be an issue, plaintiff's credibility, that cannot be resolved as a matter of law.

(C) is not the best response,

because in this situation no sworn affidavit was required to be submitted by the plaintiff.

There are certainly situations in which the nonmovant's failure to submit an affidavit will cause the nonmovant to have summary judgment entered against him. But here, as is discussed further in Choice (A), the owner's affidavit *itself* shows the existence of a genuine dispute (plaintiff's credibility) that cannot be resolved except by a trial. Because that is so, the plaintiff survives the motion even without having submitted an affidavit. But if the fact pattern were one in which there were no issues of mental state or credibility (e.g., a suit to collect on a negotiable instrument), the nonmovant's failure to submit an affidavit or any other piece of admissible evidence *would* likely be fatal—it's only the fact that the defendant inadvertently injected a credibility issue that allows the plaintiff here to avoid summary judgment without having submitted an affidavit or other admissible piece of evidence.

(D) is incorrect,

because there is no such thing as an automatic "default" in response to a motion for summary judgment.

The Advisory Committee Note on the 2010 amendments to Rule 56 says that "summary judgment cannot be granted by ***default*** even if there is a complete failure to respond to the motion[.]" Rather, the court may grant summary judgment only "if ***the motion and supporting materials*** – including the facts considered undisputed—***show that the movant is entitled to it***[.]" (Rule 56(e)(3)). In other words, the mere fact that the nonmovant (the plaintiff) here didn't file papers in opposition to the motion does not mean that every fact asserted by the movant should be accepted as undisputed by the court—the judge was required to examine all evidence called to the court's attention, including the ***movant's own affidavit*** (with its accusation that the plaintiff was lying), and to notice that that affidavit itself demonstrated the existence of a triable issue (the credibility of the plaintiff). Given that the judge was required to review this evidence from sources other than the plaintiff, no submission by the plaintiff in opposition to the motion was required in order for the plaintiff to be entitled to have the motion denied.

Answer 11

(B) is the best response,

because Rule 35 orders for medical examinations may be rendered only against parties or those under a party's control.

FRCP 35(a)(1) specifies which persons may be ordered to undergo a physical or mental examination: "The court where the action is pending may ***order a party*** whose mental or physical condition—including blood group—is in controversy to submit to a physical or mental examination by a suitably licensed or certified examiner. The court has the same authority to ***order a party*** to produce for examination ***a person who is in its custody or under its legal control.***" The facts tell you that Driver is not a party to the action. And while Plaintiff might point to Driver's status as an employee of Defendant at the time of the accident in support of an argument that Driver is "under [Defendant's] legal control," this argument would almost certainly fail—the facts tell you that Driver is ***no longer employed*** by defendant, so he is no longer under Defendant's "legal control" even if he was under that control while employed. (Furthermore, it's doubtful that even if Driver *were* still employed by Defendant, this would be enough to put him under Defendant's "legal control." The courts have interpreted the sole purpose of the "under legal control" clause as being to help in cases where a parent or guardian is suing to recover for injuries to a ***minor***; the clause "allows the court to order that the parent or guardian makes a good faith effort to produce the minor for examination." *Scharf v. U.S. Atty. Gen.*, 597 F.2d 1240, 1244 (9th Cir. 1979). That purpose obviously does not apply here.)

(A) is not the best response,

because Rule 35 does not authorize in order to compel a non-party to submit to a physical or mental examination, even if the examinee's medical condition is relevant to a claim or defense in the action.

As is more fully discussed in the treatment of choice (B) above, only a party (or a person under the legal control of a party) may be the subject of a Rule 35 order.

(C) is not the best response,

because the court would be required to deny the discovery request even if the plaintiff *had* shown good cause for the examination.

It's true that even in the core situation to which Rule 36 applies—a request for an order compelling a party to submit to a physical or mental examination—the person requesting the order must show good cause. See Rule 35(a)(2)(A), which provides that the order for an examination may be made "only ***on motion for good cause*** and on notice to all parties and the person to be examined." But a showing of good cause is necessary ***but not sufficient*** for the order—no matter how strong the movant's need is for a physical examination of a non-party, Rule 35 does not authorize the court to order that examination. By implying that a showing of good cause would justify the court in ordering the examination, Choice (C) incorrectly states how Rule 35 works.

(D) is not the best response,

because it misstates the rule that applies to requests for physical examinations.

As is discussed in Choice (B), Rule 35 authorizes the court to order a party to produce a non-party for examination only if that party has "legal control" over the non-party, a situation that does not exist here, since Driver no longer works for Defendant.

Answer 12

(C) is the best explanation,

because it recognizes that ***an untimely amended claim will "relate back" to the date of the original pleading only if it arises out of the same transaction or occurrence as the original claim.***

The facts tell you that the tort claim would be time-barred if it were brought as a new state-court action. The federal courts in diversity cases are required to treat a state-law-based claim as time-barred if it would be time-barred in a state-court action. Therefore, the tort claim will also have to be time-barred in the federal diversity action unless there is some procedural rule that allows the tort claim to "relate back" to the earlier-filed contract claim. In federal actions—whether ones asserting federal-question claims or state-law claims asserted in diversity—the availability of the relation-back doctrine is controlled by Rule 15(c). Assuming that all defendants to the newly-asserted claim are ones who were named in the previously-filed claims (and that's the situation here, where only Defendant is named in both the old contract claim and the new tort claim), Rule 15(c)(1) recognizes two situations in which relation back will apply. 15(c)(1) says that:

"An ***amendment*** to a pleading ***relates back to the date of the original pleading*** when:

(A) the ***law that provides the applicable statute of limitations allows relation back***; [or]

(B) the ***amendment asserts a claim or defense*** that ***arose out of the conduct, transaction, or occurrence set out***—or attempted to be set out—in the ***original pleading***[.]"

As to 15(c)(1)(A), the "law that provides the applicable statute of limitations" is, of course, the substantive law of State A, since the new claim is based on state tort law. The facts tell you that under State A law, "relation back" applies where the new and old claim not only arise out of the same conduct or transaction but are supported by identical or near-identical legal theories. Here, the old claim is a pure breach-of-contract claim, and the new claim is a pure tort claim, so it is very unlikely that the federal court would find that State A law would allow relation back in this circumstance. This fact means that Plaintiff's only hope of getting relation back applied will have to come from convincing the court that the requirements of 15(c)(1)(B) are satisfied here—i.e., that the breach-of-contract claim and the tortious-interference claim arise out of the same "conduct, transaction or occurrence." Plaintiff is unlikely to succeed in convincing the court of this. But you don't have to decide whether plaintiff will succeed with that argument—you just have to realize that *if* we start from the assumption that Defendant wins on its motion (i.e., gets the tort claim dismissed as time-barred), the only one of the four choices that asserts a legal theory that would deliver a victory to Defendant is the choice that turns on whether both claims involved the same conduct or transaction. Because of 15(c)(1)(B), a conclusion by the court that they involve different conduct/transactions will deliver a victory to defendant; and as we'll see in the discussion of the other choices, none of those makes a legal argument that could deliver a victory to Defendant.

(A) is not correct,

because it misstates the significance of the law of State A.

As discussed in Choice (C) above, Rule 15(c)(1) allows the pleader to get the benefit of relation back if either of two standards is satisfied, one of which (given in 15(c)(1)(A)) is that in a diversity case, the law of the state that supplies the rule of decision would allow relation-back. So if State A law allowed relation back on these facts, Plaintiff would get the benefit of relation back here, without any need to consider the other (federal-law) standard listed in 15(c)(1). But the converse is not true—even if the law of the state that supplies the rule of decision doesn't allow relation back, the pleader gets the benefit if the test of 15(c)(1)(B) (the old claim and new claim arose out of the same transaction or occurrence) is satisfied. Choice (A) asserts that Defendant automatically wins (i.e., there's no relation back) if State A law doesn't allow relation back; since Plaintiff could still win based on same-transaction-or-occurrence even if State A law didn't allow relation back, Choice (A) is legally incorrect.

(B) is not correct,

because a difference in legal theory between the two claims does not necessarily prevent relation back from operating.

Remember that regardless of what the relevant state law says about the availability of relation back, Rule 15(c)(1)(B) says that Plaintiff can get the benefit of relation back based *solely* on whether the old claim and the new claim arise out of the same transaction or occurrence. In other words, for purposes of meeting the 15(c)(1)(B) federal standard, there is no requirement that the old claim and the new claim be based on the same legal theory. Since Choice (B) says that a difference in legal theory would cause Defendant to win (i.e., would cause relation back not to apply), that choice is legally incorrect.

(D) is not correct,

because any delay by Plaintiff in amending would be irrelevant to the issue of whether relation back is allowed.

It's true that in some circumstances, a federal court may use its discretion to deny leave to amend a pleading because the pleader delayed his attempt to amend unduly and without good cause. However, the issue here is solely the one raised by Defendant on its motion; whether the tort claim is *time-barred*, i.e., foreclosed by the statute of limitations. Any delay by the Plaintiff in amending would not bear on whether the statute of limitations has run—only successful use of the relation-back doctrine will allow plaintiff to avoid being time-barred, and a delay by plaintiff in amending will not prevent use of relation back if the requirements imposed by Rule 15(c)(1) for that doctrine are otherwise satisfied. *See Arthur v. Maersk, Inc.*, 434 F.3d 196, 203 (3d Cir. 2006) ("There is no allowance in Rule 15(c) for inquiry into a party's delay in moving for leave to amend.").

Answer 13

(C) is the best response,

because it properly applies the federal-court standard governing a motion to dismiss on grounds of *forum non conveniens* when the plaintiff is not a U.S. citizen.

The doctrine of *forum non conveniens* authorizes a trial court, in its ***discretion***, to decline to exercise jurisdiction and to dismiss the action in favor of an alternative forum if that forum is adequate. The decision to grant such a motion is governed by a number of public and private considerations, including which state or country's substantive law will govern the case, the forum state's interest in trying the case, the location of witnesses, and the burdensomeness of jury duty. *See Gulf Oil Corp. v. Gilbert*, 330 U.S. 501 (1947). A foreign plaintiff's forum choice is ***not entitled to deference*** *(see Piper Aircraft Co. v. Reyno*, 454 U.S. 235 (1981)), and the key question is whether an alternative forum that would be adequate to hear the claim is available. The contract for sale specifies that the laws of China will govern any dispute between the parties, which suggests (but does not dictate) that the remedy offered by a Chinese forum is not "clearly inadequate or unsatisfactory"; if the federal court decides that the suit may indeed appropriately be tried in China, the court may use its discretion to dismiss so that the case may be tried there. *Id.* at 254. If the federal judge here cannot find any strong reasons to honor Plaintiff's forum choice (and none are apparent from the facts as presently stated), the court should exercise its discretion to grant the motion, leaving Plaintiff to re-file the case in China.

(A) is not the best response,

because the federal statute does not allow transfer to a foreign court.

The federal transfer-of-venue statute, 28 U.S.C. § 1404, permits either plaintiff or defendant to move to transfer an action that is pending in a federal district court to ***any other district in the United States*** "[f]or the convenience of parties and witnesses, in the interest of justice." Transfers under § 1404 can be made ***only between different federal district courts***, not to a foreign court. Furthermore, transfer under the statute does not result in a ***dismissal*** of the action, just a transfer (and the facts tell you that Defendant is seeking to ***dismiss*** the action). Plus, Defendant is urging that the action would be better heard in China (not in some other federal district court). So the use of § 1404 would be inappropriate for two distinct reasons—the lack of a transfer and the fact that the proposed alternative forum is not another federal district court. Thus, although this choice reaches the correct outcome (that the motion should be granted), its reliance on the transfer-of-venue statute as the reason for granting the motion is incorrect.

(B) is not the best response,

because it misstates the standard used in a federal case to decide whether an action should be dismissed on grounds of *forum non conveniens*.

The motion is directed to the district court's discretion, and it is not an abuse of discretion to grant such a motion even if the grant will result in an unfavorable change in the law for the plaintiff. This principle is illustrated by the Supreme Court's decision in *Piper Aircraft Co. v. Reyno*, 454 U.S. 235 (1981), where plaintiff (an American administratrix representing the estates of foreign individuals killed in an airplane crash in Scotland) opposed a *forum non conveniens* dismissal on the ground that Scotland, the alternative forum, would apply law less favorable to plaintiff (for example, by refusing to apply strict tort liability). The Supreme Court rejected this argument, holding that a change in law would defeat such a motion only when the remedy in the alternative forum is "so clearly inadequate or unsatisfactory that it is no remedy at all." *Id.* at 254. Here, the parties themselves contracted to be bound by the law of China, so it would be difficult for Plaintiff to argue that the law is inadequate.

(D) is not the best response,

because jurisdiction is not a pre-condition to the court's power to dismiss for *forum non conveniens*.

The Supreme Court has made clear that district courts have authority to dismiss a federal action on grounds of *forum non conveniens* without first determining that they have jurisdiction over the case. *See Sinochem Intern Co. Ltd. v. Malaysia International Shipping Corp.* 549 U.S. 422, 435-36 (2007) ("[W]here subject matter jurisdiction or personal jurisdiction are difficult to determine, and *forum non-conveniens* weighs heavily in favor of dismissal, the court properly takes the less burdensome course."). So there is no bright-line rule stating that a federal court must first consider dismissal on jurisdictional grounds before reaching the question of *forum non conveniens*.

Answer 14

(B) is the best response,

because the default judgment was void for invalid service, and the court must therefore set aside the judgment.

Solving this problem requires multiple steps. Probably the best way is to start at the "back end," by first looking at whether there is a procedural mechanism whereby the court can be induced to consider setting aside the judgment. Where a judgment has become final (as it is here), the mechanism for relief is given in FRCP 60(b). 60(b) says that "On motion and just terms, the court ***may relieve a party*** or its legal representative ***from a final judgment***, order, or proceeding for the following reasons," and then lists six categories of reasons, of which the fourth is because "the judgment is void." So if the musician can show that the judgment is "void," he will be entitled to have it set aside under Rule 60(b).

All federal courts agree that if a court enters an *in personam* judgment against the defendant without the court's having personal jurisdiction over the defendant, the judgment is void. *See, e.g., Combs v. Nick Garin Trucking*, 825 F.2d 437, 442 (D.C. Cir. 1987) ("Of course, *an in personam* judgment entered without personal jurisdiction over a defendant is void as to that defendant."). All courts also agree that where the requirements for effective service of process on a defendant have not been met (and have not been waived by the defendant), the court does not gain personal jurisdiction over that defendant. *See id.* at 442: "[S]ince service of process is the means by which a court asserts jurisdiction to adjudicate the rights of a party, it is uniformly held that a judgment is void where the requirements for effective service have not been satisfied." So the musician will be entitled to have the default judgment set aside as void if he can show that service of process on him was not effective (assuming he is not found to have waived service).

The valid procedures for making service of a summons and complaint on an individual within the United States are forth in FRCP 4(e), which reads as follows:

"(e) Unless federal law provides otherwise, an ***individual***—other than a minor, an incompetent person, or a person whose waiver has been filed—may be served in a judicial district of the United States by:

(1) ***following state law for serving a summons*** in an action brought in courts of general jurisdiction in the state where the district court is located or where service is made; or

(2) doing ***any of the following***:

(A) ***delivering a copy of the summons and of the complaint to the individual personally***;

(B) ***leaving a copy of each at the individual's dwelling or usual place of abode with someone of suitable age and discretion who resides there***; or

(C) delivering a copy of each to an agent authorized by appointment or by law to receive service of process."

Here, the facts tell you that the two states whose law might apply (State A, where the service is being attempted, or State B, where the federal court hearing the suit is located) do not have laws allowing any possibly relevant method of service, such as service by mail. Therefore, Rule 4(e)(1)'s grant of the right to make service by "following state law for serving a summons" does not apply here. Consequently, you know that if service here was valid, it would have to have been done pursuant to Rule 4(e))(2), which lists three methods (in 2(A), (B), and (C) respectively, quoted above) that are always available based on "federal law," regardless of whether they are allowed under state law.

But all three of these methods (service on the individual defendant personally, service by leaving a copy at the defendant's dwelling with an adult co-resident, and service by delivery to an agent) all require "in person" delivery. That is, although Rule 4(e)(2) doesn't expressly say that the delivery must be "in person" as opposed to, say, by registered mail, courts have universally interpreted the Rule to require in-person service. So the attempted service here, in which the mails were used, does not meet the requirements for any of the three branches of Rule 4(e)(2).

Now, it so happens that the federal courts recognize—and, indeed, encourage—litigants to use an alternative non-physical-service notification method, namely the "request for waiver of service" method authorized by Rule 4(d), in which a copy of the summons and complaint can be sent by "first-class mail or other reliable means," together with a request that the defendant waive personal service. But even when a plaintiff attempts to use the request-for-waiver method, the attempt does not eliminate the need for personal service unless the defendant ***signs and returns the waiver form*** (and the plaintiff files the signed form with the court). Here, it's clear that even if the envelope that was sent to the musician met the standards for a Rule 4(d) request for waiver (which it probably did not, since there is no mention in the facts of a waiver form or a pre-paid method for the defendant to return it), the musician never signed and returned any form. Therefore, no waiver-of-service ever occurred. Putting it all together, there never occurred either a valid service or a valid waiver of the need for service. Consequently, the federal court never gained personal jurisdiction over the musician, and the default judgment against him was a nullity. Therefore, the court can—and, indeed, must—set power to set aside "void" judgments. (By the way, strictly speaking, this result would be true even if the musician had actually opened the envelope and learned of the suit in a timely way; however, the fact that the musician asserts—without proof to the contrary—that he never received actual notice of the suit until recently, makes it even easier for the court to conclude that it never had personal jurisdiction over him.)

(A) is not the best response,

because service was improper even if the musician was negligent in failing to open the envelope.

As is discussed more extensively as to Choice (B) above, the sending of the summons and complaint by certified mail was not a valid way to carry out service under these circumstances. And, according to most courts, that would be true even if the musician *had* in fact opened the envelope and learned of the suit in a timely manner. But certainly, the mere fact that the musician was negligent in failing to open the letter would not be enough to convert the mail service into a valid method of service, assuming that the musician did not in fact gain timely actual knowledge of the suit.

(C) is not the best response,

because the musician's right to move to set aside the default was not limited to a one-year period.

It's true that for *some* types of relief from a judgment available under Rule 60, there is a one-year time limit. Rule 60(c)(1) says that, "A motion under Rule 60(b) must be made within a reasonable time—and for ***reasons (1), (2),*** and ***(3) no more than a year after the entry of the judgment*** or order or the date of the proceeding." But relief from a judgment because it is "void" is made for reason (4) in 60(b), not reasons (1), (2), or (3). Therefore, there is no one-year limit, though the motion must be made "within a reasonable time." Here, where the facts tell you that the musician made his motion "immediately" after discovering the judgment's existence, the "within a reasonable time" requirement would certainly be deemed satisfied (at least assuming that there is no contrary evidence that the musician unreasonably ignored other evidence of the judgment's existence, and nothing in the facts here suggests that there was such evidence).

(D) is not the best response,

because whatever authority the fiancée might have been given would not be relevant to papers that were attempted to be served by mail.

There can indeed be situations, as this choice suggests, in which it matters whether the summons and complaint were or were not left with a person whom the defendant had "authorized" to receive them. In particular, where the plaintiff is relying on federal-law-based rather than state-law-based methods of service, Rule 4(e)(2)(C) make service valid if it is accomplished by "delivering a copy of [the summons and complaint] to an ***agent*** authorized by appointment ***or by law*** to receive service of process." (And at least some cases say that "by law" can include an authorization that occurs pursuant to the common-law of agency, whereby the defendant might confer on, say, a family member actual authority to accept papers on his behalf.) But 4(e)(2)(C), like the other two branches of 4(e)(2), applies *only* where the papers are ***hand-delivered*** by a person purporting to make service Here, where the papers arrive via the U.S. Postal Service, the fact that the defendant might have authorized someone else to "receive service of process" will not be enough to make the mail service valid merely because the mail carrier hands the document to that authorized person.

Answer 15

(B) is the best response,

because the federal courts presume that a direct financial relationship between a juror and a party will interfere with the juror's ability to be impartial.

Most American courts, including the federal system, apply a *per se* presumption that a prospective juror who owns even a small amount of stock in a party must be discharged for cause. *See, e.g., Chestnut v. Ford Motor Company*, 445 F.2d 967, 971-72 (4th Cir. 1971): "That a stockholder in a company which is a party to a lawsuit is incompetent to sit as juror is so well settled as to be black letter law." In fact, most state and federal courts hold that a trial judge's refusal to strike a juror for cause who owns any stock at all in a party is reversible error. *Id.*

In the federal system, there is no statute or Federal Rule that expresses this presumption—it is merely a policy applied as a matter of judge-made law. But the strength of the policy is demonstrated in an analogous area in which there *is* a federal statute that imposes a similar *per se* restriction: 28 U.S.C. § 455(b)(4) requires a federal ***judge*** to disqualify himself from any case in which he, his spouse, or his minor child residing in the judge's household has a financial interest in a party (including even a small amount of publicly-traded stock in the party). In fact, the presumption of conflict is so strong that under § 455(e), the judge may not participate in the case even if both parties are willing to ***waive*** the disqualification.

Neither (A), (C), or (D) is the best response,

because each of them is flatly inconsistent with the *per se* rule discussed in Choice (B) that any ownership stake by a juror in a party, no matter how small, and no matter how convincing the juror's testimony that she can be impartial, is automatically grounds for disqualifying the juror for cause.

Answer 16

(A) is the best response,

because these decisions are both required to protect various constitutional rights.

First, let's consider Motion 1. If a federal-court claim is one that would have been "at common law" at the time the Seventh Amendment was adopted in 1791, that Amendment guarantees the plaintiff the right to have the claim heard by a jury. Where a federal court suit involves both a "legal" claim (roughly speaking, one that in 1791 would have been a claim "at common law") and an "equitable" claim (one that could not have been brought "at common law" in 1791, and thus would have had to be brought before a court of equity), various Supreme Court decisions require the federal judge to manage trial of the case so that the plaintiff's right to have the legal claim heard by a jury is not impaired. Because of the rules of "former adjudication" (claim preclusion and collateral estoppel), safeguarding the plaintiff's practical ability to have the legal claim heard by a jury generally requires that any issue of law or fact that is common to the legal and equitable claims be tried *first* to (and decided by) the jury—only then may the judge decide the equitable claims. *See Beacon Theatres, Inc. v. Westover*, 359 U.S. 500 (1959), so holding. Here, this principle means that since the cook has a Seventh Amendment right to have a jury determine whether her firing was a gender-discriminatory act and, if so, what compensatory damages she is entitled to, the jury must decide these two issues before the judge may rule on whether the cook is also entitled to an order reinstating her at her job. (Furthermore, whichever way the jury rules on whether the defendant discriminated, the rules of former adjudication mean that the trial court probably has to accept and apply that ruling in deciding the reinstatement issue.) So the motion, which asks the court to make the first ruling on whether there was discrimination and, if so, on whether reinstatement is required, cannot be granted without violating the cook's Seventh Amendment right to have her damages claim decided by a jury.

Now, let's look at Motion 2. The Supreme Court has held repeatedly that neither state nor federal courts may permit a private litigant (or for that matter a government litigant) to use peremptory challenges to exclude civil jurors on the basis of either their race or their gender—allowing such challenges violates the excluded jurors' equal protection rights, and the opposing litigant is given standing to assert these rights. *See, e.g., J. E. B. v. Alabama Ex Rel. T. B.*, 511 U.S. 127, 146 (1994): "[T]he Equal Protection Clause prohibits discrimination in jury selection on the basis of gender, or on the assumption that an individual will be biased in a particular case for no reason other than the fact that the person happens to be a woman or happens to be a man"; *Edmonson v. Leesville Concrete Co.*, 500 U.S. 614 (1991): Even in civil litigation, allowing racially-discriminatory peremptory challenges constitutes state action because the government-run court system becomes a party to the discrimination.

It is usually not easy for one party to demonstrate that the other party has indeed used its peremptory strikes in a race- or gender-discriminatory way. But the facts here are so egregious that the challenger (the cook) will succeed with her motion. To make a challenge to the discriminatory use of peremptory challenges, the challenger must first show a "pattern" of discriminatory peremptory strikes; the two strikes here, coupled with the defendant's bald-faced (and tactically stupid) explicit reference to gender as being the reason, will be enough to satisfy this first step. If the defendant had succeeded in giving a "facially neutral" explanation for the strikes (i.e., one that avoided expressly referring to gender as the reason for the strikes, such as an explanation like "I didn't like the way either juror refused to look me in the eye when I was questioning her"), then the burden would have shifted to the cook to show that this neutral explanation was a mere pretext. But here, where the defendant has not even been able to come up with a facially-neutral-though-unconvincing explanation, the judge should deny the peremptory strikes out-of-hand, without even shifting back on the cook the burden of showing pretext.

Neither (B), (C), nor (D) is the best response,

because each reaches the wrong outcome as to at least one of the two motions (and (B) gets *both* outcomes wrong).

Answer 17

(D) is correct,

because multiple plaintiffs are not permitted to aggregate their claims to meet the jurisdictional amount unless they are suing to enforce their common interest in a single undivided right.

First, pay attention to the obvious fact that here, ***no single plaintiff*** has claims aggregating more than $75,000. (If one plaintiff *did* have claims aggregating more than $75,000 against a single defendant, that would pose a very different situation, discussed at the end of this discussion of Choice (D).) It has long been the case that where no single plaintiff has claims against any defendant for more than the jurisdictional amount, the court will not combine the dollar amounts of multiple plaintiffs' claims for purposes of determining whether more than the jurisdictional amount is at stake, except in the uncommon situation where all plaintiffs share a "single title or right." *See, e.g., Snyder v. Harris,* 394 U.S. 332, 334-335 (1969): "[T]he separate and distinct claims of ***two or more plaintiffs cannot be aggregated*** in order to satisfy the jurisdictional amount requirement. Aggregation has been permitted ***only*** (1) in cases in which ***a single plaintiff seeks to aggregate two or more of his own claims against a single defendant*** and (2) in cases in which ***two or more plaintiffs*** unite to enforce a ***single title or right in which they have a common and undivided interest***."

The "single title or right [with] a common and undivided interest" standard is very rarely met—an example where it would be met is that four individuals are each bequeathed an "undivided interest" in a piece of property (so that if the plaintiffs all sued a defendant over title to the property, the amount-in-controversy requirement would be satisfied if the property was worth more than $75,000, even if no one person's interest would be worth $75,000 if the property were partitioned). The fact that the defendant may have committed the "same" wrong towards each plaintiff by violating a single rule of law in the same way at the same time, is *not* enough to give the plaintiffs the requisite "single undivided title or right" status. So here, the fact that the brokerage firm violated the ECA statute by the same type of act, at the same time, as to each employee would not be enough to permit aggregation of their claims.

Note, however, that where there is ***at least one plaintiff*** whose own claim (or claims) against a single defendant is/are valued at ***more than $75,000***, the doctrine of ***supplemental jurisdiction***, as enacted in 28 U.S.C. § 1367 and then interpreted by the U.S. Supreme Court in *Exxon Mobil Corp. v. Allapattah Services, Inc.*, 545 U.S. 546 (2005), applies. In that situation, supplemental jurisdiction *does* permit the federal court to hear the claims of certain other plaintiffs with claims that are transactionally related to the "main" plaintiff's claim, even though each of these "minor" plaintiffs has less than $75,000 at stake—and that's true whether the way the multiple plaintiffs are together in the case is via a class action or via a Rule 20 joinder. So on our facts, if one employee had received 76 checks so that his claims against the firm amounted to $76,000, the court *would* have supplemental jurisdiction to hear the transactionally related claims of the other 19 employees, each of whom had less than $76,000 at stake. In other words, the key point here is that ***no single plaintiff*** has claims against any defendant totaling more than $75,000. But nothing in the supplemental jurisdiction statute changes the main "no-aggregation-of sub-$75,000-plaintiffs" result we've been discussing above—supplemental jurisdiction can *only* kick in when there is at least one single plaintiff-vs-defendant pairing as to which there is both diversity and more than $75,000 at stake.

(A) is not the best response,

because supplemental jurisdiction does not apply to the situation in which no single plaintiff has more than $75,000 at stake.

As is further explained in the discussion of choice (D) above, the supplemental jurisdiction statute (28 U.S.C. § 1367(a)) does not apply where no single plaintiff has claims against a single defendant aggregating more than $75,000. And that's true even though the various plaintiffs have claims that all derived from the same transaction or series of transactions (which is the case here). (But if at least one employee had claims totaling more than $75,000 against the defendant, then the court *could* use supplemental jurisdiction to hear the other employees' claim as well, assuming these other plaintiffs were diverse with the defendant.)

(B) is not the best response,

because it is an incorrect statement of how the case law of aggregation has developed.

As is further explained in the discussion of choice (D) above, Supreme Court cases like *Snyder v. Harris*, 394 U.S. 332, 334-335 (1969) have expressly rejected the argument that where multiple plaintiffs have claims arising out of the same transaction or series of related transactions, aggregation of the various claims should be permitted for purposes of determining whether the $75,000 amount-in-controversy requirement is satisfied. It is only in the very unusual case where all plaintiffs have a common or undivided interest in a "single right" that the dollar value of each plaintiff's interest may be aggregated in determining whether the $75,000 requirement is satisfied.

(C) is not the best response,

because an objection to the court's lack of subject matter jurisdiction is never waived.

Where the defendant has improperly removed from state to federal court, the plaintiff or plaintiffs normally have a limited time in which to move to have the case remanded back to state court: 28 U.S.C. § 1447(c) says that "A motion to remand the case on the basis of any defect other than lack of subject matter jurisdiction must be made ***within 30 days after the filing of the notice*** of removal[.]" But where the motion is based upon the lack of subject matter jurisdiction, the next sentence of § 1447(c) shows that there's no time limit: "If at any time before a final judgment it appears that the district court lacks subject matter jurisdiction, the case shall be remanded." (And notice that the remand can happen even if no party moves for it—so if the federal judge suddenly notices the lack of, say, complete diversity or amount-in-controversy, the judge not only may but *must* remand the case no matter how far it has proceeded on the merits, as long as final judgment has not yet been entered.)

Answer 18

(D) is the best response,

because a third-party defendant may assert against the plaintiff any defenses that the third-party plaintiff has to the plaintiff's claim.

Once a person is brought in as a third-party defendant, Rule 14(a)(2)(C) says that that person "may assert against the plaintiff any defense that the third-party plaintiff has to the plaintiff's claim[.]" By allowing the third-party defendant to raise defenses that the third-party plaintiff might have failed to raise, the Rule 14(a)(2)(C) "protects the impleaded third-party defendant where the third-party plaintiff ***fails or neglects to assert a proper defense*** to the plaintiff's action." *Lindner v. Meadow Gold Dairies, Inc.*, 515 F. Supp. 2d 1141, 1149 (D. Haw. 2007) (quoting Advisory Committee Notes to 1946 Amendments to FRCP 14(a)). While it is unclear from the fact pattern whether a statute of limitations defense would be meritorious, the trucker is entitled to assert it as a way of showing that he has no third-party liability.

(A) is not the best response,

because it's irrelevant for impleader whether the third-party defendant is or could be directly liable to the original plaintiff.

Impleader does not require that the third-party defendant be liable directly to the original plaintiff; rather, it requires that the third-party defendant "is or may be liable" to ***the original defendant***. Impleader thus is based on the ***theory of derivative or secondary liability***. "It is well established that a defendant may, as third-party plaintiff, implead a party that the plaintiff could not sue directly, [so that] the claim against the third-party defendant inur[es] to the benefit of the third-party plaintiff and not to the original plaintiff." *Parks v. United States*, 784 F.2d 20, 24 (1st Cir. 1986). So here, even though it is probably true as a matter of substantive law that the construction company could not recover directly against the trucker (because the trucker's promise of performance ran only to the benefit of the distributor, and the construction company was not an intended third-party beneficiary of that promise), this would be completely irrelevant to the key issue in the third-party suit of whether the trucker is liable to the distributor. Consequently, the court will not permit the trucker to raise as a defense that the construction company couldn't recover directly against the trucker.

(B) is not the best response,

because impleader does not have to await judgment on the main claim.

Federal Rule 14(a)(1) allows impleader against a party who "is or ***may be liable"*** to the third-party plaintiff, and this use of "may be" indicates that the impleader claim is permitted before the third-party plaintiff's liability has been determined by the court in the main action. In other words, the Rule does ***not*** require that the court first adjudicate the third-party plaintiff's liability. (In fact, Rule 14's strong preference that impleader occur very early in the litigation of the main claim is demonstrated by the last sentence of Rule 14(a)(1), which says that if the third-party plaintiff will be filing the third-party complaint "more than 14 days after serving its original answer," the third-party plaintiff must move to obtain leave of court to allow this later-than-usual filing.)

(C) is not the best response,

because although the federal rule permits a third-party defendant to assert most defenses that the third-party plaintiff may have against the original plaintiff, there is an exception for "personal defenses" like venue.

As is discussed more fully in the explanation of choice (D) above, as a ***general*** rule the third-party defendant may assert against the original plaintiff any defense that the third-party plaintiff would have to the original plaintiff's claim. But the federal courts have recognized an exception to this general rule for any defense held by the third-party plaintiff that is classified as a ***"personal defense,"*** and venue (like lack of personal jurisdiction and improper service) is one of these personal defenses. *See* W,M&K (3d Ed.), Vol. 6, § 1457, p. 518: "[T]he third-party defendant may not object to the court's lack of personal jurisdiction over the defendant . . . [or] its lack of venue over the original action . . . even if the original defendant has not waived these defenses . . . . These matters are considered the original defendant's personal defenses and are therefore not available to the third-party defendant."

Answer 19

(D) is the best response,

because a third-party complaint is proper only where any liability it alleges would be derivative of the main plaintiff's claim against the third-party plaintiff.

First, let's take care of several pieces of nomenclature: The electrician's claim against the plumber is a "third-party complaint"; the electrician is the "third-party plaintiff" (or "TPP"), and the plumber is the "third-party defendant" (or "TPD"). Now, then: The mechanism by which a third-party plaintiff may bring a third-party complaint against a third-party defendant is specified by FRCP 14. Rule 14(a)(1) says that "A defending party may, as third-party plaintiff, serve a summons and complaint on a nonparty ***who is or may be liable to it for all or part of the claim against [the third-party plaintiff].***" So the Rule 14 impleader procedure applies where, and only where, the third-party plaintiff is alleging that the third-party defendant "is or may be liable to [the third-party plaintiff] ***for all or part of the claim against" that third-party plaintiff.*** In other words, the third-party complaint must assert some sort of ***derivative*** liability, whereby the TPD is alleged to be liable *not directly* to the original plaintiff, but ***to the TPP*** in the event that the TPP is found liable to the original plaintiff. *See* W,M&K (2d Ed.): "A third-party claim may be asserted under Rule 14(a) only when the third party's liability is in some way ***dependent on the outcome of the main claim*** or when the third party is ***secondarily liable to defendant***."

Consequently, one type of claim that ***cannot*** be made in the form of a Rule 14 third-party claim is a so-called "claim" (which is really a "defense" rather than a claim) of the form, "If any party is liable to the main plaintiff, it's X, not me." *See, e.g., Toberman v. Copas*, 800 F. Supp. 1239, 1242 (M.D. Pa. 1992): "A theory that another party is the correct defendant is not appropriate for a third party complaint." And that's what's going on here: The electrician is claiming that the driver who hit the messenger (the messenger being the original plaintiff) is not the electrician, but rather the plumber, so that only the plumber, not the electrician, could possibly be liable to the messenger. This claim is not a valid third-party claim, because any liability that the plumber might have for negligent driving is ***completely separate*** from the electrician's conduct and does not derive from any liability that the electrician might have to the messenger. Since the claim is not a valid third-party claim, the court should (indeed must) dismiss the third-party complaint under Rule 12(b)(6) for failure to state a claim on which relief can be granted.

(A) is not the best response,

because if the electrician-vs-plumber complaint here were an otherwise-valid third-party complaint, the doctrine of supplemental jurisdiction would remove any subject-matter jurisdiction problem.

Supplemental jurisdiction is granted by 28 U.S.C. § 1367. § 1367(a) says that "in any civil action of which the district courts have ***original jurisdiction***, the district courts shall have ***supplemental jurisdiction*** over ***all other claims that are so related to claims in the action within such original jurisdiction that they form part of the same case or controversy*** under Article III of the United States Constitution. Such supplemental jurisdiction ***shall include claims that involve the joinder or intervention of additional parties.***" So if the original claim by the plaintiff against the defendant falls within the district court's "original jurisdiction," then a third-party claim falls within supplemental jurisdiction as long as that third-party claim is "so related to" the original claim(s) that the original claim and the third-party claim can be said to be "part of the same case or controversy" for Article III constitutional purposes. And because of the derivative nature of a valid third-party claim (i.e., the fact that by definition it derives from the defendant's liability to the original plaintiff), the third-party claim will virtually *always* be "so related" to the main claim as to make them part of the "same case or controversy," as § 1367(a) requires. In other words, ***as a practical matter a valid Rule 14 third-party claim will virtually always fall within the court's supplemental jurisdiction.*** *See* W,M,C&F (3d Ed.), Vol. 13D, § 3567.1, p. 347: "[I]mpleader claims routinely satisfy § 1367(a) because they concern the ultimate liability for the very transaction that is the basis of the underlying suit." Therefore, if the electrician's claim against the plumber were a valid third-party claim under Rule 14 (which it isn't), the applicability of supplemental jurisdiction under 28 U.S.C. § 1367(a) would mean that the fact that the electrician and the plumber are not diverse to each other would be irrelevant. That makes Choice (A) incorrect as an argument for why the court should dismiss the third-party complaint.

(B) is not the best response,

because the "100-mile bulge" provision of Rule 4(k)(1)(B) gives the court personal jurisdiction over the plumber.

Rule 4(k)(1) says that "Serving a summons or filing a waiver of service establishes personal jurisdiction over a defendant: . . . (B) who is a ***party joined under Rule 14*** or 19 and is ***served within a judicial district of the United States and not more than 100 miles from where the summons was issued***[.]" This is the so-called ***"100-mile bulge" provision***, which grants a federal court personal jurisdiction over a third-party defendant if that party can be found and served within a 100-mile radius of the courthouse in which the federal court hearing the case sits. And that's true even if the third-party defendant does not have minimum contacts (or, indeed, *any* contacts whatsoever) with the state where the action is pending, as long as that third-party defendant has minimum contacts with the state where he was served. The service on the plumber here meets this requirement, because: (1) the underlying case is pending at the federal courthouse located in State A; (2) service of the third-party complaint was made in person on the plumber at a place in State C less than 100 miles from the State A federal courthouse; and (3) the facts tell you that the plumber was performing a multi-week project at the site in State C where he was served, enough of a contact with State C to constitute the constitutionally-required minimum contacts with State C. So if the complaint were a valid third-party complaint as defined in Rule 14, the 10-mile bulge provision would apply, furnishing the State A federal court with personal jurisdiction over the plumber and making this choice an incorrect argument for why the claim against the plumber should be dismissed.

(C) is not the best response,

because service of the complaint on plumber was quick enough to meet the "of right" requirements.

FRCP 14, in addition to specifying what types of claims may be made by impleader, specifies the time limits for making service of a Rule14 impleader claim. Rule 14(a)(1) starts by articulating the general principle that "A defending party may, as third-party plaintiff, serve a summons and complaint on a nonparty who is or may be liable to it for all or part of the claim against [the third-party plaintiff]." Then, the next sentence of 14(a)

(1) says, "But the third-party plaintiff must, by motion, obtain the court's leave ***if it files the third-party complaint more than 14 days after serving its original answer***[.]" Reading these first two sentences of Rule 14(a)(1) together, the scheme is that as long as the defending party serves the third-party complaint within 14 or fewer days after that defending party served its "original answer," no leave of court is required (i.e., the third-party claim can be served "of right"). The facts here tell you that the electrician served his purported third-party complaint against the plumber 11 days after the electrician had served his original answer to the messenger's complaint. So the service of the third-party complaint occurred less than 14 days after service of the original answer, obviating the need for the electrician to obtain leave of court. That means that the electrician's failure to get leave of court is not a reason for dismissing the third-party claim.

Answer 20

(B) is the best response,

because where the defendant being served is an individual, the papers may not be left at the person's usual place of business.

This question is mildly tricky because it involves service of process on an individual who is in business, so in a sense it falls half-way between the situation of service on an individual arising out of a non-business matter (e.g., an auto accident) and the situation of service on a corporation arising out of a business matter. The key insight is to know that when an individual is being served, even if the individual operates a business, he or she cannot be served by leaving the papers with a third person found at the individual's usual place of business (at least assuming that there is no special provision of state law that allows this).

Let's review the FRCP provisions governing service on an individual found within the United States. These provisions are given in Rule 4(e). Since we can't conclude that a particular form of service was invalid unless we look at *all* the allowable methods, we have to look at the full text of this provision:

"Unless federal law provides otherwise, an ***individual***—other than a minor, an incompetent person, or a person whose waiver has been filed—may be served in a judicial district of the United States by:

(1) ***following state law*** for serving a summons in an action brought in courts of general jurisdiction in ***the state where the district court is located*** or ***where service is made***; or

(2) doing ***any of the following***:

(A) delivering a copy of the summons and of the complaint ***to the individual personally***;

(B) ***leaving a copy*** of each at the individual's ***dwelling or usual place of abode*** with ***someone of suitable age and discretion who resides there***; or

(C) delivering a copy of each to an ***agent*** authorized by appointment or by law to receive service of process."

So, putting aside for the moment the possibility that state law may supply an additional method, if the plaintiff is relying only on the federal methods specified in Rule 4(e)(2), then other than handing the papers to the "individual personally" (4(e)(2)(A)) or to an authorized "agent" (4(e)(2)(C)), the only way service can be made by leaving the papers with someone other than the individual being served is by leaving them at the individual's "***dwelling or usual place of abode*** with ***someone of suitable age and discretion who resides there.***" In other words, there's no way to make service by showing up at the individual's usual ***place of business*** and leaving the papers with a co-worker or employee of the individual defendant. So on our facts, even if the accountant still worked at the 123 Main Street address, and even if the receptionist who took the papers was the accountant's employee, the service would *still* have been improper under Rule 4(e)(2).

Notice that 4(e)(2)(C) allows service on an individual without regard to the location (and thus possibly allows service at the person's place of business) if the papers are left with "an ***agent*** authorized by ***appointment or by law*** to receive service of process." But this provision is interpreted pretty narrowly; unless the defendant has, according to common-law "agency" principles, conferred on the third person the power to accept service (and merely conferring the general power to "act as my assistant when I'm not around" would *not* be sufficient), a co-worker or employee of the individual would not count as an agent. Here, where the defendant doesn't even work at those premises any more, and there's nothing to suggest that he has authorized the receptionist to act on his behalf to receive papers, the receptionist would certainly not be an "agent authorized by appointment or by law to receive service of process."

There's one last possibility that you have to rule out before you can be confident that the service method here was improper. Under Rule 4(e)(1), if either State A (the "state where the district court [in which the suit is pending] is located") or State B (the state "where service is made") had passed a statute allowing service on an individual by leaving the papers with a third person at the individual's place of business, that state provision would have made the service here valid. But the facts tell you that States A and B have no method-of-service provisions beyond those provided directly by the FRCP (i.e., those listed in 4(e)(2)), so this escape-hatch allowing the use of state-law service methods is not available to save the method used here.

(A) is not the best response,

because it reaches the right result but on incorrect legal reasoning.

This choice suggests that the only reason service was invalid was that the accountant was no longer using 123 Main St. as his usual place of business at the time the service occurred. But as the analysis of choice (B) above demonstrates, federal law does not allow service on an individual by leaving papers with a third person at the individual's place of business (or, indeed, any location other than the individual's "dwelling or usual place of abode"), even if that place of business is current. So even if the accountant customarily showed up at 123 Main St. as his place of business every day, service would still have been improper, making this choice a much less good explanation of the result than Choice (B).

(C) is not the best response,

both because it reaches the incorrect result and because it does so by an incorrect legal analysis.

As the analysis of choice (B) above demonstrates, federal law does not allow service on an individual by leaving papers with a third person at the individual's place of business. So even if the 123 Main St. address were the accountant's actual place of business (rather than merely being a place he falsely identified on his website as being his place of business), the service here would still have been improper.

(D) is not the best response,

because it is based on an incorrect legal rule about when a waiver of the right to object to improper service occurs.

It's certainly true that under federal law, a defendant can easily be found to have waived, by mere inaction, his right to object to improper service. The relevant provisions are found in FRCP 12. Rule 12(b)(5) effectively gives a defendant a choice of two ways of raising the defense of "insufficient service of process": (1) by raising the defense in that defendant's "responsive pleading" (which is of course the answer) or (2) by motion. And Rule 12(h)(1) says that the defenses listed in Rule 12(b)(2)-(5) (which as just noted include the 12(b)(5) "insufficient service of process" defense) are waived if made in neither a pre-answer Rule 12 motion nor in the answer itself. But the facts here tell you that after receiving the papers from the receptionist, the accountant "immediately" filed an answer that included the insufficient-service defense. "Immediately" implies that the accountant did not file a Rule 12(b) motion prior to the answer (which, if he had so filed without raising the insufficient-service defense as part of the motion, *would* have been an automatic waiver), so by raising the defense in his answer the accountant properly and timely asserted it. In other words, this choice, by suggesting that the insufficient-service defense must be made by a pre-answer motion rather than in the answer itself, is making an incorrect statement of law. (But keep in mind that if the accountant had made a Rule 12(b) motion for any other reason—such as, say, a 12(b)(6) motion for failure to state a claim on which relief can be granted—his failure to assert the insufficient-service objection as part of that 12(b) motion *would* have resulted under Rule 12(h)(1)(A) in a waiver of the objection, so that it could no longer later be asserted as part of even a timely-filed answer.)

Answer 21

(B) is correct,

because the *Erie* doctrine requires the federal court to follow the substantive policy embedded in the additur technique.

The principle embodied by *Erie v. Tompkins*, 304 U.S. 64 (1938) is that when a federal court is sitting in diversity, the court must apply *state*—not federal—substantive law. So the issue here is whether State A's common-law rule allowing a trial judge to use the "additur" conditional-new-trial technique if the judge believes a jury verdict to be manifestly and excessively low is a "substantive" principle that is binding on the federal judge. It's very likely that the Supreme Court would hold that State A's endorsement of the additur technique represents an attempt by the state to achieve the substantive goal of ensuring that jury verdicts are not unreasonably low. The Supreme Court has never expressly decided whether *Erie* doctrine applies to additur, but the Court has decided a case involving a closely analogous state-law technique for controlling the size of jury verdicts. In *Gasperini v. Center For Humanities, Inc.*, 518 U.S. 415 (1996), the Court had to decide whether a federal judge sitting in diversity must apply a New York statute under which the trial judge should order a new trial if the jury's award "deviates materially from what would be reasonable compensation." The Court held that the answer was yes: Although the statute may have had a procedural aspect, the state was pursuing the obviously substantive goal of controlling the size of jury verdicts, so the federal court was required to follow a similar policy of ordering a new trial if the jury verdict was a material deviation from compensation that would be reasonable. Here, by recognizing additur, State A is, similarly, pursuing the substantive objective of using conditional new trial orders to make sure that a clearly-inadequate jury verdict does not stand; therefore, the federal court should (and indeed under *Erie* must) pursue the same objective.

There is an additional complication in this case: The Seventh Amendment guarantees a litigant in a federal trial a right to a jury trial, and there is some older Supreme Court precedent suggesting that use of additur may violate the Seventh Amendment by leading the judge to award a damage amount greater than was ever awarded by the jury. But as is discussed more fully in the treatment of choice (D) below, use of additur in the circumstances here would be very unlikely to be found to be a violation of the Seventh Amendment, because the $200,000 hospital-bill payment was not genuinely in dispute.

(A) is not the best response,

because the movant must, as a pre-condition to a post-verdict motion for judgment as a matter of law, make the motion at the close of evidence.

The making of a motion for judgment as a matter of law or "JML" (the federal equivalent of the common-law motion for "JNOV," or "judgment notwithstanding the verdict") is governed by FRCP 50(a). Rule 50(a)(2) says that "A motion for judgment as a matter of law may be made at any time ***before the case is submitted to the jury***." In other words, by negative implication once the case is submitted to the jury, the motion is no longer timely. Assuming that the motion was timely made, then after the jury hands down a verdict with which the movant is unhappy, Rule 50(b) says that "No later than 28 days after the entry of judgment . . . The movant may file a ***renewed*** motion for judgment as a matter of law[.]" Here, the facts tell you that the case was submitted to the jury "without any motion having been made by either side"—therefore, you know that the skydiver did not move for JML before the case was sent to the jury and that he therefore lost the right to make (or renew) such a motion after the verdict. (But if the skydiver *had* moved for JML before the case went to the jury, this choice would be correct: The skydiver would have had 28 days after entry of the judgment in which to renew his JML motion, and the court would have been justified in granting the motion—i.e., awarding judgment for $200,000—since that amount would be correct as a matter of law in the sense that there would have been uncontested proof of the $200,000 in hospital-bill damages.)

(C) is not the best choice,

because it states a legally-incorrect rule.

The case for using additur is actually weaker in federal-question cases than in diversity cases. That's because in a federal question case, *Erie* doctrine is irrelevant, so there's no state-law substantive policy that the federal court might be required to implement, as would arguably be the situation in a diversity case where the relevant state law encourages the use of additur to prevent unreasonably low jury verdicts. But in any event, this choice is wrong in asserting that additur may not be applied in diversity cases, as is explained in the discussion of Choice (B).

(D) is not the best choice,

because the use of additur here would be the equivalent of a grant of summary judgment on damages and would therefore not invade the province of the jury.

It's true that in an old case, the Supreme Court seemed to hold that the use of additur violated the plaintiff's Seventh Amendment right to a jury trial. That case was *Dimick v. Schiedt*, 293 U.S. 474, 486-87 (1935), in which the majority said that "where the verdict is too small, an increase by the court [by use of additur] is a bald addition of something which in no sense can be said to be included in the verdict," thereby violating the right of the *plaintiff* (not the defendant) to have a jury determine the correct damage amount. It's not at all clear that *Dimick* would turn out the same way today, i.e., that the present Supreme Court would find *any* use of additur to be a violation of the Seventh Amendment. But in any event, the lower federal courts have, post-*Dimick*, always recognized that there is no Seventh Amendment problem with the use of additur in one particular situation: that in which the trial demonstrates that if the defendant is liable at all, he is liable for at least some particular amount ***as proven by the uncontested evidence***. *See, e.g., Roman v. Western Manufacturing, Inc.*, 691 F.3d 686, 702 (5th Cir. 2012): "[T]he constitutional rule against additur is not violated in a case where the jury ha[s] properly determined liability and there is ***no valid dispute as to the amount of damages***. In such a case the court is in effect simply ***granting summary judgment*** on the question of damages." That's the situation here: The jury has found liability (a defective product that caused the injury), and the manufacturer never contested the skydiver's evidence that the hospital bill for the resulting injuries totaled $200,000 and was paid. Therefore, the trial judge's use of additur—i.e., the judge's grant of a new trial conditioned upon the manufacturer's refusal to agree to pay $200,000—was functionally no different from the judge's granting post-trial summary judgment of $200,000 as the amount of damages about which there was no genuine issue of law or fact; and no court would consider a grant of summary judgment to be a violation of a litigant's Seventh Amendment right to jury trial.

Answer 22

(C) is the best response,

because in a diversity action, the federal court must follow the conflict-of-laws principles of the state in which the federal court sits.

The underlying claim here is based on state law of product liability. In that situation, there is no federal statute or rule that governs what test is to be used in determining whether the product's design was defective (and the product would have to be defective in order for the landscaper to recover). Since there is no federal statute or rule on point, the case is governed by the basic rule of *Erie v. Tompkins*, 304 U.S. 64 (1938), that the federal court must follow the state's substantive law. The question then becomes, *which* state's substantive law must the federal court follow? The answer has always been, since soon after *Erie* itself was decided, that the federal court must follow the substantive law of whichever state the state court where the federal court sits would follow had the case been filed in state court. In other words, the federal court must ***follow the conflict of laws principles of the state in which the federal court sits***. *See Klaxon Co. v. Stentor Co.*, 313 U.S. 487, 496 (1941), a diversity case filed in Delaware federal court: "The conflict of laws rules to be applied by the federal court [sitting] in Delaware must conform to those prevailing in Delaware's state courts." (If the federal court were free to make its own conflict-of-laws decision about which state's substantive law to apply, then the plaintiff could "forum shop" between the state and federal courts in a particular state, by picking whichever court she thought would use a conflicts rule that would lead to use of the most favorable-to-the-plaintiff substantive law, thereby defeating *Erie*'s anti-forum-shopping purpose.)

(A) is not the best response,

because it leads to the wrong result in those cases where State C's conflict principles would lead that state to apply another state's design-defect test.

If State C's conflict principles would cause State C to use, say, the design-defect test applied by the state where the product was designed and manufactured (State B), then this choice would result in the federal court's using a different substantive rule than would be used by the courts of the state where the federal court sits (State C). And, for the reasons discussed in the analysis of Choice (C) above, such an approach would encourage plaintiffs to forum-shop. The correct approach is for the federal court to use the conflict-of-law rules of the state where the federal court sits, rather than necessarily the substantive law of that state.

(B) is not the best result,

because *Erie* principles require a federal court sitting in diversity to apply state, not federal, substantive law.

It is probably true that there are design-defect standards developed by the federal courts for use in suits where the federal law supplies the rule of decision (e.g., in a suit by a member of the Armed Forces who is injured by a defective product purchased by the military from the company now being sued). But the basic principle behind *Erie* doctrine is that where the right sued upon is created by a state, a federal court hearing a suit on that right is required to consult state law, not federal common-law principles developed in connection with analogous federally-created rights.

(D) is not the best response,

because it is not up to the federal court to select what it thinks is the best conflict-of-laws approach to the controversy.

Erie requires that a federal court sitting in diversity apply "state substantive law." The object of *Erie* doctrine is principally to ensure that insofar as the outcome of a suit is dependent on substantive rules, a diversity suit should reach the same outcome as a suit brought in the courts of the state where the federal court sits, so as to reduce forum-shopping. The Supreme Court has interpreted this rationale to require that the federal court apply the conflict-of-laws rule of the state where the federal court sits, rather than permitting the federal court to use "federal conflict-of-law principles," which might include the federal judge's own judgment about which state has the strongest interest in having its substantive law apply. This "follow state conflict-of-laws principles" approach was announced by the Supreme Court in *Klaxon Co. v. Stentor Co.*, 313 U.S. 487, 496 (1941) (quoted in Choice (C) above), and has remained good law despite some criticisms.

Answer 23

(D) is correct,

because it correctly applies the federal rule governing a request for a waiver of service.

Under the waiver-of-service procedure laid out in Federal Rule 4(d)(1), a plaintiff can send "by first-class mail or other reliable means" notice to a corporate (or for that matter an individual) defendant of the commencement of the suit and request that the defendant "waive service of a summons." Then, if the defendant complies with the request by signing and returning the waiver form to the plaintiff, the plaintiff can file the waiver with the court and avoid having to make service. See Rule 4(d)(4), entitled "Results of Filing a Waiver": "When the plaintiff ***files a waiver***, proof of service is not required and ***these rules apply as if a summons and complaint had been served at the time of filing the waiver***." But the request-for-waiver process does not obviate the need for actual service unless and until the plaintiff receives the signed waiver and files it with the court. See the Advisory Committee Notes to the 1993 Amendments on Rule 4: "[i]f the waiver is not returned ***and filed***, . . . the action will not otherwise proceed until formal service of process is effected." *See also Cambridge Holdings Group, Inc. v. Federal Insurance Company,* 489 F.3d 1356 (D.C. Cir. 2007): "if the defendant does not waive, the rule does not suggest that service is nonetheless effective." So service was not deemed complete until Plaintiff filed the signed return with the court on August 22.

(A) is incorrect,

because it misstates the requirements for the waiver-of-service procedure to be proper.

As is more fully described in the treatment of Choice (D) above, the waiver procedure does not result in the complaint's being deemed served unless and until the plaintiff has received back from the defendant the signed waiver and filed it with the court.

(B) is incorrect,

because it misstates how the waiver-of-service procedure works.

It's true that according to Rule 4(d)(1)(F), the plaintiff, when he mails the defendant a request for waiver of service, is not required to give the defendant more than 30 days in which to sign and return the form to the plaintiff. But once the plaintiff does that, the fact that the defendant does not comply with the request within the allotted 30 days does not entitle the plaintiff to file a statement with the court or otherwise treat the requirement of service as having been satisfied. Indeed, there is no period of time so lengthy that the defendant's failure to return the requested signed form is deemed to be a waiver of service. Unless and until the defendant returns the signed form and the plaintiff files the form with the court, service is not deemed to have been carried out—so by declining to sign, the defendant can effectively require the plaintiff to make actual service. (The only "teeth" contained in the Rule 4(d)(1) request-for-waiver mechanism is that if the defendant does not grant the waiver, the court is *required* to make the defendant pay for the plaintiff's expenses in making service, as well as plaintiff's attorney's fees for any motion that plaintiff makes in order to collect the service expenses.)

(C) is incorrect,

because it misstates the point at which the waiver-of-process mechanism substitutes for actual service.

Plaintiff's receipt of the signed waiver form from the defendant is certainly a *necessary* condition to Plaintiff's ability to avoid making service, but that receipt is *not* also a *sufficient* condition for that ability—the need for actual service on defendant is not extinguished unless and until Plaintiff files the signed waiver with the court. See the explanation of Choice (D) for more about this process.

Answer 24

(B) is the best response,

because the federal court must follow the preclusion rule of State A, and that rule would deny issue preclusion because the issue was not actually litigated.

To solve this problem, you first have to decide whether the federal court is required to follow the relevant state law of "issue preclusion" (also called "collateral estoppel"). The answer is "yes," because a federal statute so specifies. 28 U.S.C. § 1738, partly entitled "full faith and credit," says that judgments rendered by any state court "***shall have the same full faith and credit in every [federal] court***" as the judgment would have in the courts of the state that rendered it. And as the Supreme Court has explained, § 1738 "has long been understood to encompass the doctrines of res judicata, or 'claim preclusion,' and collateral estoppel, or 'issue preclusion.'" *San Remo Hotel, LP v. City and County of San Francisco*, 545 U.S. 323, 336 (2005). So whatever issue-preclusive effect the plea bargain would have in the State A courts in a later suit between the husband and a private adversary like the insurer, the federal court must give that plea bargain the same issue-preclusive effect, regardless of whether the federal court thinks the State A approach is correct.

Therefore, you next have to figure out *what* issue-preclusive effect, if any, a State A court would give to the plea bargain here if the question arose in the context of a civil suit in that court between the insurer and the husband. The facts tell you that the State A courts "follow the prevailing national approach" to issue preclusion. Therefore, you have to decide what the prevailing national approach would be as to the use of issue preclusion here.

A good source of doctrine on the issue is the Second Restatement of Judgments. § 27 of the Restatement gives the following "General Rule" for when an issue of law or fact should be given issue-preclusive effect in a subsequent suit between the *same parties* (which is not the situation here, but in a minute you'll see why the same-party rule is relevant here): "When an ***issue of fact or law*** is ***actually litigated and determined*** by a valid and ***final judgment***, and the ***determination is essential to the judgment***, the determination is conclusive in a subsequent action between the parties, ***whether on the same or a different claim***." Then, § 29 deals with the issue of when a person who would be subject to issue preclusion under § 27 in a suit with the same opponent as the first suit should also be subject to preclusion in a suit with a ***different opponent***: "A party precluded from relitigating an issue with an opposing party, in accordance with [§ 27], is ***also precluded*** from doing so with ***another*** person ***unless the fact that he lacked full and fair opportunity to litigate the issue in the first action or other circumstances justify affording him an opportunity to relitigate the issue***." (§ 29 then continues on, by giving a list of various factors that might as a matter of policy justify not applying issue preclusion even though the preclusion doctrine would apply if the second case involved the same adversary.) For our present purposes, all we need to take away from the combination of § 27 (rules for where the parties are the same in the second as in the first suit) and § 29 (how the rules are different if the party who lost on the issue in the first suit is facing a different adversary in the second suit) is this simple rule: If issue preclusion *wouldn't apply* even if the two parties were the same in both suits, it ***cannot possibly apply*** where the party seeking to make use of preclusion was ***not*** a party to the first suit. So if we can find some requirement for issue preclusion that because it wasn't met in the first suit would prevent the government of State A from using issue preclusion against the husband in a later civil suit between the government and the husband, we can be confident that that same unmet requirement will prevent the insurer from using issue preclusion.

As you can see from the language of Rest. 2d § 27 quoted above, the determination on an issue of fact or law is "conclusive" (i.e., issue-preclusion will apply), even in a later suit between the same parties, only if ***three distinct requirements*** are all satisfied:

(1) the issue was ***"actually litigated"***;

(2) the issue was ***"determined by a final judgment"***; and

(3) the determination of the issue was ***"essential to the judgment."***

Here, a careful reading of the homicide clause shows that the insurer can deny payment under that clause only if (a) the wife's death was the result of a voluntary act by the wife or the husband; and (b) that voluntary act was committed with the intent of causing the death. The husband's best chance of avoiding issue-preclusion as to issues (a) and (b) (and he will avoid the bad effects of preclusion if he can avoid it as to *either* (a) or (b), since the insurer has to prove *both*) is to show that whether or not the plea-bargain establishes that his shot was a "voluntary act," the plea-bargain does not satisfy the three requirements for issue-preclusion on the issue of whether the husband by firing the shot ***intended to cause the wife's death***. (Since it's pretty clear that requirements for issue-preclusion are not met as to intent-to-cause-death, that's the only fact we'll focus on here.)

Well, can we say that the issue of whether the husband intended to kill the wife when he fired the shot was "actually litigated" in the State A criminal proceeding that ended in the plea bargain? Clearly, the answer is "no": The husband's precise state of mind in firing the shot was not "actually litigated" in the proceeding that ended in the guilty plea. Indeed, the facts tell you that when the husband was required to make his "allocution" (oral explanation of why and how there was a "factual basis" for the guilty plea), the husband expressly denied that he intended for his shot to strike the wife. Where the defendant is permitted to plead guilty while maintaining his innocence of some aspect of the crime—a so-called "*Alford* plea"—the vast majority of courts have held that a fact denied by the defendant during the course of the allocution should not be deemed to have been "actually litigated," and therefore not subject to later issue preclusion.

Furthermore, recall that an issue can be subjected to issue preclusion only if determination of that issue was ***"essential to the judgment."*** Here, the facts tell you that in State A, there are two different mental states that can suffice for voluntary manslaughter: an intent to kill, or reckless behavior that leads to a killing. All we know from the guilty plea—even if we treat it as establishing all required elements of the crime—is that the defendant had one of the two required mental states, intent to kill *or* recklessness. But the insurance policy's homicide clause kicks in only if the killing by the spouse of the insured was ***intentional***—there is no mention of a reckless killing as sufficing. Since the insurer isn't entitled to summary judgment unless it can show that the husband is precluded from relitigating every factual issue needed to satisfy the homicide clause, it cannot be said that a determination of the required mental state was "essential to the judgment" entered by the State A court under the plea bargain. Therefore, we can be confident that the State A courts—following prevailing national principles—would not preclude the husband from relitigating all issues required to trigger the homicide clause, and the federal court must follow suit by declining issue preclusion and letting the case go to trial (at least with respect to the husband's mental state when he fired).

(A) is not the best response,

because the State A court would not apply issue preclusion, so the federal court cannot do so either.

Under the prevailing approach, an issue will not be subject to issue preclusion unless it was both "actually litigated" in the prior case and the finding on that issue was "essential to the judgment." (See the discussion of Choice (B) above.) Here, the handling in the criminal case of the issue of whether the husband intended for his shot to strike the wife does not satisfy either of these requirements, so we can be confident that the State A courts (which we're told follow the "prevailing national approach" to the relevant issues) would not apply issue preclusion here. Therefore, even though this choice correctly states that the federal court must follow State A's approach, this choice incorrectly states what that state-law approach would be.

(C) is not the best response,

because it wrongly states that the federal court should follow the Court of Appeals case law on when issue preclusion should apply.

As is described in the explanation of choice (B), the full-faith-and-credit principle of a federal statute, 28 U.S.C. § 1738, requires a federal court to give to a prior state-court judgment the same res judicata effect (including the same issue-preclusion or collateral-estoppel effect) as that judgment would have in the courts of the state that rendered it, which in this case is State A. Therefore, even though this choice is correct in stating that, because a federal court that follows prevailing rules would not apply issue preclusion to an issue that was not actually litigated, the court here should not apply issue preclusion. This choice incorrectly states how the federal court here must reach its decision; the federal court must apply whatever rule of issue preclusion that the State A courts would apply and is not free to consult opinions written by the federal Court of Appeals for the circuit in which the federal court sits.

(D) is not the best response,

for the same basic reason that choice (C) is incorrect: The federal court is required to follow whatever approach to issue preclusion would be applied by the State A courts and is not free to consult federal Court of Appeals opinions. (The choice is also wrong for a second reason: The "prevailing national approach" that you are told is applied by the federal Court of Appeals would not regard the issue of the husband's intent in firing the shot as having been conclusively determined, due to the fact that the husband's intent was neither "actually litigated" nor decided in a way that was "essential to the judgment" of conviction.)

Answer 25

(B) is the correct answer,

because it correctly states the standard that governs amendment under the federal rules when a responsive pleading omits an affirmative defense.

Under the fairly liberal amendment procedure of Federal Rule 15, a party (call that party "*A*," and the opposing party "*B*" for clarity) may amend his pleading ***once as a matter of right*** in either of these two situations: (1) within ***21 days of when A served his original pleading*** (see Rule 15(a)(1)(A)) or (2) if *A*'s pleading was one that required a ***responsive pleading*** by *B*, within ***21 days*** of when B either (i) ***served that responsive pleading*** or (ii) made a ***motion*** under Rule 12(b), (e), or (f) (with the 21 days starting on whichever of two events mentioned in (i) and (ii) happened earlier) (see Rule 15(a)(1)(B)).

In our situation, Defendant's answer did not assert any counterclaims. Therefore, the service of that answer did not require a "responsive pleading" (the way, for instance, an answer that included a counterclaim would have required that Plaintiff filed an answer to the counterclaim). Since no responsive pleading was required, the scenario covered in sub-section (2) in the prior paragraph (the situation governed by Rule 15(a)(1)(B)) does not apply. Consequently, the only scenario in which defendant had a period in which to amend "of right" was the scenario covered in sub-section (1) above, the garden-variety scenario in which Defendant had the right to amend once if he acted within the 21 days following his service of his original answer (with that original service having happened on March 15). Therefore, once 21 days passed after March 15 (i.e., once April 7 or thereabouts arrived), Defendant ***lost the right to amend even once as of right.*** So by April 20, defendant was in a position where he could amend only "with the opposing party's written consent or the court's leave." (Rule 15(a)(2).) Since we know from the facts that Defendant did not request (and thus did not receive) Plaintiff's consent to the amendment, the only route left to Defendant was to seek the court's permission to amend. (And, by the way, Rule 15(a)(2) says that "the court should ***freely give leave*** when justice so requires"; since the case is still in its early stages, and there is no apparent prejudice to Plaintiff that would result from an amendment, the court is very likely to grant the leave to amend if asked to do so.)

(A) is not correct,

because it misstates the timing requirement of the federal rule with respect to amendment.

A party has an ***automatic right to amend his or her pleadings, but only if 21 days have not elapsed since service of the paper.*** *See* FRCP 15(a). Putting aside special provisions for the situation in which that party's pleading required a responsive pleading (not applicable here), once 21 days passed from when Defendant filed his original answer on March 15, Defendant could *only* amend by successfully requested leave of court. (See more about this in the discussion of Choice (B) above.) It's true that Defendant, as one who granted a requested waiver of service, was *originally* entitled to 60 days from the day Plaintiff sent the waiver request (i.e., until about May 3) in which to answer, a time period that has still not elapsed. But once Defendant filed his first answer, the relevant time limit became 21 days after that filing, not the originally available 60-days-following-service-of-waiver-request; that's why a defendant should take care before filing a first version of his or her answer.

(C) is not correct,

because the doctrine of waiver does not operate in the automatic manner described in this choice.

It's true that, generally, a defendant's failure to plead an affirmative defense, such as the statute of limitations, will *eventually* act as a waiver of that defense. However, a party that fails to include an affirmative defense in its answer may ***amend*** the answer as of right if 21 days have not passed since service of that answer (and may also amend on consent of the opposing party or with leave of court). So Choice (C), by saying that Defendant's failure to include the defense in his answer constituted an "automatic" waiver that could not be cured by amendment-of-right, is legally incorrect.

(D) is incorrect,

as a matter of law.

There *are* certain defenses that may be asserted by motion rather than as part of the answer; they are the seven defenses specified in Rule 12(b)(1)-(7), which include lack of subject-matter or personal jurisdiction, failure to state a claim on which relief can be granted, etc. But unless a defense is one of the seven special ones listed in 12(b)(1)-(7), the defense may *only* be asserted as part of the answer, not by motion. The statute of limitations is not one of the seven, so it may not be asserted by motion. (Indeed, statute of limitations is an "affirmative defense," and as such must, according to Rule 8(c)(1), be affirmatively stated in the "responsive pleading" filed by the one asserting it, which in this case is the answer.)

Answer 26

(C) is correct,

because it correctly recognizes that partial summary judgments are normally not final and that the judgment here does not fall within any exception that would make the judgment here final.

Federal courts of appeal "have jurisdiction of appeal from all ***final decisions*** of the district courts of the United States" (28 U.S.C. § 1291). But the appeals courts do ***not*** have jurisdiction to hear appeals from ***non-final*** orders, except for a few special situations specified in 28 U.S.C. § 1292 (most importantly, cases involving injunctions), none of which exists here. So the Court of Appeals has power to hear the appeal *only* if the district court's grant of partial summary judgment (i.e., its judgment on the contract claim) is deemed to be a final judgment rather than an interlocutory order. FRCP 54(b) deals with the finality of claims in actions that present more than one claim by stating the general rule that "any order or other decision, however designated, that adjudicates fewer than all the claims . . . does not end the action." However, 54(b) recognizes one exception to this "no final judgment" rule: "[T]he [district] court ***may direct entry of a final judgment as to one or more, but fewer than all***, claims or parties ***only if the court expressly determines that there is no just reason for delay***[.]" Here, the facts tell you that the district court's order granting the partial summary judgment was silent about "whether the judgment was deemed final, or whether there was any reason to allow an immediate appeal from it." From this, you can infer that the district court did ***not*** "expressly determine that there [was] no just reason for delay," the pre-condition for the partial summary judgment to be deemed final. Since the partial judgment was not final and did not fall within any special exception to the general rule stating that appeals from non-final judgments are not allowed in federal practice, the court of appeals does not have jurisdiction to hear the appeal even if it would like to do so.

(A) is not correct,

because ***the grant of partial summary judgment is normally not a final judgment.***

As is described more fully in the discussion of Choice (C) above, under FRCP 54(b) an entry of judgment on fewer than all claims is ***not*** deemed final unless the district court "expressly determines that there is no just reason for delay" (which didn't happen here). Since Choice (A) says that the grant of partial summary judgment is automatically a final judgment, this choice is an incorrect statement of law (and also incorrectly predicts the outcome).

(B) is not correct,

because immediate appellate review is not available on the facts presented.

Federal law under 28 U.S.C. § 1292(b) allows for ***appeals of interlocutory orders only in limited circumstances,*** none of which applies on the present facts. Since Choice (B) asserts that grants of partial summary judgment are immediately appealable at the discretion of the appeals court—and implies that that's true whether or not the district court took any action to make the judgment immediately appealable—Choice (A) is wrong as a matter of law.

(D) is not correct because,

although there is a rule which makes an appeal filed within 10 days a relevant fact, the rule does not apply in the present situation.

Under 28 U.S.C. § 1292(b), if a district court includes in an otherwise non-appealable order a statement that the order involves a "controlling question of law as to which there is substantial ground for difference of opinion and that an immediate appeal from the order may materially advance the ultimate termination of the litigation," the court of appeals may, "in its discretion" permit an appeal. In that special circumstance, the appealing party must apply for leave to appeal within 10 days of when the district court entered its order. 28 U.S.C. § 1292(b). Here, however, the facts tell you that the District Court said nothing about an immediate appeal, so the special situation referred to in the prior sentence could not have arisen, making the presence or absence of a consent to appeal within 10 days irrelevant to this problem.

Answer 27

(B) is the best response,

because full faith and credit principles do not require a court to apply procedural rules of another court that has rendered a judgment.

When a state court has rendered a judgment, whatever obligation is imposed on a federal court to honor and enforce that judgment derives not from the U.S. Constitution's "Full Faith & Credit Clause" (which only requires a *state* court to honor another state's judgments), but from a federal statute. That statute, 28 U.S.C. § 1738, says that the "records and judicial proceedings of any court of any . . . State . . . shall have ***the same full faith and credit in every [federal] court*** as they have by law or usage in the courts of [the rendering] State[.]" But the present question doesn't involve enforcement of a typical out-of-state judgment (say, an award of money damages); rather, it involves an issue of ***admissibility of evidence***. And to answer the question, you have to decide whether the federal full faith and credit statute requires the State B federal court to refuse to allow the engineer's testimony if the State A courts would so refuse on account of the injunction. The answer to that question is not completely obvious just looking at the text of the federal statute.

However, precisely this issue of statutory interpretation has come before the U.S. Supreme Court, and the Court held unanimously that the full faith and credit statute does ***not*** require the federal court to honor any rule of evidence-admissibility imposed by such an injunction. The facts here are modeled on *Baker v. General Motors Corp.*, 522 U.S. 222 (1998), in which all nine Justices agreed that a Missouri federal court hearing a consumer suit against G.M. was not required by the full faith and credit statute to exclude evidence from the former G.M. engineer merely because a Michigan state court had entered an injunction against the engineer barring the engineer from giving testimony against G.M. in any third-party suit. The Court in *Baker* agreed that the full faith and credit statute would require non-Michigan courts to honor the ***true res judicata effects*** of the Michigan judgment in the same way that the Michigan courts themselves would honor those effects; so, for instance, since as the result of the Michigan settlement and injunction G.M. and the engineer would be prevented from bringing new suits against each other for the claims that were resolved in the Michigan settlement, the Missouri federal court would similarly be required not to hear such a suit brought by one of those parties against the other. But full faith and credit principles did ***not*** allow Michigan to preclude other states from hearing suits brought by ***strangers*** to the Michigan litigation, or to tell these other states what ***procedural rules*** they should follow in such "stranger" suits. Therefore, the Court held, Michigan "lacks authority to ***control courts elsewhere*** by precluding them, in ***actions brought by strangers to the Michigan litigation***, from ***determining for themselves what witnesses are competent to testify*** and ***what evidence is relevant and admissible*** in their search for the truth." That principle applies here: The suit in State B federal court was brought by a stranger to the State A litigation and injunction, and the concept of full faith and credit does not require the federal court (or indeed *any* state or federal court outside of the State A state-court system) to apply a rule or policy of evidence admissibility or witness competence just because that rule would be followed in the State A courts.

By the way, it's important to note that on our facts here (as in *Baker*, *supra*), the "stranger" to the first litigation (i.e., the injured consumer who had nothing to do with the earlier suit) is the one trying to bring about the engineer's testimony, by means of a subpoena. If instead the issue arose because the engineer wanted to ***volunteer*** to testify on behalf of the stranger/consumer, then in all probability the federal court *would* have to "honor" the State A injunction, by holding that the State A suit, settlement, and injunction had definitively foreclosed the engineer's own right to volunteer testimony.

(A) is not the best response,

because the reason the federal court need not exclude the testimony has nothing to do with the strength or existence of any policy interest on the part of State B.

This choice correctly states the outcome (that the federal court does not have to exclude the engineer's testimony even if the State A courts would do so in a comparable suit). But the choice reaches this correct result by incorrect legal reasoning. As is discussed more fully in the treatment of Choice (B), the full faith and credit statute simply does not require the federal courts to follow the evidence-admissibility or witness-competence rules of State A. And that's true whether the state in which the federal court sits (here, State B) has a countervailing policy in favor of making testimony available, or not—in fact, even if the State B courts would choose, for policy reasons, to honor the State A "no testimony" ruling, the federal court is free to follow federal procedures and policies for determining whether to enforce the subpoena and admit the engineer's testimony.

(C) is not the best response,

because the full faith and credit statute does not require the State B federal court to enforce the injunction in the way this choice asserts.

This choice articulates the argument actually made by G.M. in the *Baker* case (see Choice (B)), that the full faith and credit statute requires the federal court to "enforce" the earlier state court injunction by refusing to hear the engineer's testimony. But the Supreme Court unanimously rejected this argument in *Baker*—the full faith and credit principle, the Court said, does *not* extend to the point of requiring the second court to follow the first court's litigation procedures, such as matters of witness competency and evidence admissibility.

(D) is not the best response,

because the likely willingness of the State A judge who originally entered the injunction to modify it is irrelevant.

As is discussed more extensively in connection with Choice (B), the full faith and credit statute does not require the federal court to support the policy embodied in the State A judge's decision to impose an injunction on future testimony by the engineer. So even if the federal judge is certain that the State A judge would ***not***, in the event of a new State A action brought by a stranger against the manufacturer, consent to modify the injunction to allow the engineer's testimony to be subpoenaed by the stranger, the State A judge's unwillingness to compel the testimony would not prevent the federal judge from making his or her own independent decision about whether to enforce the subpoena and allow the testimony.

Answer 28

(C) is the best response,

because Plaintiff's claim against Distributor is not within the court's diversity jurisdiction, supplemental jurisdiction cannot be exercised over Distributor, and the facts do not suggest that any other jurisdictional basis is available.

When faced with a multi-party and multi-claim action, it helps to diagram the action:

Plaintiff (State A) v. Defendant (State B)
↓ (third-party claim under FRCP 14)
Distributor (State A)

Here, Plaintiff is seeking to sue Distributor, who has been joined in the action as a third-party defendant. *See* FRCP 14. However, in order to bring a claim against a third-party defendant, the court must be able to exercise subject-matter jurisdiction. One form of subject-matter jurisdiction is ordinary diversity jurisdiction under 28 U.S.C. § 1332(a), by which the court can hear the case if the plaintiff and the defendant are "citizens of different States" and "the matter in controversy exceeds the sum or value of $75,000 exclusive of interests and costs." 28 U.S.C. § 1332(a)(1). Since Plaintiff and Distributor are citizens of the same state (State A), ordinary diversity jurisdiction is not present as between them. The Plaintiff-vs-Distributor claim could still be heard if that claim fell within a second type of jurisdiction, ***supplemental jurisdiction***. But the Plaintiff-vs-Distributor claim does ***not*** qualify for supplemental jurisdiction. That's because 28 U.S.C. § 1367(b) says that when the anchor claim (here, Plaintiff-vs-Defendant) is grounded in ***diversity*** jurisdiction, there is ***no*** supplemental jurisdiction over any claim "by plaintiffs against ***persons made parties*** under Rule ***14***, 19, 20, or 24 of the Federal Rules of Civil Procedure. . . . " 28 U.S.C. § 1367(b). In federal actions, third-party claims are governed by Rule 14; the defendant's right to claim against the third-party-defendant is covered by 14(a)(1), and the original plaintiff's right to claim against the third-party-defendant is covered by 14(a)(3). In other words, in this case Distributor is a "person made party under Rule 14," and as such, § 1367(b) says that there is no supplemental jurisdiction over any claim "by [a] plaintiff against [that] person made party under Rule 14." So Plaintiff's third-party claim against Distributor is not supported by either basic diversity or supplemental jurisdiction and must be dismissed.

On the other hand, the court ***has*** subject matter jurisdiction over both (1) Plaintiff's original claim against Defendant; and (2) Defendant's third-party claim against Distributor. As to (1), Plaintiff and Defendant are citizens of different states, so that's an easy situation for ordinary diversity. As to (2), since Plaintiff and Distributor are not diverse (and "complete diversity" is ordinarily required), Distributor's presence in the case (to defend against Defendant's third-party claim against him) might be viewed as destroying the required complete diversity. But the Defendant-vs-Distributor claim *does* fall within the court's *supplemental* jurisdiction. That happens because of 28 U.S.C. § 1367(a), the main provision creating supplemental jurisdiction. Section 1367(a) says that in general, "[i]n any civil action of which the district courts have original jurisdiction, the district courts shall have ***supplemental jurisdiction*** over ***all other claims that are so related to claims in the action within such original jurisdiction that they form part of the same case or controversy*** under Article III of the United States Constitution . . . . Such supplemental jurisdiction shall ***include claims that involve the joinder or intervention of additional parties***." Since the court started by having jurisdiction over the Plaintiff-vs-Defendant "anchor" claim, supplemental jurisdiction included any claim that was "so related" to the Plaintiff-vs-Defendant claim as to be part of the "same case or controversy" as the Plaintiff-vs-Defendant claim. And since Defendant's third-party claim against Distributor ("If I'm liable to Plaintiff, you have to indemnify me because you caused the accident by leasing defective equipment") arose out of the ***same accident*** as the one giving rise to the anchor claim (Plaintiff-vs-Defendant), the third-party claim is easily sufficiently closely-related to the anchor claim as to make the two claims part of the same "case or controversy" (as that term is used in Article III of the U.S. Constitution). Since there is no provision, in § 1367 or elsewhere, that specifically withholds supplemental jurisdiction as to a third-party claim by the original defendant against the third-party defendant, that third-party claim stays in the case. (Indeed, this type of claim—a garden-variety third-party claim by the original defendant against a third-party defendant claiming indemnification or contribution as to the main claim—is the prototypical claim that Congress had in mind when it drafted the clause of § 1367(a) allowing supplemental jurisdiction over "claims that involve the joinder or intervention of additional parties.")

(A) is not the best response,

because, of the three claims in the case, the *only* claim that lacks subject-matter jurisdiction is Plaintiff's claim against Distributor, for the reason described in the explanation to Choice (C).

Diversity jurisdiction exists over Plaintiff's claim against Defendant because both parties are citizens of different states and the amount-in-controversy requirement is met. And as is discussed more fully in the explanation of Choice (C), supplemental jurisdiction exists over Defendant's third-party claim against Distributor. So the fact that Distributor and Plaintiff are not diverse does not oust the district court of power to hear the anchor claim or the third-party claim. Since the court will grant the dismissal motion only as to the Plaintiff-v-Distributor claim, this choice's statement that all three motions should be granted is incorrect.

(B) is not the best response,

because Distributor's motion to dismiss Defendant's third-party claim for lack of subject-matter jurisdiction should not be granted.

When the anchor claim (here, Plaintiff's claim against Defendant) is grounded in diversity jurisdiction, federal law permits the exercise of supplemental jurisdiction over a third-party claim brought by Defendant against a party joined by FRCP 14, as is more fully explained as to Choice (C). So Distributor's motion will be granted only as to Plaintiff's claim against it, not as to Defendant's "main" third-party claim against it.

(D) is not the best response,

because the court may exercise diversity jurisdiction over Plaintiff's claim against Defendant.

The complaint alleges that the parties to the main claim are citizens of different states (Plaintiff is a citizen of State A and Defendant is a citizen of State B) and that the amount in controversy exceeds $75,000; therefore, both conditions of diversity jurisdiction are present. *See* 28 U.S.C. § 1332(a)(1). Consequently, Defendant's motion to dismiss Plaintiff's complaint will be denied. (Furthermore, the court will grant Distributor's motion to dismiss Plaintiff's claim against it, making this choice doubly wrong.)

Answer 29

(A) is the best response,

because it is the only one of the choices that is guaranteed to occur early enough in the case that there could be no waiver of the right to make the jury-trial demand.

The time for demanding a jury trial in federal actions is specified in FRCP 38. Rule 38(b) says that a party may demand a jury trial on any issue triable by right by a jury, if the demanding party does so by "(1) serving the other parties with a written demand—which may be included in a pleading—no later than 14 days after the last pleading directed to the issue is served[.]" (The party must also then file the demand with the court within "a reasonable time after service"; see the combination of Rules 38(b)(2) and 5(d)(1).) Since Rule 38(b) allows the demand to be "included in a pleading," this choice states a method and time for serving the demand that is guaranteed not to exceed the "no later than 14 days after the last pleading" deadline. And this method also turns out to be the latest stage that's guaranteed to be timely, since the other three choices may involve missing the deadline.

(B) is not the best response,

because the time it specifies may fall after the appropriate deadline.

As is noted in the explanation of Choice (A), a party's right to demand a jury trial on an issue ends unless service of the demand is made "no later than 14 days after the last pleading directed to the issue is served." This choice requires you to assume that the answer does not contain a counterclaim, since on that assumption the answer *is* the "last pleading directed to the issue [of infringement]." On that assumption, the screenwriter's time to serve the demand will end 14 days after the studio serves its answer on him. Since Choice (B) purports to give the screenwriter 60 days after service of the answer, it overstates the amount of time available.

(C) is not the best response,

for the same reason that (B) is not the best response.

The parties are required by Rule 26(f) to hold a conference at which they discuss the claims, possibilities of settlement, initial disclosure, etc. "as soon as practicable." This conference may—and in the majority of cases will—occur more than 14 days after service of the last pleading. Therefore, if as this choice suggests the screenwriter waits until the conference to serve his demand for jury trial, he cannot count on his demand still being timely.

(D) is not the best response,

for the same reasons that (B) and (C) are incorrect.

Rule 16 sets out the procedures by which the judge will hold one or more pretrial conferences. Normally, the judge will not even issue a scheduling order until after he or she has received a report by the parties outlining their discovery plan, which Rule 26(f) requires them to prepare. And the discovery plan cannot possibly be filed with the court until sometime after the discovery conference between the parties, referred to in Choice (C), has occurred. Since as is explained in the discussion of Choice (C) the day of the discovery conference will itself be too late for service of the jury trial demand, the date on which the judge holds the initial pretrial conference is guaranteed to fall even further past the deadline for filing of the jury-trial demand.

Answer 30

(C) is the best response,

because the defendant has not made the showing required to overcome the qualified work-product immunity that applies on these facts.

Rule 26 confers a limited immunity from discovery (colloquially called ***"work-product immunity,"*** though that term is not used by the FRCP) for materials prepared in anticipation of litigation. The main provision that does this is the first sentence of Rule 26(b)(3)(A): "Ordinarily, a party ***may not discover documents and tangible things that are prepared in anticipation of litigation or for trial by or for another party or its representative*** (including the other party's attorney, consultant, surety, indemnitor, insurer, or agent)." But the Rule goes on to explain that this immunity is limited, in the sense that even materials that are prepared in anticipation of litigation may be discovered if (i) the materials otherwise meet the requirements for discoverability set out in Rule 26(b)(1) (i.e., they are "nonprivileged matter that is relevant to any party's claim or defense and proportional to the needs of the case"), and (ii) the party seeking discovery "shows that it has ***substantial need*** for the materials to prepare its case and ***cannot, without undue hardship, obtain their substantial equivalent by other means***."

Let's see how these work-product provisions apply to the musician's statement here. First, the statement certainly falls within the broad definition of work-product given by the first sentence of Rule 26(b)(3)(A), in that it is a "document ***prepared in anticipation of litigation*** or for trial by or ***for another party or its representative*** (including the other party's attorney, consultant, surety, indemnitor, insurer, or agent)." This is so because: (1) the document was prepared for a "representative" of "another party," since the investigator is a "consultant" to, or "agent of" (either of which statuses count as being a "representative" of) the plaintiff; and (2) the investigator was hired to find the musician and take her statement after the plaintiff had filed suit, and it's clear from context that the plaintiff's lawyer's purpose in trying to get the statement was to prepare for trial. Therefore, the plaintiff will be entitled to keep the statement out of discovery unless the defendant makes two showings: (i) "that it has ***substantial need*** for the materials to prepare its case" and (ii) that it (the defendant) "***cannot, without undue hardship, obtain their substantial equivalent by other means***." The courts have held that the party seeking discovery bears the burden of production and persuasion as to both of these showings.

The defendant might be able to making showing (i), that he has "substantial need" for the statement to prepare his case; he can plausibly argue that by the plaintiff's own assertion, the statement contains something the musician knows about the case, and if so, the defendant will be materially helped by learning what that information is, so he can counter or explain it at trial. (It's not clear that the defendant will succeed in making this showing, but he's at least got a plausible chance of doing so.) But it's very ***unlikely*** that the defendant can make showing (ii), that he "***cannot, without undue hardship, obtain their substantial equivalent by other means***." That's because the privilege log has given the defendant the identity of the musician, and the defendant has not demonstrated why his legal team can't simply approach the musician on its own and ask her to tell them the contents of the statement. Nor has the defendant indicated that the defense team has already tried and failed to get this information from the musician. The courts have generally held, in cases where a party tries to obtain witness statements given to the other party, that unless the party seeking discovery shows that it ***has already made significant efforts to get equivalent information*** from the witness and failed, that party has failed to carry its burden of making the requisite showing of inability to get the "substantial equivalent by other means." (Later in the case, if the defendant shows that his team approached the musician for the information, was rejected, tried to get the information by deposing the musician and failed, this showing might now be enough to show the required inability to obtain equivalent materials.)

By way of background, keep in mind that Rule 26 effectively recognizes two levels of work-product immunity, what might be called ***"fact"*** work product and ***"opinion"*** work product. "Fact" work product is "ordinary" work product, work product that represents real-world events; "opinion" work product reveals a ***lawyer's mental processes***. Both types of work product receive at least some protection under the FRCP, but "fact" work product receives much less. Fact work product is the ordinary material we've already talked about in this answer, as to which Rule 26(b)(3) says that the immunity can be overcome if the party seeking discovery "shows that it has ***substantial need*** for the materials to prepare its case and ***cannot, without undue hardship, obtain their substantial equivalent by other means***." So fact work product can be described as being protected by a "qualified immunity" (though the Federal Rules don't use this phrase). By contrast, "opinion" work product is given ***virtually absolute immunity***; that's done by Rule 23(b)(3)(A), which says that even where the court finds that the qualified immunity for factual materials has been overcome and orders discovery of those materials, the court "must protect against disclosure of the ***mental***

impressions, conclusions, opinions, or legal theories of a party's attorney or other ***representative concerning the litigation***." So if, for instance, in our case the investigator had written out the substance of the musician's statement and added his own comment that "the witness seems very credible, and we should consider using her testimony at trial," this narrative of "mental impression" or "opinion" would not have to be disclosed to the defendant even if the court ordered that the text of the musician's own statement be disclosed because the defendant had substantial need of it and couldn't obtain the substantial equivalent otherwise. So whenever you encounter a work-product immunity question, be sure to ***distinguish*** between ordinary factual matters in the work-product document (which get only qualified immunity, i.e., can be ordered to be disclosed if the other party has substantial need and can't get the equivalent otherwise) and mental impressions, conclusions, opinions, and legal theories by the team of litigation professionals (which are absolutely privileged against discovery).

(A) is not the best response,

because the statement being sought here is not a copy of the defendant's own prior admissions.

This choice is referring to an actual provision of the discovery rules, but mis-applies that provision. Rule 26(b)(3)(C) says that "Any party or other person may, on request and without the required showing, ***obtain the person's own previous statement*** about the action or its subject matter." So if what the defendant were seeking is a copy of a statement he had directly made to the plaintiff's investigator about, say, his sobriety at the time of the accident, the defendant *would* be entitled to that disclosure. But the sentence just quoted does not apply to a statement made by someone other than the person seeking disclosure, which statement in turn quotes a statement made by the seeking party. And that's what's happening here; the statement being sought is the musician's statement, and the fact that the musician is repeating something said by the defendant is not enough to make the 26(b)(3)(C) "own previous statement" applicable to this disclosure request by the defendant. (If it were the *musician* who was seeking to make the plaintiff's team give the musician a copy of her own signed statement, the musician *would* be entitled to use 26(b)(3)(C), and she could then pass that copy on to the defendant—but the defendant does not have standing to make the request on his own.)

(B) is not the best response,

because the fact that it cites does not have the legal consequence that the choice asserts it to have.

This choice correctly draws a distinction between the words spoken by an occurrence witness (in this case, "the musician's own words"), and what's usually called "opinion work product" (here, "mental impressions or legal theories" of the plaintiff's legal team). As is more fully discussed in the last paragraph of the explanation of choice (C) above, "opinion work product" is indeed absolutely protected, whereas ordinary "factual" work product (like the musician's own words) gets only qualified immunity, which can be overcome by a suitable showing of need. But for the reasons explained in the treatment of Choice (C), even the qualified immunity applicable to the musician's own statement would not be overcome on these facts—so the distinction between qualified and absolute immunity that this choice is referring to does not produce the outcome that the defendant would be granted the requested discovery.

(D) is not the best response,

because how the plaintiff intends to use the statement is irrelevant to the outcome of the motion.

This choice in effect asserts that where an item of work product would only be used by the discovering party for a credibility-related purpose, that fact makes a difference to whether the item is discoverable. Actually, it's true that in *some* circumstances, the fact that the item will or will not be used solely for its effect on witness credibility *is* relevant; but the facts here do not involve such a circumstance. Two provisions of Rule 26 say that an item that would otherwise be discoverable will not be discoverable if it is expected to be used at trial ***"solely for impeachment."*** For example, Rule 26(a)(3)(A) requires one party to make automatic disclosure shortly before trial to the other of certain types of materials (e.g., the names of witnesses expected to be called at trial, or the contents of documents), but says that the disclosure is not required where the evidence will be used at trial "***solely for impeachment***." So if the only way in which the plaintiff were planning to use the musician's out-of-court signed statement (or, for that matter, the musician's live testimony repeating the contents of the statement) were as a method of impeaching the defendant's anticipated trial testimony that "I did not have anything to drink," this choice would correctly articulate a reason the plaintiff could decline to release the statement. But here, the statement's likely use by plaintiff is not just for impeachment—it would be admissible (and the plaintiff would probably want to use it) as substantive evidence that the defendant was drunk, a use that would apply even if the defendant never took the stand. So while this choice correctly states the outcome of the motion—that the court will deny the motion to compel—it does so for a reason that would probably not apply under these circumstances.

Answer 31

(C) is correct,

because service on an in-state agent followed by mail notice meets due process requirements.

Constructive notice to an out-of-state defendant made through service on a state official "appointed by law" to fulfill that function is constitutionally adequate if authorized by a state statute, so long as notice by mail is also required to be given to the defendant. *See Hess v. Pawloski*, 274 U.S. 352 (1927). The Due Process Clause of the Fourteenth Amendment requires that defendant receive notice of an action before the court can proceed. The requirement of notice is in addition to, not a substitute for, the requirement that a court have personal jurisdiction over defendant. Although personal in-hand service to defendant has traditionally been required in most situations, alternative forms of notice will satisfy Due Process if they are ***"reasonably calculated, under all the circumstances,*** to apprise interested parties of the pendency of the action and afford them an opportunity to present their objections." *Mullane v. Central Hanover Bank & Trust Co.*, 339 U.S. 306 (1950).

The Supreme Court has implicitly held on various occasions that a scheme in which an out-of-state individual or business is deemed to appoint an in-state official as agent for service of process meets due process requirements, provided that the state official is required to notify the defendant that the action has commenced. *See, e.g., Wuchter v. Pizzutti*, 276 U.S. 13, 18-19 (1928), in which the Supreme Court discussed the question "whether a statute, making the Secretary of State the person to receive the process, ***must***, in order to be valid, contain a provision making it reasonably probable that ***notice of the service on the Secretary will be communicated to the non-resident defendant*** who is sued." The Court answered "yes" to the question, but in so doing indicated by negative implication that if the service-on-the-Secretary-of-State scheme *does* include a requirement that the state official in turn give notice of service to the non-resident defendant, the scheme *is constitutionally adequate*. Since Choices (A) and (B)—each of which mentions steps less likely than mail notice to give the non-resident actual notice—are constitutionally insufficient for the reasons discussed below as to those choices, Choice (C) is the "least effective" method that still meets the requirements of due process.

(A) is not the best response,

because mere service on the Secretary was not reasonably calculated to result in the defendant's timely receipt of actual notice of the suit.

In *Wuchter v. Pizzutti*, 276 U.S. 13, 18-19 (1928), the Supreme Court asked itself "whether a statute, making the Secretary of State the person to receive the process, ***must***, in order to be valid, contain a provision making it reasonably probable that ***notice of the service on the Secretary will be communicated to the non-resident defendant*** who is sued." The Court then answered this question in the ***affirmative***, reasoning that "where the service of summons is limited to a service on the Secretary of State or some officer of the state, without more, it will be entirely possible for a person injured to sue any non-resident he chooses . . . [leaving] open . . . a clear opportunity for the commission of fraud[.]" Therefore, the Court concluded, such a provision not calling for the Secretary to notify the non-resident defendant "is not a reasonable provision, and . . . would certainly be ***depriving a defendant of his property without due process of law.***"

(B) is not the best response,

because newspaper publication does not satisfy the requirement that the best reasonably-available notice method be used.

The Supreme Court has held that "[t]he means [of notice] employed must be such as one desirous of ***actually informing*** the absentee might ***reasonably adopt*** to accomplish it." *Mullane v. Central Hanover Bank & Trust Co.*, 339 U.S. 306, 314-15 (1950). In the case of a defendant whose name and address are known to the plaintiff, or can be determined with reasonable diligence, *Mullane* holds that ***publication will not suffice***, and that nothing less than notice by mail to that address will be adequate. Cf. F,K&M (5th Ed.) § 3.20, p. 176. Since Plaintiff has learned Defendant's street address, mere publication (even together with service on the Secretary of State) will not suffice—either Plaintiff or the Secretary must give at least mail notice to Defendant.

(D) is not the best response,

because Choice (C—calling for mail notice—is a less-good method that will nonetheless be constitutionally sufficient.

The question asks you to choose the LEAST effective notice method listed that will nonetheless be constitutionally adequate. For the reasons discussed as to Choice (C), the mail notice listed in that choice is sufficient to satisfy due process. Therefore, Choice (D) is not the least effective method that is nonetheless constitutionally sufficient.

Answer 32

(C) is the best response,

because supplemental jurisdiction applies.

This situation illustrates a situation in which (1) the district court has power to exercise ***supplemental jurisdiction*** and (2) there is no reason for the court to use its discretion to decline to exercise that power. Supplemental jurisdiction is authorized under a federal statute, 28 U.S.C. § 1367. Under the key portion of that statute, § 1367(a), when a federal court has original jurisdiction over a claim, the court has supplemental jurisdiction over "all other claims that are ***so related to claims in the action*** within such original jurisdiction that ***they form part of the same case***

or controversy under Article III of the United States Constitution." Then, the last sentence of § 1367(a) goes on to say that § 1367(a)'s grant of supplemental jurisdiction "shall include claims that involve the ***joinder*** or intervention of ***additional parties.***" In those cases where § 1367(a) gives the district court power to exercise supplemental jurisdiction, the court then has the power to "decline to exercise supplemental jurisdiction" if any of the special factors set out in § 1367(c) is present.

Here, the court has original jurisdiction over the ABA claim against Employer, since that claim "arises under" federal law, namely the ABA statute. The breach-of-contract claim against Employer and Manager is in turn related to the ABA claim, because both claims concern the conditions of Plaintiff's firing. § 1367(a) therefore gives the court power to exercise supplemental jurisdiction over the state-law claim, including any "additional" party added on account of that state-law claim. But, as noted above, the court may ***decline to exercise*** that supplemental jurisdiction if any of the special factors listed in § 1367(c) is present. Factors listed in § 1367(c) include: that the state-law claim (against Manager and Employer) involves a novel or complex state law issue; that the state-law claim "substantially predominates" over the federal claim; that the federal claim has been dismissed; or that there are some "exceptional circumstances" that present a compelling reason for declining jurisdiction. Here, none of the discretionary factors seems to tilt against the exercise of power: the contract claim is not novel or complex; that claim is not likely to predominate over the federal law claim; and, so far the federal claim has not been dismissed. Finally, there seem to be no exceptional circumstances or compelling reasons to deny supplemental jurisdiction. Therefore, there is no reason for the court to decline to exercise the supplemental jurisdiction that it has over the state-law claim (and over all parties to that claim).

(A) is not the best response,

because the claim against Manager does not itself arise under federal law.

Plaintiff's claim against *Manager* does not arise under the ABA Act or, indeed, under *any* federal statute, preventing jurisdiction over that claim from being present under the statute granting federal-question jurisdiction, 28 U.S.C. § 1331. Plaintiff's claim against Manager is a garden-variety state-law contract claim, and no federal issue is alleged as part of the well-pleaded complaint relating to that claim (a requirement for federal-question jurisdiction made clear by *Louisville & Nashville R. Co. v. Mottley*, 211 U.S. 128 (1908), as well as by 28 U.S.C. § 1331). This choice reaches the right outcome (motion denied, because the court has subject-matter jurisdiction), but reaches it on incorrect reasoning by asserting that the reason the court has jurisdiction for the claim against Manager is "since the ABA claim arises under a federal statute." (The correct choice would have to somehow point to supplemental jurisdiction, which choice (C) does.)

(B) is not the best response,

because it incorrectly applies the test for federal diversity jurisdiction.

Federal courts can invoke diversity jurisdiction to adjudicate claims alleged to be valued at more than $75,000 between citizens of different states. *See* 28 U.S.C. § 1332. Both Plaintiff and Manager are citizens of the same state, State A, so diversity of citizenship is not present. Remember that for diversity jurisdiction, ***complete*** diversity is required—no plaintiff may be a citizen of the same state as any defendant. So the fact that there is diversity as between the sole plaintiff and *one* of the defendants to the state-law claim (Employer) is not enough to give the court diversity jurisdiction over that state-law claim.

(D) is not the best response,

because the court can exercise jurisdiction over Manager, based on supplemental jurisdiction and the power to add additional parties pursuant to that jurisdiction.

Federal statute authorizing the exercise of supplemental jurisdiction explicitly provides that the scope of such jurisdiction "shall include claims that involve the ***joinder*** or intervention of ***additional parties.***" (See the last sentence of 28 U.S.C. § 1367(a).) There are certain exclusions to supplemental jurisdiction (specified in § 1367(b)) that apply when the anchor claim is based solely on diversity jurisdiction. But the anchor claim here (the ABA claim) is based on a federal question, not solely diversity, so these exclusions don't apply.

Answer 33

(B) is the best response,

because situations involving derivative liability represent an exception to the general rule preventing a stranger to the first action from invoking the benefits of claim preclusion.

"Claim preclusion" involves twin doctrines, the doctrine of "merger" and that of "bar." Depending on whether the plaintiff wins or loses the first suit, either merger or bar will prevent a second litigation by that plaintiff on the same claim. If the plaintiff wins the first suit (i.e., gets a favorable judgment against the defendant), "merger" prevents the plaintiff from bringing a second suit on the claim against the same defendant; if the plaintiff loses the first suit, "bar" prevents her from bringing a second suit on the claim against the same defendant. Obviously here, the two actions are not against the same defendant, so neither "merger" nor "bar" would seem to apply, but as we'll soon see, to analyze some scenarios we have to first figure out whether merger or bar would apply had the second suit been against the same plaintiff as the first suit.

Here, the judgment in the first suit by the plaintiff (the accountant) was against her; therefore, she would be "barred" from bringing another suit on the "same claim" against the cab driver. *See* Rest. 2d Judgments, § 19: "A valid and final personal judgment rendered in favor of the defendant ***bars another action*** [against that defendant] ***by the plaintiff on the same claim***." But we next have to figure out whether a suit by the accountant against that same defendant (the cab driver) for her personal injuries would be deemed to be on the "same claim" as the first suit for property damage. The answer is "yes." That's because modern courts nearly always apply a "transactional" test for determining whether two suits involve a single claim, and the transactional test would be satisfied here. Here's how the Restatement of Judgments 2d defines the dimensions of a claim for purposes of the doctrines of merger or bar:

> "(1) When a valid and final judgment rendered in an action extinguishes the plaintiff's claim pursuant to the rules of merger or bar . . . , the claim extinguished includes ***all rights of the plaintiff to remedies against the defendant*** with respect to ***all or any part of the transaction, or series of connected transactions, out of which the action arose***.
>
> "(2) What factual grouping constitutes a 'transaction,' and what groupings constitute a 'series,' are to be determined pragmatically, giving weight to such considerations as ***whether the facts are related in time, space, origin, or motivation***, whether they ***form a convenient trial unit***, and whether their treatment as a unit ***conforms to the parties' expectations or business understanding or usage***."
>
> Rest. 2d of Judgments § 24.

Where both suits involve a single physical accident, courts almost universally treat ***property damage and personal injuries from that accident*** as both involving a single claim. Thus, Rest. 2d Judgments, Illustration 1 to § 24, reaches exactly this conclusion: "*A* and *B*, driving their respective cars, have a collision injuring *A* and damaging his car. The occurrence is single, and so is *A*'s claim. If *A* obtains a judgment against *B* on the ground of negligence for the damage to the ***car***, he is prevented by the doctrine of merger from subsequently maintaining an action for the ***harm to his person***." So in our question, the accountant has a single claim covering both property damage to her painting and injuries to her person, and the judgment against her in the property-damage suit would cause her to be "barred" from bringing a personal-injury suit against the same defendant, the cab driver.

Then, a separate rule of law provides that where one person (call him *A*) is vicariously responsible for the conduct of another person (*B*), then if an injured person sues *B,* the merger or bar consequences are normally the same for purposes of a second suit by the injured person against *A* as they would be for a second suit against the original defendant *B*. Here's how Rest. Judgments 2d, § 51, expresses the rule:

> "If two persons have a relationship such ***that one of them is vicariously responsible for the conduct of the other***, and an action is brought by the injured person ***against one of them***, the judgment in the action has the following preclusive effects against the injured person in a subsequent action against the other.
>
> (1) A judgment against the injured person that ***bars him from reasserting his claim against the defendant in the first action extinguishes any claim he has against the other person responsible for the conduct unless***:
>
> (a) The claim asserted in the second action is based upon grounds ***that could not have been asserted*** against the defendant in the first action; or
>
> (b) The judgment in the first action was ***based on a defense that was personal*** to the defendant in the first action."

Here, under the common-law principle of *respondeat superior*, the cab company was vicariously responsible for negligent conduct of its employee, the cab driver, that occurred during the course of the employment. Therefore, unless one of the two exceptions mentioned in (a) and (b) of Rest. 2d § 51 above applies, when the accountant sued the driver and lost on the property claim her personal injury suit against the cab company would be barred exactly the same way her personal injury suit against the driver would be barred (since the property damage and personal injury suits involved a single claim, as we saw above). And neither of the exceptions applies here; the claim for personal injuries could have been asserted as part of the initial suit in city court, and there was no plausible defense that could have been asserted by the cab driver in the first suit that would have been "personal" to him and inapplicable to the company as vicariously liable for the driver's negligence.

In sum, the accountant's personal injury suit against the company is barred by the judgment against her in the property suit, just as any personal injury suit by her against the cab driver would have been barred by that same judgment. And since the doctrine of "bar" is a species of claim preclusion, Choice (B) is the correct explanation for why the judge would dismiss the suit.

(A) is not the best response,

because collateral estoppel would not apply since we cannot say what issues were actually litigated and decided in the first suit.

"Issue preclusion" (a/k/a "collateral estoppel") applies to prevent relitigation of an issue only when the issue (whether of fact or law) is "***actually litigated*** and determined . . . and the determination is ***essential to the judgment***." Rest. 2d, Judgments, § 27. Here, the cab company might argue that the judgment against the accountant in the first suit demonstrates that the cab driver must not have been negligent, because otherwise judgment would have been for the accountant in at least some amount. But that argument wouldn't work: collateral estoppel applies only where we can say ***authoritatively*** that the issue in question was actually litigated and that that determination was essential to the judgment—doubts about what happened in the first suit get resolved against the use of preclusion. Here, the jury might have issued its verdict against the accountant because it found that the painting wasn't damaged at all, or that the damage did not come from the collision but from some conduct by the accountant or a third-party—in other words, we simply don't know that the jury in fact rested its verdict on a finding that the cab driver was not negligent. Since we can't say that the first judgment rested on a factual finding of non-negligence by the driver, the court will not use collateral estoppel at all. So this choice reaches the correct result (dismissal granted), but based on incorrect legal reasoning (use of collateral estoppel instead of claim preclusion).

(C) is not the best result,
because the mutuality principle it implicitly refers to would not apply in this situation of vicarious liability.

Traditionally, a party to the second suit who was a "stranger" to the first suit was prevented from gaining the benefit of either claim preclusion or issue preclusion on the theory that the stranger could not have been bound by an favorable result in the first suit, so the concept of "mutuality" dictated that the stranger not be given the benefit of a favorable result either. Modern courts no longer have an absolute rule against non-mutual use of either claim preclusion or issue preclusion, so even if the company would not have been bound by any judgment *against* its employee in the first suit, this fact would not automatically prevent the company from obtaining the *benefit* of claim preclusion or issue preclusion if those doctrines otherwise applied. For the reasons discussed in the analysis of Choice (B), the fact that the cab company would be vicariously liable for on-the-job negligence by its driver means that the cab company is not treated as a "stranger" to the first action, and therefore will be able to get the benefit of claim preclusion even in a jurisdiction that would otherwise forbid non-mutual use of claim preclusion as a general matter.

(D) is not the best result,
because the fact that the first court was of limited jurisdiction is irrelevant on these facts.

In some circumstances, the fact that the first suit is in a court of limited jurisdiction or whose procedures are significantly limited may indeed make it unfair to bind the loser to the results of that first suit for purposes of a second suit in a court that does not have the limitation. Thus, Rest. 2d of Judgments, § 26, says that the usual rules of merger and bar do not apply where "(c) The plaintiff was unable to . . . seek a certain remedy . . . in the first action because of ***the limitations on the subject matter jurisdiction of the courts*** . . . and the plaintiff desires in the second action to . . . seek that remedy or form of relief[.]" So, for instance, if the "city court" had had a cap on available damages lower than the combined property and personal-injury damages that the accountant was seeking, that fact might have been enough to prevent the accountant's failure to add the personal-injury claim to the first suit from barring her second suit. But here, the two claims together sought only $220,000 (i.e., less than the $250,000 limit on the city court's cap on recovery), so this rationale would not apply to give the accountant a "second bite at the apple."

Answer 34

(C) is the best response,
because the State A notice-of-claim rule expresses a strong state substantive policy that must be respected by the federal court under *Erie* principles.

When a federal court hears a claim based solely on state law (i.e., a diversity case), the doctrine of *Erie v. Tompkins,* 304 U.S. 64 (1938), requires the federal court to apply any state statutes, rules, or judicial decisions that are mostly substantive, but not state-law principles that are essentially procedural. However, before you can even know whether *Erie* doctrine applies to a particular set of facts, you have to first determine whether there is a valid ***federal rule or statute governing the matter in question***, which if applied would be ***inconsistent*** with the state principle; if there is, the federal rule or statute ***must be applied***, and *Erie* never even gets triggered. (Notice that this is one of the tricky things about applying *Erie* doctrine—you first have to *know* that there doesn't exist any federal rule or statute conflicts with the state rule in question, and to do that you in turn theoretically have to know "everything" about which federal rules and statutes exist! But for MBE purposes, you can usually safely *assume* that there is no such inconsistent federal principle unless you specifically recall it from studying the FRCP or the core Civil Procedure provisions of Title 28 of the U.S. Code, or the examiners call the conflict to your attention somehow.)

In this case, there is ***no federal statute or rule applicable to these facts*** that would be inconsistent with having the federal court honor the state notice-of-claim requirement. Therefore, this is indeed a situation in which classic *Erie* analysis is required.

The question then becomes, does the state-law requirement of notice-of-claim embody a sufficiently strong state ***substantive interest*** that *Erie* principles require the federal court to defer to state law by applying that requirement? The extent to which the state rule is ***outcome-determinative*** is an important part of the analysis. That's because "[W]here a federal court is exercising jurisdiction solely because of the diversity of citizenship of the parties, the ***outcome*** of the litigation in the federal court ***should be substantially the same***, so far as ***legal rules determine the outcome*** of a litigation, as it would be if tried in a State court." *Guaranty Trust Co. v. York*, 326 U.S. 99, 109 (1945). Otherwise, the federal courts will be encouraging ***"forum shopping,"*** in which one party (sometimes the plaintiff, and sometimes the non-resident defendant deciding whether to remove a state-filed case to federal court) gets the chance to choose between having the case heard in state court or having it heard it a federal court located in that same state, based on which one will give him better odds of winning.

Here, the choice to apply or not apply the state notice-of-claim rule is ***quite strongly outcome-determinative***: If the rule is applied, the plumber doesn't even get a chance to have his claim heard at all; without the rule, the plumber may well win. The notice-of-claim requirement is similar to a state statute of limitations rule, and the Supreme Court has long held that such limitations rules are highly outcome-determinative and must be applied by courts sitting in diversity. Thus, in *Guaranty Trust v. York*, *supra*, the Supreme Court held that a federal court sitting in diversity must apply the state statute of limitations because the federal court "cannot afford recovery if the right to recover is made unavailable by the State[.]"

But the fact that the choice between state and federal court would be somewhat outcome-determinative is ***not the sole factor*** the federal court must consider. Beyond considering the degree to which following the state law (or not doing so) will be outcome-determinative, the federal court must perform a type of ***interest-balancing***; the court must weigh the ***strength of the state's interest*** in using its rule to ***affect the substantive rights of the parties*** against the strength of the federal judicial system's interest in ***applying uniform procedures nationally***. Here, that interest balancing cuts in favor of ***applying State A's notice-of-claim rule***. The facts tell you that the object of the notice-of-claim requirement was to reduce malpractice claims and thus the cost of malpractice insurance; this is a strongly substantive goal, one tied up with parties' rights beyond how the actual litigation will be conducted. So the state interest in having its policy applied by the federal courts is quite strong. Conversely, there is no strong federal interest in having nationally uniform procedures that would be jeopardized by applying the notice-of-claim rule in just those states that have such a rule. So the federal-versus-state interest-balancing analysis, like the outcome-determinative analysis, cuts strongly in favor of requiring the federal court to apply the state's notice-of-claim rule. Therefore, *Erie* principles almost certainly require the federal court to dismiss the suit because that's what the State A courts would do.

(A) is not the best response,

because the notice-of-claim provision is not a mere procedural rule and is therefore binding on the federal court.

While the notice provision is in a sense "procedural" (it deals with the "procedures" for bringing a malpractice claim against the hospital), that label is not dispositive when the federal court is deciding whether *Erie* principles require that the state rule be followed. As is more fully described in the discussion of choice (C) above, the decision whether to apply the state rule is heavily outcome-determinative, and the state has manifested a strong interest in using its rule to pursue the substantive state interest in reducing malpractice insurance rates. Therefore, the court must apply the state notice rule, making this choice legally incorrect. (And given that fact, the issue of whether diversity exists is irrelevant.)

(B) is not the best response,

because it misstates the time as of which a party's state citizenship is to be determined for diversity purposes.

It's true that if the plumber and the hospital had both been citizens of State A at the relevant time, there would be no diversity. But the time as of which each party's citizenship is to be determined is the ***moment the suit is filed***, not the moment the cause of action arose. *See Freeport-McMoRan, Inc. v. K. N. Energy, Inc.*, 498 U.S. 426, 428 (1991), referring to "the well-established rule that diversity of citizenship is assessed at the time the action is filed." Here, the plumber's state of citizenship (i.e., his state of "domicile") changed when he moved permanently from State A to State B. Once that happened, he became diverse with the hospital, and remained so at the moment he filed the suit, which is what counts for jurisdiction purposes. (Also, as long as his move was intended to be permanent, the fact that it may have been motivated in part by a desire to be able to sue the hospital in diversity is irrelevant.)

(D) is not the best response,

because it gives an unduly simplistic explanation of why the federal court must follow the state notice-of-claim rule.

It's true that the degree to which the federal court's decision to follow or not follow the state rule might affect the outcome of the suit is *one* of the factors that the federal court must consider in deciding whether *Erie* principles require the court to apply the state rule. But it's not the only factor. As the Court said in *Hanna v. Plumer*, 380 U.S. 460, 466-67 (1965), "'Outcome-determination' analysis was never intended to serve as a talisman." As is discussed more extensively in the analysis of choice (C) above, even where there is *some* chance that the decision on whether to follow the state rule will affect the outcome, the federal court need not follow the state rule if the state's choice of rule does not manifest a strong substantive policy, and requiring the federal court to follow the state rule would significantly interfere with a strong federal interest in having uniform national procedures. So while this choice correctly predicts the outcome (that the case must be dismissed because the plumber did not follow the state notice rule), it explains the reason for that outcome less precisely than does Choice (C).

Answer 35

(C) is correct,

because the fact that the suit arises under a federal statute means that there is no minimum amount in controversy and that the presence or absence of diversity is irrelevant.

When you are told that the defendant has moved to dismiss for "lack of subject-matter jurisdiction," you know that the motion can be successful only if the defendant demonstrates one of two defects in the suit: (1) that there was neither diversity of citizenship nor a "federal question claim"; or (2) that there was an amount in controversy requirement applicable to the type of suit in question, which amount was not satisfied. Here, neither of these potential defects exists, so the motion will be denied.

As to (1), start with the basic idea that the federal courts have original jurisdiction over two broad categories of claims: (a) those involving "diversity of citizenship" (or its close cousin "alienage" jurisdiction, which we'll ignore here); and (b) those raising what is loosely referred to as a "federal question." Here, the case falls into category (b): 28 U.S.C. § 1331, entitled "Federal Question," gives the federal district courts "original jurisdiction of all civil actions arising under the Constitution, ***laws***, or treaties ***of the United States***." Section 1331 means that if the plaintiff's claim is based upon a federal statute (which is of course a "law . . . of the United States"), there is subject-matter jurisdiction under § 1331, regardless of which states or countries the parties are citizens of. Since the woman's suit is based on a federal employment-discrimination statute, § 1331 gives the court federal-question jurisdiction, and you can and should ignore entirely the citizenship of the parties.

But what about potential defect (2), failure to meet an amount-in-controversy requirement? The very modest "trick" in this question, if there is one, is that ***there is no minimum amount-in-controversy requirement for federal-question suits.*** So while the "matter in controversy" in a suit based solely on *diversity* must exceed $75,000 in value (*see* 28 U.S.C. § 1332(a)), a suit raising a federal question may proceed even if the matter is worth, say, $1, or involves an intangible stake with no specific financial value (e.g., a request for an injunction). Therefore, when you analyze this question, as soon as you can see that the complaint raises on its face an allegation that the defendant violated a federal statute, you can be confident that the court has subject-matter jurisdiction over the claim regardless of the parties' citizenship and regardless of the amount at stake.

(A) is not the best response,

for two different reasons: (1) As explained in Choice (C), the citizenship of the parties never matters at all for purposes of determining the existence of subject-matter jurisdiction in a federal-question suit; and (2) this choice incorrectly states the rule that would apply if the parties' citizenship *were* relevant. A corporation is deemed to be a citizen both of its state of incorporation and the state in which it has its "principal place of business," which is considered to be the location from which the company's officers direct business affairs (generally, and in this case, the company's "headquarters"); it is not the case that a corporation is also a citizen of the state in which it has a majority of its employees. Therefore, the defendant here is not a citizen of State A (just of States B and C), which means that there *would* be complete diversity between plaintiff and defendant if the case were based on diversity rather than the existence of a federal question.

(B) is not the best response,

because, as discussed in the analysis of Choice (C), where the plaintiff's claim raises a federal question (as it does here), there is no amount in controversy requirement, and the existence or non-existence of diversity of citizenship is irrelevant.

(D) is not the best response,

because an objection to lack of subject-matter jurisdiction can never be waived.

It's true that there are *some* objections to matters involving jurisdiction, service, venue, or the like that will be waived if the defendant fails to assert them in either a pre-answer motion or in the answer itself. *See* FRCP 12(h), saying that the four defenses listed in Rule 12(b)(2)-(5) (lack of personal jurisdiction, improper venue, insufficient process, and insufficient service of process) are waived if the party fails to make them in either a "responsive pleading" (here, the answer) or in a timely motion made before the responsive pleading. But because the drafters of the FRCP feared that allowing the federal district courts to hear a case for which there was no subject-matter jurisdiction would exceed the limited powers given to the federal judiciary by the Constitution, the FRCP provide that the defense of lack of subject-matter jurisdiction is *never* waived. (Indeed, Rule 12(h)(3) says that "if the court determines ***at any time*** that it lacks subject-matter jurisdiction, the court ***must dismiss*** the action.")

Answer 36

(B) is the best response,

because Defendant's voluntary contacts with State A in connection with the contract were sufficiently great as to constitute "minimum contacts" and to render it not unfair to require Defendant to defend an action related to the contract in that State.

For the forum state to have personal jurisdiction over the defendant for purposes of a suit relating to activities occurring in the forum state, it must as a general rule be the case that (a) the defendant had "minimum contacts" with the forum state; and (b) it would not be "fundamentally unfair" to require the defendant to defend suit in the forum state. *See Burger King Corp. v. Rudzewicz*, 471 U.S. 462 (1985).

The facts of this problem are quite close to those of *Burger King, supra*, where the Supreme Court found both that the defendant had "minimum contacts" with the forum state (the plaintiff franchisor's home state) and that it would not be unfair to make him defend a franchise-agreement-related suit there. In *Burger King*, unlike here, the defendant didn't even travel to the franchisor's forum-state headquarters state to receive training (or for anything else), but his prospective partner did so. Also in *Burger King*, the defendant understood (as Defendant here understood) that much of the franchisor's contractually obligated work to support the defendant, and the regulation by the franchisor of the defendant's performance under the franchise agreement, would occur from the franchisor's forum-state headquarters. Finally, as is the case here, the franchise agreement in *Burger King* specified that the law of the forum state (the franchisor's home state) would apply. The Supreme Court therefore held that the defendant had "established a substantial and continuing relationship with [the franchisor's forum-state] headquarters, received fair notice from the contract documents and the course of dealing that he might be subject to suit in [the forum state], and . . . failed to demonstrate how jurisdiction in that forum would otherwise be fundamentally unfair[.]" Thus, the Supreme Court concluded, it did not "offend due process" for the forum state to exercise jurisdiction over him for an action on the franchise agreement. Here, given that Defendant had the same basic forum-state contacts as the defendant did in *Burger King,* but also traveled twice to the forum state before signing the agreement, a court would almost certainly conclude that (1) Defendant had minimum contacts with State A, and (2) it would not be "fundamentally unfair" to require Defendant to defend a suit relating to the franchise agreement in State A.

It's important to note, by the way, that the suit here was on a claim that arose from the Defendant's activities ***connected with the forum state*** (i.e., from a contract whose negotiation included the trips by Defendant to the forum state, and the performance of which from plaintiff's side would be done mostly in the forum state). In other words, the suit here was based on ***"specific jurisdiction,"*** the label applied to suits on claims related to whatever in-forum-state activities the defendant may have had. That's why all that was required for personal jurisdiction over Defendant was minimum contact with the forum state and a lack of "unfairness" in requiring Defendant to come to the forum state to defend an action. Suppose, however, that the suit had involved a claim having nothing to do with whatever connections Defendant had with the forum state—for instance, suppose Plaintiff's claim in State A federal court was a libel action claiming that Defendant had, in Canada, published a libel about some other business owned by Plaintiff in Mexico, having nothing to do with the brake-repair business or with Defendant's franchise agreement. In this hypothetical example, personal jurisdiction would have to have been what is called ***"general jurisdiction"*** (jurisdiction not relating to the defendant's forum-state-connected activities). And the Supreme Court has required ***much greater voluntary contacts*** between the defendant and the forum state for general jurisdiction than for specific jurisdiction; for instance, if Defendant had been a corporation, a suit based on general jurisdiction could have been brought against it only if Defendant was "found in" State A, defined as being either incorporated in State A or with its principal place of business in State A. So when you analyze a problem requiring you to decide whether the defendant can be required to defend an action in a particular jurisdiction, first check whether the suit relates to defendant's activities connected to the forum state, so that you'll know whether to apply the easy-to-satisfy minimum-contact standard for specific jurisdiction, or instead the hard-to-satisfy "found in the forum state" standard for general jurisdiction.

(A) is not the best response,

because when the defendant properly seeks dismissal for lack of jurisdiction and loses, the right to raise the issue on appeal is preserved.

A defendant is permitted—indeed, encouraged—to assert the defense of lack of personal jurisdiction in a federal court case by making a motion on that grounds before serving an answer. *See* Rule 12(b)(2). That's what the facts tell you that Defendant did here. Once a defendant has raised the jurisdiction objection in this way and loses, he does not forfeit or waive the right to argue on direct appeal that the district court was incorrect in denying the motion.

For clarification, though, distinguish the situation here (where the defendant is trying in a *direct* appeal to contest the trial court's denial of his lack-of-jurisdiction defense) from the quite different ***"collateral attack"*** scenario. In this second scenario, the defendant raises the jurisdiction defense in the first action, loses, and then either tries the case and loses, or defaults immediately after losing on the jurisdiction argument; then, we'll assume, because the defendant has no assets in the state where the initial suit took place, the plaintiff "sues on the judgment," i.e., brings a second suit to "enforce" the judgment in a place where the defendant *does* have assets, such as his home state. Now, when the defendant argues in the second suit (the one brought to enforce the earlier judgment) that the first court lacked personal jurisdiction, this is called a "collateral attack." And in the collateral-attack scenario, the defendant *does* have a fatal waiver problem; merely by having raised the jurisdiction defense in the first action and losing, the defendant will be found to have already had and used his chance to litigate the jurisdiction issue, so the second court will not permit him to re-litigate this issue by way of collateral attack. But that's not a problem in our question, since Defendant is re-raising the jurisdiction issue in his direct appeal from the judgment.

(C) is not the best response,

because requiring Defendant to defend the case in State A on these facts would not violate traditional notions of fair play and substantial justice.

This choice is partially correct, in the sense that it correctly suggests that there may be cases in which the defendant has just enough "minimum contacts" with the forum state to make it not a violation of his due process rights to force him to defend in the forum state, but in which these contacts are so attenuated, and the burden on the defendant to having to defend in the forum state so great, that the court will decide that it would "offend 'traditional notions of fair play and substantial justice'" for the court to exercise jurisdiction over him. *See Asahi Metal Indus. Co. v. Superior Court*, 480 U.S. 102 (1987), where the Court found that in the very unusual facts there (involving impleader of a foreign corporation as a third-party defendant, followed by a settlement of the main claim between the original plaintiff and the third-party plaintiff), it would be unfair for the forum-state court to require the third-party defendant to defend the case. But this choice is incorrect in asserting that the case here is one of those unusual situations—here, Defendant's trips to the forum state, his understanding that the other party to the contract would perform extensive services from its headquarters in the forum state, and his voluntary agreement to a contract that provided that forum-state law would apply, taken together, meaning that it would *not* "offend traditional notions of fair play and substantial justice" to require Defendant to defend in the forum state.

(D) is not the best response,

because Defendant *did* voluntarily avail himself of the privilege of doing business in State A.

It's true that after the signing of the contract, Defendant never took any voluntary action directed at State A, beyond dealing with some of Plaintiff's personnel based there. But that fact is not inconsistent with a conclusion that Defendant "voluntarily avail[ed] himself of the privilege of doing business" in State A. On facts very similar to the ones here, the Supreme Court in *Burger King Corp. v. Rudzewicz* (see the discussion of Choice (B) above) found that the defendant's limited contacts with the forum state—the headquarters state of the plaintiff/franchisor—were enough to constitute "purposeful availment" of the privilege of doing business relating to the forum state. (For instance, the defendant in *Burger King* knew that the services provided to him by the plaintiff under the contract would be rendered from the forum state, and he agreed that the forum state's substantive laws would govern any dispute about the contract.) So on our facts, it's clear that Defendant would be found to have purposely availed himself of the privilege of doing business connected with State A sufficient to give him minimum contacts with that state.

Answer 37

(D) is the correct answer,

because the federal discovery rules recognize only one situation in which a person may be permitted to conduct discovery before any suit involving that person has been filed; that's the situation in which, under Rule 27, a person may seek a court order to ***"perpetuate testimony."*** Under the Rule 27 procedure, a person "who wants to perpetuate testimony about any matter cognizable in a United States court" may, even before any suit has been filed, file a "verified petition" showing, among other things:

"(A) that the petitioner ***expects to be a party*** to [a federal-court action] but cannot presently bring it or cause it to be brought;

(B) the subject matter of the expected action and the petitioner's interest;

(C) the ***facts*** that the petitioner ***wants to establish*** by the proposed testimony and the ***reasons to perpetuate it***; . . .

(E) the name, address, and expected substance of the testimony of each deponent."

Rule 27(a)(1). Courts have interpreted Rule 27 as applying only where a delay in discovery (e.g., a delay until the case is filed and the usual post-filing discovery methods can be used) is ***likely to result in a loss of evidence***. *See, e.g., Ash v. Cort*, 512 F.2d 909 (3d Cir. 1975). The facts here supply no reason to believe that if Company has to wait until Plaintiff files the expected suit and Company can use ordinary discovery methods, the state trooper's testimony is likely to become lost or unavailable. (For instance, Company does not allege that the state trooper is ill or planning soon to leave the country or that he plans to destroy or conceal evidence.) Furthermore, Company has not specified any "facts that [it] wants to establish by the proposed testimony" (let alone any "reasons to perpetuate" that testimony) as 27(a)(1)(C) requires; it simply wishes to learn more about the accident. So Company has not met the requirements for the Rule 27 pre-filing deposition procedure, and there is no other procedure in the federal rules allowing for discovery before a case has been filed.

(A) is not correct,

because it asserts a legal rule that is broader than the actual rule.

As discussed in the explanation for Choice (D) above, FRCP 27 explicitly allows for a deposition before commencement of a suit, as long as the party seeking discovery can show that it expects a suit to be brought, and that the testimony it seeks is at risk of being lost or destroyed. So although Choice (A) reaches the right outcome (that the request should be denied), the choice cites an absolute ban on taking discovery from nonparties before commencement of a suit, and no such ban exists.

(B) is not correct,

because is misstates the requirements of the relevant federal rule.

A party seeking pre-complaint discovery must, according to Rule 27, file a ***verified petition*** with the district court, as explained in the discussion of Choice (D). But Rule 27 does not require that a draft complaint be attached to the petition, only that the petitioner show that it expects to be a party in a lawsuit. Thus, though Company's request should be denied, it is not for this reason, but rather the reason given in Choice (D).

(C) is not correct,

because no rule of the sort cited exists.

If a suit ***had already been filed***, this choice would be essentially correct in stating what information Company could obtain via a deposition of the nonparty state trooper. (Note, however, that even then, the formulation in Choice (C) is a little too broad; Rule 26(b)(1), in addition to requiring that the information be relevant to a claim or defense, also requires that the information be "proportional to the needs of the case[.]") But where, as here, no case has yet been filed, discovery is narrowly limited to the situation in which there is a special need to "perpetuate testimony," as covered in the discussion of Choice (D).

Answer 38

(C) is the correct answer,

because it recognizes the special requirements imposed on a stakeholder in a statutory interpleader action.

Interpleader is a procedure that allows a party—called the stakeholder—***to join in one lawsuit all claimants to whom he is or might be liable.*** Federal law recognizes two different kinds of interpleader actions: "Rule 22" interpleader (*see* FRCP 22) and "statutory" interpleader (*see* 28 U.S.C. § 1335). Although the procedures serve the same purpose—to enable a party to avoid the risk of multiple and conflicting liability—statutory and rule interpleader differ in their procedural requirements. Statutory interpleader requires that the plaintiff ***deposit the stake*** "into the registry of the court . . . or [furnish a] bond payable to the clerk of the court in such amount and with surety as the court or judge may deem proper." 28 U.S.C. § 1335(a)(2). In the situation in which the stake is an insurance policy sought by multiple claimants who assert claims that aggregate more than the policy limit, the court will normally require that cash or a bond for the full policy limit (here, $3 million) be deposited. If the court issues such an order (as it will almost certainly do here) and Plaintiff declines to post that amount in cash or via a surety bond, the court will lack subject matter jurisdiction over the interpleader action and will have no choice but to dismiss the action. *See, e.g., United States Fire Insurance Co. v. Asbestospray, Inc.*, 182 F.3d 201, 210 (3d Cir. 1999) ("A proper deposit or bond is a jurisdictional prerequisite . . . . The stakeholder . . . must deposit the largest amount for which it may be liable in view of the subject matter of the controversy." (By the way, *Rule 22* interpleader does *not* have an explicit deposit or bond requirement.)

(A) is not correct,

because it misstates the subject-matter jurisdiction requirements for a statutory interpleader action.

Statutory interpleader requires only diversity of citizenship between any two of the claimants—what is known as "minimal diversity." The statute explicitly provides that subject to a special amount-in-controversy requirement, "[t]he district court shall have original jurisdiction of any action of interpleader . . . ***if [t]wo or more adverse claimants, of diverse citizenship*** as defined in subsection (a) or (d) of section 1332 of this title, ***are claiming*** or may claim to be entitled to such money or property . . . ." 28 U.S.C. § 1335(a)(1). The U.S. Supreme Court has recognized that this statutory provision requires only "'minimal diversity,' that is, diversity of citizenship between two or more claimants, without regard to the circumstance that other rival claimants may be co-citizens." *State Farm Fire & Casualty Co. v. Tashire*, 386 U.S. 523, 530 (1967). Since the facts tell you that there are at least two claimants of diverse citizenship (more precisely, that the claimants include citizens of seven different states, State A through State G), you know that the requirement of minimal diversity is satisfied here. Contrary to the statement in Choice (A), the citizenship of the *stakeholder* (here, Plaintiff) is ***irrelevant*** to this determination—so it wouldn't matter, say, if every claimant but one was a citizen of State A, the same state of citizenship as Plaintiff.

(B) is not correct,

because it misstates the special amount-in-controversy requirement that applies to statutory interpleader in a diversity suit.

Statutory interpleader requires only that a claim of at least $500 be in controversy, as measured by the stake. *See* 28 U.S.C. § 1335(a) ("The district courts shall have original jurisdiction of any civil action of interpleader . . . filed by any person . . . having in his . . . custody or possession money or property of the value of $500 or more. . . ."). By contrast, in "Rule 22" interpleader, the amount-in-controversy must exceed $75,000 if the suit is based solely on diversity.

(D) is not correct,

because it misstates the federal court's power to issue the requested injunction.

The whole purpose of statutory interpleader is to protect the stakeholder from multiple and/or inconsistent judgments. And that purpose would be defeated if the federal court hearing the interpleader suit couldn't ***enjoin the claimants*** from trying to collect the stake in other lawsuits, whether federal or state ones. Therefore, 28 U.S.C. § 2361 provides that as part of any statutory interpleader action, "a district court may issue its process for all claimants and ***enter its order restraining them from instituting or prosecuting any proceeding in any State or United States court affecting the . . . obligation*** involved in the interpleader action[.]" (But this language does not authorize the federal court to enjoin the individual state-court suits from continuing against *Defendant*. So the claimants can continue to litigate in their state-court suits whether Defendant is liable, and for how much; what the claimants *can't* do in the state-court suits is to try to collect from Plaintiff, the insurer, insurance proceeds to cover any judgment against Defendant.)

Answer 39

(A) is the best response,

because a partnership is deemed to be a citizen of the state or foreign country of EACH of its partners, and the existence of diversity is to be determined as of the time the suit is filed.

First, let's figure out the citizenship of the plaintiff, a limited partnership. A limited partnership—like other artificial entities such as general partnerships, labor unions, and business trusts (but not corporations)—is considered an "unincorporated association." And the rule has always been that an unincorporated association, for diversity purposes, is deemed to be a citizen of ***every state or nation in which any member of the association is a citizen***. *See Carden v. Arkoma Assocs.*, 494 U.S. 185, 195-196 (U.S. 1990), involving exactly our present question of the citizenship of a limited partnership, where the Supreme Court said that "[D]iversity jurisdiction in a suit by or against the [artificial] entity depends on the ***citizenship of . . . 'each of its members[.]'"*** Therefore, if the plaintiff limited partnership as of a particular moment had as its partners a general partner that was a citizen of Canada, eight individuals as limited partners who were citizens of Canada, and two individuals as limited partners who were citizens of State A, the limited partnership as a whole would be deemed to have been a citizen of both Canada and State A at that time. (The only type of artificial entity to which a different rule for determining citizenship applies is the standard "corporation," whose place of incorporation and principal place of business are the *only* sources of citizenship—in other words, the citizenship of the individual stockholders is irrelevant. And that different rule exists only because Congress expressly so provided, in 28 U.S.C. 1332(c)(1).)

The second rule you need to know to solve this problem is that the relevant time for measuring a litigant's citizenship is the ***moment the complaint was filed***, not some later moment such as the commencement of the trial. As the Supreme Court put it in *Grupo Dataflux v. Atlas Global Group*, L.P., 541 U.S. 567, 570-571 (2004), "It has long been the case that . . . 'the jurisdiction of the court depends upon the state of things at the time of the action brought.' . . . This time-of-filing rule . . . measures all challenges to subject-matter jurisdiction premised upon diversity of citizenship against the state of facts that existed at the time of filing—whether the challenge be brought shortly after filing, after the trial, or even for the first time on appeal." The Supreme Court in *Grupo Dataflux* explicitly rejected even a modest proposed exception to this general rule, under which if neither the parties nor the judge raised the lack-of-diversity problem until after a jury verdict had been rendered, and due to intervening developments the litigants became completely diverse before the verdict was rendered, the court could treat subject-matter jurisdiction as existing and preserve the verdict. So in *Grupo Dataflux*, where the factual situation was virtually identical to the one in our question (the only two limited partners who had the same citizenship as the defendant had left the partnership between the moment of filing and the start of trial), the Supreme Court nonetheless concluded that the general rule—existence of diversity is determined at the moment of filing, and changes in any litigants' citizenship post-filing are irrelevant—should apply and required that the case and the jury verdict be dismissed.

So here, these two rules combine to make it be the case that the federal court does not have subject-matter jurisdiction over the case. In suits in which one of the parties is a citizen of a foreign nation, diversity jurisdiction would have to be of the "alienage" variety, specified in 28 U.S.C. § 1332(a)(2). Section 1332(a)(1) provides for jurisdiction in suits that are between "citizens of a State and citizens or subjects of a foreign state" (as long as the citizen of the foreign state is not also a permanent resident in the same U.S. state as any opposing party). Since the defendant corporation here is deemed a citizen of State A (remember, a corporation is a citizen of any state in which it was incorporated, plus the state of its principal place of business, which is the state from which its executives direct the company's business), diversity is measured as of the moment of filing, and the requisite complete diversity could exist only if no partner in the plaintiff limited partnership was a citizen of State A. Thus, the fact that two of the limited partners in the plaintiff, as of the moment the suit was filed, were citizens of State A means that the requisite complete diversity between the plaintiff limited partnership and the defendant corporation never existed. The fact that the citizenship of the limited partnership changed after filing and before commencement of the suit (by the exit of the two State A limited partners), making the partnership a citizen solely of Canada, is irrelevant. It would also be irrelevant (if it were true, which we don't know) that the defendant knew of the lack-of-diversity problem at all times and purposely tried to play "heads I win, tails you lose" by waiting until after the verdict and deciding that it would point out the diversity problem only if it lost at trial.

You should keep in mind one other rule about determining diversity that might sound inconsistent with the above "time of filing controls" rule, but that the Supreme Court has found to be distinguishable from the time-of-filing rule. If after filing of the suit and before judgment, ***the lineup of the litigant parties changes***, in that an existing plaintiff or defendant leaves the suit, or a new party joins the suit, we ***do*** analyze the existence of diversity immediately after the change. So, for instance, suppose P (a citizen of State A) files suit against D1 (a citizen of State A) and D2 (a citizen of State B), based solely on diversity. Then, after both Ds object to the lack of the required complete diversity, P voluntarily dismisses her claim against D1, and continues only against D2. In this situation, assuming that D1 is not an indispensable party, the suit ***may*** continue, because the change of party "cures the lack of complete diversity." But the Supreme Court has decided that this "change in the party lineup" situation is conceptually different from the "change in the citizenship of a continuing party" scenario posed by our problem—in the former, the change in citizenship due to the change in the party lineup dictates a re-evaluation of the existence of diversity post-change, whereas in the latter, the change in the citizenship of a continuing party does not dictate a re-evaluation. *See Grupo Dataflux, supra,* making this distinction between the two situations.

(B) is not the best response,

because the state of the defendant's knowledge or motive concerning the diversity issue is irrelevant.

This choice asserts that the critical fact is whether the defendant knew (or at least should have known) that there was a lack of the required diversity prior to the start of trial. But the state of the defendant's knowledge is completely irrelevant here. As is more fully discussed in the analysis of choice (A), the only critical issue is whether the requisite diversity existed at the moment the suit was filed; if diversity was not present then, then even if the defendant knew about the problem and remained silent in the hopes of getting a "free bite at the apple" (i.e., planned to try the case and raise the diversity issue only if it lost at trial), no rule prevented the defendant from using this tactic.

(C) is not the best response,

because a lack of diversity as of the moment the suit was filed cannot be cured by a later change to a party's citizenship.

As is discussed in the analysis of choice (A), the existence of diversity is determined by looking at the parties' citizenship at the moment the suit is filed. If as of that moment there is an overlap between the state(s) of which any plaintiff is a citizen and the states of which any defendant is a citizen, that overlap prevents the requisite diversity from existing no matter what happens post-filing. But distinguish this situation from one in which there are multiple parties on one side, and as the result of post-filing changes in the lineup of the parties (e.g., a party is dismissed from the case) there is a change in citizenship; in this new situation, the existence of diversity is determined by looking at the new lineup (though the citizenship of each of the remaining parties is still measured as of the initial filing)—thus, if P is diverse with D1 but not diverse with D2 as of filing, the problem can be cured by dropping D2. (For more about that scenario, see the last paragraph discussing Choice (A) above.) But the "change of party lineup" scenario in the prior sentence is the *only* situation in which a post-filing change relating to diversity can matter. If the party lineup *doesn't* change—and the only thing that changes post-lineup is the citizenship of a continuing party—that change never affects the diversity analysis. So here, where the suit has continued to be solely between the original limited partnership plaintiff and the original corporate defendant, the fact that two limited partners of the plaintiff departed post-filing (thereby converting the partnership from being a citizen of both Canada and State A to a citizen only of Canada) does *not* "cure" the lack of subject-matter jurisdiction, as this choice says it does.

(D) is not the best response,

because it is an incorrect statement of the rules for determining the citizenship of a partnership.

As is more fully discussed in the treatment of choice (A), the only "artificial entity" whose citizenship is determined without reference to the citizenship of the constituent members or owners is a true corporation (as to which Congress has specially provided that the citizenship of the stockholders is to be ignored). For a limited partnership (as well as for other types of "unincorporated associations," like labor unions, general partnerships, business trusts, etc.), the judge-made rule is and has always been that the entity is deemed a citizen of every state and/or foreign nation of which any constituent member is a citizen. So if, as is the case here, a limited partnership has as its partners a general partner and multiple limited partners, it must be the case that none of this whole set of partners may be a citizen of the same state or nation as any defendant.

Answer 40

(A) is the best response,

because transfer based on convenience is allowed to any district where the action might have originally been brought.

The general federal change-of-venue statute, 28 U.S.C. § 1404(a), permits the district court to ***transfer*** "any civil action to any other district or division ***where it might have been brought***," on consideration of ***"the convenience of parties and witnesses, in the interest of justice."*** The statutory language "where it might have been brought" has been interpreted to require, at the least, that transfer be to a district in which ***venue would have been proper***. (Some courts *also* require that the transfer be to a district from which personal jurisdiction over the defendant could be asserted, which in a diversity case might mean that transfer cannot be made to a district in a state with which the defendant did not have minimum contacts.) In any event, you don't have to interpret the precise meaning of the phrase "where it might have been brought" to evaluate Choice (A), since that choice echoes the phrase by adding the condition that plaintiff "could initially have brought the action" in W.D. State B. Since the facts tell you to assume that the court has found that litigation in W.D. State B would be more convenient overall than litigation in State A, § 1404(a)'s requirement that the transferring judge consider the "convenience of parties and witnesses" is also satisfied.

(B) is not the best response,

because it misstates the governing law on the right to transfer an action.

A plaintiff may move to transfer an action despite the fact that plaintiff chose the action's initial venue. The transfer statute "says nothing about affording plaintiffs different treatment from defendants," *Ferens v. John Deere Co.*, 494 U.S. 516, 522 (1990), and transfer under the general federal venue statute is not limited to defendants. Thus, Plaintiff is free to seek to change the venue of the action even though he was the one who made the original choice of where to sue.

(C) is not correct,

because it misstates the relationship of venue to state boundaries in the federal system even when the federal court sits in diversity jurisdiction.

Although it is true that individual circuits and districts in the federal system generally do not cross state boundaries, there is nothing in the federal change-of-venue provisions that prohibits a transfer across state lines. And that is true whether the action is based solely on diversity or involves a federal-question claim. (Notice, by the way, that a party who seeks to transfer an action from one district to another, when the districts are in different states, will not get the benefit of a change in law; the transferee court must apply the law of the transferor court. *See Van Dusen v. Barack*, 376 U.S. 612 (1964) and *Ferens v. John Deere Co.*, 494 U.S. 516 (1990).)

(D) is not the best response,

because the fact that venue wasn't proper does not require the court to dismiss the action.

The court in which the case was originally brought ***may transfer it to another district, even if venue was improper in the original (transferor) court.*** In that situation, the correct statutory procedure to use is not the generally used § 1404(a) (discussed in Choice (A) above), but a special provision for cases in which the original choice of venue is improper, 28 U.S.C. § 1406. Section 1406 lets the original court make the transfer (assuming venue in the transferee district is proper and that convenience will be served), even though because of the venue error that original court could not have heard the action over the defendant's objection.

STRATEGIES AND TACTICS

CONSTITUTIONAL LAW

If you think for a minute about Constitutional Law, it's a strange subject to appear on the MBE—it's more theoretical than the other subjects covered on the exam.

In a way, the unique nature of Constitutional Law can ***help*** you on the MBE. With a multiple-choice test like the MBE, it's impossible to have the type of open-ended discussions that your Constitutional Law class in law school probably involved, discussions such as how this justice or that justice might decide a case. Instead, you have to treat Constitutional Law as you do every other subject on the MBE—apply rules. Given the nature of Constitutional Law, though, you should be familiar with case law in order to see how various rules have been applied in different contexts. Why? You really can't be asked "pure" hypotheticals, because you're expected to know the law, not to read the minds of the Supreme Court justices. In many cases you simply can't know how a test applies to a given set of facts unless the Supreme Court has ***already considered*** that set of facts.

You'll notice that the discussion on Study Strategies is considerably longer for this subject than it is for any other (except for the newly added Civil Procedure discussion). Our goal here is to get you to think about constitutional concepts in such a way that you can apply them to multiple-choice questions. Keep in mind, however, that the sole purpose of this is to alert you to tricky topics you might otherwise overlook. This section is ***not*** intended to be an exhaustive, substantive review of Constitutional Law; you should rely on other materials for that. (The *Law in a Flash* set on *Constitutional Law*, for example, is an excellent tool for learning how constitutional principles apply to hundreds of different fact patterns.)

OUTLINE OF COVERAGE

You will face about 28 or 29 questions on Constitutional Law on the MBE (though only 27 will be scored, and you won't know which ones won't). (Note that the terms "Constitution," "constitutional," and "unconstitutional" refer to the federal Constitution, unless otherwise indicated.)

The following outline for the Constitutional Law portion of the MBE has been adopted by the Bar Examiners for all MBEs given on or after February 2016. It was designed to clarify what's covered on the Con Law portion of the exam. This is the most up-to-date outline of coverage released by the Bar Examiners, and your substantive study for Constitutional Law should be centered around it.

Here's what you need to know:

- I. The nature of judicial review
  - A. Organization and relationship of state and federal courts in a federal system
  - B. Jurisdiction
    - 1. Congressional power to define and limit
    - 2. The Eleventh Amendment and state sovereign immunity
  - C. Judicial review in operation
    - 1. The "case or controversy" requirement, including the prohibition on advisory opinions, standing, ripeness, and mootness
    - 2. The "adequate and independent state ground"
    - 3. Political questions and justiciability
- II. The separation of powers
  - A. The powers of Congress
    - 1. Commerce, taxing, and spending powers
    - 2. War, defense, and foreign affairs powers
    - 3. Power to enforce the 13th, 14th, and 15th Amendments
    - 4. Other powers

B. The powers of the President
   1. As chief executive, including the "take care" clause
   2. As commander-in-chief
   3. Treaty and foreign affairs powers
   4. Appointment and removal of officials

C. Federal interbranch relationships
   1. Congressional limits on the executive
   2. The presentment requirement and the President's power to veto or to withhold action
   3. Non-delegation doctrine
   4. Executive, legislative, and judicial immunities

III. The relation of nation and states in a federal system
   A. Intergovernmental immunities
      1. Federal immunity from state law
      2. State immunity from federal law, including the 10th Amendment
   B. Federalism-based limits on state authority
      1. Negative implications of the commerce clause
      2. Supremacy clause and preemption
      3. Authorization of otherwise invalid state action

IV. Individual rights
   A. State action
   B. Due process
      1. Substantive due process
         a. Fundamental rights
         b. Other rights and interests
      2. Procedural due process
   C. Equal protection
      1. Fundamental rights
      2. Classifications subject to heightened scrutiny
      3. Rational basis review
   D. Takings
   E. Other protections, including the Privileges and Immunities Clauses, the Contracts Clause, unconstitutional conditions, bills of attainder, and ex post facto laws
   F. First Amendment freedoms
      1. Freedom of religion and separation of church and state
         a. Free exercise
         b. Establishment
      2. Freedom of expression
         a. Content-based regulation of protected expression
         b. Content-neutral regulation of protected expression
         c. Regulation of unprotected expression
         d. Regulation of commercial speech
         e. Regulation of, or impositions upon, public school students, public employment, licenses, or benefits based upon exercise of expressive or associational rights
         f. Regulation of expressive conduct
         g. Prior restraint, vagueness, and overbreadth
      3. Freedom of the press
      4. Freedom of association

WHAT TO EXPECT

About half of the Constitutional Law questions on the exam will come from category IV—Individual Rights; the other half will come from categories I, II, and III. There will be questions from each of the Roman numeral topics on the exam, but not necessarily from each of the subtopics.

There are two common types of Constitutional Law MBE questions:

1. You're asked about the ***validity of a statute***; or
2. You're asked to identify the ***best or worst argument*** for upholding or overturning a statute.

STUDY STRATEGIES

1. Determine what the various constitutional clauses do.

First, you have to make two determinations:

1. ***To whom does the clause apply?*** Federal government, states, or both?
2. ***What does the clause do?*** Is it a source of power—or does it prohibit something?

Here's a rundown on some major clauses you should remember. Other major clauses, such as equal protection and due process, will be addressed separately.

A. Commerce Clause, Article I, § 8, Clause 3.

Applies to: Federal Government.
Source or prohibition: Source.

The Commerce Clause power is exceptionally broad. Congress can regulate ***four categories*** of activities involving interstate commerce: (1) ***channels*** of interstate commerce, (2) ***instrumentalities*** of interstate commerce, (3) ***articles*** moving in interstate commerce, and (4) activities ***"substantially affecting"*** commerce. What does this mean on the MBE? Basically, in determining whether Congress can regulate an activity, you need only determine that (1) the activity is ***commercial,*** and (2) the activity "substantially affects" interstate commerce or the activity is part of a general class of activities that, collectively, substantially affect interstate commerce. If both are true, then the statute is valid under the Commerce Clause. Note that most Commerce Clause questions on the MBE involve the ***sale*** or ***distribution*** of an item, usually in a ***commercial*** setting. (If, on the other hand, the activity involves a non-commercial activity, the test is stricter: You must find a "pretty obvious connection" between the activity and interstate commerce for the statute to be valid under the Commerce Clause.)

You may remember discussing the somewhat surprising *U.S. v. Lopez* decision in your Constitutional Law class. In *Lopez*, the Supreme Court actually ***struck down*** a federal "no guns in schools" statute on the grounds that it went ***beyond*** Congress's Commerce Clause power! Amazing, huh? Don't worry; since most MBE Commerce Clause questions focus on the ***sale or distribution*** of an item at the end of the stream of interstate commerce (not its ***use*** once it's ***left*** the stream of interstate commerce, which the *Lopez* statute did), you shouldn't have to worry about *Lopez* at all.

You may also remember the startling 2012 decision in *Nat'l Federation of Indep. Business v. Sebelius*, on the Affordable Care Act. In *Nat'l Federation*, five members of the Court said that requiring people to ***buy health insurance*** or else pay a penalty went beyond Congress's Commerce Clause powers, because that Clause did not authorize Congress to require someone not involved in commerce to enter into a commercial transaction. You shouldn't be surprised to see an MBE question in which Congress tries to make someone who is not presently in the market for a good (e.g., broccoli) buy the good or pay a penalty; you should answer that this isn't authorized by the Commerce Clause (but might be authorized by Congress's power to ***tax and spend,*** if the money is collected by the IRS, as in the Affordable Care Act situation).

On the other hand, where a person is ***already involved*** in a relevant aspect of commerce, Congress's power to regulate the person's commercial behavior is very broad. Here's an example. Say Old Mac—a farmer—grows corn on his farm to feed only himself and his pigs. You're likely to think, "Well, there's no impact on interstate commerce whatsoever, so Congress can't regulate Old Mac's corn production, right?" ***Wrong.*** The commerce power would allow Congress to regulate Old Mac's production: Old Mac is already engaged in an activity (farming), the activity is commercial, and the cumulative (or aggregate) effect of many farmers' production could substantially affect the supply and demand of commodities interstate. (You may remember these facts from *Wickard v. Filburn* (1942)).

CAVEAT: State power under the Commerce Clause.
Just as the Commerce Clause is a ***source*** of power for the federal government, it's also a ***limitation*** on the power of the states. No need to worry, though; the only time you analyze state statutes' impact on interstate commerce under the Commerce Clause is when there's ***no relevant federal legislation.*** Then you have to determine if a state regulation unduly burdens interstate commerce (see the discussion on validity of state statutes under item 3 below). If relevant federal legislation exists, then your analysis falls under the ***Supremacy Clause.*** There are two questions you have to ask:

1. Did Congress expressly authorize or prohibit state regulation? If so, that controls. If ***not***—
2. With no express authorization or prohibition by Congress, you have to determine if the federal law ***preempts*** the state law. If the state law ***directly contradicts*** the federal law, it will be preempted. If

there's no direct conflict, you have to determine if Congress intended the federal law to occupy the ***entire*** field. Look at four factors to determine if that is the case: (1) whether the subject matter is traditionally classified as local or federal; (2) how pervasive the federal regulation is; (3) how similar the state and federal laws are (the more they coincide, the more likely it is that federal law was intended to supersede state law); and (4) whether there's a need for uniform federal regulation. You can remember this with a mnemonic—**PUSH** (**P**ervasiveness, **U**niformity, **S**imilarity, **H**istory).

Note that preemption is an issue ***any*** time a state law conflicts with a federal law (or is in the same field). However, it's most likely to be applied in the area of interstate commerce.

B. Welfare Clause, Article I, § 8.

Applies to: Federal government.
Source or prohibition: Source.

The Welfare Clause gives Congress the power to ***tax and spend*** for the general welfare. Any federal legislation reasonably related to this power will be valid (assuming it doesn't violate some other Constitutional provision, such as Equal Protection). Pretty straightforward. So why is it here at all? Because it's easy to forget the limitations on the welfare power. Tax and spend. That's it. Congress does ***not*** have the power to enact any legislation that promotes the general welfare of the nation under the Welfare Clause, even though that's what you'd expect from its name. Just remember—tax and spend is the scope of the power.

Incidentally, keep in mind that ***states*** do have the power to legislate for the general welfare, but only under their ***police*** power, not under the Welfare Clause. (Don't forget that there is no ***federal*** police power—see item 2B, below.)

C. Contracts Clause, Article I, § 10.

Applies to: States ***only.***
Source or prohibition: Prohibition.

The Contracts Clause, or "Obligations of Contracts" Clause, prohibits states from passing any law that impairs the obligations of contracts. It's usually correctly applied when the state seems to be trying to ***escape its own obligations.***

The most important thing to remember here is that, as a prerequisite for protection under this clause, the contract must have existed when the statute was passed. States ***can*** regulate contract formation ***prospectively.*** Thus, when the "Contracts Clause" is an answer choice, the first thing you should do is check to see if the contract in question predates the offending statute. If not, then the Contracts Clause is irrelevant.

That's the most important thing to remember, but there are a couple of other points to keep in mind. First, not ***all*** contract impairments are invalid under the Contracts Clause. If they ***were,*** people could insulate themselves from state regulation simply by entering into contracts. Instead, state modifications of contracts ***will*** be permissible if the modifications (1) serve an ***important and legitimate public interest*** and (2) are necessary to achieve that public interest; and if (3) the contract impairment is ***reasonable*** under the circumstances.

Also, keep in mind that the state has more leeway when the state ***itself*** was a party to the contract. Beyond the rules on modification applicable to ***all*** contracts (see last paragraph) the state needn't adhere to a contract where it surrenders, from the start, an "essential attribute" of its sovereignty (such as the police power or eminent domain).

Here's an example of the Contracts Clause "in action":

> A state statute made it a misdemeanor to construct any building of more than five stories without an automatic fire sprinkler system.
>
> A local construction company built a ten-story federal office building in the state. It constructed the building according to the precise specifications of a federal contract authorized by federal statutes. Because the building was built without the automatic fire sprinkler system required by state law, the state has prosecuted the private contractor.
>
> Which of the following is the company's strongest defense to that prosecution?
>
> A. The state sprinkler requirement denies the company property or liberty without due process.
> B. The state sprinkler requirement denies the company equal protection of the laws.

C. As applied, the state sprinkler requirement violates the supremacy clause.
D. As applied, the state sprinkler requirement violates the obligations of contracts clause.

Remember, when you're considering the obligations of a contracts issue, the first thing you have to do is see if the contract predates the statute. Here, it apparently doesn't. That means that the contracts clause does not invalidate the statute, and D can't be the best response. (In fact, choice C is the best response.)

D. Privileges and Immunities Clauses—*both of them.*

Privileges & Immunities of the Fourteenth Amendment.
Applies to: States.
Source or Limitation: Limitation.
"Interstate" Privileges & Immunities Clause, Article IV, § 2.
Applies to: States.
Source or Limitation: Limitation.

It's important to keep these two clauses separate in your mind, because one of them has more practical effect than the other. When the MBE refers to either, it'll be distinguishable by the language used; the MBE will tell you their source: "Privileges and Immunities Clause of the Fourteenth Amendment" or "Privileges & Immunities Clause of Article IV."

1. Privileges & Immunities Clause of the Fourteenth Amendment.

This voids state enactments which clearly infringe on the privileges of ***national citizenship.*** The protection is limited to the fundamental rights shared by all citizens, namely the right to travel freely from state to state, to petition Congress for redress of grievances, to vote for national officers, to assemble peaceably, and to discuss matters of national legislation.

To say that this clause is construed narrowly is understating the matter (it's like saying law students do a little studying). In fact, reliance on this clause usually yields a ***wrong*** answer on the MBE. Here's why: These same rights are protected against state encroachment by the Due Process and Equal Protection Clauses of the Fourteenth Amendment, so, wherever Privileges and Immunities seems to apply, Due Process or Equal Protection would be a stronger argument against the constitutionality of the state action in question. Consequently, though there may be no such thing as a guarantee on the MBE, when you see "Privileges and Immunities Clause of the Fourteenth Amendment" as a possible answer for invalidating a state statute, you can be pretty sure it's just a distractor.

2. "Interstate" Privileges & Immunities Clause (Article IV).

Unlike its Fourteenth Amendment counterpart, ***this*** clause has some teeth. Here's what it does: It prevents states from discriminating against out-of-state citizens and residents in matters concerning ***"essential activities"*** (e.g., pursuing one's livelihood, owning property) and "basic rights" (e.g., medical care, court access), unless the discrimination is closely related to a substantial state purpose (e.g., protecting natural resources by the state) and there are no less restrictive means available to achieve the purpose. It's important to remember that this provision doesn't protect corporations or aliens—just out-of-state, human, U.S. citizens.

E. Eleventh Amendment.

Applies to: Individuals.
Source or Limitation: Limitation.

The important thing to remember about the Eleventh Amendment is how **narrow** it is, although recently the Court has interpreted it more broadly. It forbids most actions in federal court by private citizens for damages against the states. You should remember what the Eleventh Amendment **doesn't** cover. It **doesn't,** for instance, prevent suits by the federal government against states; or suits by anyone against state subdivisions (e.g., cities or counties); or equity suits in federal court where a state official has violated the claimant's federal constitutional rights; or suits against a state **official** for money damages, as long as the damages are to be paid out of the official's own pocket.

Congress may not abrogate the Eleventh Amendment (*Seminole Tribe of Florida v. Florida* (1996)) except where it passes a statute giving private citizens the right to sue a state under the post-Civil War Amendments. (Even within this area, Congress's power is limited—when Congress purports to use its §5 remedial powers under the Fourteenth Amendment, it's limited to measures that are fitted to the remedying of ***actual constitutional violations*** by the states. *Kimel v. Florida Bd. of Regents* (2000); *Bd. of Trustees of Univ. of Alabama v. Garrett* (2001).)

F. Thirteenth Amendment.

Applies to: Anyone—government or private individual.
Source or Limitation: Limitation.

The Thirteenth Amendment outlaws any "badges or incidents" of slavery. It gives Congress the power to prohibit virtually ***any*** discrimination against blacks, or whites (and it may cover other kinds of discrimination). The thing to remember about the Thirteenth Amendment is that it's the ***only*** constitutional provision ***explicitly limiting private acts by individuals.*** No state action is required. Contrast this with the Fourteenth Amendment, which also prohibits discrimination under its Equal Protection Clause but only limits ***state*** action—not private action.

2. Determining the validity of statutes.

Many Constitutional Law questions on the MBE ask you to determine if a given statute is valid. Here's a logical way for you to attack these questions:

A. Determine first if the statute is a federal statute or a state statute.

This isn't difficult to determine—the question will tell you.

B. Analyze the validity of federal statutes or actions.

Congress can act only pursuant to its enumerated powers under the Constitution. Thus, any valid federal statute must be ***rationally related to an enumerated power***, or it must be ***necessary and proper to effectuate an enumerated power.***

As a result, you'll probably find it useful to keep in mind the following major powers of Congress:

Civil **R**ights
Elections (Congressional)
Admiralty
Taxation
Eminent Domain
Spending/Taxing for General Welfare
Defense
Interstate Commerce
Citizenship
External (Foreign) Affairs

Here's a mnemonic for this: **CREATES DICE.**

Keep in mind that this is not an ***exhaustive*** list. For instance, Congress has virtually exclusive power over federally owned lands under the Property Clause; it controls bankruptcy. Furthermore, Congress has ***"state-like" powers over the District of Columbia*** (where, for instance, it could regulate marriages, education, and other state-oriented areas). This list does, however, represent the major congressional powers, and so, in the vast majority of cases, any valid federal law will have to be rationally related to one of these powers (or necessary and proper to effectuate one of them).

If Congress tries to legislate ***beyond*** its powers, it violates the Tenth Amendment. The Tenth Amendment reserves to the states (and the people) those powers not expressly delegated to Congress by the Constitution, nor prohibited to the States.

Note that the list above is interesting for what's missing: a police power. ***There is no federal police power!*** Only the states have police powers. Congress can use its commerce power to do "police-like" things—e.g., prohibiting interstate transportation of stolen property, misbranded goods, lottery tickets, etc.—but this doesn't change the fact that Congress doesn't have police powers. Don't forget this!

C. Determine the validity of state statutes.

In order to be valid, a state enactment must meet a three-part test:

1. The law must be enacted within the state's powers (e.g., police powers);

2. It must not violate any person's constitutional rights; and
3. It must not unduly burden interstate commerce.

If a state statute passes this test, it's valid. Let's look at each element a little more closely.

1. State powers.

The police powers are the most common source of state authority. State legislation is enacted under the police powers if it involves the ***public health, safety, welfare, or morals.*** As you can see, this is a pretty broad spectrum of authority: it covers everything from family issues to education to a whole variety of economic and social legislation. Of course, states have other powers, such as controlling in-state property, but police powers are the ***most*** significant.

2. Constitutional rights: due process and equal protection.

The two most frequent ways in which a state statute can violate the Constitution involve due process and equal protection. These will be discussed in detail below in their own section.

3. Interstate commerce.

As discussed earlier, Congress has a complete lock on interstate commerce. This doesn't mean, however, that a state can't place ***any*** burden on interstate commerce—it just can't ***unduly*** burden interstate commerce. Determining if an undue burden exists requires the application of a balancing test: Is the burden on interstate commerce outweighed by ***legitimate interests*** of the state in protecting its citizens, taking into account less burdensome alternatives? Also, the regulation must be ***non-discriminatory,*** unless the state has no reasonable, non-discriminatory alternatives in its effort to protect health and safety.

We'll look at some examples. For instance, a state statute forbidding tandem trucks on its highways, in the light of proof that such trucks are more dangerous than tractor-trailers, has been found to be an ***impermissible*** burden on interstate commerce. *Raymond Motor Transport v. U.S.* (1978). Change the facts a bit; say the statute only barred tandem trucks on ***local*** roads (***not*** highways). This would impose a lesser burden on interstate commerce and thus ***could*** be valid.

Here's another one. Say a state charges trucks involved in interstate commerce $25/year for the privileges of using state highways. The revenues are used to defray the costs of maintaining the roads. This is a ***permissible*** burden on interstate commerce, because the state interest is substantial and the burden is slight. Say instead that the fee was the same, but it was applied only against out-of-state truckers and was intended to protect in-state truckers by making it more expensive for out-of-state truckers to operate in the state. This would be ***impermissible.*** Even though the amount of the burden is the same, the regulation is ***discriminatory,*** and, since there are other, non-discriminatory ways to raise revenue, the statute would be an invalid burden on interstate commerce.

3. Due Process and Equal Protection.

These two constitutional clauses show up with such frequency, both as correct responses and as distractors, that we'll go into each one in depth.

A. Distinguishing due process problems from equal protection problems.

On the MBE, you'll face questions that ask you for the clearest constitutional violation posed by a set of facts. Even though due process and equal protection can overlap, there's a simple test you can use to determine which of the two applies: ***See if a classification is built into the statute*** (such as residents vs. non-residents, men vs. women, legitimate children vs. illegitimate children). Here's an example:

> A state has enacted a new election code designed to increase voter responsibility in the exercise of the franchise and to enlarge citizen participation in the electoral process. None of its provisions conflicts with federal statutes.
>
> Which of the following is the strongest reason for finding unconstitutional a requirement in the state election code that each voter must be literate in English?
>
> A. The requirement violates Article I Section 2 of the Constitution, which provides that representatives to Congress be chosen "by the People of the several States."
> B. The requirement violates Article I, Section 4 of the Constitution, which gives Congress the power to "make or alter" state regulations providing for the "Times" and "Manner" of holding elections for senators and representatives.
> C. The requirement violates the Due Process Clause of the Fourteenth Amendment.
> D. The requirement violates the Equal Protection of the Laws Clause of the Fourteenth Amendment.

Remember: Look for a ***classification.*** Is there one here? Sure—English-speakers vs. non-English-speakers. A classification is the hallmark of an equal protection problem. (Incidentally, the correct answer is, in fact, D.)

1. If there's a classification: how to analyze equal protection problems.

Once you've determined there's a classification, you have to determine on what principle that classification is based. Why? Because the nature of the classification determines the level of scrutiny to which the statute will be subjected in order to determine its validity—and the level of scrutiny, to a large extent, will determine if the statute will be upheld.

However, there is a threshold issue to address first. If the statute is a federal statute, there's no equal protection problem *per se*, ***because the Equal Protection Clause, as part of the Fourteenth Amendment, does not apply to the federal government.*** (But equal protection *principles* are made applicable to the federal government through the Fifth Amendment's Due Process Clause—anything that would violate the Equal Protection Clause if done by a state government would violate the Fifth Amendment Due Process Clause if done by the federal government.)

Another threshold to remember: The Equal Protection Clause applies only to ***government action*** (also called ***"state action,"*** even when applied to federal action), not to actions taken by purely private parties and in which government played no substantial role. On the MBE, you'll have to be able to decide quickly which activities constitute state action and which don't. If a state or federal government is enacting a law (which is usually the case in MBE questions), then, obviously, you have state action. If a private individual or group of individuals is involved, you need to look for two things. First, ask yourself if there's a significant "nexus" of government involvement (i.e., whether the government encourages or benefits from the private conduct). Second, ask yourself if the private conduct has a "public function" that's normally exclusively reserved to the state. If you answer "yes" to either, then there's state action.

Where ***discrimination*** is the issue, you also need to remember that, in order for a statute to be held invalid, it must be found to be discriminatory in one of the following ways: It must be discriminatory on its face, or be facially neutral but unequally administered, or have an impermissible motive—the intent to discriminate. The statute won't be found invalid if the discrimination results merely ***from its impact***. Given these requirements, if you're faced with a newly enacted statute but you're not told anything about its background, it can be held invalid ***only*** because it's invalid on its face (since it hasn't been applied, evenly or unevenly, and since you know of no improper motive).

LEVELS OF SCRUTINY:

a. Strict scrutiny.

This applies ***only*** to these types of classifications.

1. The classification is "suspect"—that is, it's based on race or alienage; ***OR***
2. The classification relates to ***who may exercise a fundamental right.***

The fundamental rights, for purposes of equal protection, are:

1. Freedom of association
2. Interstate travel (look for ***residency*** requirements as conditions to receipt of welfare benefits, medical care, or voting rights—***vital*** governmental services only—*not* tuition reduction or the right to a divorce)
3. Privacy (marriage, procreation, abortion)
4. Voting (requirements other than age, residency, and citizenship)

Note that freedom of expression ***is*** also a fundamental right, but, because it's riddled with so many rules, it is discussed separately below. Religion is also addressed separately.

Where a classification involves these fundamental rights, it's generally subject to strict scrutiny—the "compelling interest" test: It must be ***necessary*** to promote a compelling governmental interest. This is pretty much the kiss of death for a statute, since laws almost never survive this test.

You should keep one element in mind when considering a problem where alienage (i.e., non-citizenship) is the basis of the classification. A state needs only a rational basis for discriminating against non-citizens in the context of essential state functions. Thus, a state can require that state police, public school teachers, probation officers, and others be U.S. citizens.

b. Intermediate scrutiny.

This applies to the following "quasi-suspect" classifications:

Gender
Legitimacy

Under intermediate scrutiny, a law must be ***substantially*** related to an ***important state interest*** in order to be valid.

The only real way to know what a "substantial relation" is or to know which state interests are "important" is to examine the kinds of statutes that have passed muster in the past. For instance, say a state statute prohibits illegitimate children from inheriting from their father in intestacy, unless paternity was established during the father's lifetime. The state's interest in promoting orderly property distribution has been held to justify such a statute. *Lalli v. Lalli* (1978).

Take another example: A state statute requires that a paternity suit, for the purpose of obtaining support from the father, must be brought before the child is two years old. This is unconstitutional as a burden on equal protection. Although the state's interest is important—preventing stale or fraudulent claims—the "substantial relation" is missing; two years doesn't allow a reasonable opportunity to bring a claim, and the threat of stale or fraudulent claims isn't sufficiently great to justify a two-year deadline.

c. Rational relation.

This level of scrutiny will be applied to ***everything*** else. When faced with an equal protection question, you should methodically run through the suspect and quasi-suspect categories. If the classification you're examining doesn't fit one of those classifications, then it's subject to the rational relation test: If there is a set of facts imaginable that would make the law a reasonable way to achieve a legitimate governmental purpose, the law is valid. Given that test, if you correctly identify that a statute should be reviewed under this test, the statute should almost certainly be upheld.

Needless to say, there's a whole world of classifications that are analyzed under rational relation. All purely economic and social legislation is usually subject to the rational relation test. So are some classifications you might be tempted to classify as suspect or quasi-suspect; classifications based on poverty/wealth, age, and mental retardation, for instance, are subject only to the rational relation test.

d. Same-sex marriage—level of scrutiny unclear.

For one very important type of classification, it's unclear what level of scrutiny applies: classifications that treat couples differently with regard to marriage depending on whether the couple is *same-sex or opposite-sex.* As the result of *Obergefell v. Hodges* (2015), we know that state laws forbidding same-sex marriages violate equal protection. But be-cause of the ambiguous wording of the majority opinion in *Obergefell*, we don't know *what level of scrutiny* is to be applied to laws forbidding or disadvantaging marriages between same-sex couples. So for MBE purposes, you should assume that any law that either forbids or materially disadvantages same-sex marriages (compared with opposite-sex marriages) violates equal protection; unless/until there is further clarification from the Supreme Court, you will presumably not be asked to say what level of scrutiny is to be used in reviewing such laws.

2. Where there's no classification—due process problems.

Both federal and state governments are subject to due process constraints. There are two types of due process problems: procedural and substantive.

a. Procedural due process.

This addresses the fairness of the procedure used to deprive someone of a significant interest, typically in property, but also in life (e.g., capital punishment) or liberty (e.g., incarceration). In general, when you're dealing with procedural due process, you'll ask if ***notice and a hearing*** are necessary when a right is removed.

When dealing with procedural due process, keep in mind, first, that "property," in this context, doesn't necessarily mean actual, tangible land or chattels—"property" can also mean an interest already acquired in specific benefits. For instance, a doctor has a property right in his license to practice medicine; a welfare recipient has a property right in continued benefits. The most common "property" question on the MBE involves ***government jobs.*** People typically ***don't*** have a property right in continued public employment—unless something in the facts of a question suggests otherwise (such as mention of tenure or of a contract provision requiring that an employee can only be fired for "cause"). Note that a person's mere ***expectations*** of maintaining benefits or a job aren't enough to make their expectations into a property right—there must be a law—whether federal, state, or local—under which the person has a ***legitimate claim*** to the benefits.

b. Substantive due process.

Substantive due process is a much more likely source of difficulty on the MBE than procedural due process. Substantive due process becomes an issue when state action substantially interferes with a ***"fundamental"*** right. If the right interfered with is "fundamental," a statute must meet the same "strict scrutiny" test as in equal protection law or it won't be upheld. If the right is ***not*** fundamental, the statute is subject to the same "rational relation" test as in equal protection law. Remember, though, that only ***personal*** rights are considered "fundamental" under substantive due process: First Amendment rights (in general; note that, as to the right to vote, restrictions as to age, residency, and citizenship are valid), the right of privacy (contraception, procreation, marriage, abortion), and the right to interstate (and probably international) travel.

One end-run the Bar Examiners like to do around your knowledge of substantive due process is to ask you who has the ***burden of persuasion*** in a due process problem. Here's the rule: If the impaired right is fundamental, then the burden of persuasion is on the ***government*** to defend its action; if the right is non-fundamental, then the burden of persuasion is on the ***person attacking*** the government's action. We'll discuss this in item 6, below.

3. Putting it all together.

Here are a few examples to show you how due process and equal protection relate to each other.

Say there's a state statute that forbids unmarried people from buying contraceptives. Equal protection or due process problem? It's equal protection. There's a classification—married vs. unmarried people. What does the classification do? It limits who may use contraceptives, which falls under the right of privacy—a fundamental right. Because the classification defines who may exercise a fundamental right, it's subject to strict scrutiny, and on that basis, it will likely fail. Note, incidentally, that the problem is also, theoretically, a due process problem, because it infringes on the fundamental right to privacy. The important thing for you to remember, in terms of the MBE, is that the existence of a classification makes it more obviously an equal protection problem.

Change the above facts so that it's a federal statute instead of a state statute. Still a Fourteenth Amendment Equal Protection problem? It ***can't*** be—the Equal Protection Clause applies only to the states. In any case, the statute isn't likely to be valid, because the Due Process Clause of the Fifth Amendment invalidates pretty much any federal-government discrimination that, if practiced by a state, would violate the Equal Protection Clause. In addition, it's not clear what enumerated power would authorize Congress to enact such legislation. Compare the statute to the list of congressional powers, above, and see for yourself.

Back to the state statute. Say, instead of only forbidding unmarried people from using contraceptives, the statute stopped ***everyone*** from using them. Equal protection or due process? It can't be equal protection, because there's no classification involved; however, such a statute ***does*** infringe a personal right, so there's a due process problem. Since contraceptives involve the right of privacy, the right is "fundamental," and, as in the equal protection analysis, the statute will be subject to strict scrutiny—and will probably fail.

4. Freedom of expression.

You may think, "Wait a minute. Freedom of expression is a fundamental right. Why not just lump it together with the other fundamental rights?" You can't really do that, though, because what we're focusing on here is applying general constitutional principles on the MBE, and there are so many special rules that apply to freedom of expression that considering it as just another fundamental right would confuse you more than it would help you. If the only thing you remember is that any statute impinging on freedom of expression must pass the "strict scrutiny" test, you'll be in trouble.

Keep in mind, first of all, that "freedom of expression" actually covers several distinct yet related rights: the freedoms of ***speech, press, assembly,*** and ***association.***

Also keep in mind that any statute regulating freedom of speech (or association) must contain ***narrow and definite standards*** in order to be upheld. This involves the twin doctrines of ***overbreadth*** and ***vagueness.*** If a statute prohibits not only unprotected speech, but some ***protected*** speech as well, it's unconstitutionally ***overbroad.*** If the conduct prohibited by a statute is so unclearly defined that a reasonable person would have to ***guess at its meaning,*** it's unconstitutionally ***vague.*** Note that statutes that are unconstitutionally overbroad are usually unconstitutionally vague, too.

Here's an example of overbreadth and vagueness:

A newly enacted state criminal statute provides, in its entirety, "No person shall utter to another person in a public place any annoying, disturbing, or unwelcome language." A man followed a woman for three blocks down a public street, yelling offensive four-letter words in her ear. The woman repeatedly asked the man to leave her alone, but he refused.

In the subsequent prosecution of the man, the first under this statute, the man

A. can be convicted.
B. cannot be convicted, because speech of the sort described here may not be punished by the state because of the First and Fourteenth Amendments.
C. cannot be convicted, because, though his speech here may be punished by the state, the state may not do so under this statute.
D. cannot be convicted, because the average user of a public street would think his speech/action here was amusing and ridiculous rather than "annoying," etc.

Under the Constitution, language can be annoying without being subject to prohibition. Thus, even if the man's language could constitutionally be prohibited on some grounds (as, for instance, with obscenity), it can't be prohibited under the statute here, which is both overbroad and vague. Thus, C is the best response. (Incidentally, note the fact that this prosecution is the ***first under this statute.*** A statute that is otherwise unconstitutionally vague and overbroad could be saved by a judicial interpretation that limited it enough to make it valid. The question here avoids this issue by stating that there's never been a judicial interpretation of the statute.)

So much for what any statute limiting speech must do to be valid. Let's look at a few special situations.

A. Defamation, obscenity, and "fighting words."

As shown by case law, these types of language are not considered to be "speech" protected by the First Amendment. Defamation is covered in detail in the Torts section of this book. Fighting words are those personally abusive epithets likely to incite immediate physical retaliation in the ordinary citizen. Obscenity—well, use your imagination or rent a George Carlin video (after all, he's quite famous for his seven dirty words). In any case, since none of these constitute "speech," they don't get First Amendment protection; as long as a statute contains narrow and definite standards, such speech can be prohibited without meeting the "compelling interest" test.

B. Advocacy of unlawful conduct—the "clear and present danger" test.

Government action ***can*** prohibit advocacy of illegal conduct if it meets the "clear and present danger" test from *Brandenberg v. Ohio*: If (1) the advocacy is ***intended*** to produce or incite ***imminent*** illegal action, and (2) the advocacy is ***likely*** to produce or incite such action, then it can be prohibited.

C. Prior restraints.

A prior restraint is a governmental action that prohibits speech before it takes place. As you can imagine, these actions are ***presumptively invalid,*** due, generally, to their vagueness or to their placing too much discretion in the hands of the public officials (those responsible, say, for granting licenses to hold demonstrations). Prior restraints can be valid, though, where the mere existence of the communication is proven to create some ***special harm to society*** (e.g., prohibiting publication of planned army movements in wartime would be valid). Otherwise, in the licensing situation, you should apply the time, place, and manner standards discussed in **E,** below.

D. Commercial speech.

Commercial speech is speech whose primary goal is a ***commercial transaction.*** The thing to remember about commercial speech is that, although it's somewhat protected, it can be subject to ***greater regulation*** than non-commercial speech (e.g., it's permissible to prohibit misleading ads).

E. Public speech—time, place, and manner regulations.

If you determine that the speech in a given fact pattern is constitutionally protected, don't stop there; constitutionally protected speech ***is*** subject to ***reasonable time, place, and manner regulations.*** In order to be valid, such a regulation:

1. Must be ***neutral*** as to the content of the speech, both on its face and as applied (this is referred to as the requirement that the speech be "content-neutral");
2. Must further a ***significant governmental interest*** not capable of accomplishment by less restrictive means (e.g., maintaining traffic flow); and
3. Must allow for adequate ***alternative channels*** for communicating the information.

Here's an example:

> The owner of a milk container manufacturing firm sought to focus public attention on the milk packaging law of a state in order to have it repealed. On a weekday at 12:00 p.m., the owner delivered an excited, animated, and loud harangue on the steps of the State Capitol in front of the main entryway. An audience of 200 onlookers, who gathered on the steps, heckled him and laughed as he delivered his tirade. The owner repeatedly stated, gesturing expressively and making faces, that "the g-d damned milk packaging law is stupid," and that "I will strangle every one of those g-d damned legislators I can get hold of because this law they created proves they are all too dumb to live." After about fifteen minutes, the owner stopped speaking, and the amused crowd dispersed. A relevant statute of the state prohibits "all speech making, picketing, and public gatherings of every sort on the Capitol steps in front of the main entryway between 7:45 a.m.-8:15 a.m., 11:45 a.m.-12:15 p.m., 12:45 p.m.-1:15 p.m., and 4:45 p.m.-5:15 p.m., on Capitol working days."
>
> This statute is probably
>
> A. constitutional both on its face and as applied to the owner.
> B. constitutional on its face but unconstitutional as applied to the owner.
> C. unconstitutional on its face, because it applies to all working days.
> D. unconstitutional on its face, because it concerns the State Capitol.

Here, public speech is involved, since the Capitol steps would be considered a public forum. Public speech can be subject to time, place, and manner restrictions. Here, the statute is content-neutral (all speech-making, etc., is prohibited, regardless of the topic or point of view espoused). The statute is addressed to a governmental concern with traffic flow, since the statute only forbids speech during "peak periods" or "rush" times at the building; that's a significant interest that can't readily be accomplished by less-restrictive means. And adequate alternative means of communication are left open (e.g., speech-making that's not right in front of the main entryway, or that's outside of these narrow rush-hour periods). Therefore, the statute meets the three requirements for time-place-and-manner regulations, and is a valid restriction on speech, constitutional both on its face and as applied to the owner (making A the best response).

MBE questions will sometimes involve an attempt by a group or an individual to obtain a ***permit or license,*** as required by an ordinance or regulation, before that group or individual can speak or demonstrate. Be sure to apply the three-part test in this situation. Note that the ordinance or regulation must set out the grounds for ***denying*** a permit in ***narrow and specific*** language that curtails the discretion of local officials. (If it doesn't, the ordinance or regulation is probably overbroad.)

5. Freedom of religion.

Freedom of religion, like freedom of expression, is a fundamental right. It's considered separately here, because, as with freedom of expression, courts apply special rules to it.

Under the First Amendment, the government can neither ***outlaw nor seriously burden*** a person's pursuit of religion (the Free Exercise Clause), nor ***endorse or support*** a particular religion (the Establishment Clause). The upshot is that the government has to be ***religion-neutral.*** Your analysis of religion questions will differ slightly depending on whether a statute ***hurts*** religion or ***helps*** it. In general, any government action must conform with the following test, from *Lemon v. Kurtzman* (1971):

1. the government action must have a ***secular (i.e., non-religious) purpose***;
2. the ***primary or principal effect of the action must not be the advancement of religion***; and
3. the government action must ***not foster excessive governmental entanglement*** with religion.

In general, when a law ***burdens*** the free exercise of religion, you have to perform a ***balancing*** test to determine if the statute is valid. Weigh the magnitude of the burden against the strength of the state interest, taking into account whether there are less burdensome means of accomplishing the state's goal.

Here are a couple points to remember about freedom of religion.

A. The government can only regulate the *practice* of religion.

You can't be told what to believe—for instance, the government can't prohibit you from believing in a specific religion. The government may, however, burden the ***practice*** of your beliefs, if the burden meets the balancing test described above.

B. Only selected kinds of beliefs are covered.

The First Amendment's religion clauses only protect those beliefs paralleling traditional religious views. Thus, a mere political or philosophical view won't be protected, whereas something as bizarre as devil worship will be.

Why is this important? Because it limits what a court can look into when deciding a religion case. If your belief parallels a traditional religion, it doesn't matter if your deities are Coca-Cola bottles—your belief will be protected to the same extent as, say, Roman Catholicism. The court simply cannot investigate the reasonableness of your religious views. Note, though, that in applying the balancing test—strength of state interest vs. magnitude of burden on free exercise—the court can determine how important a particular practice is to the exercise of a religion.

C. Aid to private, religious schools.

There's a potential Establishment Clause problem any time the government helps out ***private, religious schools,*** even if that help is the same as that given to public schools. (Remember that the *Lemon v. Kurtzman* test applies to these situations.) There are two specific guidelines that will help you: First, the aid ***must*** be for secular (non-religious) instruction; second, aid to post-secondary schools (e.g., colleges) is more likely to be upheld than aid to elementary or secondary schools, because there's less perceived risk of religious indoctrination of college-aged people.

Beyond that, there are very few guidelines as to exactly which aid programs will be permissible and which won't. In fact, MBE questions on this topic tend to stay very close to actual cases, since that's the only sure way to know if a particular kind of aid to religious-oriented schools is valid. When in doubt, guess that the particular kind of aid is valid, since in recent years the Court has become much more inclined to find aid OK (e.g., vouchers for private-school tuition, even though 96 percent of participants use them for religious schools—*Zelman v. Simmons-Harris* (2002)).

Something you should watch for particularly is the "no fostering of excessive government entanglement" element of the *Lemon v. Kurtzman* test. For instance, where any kind of government aid to a parochial school would require that the government keep close surveillance on how the funds are dispensed (e.g., grants for salaries of teachers of secular subjects only), the entanglement required to monitor such a program—even though it would otherwise be constitutional—would make the grant impermissible.

6. Burden of persuasion.

To wrap up the area of fundamental rights, remember our discussion of who has to prove what in these cases. To recap, the rule is this: If the validity of a statute will be determined by the "rational relation" test, the plaintiff—that is, the one whose rights have ostensibly been violated—bears the burden of persuasion. ***If***, however, the validity of the statute is determined by the "strict scrutiny" test, once the right has been shown to be impacted, ***the government bears the burden of proving that the statute is valid.*** This is important to remember, because it's counterintuitive; in a normal civil case, the plaintiff typically bears the burden of persuasion. Of course, the fact that this isn't true for cases addressing fundamental rights is what makes it such an attractive issue for the MBE.

7. Standing.

Standing is a sneaky little issue that can come up and torpedo you. Keep in mind that standing is a prerequisite for ***every*** case; if the plaintiff doesn't have it, it doesn't matter how worthwhile his claim is; the case must be dismissed. There is a section on standing in the "Tactics" section, below, but here's the test for standing itself: Standing exists only if the action challenged has caused, or is imminently likely to cause, an injury to the party seeking review. That's all there is to it.

You are likely to encounter this problem on the MBE in the area of ***taxpayer standing.*** As a general rule, taxpayers don't have standing. There is a very narrow exception to this rule, which typically only applies to cases involving religion based on the Establishment Clause. Technically, a federal taxpayer can gain standing to challenge spending matters if he can show two things: that the federal tax was invalidly applied to him, making the injury personal, ***or*** that the expenditures in question ***both*** exceeded a specific constitutional limitation on the taxing and spending powers, ***and*** that they were part of a federal spending program. This, as a rule, restricts taxpayer standing to ***religion*** cases. (Note that this is the rule for federal taxpayers. For state and municipal taxpayers, the outcome is similar: They can normally challenge state or municipal expenditures, limited typically to religion cases, e.g., local busing of parochial school students.)

You should also know when a plaintiff has standing to assert ***someone else's*** constitutional rights in federal court. In general, this is possible only where the plaintiff is injured because someone else's constitutional rights have been violated, or where those who are injured simply cannot assert their own rights. For instance, a beer distributor could challenge a state law that prohibits the sale of beer to men under 21 while allowing women as young as 18 to purchase it, since the equal protection violation to the 18- to 21-year-old men adversely impacts the distributor's business. Similarly, say a state law unconstitutionally compels disclosure of NAACP membership lists. The NAACP would have standing to file suit on behalf of its members, claiming breach of the members' freedom of association rights, because, if the members themselves filed suit, they'd have to reveal their identities—which is what they wanted to avoid in the first place.

8. Jurisdiction.

Jurisdiction brings back happy memories of Civil Procedure for you, doesn't it? There are several facets of jurisdiction (principally federal court jurisdiction) that you should keep in mind on the Constitutional Law questions of the MBE.

First, keep in mind that Congress has the power to create courts inferior to the Supreme Court, and, as a result, Congress can control the jurisdiction of those lower federal courts, as long as it stays within the boundaries of Article III (e.g., Congress couldn't give federal courts the power to render ***advisory opinions***). Congress can also control the appellate jurisdiction of the Supreme Court. For instance, Congress could stop the Supreme Court from hearing abortion cases. The only thing it really couldn't do, in this arena, is monkey with the Supreme Court's ***original jurisdiction*** (e.g., where an Ambassador, a state, or the United States itself is a party).

Second, remember that diversity jurisdiction isn't the only basis of federal court jurisdiction. Diversity cases—i.e., cases between citizens of different states in which at least $75,000 (exclusive of interest or costs) is at stake—are probably the most common federal court cases, but there are several other kinds. You undoubtedly remember federal question jurisdiction from Civil Procedure. Under federal question jurisdiction, if a case arises under a federal statute, a treaty, or the Constitution, a federal court has jurisdiction over the case. There are other kinds of federal jurisdiction, too—e.g., cases between a state and a citizen of another state—but diversity and federal question jurisdiction are the two biggies.

Third, remember which types of lower-court decisions the Supreme Court can hear. In brief, the Supreme Court can hear lower-court cases that decide a matter of federal statutory or federal constitutional law. So, for instance, the Court has power to hear:

1. Appeals from a state's highest court:
   Cases where a state's highest court has held a federal statute/treaty invalid or held a state statute valid in the face of a claim of invalidity under the Constitution or a federal law.
2. Appeals from a lower federal court:
   Cases where a lower federal court decided an issue of federal statutory law, or an issue of federal constitutional law.

But there's a special sub-rule that can deprive the Court of jurisdiction to review even a state-court decision on a federal-law or federal-constitutional issue: The Supreme Court may not hear the case if there was an ***"independent and adequate"*** state-law ground for the decision. That is, suppose a state court opinion rests on *two independent grounds*, one of which is based on federal law and the other on state law. The Supreme Court does not have jurisdiction to hear the appeal if the state-law portion of the opinion is by itself *sufficient to sustain* the judgment.

For instance, let's suppose that a state enacts a statute requiring all pregnant women to have trans-vaginal ultrasounds before any abortion may be performed, and let's assume that the state court says that this provision violates both the federal Constitution's Fourteenth Amendment right to substantive due process, and a separate right of reproductive autonomy given by the state constitution. The state court's conclusion that the statute violates state law supplies an independent and adequate state ground for invalidating the statute, and the existence of that ground deprives the Supreme Court of jurisdiction to review even the federal-constitutional-law portion of the opinion. That's because the federal question is moot—the case would turn out the same way (victory for the party attacking the statute) regardless of whether how the Supreme Court decided the federal-constitutional issue.

Fourth, federal courts will not address ***"political questions."*** Political questions are those issues the Constitution commits to other governmental branches, as well as issues the judicial process is inherently incapable of resolving and enforcing. Foreign affairs are the most obvious example. Foreign affairs are the domain of Congress and the President; thus, a lawsuit by any person or organization that challenged the handling of foreign affairs would not be heard by a federal court.

Fifth, federal courts will not issue ***"advisory opinions."*** An advisory opinion is one that answers a legal question when none of the parties before the court either has suffered or will face specific injury related to that question; remember, a federal court has jurisdiction only over "cases and controversies."

Sixth, keep in mind other factors that contribute to whether a federal court will hear a claim: Specifically, the issue can be neither ***moot*** nor ***unripe.*** A case is moot if it's been resolved or rendered academic before it reaches the court. There are, however, lots of exceptions to this rule—for instance, say a pregnant woman challenges a state's restrictions on abortion. By the time her case winds its way up to federal court, she probably won't be pregnant any more. The issue is, therefore, moot, but this type of case fits into one of the exceptions to the "moot" rule: If an event is recurring but ***will always evade review,*** the court will address the issue anyway (otherwise, the issue may never be resolved). Class actions, too, can proceed so long as any of the claim remains valid, even if the claim of the representative of the class becomes moot (e.g., because it's settled). You get the idea.

"Ripeness" is really an aspect of standing. A case is "unripe" if it doesn't present an ***immediate*** threat of harm. Here's an example:

> A state enacts the Young Adult Marriage Counseling Act, which provides that, before any persons less than 30 years of age may be issued a marriage license, they must receive at least five hours of marriage counseling from a state-licensed social worker. This counseling is designed to insure that applicants for marriage licenses know their legal rights and duties in relation to marriage and parenthood, that they understand the "true nature" of the marriage relationship, and that they understand the procedures for obtaining divorce.
>
> A man, aged 25, contemplated marrying a woman, also aged 25. Both are residents of the state. The man has not yet proposed to the woman because he is offended by the counseling requirement.
>
> The man sues in federal court, seeking a declaratory judgment that the Young Adult Marriage Counseling Act is unconstitutional.
>
> Which of the following is the clearest ground for dismissal for this action by the court?
>
> A. The man and the woman are residents of the same state.
> B. No substantial federal question is presented.
> C. The suit presents a nonjusticiable political question.
> D. The suit is unripe.

Here, you can see that the man hasn't even proposed to the woman, and so there is no immediate threat of harm, which makes the issue "unripe" and, therefore, D is the best response. (Note that this question also addresses two issues of jurisdiction we've already discussed: Choice A impliedly addresses federal court diversity jurisdiction and suggests that, if the parties are residents of the same state, there can't be federal court jurisdiction at all. This choice incorrectly ignores the existence of federal question jurisdiction, which would exist here, because the man is questioning the validity of a state statute ***under the federal Constitution.*** That also knocks out choice B, since it ignores the existence of a federal constitutional question.)

9. Separation of powers.

You may find this a bit bewildering on the MBE, because it's unlikely your Constitutional Law professor spent much time on this issue in law school. While a complete review of the powers of each governmental branch is best left to your substantive review, don't forget the basics: Congress makes the laws, the President executes the laws, and the judiciary interprets the laws. For instance, Congress can't determine the constitutionality of its enactments, and it can't institute or enforce its own laws; the President, who has executive powers, only has legislating abilities to the extent that Congress delegates such powers to him.

On the MBE, you're most likely to see separation-of-powers questions involving Congressional attempts to evade its obligation to pass laws by both Houses, and present the bill to the President for his signature. For instance, the ***"legislative veto"*** is often tested, and represents a violation of both the Bicameral-Passage and Presentation Clauses. *Example:* Congress sets up a Commission to review every application for a new airport. The Commission's approval of a new airport takes effect unless either House of Congress passes a resolution cancelling the approval within 30 days of the approval. This is an illegal "legislative veto"—the cancellation is the equivalent of "making a law," so it can be done only by the vote of *both* Houses, and presentation of the bill to the President for his signature or veto.

10. Bills of attainder.

A "bill of attainder" is a law, either federal or state, that punishes, without a trial, past or future conduct of specifically named individuals or ascertainable groups. Bills of attainder are ***impermissible.*** Bills of attainder are an occasional answer choice on the MBE. Just remember the hallmark of a bill of attainder:

punishment on the basis of political beliefs or activities. For instance, a statute that bans members of the Communist Party from taking leadership positions in labor unions would be an invalid bill of attainder. *United States v. Brown* (1965).

EXAM TACTICS

1. When asked the validity of a law, check first to see if it's a federal or a state law.

As noted in the "Study Strategies" section, it's important to distinguish federal laws from state laws. If you do this, you'll frequently be able to eliminate at least one distractor. Here's an example:

> The strongest constitutional basis for the enactment of a federal statute requiring colleges and universities receiving federal funds to offer student aid solely on the basis of need is the
>
> A. police power.
> B. war and defense power.
> C. power to tax and spend for the general welfare.
> D. power to enforce the privileges and immunities clause of the Fourteenth Amendment.

Here, take note of the fact that this is a ***federal*** statute. You know that the federal government has no police powers, so choice A can't be the best response. (In fact, the correct answer is C. Incidentally, this indicates how Congress can use its strongest powers—namely, spending and interstate commerce—to legislate in areas not delegated to it by the Constitution. In this case, that's education—a traditional state function.)

2. When asked about a plaintiff's standing, ignore substance.

If you're asked about a plaintiff's standing, remember what standing requires: The plaintiff must either have suffered or be imminently likely to suffer an injury due to the challenged action. What you must do is focus on that requirement and ***ignore issues of substance*** in the plaintiff's claim. Here's an example:

> As part of a comprehensive federal aid-to-education program, Congress included the following provision as a condition for state receipt of federal funds: Whenever textbooks are provided to students without charge, they must include no religious instruction and must be made available on the same terms to students in all public and private schools accredited by the state educational authority.
>
> A federal taxpayer challenges the free-textbook provision insofar as it allows the distribution of free textbooks to students in a private school where religious instruction is included in the curriculum. On the question of the adequacy of the plaintiff's standing to raise the constitutional question, the most likely result is that standing will be
>
> A. sustained, because any congressional spending authorization can be challenged by any tax payer.
> B. sustained, because the challenge to the exercise of congressional spending power is based on a claimed violation of specific constitutional limitations on the exercise of such power.
> C. denied, because there is insufficient nexus between the taxpayer and the challenged expenditures.
> D. denied, because, in the case of private schools, no state action is involved.

Here, choice D depends on a substantive issue in the case; that is, whether there is state action involved. The question only asked about standing, though. To determine standing, a court looks solely at whether the plaintiff is legally qualified to press a claim, not whether his claim has merit. Thus, D can't be the best response. (In fact, B is the best response.)

3. Avoid answers which state that a statute is constitutional because the plaintiff's interest is a "privilege, not a right."

Sometimes an answer choice will suggest that a statute is valid, in the face of a due process challenge, because plaintiff's interest is a "privilege" and not a "right." This is a distinction without a difference. If a governmental action impinges on a plaintiff's personal, fundamental interest, it doesn't matter if the interest is characterized as a privilege instead of a right. As a result, the "privilege and not a right" answer choice is almost certainly a distractor.

4. What to do with economic legislation.

When you're faced with a purely economic or social statute, remember that there's probably ***no serious due process or equal protection problem***, because the statute will be subject only to the "rational relation" test. It's easy to read too much into such a question; don't be tempted to do so. For instance, say a state, as an environmental protection measure, bans plastic, non-returnable milk cartons but allows milk to be sold in cardboard milk cartons. There's no serious due process or equal protection problem here. *Minnesota v. Cloverleaf Creamery Co.* (1981).

QUESTIONS
CONSTITUTIONAL LAW

QUESTIONS

CONSTITUTIONAL LAW

Question 1

A state law provides that a person who has been divorced may not marry again unless he or she is current on all child-support payments. A woman who was refused a marriage license pursuant to this law sued the appropriate state officials.

What standard should the court apply in reviewing the constitutionality of this law?

(A) The state must show that the law is necessary to serve a compelling government interest.

(B) The state must show that the law is substantially related to an important government interest.

(C) The woman must show that the law serves no important public purpose.

(D) The woman must show that the legislature did not have a rational basis for enacting the law.

Question 2

Congress enacted a statute prohibiting discrimination in the rental of residential property anywhere in the United States on the basis of sexual orientation or preference by any person or entity, public or private.

Which of the following provisions provides the strongest basis for Congress's authority to enact this statute?

(A) The Enforcement Clause of the Fourteenth Amendment.

(B) The Privileges and Immunities Clause of Article IV.

(C) The Commerce Clause of Article I, Section 8.

(D) The General Welfare Clause of Article I, Section 8.

Question 3

A state law made it a criminal offense for any state employee to "knowingly provide educational services or extend welfare benefits" to a foreign national who was in the United States in violation of U.S. immigration laws. The principal of a public elementary school was prosecuted under the law for enrolling and providing education to several foreign nationals he knew to be in the country illegally. All of these actions took place before the new law was adopted. No federal statute applied to the principal's actions.

What constitutional provision would be most helpful to the principal's defense?

(A) The Due Process Clause of the Fourteenth Amendment.

(B) The Equal Protection Clause of the Fourteenth Amendment.

(C) The Ex Post Facto Clause of Article I, Section 10.

(D) The Privileges or Immunities Clause of the Fourteenth Amendment.

Question 4

An unconstrued state law prohibited the distribution within the state of "seditious propaganda." The state prosecuted United States Post Office letter carriers under this law for delivering propaganda from a foreign country to state residents.

Which of the following statements is an INACCURATE description of the state's law as applied to the letter carriers?

(A) It is an unconstitutional bill of attainder.

(B) It is void for vagueness.

(C) It may not be applied to the letter carriers, because they are employees of a federal instrumentality carrying out an authorized function.

(D) It unconstitutionally abridges rights protected by the First and Fourteenth Amendments.

Question 5

A protester entered an IRS office during business hours. He denounced the income tax and set fire to pages from his copy of the Internal Revenue Code. The fire was extinguished before it caused any other damage. The protester was arrested and charged with violating a state law that prohibited igniting a fire in a public building. He claimed that his prosecution was unconstitutional under the First Amendment.

May the protester constitutionally be convicted?

(A) No, because he was exercising his right to freedom of speech by burning a copy of the code.

(B) No, because the copy of the code belonged to him, and thus burning it did not infringe upon a legitimate government interest.

(C) Yes, because the burning of the code was conduct rather than speech.

(D) Yes, because the state law is narrowly drawn to further a substantial government interest in prohibiting the noncommunicative aspects of the act in question.

Question 6

A private university is owned and operated by a religious organization. The university is accredited by the department of education of the state in which it is located. This accreditation certifies that the university meets prescribed educational standards. Because it is accredited, the university qualifies for state funding for certain of its operating expenses. Under this funding program, 25 percent of the university's total operating budget comes from state funds.

A professor at the university was a part-time columnist for the local newspaper. In one of her published columns, the professor argued that "religion has become a negative force in society." The university subsequently discharged the professor, giving as its sole reason for the dismissal her authorship and publication of this column.

The professor sued the university, claiming only that her discharge violated her constitutional right to freedom of speech.

The university moved to dismiss the professor's lawsuit on the ground that the U.S. Constitution does not provide the professor with a cause of action in this case.

Should the court grant the university's motion to dismiss?

(A) Yes, because the First and Fourteenth Amendments protect the right of the university to employ only individuals who share and communicate its views.

(B) Yes, because the action of the university in discharging the professor is not attributable to the state for purposes of the Fourteenth Amendment.

(C) No, because the accreditation and partial funding of the university by the state are sufficient to justify the conclusion that the state was an active participant in the discharge of the professor.

(D) No, because the U.S. Constitution provides a cause of action against any state-accredited institution that restricts freedom of speech as a condition of employment.

Question 7

A state law that restricted abortion was challenged in state court as a violation of the Due Process Clause of the Fourteenth Amendment to the U.S. Constitution and as a violation of a similar due (though not identical) process provision of the state constitution. The case made its way to the state's highest court, which ruled that the law violated the due process provisions of both the U.S. and the state constitutions.

If petitioned to do so, may the U.S. Supreme Court exercise jurisdiction to review the state court decision?

(A) No, because the state court's decision in this case rests on adequate and independent state law grounds.

(B) No, because the U.S. Supreme Court has appellate jurisdiction only over state court decisions that determine the constitutionality of federal laws.

(C) Yes, because the U.S. Supreme Court has appellate jurisdiction over any ruling of a state's highest court based on an interpretation of federal law.

(D) Yes, because the U.S. Supreme Court has appellate jurisdiction over decisions that find state laws in violation of the federal Constitution.

Question 8

A recently enacted federal statute requires the President to make each appointment of a United States ambassador to a foreign country from a list of three individuals. The list is to be compiled by the Senate Foreign Relations Committee and approved by the full Senate in advance of the appointment. The statute also provides that Senate confirmation of the appointment is deemed to occur automatically 30 days after the time the President names an appointee from the list, unless the full Senate determines otherwise within the 30-day period.

Is this statute constitutional?

(A) No, because the statute violates the constitutional requirements for appointment of principal officers of the United States.

(B) No, because the statute impermissibly restricts the plenary foreign affairs powers of the President.

(C) Yes, because the statute is consistent with the constitutional requirement that the presidential appointment of ambassadors be with the advice and consent of the Senate.

(D) Yes, because the statute is a necessary and proper measure in furtherance of Congress's power to regulate commerce with foreign states.

Question 9

Under a state law, a drug company that makes a false factual claim about a prescription drug is strictly liable in tort to any user of the drug.

In an advertisement promoting sales of a particular drug, a drug company claimed that the drug was safe for children. Suit was filed against the company on behalf of a child who allegedly was harmed as a result of taking the drug. At the time the child took the drug, the available medical studies supported the company's claim that the drug was safe for children, but later research proved that the drug actually was harmful to children. The company has moved to dismiss the suit on First Amendment grounds.

Should the court grant the motion?

(A) No, because false or misleading commercial speech is not constitutionally protected.

(B) No, because the drug business is subject to extensive health and safety regulation.

(C) Yes, because liability cannot be imposed for false statements without a showing of actual malice.

(D) Yes, because the company's claims about the drug were a matter of public concern.

Question 10

A state owned a large natural gas field and took bids for its exploitation. The highest bid came from an interstate pipeline company that distributed natural gas to providers throughout the country. A local gas company submitted the next highest bid, which included the commitment that it would pass along to local customers any savings if it was awarded the contract. The state awarded the contract to the local company. The interstate company sued to overturn this decision.

Should the interstate company prevail?

(A) No, because the state has a compelling interest in reducing the cost of gas for state citizens.

(B) No, because the state acted as a market participant.

(C) Yes, because the state acted irrationally by not choosing the highest bidder and thus denied the interstate company due process of law.

(D) Yes, because the state discriminated against interstate commerce.

Question 11

Congress enacted a statute authorizing the denial of all federal funding to public school districts in which a specified percentage of the students enrolled in the public schools fail to pass a national achievement test. According to the terms of the federal statute, the first national achievement test was scheduled for administration five years from the effective date of the statute.

After reviewing then-current levels of public school student performance, the officials of a state became concerned that several of its public school districts would lose their federal funding after the administration of the first national achievement test. Then-current levels of private school student performance were substantially higher.

In order to improve the chances of those school districts retaining their federal funding, the state recently enacted a law that requires all children of elementary and secondary school age to attend the schools operated by their respective local public school districts. The law is to take effect at the beginning of the next school year.

Parents of children enrolled in private schools within the state have filed suit to challenge the constitutionality of this state law.

Should the court uphold the law?

(A) Yes, because it is rationally related to a legitimate state interest.

(B) Yes, because it is necessary to further a compelling state interest.

(C) No, because it is not rationally related to a legitimate state interest.

(D) No, because it is not necessary to further a compelling state interest.

Question 12

Congress enacted a statute establishing a program to protect areas in the United States that are rich in biological diversity. The program is consistent with the terms of an environmental treaty that the President objected to and did not sign.

The statute creates an executive agency and authorizes it to designate parts of federal lands for inclusion in the program in accordance with criteria taken from the treaty. In an inseverable provision, the statute further provides that the agency must report each designation to a committee of Congress and that the committee may overturn the agency's designation by a majority vote.

Why is the statute unconstitutional?

(A) It constitutes an invalid delegation of legislative authority to an executive agency.

(B) It interferes with the exercise of the President's paramount authority in foreign affairs.

(C) It requires an executive agency to report its decisions to Congress.

(D) It authorizes a committee of Congress to overturn an executive decision.

Question 13

A city ordinance prohibited individuals from picketing in residential neighborhoods unless the picketing related to the neighborhood zoning requirements. This exception to the ordinance was adopted in response to local citizens' strong views about proposed rezoning of residential neighborhoods.

A group that wished to picket in front of a business owner's home because of the business owner's employment practices challenged the ordinance as unconstitutional under the First Amendment.

Will the group's challenge likely prevail?

(A) No, because the ordinance is a content-neutral regulation of speech.

(B) No, because the ordinance regulates conduct rather than speech.

(C) Yes, because the ordinance irrationally discriminates between different types of protesters.

(D) Yes, because the ordinance is a content-based regulation of speech.

Question 14

A state law prohibits the withdrawal of groundwater from any well within the state for use in another state. The express purpose of the law is to safeguard the supply of water for state citizens. Adoption of this state law followed enactment of a federal statute providing that "the transport of groundwater from one state to another may be restricted or prohibited in accordance with the laws of the state in which the water originates."

An association of water users in a neighboring state has filed suit to have the state law declared unconstitutional and enjoined on the ground that it violates the negative implications of the Commerce Clause.

Which of the following is the best argument supporting a motion to dismiss the lawsuit?

(A) The law promotes a compelling state interest that outweighs any burden on interstate commercial activity that might result from this state regulation of its groundwater.
(B) Groundwater located within a state is not itself an article of interstate commerce, and therefore state regulation of the withdrawal of such groundwater does not implicate the Commerce Clause.
(C) The Tenth Amendment reserves to the states plenary authority over the regulation of the natural resources located within their respective borders.
(D) The federal statute explicitly consents to a state's regulation of its groundwater in a way that would otherwise violate the negative implications of the Commerce Clause.

Question 15

Congress passed a statute providing that parties could no longer seek review in the U.S. Supreme Court of final judgments in criminal matters made by the highest court in each state.

What is the best argument supporting the constitutionality of the statute?

(A) Congress has the power to make exceptions to the appellate jurisdiction of the Supreme Court.
(B) Criminal matters are traditionally governed by state law.
(C) The proper means of federal judicial review of state criminal matters is by habeas corpus.
(D) The review of state court judgments is not within the original jurisdiction of the Supreme Court.

Question 16

A state adopted a rule denying admission to its bar to anyone who was currently or had previously been a member of a subversive group. The state's bar application form was modified to ask applicants whether they were or had previously been members of any subversive organization. An applicant refused to answer the question and was denied bar admission on that basis. The applicant challenged the decision, arguing that the question infringed upon his freedom of association.

Is the applicant likely to prevail?

(A) No, because membership in a subversive group constitutes endorsement of the group's illegal activities.
(B) No, because the Constitution does not apply to the bar.
(C) Yes, because denying bar admission based on any association with a subversive organization violates the First Amendment.
(D) Yes, because denying bar admission based solely on past membership in a subversive organization violates the First Amendment.

Question 17

A state statute prohibits any retailer of books, magazines, pictures, or posters from "publicly displaying or selling to any person any material that may be harmful to minors because of the violent or sexually explicit nature of its pictorial content." Violation of this statute is a misdemeanor.

A store displays publicly and sells magazines containing violent and sexually explicit pictures. The owner of this store is prosecuted under the above statute for these actions. In defending against this prosecution in a state trial court, the argument that would be the best defense for the store is that the statute violates the

(A) First Amendment as it is incorporated into the Fourteenth Amendment, because the statute is excessively vague and overbroad.
(B) First Amendment as it is incorporated into the Fourteenth Amendment, because a state may not prohibit the sale of violent or sexually explicit material in the absence of proof that the material is utterly without any redeeming value in the marketplace of ideas.
(C) Equal Protection of the Laws Clause, because the statute irrationally treats violent and sexually explicit material that is pictorial differently from such material that is composed wholly of printed words.
(D) Equal Protection of the Laws Clause, because the statute irrationally distinguishes between violent and sexually explicit pictorial material that may harm minors and such material that may harm only adults.

Question 18

Congressional legislation authorizing marriages and divorces as a matter of federal law on prescribed terms and conditions could most easily be upheld if it

(A) applied only to marriages and divorces in which at least one of the parties is a member of the armed forces.
(B) applied only to marriages performed by federal judges and to divorces granted by federal courts.
(C) implemented an executive agreement seeking to define basic human rights.
(D) applied only to marriages and divorces in the District of Columbia.

Question 19

A purchaser bought land in the mountain foothills just outside a resort town and planned to build a housing development there. Soon thereafter, the county in which the land was located unexpectedly adopted a regulation that, for the first time, prohibited all construction in several foothill and mountain areas, including the area of the purchaser's property. The purpose of the county's regulation was "to conserve for future generations the unique natural wildlife and plant habitats" in the mountain areas. Since the adoption of the regulation, the purchaser has been unable to lease or sell the property at any price. Several realtors have advised the purchaser that the property is now worthless. The purchaser sued the county, claiming that the regulation has taken the purchaser's property and that the county therefore owes the purchaser just compensation.

Is the court likely to rule in favor of the purchaser?

(A) No, because the county did not take title to the property from the purchaser.

(B) No, because the regulation has not caused or authorized any uninvited physical invasion or intrusion onto the property.

(C) Yes, because the conservation objective of the county ordinance is not sufficiently compelling to justify the substantial diminution in the property value.

(D) Yes, because the effect of the county's regulation is to deny the purchaser's investment-backed expectation and essentially all economically beneficial use of the property.

Question 20

Congress recently enacted a statute imposing severe criminal penalties on anyone engaged in trading in the stock market who, in the course of that trading, takes "unfair advantage" of other investors who are also trading in the stock market. The statute does not define the term "unfair advantage." There have been no prosecutions under this new statute. The members of an association of law school professors that is dedicated to increasing the clarity of the language used in criminal statutes believe that this statute is unconstitutionally vague. Neither the association nor any of its members is currently engaged in, or intends in the future to engage in, trading in the stock market. The association and its members bring suit against the attorney general of the United States in a federal district court, seeking an injunction against the enforcement of this statute on the ground that it is unconstitutional.

May the federal court determine the merits of this suit?

(A) Yes, because the suit involves a dispute over the constitutionality of a federal statute.

(B) Yes, because the plaintiffs seek real relief of a conclusive nature—an injunction against enforcement of this statute.

(C) No, because the plaintiffs do not have an interest in the invalidation of this statute that is adequate to ensure that the suit presents an Article III controversy.

(D) No, because a suit for an injunction against enforcement of a criminal statute may not be brought in federal court at any time prior to a bona fide effort to enforce that statute.

Question 21

A certain mineral is added to bodies of fresh water to prevent the spread of certain freshwater parasites. The presence of those parasites threatens the health of the organisms living in rivers and streams throughout the country and imperils the freshwater commercial fishing industry. The mineral is currently mined only in one state.

In order to raise needed revenue, Congress recently enacted a statute providing for the imposition of a $100 tax on each ton of the mineral mined in the United States. Because it will raise the cost of the mineral, this tax is likely to reduce the amount of the mineral added to freshwater rivers and streams and, therefore, is likely to have an adverse effect on the interstate freshwater commercial fishing industry. The producers of the mineral have filed a lawsuit in federal court challenging this tax solely on constitutional grounds. Is this tax constitutional?

(A) No, because producers in only one state will pay the tax and, therefore, it is not uniform among the states and denies the producers of the mineral the equal protection of the laws.

(B) No, because it is likely to have an adverse effect on the freshwater commercial fishing industry and Congress has a responsibility under the Commerce Clause to protect, foster, and advance such interstate industries.

(C) Yes, because the tax is a necessary and proper means of exercising federal authority over the navigable waters of the United States.

(D) Yes, because the power of Congress to impose taxes is plenary, this tax does not contain any provisions extraneous to tax needs or purposes, and it is not barred by any prohibitory language in the Constitution.

Question 22

The U.S. government demonstrated that terrorist attacks involving commercial airliners were perpetrated exclusively by individuals of one particular race. In response, Congress enacted a statute imposing stringent new airport and airline security measures only on individuals of that race seeking to board airplanes in the United States.

Which of the following provides the best ground for challenging the constitutionality of the statute?

(A) The Commerce Clause of Article I, Section 8.

(B) The Due Process Clause of the Fifth Amendment.

(C) The Privileges and Immunities Clause of Article IV.

(D) The Privileges or Immunities Clause of the Fourteenth Amendment.

Question 23

A recently enacted state law forbids aliens from owning more than 100 acres of land within the state and directs the state attorney general to bring an action of ejectment whenever an alien owns such land.

A farmer, who was a resident alien, located and purchased 200 acres of land in the state after passage of that law. He brings an action in federal court to enjoin the state attorney general from enforcing the statute against him. The defendant moves to dismiss the complaint. The federal court should

(A) dismiss the action, because under the Constitution aliens may not sue in federal court.
(B) dismiss the action, because a state has unlimited power to determine the qualifications for landholding within its boundaries.
(C) hear the action, because the United Nations Charter forbids such discrimination.
(D) hear the action, because a federal question is presented.

Question 24

As a part of the practice of the religious beliefs of a small cult of Satan worshippers, the worshippers' high priest was required to sacrifice a cat to the glory of Satan after a live dissection of the animal in which it endured frightful pain. In the course of such religious sacrifice, the priest was arrested on the complaint of the local Humane Society and charged under a statute punishing cruelty to animals. On appeal, a conviction of the priest probably will be

(A) sustained on the grounds that belief in or worship of Satan does not enjoy constitutional protection.
(B) sustained on the grounds that sincere religious belief is not an adequate defense on these facts.
(C) overturned on the grounds that the constitutionally guaranteed freedom of religion and its expression was violated.
(D) overturned on the grounds that the beliefs of the cult members in the need for the sacrifice might be reasonable, and their act was religious.

Question 25

A state employee grievance system requires any state employee who wishes to file a grievance against the state to submit that grievance for final resolution to a panel of three arbitrators chosen by the parties from a statewide board of 13 arbitrators. In any given case, the grievant and the state alternate in exercising the right of each party to eliminate five members of the board, leaving a panel of three members to decide their case. At the present time, the full board is composed of seven male arbitrators and six female arbitrators.

A female state employee, filed a sexual harassment grievance against her male supervisor and the state. The state's attorney exercised all of her five strikes to eliminate five of the female arbitrators. At the time she did so, the state's attorney stated that she struck the five female arbitrators solely because she believed women, as a group, would necessarily be biased in favor of another woman who was claiming sexual harassment. Counsel for the employee eliminated four males and one female arbitrator, all solely on grounds of specific bias or conflicts of interest. As a result, the panel was all male. When the panel ruled against the employee on the merits of her case, she filed an action in an appropriate state court, challenging the panel selection process as a gender-based denial of equal protection of the laws. In this case, the court should hold that the panel selection process is

(A) unconstitutional, because the gender classification used by the state's attorney in this case does not satisfy the requirements of intermediate scrutiny.
(B) unconstitutional, because the gender classification used by the state's attorney in this case denies the grievant the right to a jury made up of her peers.
(C) constitutional, because the gender classification used by the state's attorney in this case satisfies the requirements of the strict scrutiny test.
(D) constitutional, because the gender classification used by the state's attorney in this case satisfies the requirements of the rational basis test.

Question 26

A city is a center for businesses that assemble personal computers. Components for these computers are manufactured elsewhere in the state in which the city is located and in other states and are then shipped to the city, where the computers are assembled. A city ordinance imposes a special license tax on all of the many companies engaged in the business of assembling computers in the city. The tax payable by each such company is a percentage of the company's gross receipts.

A state statute that authorizes municipalities to impose this license tax has a "state content" provision. To comply with this provision of state law, the city license tax ordinance provides that the tax paid by any assembler of computers subject to this tax ordinance will be reduced by a percentage equal to the proportion of computer components manufactured in the state. A company assembles computers in the city and sells them from its offices, also in the city, to buyers throughout the United States. All of the components of its computers come from outside the state. Therefore, the company must pay the city license tax in full without receiving any refund. Other city computer assemblers use components manufactured in the state in varying proportions and, therefore, are entitled to partial reductions of their city license tax payments. Following prescribed procedure, the company brings an action in a proper court asking to have the city's special license tax declared unconstitutional on the ground that it is inconsistent with the negative implications of the Commerce Clause. In this case, the court should rule

(A) against the company, because the tax falls only on companies resident in the city and, therefore, does not discriminate against or otherwise adversely affect interstate commerce.
(B) against the company, because the Commerce Clause does not interfere with the right of a state to foster and support businesses located within its borders by encouraging its residents to purchase the products of those businesses.
(C) for the company, because any tax on a company engaged in interstate commerce, measured in whole or in part by its gross receipts, is a per se violation of the negative implications of the Commerce Clause.
(D) for the company, because the tax improperly discriminates against interstate commerce by treating in-state products more favorably than out-of-state products.

Question 27

A federal statute required a federal agency to establish minimum quality standards for all beer sold in the United States. The statute also provided that public proceedings must precede adoption of the standards, and that once they were adopted, the standards would be subject to judicial review. No standards have yet been adopted. Several officials of the agency have indicated their personal preference for beer produced by a special brewing process commonly referred to as pasteurization. However, these officials have not indicated whether they intend to include a requirement for pasteurization in the minimum beer quality standards to be adopted by the agency. A brewery that produces an unpasteurized beer believes that its brewing process is as safe as pasteurization. The brewery is concerned that, after the appropriate proceedings, the agency may adopt quality standards that will prohibit the sale of any unpasteurized beer. As a result, the brewery sued in federal district court to enjoin the agency from adopting any standards that would prohibit the sale of unpasteurized beer in this country.

How should the district court dispose of the suit?

(A) Determine whether the agency could reasonably believe that pasteurization is the safest process by which to brew beer, and if the agency could reasonably believe that, refuse to issue the injunction against the agency.
(B) Determine whether the process used by the brewery is as safe as pasteurization and, if it is, issue the injunction against the agency.
(C) Refuse to adjudicate the merits of the suit at this time and stay the action until the agency has actually issued beer quality standards.
(D) Refuse to adjudicate the merits of the suit, because it does not involve a justiciable case or controversy.

Question 28

As part of a comprehensive, federal aid-to-education program, Congress included the following provisions as conditions for state receipt of federal funds: (1) whenever textbooks are provided to students without charge, they must include no religious instruction and must be made available on the same terms to students in all public and private schools accredited by the state educational authority; (2) salary supplements can be paid to teachers in public and private schools, up to 10 percent of existing salary schedules, where present compensation is less than the average salary for persons of comparable training and experience, provided that no such supplement is paid to any teacher who instructs in religious subjects; and (3) construction grants can be made toward the cost of physical plant at private colleges and universities, provided that no part of the grant is used for buildings in which instruction in religious subject matters is offered.

A federal taxpayer challenges the construction grants to church-operated private colleges and universities. The most likely result is that the construction grants will be

(A) sustained, because aid to one aspect of an institution of higher education not shown to be pervasively sectarian does not necessarily free it to spend its other resources for religious purposes.
(B) sustained, because bricks and mortar do not aid religion in a way forbidden by the Establishment Clause of the First Amendment.
(C) held unconstitutional, because any financial aid to a church-operated school strengthens the religious purposes of the institution.
(D) held unconstitutional, because the grants involve or cause an excessive entanglement with religion.

Question 29

The governor of a state proposes to place a Christmas nativity scene, the components of which would be permanently donated to the state by private citizens, in the rotunda of the state capitol building, where the state legislature meets annually. The governor further proposes to display this state-owned nativity scene annually from December 1 to December 31, next to permanent displays that depict the various products manufactured in the state. The governor's proposal is supported by all members of both houses of the legislature.

If challenged in a lawsuit on Establishment Clause grounds, the proposed nativity scene display would be held

(A) unconstitutional, because the components of the nativity scene would be owned by the state rather than by private persons.
(B) unconstitutional, because the nativity scene would not be displayed in a context that appeared to depict and commemorate the Christmas season as a primarily secular holiday.
(C) constitutional, because the components of the nativity scene would be donated to the state by private citizens rather than purchased with state funds.
(D) constitutional, because the nativity scene would be displayed alongside an exhibit of various products manufactured in the state.

Question 30

A city owns and operates a large public auditorium. It leases the auditorium to any group that wishes to use it for a meeting, lecture, concert, or convention. Each user must post a damage deposit and pay rent, which is calculated only for the actual time the building is used by the lessee. Reservations are made on a first-come, first-served basis.

A private organization that permits only males to serve in its highest offices rented the auditorium for its national convention. The organization planned to install its new officers at that convention. It broadly publicized the event, inviting members of the general public to attend the installation ceremony at the city auditorium. No statute or administrative rule prohibits the organization from restricting its highest offices to men. An appropriate plaintiff sues the private organization seeking to enjoin it from using the city auditorium for the installation of its new officers. The sole claim of the plaintiff is that the use of this auditorium by the organization for the installation ceremony is unconstitutional because the organization disqualifies women from serving in its highest offices. Will the plaintiff prevail?

(A) Yes, because the Fourteenth Amendment prohibits such an organization from discriminating against women in any of its activities to which it has invited members of the general public.
(B) Yes, because the organization's use of the city auditorium for this purpose subjects its conduct to the provisions of the Fourteenth Amendment.
(C) No, because the freedom of association protected by the Fourteenth Amendment prohibits the city from interfering in any way with the organization's use of city facilities.
(D) No, because this organization is not a state actor and, therefore, its activities are not subject to the provisions of the Fourteenth Amendment.

Question 31

A county is located adjacent to the border of a neighboring state. The communities located in the county are principally suburbs of a large city located in the neighboring state, and therefore there is a large volume of traffic between that city and the county. While most of that traffic is by private passenger automobiles, some of it is by taxicabs and other kinds of commercial vehicles.

A county ordinance, the stated purpose of which is to reduce traffic congestion, provides that only taxicabs registered in the county may pick up or discharge passengers in the county. The ordinance also provides that only residents of the county may register taxicabs in the county. Which of the following is the proper result in a suit brought by taxicab owners who reside in the city challenging the constitutionality of the county ordinance?

(A) Judgment for the taxicab owners, because the fact that private passenger automobiles contribute more to the traffic congestion problem in the county than do taxicabs indicates that the ordinance is not a reasonable means by which to solve that problem.
(B) Judgment for the taxicab owners, because the ordinance unduly burdens interstate commerce by insulating county taxicab owners from out-of-state competition without adequate justification.
(C) Judgment for the county, because the ordinance forbids taxicabs registered in other counties of the state as well as in other states to operate in the county and, therefore, it does not discriminate against interstate commerce.
(D) Judgment for the county, because taxicab owners do not constitute a suspect class and the ordinance is reasonably related to the legitimate governmental purpose of reducing traffic congestion.

Question 32

A city enacted an ordinance banning from its public sidewalks all machines dispensing publications consisting wholly of commercial advertisements. The ordinance was enacted because of a concern about the adverse aesthetic effects of litter from publications distributed on the public sidewalks and streets. However, the city continued to allow machines dispensing other types of publications on the public sidewalks. As a result of the ordinance, 30 of the 300 sidewalk machines that were dispensing publications in the city were removed.

Is this ordinance constitutional?

(A) Yes, because regulations of commercial speech are subject only to the requirement that they be rationally related to a legitimate state goal, and that requirement is satisfied here.

(B) Yes, because the city has a compelling interest in protecting the aesthetics of its sidewalks and streets, and such a ban is necessary to vindicate this interest.

(C) No, because it does not constitute the least restrictive means with which to protect the aesthetics of the city's sidewalks and streets.

(D) No, because there is not a reasonable fit between the legitimate interest of the city in preserving the aesthetics of its sidewalks and streets and the means it chose to advance that interest.

Question 33

A barber is licensed in a state where the state barber licensing statute provides that the Barber Licensing Board may revoke a barber license if it finds that a licensee has used his or her business premises for an illegal purpose.

The barber was arrested by federal narcotics enforcement agents on a charge of selling cocaine in his barbershop in violation of federal laws. However, the local U.S. attorney declined to prosecute and the charges were dropped.

Nevertheless, the Barber Licensing Board commenced a proceeding against the barber to revoke his license on the ground that he used his business premises for illegal sales of cocaine. At a subsequent hearing before the board, the only evidence against the barber was affidavits by unnamed informants, who were not present or available for cross-examination. Their affidavits stated that they purchased cocaine from the barber in his barbershop. Based solely on this evidence, the board found that the barber used his business premises for an illegal purpose and ordered his license revoked.

In a suit by the barber to have this revocation set aside, his best constitutional argument is that

(A) the barber's inability to cross-examine his accusers denied him a fair hearing and caused him to be deprived of his barber license without due process of law.

(B) the administrative license revocation proceeding was invalid, because it denied full faith and credit to the dismissal of the criminal charges by the U.S. attorney.

(C) Article III requires a penalty of the kind imposed on him to be imposed by a court rather than an administrative agency.

(D) the existence of federal laws penalizing the illegal sale of cocaine preempts state action relating to drug trafficking of the kind involved in this case.

Question 34

An attorney contracted for expensive cable television service for a period of six months solely to view the televised trial of a suspect, who was on trial for murder in a state court.

In the midst of the trial, the judge prohibited any further televising of the suspect's trial because he concluded that the presence of television cameras was disruptive.

The attorney brought an action in a federal district court against the judge in the suspect's case, asking only for an injunction that would require the judge to resume the televising of the suspect's trial. The attorney alleged that the judge's order to stop the televising of the suspect's trial deprived him of property—his investment in cable television service—without due process of law.

Before the attorney's case came to trial, the suspect's criminal trial concluded in a conviction and sentencing. There do not appear to be any obvious errors in the proceeding that led to the result in the suspect's case. After the suspect's conviction and sentencing, the defendant in the attorney's case moved to dismiss that suit.

The most proper disposition of this motion by the federal court would be to

(A) defer action on the motion until after any appellate proceedings in the suspect's case have concluded, because the suspect might appeal, his conviction might be set aside, he might be tried again, and television cameras might be barred from the new trial.

(B) defer action on the motion until after the state supreme court expresses a view on its proper disposition, because the state law of mootness governs suits in federal court when the federal case is inexorably intertwined with a state proceeding.

(C) grant the motion, because the subject matter of the controversy between the attorney and the suspect has ceased to exist and there is no strong likelihood that it will be revived.

(D) deny the motion, because the attorney has raised an important constitutional question: whether his investment in cable service solely to view the suspect's trial is property protected by the Due Process Clause of the Fourteenth Amendment.

Question 35

A state imposes a tax on the "income" of each of its residents. As defined in the taxing statute, "income" includes the fair rental value of the use of any automobile provided by the taxpayer's employer for the taxpayer's personal use. The federal government supplies automobiles to some of its employees who are resident in the state so that they may perform their jobs properly. A federal government employee supplied with an automobile for this purpose may also use it for the employee's own personal business.

Assume there is no federal legislation on this subject. May the state collect this tax on the fair rental value of the personal use of the automobiles furnished by the federal government to these employees?

(A) No, because such a tax would be a tax on the United States.
(B) No, because such a tax would be a tax upon activities performed on behalf of the United States, since the automobiles are primarily used by these federal employees in the discharge of their official duties.
(C) Yes, because the tax is imposed on the employees rather than on the United States, and the tax does not discriminate against persons who are employed by the United States.
(D) Yes, because an exemption from such state taxes for federal employees would be a denial to others of the equal protection of the laws.

Question 36

A city ordinance requires a taxicab operator's license to operate a taxicab in the city. The ordinance states that the sole criteria for the issuance of such a license are driving ability and knowledge of the geography of the city. An applicant is tested by the city for these qualifications with a detailed questionnaire, written and oral examinations, and a practical behind-the-wheel demonstration.

The ordinance does not limit the number of licenses that may be issued. It does, however, allow any citizen to file an objection to the issuance of a particular license, but only on the ground that an applicant does not possess the required qualifications. City licensing officials are also authorized by the ordinance to determine, in their discretion, whether to hold an evidentiary hearing on an objection before issuing a license.

An applicant applied for a taxicab operator's license and was found to be fully qualified after completing the usual licensing process. Her name was then posted as a prospective licensee, subject only to the objection process. A licensed taxicab driver filed an objection to the issuance of such a license to the applicant solely on the ground that the grant of a license to the applicant would impair the value of his taxicab driver's existing license. The driver demanded a hearing before a license was issued to the applicant so that he could have an opportunity to prove his claim. City licensing officials refused to hold such a hearing, and they issued a license to the applicant. The taxicab driver has now petitioned for review of this action by city officials in an ap-propriate court, alleging that the Constitution requires city licensing officials to grant his request for a hearing before issuing a license to the applicant.

In this case, the court should rule for

(A) The taxicab driver, because the Due Process Clause of the Fourteenth Amendment requires all persons whose property may be adversely affected by governmental action to be given an opportunity for a hearing before such action occurs.
(B) The taxicab driver, because the determination of whether to hold a hearing may not constitutionally be left to the discretion of the same officials whose action is being challenged.
(C) The city officials, because the taxicab driver had the benefit of the licensing ordinance and, therefore, may not now question actions taken under it.
(D) The city officials, because the licensing ordinance does not give the taxicab driver any property interest in being free of competition from additional licensees.

Question 37

Current national statistics show a dramatic increase in the number of elementary and secondary school students bringing controlled substances (drugs) to school for personal use or distribution to others. In response, Congress enacted a statute requiring each state legislature to enact a state law that makes it a state crime for any person to possess, use, or distribute, within 1,000 feet of any elementary or secondary school, any controlled substance that has previously been transported in interstate commerce and that is not possessed, used, or distributed pursuant to a proper physician's prescription.

This federal statute is

(A) unconstitutional, because Congress has no authority to require a state legislature to enact any specified legislation.
(B) unconstitutional, because the possession, use, or distribution, in close proximity to a school, of a controlled substance that has previously been transported in interstate commerce does not have a sufficiently close nexus to such commerce to justify its regulation by Congress.
(C) constitutional, because it contains a jurisdictional provision that will ensure, on a case-by-case basis, that any particular controlled substance subject to the terms of this statute will, in fact, affect interstate commerce.
(D) constitutional, because Congress possesses broad authority under both the General Welfare Clause and the Commerce Clause to regulate any activities affecting education that also have, in inseverable aggregates, a substantial effect on interstate commerce.

Question 38

Congress enacts a criminal statute prohibiting "any person from interfering in any way with any right conferred on another person by the equal protection clause of the Fourteenth Amendment."

Application of this statute to a private citizen, would be most clearly constitutional if the citizen, with threats of violence, coerces

(A) a public school teacher to exclude black pupils from her class, solely because of their race.

(B) black pupils, solely because of their race, to refrain from attending a privately owned and operated school licensed by the state.
(C) the bus driver operating a free school bus service under the sponsorship of a local church to refuse to allow black pupils on the bus, solely because of their race.
(D) the federal office in charge of distributing certain federal benefits directly to students from distributing them to black pupils, solely because of their race.

Question 39

The vaccination of children against childhood contagious diseases (such as measles, diphtheria, and whooping cough) has traditionally been a function of private doctors and local and state health departments. Because vaccination rates have declined in recent years, especially in urban areas, the President proposes to appoint a Presidential Advisory Commission on Vaccination, which would be charged with conducting a national publicity campaign to encourage vaccination as a public health measure. No federal statute authorizes or prohibits this action by the president. The activities of the Presidential Advisory Commission on Vaccination would be financed entirely from funds appropriated by Congress to the office of the president for "such other purposes as the President may think appropriate."

May the President constitutionally create such a commission for this purpose?

(A) Yes, because the President has plenary authority to provide for the health, safety, and welfare of the people of the United States.
(B) Yes, because this action is within the scope of executive authority vested in the President by the Constitution, and no federal statute prohibits it.
(C) No, because the protection of children against common diseases by vaccination is a traditional state function and, therefore, is reserved to the states by the Tenth Amendment.
(D) No, because Congress has not specifically authorized the creation and support of such a new federal agency.

Question 40

Congress enacts a statute punishing "each and every conspiracy entered into by any two or more persons for the purpose of denying black persons housing, employment, or education, solely because of their race." Under which of the following constitutional provisions is the authority of Congress to pass such a statute most clearly and easily justifiable?

(A) The obligation of Contracts Clause.
(B) The General Welfare Clause of Article I, Section 8.
(C) The Thirteenth Amendment.
(D) The Fourteenth Amendment.

Question 41

An independent municipal water-supply district was incorporated under the applicable laws of a state. The district was created solely to supply water to an entirely new community in a recently developed area of the state. That new community is racially, ethnically, and socioeconomically diverse, and the community has never engaged in any discrimination against members of minority groups.

The five-member, elected governing board of the newly created water district contains two persons who are members of racial minority groups. At its first meeting, the governing board of the water district adopted a rule unqualifiedly setting aside 25 percent of all positions on the staff of the district and 25 percent of all contracts to be awarded by the district to members of racial minority groups. The purpose of the rule was "to help redress the historical discrimination against these groups in this country and to help them achieve economic parity with other groups in our society." Assume that no federal statute applies. A suit by appropriate parties challenges the constitutionality of these set-asides. In this suit, the most appropriate ruling on the basis of applicable United States Supreme Court precedent would be that the set-asides are

(A) unconstitutional, because they would deny other potential employees or potential contractors the equal protection of the laws.
(B) unconstitutional, because they would impermissibly impair the right to contract of other potential employees or potential contractors.
(C) constitutional, because they would assure members of racial minority groups the equal protection of the laws.
(D) constitutional, because the function and activities of the water district are of a proprietary nature rather than a governmental nature and, therefore, are not subject to the usual requirements of the Fourteenth Amendment.

Question 42

A state legislature enacts a statute that it believes reconciles the state's interest in the preservation of human life with a woman's right to reproductive choice. That statute permits a woman to have an abortion on demand during the first trimester of pregnancy but prohibits a woman from having an abortion after that time unless her physician determines that the abortion is necessary to protect the woman's life or health.

If challenged on constitutional grounds in an appropriate court, this statute will probably be held

(A) constitutional, because the state has made a rational policy choice that creates an equitable balance between the compelling state interest in protecting fetal life and the fundamental right of a woman to reproductive choice.

(B) constitutional, because recent rulings by the United States Supreme Court indicate that after the first trimester a fetus may be characterized as a person whose right to life is protected by the Due Process Clause of the Fourteenth Amendment.

(C) unconstitutional, because the state has, without adequate justification, placed an undue burden on the fundamental right of a woman to reproductive choice prior to fetal viability.

(D) unconstitutional, because a statute unqualifiedly permitting abortion at one stage of pregnancy, and denying it at another with only minor exceptions, establishes an arbitrary classification in violation of the Equal Protection Clause of the Fourteenth Amendment.

Question 43

Congress enacts a law providing that all disagreements between the United States and a state over federal grant-in-aid funds shall be settled by the filing of a suit in the federal district court in the affected state. "The judgment of that federal court shall be transmitted to the head of the federal agency dispensing such funds, who, if satisfied that the judgment is fair and lawful, shall execute the judgment according to its terms." This law is

(A) constitutional, because disagreements over federal grant-in-aid funds necessarily involve federal questions within the judicial power of the United States.

(B) constitutional, because the spending of federal monies necessarily includes the authority to provide for the effective settlement of disputes involving them.

(C) unconstitutional, because it vests authority in the federal court to determine a matter prohibited to it by the Eleventh Amendment.

(D) unconstitutional, because it vests authority in a federal court to render an advisory opinion.

Question 44

The president of the United States recognizes a new country and undertakes diplomatic relations with its government through the secretary of state. The country is governed by a repressive totalitarian government.

In an appropriate federal court, a researcher brings a suit against the president and the secretary of state to set aside this action on the ground that it is inconsistent with the principles of our constitutional form of government. The researcher has a lucrative contract with the U.S. Department of Commerce to provide commercial information about the new country. The contract expressly terminates, however, "when the president recognizes the new country and undertakes diplomatic relations with its government." Which of the following is the most proper disposition of the researcher's suit by federal court?

(A) Suit dismissed, because the researcher does not have standing to bring this action.

(B) Suit dismissed, because there is no adversity between the researcher and the defendants.

(C) Suit dismissed, because it presents a non-justiciable political question.

(D) Suit decided on the merits.

Question 45

A generally applicable state statute requires an autopsy by the county coroner in all cases of death that are not obviously of natural causes. The purpose of this law is to ensure the discovery and prosecution of all illegal activity resulting in death. In the 50 years since its enactment, the statute has been consistently enforced.

A man's parents are sincere practicing members of a religion that maintains it is essential for a deceased person's body to be buried promptly and without any invasive procedures, including an autopsy. When the man died of mysterious causes and an autopsy was scheduled, his parents filed an action in state court challenging the constitutionality of the state statute, and seeking an injunction prohibiting the county coroner from performing an autopsy on their son's body. In this action, the parents claimed only that the application of this statute in the circumstances of their son's death would violate their right to the free exercise of religion as guaranteed by the First and Fourteenth Amendments. Assume that no federal statutes are applicable. As applied to the parents' case, the court should rule that the state's autopsy statute is

(A) constitutional, because a dead individual is not a person protected by the Due Process Clause of the Fourteenth Amendment.

(B) constitutional, because it is a generally applicable statute and is rationally related to a legitimate state purpose.

(C) unconstitutional, because it is not necessary to vindicate a compelling state interest.

(D) unconstitutional, because it is not substantially related to an important state interest.

Question 46

A federal statute appropriated $7 million for a nationwide essay contest on "How the United States Can Best Stop Drug Abuse." The statute indicates that its purpose is to generate new, practical ideas for eliminating drug abuse in the United States.

Contest rules set forth in the statute provide that winning essays are to be selected on the basis of the "originality, aptness, and feasibility of their ideas." The statute expressly authorizes a first prize of $1 million, 50 second prizes of $100,000 each, and 100 third prizes of $10,000 each. It also states that judges for the contest are to be appointed by the president of the United States with the advice and consent of the Senate, and that all residents of the United States who are not employees of the federal government are eligible to enter and win the contest. A provision of the statute authorizes any taxpayer of the United States to challenge its constitutionality. In a suit by a federal taxpayer to challenge the constitutionality of the statute, the court should

(A) refuse to decide its merits, because the suit involves policy questions that are inherently political and, therefore, non-justiciable.
(B) hold the statute unconstitutional, because it does not provide sufficient guidelines for awarding the prize money appropriated by Congress and, therefore, unconstitutionally delegates legislative power to the contest judges.
(C) hold the statute unconstitutional, because its relationship to legitimate purposes of the spending power of Congress is too tenuous and conjectural to satisfy the Necessary and Proper Clause of Article I.
(D) hold the statute constitutional, because it is reasonably related to the general welfare, it states concrete objectives, and it provides adequate criteria for conducting the essay contest and awarding the prize money.

Question 47

A senator makes a speech on the floor of the U.S. Senate in which she asserts that a federal civil servant with minor responsibilities was twice convicted of fraud by the courts in his home state. In making this assertion, the senator relied wholly on research done by her chief legislative assistant. In fact, it was a different man of the same name, and not the civil servant, who was convicted of these crimes in the state court proceedings. This mistake was the result of carelessness on the legislative assistant's part.

No legislation affecting the appointment or discipline of civil servants or the program of the federal agency for which the civil servant works was under consideration at the time the senator made her speech about him on the floor of the Senate. The civil servant sues the senator and his legislative assistant for defamation. Both defendants move to dismiss the complaint. As a matter of constitutional law, the court hearing this motion should

(A) grant it as to the legislative assistant, because he is protected by the freedom of speech guarantee against defamation actions by government officials based on his mere carelessness; but deny it as to the senator, because, as an officer of the United States, she is a constituent part of the government and, therefore, has no freedom of speech rights in that capacity.
(B) grant it as to both defendants, because the senator is immune to suit for any speech she makes in the Senate under the Speech or Debate Clause of Article I, Section 6, and his legislative assistant may assert the senator's immunity for his assistance to her in preparing the speech.
(C) deny it as to both defendants, because any immunity of the senator under the Speech or Debate Clause does not attach to a speech that is not germane to pending legislative business, and the legislative assistant is entitled to no greater immunity than the legislator he was assisting.
(D) deny it as to the legislative assistant, because he is not a legislator protected by the Speech or Debate Clause; but grant it as to the senator, because she is immune from suit for her speech by virtue of that clause.

Question 48

Three states are located next to one another, from west to east. The farthest east and farthest west of the states permit the hunting and trapping of snipe, but the state between them strictly forbids it in order to protect snipe, a rare species of animal, from extinction. The state in the middle has a state statute that provides, "Possession of snipe traps is prohibited. Any game warden finding a snipe trap within the state shall seize and destroy it." Snipe traps cost about $15 each.

A hunter is a resident of the westernmost of the three states and is an ardent snipe trapper. She drove her car to the easternmost of the states to purchase a new, improved snipe trap from a manufacturer there. In the course of her trip back across the middle state with the trap in her car, she stopped in a state park to camp for a few nights. While she was in the park, a state game warden saw the trap, which was visible on the front seat of her car. The warden seized the trap and destroyed it in accordance with the middle state's statute after the hunter admitted that the seized item was a prohibited snipe trap. No federal statutes or other federal administrative regulations apply. The hunter challenges the application of the middle state's statute to her. She demonstrates to the court that common carriers are permitted to transport snipe traps as cargo across the middle state for delivery to another state and that in practice, the middle state's statute is enforced only against private individuals transporting those traps in private vehicles. If the hunter's challenge is based only on a theory of denial of equal protection, this application of the statute will probably be found

(A) constitutional, because the traps constitute contraband in which the hunter could have no protected property interest.
(B) constitutional, because there is a rational basis for differentiating between the possession of snipe traps as interstate cargo by common carriers and the possession of snipe traps by private individuals.
(C) unconstitutional, because the state cannot demonstrate a compelling public purpose for making this differentiation between common carriers and such private individuals.
(D) unconstitutional, because interstate travel is a fundamental right that may not be burdened by state law.

Question 49

Until 1954, a state required segregation in all public and private schools, but all public schools are now desegregated. Other state laws, enacted before 1954 and continuing to the present, provide for free distribution to all public and private schools of particular textbooks on secular subjects for use by students in those schools; the same textbooks are distributed to the two types of schools. In addition, the state accredits schools and certifies teachers.

A private school that offers elementary and secondary education in the state denies admission to all non-Caucasians.

Which of the following is the strongest argument against the constitutionality of free distribution of textbooks for use by the students at the private school?

(A) No legitimate educational function is served by the free distribution of the textbooks.
(B) The state may not in any way aid private schools.
(C) The Constitution forbids private bias of any kind.
(D) Segregation is furthered by the distribution of textbooks to these students.

Question 50

A mathematician was hired as an assistant professor of mathematics at a state college and is now in his third consecutive one-year contract. Under state law he cannot acquire tenure until after five consecutive annual contracts. In his third year, the mathematician was notified that he was not being rehired for the following year. Applicable state law and college rules did not require either a statement of reasons or a hearing, and in fact neither was offered to him.

Which of the following, if established, sets forth the strongest constitutional argument the mathematician could make to compel the college to furnish him a statement of reasons for the failure to rehire him and an opportunity for a hearing?

(A) There is no evidence that tenured teachers are any more qualified than he is.
(B) He leased a home in reliance on an oral promise of reemployment by the college president.
(C) He was the only teacher at the college whose contract was not renewed that year.
(D) In the expectation of remaining at the college, he had just moved his elderly parents to the town in which the college is located.

Question 51

A city passed an ordinance requiring individuals to obtain a license in order to care for children under the age of 12 for pay. To receive such a license, the ordinance required the individuals to complete ten hours of instruction in child care, undergo a background check, and pay a $100 fee. The ordinance affected women disproportionately to men, because female babysitters far out-numbered male babysitters in the city. City officials who promoted the measure said that the certification process would ensure that babysitters were adequately regulated for the health and safety of the city's children.

Is the ordinance constitutional?

(A) No, because it has a disparate impact on women without a showing that the ordinance is necessary to advance a compelling government interest.
(B) No, because it infringes on the freedom of contract without a compelling government interest.
(C) Yes, because any burden it imposes is clearly outweighed by an important government objective.
(D) Yes, because it is rationally related to a legitimate government objective.

Question 52

A federal statute required that any individual or entity owning more than 100 cars had to ensure that at least 10 percent of those cars were electric powered.

A city filed suit in federal district court against the federal official who enforced this requirement. The city sought an injunction prohibiting enforcement of the statute on the ground that it was unconstitutional.

Should the court grant the injunction?

(A) No, because the statute is valid under the Commerce Clause and does not violate the Tenth Amendment.

(B) No, because the federal government has sovereign immunity and cannot be sued without its explicit consent.

(C) Yes, because the statute violates the reserved rights of the states under the Tenth Amendment.

(D) Yes, because as applied to state and local governments, the statute exceeds Congress's power under the Commerce Clause.

ANSWERS

CONSTITUTIONAL LAW

Answer Key

Use this Answer Key to quickly identify the correct answer to each question.

(1) A	(11) D	(21) D	(31) B	(41) A	(51) D
(2) C	(12) D	(22) B	(32) D	(42) C	(52) A
(3) C	(13) D	(23) D	(33) A	(43) D	
(4) A	(14) D	(24) B	(34) C	(44) C	
(5) D	(15) A	(25) A	(35) C	(45) B	
(6) B	(16) D	(26) D	(36) D	(46) D	
(7) A	(17) A	(27) D	(37) A	(47) B	
(8) A	(18) D	(28) A	(38) A	(48) B	
(9) A	(19) D	(29) B	(39) B	(49) D	
(10) B	(20) C	(30) D	(40) C	(50) B	

ANSWERS

CONSTITUTIONAL LAW

Answer 1

(A) is the best response,

because this choice correctly states the test for strict scrutiny, which the statute will have to survive.

The woman's suit would be brought on a substantive due process theory. The Supreme Court held in *Zablocki v. Redhail*, 434 U.S. 374 (1978), that marriage is a "fundamental right" for substantive due process purposes. That case, like the fact pattern here, involved a state statute making a marriage license conditional upon the payment of all court-ordered child support. The Court concluded that the statute "substantially" interfered with this fundamental right of marriage, triggering strict scrutiny of the statute. When a statute is strictly scrutinized, the defender of the statute (here, the state) bears the burden of proving that the law is necessary to serve a compelling governmental interest.

(B) is not the best response,

because it does not represent the correct test for strict scrutiny.

The statute here substantially interferes with the right to marry, which the Supreme Court has found to be a fundamental right, as discussed in Choice A. Where a fundamental right is being substantially interfered with, the statute will be strictly scrutinized by the court. The standard recited in this choice—"substantially related to an important government interest"—is not the strict scrutiny standard, but is rather the standard for mid-level review, used, for example, in equal protection cases involving gender classifications.

(C) is not the best response,

because it does not represent the correct test for strict scrutiny.

The statute here substantially interferes with the right to marry, which the Supreme Court has found to be a fundamental right. Any substantial interference with a fundamental right triggers strict judicial scrutiny. In strict scrutiny, the burden of proof is placed on the defender of the statute, not on the person attacking it. Since this choice imposes the burden of proof on the woman (the person attacking the statute), it cannot correctly state the strict scrutiny standard.

(D) is not the best response,

because it does not represent the correct test for strict scrutiny.

The statute here substantially interferes with the right to marry, which the Supreme Court has found to be a fundamental right. Any substantial interference with a fundamental right triggers strict judicial scrutiny. In strict scrutiny, the burden of proof is placed on the defender of the statute, not on the person attacking it. Like Choice C, this choice imposes the burden of proof on the person attacking the statute, so it cannot correctly state the strict scrutiny standard.

Answer 2

(C) is the best response,

because rental activities have a substantial effect on interstate commerce.

Congress of course has the power to "regulate commerce . . . among the several states." But the issue raised by this choice is that Congress has attempted to prohibit sexual-orientation discrimination by "any person," in connection with any residential property, no matter how local the transaction. For instance, the statute would apply to one private individual's refusal, on sexual-orientation grounds, to rent out a room in her owner-occupied house, an essentially *intra*state transaction. But the Supreme Court has long held that even purely intrastate commercial acts may be regulated under the commerce power, if such intrastate acts, taken in the aggregate, have a substantial effect on interstate commerce. For instance, in *Wickard v. Filburn*, 317 U.S. 111 (1942), the Court famously held that Congress could regulate the amount of wheat that could be grown by a farmer, even where all of the wheat would be consumed by the farmer's family rather than sold—home-grown wheat competed with wheat sold in interstate commerce, so the home-growing taken in the aggregate had a substantial effect on interstate commerce. Here, similarly, rentals of single rooms even in local transactions are commercial activities that collectively affect the *inter*state market for accommodations, and may thus be regulated under the commerce power.

(A) is not the best response,

because Congress is attempting to regulate purely private conduct.

The Enforcement Clause of the Fourteenth Amendment is § 5, which gives Congress "power to enforce [this Amendment] by appropriate legislation." But the entire Fourteenth Amendment limits only *"state action,"* that is, conduct by state and local governments rather than by private individuals.

Consequently, the Supreme Court has held that Congress's § 5 enforcement power, too, applies only where Congress is regulating state action rather than purely private conduct. See, e.g., *U.S. v. Morrison*, 529 U.S. 598 (2000), where the Court held that Congress could not use its § 5 enforcement powers to regulate gender-motivated violence against women committed by private persons. Here, since Congress is purporting to prohibit purely private discrimination based on sexual orientation, Congress cannot use its Fourteenth Amendment enforcement powers to do so.

(B) is not the best response,

because the Article IV Privileges and Immunities Clause does not serve as a source of congressional power.

The Privileges and Immunities Clause of Article IV prohibits any state from engaging in certain types of discrimination against citizens of other states. It is not a source of congressional power.

(D) is not the best response,

because the General Welfare Clause is not a free-standing source of congressional power.

It's true that Article I, § 8, cl. 1, gives power to Congress in connection with the "general welfare" of the United States. But this is not a grant of free-standing congressional power. Rather, the clause gives Congress the power to *tax and spend* for the purpose of achieving the general welfare. So where all Congress is doing is to *regulate*, rather than to tax and spend, the General Welfare Clause does not act as a source of authority.

Answer 3

(C) is the best response,

because the statute criminalized conduct that took place before the statute's enactment.

Article I, § 10 of the Constitution prohibits the states from passing any "*ex post facto* Law." An *ex post facto* law is a law that imposes a punishment for an act that, at the time it occurred, was not punishable. That's what the state is doing here, by prosecuting the principal for actions he took before the new statute was enacted. (The statute would not pose an *ex post facto* problem if it were applied to actions taken by a state employee *after* the date of the statute's enactment.)

(A) is not the best response,

because the restriction would only have to pass "mere rationality" review to be valid under the Due Process Clause.

The principal would indeed have a plausible due process claim, since he has been deprived of a liberty interest, namely, his freedom to give schooling to certain people. But not all governmentally imposed restrictions on liberty violate the Due Process Clause. Where the liberty interest being restricted is not a "fundamental" one, the government may infringe on it without violating the Due Process Clause, as long as the means chosen is rationally related to the fulfillment of a legitimate state objective, an easy-to-satisfy test. There is no reason to believe that a person's right to help others get schooling is a "fundamental" interest for due process purposes. The state has a very plausible argument that it is pursuing a "legitimate" interest (keeping its employees from aiding and abetting violations of U.S. immigration law), and that the means it has chosen are at least rationally related to the achievement of this objective. It is not certain that this argument will be victorious, but the principal is far more likely to lose with this due process argument than with the *ex post facto* claim covered by choice C.

(B) is not the best response,

because the law does not create a suspect classification or burden a fundamental right.

The state has indeed made a classification—it treats state employees who facilitate the schooling of known illegal immigrants differently from non-state-employees who do the same thing. So the principal has at least a plausible equal protection claim. But unless a governmental classification either involves a suspect class, or burdens an interest that is deemed fundamental for equal protection purposes, the classification is subject only to the easy-to-satisfy mere-rationality standard: it just has to be rationally related to the achievement of a legitimate state objective. The classification scheme here—which treats state employees differently from all other people—does not create a suspect class (as, say, a classification based on race or national origin would do). Nor does the classification burden any fundamental right, since neither the right to be a state employee nor the right to help others become educated has ever been found to be fundamental for equal protection purposes. So the principal will have to show either that the state is not pursuing a legitimate governmental interest, or that the means the state has chosen is not rationally related to such an interest. The principal probably cannot make either of these showings: The state's interest in not making it easier for immigration-violators to remain in the country is probably at least "legitimate," and a ban on state employees' rendering educational assistance to such violators is probably at least rationally related to the fulfillment of that interest. The principal's equal protection argument is not certain to fail, but it is clearly a weaker argument than the *ex post facto* argument covered by choice C.

(D) is not the best choice,

because the case does not involve any right of national citizenship, and is thus not covered by the Privileges or Immunities Clause.

The Fourteenth Amendment's Privileges or Immunities Clause prevents a state from impairing certain rights held by U.S. citizens. But the clause has always been interpreted to protect only certain rights of *"national,"* as opposed to state, citizenship. The list of rights protected by the clause is a very short one, essentially limited to the right to travel from state to state and to relocate to a new state without penalty, the right to vote in national elections, and a few other narrowly-defined rights. The principal would have to show that his "right" to help others gain an education was covered by the clause. But the right to help others obtain an education is certainly not a right of "national" citizenship of the sort that would be found to be protected by the Fourteenth Amendment's Privileges or Immunities Clause.

Answer 4

(A) is the best response,

because the bill does not single out a named person or easily-ascertained group.

A bill of attainder is a legislative act that applies either to named individuals or to easily-ascertainable members of a group, in such a way as to inflict punishment on them without a judicial trial. *U.S. v. Lovett*, 328 U.S. 303 (1946). Since the statute here makes it a crime for *anyone* to engage in the forbidden distribution, it does not single out named individuals or easily-ascertained members of a group. Therefore, it is not a bill of attainder.

(B) is not the best response,

because the statute fails to give individuals reasonable notice of whether their conduct would or would not violate the statute.

A statute will be held void for vagueness if the conduct that it forbids is so unclearly defined that persons of reasonable intelligence must necessarily guess at its meaning. The idea is that a statute is unconstitutionally vague if it does not give fair notice of the dividing line between forbidden and non-forbidden behavior. Given that the term "seditious propaganda" is not defined in the statute, and its meaning is non-obvious, the statute indeed fails to give fair notice of what is forbidden. Therefore, this choice is not an inaccurate description of the law.

(C) is not the best response,

because the letter carriers fall within the federal immunity from state regulation.

The federal government is essentially immune from state regulatory interference. A federal employee is also immune from state regulation that would substantially interfere with his ability to carry out his officially-authorized functions. Since the letter carriers are, when delivering foreign propaganda to the addressee, carrying out their authorized federal functions, the carriers are immune from a state prosecution that would interfere with those deliveries. Therefore, this choice is not an inaccurate description of the law.

(D) is not the best response,

because the state law violates the free-speech rights of the addressees and the letter carriers.

Core political speech is especially rigorously protected under the First Amendment (as made applicable to the states by the Fourteenth Amendment). Even speech advocating force or crime may not be forbidden on the grounds that it is subversive, unless the government proves that (1) the speech is intended to incite or produce imminent lawless action; and (2) such imminent lawless action is in fact likely to occur. *Brandenburg v. Ohio*, 395 U.S. 444 (1969). There is no indication here that the state government has succeeded in making either of these showings as to the letter carriers. Therefore, this choice is an accurate description of the state law, making it not the best choice.

Answer 5

(D) is the best response,

because it correctly states the standard for judging non-content-based restrictions on speech.

Where a regulation has a significant impact on protected expression, but is "content neutral" (i.e., not related to the message being communicated), the regulation is subject to mid-level review: It must be "narrowly tailored" to further a "significant governmental interest." *Clark v. Community For Creative Non-Violence*, 468 U.S. 288 (1984). The protester's conduct in setting the fire receives First Amendment protection, because he was intending to deliver a message (a protest), and the audience was likely to understand that message. But the statute here is content-neutral: All setting of fires in public buildings is prohibited, regardless of the content of any message being delivered by the fire-setter. So the "narrowly tailored to further a significant governmental interest" standard is the applicable standard. (It is highly likely that the ban here satisfies this mid-level standard, since there is obviously a significant governmental interest in avoiding the danger posed by fires in public buildings, and a ban on intentionally setting such fires is a narrowly tailored means of avoiding this danger.)

(A) is not the best response,

because, while it states a correct premise, it draws an incorrect conclusion from that premise.

It's true that the protester's conduct in setting the fire receives First Amendment protection, because he was intending to deliver a message (a protest), and the audience was likely to understand that message. But the mere fact that a person is exercising free speech does not automatically prevent the government from regulating, or even forbidding, that speech in particular circumstances. As explained further in Choice D above, where the government restricts speech but does so in a content-neutral way, the restriction will be valid as long as it is narrowly tailored to further a significant governmental interest. Since this choice suggests that the restriction is automatically invalid merely because it restricts the protester's exercise of his right to free speech, the choice is incorrect.

(B) is not the best response,

because it draws a legally incorrect conclusion from a correctly-stated fact.

It's of course true that the protester owned the copy of the material being burned. But it certainly does not follow from this fact that the burning "did not infringe upon a legitimate government interest." The government has a substantial interest in avoiding dangerous fires in public places, and that interest applies whether or not the materials being burned belonged to the burner. Since the anti-burning restriction here is content-neutral (it does not depend on the particular message, if any, being communicated by the burning), the restriction will be upheld even though it significantly infringes speech, as long as the restriction is narrowly tailored to achieve a substantial governmental interest. Note that not only does this choice incorrectly assert that the burning didn't infringe on a legitimate governmental interest, but the choice also incorrectly asserts that the governmental interest must merely be "legitimate"—for content-neutral restrictions that significantly infringe on protected speech, the governmental interest being pursued must be "substantial," not just "legitimate."

(C) is not the best response,

because it is based on an irrelevant distinction.

It is of course true that the protester's act of burning the code was "conduct," not pure speech. But the conduct/speech distinction is essentially irrelevant in First Amendment law: If conduct is motivated by an intent to communicate a message (and the audience is likely to understand the message), the conduct receives First Amendment protection. However, even conduct that receives First Amendment protection because it is communicative may nonetheless be subjected to significant governmental restriction; where the restriction is content neutral, the restriction will be upheld if it is narrowly tailored to achieve a significant governmental interest. Since this choice asserts that the protester automatically loses because his code-burning was conduct rather than speech, it is incorrect as a matter of law.

Answer 6

(B) is the best response,

because it correctly identifies the state-action issue.

The professor's suit would have to have been based on the First Amendment, as made applicable to the states by means of the Fourteenth Amendment's Due Process Clause. The Fourteenth Amendment applies only where there is "state action," that is, some sort of participation in the challenged action by a state or local government entity. So purely private action cannot be the basis for a First Amendment or Fourteenth Amendment claim. Here, the university whose conduct is alleged to have violated the professor's free-speech rights is a private university. Unless the state has somehow participated in that conduct, the absence of state action will automatically defeat the professor's claim. The mere fact that a substantial portion of the university's operating budget comes from state funds is not sufficient to cause the university's conduct to be deemed state action. *See, e.g., Rendell-Baker v. Kohn*, 457 U.S. 830 (1982) (even though a private high school received public funds amounting to 90% of the school's budget, this was not enough to transform the school's employment decisions into state action).

(A) is not the best response,

because it is wrong as a proposition of law.

If the university here were a public university, it would normally not have an untrammeled right to discharge an employee for not sharing or communicating the university's views—the employee's free-speech rights would protect against such a dismissal. At least where the speech is on a matter of public concern (as is the case here), the speech may be grounds for dismissal only if the employer's interest in promoting the efficiency of its operations is found to outweigh the employee's free speech rights, a standard that the university would probably not be able to meet here. What entitles the university to victory is the school's status as a private actor, as discussed in Choice B.

(C) is not the best response,

because the factors it cites are not sufficient to convert the university's action into state action.

It's true that in some instances, the government may be so involved with the conduct of an otherwise-private actor that the latter's conduct is converted to state action for constitutional purposes. But the mere fact that the government regulates a privately-conducted activity, or supplies funding for such an activity, will not by itself be enough to convert the activity into state action. So the fact that the government accredits the university, and supplies funding for some of its activities, is not enough state involvement to convert the university's hiring decisions into state action. *See, e.g., Rendell-Baker v. Kohn* (cited in Choice B above).

(D) is not the best response,

because it misstates what kind of state involvement would be needed to satisfy the requirement of state action.

There is no provision of the U.S. Constitution that supplies a cause of action against a *private* institution for conditioning a job on a restriction of the worker's free speech. Any constitutional claim premised on a free-speech violation would have to be brought under the First Amendment, as made applicable to the states by the Fourteenth Amendment. But the First or Fourteenth Amendments apply only to "state action," and the conduct of a private actor cannot constitute a violation of either Amendment if the government is not extensively involved in that conduct. The mere fact that the state accredits the university, or otherwise regulates it, would not be enough to convert the university's employment decisions into the requisite state action. (If, by contrast, the state *ordered* the university to, say, impose a loyalty oath on all of its employees as a condition of a job, such an order *would* constitute such extensive state involvement in the university's conduct as to transform the loyalty-oath requirement into state action.)

Answer 7

(A) is the best response,

because it explains why the U.S. Supreme Court does not have jurisdiction to review the decision.

Any jurisdiction the U.S. Supreme Court would have over this case would have to be under the constitutional provision giving the Court jurisdiction over cases involving "federal questions," i.e., cases "arising under this Constitution [and] the laws of the United States[.]" (Art. III, § 2, cl. 1.) The state court decision here, since it finds that the state statute violated the due process provisions of the U.S. Constitution, would seem to qualify as a case "arising under this Constitution." But where a state court opinion rests on *two independent grounds*, one of which is based on federal law and the other on state law, the Supreme Court does not have jurisdiction to hear the appeal if the state-law portion of the opinion is by itself sufficient to sustain the judgment. (If the Court were to hear the appeal, it would in effect be rendering an advisory opinion, since its opinion on the federal law issue would not make a difference to the outcome.) In this situation, there is said to be an "independent and adequate state ground."

That's the situation here. We're told that the state supreme court decided that, apart from whether the state law restricting abortion violated the *federal* Constitution's due process provisions, the provision also violated the *state's* similar (but presumably not identical) due process provision. There is no indication that the state court, in reaching this conclusion about state law, relied in any way on its interpretation of the federal constitutional provision. Therefore, the state court's conclusion that the statute violates state due process law supplies an independent and adequate state ground for invalidating the statute. The existence of that ground deprives the Supreme Court of jurisdiction to review even the federal-law portion of the opinion on appeal.

(B) is not the best response,

because, while it reaches the correct outcome, it does so by misstating the scope of the Supreme Court's appellate jurisdiction.

The U.S. Supreme Court has appellate jurisdiction not only over state court decisions that determine the constitutionality of federal laws, but also over state court decisions that construe the meaning of federal statutes. So this choice is not a factually accurate statement about the Supreme Court's appellate jurisdiction. But this choice does hint, however clumsily, at the real reason why the Supreme Court can't hear the case: The Supreme Court has no jurisdiction to review a state court decision whose result can be fully supported by state-law considerations alone. As is discussed further in Choice A, if a state court decision is based on two grounds, and one of those grounds is an "independent and adequate" state-law ground, the Supreme Court must treat the case as if the state-law ground were the sole one present, thereby depriving the Supreme Court of jurisdiction to hear the federal-law portion of the state opinion.

(C) is not the best response,

because it overlooks the significance of the "independent and adequate" state ground.

It is not factually correct to say, as this choice does, that the Supreme Court has appellate jurisdiction "over any ruling of a state's highest court based on an interpretation of federal law." This statement is incorrect in those situations where the state court decision rests upon two independent grounds, one of which is based on state law and the other on federal law. Because the outcome of the case here is fully supported by the state-law portion of the opinion (the statute is invalidated, whether or not it violates federal law), the federal-law portion of the opinion does not make any difference, a fact that deprives the Supreme Court of jurisdiction to review that federal-law portion.

(D) is not the best response,

because, while it is generally a true statement, it overlooks the significance of the "independent and adequate" state ground.

Generally, the Supreme Court indeed has appellate jurisdiction over decisions that find state law to be in violation of the federal Constitution. But if a state court decision is based on two grounds, and one of those grounds is a state-law ground that is by itself sufficient to sustain the judgment (an "independent and adequate" state-law ground), a special rule applies: The Supreme Court must treat the case as if the state-law ground were the sole one present, thereby depriving the Supreme Court of jurisdiction to hear the federal-law portion of the state opinion.

Answer 8

(A) is the best response,

because both the listing requirement and the automatic confirmation requirement violate the Appointments Clause.

The Appointments Clause (Art. II, § 2, cl. 2) provides that the President shall "nominate, and by and with the Advice and Consent of the Senate, shall appoint Ambassadors . . . Judges of the Supreme Court, and all other Officers of the United States[.]" The statute here violates this Clause in two respects. First, by saying that the President may appoint an ambassador only from among the names appearing on a congressionally-generated list, the statute violates the principle, expressed in the Appointments Clause, that the President may nominate anyone he or she wishes as an ambassador or other principal federal officer (subject, of course, to Senate confirmation). Second, the phrase "by and with the advice and consent of the Senate" means that a presidential appointment of an ambassador or other principal federal officer must be affirmatively approved by a vote of the Senate; the Senate is not permitted to abdicate its duty to consent (or not consent) to such an appointment by means of a statute stating that lack of disapproval within 30 days shall be the equivalent of approval.

(B) is not the best response,

because it reaches the right result for the wrong reason.

The President does not have "plenary foreign affairs powers." For instance, the President may make a treaty only if two thirds of the Senate approves. And in any event, the statute here does not generally curtail the President's broad role in foreign affairs—the statute affects only the appointment of ambassadors. The only problems posed by the statute are caused by the Appointments Clause, as described in Choice A.

(C) is not the best response,

because it misstates the effect of the advice-and-consent portion of the Appointments Clause.

The requirement in the Appointments Clause that the Senate advise and consent to the appointment of ambassadors and other principal federal officers means that the Senate must affirmatively vote to confirm. So a provision saying that the Senate is deemed to have approved an appointment merely by failing to object within 30 days violates this obligation of an affirmative vote.

(D) is not the best response,

because it ignores the Appointments Clause problem.

First, although the Necessary and Proper Clause gives Congress broad ranging authority to implement its enumerated powers, it is unlikely that restricting the President's power to appoint ambassadors to names on a congressionally-generated list would be found to be a "necessary" means of regulating foreign commerce—the connection between foreign commerce and the choice of ambassador is simply too tenuous to qualify under the Necessary and Proper Clause. The second, and more direct, problem is that the Necessary and Proper Clause applies only to congressional actions that do not violate some independent constitutional provision, and the provision here directly violates the Appointments Clause (as described in Choice A). Thus, the statute is not a "proper" means of carrying out any power granted to Congress.

Answer 9

(A) is the best response,

because it correctly states one of the limits that may be constitutionally imposed on commercial speech.

The drug company's claim that the product is safe for children was made as part of speech promoting the sale of a product; therefore, the claim constituted commercial speech. Commercial speech receives First Amendment protection, but to a somewhat lesser extent than, say, core political speech. One of the limitations is that commercial speech that is misleading or deceptive is not entitled to *any* First Amendment protection at all. *See, e.g., Central Hudson Gas v. Public Service Comm.*, 447 U.S. 557 (1980): "[T]here can be no constitutional objection to the suppression of commercial messages that do not accurately inform the public about lawful activity. The government may ban forms of communication more likely to deceive the public than to inform it[.]" Since there is ample evidence that the drug in fact harms children, the speech here was deceptive speech that was not entitled to any constitutional protection.

(B) is not the best response,

because, although it states a true proposition, it reaches an unjustified conclusion.

It's true that the drug business is subject to extensive health and safety regulation. But the existence and validity of such regulation does not mean that the government can restrict all commercial speech related to the regulated activity. For instance, regulations that significantly restrict truthful advertising of a lawfully-offered product are subjected to mid-level review (so that the restriction must directly advance a substantial governmental interest, in a narrowly tailored way). What makes the speech restriction here constitutional is that the speech in question is false or misleading, as described in Choice A.

(C) is not the best response,

because it adopts a test that does not apply to the regulation of commercial speech.

The "actual malice" requirement applies in tort cases that allege defamation by public officials or public figures. The requirement has no role to play in cases where a state regulates commercial speech. Government may restrict false or misleading commercial speech without respect to the mental state of the speaker.

(D) is not the best response,

because it ignores the significance of the fact that the speech here is false or misleading.

Truthful commercial speech is entitled to substantial First Amendment protection, and that is true whether the speech is about a matter of public concern or not. So if the speech here were not false or misleading, the regulation would have to survive a form of mid-level review, even if the speech was not a matter of public concern. What gives the state the right to forbid the speech here is the fact that the speech is false or misleading, as is discussed further in Choice A.

Answer 10

(B) is the best response,

because it correctly states why the dormant Commerce Clause does not apply.

The interstate company's suit would have to have been brought under a dormant Commerce Clause theory. That is, the plaintiff's argument would be that when the state awarded the contract to the local gas company, it was preferring an in-state supplier over an out-of-state supplier, and thus impermissibly favoring local economic interests. But the Supreme Court has long recognized a "market participant" exception to the dormant Commerce Clause: When a state acts as a market participant (rather than as a pure regulator), the state may give a preference to in-staters without violating the dormant commerce clause. *See, e.g., Reeves v. Stake*, 426 U.S. 794 (1976) (state-owned cement plan may choose to sell preferentially to in-state customers in times of shortage, because the dormant commerce clause does not apply where the state is a market participant). Here, since the state owned the gas field, it was entitled to award a local company the contract to do business with the state-owned entity even if the state was acting for the purpose of preferring local economic interests over out-of-state interests.

(A) is not the best response,

because it states the wrong test.

If this were a standard dormant Commerce Clause scenario involving "protectionism"—in which the state, acting as regulator, intentionally discriminates against out-of-staters in favor of local economic interests—then the court would employ a variant of strict scrutiny, under which one of the issues would indeed be whether the state had a compelling interest in reducing its own citizens' gas costs. (Even then, it's unlikely that this objective would be found to be sufficiently "compelling" to justify the preference.) But because the state is acting as a market participant, standard dormant Commerce Clause analysis does not apply, and the state is permitted to prefer local economic interests over out-of-state interests.

(C) is not the best response,

because it incorrectly asserts that the state has acted irrationally.

Where the state is acting as a market participant, the state is relatively free to choose to protect local economic interests at the expense of out-of-state interests. Even in this market-participant scenario, the state may probably not "irrationally" favor local interests. But the state here has not acted irrationally—giving the contract to a local company that's more expensive, in exchange for that company's promise to pass the extra proceeds back to local consumers, is not irrational, since promoting local citizens' economic interests is at least a sensible (though not necessarily the only plausible) legislative decision.

(D) is not the best response,

because even if the state has discriminated against interstate commerce, it was permitted to do so.

When the state acts as a pure regulator, the dormant Commerce Clause prevents the state from intentionally favoring local economic interests over out-of-state interests. So if the state merely passed a regulation that, say, required *any* in-state gas-field owner to contract with an in-state company to transport the gas, this would be a protectionist measure that would virtually automatically be found to violate the dormant Commerce Clause. But because the state, as owner of the gas field in question, was a market participant, the state was not bound by the usual principles of the dormant Commerce Clause. Therefore, the state was permitted to intentionally favor local consumers over out-of-staters, making it irrelevant that the state may have been essentially "discriminating against interstate commerce," if indeed that's what the state was doing.

Answer 11

(D) is the best response,

because strict scrutiny would apply, and the statute would not survive that scrutiny.

The parents would sue on a Fourteenth Amendment substantive due process theory. Under substantive due process analysis, any governmental action that is found to substantially impair a "fundamental liberty interest" must be subjected to strict scrutiny. The Supreme Court has long held that a parent has a fundamental liberty interest in controlling his or her child's education, and that a state requirement that the parent use the public schools violates that liberty interest. *See Pierce v. Society of Sisters*, 268 U.S. 510 (1925) (statute requiring children to attend public schools violates "the liberty of parents and guardians to direct the upbringing and education of children under their control"). To survive the requisite strict scrutiny, the state would have to prove that the means it chose were "necessary" to fulfill a "compelling" state interest. The law here would not survive that strict scrutiny: Even if the state had a compelling interest in raising test scores in order to continue receiving federal money, requiring parents to send their children to public schools rather than private schools would not be found to be a "necessary" means of raising the scores (since other measures, like better teaching, would be likely to suffice).

(A) is not the best response,

because it states the wrong test for reviewing the state law.

If no fundamental liberty interest were at stake here in the parents' substantive due process claim, this choice would probably correctly state the test and the outcome: Governmental regulation of a matter that does not involve a fundamental right merely needs to be rationally related to the achievement of a legitimate state objective, an easy-to-satisfy standard that would likely be met here. But because the right to control the education of one's children is a right that has long been held "fundamental" for substantive due process purposes, strict scrutiny, not the mere-rationality standard, would be the appropriate standard of review.

(B) is not the best response,

because although it states the correct test, it incorrectly predicts how that test would be resolved.

Since the right to control the education of one's children is a "fundamental" liberty interest, any substantial governmental restriction on that right would be subjected to strict scrutiny, under which the state would have the burden of establishing that the means chosen were necessary to further a compelling state interest. So this choice correctly recites that strict scrutiny would be the applicable standard of review. But there are many less-intrusive ways of achieving the state's interest in keeping the federal funds (which may or may not be a compelling interest): For instance, better classroom preparation or test preparation would have a good chance of increasing test scores sufficiently. Therefore, it cannot be said that forcing parents to send their children to public schools is a "necessary" means (i.e., the only effective means) of achieving the stated interest.

(C) is not the best response,

because it not only states the wrong test, it also incorrectly applies that test.

If the liberty interest at stake here were not one that is "fundamental" for substantive due process purposes, it would be correct to say that the test would be whether the means chosen by the state was rationally related to the achievement of a legitimate state interest. But because the freedom to control one's children's education is considered fundamental (see Choice D above), strict scrutiny rather than the mere-rationality standard controls. Therefore, it would not be enough that the means chosen by the state was "rationally related" to the achievement of a "legitimate" state objective. Furthermore, even if this was a case in which the mere-rationality test was to be used, this choice would be a misstatement of how the test would come out: the state probably *has* a legitimate (though not compelling) interest in keeping the federal funds, and coercing all private students to enter the public schools would be at least "rationally related to" (though not "necessary for") the achievement of that interest.

Answer 12

(D) is the best response,

because Congress may overturn an executive action only by passing a statute.

Here, Congress has correctly set up an executive agency, and has correctly given to that agency the power to make certain executive decisions in furtherance of an enumerated congressional power (the power to regulate the use of federal lands). But once the agency has used its delegated powers to make a decision, Congress may only overturn that decision by *enacting a statute*, that is, by (1) having both Houses vote to pass the statute, and (2) presenting the statute for the President's signature or veto. What Congress has tried to do here, instead, is to enact a *"legislative veto,"* by which one House (or a committee of one House) purports to single-handedly overturn an executive decision. And the legislative-veto technique has been held to be a violation of both the requirement that any "legislative act" (i.e., any statute affecting persons beyond the legislative branch) be approved by vote of both Houses, and the requirement that such an act be presented to the President for the President's signature or veto. *See INS v. Chadha*, 462 U.S. 919 (1983) (Congress cannot give the Attorney General the authority to suspend certain deportations of aliens, while retaining to itself the power to reverse such a suspension decision by means of a one-House resolution).

(A) is not the best response,

because the delegation here was proper.

Congress is free to delegate legislative (i.e., lawmaking) power to an executive agency, provided that Congress provides adequately-specific standards for the exercise of that power by the agency. Here, Congress has provided such standards, since the agency is directed to use particular criteria set forth in the treaty. Thus there is no problem of improper, i.e., standardless, delegation.

(B) is not the best response,

because the statute here does not materially affect the President's foreign-affairs authority.

It's true that the statute here incorporates elements from the never-enacted treaty. But the use of such elements does not interfere in any meaningful way with the President's authority to conduct the nation's foreign affairs—the statute simply says that certain criteria that would have been part of the never-enacted treaty shall be used for another purpose, namely, a domestic regulation to protect certain federal land from environmental harm. Congress has authority to control the use of federal lands, and properly delegated that authority here to an executive agency. (The problem is the veto power retained by Congress.)

(C) is not the best response,

because there is nothing wrong with Congress's requiring the agency to report to it.

Where Congress has correctly delegated lawmaking authority to an executive agency (which it has done here), Congress has the additional power to supervise the agency's use of that power, by requiring the agency to report to Congress on how the agency is exercising the power. Congress possesses this additional power by means of the Necessary and Proper Clause; that clause has been interpreted to mean that as long as Congress is acting in furtherance of one of its enumerated powers (here, the power to control federal lands), Congress may use any means that are rationally related to the carrying out of that enumerated power, if no independent constitutional provision is violated. Requiring an agency to report on how it is using its delegated powers is certainly a rational means of carrying out Congress's power to make that delegation.

Answer 13

(D) is the best response,

because the city is prohibiting some types of picketing but not others based on the message conveyed.

Picketing is an expressive activity, so it receives First Amendment protection. The ordinance here allows one type of picketing, but forbids other types, based on the content of the message being expressed: Picketing having to do with neighborhood zoning requirements is allowed, but picketing on other topics is forbidden. Therefore, the ordinance is a content-based restriction on speech. When the government restricts speech on the basis of its content, the restriction will be *strictly scrutinized*: It will be struck down unless the government can bear the burden of proving that the restriction is a necessary means of achieving a compelling governmental objective. Speech restrictions rarely survive such scrutiny, and the one here certainly would not: There is almost certainly no compelling governmental interest being served by a general ban on picketing in residential neighborhoods, and even if there were, distinguishing between picketing concerning zoning requirements and picketing on other topics would not be a necessary means of achieving that objective. For a similar case in which a ban on certain picketing messages was struck down, see *Boos v. Barry*, 485 U.S. 312 (1988) (ordinance prohibiting the display of any sign within 500 feet of a foreign embassy if that sign tends to bring the foreign government into "public disrepute" was struck down as not being a necessary means of protecting the interest in preserving the dignity of foreign diplomats).

(A) is not the best response,

because it is factually incorrect.

The ordinance here allows one type of picketing, but forbids other types, based on the content of the message being expressed: Picketing having to do with neighborhood zoning requirements is allowed, but picketing on other topics is forbidden. Therefore, the ordinance is a content-based restriction on speech, not a content-neutral restriction. (By the way, even if the ordinance restricting picketing *were* content neutral—such as a total ban on picketing in residential neighborhoods—the ordinance would be subjected to mid-level review, whereby it would be struck down if it was not narrowly tailored to achievement of an important governmental interest.)

(B) is not the best response,

because it makes a meaningless distinction.

Conduct that contains a significant expressive element receives First Amendment freedom of speech protection. So the distinction between "conduct" and "speech" drawn by this choice is essentially meaningless for First Amendment purposes.

(C) is not the best response,

because it states the wrong test for judging the ordinance.

If the correct test for judging the ordinance were indeed whether it drew a rational distinction between the types of picketers, the ordinance would survive (not fail, as this choice suggests). That's because, given local citizens' strong views about the proposed rezoning of residential neighborhoods, it is not irrational for the town to allow picketing on that topic in residential neighborhoods while forbidding such picketing on less-controversial topics (or on topics not so closely tied to residential neighborhoods). However, because the government is drawing a distinction based on the content of the speech, the test is not whether the distinction is rational, but whether it is necessary to achieve a compelling governmental objective, a far tougher test that the ordinance will certainly fail, as discussed in Choice D.

Answer 14

(D) is the best response,

because it correctly explains why the law does not violate the dormant Commerce Clause.

The phrase "negative implications of the Commerce Clause" is a synonym for "the dormant Commerce Clause." That is, a state regulation that significantly affects interstate commerce may be found to violate Congress's power to regulate commerce, if the court believes that the regulation discriminates against (or unduly burdens) out-of-state economic interests in favor of in-state interests. But even where a state takes an action that would ordinarily be held to violate dormant Commerce Clause principles, Congress is always free to affirmatively *consent* to the state action, in which case there is no violation. That's what happened here: When Congress said that interstate groundwater transportation may be restricted or prohibited by the law of the state where the water originates, Congress was expressly permitting the home state of the water to discriminate against out-of-staters; that permission conclusively nullifies any dormant Commerce Clause claim.

(A) is not the best response,

because it both states the wrong test for dormant Commerce Clause cases, and ignores the significance of congressional consent.

First, imagine that the federal statute did not exist. In that event, this choice would still be wrong, because, by requiring a "compelling state interest," it more or less applies strict scrutiny to claimed dormant commerce clause violations. The actual test used is more forgiving: The state regulation must merely pursue a legitimate (not compelling) state objective, the means chosen must be rationally related to that legitimate objective, and there must not have been available means that were materially less burdensome to, or discriminatory against, interstate commerce. In any event, since Congress has expressly consented to the type of burden on commerce here, the dormant commerce clause does not apply at all, and there is no need to consider what test to use.

(B) is not the best response,

because it is based on a false factual premise.

Any item that can be bought, sold or transported over state lines is an article of interstate commerce, for purposes of dormant Commerce Clause analysis. So the groundwater here could certainly be the subject of a valid dormant Commerce Clause claim, but for the fact that Congress has expressly given its consent to the type of restriction here.

(C) is not the best response,

because the Tenth Amendment does not validate a state law that would otherwise violate a federal constitutional provision.

The Tenth Amendment has relatively little scope under modern law; virtually its only function is to prevent Congress from commanding the states to enact or enforce federal policies. The Tenth Amendment can never validate a state law that violates some other Federal constitutional provision. Therefore, the Tenth Amendment would not save the state statute here from attack on the grounds that the statute intentionally discriminates against, and unduly burdens, interstate commerce, and thereby violates the dormant Commerce Clause. (It's only the congressional consent to such a statute that, as described in Choice D, insulates the state statute from dormant Commerce Clause attack.)

Answer 15

(A) is the best response,

because it correctly reflects Congress's power to modify the Supreme Court's appellate jurisdiction.

Article III, § 2, of the Constitution says that in all cases falling within the federal judicial power, and not falling within the Supreme Court's original jurisdiction, the Supreme Court "shall have appellate jurisdiction . . . with such *exceptions*, and under such *regulations* as the Congress shall make." Supreme Court cases have interpreted this language as meaning that Congress may remove an entire subject area from the Supreme Court's appellate jurisdiction, as long as Congress is acting in a substantively neutral way (rather than, say, trying to dictate the outcome in a particular type of case). *See, e.g., Ex parte McCardle*, 74 U.S. 506 (1869) (Congress may constitutionally prevent the Court from hearing all *habeas corpus* appeals from the federal circuit courts). Since the statute here prevents *either* side from appealing criminal decisions made by a state's highest court, the statute is probably sufficiently neutral. It's possible that the Supreme Court might conclude that the statute here is so broad that it went beyond Congress's power to modify the Court's appellate jurisdiction, but of the four arguments for the statute's constitutionality, this one is clearly the most likely to succeed.

(B) is not the best response,

because it states a fact that, while true, is irrelevant.

It's true that criminal matters are traditionally governed by state law. But when a decision by a state's highest court in a criminal case turns on a matter of federal law (including a federal statute or a federal constitutional provision), the case falls within the federal judicial power. Therefore, the Supreme Court has the constitutional right to hear an appeal from such a decision, unless Congress has made proper use of its constitutional power to curtail the Supreme Court's appellate jurisdiction in the type of case in question.

(C) is not the best response,

because it is a misstatement of law.

It's true that, under some circumstances, a prisoner convicted of state criminal charges may bring a federal *habeas corpus* proceeding. But such a proceeding is a separate civil suit brought by a wrongfully-convicted criminal, and is not the only method of having a state-court conviction reviewed by the federal courts. Where a state court criminal conviction has been heard and upheld by the state's highest court, if there is a substantial federal claim present in the case (e.g., a claim that the conviction violates the federal Constitution), the case falls within the federal judicial power, and may be heard by the Supreme Court under the latter's appellate jurisdiction. (The correct answer turns on the fact that Congress has the power to limit the Supreme Court's appellate jurisdiction.)

(D) is not the best response,

because it states a fact that is true, but irrelevant.

When the Constitution puts a particular type of case within the Supreme Court's "original jurisdiction," this phrase means that the Court has the constitutional power to hear the case in the first instance as a trier of fact. It is true that state-court criminal charges do not fall into one of the few categories of cases that are within the Supreme Court's original jurisdiction (e.g., suits in which a state is a party). But where a state-court criminal proceeding turns on a matter of federal law, and has been decided by the state's highest court, the case can normally be heard by the Supreme Court pursuant to the latter's "appellate" (as opposed to "original") jurisdiction, assuming that Congress has not invoked its power to prevent the Court from hearing appeals in that type of case.

Answer 16

(D) is the best response,

because it correctly suggests that denial of bar admission based on membership in a subversive group must be based upon the candidate's intent to further the group's illegal aims.

First, the Supreme Court has repeatedly held that the First Amendment freedom of association prevents the government from denying a privilege or benefit, such as bar membership, based *solely on membership* in an organization. *See, e.g., Baird v. State Bar of Arizona*, 401 U.S. 1 (1971) (Stewart, J., concurring): "[M]ere membership in an organization can never, by itself, be sufficient ground for a State's imposition of civil penalties or criminal punishment." Second, the state cannot deny a privilege or benefit based upon the applicant's refusal to *disclose* her mere membership in an organization—if a membership could not by itself be the basis for denying a privilege, the government cannot require disclosure of the membership as a condition of receiving the privilege, either. On the other hand, the government *may* withhold a benefit or privilege (such as bar membership) based on the applicant's membership in an organization that the applicant *knows* advocates the overthrow of the government by force or violence, if the applicant *shares the specific intent* to further the organization's illegal goals. *Baird*, *supra*. And the government is permitted to (1) ask questions sufficient to find out whether the applicant has such a specific intent; and (2) deny membership to an applicant who will not answer such questions about her intent. But since on the facts here, the government is asking about mere membership in a subversive group, without defining "subversive," without asking anything about the organization's possibly-illegal objectives, and without asking whether the applicant shares those objectives, the denial of membership based on refusal to answer violates the applicant's freedom of association.

(A) is not the correct response,

because it is factually incorrect, and leads to an incorrect legal conclusion.

Mere membership in a "subversive group" does not by itself demonstrate that the member shares or endorses any illegal goals that the group might have, or even demonstrate that the member is aware of those goals. Therefore, the Supreme Court has repeatedly held that, on account of the First Amendment freedom of association, mere membership in an organization can never by itself be sufficient for denial of a government benefit, and refusal to answer questions about mere membership cannot by itself be the basis for such a denial. (See the more detailed discussion in Choice D above.)

(B) is not the correct response,

because it is an incorrect statement of law.

The rule at issue in this case was adopted by a state, and governs the award of a right or benefit furnished by state law (bar membership). Therefore, the rule constitutes state action, and must be analyzed to determine whether it violates the First Amendment freedom of speech and association, made applicable to the states by the Fourteenth Amendment's Due Process Clause. For the reasons specified in the discussion of Choice D above, the rule in fact violates those First Amendment rights.

(C) is not the correct response,

because it overstates the relevant legal principles.

It's not accurate to say that the denial of bar admission may not be premised on "any association with a subversive organization." The government *may* withhold a benefit or privilege (such as bar membership) based on the applicant's membership in an organization that the applicant *knows* advocates the overthrow of the government by force or violence, if the applicant *shares the specific intent* to further the organization's illegal goals. And the government is permitted to (1) ask questions sufficient to find out whether the applicant has such a specific intent; and (2) deny membership to an applicant who will not answer such questions about her intent. (See the further discussion in Choice D above.) So this choice, by asserting that *any* association with a subversive organization is irrelevant to the bar admission scenario, overstates the breadth of the relevant legal principles.

Answer 17

(A) is the best response,

because the statute bars some protected conduct, and leaves the public uncertain about what conduct is and is not forbidden.

A statute is *overbroad* if, in addition to proscribing activities that may be constitutionally forbidden, it also sweeps within its coverage a substantial amount of speech or conduct that is protected by the guarantees of free speech. The doctrine of vagueness is similar but not identical to that of overbreadth: A statute will be void for vagueness if the conduct forbidden by it is so unclearly defined that persons of common intelligence would have to guess at its meaning and would differ as to its application.

The statute here is both overbroad and vague. It is overbroad because it covers (or appears to cover) a substantial amount of conduct protected by the First Amendment. One big problem is that the way the statute is written, if the material might be harmful to minors, it may not be sold to (or displayed to) *adults*, either. And adults have a First Amendment right to read even sexually explicit materials, if they are not "obscene." So the statute probably denies to adults massive amounts of non-obscene—and thus protected—sexually explicit materials (e.g., *Playboy* magazine), since these "may" be harmful to minors. That makes the statute overbroad.

And the statute is vague, as well, because it does not give even an approximate definition of either the term "sexually explicit nature" or the term "harmful." So a reader of the statute would be left to guess just how great the degree of sexual explicitness (are topless women covered, no pun intended?), or how great the likelihood of harm needs to be (chance that one in 1,000 minor readers would have a nightmare?).

(B) is not the best response,

because this is a corrupted version of a now-outmoded test for obscenity, and is therefore not the relevant test.

At one time, to sustain an obscenity prosecution, prosecutors had to prove that the material was utterly without "the slightest redeeming social importance," a standard somewhat similar to the one in this choice. But that's no longer the test for obscenity: Now, a "patently offensive" portrayal of "sexual conduct" that is "specifically defined" by state law may be prohibited, provided only that the work, taken as a whole, lacks "serious literary, artistic, political, or scientific value." (*Miller v. Cal.* (1973)). So the presence of the smallest "redeeming value in the marketplace of ideas" (as this choice states) wouldn't protect against a finding of obscenity.

But even if this choice had the right test for obscenity, it would miss the fact that, as the Court held in *Ginsberg v. N.Y.* (1968), states *may* prohibit the sale to *minors* of sexually explicit material that doesn't meet the definition of obscenity. The big problem with the statute is that (as described in choice A) it bars adults from seeing or buying non-obscene materials on the ground that these might harm minors, and choice B doesn't capture this difficulty at all.

(C) is not the best response,

because the distinction between written and pictorial material would not be found to be wholly irrational.

Where a statute treats two different classes of things or people in two different ways, unless a suspect category or fundamental right is involved, only a completely irrational classification will be found to violate equal protection. So here, if a plaintiff could convince the court that it is irrational to treat people who want to buy sexually explicit pictorial materials differently from those who want to buy sexually explicit materials consisting solely of words, the plaintiff might prevail with an equal protection argument.

The problem is that it is very unlikely that a court would agree that it's completely irrational to distinguish between pictures and words. It might be rational, for example, for a state to conclude that the harmful impact of sexually explicit pictures on men with a latent tendency to impose sexually sadistic violence on women is greater than the impact on the same men of works consisting solely of words. In summary, the equal protection argument is far less likely to succeed than the overbreadth and vagueness arguments used in choice A.

(D) is not the best response,

because there is a rational distinction that may be made between minors and adults.

Where a statute treats two different classes of things or people in two different ways, unless a suspect category or fundamental right is involved, only a completely irrational classification will be found to violate equal protection. So here, if a plaintiff could convince the court that it is wholly irrational to treat violent or sexually explicit pictorial materials differently depending on whether they harm minors or just adults, the claim might work.

But a plaintiff would be exceptionally unlikely to succeed in making such a showing. The Court has previously held (in *Ginsberg v. N.Y.* (1968), a First Amendment case), that the states may prohibit the sale to minors of sexually explicit material that doesn't meet the definition of obscenity, on the grounds that minors are more impressionable. So a court now would be unlikely to conclude that it's wholly irrational for materials that might harm minors in this way to be distinguished from those that would "only" harm adults. (Besides, any materials that would harm adults would be likely to harm minors as well, making the statute's distinction even less irrational.)

Answer 18

(D) is the best response,

because it recognizes an area over which Congress would clearly have authority to legislate marriages and divorces.

The central obstacle under this problem is that the states have the general power to legislate regarding marriage and divorce, because family oriented legislation is not within Congress's enumerated powers. Congress only has power to the extent of its enumerated powers under the Constitution. In order to be valid, a federal statute must be rationally related to an enumerated power, or be a necessary and proper means of effectuating such power. These are the major powers of Congress: civil rights, elections (congressional), admiralty, taxation, eminent domain, spending for general welfare, defense, interstate commerce, citizenship, and external (foreign) affairs.

What choice D does is to avoid the whole issue of congressional power vis-à-vis state power. Under Article I, §8, of the Constitution, Congress is expressly given the power to govern the District of Columbia. This, in effect, gives it "state-like" control over the District of Columbia, and this neatly avoids the obstacle in this problem—namely, that marriage and divorce is neither one of Congress's enumerated powers, nor is its legislation necessary and proper to effectuating an enumerated power. Since legislation concerning marriage and divorce would clearly be part of "governing" the District of Columbia, such congressional legislation would be valid. This is admittedly a bit of a tricky question, since you don't often come across questions concerning Congress's power over the District of Columbia. However, under these facts, this power provides the best means of regulating marriages and divorces, and since D recognizes this, it's the best response.

(A) is not the best response,

because although Congress has power over the military, legislating marriages of members of the armed forces would not be sufficiently close to the military power to merit congressional control.

Congress only has power to the extent of its enumerated powers under the Constitution. In order to be valid, a federal statute must be rationally related to an enumerated power, or be a necessary and proper means of effectuating such a power. These are the major powers of Congress: civil rights, elections (congressional), admiralty, taxation, eminent domain, spending for general welfare, defense, interstate commerce, citizenship, and external (foreign) affairs. The central focus of the legislation here—marriage and divorce—is a family law matter traditionally reserved to the states. The military power, found in Article I, § 8, of the Constitution, grants Congress the power, in general, to declare war, raise armies, maintain a navy, create rules regulating the armed forces, and otherwise organize, discipline, arm, and call forth the militia. Regulating the marriages of military personnel could only be tenuously related to this power. Thus, the military power would not be a good basis on which Congress could regulate marriage and divorce. Since A doesn't recognize this, it's not the best response.

(B) is not the best response,

because Congress's power over the jurisdiction of federal courts would not be a strong basis on which to uphold legislation concerning marriages and divorces.

Congress only has power to the extent of its enumerated powers under the Constitution. In order to be valid, a federal statute must be rationally related to an enumerated power, or be a necessary and proper means of effectuating such a power. These are the major powers of Congress: civil rights, elections (congressional), admiralty, taxation, eminent domain, spending for general welfare, defense, interstate commerce, citizenship, and external (foreign) affairs.

The central focus of the legislation here—marriage and divorce—is a family law matter traditionally reserved to the states. It's true that Congress has great control over the jurisdiction of the lower federal courts, since it was given the power to create such lower courts in Article III, § 2, of the Constitution. This theoretically would give Congress the power to regulate marriages performed by federal judges and divorces granted by federal courts. However, due to Congress's lack of enumerated power over marriage and divorce, this argument would not be tremendously strong, especially in light of the fact that there's another choice—D, which provides a clear area of congressional power. As a result, B is not the best response.

(C) is not the best response,

because it does not overcome the central obstacle here—that is, that marriage and divorce is an area traditionally controlled by the states, not the federal government.

Congress only has power to the extent of its enumerated powers under the Constitution. In order to be valid, a federal statute must be rationally related to an enumerated power, or be a necessary and proper means of effectuating such a power. These are the major powers of Congress: civil rights, elections (congressional), admiralty, taxation, eminent domain, spending for general welfare, defense, interstate commerce, citizenship, and external (foreign) affairs.

While Congress has considerable power over human rights under amendments like the Fourteenth Amendment, this wouldn't as a general matter give it the power to legislate concerning marriage and divorce. The fact that there's an executive agreement involved doesn't create for Congress power it doesn't otherwise have. Since choice C doesn't recognize this, it's not the best response.

Answer 19

(D) is the best response,

because the county's regulation resulted in a taking of the purchaser's land.

The Fifth Amendment to the Constitution prohibits the government from taking private property "without just compensation." The Supreme Court has held that a land use regulation may constitute a regulatory taking when the regulation deprives the owner of all economically viable use of his land (*Lucas v. South Carolina Coastal Council*). The purchaser in this problem bought the land with the expectation of developing it. However, the county's regulation, enacted after the purchase, barred him from doing so. The blanket prohibition on any sort of development deprived the purchaser of any means of recouping any part of his investment and was therefore a regulatory taking of the purchaser's land. As a result, the Taking Clause requires that the county pay just compensation to the purchaser.

(A) is not the best response,

because the government does not have to take possession of an individual's property in order for there to be a taking.

The Fifth Amendment's Taking Clause requires just compensation to be paid to landowners not only when they have been deprived of possession of their land because of government action, but also when a land use regulation denies the landowner of any economically viable use of the land. In this case, the county's regulation prohibited the purchaser from building anything on his land. Although the county did not appropriate the parcel, the regulation so significantly interfered with the purchaser's investment-backed expectations that it constituted a regulatory taking.

(B) is not the best response,

because physical occupation of an individual's land is sufficient to result in a taking, it is not necessary.

The Fifth Amendment's Taking Clause requires just compensation to be paid to landowners not only when they have been deprived of possession of their land because of government action, but also when a land use regulation denies the landowner of any economically viable use of the land. In this case, the county's regulation prohibited the purchaser from building anything on the purchased land. Although the county did not appropriate the parcel, the regulation so significantly interfered with the purchaser's investment-backed expectations that it constituted a regulatory taking.

(C) is not the best response,

because courts do not consider the goals of a governmental entity when determining whether a taking has occurred.

The Taking Clause of the Fifth Amendment applies when a governmental entity either interferes with an individual's right to possess his land (either by physically occupying or taking possession of the land) or enacts a land use regulation that effectively removes any economically viable use of the land. The legislative purpose of the zoning may be relevant if the regulation's constitutionality is challenged, but is irrelevant to the issue of whether compensation is due to the landowner.

Answer 20

(C) is the best response,

because none of the members of the association has been injured or will be injured, meaning the organization lacks standing.

Standing is an interest in the outcome of a controversy. An organization has standing to challenge government actions that cause an injury in fact to its members if the organization can demonstrate the following: (1) that there is an injury in fact to some members of the organization that would give these individual members a right to sue on their own behalf; (2) that the injury to the members is related to the organization's purpose; and (3) that neither the nature of the claim nor the relief requested requires participation of the individual members in the lawsuit. *Hunt v. Wash. Apple* (1977).

Here, the organization cannot satisfy (at least) requirement (1). The facts carefully specify that no member currently trades or expects to do so in the future. Consequently, no member could be prohibited by the statute from conduct they would otherwise engage in or benefit from the statute's protections. Therefore, no member has standing to bring an individual action, and thus the organization does not have standing either.

(A) is not the best response,

because the mere fact that a suit involves a "dispute over the constitutionality of a federal statute" does not dispense with the need for standing.

It's true that, as this choice suggests, a federal suit (at least one not based on diversity) must involve a federal question, that is, a question arising under the Constitution or under a federal statute. So, the fact that the constitutionality of a federal statute is at issue certainly satisfies the "must pose a federal question" requirement. But there is an additional requirement that the plaintiffs have standing, and for the reasons discussed in choice C above, that requirement is not satisfied.

(B) is not the best response,

because the fact that the suit seeks "relief of a conclusive nature" is irrelevant.

Where plaintiffs lack standing, the fact that they are seeking "relief of a conclusive nature" does not nullify the non-justiciability of their claim. This organization lacks standing for the reasons discussed in choice C above. If choice B were correct, it would follow that any person or organization, no matter how little their practical stake in the outcome, could sue for an injunction against any statute's enforcement. This would make a mockery of the constitutional requirement that each federal suit involve a "case or controversy."

(D) is not the best response,

because a suit for an injunction preventing enforcement of the statute *could* be brought.

It's true that if the court were convinced that enforcement of the statute was extremely unlikely to occur in the reasonable future, the court might exercise its discretion to conclude that the suit shouldn't be heard because it wasn't ripe. But this choice says far more than that—it asserts that the mere fact that there has not yet been a "bona fide effort" to enforce the statute means an injunction suit can't be brought. And that's clearly not true. *See, e.g., Epperson v. Arkansas* (1968) (involving a ban on teaching evolution, which ban had never been enforced during its entire 40 years on the books).

Answer 21

(D) is the best response,

because the purpose of the tax is to raise revenue.

Article I, § 8, cl. 1, of the Constitution gives Congress the power to "lay and collect Taxes . . . and Excises, to pay the Debts and provide for the Common Defence and general Welfare of the United States." So Congress can tax for the purpose of "provid[ing] for the . . . general Welfare." That's what it is doing here. Because the power is plenary (i.e., complete) a tax measure will be upheld so long as it bears some reasonable relationship to revenue production and does not violate any specific constitutional provision.

Here, the purpose of the tax is to raise revenue, so the requirement of "reasonable relationship to revenue production" (expressed in the choice as not having any "provisions extraneous to tax needs or purposes") is satisfied. There is no provision in the Constitution that this tax would violate. Therefore, it's valid.

(A) is not the best response,

because the tax is uniform in its application.

It's true that Article 1, § 8, cl. 1, which grants the power to tax, also requires that "all Duties, Imposts and Excises shall be uniform throughout the United States." However, this requirement merely means that any excise tax (and this is one, since it's imposed on the sale or production of a particular product) may not discriminate among states—it does not matter that only some individuals (and only residents of one state) pay the tax because they are the ones who produce or sell the product.

The tax on the mineral here meets the requirement of uniformity, because it applies the same way on each ton of the mineral mined in the country—so while it is currently mined only in one state, if it is ever mined in another state the tax will also apply there.

(B) is not the best response,

because it misstates the operation of the "Commerce Clause."

If the phrase "Commerce Clause" is intended to mean "commerce power," the fact that Congress has the power to regulate interstate commerce doesn't impose on Congress any affirmative *obligation* to do any regulating of any sort, so Congress is free to take an action that would inhibit (rather than foster) a particular "interstate industry." If the phrase "Commerce Clause" is intended to mean the "dormant Commerce Clause," this is a limitation on what the states may do, not an affirmative requirement on Congress. So there is no plausible meaning for the phrase "Commerce Clause" that would impose on Congress an obligation to "protect . . . such interstate industries."

(C) is not the best response,

because the issue is the power to tax, not navigable waterways.

Congress has no special authority over the "navigable waters" of the United States. (The federal judicial power extends to "all Cases of admiralty and maritime Jurisdiction," but this doesn't add anything to Congress's powers.) While it's true that Congress's commerce power would probably give it authority to regulate navigable waters because they affect commerce, this power is far more tangential to the problem here than is Congress's power to tax for the general welfare. So choice C reaches the correct conclusion, but for the wrong reason.

Answer 22

(B) is the best response,

because it correctly recognizes that the Equal Protection Clause of the Fourteenth Amendment applies to the federal government through the Due Process Clause of the Fifth Amendment.

The Equal Protection Clause, operating on the federal government through the Due Process Clause of the Fifth Amendment, provides a strong basis for challenging the statute because the statute draws distinctions on racial lines. In order to determine whether a statute is valid under equal protection, you have to determine the basis of the classification, and then apply the appropriate level of scrutiny (strict, intermediate, or rational basis) to the statute. When a statute classifies individuals based on their race, which is a "suspect classification," a court will review the statute using strict scrutiny. This means that in order for the statute to be valid, the classification must be necessary to promote a compelling governmental interest. Because this test is so difficult to pass, the application of strict scrutiny will generally result in a statute being ruled invalid. Since choice B recognizes this, it is the best response.

Note that the application of strict scrutiny does not *guarantee* that a statute will be held invalid. Rather, it puts a very heavy burden on the government that makes the argument in favor of upholding the statute unlikely to succeed. Remember, the examiners asked for the best "of the following" bases for challenging the statute. This does not necessarily mean that the best answer will support a successful challenge.

(A) is not the best response,

because, although the Commerce Clause may provide Congress with the power to pass such a statute, it does not limit the power of Congress to classify individuals based on their race.

The Commerce Clause gives Congress the right to regulate interstate commerce. This is interpreted extremely broadly. Since commercial airliners move people across state and national borders, they are within Congress's power to regulate since interstate and international travel are forms of commerce. However, choice A provides a basis for supporting the validity of the statute, not challenging it.

(C) is not the best response,

because the statute was passed by Congress, not a state.

The Privileges and Immunities Clause of Article IV prohibits states from acting in ways that discriminate against the citizens of other states. Since the statue in this question was neither passed by a state nor was aimed at privileging state citizens over non-state citizens, the Privileges and Immunities Clause has not been violated.

(D) is not the best response,

because the statute was passed by Congress, not a state.

Although the Privileges or Immunities Clause of the Fourteenth Amendment does protect the right to travel as one of the fundamental rights of U.S. citizenship, it only applies to actions by one state that deprive non-state citizens of their rights as citizens. Even if one can make the argument that this statute impinges on some citizens' right to travel, a statute passed *by Congress* cannot be successfully challenged on this basis, since the Supreme Court has never applied the Privileges or Immunities Clause to actions of the federal government.

Answer 23

(D) is the best response,

because it correctly identifies the basis of the federal court's jurisdiction.

What this question impliedly addresses is whether the federal court can hear the case. The jurisdiction of the federal courts is addressed in Article III, § 2, of the Constitution. Among other cases, federal courts may hear cases between citizens of different states ("diversity" jurisdiction), cases arising under the Constitution or a federal law or treaty ("federal question" jurisdiction), and those where the United States is a party.

Choice D suggests that there's federal question jurisdiction under these facts. If you look at the farmer's claim, you can deduce that it will address an equal protection violation, since the statute under which the farmer has been injured creates a suspect classification: It forbids aliens from owning more than 100 acres of land, and alienage is a suspect classification. Equal protection is protected by the federal Constitution, so the farmer's claim would "arise" under the Constitution, giving the federal court federal question jurisdiction over the case. Since choice D recognizes this, it's the best response.

(A) is not the best response,

because it misstates federal court jurisdiction.

Article III, § 2, of the Constitution gives the Supreme Court original jurisdiction over cases where a state is a party, as here. Congress has the power to create lower federal courts, and give them jurisdiction concurrent with the Supreme Court. In fact, Congress specifically authorized federal courts to hear cases brought by aliens against states. As a result, A is incorrect in stating that aliens may not sue in federal court, making it not the best response.

(B) is not the best response,

because while the state typically has power over in-state land, this power is not unlimited.

In order to be valid, a state law—like the one here must meet three requirements:

1. It must be enacted within the state's powers (e.g., police powers);
2. It must not violate any person's constitutional rights; and
3. It must not improperly burden interstate commerce.

While regulating in-state land is one of the state's powers, this regulation must still meet the other two requirements. Here, the statute is an impermissible regulation principally because it violates the Equal Protection Clause, by setting up a classification based on alienage. Since choice B incorrectly states that the state's right to regulate in-state land is unlimited, it's not the best response.

(C) is not the best response,

because violation of the U.N. charter, by itself, would not give the federal court power to hear the lawsuit.

The jurisdiction of the federal courts is determined in Article III, § 2, of the Constitution, and as provided by Congress (which can regulate the appellate jurisdiction of federal courts). One source of federal court jurisdiction is "federal question" jurisdiction, which gives federal courts the power to hear cases arising under the Constitution or a federal law or treaty. If you chose this response, you may have thought of the U.N. charter as a treaty; in fact, it's not, and there's nothing under these facts to suggest that it's been adopted as a treaty. On the other hand, you may have been taking a wild stab in the dark in choosing this response, which is unavoidable once in awhile. In any case, there is a federal question presented by these facts, which is what gives the court jurisdiction to hear the case. The farmer would most likely be arguing that the state statute violated the federal Constitution, by violating the Equal Protection Clause. Since choice C doesn't recognize this, it's not the best response.

Answer 24

(B) is the best response,

because it impliedly recognizes that the statute is a reasonable restriction on the free exercise of religion.

The "free exercise" part of the First Amendment's Religion Clause guarantees the right to free exercise of religion. However, as with the First Amendment rights of speech, assembly, and association, this right is not absolute. Instead, reasonable regulation is permissible. And, in fact, if government enacts a "neutral law of general applicability" that forbids a certain type of conduct, the free exercise clause "does not relieve an individual of the obligation to comply" with that neutral law. *Employment Div. v. Smith*, 494 U.S. 872 (1990).

Here, the statute which the priest was convicted of violating is a "neutral" and "generally applicable" law prohibiting cruelty to animals—in other words, it does not forbid particular conduct if done as part of a religious observance while allowing the conduct if not religiously-motivated. (If the law made that distinction, it would not be a "generally applicable" law, and the rationale of *Employment Div. v. Smith* wouldn't apply, so the law would violate the free exercise right.) Therefore, the fact that the priest was motivated to perform the act by a sincere religious belief *would* not furnish a defense.

(A) is not the best response,

because a belief in Satan *could* enjoy constitutional protection, and A makes the blanket statement that it cannot.

The "free exercise" part of the First Amendment's Religion Clause guarantees the right to free exercise of religion. In order to gain protection a religious belief must be held in good faith, and it must parallel an orthodox religious belief; it cannot be merely a political or philosophical view. *United States v. Seeger* (1965). Thus, a belief in Satan could constitute a religious belief. If the priest, in fact, had a religious belief in Satan, and the statute here violated the priest's right to the free exercise of religion (e.g., by forbidding *any* worship of Satan), his conviction would be overturned. Since A doesn't recognize this, it's not the best response.

(C) is not the best response,

because applying this statute to the priest would not violate his right to freedom of religion.

The "free exercise" part of the First Amendment's Religion Clause guarantees the right to free exercise of religion. However, as is further explained in the discussion of Choice (B), the free exercise clause does not relieve a person of the obligation to obey a valid, neutral, and "generally applicable" prohibition of particular conduct. Since the prohibition on animal cruelty constitutes such a neutral and generally applicable prohibition, the priest's conviction does not violate his freedom of religion.

Incidentally, note that while the conduct of religion can be regulated, the beliefs themselves cannot. The right to *hold* religious beliefs is considered absolute. But since the priest is not being punished for believing in Satan, his conviction does not violate this principle.

(D) is not the best response,

because it does not apply the correct test to these facts.

The statute here impacts the priest's exercise of his religious beliefs. Thus, the "free exercise" part of the First Amendment's Religion Clause, guaranteeing the right to free exercise of religion, is called into question. This right, as with the First Amendment rights of speech, assembly, and association, is not absolute.

However, as is further explained in the discussion of Choice (B), the free exercise clause does not relieve a person of the obligation to obey a valid, neutral, and "generally applicable" prohibition of particular conduct. Since the prohibition on animal cruelty constitutes such a neutral and generally applicable prohibition, the priest's conviction does not violate his freedom of religion. *Employment Div. v. Smith*, 494 U.S. 872 (1990). So even if the court believed that the cult members' belief in the need for pain-inducing animal cruelty was "reasonable" (not a likely conclusion by the court), under *Employment Div. v. Smith* the priest would not be relieved of the obligation to obey the anti-animal-cruelty statute.

Answer 25

(A) is the best response,

because peremptory challenges based on gender violate equal protection.

Gender-based classifications are subject to intermediate scrutiny, which requires the government to show that the classification be substantially related to an important government objective. The use of peremptory challenges to exclude all women from a jury cannot survive mid-level review because it fails to further the state's legitimate interest in achieving a fair trial, while reinforcing stereotypical assumptions about women. *J.E.B. v. Alabama* (1994).

This rationale should apply to invalidate the state's action here, even though a non-jury adjudication method has been used. The state's attorney used all of her peremptory challenges to eliminate women from the arbitrator's panel because she believed that they would necessarily be biased in favor of another woman claiming sexual harassment. Her reasoning reinforced the stereotypical assumption about women. By removing only women from the panel she did not substantially further the state's legitimate interest in ensuring the employee grievance system provides a fair trial for employers and employees; therefore her actions were unconstitutional.

(B) is not the best response,

because a participant in an arbitration does not have a constitutional right to have the arbitration panel made up of the participant's peers; that is a right limited to formal jury trials.

(C) is not the best response,

because gender-based classifications are examined under intermediate scrutiny, not strict scrutiny, and the state's action could not survive strict scrutiny.

Gender-based classifications are subject to intermediate scrutiny, which requires the government to show that the classification is substantially related to an important government objective. As described in the analysis of choice A, the state's strike-all-female-arbitrators action here does not satisfy this intermediate-level standard.

Choice C is wrong for two reasons. First, it applies the wrong standard, strict scrutiny instead of the proper intermediate-level scrutiny. Second, the state's action cannot even survive the intermediate-level scrutiny (see the analysis of choice C for why), so it certainly couldn't survive strict scrutiny, as choice C says it could.

(D) is not the best response,

because gender-based classifications are examined under intermediate scrutiny, not rational-basis review.

Gender-based classifications are subject to intermediate scrutiny, which requires the government to show that the classification be substantially related to an important government objective. Thus rational-basis review (under which the action will be upheld if the means chosen are "rationally related" to the achievement of a "legitimate" state interest) is not the right standard. (It probably is true that if rational-basis review were the correct standard, the state would survive that review here, though this is not absolutely certain.)

Answer 26

(D) is the best response,

because the tax discriminates against out-of-state manufacturers.

Congress's power over interstate commerce is nonexclusive. If Congress has not enacted laws regarding the subject, a state or local government may regulate aspects of interstate commerce if (and only if) the regulation: (1) does not discriminate against out-of-state competition to benefit local economic interests; and (2) does not unduly burden interstate commerce. This limit on the powers of state or local governments to regulate or affect interstate commerce is sometimes called the "dormant Commerce Clause."

By reducing the amount of taxes paid by assemblers of computers in an amount equal to the portion of computer components manufactured in the state, the city is discriminating against out-of-state competition to benefit local economic interests. This discrimination causes the tax measure to violate test (1) above. Consequently, the ordinance violates the dormant Commerce Clause principle.

(A) is not the best response,

because the ordinance has the effect of making parts manufactured outside of the state more expensive.

It is true that the tax falls only on companies resident in the city. But the *effect* of the tax is to make components manufactured in the state less expensive than those manufactured outside of the state. Consequently, companies are induced to favor in-state component-makers over out-of-state ones. This intentional discrimination against out-of-staters violates the no-discrimination-against-out-of-staters component of dormant Commerce Clause principles (described more fully in the discussion of choice D above).

(B) is not the best response,

because the dormant Commerce Clause places limits on a state's right to foster resident corporations.

Although a state may sometimes foster local businesses by encouraging its residents to "buy local," some methods of encouragement violate the dormant Commerce Clause. Where a state uses its tax system to confer a direct financial benefit to those who buy locally manufactured goods, at the expense of out-of-state makers of goods, the state crosses the line into forbidden "economic protectionism," and violates the dormant Commerce Clause. That's what the tax here does.

(C) is not the best response,

because taxes based on gross receipts are not a per se violation of dormant Commerce Clause principles.

Some tax schemes violate the dormant Commerce Clause because they either discriminate against, or unduly burden, interstate commerce. But the mere fact that a tax is "measured in whole or in part by [the taxpayer's] gross receipts" does not automatically mean that either forbidden discrimination or an undue burden on commerce is present.

It's true that if a state enacted a tax on a multi-state taxpayer's gross receipts, and made no distinction between receipts from in-state activities and those from out-of-state activities, that tax might well be found to be an undue burden on commerce, and thus a violation of the dormant Commerce Clause. But choice C goes way beyond this principle and doesn't tie in to the problem with the tax here (which is that it intentionally discriminates against out-of-state component makers).

Answer 27

(D) is the best response,

because the case is not ripe for adjudication.

In order for a case to be heard in federal court, it must meet a series of justiciability requirements. In particular, to be heard the plaintiff must have standing and the case must (1) not call for an advisory opinion, (2) be ripe for adjudication, (3) not be moot, and (4) not call for the courts to decide a non-justiciable "political question." The court in this problem should refuse to hear the case because the controversy is not yet ripe for decision. A case is considered not yet ripe when the controversy is not yet sufficiently concrete as to allow effective adjudication. In particular, when a plaintiff sues for some anticipated harm, that harm must be reasonably likely and specific. When it is unclear whether or not harm will ever come to the plaintiff, the case is not ripe.

In this problem, the brewery is not facing imminent harm resulting from a regulation because the regulation has not yet been enacted. Since, at this point in time, we cannot be reasonably certain about what standards the agency will adopt, we do not know if the anticipated harm will ever come to the brewery. It is possible that the agency will adopt standards that allow the brewery to continue to sell unpasteurized beer. Accordingly, the case is not yet ripe for adjudication, and the court should refuse to hear the case.

(A) is not the best response,

because the federal district court should refuse to hear the case.

As discussed in the analysis of choice D above, a federal court will refuse to hear cases that are non-justiciable because they call for advisory opinions, are not yet ripe, are moot, or involve "political questions." The brewery's claim is not ripe because there is no presently existing risk of harm. The claim will only become ripe if the agency actually adopts a standard that, if enforced, would harm the brewery's economic interests. At this point, we can only speculate as to what standards will be adopted and so the possibility of harm to the brewery is too remote.

(B) is not the best response,

because the federal district court should refuse to hear the case.

As discussed in the analysis of choice D above, a federal court will refuse to hear cases that are non-justiciable because they call for advisory opinions, are not yet ripe, are moot, or involve "political questions." The brewery's claim is not ripe because there is no presently existing risk of harm. The claim will only become ripe if the agency actually adopts a standard that, if enforced, would harm the brewery's economic interests. At this point, we can only speculate as to what standards will be adopted and so the possibility of harm to the brewery is too remote.

(C) is not the best response,

because the federal district court will dismiss a suit when the controversy is not yet ripe for adjudication.

This choice correctly states that the federal court should refuse to hear the case since, as discussed in the analysis of choice D above, the dispute is not yet ripe. However, the proper response to an unripe suit is dismissal, not staying the action. Federal courts will dismiss any suit that fails to meet the five justiciability requirements (standing, case or controversy, ripeness, mootness, and "political questions"). If the agency subsequently adopts a regulation that prohibits the sale of unpasteurized beer, the brewery will then have a ripe claim, and may file a new action to enjoin enforcement of the standard.

Answer 28

(A) is the best response,

because it recognizes the central reason the provision for construction of buildings to be used for secular purposes, at religious colleges and universities, is constitutional.

Under the First Amendment, the government must be "religion neutral"; that is, it can't respect an establishment of religion, and it can't prohibit the free exercise of religion. Here, you have Congress subsidizing construction of buildings at private, and potentially religious, colleges and universities. Thus, there's a potential Establishment Clause problem. In such situations, the test used to determine if the enactment is constitutional is from *Lemon v. Kurtzman* (1971):

1. The statute must have a secular purpose;
2. It must have as its principal or primary effect neither the advancement nor inhibition of religion; and
3. It must not foster excessive government entanglement with religion.

Choice A implicitly recognizes that this test is met. The central issue here is the third element, "excessive entanglement," because it is purely judgmental—the only real way to know if a particular provision constitutes excessive entanglement is to see if the Supreme Court has already addressed the issue. And, by gum, with this one, it has. The issue of government grants for construction of buildings to be used exclusively for secular education, at religious colleges and universities, was addressed in *Tilton v. Richardson* (1971). The grants were upheld, on the basis that, as long as the schools involved were not "permeated with religion," the grants didn't involve excessive entanglement with religion. Choice A correctly addresses this.

(B) is not the best response,

because it does not identify the central reason the building grant will be constitutional.

Under the First Amendment, the government must be "religion neutral"; that is, it can't respect an establishment of religion, and it can't prohibit the free exercise of religion. Here, you have Congress subsidizing construction of buildings at private, and potentially religious, colleges and universities. Thus, there's a potential Establishment Clause problem. In such situations, the test used to determine if the enactment is constitutional is from *Lemon v. Kurtzman* (1971):

1. The statute must have a secular purpose;
2. It must have as its principal or primary effect neither the advancement nor inhibition of religion; and
3. It must not foster excessive government entanglement with religion.

Here, choice B states that the bricks and mortar themselves do not foster religion. However, say the facts were different, and the bricks and mortar were to be used to build a chapel. This would clearly violate the Establishment Clause, although the reasoning in B would still make the grant valid.

Instead, the reason the grants here will be valid is that they are to be used for secular education only and, thus, don't respect an establishment of religion or involve excessive government entanglement with religion. While the "excessive entanglement" issue involves line-drawing, the Supreme Court addressed this specific issue in *Tilton v. Richardson* (1971), and decided such grants were valid. Since B does not recognize the specific reason the grants will be valid, it's not the best response.

(C) is not the best response,

because it fails to recognize that aid for secular purposes can be constitutional even if the recipient is a private, religious school.

Under the First Amendment, the government must be "religion neutral"; that is, it can't respect an establishment of religion, and it can't prohibit the free exercise of religion. Here, you have Congress subsidizing construction of buildings at private, and potentially religious, colleges and universities. Thus, there's a potential Establishment Clause problem. In such situations, the test used to determine if the enactment is constitutional is from *Lemon v. Kurtzman* (1971):

1. The statute must have a secular purpose;
2. It must have as its principal or primary effect neither the advancement nor inhibition of religion; and
3. It must not foster excessive government entanglement with religion.

The key point here is that financial aid to church-operated schools can be valid if it meets this test, because it's possible to aid the secular goals of schools without violating the *Lemon v. Kurtzman* test. While this would, tangentially perhaps, strengthen the religious purposes of the school, this would be sufficiently outweighed by the government's interest in the general welfare of students to allow limited financial aid to religious schools.

There is a caveat to this, in the sense that almost no direct aid to primary and secondary religious schools would be permissible, since such aid is considered "excessive entanglement" (in that religious indoctrination of younger students is more of a problem than with older, university-age students). In any case, since C would prohibit any financial help to religious schools, when in fact there are limited circumstances (including those here) where such aid would be permissible, C cannot be the best response.

(D) is not the best response,

because the aid here would not be considered "excessive entanglement," and the grants would, in fact, be considered constitutional.

Under the First Amendment, the government must be "religion-neutral"; that is, it can't respect an establishment of religion, and it can't prohibit the free exercise of religion. Here, you have Congress subsidizing construction of buildings at private, and potentially religious, colleges and universities. Thus, there's a potential Establishment Clause problem. In such situations, the test used to determine if the enactment is constitutional is from *Lemon v. Kurtzman* (1971):

1. The statute must have a secular purpose;
2. It must have as its principal or primary effect neither the advancement nor inhibition of religion; and
3. It must not foster excessive government entanglement with religion.

It's the third element that choice D calls into question. In fact, if you chose this response, this is a perfectly understandable mistake to make, because the "excessive entanglement" issue is purely judgmental—the only real way to know if a particular provision constitutes excessive entanglement is to see if the Supreme Court has already addressed the issue. And, with this one, it has. The issue of government grants for construction of buildings to be used exclusively for secular education, at religious colleges and universities, was addressed in *Tilton v. Richardson* (1971). The grants were upheld, on the basis that, as long as the schools involved were not "permeated with religion," the grants didn't involve excessive entanglement with religion. Since D states otherwise, it's not the best response.

Answer 29

(B) is the best response,

because based on the facts, a reasonable observer would likely believe the state government was endorsing the nativity scene as a religious symbol.

The constitutionality of the display of a religious symbol such as a nativity scene will be a question of fact. The most important single factor seems to be the context in which the religious symbol is displayed: If the religious symbol is presented by itself in what is clearly a space reserved by the government for its own property and its own messages, the Court is likely to conclude that a reasonable observer would believe that the government was endorsing the religious message. Conversely, the presence of other non-religious symbols nearby, or the existence of a sign indicating that the display was furnished by private parties, may well be enough to lead a reasonable observer to the conclusion that the government was not endorsing religion. *See Allegheny County v. ACLU* (1989) (nativity scene displayed in a courthouse violated the Establishment Clause, in part because the absence of any nearby non-religious symbols as part of the display would lead a reasonable observer to conclude that the city was endorsing a religious observance, not merely celebrating the secular holiday season).

On this standard, the proposed display of the nativity scene would be unconstitutional. The nativity scene would not be surrounded by non-religious symbols having to do with the holiday season, a fact that would rebut the implication that the nativity scene was just part of a secular celebration of the holiday season.

The whole presentation (and the fact that the governor and legislature supported it) would create in a reasonable observer the impression that the government was endorsing a religious message.

(A) is not the best response,

because the ownership of the display would not be dispositive on the issue of whether the government seemed to be endorsing religion.

If the scene here seemed to be a celebration of Christmas as a primarily secular holiday, the fact that the government owned the display would not be fatal.

But (for the reasons discussed in choice B above), the context of the display here would suggest to a reasonable observer that the state was endorsing religion. Consequently, the display violates the Establishment Clause. Thus choice A reaches the correct result, but for the wrong reason.

(C) is not the best response,

because donation would be only one element considered in the total context of the display.

If the display made it clear to the public that private citizens had donated the components, this would indeed be one factor (but just one) tending to demonstrate that the display was not a forbidden government endorsement of religion. But there's no indication that the fact of private donations would be disclosed to the public. Furthermore, this fact, even if disclosed, probably wouldn't be enough to overcome the otherwise-powerful impression that the government is endorsing a religious message.

(D) is not the best response,

because displaying the scene next to the products would not rebut the impression that the state was endorsing the nativity scene's religious message.

When a religious symbol such as a nativity scene is displayed in a public place, the issue is whether a reasonable observer would believe that the government is endorsing a religious method. Context is all-important. If the nativity scene were displayed next to other objects that pertain to December as a primarily secular holiday (e.g., a Santa Claus figure), the impression of an endorsement of religion would be rebutted. But putting the scene next to the year-round display of in-state-manufactured products would not rebut the impression of an endorsement of religion, because an observer would realize that the two displays were separate, and that the nativity scene was its own stand-alone display on an explicitly religious topic.

Answer 30

(D) is the best response,

because there is no evidence of the city's involvement with the private organization beyond the renting of the auditorium.

The Fourteenth Amendment provides that no state shall make or enforce any law that shall deny to any person within its jurisdiction the equal protection of the laws. This Amendment, and thus the Equal Protection Clause contained in it, applies *only to government action*, not to action by private citizens. This is known as the requirement of "state action," and whenever you have an equal protection or due process question, you should check to see that it's satisfied.

There are several ways in which the state can become so involved with private citizens' discriminatory actions that the discrimination will be attributable to the state for state-action purposes. For instance, perhaps the state has become so involved with the private action that the two become symbiotic, which is to say there is a mutually beneficial relation between the state and the private discriminator (e.g., the state gets revenue from leasing space in a public parking garage to a discriminatory restaurant; *Burton v. Wilmington Parking Auth.* (1961)). Or, perhaps the state has somehow encouraged the private discrimination.

But here, the state involvement with the private action is so limited, and so independent of the discrimination, that no state action will be found. The state will rent to anyone, and charges the same hourly rate to everyone, so the fact that the state is renting to the all-male organization here does not constitute any kind of endorsement or encouragement by the state of (or unusual benefit to the state from) the discrimination. Consequently, there is no state action, and the organization's conduct will not be subject to the Fourteenth Amendment.

(A) is not the best response,

because inviting members of the general public does not make a private organization a state actor.

It's probable that if this organization were a public organization (e.g., organized by and run by a city), the all-male-officers rule would violate the Fourteenth Amendment. But as described in choice D above, there is no state action here. Therefore, choice A cannot be correct in suggesting that the Fourteenth Amendment applies. And that's true even though this private organization has invited members of the public to some of its activities.

(B) is not the best response,

because renting the auditorium does not make the private organization a state actor.

As is described in choice D above, the mere occasional first-come-first-served rental of a city auditorium to a discriminatory private group is not enough to transform the private group's conduct into the requisite state action. If the city encouraged, or substantially benefitted from, the discrimination in some way, that might be enough to constitute state action. But the rental here—which is on the same basis as it would be for any other group, discriminatory or not—does not come close to being state action.

(C) is not the best response,

because the absence of state action prevents the court from even getting to the Fourteenth Amendment issue.

First of all, this choice is wrong because although there is a constitutionally protected interest in freedom of association, it's conferred by the First Amendment (as a variant of the freedom of expression), not by the Fourteenth Amendment. Second, whatever freedom-of-association claim the organization might have would not be strong enough to prohibit interference "in any way" with the organization's use of city facilities. (The organization's freedom-of-association rights might be strong enough to interfere with some efforts by the city to reduce discrimination. *See, e.g., Boy Scouts of America v. Dale* (2002), holding that because opposition to homosexuality is part of the Scouts' "expressive message," the Scouts' freedom of association was violated by a state anti-discrimination law that barred the group from excluding gay members.)

But the biggest reason why this choice is wrong is that due to the lack of "state action" here (see choice D above), the court would never even get to the point of analyzing whether the freedom of association issue blocked the application of the Fourteenth Amendment.

Answer 31

(B) is the best response,

because lessening congestion by allowing only county-based cabs to do business is an undue burden on interstate commerce.

Under the dormant commerce clause, a state regulation that substantially affects interstate commerce must meet each of the following requirements to be upheld:

(1) The regulation must pursue a legitimate end;
(2) The regulation must be rationally related to that legitimate end; and
(3) The regulatory burden imposed by the state on interstate commerce, and any discrimination against interstate commerce, must be outweighed by the state's interest in enforcing the regulation.

Protection of a state's economic interests is generally not considered to be a legitimate state objective, where the pursuit of that objective materially affects interstate commerce.

The stated purpose of the regulation, reducing traffic congestion in the county, is a general welfare and safety concern that would be provisionally considered by the Court to be a legitimate state end, pending the rest of the analysis. The ordinance is also rationally related to that legitimate state end. The ordinance fails, however, in that its effect imposes an *undue burden* on interstate travel. The practical effect of this ordinance is to preclude taxicab drivers from the neighboring state from doing business in the county or in the state in which the county is located—they can neither pick up passengers nor drop off passengers in the county, even passengers who originated in the neighboring state. So the ordinance functionally eliminates from the competition for business anyone not from the county. Reduction of some degree of traffic congestion would not be enough of a benefit to justify this sort of protectionism against out-of-staters. (And the fact that the governmental body is a county rather than state, or the fact that in-staters from outside the county are also discriminated against, makes no difference.)

(A) is not the best response,

because there is no requirement that the means used be the best way of achieving the ends.

Under the dormant Commerce Clause, a state regulation which affects interstate commerce must meet each of the following requirements to be upheld: (1) the regulation must pursue a legitimate end; (2) the regulation must be rationally related to that legitimate end; and (3) the regulatory burden imposed by the state on interstate commerce, and any discrimination against interstate commerce, must be outweighed by the state's interest in enforcing the regulation.

The fact that the means used is not the "best" means of solving the problem—i.e., is not the means having the tightest possible fit with the governmental objection—is irrelevant under this test. (Factor (2) above requires just a "rational relation" between means and end, a very easy-to-satisfy test.) So the fact that the county has tried to solve its congestion problem "one step at a time" (by eliminating some sources of congestion but not the biggest source) is also irrelevant—as long as the county has eased the problem somewhat, that's all that is required as to the means-end fit.

(C) is not the best response,

because unlawful discrimination against interstate commerce is not rebutted by showing that in-staters from a different part of the state are also being discriminated against.

Under the dormant Commerce Clause, as long as the business efforts of out-of-staters are being discriminated against or unduly burdened, the fact that in-staters from other parts of the state (in this case, those living in the state containing the county but not in the county itself) are also being discriminated against is irrelevant.

(D) is not the best response,

because the answer applies a due process analysis to a dormant Commerce Clause issue.

Suspect classes are part of a due process analysis. The issue here is whether the restriction violates the dormant Commerce Clause. The appropriate analysis under the dormant Commerce Clause is the balance between the burden on interstate commerce imposed by the state, and the state's interest in enforcing the regulation. Suspect classes have nothing to do with that analysis.

Answer 32

(D) is the best response,

because the ordinance removes only one box in ten from the streets.

Commercial speech, if it is not misleading or concerning unlawful activity, is covered by the First Amendment and may be regulated only if the state shows that the regulation (1) directly advances, (2) a substantial governmental interest, (3) in a way that is reasonably tailored to achieve that objective. *Central Hudson Gas v. Public Serv. Comm.*, 447 U.S. 557 (1980)

While the ordinance here directly advances the city's governmental interest in preventing the adverse effects of publication-caused litter on public sidewalks and streets, the ordinance fails the last part of the Court's test. The facts state that the city's ordinance removed just 30 of the existing 300 sidewalk machines that were dispensing publications. And there's no indication that publications containing solely advertising will result in more litter per-publication than those that have some non-advertising content. An ordinance that removes only one box in ten, and with no indication why that one poses more of a litter problem, is not reasonably tailored to achieving the city's legitimate interest of combatting litter.

(A) is not the best response,

because this choice states the wrong test.

As is described in the discussion of choice D above, the Court applies what is essentially mid-level review to regulations of commercial speech. Since choice A says that the review is the easy-to-satisfy rational-relation standard, it's wrong.

(B) is not the best response,

because the answer is based on a test that is inapplicable to the facts.

This choice propounds the strict-scrutiny standard used for content-based restrictions. What's at issue here, however, is a time-place-and-manner regulation aimed at the secondary effects (litter) of a certain method of disseminating written material. The appropriate standard is the intermediate-level review described in the discussion of choice D. Furthermore, if strict-scrutiny *were* the correct standard, the ordinance here would clearly not satisfy the standard, since it's attacking only one-tenth of the problem (by removing only one-tenth of the boxes), meaning that the means chosen are not a very good method of achieving the objective.

(C) is not the best response,

because the applicable test is reasonable fit, not least restrictive means.

Commercial speech, if it is not misleading or concerning unlawful activity, is covered by the First Amendment and may be regulated only if the state shows that the regulation (1) directly advances, (2) a substantial governmental interest, (3) in a way that is reasonably tailored to achieve that objective.

The Court has indicated that showing (3) does not require that there *not* be any less-restrictive alternative, merely that there be a fairly close relationship between means and end. In fact, the scheme here doesn't even meet this reasonably tailored test, but choice C is wrong because it states an incorrectly strict test for the means-end fit.

Answer 33

(A) is the best response,

because the defendant's barber license was "property," which the state could not take away from him without due process.

Where a state-issued license is required to pursue a business or profession, a person who has already obtained the license has a "property" interest in that license for Fourteenth Amendment due process purposes. Consequently, that property may not be taken away without due process of law.

Precisely what procedural safeguards the barber is entitled to is not certain, but the more serious the threatened loss of property or liberty, the wider the array of procedural safeguards required. *Mathews v. Eldridge,* 425 U.S. 319 (1976). Here, the threatened loss (the right to practice one's profession) is serious, so extensive safeguards ought to be given. Since the proceeding is analogous to a criminal trial—the Board is determining whether the barber used his premises to commit a crime—he has a strong claim of entitlement to the sorts of procedures used in criminal trials, including the right to cross-examine his accusers. There's no guarantee that he would win with this due process argument, but it's clearly the most likely to succeed of the four choices.

(B) is not the best response,

because the U.S. attorney dropped the case before a judgment was entered.

Article IV, § 1, states that full faith and credit shall be given by each state to public acts and judicial proceedings of every other state. By extension of this principle, the states must give full faith and credit to federal proceedings as well.

However, the decision by the local U.S. attorney not to prosecute the barber was not a judicial decision deserving full faith and credit, because it was not the final outcome of a judicial proceeding. (The case was dropped, not decided, and so there would be nothing to give full faith and credit to.) Consequently, choice B is not correct.

(C) is not the best response,

because Article III has nothing to do with state proceedings, and, anyway, this is not the sort of "penalty" that must be conferred by a court rather than an agency.

Article III prescribes the judicial power of the United States, i.e., the limits of the power of the *federal* judiciary. It says nothing about how the states must exercise their judicial power. Since this is a state proceeding, Article III is irrelevant.

Furthermore, even if this were a federal license-revocation proceeding, nothing in Article III specifies that the license could only be revoked by an Article III court rather than an administrative agency. If this were a truly "penal" proceeding (e.g., a proceeding to institute a criminal conviction or a fine intended to punish), it would have to be in an Article III court (i.e., before a judge with a lifetime term). But this is a non-penal administrative proceeding, so it need not be before an Article III court.

(D) is not the best response,

because federal drug laws are not so extensive as to force aside state laws.

Under the Supremacy Clause of Article IV, § 2, even absent explicit language, Congress's intent to supersede state law altogether may be found from a scheme of federal regulation so pervasive as to make reasonable the inference that Congress left no room to supplement it.

However, there's nothing in the facts here to suggest that when Congress made it a federal crime to sell cocaine, it intended to preempt the states from also criminalizing cocaine sales. (Indeed, as to virtually all federal drug crimes, the states have concurrent jurisdiction to criminalize the same conduct.) So the state would even be free to prosecute the barber for the state crime of cocaine selling. Beyond that, the state proceeding here is a non-penal civil proceeding, so it certainly wouldn't be preempted by the existence of a federal statute criminalizing the same conduct.

Answer 34

(C) is the best response,

because the case is now moot.

A case is moot if it raised a justiciable controversy at the time the complaint was filed but events occurring after the filing have deprived the litigant of an ongoing stake in the controversy and it is not likely that the case will be revived.

The attorney was seeking only an injunction (not, for instance, damages). And the facts tell us that this is the only criminal trial he was counting on seeing via cable television. So unless this criminal trial has a significant likelihood of continuing, there is no ongoing damage to the attorney, and thus no need for an injunction. The facts tell us that there were no obvious errors in the trial, so it's unlikely that the case will be reversed and remanded for a new trial. Consequently, there is virtually no possibility of new proceedings that could be televised, and thus no live controversy about whether the injunction sought by the attorney should be granted.

(A) is not the best response,

because the likelihood of a live controversy is remote, thus dictating dismissal rather than deferral.

It is appropriate for a court to defer decision in a case where later events will or may likely occur that would make the case more suitable for decision than it is now. So if there were a good likelihood that a new trial would occur, deferral might be the right course. But here, we're told that there are no obvious errors, so it's unlikely that there will be an appellate reversal and a new criminal trial. Since likelihood of a new trial that would raise the "do we televise?" issue is remote, the court should dismiss rather than merely defer.

(B) is not the best response,

because the state supreme court will not have occasion to say anything about the case's merits.

The attorney's case presents a pure question of federal (constitutional) law. While principles of concurrent jurisdiction would probably have permitted him to bring the case in state court, he didn't choose to do that. Therefore, the state supreme court will never have occasion to express an opinion. In any event, this choice's statement that "state law of mootness governs suits in federal court . . ." is basically gibberish—it's up to the federal courts to say, as a federal constitutional matter, when a controversy is moot.

(D) is not the best response,

because however important the constitutional question raised by the attorney, it's moot due to the fact that there's no longer a criminal trial about which to grant the requested injunctive relief.

A case will be dismissed as moot if the relief sought no longer makes sense. That's true even if, in the abstract, the case presents "an important constitutional question." So choice D, by ignoring the mootness problem and relying solely on the importance of the issue, is wrong.

Answer 35

(C) is the best response,

because employees of the federal government are not immune from state taxes.

The federal government is immune from taxation by any state. Federal immunity from state taxation exists only in these situations where the "legal incidence" of the tax is on the United States. Employees of the federal government are not immune from state taxation. *Graves v. New York Ex Rel. O'Keefe,* 306 U.S. 466 (1939). Since the legal incidence of the tax here is on the employee, not the government, there is no immunity from the tax. (If the tax were on the deemed value of the business use of the auto, so that the United States was in effect being taxed, the result might be different. But the facts make it clear that it's only the employee's personal use that's being taxed, so the case is an easy one.)

(A) is not the best response,

because a tax on federal employees is not a tax on the U.S. government.

The federal government is immune from taxation by any state. Federal immunity from state taxation exists only in these situations where the "legal incidence" of the tax is on the United States. The tax here is not on the government or a government entity, but upon employees of the federal government, and they are not immune from state taxation.

(B) is not the best response,

because only the value of the personal use is taxed, not the value of the use generally.

The federal government is immune from taxation by any state. Federal immunity from state taxation exists only in these situations where the "legal incidence" of the tax is on the United States. Employees of the federal government are not immune from state taxation.

The state probably could not tax government employees for the use of automobiles in discharge of government duties, because in that case the legal incidence of the tax would be on the United States. But the tax here applies only to the fair value of the personal use, not the use for the United States' benefit. (The fact that the car is primarily used for federal government purposes is irrelevant, since it's only the value of the personal use that's being taxed.)

(D) is not the best response,

because it reaches the right result but for the wrong reason.

If the state were to give federal employees a total tax exemption on the value of the personal use of the car, this would probably *not* be an equal protection violation. That's because the standard would be whether there was a rational relation between the means chosen by the state (exemption) and some legitimate state objective. A court would probably hold that it's rational for a state to conclude that state-federal relations would benefit from this sort of exemption.

Answer 36

(D) is the best response,

because there is no right to a hearing unless one has been deprived of liberty or property, and the driver hasn't been so deprived.

A person who is affected by governmental action doesn't thereby automatically get the right to a hearing. Instead, only those whose "property" or "liberty" are being affected have the right to due process (and even then, these due process rights won't necessarily entail the right to a formal hearing). Here, nothing the city has ever done has created in the driver a property interest in being free of additional taxi competition. Indeed, the facts demonstrate the contrary—there is no limit to the number of licenses that may be issued, and the only required qualifications are driving ability and geographic knowledge. So the driver has not been deprived of a property (or liberty) interest, and the court will never even reach the issue of what procedures (such as a hearing) were due to him—none were.

(A) is not the best response,

because this is not a correct statement of who gets the protection of due process.

For the reason stated in the discussion of choice D above, choice A is exactly wrong about when the due process clause applies—only those deprived of "property" or "liberty" by the government, not all those "adversely affected by government action," have a due process interest.

(B) is not the best response,

because the driver never had a right to a hearing at all.

For the reasons stated in the discussion of choice D above, the driver had no due process rights that were implicated here, and therefore had no right to a hearing. Thus, the court would never reach the issue of who may decide whether he gets a hearing

(C) is not the best response,

because the fact that the driver once got the benefit of the ordinance has nothing to do with whether his due process rights have been violated here.

The licensing ordinance might have been written in such a way that the driver would get a property interest in not having new competition. (For instance, this would probably be so if the ordinance set the number of licenses at a fixed total, and charged a substantial fee for each one.) In that event, he would be permitted to assert his due process claim even though he originally benefitted from the same ordinance. The reason the driver loses is because he had no property interest in being free from additional competition (see the discussion of choice D above), not because he previously benefitted from the ordinance.

Answer 37

(A) is the best response,

because any attempt by Congress to force a state to enact particular legislation would violate the Tenth Amendment.

Although the Tenth Amendment today doesn't pose much of a limit for Congress, it does prevent Congress (or any other part of the federal government) from compelling a state to enact or enforce a particular law. *See N.Y. v. U.S.* (1992): Under the Tenth Amendment, Congress may not "commandee[r] the legislative processes of the States by directly compelling them to enact and enforce a federal regulatory program." That's what Congress has purported to do here, by requiring each state to make certain conduct a crime. (Congress could use the power of the purse to coerce states into acting by denying federal funds to states that don't pass the statute. But that's not what Congress is doing here.)

(B) is not the best response,

because banning controlled substances that had moved in interstate commerce *does* have a sufficient nexus with commerce to allow congressional regulation.

The examiners are trying to trick you by making you think that *U.S. v. Lopez* (1995) (Congress can't ban guns near schools, because there's not enough connection to interstate commerce) applies. But the federal statute in *Lopez* banned *all* guns—even those that had never travelled in interstate commerce. Had it banned just guns that had moved in interstate commerce, the result in *Lopez* would almost certainly have been different.

However, in this question you don't need to determine whether a direct ban by Congress on drug possession or sale near schools (i.e., Congress passes a statute making such possession a federal crime) would be valid under *Lopez*. That's because in the fact pattern here, Congress hasn't done the banning directly — instead, it has tried to force the states to do it. And such a "commandeering" of a branch of state government to achieve a federal objective violates the Tenth Amendment, as described in choice A.

(C) is not the best response,

because the jurisdictional statement doesn't take care of the fact that Congress is unconstitutionally ordering states to enact statutes.

If Congress were passing a statute that made the drug-related conduct here a federal crime, the jurisdictional provision would indeed be enough to create a sufficient nexus to interstate commerce. (See the discussion of *Lopez* in choice B above.)

But that's not what Congress is doing. Instead, it's ordering states to enact statutes containing the jurisdictional provision. And with or without jurisdictional provisions, ordering a state to enact a statute violates the Tenth Amendment, as discussed in the analysis of choice A above.

(D) is not the best response,

because it ignores the Tenth Amendment problem, and also incorrectly asserts that there is a "General Welfare Clause."

First, as discussed in choice A above, Congress violates the Tenth Amendment when it orders a state to enact a particular statute. Second, choice D suggests that there is an independent congressional power to act for "the general welfare." This is not so—there's a power to "*tax and spend* . . . for the general welfare," but that's not what's at issue here (because Congress is doing pure regulating, not taxing or spending). So this choice is wrong in both result and reasoning, and the reasoning is wrong in two different respects.

Answer 38

(A) is the best response,

because it identifies most closely the situation in which "state action" is involved.

The question here asks you for the facts under which the statute is most likely to be constitutional. To determine this, you have to identify first why the statute might not be constitutional. The problem is the "state action" requirement of the Fourteenth Amendment. That is, the Fourteenth Amendment only addresses *governmental* action. Specifically, the Equal Protection Clause forbids governmental discrimination, not private discrimination. Thus, the correct response would have to involve "state action" in promoting discrimination.

That's what choice A does. A public school is an agency of the state, and as such any action taken by it would be considered "state action." Here, as an agent of the school, a teacher's discrimination on the basis of race would be considered an equal protection violation. The citizen's actions, in threatening the teacher with violence if she didn't comply, would satisfy the "interference" part of the statute. As a result, the statute could be applied to the citizen, making A the best response.

(B) is not the best response,

because the acts the citizen encouraged would not involve "state action."

The question here asks you for the facts under which the statute is most likely to be constitutional. To determine this, you have to identify first why the statute might not be constitutional. The problem is the "state action" requirement of the Fourteenth Amendment. That is, the Fourteenth Amendment only addresses *governmental* action. Specifically, the Equal Protection Clause forbids governmental discrimination, not private discrimination. Thus, the correct response would have to involve "state action" in promoting discrimination.

Here, the actions of the black students, in refraining from attending a private school, would not be considered "state action." Thus, the citizen's actions, in threatening them with violence if they attended class, would not be promoting an equal protection violation, and the statute would not apply. Since B doesn't recognize this, it's not the best response.

(C) is not the best response,

because the acts the citizen encouraged would not involve "state action."

The question here asks you for the facts under which the statute is most likely to be constitutional. To determine this, you have to identify first why the statute might not be constitutional. The problem is the "state action" requirement of the Fourteenth Amendment. That is, the Fourteenth Amendment only addresses *governmental* action. Specifically, the Equal Protection Clause forbids governmental discrimination, not private discrimination. Thus, the correct response would have to involve "state action" in promoting discrimination.

Here, the bus driver works for a local church. The actions of the church would not constitute "state action." Thus, the citizen's coercing the bus driver into refusing to allow black children onto his bus would not be "interfering" with a right conferred by the Equal Protection Clause. Since C doesn't recognize this, it's not the best response.

(D) is not the best response,

because the acts the citizen encouraged would not involve "state action."

The question here asks you for the facts under which the statute is most likely to be constitutional. To determine this, you have to identify first why the statute might not be constitutional. The problem is the "state action" requirement of the Fourteenth Amendment. That is, the Fourteenth Amendment only addresses *governmental* action. Specifically, the Equal Protection Clause forbids governmental discrimination, not private discrimination. Thus, the correct response would have to involve "state action" in promoting discrimination.

Here, the official coerced was a *federal* official, not a state official, and the Equal Protection Clause only applies to states, not the federal government. Thus, any action taken by the federal official could not be considered an equal protection violation. Had the facts been different, and the official was a state official instead of a federal official, the "state action" requirement would be met, and the citizen could be convicted under the statute. However, since the "state action" requirement is missing, D is not the best response.

Answer 39

(B) is the best response,

because the Commission is a temporary agency set up for a specific purpose.

Creation of an advisory commission, such as the one here, falls within the President's executive powers. Congress has the right to earmark specified federal monies to be spent as the President shall determine. Therefore, nothing about this arrangement violates any Constitutional provision.

(A) is not the best response,

because it is not a correct statement of law.

The President does not have "plenary power to provide for the health, safety, and welfare of the people . . . ." For instance, the President does not have power to spend federal money for what he determines to be the health needs of "the people." This answer ignores both the source of the President's authority (the executive power, that is, the power to see that the laws are carried out) and the need for all funding to be appropriated by Congress.

(C) is not the best response,

because it incorrectly states the effect of the Tenth Amendment.

The Tenth Amendment states that the powers not delegated to the federal government by the Constitution, and not prohibited to the states, are reserved to the states. The Tenth Amendment has relatively little force today as a limit on federal power. (About the only force it has as a limit on federal powers is to prevent Congress from directly forcing the states to enact or enforce federal policies).

The Amendment does not mean that the federal government may not exercise power over a "traditional state function." So the fact that vaccination has traditionally been a function handled by the states does not mean that the Tenth Amendment bars the federal government from taking action with respect to vaccinations.

(D) is not the best response,

because Congress does not need to authorize the creation of a temporary commission.

An Advisory Commission on Vaccination is not a new federal agency. It is an advisory group, set up for a specific purpose and having a temporary existence. The President does not need congressional approval to create such an organization. Nor has Congress prohibited its creation because, as the facts state, no federal statute authorizes or prohibits this action.

Answer 40

(C) is the best response,

because the Thirteenth Amendment addresses *private* acts.

Here, Congress is trying to eliminate private discrimination through this statute. That's the central obstacle to the validity of the statute, because the most likely source of constitutionality for statutes eliminating discrimination is the Fourteenth Amendment, which, problematically, only eliminates *state* action in promoting or authorizing discrimination. The Thirteenth Amendment is, in fact, the only constitutional provision explicitly limiting private acts by individuals. Under it, if Congress could rationally determine that the conduct it is prohibiting imposes a "badge or incident" of slavery on a victim, the statute will be valid. *Jones v. Alfred H. Mayer Co.* (1968). This provision is exceptionally broad, giving Congress the power to prohibit virtually all racial discrimination against blacks, and whites, for that matter.

Here, the statute will serve to eliminate racial discrimination against blacks, and Congress could rationally determine that when people conspire to deny blacks housing, employment, or education due to their race, this constitutes a "badge or incident" of slavery. As a result, the statute will be valid, and the Thirteenth Amendment will be the source of the validity. Since C recognizes this, it's the best response.

(A) is not the best response,

because the Contracts Clause is a limitation on the states, not a source of power for the federal government.

The Contracts Clause, Article I, § 10, of the Constitution, prohibits states from passing any law that impairs the obligations of existing contracts. A law "impairs" contracts by substantially invalidating, releasing, or extinguishing obligations under a contract, or, alternatively, derogating rights under a contract that are substantial.

Here, there is a federal law involved, not a state law. Furthermore, the question is asking you for a basis on which the statute is *justifiable*, not one on which it is unconstitutional. As a result, the Contracts Clause cannot be the right answer, making A not the best response.

(B) is not the best response,

because the Welfare Clause could not be a source of constitutionality for this statute.

The Welfare Clause, Article I, § 8, of the Constitution, empowers Congress to collect taxes and spend money and to provide for the general welfare, and to make all laws that are necessary and proper to implement those powers. The statute here is designed to eliminate discrimination through regulating behavior. It doesn't address taxing or spending, so the Welfare Clause cannot be a source of power for it. Since B doesn't recognize this, it's not the best response.

(D) is not the best response,

because the Fourteenth Amendment doesn't address *private* discrimination.

Under the Fourteenth Amendment, the states are forbidden from, among other things, discriminating on the basis of race. If a state does so, an equal protection violation exists. However, one of the requirements of the Fourteenth Amendment is *state action*. Here, on the other hand, Congress is trying to eliminate *private* discrimination, which is not covered by the Fourteenth Amendment. Furthermore, the Fourteenth Amendment Equal Protection Clause only addresses state action, not *federal* action. As a result, the Fourteenth Amendment is not a good source of constitutionality for the statute, making D not the best response.

Answer 41

(A) is the best response,

because the rule would not survive strict scrutiny.

Equal protection requires race-based affirmative action plans to be subject to the same strict scrutiny as are governmental actions that intentionally discriminate against racial minorities. Any governmental action that is explicitly race-based must be "necessary" to achieve a "compelling" governmental interest. Minority set-aside programs enacted by a city or state will be subjected to strict scrutiny and will usually be found unconstitutional on equal protection grounds. *Richmond v. J.A. Croson Co.* (1989).

The set-aside plan here is unconstitutional. Although the water district claims to be pursuing the objective of overcoming past discrimination, *Richmond* establishes that a desire to overcome broad, historical, "societal" discrimination is not a compelling governmental interest. Therefore, the fact that racial minorities have been discriminated against "in this country" does not suffice (and the facts make it very clear that the community to be served by the water district has never discriminated).

(B) is not the best response,

because the Contracts Clause has nothing to do with the set-aside here.

The Contracts Clause protects solely against governmental actions that have the effect of interfering with contractual obligations that were undertaken *before the governmental* action. Nothing in the Clause prevents the government from making it harder for people to make a certain kind of contract after the enactment. Since the set-aside here would apply only to hiring and contracting occurring after the set-aside was enacted, the Contracts Clause would have no application to these facts.

(C) is not the best response,

because racial set-asides have to pass a strict scrutiny test.

Equal protection requires race-based affirmative action plans to be subject to the same strict scrutiny as are governmental actions that intentionally discriminate against racial minorities. (See the discussion of choice A above.) In other words, the Supreme Court takes the view that when minority groups are given express, racially oriented preferences, they are not receiving "equal protection"—they are instead receiving a preference, one that may well constitute a denial of equal protection to the members of the non-favored (majority) racial group. Here, because the government entity giving the preference has not been shown to have discriminated in the past, the preference would fail the required strict scrutiny. So choice C is wrong both as to the theory it espouses and as to the result it predicts.

(D) is not the best response,

because state actions, whether involving governmental or proprietary functions, are reviewed under strict scrutiny.

The examiners are hoping you'll think about the equal protection voting cases (e.g., *Ball v. James* (1981)) holding that where a governmental unit has a limited purpose which disproportionately affects only one group (e.g., landowners), the right to vote for positions governing that unit may be limited to the affected group. So here, the right to elect members of the water district's governing board may indeed be limited to landowners.

But once the district is formed, it can't give out "goodies" (staff positions and private-sector contracts) on a racially discriminatory basis unless the scheme survives strict scrutiny. For the reasons described in choice C, the scheme here would fail that strict scrutiny. The fact that this was a special-purpose body whose governors could be elected solely by landowners doesn't change this result in the slightest.

Answer 42

(C) is the best response,

because the state may not, up to the point where the fetus is viable, unduly burden a woman's fundamental right to choose whether to continue the pregnancy.

The Court has held that the right of privacy includes the right of a woman to have an abortion under certain circumstances without undue interference from the state. Up until the time the fetus is viable, a state may adopt regulations protecting the mother's health and the life of the fetus only if the regulation does not impose an undue burden or substantial obstacle to the woman's right to have an abortion. Then, once the fetus becomes viable, the state's interest in the fetus's life can override the woman's right to choose an abortion. *Planned Parenthood v. Casey* (1992).

The fetus is not yet viable in many pregnancies that have gone beyond the first trimester. (Typically, viability occurs late in the second or early in the third trimester.) Since the statute here forbids the mother from ending such a post-first-trimester-but-not-yet-viable pregnancy unless her life or health is in danger, a court would almost certainly hold that the statute "unduly burdens" the mother's fundamental rights.

(A) is not the best response,

because, prior to viability, the state does not have a compelling state interest in preserving fetal life.

Under *Planned Parenthood v. Casey* (1992), a woman's right to reproductive choice—and to not be "unduly burdened" in the exercise of that reproductive choice—extends beyond the first trimester, all the way to viability. Before viability, the state's interest in fetal life is not compelling. Therefore, choice A's statement that before viability the state can seek an "equitable balance" between its compelling interest in protecting fetal life and the woman's fundamental right to reproductive choice is inconsistent with *Casey*, and thus wrong.

(B) is not the best response,

because the fetus doesn't become a "person" after the first trimester, merely a potential life that the state has an interest in protecting.

Even after the point of viability, the Supreme Court has never said that the fetus is a "person" whose right to life is protected by the Due Process Clause. Furthermore, even if the Court had said this, choice B would still be wrong, because that choice falsely states that the fetus is a person when the first trimester is over even if the fetus is not yet viable. (As applied to such cases the statute is in fact *un*constitutional, because the woman's right to abort a non-viable fetus can't be "unduly burdened," and an outright prohibition of pre-viability abortions not needed to protect that woman's life or health would certainly be an undue burden.)

(D) is not the best response,

because the answer is based on equal protection analysis, rather than the proper substantive-due-process analysis.

The Court has never used equal protection analysis in abortion cases. If it did, the statute here would probably be constitutional, because it would not be irrational for a state to decide that abortions after the end of the first trimester harm the state's interest in protecting fetal life more than those that occur during the first trimester. The essence of the Court's analysis of abortion rights has always been substantive due process, not equal protection. And, under that substantive due process analysis, it's the existence of a fundamental right to reproductive choice prior to viability that is the focus of the analysis.

Answer 43

(D) is the best response,

because it correctly identifies a flaw in the statute: Congress cannot enlarge federal court jurisdiction to include advisory opinions.

Article III, § 2, of the Constitution gives Congress the power to create federal courts beneath the Supreme Court, and also the power to determine the jurisdiction of those courts. However, there is a limitation on this power: Congress cannot expand federal court jurisdiction beyond the boundaries prescribed by Article III. The "case and controversy" requirement is one such boundary. Federal courts can only render opinions where there is an actual controversy—they cannot offer advisory opinions. That is, the matter in controversy must be definite and concrete, touching the legal relations of parties having adverse legal interests, and—here's the problem—there must be a real and substantial controversy capable of specific relief through a decree of a conclusive character. *Aetna Life Insurance Co. v. Haworth* (1937).

Here, an advisory opinion is exactly what the statute calls for. The federal courts are not being used to resolve disputes—rather, they are rendering opinions that will be taken under advisement by the administrator of the federal agency that is dispersing the funds in question. Such advisory opinions are prohibited, and since choice D recognizes this, it's the best response.

(A) is not the best response,

because it fails to recognize that the statute expands federal court jurisdiction beyond the bounds of Article III, and thus is invalid.

Article III, § 2, of the Constitution gives Congress the power to create federal courts beneath the Supreme Court, and also the power to determine the jurisdiction of those courts. As choice A implicitly recognizes, one of the bases of federal court jurisdiction is "federal question" jurisdiction—that is, cases that arise under the Constitution, or a federal law or treaty. Where federal grant-in-aid funds are in question, "federal question" jurisdiction would, in fact, exist. However, this alone doesn't determine if the federal court can hear the case. For instance, the plaintiff must have standing to present the claim in question, and there must be a "case or controversy." This is where choice A falls down, because the statute here improperly authorizes federal courts to render advisory opinions. Under this statute, the federal courts are not being used to resolve disputes—rather, they are rendering opinions that will be taken under advisement by the administrator of the federal agency which is dispersing the funds in question. Since choice A doesn't recognize that this makes the statute invalid, it's not the best response.

(B) is not the best response,

because it misstates the law.

Congress has the power to legislate, and this power includes the power to decide how federal funds will be spent. The President has the power to execute such appropriations. However, the power to resolve disputes about how funds are distributed would not, contrary to what choice B suggests, give Congress the power to use federal courts as tribunals. While Congress can set up tribunals to resolve disputes, it cannot use Article III courts for this purpose. To do so would require federal courts to render advisory opinions, which is something prohibited by Article III. Since choice B doesn't recognize this, it's not the best response.

(C) is not the best response,

because the Eleventh Amendment would not bar suits under this statute.

The Eleventh Amendment, as a general matter, bars a citizen from suing a state in federal court without that state's consent. One of the exclusions to the Amendment is a suit by the federal government against a state. Here, the lawsuits covered by the statute are between states and the federal government. The Eleventh Amendment does not bar federal court suits by the federal government against the states. Thus, the statute here cannot be unconstitutional due to operation of the Eleventh Amendment. Instead, what makes this statute unconstitutional is that it authorizes federal courts to render advisory opinions, which they are prohibited from doing under Article III of the Constitution. Since choice C doesn't recognize the correct basis for the statute's unconstitutionality, it's not the best response.

Answer 44

(C) is the best response,

because it recognizes the central reason for dismissing the suit: it involves a non-justiciable issue.

There are several limitations on the jurisdiction of federal courts. For instance, the plaintiff must have standing to press his claim, there must be some basis for federal court jurisdiction (e.g., diversity, federal question), there must be a "case or controversy," and the issue that's involved here—a "political question"—cannot be presented.

A "political question" is one that the Constitution commits to another governmental branch, which the judicial process is inherently incapable of resolving and enforcing. These are the criteria for determining political questions:

1. A "textually demonstrable" constitutional commitment of the issue to the political branches;
2. Lack of manageable standards for judicial resolution;
3. A need for finality in the action of the political branches; and
4. Difficulty or impossibility of devising effective judicial remedies.

Foreign relations is a classic source of "political questions." Congress and the President control foreign affairs exclusively, and the nature of foreign affairs is such that the judiciary cannot intrude. Here, the researcher is seeking to forbid the President from recognizing a new country, due to its totalitarian government. This is a purely political question, and as such the court should dismiss the suit. Since C recognizes this, it's the best response.

(A) is not the best response,

because the researcher *does* have standing to bring the action.

In order to press a claim, a plaintiff requires standing. Standing requires that the action challenged must have caused, or is imminently likely to cause, an injury to the party seeking review. Here, if the President recognizes the new country (which he is empowered to do), the researcher's contract with the Department of Commerce will terminate. Thus, the researcher is imminently likely to suffer an injury due to the action he's challenging, and he will have standing on that basis. Since A doesn't recognize this, it's not the best response.

(B) is not the best response,

because there *is* adversity between the parties.

Here, the researcher is bringing suit in federal court. The federal court requirements for jurisdiction, found in Article III of the Constitution, include the requirement that the federal courts can only hear "cases and controversies." One element of a "case and controversy" is that the parties must have adverse legal interests. Thus, B is correct in implying that adversity is a requirement of a federal court suit—but it's not correct in stating that there's no adversity here. The President wants to recognize the new country, and the researcher doesn't want him to do so. Thus, it can't be the lack of adversity that makes the suit improper. Rather, it's the fact that the conduct of foreign relations is the basis of the suit, and this is a non-justiciable "political question" that will require that the suit be dismissed. Since B doesn't recognize that adversity exists here, and it ignores the real reason for dismissing the suit, it's not the best response.

(D) is not the best response,

because the federal court will not hear the case on its merits.

There are several limitations on the jurisdiction of federal courts. For instance, the plaintiff must have standing to press his claim, there must be some basis for federal court jurisdiction (e.g., diversity, federal question), there must be a "case or controversy," and the issue that's involved here—a "political question"—cannot be presented.

A "political question" is one that the Constitution commits to another governmental branch, which the judicial process is inherently incapable of resolving and enforcing. These are the criteria for determining political questions:

1. A "textually demonstrable" constitutional commitment of the issue to the political branches;
2. Lack of manageable standards for judicial resolution;
3. A need for finality in the action of the political branches; and
4. Difficulty or impossibility of devising effective judicial remedies.

Foreign relations is a classic source of "political questions." Congress and the President control foreign affairs exclusively, and the nature of foreign affairs is such that the judiciary cannot intrude. Here, the researcher is asking the court to forbid the president from recognizing a new country. This is a purely political question, and as such the court should dismiss the suit. Since D doesn't recognize this, it's not the best response.

Answer 45

(B) is the best response,

because free exercise rights must yield to a rational and generally applicable law even if that law proscribes conduct required by religion.

This case is governed by *Employment Div. v. Smith* (1990), in which the Court held that "the right of free exercise does not relieve an individual of the obligation to comply with a *valid and neutral law of general applicability* on the ground that the law proscribes . . . conduct that his religion prescribes." Here, the law states that "there must be an autopsy" (in certain cases), and the parents claim that their religion prohibits autopsies. So *Smith* applies: We have a "valid and neutral law of general applicability" (i.e., a law that's not motivated by anti-religious bias, that applies to all cases of non-natural death, and that's rationally related to the legitimate state purpose of detecting illegal activity). That law is proscribing certain conduct (refusing an autopsy), and it's applicable to conduct that the plaintiff's religion prescribes, or requires (refusing an autopsy). So *Smith* requires that the law be enforced notwithstanding the parents' objection, even though the effect would be to impair their free exercise of their religion.

(A) is not the best response,

because while the statute is constitutional, it is not constitutional for the reason stated in this choice.

It's in a sense true that a "dead individual is not a person protected by the due process clause. . . ." But the parents' claim is not based on their son's due process rights, but on their own free-exercise rights (as made applicable to the states through the Fourteenth Amendment's Due Process Clause). So the fact that their son has no relevant rights is irrelevant. Instead, the statute is constitutional for the reason discussed in the analysis of choice B above.

(C) is not the best response,

because strict scrutiny is not the appropriate standard for the statute here.

Employment Div. v. Smith (1990) says that where a valid, generally applicable statute requires certain conduct, the statute must be obeyed even by a person whose religion proscribes that conduct. So the Court does not strictly scrutinize the statute, as this choice implies that it should. Instead, the Court gives just the lowest-level, mere-rationality review, which the statute here easily passes.

(D) is not the best response,

because mid-level review is not the appropriate standard for the statute here.

Employment Div. v. Smith (1990) says that where a valid, generally applicable statute requires certain conduct, the statute must be obeyed even by a person whose religion proscribes that conduct. So the Court does not give mid-level review to the statute, as this choice implies that it should. Instead, the Court gives just the lowest-level, mere-rationality review, which the statute here easily passes.

Answer 46

(D) is the best response,

because Congress provided clear standards for the contest.

The General Welfare Clause, Article I, § 8, states that Congress shall have power to "lay and collect Taxes . . . to pay the Debts and provide for the . . . general Welfare of the United States." This clause gives Congress the substantive power to tax and spend, limited only by the requirement that the taxing and spending be for the general welfare. Congress may delegate its legislative power as long as the person or body receiving the delegated power is directed to conform to an intelligible principle set forth by Congress.

The statute here is valid under these rules: (1) eradication of drug abuse would contribute to the "general welfare," and the contest is a rational way of using federal funds to generate ideas for doing this (it is exceptionally rare for the Court to conclude that a particular taxing or spending scheme doesn't bear the requisite connection to "the general welfare"); and (2) the contest rules, and the structure for running the contest, are sufficiently specific that the requirement of an "intelligible principle" guiding the delegation would be found to be satisfied.

(A) is not the best response,

because the contest's constitutionality is a simple matter to decide.

The requirement of a justiciable Article III controversy is deemed to carry with it a limitation against the deciding of purely "political questions." The court will leave the resolution of such political questions to the other departments of government. The primary earmarks of a non-justiciable political question are: (1) the presence of a "textually demonstrable" constitutional commitment of the issue to the political branches (Congress and the executive branch) for resolution; (2) a need for the political branches' decision on the issue to be final, and not subject to judicial second-guessing; (3) a lack of adequate standards for judicial resolution of the issue; and (4) the presence of issues that are too controversial or could involve enforcement problems.

None of these factors are present here. There is no reason why the court cannot quickly determine that the spending here is rationally related to pursuit of the general welfare, and that the guidance given to the contest administrators is reasonably specific.

(B) is not the best response,

because the statute sets out very clear standards.

Congress may delegate its legislative power (here, the spending power) as long as the person or body receiving the delegated power is directed to conform to an intelligible principle set forth by Congress. Here, the guidelines for awarding the prize money appropriated by Congress are very clearly set out in the statute, so there is no problem of inappropriately vague delegation.

(C) is not the best response,

because the statute is a legitimate use of Congress's power to appropriate funds to end drug abuse.

The General Welfare Clause, Article I, § 8, states that Congress shall have power to "lay and collect Taxes . . . to pay the Debts and provide for the . . . general Welfare of the United States." This Clause gives Congress the substantive power to tax and spend, limited only by the requirement that the taxing and spending be reasonably related to the pursuit of the general welfare. The requirement that the taxing and spending have a rational relation to the attainment of the general welfare has very little "bite"—the Court rarely (if ever) concludes that a particular taxing or spending scheme doesn't bear the requisite connection to "the general welfare." Here, given the size of the drug abuse problem, and the relatively small sum proposed, it's wildly unlikely that the court would conclude that the relationship between the contest and the elimination of drug abuse is "too tenuous and conjectural" to pass muster.

Answer 47

(B) is the best response,

because the statements were made during the legislative process.

Article I, § 6, states that for any speech or debate in either the House of Representatives or the Senate, members of Congress shall not be questioned in any other place. This is the "Speech and Debate Clause." The clause clearly applies to the senator's statement: The statement was made on the floor of the Senate, so it falls within even the most narrowly defined construction of the Speech and Debate Clause. (The fact that the speech didn't relate to current legislation is irrelevant—as long as the words were spoken on the floor during the session, that's enough.)

With respect to the senator's legislative assistant, the Clause itself, by its literal terms, seems not to apply. But the Court has held that the clause applies "not only to a Member but also to his aides insofar as the conduct of the latter would be a protected legislative act if performed by the Member himself." *Gravel v. U.S.* (1972). Thus, since the senator is covered, so is his legislative assistant.

Neither (A), (C), nor (D) is the best answer, since each asserts that at least one of the defendants is not covered by the Speech and Debate Clause. Both defendants are in fact covered, as explained in the discussion of choice B above.

Answer 48

(B) is the best response,

because it correctly recognizes that the statute here will be valid under the "rational relation" test.

Here, the statute is a state statute. In order to be valid, a state statute must be enacted within the state's powers (e.g., police powers), it must not improperly burden a person's constitutional rights, and it must not unduly burden interstate commerce.

The hunter's claim asserts that the statute is an equal protection violation. Equal protection is triggered by the existence of a classification that determines people's rights. If the classification is "suspect," or determines who may exercise a fundamental right, it's subject to strict scrutiny. Suspect classifications are race and alienage; the fundamental rights are the First Amendment rights, interstate travel, voting, and privacy. Where the statute instead consists of only economic or social legislation not involving a suspect classification or fundamental right, the "rational relation" test will be used.

Here, the statute as applied distinguishes between those who may and may not transport snipe traps through the middle state: common carriers are not prohibited from carrying snipe traps, and private individuals are. This does not involve a suspect classification or a fundamental right, so it will be subject to the rational relation test. Here, there is a rational basis on which to make the distinction, since it's likely that common carriers would not have the middle state as their destination, where a private person quite possibly could. Furthermore, prohibiting common carriers from transporting snipe traps through the middle state would be an impermissible burden on interstate commerce, so the state *could not* constitutionally prohibit common carriers from transporting snipe traps. Since choice B recognizes that the distinction is constitutional, due to the rational basis for distinguishing common carriers from private individuals, it's the best response.

(A) is not the best response,

because it doesn't address the constitutionality of the statute as applied to the hunter.

Here, the statute is a state statute. In order to be valid, a state statute must be enacted within the state's powers (e.g., police powers), it must not improperly burden a person's constitutional rights, and it must not unduly burden interstate commerce.

The hunter's claim suggests that the statute is an equal protection violation. Equal protection is triggered by the existence of a classification that determines people's rights. If the classification is "suspect," or determines who may exercise a fundamental right, it's subject to strict scrutiny. Suspect classifications are race and alienage; the fundamental rights are the First Amendment rights, interstate travel, voting, and privacy. Where the statute instead is only economic or social legislation, the "rational relation" test will be used. Here, the statute as applied distinguishes between who may transport snipe traps through the middle state: common carriers are not prohibited from carrying snipe traps, and private individuals are. This does not involve a suspect classification or a fundamental right, so it will be subject to the rational relation test. Here, there is a rational basis on which to make the distinction, since it's likely that common carriers would not have the middle state as their destination, where a private person quite possibly could. More importantly, prohibiting common carriers from transporting snipe traps through the middle state would be an impermissible burden on interstate commerce, so the state *could not* constitutionally prohibit common carriers from transporting snipe traps. As a result, it's not the lack of permissible reasons why the hunter might have the snipe trap that makes the statute constitutional, but rather the rational reason for distinguishing between common carriers and individuals transporting snipe traps. Since choice A doesn't recognize this, it's not the best response.

(C) is not the best response,

because it overstates the level of scrutiny to which the statute will be subject.

Here, the statute is a state statute. In order to be valid, a state statute must be enacted within the state's powers (e.g., police powers), it must not improperly burden a person's constitutional rights, and it must not unduly burden interstate commerce.

The hunter's claim suggests that the statute is an equal protection violation. Equal protection is triggered by the existence of a classification that determines people's rights. If the classification is "suspect," or determines who may exercise a fundamental right, it's subject to strict scrutiny. Suspect classifications are race and alienage; the fundamental rights are the First Amendment rights, interstate travel, voting, and privacy. Where the statute instead is only economic or social legislation, the "rational relation" test will be used. Here, the statute as applied distinguishes between who may transport snipe traps through the middle state: common carriers are not prohibited from carrying snipe traps, and private individuals are. This does not involve a suspect classification or a fundamental right, so it will be subject to the rational relation test.

If you chose this response, you may have thought that the statute impermissibly burdens private individuals' fundamental right to interstate travel. However, the statute doesn't burden interstate travel, just the transportation of snipe traps. The hunter was free to travel interstate, it's just that she couldn't possess a snipe trap in the middle state. As a result, the right to interstate travel would not be called into question. Since the rational basis test would be the appropriate test here, and choice C doesn't recognize this, it's not the best response.

(D) is not the best response,

because the statute here doesn't burden the right to interstate travel.

Here, the statute is a state statute. In order to be valid, a state statute must be enacted within the state's powers (e.g., police powers), it must not improperly burden a person's constitutional rights, and it must not unduly burden interstate commerce.

The hunter's claim suggests that the statute is an equal protection violation. Equal protection is triggered by the existence of a classification that determines people's rights. If the classification is "suspect," or determines who may exercise a fundamental right, it's subject to strict scrutiny. Suspect classifications are race and alienage; the fundamental rights are the First Amendment rights, interstate travel, voting, and privacy. Where the statute instead is only economic or social legislation, the "rational relation" test will be used. Here, the statute as applied distinguishes between who may transport snipe traps through the middle state: common carriers are not prohibited from carrying snipe traps, and private individuals are. This does not involve a suspect classification or a fundamental right, so it will be subject to the rational relation test.

If you chose this response, you may have thought that since the statute burdened the hunter's right to travel through the state with snipe traps, it unconstitutionally burdened her fundamental right to interstate travel. However, the statute doesn't really burden her right to interstate travel at all. When you're talking about impermissible burdens on interstate travel, you're generally talking about waiting periods before new residents may receive crucial governmental benefits or services. Here, the hunter is free to move in and out of the middle state—she just can't have a snipe trap while she's there. Since choice D incorrectly states that the hunter's right to interstate travel is burdened by this statute, it's not the best response.

Answer 49

(D) is the best response,

because it correctly identifies the central reason the distribution is invalid: It amounts to a state authorization of discrimination.

In order to be valid, a state law must meet a three-part test:

1. It must be enacted within the state's powers (e.g., police powers);
2. It must not violate any person's constitutional rights; and
3. It must not improperly burden interstate commerce.

The distribution of free textbooks satisfies (1) above: The distribution would be an exercise of the state's police power, since it aids the welfare of the public. The problem is the second element: The distribution to the private school is a violation of the equal protection provision of the Fourteenth Amendment. Equal protection is triggered by a classification that determines people's rights. Here, the classification is on the basis of color. While a state need not outlaw private acts of racial discrimination, the state cannot authorize or encourage such acts; if they do, they are considered to have committed state action in support of the private act, constituting a Fourteenth Amendment equal protection violation. *See, e.g., Reitman v. Mulkey*, 387 U.S. 369 (1967) (where a state amends its constitution to repeal local governments' prior right to ban private individuals' right to discriminate on racial or other grounds in the sale or lease of residential real estate, and where both the purpose and effect of the amendment are to "encourage" such discrimination, the amendment constitutes state action, making the amendment a violation of the Fourteenth Amendment).

Here, the state's distribution of free textbooks to a racially-segregated school would constitute state encouragement of racial discrimination in violation of the Equal Protection Clause of the Fourteenth Amendment. Thus, the distribution will be invalid. Since D recognizes this, it's the best response.

(A) is not the best response,

because it's not factually true; education *is* aided by the free distribution of textbooks.

In order to be valid, a state law must meet a three-part test:

1. It must be enacted within the state's powers (e.g., police powers);
2. It must not violate any person's constitutional rights; and
3. It must not improperly burden interstate commerce.

Choice A addresses the first element—a legitimate goal of government. The distribution of free textbooks would be an exercise of the state's police power, because it aids the welfare of the public. The problem is the second element: The distribution to the private school is an equal protection violation. Equal protection is triggered by a classification that determines people's rights. Here, the classification is on the basis of race. While states need not outlaw racial discrimination, they cannot authorize or encourage it.

The state's distribution of free textbooks to a racially-segregated school would constitute state encouragement of private discrimination. Thus, the distribution will be invalid. Since choice A mischaracterizes the facts and ignores the central reason the distribution is unconstitutional, it's not the best response.

(B) is not the best response,

because it misstates the law. States *may* aid private schools; the problem here is that such a distribution would foster discrimination, and thus would constitute an equal protection violation.

In order to be valid, a state law must meet a three-part test:

1. It must be enacted within the state's powers (e.g., police powers);
2. It must not violate any person's constitutional rights; and
3. It must not improperly burden interstate commerce.

The distribution of free textbooks would be an exercise of the state's police power, because it aids the welfare of the public. The problem is the second element: The distribution to the private school is an equal protection violation. Equal protection is triggered by a classification that determines people's rights. Here, the classification is on the basis of color. While states need not outlaw discrimination, they cannot authorize or encourage it. Distributing free textbooks to a racially segregated school would encourage discrimination. Thus, the distribution will be invalid.

It's not the fact that the state is giving some sort of aid to a private school that makes the distribution invalid, but the fact that the state is encouraging racial segregation by means of the distribution. Since B doesn't recognize this, it's not the best response.

(C) is not the best response,

because it misstates the law.

The Constitution does not forbid *private* bias; it only prevents states from enforcing, facilitating, encouraging, or authorizing discrimination. *Shelly v. Kraemer* (1948).

In order to be valid, a state law must meet a three-part test:

1. It must be enacted within the state's powers (e.g., police powers);
2. It must not violate any person's constitutional rights; and
3. It must not improperly burden interstate commerce.

The distribution of free textbooks would be an exercise of the state's police power, because it aids the welfare of the public. The problem is the second element: The distribution to the private school is an equal protection violation. Equal protection is triggered by a classification that determines people's rights. Here, the classification is on the basis of color. While states need not outlaw discrimination, they cannot authorize or encourage it. Distributing free textbooks to a racially segregated school would encourage discrimination. Thus, the distribution will be invalid. Since C doesn't recognize this, and misstates the law, it's not the best response.

Answer 50

(B) is the best response,

because it's the only choice that adds a fact making the mathematician's claim valid.

Under these facts, you have a state activity that is depriving the mathematician of what looks like some interest or right. Thus, what's involved here is, at least on its face, a *due process* issue. Since what the mathematician is contesting is the lack of some process before he was not rehired, the issue is more specifically *procedural* due process. (Substantive due process involves a law limiting a right, where, depending on whether the right is fundamental, either the "compelling interest" or "rational relation" test will be used to determine the law's validity.)

Under procedural due process, there need only be fair process if the right being deprived is a *property* right (or life or liberty). Thus, in order for the mathematician to prevail, he'd have to claim he had a property right in his state employment. This demands more than the mere enjoyment of a benefit; an applicable federal, state, or municipal law must recognize a legitimate claim to the benefit. (For instance, there's a property interest in receiving a public education through high school and in receiving continuing welfare benefits.) As to public employment—the issue under these facts—the existence of a property interest will similarly be determined by applicable law.

There is a Supreme Court case that involves facts nearly identical to the ones here, and that shows why the mathematician's "oral promise of reemployment" argument might work. In *Perry v. Sindermann*, 408 U.S. 593 (1972), P was a professor at a public college that by state statute was not allowed to award anyone official tenure. You would think that the statute would automatically prevent P from establishing that he had a property right in continued employment. But the Court held that if P could show that under the unwritten "common law" of the state where the college was located, employees in a particular college have the unofficial equivalent of tenure, this would be enough to give P a "legitimate claim of entitlement" to reemployment. And, the Court said, if P indeed had such a legitimate claim of entitlement to reemployment (a matter to be determined at trial), he was entitled to procedural due process before being fired. So under *Perry*, the mathematician here could argue that under state law (in this case, the common-law contract doctrine of *promissory estoppel*), the oral promise of reemployment by the president gave the mathematician a "legitimate claim of entitlement" to that reemployment, thereby triggering an obligation to give him procedural due process. It's not clear that this argument will work (e.g., because state law might not recognize promissory estoppel on these facts), but of the four choices, it's the only one that furnishes the mathematician with a plausible argument about why state-law principles gave him a legitimate claim of entitlement to continue in his job for another year.

(A) is not the best response,

because it relies on an irrelevant fact.

Under these facts, you have a state activity that is depriving the mathematician of what looks like some interest or right. Thus, what's involved here is a *due process* issue. Since what the mathematician is contesting is the lack of some process before he was not rehired, the issue is more specifically *procedural* due process.

Under procedural due process, there need only be fair process if the right being deprived is a *property* right (or life or liberty). Thus, in order for the mathematician to prevail, he'd have to claim he had a property right in his state employment. The fact that tenured teachers are no more qualified than the mathematician does not make the mathematician's continued employment into a property right, and as a result the choice relies on an irrelevant fact. Therefore, Choice A is not the best response.

(C) is not the best response,

because it doesn't address the central issue here whether the mathematician had a property right in his public employment.

Under these facts, you have a state activity that is depriving the mathematician of what looks like some interest or right. Thus, what's involved here is a *due process* issue. Since what the mathematician is contesting is the lack of some process before he was not rehired, the issue is more specifically *procedural* due process.

Under procedural due process, there need only be fair process if the right being deprived is a *property* right (or life or liberty). Thus, in order for the mathematician to prevail, he'd have to claim he had a property right in his state employment. The fact that the mathematician was the only teacher not rehired would not transform the mathematician's interest in his job into a property right. Therefore, Choice C is not the best response.

(D) is not the best response,

because it relies on an irrelevant fact.

Under these facts, you have a state activity that is depriving the mathematician of what looks like some interest or right. Thus, what's involved here is a *due process* issue. Since what the mathematician is contesting is the lack of some process before he was not rehired, the issue is more specifically *procedural* due process.

Under procedural due process, there need only be fair process if the right being deprived is a *property* right (or life or liberty). Thus, in order for the mathematician to prevail, he'd have to claim he had a property right in his state employment. To have a property right in a benefit, you have to have more than the mere present enjoyment of that benefit; an applicable federal, state, or municipal law must recognize a legitimate claim to the benefit. (For instance, there's a property interest in receiving a public education or in continuing to receive welfare benefits.) As to public employment—the issue under these facts—the existence of a property interest will similarly be determined by applicable law. As is discussed further in the treatment of Choice B, the Supreme Court has held that a public worker would have a property right in continued employment if he could show that under unwritten common-law principles, he had a "legitimate claim of entitlement" to that continued employment. But the special facts recited in this choice—that the mathematician expected to remain at the college, and acted in reliance on that expectation by moving his parents—would not be enough to give the mathematician a "legitimate claim of entitlement" to reemployment under common-law principles. The only common-law doctrine that's plausibly relevant here is promissory estoppel, but nothing in this choice indicates that the college made any sort of promise that would have reasonably justified the mathematician's reliance, a requirement for that doctrine. So even though the argument in Choice D involves reliance, the argument is far less likely to produce a "legitimate" entitlement than the promise-based argument in Choice B.

Answer 51

(D) is the best response,

because it correctly identifies the standard of review for this ordinance.

The ordinance is facially neutral since it does not, in its text, single out women for disparate treatment. The issue is whether the fact that the disparate effect that the law has on women, based on their percentage of the child-care workforce, renders the ordinance unconstitutional. Absent evidence that the city *intended* to discriminate against women, this licensing scheme will not be subject to any heightened level of review. Accordingly, a court will assess the ordinance under rationality review and uphold it unless it is not rationally related to a legitimate government interest. Since the protection of children is a legitimate city interest and the city could rationally believe that the licensing requirements will help further that interest, the ordinance is constitutional.

(A) is not the best response,

because disparate impact, standing alone, does not cause a court to use a heightened level of review.

In order to trigger a heightened level of scrutiny, as implied by choice A, a government action that has disparate impact on women must constitute sex discrimination. However, *disparate impact*, absent *intent* to discriminate, does not rise to the level of sex discrimination. Accordingly, a court assessing the constitutionality of this ordinance will apply rational basis review and will uphold the statute if it is rationally related to a legitimate government interest.

(B) is not the best response,

because freedom to contract is not a fundamental right triggering heightened scrutiny.

Although this regulation will restrict the caregivers' ability to contract freely for their babysitting services, a court assessing the constitutionality of the ordinance will apply rationality review because the freedom to contract is not a fundamental right. If you chose this response, you were probably thinking of the Constitution's Contracts Clause, which bars the government from passing laws that retroactively affect existing contractual rights. Since the effect of this ordinance will only be felt prospectively, the Contracts Clause is not implicated.

(C) is not the best response,

because a burden-balancing test is the incorrect method of review for this ordinance.

The proper level of review in this case is rational basis review. The issue is whether the fact that the disparate effect that the law has on women, based on their percentage of the child-care workforce, renders the ordinance unconstitutional. Absent evidence that the city intended to discriminate against women, this licensing scheme will not be subject to any heightened level of review. Accordingly, a court will assess the ordinance under rationality review and uphold it unless it is not rationally related to a legitimate government interest. Since the protection of children is a legitimate city interest and the city could rationally believe that the licensing requirements will help further that interest, the ordinance is constitutional.

Answer 52

(A) is the best response,

because the purchase of cars is a commercial activity.

For a congressional statute to be constitutional, it must be enacted pursuant to one of Congress's enumerated powers under Article I of the Constitution. Choice A identifies the Commerce Clause as the source of the power to enact this statute. Under the Commerce Clause (Article I, § 8, cl. 3), Congress has the power to "regulate commerce with foreign nations, and among the several states." Congress's powers under the Commerce Clause are read quite broadly by courts, and on the MBE it should always be the first of the enumerated powers you consider when approaching a problem. Here, the statute falls within the commerce power because the large-scale purchase of cars has a significant effect on interstate commerce.

Now, what about the Tenth Amendment? Essentially the only real-world effect of the Tenth Amendment is to prohibit the federal government from commandeering the lawmaking power of state or local legislatures. So, for example, Congress could not pass an act requiring all of the states to pass laws mandating the purchase of electric cars. However, the directive in this statute is generally applicable since it applies to all owners of large fleets of cars, not only to governmental owners. Since it is a direct regulation that is generally applicable, and does not commandeer the legislative function of the local government, it does not violate the Tenth Amendment.

(B) is not the best response,

because the city is seeking an injunction.

The federal government has sovereign immunity from suits seeking compensatory damages. However, there is no bar against a plaintiff seeking injunctive relief against the federal government or its officers. Here, we are told that the city "sought an *injunction* prohibiting enforcement of the statute." Since the city is not seeking monetary relief, its suit is not barred by the federal government's sovereign immunity.

(C) is not the best response,

because the statute is applicable to both private and governmental entities.

Essentially the only real-world effect of the Tenth Amendment is to prohibit the federal government from commandeering the lawmaking power of state or local legislatures. So, for example, Congress could not pass an act requiring all of the states to pass laws mandating the purchase of electric cars. However, the directive in this statute is generally applicable since it applies to all owners of large fleets of cars, not only to governmental owners. Since it is a direct regulation that is generally applicable, and does not commandeer the legislative function of the local government, it does not violate the Tenth Amendment.

(D) is not the best response,

because this exercise of commerce power is not in violation of the Tenth Amendment.

The Tenth Amendment reserves to the states all legislative power not specifically provided to the federal government in the Constitution. However, the commerce power is a specifically enumerated power of Congress (Article I, § 8, cl. 3). Essentially the only real-world effect of the Tenth Amendment is to prohibit the federal government from commandeering the lawmaking power of state or local legislatures, but that has not occurred in this situation. The directive in this statute is generally applicable since it applies to all owners of large fleets of cars, not only to governmental owners. Since it is a direct regulation that is generally applicable and does not commandeer the legislative function of the local government, it does not violate the Tenth Amendment.

STRATEGIES AND TACTICS

CONTRACTS

Contracts and Sales questions are alike in every way on the MBE except one: the ***source of law*** involved. Contracts questions rely on the common law, but Sales questions rely on the UCC. Because of their similarities, we'll address them together here. For simplicity, we'll use "Contracts" to refer to both Contracts and Sales.

OUTLINE OF COVERAGE

You should be familiar with the provisions of Articles 1 and 2 of the Uniform Commercial Code (UCC) and assume that they have been adopted for the purpose of answering Contracts questions on the MBE. As we'll discuss below, approximately 25 percent of the Contracts questions on the MBE will involve the UCC.

The following outline of coverage for the Contracts portion of the MBE was adopted by the Bar Examiners for all MBEs given on or after February 2016. It was designed to clarify what's covered on the Contracts portion of the exam. This is the most up-to-date outline of coverage released by the Bar Examiners, and your substantive study for Contracts should be focused on this outline.

Here's what you need to know:

I. Formation of contracts
   A. Mutual assent
      1. Offer and acceptance
      2. Indefiniteness or absence of terms
      3. Implied-in-fact contract
      4. "Pre-contract" obligations based on reliance
   B. Consideration
      1. Bargain and exchange and substitutes for bargain: "moral obligation," reliance, and statutory substitutes
      2. Modification of contracts: preexisting duties
      3. Compromise and settlement of claims
II. Defenses to enforceability
   A. Incapacity to contract
   B. Duress
   C. Undue influence
   D. Mistake, misunderstanding
   E. Fraud, misrepresentation, and nondisclosure
   F. Illegality, unconscionability, and public policy
   G. Statute of frauds
III. Parol evidence and interpretation
IV. Performance, breach, and discharge
   A. Conditions
      1. Express
      2. Constructive
      3. Obligations of good faith and fair dealing in performance and enforcement of contracts
      4. Suspension or excuse of conditions by waiver, election, or estoppel
      5. Prospective inability to perform: effect on other party
   B. Impracticability and frustration of purpose
   C. Discharge of contractual duties
   D. Express and implied warranties in sale-of-goods contracts
   E. Substantial and partial breach and anticipatory repudiation

V. Remedies
   A. Measure of damages for breach; protecting the expectation interest
   B. Consequential damages: causation, certainty, and foreseeability
   C. Liquidated damages and penalties
   D. Avoidable consequences and mitigation of damages
   E. Rescission and reformation
   F. Specific performance; injunction against breach; declaratory judgment
   G. Restitutionary and reliance recoveries
   H. Remedial rights of breaching parties
VI. Third-party rights
   A. Third-party beneficiaries
      1. Intended beneficiaries
      2. Incidental beneficiaries
      3. Impairment or extinguishment of third-party rights
      4. Enforcement by the promise
   B. Assignment of rights and delegation of duties

WHAT TO EXPECT

There will be about 29 or 30 questions on Contracts on the MBE (though only 28 will be scored, and you won't know which ones won't). Approximately 50 percent of the questions will cover categories I and IV above (Formation of Contracts; Performance, Breach and Discharge), and approximately 50 percent will cover the remaining categories.

Important note: Remember that ***approximately 25 percent*** of the Contracts questions on each MBE will be based on the UCC, Articles 1 and 2 (in other words, they'll be Sales questions).

Types of questions

You should also be aware that you may be asked many types of contract questions. These include:

1. Plaintiff's or defendant's best argument or theory for recovery
2. How contractual terms should be construed (e.g., as conditions)
3. How to characterize facts (e.g., if certain acts constitute an offer, acceptance, contract)
4. Whether plaintiff will succeed
5. Legal effect of additional facts
6. If court decides for a specified party, the reason why
7. How a goal could be accomplished (e.g., offer accepted or revoked)
8. Which of two or three alternatives are correct, or would influence the outcome of the case

STUDY STRATEGIES

1. Common law vs. UCC.

Remember the ***distinctions between the common law and the UCC.*** For example, look at the subject of contract ***modifications:*** At common law, modifications require consideration. Under the UCC, modifications require only good faith. ***Irrevocable offers*** are also different under common law and the UCC. At common law, an offer can be made irrevocable only with consideration; in general, the offeree must pay for the irrevocability and thus create an option contract. Under the UCC, merchants (not non-merchants) can make irrevocable, or "firm," offers without consideration, so long as the offers are in writing and signed. A firm offer made under this rule cannot be made irrevocable for a period longer than three months.

Another difference to watch for is ***delays.*** At common law, a reasonable delay is only a minor breach of contract unless the contract provides that time is of the essence—or unless the breaching party knew, when the contract was created, of some extraordinary fact that made the deadline essential. If time is of the essence, any delay is a major breach (the difference being that, with a minor breach, the other party must perform and sue for damages; with a major breach, the other party needn't perform and can still sue for damages). Under the UCC's "perfect tender" rule, every deadline must be met precisely, and any delay is a major breach. Note, however, that the exceptions to the UCC rule make it considerably less harsh in practice (e.g., with notice to the buyer, a seller can cure defective performance if there's time left for performance; also, even if the time for performance has passed, the seller can still cure if the buyer rejected a non-conforming tender that the seller had reasonable grounds to believe the buyer would accept. UCC § 2-508(2)).

These kinds of distinctions are easy to overlook and are, thus, attractive targets for MBE questions.

2. Unilateral vs. bilateral contracts.

In real life, an offeror rarely desires ***only*** a unilateral contract; almost every contract offer could be interpreted as seeking a bilateral contract, as well. Remember, however, that you're preparing not only for real life but also for the MBE; you will need to know and apply the distinctions between offers for bilateral and for unilateral contracts:

- ➡ An offer for a bilateral contract seeks a promise in return, not performance. The offer is accepted when the offeree provides a return promise.
- ➡ An offer for a unilateral contract seeks performance in return, not a promise.

As an example, let's talk about a typical reward offer. The offeror isn't interested in obtaining a promise from someone that he'll perform some act (such as, "I promise I'll try to find your dog if you pay me the reward"); the offeror is interested only in the performance (the actual return of the dog, instead of a promise to look). Thus, a reward offeror must be seeking a unilateral contract. (Incidentally, the modern view is that the offeree need only complete performance with knowledge of a reward offer (or a public offer of any kind), in order to earn the reward. Contrast this with the traditional rule—that the public offer must have provoked the offeree's performance.)

Look at another example: Say that an offeror states, "I'll pay you $50 if you paint my house." Because either a promise to paint or the actual painting of the house would suffice, this offer could be interpreted as seeking either a bilateral or a unilateral contract. When in doubt, a court will construe an offer as a bilateral offer.

Here's a less obvious example from the MBE:

> A doctor and a lawyer, who lived in different suburbs twenty miles apart, were golfing acquaintances at a country club. The doctor wrote to the lawyer by U.S. mail on Friday, October 8:
>
> > I need a motorcycle for transportation to the country club, and will buy your Suzuki for $1,200 upon your bringing it to my home address above [stated in the letterhead] on or before noon, November 12 next. This offer is not subject to countermand.
> >
> > Sincerely,
> >
> > [signed by the doctor]
>
> The lawyer replied by mail the following day:
>
> > I accept your offer, and promise to deliver the bike as you specified.
> >
> > Sincerely,
> >
> > [signed by the lawyer]
>
> This letter, although properly addressed, was misdirected by the postal service and not received by the doctor until November 10. The doctor had bought a different Suzuki bike, from a farmer, for $1,050 a few hours before.
>
> The farmer saw the lawyer at the country club on November 11 and mentioned in passing: "I sold my Suzuki to [the doctor] yesterday for $1,050."
>
> On November 12, the lawyer took his Suzuki to the doctor's residence; he arrived at 11:15 a.m. The doctor was asleep and did not answer the lawyer's doorbell rings until 12:15 p.m. The doctor then rejected the lawyer's bike on the ground that he had already bought the farmer's.
>
> In a lawsuit by the lawyer against the doctor for breach of contract, what would the court probably decide regarding the lawyer's letter of October 9?
>
> A. The letter bound both parties to a unilateral contract as soon as the lawyer mailed it.
> B. Mailing of the letter by the lawyer did not, of itself, prevent a subsequent, effective revocation by the doctor of his offer.
> C. The letter bound both parties to a bilateral contract, but only when received by the doctor on November 10.
> D. Regardless of whether the doctor's offer had proposed a unilateral or a bilateral contract, the letter was an effective acceptance upon receipt, if not upon dispatch.

Look at the doctor's original letter. He didn't say, "I'll buy your Suzuki for $1,200 if you promise to bring it to my home address. . . . " He was looking only for performance in return: the lawyer's bringing the Suzuki to the doctor's house before noon on November 12. Since the doctor was seeking ***return performance,*** he made an offer for a unilateral contract; thus, the lawyer's ***promise*** to perform couldn't constitute acceptance—the lawyer could accept the offer only by performing. As a result, the lawyer's promise was meaningless, so the unaccepted offer remained revocable (and was revoked when the lawyer learned from the farmer that the doctor had bought another Suzuki, thus behaving inconsistently with the offer remaining open). (Choice B recognizes this, making it the best response.)

3. Issues of consideration.

A. Consideration itself.

Let's get back to basics for a minute. Any enforceable agreement requires consideration or a substitute for consideration (such as promissory estoppel). You also undoubtedly remember the definition of consideration: a bargained-for exchange, plus either detriment to the promisee or benefit to the promisor (and typically both).

The key here is the ***bargain.*** Both parties must view the return promise (or performance) as the "price" of the contract. If they don't, there's no consideration.

The most important function of the "bargain" element is that ***it makes promises to make a gift unenforceable.*** The best way to distinguish a gift from a bargain is to look at whether or not the promisor is ***getting something in return*** for his/her promise or action. If not, then it's a gift, and the promise is unenforceable (unless promissory estoppel applies (see item **D,** below)).

B. Consideration in the form of surrendering a legal claim.

Okay, here's the situation. Larry and Curly are painters. In a fit, Larry hits Curly on the head with a paintbrush. Curly threatens to sue Larry for assault and battery. Larry tells him, "If you promise not to sue me, I'll give you $500." Curly agrees. Consideration for the agreement? Curly's surrendering his claim! It was bargained for, and it constitutes a detriment to him (as promisee) and a benefit to Larry (as promisor). That's pretty straightforward.

What's trickier is the situation where the claim is ***invalid.*** Although it seems strange, surrendering an invalid claim can ***still*** be consideration, if two requirements are met:

1. A reasonable person could believe the claim is well-founded; and
2. The claim could be pursued in good faith.

Note that the mindset of the one who's surrendering the claim is all-important ***and that the other party's belief is irrelevant.*** Say Curly's claim against Larry is no good, but Curly reasonably believes it's valid even though Larry believes it isn't. Larry's belief is unimportant, since the two requirements for consideration—reasonableness and good faith—are met. If the situation were ***reversed***—that is, it's reasonable to believe the claim is well-founded, Larry believes it's good, but Curly knows it isn't—there's ***no consideration,*** since Curly, knowing the claim is invalid, couldn't pursue it in good faith. Here's another example, this time from the MBE:

> A man and a woman owned adjoining residences. In 2009, they hired the same contractor to lay sidewalks in front of both of their homes. Each owner was to pay the contractor for that part of the work attributable to his or her property. In early 2010, after the man had paid the bill which the contractor had submitted to him, the man became convinced that the contractor had erred and had charged him for labor and materials which were used for part of the sidewalk in front of the woman's property. In reality, the contractor had made no error, and the man had paid only for labor and materials for the walk in front of his own property.
>
> Still in early 2010, the man asked the woman to reimburse him for the amount which the man believed he had erroneously paid the contractor. After a lengthy discussion, and although she was still convinced that she owed the man nothing, the woman finally said: "I want to avoid trouble, and so if you agree not to sue for reimbursement, I'll employ a handyman to keep our sidewalks free of ice and snow for this November and December plus for November/December of next year."
>
> Although she could have hired the man for two seasons, the woman hired a handyman only for November and December of 2010. During the early fall of 2011, the woman decided to go to Florida for the winter.
>
> During November and December of 2011, the man noticed that no one was shoveling the ice and snow in front of either property. Therefore, the man kept his own walks clean. In early 2012, the man sued

the woman for breach of her promise to have the walks cleaned for the prior November and December, seeking the fair value of that work. Will the man prevail?

A. Yes, because the man reasonably believed that he was settling a valid claim for reimbursement against the woman.
B. No, because the woman did not believe that what she was settling was a valid claim by the man.
C. No, because the man's claim was in fact invalid.
D. No, because the woman's promise to employ the caretaker was aleatory.

If you apply the rule on invalid claims, you can see that it's the man's belief in the validity of his own claim that counts, as long as it's reasonable for him to believe the claim is valid. Both of these requirements for consideration are satisfied here, regardless of what the woman believes. Thus, the correct response is A.

C. Consideration in a unilateral contract.

Remember that, in a unilateral contract, the offeror seeks return performance, not a return promise. Under such circumstances, it can be difficult to figure out the consideration for the agreement. In fact, the consideration is the offeree's performance. That's all there is to it.

D. Promissory estoppel.

An agreement can be enforceable without consideration as long as there's a substitute for consideration—typically, promissory estoppel. Promissory estoppel is a last resort. It can act as a substitute for consideration in order to avoid injustice. It's triggered by a gratuitous promise that is likely to, and does, induce the promisee's reliance. It's not true consideration, because there's no bargain, but it does result in the promise's being ***enforceable.*** The most important thing to remember is that the ***lack of an otherwise enforceable contract*** is a prerequisite for promissory estoppel; if there's an enforceable contractual promise, there ***can't*** be promissory estoppel!

E. Quasi-contract.

Quasi-contract, like promissory estoppel, requires that there be ***no enforceable contract.*** If there ***is*** one, quasi-contract can't apply.

Courts typically apply quasi-contract rules if a plaintiff has conferred a benefit on the defendant under circumstances where the defendant would be ***unjustly enriched*** if he were allowed to retain the benefit without paying for it. Thus, once you've established that there's no enforceable contract, you have to determine if there's unjust enrichment. If you find enrichment, but it's not unjust, you can't have a quasi-contractual recovery. Keep in mind, also, that there can't be unjust enrichment if the performing party suffered no detriment.

4. Conditions.

The bar exam frequently tests conditions, because it's easy to confuse the different types. Remember the basic definition of a condition: an event, other than the mere passage of time, that triggers, limits, or extinguishes an absolute duty to perform of one party to a contract.

There are two different ways to categorize conditions. The first is to categorize them according to how the condition came about; there are three types: ***express, implied,*** and ***constructive*** conditions. The most important thing to remember here is the level of compliance required by each type. If a condition is ***express***—that is, the parties explicitly included it in the contract—the parties must ***comply strictly*** with the terms of that condition. Substantial performance won't suffice, so, if there's substantial, but not complete, performance, the nonbreaching party doesn't have to perform at all. On the other hand, with implied and constructive conditions, substantial performance is sufficient. (Note that if performance isn't complete, the other party will still have to pay the contract price, but may deduct his actual damages from it.)

The second way to categorize conditions is by the time of performance. This is the part of the law of conditions that you're likely to find confusing. There are two important categories here: ***conditions precedent and conditions concurrent.*** (Conditions subsequent rarely figure on the MBE.) We'll look at each one separately.

A. Conditions precedent.

A condition precedent is an event or act that must occur first in order to trigger a party's absolute duty of performance. These are easy to spot. Just ask this question: Is there an enforceable duty before the required event happens? If you answer no, that's a condition precedent. For example, let's say I tell you, "If the Yankees make it to the World Series, I'll buy your tickets for $500." You agree. Ask yourself, do I owe you any duty if the Yankees don't make it to the World Series? No. Thus, the Yankees making it to the World Series is a ***condition precedent*** to my duty to perform (and to your duty to tender tickets, as well). The Yankees making it to the World Series triggers my duty to pay, as well as your duty to tender tickets.

B. Concurrent conditions.

Concurrent conditions exist where each party's duty to perform is conditioned on the other party's performance. Say, for instance, Laurel offers to sell Hardy his piano for $200. Hardy agrees. Hardy's tendering the piano is a condition to Laurel's duty to pay; Laurel's tendering the $200 is a condition to Hardy's duty to hand over the piano. The thing to remember about concurrent conditions is that they have to be capable of simultaneous performance. With the Laurel and Hardy agreement, this requirement is satisfied, since a transfer is physically possible, and the parties didn't provide for any special order of performance.

Let's change the facts: Say Dorothy agrees to whitewash Auntie Em's fence for $100. Whitewashing the fence and tendering the cash can't be concurrent conditions, because they can't be accomplished at the same time. Whitewashing the fence will always take longer (even with a very small fence!) than handing over cash will take. (In fact, because Dorothy's performance will take time to complete and Em's won't, Dorothy's performance would impliedly have to precede Em's duty to perform—that is, Dorothy's performance would be an implied condition precedent to Em's duty to perform. If Dorothy doesn't perform, Em has no duty to pay.)

Let's change the facts again: Say David agrees to sell his golden gun to Glenn for $1,000. David is to deliver the gun on February 1, and Glenn is to pay on February 15. No concurrent conditions here, since the parties can't perform simultaneously. But say, instead, that the two make no provision about when Glenn is to pay; they provide only that David is to deliver the gun on February 1. A court would imply concurrent conditions, because time is set for one performance—David's—and the parties ***can*** perform simultaneously. Finally, assume no time is set for either party to perform (this is analogous to the original Laurel and Hardy example, where performance could be simultaneous)—there would be implied concurrent conditions.

5. Interpretation.

Some MBE questions require you to interpret contract provisions. The general rule is that contract terms are to be interpreted ***objectively***, by determining what interpretation a reasonable person, knowing the same things that the parties know, would place on the terms. You want to avoid any extraordinary or unusually strict interpretation of contract language. Here's an example:

> A teacher applied for a life insurance policy. In the application, the teacher answered in the negative the question, "Have you ever had any heart disease?" Both the application and the insurance policy that was issued provided: "Applicant warrants the truthfulness of the statements made in the application and they are made conditions to the contract of insurance." Unknown to the teacher, she had had heart disease at a very early age. The teacher died of a sudden (and unforeseeable) heart attack two months after the policy was issued. The insurer refused to pay. The teacher's personal representative sued the insurer on the policy, and the insurer defended on the grounds that the policy was unenforceable because the teacher had made a material false statement in the application. The court will probably decide that
>
> A. the clause is a condition, and because the condition was not met, the company is not liable.
> B. the clause is a condition, but it should be interpreted to mean, "truthfulness to the best of my knowledge."
> C. the clause is not a condition, and therefore the company will be liable even though the teacher's statement was not true.
> D. the clause is not a condition but is a promise, and therefore the company will have a cause of action against the teacher's estate for any losses it suffered because of the teacher's misstatement.

Here, it wouldn't be reasonable for the insurance company to expect people to disclose diseases they didn't know about, so a court would adopt a ***reasonable*** interpretation of the clause and require truthfulness only to the best of an applicant's knowledge. That makes B the best response.

6. The Statute of Frauds.

If a contract falls within the Statute of Frauds (SOF), it must be ***in writing*** to be enforceable. Thus, the first thing you have to know is which kinds of contracts are covered by the SOF; then, when you encounter a problem on the MBE in which the enforceability of an oral contract is in question, check it against your list of SOF rules ***methodically.*** Overcome the temptation to put contracts ***within*** the SOF even though they don't belong there. If a contract doesn't fall within the SOF, it's enforceable even though it's oral. That's all there is to it.

The SOF coverage varies from state to state, but here are seven basic types of contracts that generally fall within the SOF (of course, an MBE question could offer a Statute of its own, and that statute could vary from the usual SOF):

1. Contracts of ***suretyship*** (i.e., a contract to answer for another's debt or default—a guarantee of performance);
2. Contracts for the ***sale of an interest in land*** (including leases of one year or longer);
3. Contracts for the ***sale of goods worth more than $500*** (UCC § 2-201) (except specially manufactured goods, or where there is partial performance);
4. Contracts that ***cannot possibly be performed within a year;***
5. Contracts for the sale of securities (UCC § 8-319);
6. Regardless of cost, contracts for the sale of personal property other than goods with a value of more than $5,000, e.g., royalty rights (UCC § 1-206); and
7. Contracts in consideration of marriage.

Here's a mnemonic to help you remember this list: **MP SIGNS** (**M**arriage; **P**ersonal property more than $5,000; **S**uretyship; **I**nterest in land; **G**oods more than $500; **N**ot performable within a year; **S**ecurities). Of these seven types, only numbers 1 through 4 appear with regularity on the MBE.

You also need to know when the need for a writing will be excused. At common law, there are five circumstances under which a contract within the SOF will be enforceable even without a writing:

1. Full performance by both sides;
2. Seller conveys property to buyer;
3. Buyer pays all or part of the purchase price AND performs some act explainable only by the contract's existence (e.g., constructing buildings on land);
4. Promissory estoppel; and
5. Waiver (e.g., by not affirmatively pleading the Statute of Frauds as a defense).

Under the UCC, courts will excuse the necessity for a writing under several circumstances. Where a transaction in goods is involved, part performance removes the writing requirement (but only to the extent of the actual performance), as does an admission in court by the party denying the contract's existence. In addition, specially manufactured goods don't require a writing once the seller has begun manufacture or made commitments to procure the goods (§ 2-201(3)(a)) and a letter of confirmation can also satisfy the SOF if the transaction is between merchants.

You should also remember the "main purpose" exception to the SOF as regards contracts of suretyship (where one person promises to pay for the debts of another): if the surety's ***main purpose*** is to further his ***own interest,*** then the promise does ***not*** fall within the SOF.

Here's an example of a Statute of Frauds issue from the MBE:

> In September 2010, a student, 23 years old and unmarried, was beginning his third year of law school. One night that month, the student called his father and told him that he did not have the money with which to pay his tuition for the second semester or any spending money. The student's father told the student that if he agreed not to marry until he finished law school, he would pay his tuition and $200 a month spending money until the student graduated. The student, who was engaged to be married at that time, agreed that he would not marry until after he graduated.
>
> The student's father died suddenly on January 26. The student did not marry and graduated from law school. His father had previously paid the student's tuition for the spring semester, but had paid no spending money to the student. The student's claim against his father's estate having been denied by the executor, the student brought suit against the estate in June 2011, asking for a judgment of $800 ($200 spending money for each of the months, February through May). In this action, the student probably will be
>
> A. successful.
> B. unsuccessful, because his contract with his father was illegal.
> C. unsuccessful, because the father's death terminated the offer.
> D. unsuccessful, because his contract with his father was not in writing and signed by the father.

The specific agreement on which the student is suing—the $200-per-month spending money—doesn't fit into any of the SOF categories—not even the "made in consideration of marriage" category, because this promise was to delay marriage. (A contract in consideration of marriage would arise, say, if the student had promised to pay his fiancee's tuition if she agreed to marry him.) Because the student's agreement isn't covered by the SOF, it's enforceable without a writing, so choice D can't be right. That's all there is to the SOF analysis. (Choice A is the best response.)

Remember, even if a contract fails for non-compliance with the SOF, a party may be entitled to quasi-contractual recovery for the reasonable value of his part performance, and to restitution of any other benefits he may have conferred.

7. Third-party beneficiaries.

If the promisee of a contractual promise intends that her performance should benefit someone outside the contract, that other person is called the "intended third-party beneficiary." As you know, only intended, not incidental, beneficiaries have enforceable rights. Remember, though, that a beneficiary's rights aren't enforceable until those rights vest. Why is that a big deal? Because, before that, the parties to the contract can modify or even rescind it ***without regard to the beneficiary.*** Once the rights vest, however, any modification ***requires the beneficiary's consent.***

Traditionally, determining when the beneficiary's rights vest depends on whether a beneficiary is a creditor beneficiary or a donee beneficiary; most modern courts, however, agree with the Rest. 2d of Contracts § 311, which ignores the donee/creditor distinction and views the beneficiary's rights as vesting when one of three events occurs:

1. The beneficiary manifests assent to the promise;
2. The beneficiary sues to enforce the promise; or
3. The beneficiary justifiably relies on the promise to his detriment.

Remember, the ***third-party beneficiary's rights can't vest until he knows about the contract.*** Thus, before a third-party beneficiary finds out about a contract, it can be modified or rescinded, with no regard for the beneficiary's rights.

8. Assignment and delegation.

You need to remember two things about assignment and delegation: first, what can/can't be assigned or delegated; second, the effect of contract prohibitions on assignment and delegation.

A. Assignment—what *can* be assigned.

Under both the common law and the UCC, the only rights that ***can't*** be assigned are those that would materially change the other party's duty, risk, or chance of receiving return performance. That includes things like personal services, rights under future contracts, requirements and output contracts, and assignments contrary to public policy (such as government pensions and alimony payments). All other rights can be assigned.

B. Delegation—what can be delegated.

Determining which duties can be delegated is a bit more complicated. The easiest way to do this is with a two-tier analysis:

1. Ask if the duty is "impersonal." If not—it can't be delegated.

   An "impersonal" duty is one in which the one receiving performance has no particular interest in limiting performance only to the one from whom he expected performance. Personal duties include services of people like lawyers, doctors, architects, and portrait painters—where the identity of the person performing the duty matters.
2. If you determine that the duty is impersonal, ask if the delegation ***materially alters*** the nature of the performance or the risks and burdens to the party who would receive the performance. If not—it's delegable.

Keep in mind that an "assignment of the contract" ***impliedly*** includes a delegation of duties as well, unless circumstances suggest otherwise (e.g., the contract is only assigned as security for a loan, which would indicate that the duties weren't delegated as part of the assignment of the contract). Unless the obligee expressly agrees to release the delegator (a "novation"), the delegator remains liable to the obligee even after delegating his duties under the contract.

C. Contract prohibitions on assignments and delegations.

The rules in (A) and (B) on assignments and delegations apply when the contract contains nothing ***preventing*** transfer. A contract prohibition throws a wrench into the works, but exactly what the prohibition does is totally dependent on how the prohibition is worded. Look at these examples:

1. **"Assignment of rights under this contracted is prohibited," or similar language.**

The assignment is valid. The other party can sue only for damages for breach of covenant.

Note that, under the UCC § 9-406(d), assignment of the right to receive payment generally ***cannot*** be prohibited (and any prohibition is invalid).

2. **"Assignment of rights under this contract is void," or similar language.**

The assignment is voidable at the other party's option. Note that, under the UCC § 9-406(d), assignment of the right to receive payment generally cannot be prohibited (and any prohibition is invalid).

3. **The contract prohibits assignment "of the contract."**

This bars only delegation of duties, not assignment of rights. Although such provisions are upheld, they are narrowly construed. UCC § 2-210(4) and common law.

9. Integration and the parol evidence rule.

These two concepts are flip sides of the same coin: In order to determine if the parol evidence rule bars evidence of contract terms, you have to determine if the contract is "completely integrated."

Under the parol evidence rule, a writing that is "completely integrated" cannot be contradicted or supplemented by prior written or oral agreements, or by contemporaneous oral agreements. A "completely integrated" agreement is one that the parties intended to be a ***final and complete statement*** of their agreement.

You need to know two things here: first, what the exceptions to parol evidence are, and second, what happens if an agreement ***isn't*** completely integrated.

First—the exceptions: The parol evidence rule doesn't bar evidence of defects in contract formation, such as lack of consideration, fraud, and duress. Also, when a contract's effectiveness is subject to an oral or earlier written ***condition*** (e.g., "This construction contract will not be binding on either party until Owner's architect approves Builder's plans"), the parol evidence rule doesn't bar proof of the condition's existence.

Second—the ramifications of an incomplete, or partial, integration: A partially integrated agreement is one that doesn't reflect the ***complete*** agreement of the parties. Even if a court determines that a contract is only partially integrated, though, it's not open season on evidence of other terms. The written agreement will be considered final as to the terms it states, but the agreement may be ***supplemented*** by consistent, additional terms. Say, for example, that Bluto agrees to loan Wimpy $500, at 15 percent interest, to buy hamburgers, with a due date of Tuesday on the loan. They reduce the agreement to a writing that mentions their names, the amount, and the term of the loan, but not the interest rate. They couldn't have intended the writing to reflect their complete agreement, because they agreed on interest, and it's not in the writing. Thus, the agreement can be only partially integrated (assuming they intended it to be final as to the terms it ***does*** state). If they end up in court, either one can offer evidence, in the form of oral testimony or other notes, as to their agreement on the interest rate, since that's a consistent additional term. They could not, however, dispute the amount of the loan, since that was fully integrated in the writing and thus can't be contradicted.

In real life, there are several different, rather complex, rules for determining if an agreement is "completely integrated." On the MBE, your job is made easier by the limited number of answer choices. Typically, the examiners will set up the problem so that you ***don't have to decide whether the integration is total.*** For instance, if a party wants to prove an oral term that flatly ***contradicts*** a written term, you don't have to worry about whether the integration is partial or total, because *in either case* the contradictory oral term can't be proved.

Here is an example from the MBE:

> A corporation, through its president, requested from a bank a short-term loan of $100,000. On April 1, the president and the bank's loan officer agreed orally that the bank would make the loan to the corporation on the following terms: (1) the loan would be repaid in full on or before the following July 1 and would carry interest at an annual rate of 15 percent (a lawful rate under the applicable usury law); and (2) the president would personally guarantee repayment. The loan was approved and made on April 5. The only document evidencing the loan was a memorandum, written and supplied by the bank and signed by the president on behalf of the corporation, that read in its entirety:
>
> April 5
>
> In consideration of a loan advanced on this date, [the corporation] hereby promises to pay [the bank] $100,000 on September 1.
>
> [the corporation]
>
> by /s/ [the president]

The corporation did not repay the loan on or before July 1, although it had sufficient funds to do so. On July 10, the bank sued the corporation as principal debtor and the president individually as guarantor for $100,000, plus 15 percent interest from April 5.

At the trial, can the bank prove the president's oral commitment to repay the loan on or before July 1?

A. Yes, because the oral agreement was supported by an independent consideration.
B. Yes, because the evidence of the parties' negotiations is relevant to their contractual intent concerning maturity of the debt.
C. No, because such evidence is barred by the preexisting duty rule.
D. No, because such evidence contradicts the writing and is barred by the parol evidence rule.

Here, the element the bank wants to prove ***directly contradicts*** a term in the written agreement—the due date of the loan. Therefore, it doesn't matter whether the agreement is fully or partially integrated—no evidence will be admitted on the matter. D is, therefore, the best answer.

EXAM TACTICS

1. **Once you've determined that a question is Contracts-oriented, check immediately to see if a transaction in goods is involved.**

If the facts involve a transaction in goods, UCC Article 2 applies. You need to make this distinction early, because, when a question addresses an issue on which the common law and the UCC differ, one of the incorrect answers will inevitably try to mislead you by addressing the rule from the law that ***doesn't*** apply. Remember, approximately one in every four Contracts questions will involve a transaction in goods! Here's an example from the MBE showing the importance of noticing whether the UCC applies:

On May 1, a landowner telegraphed an investor, "Will sell you any or all of the lots in Grove subdivision at $5,000 each. Details follow in letter." The letter contained all the necessary details concerning terms of payment, insurance, mortgages, etc., and provided, "This offer remains open until June 1." On May 2, after the investor had received the telegram but before he had received the letter, the investor telegraphed the landowner, "Accept your offer with respect to lot 101." Both parties knew that there were 50 lots in the Grove subdivision and that they were numbered 101 through 150.

On May 3, the landowner telephoned the investor, saying that because he had just discovered that a shopping center was going to be erected adjacent to the Grove subdivision, he would "have to have $6,000 for each of the lots, including lot 101." During the telephone call, the investor agreed to pay him $6,000 for lot 101. On May 6, the investor telegraphed, "Accept your offer with respect to the rest of the lots." Assuming that contracts were formed covering all 50 lots, and that there is no controlling statute, the investor will most likely be required to pay

A. only $5,000 for each of the 50 lots.
B. only $5,000 for lot 101, but $6,000 for the remaining 49 lots.
C. $6,000 for each of the 50 lots.
D. $6,000 for lot 101, but only $5,000 for the remaining 49 lots.

If you failed to determine that the common law applies here, because this is a sale of an interest in land, you might mistakenly apply the UCC and select choice C, which reflects the UCC rule on modifications—that no consideration is required for modifications as long as they are made in good faith. UCC § 2-209. (Remember, the parties were modifying a pre-existing deal on lot 101.) The UCC, Article 2, can't apply here because there's ***no transaction in goods.*** The correct answer is B, which reflects the common law "pre-existing" duty rule as to modifications, that modifications require consideration. The deal for Lot 101 was already done, with no consideration offered by the landowner in return for the higher price on it, making the investor's promise to pay the extra $1000 for that lot unenforceable.

In fact, you should spot yet another common law/UCC difference here: At common law, an irrevocable offer requires consideration in order to make it a valid "option"; under the UCC, § 2-205, merchants can make irrevocable, or "firm," offers, without consideration, as long as the offer is embodied in a signed writing. Under these facts, then, the landowner's letter didn't create an irrevocable offer. (If you mistakenly applied the UCC as to this element, you'd have picked choice A).

2. **Read the facts *very carefully*.**

Although this statement is true of every MBE question, it's especially true for Contracts and Sales questions.

3. Find that a contract exists, wherever possible.

Traditionally, a contract requires an offer, acceptance, and consideration (or some consideration substitute). If a contract exists, then concepts like promissory estoppel and quasi-contract don't apply, and you have to analyze the problem under the contract: What are the parties' duties, what relieves those duties, what triggers them, etc.

4. Pay attention when you're told a seemingly meaningless detail about someone.

In most MBE questions, you're not told anything about the parties except their gender, their occupation, and their family relation to each other (if any). If a question *does* tell you something more, *watch out*—those facts are almost always relevant to the status of the person described. Here's an example from the MBE:

> In a telephone call on March 1, a retired man who had previously been a farmer said to a young woman who ran a jewelry business, "I will sell my automobile for $3,000 cash. I will hold this offer open through March 14." On March 12, the man called the woman and told her that he had sold the automobile to someone else, an accountant. The man in fact had not sold the automobile to anyone. On March 14, the woman learned that the man still owned the automobile, and on that date called the man and said, "I'm coming over to your place with $3,000." The man replied, "Don't bother, I won't deliver the automobile to you under any circumstances." The woman protested, but made no further attempt to pay for or take delivery of the automobile.
>
> In an action by the woman against the man for breach of contract, the woman probably will
>
> A. succeed, because the man had assured her that the offer would remain open through March 14.
> E. succeed, because the man had not in fact sold the automobile to the accountant.
> F. not succeed, because the woman had not tendered the $3,000 to the man on or before March 14.
> G. not succeed, because on March 12 the man had told the woman that he had sold the automobile to the accountant.

Here, the first thing you're told is that the man is "retired." This is certainly out of the ordinary as descriptions on the MBE go—and, in fact, it's significant. As you know, where the sale of goods is concerned, only a merchant in those types of goods can make an offer irrevocable without consideration. When the question tells you that the man is retired, it's really telling you that he's ***not a merchant.*** Thus, for the offer to be irrevocable, it would have to be supported by consideration (making it an enforceable "option" contract). Because the offer here wasn't supported by consideration, it was revocable, and when the man acted inconsistently with the offer—by telling the woman that he had sold the automobile to the accountant—he terminated the woman's ability to accept the offer. Thus, D is the best response. If you ignored the added information about the man, you might have believed that the man was a merchant and that the offer was ***irrevocable,*** and you'd have chosen (incorrect) choice A.

5. What to do when you're told a party wins a case, and that outcome doesn't seem correct to you.

In some Contracts and Sales questions, you'll be told a party prevailed and be asked why. If the victory doesn't make sense to you, ask yourself why—the best response will probably address your doubts. Here's an example:

> Blackacre is a three-acre tract of land with a small residence. The landowner who owned it rented it to a salesman at a monthly rental of $800. After the salesman had been in possession of Blackacre for several years, the salesman and the landowner orally agreed that the salesman would purchase Blackacre from the landowner for the sum of $96,000, payable at the rate of $800 a month for ten years, and also would pay the real estate taxes and the expenses of insuring and maintaining Blackacre. The landowner orally agreed to give the salesman a deed to Blackacre after five years had passed and $48,000 had been paid on account and to then accept from the salesman a note secured by a mortgage for the balance. The salesman continued in possession of Blackacre and performed his obligations as orally agreed. During this time the salesman, without consulting the landowner, made improvements for which he paid $4,000. When the salesman had paid $48,000, he tendered a proper note and mortgage to the landowner and demanded the delivery of the deed as agreed. The landowner did not deny the oral agreement but told the salesman that she had changed her mind, and she refused to complete the transaction. The salesman then brought an action for specific performance. The landowner pleaded the Statute of Frauds as her defense. If the landowner wins, it will probably be because
>
> A. nothing the salesman could have done would have overcome the original absence of a written agreement.
> B. the actions and payments of the salesman are as consistent with his being a tenant as with an oral contract.
> C. the salesman did not secure the landowner's approval for the improvements that he made.
> D. the landowner has not received any unconscionable benefit, and, therefore, the salesman is not entitled to equitable relief.

Here, the question's instruction to you to assume that the landowner won probably threw you for a loop. If it did, it's probably because you relied on the SOF rule that partial performance—the buyer, apart from paying part of the purchase price, does something unequivocally referable to the existence of an oral agreement—removes a land sale contract from the SOF. The salesman's $4,000 in improvements did just that. Your first reaction gives you a clue to the right response: Since the landowner won, it must be that something in the possible choices overcame the fact that the salesman spent $4,000 on improvements to the land. There's only one answer choice that addresses this problem: choice B, which is the correct response.

6. **Distinguish *third-party beneficiaries* and *assignees*.**

This is an easy distinction. Frequently, in questions dealing with third-party beneficiaries, one of the responses will mention a rule relating to assignees (and vice versa). Remember: A beneficiary is created in the contract; an assignee gains his rights only later, when a party transfers his contract rights to the assignee. Thus, a person who doesn't have rights created and arising in the contract ***can't*** be a beneficiary. Here's an example. Cleopatra contracts to sell her asp to Mark Antony for $100 and provides, in their contract, that Antony should pay the contract price to Julius Caesar. Because Caesar's rights are created in the contract, he's a third-party beneficiary. Say, instead, that the contract doesn't mention paying Caesar. After the contract is created, Cleopatra transfers her right to payment to Caesar. Did he have rights when the contract was created? No. His rights were created later. Thus, he must be an assignee.

QUESTIONS
CONTRACTS

QUESTIONS

CONTRACTS

NOTE: For ease of study, we've put all questions involving **Sales** (i.e., UCC Article 2) at the end of the section, beginning with Question 37.

Question 1

Before putting her home up for sale, a homeowner painted the living room ceiling to conceal major water damage caused by a leaking roof that had not yet been repaired. On the first day the home was offered for sale, the homeowner gave a buyer a personal tour. The homeowner made no statements at all regarding the water damage or the roof. Without discovering the water damage or the leaking roof and without consulting a lawyer, the buyer immediately agreed in writing to buy the home for $200,000.

Before the closing date, the buyer discovered the water damage and the leaking roof. The cost of repair was estimated at $22,000. The buyer has refused to go through with the purchase.

If the homeowner sues the buyer for breach of contract, is the homeowner likely to prevail?

(A) No, because no contract was formed since the buyer did not have a real opportunity to understand the essential terms of the contract.

(B) No, because the homeowner concealed evidence of the water damage and of the leaking roof.

(C) Yes, because the homeowner made no affirmative statements of fact about the water damage or the leaking roof.

(D) Yes, because the buyer acted unreasonably by failing to employ an inspector to conduct an independent inspection of the home.

Question 2

An engineer entered into a written contract with an owner to serve in the essential position of on-site supervisor for construction of an office building. The day after signing the contract, the engineer was injured while bicycling and was rendered physically incapable of performing as the on-site supervisor. The engineer offered to serve as an off-site consultant for the same pay as originally agreed to by the parties.

Is the owner likely to prevail in an action against the engineer for damages resulting from his failure to perform under the contract?

(A) No, because the engineer offered a reasonable substitute by offering to serve as an off-site consultant.

(B) No, because the engineer's physical ability to perform as on-site supervisor was a basic assumption of the contract.

(C) Yes, because the engineer breached the contract by disappointing the owner's expectations.

(D) Yes, because the engineer's duty to perform was personal and absolute.

Question 3

An experienced rancher contracted to harvest his neighbor's wheat crop for $1,000 "when the crop [was] ripe." In early September, the neighbor told the rancher that the crop was ripe. The rancher delayed because he had other customers to attend to. The neighbor was concerned that the delay might cause the crop to be lost, for hailstorms were common in that part of the country in the fall. In fact, in early October, before the crop was harvested, it was destroyed by a hailstorm.

Is the rancher liable for the loss?

(A) No, because no time for performance was established in the contract.

(B) No, because the neighbor failed to tell the rancher that the crop might be destroyed by a hailstorm.

(C) Yes, because at the time the contract was made, the rancher had reason to foresee the loss as a probable result of his breach.

(D) Yes, because a party who undertakes a contractual obligation is liable for all the consequences that flow from his breach.

Question 4

A niece had worked in her aunt's bookstore for many years. The bookstore business, which was housed in a building that the aunt leased, was independently appraised at $200,000. The aunt decided to retire. She wrote to the niece, expressing her affection for the niece and offering to sell her the bookstore business for $125,000 if the landlord would agree to a transfer of the lease. The letter also specified when the aunt would transfer the business. The niece wrote back accepting her aunt's offer. In a phone call to the niece, the aunt stated that the landlord had approved the transfer of the lease and that she would now ask her attorney to draft a written contract so that there would be a record of the terms. Before the attorney had finished drafting the document, the aunt changed her mind about selling the business and informed the niece of her decision.

In an action for breach of contract brought by the niece against her aunt, is the niece likely to prevail?

(A) No, because the motivation for the transfer of the business was the aunt's affection for her niece, not the price.
(B) No, because the promised consideration was inadequate in light of the market value of the business.
(C) Yes, because the condition concerning the landlord's assent to the transfer of the lease was beyond the control of either party.
(D) Yes, because the document being drafted by the attorney was merely a record of an agreement already made, not a condition to it.

Question 5

An actor straight out of drama school and an agent entered into a one-year written contract that described the services the agent would provide. Because he was eager for work, the actor agreed, in the contract, to pay the agent 15 percent of his yearly earnings. At the end of the year, the actor was so pleased with his many roles that he gave the agent 20 percent of his earnings. After the first contract had expired, the actor and the agent decided to continue working together. They photocopied their old contract, changed the date, and signed it. At the end of the year, a dispute arose as to what percentage of earnings the actor owed. It is a trade practice in the acting profession for actors to pay their agents 10 percent of their yearly earnings, payable at the end of the year.

What percentage of the actor's earnings is a court most likely to award the agent?

(A) 20 percent, because course of dealing is given greater weight than trade usage.
(B) 15 percent, because it was an express term of the contract.
(C) 10 percent, because trade usage is the applicable default rule.
(D) Nothing, because the contract is too indefinite.

Question 6

A bank agreed to lend a merchant $10,000 for one year at 8% interest. The loan proceeds were to be disbursed within two weeks. The merchant intended to use the loan proceeds to purchase a specific shipment of carpets for resale at an expected profit of $5,000 but said nothing about these plans to the bank. The bank failed to disburse the proceeds and refused to assure the merchant that it would do so. The merchant was able to secure a loan from another lender at 10% interest for one year. However, by the time the merchant started the application process for a substitute loan, it was too late to pursue the opportunity to buy the shipment of carpets.

In an action against the bank for breach of contract, which of the following amounts is the merchant likely to recover?

(A) Nothing, because lost opportunities are not foreseeable.
(B) Nothing, because the parties failed to tacitly agree that the merchant would be entitled to damages in the event of a breach by the bank.
(C) The difference in cost over time between a loan at 10 percent and a loan at 8 percent.
(D) $5,000, the merchant's foreseeable loss.

Question 7

A janitorial service contracted in writing with a hospital for a one-year term. Under the terms of the contract, the janitorial service agreed to clean the hospital daily in accordance with the hygiene standards of the city's health code. Because the janitorial service did not clean a patient's room in accordance with the required hygiene standards, the patient contracted an infection that required continued hospitalization. In addition to suing the hospital, the patient sued the janitorial service for breach of contract.

Which of the following statements is most accurate with respect to the breach of contract claim against the janitorial service?

(A) The janitorial service is liable to the patient as a matter of public policy, because it violated the city's health code.
(B) The patient is an intended third-party beneficiary under the contract, because the janitorial service's promise was intended to benefit all hospital patients.
(C) The patient has no claim for breach of contract against the janitorial service, because she is an incidental beneficiary.
(D) The patient cannot sue on the contract, because she was not named in the contract.

Question 8

A developer contracted in writing to sell to a buyer a house on a one-acre lot for $100,000. The developer told the buyer that the lot abutted a national park and that the water for the house came from a natural artesian spring. The developer knew that both of these representations were important to the buyer and that both were false. The buyer moved into the house and eight months later learned that a private golf course was being constructed on the adjacent land and that the water for his house was piped in from the city reservoir. The buyer immediately sued the developer to avoid the contract.

The construction of the golf course will probably increase the market value of the buyer's property, and the water from the city reservoir exceeds all established standards for drinking water.

Is the buyer likely to prevail?

(A) No, because eight months exceeds a reasonable time for contract avoidance.
(B) No, because the developer's misstatements caused no economic harm to the buyer.
(C) Yes, because the contract was void ab initio.
(D) Yes, because the buyer retained the power to avoid the contract due to fraud.

Question 9

A seller entered into a contract to sell to a buyer a house for a price of $150,000. The contract contained the following clause: "This contract is conditional on the buyer's securing bank financing at an interest rate of 7% or below." The buyer did not make an application for bank financing and therefore did not secure it, and refused to proceed with the purchase. The seller sued the buyer for breach of contract.

Is the seller likely to prevail?

(A) No, because the buyer did not secure bank financing.
(B) No, because the contract did not expressly impose on the buyer any obligation to apply for bank financing.
(C) Yes, because a court will excuse the condition to avoid a disproportionate forfeiture.
(D) Yes, because a court will imply a term imposing on the buyer a duty to use reasonable efforts to secure bank financing.

Question 10

A computer retail outlet contracted to service a bank's computer equipment for one year at a fixed monthly fee under a contract that was silent as to assignment or delegation by either party. Three months later, the retail outlet sold the service portion of its business to an experienced and well-financed computer service company. The only provision in the agreement between the retail outlet and the computer service company relating to the outlet's contract with the bank stated that the outlet "hereby assigns all of its computer service contracts to [the computer service company]."

The computer service company performed the monthly maintenance required under the service contract. Its performance was defective, however, and caused damage to the bank's operations.

Whom can the bank sue for damages arising from the computer service company's defective performance?

(A) The retail outlet only, because the computer service company made no promises to the bank.
(B) Either the retail outlet or the computer service company, because the bank has not released the outlet and the bank is an intended beneficiary of the outlet's agreement with the computer service company.
(C) Either the retail outlet or the computer service company, because since each has the right to enforce the bank's performance of its contract with the retail outlet, mutuality of remedy renders either potentially liable for the defective performance.
(D) The computer service company only, because it is a qualified and a financially responsible supplier of computer services.

Question 11

The mother of a son and a daughter was dying. The daughter visited her mother in a hospice facility and said, "You know that I have always been the good child, and my brother has always been the bad child. Even so, you have left your property in the will to us fifty-fifty. But it would be really nice if you would sell me the family home for $100,000."

"I don't know," said the mother. "It is worth a lot more than that—at least $250,000."

"That is true," said the daughter. "But I have always been good and visited you, and my brother has never visited you, so that ought to be worth something. And besides, if you won't sell me the house for that price, maybe I won't visit you anymore, either."

"Oh, I wouldn't want that," said the mother, and she signed a contract selling the house to her daughter for $100,000.

Shortly thereafter, the mother died. When her son found out that the house had been sold and was not part of his mother's estate, he sued to have the contract avoided on behalf of the mother.

On what ground would the contract most likely be avoided?

(A) Duress.
(B) Inadequate consideration.
(C) Mistake.
(D) Undue influence.

Question 12

A borrower owed a lender $50,000 due on March 1. On January 10, the lender telephoned the borrower and said that he would discharge the debt if the borrower would promise to pay the lender $45,000 by January 15. The borrower responded, "I will attempt to get the money together." On January 11, the lender again telephoned the borrower and said that he had changed his mind and would expect the borrower to make full payment on March 1. On January 15, the borrower tendered $45,000 as full payment, which the lender refused to accept. On March 1, the borrower refused the lender's demand for $50,000, and the lender sued for that amount.

Which of the following statements best supports the lender's position?

(A) The borrower's January 10 statement was not a return promise, and therefore the lender effectively revoked his offer on January 11.
(B) The January 10 telephone conversation between the lender and the borrower created an executory accord and therefore did not operate as a discharge of the $50,000 debt.
(C) The lender's offer to discharge the debt was a gift promise and therefore was not binding on the lender.
(D) The lender's promise to discharge the $50,000 debt was not enforceable because it was not in writing.

Question 13

A famous chef entered into a written agreement with a well-known interior decorator, who was respected for his unique designs. In that agreement, the decorator agreed, for a fixed fee, to design the interior of the chef's new restaurant and, upon the chef's approval of the design plan, to decorate and furnish the restaurant accordingly. The agreement was silent as to assignment or delegation by either party. Before beginning work, the decorator sold his business to his son under an agreement in which the decorator assigned to his son. The son agreed to complete the chef-decorator contract. The son was also an experienced decorator of excellent repute, advised the chef of the assignment, and supplied the chef with information confirming both the son's financial responsibility and past commercial success.

Is the chef obligated to permit the decorator's son to perform the chef-decorator agreement?

(A) Yes, because the agreement contained no prohibition against assignment or delegation.
(B) Yes, because the chef received adequate assurances of the decorator's son's ability to complete the job.
(C) No, because the decorator's duties were of a personal nature, involving his reputation, taste, and skill.
(D) No, because the decorator's purported delegation to his son of his obligations to the chef effected a novation.

Question 14

In a written contract, an architect agreed to draw up plans for and to supervise construction of a client's new house. In return, the client agreed to pay the architect a fee of $10,000 to be paid upon the house's completion. After completion, the client claimed erroneously but in good faith that the architect's plans were defective. The client orally offered to pay the architect $7,500 in full settlement of the claim for the fee. The architect orally accepted that offer despite the fact that the reasonable value of his services was in fact $10,000. The client paid the architect $7,500 pursuant to their agreement.

The architect subsequently sued the client for the remaining $2,500. In a preliminary finding, the trier of fact found that there were no defects in the architect's plans. Will the architect be likely to prevail in his action against the client for $2,500?

(A) Yes, because payment of $7,500 cannot furnish consideration for the architect's promise to surrender his claim.
(B) Yes, because the oral agreement to modify the written contract is not enforceable.
(C) No, because the architect's promise to accept $7,500 became binding when the client made the payment.
(D) No, because the architect's acceptance of partial payment constituted a novation.

Question 15

A homeowner and a contractor entered into a contract for the construction of a home for the price of $300,000. The contractor was to earn a profit of $10,000 for the job. After the contractor had spent $45,000 on labor and materials, including $5,000 on oak flooring not yet installed, the homeowner informed the contractor that the homeowner had lost his job and could not pay for any services. The homeowner told the contractor to stop working immediately. The reasonable market value of the labor and materials provided by the contractor at that point, including the oak flooring, was $40,000. The contractor used the $5,000 worth of oak flooring on another job.

In an action by the contractor against the homeowner for damages, which of the following would be the largest amount of damages recoverable by the contractor?

(A) $40,000, the reasonable value of the services the contractor had provided.
(B) $40,000, the contractor's construction costs.
(C) $50,000, the contractor's construction costs of $45,000 plus the $10,000 profit minus the $5,000 saved by reusing the oak flooring on another job.
(D) $55,000, the contractor's construction costs of $45,000 plus the $10,000 profit.

Question 16

A vendor and a purchaser each signed a memorandum which stated that the vendor agreed to sell and the purchaser agreed to purchase a tract of land and that the contract should be closed and conveyance made and accepted "by tender of general warranty deed conveying a good and marketable title" on a date specified. The memorandum signed by the parties contains all of the elements deemed essential and necessary to satisfy the Statute of Frauds applicable to the transaction except that there was omission of a recitation of the agreed-upon purchase price. The vendor has refused to perform the contract, and in action by the purchaser for specific performance, the vendor relies upon the Statute of Frauds as a defense. If the purchaser offers evidence, in addition to the written memorandum, that the parties discussed and agreed upon a purchase price of $35,000 just prior to signing, the purchaser should

(A) succeed, because the vendor is estopped to deny that such agreed-upon price is a fair and equitable one, which will be implied by law as a term of the written memorandum.
(B) succeed, because the law implies that the parties contracted for the reasonable market value of the land, although the price paid may not necessarily be that orally agreed upon.
(C) fail, because the price agreed upon is an essential element of the contract and must be in writing.
(D) fail, because the evidence does not show that the agreed-upon price is in fact the reasonable market value of the land.

Question 17

In a single writing, a painter contracted with a farmer to paint three identical barns on her rural estate for $2,000 each. The contract provided for the farmer's payment of $6,000 upon the painter's completion of the work on all three barns. The painter did not ask for any payment when the first barn was completely painted, but she demanded $4,000 after painting the second barn.

Is the farmer obligated to make the $4,000 payment?

(A) No, because the farmer has no duty under the contract to pay anything to the painter until all three barns have been painted.
(B) No, because the painter waived her right, if any, to payment on a per-barn basis by failing to demand $2,000 upon completion of the first barn.
(C) Yes, because the contract is divisible.
(D) Yes, because the painter has substantially performed the entire contract.

Question 18

While waiting in line to open an account with a bank, a customer read a poster on the bank's wall that said, "New Customers! $25 FOR 5 MINUTES. If you stand in line for more than five minutes, we will pay you $25! We like happy customers! (This offer may be withdrawn at any time.)" The customer started timing his wait and just as five minutes was about to pass, the bank manager tore the poster down and announced, "The $25 stand-in-line promotion is over." The customer waited in line for ten more minutes before being served.

In the customer's action against the bank for $25, will the customer prevail?

(A) No, because the bank withdrew its offer before the customer completed the requested performance.
(B) No, because the bank's statement was a non-binding gift promise.
(C) Yes, because the bank could not revoke its offer once the customer had commenced performance.
(D) Yes, because the customer's presence in line served as notice to the bank that he had accepted.

Question 19

In September 2010, a student, 23 years old and unmarried, was beginning his third year of law school. At that time he entered into a written lease with a landlord for the lease of an apartment for the nine-month school year ending on May 31, 2011, at $650 a month, payable in advance on the first day of each month. The student paid the rent through December 1, but did not pay the amount due on January 1, nor has he paid any since.

On January 15, 2011, the landlord threatened to evict the student if he did not pay the rent. That night the student called his father and told him that he did not have the money with which to pay the rent nor did he have the money with which to pay his tuition for the second semester. The student's father told the student that if he agreed not to marry until he finished law school, he would pay his tuition, the $650 rent that was due January 1, the rent for the rest of the school year, and $200 a month spending money until the student graduated. The student, who was engaged to be married at that time, agreed that he would not marry until after he graduated. On January 16, the student's father wrote to the landlord the following signed letter, which the landlord received on January 17: "Because of the love and affection that I bear my son, if you do not evict him, I will pay the rent he now owes you and will pay you his $650 rent on the first day of each month through May 2011. If I do not hear from you by January 25, I will assume that this arrangement is all right with you." The landlord did not reply to the father's letter and he did not evict the student. The student's father died suddenly on January 26. The student continued to live in the apartment through May 31, 2011, but paid no more rent. He did not marry and graduated from law school. His father had paid the student's tuition for the spring semester, but had paid no money to either the landlord or the student. The student's claim against his father's estate having been denied by the executor, the student brought suit against the estate in June 2011, asking for a judgment of $800 ($200 spending money for each of the months, February through May). In this action, the student probably will be

(A) successful.
(B) unsuccessful, because the student's contract with his father was illegal.
(C) unsuccessful, because the student's father's death terminated the offer.

(D) unsuccessful, because the student's contract with his father was not in writing and signed by his father.

Question 20

A chef purchased the front portion of the land needed for a restaurant he desired to build and operate, but the back portion was the subject of a will dispute between a brother and his sister. The sister's attorney advised her that her claim was doubtful. The chef, knowing only that the unresolved dispute existed, agreed in a signed writing to pay the sister $6,000, payable $1,000 annually, in exchange for a quitclaim deed (a deed containing no warranties) from the sister, who promptly executed such a deed to the chef and received the chef's first annual payment. Shortly thereafter, the probate court handed down a decision in the brother's favor, ruling that the sister had no interest in the land. This decision has become final. The chef subsequently defaulted when his second annual installment came due.

In an action against the chef for breach of contract, the sister will probably

(A) lose, because she was aware at the time of the agreement with the chef that her claim to the property quitclaimed was doubtful.
(B) lose, because the sister suffered no legal detriment in executing the quitclaim deed.
(C) win, because the chef bargained for and received in exchange a quitclaim deed from the sister.
(D) win, because the chef, by paying the first $1,000 installment, is estopped to deny that his agreement with the sister is an enforceable contract.

Question 21

A manager, aged 60, who had no plans for early retirement, had worked for a company for 20 years as a managerial employee-at-will when he had a conversation with the company's president about the manager's postretirement goal of extensive travel around the United States. A month later, the president handed the manager a written, signed resolution of the company's board of directors stating that when and if the manager should decide to retire, at his option, the company, in recognition of his past service, would pay him a $2,000-per-month lifetime pension. (The company had no regularized retirement plan for at-will employees.) Shortly thereafter, the manager retired and immediately bought a $30,000 recreational vehicle for his planned travels. After receiving the promised $2,000 monthly pension from the company for six months, the manager, now unemployable elsewhere, received a letter from the company advising him that the pension would cease immediately because of recessionary budget constraints affecting in varying degrees all managerial salaries and retirement pensions.

In a suit against the company for breach of contract, the manager will probably

(A) win, because he retired from the company as bargained-for consideration for the company's promise to him of a lifetime pension.
(B) win, because he timed his decision to retire and to buy the recreational vehicle in reasonable reliance on the company's promise to him of a lifetime pension.
(C) lose, because the company's promise to him of a lifetime pension was an unenforceable gift promise.
(D) lose, because he had been an employee-at-will throughout his active service with the company.

Question 22

In exchange for a valid and sufficient consideration, a man orally promised his neighbor, who had no car and wanted a minivan, "to pay to anyone from whom you buy a minivan within the next six months the full purchase-price thereof." Two months later, the neighbor bought a used minivan on credit from a dealership for $8,000. At the time, the dealership was unaware of the man's earlier promise to the neighbor, but learned of it shortly after the sale.

Can the dealership enforce the man's promise to the neighbor?

(A) Yes, under the doctrine of promissory estoppel.
(B) Yes, because the dealership is an intended beneficiary of the man-neighbor contract.
(C) No, because the man's promise to the neighbor is unenforceable under the suretyship clause of the Statute of Frauds.
(D) No, because the dealership was neither identified when the man's promise was made nor aware of it when the minivan sale was made.

Question 23

When a student finished college, her father handed her a signed memorandum stating that if she would go to law school for three academic years, he would pay her room, board, and tuition and would "give her a $1,000 bonus" for each "A" she got in law school. Her father paid her tuition, room, and board for her first year but died just before the end of that year. Subsequently, the student learned that she had received two "A's" in the second semester. The executor of her father's estate has refused to pay her anything for the two "A's" and has told her that the estate will no longer pay her tuition, room, and board in law school.

In an action against her father's estate for $2,000 on account of the two "A's," if the only defense raised is lack of consideration, the student probably will

(A) succeed under the doctrine of promissory estoppel.

(B) succeed on a theory of bargained-for exchange for her father's promise.
(C) not succeed, because the $1,000 for each "A" was promised only as a bonus.
(D) not succeed, because a student was already legally obligated to use her best efforts in law school.

Question 24

A wealthy widow, wishing to make a substantial and potentially enduring gift to her beloved adult stepson, established with a bank a passbook savings account by an initial deposit of $10,000.

The passbook was issued solely in the stepson's name; but the widow retained possession of it, and her stepson was not then informed of the savings account. Subsequently, the widow became disgusted with her stepson's behavior and decided to give the same savings account solely to her beloved adult daughter. As permitted by the rules of the bank, the widow effected this change by agreement with the bank. This time she left possession of the passbook with the bank. Shortly thereafter, the stepson learned of the original savings account in his name and the subsequent switch to the daughter's name. If the stepson now sues the bank for $10,000 plus accrued interest, will the action succeed?

(A) Yes, because the stepson was a third-party intended beneficiary of the original widow-bank deposit agreement.
(B) Yes, because the stepson was a constructive assignee of the widow's claim, as depositor, to the savings account.
(C) No, because the stepson never obtained possession of the passbook.
(D) No, because the stepson's rights, if any, to the funds on deposit were effectively abrogated by the second widow-bank deposit agreement.

Question 25

A fifty-year-old uncle wrote to his adult, unemployed niece and said: "If you come and live with me and take care of me and my farm for the rest of my life, I will leave the farm to you in my will." The niece immediately moved in with her uncle and took care of him and the farm until the uncle was killed instantly in an automobile accident two weeks later. By his will, the uncle left his entire estate, including the farm, to his unmarried sister. The farm was reasonably worth $75,000.

Which of the following best states the rights of the niece and the uncle's estate (or sister)?

(A) The niece is entitled to receive the reasonable value of her two weeks services only, because two weeks service would be inadequate consideration for the conveyance of the farm.
(B) The niece is entitled to receive the reasonable value of her two weeks services only, because the uncle's letter was an invalid promise to make a will.
(C) The niece is entitled to receive a conveyance of the farm, because the letter and her services created a valid contract between her and her uncle.
(D) The estate (or sister) has the right to rescind the contract, if any, because the uncle's death within two weeks after the agreement was a circumstance apparently unforeseen by the parties at the time they entered into the agreement.

Question 26

In March, when a student was 17, an electronics store delivered to him a television set. At that time the student agreed in writing to pay $400 for the set on July 1 when he would reach his eighteenth birthday. Eighteen is the applicable statutory age of majority, and on that date the student was to receive the proceeds of a trust. On July 1, when the reasonable value of the television set was $250, the student sent the electronics store a signed letter stating, "I'll only pay you $300; that is all the set is worth."

In an action against the student for money damages on July 2, what is the maximum amount that the electronics store will be entitled to recover?

(A) Nothing.
(B) $250, the reasonable value of the set.
(C) $300, the amount the student promised to pay in his letter of July 1.
(D) $400, the original sale price.

Question 27

On April 1, a landowner and an investor signed a writing in which the landowner, "in consideration of $100 to be paid to the landowner by the investor," offered the investor the right to purchase the landowner's farm for $100,000 within 30 days. The writing further provided, "This offer will become effective as an option only if and when the $100 consideration is in fact paid." On April 20, the landowner, having received no payment or other communication from the investor, sold and conveyed the farm to a developer for $120,000. On April 21, the landowner received a letter from the investor enclosing a cashier's check for $100 payable to the landowner and stating, "I am hereby exercising my option to purchase the farm and am prepared to close whenever you're ready."

Which of the following, if proved, best supports the investor's suit against the landowner for breach of contract?

(A) The investor was unaware of the sale to the developer when the landowner received the letter and check from the investor on April 21.

(B) On April 15, the investor decided to purchase the farm, and applied for and obtained a commitment from a bank for a $75,000 loan to help finance the purchase.
(C) When the April 1 writing was signed, the landowner said to the investor, "Don't worry about the $100; the recital of '$100 to be paid' makes this deal binding."
(D) The landowner and the investor are both professional dealers in real estate.

Question 28

A landowner and a contractor entered into a written contract under which the contractor agreed to build a building and pave an adjacent sidewalk for the landowner at a price of $200,000. Later, while construction was proceeding, the landowner and the contractor entered into an oral modification under which the contractor was not obligated to pave the sidewalk, but still would be entitled to $200,000 upon completion. The contractor completed the building. The landowner, after discussions with his landscaper, demanded that the contractor pave the adjacent sidewalk. The contractor refused.

Has the contractor breached the contract?

(A) No, because the oral modification was in good faith and therefore enforceable.
(B) Yes, because a discharge of a contractual obligation must be in writing.
(C) Yes, because the parol evidence rule bars proof of the oral modification.
(D) Yes, because there was no consideration for the discharge of the contractor's duty to pave the sidewalk.

Question 29

On May 1, an uncle mailed a letter to his adult nephew that stated: "I am thinking of selling my pickup truck, which you have seen and ridden in. I would consider taking $7,000 for it." On May 3, the nephew mailed the following response: "I will buy your pickup for $7,000 cash." The uncle received this letter on May 5 and on May 6 mailed a note that stated: "It's a deal." On May 7, before the nephew had received the letter of May 6, he phoned his uncle to report that he no longer wanted to buy the pickup truck because his driver's license had been suspended.

Which of the following statements concerning this exchange is accurate?

(A) There is a contract as of May 3.
(B) There is a contract as of May 5.
(C) There is a contract as of May 6.
(D) There is no contract.

Question 30

An innkeeper, who had no previous experience in the motel or commercial laundry business and who knew nothing about the trade usages of either business, bought a motel and signed an agreement with a laundry company for the motel's laundry services. The one-year agreement provided for "daily service at $500 a week." From their conversations during negotiation, the laundry company knew that the innkeeper expected laundry services seven days a week. When the laundry company refused to pick up the motel's laundry on two successive Sundays and indicated that it would not ever do so, the innkeeper canceled the agreement. The laundry company sued the innkeeper for breach of contract. At trial, clear evidence was introduced to show that in the commercial laundry business "daily service" did not include service on Sundays.

Will the laundry company succeed in its action?

(A) No, because the laundry company knew the meaning the innkeeper attached to "daily service" and, therefore, the innkeeper's meaning will control.
(B) No, because the parties attached materially different meanings to "daily service" and, therefore, no contract was formed.
(C) Yes, because the parol evidence rule will not permit the innkeeper to prove the meaning she attached to "daily service."
(D) Yes, because the trade usage will control the interpretation of "daily service."

Question 31

On May 1, a seller and a buyer entered into a written contract, signed by both parties, for the sale of a tract of land for $100,000. Delivery of the deed and payment of the purchase price were scheduled for July 1. On June 1, the buyer received a letter from the seller repudiating the contract. On June 5, the buyer bought a second tract of land at a higher price as a substitute for the first tract. On June 10, the seller communicated a retraction of the repudiation to the buyer.

The buyer did not tender the purchase price for the first tract on July 1, but subsequently sued the seller for breach of contract.

Will the buyer likely prevail?

(A) No, because the seller retracted the repudiation prior to the agreed time for performance.
(B) No, because the buyer's tender of the purchase price on July 1 was a constructive condition to the seller's duty to tender a conveyance.
(C) Yes, because the seller's repudiation was non-retractable after it was communicated to the buyer.
(D) Yes, because the buyer bought the second tract as a substitute for the first tract prior to the seller's retraction.

Question 32

A carpenter contracted with a homeowner to remodel the homeowner's home for $10,000, to be paid on completion of the work. On May 29, relying on his expectation that he would finish the work and have the homeowner's payment on June 1, the carpenter contracted to buy a car for "$10,000 in cash, if payment is made on June 1; if payment is made thereafter, the price is $12,000." The carpenter completed the work according to specifications on June 1 and demanded payment from the homeowner on that date. The homeowner, without any excuse, refused to pay. Thereupon, the carpenter became very excited, suffered a minor heart attack, and, as a result, incurred medical expenses of $1,000. The reasonable value of the carpenter's services in remodeling the homeowner's home was $13,000.

In an action by the carpenter against the homeowner, which of the following should be the carpenter's measure of recovery?

(A) $10,000, the contract price.
(B) $11,000, the contract price plus $1,000 for the medical expenses incurred because the homeowner refused to pay.
(C) $12,000, the contract price plus $2,000, the bargain that was lost because the carpenter could not pay cash for the car on June 1.
(D) $13,000, the amount the homeowner was enriched by the carpenter's services.

Question 33

During negotiations to purchase a used car, a buyer asked a dealer whether the car had ever been in an accident. The dealer replied: "It is a fine car and has been thoroughly inspected and comes with a certificate of assured quality. Feel free to have the car inspected by your own mechanic." In actuality, the car had been in an accident and the dealer had repaired and repainted the car, successfully concealing evidence of the accident. The buyer declined to have the car inspected by his own mechanic, explaining that he would rely on the dealer's certificate of assured quality. At no time did the dealer disclose that the car had previously been in an accident. The parties then signed a contract of sale. After the car was delivered and paid for, the buyer learned about the car's involvement in a major accident.

If the buyer sues the dealer to rescind the transaction, is the buyer likely to succeed?

(A) No, because the buyer had the opportunity to have the car inspected by his own mechanic and declined to do so.
(B) No, because the dealer did not affirmatively assert that the car had not been in an accident.
(C) Yes, because the contract was unconscionable.
(D) Yes, because the dealer's statement was intentionally misleading and the dealer had concealed evidence of the accident.

Question 34

An elderly widower lived alone on a small farm, which he owned. Except for the farm, including the house and its furnishings, and the usual items of personal clothing and similar things, the widower owned substantially no property. Under proper management, the farm was capable of producing an adequate family income. Because of the usual deterioration accompanying old age, the widower was unable to do farm work or even to provide for his own personal needs. The widower entered into an oral contract with his nephew by which the widower agreed to convey the farm to his nephew and his nephew agreed to move into the house with the widower, operate the farm, and take care of the widower for the rest of his life. The oral contract was silent as to when the land was to be conveyed. The nephew, who lived about 50 miles away where he was operating a small business of his own, terminated his business and moved in with the widower. With the assistance of his wife, the nephew gave the widower excellent care until the widower died intestate about five years after the date of the contract. In his final years the widower was confined to his bed and required much personal service of an intimate and arduous sort. The widower was survived by his only son, who was also the widower's sole heir and next of kin. The son resided in a distant city and gave his father no attention in his father's final years. The son showed up for the widower's funeral and demanded that the nephew vacate the farm immediately. Upon the nephew's refusal to do so, the widower's son brought an appropriate action for possession. The nephew answered by way of a counterclaim to establish his right to possession and title to the farm.

If the court's decision is in favor of the nephew, it will be because

(A) the land is located in a state where the Statute of Frauds will not be applied if there has been such part performance as will result in an irreparable hardship if the contract is not performed.
(B) the land is located in a state where the Statute of Frauds will not be applied if there has been such part performance that is by its very nature unequivocally referable to the contract.
(C) the brother is precluded by the "clean hands" doctrine from enforcing his claim against the nephew.
(D) the blood relationship of uncle–nephew is sufficient to remove the necessity for any writing to satisfy the Statute of Frauds.

Question 35

A seller and a buyer entered into a contract obligating the seller to convey title to a parcel of land to the buyer for $100,000. The agreement provided that the buyer's obligation to purchase the parcel was expressly conditioned upon the buyer's obtaining a loan at an interest rate no higher than ten percent. The buyer was unable to do so, but did obtain a loan at an interest rate of 10.5 percent and timely tendered the purchase price. Because the value of the land had increased since the time of contracting, the seller refused to perform. The buyer sued the seller.

Will the buyer prevail?

(A) No, because an express condition will only be excused to avoid forfeiture.

(B) No, because the contract called for a loan at an interest rate not to exceed ten percent and it could not be modified without the consent of the seller.

(C) Yes, because the buyer detrimentally changed position in reliance on the seller's promise to convey.

(D) Yes, because the buyer's obtaining a loan at an interest rate no higher than ten percent was not a condition to the seller's duty to perform.

Question 36

A manufacturer of computers pays its salespeople a salary of $1,000 per month and a commission of five percent on billings actually rendered for machines they sell. The manufacturer's sales people are employed at will under written agreements that provide that in order to receive a commission the sales person must be in the employment of the manufacturer when the bill is sent to the customer.

In 2010, a salesman worked for eight months to get an order from a customer for a large $750,000 computer. He consulted extensively with the customer's top executives and worked with its operating personnel to develop detailed specifications for the new equipment. He also promised the customer, with the manufacturer's knowledge and approval, to assist the customer for six months after installation in order to make the equipment work.

On January 1, 2011, the customer signed an order, and on March 1 the computer was installed. On March 15, the manufacturer fired the salesman on the stated ground that he had failed to meet his 2009 and 2010 sales quotas. The salesman thought that the manufacturer was correct in this statement. A replacement salesperson was thereupon assigned to service the customer's account. On March 31, the manufacturer billed the customer for the computer.

Assuming that the manufacturer's termination of the salesman's employment was not wrongful, if he, after demand and refusal, sues the manufacturer for the customer's sale commission, which of the following is the most likely to result?

(A) The salesman will win, because he had procured the sale of the computer.

(B) The salesman will win, because he had promised the customer to assist in making the equipment work.

(C) The manufacturer will win, because the replacement salesperson is entitled to the commission on a *quantum meruit* basis.

(D) The manufacturer will win, because the salesman was not employed by the manufacturer when the customer was billed for the computer.

Question 37

A wholesaler contracted in a signed writing to sell to a bakery 10,000 pounds of flour each week for 10 weeks, the flour to be delivered to the bakery on Mondays and payment to be made on Wednesdays of each week. The bakery did all of its weekly bread baking on Tuesdays. On Monday morning of the first week, the wholesaler tendered delivery of 8,000 pounds of flour to the bakery, and the bakery accepted it on the wholesaler's assurance that the remaining 2,000 pounds would be delivered later that evening, which it was. The bakery paid for both deliveries on Wednesday. On Monday of the second week, the wholesaler tendered delivery of 5,000 pounds of flour to the bakery and said that the remaining 5,000 pounds could not be delivered on Monday but would be delivered by Wednesday. The bakery rejected the tender.

Was the bakery legally justified in rejecting the tender of the 5,000 pounds of flour?

(A) Yes, because the bakery was legally entitled to reject any tender that did not conform perfectly to the contract.

(B) Yes, because the tender was a substantial impairment of that installment and could not be cured.

(C) No, because the tender was not a substantial impairment of the entire contract, and the wholesaler had given assurance of a cure.

(D) No, because by accepting the first 8,000 pounds on Monday of the first week, the bakery had waived the condition of perfect tender and had not reinstated it.

Question 38

A buyer sent a seller an offer to buy 50 tons of cotton of a specified quality. The offer contained no terms except those specifying the amount and quality of the cotton. The seller then sent an acknowledgment by fax. The acknowledgment repeated the terms of the buyer's offer and stated that shipment would occur within five days. Among 12 printed terms on the acknowledgment was a statement that any dispute about the cotton's quality would be submitted to arbitration. Neither the buyer nor the seller said anything further about arbitration. The seller shipped the cotton, and it was accepted by the buyer. A dispute arose between the buyer and the seller as to the quality of the cotton, and the seller asserted that the dispute had to be submitted to arbitration. The buyer instead sued the seller in court.

In that suit, which of the following arguments best supports the seller's position that the buyer must submit the dispute to arbitration?

(A) Arbitration is a more efficient method of resolving disputes than resolving them in court.
(B) The provision for arbitration did not contradict any term in the buyer's offer.
(C) The provision for arbitration did not materially alter the parties' contract.
(D) The seller's acknowledgment containing a provision for arbitration constituted a counteroffer that was accepted by the buyer when it accepted delivery of the cotton.

Question 39

A lawn service company agreed in writing to purchase from a supplier all of its requirements for lawn care products during the next calendar year. In the writing, the supplier agreed to fulfill those requirements and to give the company a 10 percent discount off its published prices, but it reserved the right to increase the published prices during the year. After the parties had performed under the agreement for three months, the supplier notified the company that it would no longer give the company the 10 percent discount off the published prices.

Does the company have a viable claim against the supplier for breach of contract?

(A) Yes, because part performance of the agreement by both parties made it enforceable for the full year.
(B) Yes, because the company's agreement to buy all of its lawn care products from the supplier made the agreement enforceable.
(C) No, because the supplier could, and did, revoke its offer with respect to future deliveries.
(D) No, because the absence of a minimum quantity term rendered the company's promise illusory.

Question 40

On June 1, a general contractor and a subcontractor entered into a contract under which the subcontractor agreed to deliver all of the steel joists that the general contractor required in the construction of a hospital building. The contract provided that delivery of the steel joists would begin on September 1.

Although the general contractor had no reason to doubt the subcontractor's ability to perform, the general contractor wanted to be sure that the subcontractor was on track for delivery in September. He therefore wrote a letter on July 1 to the subcontractor demanding that the subcontractor provide assurance of its ability to meet the September 1 deadline. The subcontractor refused to provide such assurance.

The general contractor then immediately obtained the steel joists from another supplier.

If the subcontractor sues the general contractor for breach of contract, is the subcontractor likely to prevail?

(A) No, because the subcontractor anticipatorily repudiated the contract when it failed to provide adequate assurance.
(B) No, because the contract failed to specify a definite quantity.
(C) Yes, because a demand for assurance constitutes a breach of contract when the contract does not expressly authorize a party to demand assurance.
(D) Yes, because the subcontractor's failure to provide assurance was not a repudiation since there were no reasonable grounds for the general contractor's insecurity.

Question 41

A farmer contracted to sell 100,000 bushels of wheat to a buyer. When the wheat arrived at the destination, the buyer discovered that the farmer had delivered only 96,000 bushels. The buyer sued the farmer for breach of contract. At the trial of the case, the court found that the written contract was intended as a complete and exclusive statement of the terms of the agreement. The farmer offered to prove that in the wheat business, a promise to deliver a specified quantity is considered to be satisfied if the delivered quantity is within 5 percent of the specified quantity. The buyer objected to the offered evidence.

Is the court likely to admit the evidence offered by the farmer?

(A) No, because the offered evidence is inconsistent with the express language of the agreement.
(B) No, because the written contract was totally integrated.
(C) Yes, because the offered evidence demonstrates that the farmer substantially performed the contract.
(D) Yes, because the offered evidence explains or supplements the agreement by usage of trade.

Question 42

A seller entered into an agreement to sell a machine to a buyer for $5,000. At the time of the order, the buyer gave the seller a down payment of $1,000. The buyer then built a foundation for the machine at a cost of $250. The seller failed to deliver the machine. The buyer made reasonable efforts to find a similar machine and bought one for $5,500 that did not fit on the foundation. The buyer sued the seller for breach of contract.

Which of these amounts claimed by the buyer, if any, could best be described as restitution?

(A) The $250 cost of the foundation.

(B) The $500 difference in price.

(C) The $1,000 down payment.

(D) None of the claimed amounts.

Question 43

On December 15, a lawyer received from a stationer an offer consisting of its catalog and a signed letter stating, "We will supply you with as many of the items in the enclosed catalog as you order during the next calendar year. We assure you that this offer and the prices in the catalog will remain firm throughout the coming year."

No other correspondence passed between the stationer and the lawyer until the following April 15 (four months later), when the stationer received from the lawyer a faxed order for "100 reams of your paper, catalog item #101." Did the lawyer's April 15 fax constitute an effective acceptance of the stationer's offer at the prices specified in the catalog?

(A) Yes, because the stationer had not revoked its offer before April 15.

(B) Yes, because a one-year option contract had been created by the stationer's offer.

(C) No, because under applicable law the irrevocability of the stationer's offer was limited to a period of three months.

(D) No, because the lawyer did not accept the stationer's offer within a reasonable time.

Question 44

A buyer and a seller entered into a contract for the sale of 10,000 novelty bracelets. The seller had the bracelets in stock. The contract specified that the seller would ship the bracelets by a third-party carrier. However, the contract did not specify either who was to pay the costs of carriage or the place of tender for the bracelets.

On the above facts, when would the risk of loss of the bracelets pass to the buyer?

(A) When the contract was made.

(B) When the bracelets were identified to the contract by the seller, assuming the goods conformed to the contract.

(C) When the bracelets were delivered to a carrier and a proper contract for their carriage was made.

(D) When the bracelets were unloaded on the buyer's premises by the carrier.

Question 45

On July 15, in a writing signed by both parties, a furniture store agreed to deliver to a pharmacist on August 15 five storage cabinets from inventory for a total price of $5,000 to be paid on delivery. On August 1, the two parties orally agreed to postpone the delivery date to August 20. On August 20, the furniture store tendered the cabinets to the pharmacist, who refused to accept or pay for them on the ground that they were not tendered on August 15, even though they otherwise met the contract specifications.

Assuming that all appropriate defenses are seasonably raised, will the furniture store succeed in an action against the pharmacist for breach of contract?

(A) Yes, because neither the July 15 agreement nor the August 1 agreement was required to be in writing.

(B) Yes, because the August 1 agreement operated as a waiver of the August 15 delivery term.

(C) No, because there was no consideration to support the August 1 agreement.

(D) No, because the parol evidence rule will prevent proof of the August 1 agreement.

Question 46

A farmer contracted in writing to deliver to a baker 100 bushels of wheat on August 1 at $3.50 a bushel. Because his suppliers had not delivered enough wheat to him by that time, the farmer on August 1 only had 95 bushels of wheat with which to fulfill his contract with the baker.

If the farmer tenders 95 bushels of wheat to the baker on August 1, and the baker refuses to accept or pay for any of the wheat, which of the following best states the legal relationship between the farmer and the baker?

(A) The farmer has a cause of action against the baker, because the farmer has substantially performed his contract.

(B) The farmer is excused from performing his contract because of impossibility of performance.

(C) The baker has a cause of action against the farmer for the farmer's failure to deliver 100 bushels of wheat.

(D) The baker is obligated to give the farmer a reasonable time to attempt to obtain the other five bushels of wheat.

Question 47

On June 1, a seller received a mail order from a buyer requesting prompt shipment of a specified computer model at the seller's current catalog price. On June 2, the seller mailed to the buyer a letter accepting the order and assuring the buyer that the computer would be shipped on June 3. On June 3, the seller realized that he was out of that computer model and shipped to the buyer a different computer model and a notice of accommodation. On June 5, the buyer received the seller's June 2 letter and the different computer model, but not the notice of accommodation.

At that juncture, which of the following is a correct statement of the parties' legal rights and duties?

(A) The buyer can either accept or reject the different computer model and in either event recover damages, if any, for breach of contract.

(B) The buyer can either accept or reject the different computer model, but if he rejects it, he will thereby waive any remedy for breach of contract.

(C) The seller's prompt shipment of nonconforming goods constituted an acceptance of the buyer's offer, thereby creating a contract for sale of the replacement computer model.

(D) The seller's notice of accommodation was timely mailed and his shipment of the different computer model constituted a counteroffer.

Question 48

By the terms of a written contract signed by both parties on January 15, a computer retailer agreed to sell from its inventory a particular ICB personal computer to a law firm for $3,000, and the law firm agreed to pick up and pay for the computer at the company's store on February 1. The law firm unjustifiably repudiated on February 1. Without notifying the law firm, the retailer subsequently sold at private sale that same ICB computer to a bank, who paid the same price ($3,000) in cash. The ICB computer model in question is a popular product. The retailer can buy from the manufacturer more ICB units than the retailer can sell.

If the retailer sues the law firm for breach of contract, the retailer will probably recover

(A) nothing, because it received a price on resale equal to the contract price that the law firm had agreed to pay.

(B) nothing, because the retailer failed to give the law firm proper notice of the retailer's intention to resell.

(C) the retailer's anticipated profit on the sale to the law firm plus incidental damages, if any, because the retailer lost that sale.

(D) $3,000 (the contract price), because the law firm intentionally breached the contract by repudiation.

Question 49

A plumbing company, in a signed writing, contracted with a landlord for the sale to the landlord of 50 identical sets of specified bathroom fixtures, 25 sets to be delivered on March 1, and the remaining 25 sets on April 1. The agreement did not specify the place of delivery, or the time or place of payment.

Which of the following statements is correct?

(A) The plumbing company must tender 25 sets to the landlord at the landlord's place of business on March 1, but does not have to turn them over to the landlord until the landlord pays the contract price for the 25 sets.

(B) The plumbing company has no duty to deliver the 25 sets on March 1 at the plumbing company's place of business unless the landlord tenders the contract price for the 25 sets on that date.

(C) The plumbing company must deliver 25 sets on March 1, and the landlord must pay the contract price for the 25 sets within a reasonable time after their delivery.

(D) The plumbing company must deliver 25 sets on March 1, but the landlord's payment is due only upon the delivery of all 50 sets.

Question 50

A dry goods retailer telephoned a towel manufacturer and offered to buy for $5 each a minimum of 500 and a maximum of 1,000 large bath towels, to be delivered in 30 days. The manufacturer orally accepted this offer and promptly sent a letter to the retailer, which the retailer received two days later. The letter read: "This confirms our agreement today by telephone to sell you 500 large bath towels for 30-day delivery." The letter was signed by the manufacturer. Twenty-eight days later, the manufacturer tendered to the retailer 1,000 (not 500) conforming bath towels, all of which the retailer rejected because it had found a better price term from another supplier. Because of a glut in the towel market, the manufacturer cannot resell the towels except at a loss.

In a suit by the manufacturer against the retailer, which of the following will be the probable decision?

(A) The manufacturer can enforce a contract for 1,000 towels, because the retailer ordered and the manufacturer tendered that quantity.

(B) The manufacturer can enforce a contract for 500 towels, because the manufacturer's letter of confirmation stated that quantity term.

(C) There is no enforceable agreement, because the retailer never signed a writing.

(D) There is no enforceable agreement, because the manufacturer's letter of confirmation did not state a price term.

Question 51

A buyer mailed a signed order to a seller that read: "Please ship us 10,000 widgets at your current price." The seller received the order on January 7 and that same day mailed to the buyer a properly stamped, addressed, and signed letter stating that the order was accepted at the seller's current price of $10 per widget. On January 8, before receipt of the seller's letter, the buyer telephoned the seller and said, "I hereby revoke my order." The seller protested to no avail. The buyer received the seller's letter on January 9. Because of the buyer's January 8 telephone message, the seller never shipped the goods.

Under the relevant and prevailing rules, is there a contract between the buyer and the seller as of January 10?

(A) No, because the order was an offer that could be accepted only by shipping the goods; and the offer was effectively revoked before shipment.

(B) No, because the buyer never effectively agreed to the $10 price term.

(C) Yes, because the order was, for a reasonable time, an irrevocable offer.

(D) Yes, because the order was an offer that the seller effectively accepted before the buyer attempted to revoke it.

Question 52

A buyer ordered a new machine from a manufacturer. The machine arrived on time and conformed in all respects to the contract. The buyer, however, rejected the machine because he no longer needed it in his business and returned the machine to the manufacturer. The manufacturer sold many such machines each year and its factory was not operating at full capacity.

In an action by the manufacturer against the buyer for breach of contract, which of the following is NOT a proper measure of the manufacturer's damages?

(A) The contract price of the machine.

(B) The difference between the contract price and the market price of the machine.

(C) The difference between the contract price and the price obtained from a proper resale of the machine.

(D) The profit the manufacturer would have made on the sale of the machine to the buyer.

Question 53

A new business enterprise about to commence the manufacture of clothing, entered into a written agreement to purchase all of its monthly requirements of a certain elasticized fabric for a period of three years from a textile mill at a specified unit price and agreed-upon delivery and payment terms. The agreement also included a covenant that the parties not assign this contract.

The textile mill promptly made an "assignment of the contract" to a bank as security for a $100,000 loan. The clothing company subsequently ordered, took delivery of, and paid the mill the agreed price ($5,000) for its requirement of the fabric for the first month of its operation.

Which of the following accurately states the legal effect of the covenant not to assign the contract?

(A) The covenant made the assignment to the bank ineffective.

(B) The covenant had no legal effect.

(C) The textile mill's assignment was a breach of its contract with the clothing company but was nevertheless effective to transfer to the bank the mill's rights against the clothing company.

(D) By normal interpretation, a covenant against assignment in a sale-of-goods agreement applies only to the buyer, not the seller.

ANSWERS

CONTRACTS

Answer Key

Use this Answer Key to quickly identify the correct answer to each question.

(1) B	(11) D	(21) B	(31) D	(41) D	(51) D
(2) B	(12) A	(22) B	(32) A	(42) C	(52) A
(3) C	(13) C	(23) B	(33) D	(43) A	(53) B
(4) D	(14) C	(24) D	(34) A	(44) C	
(5) B	(15) C	(25) C	(35) D	(45) B	
(6) C	(16) C	(26) C	(36) D	(46) C	
(7) C	(17) A	(27) A	(37) B	(47) A	
(8) D	(18) C	(28) D	(38) C	(48) C	
(9) D	(19) A	(29) C	(39) B	(49) B	
(10) B	(20) C	(30) A	(40) D	(50) B	

ANSWERS

CONTRACTS

Answer 1

(B) is the best response,

because it expresses the reason for which the buyer is entitled to rescind the contract.

If one party's assent to a contract is induced by a *material misrepresentation* by the other, on which the recipient is justified in relying, the contract is *voidable* by the recipient. Rest. 2d of Contracts § 164(1). Normally, a party's silent failure to mention a fact will not constitute a misrepresentation as to that fact. But intentional acts of *concealment* are deemed to be equivalent to misrepresentations. *See* Rest. 2d § 160: "Action intended or known to be likely to *prevent another from learning a fact* is *equivalent to an assertion* that the fact does not exist." So when the homeowner painted the ceiling for the purpose of concealing the water damage, this was affirmative conduct intended to prevent the buyer from learning about the damage, and therefore was the equivalent of an affirmative statement that there was no water damage. Consequently, the buyer is entitled to avoid the contract for misrepresentation, either in his own action to rescind the contract, or (as here) as a defense to the homeowner's damage action.

(A) is not the best response,

because it is not factually or legally correct.

Factually, there is no evidence that the buyer did not "understand the essential terms" of the contract. Furthermore, even if the buyer *didn't* understand the essential terms, this fact would not necessarily be grounds for the buyer to avoid the contract—for instance, if the buyer failed to understand the essential terms because he was given the contract and failed to read it closely, this would not entitle him to avoid the contract. The real problem here is misrepresentation.

(C) is not the best response,

because the lack of an affirmative misstatement in words is not dispositive.

It's true that, normally, *A*'s right to avoid a contract on account of *B*'s misrepresentation requires that *B* have made an explicit misrepresentation, and *B*'s mere failure to disclose a known fact will not constitute a misrepresentation. But where *B* takes a physical act for the purpose of *concealing* a fact, the act is considered to be the equivalent of an affirmative representation that the fact does not exist. (See the fuller discussion of this principle in Choice B.) So the homeowner, by painting over the water damage for the purpose of concealing it, will be treated as having in effect made a representation that there was no such damage, triggering the buyer's right to avoid for misrepresentation.

(D) is not the best response,

because the buyer's failure to inspect does not make a legal difference to the outcome.

When one party makes a misrepresentation that induces the other to enter a contract, the latter does not lose the right to avoid the contract for misrepresentation merely because he failed to take advantage of an opportunity to investigate. *See* Rest. 2d § 172, Comment b (in case of a misrepresentation, "The recipient is generally entitled to rely on the maker's assertions . . . *without undertaking an investigation* as to their truthfulness."). So even though the buyer had the opportunity to employ an inspector, his failure to do so did not affect his right to rescind for misrepresentation. (As discussed in Choice B, the homeowner's concealment of the damage was equivalent to a misrepresentation that no such damage existed.)

Answer 2

(B) is the best response,

because it correctly applies the defense of impracticability.

The facts here present a classic scenario for the defense of impracticability. As the Restatement puts it, "Where, after a contract is made, a party's performance is made *impracticable* without his fault by the occurrence of an event the *non-occurrence of which was a basic assumption* on which the contract was made, his duty to render that performance is *discharged*, unless the language or the circumstances indicate the contrary." Rest. 2d of Contracts § 261. Here, at the time the contract was made, it was a basic assumption on the part of both parties that the engineer would continue to be physically capable of performing the job according to the contract specifications. His injury, by making him physically incapable of doing the job, was therefore an event the non-occurrence of which was a basic assumption on which the parties contracted. Since there are no "language or circumstances indicat[ing] the contrary" (i.e., indicating that the parties *didn't* intend for impracticability to operate in circumstances like these), the engineer is discharged from his duty to perform, and will not be liable for breach.

Notice, by the way, that this answer choice correctly indicates that the defense of impracticability applies, even though the choice never mentions the word "impracticability." It's *up to you to notice* that this choice includes the key phrase "basic assumption of the contract," which is always an essential element of the impracticability defense.

(A) is not the best response,

because the engineer's offer did not solve the problem posed by his inability to perform.

The parties contracted for the engineer to provide on-site services. A post-contract offer by one party to perform less than is required by the original contract does not excuse that party's failure to perform as originally specified. And that's true even if the proposed substituted performance is perfectly reasonable—the other party is entitled to insist on the contracted-for performance, unless some special doctrine provides otherwise. (Here, what gets the engineer off the hook is not his offer of a substituted performance, but the doctrine of impracticability.)

(C) is not the best response,

because the engineer was not in breach.

This choice is not correct for the same reason that choice B *is* correct—the defense of impracticability prevents the engineer from being in breach even though the engineer's inability to perform the contracted-for services has disappointed the reasonable expectations that the owner had when entering the contract.

(D) is not the best response,

because it falsely suggests that the engineer breached by trying to delegate.

In this choice, by referring to the engineer's duty as "personal," the examiners are trying to make you think of the rule that says that a contract to perform personal services is normally not delegable by the person who is to perform the services. And it's true that the engineer would not have been permitted to delegate performance of the duties to some other engineer, no matter how well qualified, unless the owner consented. But the engineer here was not trying to delegate, so the non-delegability of his services is irrelevant. Furthermore, this choice is inaccurate in stating that the engineer's duty was "absolute"—the doctrine of impracticability, since it applies, prevents the duty from being absolute.

Answer 3

(C) is the best response,

because the foreseeability of the loss is what makes the loss recoverable.

This question involves application of an aspect of the *Hadley v. Baxendale* doctrine. As the Restatement puts the general *Hadley* principle, "Damages are not recoverable for loss that the party in breach *did not have reason to foresee* as a *probable result* of the breach when the contract was made." Rest. 2d of Contracts § 351(1). That section goes on to specify the two situations in which loss will be deemed foreseeable. One of these two situations is where the loss follows from the breach "as a result of *special circumstances*, beyond the ordinary course of events, that the party in breach *had reason to know*." Section 351(2)(b). This "had reason to know of special circumstances" provision applies here. That's because (1) we're told that the rancher was "experienced" (and the matters in which he's experienced include the local conditions, since what he's agreed to harvest is his neighbor's crop, not some far-away crop); and (2) we're told that autumn hailstorms are "common" in that area of the country. So the fact that the neighbor didn't expressly warn the rancher of the hailstorm danger doesn't matter—the rancher still had "reason to know of the special circumstances."

(A) is not the best response,

because the contract *did* establish a time for performance.

It's true that the contract did not specify a particular date for the harvest. But the clause saying that the work was to be done "when the crop [was] ripe" gave sufficient guidance about the time for performance.

(B) is not the best response,

because it cites a fact that is not dispositive.

It's true that under the doctrine of *Hadley v. Baxendale*, the non-breaching party may not recover losses that the breaching party did not have reason to foresee, as of the time the contract was made, would be a probable result of breach. Rest. 2d of Contracts § 351(1). But there are multiple ways in which the breaching party may have reason to foresee a particular type of loss, and a warning from the non-breaching party is only one of these. Thus, Rest. § 351(2)(b) imposes liability for losses stemming from breach "as a result of special circumstances, beyond the ordinary course of events, that the party in breach had *reason to know*." And the breaching party may have "reason to know" of the special circumstances even without a warning from the non-breaching party. As is discussed in more detail in Choice C, here the rancher, because of his experience, had reason to know about the hailstorm danger, even though the neighbor didn't warn him of it.

(D) is not the best response,

because it overstates the scope of a breaching party's liability.

It's true that normally, the breaching party will be liable for the consequences flowing from his breach. But under the doctrine of *Hadley v. Baxendale*, the non-breaching party may not recover losses that the breaching party did not have *reason to foresee*, as of the time the contract was made, would be a probable result of breach. Rest. 2d of Contracts § 351(1). This choice, by indicating that a contracting party is liable for "*all* the consequences" of his breach, overstates such a party's liability. So even though this choice reaches the correct outcome (rancher is liable), it does so by overly broad reasoning.

Answer 4

(D) is the best response,
because it correctly indicates that the original informal agreement is enforceable.

If the parties reach (perhaps orally) what would otherwise be a binding agreement, the fact that they further agree that the contract will be embodied in a not-yet-drafted writing does not prevent the original agreement from being binding. And that's true even if the anticipated writing is never prepared. *See* Rest. 2d of Contracts § 27: "Manifestations of assent that are in themselves sufficient to conclude a contract will not be prevented from so operating by the fact that the parties also manifest an intention to prepare and adopt a *written memorial thereof*; but the circumstances may show that the agreements are preliminary negotiations." Here the very detailed back-and-forth discussions between the parties indicate that the parties intended to be bound as of the time of the phone call; there is nothing in the circumstances to show that the "manifestations of assent" were merely "preliminary negotiations."

(A) is not the best response,
because the presence of a discounted price does not affect the enforceability of the agreement.

If the aunt had promised to make a true gift of the business to the niece, the absence of consideration would prevent the promise from being enforceable. But as long as there is *some sort of a bargain*, the fact that one party was in part motivated by affection for the other party does not prevent consideration from existing. *See* Rest. 2d of Contracts § 79, Comment c: "Ordinarily . . . courts do not inquire into the adequacy of consideration. . . . [This principle] is also applied even when it is clear that the transaction is a *mixture of bargain and gift*." If the discount from market value had been so great that it indicated that there was merely a pretense of a bargain (e.g., sale of a $200,000 business for $2), the promise would be unenforceable for lack of consideration. But the 37 percent percent discount here is not nearly great enough to indicate the total absence of a bargained-for exchange, so the consideration requirement was satisfied.

(B) is not the best choice,
because the court will not inquire into the relative equivalence between the business's market value and the price agreed upon.

Ordinarily, courts do not inquire into whether the values being exchanged are even approximately equal—that's what is meant by the (correct) saying that "courts don't inquire into the adequacy of the consideration." *See* Rest. 2d of Contracts § 79: "If the requirement of consideration is met, there is no additional requirement of . . . (b) equivalence in the values exchanged[.]" The aunt clearly bargained for the exchange of her business for a $125,000 payment, and that bargain was enough to satisfy the consideration requirement, even though the market value of what the aunt gave up was greater than the value of what she received. If the discount from market value had been so great that it indicated that there was merely a pretense of a bargain (e.g., a 99.9% discount), that fact might demonstrate a lack of consideration, which would make the agreement unenforceable. But the discount here is not nearly great enough to indicate the total absence of a bargained-for exchange.

(C) is not the best choice,
because it cites a legally-irrelevant fact.

It's true that the effectiveness of the deal proposed by the aunt's original offer was conditional on the landlord's approval. But the fact that this condition (which was not within the control of either party) had not yet been satisfied when the niece wrote her letter did not prevent that letter from acting as an acceptance. Binding contracts are often entered into but made subject to the fulfillment of a later condition that is not within the control of either party. Once the landlord approved, the condition was satisfied, and the aunt lost her right to undo the arrangement.

Answer 5

(B) is the best response,
because express terms control over terms of usage.

First, notice that this is not a contract governed by the UCC, which contains very specific rules about priority among express terms, trade usage, etc. But in non-UCC cases, courts tend to follow the same priority rules as used in the UCC. Those rules attach the most weight to express terms. *See* Rest. 2d of Contracts § 203(b): "In the interpretation of a promise or agreement or a term thereof, the following standards of preference are generally applicable: . . . (b) express terms are given greater weight than course of performance, course of dealing, and usage of trade[.]" Since the first contract contained the 15 percent figure as an express term, and since the parties photocopied that contract to make the template for the present contract, the 15 percent figure became an express term of the present contract. Therefore, that 15 percent express term prevails over any alternative meaning, including course of dealing (which probably doesn't apply anyway; see the discussion of Choice A below) or trade usage.

(A) is not the best choice,

because no course of dealing has been established here, and even if it had been, it would have yielded to the express term.

A "course of dealing" is "a *sequence* of previous conduct between the parties to an agreement which is fairly to be regarded as establishing a common basis of understanding for interpreting their expressions and other conduct." Rest. 2d of Contracts § 223(1). As the reference to "sequence" indicates, a single prior instance of conduct would not suffice to create a course of dealing. And there's nothing to indicate that the parties were "establishing a common basis of understanding" that future payments would also be 20 percent. Furthermore, since the parties photocopied the prior agreement, and the prior agreement contained the 15 percent clause, the 15 percent became an express term, which would have given that term priority even if the 20 percent was a course of dealing (which it wasn't).

(C) is not the best choice,

because trade usage would not be controlling usage on these facts.

As among express terms, course of performance, course of dealing, and trade usage, trade usage has the *lowest* (not highest) priority. Rest. 2d of Contracts § 203(b). So if the case involves either an express term, a course of performance or a course of dealing, the presence of a trade usage on the same issue will be irrelevant. That's the case here, since the parties' use of the first agreement as a template meant that the express 15 percent term from that first agreement became an express term in the new contract.

(D) is not the best choice,

because the contract has enough detail to avoid being too indefinite.

It's true that even though the parties have intended to contract, their agreement will be unenforceable if its terms are unduly indefinite. Or, as the Restatement puts it, to be enforceable the contract's terms must be "reasonably certain." Rest. 2d of Contracts § 33(1). The terms are "reasonably certain" if they "provide a basis for determining the existence of a breach and for giving an appropriate remedy." *Id*. at § 33(2). This is a fairly easy-to-satisfy requirement, and it is certainly met here. The writing specifies the duration, describes the services to be rendered, and sets forth the method of computing the agent's fee (15% of the actor's earnings); those details are sufficient to allow a court to determine whether the agent has performed the specified services, and to calculate damages if the actor breaches by not paying.

Answer 6

(C) is the best response,

because it correctly states the limits on a borrower's right to recover damages for breach of a loan commitment.

The non-breaching party's right to recover damages is limited by the doctrine of *Hadley v. Baxendale*. As the *Hadley* doctrine is articulated by the Restatement, "Damages are not recoverable for loss that the party in breach did not have reason to foresee as a probable result of the breach when the contract was made." Rest. 2d of Contracts § 351. In the case of a contract to lend money, the lender is usually entitled to presume that an alternative source of loan money is readily available, unless the borrower has brought home to the lender at the time of the loan contract the borrower's likely inability to borrow elsewhere. Nothing in these facts indicates that the merchant gave the bank reason to believe that the merchant wouldn't be able to promptly borrow elsewhere. Furthermore, the merchant didn't mention to the bank the entire proposed carpet-resale transaction that the merchant intended, so the bank had no idea of the probability that these profits would be lost if the bank breached. So for two different reasons, the damages from the lost resale profits are ones that the bank "did not have reason to foresee as a probable result of the breach." On the other hand, it *was* reasonably foreseeable to the bank that if it breached, the best available alternative lender might charge a higher rate of interest, so the extra interest cost to the merchant *is* recoverable.

(A) is not the best response,

because, although the statement it makes is often correct, this choice does not deal with the "extra interest cost" problem.

It is true that often, the value of a "lost opportunity" to make a profit will be found to be too speculative to be recovered, or will alternatively be found to be the sort of special damage that is not recoverable because the breaching party was not aware of the likelihood that it would occur in the event of breach. In the case of a contract to lend money, the lender is ordinarily entitled to presume that the borrower will find an alternative source of funding, so that no loss of opportunity will occur in the event the lender breaches. That's the case here. On the other hand, the lender *should* reasonably expect that an alternative loan would cost a higher rate of interest, so the lender will be responsible for these increased interest costs. Since this choice does not contemplate recovery of the increased interest costs, it's not the best choice.

(B) is not the best response,

because courts reject the tacit agreement test.

There was a time when some courts held that a party should not be held liable for consequential damages unless, at the time he made the contract, he was found to have made a "tacit agreement" to assume the risk of that liability. Farnsworth, § 12.14. But modern courts (and the UCC, by the way) have generally rejected the tacit-agreement test. *Id*. Therefore, if there is no evidence either way about whether the parties intended the non-breaching party to be able to recover consequential damages, that party is entitled to do so (subject, of course, to the foreseeability limitations of *Hadley v. Baxendale*).

(D) is not the best response,

because the $5,000 loss was not a "foreseeable loss."

Under the principle of *Hadley v. Baxendale*, the breaching party is responsible only for those types of damages that, as of the making of the contract, he had reason to foresee as a likely result of breach. In the case of a contract to lend money, the lender is usually entitled to presume that an alternative source of loan money will be readily available, unless the borrower has brought home to the lender at the time of the loan contract the borrower's likely inability to borrow elsewhere. Nothing in these facts indicates that the merchant gave the bank reason to believe that the merchant wouldn't be able to promptly borrow elsewhere. Furthermore, the merchant didn't mention to the bank the entire proposed carpet-resale transaction, so the bank had no reason to foresee that the resale profits would be lost if the bank breached. Therefore, the $5,000 in lost profits was, for two different reasons, not foreseeable to the bank, preventing the bank from being liable for the merchant's loss of those profits.

Answer 7

(C) is the best response,

because there is no affirmative evidence that the hospital intended the contract to benefit hospital patients.

Since the patient was not a party to the contract between the janitorial service and the hospital, she would have to recover, if at all, on a *third-party-beneficiary* theory. A non-party who is found to be an "intended beneficiary" of the contract may recover, but a non-party who is found to be merely an "incidental beneficiary" may not recover. According to the Restatement and the prevailing modern view, the decision whether the beneficiary was intended or incidental is to be made principally by looking at the intent of the promisee (here, the hospital). *See, e.g.*, Rest. 2d of Contracts § 302(b): putting aside the creditor-beneficiary scenario (not present here), the beneficiary is an intended one only if "the circumstances indicate that the promisee intends to give the beneficiary the benefit of the promised performance." So, unless there is affirmative evidence that the hospital intended to give its patients the benefit of the promise (an intent that would presumably have to include an intent to give the patient the right to sue the janitorial service if it didn't perform), each patient would merely be an incidental beneficiary.

Here, the only circumstances we're told about suggest that the hospital was mainly or exclusively concerned with fulfilling its duty of hygiene under the city's health code, not with giving patients a right of action if the janitorial service did not perform. While the question is a close one—there is a plausible argument that the hospital had a secondary desire to make sure that its patients benefited from hygienic rooms—the slightly-better prediction-of-outcome is the one made in this choice. (In any event, we can say that this is the choice that the National Conference of Bar Examiners, the drafters of this question, say is the right answer.)

(A) is not the correct response,

because it is not a legally-correct statement.

As between the original parties to the contract, the fact that the janitorial service violated the health code would demonstrate a breach by the service, since it expressly contracted to do the cleaning in the manner specified by the health code. But in a suit by a stranger to the contract, it would not be enough for the plaintiff to show a breach—the plaintiff would have to show that, even though she was a non-party, she is entitled to sue as an *intended beneficiary* under the law of third-party beneficiaries. Since this choice does not refer to the rules governing third-party beneficiaries, it cannot be the best choice.

(B) is not the correct response,

because it draws a factual assertion that is not justified by the statement of facts.

If the circumstances justified the conclusion that the hospital, in making the contract, intended to supply a benefit to all hospital patients, this would be the correct answer—each patient would be an "intended" beneficiary (rather than an "incidental" one), and intended beneficiaries may sue for breach. But for the reasons discussed more fully in Choice C, a court would be (slightly) more likely to conclude that there is insufficient evidence that the hospital had a conscious intent to benefit patients, as opposed to an intent to satisfy the requirements of the health code.

(D) is not correct,

because it overlooks the possibility that an unnamed person can nonetheless be an intended beneficiary.

It simply is not correct to state, as this choice does, that a party who is "not named in the contract" is automatically stripped of the right to sue. A person may be an "intended beneficiary" even though she is not specifically named in the contract, if the circumstances are such that it can be inferred that the promisee intended to benefit either that person or members of a class to which that person belonged. *See* Rest. 2d of Contracts § 308: "It is not essential to the creation of a right in an intended beneficiary that he be identified when a contract containing the promise is made." So, for instance, if there were affirmative evidence that the hospital intended to benefit all of its patients, the fact that this particular patient was not named would not be fatal to her third-party-beneficiary claim. The problem, rather, is that there is (probably) not sufficient evidence that the hospital intended to benefit patients as a class when it made the contract.

Answer 8

(D) is the best response,

because a person who is induced to enter a contract by means of a fraudulent misrepresentation has the power to avoid the contract.

Where one party induces the other to enter into a contract by making a fraudulent or material misrepresentation, the latter may avoid the contract. Thus the Restatement says that "If a party's manifestation of assent is *induced* by either a *fraudulent or a material misrepresentation* by the other party upon which the recipient is *justified in relying*, the contract is voidable by the recipient." Rest. 2d of Contracts § 164(1). Here, all the required elements are present: (1) We know that the buyer was "induced" by the misrepresentations, because we are told that these representations "were important" to the buyer. (It's not necessary that the misrepresentations have been the "but for" cause of the plaintiff's decision to enter the contract; all that's required is that the misrepresentation "substantially contributed" to the plaintiff's decision. Rest. 2d § 167.) (2) We know that the representations here were fraudulent, because we're told that the developer knew that they were false. (Therefore, under the Restatement test the misrepresentations do not even have to be "material," though the ones here pretty clearly *are* material.) (3) The buyer was "justified" in relying on the statements, because the case does not involve any of the special situations that pose problems of the justifiability of reliance (e.g., certain assertions of opinion, assertions as to matters of law, etc.), and there is nothing in the facts to indicate that the buyer was foolish to rely on the assertions. So the buyer was entitled to avoid the contract for fraud.

The fact that the buyer did not suffer pecuniary harm is irrelevant, as is discussed in Choice B.

(A) is not the best response,

because the buyer acted promptly upon learning of the statements' falsity.

It's true that where a person is fraudulently induced to enter a contract, that person's power of avoidance can be lost by *undue delay*. However, the "avoidance clock" does not start to run until the time when the victim learns of the fraud. *See* Rest. 2d of Contracts § 381(2): "The power of a party to avoid a contract for misrepresentation or mistake is lost if *after he knows* of a fraudulent misrepresentation . . . he does not within a *reasonable time* manifest to the other party his intention to avoid it." Since the buyer here sued for avoidance "immediately" upon learning of the fraud, the fact that eight months elapsed between the fraud and the suit doesn't matter.

(B) is not the best response,

because economic harm is not a requirement for an action to avoid on account of fraud.

The requirements for avoidance of a contract for fraud are as stated in the discussion of Choice (D). These requirements do not include a requirement that the victim have suffered economic harm. In fact, the person seeking avoidance does not need to show any sort of harm at all, economic or otherwise. *See* Rest. 2d § 164, Comment c.

(C) is not the best response,

because the contract was not void, merely voidable.

"Void ab initio" means "void from the outset." Where a party is induced to make a contract on account of a misrepresentation that meets the requirements stated above, the contract is merely "voidable" at the victim's option, not "void from the outset." So, for instance, if the buyer here had decided that he wanted to go through with the contract, the developer would not have been permitted to escape the contract by claiming that it was void ab initio.

Answer 9

(D) is the best response,

because the buyer lost the right to rely on non-occurrence of the condition due to his failure to make reasonable efforts to obtain the financing.

To begin with, "Every contract imposes upon each party a duty of good faith and fair dealing in its performance and its enforcement." Rest. 2d of Contracts § 205. Where a duty of one party is subject to the occurrence of a condition and that party's cooperation is necessary for the condition to occur, a court will typically conclude that such cooperation is part of that party's duty of good faith. *See* Rest. 2d § 245, Comment a. That's the case here: The buyer's duty was conditional upon receipt of financing, and that financing could not occur without the cooperation of the buyer (by his making an application). So the court will find an implied term requiring the buyer to make a good-faith application for the financing. Since the buyer did not fulfill this duty to make good-faith efforts, he has breached. Furthermore, "Where a party's breach by non-performance contributes materially to the non-occurrence of a condition of one of his duties, the non-occurrence is excused." Rest. 2d § 245. See also Illustr. 3 to § 245, which is exactly on point (buyer's failure to make mortgage application causes him to lose the benefit of the mortgage-financing contingency in the contract). So when the buyer failed to make reasonable efforts to get financing, he lost the right to assert the lack of bank financing as the non-occurrence of a condition to his duty to close.

(A) is not the best response,

because it ignores the significance of the buyer's failure to make good faith efforts to get the financing.

A performance that is subject to an express condition cannot become due unless the condition is either satisfied or excused. Here, because the buyer will be held to have owed a duty to make good-faith efforts to obtain the financing, his lack of such efforts will cause the condition to be excused. The problem with this choice is that it ignores the fact that the lack of financing would be excused due to the buyer's conduct.

(B) is not correct,

because even though no obligation to apply for the financing was expressly stated in the contract, the buyer had an implied obligation to apply for it.

As is more extensively discussed in Choice D, every contract contains an implicit obligation of good faith. Where a party's duty is conditional upon the occurrence of an event, that party's duty of good faith will typically be held to include an implied obligation to make reasonable efforts to see that the condition is satisfied. That's the case here. So even though the contract did not expressly impose on the buyer an obligation to seek bank financing, the contract will be found to contain an implied obligation on the buyer's part to do so.

(C) is not correct,

because it reaches the right result based on incorrect legal reasoning.

It's true that courts can and often do excuse the non-occurrence of a condition in order to avoid forfeitures. *See, e.g.,* Rest. 2d § 229: "To the extent that the non-occurrence of a condition would cause disproportionate forfeiture, a court may excuse the non-occurrence of that condition unless its occurrence was a material part of the agreed exchange." But here, excusing the non-occurrence of the financing condition would not subject the seller to any significant forfeiture—there's no indication that depriving the seller of the right to insist on a closing would cause him any disproportionate loss. (He can sell the house to someone else, presumably for about the same price.) The non-occurrence of the financing condition will indeed be excused, but this will happen because the buyer breached his implied duty to try to satisfy the condition (by applying for financing), not because the court's refusal to excuse the condition would cause the seller to suffer a forfeiture.

Answer 10

(B) is the best response,

because a delegation does not release the delegator, and the delegate is deemed to have promised to perform the delegated services.

First, let's look at whether the *retail outlet* may be sued. The outlet effectively delegated to the computer service company the outlet's duty to perform for the bank. This happened automatically when the outlet said that it "assigns all of its computer service contracts[.]" That's because an assignment "of the contract" automatically includes a delegation of duties. *See* Rest. 2d § 328(1): "Unless the language or the circumstances indicate the contrary . . . an assignment of 'the contract' or of 'all my rights under the contract' or an assignment in similar general terms is an assignment of the assignor's rights *and a delegation of his unperformed duties* under the contract." But a delegation of duties does *not*, unless the obligee expressly agrees, *release* the assignor/delegator. *See* Rest. 2d § 318(3): "Unless the obligee agrees otherwise, *neither delegation of performance* nor a *contract to assume the duty* made with the obligor by the person delegated *discharges any duty or liability of the delegating obligor*." So even though the outlet successfully delegated its duties, and the service company assumed them, the outlet remained liable to the bank, because the bank did not specifically agree to release the outlet from these liabilities.

Now, let's look at whether the *service company* is liable. When a contracting party assigns "the contract" to an assignee, and the assignee accepts the assignment, the assignee is deemed to have promised to perform the assignor's duties, and the obligee is an intended beneficiary of that implied promise. Rest. 2d § 328(2). So when the outlet assigned all of its service contracts, and the service company accepted the assignment, the service company was deemed to have made a promise to perform the outlet's not-yet-performed services under those contracts, and the bank was deemed to be an intended beneficiary of that promise of performance by the service company. Since an intended beneficiary of a promise may sue the promisor for breach, the bank may recover against the service company.

(A) is not the best response,

because it incorrectly concludes that the service company made no promise to the bank.

As is discussed more fully in Choice B, when the service company accepted the assignment of the contracts, it was deemed to have promised to perform the assignor's (the outlet's) duties under those contracts, and the obligee (the bank) was an intended beneficiary of that promise.

(C) is not the best response,

because the retail outlet lost its right to enforce the bank's performance, and in any event there is no relevant doctrine of "mutuality of remedy" applicable here.

First, this choice is not correct in saying that the retail outlet still has the right to enforce the bank's performance of the contract. The outlet lost its right to enforce performance when it made the assignment. *See* Rest. 2d § 317(1): "An assignment of a right is a manifestation of the assignor's intention to transfer it by virtue of which the *assignor's right to performance by the obligor is extinguished* in whole or in part and the assignee acquires a right to such performance." Second, even as to the rights and obligations of the service company, it is not because the service company is liable to the bank that the bank therefore gets the right to sue the service company by virtue of "mutuality of remedy"—the reason the bank can recover against the service company is because the bank is an intended beneficiary of the service company's implied promise to the outlet that it would perform the outlet's remaining duties.

(D) is not the best response,

because it incorrectly concludes that the outlet does not remain liable.

When an existing party with remaining obligations makes an assignment and delegation, that party remains liable if the assignee/delegate doesn't perform. The fact that the assignee/delegate is qualified and financially responsible is part of what makes the contract assignable in the first place, but this fact does nothing to change the general rule that an assignment does not release the assignor from liability to the obligee, except in the special situation where the obligee expressly agrees to such a release (which didn't happen here).

Answer 11

(D) is the best response,

because the daughter used her domination of the mother in order to unfairly persuade her to make the sale.

One of the grounds for avoiding a contract is that it has been induced by undue influence. Undue influence exists where one party to the contract is subjected to "unfair persuasion," which can stem either from the "domination" of the victim by the persuader, or from the fact that the victim is "by virtue of the relation between [the victim and the persuader] . . . justified in assuming that [the persuader] will not act in a manner inconsistent with [the victim's] welfare." Rest. 2d of Contracts § 177(1). Here, both sources of unfair persuasion were arguably present: (1) the mother's illness, together with the daughter's threat not to visit her when the mother was vulnerable, allowed the daughter to "dominate" the mother; and (2) the mother-daughter relationship justified the mother in assuming that the daughter would not act in a way inconsistent with the mother's welfare (welfare that arguably included treating the two children equally). It's not certain that the undue influence ground will succeed, but it is the only one that has a reasonable prospect of success.

(A) is not the best response,

because duress requires an improper threat.

Duress in inducing a contract is certainly a ground for avoiding a contract. However, duress as a grounds for avoidance will be found to exist only where the victim's agreement to make the contract was "induced by an improper threat by the other party that leaves the victim no reasonable alternative." Rest. 2d § 175(1). Various types of threats may be "improper," including, inter alia, threats to commit what would be a crime or tort, threats to bring a criminal prosecution, and threats to do something that is a "use of power for illegitimate ends." Rest. 2d § 176. But the only threat made here was the daughter's threat not to visit her mother anymore. And that threat, while inconsiderate, would probably not be deemed sufficiently "improper." (Also, the threat was not so coercive as to leave the mother with "no reasonable alternative.")

(B) is not the best response,

because a bargained-for exchange was present.

As is often said, "Courts do not inquire into the adequacy of the consideration." That is, as long as there is a real bargain, the fact that the two things being exchanged are of materially different market value does not prevent consideration from being present. Therefore, a sale for less than market value, brought about by a mixture of bargain and gift, will not reflect a lack of consideration.

(C) is not the best response,

because no mistake was present here.

A contract can indeed be avoided for either mutual or unilateral mistake, under the right circumstances. However, a "mistake" is defined as "a belief that is not in accord with the facts." Rest. 2d § 151. There is no indication here that the mother's decision to accede to the sale request was brought about by any belief on the mother's part that was not in accordance with the facts.

Answer 12

(A) is the best response,

because the borrower's response was too equivocal to constitute an acceptance.

The lender made an offer that sought acceptance in the form of the borrower's *promise* to make early payment, not an acceptance in the form of *performance* (i.e., the actual *making* of the early payment).

Therefore, the offer could only be accepted by a promise. (I.e., in classical terms, the offer was for a bilateral contract, not for a unilateral one). When the borrower responded, "I will attempt to get the money together," this was not a promise of early payment—it did not represent the type of clear commitment required for an acceptance. Consequently, the offer remained revocable unless and until it was accepted by a promise of early payment. On January 11, the lender rightfully exercised his power of revocation, by saying that he had changed his mind. Therefore, no contract requiring the lender to take the lesser sum ever came into existence, and the borrower's January 15 tender of the lesser sum had no effect.

(B) is not the best response,

because no executory accord ever came into existence.

An executory accord is a type of contract: One party promises to render a substitute performance in lieu of the one originally promised, and the other party agrees to accept that substitute performance in discharge of the original duty. An executory accord requires the same process of mutual assent as any other contract or modification of a contract. No such mutual assent occurred here, because although the lender offered to take the lesser amount in return for an earlier payment, the borrower never accepted that offer (as is discussed more fully in choice A).

(C) is not the best response,

because the lender's promise would have been supported by consideration had it been accepted.

In this choice, the examiners are trying to make you think that this fact pattern involves the pre-existing duty rule: The idea is that the borrower is merely promising to pay what he already owes (indeed, less than he already owes), and under the pre-existing duty rule a promise to do what one is already obligated to do cannot be consideration for the other party's promise of a modification. But in the scenario in which a creditor promises to take a smaller amount than already due, there is an important exception to the pre-existing duty rule: If the debtor promises to make payment *earlier* than required, that promise of early repayment *does* constitute consideration for the creditor's promise to accept the lesser amount. So if the borrower had in fact promised to make payment earlier than originally required, the pre-existing duty rule would not have applied, and there would have been consideration for the lender's promise to take the lesser amount. What prevents the lender from being bound is not lack of consideration, but the fact that the borrower never actually promised to make earlier payment.

(D) is not the best response,

because nothing required that the lender's promise be in writing.

If there had been a contract between the borrower and the lender for earlier payment of the lesser amount, that contract would not have fallen within any Statute of Frauds provision. It would not, for instance, have involved a suretyship arrangement, the sale of an interest in land, a promise that could not be fully performed within a year, or the sale of goods having a value of more than $500. Therefore, had there been mutual assent to the lesser-but-earlier-payment arrangement, the fact that the arrangement was oral would not have prevented it from being enforceable. (The problem, as discussed in choice A, is that the borrower never accepted the lender's offer.)

Answer 13

(C) is the best response,

because contracts involving artistic services are not delegable.

Delegation is a transfer of one's duties under a contract. Assignment is a transfer of one's rights under a contract. If a party to a contract wishes to have another person perform his duties under the contract, he delegates them. There are certain kinds of duties that are non-delegable. In general a duty or performance is delegable unless the obligee has a substantial interest in having the delegator perform. Rest. 2d of Contracts § 318(2). (See also UCC § 2-210(1) for contracts involving the sale of goods.) Contracts that call for the promissor's use of his own particular skills are normally not delegable. Rest. 2d of Contracts § 318(2), cmt. C. Thus, contracts involving artistic performances or professional services are generally not delegable.

Here, the chef hired the decorator because of his own particular, personal skills. Therefore, the rule that duties involving performance by a specified skilled person are not delegable applies. Thus, when the decorator sold his decorating business to his son, the chef was not obligated to permit the decorator's son to perform the chef-decorator contract, even though the decorator's son was also an experienced decorator of excellent repute.

(A) is not the best response,

because there would be no need for a non-delegation clause.

Delegation is a transfer of one's duties under a contract. There are certain kinds of duties that are non-delegable, including tasks that call for the promissor's use of his own particular skills. Thus, contracts involving artistic performances or professional services are not delegable.

The agreement between the chef and the decorator would not have to contain a prohibition on delegation, because contracts involving the use of particular skills or artistic performances, such as the design of the interior of the chef's new restaurant, are not delegable.

(B) is not the best response,
because the choice would be the chef's.

Delegation is a transfer of one's duties under a contract. There are certain kinds of duties that are non-delegable. In general a duty or performance is delegable unless the obligee has a substantial interest in having the delegator perform. Contracts that call for the promissor's use of his own particular skills, such as contracts involving artistic performances or professional services, are normally not delegable.

Under this rule, the chef is not obligated to permit the decorator's son to perform the chef-decorator agreement. And that's true no matter how great the son's ability to do the job.

(D) is not the best response,
because only the chef, not the decorator, could effect a novation.

Delegation is a transfer of one's duties under a contract. If a party to a contract wishes to have another person perform his duties under the contract, he delegates them. If the obligee under the original contract, the person to whom the duty was owed, agrees to relieve the obligor of all liability after the delegation, a novation is said to have occurred. The effect of a novation is to substitute for the original obligor a stranger to the original contract.

Here, the decorator's purported delegation to his son of his obligations did not effect a novation. For a novation to occur, the chef, who was the person to whom the decorator's duty of design was owed, would have had to agree to relieve the decorator—the obligor—of all liability. It would not be in either the decorator's or his son's power to effect a novation by themselves.

Answer 14

(C) is the best response,
because it correctly states that the architect's acceptance of the $7,500 payment prevents him from any further recovery.

The doctrine of accord and satisfaction will prevent the architect from further recovery. An "accord" is an agreement under which a party to a contract agrees to accept, as complete satisfaction of the contract, some performance different from that originally due under the contract. "Satisfaction" is performance of the accord, and once satisfaction takes place, both the accord and the original contractual duty are discharged. Here, there was a good-faith (although mistaken) dispute as to whether the architect had produced defective plans. The "accord" was the client's offer to pay $7,500 for the settlement of the claim. "Satisfaction" of the accord occurred when the architect accepted the payment. As a result, the original obligations under the contract were discharged, and the client is not liable for the remaining $2,500.

(A) is not the best response,
because the debt was subject to a good-faith dispute.

The pre-existing duty rule will prevent partial payment of a liquidated debt from discharging the obligation to pay the remainder of the debt. However, because the debt in this situation is subject to a good-faith dispute, the client's promise not to pursue his claim provides the consideration required to support the architect's acceptance of a lesser fee. The compromise of the claim in this manner constitutes accord and satisfaction, as discussed in the analysis of choice C, above.

(B) is not the best response,
because the contract was fully performed.

The Statute of Frauds, which requires certain contracts and modifications to be in writing to be enforceable, can be used as a defense by a party seeking to avoid performing under an oral contract. However, since this defense is a challenge to enforceability, it may no longer be asserted once the performances due under the contract are complete. Here, all performances due are complete: the plans are done and money has already changed hands. As a result, the Statute of Frauds may no longer be asserted as a defense by the architect.

(D) is not the best response,
because there has been no novation.

A novation occurs when the parties to a contract agree that one of them will be replaced by a third party (or potentially that both will be replaced by other parties). Since there has been no substitution of a third party for either the architect or the client, no novation has occurred.

Answer 15

(C) is the best response,
because it correctly calculates the contractor's expectation damages.

The most common measure of damages sought by a party as the result of the other party's breach is expectation damages, which seek to put the non-breaching party in the same position as he would have been had there been no breach. What the contractor expected from this job was to make a profit of $10,000. To find the amount of damages, we must first figure out where the contractor stands now. At the moment, he has already expended $40,000 on labor and $5,000 on the oak flooring, for a total of $45,000 in construction costs. However, he has saved $5,000 on another job by using the flooring there. As a result, the contractor has expended a net of $40,000. In order to put him in the same position as he would have been had there been no breach ($10,000 ahead), he will need to be awarded $50,000.

Alternatively, this result can be derived using the formula for expectation damages:

Expectation Damages = Amount of loss (expenditures and other loss) + Expected profit – Amount saved as a result of the breach

Here, the formula would work out as follows:

$50,000 = $45,000 loss (the expenditures) + $10,000 (expected profit) – $5,000 (saved by reusing the flooring)

(A) is not the best response,

because restitution does not provide as great a recovery as expectation damages.

A non-breaching party may sue for restitution, which is measured by the amount of benefit that has been conferred on the breaching party. Notably, this does not allow the plaintiff to recover expected profits, so it is unlikely to afford the plaintiff the greatest measure of damages when expectation damages are available (a possible exception being when the contract would have resulted in the non-breaching party losing money). Here, the homeowner (the breaching party) has received a benefit of $40,000 (the reasonable value of the labor provided to the homeowner). However, this is less than the amount recoverable in expectation damages (see the discussion of choice C above), so it is an incorrect answer to this question.

(B) is not the best response,

because reliance damages do not provide as great a recovery as expectation damages.

A non-breaching party may seek reliance damages, which aim to repay the plaintiff for expenses that he has undergone in reliance on the breaching party's promise. Notably, this does not allow the plaintiff to recover expected profits, so it is unlikely to afford the plaintiff the greatest measure of damages when expectation damages are available. Here, the contractor has expended $45,000 in costs (labor plus materials), but has recouped $5,000 of that cost by using the flooring on another job. As a result, reliance damages would be $40,000. However, as discussed in the analysis of choice C above, expectation damages are available and would result in the contractor obtaining a greater award.

(D) is not the best response,

because it miscalculated expectation damages.

The most common measure of damages sought by a party as the result of the other party's breach is expectation damages, which seek to put the non-breaching party in the same position as he would have been had there been no breach. What the contractor expected from this job was to make a profit of $10,000. To find the amount of damages, we must first figure out where the contractor stands now. At the moment, he has already expended $40,000 on labor and $5,000 on the oak flooring, for a total of $45,000 in construction costs. However, he has saved $5,000 on another job by using the flooring there. As a result, the contractor has expended a net of $40,000. In order to put him in the same position as he would have been had there been no breach ($10,000 ahead), he will need to be awarded $50,000.

Answer 16

(C) is the best response,

because it correctly identifies that the missing price term will render the agreement unenforceable.

Contracts for the sale of an interest in land fall within the Statute of Frauds, and thus require a writing in order to be enforceable (unless they are partially performed). In order to suffice, the writing must specify with reasonable certainty:

1. the contract's subject matter;
2. the parties' identities;
3. promises, by whom and to whom made, and essential terms and conditions; and
4. the signature of the party to be charged (the one who denies the contract's existence).

In many states, the contract requires a recital of consideration as well.

Under these facts, the price would be considered an essential term, so the written agreement would be unenforceable without it. Since C recognizes this, it's the best response.

(A) is not the best response,

because the price term, since it's "essential," would not be implied by the court.

Contracts for the sale of an interest in land fall within the Statute of Frauds, and thus require a writing in order to be enforceable (unless they're partially performed). In order to suffice, the writing must specify with reasonable certainty:

1. the contract's subject matter;
2. the parties' identities;
3. promises, by whom and to whom made, and essential terms and conditions; and
4. the signature of the party to be charged (the one who denies the contract's existence).

In many states, the contract requires a recital of the consideration, as well.

Under these facts, the price would be considered an essential term, so the written agreement would be unenforceable without it.

If you chose this response, you were probably thinking of the modern trend concerning *reliance*. In a growing number of states, and under the Restatement, the court will estop a party from asserting the Statute of Frauds as a defense due to the other party's reliance. Rest. 2d of Contracts § 139. According to the Restatement, enforcing a promise that is within the Statute of Frauds, due to reliance, depends on several factors:

1. the availability of other remedies (in particular, restitution);
2. the extent to which the promisee's detrimental reliance was foreseeable and reasonable, and how substantial the reliance was; and
3. the extent to which the reliance itself, and other evidence, agrees with the oral agreement.

Under these facts, there's no evidence of any reliance at all; and if there were, and the majority of states followed the rule on reliance, the court would have to determine what the agreed price was, not whether it was fair and equitable.

Since A fails to realize that the contract is not enforceable without the price term, it's not the best response.

(B) is not the best response,

because it reflects the UCC rule, not the common law.

Here, a contract for the sale of an interest in land is involved. Article 2 of the UCC only covers transactions in goods. Thus, the common law controls.

Contracts for the sale of an interest in land fall within the Statute of Frauds, and thus require a writing in order to be enforceable (unless they are partially performed). In order to suffice, the writing must specify with reasonable certainty:

1. the contract's subject matter;
2. the parties' identities;
3. promises, by whom and to whom made, and essential terms and conditions; and
4. the signature of the party to be charged (the one who denies the contract's existence).

In many states, the contract requires a recital of consideration as well.

Under these facts, the price would be considered an essential term, so the written agreement would be unenforceable without it.

If you chose this response, you were thinking of the UCC Statute of Frauds, which is considerably more liberal than the common law. Under UCC § 2-201, the writing must:

1. be evidence of a contract (i.e., it must provide a basis for believing that the offered oral evidence rests on a real transaction);
2. be signed; and
3. show quantity.

Thus, price; time and place of payment or delivery; warranties; and quality of goods may all be missing, leaving the contract enforceable nonetheless, although the more missing terms there are, the less likely it is the parties intended to be bound.

Here, under the UCC, the contract would be enforceable, although the court would include the price as the parties intended it (not reasonable market value). However, B fails to recognize that the UCC does not apply to these facts, and since the controlling rule at common law is different, B is not the best response.

(D) is not the best response,

because although its result is correct, its reasoning is irrelevant.

As a general rule, parties are free to set the terms of their agreement as they see fit. Barring fraud, their agreed-upon price may represent a bargain to one party, while leaving the agreement enforceable.

Choice D, in fact, reaches the correct conclusion, but the reason for the conclusion is that, since price is an essential term and the contract is covered by the Statute of Frauds, the contract will be unenforceable without a writing.

Contracts for the sale of an interest in land fall within the Statute of Frauds, and thus require a writing in order to be enforceable (unless they are partially performed). In order to suffice, the writing must specify with reasonable certainty:

1. the contract's subject matter;
2. the parties' identities;
3. promises, by whom and to whom made, and essential terms and conditions; and
4. the signature of the party to be charged (the one who denies the contract's existence).

In many states, the contract requires a recital of consideration as well.

Under these facts, the price would be considered an essential term, so the written agreement would be unenforceable without it. Since D ignores this, it's not the best response.

Answer 17

(A) is the best response,

because the contract did not alter the default rule that where one performance takes time and the other doesn't, the former must be completed before the latter.

Rest. 2d § 234(2), on order of performances, says that "where the performance of only one party under . . . an exchange [of promises] *requires a period of time*, his performance is *due at an earlier time* than that of the other party, unless the language or circumstances indicate the contrary." Since the painter's performance (painting) took a "period of time," and the farmer's performance (payment) didn't, this rule applies, and meant that the painter had to fully perform before the farmer's performance was due, unless "the language or circumstances indicate the contrary." Nothing in the contract language or the circumstances indicated the contrary. (Indeed, the document says explicitly that payment is due upon "completion of the work on all three barns," making the case especially easy.)

(B) is not the best response,

because (1) nothing in these circumstances indicates that the painter ever had a right to payment on a per-barn basis; and (2) even if the painter had such a right, her failure to demand payment after the first barn would not be a waiver of her right to demand payment after the second barn.

Under the analysis of choice A above, the painter never had a right to payment on a per-barn basis. (She might have negotiated such a right, of course, but she didn't.) So there couldn't have been any waiver.

Furthermore, even if the painter did have such a right, it's unlikely that her failure to exercise it after the first barn would cost her the right to demand payment after the second. That's so because even if the painter was held to have "waived" the right to demand payment on a barn-by-barn basis when she didn't demand payment after the first one and went on working, that waiver was *revocable* at any time before the farmer materially relied on it. Therefore, when the painter demanded full payment for two barns after the second one was done, she would have been making an enforceable revocation of any waiver that might have occurred (since there's no indication that the farmer could have materially relied on the waiver).

(C) is not the best response,

because the contract is not divisible, since the parties did not agree that painting of a single barn and payment of $2,000 were agreed equivalents.

If indeed this contract was "divisible," this choice would be correct. As the Restatement puts the idea (while not using the word "divisible"), "If the performances to be exchanged under an exchange of promises can be apportioned into corresponding pairs of part performances so that the parts of each pair are properly regarded as agreed equivalents, a party's performance of his part of such a pair has the same effect on the other's duties to render performance of the agreed equivalent as it would have if only that pair of performances had been promised." Rest. § 240.

The problem for the painter is that, here, the painting of each barn and payment for that barn are not "properly regarded as agreed equivalents," because the contract established that payment was due after the painting of all three barns. In other words, the contract was not in fact set up by the parties as a divisible one.

(D) is not the correct response,

because performance of two-thirds of the work would not constitute substantial performance.

If the painter had truly "substantially performed," she would indeed be entitled to the contract price, less damages for her less-than-perfect performance. But two-thirds performance is very unlikely to be found to constitute substantial performance. Furthermore, the question asks you whether she's entitled to be paid $4,000, not whether she's entitled to payment of any amount. So even if the court found that she'd substantially performed, the painter would be entitled only to the contract price less damages for the non-performance, and that wouldn't necessarily come out at the full $6,000 amount less exactly $2,000 for the unpainted last barn. (For instance, the farmer might now have to spend more than $2,000 to get the last barn painted by itself, leading to damages equaling this greater amount.)

Answer 18

(C) is the best response,

because the bank's unilateral offer was irrevocable once the customer started to stand in line.

An offer is unilateral if it allows acceptance only by performing the requested act. Here, the bank's offer of $25 is unilateral since it is only acceptable by actually standing in line for five minutes, not by promising to do so. A unilateral offer becomes irrevocable once the offeree begins performance. As a result, the offer from the bank to the customer became irrevocable the moment the customer got in line. Since the offer was irrevocable, the bank manager's attempt to revoke it was ineffective. The statement on the sign that "This offer may be withdrawn at any time" has no effect.

(A) is not the best response,

because the bank could not revoke its offer after the customer began to stand in line.

An offer is unilateral if it allows acceptance only by performing the requested act. Here, the bank's offer of $25 is unilateral since it is only acceptable by actually standing in line for five minutes, not by promising to do so. A unilateral offer becomes irrevocable once the offeree begins performance. As a result, the offer from the bank to the customer became irrevocable the moment the customer got in line. Since the offer was irrevocable, the bank manager's attempt to revoke it was ineffective. Whether the customer had completed his five minutes of waiting is irrelevant, since the period of irrevocability began when he commenced performance.

(B) is not the best response,

because the bank's offer was not a gift promise.

In order to be enforceable, a contract must be supported by consideration. A party to a contract can provide consideration by either doing something he is not legally obliged to do, or by refraining from doing something he is legally permitted to do. There is no requirement that the bargained-for consideration provide any benefit to the other party. Here, the customer furnished consideration by standing in line, which he was not obliged to do. As a result, the contract between the bank (promising $25 to customers who stand in line for more than five minutes) and the customer (standing in line) was binding.

(D) is not the best response,

because a unilateral offer can only be accepted by full performance.

An offer is unilateral if it allows acceptance only by performing the requested act. Here, the bank's offer of $25 is unilateral since it is only acceptable by actually standing in line for five minutes, not by promising to do so. A unilateral offer becomes irrevocable once the offeree begins performance. As a result, the offer from the bank to the customer became irrevocable the moment the customer got in line. Since the offer was irrevocable, the bank manager's attempt to revoke it was ineffective. While this answer comes to the right conclusion, the timing is incorrect. The unilateral offer is only accepted by completing the requested performance (standing in line for five minutes). At the time the bank manager attempted to revoke the offer, five minutes had not passed, so the offer had not yet been accepted. However, as discussed above, it was irrevocable, and when the customer completed his five-minute wait, his acceptance was complete.

Answer 19

(A) is the best response,

because it's the only option that recognizes that the student's claim will succeed.

Under these facts, there are a few major obstacles the student's claim would have to overcome. First, you may have noticed the unconventional consideration in the contract—the father gets nothing but peace of mind out of the deal. Second, the contract involves delaying marriage, and that brings up public policy concerns. Finally, there's a Statute of Frauds gloss, since the payment of another's debts is involved (to the extent of the rent provision, *not* the spending-money provision).

As to the consideration issue, consideration requires a bargained-for exchange, as well as either detriment to the promisee or benefit to the promisor (or typically both). While the student (as promisee) clearly suffered a detriment by delaying his wedding, it's not as clear what the benefit to his father (as promisor) was. As a matter of fact, peace of mind or personal satisfaction is sufficient to qualify as a benefit. Thus, the student's father's ensuring that his son complete school before being distracted by a wedding would be sufficient to support a contract. Furthermore, since the student delayed the marriage at his father's request, it was "bargained for." As a result, there's no problem with consideration.

As to the public policy concerns, it's only contracts in *derogation* of marriage that are considered illegal (and thus enforceable). If his father had offered to pay the student to *divorce*, instead of to delay his marriage, such an agreement would be unenforceable. As it is, there's no public policy problem with the contract.

Finally, there's no Statute of Frauds problem, because the spending-money agreement doesn't fall within the Statute of Frauds, and thus is enforceable without a writing. It's the promise to pay the student's rent that's within the Statute of Frauds, as a promise to pay the debt of another. But that's not the issue here, so the contract is enforceable without a writing.

Since choice A correctly characterizes the contract as enforceable, it's the best response.

(B) is not the best response,

because the contract was not illegal.

A contract is illegal if it is contrary to public policy when made (it need not involve criminal or tortious conduct). Such contracts include contracts that are usurious, or obstruct justice, defraud a third party, involve the commission of crimes or torts, or—the one you probably thought of if you chose this response—contracts in derogation of marriage. However, contracts in derogation of marriage involve a divorce (e.g., "Divorce that bum and I'll give you $100,000"). Here, the student's father only wanted the student to postpone his wedding until graduation. Thus, the contract was not illegal and, in fact, was enforceable. Since there was a bargained-for exchange, and detriment to the promisee (the student—in terms of delaying his marriage) and benefit to the promisor (his father—in terms of personal satisfaction), the contract was supported by consideration. Furthermore, it didn't fall within the Statute of Frauds (as to the spending-money provision), so it would be enforceable without a writing. Since B incorrectly states that the contract was illegal and thus unenforceable, it's not the best response.

(C) is not the best response,

because although it correctly states a *theoretical* rule—death of an offeror terminates the offer—it does not apply here, because there was already an enforceable contract when the student's father died, and so the enforceability of the offer is irrelevant.

A contract requires an offer, acceptance, and consideration (or some substitute for consideration). Here, the student's father offered to pay the student's rent and give him spending money if he delayed his marriage. The student did so, and this was his detriment (and his father's benefit, in terms of personal satisfaction), so the contract was supported by consideration and, thus, enforceable. The student's father's death *after* the contract was created would not discharge his (or his estate's) duty of performance, because his estate can carry out the payment—his personal contribution is not necessary to the contract. (If it *were*, as, say, he was to paint the student's portrait, it *would* be discharged by his death.) Since choice C mischaracterizes the contract as being only at the offer stage, and not an intact contract, it's not the best response.

(D) is not the best response,

because the contract is enforceable without a writing.

Choice D suggests that the contract is not enforceable because it falls within the Statute of Frauds, and thus, in general, requires a writing. This is a bit sneaky because the part of the contract to which the student's claim refers—the agreement to provide $100 spending money every month—does *not* fall within the Statute of Frauds, and thus is enforceable without a writing! It's the part of the contract addressing the student's father's agreement to pay the student's rent which must be in writing to be enforceable, since it's an agreement to pay the debt of another, and as such falls within the Statute of Frauds.

Since the agreement that forms the basis of the student's claim, the spending-money agreement, does not fall within the Statute of Frauds, and D fails to recognize this, it's not the best response.

Answer 20

(C) is the best response,

because the chef's promise of payment to the sister was supported by consideration.

When the sister issued the quitclaim deed, she was effectively settling—by assigning to the chef—her claim against the property. So the question is whether one who promises to make payment in exchange for the surrender of an invalid claim has received consideration. (If the chef didn't receive consideration in return for his promise, that promise wouldn't be enforceable.)

The answer is that the surrender of the claim that turns out to be invalid nonetheless constitutes consideration if *either* (1) the claim is *in fact doubtful* because of uncertainty as to the facts or the law; or (2) the surrendering party *believes* that the claim may be valid. Rest. 2d § 74(1). Here, (1) was the case (since the sister's attorney told her that her claim was doubtful, not that it was definitely invalid). Since the sister's surrender of the claim in a bargained-for exchange in return for the chef's promise of payment constituted consideration, the chef's promise is enforceable.

(A) is not the best response,

because surrender of a claim that the claimant believes to be doubtful (but not definitely invalid) constitutes consideration.

If the sister had *known* that her claim was totally invalid at the time she surrendered it (by issuing the quitclaim deed), her surrender would not be consideration for the chef's promise, and his promise would therefore be unenforceable. But the mere fact that the sister knew that her claim was doubtful—as opposed to invalid—is not enough to prevent her surrender from being consideration. For a more complete discussion of when surrender of an invalid claim will be consideration, see the analysis of choice C above.

(B) is not the best response,

because surrender of a possibly valid claim does constitute legal detriment.

If the sister had surrendered a claim that she knew was definitely invalid, that surrender (by issuance of the quitclaim deed) would indeed not be a "legal detriment"—she would not have worsened her legal position. But because what the sister surrendered was a "doubtful" claim rather than a claim she knew to be invalid, her surrender is deemed to constitute consideration. See the complete analysis in the discussion of choice C above.

(D) is not the best response,

because there would be no estoppel here.

This choice seems to be suggesting that there is no consideration to support the chef's promise, but that the doctrine of promisory estoppel would apply to make the promise binding without consideration. However, this analysis is wrong for two reasons: (1) as described in choice C, the sister's surrender of her doubtful claim *was* consideration for the chef's return promise; and (2) if the surrender of the claim wasn't consideration, promissory estoppel wouldn't apply because there's no indication that the sister relied to her detriment on the promise (and reasonable reliance is a pre-condition to the application of promissory estoppel).

Answer 21

(B) is the best response,

because the manager's reasonable reliance caused the company's promise, though not supported by consideration, to be binding under the doctrine of promissory estoppel.

The company's promise was not supported by consideration, since the manager didn't confer any benefit to the company, or undergo any legal detriment, in exchange for the promise. (See the discussion of choice A below for more details about why this is so.) However, the doctrine of promissory estoppel applies to make the company's promise enforceable even without consideration.

Rest. 2d § 90(a) (the most famous section in the entire Restatement) says that "[a] promise which the promisor should *reasonably* expect to induce action or forbearance on the part of the promisee or a third person and which *does* induce such action or forbearance is *binding if injustice can be avoided* only by enforcement of the promise." This section applies here.

It was reasonably foreseeable to the company that, when it made the "you'll get a pension if you retire" offer to the manager, he would or might rely on it by retiring, rather than staying on or taking another job. The promise, then, did in fact induce the foreseeable reliance: The manager relied by not only retiring but by buying the RV and not taking another position somewhere else. Furthermore, that reliance has made the manager unemployable elsewhere, so that without enforcement of the promise the manager won't have any means of support. Consequently, all the requirements of promissory estoppel are satisfied, making the promise enforceable despite the lack of consideration.

Notice, by the way, that neither the correct choice nor any other choices here mentions the doctrine of promissory estoppel. That's typical of MBE fact patterns where the correct answer is promissory estoppel: The examiners try to allude to the doctrine without mentioning it explicitly, because they believe that mentioning it will tip you off and make the question too easy.

(A) is not the best response,

because the company did not bargain to have the manager retire.

A promise or act (here, the manager's retirement) can be consideration for a counter-promise only if the promise or act was "bargained for or given in exchange" for the counter-promise. So here, the manager's retirement would be consideration for the promise of a pension only if the company bargained for that retirement, or received it in exchange for the promise. But here, there is no indication that the company was bargaining for his retirement, or that it promised the pension in exchange for that retirement. (Apparently the board of directors didn't care too much whether the manager stayed on the job or retired, as evidenced by the fact that the resolution said that the pension would be payable whenever the manager, at his own option, made the decision to retire.) Consequently, the manager's retirement was not consideration for the company's pension promise, making choice A wrong. (In reality, the promise is enforceable even without consideration, as described in choice B.)

(C) is not the best response,

because although the promise of a pension was an otherwise-unenforceable promise to make a gift, it became enforceable under the doctrine of promissory estoppel once the manager relied on it to his detriment.

A promise to make a gift can become enforceable when the promisee foreseeably relies on it to his detriment, and injustice can be avoided only by enforcing the promise. (See the discussion of choice B above.) Since choice C asserts that the promise is unenforceable, it's wrong.

(D) is not the best response,

because the promise became enforceable via the doctrine of promissory estoppel, notwithstanding the manager's at-will status.

It's true that the company could simply have fired the manager at any time without any pension payments or other payments. But once the company made its promise to pay a pension and the manager reasonably relied on it, the fact that the manager was an at-will employee ceased to matter—the doctrine of promissory estoppel made the promise binding.

Answer 22

(B) is the best response,

because the dealership meets all the requirements necessary to be an intended beneficiary.

For a third party to be an intended beneficiary, it must first of all be the case that giving him the right to sue would be appropriate to effectuate the intentions of the parties. If he meets this test, he must further fit into one of the two following categories: (1) either the performance of the promise will satisfy an obligation of the promisee to pay money to the beneficiary; or (2) the circumstances indicate that the promisee intends to give the beneficiary the benefit of the promised performance.

The dealership meets these requirements, and is thus an intended beneficiary of the man's promise. First, giving the dealership the right to sue would effectuate the intentions of the parties—the man intended to help his neighbor get a minivan by his promise to pay, and letting the seller sue on the promise is consistent with that intention. Next, the neighbor (the promisee), has promised to pay money to the dealership (the beneficiary), so enforcing the promise satisfies alternate test (1) above. Having met the requirements of an intended beneficiary, the dealership can enforce the man's promise to his neighbor.

(A) is not the best response,

because the dealership was not a party to the man's promise to his neighbor.

The essence of the promissory estoppel idea is that the maker of a promise may be bound by that promise, even though it is not supported by consideration, if the promisee relies upon that promise to his detriment, and the promisor should have foreseen the reliance. The doctrine gives only the promisee the right to sue.

For the dealership to enforce the man's promise to his neighbor under a promissory estoppel theory, some promise would have to have been made *to the dealership*, since only the promisee may sue. The man's promise was made only to his neighbor, not to the neighbor and the dealership. (In fact, the dealership did not even learn of the promise made by the man until it sold the minivan to the neighbor.) So while the dealership can enforce the man's promise, it cannot do so for the reasons stated.

(C) is not the best response,

because the man made no promise to the dealership.

The Statute of Frauds requires that certain types of contracts be in writing. One type of agreement that has to be in writing in order to be enforceable is a suretyship agreement, which is the promise to pay the debt of another.

The man's promise does not fall within the suretyship clause of the Statue of Frauds, because he did not make a promise to the dealership. For the man to be a surety of the neighbor, he would have had to make a promise *to the dealership* (the creditor), which he didn't do. So the fact that he promised the neighbor (the debtor) that he would make good on the debt is irrelevant for purposes of the suretyship provision.

(D) is not the best response,

because intended beneficiaries do not have to be identified or aware that a promise was made.

For a third party to be an intended beneficiary, it must first of all be the case that giving him the right to sue would be appropriate to effectuate the intentions of the parties. If he meets this test, he must further fit into one of the two following categories: either (1) the performance of the promise will satisfy an obligation of the promisee to pay money to the beneficiary; or (2) the circumstances indicate that the promisee intends to give the beneficiary the benefit of the promised performance.

There is no requirement that the intended beneficiary be identified when the promise is made, or that he be aware that it was made at any particular moment. Therefore, the fact that the dealership was neither identified nor aware of the promise when it was made, is irrelevant—the dealership meets all the requirements of an intended beneficiary and so would be able to sue to enforce the man's promise to his neighbor.

Answer 23

(B) is the best response,

because it correctly identifies that the "A" provision is an enforceable promise.

In order to be enforceable, an agreement must be supported by consideration, or a substitute for consideration (e.g., promissory estoppel). Consideration requires a bargained-for exchange, and either detriment to the promisee or benefit to the promisor (and typically both). Here, the father made an offer to the student proposing a unilateral contract—that is, he requested in return her *performance*, in the form of attending law school for three years. The student, as promisee, suffered a detriment by doing something she wasn't legally obligated to do—attending law school. Her father enjoyed a benefit, in the form of personal satisfaction due to his daughter's attending law school, and presumably being able to brag about this to all of his buddies. Finally, by performing at her father's request, the student satisfied the bargain element of consideration.

Note that the father's promise had two elements—paying expenses and paying $1,000 for every "A." The father's calling the "A" provision a bonus doesn't make it a gratuitous promise. The fact is, it was part and parcel of the offer the student accepted by attending law school and earning "A's." Presumably, the student worked harder at law school than she might have otherwise, knowing each "A" would mean $1,000 to her, in response to her father's promise. Her extra effort alone would be sufficient to provide consideration for the "A" provision. Since B recognizes this, it's the best response.

(A) is not the best response,

because there's consideration to support a contract, and as a result there's no need to turn to promissory estoppel.

To be enforceable, an agreement must be supported by consideration (or a substitute for consideration). Promissory estoppel is a substitute for consideration, used to avoid injustice. It is triggered by a gratuitous promise that is likely to, and does, induce the promisee's detrimental reliance. What distinguishes promissory estoppel from consideration is the bargained-for exchange. Here, the father bargained for—and got—the student to attend law school. Stated differently, the student's detriment, going to law school, was at her father's request. Thus, there was detriment to the student, in attending law school, and benefit to her father, in the form of personal satisfaction, thus satisfying the detriment and/or benefit element of consideration. Say the facts had been different, and her father had promised to give the student $10,000 as a gift, knowing she wanted to go to law school. Relying on the promise, the student enrolled in law school. Here, there's no bargain, but her father's promise to give the student $10,000 would be enforceable on promissory estoppel grounds, since his promise was likely to, and did, result in the student's reliance.

However, the facts as presented in the question indicate a bargain. Since the presence of consideration *precludes* application of promissory estoppel, A isn't the best response.

(C) is not the best response,

because the bonus for the "A's" was part of what the student bargained for, and thus the promise to pay for the "A's" would be supported by consideration.

In order to be enforceable, an agreement must be supported by consideration (or some substitute for consideration). Consideration requires bargained-for exchange and either detriment to the promisee or benefit to the promisor (and typically, both).

Here, the father made an offer to the student proposing a unilateral contract—he wanted the student to perform in return for his promise, namely, to attend law school for three years.

The promise the father made had two elements: paying the student's expenses, and paying her $1,000 for every "A." The father's calling the "A" provision a bonus doesn't make it a gratuitous promise. The fact is, it was part and parcel of the offer the student accepted by attending law school, and earning "A's."

What C suggests is that the "A" bonus was a gratuitous promise. Say, however, the facts were different, and her father didn't make *any* promise to the student until after the first year of law school, during which she earned two A's. At a party shortly after the first year, her father told the student, "In consideration of your earning two A's, I promise to give you $2,000." This *would* be gratuitous because there was no bargain, and it didn't induce any requested detriment in the student, as promisee.

In the facts in the question, the student's attending law school and earning the "A's" was in response to her father's entire promise, including the "A" bonus. Since C doesn't recognize this, it's not the best response.

(D) is not the best response,

because the student was under no duty to use her best efforts in law school.

What choice D suggests is that the student was under a pre-existing duty to perform, and thus she didn't suffer any detriment in response to her father's promise, making the promise "illusory" (unsupported by consideration). In fact, no such duty existed; the student hadn't even *applied* to law school when her father made his offer.

In order to be enforceable, an agreement must be supported by consideration, or a substitute for consideration (e.g., promissory estoppel). Consideration requires a bargained-for exchange, and either detriment to the promisee or benefit to the promisor (and typically, both). Here, the father made an offer to the student proposing a unilateral contract—that is, he requested her *performance* in return, in the form of attending law school for three years. The student, as promisee, suffered a detriment by doing something she wasn't legally obligated to do—attending law school. Her father enjoyed a benefit, in the form of personal satisfaction due to his daughter's attending law school, and presumably being able to brag about this to all of his buddies. Finally, by performing at her father's request, the student satisfied the bargain element of consideration.

Say the facts were different, and once the student was in law school, her father told her, "I'll only continue to pay your expenses if you maintain a 4.0 average." Here, her father was already contractually bound by his first promise, and since there's no additional consideration for this latter request, it's unenforceable due to a pre-existing duty. (Under the UCC, the rule is different: modifications are enforceable, without consideration, as long as they're made in good faith.)

Incidentally, the "best efforts" language of choice D is the language sometimes used to make an otherwise illusory promise enforceable. Say the student quit law school and decided to become a stand-up comic. Her father agreed to use his best efforts to promote her, in return for 10 percent of her earnings. Without the "best efforts" provision, her father would have a completely unrestricted right to renege on his promise, and thus there'd be no consideration. The "best efforts" provision restricts his freedom of action, and thus supplies consideration.

In any case, under the facts in the question, the student performed in response to her father's request, which forms the basis of an enforceable contract. Since D ignores this, it's not the best response.

Answer 24

(D) is the best response,

because it implicitly recognizes that the stepson's rights as an intended third-party beneficiary under the original widow-bank agreement hadn't "vested," so he couldn't block the modification.

When two parties form an agreement, two types of third-party beneficiaries may be created: intended beneficiaries and incidental beneficiaries. Only intended beneficiaries have enforceable rights. An intended beneficiary is one whom the promisee (here, the widow) intends to benefit from the promisor's (here, the bank's) performance; all others are incidental beneficiaries. Here, since the widow intended her stepson to benefit from the savings account at the bank, the stepson was an intended beneficiary.

Having established that, you have to determine when the stepson's rights would "vest," such that the agreement couldn't be modified or rescinded without his consent. This traditionally depended on whether the stepson was a donee or creditor beneficiary. Since the widow didn't owe her stepson a prior duty that setting up the savings account would discharge, he was a donee beneficiary. Traditionally, a donee beneficiary's rights only vested on justified detrimental reliance *or* when he manifested assent to the agreement, which could be implied to occur as soon as he had knowledge of it. However, most modern courts agree with the Rest. 2d of Contracts § 311, which ignores the donee/creditor distinction and, rather, views the rights of both as vesting when one of these three events occurs:

1. The beneficiary manifests assent to the promise;
2. The beneficiary sues to enforce the promise; or
3. The beneficiary justifiably relies on the promise to his detriment.

Here, the stepson didn't even know about the contract when it was modified, so he can't contest the modification.

Note that even if the widow had transferred the account to him *after* she created it—thus making him an assignee—she could *still* have rescinded it, because the assignment was revocable. The things most likely to make it irrevocable—foreseeable reliance by the stepson, or transferring to him the bank book, or his paying for the assignment, or his receiving performance from the bank as obligor—hadn't occurred. Thus, even if you mischaracterized the stepson as an assignee, you'd *still* select choice D, the correct response.

(A) is not the best response,

because even if the stepson is an intended beneficiary to the original widow-bank deposit agreement, his rights under the contract did not "vest" before the account was transferred to the daughter. Thus, the stepson couldn't stop the transfer.

Under these facts, the original agreement, under which the stepson would gain any rights, was between the widow and the bank. There are two ways a third party can gain rights under a contract: as an intended beneficiary, or as an assignee. The difference is that the rights of third-party beneficiaries are created in the contract, whereas an assignment involves a subsequent transfer of rights under a contract.

Since the original passbook account was entered in the stepson's name, he could be considered an intended beneficiary. That's because, as to the bank's duty, the widow is the promisee, and her intent was that her stepson benefit from the bank's performance under the contract. As an intended beneficiary, the stepson had enforceable rights under the contract, such that once his rights vested, the contract couldn't be modified or rescinded without his consent. "Vesting" is the key here. Traditionally, the time of vesting depends on whether the beneficiary is a *creditor* or a *donee* beneficiary. One is a creditor beneficiary only if the promisor's duty (here, the bank's) will discharge a duty the promisee (the widow) previously owed the beneficiary. Here, the widow owes her stepson nothing, so if he's an intended beneficiary at all, he must be a donee beneficiary.

Traditionally, the rule on vesting for a donee beneficiary is that his rights only vest on justified detrimental reliance *or* when he manifests assent to the agreement, which can be implied to occur as soon as he has knowledge of it. However, most modern courts agree with the Rest. 2d of Contracts § 311, which ignores the donee/creditor distinction and, rather, views the rights of both as vesting when one of these three events occurs:

1. The beneficiary manifests assent to the promise;
2. The beneficiary sues to enforce the promise; or
3. The beneficiary justifiably relies on the promise to his detriment.

Here, the widow modified the contract—to make her daughter the beneficiary—before her stepson even *knew* about the account. Thus, he couldn't prevent the transfer, and is left with no rights under the contract. Since choice A ignores the vesting issue, it's not the best response.

(B) is not the best response,

because the stepson could not be considered an assignee of any kind of the savings account, and even if he could, his right was validly revoked by the transfer to the widow's daughter.

A constructive assignment occurs when a fraudulent or preferential transfer is converted, pursuant to statute, into an assignment that benefits creditors. Here, since the stepson was not a creditor of the widow, there could be no constructive assignment to him.

What choice B seeks to do with the "constructive" language is to avoid a missing element of a regular assignment under these facts. In order to transfer rights under an existing contract, the assignor (here, the widow) must clearly intend to transfer her rights to a third party, the rights must be identified, and the intent must be addressed to the assignee or his representative, who must accept the assignment (although acceptance of a beneficial assignment is normally presumed). Here, the stepson didn't *know* about the transfer, so there's no assignment. Apart from that, the transfer here would not be an assignment, because an assignment involves the transfer of rights under an already-existing contract. Here, the stepson's rights were created in the original agreement between the widow and the bank. Thus, if he has any rights at all, they're due to his status as an intended third-party beneficiary, *not* as an assignee.

In fact, the stepson will not prevail in his claim, because his rights under the agreement had not vested before the widow modified it. As a donee beneficiary (since the widow owed him no preexisting duty, which the deposit would discharge), he would at least have had to *know* about the contract in order for his rights to vest, and here, he didn't, when the modification took place. Since choice B mischaracterizes the stepson, and arrives at the wrong result, it's not the best response.

(C) is not the best response,

because it presupposes the stepson was an assignee, where in fact he was only a third-party beneficiary to the widow-bank agreement.

What choice C impliedly addresses is the revocability of an assignment. In general, assignments are revocable, unless:

1. The assignee gave valuable consideration for the assignment;
2. The assignee has relied on the assignment to his detriment, and such reliance should have been foreseeable to the assignor;
3. The assignee has received payment or performance from the obligor; or
4. A symbol of the assignment (e.g., a bank book) has been transferred.

Thus, if the transaction here *had* involved an assignment to the stepson, the widow's failure to give him the passbook would make the assignment revocable. However, what makes choice C incorrect is that the stepson wasn't an assignee under the widow-bank contract. In order to transfer rights under an existing contract, the assignor (here, the widow) must clearly intend to transfer her rights to a third party, the rights must be identified, and the intent must be addressed to the assignee or his representative, who must accept the assignment (although acceptance of a beneficial assignment is normally presumed). Here, the stepson didn't *know* about the transfer, so there's no assignment. Apart from that, the transfer here would not be an assignment, because an assignment involves the transfer of rights under an already-existing contract. Here, the stepson's rights were created in the original agreement between the widow and the bank. Thus, if he has any rights at all, they're due to his status as an intended third-party beneficiary, *not* as an assignee.

In fact, the stepson will not prevail in his claim, because his rights under the agreement had not vested before the widow modified it. As a donee beneficiary (since the widow owed him no preexisting duty, which the deposit would discharge), he would at least have had to *know* about the contract in order for his rights to vest, and here, he didn't, when the modification took place.

Thus, even though C arrives at the correct result, it mischaracterizes the stepson, so it can't be the best response.

Answer 25

(C) is the best response,

because it correctly identifies that the niece will be entitled to the farm due to a valid, enforceable contract with her uncle.

Under these facts the uncle made his niece an offer, in his letter—that is, a promise to do something in return for something else. He promised to will the farm to his niece in return for her caring for him and the property for the rest of his life. Since he sought performance in return, not a promise, he proposed a unilateral, not a bilateral, contract. By moving in with him and commencing taking care of him and the property, his niece accepted his offer. By remaining at the farm until his death, she fully performed under the contract, thus entitling her to the uncle's return performance: transferring the farm to her. Since C identifies this, it's the best response.

(A) is not the best response,

because the consideration would be adequate to support the contract.

In order to be enforceable, an agreement must be supported by consideration, or some substitute for consideration (e.g., promissory estoppel). Consideration requires a bargained-for exchange and either detriment to the promisee or benefit to the promisor, and typically both. Here, as to the promise to transfer the farm, the uncle is the promisor and the niece is the promisee. By coming to take care of the uncle, the niece created a binding, unilateral contract. However, the issue here isn't whether there was consideration at all—the niece clearly suffered *some* detriment and the uncle enjoyed a benefit—but whether the consideration was adequate to support a transfer of the farm.

Consideration is only inadequate if it doesn't represent the "price" of the bargain; that is, there's a donative promise in the guise of a legal, enforceable one. That's not the case here. The uncle intended to will the farm to his niece only if she moved in, cared for him, and maintained the property for the rest of his life. Both of them clearly saw her performance as the "price" of the bargain. The fact that he lived only two weeks doesn't make otherwise satisfactory consideration, unsatisfactory. Since A doesn't recognize this, it's not the best response.

(B) is not the best response,

because the uncle's promise was not an invalid promise to make a will, but an enforceable, contractual promise.

Here, the uncle made his niece an offer—that is, a promise to do something in return for something else. He promised to will the farm to her in return for her caring for him and the property for the rest of his life. Since he sought performance in return, not a promise, he proposed a unilateral contract. The niece accepted by moving in with him and taking care of him and the farm. By remaining at the farm until his death, the niece was entitled to return performance: conveyance of the farm. Thus, what makes the promise binding is that it was performance owed to the niece under a contract—it wasn't just a promise to make a will. Since B doesn't recognize this, it's not the best response.

(D) is not the best response,

because the uncle's untimely demise would not make an otherwise enforceable contract unenforceable.

One of the underlying purposes of a contract is the allocation of risk. Here, by entering into a contract to take care of the uncle for the rest of his life, the niece took on the risk that her uncle might live for many decades to come. By the same token, the uncle ran the risk that he might die imminently, making the deal for the farm a much less attractive one for his estate. While the parties may not have foreseen the uncle's death two weeks hence when they made the contract, death is not an event that could be considered unforeseeable, so as to excuse performance under the contract.

The language in choice D concerning "unforeseen" circumstances is the language of impossibility and frustration, two means of discharging contractual duties.

Under the doctrine of impossibility, where circumstances unanticipated by the parties make contract performance vitally different from what the parties contemplated, their duties under the contract are discharged, unless the adversely affected party assumed the risk the contingency might happen. Frustration of purpose relieves a duty to perform if the purpose of the contract is destroyed by a supervening act or event that was unforeseeable when the parties entered into the contract. Here again, if the risk is considered foreseeable, a court would assign the risk to one party or the other. Neither of these would apply here, because the niece was able to perform under the contract; it's only that her length of service was briefer than either party anticipated. However, she contracted to take care of her uncle for the rest of his life, and she did so, so she's entitled to the farm.

Even if the uncle's death *was* unforeseeable, assuming the contract itself was valid, rescission by the estate would not be an available remedy. Rescission by one party requires, in general, mistake (under limited circumstances), fraud, or duress. None of these exist here. The closest ground would be mutual mistake, whereby the parties made some mistake as to a basic assumption of fact. However, the length of the uncle's life would be a matter of prediction, not fact, when the contract was entered into. Thus, unilateral rescission would not be a remedy.

In fact, the niece is entitled to the farm because she performed under the contract. Since D doesn't recognize this, it's not the best response.

Answer 26

(C) is the best response,

because it correctly identifies that the electronics store can only recover to the extent the student ratified the contract when he reached age 18: $300.

Under these facts, the student entered into a contract for a non-necessary item—a television set—when he was a minor. As a result, his initial promise was voidable at his option due to his incapacity to contract. Thus, had the student not ratified the contract when he reached the age of majority, he could have avoided the contract all together (although the electronics store could seek return of the set via restitution, if it was still in the student's possession when he disaffirmed the contract). By ratifying the contract when he reached 18, the student made the original promise to pay enforceable, *but only to the extent he ratified it*: $300.

Incidentally, note that the student wrote the letter to the electronics store on his eighteenth birthday. This is relevant, in that, had he kept the television for some time thereafter, this could be considered ratification by conduct manifesting such an intent, and he could have been liable for the entire $400. Similarly, had he failed to disaffirm within a reasonable time after reaching 18, this could be considered a ratification of his original promise. Thus, by sending the letter, the student avoided the promise to pay $400. Since C recognizes this, it's the best response.

(A) is not the best response,

because the electronics store will be able to recover damages to the extent the student ratified the contract when he reached 18: $300.

Under these facts, the student entered into a contract for a non-necessary item—a television set—when he was a minor. As a result, his initial promise was voidable at his option due to his incapacity to contract. Thus, had the student not ratified the contract when he reached the age of majority, he could have avoided the contract all together (although the electronics store could seek return of the set via restitution, if it was still in the student's possession when he disaffirmed the contract).

However, what this ignores is that the student ratified the contract when he reached 18. Thus, the promise to pay would be enforceable without consideration or promissory estoppel, but only to the extent the student ratified the contract—that is, $300. Since A ignores the fact that the student ratified the contract when he reached 18, it's not the best response.

(B) is not the best response,

because it understates the electronics store's damages: it will be able to recover to the extent the student ratified the contract at age 18—that is, $300.

Under these facts, the student entered into a contract for a non-necessary item—a television set—when he was a minor. As a result, his initial promise was voidable at his option due to his incapacity to contract. Thus, had the student not ratified the contract when he reached the age of majority, he could have avoided the contract all together (although the electronics store could seek return of the set via restitution, if it was still in the student's possession when he disaffirmed the contract). However, by ratifying the contract when he reached 18, the student made the original promise to pay enforceable to the extent he reaffirmed it: $300.

If you chose this response, you were thinking of the rule relating to "necessaries." When a minor contracts to purchase necessaries, he may be bound to pay for the reasonable value of those items. Necessaries are those things, including clothing, shelter, food, or other items, necessary to sustain the minor, considering his age and station in life. If you chose this response, it's fair to say that a lot of people would agree that a television would be *more* necessary than food, shelter, or clothing—especially if it has a remote control. Alas, the law wouldn't consider a television a "necessary," so the reasonable value rule wouldn't apply. Since choice B doesn't recognize this, it's not the best response.

(D) is not the best response,

because it overstates the electronics store's damages; the student is only liable to the extent he ratified the contract: $300.

Under these facts, the student entered into a contract for a non-necessary item—a television set—when he was a minor. As a result, his initial promise was voidable at his option due to his incapacity to contract. Thus, had the student not ratified the contract when he reached the age of majority, he could have avoided the contract all together (although the electronics store could seek return of the set via restitution, if it was still in the student's possession when he disaffirmed the contract). If you chose this response, you probably thought that ratification means the whole obligation is revivified—however, that's not the rule. Say the facts were different, and the student didn't disaffirm the contract within a reasonable time after reaching 18. *This* would be considered a ratification of the original promise, and he'd be obligated to pay the $400. In other words, a ratification needn't be express; conduct manifesting intent, or failure to disaffirm within a reasonable time after reaching majority, can do the trick as well. Since D overstates the actual damages here, it's not the best response.

Answer 27

(A) is the best response,

because the investor still had the power of acceptance on April 21.

The statement in the document that the offer "will become effective as an option only if and when the $100 consideration is in fact paid" will be enforced. However, even before payment of the $100, the landowner had made both an offer to sell the property, and an offer to grant an option. Each of those offers remained open unless something happened to either terminate it or cause it to be accepted.

The landowner's sale of the property to the developer on April 20 did not terminate either offer, because this inconsistent sale could terminate the offers only if it was a revocation, and a revocation does not become effective until received by the offeree. So the revocation could not have become effective until the investor learned of the inconsistent sale, which (according to choice A) had not yet happened by the time the investor accepted the option offer by delivering his check to the landowner. Once that happened, the offer to sell the property became temporarily irrevocable under the option.

(B) is not the best response,

because actions taken in preparation to perform cannot keep open a revoked offer.

An offeree can make an offer temporarily irrevocable if the offeree makes preparations that are not explicitly required by the contract but that are necessary before performance can begin. The Restatement (in § 87(2)) provides that an offer which the offeror should reasonably expect to induce action or forbearance of substantial character on the part of the offeree before acceptance, and which does induce such action or forbearance, is binding as an option contract to the extent necessary to avoid injustice. But there are two problems for the investor with this approach: (1) it's highly unlikely that the effort in applying for a loan constitutes action of a "substantial character"; and (2) it's also highly unlikely that enforcing the contract at all would be "necessary to avoid injustice," in view of the trivial reliance interest that the investor has here.

(C) is not the best response,

because the investor's evidence would not change the requirement of the contract.

In general, a party's oral statement, made prior to or simultaneously with the signing of the document, that a clause of the document doesn't mean what it seems to mean won't be effective to vary the contract. (This stems from the parol evidence rule.) Since the document clearly says that the option won't be binding without actual payment of the $100, the landowner's statement to the contrary won't change this. (If the investor can show that the landowner intentionally mislead him, the investor might have a claim for fraud. But if the landowner was simply mistaken about the law on recitals of consideration, his oral statement will have no legal effect.)

The examiners are trying to confuse you, thinking that you may remember the general rule that where a contract recites the existence of consideration, the court won't ordinarily insist on proof that the recited consideration wasn't paid. But here, the document deals expressly with the issue by not simply reciting that consideration "has been paid," but by explicitly saying that "consideration hasn't been paid and the option contract won't be binding until consideration *is* paid." So here, the general rule that the court will not go behind recitations of consideration won't apply.

(D) is not the best response,

because option contracts for the sale of real estate need consideration to be binding.

The examiners are trying to trick you, by inducing you to think that this contract is covered by the special UCC rule on firm offers. It's true that UCC § 2-205 says that "[a]n offer by a merchant to buy or sell goods in a signed writing which by its terms gives assurance that it will be held open is not revocable, for lack of consideration, during the time stated. . . ." But the UCC applies only to contracts for the sale of goods, not real estate. There's no comparable firm-offer provision in the general common-law principles that deal with real estate. Therefore, the fact that both parties are "professional dealers in real estate" makes no difference.

Answer 28

(D) is the best response,

because the modification is ineffective.

At common law, in order to be effective, a modification must be supported by consideration. In this case, the modification would allow the contractor to reap an additional benefit (the release of his obligation to pave the sidewalk) without offering any return promise. Since the contractor has not provided consideration for the release, the modification will be ineffective under the pre-existing duty rule, and the landowner may elect to enforce the original contract as written.

(A) is not the best response,

because the contract is not for the sale of goods.

At common law, a modification must be supported by consideration in order to be effective. An exception exists for sales of goods, where the UCC provides that, under certain circumstances, a good-faith modification may be effective even absent consideration. However, the UCC is inapplicable to this situation since the construction contract primarily calls for the provision of a service, not the sale of goods. Accordingly, since the contractor has not provided any consideration for the release of his obligation to pave the sidewalk, the modification relieving him of that duty is ineffective, and the landowner can insist on full performance.

(B) is not the best response,

because it is too broad.

In general, contracts or modifications do not need to be in writing in order to be enforceable. The exception is for contracts that fall within the Statute of Frauds (suretyship, interests in land, promises in consideration of marriage, performance impossible within one year, and sales of goods valued over $500). A modification must be in writing if, as modified, the contract is within the statute of frauds. Since the landowner-contractor agreement does not fall within any of these categories, the contract and its modifications do not need to be in writing.

(C) is not the best response,

because the attempted modification occurred after the original written agreement.

The parol evidence rule generally bars introduction of evidence of prior oral understandings to interpret a later written agreement. While there are many exceptions and nuances to this rule, they do not need to be reached here because of the timing of the attempted oral modification. The statements at issue were made *after* the written contract was entered into, so introduction of the oral statements will not be barred by the parol evidence rule. However, as noted in the explanation of choice D above, the modification will still be ineffective because it was unsupported by consideration.

Answer 29

(C) is the best response,

because acceptances are effective when mailed.

In order to analyze questions that ask you to determine the time at which a contract becomes effective, it is important to examine each communication one at a time. The uncle's May 1 letter, which said he was "thinking of selling" his pickup truck, is not an offer, because it does not create a power of acceptance in his nephew. Instead, it is more accurately categorized as a solicitation for an offer, because it indicates that he would only "consider" a $7,000 offer, not that he would certainly accept it. The nephew's May 3 letter stating, "I will buy your pickup for $7,000 cash," is an offer, because the uncle would reasonably believe that he has the power to say "it's a deal" and form a binding contract. This is exactly what he did in his letter of May 6, which accepted the nephew's offer. Under the mailbox rule, an acceptance is effective as soon as the offeree places the letter in the mail. As a result, the contract was formed on May 6.

(A) is not the best response,

because the May 1 letter was not an offer.

In order to analyze questions that ask you to determine the time at which a contract becomes effective, it is important to examine each communication one at a time. The uncle's May 1 letter, which said he was "thinking of selling" his pickup truck, is not an offer, because it does not create a power of acceptance in his nephew. Instead, it is more accurately categorized as a solicitation for an offer, because it indicates that he would only "consider" a $7,000 offer, not that he would certainly accept it. The nephew's May 3 letter stating, "I will buy your pickup for $7,000 cash," is an offer, because the uncle would reasonably believe that he has the power to say "it's a deal" and form a binding contract. This is exactly what he did in his letter of May 6, which accepted the nephew's offer. Under the mailbox rule, an acceptance is effective as soon as the offeree places the letter in the mail. As a result, the contract was formed on May 6.

(B) is not the best response,

because on May 5 the uncle had not yet accepted the nephew's offer.

In order to analyze questions that ask you to determine the time at which a contract becomes effective, it is important to examine each communication one at a time. The uncle's May 1 letter, which said he was "thinking of selling" his pickup truck, is not an offer, because it does not create a power of acceptance in his nephew. Instead, it is more accurately categorized as a solicitation for an offer, because it indicates that he would only "consider" a $7,000 offer, not that he would certainly accept it. The nephew's May 3 letter stating, "I will buy your pickup for $7,000 cash," is an offer, because the uncle would reasonably believe that he has the power to say "it's a deal" and form a binding contract. This is exactly what he did in his letter of May 6, which accepted the nephew's offer. Under the mailbox rule, an acceptance is effective as soon as the offeree places the letter in the mail. As a result, the contract was formed on May 6.

(D) is not the best response,

because the nephew did not attempt to revoke his offer until after it had been accepted.

In order to analyze questions that ask you to determine the time at which a contract becomes effective, it is important to examine each communication one at a time. The uncle's May 1 letter, which said he was "thinking of selling" his pickup truck, is not an offer, because it does not create a power of acceptance in his nephew. Instead, it is more accurately categorized as a solicitation for an offer, because it indicates that he would only "consider" a $7,000 offer, not that he would certainly accept it. The nephew's May 3 letter stating, "I will buy your pickup for $7,000 cash," is an offer, because the uncle would reasonably believe that he has the power to say "it's a deal" and form a binding contract. This is exactly what he did in his letter of May 6, which accepted the nephew's offer. Under the mailbox rule, an acceptance is effective as soon as the offeree places the letter in the mail (rather than when it is received). As a result, the contract was formed on May 6. Generally, an offer can be revoked at any time before it is accepted. Since there was already a binding contract on May 6, the nephew's attempt to revoke the offer on May 7 was too late, and therefore ineffective.

Answer 30

(A) is the best response,

because the laundry company knew of the meaning the innkeeper attached to the term "daily service."

Generally the parol evidence rule prohibits consideration of prior extrinsic evidence when the parties have entered into a final written agreement. However, when there is an ambiguity in the meaning of a material term in a contract, a court may consider extrinsic evidence in determining the proper meaning. This may take the form of usage of trade, course of dealing, or course of performance, with the most specific form being preferred. However, when the two parties attach different meanings to the term at the time the agreement was made — in this instance, the first knew the meaning attached by the second while the second did not know the meaning intended by the first — the meaning attached by the party unaware of the difference (here, the second party) will control. In this case, the innkeeper did not know of the custom in the industry that "daily service" did not include Sundays. However, the laundry company was aware that the innkeeper expected service on Sundays. As a result, the innkeeper's interpretation will control and the laundry company's action will fail.

(B) is not the best response,

because a contract was formed.

In order for a contract to be formed, there must be a meeting of the minds between the parties regarding the material terms of the contract. Therefore, in cases where there is a mutual mistake about the meaning of a material term to the contract, it may be that no meeting of the minds has occurred and no contract was formed. *Raffles v. Wichelhaus* (1864). However, in this case, the misunderstanding was unilateral. While the innkeeper had no knowledge of the meaning attached to the term "daily service" by the laundry company, the converse was not true. When two parties to a contract attach different meanings to a material term in the contract, and only one party knows of the difference, a contract will be formed and the meaning of the disputed term will be that supplied by the unaware party. In this case, the result is that there is a contract for laundry service and Sundays are included within the term "daily service."

(C) is not the best response,

because the parol evidence rule does not prohibit introduction of extrinsic evidence when there is an ambiguity concerning the meaning of a material term in a written contract.

Generally the parol evidence rule prohibits consideration of prior extrinsic evidence when the parties have entered into a final written agreement. However, when there is an ambiguity in the meaning of a material term in a contract, a court may consider extrinsic evidence in determining the proper meaning. This may take the form of usage of trade, course of dealing, or course of performance, with the most specific form being preferred. However, when the two parties attach different meanings to the term at the time the agreement was made — in this instance, the first knew the meaning attached by the second while the second did not know the meaning intended by the first — the meaning attached by the party unaware of the difference (here, the second party) will control. In this case, the innkeeper did not know of the custom in the industry that "daily service" did not include Sundays. However, the laundry company was aware that the innkeeper expected service on Sundays. As a result, the innkeeper's interpretation will control and the laundry company's action will fail.

(D) is not the best response,

because, while trade usage may be used to resolve an ambiguity in the definition of a material term in a written contract, the innkeeper will be able to introduce the more specific evidence that indicates that her meaning of the term "daily service" should control.

Generally the parol evidence rule prohibits consideration of prior extrinsic evidence when the parties have entered into a final written agreement. However, when there is an ambiguity in the meaning of a material term in a contract, a court may consider extrinsic evidence in determining the proper meaning. This may take the form of usage of trade, course of dealing, or course of performance, with the most specific form being preferred. However, when the two parties attach different meanings to the term at the time the agreement was made — in this instance, the first knew the meaning attached by the second while the second did not know the meaning intended by the first — the meaning attached by the party unaware of the difference (here, the second party) will control. In this case, the innkeeper did not know of the custom in the industry that "daily service" did not include Sundays. However, the laundry company was aware that the innkeeper expected service on Sundays. As a result, the innkeeper's interpretation will control and the laundry company's action will fail.

Answer 31

(D) is the best response,

because the buyer purchased the second tract.

Generally, when a party repudiates, that party may retract that repudiation at any time. However, the right to retract the repudiation ends once the non-repudiating party has materially changed its position in reliance on the repudiation. In this problem, the buyer learned of the seller's repudiation on June 1st and four days later purchased a substitute tract. The buyer would not have done so but for the seller's indication that he did not intend to go through with his obligations under the contract. At the point the buyer purchased the substitute plot, he had materially changed his position, and the seller's repudiation became non-retractable. Since the seller's attempted retraction was not until five days after the substitute tract, the retraction was ineffective.

(A) is not the best response,

because the seller's repudiation became final when the buyer purchased the substitute tract.

Generally, when a party repudiates, that party may retract that repudiation at any time. However, the right to retract the repudiation ends once the non-repudiating party has materially changed its position in reliance on the repudiation. In this problem, the buyer learned of the seller's repudiation on June 1st and four days later purchased a substitute tract. The buyer would not have done so but for the seller's indication that he did not intend to go through with his obligations under the contract. At the point the buyer purchased the substitute plot, he had materially changed his position, and the seller's repudiation became non-retractable. Since the seller's attempted retraction was not until five days after the substitute tract, the retraction was ineffective.

(B) is not the best response,

because the seller's repudiation relieved the buyer of his obligation to tender payment.

Generally, the obligations to tender payment and convey land in a real estate conveyance contract are conditions simultaneous to each other. However, in this problem, the buyer was relieved of his obligation to perform his obligations since the seller had repudiated (anticipatorily breached) the contract. The seller's repudiation combined with the buyer's purchase of the substitute tract made the seller's repudiation final. From that point onward, the buyer had the right to sue the seller for breach and the buyer's obligation to tender payment on the closing date was discharged.

(C) is not the best response,

because the repudiation was retractable until the buyer purchased the substitute tract.

Generally, when a party repudiates, that party may retract that repudiation at any time. However, the right to retract the repudiation ends once the non-repudiating party has materially changed its position in reliance on the repudiation. In this problem, the buyer learned of the seller's repudiation on June 1st and four days later purchased a substitute tract. The buyer would not have done so but for the seller's indication that he did not intend to go through with his obligations under the contract. At the point the buyer purchased the substitute plot, he had materially changed his position, and the seller's repudiation became non-retractable. Since the seller's attempted retraction was not until five days after the substitute tract, the retraction was ineffective.

Answer 32

(A) is the best response,

because the other harms to the carpenter are unrecoverable in a contract action.

The homeowner breached the contract by not paying promptly upon the carpenter's completion of the work. As a result, the carpenter can sue for the contract price (here $10,000) plus any damages that would have been foreseeable by the homeowner at the time of the breach. Aside from non-payment, the carpenter has suffered two harms: the medical bills and the lost discount on the car he had contracted to purchase. However, neither of these is recoverable because the homeowner could not have foreseen them. A reasonable person would not expect non-payment on a contract to cause the payee to have a heart attack, and the homeowner was not on notice of the prompt payment provision in the carpenter's contract to purchase the car. As a result, the only item for which the carpenter can recover is the amount due under the terms of the contract with the homeowner.

(B) is not the best response,

because the carpenter's heart attack was not foreseeable.

The homeowner breached the contract by not paying promptly upon the carpenter's completion of the work. As a result, the carpenter can sue for the contract price (here $10,000) plus any damages that would have been foreseeable by the homeowner at the time of the breach. Assuming that the carpenter could show that his heart attack was a result of the homeowner's breach, his medical bills would still not be recoverable since the heart attack was not foreseeable. A reasonable person would not expect non-payment on a contract to cause the payee to have a heart attack. As a result, the only item for which the carpenter can recover is the amount due under the terms of the contract with the homeowner, and he should recover $10,000.

(C) is not the best response,

because the homeowner did not know of the discount provision.

The homeowner breached the contract by not paying promptly upon the carpenter's completion of the work. As a result, the carpenter can sue for the contract price (here $10,000) plus any damages that would have been foreseeable by the homeowner at the time of the breach. Although the fact that the carpenter was unable to take advantage of the prompt payment discount in the contract for the purchase of the car was a direct result of the homeowner's non-payment, it will still not be recoverable, since the homeowner was not on notice of the provision. As a result, the only item for which the carpenter can recover is the amount due under the terms of the contract with the homeowner, and he should recover $10,000.

(D) is not the best response,

because the claim is liquidated.

If you chose this response, you likely based your choice on the amount of benefit received by the homeowner as a result of the carpenter's work. This would be an appropriate measure of damages in a case in which an unjust enrichment claim is available. However, an important limitation on the scope of unjust enrichment claims is that the amount recovered cannot exceed the contract price when the only obligation under the contract left unperformed is the payment of a liquidated sum. Since the carpenter has completed his work, the only action that the contract still obliges anyone to perform is the homeowner's payment of the contract price. Here, the contract price ($10,000) is lower than the value received by the homeowner ($13,000), so the carpenter will be limited in his suit to a recovery of $10,000.

Answer 33

(D) is the best response,

because the dealer intentionally misled the buyer.

In the event that a seller convinces a buyer to purchase goods based on the seller's intentional material misrepresentation, the buyer may elect to void the contract of sale. Here, the buyer specifically asked the dealer whether the car had been in any accidents and the dealer made statements that were clearly intended to cause the buyer to believe that it had not, even though the dealer knew that was not the case. Although the seller did not explicitly state that the car had never been in an accident, the context of his statements (in response to a direct question) would cause a reasonable person hearing them to believe that the car was accident-free. The context also indicates that the dealer's silence was an intentional deception, since he had also repaired and repainted the car to conceal evidence of the past accident.

As to the materiality requirement, the fact that a car had been in an accident would clearly be a piece of information that would be an important concern to an individual deciding whether or not to purchase a car. Accordingly, the buyer may void the contract and rescind the sale.

(A) is not the best response,

because the seller made a material misrepresentation in an effort to induce the buyer to purchase the car.

In the event that a seller convinces a buyer to purchase goods based on the seller's intentional material misrepresentation, the buyer may elect to void the contract of sale. Here, the buyer specifically asked the dealer whether the car had been in any accidents and the dealer made statements that were clearly intended to cause the buyer to believe that it had not, even though the dealer knew that was not the case. Although the seller did not explicitly state that the car had never been in an accident, the context of his statements (in response to a direct question) would cause a reasonable person hearing them to believe that the car was accident-free. The context also indicates that the dealer's silence was an intentional deception, since he had also repaired and repainted the car to conceal evidence of the past accident. Although the seller offered the buyer the opportunity to have his own mechanic examine the car, there was no obligation for her to do so. Absent such an obligation, the buyer is entitled to rely on the seller's statements regarding the condition of the car. As to the materiality requirement, the fact that a car had been in an accident would clearly be a piece of information that would be an important concern to an individual deciding whether or not to purchase a car. Accordingly, the buyer may void the contract and rescind the sale.

(B) is not the best response,

because the dealer's statements, taken in context, were intended to imply that the car had never been in an accident.

In the event that a seller convinces a buyer to purchase goods based on the seller's intentional material misrepresentation, the buyer may elect to void the contract of sale. Here, the buyer specifically asked the dealer whether the car had been in any accidents and the dealer made statements that were clearly intended to cause the buyer to believe that it had not, even though the dealer knew that was not the case. Although the seller did not explicitly state that the car had never been in an accident, the context of his statements (in response to a direct question) would cause a reasonable person hearing them to believe that the car was accident-free. The context also indicates that the dealer's silence was an intentional deception, since he had also repaired and repainted the car to conceal evidence of the past accident. As to the materiality requirement, the fact that a car had been in an accident would clearly be a piece of information that would be an important concern to an individual deciding whether or not to purchase a car. Accordingly, the buyer may void the contract and rescind the sale.

(C) is not the best response,

because the evidence is insufficient to support a claim that the contract was unconscionable.

In order for a contract to be unconscionable, it must have unfair terms that were agreed to as a result of an unfair bargaining process. In general, more than mere misrepresentation on the part of one party is needed to show unconscionability. Unconscionability will generally be found only in cases where no reasonable person would have agreed to the terms of the contract after fair negotiations. There will normally have to be grossly unfair terms in the contract and the bargaining process would have to be characterized by a substantial inequality in bargaining power. Here, the buyer could have had his own mechanic examine the car, so there was a procedural safeguard to protect the buyer from the dealer's advantage in knowledge. On the MBE, you should be very careful before selecting unconscionability as a justification for voiding a contract because of the high hurdles that must be cleared in order to prove the defense. It is much more likely that an easier–to–prove defense to enforcement, such as inducement by fraud, is available.

Answer 34

(A) is the best response,

because it provides a sound basis for enforcing the oral contract.

The principal obstacle for the nephew under these facts is finding a way to enforce the land sale contract even though it was oral. That is, he wants to prove that when the widower *bought* the farm, the nephew *got* the farm. The problem is, land sale contracts are within the Statute of Frauds, meaning that they must be in writing to be enforceable. (While Statutes of Frauds vary from state to state, land sale contracts are traditionally covered.)

Since the contract here required a writing, if the nephew prevailed, it means he offered some basis on which the writing requirement would be excused. Furthermore, note that the nephew would want the contract *enforced,* not just quasi-contractual recovery (which would give him only the reasonable value of his services).

Choice A offers just such a basis, by providing reasoning that some states view as a valid excuse from complying with the Statute of Frauds. Courts are becoming more willing to apply the reliance doctrine to Statute of Frauds problems, such that where a buyer relies on the contract and performs under it on that basis, the other party is *estopped* from pleading the Statute of Frauds, and the performing party (here, the nephew) can recover *on the contract.* Thus, while land sale contracts traditionally required payment *plus* some action explainable only by the contract's existence, modern courts *are* allowing payment to suffice based on *reliance.* While you couldn't say this was a *general* rule, choice A specifically conditions the recovery on the action being in a state that *does* recognize the reliance doctrine. This, coupled with the fact that no other choice would result in the nephew's being able to enforce the contract, makes A the best response.

(B) is not the best response,

because although it states a theoretically correct rule of law, it would not apply to these facts; and beyond that, it wouldn't give the nephew the remedy he wants (enforcing the contract) but rather would result in recovery under quasi-contract (the reasonable value of his services).

Under the Statute of Frauds, certain types of contracts must be in writing in order to be enforceable. While the contracts covered vary somewhat from state to state, such contracts typically include, among others, those contracts incapable of performance in less than one year; contracts in consideration of marriage; contracts for the sale of an interest in land; and sale of goods and securities as covered by the UCC. As a contract for the sale of an interest in land, the contract between the widower and his nephew would have to comply with the Statute of Frauds.

However, there *are* circumstances where compliance with the Statute of Frauds will be *excused.* Typically, this will occur where excuse is the only way to avoid undue hardship or fraud. Choice B states the *traditional* rule: Under a land sale contract, where the buyer pays in whole or in part, the seller's promise to sell is only enforceable if there is other conduct unequivocally referable to the agreement — that is, the only explanation for the payment and acts is the contract's existence. For instance, if a buyer pays and constructs buildings on the land, this would unequivocally suggest a land sale contract. However, under these facts, the nephew could have performed services for the widower with the expectation of payment, not necessarily conveyance of the land. Thus, the "unequivocal referability" would be missing. Not only *that,* but using this argument would only give the nephew the reasonable value of his services, *not* the farm itself (and it's the farm he wants). Since B doesn't recognize this, it's not the best response.

(C) is not the best response,

because the "clean hands" doctrine is irrelevant to these facts.

The "clean hands" doctrine is only relevant where a plaintiff seeks specific performance of a contract. Under that doctrine, a plaintiff will be denied specific performance if he's guilty of any inequitable conduct with respect to the transaction in controversy. There are two reasons why this won't apply here. First, the widower's son is not seeking specific performance of a contract; instead, his is a standard legal claim for possession of land. Second, while the son may have been something of a jerk for ignoring his father in his twilight years, this wouldn't rise to the level of inequity. Thus, the "clean hands" doctrine wouldn't be relevant to a court's decision in the nephew's favor. Since C doesn't recognize this, it's not the best response.

(D) is not the best response,

because it offers an exception to the Statute of Frauds that does not, in fact, exist.

Under the Statute of Frauds, certain types of contracts must be in writing to be enforceable. While the contracts covered vary from state to state, contracts for the sale of interests in land are traditionally covered. Thus, the contract between the widower and his nephew would be within the Statute of Frauds, and would generally require a writing to be enforceable.

However, there *are* circumstances where compliance with the Statute of Frauds will be *excused.* Typically, this will occur where excuse is the only way to avoid undue hardship or fraud. The mere existence of *any* familial relationship would *not* provide an excuse from satisfying the Statute of Frauds. Instead, the source of the excuse under these facts is that the nephew would suffer undue hardship if the contract weren't enforced. Since choice D doesn't recognize this, it's not the best response.

Answer 35

(D) is the best response,

because the interest rate condition was intended to only benefit the buyer.

While the general rule is that express conditions in a contract will be strictly enforced, there is an important exception for cases in which a condition is only intended to benefit one party to the contract. In such cases, that party always has the power to waive the condition. The waiver need not be express, but rather may be inferred by the circumstances. Here, the provision that made the buyer's obligation to purchase the parcel conditional on his obtaining a loan at an interest rate no higher than ten percent was designed to protect the buyer in the event that he could not obtain such a loan. (The seller has no reason to care what interest rate the buyer gets.) Since the buyer tendered the purchase price, he was clearly willing to go through with the sale even though he was unable to get a loan at a specified rate. From this conduct, a court would certainly infer that the buyer intended to waive the condition. Accordingly, the seller cannot use the failure of the condition as a means of avoiding the contract.

(A) is not the best response,

because it is an incorrect statement of law.

The problem with choice A is the word "only." It is true that a court will avoid applying the "strict compliance" rule in situations where a forfeiture would result (i.e., one party has relied on the bargain and insisting on strict compliance would cause him to fail to receive the expected benefit of his bargain). However, this is not the only case in which a court will not enforce strict compliance. In particular, as is the situation in this case, a court will allow a party to waive a condition if the condition was included in the contract solely to benefit the party seeking to waive it. The waiver need not be express, but rather may be inferred by the circumstances.

(B) is not the best response,

because there was no attempt to modify the contract.

The issue of this problem is not modification of the contract, but rather the waiver of an express condition. A modification is a change in the obligations of one or both of the parties to a contract. Here, the parties are not disputing whether or not the obligations under the contract have been changed. Instead, the dispute is over whether the seller can refuse to perform because the buyer was unable to obtain a loan at or below a ten percent interest rate, which was an express condition in the contract. The seller is unable to enforce this condition because it was included in the contract solely for the benefit of the buyer (to protect him in case he could not get a satisfactory loan). When an express condition protects only one party to a contract, that party may elect to waive the condition and insist on the other party's performance even if the condition has not been satisfied.

(C) is not the best response,

because it raises an irrelevant concern.

The issue in this case is whether the seller can refuse to perform because the buyer was unable to obtain a loan at or below a ten percent interest rate, which was an express condition in the contract. The seller is unable to enforce this condition because it was included in the contract solely for the benefit of the buyer (to protect him in case he could not get a satisfactory loan). When an express condition protects only one party to a contract, that party may elect to waive the condition and insist on the other party's performance even if the condition has not been satisfied. While it is certainly true that the buyer detrimentally changed his position in reliance on the seller's promise to convey (by taking a loan), that is irrelevant to whether or not the contract is enforceable. If the contract was not enforceable, and the buyer was attempting to sue under a promissory estoppel theory, then the concern would be relevant. However, since the buyer will be able to enforce the contract, he will not have to rely on promissory estoppel.

Answer 36

(D) is the best response,

because it addresses the central reason that the salesman will not be entitled to the commission.

There are two key points here: the provisions of the original contract, and the fact that the termination wasn't wrongful.

Under the original contract, the manufacturer was free to terminate the salesman at any time. Furthermore, the salesman's being employed *when the bill was sent to the customer* was an express condition of the duty to pay the commission. As a result, in the absence of a bad-faith termination, the contract terms would control in determining the salesman's right to the commission. Here, you're told specifically that the termination wasn't wrongful. Thus, the termination was within the manufacturer's rights, and it can't be a source of liability for the company.

Furthermore, the salesman *was* paid a salary for the time he put in, and thus the manufacturer didn't receive something for nothing. A primary purpose of contracts is to allocate risks. Here, the salesman knew what he bargained for and undertook the risk he might be rightfully terminated before the bill was sent. The thing that makes this question tough is that your gut feeling is that the salesman deserves the commission. This answer indicates, as do so many MBE questions, why it's so important to analyze MBE questions coldly and impartially. Since D recognizes that the salesman isn't entitled to the commission and the central reason why, it's the best response.

(A) is not the best response,

because it ignores the existence of an express condition that was not satisfied under these facts.

The contract between the manufacturer and the salesman required that the salesman be employed *when the bill is sent to a customer* in order to receive a commission from that sale. Thus, eligibility to receive a commission is *expressly* conditioned on the salesman's being employed when the bill is sent. Here, the salesman was fired on March 15, and the bill was sent on March 31. Thus, an express condition was not met, and the salesman is not entitled to the commission. (Note that the salesman is trying to recover under the contract, since he's seeking the sales commission, *not* the reasonable value of his services.)

If you chose this response, it's probably because your gut feeling is that the salesman *should* be paid. Probably, if you were the salesman, you'd stuff a raw potato up the exhaust pipe of your former boss's Mercedes — right? If you feel this way, there's an important fact you overlooked: The termination wasn't wrongful. Had the manufacturer acted in bad faith, the result would have been entirely different. In fact, another significant point is that the salesman was *also* receiving a salary. Thus, when the salesman entered the employment agreement, terminable at the manufacturer's will and with the commission-only-when-billed provision, he got what he bargained for. Since A mistakenly states that the salesman should recover the sales commission, it's not the best response.

(B) is not the best response,

because the salesman's promise to help the customer will not be relevant to his claim against the manufacturer.

The salesman's promise to the customer will not determine his right to the sales commission. Instead, you have to look at the manufacturer's and the salesman's rights and duties under the employment contract and determine if there is some basis on which the salesman is entitled to the sales commission. The original contract was terminable at will, so the manufacturer could fire the salesman on the spot, anytime. Furthermore, the contract makes employment on the date the customer is sent a bill an *express condition* of the duty to pay the salesman a commission. Of course, if the manufacturer acted wrongfully or in bad faith, the salesman would prevail. But this question tells you specifically that the termination wasn't wrongful. The salesman was terminated March 15, and the bill was sent March 31; thus, he's not entitled to the sales commission.

A wrinkle here is that the manufacturer knew the salesman promised the customer that he'd assist for six months after installation in getting the system going. Thus, the salesman could argue that the manufacturer was estopped from firing him for that period. However, the facts specifically tell you that the termination was within the manufacturer's rights, so estoppel can't apply. Since B attaches significance to the salesman's promise to the customer, where little actually exists, B isn't the best response.

(C) is not the best response,

because it misstates the facts. If *quantum meruit* were applicable (which it isn't), it would mean *the salesman* should get paid, not *his replacement.*

Quantum meruit ("what the thing's worth") is the measure of recovery under quasi-contract. Quasi-contract is typically applied where plaintiff confers a benefit on the defendant, under circumstances where defendant would be unjustly enriched if he were allowed to retain the benefit without paying for it. The problem with applying this here is that there *is* a contractual provision that controls, and so there is no basis for referring to quasi-contract. Under the contract here, the manufacturer was entitled to fire the salesman at any time. The salesman's employment at the time a customer is billed is an express condition to his being paid a commission. Most importantly, you're told that the salesman's termination wasn't wrongful. Thus, the salesman's right to the commission can be determined within the four corners of the contract, without falling back on quasi-contract.

Assuming *arguendo* that quasi-contract were applicable, it would result in the salesman being paid, not his replacement, since it's the salesman's work with the customer that resulted in the benefit to the manufacturer. Thus, even if quasi-contract were appropriate here, choice C misapplies it, so it's not the best response.

Answer 37

(B) is the best response,

because it correctly captures the rule on when defective installments may be rejected.

In sale-of-goods cases, it is actually harder for the buyer under an installment contract to reject a non-conforming tender than for the buyer in a one-shot (non-installment) contract. Rejection in installment contracts is handled by a special code section, § 2-612(2), which begins by saying that "the buyer may reject any installment which is non-conforming *if* the non-conformity *substantially impairs* the *value* of that installment and *cannot be cured*[.]" The final clause of that section then adds a proviso dealing further with cure: If the non-conformity of the installment *does not substantially impair the value of the whole contract*, then "if . . . the seller *gives adequate assurance* of [the non-conformity's] *cure* the buyer *must accept that installment*."

Applying § 2-612(2) to these facts: (1) The non-conformity certainly substantially impaired the value of the installment, since 50 percent of the required poundage was missing. (2) The non-conformity couldn't be "cured" here, since a cure would require that the shortfall be made up by the time of the weekly baking on Tuesday morning, and the seller was merely committing to make up the shortfall on Wednesday, which would be too late to be useful. (3) For the same reason as (2), the seller's assurances of cure were not "adequate," since the make-up delivery would arrive too late for the week's baking. So Choice B correctly explains why the requirements for the buyer to reject under § 2-612(2), first clause, are satisfied.

(A) is not the best choice,

because the perfect tender rule that it recites does not apply to these facts.

In one-shot (non-installment) cases, UCC § 2-601 essentially applies (though with some important exceptions) the "perfect tender" rule — the buyer can reject the whole delivery, or any commercial units, if the goods "fail *in any respect* to conform to the contract[.]" But § 2-601 explicitly says that it does not apply to installment contracts, and the contract here is an installment contract. As is described in Choice B, in installment contracts the buyer may reject the installment only if the non-conformity "substantially impairs" the value of the installment.

(C) is not the best choice,
because it relies on two irrelevant facts.

First, the installment buyer is permitted, by § 2-601(2), to reject a non-conforming installment if the non-conformity substantially impairs the value of *that installment*—there is *no* requirement that the non-conformity also impair the value of the *entire contract*. (Impairment of the value of the entire contract matters only if the buyer wants to cancel the whole contract, not merely reject the installment; see § 2-601(3).) Second, the wholesaler's assurances of cure are irrelevant here—to be a true "cure," the promised delivery would have to be in time for the weekly baking session, and here the promised delivery would, even if it happened, be a day too late. Therefore, the assurances of cure were not "adequate," as § 2-601(2) requires.

(D) is not the best choice,
because the bakery's acceptance of the non-conformity of the first installment did not affect its right to reject the second installment.

It's true that even where a non-conformity in one installment substantially impairs the value of the whole contract, the buyer loses his right to cancel the whole contract (and is deemed to "reinstate the contract") if he accepts the non-conforming installment without promptly notifying the seller of the cancellation. UCC § 2-612(3). So here, if the shortage in the first installment had substantially impaired the value of the whole contract (which it probably did not), the bakery's willingness to accept the late evening delivery would have wiped out any right the bakery might have had to cancel the whole contract at that point. But acceptance of *one* non-conforming installment does not constitute a waiver of the buyer's right to reject any *later* installment whose nonconformity substantially impairs the value of that installment. So nothing the bakery did in connection with the first installment limited its right to reject the second non-conforming installment.

Answer 38

(C) is the best response,
because the arbitration clause was a proposal for an additional term, which automatically became part of the contract if it was not a material alteration.

This is a classic battle-of-the-forms problem under the UCC. Because the buyer's offer was silent on the issue of whether disputes were to be arbitrated, the arbitration clause contained in the seller's acknowledgment (i.e., the seller's acceptance) was what the UCC refers to as an "additional" term. Under § 2-207(2), in a contract between merchants, the acceptance's proposed additional terms become part of the contract unless one of three things happens: (1) the offer expressly limits acceptance to the term of the offer; (2) the proposed term materially alters the contract; or (3) the offeror promptly notifies the offeree of an objection to the proposed term. (It's clear that both parties are "merchants," because non-merchants don't buy or sell 50 tons of cotton.)

Here, it's clear that event (1) didn't happen (the buyer's offer said nothing to indicate that the seller could only accept by agreeing to the terms of the offer and making no other changes or proposals). Similarly, it's clear that (3) didn't happen, since the buyer never responded with an objection (or any other comment) about the proposed arbitration clause. So the arbitration clause became part of the contract as long as (2) didn't happen, i.e., as long as the clause is not deemed to have materially altered the contract. Courts have generally split on the issue of whether an arbitration clause materially alters a contract. But this choice is correct in stating that the seller's *best argument* is to assert that the arbitration clause did not pose a material alteration—the seller has a plausible chance of convincing the court that this is true, and if the seller is able to do so, he automatically wins the case (i.e., he's entitled to arbitration). By contrast, none of the other arguments, even if factually correct, will result in victory for the seller on this point.

(A) is not the best response,
because it states a fact that, even if true, is irrelevant.

Even if arbitration were a more efficient dispute resolution mechanism (which may or may not be true), arbitration's relative efficiency is not the governing standard for assessing whether the arbitration provision became a term of the parties' agreement. Rather, the issue is determined by UCC § 2-207(2)'s detailed provisions about when a proposed "additional" term in the acceptance becomes part of the agreement. And the relative efficiency of the proposed additional term is not one of the factors to be considered under § 2-207(2).

(B) is not the best response,
because, while it correctly states a fact, it draws an unwarranted conclusion from that fact.

It's true that the provision for arbitration did not contradict any term in the buyer's offer, since the buyer's offer was entirely silent about whether there should be arbitration. But this choice falsely implies that where the acceptance proposes a term that does not contradict any term in the offer, the term proposed in the acceptance automatically becomes part of the contract. UCC § 2-207(2) contains detailed provisions about when a proposed "additional" (i.e., non-contradicting) term in the acceptance becomes part of the agreement; sometimes the additional term does not do so.

(D) is not the best response,
because it is based on the incorrect premise that the seller's response was a counter-offer.

If the case was to be resolved by common-law principles, this choice's assertion that the seller's response was a counter-offer would be factually correct. That's because, under the common law's "mirror image" rule, an additional material term in a response to an offer constitutes a counter-offer. However, UCC Article 2 governs this transaction because it involves a sale of goods. Under UCC § 2-207, the presence of an additional term does not turn what would otherwise be an acceptance into a counter-offer: § 2-207(1) says that "A definite and seasonable expression of acceptance or a written confirmation which is sent within a reasonable time operates as an acceptance even though it states terms additional to or different from those offered or agreed upon, unless acceptance is expressly made conditional on assent to the additional or different terms." Since the "acceptance . . . expressly made conditional on assent" language does not apply here, the presence of the proposed additional term did not stop the seller's acknowledgment from serving as an acceptance and forming a contract. Furthermore, the buyer's silent acceptance of the goods does not, under § 2-207, mean that the buyer is deemed to have accepted the arbitration clause. The agreement was complete as soon as the seller's acknowledgment clause was sent, and no later conduct by the buyer (e.g., his "accepting" the delivery by not sending the goods back) changed the terms of that already-completed agreement.

Answer 39

(B) is the best response,
because the contract qualifies as an enforceable requirements contract under the UCC.

UCC § 2-306 authorizes requirements and output contracts. The contract here is enforceable, because the company's promise to buy all of its requirements for lawn care products during the coming year furnished consideration for the supplier's promise to give it a 10 percent discount off its published prices. Although the terms of the agreement gave the supplier the discretion to increase the published prices during the year, nothing in the contract gave the supplier the right to discontinue the 10 percent discount from the published prices. Therefore, the supplier's refusal to continue giving the discount was a breach.

(A) is not the best response,
because the fact that the parties partly performed is irrelevant.

The fact that the parties have partly performed an agreement matters in some scenarios. For instance, an oral agreement that would normally fall within the Statute of Frauds and thus be unenforceable may become enforceable based on part performance. But the contract here was in writing, and met the criteria for a requirements contract under the UCC. Therefore, the supplier was required to honor the 10 percent discount throughout the coming year. And that is true without respect to whether there had been any part performance.

(C) is not the best response,
because the supplier had no right of revocation at the time in question.

"Revocation" refers to the offeror's right to cancel his offer up until the time a contract has been formed by mutual assent (i.e., by acceptance). Once the contract is formed, the offeror no longer has a right of revocation. If the agreement here could properly be construed as a series of offers to make individual one-delivery contracts, then the supplier might indeed have had the right of revocation described in this choice. But this "series of offers" interpretation is not correct here; the parties made a single contract to cover all of the company's requirements for lawn care products during the coming year, not a series of possible future contracts.

(D) is not the correct response,
because the absence of a minimum quantity term did not affect the enforceability of the contract.

UCC § 2-306(1) makes requirements (and output) contracts enforceable. If the parties choose to impose a minimum-quantity term in a requirements contract, that term will be enforced. But as long as the buyer is promising to buy all his requirements for a certain type of product, the fact that the contract does not establish a minimum quantity does not prevent the contract from being enforceable. (§ 2-306(2) imposes on the buyer an obligation to "use best efforts to promote the sale of the goods," thus preventing the buyer's promise from being illusory and therefore preventing the seller from having a lack-of-consideration defense.)

Answer 40

(D) is the best response,
because it correctly construes the limits on the general contractor's right to demand assurances of performance.

This is a contract for the sale of goods, so the scope of a party's right to demand assurances of performance is specified in UCC § 2-609(1). That section says, in part, that "*When reasonable grounds for insecurity arise* with respect to the performance of either party the other may in writing demand adequate assurance of due performance and until he receives such assurance may if commercially reasonable suspend any performance for which he has not already received the agreed return." By negative implication, if reasonable grounds for insecurity concerning the performance of the other party have not yet arisen, the first party does not have a right to demand assurances. Since we're expressly told that "the general contractor had no reason to doubt the subcontractor's ability to perform," we know that reasonable grounds for insecurity had not yet arisen. Therefore, the general contractor had no right to demand assurances, and the subcontractor was not required to provide them. When he didn't provide them, this was not a repudiation or breach of the contract, so the general contractor had no right to suspend (let alone cancel) the contract or obtain the supplies from someone else.

(A) is not the best response,

because the subcontractor was not required to provide assurances.

There are indeed circumstances in which a contracting party's failure to provide adequate assurance of performance upon request by the other party will constitute an anticipatory repudiation. But under UCC § 2-609(1), the party who wishes to demand assurances may do so only "when reasonable grounds for insecurity arise with respect to the performance of [the other] party." Since we're told that the general contractor had no reason to doubt the subcontractor's ability to perform, the general contractor had no right to demand assurances, and the subcontractor's failure to provide them was therefore not an anticipatory repudiation.

(B) is not the best response,

because the absence of a stated quantity did not matter in this requirements contract.

The subcontractor promised to deliver all of the general contractor's requirements for steel joists that would be required in the construction of the building. Therefore, this was a valid requirements contract under UCC § 2-306(1), and that's true even though the contract did not state a definite quantity or even a minimum quantity.

(C) is not the best response,

because, although it reaches the correct conclusion, it misstates the legal effect of the contract's silence on the right to demand assurances.

Both at common law and under the UCC, if the contract is silent on the issue, either party has the right to demand assurances of performance from the other, if (and only if) the demanding party has reasonable grounds for feeling insecure about whether the other party will perform. So if the general contractor had had reasonable grounds for insecurity about whether the subcontractor would perform, the fact that the contract document did not expressly give the general contractor a right to demand assurances would not have transformed his demand into a breach. The problem with the general contractor's demand here is that he did not in fact have reasonable grounds for insecurity.

Answer 41

(D) is the best response,

because even a total integration may be supplemented or explained by a trade usage.

First, notice that this agreement, since it is for the sale of goods, is governed by Article 2 of the UCC. Article 2's version of the parol evidence rule makes it clear that even a term in a total integration may be supplemented or explained by a trade usage. When the sub-sections of § 2-202 are viewed together, the result is that even where the writing is a total integration (i.e., it was "intended . . . as a complete and exclusive statement of the terms of the agreement," § 2-202(b)), the meaning of terms in it may still be "explained or supplemented (a) by course of performance, course of dealing, or usage of trade[.]" (But express terms in the total integration may not be "contradicted" by evidence of prior agreements, or of simultaneous oral agreements; also, even "consistent additional terms" may not be shown if the integration is total.)

According to most courts, a trade usage will be viewed as permissibly "explaining" or "supplementing" a term in a total integration, as long as the usage doesn't represent a "total negation" of the writing. The 5%-leeway trade usage would likely not be found to "totally negate" the quantity term of the writing, but rather, to merely "explain" the precise meaning of that term.

(A) is not the best response,

because the offered evidence is not inconsistent with the express language of the agreement.

Under UCC § 2-202, evidence of trade usage may be used to "explain" or "supplement" the meaning of a term, even a term contained in a total integration. However, that provision says that no form of evidence (trade usage or otherwise) may "contradict" such a writing. But by the prevailing view, only evidence that "totally negates" a written term will be deemed to be contradictory. Here, the writing contains the quantity term, but does not say anything about how one is to interpret the meaning of the stated quantity. So it's likely that the court would conclude that the 5 percent-leeway usage is a non-contradictory and permissible "explanation" of the quantity term.

(B) is not the best response,

because the fact that the agreement was totally integrated doesn't prevent admission of the proposed evidence.

UCC § 2-202 says that although a writing is either partly or totally integrated (i.e., the writing is what the section calls a "writing intended by the parties as a final expression of their agreement with respect to such terms as are included therein"), a term in it may be "explained" or "supplemented" (though not "contradicted") by a trade usage. And even the fact that the writing was a *total* integration (i.e., was, as we're told, "intended as a *complete and exclusive* statement of the terms of the agreement," mirroring language in § 2-202(b)) doesn't preclude the court from considering a trade usage that merely "explains" a written term. As is discussed in Choice A, since the trade usage here does not "totally negate" the written quantity term, it's admissible as an explanation of the written term's meaning.

(C) is not the best response,

because substantial performance by the farmer would not be sufficient.

This is a non-installment contract (i.e., a "one-shot" contract). UCC § 2-601, which applies to non-installment contracts, says that "if the goods or the tender of delivery fail in any respect to conform to the contract," the buyer may "reject the whole." This section thus applies the "perfect tender" rule, not the more-forgiving substantial-performance standard. So even though the farmer probably did substantially perform, that fact alone will not entitle him to establish that the buyer breached by rejecting the shipment. Furthermore, the question asks you whether the proffered trade-usage evidence will be admitted, and the fact that the farmer may or may not have substantially performed is irrelevant to that question.

Answer 42

(C) is the best response,

because restitution is designed to reverse unjust enrichment.

A party's "restitution interest" is defined as his "interest in having restored to him any *benefit that he has conferred* on the other party." Rest. 2d of Contracts § 344(c). Of the three sums laid out by the buyer, the only one that took the form of a benefit conferred on the other party was the $1,000 down payment. Under UCC § 2-711(1), if the seller fails to make delivery, the buyer is entitled to various items of damage "in addition to recovering so much of the price as has been paid[.]" So in addition to such expectation-interest damages as the cost of cover, the buyer will be entitled to restitution of the down payment.

(A) is not the best response,

because it does not represent any benefit conferred on the seller.

A party's restitution interest is the party's interest in having restored to him any benefit that he has conferred on the other party. Rest. 2d § 344(c). The cost of the foundation was not a sum that was paid to the seller, and it did not benefit the seller. Therefore, it is not part of the buyer's restitution interest (though it would be recoverable as a component of his expectation interest).

(B) is not the best response,

because it does not represent any benefit conferred on the seller.

A party's restitution interest is the party's interest in having restored to him any benefit that he has conferred on the other party. Rest. 2d § 344(c). The $500 price differential, although paid out by the buyer, did not confer any benefit on the seller, so it can't be part of the buyer's restitution interest (though it would be recoverable as a component of his expectation interest).

(D) is not the best response,

because the buyer's restitution interest includes the $1,000 down payment.

This choice is wrong because choice C is correct—the buyer's restitution interest consists of his interest in recovering any benefit he conferred on the other party, an interest that would encompass the $1,000 down payment.

Answer 43

(A) is the best response,

because, although the offer was no longer irrevocable on April 15, it had not been revoked, and was therefore capable of being accepted.

UCC § 2-205 allows merchants to make "firm offers," i.e., offers that are irrevocable for a limited period even without consideration. Section 2-205 says that the period of irrevocability "in no event may . . . exceed three months." So by April 15, the offer was no longer irrevocable, and the stationer was therefore free to revoke it.

But the stationer did not in fact revoke. (The revocation could only have occurred if the lawyer had learned that the stationer was no longer sticking to the offer.) Nor did the offer lapse on account of the passage of time, because the circumstances indicate that a "reasonable time for acceptance" was any time during the following year. There is no other event that caused the offer to terminate. Consequently, the lawyer's fax was a valid acceptance.

(B) is not the best response,

because at the time of acceptance this was not an option contract any more.

For the reasons stated in the analysis of choice A above, the period of irrevocability—i.e., the period during which there was an option contract—was only three months, not one year. So the lawyer's acceptance was effective not because there was an option contract at the time he accepted, but because the non-option-contract offer was unrevoked as of the moment of his acceptance (as described in the discussion of choice A above).

(C) is not the best response,

because although the stationer's offer was irrevocable for only three months, it was still in force (though revocable) when the lawyer accepted.

It's true that, as this choice states, an offer by a merchant under § 2-205 may remain "firm," i.e., irrevocable, only for three months, at a maximum. But after that time expires, a firm offer doesn't automatically terminate, it merely becomes revocable. The stationer didn't exercise its right to terminate the offer, so it was still in force when the lawyer accepted it on April 15.

(D) is not the best response,

because in this case a reasonable time for acceptance was the entire year.

It's true that, as this choice suggests, an offer that has no express acceptance deadline will lapse after a "reasonable time." But here, the letter's reference to "the next calendar year" indicates that a reasonable time for acceptance was the entire next year. After three months, the stationer had the right to termination by revocation, but it didn't do so. Since there was no termination by lapse of a reasonable time for acceptance, the April 15 acceptance occurred while the offer was still open, and was therefore effective.

Answer 44

(C) is the best response,

because unless a sales contract expressly provides otherwise, the risk of loss passes when the goods are shipped.

Because the subject of this contract is the sale of goods (the bracelets), Article 2 of the UCC applies. UCC § 2-509 provides that, as a default rule, when a third-party carrier is used, the risk of loss of the goods passes to the buyer upon the seller's delivery of the goods to the carrier. The parties to the contract are free to alter this allocation of risk by providing otherwise in the contract. However, since the contract of sale is silent on this matter, § 2-503 will apply, and the risk of loss passed when the bracelets were delivered to the carrier.

(A) is not the best response,

because the risk of loss passed when the seller delivered the bracelets to the carrier.

Because the subject of this contract is the sale of goods (the bracelets), Article 2 of the UCC applies. UCC § 2-509 provides that, as a default rule, when a third-party carrier is used, the risk of loss of the goods passes to the buyer upon the seller's delivery of the goods to the carrier. The parties to the contract are free to alter this allocation of risk by providing otherwise in the contract. However, since the contract of sale is silent on this matter, § 2-503 will apply, and the risk of loss passed when the bracelets were delivered to the carrier.

(B) is not the best response,

because identification of goods to the contract does not cause the risk of loss to shift from seller to buyer.

Because the subject of this contract is the sale of goods (the bracelets), Article 2 of the UCC applies. UCC § 2-509 provides that, as a default rule, when a third-party carrier is used, the risk of loss of the goods passes to the buyer upon the seller's delivery of the goods to the carrier. The parties to the contract are free to alter this allocation of risk by providing otherwise in the contract. However, since the contract of sale is silent on this matter, § 2-503 will apply, and the risk of loss passed when the bracelets were delivered to the carrier.

(D) is not the best response,

because the risk of loss had already passed to the buyer when the seller delivered the bracelets to the carrier.

Because the subject of this contract is the sale of goods (the bracelets), Article 2 of the UCC applies. UCC § 2-509 provides that, as a default rule, when a third-party carrier is used, the risk of loss of the goods passes to the buyer upon the seller's delivery of the goods to the carrier. The parties to the contract are free to alter this allocation of risk by providing otherwise in the contract. However, since the contract of sale is silent on this matter, § 2-503 will apply, and the risk of loss passed when the bracelets were delivered to the carrier.

Answer 45

(B) is the best response,

because the UCC allows the attempt at modification to serve as a waiver.

Waiver is a party's manifestation of willingness to forego the benefit of a condition that occurs after the contract is formed but before the condition fails to occur. So here, the pharmacist's oral agreement on August 1 that the cabinets didn't have to be delivered until August 20 meets the requirement of a waiver.

The real issue in this question is the effect of the Statute of Frauds. Under § 2-201(1), a sales contract for $500 or more must be supported by a signed writing.

The question is whether, in a contract that falls within § 2-201(1)'s Statute of Frauds requirement (because it's for more than $500) and that initially satisfies that requirement, any modification must be in writing. Section 2-209(3), on modifications, says that "the requirements of the statute of frauds section . . . must be satisfied if the contract as modified is within its provisions." Courts are in confusion about whether and when this sentence requires the modification itself to be in writing. But on these facts it doesn't matter, because, according to § 2-209(4), "[a]lthough an attempt at modification or rescission does not satisfy the requirements of [the Statute of Frauds], it can operate as a waiver." So the pharmacist's oral promise to take a later delivery, although oral, will still act as a waiver. Although the pharmacist might have had the power to retract the waiver (see § 2-209(5), allowing retraction unless retraction would be "unjust in view of a material change of position in reliance on the waiver"), there's no indication in these facts that the pharmacist ever retracted. So he's bound by the waiver, and the furniture store will win.

(A) is not the best response,

because the July 15 contract would have to be in writing per the Statute of Frauds, but the oral change would nonetheless be binding as a waiver.

Under § 2-201(1), a sales contract for $500 or more must be supported by a signed writing. So this contract had to be in writing, as it was. Consequently, choice A is flatly wrong.

The furniture store will win, but not for the reason given. Instead, it will win because the August 1 agreement (whether or not it had to be in writing to be a full, non-retractable change to the agreement) served as a waiver, and, as described in the analysis of choice B above, waivers will be enforced even though they are oral.

(C) is not the best response,

because the UCC does not require consideration for agreements modifying a preexisting contract.

See § 2-209 (1): "An agreement modifying a contract within this Article needs no consideration to be binding."

(D) is not the best response,

because the parol evidence rule does not apply.

The parol evidence rule as integrated into the UCC holds that where a writing is a final expression of the parties' agreement (i.e., an integration), it may not be contradicted by evidence of any *prior* agreement, whether written or oral, nor of any oral agreement that is *contemporaneous* with the writing.

The August 1 agreement occurred after, not before or simultaneous with, the execution of the signed writing. Therefore, the parol evidence rule has no application on the issue of whether the August 1 agreement is enforceable though an oral agreement.

Answer 46

(C) is the best response,

because it correctly states that the baker has a valid claim against the farmer for breach of contract.

Under UCC § 2-601, the buyer, in a single delivery (not installment) contract, has the right to reject the goods if they "fail in any respect to conform to the contract." However, the seller will have the right to cure defects, under § 2-508, under two circumstances, as long as seller notifies buyer of his intent to cure:

1. The time for performance has not run out, and the seller can cure within that time; or
2. The seller has reason to believe that the buyer would accept non-conforming goods—in which case the seller can go reasonably *beyond* the time allowed for performance in curing the defects.

Here, neither of these exceptions will apply. The contract called for the farmer to deliver on August 1, which he did; thus, there's no time left for performance. Second, there's nothing in these facts to give the farmer a reasonable belief that the baker would accept non-conforming goods. As a result, the general rule will apply, and the baker will have a claim for breach (since the baker rightfully rejected the goods). Since C recognizes this, it's the best response.

(A) is not the best response,

because it does not reflect the UCC view on performance.

Under the UCC, the general rule is that the buyer in a single delivery contract has the right to reject the goods if they "fail in any respect to conform to the contract." UCC § 2-601. In fact this is not the panacea it seems, since the seller has a right to cure defects, pursuant to § 2-508, if he notifies the buyer of the intent to cure, and:

1. The time for performance has not run out, and the seller can cure within that time; or
2. The seller has reason to believe that the buyer would accept non-conforming goods—in which case the seller can go reasonably *beyond* the time allowed for performance in curing the defects.

Neither of these exceptions would benefit the farmer under these facts, because the time for performance expired the same day the farmer delivered the defective shipment, and there's nothing under these facts to give the farmer a reasonable belief the baker would accept non-conforming goods. Thus, the baker would have a valid claim against the farmer for failure to deliver the 100 bushels of wheat.

If you chose this response, you were thinking of the common-law rule, under which a minor contractual breach (which is what this would be considered) does not relieve the aggrieved party of his duty to perform; instead, he must perform and sue for damages. However, since a transaction in goods is involved here, the UCC controls, and since choice A doesn't reflect the UCC stance, it's not the best response.

(B) is not the best response,

because the farmer would not be excused from performing on grounds of impossibility.

Under UCC § 2-613, a seller can only avoid a contract due to impossibility if the goods are identified when the contract is made, and the goods are destroyed, through no fault of either party, before the risk of loss passes to the buyer. Here, the goods weren't identified when the contract was made; the contract was for any 100 bushels of wheat.

Instead, the farmer will be liable to the baker for failure to deliver the wheat, since the time for performance ended the day the farmer delivered the 95 bushels to the baker, and the farmer had no reason to believe the baker would give him extra time in which to cure the defect. Since B doesn't recognize this, it's not the best response.

(D) is not the best response,

because the baker had no duty to give the farmer the opportunity to cure the defect.

The general rule is that, in single delivery contracts (*not* installment contracts), the buyer has the right to reject the goods if they "fail in any respect to conform to the contract." UCC § 2-601. This isn't quite as strict as it sounds, because the seller has a right to cure defects under one of two exceptions from § 2-608, as long as the seller notifies the buyer of his intent to cure:

1. The time for performance has not run out, and the seller can cure within that time; or
2. The seller has reason to believe that the buyer would accept non-conforming goods—in which case the seller can go reasonably beyond the time allowed for performance in curing the defects.

Here, neither one of these would apply so as to give the farmer a chance to cure. First, the contract called for delivery on August 1, and the farmer delivered the defective shipment on August 1, so the time for performance had run out. Second, under these facts, the farmer had no grounds to believe the baker would accept a defective shipment. Thus, the baker had no obligation to accept the shipment.

If you chose this response, you *may* have been thinking of a buyer's obligation under an *installment* contract, not a single delivery contract like the one involved here. Where installment contracts are concerned, the buyer can *only* reject non-conforming installments if the non-conformity substantially impairs the value of that installment *and* the defect can't be cured. If the seller gives adequate assurances of cure, the buyer *must* accept the installment. Thus, under an installment contract, the farmer could have additional time to get his hands on more wheat, and the baker probably would have to accept the 95 bushels. However, since the rule for single-delivery contracts is different, and a single delivery contract is involved here, D isn't the best response.

Answer 47

(A) is the best response,

because the seller accepted the buyer's offer by promising to sell the specific computer.

In a sales contract, the UCC provides that an order (offer) can be accepted either by shipping goods (either conforming or non-conforming) or by promising to do so. UCC § 2-206(1)(b). The seller's June 2 letter, promising to ship the computer the next day, was therefore the seller's acceptance of the buyer's offer to purchase. On June 3, the seller shipped a different computer (a non-conforming good). Because the contract had been accepted on June 2, the shipment, even though it was accompanied by the letter, was not an accommodation shipment. Instead, the non-conforming shipment was a breach. In the event of a breach by shipment of non-conforming goods, the seller may accept or reject the shipment, and in either event sue for damages.

(B) is not the best response,

because the seller breached the contract.

In a sales contract, the UCC provides that an order (offer) can be accepted either by shipping goods (either conforming or non-conforming) or by promising to do so. UCC § 2-206(1)(b). The seller's June 2 letter, promising to ship the computer the next day, was therefore the seller's acceptance of the buyer's offer to purchase. On June 3, the seller shipped a different computer (a non-conforming good). Because the contract had been accepted on June 2, the shipment, even though it was accompanied by the letter, was not an accommodation shipment. Instead, the non-conforming shipment was a breach. In the event of a breach by shipment of non-conforming goods, the seller may accept or reject the shipment, and in either event sue for damages.

(C) is not the best response,

because the buyer's offer had already been accepted before the seller sent the non-conforming computer.

In a sales contract, the UCC provides that an order (offer) can be accepted either by shipping goods (either conforming or non-conforming) or by promising to do so. UCC § 2-206(1)(b). The seller's June 2 letter, promising to ship the computer the next day, was therefore the seller's acceptance of the buyer's offer to purchase. The contract was thus formed on June 2, the day before the shipment.

(D) is not the best response,

because the buyer's offer had already been accepted before the seller sent the non-conforming computer.

In a sales contract, the UCC provides that an order (offer) can be accepted either by shipping goods (either conforming or non-conforming) or by promising to do so. UCC § 2-206(1)(b). The seller's June 2 letter, promising to ship the computer the next day, was therefore the seller's acceptance of the buyer's offer to purchase. The contract was thus formed on June 2, the day before the shipment. If you selected choice D, you were probably thinking that the seller's shipment of the non-conforming computer was an accommodation shipment. Under the UCC § 2-206(1) (b), in response to an order, a seller may send non-conforming goods. If the seller also notifies the buyer that the goods are meant as an accommodation, then the shipment is not an acceptance and breach, but rather a counter-offer, which the buyer may accept by accepting the goods. This is not the case here, because the seller had already accepted the buyer's offer by sending the June 2 letter.

Answer 48

(C) is the best response,

because the retailer is a "lost volume" seller.

A "lost volume" seller is one who can obtain as many items from a supplier as she can sell. When the customer of such a seller breaches his contract, and the seller resells the item to another customer at the same price, the seller will end up making one fewer sale because of the breach. This is because the new customer would have bought the item anyway, regardless of whether the first customer had breached. Damages available to a lost volume seller under the UCC are the profits, including reasonable overhead, which the seller would have made from full performance by the buyer, together with any incidental damages. UCC § 2-708(2).

The retailer is a "lost volume" seller, because as the facts state, the company can buy more ICB personal computers than it can sell. The retailer contracted with the law firm for the sale of an ICB personal computer for $3,000. The law firm repudiated and the retailer sold at private sale the same specific computer to the bank, who paid the same price. The retailer did not lose any money on the sale of the specific computer, but as a lost volume seller, the retailer made one fewer sale. The retailer's damages would include the profit from the lost sale to the law firm plus any incidental damages.

(A) is not the best response,

because damages to a "lost volume" seller include lost profits and incidental damages.

A "lost volume" seller is one who can obtain as many items from a supplier as she can sell. When the customer of such a seller breaches his contract, and the seller resells the item to another customer at the same price, the seller will end up making one fewer sale because of the breach. This is because the new customer would have bought the item anyway, regardless of whether the first customer had breached. Damages available to a lost volume seller under the UCC are the profits, including reasonable overhead, which the seller would have made from full performance by the buyer, together with any incidental damages.

The retailer is a "lost volume" seller, because as the facts state, the retailer can buy more ICB personal computers than it can sell. So the fact that the retailer sold the unit in question to a different buyer for the same price is irrelevant—the company has still lost one net sale. Under the UCC, damages available to a "lost volume" seller include the profits from the seller's lost sale (to the law firm) plus any incidental damages.

(B) is not the best response,

because notice of intent to resell is not required where the recovery is on a "lost volume" basis.

When the seller elects the remedy of "cover"—i.e., the right to resell and collect the difference between the resale price and the (higher) contract price—and the resale is at a private sale, the seller is required to give the buyer "reasonable notification of his intention to resell." UCC § 2-706(3). Since we're told here that the retailer's sale to the bank is "at private sale," the retailer would be required to give notice of intent to resell to the law firm if the retailer wanted to recover the resale/contract-price differential under § 2-706(3).

However, the retailer is *not* recovering on this resale/contract-price basis. That's because that basis would give it $0. Instead, it's recovering its lost profits as a lost volume seller under § 2-708(2). (See the discussion of choice C above for an analysis.) There's no pre-sale notice requirement for recoveries on this lost-volume basis.

(D) is not the best response,

because the damages available to a lost volume seller are not the contract price.

As the discussion of choice C above describes, the retailer is a "lost volume" seller, who has lost one net sale and is entitled under UCC § 2-708(2) to the profits that it would have made from full performance by the buyer, together with any incidental damages. Nothing in the UCC provides for a different measure of damages—such as the full contract price—merely because the buyer has "unjustifiably repudiated." (Giving the retailer the entire contract price would obviously overcompensate it, since it has avoided having to pay the wholesale purchase price to the manufacturer.)

Answer 49

(B) is the best response,

because the answer correctly states the UCC's non-carrier rules for delivery and payment.

Under the UCC, non-carrier cases are those instances where the parties did not intend that the goods be moved by carrier. That is the case here, since there's no indication that either party thought a carrier would be used. In non-carrier cases, unless the contract provides otherwise, "payment is *due at the time* and place at which the buyer is to receive the goods." UCC § 2-310(A). In other words, this was to be a cash sale, with payment due when the goods were delivered. Furthermore, under § 2-308(a), the place for delivery was "the seller's place of business. . . ." So if the landlord didn't tender cash on March 1 at the seller's place of business, the plumbing company had no duty to deliver the goods. (Nor was the landlord entitled to wait until all 50 sets of fixtures had been delivered—see the discussion of choice D below.)

(A) is not the best response,

because delivery would not be to the landlord's place of business.

Under § 2-308(a), unless the contract provided otherwise (which it didn't) the place for delivery was "the seller's place of business. . . . " Since choice A says that the sets of fixtures must be delivered at the landlord's place of business, it's wrong.

(C) is not the best response,

because payment is due concurrently with the plumbing company's delivery.

Under UCC § 2-310(a), unless otherwise agreed, "payment is due at the time and place at which the buyer is to receive the goods even though the place of shipment is the place of delivery." Since the parties made no plans for shipment by common carrier, the place for delivery was the seller's premises (see discussion of choice A above). Therefore, payment was due concurrently with delivery—i.e., the buyer was not entitled to even brief credit. (Nor was the landlord entitled to wait until all 50 sets of fixtures had been delivered—see the discussion of choice D below.)

(D) is not the best response,

because payment is due only on the 25 sets of fixtures delivered.

Under UCC § 2-307, unless otherwise agreed, "where the circumstances give either party the right to make or demand delivery in lots the price if it can be apportioned may be demanded for each lot." Since the agreement contemplates that delivery would occur separately for each of the two lots, and since the price can easily be apportioned (because the sets of fixtures are usable independently of each other), the quoted provision applies. Therefore, the plumbing company was entitled to demand that payment for the first 25 sets be made at the time these sets were delivered.

Answer 50

(B) is the best response,

because the confirmation sent by the manufacturer became binding on the retailer when he failed to object.

In sales-of-goods cases, a writing signed by the party against whom enforcement is sought is required for contracts aggregating $500 or more. UCC § 2-201(1) (first sentence). However, there is a very important exception: A merchant who *receives a signed confirmation from the other party* will be bound by it just as if he had signed it, unless the recipient of the confirmation objects within ten days. UCC § 2-201(2).

Both the retailer, a dry goods retailer, and the manufacturer, a towel manufacturer, are merchants. The manufacturer confirmed in writing the agreement it reached with the retailer on the phone. Under § 2-201(2), if the retailer did not want to enter into a contract under those terms, the retailer was obligated to object in writing within ten days. Since the retailer did not object, the contract is enforceable under the terms listed in the confirmation.

The fact that the retailer originally offered to buy somewhere between 500 and 1,000 towels is irrelevant. Under the last sentence of § 2-201(1), where a memorandum (writing) of the agreement exists, "the contract is not enforceable . . . beyond the quantity of goods shown in such writing." Since under § 2-201(2) the confirmation serves as the type of memorandum required in § 2-201(1), the 500-unit quantity listed in the confirmation is the maximum quantity for which the contract is enforceable.

(A) is not the best response,

because the written confirmation stated a term of 500 towels.

As described more fully in the last sentence of the discussion of choice B above, the contract was not enforceable beyond the quantity stated in the confirmation. UCC §§ 2-201(1) and (2).

(C) is not the best response,

because as a confirmation between merchants, the agreement does not need to be signed.

Under UCC § 2-201(2), a merchant who receives a signed confirmation from the other party will be bound by it just as if he had signed it, unless the recipient of the confirmation objects in writing within ten days. Since both the manufacturer and the retailer were merchants, when the retailer failed to object in writing within ten days of getting the manufacturer's signed letter (a confirmation), the retailer is bound even though he never signed a writing.

(D) is not the best response,

because the absence of a price term from the memorandum will not make a contract unenforceable.

In sales-of-goods cases, a memorandum is required if the total sale amount is $500 or more. But the memorandum need not recite all terms; according to the last sentence of § 2-201(1), "[a] writing is not insufficient because it omits or incorrectly states a term agreed upon. . . . " So the fact that the price was omitted is irrelevant. (The manufacturer will be permitted to prove that the parties orally agreed on the $5 price.)

Answer 51

(D) is the best response,

because the seller's acceptance was effective on dispatch.

First, the buyer's signed order was an offer. How could this offer be accepted? Well, under UCC § 2-206(1), "[u]nless otherwise unambiguously indicated by the language or circumstances . . . (b) an order or other offer to buy goods for prompt or current shipment shall be construed as inviting acceptance either by a prompt promise to ship or by the prompt or current shipment of conforming or non-conforming goods[.]" So this order authorized the seller to accept by either promising to ship or shipping.

Next, we have to figure out whether and/or when the seller accepted that offer. Acceptance by mail was reasonable under the circumstances (see § 2-206(1)(a): Acceptance normally may be made "in any manner and by any medium reasonable in the circumstances."). The "mailbox rule" (a common-law rule that applies in the UCC context because nothing in Article 2 displaces it, and under § 1-103 common-law rules apply in the UCC unless expressly displaced by the Code) states that acceptance is effective immediately upon proper dispatch. The Second Restatement states the rule this way: "An acceptance made in a manner and by a medium invited by an offer is operative and completes the manifestation of mutual assent *as soon as put out of the offeree's possession*, without regard to whether it ever reaches the offeror." Rest. 2d § 63(A). So under this common-law rule, the seller accepted by mailing, since at that moment the acceptance document (his letter) was "put out of the offeree's possession."

Since there was a contract at the moment the seller mailed the acceptance on January 7, the buyer's purported January 8 revocation was ineffective.

(A) is not the best response,

because the offer could be accepted by a promise to ship, not just by shipment.

Under UCC § 2-206(1) (quoted more fully in the discussion of choice D above), the buyer's order authorized acceptance "either by a prompt promise to ship or by the prompt or current shipment of conforming or non-conforming goods[.]" So although the seller could have accepted by shipment, he was alternatively entitled to accept by promising to ship, which he did. Therefore, choice A is wrong. (Since acceptance occurred at the moment of promise by the seller—i.e., the mailing of the acceptance letter—the bargain was concluded before the buyer could revoke the next day.)

(B) is not the best response,

because the seller's order, although it supplied a price not previously mentioned by the buyer, was effective as an acceptance.

The buyer's offer indicated his willingness to buy at the seller's "current price." Therefore, although the seller's reply document was the first to mention the $10 price (and although the buyer never expressly committed to the $10 price), since the $10 was indeed the seller's current price, the seller's reply matched the offer well enough to qualify as an acceptance.

(C) is not the best response,

because nothing made the buyer's offer irrevocable for any length of time.

Offers ordinarily are not irrevocable. It's true that UCC § 2-205 authorizes "firm offers" (i.e., irrevocable ones) even without consideration for the irrevocability. But under § 2-205, an offer is not "firm" unless it "by its terms[,] gives assurance that it will be held open[.]" Nothing in the buyer's order "by its terms" gave that assurance. Therefore, the buyer had the usual common-law right to revoke before acceptance. (His problem was that his revocation didn't happen until after the acceptance, for the reason described in the discussion of choice D above.)

Answer 52

(A) is the best response,

because the buyer returned the machine.

A seller will have an action for the price if the buyer has accepted the goods, the goods are lost or damaged after the risk of loss has passed to the buyer, or if the seller is unable to resell the rejected goods. None of these have taken place in this situation; the buyer rejected the machine and returned it, without damage, to the manufacturer. In addition, since the manufacturer sells many identical machines each year, it should be able to resell the returned one. (*See* UCC § 2-709.)

(B) is not the best response,

because the buyer can recover the market/contract price differential.

UCC § 2-708(1) provides that if a buyer either does not accept the goods or repudiates the contract, the seller may recover "the difference between the market price at the time and place for tender and the unpaid contract price." Since the buyer has wrongfully rejected the goods, this measure of damages will be available to the manufacturer.

(C) is not the best response,

because the buyer wrongfully rejected the machine.

UCC § 2-706(1) provides that if a buyer wrongfully rejects goods, "the seller may resell the goods concerned or the undelivered balance thereof. Where the resale is made in good faith and in a commercially reasonable manner the seller may recover the difference between the resale price and the contract price." Since the buyer wrongfully rejected the machine, the manufacturer may resell the machine and recover from the buyer the difference in the price obtained for the machine and the contract price.

(D) is not the best response,

because the manufacturer is a lost volume seller.

A lost volume seller is a seller who is not operating at full capacity. As a result, if a buyer wrongfully rejects the sold item, the seller will have lost a sale. (It would not make the seller whole to resell the returned item because, had the buyer not rejected the item, the seller would have made the profit on two sales rather than only one.) UCC § 2-708(2) provides that in the event of a buyer's wrongful rejection of goods, a lost volume seller may recover the profits it would have made on the sale.

Answer 53

(B) is the best response,

because the covenant will have no legal effect—the assignment will be valid and the textile mill will not be liable for breach of contract.

Under the UCC, barring circumstances to the contrary, a prohibition against assigning the contract prevents *only* delegating duties, not assigning rights. UCC § 2-210(4). Furthermore, barring circumstances to the contrary ("as in an assignment for security"), an "assignment of the contract" is a delegation of performance of the duties of the assignor as well as an assignment of his rights. UCC § 2-210(5). Here, the mill, by "assigning the contract" to the bank as *security* for a loan, assigned only its *rights* under the contract (not its duties) — that is, its right to payment from the clothing company, in the form of a security interest to the bank.

An assignment by a seller of his right to payment, as is the case here, is automatically allowed regardless of a provision in the contract prohibiting assignment. UCC § 2-210(2), which provides for exceptions to the general rule allowing assignment in the sale of goods (such as not allowing an assignment that would materially change the duty of the other party), is now subject to § 9-406(d), which makes rights to payments for goods sold (or the creation of a security interest in the payments), whether or not earned, freely alienable notwithstanding a contrary agreement or rule of law. Section 9-406(d) provides that those anti-assignment clauses are "ineffective," meaning that "the clause is of no effect whatsoever; the clause does not prevent the assignment from taking effect between the parties and the prohibited assignment does not constitute a default" under the contract. § 9-406(d), cmt. 5.

In the case of a security interest in a seller's interest, as is the case here, UCC § 2-210(3) does provide for damages, but only where enforcement of the security interest actually resulted in the delegation of material performance by the seller, which has not occurred under these facts.

Since Choice B correctly recognizes that the covenant will not be valid, it's the best response.

(A) is not the best response,

because the assignment was effective despite the existence of the covenant.

As shown by the analysis in choice B above, the mill, by "assigning the contract" to the bank as security for a loan, assigned only its *rights* under the contract (not its duties) — that is, its right to payment from the clothing company, in the form of a security interest to the bank. As further discussed in choice B above, UCC § 9-406(d) provides that a clause prohibiting such an assignment doesn't prevent the assignment from taking effect and the prohibited assignment does not constitute a default under the contract. § 9-406(d), cmt. 5.

(C) is not the best response,

because, although it correctly states that the assignment will be effective, it incorrectly states that the mill will be liable for breach of contract.

As shown by the analysis in choice B above, the mill, by "assigning the contract" to the bank as security for a loan, assigned only its *rights* under the contract (not its duties) — that is, its right to payment from the clothing company, in the form of a security interest to the bank. As further discussed in choice B above, UCC § 9-406(d) provides that a clause prohibiting such an assignment doesn't prevent the assignment from taking effect and the prohibited assignment does not constitute a default under the contract. § 9-406(d), cmt. 5.

(D) is not the best response,

because it misstates the law.

Under the UCC, a prohibition against assignment in the contract would apply to *both* buyer and seller. UCC § 2-210. Instead, what's central to resolving this question is determining how a court would *interpret* the prohibition against assignment.

As shown by the analysis in choice B above, the mill, by "assigning the contract" to the bank as security for a loan, assigned only its *rights* under the contract (not its duties) — that is, its right to payment from the clothing company, in the form of a security interest to the bank. As further discussed in choice B above, UCC § 9-406(d) provides that a clause prohibiting such an assignment doesn't prevent the assignment from taking effect and the prohibited assignment does not constitute a default under the contract. § 9-406(d), cmt. 5.

STRATEGIES AND TACTICS

CRIMINAL LAW AND PROCEDURE

OUTLINE OF COVERAGE

The following outline for the Criminal Law portion of the MBE was adopted by the Bar Examiners for all MBEs given on or after February 2016. It was designed to clarify what's covered on the Crim Law portion of the exam. This is the most up-to-date outline of coverage released by the Bar Examiners, and your study for Criminal Law should focus on this outline.

Notice that what the Examiners refer to as "Criminal Law" also includes what's called in law school "Criminal Procedure." So you'll be responsible for major aspects of Criminal Procedure (constitutional protections of accused persons, like the Fourth Amendment's rules on searches and seizures) that you may not have covered in your basic Criminal Law course.

Here's what you need to know:

- I. Homicide
  - A. Intended killings
    - 1. Premeditation, deliberation
    - 2. Provocation
  - B. Unintended killings
    - 1. Intent to injure
    - 2. Reckless and negligent killings
    - 3. Felony murder
    - 4. Misdemeanor manslaughter
- II. Other crimes
  - A. Theft and receiving stolen goods
  - B. Robbery
  - C. Burglary
  - D. Assault and battery
  - E. Rape; statutory rape
  - F. Kidnapping
  - G. Arson
  - H. Possession offenses
- III. Inchoate crimes; parties
  - A. Inchoate offenses
    - 1. Attempts
    - 2. Conspiracy
    - 3. Solicitation
  - B. Parties to crime
- IV. General principles
  - A. Acts and omissions
  - B. State of mind
    - 1. Required mental state
    - 2. Strict liability
    - 3. Mistake of fact or law

- C. Responsibility
  1. Mental disorder
  2. Intoxication
- D. Causation
- E. Justification and excuse
- F. Jurisdiction

V. Constitutional protection of accused persons
- A. Arrest, search and seizure
- B. Confessions and privilege against self-incrimination
- C. Lineups and other forms of identification
- D. Right to counsel
- E. Fair trial and guilty pleas
- F. Double jeopardy
- G. Cruel and unusual punishment
- H. Burdens of proof and persuasion
- I. Appeal and error

There will be about 28 or 29 "Criminal Law" questions on the MBE (though only 27 will be scored, and you won't know which ones won't). Of these, approximately half will cover categories I through IV (i.e., "substantive" Criminal Law); the other half will cover category V (i.e., constitutional Criminal Procedure a/k/a constitutional protection of the accused). Because the NCBE has increased the relative percentage of Criminal Procedure questions on the MBE in recent years, fewer than half of all questions in this "archive" of questions are on Criminal Procedure, and more than half are on substantive Criminal Law.

WHAT TO EXPECT

While students typically score higher on criminal law questions than on questions in other subject areas, there is a very broad range of subjects covered, and numerous types of questions are used. Here are a few of the major types of questions:

1. You're asked whether, under the facts given, the defendant should be found guilty;
2. You're asked for the prosecutor's (or the defendant's) best argument;
3. You're asked which of four precedents is the best one for the facts given;
4. You're asked the most serious crime for which the defendant could be convicted;
5. You're asked which of four fact patterns most closely fits a certain type of crime (e.g., felony murder).

STUDY STRATEGIES

1. Learn the differences between degrees and types of homicides.

You must keep the different types of homicides clear in your mind. Keep in mind that the common law did ***not*** recognize degrees of murder; therefore, if an MBE question wants to discuss degrees of murder, it will supply an appropriate statute.

In studying homicide, begin with murder. At common law, murder is an unlawful killing (neither justifiable nor excusable) with malice aforethought. Remember, "malice" ***doesn't mean intent.*** The Bar Examiners use this as a common MBE trap. Although the malice element ***can*** be satisfied by an intent either to kill or to cause serious injury, or by felony murder, it can ***also*** be satisfied by a "depraved heart"—that is, the actor disregards an unreasonably high risk of harm to human life. Usually on the MBE, if the examiners want to indicate a depraved heart, they will give you facts from which a reasonable jury can infer that the defendant beyond doubt ***consciously disregarded*** (i.e., wasn't just unaware of) the high risk of harm. In any event, keep in mind that it's possible to be convicted of murder ***without*** intending to kill!

If a defendant satisfies the test for intentional murder, always look to see if there's sufficient ***provocation*** by the victim to knock the conviction down to voluntary manslaughter. Keep in mind that provocation is both subjective and objective: The provocation must be enough to anger this defendant, ***and*** it should be of a type that would provoke a reasonable person to kill; furthermore, this defendant must not have cooled off when the killing takes place, ***and*** a reasonable person would not have cooled off in these circumstance (a "heat of passion" killing).

If a defendant is charged with a killing that doesn't satisfy the requirements for murder, check for involuntary manslaughter; there are two types: ***criminal negligence*** and ***misdemeanor manslaughter.*** Criminal negligence means that the defendant ignores a risk of harm to human life, and that risk is ***less*** than the risk represented by depraved heart murder. Misdemeanor manslaughter is the misdemeanor equivalent of felony murder. What's important to remember here? First, don't get hung up on the difference between the mental state needed for depraved heart murder and the "gross negligence" that suffices for criminal negligence involuntary manslaughter. On the MBE, the examiners will usually set up the facts so that it's pretty clear which side of the line the case falls on.

Here's a good illustration of the difference between the mind-sets for depraved heart murder and criminal-negligence manslaughter: Two men set out in separate cars. One drives through town and shoots a gun into the window of a house where it's obvious that a crowded party is being held. He doesn't intend to kill anyone, but he does kill one of the people at the party. The other man drives out to the country and fires a gun into the window of what seems to be an abandoned hunting cabin. He doesn't intend to kill anyone, but he hits and kills a homeless person who's taken refuge in the cabin. The man who drove through the city committed depraved heart murder, due to what the jury can infer was his conscious disregard of the high probability that firing into a crowded house would hurt or kill someone. The one who drove through the country is liable for at most criminal-negligence involuntary manslaughter; the egregiousness of his conduct is much less, and there's no indication that he consciously disregarded a high risk of death or serious bodily harm.

Here's a sample question from the MBE concerning homicide:

> In which of the following situations is the defendant most likely to be guilty of common-law murder?
>
> A. Angered because his neighbor is having a noisy party, the defendant fires a rifle into the neighbor's house. The bullet strikes and kills a guest at the party.
> B. During an argument, a victim slaps the defendant. Angered, the defendant responds by shooting and killing the victim.
> C. The defendant drives his car through a red light and strikes and kills a pedestrian who is crossing the street.
> D. Using his fist, the defendant punches a victim in the face. As a result of the blow, the victim falls and hits his head on a concrete curb, suffers a concussion, and dies.

This question covers the spectrum of homicides. As outlined above, you should start with the definition of murder: an unlawful killing with malice aforethought. Keep in mind that malice doesn't mean intent, but can be satisfied by extreme negligence or depraved heart. Applying this definition, you should find that choices C and D are eliminated. Driving through a red light, in the absence of other facts, would certainly be considered negligent, but not a conscious disregard of an extremely high risk of death or serious injury (which is what depraved heart murder requires), so it's highly unlikely to be considered murder. Choice D, similarly, involves a non-intentional killing; punching someone in the face would show intent to injure, but not to injure seriously enough for intentional murder. Furthermore, D would not involve disregard of obvious high risk sufficiently great to satisfy depraved heart murder.

Your choice is now between A and B. As outlined above, the second thing you should do on a homicide question is to analyze whether there is provocation sufficient to make the killing voluntary manslaughter. Remember, the provocation must be serious enough to provoke a reasonable person to kill, not just serious enough to provoke this defendant. Applying this to A and B, you'll see provocation in both; however, in A, the provocation—a noisy party—would not be enough to cause a ***reasonable*** person to kill. The provocation in B—being slapped during an argument—could well be enough (although it's not a certainty). Thus, you wind up with one answer choice that clearly fits murder, one that doesn't fit very well, and two that definitely don't work, so the one that fits, choice A, must be the best response.

2. Know the basic definitions of crimes against people and property.

It may seem too good to be true, but many Criminal Law MBE questions require nothing more than a mechanical application in which you compare the elements of different crimes to the facts you're given. The most important crimes to know are larceny, robbery, and burglary. (The following are common law definitions—if an MBE question wants you to deal with differences found in modern rules, it will state them.) Larceny is a trespassory taking and carrying away of the personal property of another with the intent to steal it. Robbery is very similar; it's simply a larceny from a person that is accomplished by force or fear. Burglary is the breaking and entering of the dwelling house of another, at night, with the intent to commit a felony therein. Although you'll also need to know the elements of false pretenses, embezzlement, larceny by trick, and other larceny-related crimes against the person, larceny, robbery, and burglary are the main crimes to remember.

3. Appreciate "hidden" issues—causation and intent.

MBE questions rarely focus on ***obvious*** issues. That's why it's important to know elements of crimes ***flawlessly.*** Even if you do, though, it's easy to miss issues, as the following question illustrates:

An antique dealer who was a skilled calligrapher crafted a letter on very old paper. She included details that would lead knowledgeable readers to believe the letter had been written by Thomas Jefferson to a friend. The antique dealer, who had a facsimile of Jefferson's autograph, made the signature and other writing on the letter resemble Jefferson's. She knew that the letter would attract the attention of local collectors. When it did and she was contacted about selling it, she said that it had come into her hands from a foreign collector who wished anonymity, and that she could make no promises about its authenticity. As she had hoped, a collector paid her $5,000 for the letter. Later the collector discovered the letter was not authentic, and handwriting analysis established that the antique dealer had written the letter.

In a jurisdiction that follows the common-law definition of forgery, the antique dealer has

A. committed both forgery and false pretenses.
B. committed forgery, because she created a false document with the intent to defraud, but has not committed false pretenses, since she made no representation as to the authenticity of the document.
C. not committed forgery, because the document had no apparent legal significance, but has committed false pretenses, since she misrepresented the source of the document.
D. not committed forgery, because the document had no apparent legal significance, and has not committed false pretenses, since she made no representation as to authenticity of the document.

The subtle issue here relates to the definition of forgery. Forgery can occur only with respect to a document that has ***some apparent legal significance*** — for instance, the document represents a right to payment (e.g., a negotiable instrument), or indicates that title to property has passed (a deed), or purports to show that a contractual obligation is owed (a signed contract), or the like. Where the document when viewed on its face—and whether fake or genuine—does *not* purport to have legal significance, it can't be a "forgery" even if it's "counterfeit." Since even a genuine letter by Jefferson wouldn't have present legal significance, faking it can't be forgery. (But using the fake to exchange it for money would be false pretenses.) So because of the subtleties in the definition of forgery, (C) is the correct answer.

Another issue that can trip you up is ***intent.*** You need to remember how intent applies to the different crimes. For instance, note how intent affects conspiracy, accomplice liability, larceny, and robbery. In conspiracy, the conspirators must not only intend to agree, but must also intend the criminal goal of the conspiracy. For a defendant to be liable as an accomplice, he must intend that his principal carry out the criminal act. (Thus, if one offers help without that intent, he ***cannot*** be liable as an accomplice.) In larceny, the trespassory taking must be done with the ***intent to steal.*** If the actor intends only to ***borrow*** another's property, there's ***no intent to steal*** and thus no larceny; however, if he plans to steal when he takes the goods but changes his mind later and returns them, he's still liable—he took the goods with the requisite intent. Burglary is similar in that it requires breaking and entering another's dwelling house, at night, ***with the intent to commit a felony therein.*** If a defendant intends to go in and play Scrabble, there's no burglary. If he mistakes the house for his own, goes in, and removes jewelry, believing that's his own, there's no intent to commit a felony, and thus no burglary. Keep in mind that, where intent is concerned, ***even an unreasonable belief*** can be a defense ***if it negates intent.*** In real life, a defendant's unreasonable belief may make it far less likely a jury will believe him, but this doesn't change the legal rule that even an unreasonable belief can negate intent.

Intent is also important to remember when dealing with crimes that punish a defendant for doing one act while intending to perform another. The defendant is liable ***even if*** the second crime is not performed! This applies, of course, to the inchoate crimes of conspiracy and attempt, but also to crimes like larceny and burglary. For instance, burglary requires breaking and entering another's dwelling house, at night, with the intent to commit a felony therein. Thus, once the criminal actor has broken and entered with the appropriate intent, the crime is complete. Even if he has a change of heart once he's inside, he's still liable! Larceny requires the intent to steal. Once a person takes another's property with the intent to steal, a change of heart won't exonerate him, because the crime was ***complete*** when the taking occurred!

4. For Criminal Procedure, study cases.

In many instances, Criminal Procedure MBE questions resemble actual Supreme Court cases very closely; thus, you should become as familiar as you can with the fact patterns of ***actual cases.***

5. Distinguish types of warrantless searches.

Remember to keep the different types of warrantless searches distinct in your mind. They are: (1) search incident to arrest; (2) inventory searches; (3) exigent circumstances; (4) plain view doctrine; (5) automobile searches; (6) consent searches; (7) stop and frisk; and (8) regulatory inspections (actually, you do need a warrant for this last one, but you don't need conventional probable cause to get it). Questions involving warrantless searches show up ***a lot*** on the MBE, so study the scope of each type very carefully. Frequently,

Criminal Procedure MBE questions will involve one kind of search, but some of the answer choices will try to confuse you by relying on a ***different*** type of search.

Also, remember that the Fourth Amendment applies only to searches and seizures done by the ***police*** or by people working under the direction of the police.

Lastly, remember *Arizona v. Gant* (2009), which changed the rules on when the ***passenger compartment of a vehicle*** can be searched incident to arrest of the driver: The basic rule that a warrantless search incident to arrest must be limited to areas within the arrestee's "immediate control" now applies to searches of vehicles after the arrest of the driver. So if the police make an arrest for a ***traffic violation,*** handcuff the driver and put him in the patrol car, and then find evidence of some other crime when they search the passenger compartment, that search is ***not justified by the incident-to-arrest doctrine.***

6. **Keep in mind when *Miranda* kicks in.**

Custodial interrogations/confessions is one of the Bar Examiners' favorite Crim Pro topics, so be sure to have a really good understanding of this part of Criminal Procedure.

Also, remember that *Miranda* warnings are required only when the suspect would reasonably believe that the police intend to conduct a ***custodial*** interrogation. "Custodial" means the suspect is ***not free to leave.*** Thus, if the police question someone under circumstances not indicating that he's not free to leave (e.g., a casual street encounter, where suspicion of a particular crime has not yet focused on the person)—no *Miranda*. If the suspect volunteers a confession—no *Miranda*. Note also that a custodial interrogation ***can*** take place away from the police station, but it ***must*** be administered by the police (or an agent of the police)—not by someone who's just a civilian.

EXAM TACTICS

1. **Apply statutes.**

Some criminal law questions on the MBE will contain statutes. If you come across one of these, apply the statute to the facts ***verbatim.*** In many cases, simply doing this will lead you to the correct response. Here's an example:

> While testifying at a civil trial, a witness was asked on cross-examination if he had been convicted in a circuit court of stealing $200 from his employer on August 16, 2011. The witness said, "No, I have never been convicted of any crime." In fact, the witness had pleaded guilty to such a charge and had been placed on probation.
>
> The witness was then charged with perjury on the ground that his statement denying the conviction was false. A statute in the jurisdiction defines perjury as knowingly making a false statement while under oath.
>
> At trial, the state proved the witness's statement and the prior conviction. The witness testified that the attorney who represented him in the theft case had told him that, because he had been placed on probation, he had not been convicted of a crime. The witness had served his probationary period satisfactorily and been discharged from probation. The alleged advice of the attorney was incorrect.
>
> If the jury believes the witness, it should find him
>
> A. guilty, because his mistake was one of law.
> B. guilty, because reliance on the advice of an attorney is not a defense.
> C. not guilty, if the jury also finds that his reliance on the attorney's advice was reasonable.
> D. not guilty, because he lacked the necessary mental state.

Here, the statute states that perjury requires ***knowingly*** making a false statement while under oath. Regardless of whether the witness should or shouldn't have relied on his attorney's opinion, he ***didn't knowingly make a false statement.*** Because that's what the statute requires, the witness simply ***cannot*** be guilty; he lacks the necessary mental state. Choice D correctly identifies this. To answer this question, then, all you have to do is mechanically apply the statute.

Note also that, in questions based on statutes, the correct response must agree with the statute. If an answer refers to a common law rule that conflicts with the statute, it cannot be the best response, even if the common law rule strikes you as being more "correct." Here's an example:

> A defendant became intoxicated at a bar. He got into his car and drove away. Within a few blocks, craving another drink, he stopped his car in the middle of the street, picked up a brick, broke the display window of a liquor store, picked up a bottle, consumed more liquor, and then drove off at a high speed. He ran a red light and struck and killed a pedestrian who was crossing the street.

Relevant statutes define manslaughter as the "killing of a human being in a criminally reckless manner." Criminal recklessness is "consciously disregarding a substantial and unjustifiable risk resulting from the actor's conduct." Another statute provides that intoxication is not a defense to crime unless it negates an element of the offense.

The defendant was charged with manslaughter in the death of the pedestrian.

The defendant pleads intoxication as a defense. The state's best argument to counter the intoxication issue in the manslaughter death of the pedestrian is that

A. intoxication is no defense to the crime charged, because manslaughter is historically a general intent crime.
B. intoxication is a defense only to a specific intent crime, and no specific intent is involved in the definition of the crime of manslaughter.
C. conscious risk-taking refers to the defendant's entire course of conduct, including drinking with the knowledge that he might become intoxicated and seriously injure or kill someone while driving.
D. whether the defendant was intoxicated or not is not the crucial issue here; the real issue is whether the manner in which the defendant was operating his car can be characterized under the facts as criminally reckless.

As you can see, choices A, B, and D ignore the terms of intoxication statute given in the facts, and, as a result, cannot be correct. That leaves only one alternative—C—which is in fact the correct response.

2. **Remember causation.**

Causation is a tricky issue, because it will never "pop out" of the page at you. In some MBE questions, the causation issue is carefully masked but nonetheless central to finding the correct answer. Remember—causation is ***always*** required for criminal liability. If the defendant's conduct did not cause the victim's injury, there's no criminal liability.

3. **Remember that forgiveness or condonation by the victim, or return of stolen property, doesn't negate criminal liability.**

For example, the crime of larceny is complete once one has taken someone else's property with the intent to steal it, whether or not the actor later decides to return the property. Likewise, the crime of burglary is complete once one has broken and entered another's dwelling house at night with the intent to commit a felony therein, even if the person later reconsiders. The fact that the victim subsequently forgives the criminal actor ***does not*** erase the crime's commission, because crimes are considered wrongs against the ***state***, not against the individual (this is the primary distinction between crimes and torts).

Unfortunately, questions involving issues like this are sneaky. Your gut reaction will probably be that the defendant ***shouldn't be found guilty***, because he's either renounced his criminal purpose or settled with the victim. Beware! You have to analyze these problems coldly and apply the elements of crimes ***mechanically***. Here's an example:

A debtor took a diamond ring to a pawnshop and borrowed $20 on it. It was agreed that the loan was to be repaid within 60 days and if it was not, the pawnshop owner, the defendant, could sell the ring. A week before expiration of the 60 days, the defendant had an opportunity to sell the ring to a customer for $125. He did so, thinking it unlikely that the debtor would repay the loan and if he did, the defendant would be able to handle him somehow, even by paying him for the ring if necessary. Two days later, the debtor came in with the money to reclaim his ring. The defendant told him that he had sold the ring because he thought the debtor would not reclaim it, and offered to give the debtor $125. The debtor demanded his ring. The defendant said, "Look buddy, that's what I got for it and it's more than it's worth." The debtor reluctantly took the money. Larceny, embezzlement, and false pretenses are separate crimes in the jurisdiction. The defendant could most appropriately be found guilty of

A. Larceny
B. Embezzlement
C. False pretenses
D. None of the above

Here, your gut reaction is likely lead to choice D, because you think that the defendant should not be found guilty—after all, he gave the debtor the money he got for the ring and so didn't profit from his conduct. According to the law, though, once the defendant misappropriated property in his possession, he became liable for embezzlement, ***regardless*** of the fact that he later turned over the proceeds to the debtor. This makes B the best response. (Choices A and C identify the wrong crimes.) You can see from this example how important it is to analyze MBE problems coldly and mechanically.

4. How to handle questions that ask for a defendant's "best defense."

Seeing the words "best defense" may strike fear in your heart, because you think you'll have to do some fine line-drawing as to the quality of various defenses. Have no fear, because that's not what you'll need to do. Based on our review of many such "best defense" questions, you can rely on this: One of the answer choices will almost certainly lead to an acquittal of the defendant, and three of them ***won't.*** To figure out which is which, analyze the choices as follows:

A. Does this answer choice apply to the facts?

If the answer choice does not correctly characterize the facts—e.g., the choice states the defendant acted without the requisite intent when the facts show the opposite—it cannot be the best response, even if it's theoretically correct.

B. Is this answer choice a correct statement of the law?

This is where you have to dig into your memory bank. The answer choice must correctly reflect the law in order to be the best response.

C. Is the argument sufficient to acquit the defendant?

Apart from being faithful to the facts and citing the correct law, the answer choice must identify the ***central issue*** in the facts. It must also negate an element of the crime or provide a valid defense to it. Watch for intent, defenses, and causation, which frequently are hidden issues. Here's an example:

> A husband met a man, who was known to him to be a burglar, in a bar. The husband told the burglar that he needed money. He promised to pay the burglar $500 if the burglar would go to the husband's house the following night and take some silverware. The husband explained to the burglar that, although the silverware was legally his, his wife would object to his selling it.
>
> The husband pointed out his home, one of a group of similar tract houses. He drew a floor plan of the house that showed the location of the silverware. The husband said that his wife usually took several sleeping pills before retiring, and that he would make sure that she took them the next night. He promised to leave a window unlocked.
>
> Everything went according to the plan except that the burglar, deceived by the similarity of the tract houses, went to the wrong house. He found a window unlocked, climbed in and found silver where the husband had indicated. He took the silver to the cocktail lounge where the payoff was to take place. At that point police arrested the two men.
>
> If the husband were charged with burglary, his best argument for acquittal would be that
>
> A. there was no breaking.
> B. he consented to the entry.
> C. no overt act was committed by him.
> D. there was no intent to commit a felony.

The key fact to note here is that the mental element of burglary is missing. Burglary is breaking and entering the dwelling house of another, at night, with the intent to commit a felony therein. Thus, either the husband or the burglar had to *intend* to commit a felony. Neither did, because they both believed that the burglar entered to retrieve silverware that *belonged* to the husband; if the burglar had gone to the right house, his acts would not have been felonious. D is, therefore, the best response. The remaining three choices illustrate the other two steps in your "best defense" analysis. A and B both represent misstatements of the facts, because there *was* a breaking (opening a window), and there was *no consent* to entry (because the husband was not authorized to consent to the entry of another person's house). Choice C, although it does correctly state the facts, ignores the legal principle that even in a state requiring an overt act for conspiracy, a member of the conspiracy can be liable without an overt act of his own. That leaves D, which comports with both the facts and the law and acquits the husband.

By the same token, questions that ask for the ***prosecutor's*** best argument involve the same kind of analysis, but from the other side. That is, one of the answer choices will result in the defendant's conviction, and the other three won't. You'd simply ask whether the answer choice applies to the facts, if it's legally correct, and if it addresses a central issue that will result in the defendant's conviction.

5. In Procedure questions involving a search, determine the purpose of the search first.

Categorizing the type of search first is crucial, because what's valid in one set of circumstances—e.g., a valid custodial arrest—will differ from what's valid in another—e.g., a stop and frisk. Here's an example:

A police officer stopped a defendant for speeding late one night. Noting that the defendant was nervous, he ordered him from the car and placed him under arrest for speeding. By state law, the police officer was empowered to arrest the defendant and take him to the nearest police station for booking. He thoroughly searched the defendant's person and discovered a small soft cellophane package of heroin in the defendant's jacket pocket.

The defendant is charged with possession of heroin. At trial, the defendant's motion to prevent introduction of the heroin into evidence, on the ground that the search violated his federal constitutional rights, will most probably be

A. denied, because the search was incident to a valid custodial arrest.
B. denied, because the police officer acted under both a reasonable suspicion of criminality and a legitimate concern for his own personal safety.
C. granted, because there was no reasonable or proper basis upon which to justify conducting the search.
D. granted if the police officer was not in fear and had no suspicion that the defendant was transporting narcotics.

It may seem basic, but the important thing here is to identify that this is a search incident to a valid custodial arrest. If you do that, you should be able to eliminate both answers B and D immediately, because they deal with the standard for a "stop and frisk." Because a search incident to a valid custodial arrest is justified, C is wrong. That leaves you with A—the correct response.

6. **In Procedure questions, watch for the "hidden" issue of standing.**

Keep in mind that a person can object to a search ***only*** if he has a legitimate expectation of privacy as to the place searched. This rule is likely to be an issue if something incriminating one person is seized from someone else's home, car, office, etc. Here's an example:

A defendant was indicted in state court for bribing a public official. During the course of the investigation, police had demanded and received from the defendant's bank the records of the defendant's checking account for the preceding two years. The records contained incriminating evidence.

On the basis of a claim of violation of his constitutional rights, the defendant moves to prevent the introduction of the records in evidence. His motion should be

A. granted, because a search warrant should have been secured for seizure of the records.
B. granted, because the records covered such an extensive period of time that their seizure unreasonably invaded the defendant's right of privacy.
C. denied, because the potential destructibility of the records, coupled with the public interest in proper enforcement of the criminal laws, created an exigent situation justifying the seizure.
D. denied, because the records were business records of the bank in which the defendant had no legitimate expectation of privacy.

Standing to object to a search is a threshold issue—if a person has no legitimate expectation of privacy as to the premises searched, he has no right to challenge the search. Here, once the checking account records are in the bank's hands, the defendant doesn't have a legitimate expectation of privacy concerning them (apart from anyone else, everyone working at the bank has access to them). Thus, choice D is the best response.

7. **How to handle questions that deal with testimony and include the statement "If the jury believes him. . . ."**

If a question states that the jury believes a piece of testimony, treat that testimony as ***fact.*** Why is this something to watch out for? Two reasons. First, it will inevitably appear when the defendant is testifying on his own behalf and your gut reaction is that he's lying through his teeth. If the jury believes him, though, you have to ignore your own feelings and treat the testimony as fact. Second, the testimony will ***probably*** address the issue of state of mind, so watch for ***intent*** problems when you see such testimony. Here's an example of these principles:

A defendant and an accomplice went into a drugstore, where the defendant reached into the cash register and took out $200. The owner of the store came out of a back room, saw what had happened, and told the defendant to put the money back. The accomplice then took a revolver from under his coat and shot and killed the store owner.

The defendant claims that the store owner owed her $200 and that she went to the drugstore to try to collect the debt. She said that she asked the accomplice to come along just in case the store owner made trouble but that she did not plan on using any force and did not know that the accomplice was armed.

If the defendant is prosecuted for murder on the basis of felony murder and the jury believes her claim, she should be found

A. guilty, because her accomplice committed a homicide in the course of a felony.
B. guilty, because her taking the accomplice with her to the store created the risk of death that occurred during the commission of a felony.
C. not guilty, because she did not know that the accomplice was armed and thus did not have the required mental state for felony murder.
D. not guilty, because she believed she was entitled to the money and thus did not intend to steal.

Your first reaction to the defendant's testimony was probably, "Oh, sure, and I'm the tooth fairy." If you read the facts carefully, though, you should have noticed that you are told to assume that the ***jury believed her claim.*** That means that you have to accept, as a fact, that the defendant went to the store intending to retrieve her own money. Why is that point important? It eliminates a necessary element, her intent to steal, and thus removes the possibility of a felony; without a felony or an attempted felony, there can't be felony murder. Answer D recognizes this, so it's not only the best answer but also shows how important testimony can be in MBE questions.

8. How to handle questions asking which answer choice represents the most likely case in which the defendant will be convicted.

This type of question requires you to mechanically apply the law. If you do, you'll find that, in three of the answers, at least one element of the crime in question is missing, or that there's a valid defense, or that causation is lacking. Only one answer will satisfy all the requirements of the crime. Here's an example:

In which of the following situations is the defendant most likely to be guilty of larceny?

A. The defendant took a victim's television set, with the intention of returning it the next day. However, he dropped it and damaged it beyond repair.
B. The defendant went into a home and took $100 in the belief that the homeowner had damaged the defendant's car to that amount.
C. Mistakenly believing that larceny does not include the taking of a dog, the defendant took his neighbor's dog and sold it.
D. Unreasonably mistaking a victim's car for his own, the defendant got into the victim's car in the parking lot and drove it home.

Remember, in analyzing this problem, you'll find three answer choices that result in the defendant being acquitted and one that results in his being convicted. If you mechanically apply the elements of larceny to each choice, you'll find only one that fits the crime. Larceny requires a trespassory taking and carrying away of another's personal property, with the intent to steal it. In choice A, the defendant has no intent to steal, because he intends to return the TV set the next day. That choice is out. In choice B, the defendant has no intent to steal, because he intends the $100 to pay for damage to his own car. That choice is out. In choice D, the defendant's mistake—however unreasonable—would provide a defense, because it negates his intent to steal. That choice is out. You're left with choice C. The defendant's mistake is "ignorance of the law" (a mistaken belief that particular conduct is not defined as a crime), which, as a general principle, is not a valid defense. Otherwise, choice C satisfies the elements of larceny, so it's the best response.

QUESTIONS

CRIMINAL LAW AND PROCEDURE

QUESTIONS

CRIMINAL LAW AND PROCEDURE

NOTE: For ease of study, we've put all questions involving **Criminal Procedure** at the end of the section, beginning with Question 47.

Question 1

An executive of an accounting firm was fired and told to immediately leave the building where she worked. The executive went home, but she returned that night to retrieve personal items from her office. When she discovered that her key no longer opened a door to the building, she forced the door open and went to her former office. To avoid attracting attention, she did not turn on any lights. In the dark, she knew that she was taking some items that were not hers; she planned to sort these out later and return them.

Upon arriving home, she found that she had taken a record book and some financial papers that belonged to the firm. After thinking it over and becoming angrier over being fired, she burned the book and papers in her fireplace.

The jurisdiction has expanded the crime of burglary to include all buildings.

What crime(s) has the executive committed?

(A) Burglary and larceny.

(B) Burglary, but not larceny.

(C) Larceny, but not burglary.

(D) Neither larceny nor burglary.

Question 2

A woman and her sister took a trip to the Caribbean. When they passed through U.S. Customs inspection upon their return, the customs officials found liquid cocaine in several bottles each of them was carrying. They were arrested. Upon separate questioning by customs officers, the woman broke down and cried, "I told my sister there were too many officers at this airport." The sister did not give a statement.

The woman and her sister were indicted for conspiracy to import cocaine. They were tried separately. At the woman's trial, after the government introduced the above evidence and rested its case, her lawyer moved for a judgment of acquittal on grounds of insufficient evidence.

Should the court grant the motion?

(A) No, because the evidence shows that both the woman and her sister agreed to import cocaine.

(B) No, because the evidence shows that both the woman and her sister possessed cocaine.

(C) Yes, because the evidence shows only that the woman and her sister committed separate crimes of cocaine possession.

(D) Yes, because the evidence shows that the woman effectively withdrew from the conspiracy when she cooperated by giving a statement.

Question 3

A man and his friend were watching a televised football game at the man's home. Upset by a penalty called by the referee, the friend threw a bottle of beer at the man's television, breaking the screen. Enraged, the man picked up a nearby hammer and hit the friend on the head with it. The friend died from the blow.

The crimes below are listed in descending order of seriousness.

In a jurisdiction that follows common law principles, what is the most serious crime of which the man could properly be convicted?

(A) Murder.

(B) Voluntary manslaughter.

(C) Involuntary manslaughter.

(D) Assault.

Question 4

A man had spent the evening drinking at a local bar and was weaving down the street on his way home, singing. Suddenly, a person wearing a cartoon character mask jumped out from an alley, pointed his gun at the man, and snarled, "This is loaded, buddy, and I don't mind using it. Hand over your cash pronto." The man was so drunk that he failed to understand what was going on and started to howl with laughter at the sight of the cartoon mask. Surprised and rattled by the man's reaction, the masked gunman fled. The man soon recovered his composure and staggered home safely.

The crimes below are listed in descending order of seriousness.

What is the most serious crime of which the masked gunman may properly be charged and convicted?

(A) Attempted robbery.

(B) Attempted battery.

(C) Attempted larceny.

(D) No crime.

Question 5

A defendant was charged with battery, defined as at common law. At trial, an expert witness testified for the defense that the defendant, an athlete, was under the influence of a performance-enhancing drug at the time he committed the battery and that he would not have done so had he not been so influenced. The defendant asked for an instruction to the effect that if the jury believed that he was influenced by the drug at the time of the crime and would not have committed it otherwise, it had to acquit him.

Which of the following circumstances would most aid the defendant's argument in favor of such an instruction?

(A) Evidence that the defendant is addicted to this drug and has an overwhelming urge to consume it.

(B) Evidence that the defendant's coach, who gave him the drug, told him it was only an aspirin.

(C) Evidence that the victim of the assault taunted the defendant about his use of the drug immediately before the assault.

(D) Expert testimony that a reasonable person, on consuming this drug, may experience uncontrollable rages.

Question 6

A common law jurisdiction defines first-degree murder as any murder that is (1) committed by means of poison or (2) premeditated. All other murder is second-degree murder, and manslaughter is defined as at common law.

An employee was angry with her boss for denying her a raise. Intending to cause her boss discomfort, the employee secretly dropped into his coffee three over-the-counter laxative pills. The boss drank the coffee containing the pills. Although the pills would not have been dangerous to an ordinary person, because the boss was already taking other medication, he suffered a seizure and died.

If the employee is charged with murder in the first degree, should she be convicted?

(A) Yes, only because she used poison.

(B) Yes, only because she acted with premeditation.

(C) Yes, both because she used poison and because she acted with premeditation.

(D) No.

Question 7

A man asked his girlfriend to lend him something he could use to break into his neighbor's padlocked storage shed in order to steal a lawn mower. She handed him a crowbar. He took the crowbar but then found a bolt cutter that the neighbor had left outside the shed. Using the bolt cutter, he cut the padlock on the shed and took the mower, which he then used to mow his girlfriend's lawn. She was surprised and pleased by this gesture.

Burglary in the jurisdiction applies to any structure or building, and there is no nighttime element.

The girlfriend has been charged as an accomplice to burglary and larceny.

Of which crimes, if any, is she guilty?

(A) Burglary and larceny.

(B) Burglary, but not larceny, because she intended to assist only in the breaking.

(C) Larceny, but not burglary, because she provided no actual assistance to the breaking but received a benefit from the larceny.

(D) Neither burglary nor larceny, because she provided no actual assistance.

Question 8

A defendant was tried for armed robbery. The state introduced evidence that a man, identified by witnesses as the defendant, entered a convenience store at 11 p.m. on March 5, threatened the clerk with a gun, and took $75 from the cash register.

The defendant did not testify, but his sister did. She testified that on March 5, at the time of the robbery, the defendant was with her in a city 300 miles away. On cross-examination, the sister admitted having given a statement to the police in which she had said that the defendant was not with her on March 5, but she claimed that the earlier statement was mistaken.

The court instructed the jury that in order to convict the defendant, they had to find all of the elements of the crime beyond a reasonable doubt.

As to the defendant's claim of alibi, which of the following additional instructions would be proper?

(A) Alibi is a matter of defense and so must be established by the defendant; however, the burden of persuasion is by a preponderance of the evidence, not beyond a reasonable doubt.

(B) Before you may consider the defendant's claim of alibi, you must decide whether he has produced sufficient evidence to raise the issue.

(C) If you have a reasonable doubt as to whether the defendant was present at the convenience store at about 11 p.m. on March 5, you must find him not guilty.

(D) If the defendant's evidence has caused you to have a reasonable doubt as to whether he was the robber, you must find him not guilty.

Question 9

A state statute provides: "Aggravated robbery of the elderly consists of robbery committed against a victim who is 65 years of age or older." Another state statute provides that when a criminal statute does not designate a necessary mental state, the mental state required is recklessness. A third state statute provides that a person acts recklessly if the person "consciously disregards a substantial and unjustified risk that the material element exists or will result from the person's conduct."

The evidence at a criminal trial showed that the defendant robbed a 66-year-old man outside a senior citizens' center. The defendant testified truthfully that the robbery had occurred on a dark night, that she had had no idea how old the victim was and had not cared how old the victim was, and that she had intended to rob whomever she encountered.

Could the defendant properly be convicted of aggravated robbery of the elderly?

(A) No, because the only evidence on the issue showed that the defendant did not know, nor could she reasonably have known, the victim's age.
(B) No, because there was no evidence of a substantial risk that the victim was age 65 or older.
(C) Yes, because the evidence was clear that the victim was 66 years old, and the statute is designed to protect the elderly.
(D) Yes, because the jury could find that there was no justification for the defendant's conduct and that she was willing to take the risk that the victim was age 65 or older.

Question 10

While on their way home from a ball game, a driver and his passenger stopped at an all-night gas station. The passenger offered to pay for the gas. While the passenger pumped gas, he was surprised to see the driver enter the station, take money from the unattended cash drawer, and get back in the car. The passenger paid the attendant for the gas, and the driver drove off. The driver offered to reimburse the passenger for the gas, but the passenger declined. After discovering the missing cash, the gas station attendant called the police, and the driver was later stopped. The driver escaped with the stolen money, however, and was never prosecuted.

If the passenger is prosecuted for theft as an accomplice, should he be convicted?

(A) No, because he had no intent to promote the commission of the offense.
(B) No, because the driver, the principal, was never prosecuted.
(C) Yes, because he facilitated commission of the offense by failing to make any effort to stop it.
(D) Yes, because he paid the attendant while he knew the driver was holding the stolen money.

Question 11

A defendant watched a liquor store furtively for some time, planning to hold it up. He bought a realistic-looking toy gun for the job. One night, just before the store's closing time, he drove to the store, opened the front door and entered. He reached in his pocket for the toy gun, but he became frightened and began to move back toward the front door. However, the shopkeeper had seen the butt of the gun. Fearing a holdup, the shopkeeper produced a gun from under the counter, pointed it at the defendant, and yelled, "Stop!" The defendant ran to the door and the toy gun fell from his pocket. The shopkeeper fired. The shot missed the defendant, but struck and killed a passerby outside the store.

A statute in the jurisdiction defines burglary as "breaking and entering any building or structure with the intent to commit a felony or to steal therein." On a charge of burglary, the defendant's best defense would be that

(A) the intent required was not present.
(B) the liquor store was open to the public.
(C) he had a change of heart and withdrew before committing any crime inside the store.
(D) he was unsuccessful, and so at most could only be guilty of attempted burglary.

Question 12

Two criminals planned to break into a federal government office to steal food stamps. One of them telephoned the defendant one night and asked whether the defendant wanted to buy some "hot" food stamps. The defendant, who understood that "hot" meant stolen, said, "Sure, bring them right over." The two criminals then successfully executed their scheme. That same night they delivered the food stamps to the defendant, who bought them for $500. The defendant did not ask when or by whom the stamps were stolen. All three were arrested. The two criminals entered guilty pleas in federal court to a charge of larceny in connection with the theft. The defendant was brought to trial in the state court on a charge of conspiracy to steal food stamps.

On the evidence stated, the defendant should be found

(A) guilty, because when a new confederate enters a conspiracy already in progress, he becomes a party to it.
(B) guilty, because he knowingly and willingly aided and abetted the conspiracy and is chargeable as a principal.
(C) not guilty, because although the defendant knew the stamps were stolen, he neither helped to plan nor participated or assisted in the theft.
(D) not guilty, because the two criminals had not been convicted of or charged with conspiracy, and the defendant cannot be guilty of conspiracy by himself.

Question 13

An undercover police detective told a local drug dealer that she wanted to buy cocaine, but that she needed time to raise the necessary funds. The drug dealer said that he needed time to get the cocaine. They agreed to meet again in ten days. An hour later, without a warrant, other officers forcibly entered the drug dealer's apartment and arrested him for attempted possession of a controlled substance.

If the drug dealer is prosecuted in a common-law jurisdiction for attempted possession of cocaine, should he be convicted?

(A) No, because he had not taken sufficient acts toward commission of the crime.

(B) No, because he was illegally arrested.

(C) Yes, because by objective standards an agreement between them had occurred.

(D) Yes, because his intention to obtain the cocaine was unequivocally expressed.

Question 14

A thief and his friend planned to hold up a bank. They drove to the bank in the thief's car. The thief entered while the friend remained as lookout in the car. After a few moments, the friend panicked and drove off.

The thief looked over the various tellers, approached one and whispered nervously, "Just hand over the cash. Don't look around, don't make a false move—or it's your life." The teller looked at the fidgeting thief, laughed, flipped him a dollar bill and said, "Go on, beat it." Flustered, the thief grabbed the dollar and left. Soon after leaving the scene, the friend was stopped by the police for speeding. Noting his nervous condition, the police asked the friend if they might search the car. The friend agreed. The search turned up heroin concealed in the lid of the trunk. The friend's best defense to a charge of robbery would be that

(A) the thief alone entered the bank.

(B) the friend withdrew before commission of the crime when he fled the scene.

(C) the friend had no knowledge of what the thief whispered to the teller.

(D) the teller was not placed in fear by the thief.

Question 15

A defendant was driving his automobile at a legal speed in a residential zone. A child darted out in front of him and was run over and killed before the defendant could prevent it. The defendant's driver's license had expired three months previously; the defendant had neglected to check when it was due to expire. Driving without a valid license is a misdemeanor in the jurisdiction. On a charge of manslaughter, the defendant should be found

(A) guilty under the misdemeanor-manslaughter rule.

(B) guilty because the licensing requirements are to protect life, and failure to obey is negligence.

(C) not guilty because the offense was not the proximate cause of the death.

(D) not guilty because there was no criminal intent.

Question 16

A defendant was tried for robbery. The victim and an eyewitness were the only witnesses called to testify. The victim testified that the defendant threatened her with a knife, grabbed her purse, and ran off with it. The eyewitness testified that he saw the defendant grab the victim's purse and run away with it but that he neither saw a knife nor heard any threats. On this evidence, the jury could properly return a verdict of guilty of

(A) robbery only.

(B) larceny only.

(C) either robbery or larceny.

(D) both robbery and larceny.

Question 17

After being fired from his job, the defendant drank almost a quart of vodka and decided to ride the bus home. While on the bus, he saw a briefcase he mistakenly thought was his own, and began struggling with the passenger carrying the briefcase. The defendant knocked the passenger to the floor, took the briefcase, and fled. The defendant was arrested and charged with robbery.

The defendant should be

(A) acquitted, because he used no threats and was intoxicated.

(B) acquitted, because his mistake negated the required specific intent.

(C) convicted, because his intoxication was voluntary.

(D) convicted, because mistake is no defense to robbery.

Question 18

While browsing in a clothing store, a thief decided to take a purse without paying for it. She placed the purse under her coat and took a couple of steps toward the exit. She then realized that a sensor tag on the purse would set off an alarm. She placed the purse near the counter from which she had removed it.

The thief has committed

(A) no crime, because the purse was never removed from the store.

(B) no crime, because she withdrew from her criminal enterprise.

(C) only attempted larceny, because she intended to take the purse out of the store.

(D) larceny, because she took the purse from its original location and concealed it with the intent to steal.

Question 19

An employee decided to kill his boss, after she told him that he would be fired if his work did not improve. The employee knew his boss was scheduled to go on a business trip on Monday morning. On Sunday morning, the employee went to the company parking garage and put a bomb in the company car that his boss usually drove. The bomb was wired to go off when the car engine started. The employee then left town. At 5 a.m. Monday, the employee, after driving all night, was overcome with remorse and had a change of heart. He called the security officer on duty at the company and told him about the bomb. The security officer said he would take care of the matter. An hour later, the officer put a note on the boss' desk telling her of the message. He then looked at the car but could not see any signs of a bomb. He printed a sign saying "DO NOT USE THIS CAR," put it on the windshield, and went to call the police. Before the police arrived, a company vice-president (not the boss) got into the car and started the engine. The bomb went off, killing her.

The jurisdiction defines murder in the first degree as any homicide committed with premeditation and deliberation or any murder in the commission of a common-law felony. Second-degree murder is defined as all other murder at common law. Manslaughter is defined by the common law. The employee is guilty of

(A) murder in the first degree, because, with premeditation and deliberation, he killed whoever would start the car.

(B) murder in the second degree, because he had no intention of killing the company vice-president.

(C) manslaughter, because at the time of the explosion, he had no intent to kill, and the death of the company vice-president was in part the fault of the security officer.

(D) only attempted murder of the boss, because the death of the company vice-president was the result of the security officer's negligence.

Question 20

In which of the following situations would the defendant's mistake most likely constitute a defense to the crime charged?

(A) A local ordinance forbids the sale of alcoholic beverages to persons under 18 years of age. Relying on false identification, the defendant sells champagne to a 16-year-old high school student. The defendant is charged with illegal sale of alcoholic beverages.

(B) Mistaking the defendant for a narcotics suspect, an undercover police officer attempts to arrest him. The defendant, unaware that the person who has grabbed him is an officer, hits him and knocks him unconscious. The defendant is charged with assault.

(C) The defendant, aged 23, has sexual intercourse with a 15-year-old prostitute who tells the defendant that she is 18. The defendant is charged with the felony of statutory rape under a statute that makes sexual relations with a child under 16 a felony.

(D) Relying on erroneous advice from his attorney that, if his wife has abandoned him for more than a year, he is free to marry. The defendant remarries and is subsequently charged with bigamy.

Question 21

A student and his friend were watching a football game at the student's home when they began to argue. The friend became abusive, and the student asked him to leave. The friend refused, walked into the kitchen, picked up a knife, and said he would cut the student's heart out. The student pulled a gun from under the sofa, walked to his front door, opened it, and again told the friend to leave. The friend again refused. Instead, he walked slowly toward the student, brandishing the knife in a threatening manner. The student, rather than running out the door himself, shot in the friend's direction, intending only to scare him. However, the bullet struck the friend, killing him instantly.

Charged with murder, the student should be

(A) convicted, because the use of deadly force was unreasonable under the circumstances.

(B) convicted, because he had a clear opportunity and duty to retreat.

(C) acquitted, because he did not intend to kill the friend.

(D) acquitted, because he was acting in self-defense and had no duty to retreat.

Question 22

In a criminal trial, the evidence showed that the defendant's neighbor tried to kill the defendant by stabbing him. The defendant ran to his room, picked up a gun, and told his neighbor to back off. The neighbor did not, but continued her attack and stabbed him in the arm. The defendant then shot the neighbor twice. The neighbor fell to the floor and lay quietly moaning. After a few seconds, the defendant fired a third shot into the neighbor. The jury found that the neighbor died instantly from the third shot and that the defendant was no longer in fear of being attacked by her.

The defendant could properly be convicted of which of the following degrees of criminal homicide, if any?

(A) Attempted murder only.

(B) Manslaughter only.

(C) Murder or manslaughter.

(D) No degree of criminal homicide.

Question 23

A runaway was fifteen years old, but she appeared and acted older. When asked, she always said she was twenty-two, and she carried false identification saying she was that old. She frequented taverns and drank heavily. One evening in a bar she became acquainted with the defendant. He believed her when she told him her claimed age. They had several drinks and became inebriated. Later, they drove in the defendant's car to a secluded spot. After they had necked for a while, the defendant propositioned the runaway and she consented. Before the defendant achieved penetration, the runaway changed her mind, saying, "Stop! Don't touch me! I don't want to do it." When the defendant did not desist, the runaway started to cry and said, "I am only fifteen." The defendant immediately jumped from the car and ran away. The defendant was indicted for attempted rape, assault with intent to rape, contributing to the delinquency of a minor, and attempted statutory rape. The age of consent in the jurisdiction is sixteen. The attempted rape charge can only be sustained if

(A) the jury acquits the defendant on all other charges.

(B) the State can show that the defendant thought the runaway was over the age of consent.

(C) the jury finds that the runaway was resisting force used by the defendant to accomplish an act of intercourse.

(D) evidence of the defendant's flight is not admitted by the trial judge.

Question 24

A computer analyst admired his co-worker's wristwatch and frequently said how much he wished he had one like it. The co-worker decided to give the computer analyst the watch for his birthday the following week.

On the weekend before the computer analyst's birthday, the computer analyst and the co-worker attended a company picnic. The co-worker took his watch off and left it on a blanket when he went off to join in a touch football game. The computer analyst strolled by, saw the watch on the blanket, and decided to steal it. He bent over and picked up the watch. Before he could pocket it, however, the co-worker returned. When he saw the computer analyst holding the watch, he said, "I know how much you like that watch. I was planning to give it to you for your birthday. Go ahead and take it now." The computer analyst kept the watch. The computer analyst has committed

(A) larceny.

(B) attempted larceny.

(C) embezzlement.

(D) no crime.

Question 25

A babysitter, while babysitting one night, noticed that the neighbor, who lived next door, had left his house but that the door did not close completely behind him. The babysitter said to the 11-year-old boy she was babysitting, "Let's play a game. You go next door and see if you can find my portable television set, which I lent to the neighbor, and bring it over here." The babysitter knew that the neighbor had a portable television set, and the babysitter planned to keep the set for herself. The boy thought the set belonged to his babysitter, went next door, found the television set, and carried it out the front door. At that moment, the neighbor returned home and discovered the boy in his front yard with the television set. The boy explained the "game" he and the babysitter were playing. The neighbor took back his television set and called the police.

The babysitter is

(A) not guilty of larceny or attempted larceny, because the boy did not commit any crime.

(B) not guilty of larceny but guilty of attempted larceny, because she never acquired possession of the television set.

(C) guilty of larceny as an accessory to the boy.

(D) guilty of larceny by the use of an innocent agent.

Question 26

In which of the following situations is the defendant most likely to be guilty of the crime charged?

(A) Without the permission of the owner, the defendant takes a car with the intention of driving it three miles to a grocery store and back. The defendant is charged with larceny.

(B) The defendant gets permission to borrow a car for the evening by falsely promising to return it, although he does not intend to do so. Two days later, he changes his mind and returns the car to its owner. The defendant is charged with larceny by trick.

(C) The defendant gets permission to borrow a car for the evening by misrepresenting his identity and falsely claiming he has a valid driver's license. He returns the car the next day to the car's owner. The defendant is charged with obtaining property by false pretenses.

(D) With permission, the defendant, promising to return it by 9:00 p.m., borrows a car. Later in the evening, the defendant decides to keep the car until the next morning and does so. The defendant is charged with embezzlement.

Question 27

While testifying as a witness in a civil trial, a witness was asked on cross-examination if he had been convicted in the circuit court of stealing $200 from his employer on August 16, 1997. The witness said, "No, I have never been convicted of any crime." In fact, the witness had pleaded guilty to such a charge and had been placed on probation.

The witness was then charged with perjury on the ground that his statement denying the conviction was false. A statute in the jurisdiction defines perjury as knowingly making a false statement while under oath. At trial, the state proved the witness's statement and the prior conviction. The witness testified that the attorney who represented him in the theft case had told him that, because he had been placed on probation, he had not been convicted of a crime. The witness had served his probationary period satisfactorily and been discharged from probation. The alleged advice of the attorney was incorrect. If the jury believes the witness, it should find him

(A) guilty, because his mistake was one of law.
(B) guilty, because reliance on the advice of an attorney is not a defense.
(C) not guilty if the jury also finds that his reliance on the attorney's advice was reasonable.
(D) not guilty, because he lacked the necessary mental state.

Question 28

In which of the following situations is the defendant most likely to be guilty of common-law murder?

(A) During an argument in a bar, a drunk punches the defendant. The defendant, mistakenly believing that the drunk is about to stab him, shoots and kills the drunk.
(B) While committing a robbery of a liquor store, the defendant accidentally drops his revolver, which goes off. The bullet strikes and kills a customer in the store.
(C) While hunting deer, the defendant notices something moving in the bushes. Believing it to be a deer, the defendant fires into the bushes. The bullet strikes and kills another hunter.
(D) In celebration of the Fourth of July, the defendant discharges a pistol within the city limits in violation of a city ordinance. The bullet ricochets off the street and strikes and kills a pedestrian.

Question 29

At 11:00 p.m., a husband and his wife were accosted in the entrance to their apartment building by the defendant, who was armed as well as masked. The defendant ordered the couple to take him into their apartment. After they entered the apartment, the defendant forced the wife to bind and gag her husband and then to open a safe which contained a diamond necklace. The defendant then tied her up and fled with the necklace. He was apprehended by apartment building security guards. Before the guards could return to the apartment, but after the defendant was arrested, the husband, straining to free himself, suffered a massive heart attack and died.

The defendant is guilty of

(A) burglary, robbery, and murder.
(B) robbery and murder only.
(C) burglary and robbery only.
(D) robbery only.

Question 30

A high school student's teacher told her that she was going to receive a failing grade in history, which would prevent her from graduating. Furious, she reported to the principal that the teacher had fondled her, and the teacher was fired. A year later, still unable to get work because of the scandal, the teacher committed suicide. The student, remorseful, confessed that her accusation had been false.

If the student is charged with manslaughter, her best defense would be that she

(A) committed no act that proximately caused the teacher's death.
(B) did not intend to cause the teacher's death.
(C) did not act with malice.
(D) acted under extreme emotional distress.

Question 31

A jail inmate wanted to make some money, so she decided to sell cocaine. She asked her friend, who was reputed to have access to illegal drugs, to supply her with cocaine so she could resell it. The friend agreed and sold the inmate a bag of white powder. The inmate then repackaged the white powder into smaller containers and sold one to an undercover police officer, who promptly arrested the inmate. The inmate immediately confessed and said that her friend was her supplier.

If the friend knew the white powder was not cocaine but the inmate believed it was, which of the following is correct?

(A) Both the friend and the inmate are guilty of attempting to sell cocaine.
(B) Neither the friend nor the inmate is guilty of attempting to sell cocaine.
(C) The friend is guilty of attempting to sell cocaine, but the inmate is not.
(D) The friend is not guilty of attempting to sell cocaine, but the inmate is.

Question 32

In a jurisdiction that has abolished the felony-murder rule, but otherwise follows the common law of murder, a woman and a man, both armed with automatic weapons, went into a bank to rob it. The man ordered all the persons in the bank to lie on the floor. When some were slow to obey, the woman, not intending to hit anyone, fired about 15 rounds into the air. One of these ricocheted off a stone column and struck and killed a customer in the bank.

The woman and the man were charged with murder of the customer. Which of the following is correct?

(A) The woman can be convicted of murder, because she did the act of killing, but the man cannot be convicted of either murder or manslaughter.
(B) Neither can be guilty of murder, but both can be convicted of manslaughter based upon an unintentional homicide.
(C) The woman can be convicted only of manslaughter, but the man cannot be convicted of murder or manslaughter.
(D) Both can be convicted of murder.

Question 33

A businessman lived on the second floor of a small convenience store/gas station that he owned. One night he refused to sell a customer a six-pack of beer after hours, saying he could not violate the state laws. The customer became enraged and deliberately drove his car into one of the gasoline pumps, severing it from its base. There was an ensuing explosion causing a ball of fire to go from the underground gasoline tank into the building. As a result, the building burned to the ground and the businessman was killed.

In a common-law jurisdiction, if the customer is charged with murder and arson, he should be

(A) convicted of both offenses.
(B) convicted of involuntary manslaughter and acquitted of arson.
(C) convicted of arson and involuntary manslaughter.
(D) acquitted of both offenses.

Question 34

A defendant is charged with murder. The evidence shows that she pointed a gun at the victim and pulled the trigger. The gun discharged, killing the victim. The gun belonged to the victim.

The defendant testifies that the victim told her, and she believed, that the "gun" was a stage prop that could fire only blanks, and that she fired the gun as part of rehearsing a play with the victim at his house. If the jury believes the defendant's testimony and finds that her mistaken belief that the gun was a prop was reasonable, they should find her

(A) guilty of murder.
(B) guilty of manslaughter.
(C) guilty of either murder or manslaughter.
(D) not guilty of murder or manslaughter.

Question 35

Which of the following is most likely to be found to be a strict liability offense?

(A) A city ordinance providing for a fine of not more than $200 for shoplifting.
(B) A federal statute making it a felony to possess heroin.
(C) A state statute making it a felony to fail to register a firearm.
(D) A state statute making the sale of adulterated milk a misdemeanor.

Question 36

A law student broke into his professor's office in order to look at examination questions. The questions were locked in a drawer, and the law student could not find them. The law student believed that looking at examination questions was a crime, but in this belief he was mistaken.

Charged with burglary, the law student should be

(A) acquitted, because he did not complete the crime and he has not been charged with attempt.
(B) acquitted, because what he intended to do when he broke in was not a crime.
(C) convicted, because he had the necessary mental state and committed the act of breaking and entering.
(D) convicted, because factual impossibility is not a defense.

Question 37

A defendant, while eating in a restaurant, noticed that a departing customer at the next table had left a five-dollar bill as a tip for the waitress. The defendant reached over, picked up the five-dollar bill, and put it in his pocket. As he stood up to leave, another customer who had seen him take the money ran over to him and hit him in the face with her umbrella. Enraged, the defendant choked the customer to death.

The defendant is charged with murder. He requests the court to charge the jury that they can find him guilty of voluntary manslaughter rather than murder. The defendant's request should be

(A) granted, because the jury could find that the defendant acted recklessly and not with the intent to cause death or serious bodily harm.
(B) granted, because the jury could find that being hit in the face with an umbrella constitutes adequate provocation.
(C) denied, because the evidence shows that the defendant intended to kill or to cause serious bodily harm.

(D) denied, because the evidence shows that the defendant provoked the assault on himself by his criminal misconduct.

Question 38

A customer asked to see an expensive watch in a jewelry store. In conversation with the clerk, the customer falsely claimed to be the son of the mayor. When handed the watch, he asked if he could put it on, walk around a bit so he could see how it felt on his wrist, and then briefly step outside to observe it in natural light. The clerk agreed, saying, "I know I can trust someone like you with the merchandise." The customer walked out of the store wearing the watch and never returned. A week later, the clerk was at a gathering when she spotted the customer wearing the watch. She told him that he must either pay for the watch or give it back. He hissed, "I'll knock your block off if you mess with me." Intimidated, the clerk backed off. The following list of crimes is in descending order of seriousness.

What is the most serious crime the customer committed?

(A) Robbery.
(B) Larceny.
(C) False pretenses.
(D) Embezzlement.

Question 39

A defendant was an alcoholic who frequently experienced auditory hallucinations that commanded him to engage in bizarre and sometimes violent behavior. He generally obeyed their commands. The hallucinations appeared more frequently when he was intoxicated, but he sometimes experienced them when he had not been drinking. After the defendant had been drinking continuously for a three-day period, an elderly woman began to reproach him about his drunken condition, slapping him on the face and shoulders as she did so. The defendant believed that he was being unmercifully attacked and heard the hallucinatory voice telling him to strangle his assailant. He did so, and she died.

If the defendant is charged with second degree murder, the defendant's best chance of acquittal would be to rely on a defense of

(A) intoxication.
(B) lack of malice aforethought.
(C) self-defense.
(D) insanity.

Question 40

A husband and wife were walking to their car one evening after having seen a movie. As they were passing a dark alleyway, a defendant leaped out brandishing a gun. He pushed the wife against the wall of a nearby building, held the gun to her head, and demanded money from the man. The husband handed over his cash. The defendant grabbed the cash and ran away.

Which of the following, listed in descending order of seriousness, is the most serious crime for which the defendant may be convicted?

(A) Robbery from the husband.
(B) Larceny from the husband.
(C) Assault on the husband and his wife.
(D) Assault on the wife.

Question 41

A college student approached an undercover police officer and inquired about hiring someone to kill his girlfriend's parents. Unknown to the college student, the police officer pretended to agree to handle the job and secretly taped subsequent conversations with the college student concerning plans and payment. A few days before the payment was due, the college student changed his mind and called the plan off. Nevertheless, the college student was charged with solicitation to commit murder.

The college student should be

(A) acquitted, because he withdrew before payment.
(B) acquitted, because no substantial acts were performed.
(C) convicted, because the offense was completed before his attempt to withdraw.
(D) convicted, because the police officer agreed to commit the offense.

Question 42

A homeless young woman broke into the basement of a hotel and fell asleep. She was awakened by a security guard, who demanded that she leave. As the young woman was leaving, she cursed the security guard. Angered, the guard began to beat the young woman on her head with his flashlight. After the second blow, the young woman grabbed a fire extinguisher and sprayed the guard in his face, causing him to lose his sight in one eye.

The jurisdiction defines aggravated assault as assault with intent to cause serious bodily injury. The most serious crime for which the young woman could properly be convicted is

(A) aggravated assault.
(B) burglary.
(C) assault.
(D) trespass.

Question 43

A defendant was short of money. He decided to go into a house to take the homeowner's silverware and then to sell it. That night, while the homeowner was away, the defendant entered by picking the lock on the front door. He picked up a chest of silverware from the dining room and went out the front door of the house to his car. As he was putting the chest of silverware into the trunk, he had second thoughts and decided that he did not wish to become a thief. He reentered the house and replaced the chest of silverware where he had found it. As he came out of the house the second time, he was arrested by the police, who had been called by a neighbor.

The defendant is

(A) guilty of burglary and larceny.
(B) guilty of burglary and attempted larceny.
(C) guilty of burglary but not guilty of any larceny offense.
(D) not guilty of burglary or any larceny offense.

Question 44

Which of the following is LEAST likely to be the underlying felony in a prosecution for felony murder?

(A) Arson.
(B) Manslaughter.
(C) Attempted rape.
(D) Burglary.

Question 45

A gangster and two of his friends were members of a teenage street gang. While they were returning from a dance late one evening, their car collided with a car driven by an elderly woman. After an argument, the gangster attacked the elderly woman with his fists and beat her to death. The two friends watched, and when they saw the woman fall to the ground they urged the gangster to flee. The gangster was eventually apprehended and tried for manslaughter, but the jury could not decide on a verdict.

If the gangster's companions are subsequently tried as accomplices to manslaughter, they should be

(A) acquitted, because the gangster was not convicted of the offense.
(B) acquitted, because they did not assist or encourage the gangster to commit the crime.
(C) convicted, because they urged him to flee.
(D) convicted, because they made no effort to intervene.

Question 46

Four men are charged with conspiracy to commit a series of bank robberies. Nine successful bank robberies took place during the period of the charged conspiracy. Because the robbers wore masks and gloves and stole the bank surveillance tapes, no direct identification of the robbers by the witnesses has been made. Some circumstantial evidence ties each of the men to the overall conspiracy. During cross-examination, a prosecution witness testified that one defendant was in jail on other charges during six of the robberies. That defendant's lawyer has moved for a judgment of acquittal at the close of the government's case.

Should the motion be granted?

(A) No, because a conspirator is not required to agree to all of the objects of the conspiracy.
(B) No, because a conspirator need not be present at the commission of each crime conspired upon.
(C) Yes, provided the defendant has complied with the rule requiring pretrial notice of alibi.
(D) Yes, regardless of compliance with the alibi rule, because the government is bound by exculpatory evidence elicited during its case in chief.

Question 47

A store owner whose jewelry store had recently been robbed was shown by a police detective a photograph of the defendant, who previously had committed other similar crimes. The store owner examined the photograph and then asked the detective whether the police believed that the man pictured was the robber. After the detective said, "We're pretty sure," the store owner stated that the man in the photograph was the one who had robbed her.

The defendant was indicted for the robbery. His counsel moved to suppress any trial testimony by the store owner identifying the defendant as the robber.

Should the court grant the motion and suppress the store owner's trial testimony identifying the defendant as the robber?

(A) No, because suppression of in-court testimony is not a proper remedy, even though the out-of-court identification was improper.
(B) No, because the out-of-court identification was not improper.
(C) Yes, because the improper out-of-court identification has necessarily tainted any in-court identification.
(D) Yes, unless the prosecution demonstrates that the in-court identification is reliable.

Question 48

A defendant was charged with attempted murder. At the preliminary hearing, the presiding judge heard the testimony of four prosecution witnesses and found that the prosecution had failed to establish probable cause that the defendant had committed any offense. Accordingly, he dismissed the charge.

The prosecutor then called the same four witnesses before a grand jury. The grand jury indicted the same defendant for attempted murder.

The defendant has moved to quash the indictment on the ground of double jeopardy.

How should the court proceed?

(A) Grant the motion, because the dismissal of the first charge on the merits, whether correct or incorrect, bars any further prosecution.

(B) Grant the motion, unless the prosecution has evidence that was not presented in the first case.

(C) Deny the motion, because the defendant has not yet been in jeopardy of conviction on the attempted murder charge.

(D) Deny the motion, because the protection of the double jeopardy clause does not come into play until there has been a conviction or an acquittal.

Question 49

Police, who had probable cause to arrest a man for a series of armed robberies, obtained a warrant to arrest him. At 6 a.m. they surreptitiously entered the man's house and, with guns drawn, went to the man's bedroom, where they awakened him. Startled, the man asked, "What's going on?" and an officer replied, "We've got you now." Another officer immediately asked the man if he had committed a particular robbery, and the man said that he had. The police then informed him that he was under arrest and ordered him to get dressed.

Charged with robbery, the man has moved to suppress the use of his statement as evidence.

What is the man's best argument for granting his motion?

(A) The police did not give him the required *Miranda* warnings.

(B) The statement was not voluntary.

(C) He was not informed that he was under arrest until after he made the statement.

(D) The police did not have a search warrant authorizing entry into the house.

Question 50

Federal agents had a hunch that a local man was engaged in illegal gambling activities. An agent decided to enter the man's house while he was not at home and see what he could find. The agent discovered an envelope containing $5,000 in cash and an executive's business card. Returning the envelope to its place, the agent located and interviewed the executive, who admitted that he had paid the man $5,000 to settle a gambling debt; the executive also disclosed that the man regularly took illegal bets from the executive and several of his acquaintances. The agent then interviewed the acquaintances, who confirmed what the executive had told him. The agent then arranged to be introduced to the man at a local bar. After a few drinks, the man, unaware of the agent's identity, boasted that he was one of the biggest bookmakers in the state.

The agent testified to all of his investigation's discoveries before a grand jury, which returned an indictment against the man for illegal gambling activities, based solely on the agent's testimony. The man's attorney then filed a motion to dismiss the indictment, claiming that it rested on violations of the man's constitutional rights.

Should the court grant the motion?

(A) No, because dismissal of the indictment is not the appropriate remedy.

(B) Yes, because much of the agent's testimony before the grand jury was inadmissible hearsay.

(C) Yes, because of the agent's unlawful search of the man's home.

(D) Yes, because of the agent's violation of the man's right to counsel.

Question 51

A defendant was charged with the capital offense of first-degree murder, for which the only available penalties were death or life in prison without parole. During jury selection, the trial court, over the defendant's objection, granted the prosecution's for-cause challenge of five prospective jurors who indicated upon questioning by both parties that they personally were opposed to the death penalty and were unsure if they could ever vote to impose it. The jury convicted the defendant and, following a separate sentencing hearing, sentenced him to death.

On appeal, the defendant's only argument was that excusing the prospective jurors violated his federal constitutional right to be tried by a jury chosen from a fair cross section of the community.

How should the court of appeals rule on the conviction and the death sentence?

(A) Affirm both.

(B) Affirm the conviction, but reverse the death sentence and remand for a new sentencing hearing before a different jury.

(C) Affirm the conviction, but reverse the death sentence and remand for resentencing to life in prison.

(D) Reverse both.

Question 52

Police responded to a call that shots had been heard coming from a certain house. Upon arriving at the house, the police looked through a window and saw a man lying on the living room floor. The police opened the front door, which was not locked, and found that the man had recently been shot in the back and was unconscious. An ambulance was called. While waiting for the ambulance, one officer walked through the house to see if anyone else was present. No one else was found, but the officer did see on the kitchen table clear bags of what he believed to be cocaine. The officer seized the bags, and laboratory tests later confirmed that the contents were cocaine.

After the ambulance arrived a few minutes later and took the man to the hospital, the police went through the house and opened drawers trying to find the gun used in the shooting. No gun was found, but upon opening a drawer in an upstairs bedroom, the police found marijuana and seized it.

Later investigation led to charging a young woman, who lived in the house, with unlawful possession of the cocaine and the marijuana. The young woman has filed a motion to suppress the use of both as evidence on the ground that the entry into the house and the searches were made without a warrant.

How should the court decide the young woman's motion?

(A) Grant it as to the cocaine, but deny it as to the marijuana.
(B) Deny it as to the cocaine, but grant it as to the marijuana.
(C) Grant it as to both the cocaine and the marijuana.
(D) Deny it as to both the cocaine and the marijuana.

Question 53

An ex-convict and his cellmate planned to hold up a bank. They drove to the bank in the ex-convict's car. The ex-convict entered while the cellmate remained as lookout in the car. After a few moments, the cellmate panicked and drove off. Soon afterward, the cellmate was stopped by a police officer for speeding. The officer began to write a ticket and explained to the cellmate that he was going to issue this ticket instead of arresting the cellmate as the officer was authorized to do under local police department procedures. While writing at the ticket, the officer noted the cellmate's extreme nervousness, and therefore asked the cellmate if the officer could search the car. The cellmate agreed. The search turned up heroin concealed in the lid of the trunk, and the ex-convict was prosecuted for possessing the drug with intent to resell. In that trial, the prosecution's best argument to sustain the validity of the search of the ex-convict's car would be that

(A) the search was reasonable under the circumstances, including the cellmate's nervous condition.
(B) the search was incident to a valid arrest.
(C) The cellmate had, under the circumstances, sufficient standing and authority to consent to the search.
(D) exigent circumstances, including the inherent mobility of a car, justified the search.

Question 54

A detective received information from an informant, who had given reliable information many times in the past, that a suspect was a narcotics dealer. Specifically, the informant said that, two months before, he had visited the suspect's apartment with one of the suspect's friends and that on that occasion he saw the suspect sell that friend some heroin. The detective knew that the informant, the suspect, and the friend of the suspect were all friends. Thereafter, the detective put all this information into an affidavit form, appeared before a magistrate, and secured a search warrant for the suspect's apartment. The search turned up a supply of heroin. The suspect's motion to suppress introduction of the heroin into evidence will most probably be

(A) granted, because a search warrant cannot validly be issued solely on the basis of an informant's information.
(B) granted, because the information supplied to the detective concerned an occurrence too remote in time to justify a finding of probable cause at the time of the search.
(C) granted, because a search for "mere evidence" alone is improper and illegal.
(D) denied, because the informant had proven himself reliable in the past and the information he gave turned out to be correct.

Question 55

A defendant sold heroin to an addict. The addict was later stopped by two police officers for speeding 30 miles per hour over the speed limit. The officers required the addict to get out of the car. One of the officers told the addict he was arresting him pursuant to department policy of arresting all persons stopped for going more than 20 mph over the speed limit; that officer put the addict in handcuffs, escorted him to the patrol car, and kept watch over him there. The other officer searched the passenger compartment of the addict's car and found the heroin concealed under the rear seat. The defendant has now been charged with illegally selling the heroin found in the addict's car.

The defendant's motion to prevent introduction of the heroin into evidence will most probably be

(A) granted, because the heroin was not in plain view.
(B) granted, because the scope of the search was excessive.
(C) denied, because the defendant has no standing to object to the search.
(D) denied, because the search was proper as incident to a valid full custodial arrest.

Question 56

A thief held up a drugstore at 10:30 at night, and drove away. His car broke down in an isolated area just outside the small city in which the crime occurred. The thief walked to the nearest house and asked the homeowner if he could stay until the next morning, explaining that he had been searching for his sister's home and had run out of gas. The homeowner agreed to let him sleep on a couch in the basement. During the course of the night, the homeowner began to doubt the story the thief had told him. Early the next morning, the homeowner called the police and said he was suspicious and frightened of a stranger whom he had allowed to stay the night. The police went immediately to the house to assist the homeowner and walked through the open front door. They found the thief and the homeowner drinking coffee in the kitchen. When they saw the thief, they realized he matched the description of the drugstore robber. They arrested the thief and in his jacket they found drugs taken during the robbery.

The thief moves to suppress the evidence of the drugs. If the court finds that the police did not have probable cause to believe the man was the thief until they saw him inside the homeowner's house and realized he matched the description, the court should

(A) grant the motion, because, as a guest, the thief has sufficient standing to contest the entry of the house without a warrant.
(B) grant the motion, because, as a guest, the thief has sufficient standing to contest the lack of probable cause at the time of the entry.
(C) deny the motion, because the thief had no ownership or other possessory interest in the premises.
(D) deny the motion, because the police had the permission of the owner to enter the house.

Question 57

The police had, over time, accumulated reliable information that a drug dealer operated a large cocaine-distribution network, that he and his accomplices often resorted to violence, and that they kept a small arsenal of weapons in his home.

One day, the police received reliable information that a large brown suitcase with leather straps containing a supply of cocaine had been delivered to the drug dealer's home and that it would be moved to a distribution point the next morning. The police obtained a valid search warrant to search for and seize the brown suitcase and the cocaine and went to the drug dealer's house. The police knocked on the drug dealer's door and called out, "Police. Open up. We have a search warrant." After a few seconds with no response, the police forced the door open and entered. Hearing noises in the basement, the police ran down there and found the drug dealer with a large brown suitcase with leather straps. They seized the suitcase and put handcuffs on the drug dealer. A search of his person revealed a switchblade knife and a .45-caliber pistol. The drug dealer cursed the police and said, "You never would have caught me with the stuff if it hadn't been for that lousy snitch!" In addition to charges relating to the cocaine in the suitcase, the drug dealer is charged with unlawful possession of weapons. The drug dealer moves pretrial to suppress the use as evidence of the weapons seized by the police and of the statement he made. As to the drug dealer's statement, his motion to suppress should be

(A) granted, because the entry by forcing open the door was not reasonable.
(B) granted, because the police failed to read the drug dealer his *Miranda* rights.
(C) denied, because the statement was volunteered.
(D) denied, because the statement was the product of a lawful public safety search.

Question 58

State troopers lawfully stopped a driver on the turnpike for exceeding the speed limit by four miles per hour. One trooper approached the car to warn the driver to drive within the speed limit. The other trooper remained in the patrol car and ran a computer check of the license number of the driver's car. The computer check indicated that there was an outstanding warrant for the driver's arrest for unpaid traffic tickets. The troopers then arrested the driver. After handcuffing her, the troopers searched her and the car, and discovered ten glassine bags of heroin in a paper bag on the back seat of the car. Later it was learned that the driver had paid the outstanding traffic tickets ten days earlier and the warrant had been quashed, but the clerk of the court had failed to update the computer, which continued to list the warrant as outstanding. The driver was charged with unlawful possession of heroin. Her attorney filed a motion to suppress the use as evidence of the heroin found in the car.

Should the motion be granted?

(A) No, because the troopers could reasonably rely on the computer report and the search was incident to arrest.
(B) No, because troopers may lawfully search the passenger compartment of a car incident to a valid traffic stop.
(C) Yes, because there was no arrest for the traffic violation and no lawful arrest could be made on the basis of the warrant.
(D) Yes, because there was no probable cause or reasonable suspicion to believe drugs were in the car.

Question 59

A bank robber handed a teller a handwritten note demanding money. Shortly thereafter, the defendant was arrested for the robbery. At the police station, the defendant was required, over his protest, to write out the words of the note and have his fingerprints taken. He was then, for the first time, allowed to telephone a lawyer, who thereafter represented him.

The prosecution, after introducing the robbers' note to the teller, also offers in evidence the defendant's writing of the words on the note at the request of the police. On appropriate action, the court should rule this

(A) admissible.
(B) inadmissible, because he was not advised that his handwriting sample could be admitted into evidence against him.
(C) inadmissible, because he was not advised of his right to refuse to give a handwriting sample.
(D) inadmissible, because he had not been informed he had a right to have counsel present.

Question 60

A grand jury was investigating a bank robbery. The only information known to the prosecutor was a rumor that the defendant might have been involved. The grand jury subpoenaed the defendant. He refused to answer questions about the robbery and was granted use immunity. He then testified that he and his accomplice had robbed the bank. The grand jury indicted both the defendant and the accomplice for the bank robbery. The prosecutor had no evidence as to the identity of the robbers except the testimony of the defendant and the accomplice.

At the defendant's trial, his objections to the accomplice's being permitted to testify should be

(A) sustained, because the prosecutor may not bargain away the rights of one codefendant in a deal with another.
(B) sustained, because the accomplice's testimony was acquired as a result of the defendant's grand jury testimony.
(C) overruled, because the police suspected the defendant even before he testified in the grand jury hearing.
(D) overruled, because a witness cannot be precluded from testifying if his testimony is given voluntarily.

Question 61

A motorist was driving through an apartment building area plagued with an unusually high incidence of burglaries and assaults. Acting pursuant to a police department plan to combat crime by the random stopping of automobiles in the area between midnight and 6:00 a.m., a police officer stopped the motorist and asked him for identification. As the motorist handed the officer his license, the officer directed a flashlight into the automobile and saw what appeared to be the barrel of a shotgun protruding from under the front seat on the passenger side of the car. The officer ordered the motorist from the car, searched him, and discovered marijuana cigarettes and a shotgun.

At the motorist's trial for unlawful possession of narcotics, his motion to suppress the use of the marijuana as evidence should be

(A) sustained, because the marijuana was discovered as a result of the unlawful stopping of the motorist's automobile.
(B) sustained, because the use of the flashlight constituted a search of the interior of the motorist's automobile without probable cause.
(C) denied, because the officer's conduct was consistent with the established police plan.
(D) denied, because the discovery of the gun in plain view created the reasonable suspicion necessary to justify the arrest and search of the motorist.

Question 62

Police telephoned a friend of the suspect in a homicide committed during a robbery of a liquor store and asked if he would help locate the suspect. The friend agreed and met the police officers at headquarters later that night.

After a discussion during which police asked questions about the suspect and the homicide, the friend said that he wanted to get something "off his chest" and advised the officers that he was in on the robbery but that the suspect had shot the owner of the store without his permission or prior knowledge. The officers then for the first time gave the friend his *Miranda* warnings. The friend was indicted for felony murder. He moved to prevent the introduction of his statement into evidence. His motion should be

(A) granted, because the friend was effectively in custody and entitled to receive *Miranda* warnings at the beginning of the discussion.
(B) granted, because the friend's rights to counsel and to due process were violated by the interrogation at police headquarters.
(C) denied, because his statement was freely and voluntarily given and he was not entitled to *Miranda* warnings.
(D) denied, because by visiting headquarters voluntarily, the friend waived his right to have *Miranda* warnings at the beginning of the discussion.

Question 63

A state enacted a statute "to regulate administratively the conduct of motor vehicle junkyard businesses in order to deter motor vehicle theft and trafficking in stolen motor vehicles or parts thereof." The statute requires a junkyard owner or operator "to permit representatives of the Department of Motor Vehicles or of any law enforcement agency upon request during normal business hours to take physical inventory of motor vehicles and parts thereof on the premises."

The statute also states that a failure to comply with any of its requirements constitutes a felony.

Police officers assigned to their city's Automobile Crimes Unit periodically visited all motor vehicle junkyards in town to make the inspections permitted by the statute. A junkyard owner conducted such a business in the city at issue. One summer day, the officers asked to inspect the vehicles on her lot. The junkyard owner said, "Do I have a choice?" The officers told her she did not. The officers conducted their inspection and discovered three stolen automobiles. The junkyard owner is charged with receiving stolen property. The junkyard owner moves pretrial to suppress the evidence relating to the three automobiles on the ground that the inspection was unconstitutional. Her motion should be

(A) sustained, because the statute grants unbridled discretion to law enforcement officers to make warrantless searches.
(B) sustained, because the stated regulatory purpose of the statute is a pretext to circumvent the warrant requirement in conducting criminal investigations.
(C) denied, because the statute deals reasonably with a highly regulated industry.
(D) denied, because administrative searches of commercial establishments do not require warrants.

Question 64

A criminal was indicted in a state court in January 2015 for a robbery and murder that occurred in December 2012. He retained counsel, who filed a motion to dismiss on the ground that the criminal had been prejudiced by a 25-month delay in obtaining the indictment. Thereafter, the criminal, with his counsel, appeared in court for arraignment and stated that he wished to plead guilty. The presiding judge asked the criminal whether he understood the nature of the charges, possible defenses, and maximum allowable sentences. The criminal replied that he did, and the judge reviewed all of those matters with him. He then asked the criminal whether he understood that he did not have to plead guilty. When the criminal responded that he knew that, the judge accepted the plea and sentenced the criminal to 25 years.

Six months later, the criminal filed a motion to set aside his guilty plea on each of the following grounds. Which of these grounds provides a constitutional basis for relief?

(A) The judge did not rule on his motion to dismiss before accepting the guilty plea.
(B) The judge did not determine that the criminal had robbed and killed the victim.
(C) The judge did not determine whether the criminal understood that he had a right to jury trial.
(D) The judge did not determine whether the prosecutor's file contained any undisclosed exculpatory material.

Question 65

A marijuana farmer had been missing for several months. The sheriff's department received an anonymous tip that a rival marijuana farmer had buried the missing farmer in a hillside about 200 yards from the rival farmer's farmhouse. Sheriff's deputies went to the rival farmer's farm. They cut the barbed wire that surrounded the hillside and entered, looking for the grave. They also searched the adjacent fields on the rival farmer's farm that were within the area enclosed by the barbed wire and discovered clothing that belonged to the missing farmer hanging on a scarecrow. The rival farmer observed their discovery and began shooting. The deputies returned the fire. The rival farmer dashed to his pickup truck to escape. Unable to start the truck, he fled across a field toward the barn. A deputy tackled him just as he entered the barn.

As the rival farmer attempted to get up, the deputy pinned his arms behind his back. Another deputy threatened, "Tell us what you did with the missing farmer or we'll lock you up and you'll see your family on welfare." The rival farmer responded that he had killed the missing farmer in a fight but did not report the incident because he did not want authorities to enter his land and discover his marijuana crop. Instead, he buried him behind the barn. The rival farmer was thereafter charged with murder. If the rival farmer moves to suppress his admission about killing his neighbor, the court should

(A) grant the motion, because the rival farmer did not voluntarily waive his right to silence.
(B) grant the motion, because the statement was the product of the warrantless entry and search of the rival farmer's farm.
(C) deny the motion, because the deputy was in hot pursuit when he questioned the rival farmer.
(D) deny the motion, because the rival farmer was questioned during a police emergency search.

Question 66

A woman who is a computer whiz decided to dedicate herself to exposing persons who traffic in child pornography. She posted a number of sexually oriented photographs on her web site. The file for each photograph contained an embedded Trojan horse program. The defendant downloaded one of those photographs onto his personal computer. Using the embedded program, the woman entered the defendant's computer and found a file containing a pornographic photograph of a child. She copied the file and turned it over to a federal law enforcement agency. A federal agent told her that a successful prosecution would require more than one photograph and offered her a monetary reward for additional photos leading to a conviction of the defendant. The woman entered the defendant's computer again, and this time she found hundreds of child pornography photos, which she turned over to the federal agency.

The defendant is charged with multiple counts of violating federal statutes regarding child pornography. He moves to suppress the photographs that the woman discovered on his computer. The motion is based on both the Fourth Amendment and a federal statute forbidding interception of electronic communication without permission. The parties have stipulated that the woman's conduct in downloading photos from the defendant's computer violated the interception statute. How should the court rule on the defendant's motion to suppress?

(A) Deny it as to all photographs.

(B) Grant it as to all photographs, because the woman acted without probable cause.

(C) Grant it as to all photographs, because the woman violated the federal interception statute.

(D) Grant it only as to the second set of photographs.

ANSWERS

CRIMINAL LAW AND PROCEDURE

Answer Key

Use this Answer Key to quickly identify the correct answer to each question.

(1) C	(11) B	(21) D	(31) D	(41) C	(51) A	(61) A
(2) A	(12) C	(22) C	(32) D	(42) D	(52) B	(62) C
(3) A	(13) A	(23) C	(33) A	(43) A	(53) C	(63) C
(4) A	(14) D	(24) A	(34) D	(44) B	(54) B	(64) C
(5) B	(15) C	(25) D	(35) D	(45) B	(55) C	(65) A
(6) D	(16) C	(26) B	(36) B	(46) B	(56) D	(66) D
(7) A	(17) B	(27) D	(37) B	(47) D	(57) C	
(8) C	(18) D	(28) B	(38) B	(48) C	(58) A	
(9) D	(19) A	(29) A	(39) D	(49) A	(59) A	
(10) A	(20) B	(30) A	(40) A	(50) A	(60) B	

ANSWERS

CRIMINAL LAW AND PROCEDURE

Answer 1

(C) is the best response,

because the theory of continuing trespass made the executive guilty of larceny when she burned the materials.

First, let's consider whether the executive is guilty of *burglary*. Burglary is: (1) the breaking, (2) and entering, (3) of the dwelling, (4) of another, (5) at night time, (6) with the intent to commit a felony within. (Here, the statute has eliminated requirement (3).) No burglary occurred, because element (6) was missing. The time for measuring the existence of an "intent to commit a felony within" is the moment of the breaking and entering. Here, at the time of the breaking and entering, the executive intended to retrieve only her own personal property. So she did not have a felonious intent at the requisite moment. The fact that she *later* formed such an intent (when she was home, and decided to destroy what she knew was the property of another) doesn't count—the only thing that counts is the intent at the moment of breaking and entering.

Now, let's consider whether the executive committed *larceny*. Larceny is: (1) the taking and (2) carrying away of (3) the tangible property (4) of another, (5) by trespass or without consent, (6) with the intent to permanently deprive the other of his interest in the property. During the entire session at the office building, the executive never satisfied element (6): Since she intended to return any property not belonging to her that she might grab in the dark, she did not act "with the intent to permanently deprive the other of his interest in the property."

But the doctrine of "*continuing trespass*" applies, to make the executive guilty of trespass as soon as she burned the book and papers. Under the continuing trespass doctrine, applied by most courts, one who takes another's property, knowing that it is not his own but intending to return it, commits a "trespassory taking" at that moment; that original trespassory taking, although not coinciding with an intent to steal, is deemed to continue until the taker *does* form such an intent, at which point the larceny is complete. LaFave, § 8.5, p. 817. Here, the executive knew while in the office that she was taking property that was not her own and that she was unauthorized to take; at that moment, she had a trespassory intent, even though she had no present intent to steal and was thus not yet guilty of larceny. Then, at the moment she burned these materials at home, she had the intent to deprive the owner permanently of his interest in the property; that intent now coincided with the continuing trespass, making her guilty of larceny at the moment of burning.

Neither (A), (B), nor (D) is the best response,

because each of them is directly inconsistent with the above analysis, either by stating that burglary was present (choices A and B) or by stating that larceny was not present (choice D).

Answer 2

(A) is the best response,

because there was enough circumstantial evidence of an agreement to commit a crime to justify sending the case to the jury.

Conspiracy is an agreement between two or more persons to accomplish a crime. (Some jurisdictions also require an overt act in furtherance of the conspiracy, but any overt-act requirement is not at issue here.) The prosecution bears the burden of proving that an agreement to commit a crime was made by the two defendants. However, the existence of an agreement need not be proven by direct evidence; *circumstantial evidence* can suffice.

Now that the defendant has asked for a directed verdict, the court should deny the verdict as long as the prosecution has proved facts that, taken in a light most favorable to the prosecution, are sufficient to allow a rational jury to conclude beyond reasonable doubt that there was an agreement to smuggle cocaine. The woman's admission that she told her sister that there were "too many officers at this airport," when taken together with the fact that both defendants were carrying bottles of liquid cocaine, was enough circumstantial evidence to allow a reasonable jury to conclude that, beyond a reasonable doubt, the women agreed to import cocaine. (There is no other plausible explanation of what the "too many officers" remark could have meant in these circumstances; and all that's required is that a rational jury *could* [not *must*] conclude beyond a reasonable doubt that there was an agreement.)

(B) is not the best response,

because the mere fact of possession does not prove a conspiratorial agreement.

Conspiracy requires an *agreement* between two or more persons to accomplish a crime. The mere fact that each of the two women was found in possession of smuggled cocaine does not prove that they made an agreement to do so together—each might have formed the intent to smuggle independently from the other.

(C) is not the best response,

because it overlooks the circumstantial evidence of an agreement to smuggle.

Conspiracy requires an agreement between two or more persons to accomplish a crime. However, the existence of an agreement need not be proven by direct evidence; circumstantial evidence can suffice. Here, the woman's admission that she told her sister that there were "too many officers at this airport," when taken together with the fact that both defendants were carrying bottles of liquid cocaine, was enough circumstantial evidence to allow a reasonable jury to conclude that, beyond a reasonable doubt, the women agreed to import cocaine. So this choice is not accurate in saying that the evidence shows "only" separate crimes of cocaine possession.

(D) is not the best response,

because the woman's cooperation was not a withdrawal.

This choice is wrong for several reasons. First, the crime was complete as soon as the women agreed to commit the smuggling, so any later withdrawal would not be a defense to this already-completed crime. (Even if the jurisdiction required an overt act, the actual smuggling of the cocaine by the woman would meet the overt-act requirement, and that smuggling occurred before the withdrawal.) Apart from this timing problem, courts unanimously hold that a withdrawal requires an affirmative act bringing home the fact of withdrawal to the withdrawer's confederates (Lafave, § 6.5, p. 603), and here, the woman's confession was not even known to her sister at the time it was made, so it could not have brought the withdrawal home to the sister. Lastly, the withdrawal must consist of a voluntary and complete renunciation of the criminal purpose; a confession after one has been caught would certainly not meet the requirement of voluntariness.

Answer 3

(A) is the best response,

because one of the mental states that suffices for murder is an intent to do serious bodily harm.

At common law, a number of mental states can suffice for murder. One of these mental states is an intent to do *serious bodily injury*. The intent to do serious bodily injury, like the intent to kill, can be *inferred* from the defendant's conduct in the light of the surrounding circumstances. The defendant's choice of weapon, and the nature of the physical attack on the victim, are circumstances that can lead a reasonable jury to infer an intent to seriously injure the victim. Here, the man's choice of a hammer, and his swinging the hammer at his friend's head rather than at some other point on the body, would justify a reasonable jury in concluding beyond a reasonable doubt that the man intended to cause at least serious bodily injury to his friend. Since the friend's death directly resulted from the man's conduct, all the requirements for murder of the intent-to-do-serious-bodily-injury variety are present. (It's possible—though not likely—that the jury might accept the partial defense of reasonable provocation, which would downgrade the crime to voluntary manslaughter. But a reasonable jury *could* certainly reject the provocation defense, in which case a murder conviction would be appropriate, and you're asked to specify the most serious crime of which the defendant "could properly be convicted.")

(B), (C), and (D) are not the best responses,

because each of them is less serious than murder, and a murder conviction would be proper.

As to choice B (voluntary manslaughter or V.M.), the man could certainly raise the defense that he committed the crime under extreme provocation, entitling him to a reduction to V.M. It's unlikely that the jury would accept this defense, because hitting someone in the head with a hammer is probably not a "reasonable" response to the provocation caused by an intentional breaking of a television. But whether or not the jury *would* accept the defense, a reasonable jury *could* reject the defense, so a murder conviction on an intent-to-do-serious-bodily-injury theory would be appropriate, making V.M. not the most serious crime for which a conviction would be "proper."

As to choice C (involuntary manslaughter, or I.M.), the fact that a murder conviction would be permissible means I.M. cannot be the most serious crime of which the man could properly be convicted. Furthermore, I.M. is generally premised upon criminal negligence or recklessness, not an intent to do bodily harm, so the facts here are not appropriate ones for I.M.

As to choice D (assault), a conviction for assault would certainly be proper. But as discussed above, the murder conviction would also be proper, and obviously murder is a more serious crime than assault.

Answer 4

(A) is the best response,

because the fact that the drunk man never felt fear or believed that force was being used is irrelevant to the defendant's liability for attempted robbery.

A robbery is a larceny from a person, or in a person's immediate presence, brought about by either force or fear. The gunman would like to assert the defense of *factual impossibility*. The argument would be that the drunk man was incapable of feeling fear or even of perceiving that force was being threatened, so that it was impossible for the defendant to have succeeded with the robbery, thereby preventing him from being guilty even of an attempt to rob. But, sadly for the defendant, the defense of factual impossibility is universally *rejected*: Impossibility is no defense to attempt charges where, had the facts been as the defendant believed them to be, the defendant would have had the mental state required for the completed crime. Here, if the facts had been as the gunman believed them to be (i.e., that the victim was capable of feeling fear or at least recognizing that the gunman's threat to use the gun might well be real), the gunman would have had the mental state for robbery. So the fact that circumstances made it factually impossible for the completed crime to occur is irrelevant.

(B), (C), and (D) are not the best response,

because each lists a less serious crime than attempted robbery (or lists no crime at all), and the defendant may properly be convicted of attempted robbery.

As to choice C, the defendant could indeed be convicted of attempted larceny, since he attempted to permanently deprive the drunk man of his property; it's only the fact that attempted robbery is a more serious crime than attempted larceny that prevents C from being the right answer. As to attempted battery (choice B), it's not clear whether that crime has been committed at all—probably not, since there's no indication that the gunman had the specific intent to make a harmful or offensive bodily conduct. But whether attempted battery was or wasn't committed, it is certainly not the most serious crime for which the gunman may be convicted.

Answer 5

(B) is the best response,

because it would support the defense of involuntary intoxication.

First, although the defendant ingested a "drug" rather than alcohol, the defense he is raising is commonly called the defense of "intoxication." There are two varieties of intoxication defense, "voluntary intoxication" and "involuntary intoxication." The main circumstance covered by the involuntary intoxication defense is where the intoxication has "resulted from an *innocent mistake* by the defendant as to the *character of the substance taken*, as when another person has tricked him into taking the liquor or drugs." Lafave, § 4.10(g), p. 419. That's the case postulated by this choice, since the defendant's honest belief that what he was taking was aspirin would support the conclusion that he did not knowingly take a substance that would intoxicate him.

Once the defendant has established that his intoxication was involuntary, he would be entitled to an acquittal if the intoxication either prevented him from having the required mental state, or deprived him of the ability to *conform his conduct* to the requirements of the law. *See, e.g.,* Model Penal Code § 2.08(4): "Intoxication that (a) is not self-induced [i.e., that is involuntary] . . . is an affirmative defense if by reason of such intoxication the actor at the time of his conduct lacks substantial capacity either to appreciate its criminality [wrongfulness] or to *conform his conduct to the requirements of law*." Here, the other evidence suggests that even if the drug did not negate the defendant's intent to strike another, it may have caused him to lose the ability to conform his conduct to the law (i.e., his ability to resist the urge to strike). So if the defendant can show that his intoxication was involuntary, he will be entitled to the requested instruction.

(A) is not the best response,

because voluntary intoxication would not be a defense to battery.

A defendant who argues that his addiction to a drug has compelled him to consume that drug is nonetheless raising a version of the "voluntary intoxication" defense. If voluntary intoxication directly negates the required mental state, then in most states the defense will work. But battery is a crime that can be committed not only with the mental state of "intent to strike another," but also with the mental state of *recklessness* as to the risk of striking another. Lafave, § 4.10(a), p. 414. Nearly all courts hold that recklessness cannot be negated by voluntary intoxication. *Id.* Therefore, courts generally hold that voluntary intoxication is no defense to battery.

(C) is not the best response,

because even if the taunting occurred, this would not make a legal difference.

If there were no intoxication issue in the case, the fact that the victim taunted the defendant would not constitute a defense to a battery charge—a person is expected to have enough self-control not to strike another in response to taunts or insults. Nor would the voluntary intoxication defense change this result—as explained in choice A, voluntary intoxication is no defense to battery, and that's true whether or not taunting by the victim is also present. Since under this choice there is nothing to make the intoxication involuntary rather than voluntary, the intoxication defense would not work.

(D) is not the best response,

because uncontrollable rages would not constitute a defense if the intoxication was voluntary.

Voluntary intoxication is no defense to battery, and that's true no matter what the effects of the intoxicant are. Why? Because battery can be committed without the intent to strike another, if the defendant *recklessly disregarded* the risk of striking another. The defendant's voluntary taking of an intoxicant that produces rages would not be deemed to negate recklessness (and, indeed, the taking would itself probably *constitute* recklessness). Therefore, the voluntary intoxication would not negate all possible mental states for battery. Since under this choice there is nothing to make the intoxication involuntary rather than voluntary, the intoxication defense would not work.

Answer 6

(D) is the best response,

because the employee lacks the required mental state for murder.

Murder is an unlawful killing that is accompanied by implied or express "malice aforethought." Putting aside the special case of felony murder, malice is deemed to exist if (and only if) the defendant had any of the following three mental states at the time he committed the relevant act: (1) an intent to kill; (2) an intent to do serious bodily injury; or (3) a reckless indifference to the value of human life ("depraved heart").

The employee here, at the time she took the relevant act (dropping the laxatives into the coffee) intended only to "cause her boss discomfort." This is certainly not an intent to kill. Nor is it an intent to do serious bodily injury, since "discomfort" implies transient and non-serious harm. As to "reckless indifference to the value of human life," courts find that mental state to be present only if (at a minimum) the conduct involved what a reasonable person in the defendant's situation would regard as a *very high risk* of death or serious bodily injury to another. Lafave, § 7.4, p. 666. (Most courts would probably also require that the defendant be subjectively *aware* of the high degree of risk.) Since we're told that the pills "would not have been dangerous to an ordinary person," it cannot be said that a reasonable person in the employee's situation would have recognized a very high risk of death or serious injury from the pills. Since the employee did not have any of the mental states required for murder, she certainly cannot be guilty of "first-degree murder," which is defined so as to have "murder" as a pre-requisite. (Therefore, it doesn't matter whether the pills in this situation would be considered "poison.")

(A) is not the best response,

because this was not murder at all, let alone first-degree murder.

As is discussed in the treatment of choice D, the employee did not have any of the mental states that will suffice for murder. Therefore, even if the pills are considered to be "poison," she cannot be convicted of first-degree murder (which exists only where the crime is, at a minimum, *some sort* of murder).

(B) is not the best response,

because this was not murder at all, let alone first-degree murder.

Again, as is discussed in the treatment of choice D, the employee did not have any of the mental states that will suffice for murder. Therefore, even if her crime is deemed to have been "premeditated," it is not a premeditated "murder," and only "murders" can be first-degree murders.

(C) is not the best response,

because this was not a murder at all.

As is discussed in the answers to choices A, B, and D, the fact that the employee lacked any of the required mental states for murder means that neither her arguable use of poison nor her arguable premeditation could possibly convert her crime into "first-degree murder."

Answer 7

(A) is the best response,

because the girlfriend encouraged both the burglary and larceny.

If *A*, while having the mental state for crime *X, aids, abets, encourages or assists B* to commit crime *X*, and *B* in fact commits crime *X*, *A* is guilty of crime *X* as an accomplice. When the girlfriend lent the man her crowbar, knowing that it was to be used to break into the shed to steal the mower, she was at the very least "encouraging" the man to do the break-in. Under the plan that the girlfriend was encouraging, she intended that there be both a burglary (breaking and entering of a structure with intent to commit a felony [theft] therein) and a larceny (the theft of the mower). Therefore, the girlfriend had the mental state for both burglary and larceny, and committed an act (the giving of encouragement) in furtherance of each of these crimes. Then, when the man carried out both crimes in essentially the manner contemplated by both parties, the woman became substantively liable for both crimes just as the man did.

Because the woman gave active encouragement, the fact that any "aid" she gave turned out not to be necessary is irrelevant. *See* Lafave, § 6.7(a), p. 624: "At least where the attempted aid is known to the [principal], it may make no difference that the aid was unsuccessful or was not utilized, as it may qualify as an encouragement. On this basis, it is correct to conclude that an accessory who provides instrumentalities to a burglar for use in a particular burglary should not escape liability as an accomplice merely because the burglar found and used other instrumentalities at the crime scene."

(B) is not the best response,

because the girlfriend intended to assist in the larceny as well as the breaking.

For the girlfriend to be guilty of larceny on an accomplice theory, she must have had the intent required for larceny. Contrary to what this choice asserts, she had the required intent: A reasonable jury can infer that, beyond a reasonable doubt, the girlfriend intended to help the man carry out his complete plan, which as she knew included not just the breaking into the shed but also the stealing of the mower.

(C) is not the best response,

because the girlfriend encouraged the burglary, even though her assistance was not used in it.

If *A* is accused of being an accomplice to crime *X*, the *actus reus* requirement is satisfied as long as *A* "aided, abetted, *encouraged* or assisted" *B* to commit crime *X*. Since the girlfriend "encouraged" the man to carry out the breaking and entering with intent to commit a felony therein, she meets the *actus reus* requirement for burglary even if the court decides that the man's failure to use the crowbar prevents the girlfriend from having "aided" or "assisted" the burglary. So this choice incorrectly asserts that the woman is not guilty of burglary because of her lack of assistance with that crime.

This choice is also wrong for a second reason: The fact that the girlfriend received an unanticipated benefit (the mowing) from the completed crime does not make any difference to her liability for larceny. That's so because her status as an accomplice is judged as of the moment she rendered the aid or encouragement, which in this case occurred before the underlying crime. (She's guilty of larceny for the same reason she's guilty of burglary—she encouraged both crimes before they were committed.)

(D) is not the best response,

because the girlfriend encouraged both crimes.

As is discussed in choice A, the fact that the girlfriend arguably provided "no actual assistance" to either crime doesn't matter—whether she did or didn't supply "assistance" (and this point is debatable), she certainly provided "encouragement," and that's enough for her to have accomplice liability for the actions that she encouraged the principal to take.

Answer 8

(C) is the best response,

because the defendant's presence at that time and place was an element of the crime charged, as to which the prosecution bore the burden of proof beyond a reasonable doubt.

The Supreme Court has long held that the Due Process Clause protects the accused against conviction except upon "*proof beyond a reasonable doubt* of *every fact necessary to constitute the crime* with which he is charged." *In re Winship*, 397 U.S. 358 (1970). Given the prosecution's theory of the case here, the defendant's presence at the convenience store at 11 PM on March 5 was a "fact necessary to constitute the crime . . . charged." Therefore, the prosecution was required to prove that fact beyond a reasonable doubt. Since this instruction carefully declines to place any burden at all on the defendant with regard to the alibi defense, and all of the other instruction choices impose some burden of proof on the defendant regarding that defense, this choice is the only correct one.

(A) is not the best response,

because it incorrectly places the burden of producing some evidence on the defendant.

The Supreme Court has held that a defendant may constitutionally be required to produce some evidence in support of an "*affirmative defense*," such as the defense of self-defense. *See, e.g., Patterson v. New York*, 432 U.S. 197 (1977). (D may constitutionally be required to bear the burden of persuasion on the affirmative defense of extreme emotional disturbance.) But "affirmative defenses" are defenses that add some *new, mitigating element*, not defenses that merely tend to show that some element of the underlying crime was not present. Therefore, when the defendant raises a "defense" that merely attempts to rebut an element of the prosecution's case, the burden of proof on this defense may not be placed on the defendant. An "alibi defense" falls into this category. "Thus the burden of proof as to the 'defense' of alibi may not be placed upon the defendant, for alibi of necessity negates defendant's participation in the conduct defined as criminal." Lafave, § 1.8, p. 57.

(B) is not the best response,

because it incorrectly places the burden of production on the defendant.

This choice is wrong for the same reason that choice A is wrong: An alibi defense negates an element of the crime, rather than supplying some new fact of justification or mitigation. Therefore, the prosecution's burden of proving each element of the crime beyond a reasonable doubt prevents placing on the defendant even the burden of producing some evidence in support of his alibi.

(D) is not the correct response,

because it incorrectly imposes the burden of creating a reasonable doubt on the defendant.

This choice is wrong for the same reason that choices A and B are wrong: An alibi defense negates an element of the crime, rather than supplying some new fact of justification or mitigation; therefore, the defendant can never be required to bear the burden of proving an alibi defense. This choice suggests that it is only where "the *defendant's evidence has caused you* to have a reasonable doubt . . . " that a not-guilty verdict is required. In reality, the prosecution's *own failure to show*, beyond a reasonable doubt, that the defendant was the robber, would also require an acquittal. So by implying that the defendant had the burden to come up with evidence creating a reasonable doubt, this instruction unconstitutionally diminishes the prosecution's burden of proof.

Answer 9

(D) is the best response,

because the jury could properly find that the defendant recklessly disregarded the risk that the victim was over 65.

The issue is whether the defendant was "reckless" with respect to the risk that the victim was over 65. The statute says that she was reckless if and only if she "consciously disregard[ed] a substantial and unjustified risk" that the victim was over 65. By this formulation, the terms "substantial" and "unjustified" are to be measured objectively: Would a reasonable observer believe that the risk of the victim's being over 65 was substantial and unjustified? A reasonable jury could answer yes on both of these points: (1) a significant portion of the population is over 65, so the risk that any given person would be over 65 could certainly be found to be "substantial" (and a "substantial" risk is not one that is necessarily greater than 50-50, just one that is of non-trivial probability); (2) in view of the utter lack of social utility in the defendant's behavior, the jury could properly conclude that it was "unjustified" for the defendant to run the risk that the victim would be over 65.

But the analysis isn't finished yet: It must also be the case that a reasonable jury could conclude that the defendant "*consciously disregarded*" the risk that the victim was over 65. Here, we know various things about the defendant's mental state with regard to the victim's age, from her testimony and other circumstances: (1) the crime took place outside a senior citizen center; (2) the defendant couldn't really see the victim (and knew she couldn't see him) because of the darkness; (3) the defendant didn't have any opinion or knowledge about the victim's age; and (4) even if the defendant *had* known that the victim was elderly, she still would have robbed him, since she intended to rob "whomever she encountered." Taken together, this package of circumstances and knowledge would justify a reasonable jury in concluding that, beyond a reasonable doubt, the defendant "consciously disregarded" (rather than merely "was unaware of") the risk that the victim was over 65.

(A) is not the best response,

because it incorrectly incorporates the element of knowledge into the standard.

What matters is whether the defendant was "reckless" as to the risk of the victim's being over 65. This choice asserts that the requisite mental state was not present because the defendant neither knew nor "reasonably could have known" the victim's age. But recklessness is defined in the statute as "conscious disregard [of] a substantial and unjustified *risk*" of the element in question. So a person can be reckless as to an element even if the person neither knows nor could reasonably have known that the element was present. Since this choice incorrectly requires at least a possibility that the defendant "knew" the victim's age, it cannot be the best choice.

(B) is not the best response,

because it is false as a factual matter.

In finding the elements of a crime, the jury is entitled to make reasonable inferences. Therefore, in deciding whether there was a "substantial risk" that the victim was over 65, the jury was entitled to make reasonable inferences from the totality of the circumstances as known to the defendant. And that's true even if (as here), there was no direct evidence in the case about just how great the possibility was that this particular victim was over 65. Where a robbery takes place immediately outside of a senior citizens' center, and in the dark, it is reasonable for the jury to infer that there is a "substantial risk" that the victim may be over 65. (A risk can be "substantial" even though it has less than a 50/50 chance of eventuating; all that's required is that the risk be more than remote.)

(C) is not the best result,

because, although it reaches the right result, it does so without incorporating the elements that go into a finding of recklessness.

The defendant can be convicted only if the jury finds, beyond a reasonable doubt, that the defendant behaved "recklessly" with regard to the risk that the victim was over 65. Such a finding of recklessness in turn requires that the jury find that the defendant "consciously disregarded a substantial and unjustified risk" that the victim was over 65. This choice relies on two facts, which even when taken together do not establish the required recklessness as to age. First, the fact that the victim was in fact over 65 only very weakly supports the inference that the defendant "consciously disregarded" the risk that the victim was over 65. For instance, given the fact that the episode occurred in the dark, it may never have occurred to the defendant that the victim was over 65. Second, the fact that the statute's purpose was to protect the elderly doesn't have any bearing on whether the defendant had the required conscious disregard of the victim's age. (It's only the defendant's testimony that she knew that she didn't know the victim's age, didn't care about that age, and would have robbed him regardless of his age, that justifies the conclusion that she "consciously disregarded" the age issue; and none of these aspects of the testimony is referred to in this choice.)

Answer 10

(A) is the best response,

because it correctly applies the mental-state requirements for accomplice liability.

A conviction based on accomplice liability requires not only a showing that the accomplice aided, encouraged, or assisted the principal to commit the underlying crime, but also a showing that the accomplice had a *culpable mental state* sufficient for that underlying crime. The crime of larceny (theft) requires an intent to permanently deprive another of the latter's property. So unless the passenger is shown to have *intended* to aid, encourage or assist the driver in the taking of the station owner's property, the passenger cannot be convicted as an accomplice. And that intent must have existed before or simultaneously with the actual taking. Since the passenger had no prior knowledge that the driver intended to take the cash, and no intent to assist in or encourage the taking, the passenger did not have the required mental state for larceny.

(B) is not the best response,

because prosecution of the principal is not a prerequisite for conviction of the accomplice.

To gain a conviction of an accomplice, the prosecution must prove that the principal committed the underlying crime. But under virtually all modern approaches, the fact that the principal has not been prosecuted does not bar a successful prosecution of the accomplice, assuming, of course, that in the accomplice's trial the prosecution proves that the principal committed the crime. (Even under the traditional common-law approach, proof that the passenger was present at the scene of the crime, coupled with proof that he aided or encouraged the crime, would likely have sufficed for accomplice liability despite the lack of prosecution of the principal.)

(C) is not the best response,

because a person's failure to try to stop a crime at which he is present is not enough for accomplice liability.

A conviction based on accomplice liability requires the prosecution to prove that the accomplice had a *culpable mental state* sufficient for the underlying crime. Since larceny requires an intent to permanently take another's property, the passenger could be convicted of being an accomplice to larceny only if the prosecution proved that he intended to help bring about such a larcenous taking. Even if the passenger could readily have stopped the larceny from being completed (not at all clear), his failure to make any attempt to stop it does not establish that he intended to bring about the larceny.

(D) is not the best result,

because it cites a fact that does not establish the required intent.

This choice is incorrect for essentially the same reason that choice C is incorrect: A conviction based on accomplice liability requires the prosecution to prove that the accomplice had a culpable mental state sufficient for the underlying crime, in this case, an intent to help bring about a larcenous taking. The passenger's payment of the cost of the fuel, even while the passenger knew that the driver had taken the money, does not establish that the passenger intended to assist the driver in taking and keeping the money.

Answer 11

(B) is the best response,

because it is plausible under these facts, and negates one of the elements of burglary.

Under the statute, burglary requires breaking and entering any building or structure with the intent to commit a felony or to steal therein. However, a structure that is open to the public *cannot* be "broken and entered," at least as to areas where, and times when, the public is welcome. Since the liquor store was open to the public, and the defendant entered it during its business hours, he could not satisfy the "breaking and entering" element of burglary. Since B cites a fact that will exonerate the defendant, and it fits these facts, it's the best response.

(A) is not the best response,

because it misstates the facts.

The facts state that the defendant intended to hold up the liquor store. The statute requires that the actor intend to commit a felony or to steal something from within a building or structure. Thus, the defendant had the requisite intent, and, since A states otherwise, it's not the best response.

(C) is not the best response,

because the fact it cites occurred too late to exonerate the defendant.

The act of burglary is complete when the breaking and entry takes place—the wrongdoer need not actually commit the felony therein, under the statute given. Even if abandonment *were* a possible defense once a defendant entered the building, it would not exonerate him here, because the facts suggest that he does not satisfy the elements of the abandonment defense. In order to successfully claim abandonment, the abandonment must be completely voluntary, and not made due to problems in completing the crime or the risk of getting caught; and it must represent a full renunciation of the criminal purpose. Here, the facts tell you only that a defendant became "frightened." This does not suggest necessarily that his abandonment was completely voluntary. (A voluntary abandonment could be, for instance, a defendant's suddenly feeling sorry for the shopkeeper, and deciding against stealing from him.) Since C identifies a fact that will not exonerate the defendant, it's not his best argument, and as a result C is not the best response.

(D) is not the best response,

because the defendant's lack of success would not exonerate him.

The statute requires only that the perpetrator break and enter a building or structure with the intent to commit a felony or to steal therein. Once inside, the crime is complete, *regardless* of whether the person successfully carries out his intent. Since D cites a fact that will not exonerate the defendant, it's not his best argument, making D not the best response.

Answer 12

(C) is the best response,

because it arrives at the correct response, and correctly analyzes the central reason why the defendant will be acquitted.

A conspiracy requires an agreement between at least two people, the intent to enter into such an agreement, and the intent to achieve the agreement's unlawful objective. Here, the defendant didn't have the intent to enter into an agreement to steal food stamps, or the intent to steal food stamps; he only had the intent to buy stolen food stamps. As a result, he was not part of a conspiracy to actually steal the food stamps. Had he actually helped to plan or participated in or assisted the theft, these acts would be evidence of his agreement to take part in the conspiracy; but he didn't. Since C correctly identifies that the defendant won't be guilty, and the central reason why he'll be exonerated, it's the best response.

(A) is not the best response,

because although it states a correct rule of law, it does not apply to these facts, and arrives at an incorrect result.

Choice A states as a given that the defendant has entered the conspiracy. This overlooks the central issue under these facts: whether or not the defendant actually entered the conspiracy. A conspiracy requires an agreement, an intent to enter into such an agreement, and the intent to achieve the agreement's objectives. Here, the defendant did not conspire to actually steal the food stamps, because he didn't intend to steal the food stamps and didn't agree to enter into a plan to effect the stealing of the food stamps. As a result, he can't be liable for conspiracy to steal the food stamps, and thus A cannot be the best response.

(B) is not the best response,

because it mischaracterizes the facts, and arrives at an incorrect result.

The defendant did not knowingly and willingly aid and abet the *theft;* he had no agreement regarding the theft, no intent to enter into such an agreement, and no intent to steal the food stamps. He merely agreed to buy stolen goods. As a result, his involvement is too late for him to be considered a conspirator with respect to stealing the food stamps, since he only agreed to buy them once they actually were stolen.

Since B misstates the facts, and cites an argument which would not, in fact, result in the defendant being convicted, it cannot be the best response.

(D) is not the best response,

because it misstates the law.

A conspiracy requires that there be an agreement between at least two people, but it doesn't require that they all be charged with conspiracy. Beyond the agreement requirement, conspiracy requires that the defendant had intended to enter such an agreement, and had the intent to achieve the agreement's unlawful objective (at common law, a conspiracy could alternatively involve a lawful ultimate act, to be done unlawfully). If you chose this response, you may have mistaken these facts for a situation where there are two parties to a conspiracy who are both charged with conspiracy, and one is acquitted.

The rule under those circumstances is that the other could not be convicted, because it takes at least two guilty parties to have a conspiracy (likewise, with a conspiracy of three persons, all of whom are charged with conspiracy, if two are acquitted, the third would have to be also). However, the facts here state that *only the defendant has been charged*. Thus, this rule would not apply. Since D misstates the law, it's not the best response.

Answer 13

(A) is the best response,

because the defendant must go beyond mere preparation in order to be convicted for attempted possession.

The common law of attempt required that the defendant commit some act (beyond mere "preparation") toward bringing about the intended crime. Lafave, § 10.4, pp. 442-49. Here, the drug dealer took no act, much less any act that would qualify at common law, toward obtaining the cocaine. Indeed, the drug dealer likely would not be guilty of attempt even under the Model Penal Code's broadened standards because there was no "substantial step" toward commission of the crime. *See* MPC § 5.01(1)(c). Thus, under these facts, solely stating that you need more time and agreeing to meet again will not qualify as acts bringing about the intended crime.

(B) is not the best response,

because the legality or illegality of a defendant's arrest has nothing to do with whether the defendant was guilty of an attempt.

Thus, this answer reaches the right result for the wrong reason. Instead, the defendant will not be convicted because he must go beyond mere preparation in order to be convicted for attempted possession. The common law of attempt required that the defendant commit some act (beyond mere "preparation") toward bringing about the intended crime. Lafave, § 10.4, pp. 442-49. Here, the drug dealer took no act, much less any act that would qualify at common law, toward obtaining the cocaine. Indeed, the drug dealer likely would not be guilty of attempt even under the Model Penal Code's broadened standards because there was no "substantial step" toward commission of the crime. *See* MPC § 5.01(1)(c). Thus, under these facts, solely stating that you need more time and agreeing to meet again will not qualify as acts bringing about the intended crime.

(C) is not the best response,

because an agreement to commit a crime is neither necessary nor sufficient to constitute attempt.

The call of this question does not concern conspiracy, so the existence of an agreement is not relevant. Instead, the defendant will not be convicted because he must go beyond mere preparation in order to be convicted for attempted possession. The common law of attempt required that the defendant commit some act (beyond mere "preparation") toward bringing about the intended crime. LaFave, § 10.4, pp. 442-49. Here, the drug dealer took no act, much less any act that would qualify at common law, toward obtaining the cocaine. Indeed, the drug dealer likely would not be guilty of attempt even under the Model Penal Code's broadened standards because there was no "substantial step" toward commission of the crime. *See* MPC § 5.01(1)(c). Thus, under these facts, solely stating that you need more time and agreeing to meet again will not qualify as acts bringing about the intended crime.

(D) is not the best response,

because, even if this statement is true, attempt under common law required more than an unequivocal expression of criminal intent.

In addition, the defendant must also have committed some act toward bringing about the intended crime. Wayne R. LaFave, Principles of Criminal Law § 10.4, at 442-49 (2d ed. 2003). Here, the drug dealer took no act, much less any act that would qualify at common law, toward obtaining the cocaine. Indeed, the drug dealer likely would not be guilty of attempt even under the Model Penal Code's broadened standards because there was no "substantial step" toward commission of the crime. *See* MPC § 5.01(1)(c). Thus, under these facts, solely stating that you need more time and agreeing to meet again will not qualify as acts bringing about the intended crime.

Answer 14

(D) is the best response,

because it addresses the fact that is most likely to exonerate the friend from culpability for robbery: No robbery took place.

A robbery is a larceny from either a person or a person's presence, by either force or fear. Under the facts here, the thief did not use force, and the teller was clearly not put in fear. As a result, although there may be another crime, there's no robbery. If there's no robbery, nobody, including the friend, could be liable for robbery. This is a clever question in that it leads you down the garden path, focusing on the friend's actions, not the thief's. Thus, whenever accomplice liability is involved, check first to see if the actual crime took place. If it didn't, the accomplice can't possibly be liable. (Note that if the robbery had taken place, the friend would be liable as an accomplice, since he procured, counseled, or commanded the commission of a felony.) Since choice D states the fact that will exonerate the friend, it's the best response.

(A) is not the best response,

because the fact it states would not exonerate the friend, and thus it would not make a good defense.

The friend *could,* in theory, be convicted as an accomplice to robbery *even though* the thief was the only one who entered the bank. Robbery is a crime requiring larceny from a person or a person's presence, by either force or fear.

An accomplice is one who procures, counsels or commands the commission of a felony. (Modern courts do not recognize a difference between accessories before the fact and principals in the second degree, but instead call them both accomplices. At common law, the difference between the two is that a principal is actually or constructively present at the commission of the criminal act, and the accessory is not. Here, it's likely the friend would be considered a principal in the second degree, since he was at the bank, albeit not inside it.) Thus, it isn't necessary that the accomplice actually participate in the criminal act itself. Since choice A would condition the friend's culpability on whether or not he entered the bank, it can't be the best response.

(B) is not the best response,

because the fact it states would not exonerate the friend, and thus it would not make a good defense.

Choice B implies that the friend would have a valid defense due to withdrawal. In fact, the friend withdrew too late for withdrawal to serve as a defense, and, in any case, on these facts it is not clear that the friend's withdrawal reflects a renunciation of the criminal purpose, which a valid withdrawal requires—these facts only indicate that the friend "panicked." This suggests that he became nervous about the odds of success, which is not a valid withdrawal. As to timing, an accessory cannot withdraw once the chain of events has become "unstoppable." Here, the friend planned the crime with the thief and drove the thief to the bank. If the crime had taken place, the friend would be liable, since he did *everything* before its commission that he intended to do. Since B addresses an argument that will not exonerate the friend, it's not his best defense, and thus not the best response.

(C) is not the best response,

because the fact it states would not exonerate the friend, and thus would not make a good defense.

As an accomplice to a robbery, one must intend that the robbery be committed, and aid in its commission, but he needn't know the details of how the robbery is actually carried out. Here, the friend planned the robbery with the thief, and actually drove him to the bank. He intended that the robbery take place, and only chickened out while he was at the scene. Since the friend had the requisite intent, and helped in executing the ostensible robbery, it doesn't matter that he didn't know exactly what the thief said to the teller. As a result, C is not the best response.

Answer 15

(C) is the best response,

because it correctly identifies that the defendant will not be guilty, and it cites the central reason why.

The key here is that there's no relation between the licensing violation and the death. Apart from that, these facts indicate that *the defendant did nothing wrong*—these facts indicate that it was the child's fault that he got run over, since the facts state that *the child was killed before the defendant could prevent it.* Since the defendant was not even negligent, he couldn't be liable.

Misdemeanor manslaughter is a killing that occurs as a result of or during a *malum in se* misdemeanor, or a felony that is not sufficient for felony murder. Here, the defendant's misdemeanor—failing to renew his driver's license—neither resulted in the child's death, nor is the type of inherently bad misdemeanor appropriate for misdemeanor manslaughter. The other type of manslaughter—criminal negligence manslaughter—would require that the defendant engaged in a criminally negligent course of behavior, which resulted in the child's death. Here again, the causal connection is lacking. The simple fact is that the defendant's failure to renew his license had *no bearing* on the death of the child; in fact, under these facts, it's fairly clear that the child's own negligence resulted in his death. The defendant did not in fact behave negligently under these facts.

Since C correctly identifies that there's no causal connection between the defendant's negligence in failing to renew his license and the child's death, it's the best response.

(A) is not the best response,

because there's no causation between the defendant's misdemeanor and the death, and, beyond that, the misdemeanor involved is not the type that can be the subject of misdemeanor-manslaughter.

Misdemeanor manslaughter is a killing that occurs as a result of or during a *malum in se* misdemeanor, or a felony that is not sufficient for felony murder. Here, the defendant's misdemeanor—failing to renew his driver's license—neither resulted in the child's death, nor is the type of inherently bad misdemeanor appropriate for misdemeanor manslaughter. As a result, A is not the best response.

(B) is not the best response,

because it ignores causation, and as a result arrives at the wrong result.

It may be true that the purpose of the licensing requirement is to protect life, and that driving without a license is negligent—but this does not change the fact that there would have to be a causal connection between the defendant's negligence and the child's death in order to find him guilty of manslaughter.

Under these facts, it's fairly clear that the child's death was the fault of the child, not the defendant (as indicated by the language: "*killed before the defendant could prevent it*"). Thus, it's irrelevant that the defendant may have been negligent in failing to get his license reviewed. Look at it this way: Even if the defendant's license was valid, it would not have had a bearing on his liability for manslaughter in running over the child. Since B ignores causation, it's not the best response.

(D) is not the best response,

because it misstates the law: the defendant *could* be guilty without criminal intent.

Under these facts, it so happens he's not guilty, but it's not because he lacked criminal intent: It's because the element of causation is missing. The defendant could be liable for manslaughter without intent, since, under criminal negligence type manslaughter, he's liable for manslaughter if a killing occurs through his gross or criminal negligence, either by act or omission. Thus, his act must create an unreasonable risk of harm. This does not require intent, and since choice D states as a general principle that a manslaughter conviction is not possible without intent, it's not the best response.

Answer 16

(C) is the best response,

because it correctly identifies that the jury could find the defendant guilty of either robbery or larceny, but not both.

There are two keys here: One is realizing that larceny is a *lesser-included offense* to robbery; the second is that the jury could properly decide either way on the use of force and fear (the knife and the threats).

The jury, as finder of fact, could believe or disbelieve any testimony. The key fact here involves the use of the knife and the threats: If the jury believes the victim, it would find the defendant guilty of robbery; if it doesn't, which would be reasonable since the eyewitness wasn't aware of the knife or threats, then it would find the defendant guilty of larceny. Robbery requires a larceny from a person or a person's presence, by either force or fear. The use of the knife and/or the threats in the act described in these facts would thus satisfy robbery. Larceny is the trespassory taking and carrying away of another's personal property with intent to steal. The act described in these facts is sufficient for larceny, if the knife and threats were not used. Note, however, that the jury couldn't properly find the defendant guilty of *both* robbery and larceny, since larceny is a lesser-included offense of robbery (requiring proof of some, but not all, of the elements of robbery, and no other elements).

Since C correctly identifies that the jury could find the defendant guilty of either robbery or larceny but not both, it's the best response.

(A) is not the best response,

because it is too narrow: The jury could also properly return a verdict of guilty of larceny.

The key here is whether the jury believes the defendant used the knife and/or made the threats, because this will determine whether or not it finds him guilty of robbery or larceny. Larceny requires a trespassory taking and carrying away of another's personal property with intent to steal. Robbery additionally requires that the larceny be from a person or in the presence of a person, by either force or fear. The jury, as the finder of fact, would be entitled—under these facts—to believe the victim, and find that force and fear were used, making the defendant liable for robbery, or not to believe the victim (due to the eyewitness' testimony) and find that only a larceny took place. Since A incorrectly limits the jury to robbery only, it's not the best response.

(B) is not the best response,

because it is too narrow: The jury could also properly return a verdict of guilty of robbery.

The key here is whether the jury believes the defendant used the knife and/or made the threats, because this will determine whether or not it finds him guilty of robbery or larceny. Larceny requires a trespassory taking and carrying away of another's personal property with intent to steal. Robbery additionally requires that the larceny be from a person or in the presence of a person, by either force or fear. The jury, as the finder of fact, would be entitled—under these facts—to believe the victim, and find that force and fear were used, making the defendant liable for robbery, or not to believe the victim (due to the eyewitness's testimony) and find only a larceny took place. Since B limits the jury to finding larceny only, it's not the best response.

(D) is not the best response,

because the jury *could not* properly find the defendant guilty of both robbery and larceny, since larceny is a lesser-included offense of robbery.

A lesser included offense is one which requires proof of some but not all of the elements of another offense, and no other elements. Larceny requires a trespassory taking and carrying away of another's personal property with intent to steal. Robbery requires larceny from a person or the presence of a person, by either force or fear. As a result, the defendant *could not* properly be convicted of both charges. Furthermore, the jury could properly find that the defendant did not use a knife or threats. Since robbery requires the use of either force or fear, if the jury didn't believe the victim's testimony about those two factors, it couldn't find the defendant guilty of robbery.

Since D incorrectly states that the jury could properly find the defendant guilty of both robbery and larceny, it's not the best response.

Answer 17

(B) is the best response,

because the defendant's mistaken belief that the briefcase was his own prevented him from having the required mental state for robbery.

Robbery is the: (1) taking, (2) of personal property of another, (3) from the other's person or presence, (4) by force or intimidation, (5) with the intent to permanently deprive him of it.

The intent required for robbery is the intent to use force to take "the property of another." Therefore, if the defendant mistakenly (even unreasonably) believes that the property in question is his own, the required "intent to take the property of another" is lacking. The fact that that mistake was brought about by voluntary intoxication—and the fact that the mistake may have been "unreasonable"—makes no difference.

(A) is not the best response,

because (1) the absence of threats would not prevent this from being robbery; and (2) the intoxication would not necessarily prevent this from being robbery.

Robbery is the taking of personal property of another from the latter's person or presence, "by force or intimidation." A taking can involve force without involving threats. Here, the defendant struggled with the owner, and knocked him to the floor, so the requisite force was present even though the defendant made no threats.

Also, the fact that the defendant was drunk would not necessarily prevent him from being guilty—it was only the defendant's mistaken belief that the briefcase was his that caused him to avoid guilt. (It's true that the intoxication may have been what caused the defendant to have the mistaken belief—but no matter why the mistaken belief occurred, the defendant would have avoided guilt.) To the extent that this choice relies on an absence of threats, and the existence of the intoxication, to explain the result, it's twice-wrong even though it states the correct outcome.

(C) is not the best response,

because voluntary intoxication can still prevent the required specific intent from existing.

Robbery requires an intent to take "the property of another." If a defendant fails to have the requisite intent, whatever the reason, the crime has not been committed. Here, the defendant thought the briefcase was his, so he lacked the requisite intent to take "property of another." The fact that the intoxication was "voluntary" would not make a difference, if for any reason (including intoxication) he lacked the requisite intent.

(D) is not the best response,

because mistake *can* be a defense to specific intent crimes.

If a mistake of fact prevents the defendant from having the requisite intent for a "specific intent" crime, that mistake is indeed a defense. Here, robbery requires an intent to take "the property of another." If a mistake causes a defendant to believe (whether reasonably or not) that the property is his own rather than another's, that mistake causes the defendant not to meet the intent element for the crime.

Answer 18

(D) is the best response,

because the thief's actions satisfied all the elements of larceny.

Larceny is the: (1) taking and (2) carrying away of (3) the tangible property (4) of another, (5) by trespass or without consent, (6) with the intent to permanently deprive the person of his interest in property.

The thief committed larceny: (1) She picked up the purse, a taking. (2) She moved it from its original position when she placed it under her coat and took a few steps toward the exit, a carrying away. (3) The purse is a tangible item (4) owned by another, the clothing store. (5) The thief took it without the clothing store's consent. (6) When she picked up the purse (exerted control over it) the facts state that she did so with the intent to take it without paying for it. The thief's actions therefore satisfy all the requirements of larceny.

The fact that the thief did not exit from the store with the property is irrelevant—the crime was complete once she exerted dominion and carried the item a small distance, while intending to keep it. Nor does the fact that the thief took only a couple of steps with the purse prevent the "carrying away" element from being satisfied—even the smallest movement of the item will suffice.

(A) is not the best response,

because the thief completed the crime once she exerted dominion over the purse and carried it a small distance, while intending to keep it. See the analysis of choice D, above.

(B) is not the best response,

because the thief completed the crime when her actions matched her intent.

The crime was complete once the thief exerted dominion over the purse and carried it a small distance, while intending to keep it. Nothing she did thereafter—including "withdrawing" from the "criminal enterprise"—could undo the completed crime.

(C) is not the best response,

because the crime of larceny was complete once the thief moved the item with intent to take it.

By the analysis in choice D, above, the crime was complete once the thief exerted dominion over the purse and carried it a small distance, while intending to keep it. Since choice C says that only attempted, not completed, larceny has occurred, it's wrong.

Answer 19

(A) is the best response,

because the employee acted with the intent to kill whoever started the car, and then killed that person.

This is basically a problem involving "concurrence"—the examiners are thinking (maybe hoping) you'll reason, "The requisite intent no longer existed at the time of the explosion, therefore the requirement of concurrence between act and mental state has not been satisfied."

It's true that "concurrence" is required. But in the case of a crime defined in terms of a particular result (like murder), the requisite concurrence is between *mental state and act*, *not* between *mental state and result*. In other words, at the moment a defendant takes the act that brings about the result, the defendant must be actuated by the appropriate intent; it doesn't matter whether the defendant still has that intent when the result finally occurs.

Here, the "act" was the setting of the bomb. When the employee planted the bomb, he was actuated by an intent to kill his boss. The fact that before the bomb went off (producing death as a result) he had changed his mind is irrelevant.

There's a further element to worry about: the fact that an unintended victim (the company vice president), not the intended victim (the boss) was killed. But this makes no difference either, under the familiar doctrine of transferred intent, by which, if the type of harm intended is the type that results, the fact that a different victim ended up suffering that harm is irrelevant.

Lastly, the fact that the security guard had the opportunity to avoid the harm but failed to do so is irrelevant—the employee intended to bring about a death by bomb, and his act was the but-for cause of that death by bomb, so the fact that some other actor failed in a chance to avoid the harm makes no difference. And that's true even if the failure by the other person amounted to negligence.

(B) is not the best response,

because the employee killed with premeditation and deliberation, making him guilty of first degree murder.

Under the analysis in choice A, two things prevent this choice B from being correct: (1) the employee's intent is measured as of the moment he planted the bomb (and the fact that by the time of death he no longer intended to kill anyone is irrelevant); and (2) the employee's intent to kill his boss is deemed "transferred" to the company vice-president.

(C) is not the best response,

because, under the analysis in choice A, two things prevent this choice C from being correct: (1) the employee's intent is measured as of the moment he planted the bomb (and the fact that by the time of death he no longer intended to kill anyone is irrelevant); and (2) the fact that the security officer had a good opportunity to avoid the harm does not prevent the employee's act from being the legal cause of the harm.

(D) is not the best response,

because the employee is guilty of murder, not just attempted murder.

Under the analysis in choice A, the fact that the security officer had a good opportunity to avoid the harm does not prevent the employee's act from being the legal cause of the harm. And that's true even if the security guard's failure amounted to negligence. The employee's act of planting the bomb was clearly a "but-for" cause of the death, and was so closely connected with the death that it was certainly a "legal" or "proximate" cause of that death. (The fact that the guard's negligence may have *also* been a proximate cause [and a but-for cause] won't save the employee from guilt for the death.) Since the employee caused the death by an act that was intended to cause the death, he's guilty of murder, not just attempted murder.

Answer 20

(B) is the best response,

because the right to use self-defense is not lost where the defendant makes a reasonable mistake about the need for self-defense on the present occasion.

The defense of self-defense states that an individual who is not the aggressor may use such force as reasonably appears necessary to protect himself from the imminent use of unlawful force upon himself. The defendant does not lose the defense merely because he is reasonably mistaken about some aspect of the situation, such as the legality of the force being used against him. So here, the fact that the defendant mistakenly (but not unreasonably, so far as we're aware from the facts) believes that the person who has grabbed him is not privileged to do so, does not cause the defendant to lose the right to use a reasonable level of force to resist the attack.

(A) is not the best response,

because the offense here is a "public welfare" offense, and is thus probably a strict liability crime.

"Public welfare" offenses are generally interpreted to be strict liability offenses, because they generally involve a relatively low penalty and are not regarded by the community as involving significant moral impropriety. Ordinances forbidding the sale of alcohol to minors generally fall into this public welfare-offense category. Consequently, such ordinances typically do not recognize the defense of mistake (even reasonable mistake).

(C) is not the best response,

because statutory rape is a strict liability crime.

Most statutory rape statutes impose strict liability. In particular, they reject the defense of "I didn't know she was underage," precisely because that defense is so often asserted and so hard for the prosecution to rebut.

(D) is not the best response,

because reliance on mistaken advice about how a crime is defined is not a defense to most crimes, and certainly not to the crime of bigamy.

There are crimes that are defined to require a "knowing" violation. (Income-tax evasion falls into this category, for instance.) For such a crime, the fact that D reasonably relied on counsel's advice that the proposed conduct was legal would be a defense.

But most crimes are *not* defined to make knowledge of illegality an element of the crime. Bigamy is like most crimes in this respect—a mistaken (even reasonably mistaken) belief that the law treats abandonment as being the automatic equivalent of a divorce does not furnish a defense. The colloquial expression "ignorance of the law is no excuse" is in fact a generally correct statement, and it's correct on the facts here.

Answer 21

(D) is the best response,

because the student reasonably believed he faced death and was under no duty to retreat in his home.

A person may use deadly force in self-defense if he: (1) is confronted with unlawful force; (2) reasonably believes he is threatened with imminent death or great bodily harm; and (3) uses no greater force that he reasonably believes is required to avoid the danger.

Here, the student was certainly faced with "unlawful force" (the threatened knife attack), and reasonably believed that this attack threatened him with death or great bodily harm. In addition, the level of force used was no greater than the student reasonably believed was necessary, given that the student was not trying to actually hit his friend. (If he had shot to kill, rather than just to frighten or wound, this might have been greater force than was reasonably believed necessary, which would have been a violation of requirement (3) above.)

Notice that it's important that the student did not instigate the confrontation—if the student had been the initial aggressor, in an unlawful and physical way, he would have forfeited his right to use self-defense on that occasion.

The most interesting question in this fact pattern is whether, since the student could have run out the door, he was required to *retreat* in this way rather than use deadly force. Some courts impose a general duty to retreat if the actor can safely do so, but even these courts do not require a person to retreat in or from his *home*. Therefore, in all courts the student (since he was in his home) was permitted to use a reasonable though deadly level of force rather than retreating. Thus, the student met all the requirements for self-defense, which is a complete defense to a criminal charge.

(A) is not the best response,

because the use of deadly force here was not unreasonable.

Even when a defendant is threatened with unlawful force that threatens imminent death or great bodily harm, the defendant may only use the lowest level of force that's reasonable in the circumstances. But here, nothing in the fact pattern indicates that the student used greater (or more deadly) force than seemed to him reasonably required. First, the student tried to impose a solution (that the friend would leave) that would not have involved actual use of deadly force.

Then, the student tried to use the deadly object in a nondeadly way (aiming to frighten, not wound or kill). Given that the knife threat from the friend posed the imminent risk of death to the student, and given the absence of other solutions (apart from retreating, which the student was not required to do in his home), the student's intent here was to use no more force than reasonably appeared necessary. The fact that the student unintentionally hit and killed the friend does not retroactively transform the student's conduct into the unreasonable use of force—a defendant's act is to be evaluated by the reasonableness of his conduct and beliefs, not by reference to an unexpectedly harmful outcome.

(B) is not the best response,

because the student had no duty to retreat in his home.

As described in the analysis of choice D, above, even courts imposing a general duty to retreat before the use of deadly force do not impose that duty when the defendant is in his own home. Therefore, the student had no duty to retreat even though he may have had the clear opportunity to do so.

(C) is not the best response,

because in the absence of a defense of self-defense the student's conduct might well be extreme-indifference murder despite his lack of intent to kill.

As the analysis in choice D above shows, the defense of self-defense will result in the student's acquittal. Therefore, any choice that doesn't refer to this defense cannot be the best response.

In any event, if self-defense were not available, choice C would still not be the best response. That's because, on these facts, the fact that the student didn't have an intent to kill the friend would not necessarily entitle him to an acquittal.

There are multiple states of mind that may suffice for murder, and intent-to-kill is only one. Another is "extreme indifference to the value of human life" (sometimes called a "depraved heart.") Where a defendant fires a loaded gun in the direction of a victim, intending only to frighten him, the defendant might well be found to have exhibited extreme indifference to the value of human life, in which case he would be guilty of murder if the shot proved fatal, despite the lack of an intent to kill. So choice C, in stating that the absence of an intent to kill means that the student must be acquitted, is incorrect.

Answer 22

(C) is the best response,

because whether the defendant is guilty of murder, or guilty only of manslaughter, depends upon whether he fired the third shot in the heat of passion provoked by the neighbor's attack.

Defendant would be convicted of manslaughter in this scenario if (i) he acted in response to a provocation that would be sufficient to cause a reasonable person to lose self-control, (ii) he in fact acted in a "heat of passion," (iii) the lapse of time between the provocation and the killing was not great enough that a reasonable person would have "cooled off," and (iv) he had not in fact "cooled off" by the time he killed. Here, there is a factual question as to the defendant's state of mind in the "few seconds" between the second and third shots; the answer to that factual question will determine whether he is guilty of murder or manslaughter.

(A) is not the best response,

because the defendant killed the neighbor, so he is guilty of either murder or manslaughter of the neighbor.

Whether the defendant is guilty of murder, or guilty only of manslaughter, depends upon whether he fired the third shot in the heat of passion provoked by the neighbor's attack.

(B) is not the best response,

because while it is true that the defendant can be convicted of manslaughter, he also may be convicted for murder under these facts.

The conviction depends on whether he fired the third shot in the heat of passion provoked by the neighbor's attack. Defendant would be convicted of manslaughter in this scenario if (i) he acted in response to a provocation that would be sufficient to cause a reasonable person to lose self-control, (ii) he in fact acted in a "heat of passion," (iii) the lapse of time between the provocation and the killing was not great enough that a reasonable person would have "cooled off," and (iv) he had not in fact "cooled off" by the time he killed. Here, there is a factual question as to the defendant's state of mind in the "few seconds" between the second and third shots; the answer to that factual question will determine whether he is guilty of murder or manslaughter.

(D) is not the best response,

because the defendant was not in imminent fear of the neighbor, and therefore was not acting in self-defense, when he fired the third shot.

In order to claim self-defense, the defendant must have been resisting the present or imminent use of unlawful force. Here, after being shot twice, the "neighbor fell to the floor and lay quietly moaning." Lacking imminent fear, the defendant will not succeed in a self-defense claim. The defendant will be guilty of murder or manslaughter, depending upon whether he fired the third shot in the heat of passion provoked by the neighbor's attack.

Answer 23

(C) is the best response,

because it negates an element of attempted rape.

Note the way this question is worded: The attempted rape charge can *only be sustained if . . . .* That means that, if the facts the correct choice gives are *removed,* then the defendant *could not* be convicted. Thus, the way to analyze questions like this is actually to analyze the facts in light of removing what the choice states, and seeing if the defendant could still be convicted. If the defendant *could,* then that choice is not the best response.

Attempted rape requires proof that the defendant attempted unlawful intercourse, with one other than his wife, without the victim's consent. Here, if the runaway did not resist, coupled with the facts given in the problem, consent would be a valid defense. The thing that makes this problem tricky is that the runaway is 15; however, this question focuses on the *attempted rape* charge, not the attempted *statutory* rape charge. For statutory rape, *consent is no defense.* The question here involves a charge for which consent *could be* a valid defense. Since the facts choice C presents would exonerate the defendant, it's the best response.

(A) is not the best response,

because the defendant could be convicted of both attempted rape and at least one of the other charges.

If choice A presented a lesser included offense of the other charges, or vice versa, that would preclude conviction of both or all of the charges involved. A lesser included offense is one that requires proof of some, but not all, of the elements of another offense, based on the same conduct. At least one of the other offenses—contributing to the delinquency of a minor—could involve different elements than attempted rape, even if it involved the same conduct. Since A states otherwise, it's not the best response.

(B) is not the best response,

because it does not state the only way the defendant could be convicted of attempted rape.

In order to be convicted of attempted rape, all the state must show is that the defendant attempted to have unlawful intercourse, with one other than his wife, without the victim's consent. It's possible to be convicted of attempted rape of someone under the age of consent. (However, when the female is under the age of consent, the defendant can also be charged with statutory rape. When one is charged with statutory rape, his knowledge of the female's being under age is irrelevant.) Since B does not state a condition necessary to convicting the defendant of attempted rape, it's not the best response.

(D) is not the best response,

because the defendant could be convicted of attempted rape even if evidence of his flight is admitted.

Attempted rape requires proof of attempted unlawful intercourse, with one other than the defendant's wife, without the victim's consent. An attempt to commit a crime requires that one have the intent to commit a crime, along with an overt act done in furtherance of the intent, beyond mere preparation. Abandonment is only a valid defense to attempt when it is completely voluntary, and not made due to problems in completing the crime or the risk of getting caught, and represents a full renunciation of the criminal purpose. Under these facts, it's clear that the defendant would be liable for attempt, and that his flight would not exonerate him—since he'd already done everything necessary for attempted rape, and his flight took place too late. Since choice D states an element that would not stop the defendant from being convicted of attempted rape, it's not the best response.

Answer 24

(A) is the best response,

because the crime of larceny was complete when the computer analyst picked up the watch with an intent to steal it.

Larceny is: (1) the taking and (2) carrying away of (3) the tangible property (4) of another, (5) by trespass or without consent, (6) with the intent to permanently deprive the person of his interest in property. Under these facts the computer analyst met all the requirements of the crime of larceny as soon as he picked up the watch. The only one of the above requirements that could possibly be in doubt as of that moment was whether the computer analyst satisfied the "carrying away" requirement. However, courts hold that even a small movement of the entire object will suffice. So the fact that the computer analyst "picked up" the watch was enough.

Once he picked up the watch with intent to permanently deprive his co-worker of it, the crime was complete. Nothing that the co-worker did after that—including giving title to the computer analyst—could undo the fact of the completed crime.

(B) is not the best response,

because the computer analyst completed the crime of larceny when he picked up the watch.

Criminal attempt is an act that although done with the intent of committing a crime falls short of completing the crime. Since, according to the analysis in choice A above, the crime was complete as soon as the computer analyst picked up the watch, there has been actual larceny, not just attempted larceny.

(C) is not the best response,

because the computer analyst was never in lawful possession of the watch.

Embezzlement is the: (1) fraudulent, (2) conversion, (3) of property, (4) of another, (5) by a person in lawful possession of that property. So at the moment of the fraudulent conversion, the defendant must have been already in lawful possession of the property.

That wasn't the case here—at the moment the computer analyst picked up the watch (the moment when he arguably "converted" it), he was not already in lawful possession. That's because as of that moment, the co-worker hadn't yet relinquished possession to the computer analyst—he had merely left the watch on the blanket, intending to reserve possession to himself.

(D) is not the best response,

because the computer analyst committed larceny, as described in the analysis of choice A above.

Answer 25

(D) is the best response,

because the babysitter knowingly directed the boy to steal the television set.

Larceny is: (1) the taking and (2) carrying away of (3) the tangible property (4) of another, (5) by trespass or without consent, (6) with the intent to permanently deprive the person of his interest in property.

Anyone who intentionally acts through an innocent agent is classified as a principal.

The babysitter is guilty of larceny, even though she herself did not take the television set. She knowingly created a mistake of fact in the mind of the boy, and intentionally induced him to commit acts satisfying the first five elements of the crime of larceny. Since the boy was an innocent agent who acted at the behest of the babysitter, the boy's acts will be ascribed to the babysitter as if she had done them herself. The babysitter herself satisfies the sixth requirement (intent to permanently deprive the owner). Therefore, the babysitter is guilty of larceny.

(A) is not the best response,

because, as an innocent agent of the babysitter, the boy's actions are imputed to the babysitter.

It's true that the boy did not commit any crime. But as an innocent agent, his acts are ascribed to the principal. Therefore, his own innocence is irrelevant to whether the babysitter is guilty. See the analysis in choice D above.

(B) is not the best response,

because her innocent agent acquired possession.

When a person intentionally causes an innocent agent to perform an act, the agent's act is attributed to the principal. So once the boy took and carried away possession of the set, this act is ascribed to the babysitter as if she had done it herself. Therefore, it's not accurate to say, as this choice does, that the babysitter "never acquired possession."

(C) is not the best response,

because the boy was not guilty of larceny, and the babysitter is a principal, not an accessory.

A principal is one who, with the requisite mental state, actually engages in the act or omission that causes the criminal result. An accessory is one who aids or counsels a principal in the completion of a crime. If the boy had been a principal, then the babysitter would probably have been an accessory.

In this case, however, the babysitter is not guilty as an accessory, because she was the principal. The boy acted without criminal intent after being misled by the babysitter. Therefore (as explained more fully in the analysis of choice D above), the boy was an innocent agent and the babysitter a principal in this crime.

Answer 26

(B) is the best response,

because the defendant satisfies all the elements of larceny by trick.

The question asks the choice where the defendant is *most likely* to be convicted. This means in one choice the defendant *will* be guilty, and in the other three he *won't.* So you have to determine the elements in each choice, and apply them mechanically, to arrive at the best response.

Larceny by trick is different from larceny in the way that the property is acquired; larceny by trick involves a fraudulent taking, which negates the owner's apparent consent. Every other element is the same: The carrying away of another's personal property, with intent to steal it. Under the facts here, these elements are satisfied: The defendant obtains possession by misrepresenting his intent to return the car. The wrinkle here is that, after taking the car, the defendant decides to return it after all. However, the defendant's subsequent actions are not relevant to his guilt—once he has fulfilled all the requirements of larceny by trick, his subsequent repentance cannot exonerate him. Thus, the defendant is likely to be guilty, making B the best response.

(A) is not the best response,

because one of the elements of larceny—the intent to steal—is not satisfied, so the defendant cannot be convicted.

Larceny requires the trespassory taking and carrying away of personal property of another with the intent to steal it. Here, the defendant does not intend to steal the car—instead, he intends to borrow it and return it after driving it only six miles in total. Although every other element of larceny is satisfied, with the intent to steal element missing, the defendant will be acquitted. Since the question asks which choice states facts under which the defendant will most likely be convicted, A cannot be the best response.

(C) is not the best response,

because the defendant is not likely to be convicted of false pretenses.

False pretenses requires a misrepresentation of a material fact, which prompts the victim to pass title to his property to the defendant, who knows the misrepresentation is false and intends to defraud the victim. There is one element missing here: The victim did not pass *title* to the car, only possession for the evening. Say that the facts were different, and the defendant got the car's owner to give him the car by falsely convincing the car's owner that transferring title will result in a tax benefit to the car's owner. That *would* be false pretenses, because there *title* was involved, not just *possession*.

Under the facts in choice C, however, the defendant's lie about having a driver's license prompts the car's owner to surrender possession of the car for an evening, not the title. As a result, the defendant can't be convicted of false pretenses, meaning C is not the best response.

(D) is not the best response,

because the act of interference with the rights of the owner was not serious enough to be considered a conversion.

Embezzlement occurs when someone misappropriates property of which he has lawful possession. It requires conversion of the property. Conversion is a *serious* act of interference with the rights of the owner.

Say the facts in the problem were different, so that the defendant used the car as collateral for a bank loan and returned it. This would be an interference significant enough to be grounds for embezzlement. However, under the facts here, the defendant only kept the car a few hours longer than the car's owner intended him to have it.

This is not serious enough to constitute conversion, and thus the defendant cannot be guilty of embezzlement. Since the question here asks for the choice under which the defendant is most likely to be convicted, D cannot be the best response.

Answer 27

(D) is the best response,

because it cites the central reason the witness will be acquitted, and arrives at the correct result: not guilty.

This requires a mechanical application of the statute in the question. The statute requires that one *knowingly* make a false statement while under oath. Mistake is a valid defense where it negates an element of the crime.

That's the case here. The lawyer's erroneous advice itself is not a defense, but rather it contributed to the witness's lack of knowledge that he was lying on the witness stand, which is a defense. Since D correctly identifies that the witness will not be guilty because he lacked the requisite mental state, it's the best response.

(A) is not the best response,

because "mistake of law" is not applicable to these facts, and, in any case, the witness is not guilty.

The defendant makes a mistake of law when he either believes his acts are not proscribed, or he is simply unaware of the law proscribing his behavior. A mistake of law does *not* exonerate a defendant. Mistake of law arises only when the defendant's behavior fits the crime. Here, the witness will be exonerated because his act simply does not meet the statutory definition of perjury—he didn't *knowingly* make a false statement under oath, because he didn't know he'd been convicted of a crime. Since A mistakenly applies "mistake of law" to these facts, and erroneously finds the witness guilty, it's not the best response.

(B) is not the best response,

because although it states a correct rule of law, it does not apply to these facts and it arrives at the wrong conclusion.

It is true that reliance on erroneous advice from a lawyer is no defense. However, that's not applicable to these facts, because what exonerates the witness is the fact that he does not satisfy all the elements of the crime of perjury: He didn't *knowingly* make a false statement under oath. The issue of whether he has a valid defense due to mistake would only come into play if he *satisfied* all the elements of perjury, and needed a way out. The key is that the erroneous legal advice here is what *created* the witness's mistaken belief—but it's not the legal advice that's central to the witness's innocence but rather the fact that he lacks the mental element the crime requires. Since B states a rule that does not apply to these facts and arrives at the wrong conclusion, it's not the best response.

(C) is not the best defense,

because reasonable reliance on the erroneous advice will not exonerate the witness.

The actual rule is that reliance on erroneous advice of a lawyer is no defense, no matter how reasonable the reliance is. The key to the witness's innocence is that he lacked the requisite mental state—knowledge. Thus, the jury will find him not guilty if he lacked the requisite mental state, *regardless* of how that mental state came about. For instance, his reliance could have been *unreasonable,* and the fact would still remain that he did not knowingly make a false statement under oath. Since C focuses on an element that will not exonerate the witness and mistakenly says that it *will*, it's not the best response.

Answer 28

(B) is the best response,

because it represents the facts under which the defendant is most likely to be guilty of murder.

The key here is realizing that common-law murder does not require *intent.* Murder is an unlawful killing with malice aforethought. Malice is satisfied by either intent to kill or do serious bodily injury, depraved heart, or felony murder. The most applicable category here is felony murder. Felony murder is a killing committed during the course of a "dangerous" felony (or an attempt), even though there is *no intent* to kill or cause serious bodily harm. That's exactly the case here. Armed robbery is a classic dangerous felony. The facts explicitly state that the defendant killed a customer "while committing a robbery." Even though the killing was accidental, felony murder does not require intent, so this fact will not exonerate the defendant. Since the defendant satisfies the elements of felony murder, B is the best response.

(A) is not the best response,

because the defendant would most likely be liable for manslaughter, not murder.

While the defendant is unlikely to be exonerated from *any* liability, he'd likely be liable only for manslaughter, not murder, under the imperfect self-defense doctrine. Under that doctrine, the defendant will be liable for manslaughter instead of murder, when he intentionally kills another, if either: (1) the defendant was the aggressor in a fight (and therefore not entitled to a self defense claim), or (2) the defendant honestly but unreasonably believed deadly force was necessary. While the facts in choice A don't stipulate who started the fight or if the belief was reasonable, the facts do indicate that at most the defendant will likely be liable only for manslaughter. Since the question is looking for the choice most likely representing common-law murder, choice A is not the best response.

(C) is not the best response,

because the defendant would be unlikely to be liable for common-law murder.

Common-law murder is an unlawful killing with malice aforethought. While "malice" can be satisfied by depraved heart murder, "depraved heart" occurs when the defendant engages in extremely negligent conduct, which a reasonable man would realize creates a very high degree of risk to human life, and which results in death. While the defendant's action in choice C was negligent, it is unlikely to be considered serious enough to satisfy depraved heart murder. After all, he was in the woods, hunting deer. Were there other facts—for instance, the woods were crawling with hunters—the result might be different. As the facts are, the defendant's negligence simply would not rise to the level of depraved heart murder, but would likely be criminal negligence manslaughter. Also, the defendant did not intend to kill the other hunter and was not committing a felony, so his conduct does not satisfy other types of malice, and he cannot be guilty of common law murder. As a result, C is not the best response.

(D) is not the best response,

because the defendant's act is not serious enough to be characterized as common law murder.

Murder is an unlawful killing with malice aforethought. Malice can be intent to kill or do serious bodily injury, depraved heart, or felony murder. There are two facts of particular note here: first, the city ordinance; and second, the culpability of the defendant regardless of the ordinance. The ordinance gives rise to the issue of felony murder. However, violation of a city ordinance is typically a misdemeanor, not a felony, so felony murder could not apply. Analyzing the defendant's act without the ordinance requires focusing on depraved heart murder, since there's clearly no intent here. "Depraved heart" exists when the defendant engages in extremely negligent conduct, which a reasonable man would realize creates a very high degree of risk to human life and results in death. Here, the defendant was aiming at the street, and the bullet bounced up and killed a pedestrian. While this was undoubtedly negligent, without more facts it would be difficult to say that it was *extremely* negligent. For instance, if the pedestrian were part of a crowd, it *would* be; if he were alone, and the angle of the ricochet were unusual, it would be closer to a "freak" accident. As it stands, there are insufficient facts to conclude that the defendant would likely be guilty of murder. Rather, his conduct would most likely satisfy requirements for criminal-negligence manslaughter or misdemeanor manslaughter. Since he won't likely be guilty of murder, D isn't the best response.

Answer 29

(A) is the best response,

because the defendant can be found guilty of all three crimes. Let's take the crimes one at a time.

First, let's look at burglary. Burglary is: (1) the breaking, (2) and entering, (3) of the dwelling, (4) of another, (5) at night time, (6) with the intent to commit a felony within.

The defendant's actions satisfy all the requirements for burglary. Requirements (1) and (6) are the only ones that are even worth discussing here. As to (1) (breaking), courts recognize "constructive breaking"—if a defendant uses fraud or threat of force to induce the occupants to let him in, that counts as breaking. That's what happened here.

As to (6) (intent to commit a felony within), where a defendant commits a felony once inside the premises, courts will, in the absence of other evidence, presume that the defendant had the intent to commit that felony at the time of entry. So here, the defendant would readily be found to have intended, at the time he entered, to commit the felony of robbery once he was inside. Thus the requisite intent-to-commit-a-felony-within is satisfied.

Next, let's examine robbery. Robbery is: (1) a taking, (2) of the personal property of another, (3) from the other's person or presence, (4) by force or intimidation, (5) with the intent to permanently deprive. Here, the only interesting question is whether taking the property from the safe (rather than directly from the person) of the victim meets requirement (3). But the taking will suffice if it's from the "person or presence" of the owner, and the safe would be found to have been within the husband and wife's presence at the time the defendant took the necklace.

Finally, let's look at murder. There are of course multiple types of (ways of committing) murder. Here, the relevant type of murder is felony murder. Felony murder is a killing, even an accidental one, committed during the commission of a dangerous felony.

The defendant's actions satisfy the requirements of felony murder. The defendant was committing robbery, and robbery is one of the "dangerous" felonies recognized at common law as a predicate crime for felony murder. The interesting question is whether the fact that the defendant was arrested before the husband had his heart attack prevents the husband's death from being "during the commission of" the robbery. Notice that the husband's death was very closely, causally related to the robbery—the husband had his heart attack because he was trying to free himself from his bonds and gag, and he was bound and gagged because, and solely because, the defendant wanted to commit, and escape from, the robbery. Where there is a close causal relationship between the underlying felony (or the attempt to escape from it) and the death, the requirement of a death "during the commission of" the felony is generally deemed satisfied, even if the death doesn't come until after the felony-and-escape period is in some sense over.

(B), (C), and (D) are not the best responses,

because each fails to cover at least one of the three crimes that in fact was committed, as described in choice A.

Answer 30

(A) is the best response,

because the facts of the case make proximate cause the best defense.

Manslaughter is death caused by criminal negligence. Proximate cause is that which in a natural and continuous sequence, unbroken by any intervening cause, produces injury and without which the injury would not have occurred. The student can plausibly try to show at trial that the teacher was depressed about other things as well, not just the lack of work, so that the firing was not sufficiently closely causally related to the death to meet the requirement of proximate cause. And the student can argue that a death by suicide is not a "natural and probable consequence" of being fired or falsely accused, which is the standard for proximate cause in many jurisdictions.

Finally, the relatively long time period—about a year—between false accusation and death tends to weaken the causal connection. Indeed, notice that the facts say that the suicide occurred "a year later." If there was slightly *more* than a year between false accusation and death, then the common-law "year and a day" rule—by which a death happening more than a year and a day after the *actus reus* would be conclusively deemed not to be the proximate result of the act—might apply. (Some jurisdictions apply this rule to manslaughter cases, not just murders.)

There is no guarantee that this proximate-cause defense will work—indeed, perhaps it's not even "more likely than not" to work. But of the four choices, it's the only one that has a plausible chance. (For why each of the others won't work, read the discussions of those choices below.)

(B) is not the best response,

because the student's actual intent would not be an issue in an involuntary manslaughter case.

The prosecution here would have to be for involuntary manslaughter, not voluntary manslaughter. Involuntary manslaughter is generally defined as death caused by gross criminal negligence (or, sometimes, "recklessness").

The fact that the student did not intend to cause the teacher's death could not possibly be a defense here, because the student's subjective intent would not be the issue where the question is whether she acted with gross negligence or recklessness about the risk of death. Instead, the issue is whether a reasonable person in the student's position would have known that a false accusation like the one she made posed a great risk of the teacher's eventual suicide. (Indeed, intent-to-cause-death is almost *never* present in successful prosecutions for involuntary manslaughter, because if it were present, the case would be a murder prosecution instead.)

(C) is not the best response,

because malice is relevant to the wrong state of mind.

As described in choice B above, the relevant mental state in this involuntary manslaughter prosecution is gross negligence or recklessness. The fact that the student lacked "malice" is not relevant at all. (It's relevant to some types of murder, as in the phrase "with malice aforethought," used to describe the mental state for garden-variety intent-to-kill murder.)

(D) is not the best response,

because her emotional distress would be relevant to sentencing, but not to whether she is guilty of the substantive crime.

"Extreme emotional distress" is not generally a substantive defense to crime. Instead, it can be a mitigating factor at sentencing. Even if extreme distress *were* in theory a defense, it would not apply here, where making a false sexual-misconduct accusation would hardly be an excusable response to being upset about a failing grade.

Answer 31

(D) is the best response,

because the friend did not have the intent to sell cocaine, while the inmate did.

The prosecution of the inmate poses the classic question of whether "factual impossibility" can be a defense. Factual impossibility is not a defense. That is, impossibility is no defense to an attempt prosecution in those cases where, had the facts been as the defendant believed them to be, the defendant would have had the mental state required for the substantive crime. Here, had the facts been as the inmate believed (that the vials contained cocaine), the inmate would have had the mental state required for sale of cocaine.

Therefore, she had the mental state for attempt. And, since she carried out the physical act of selling the substance, she meets the *actus reus* requirement for attempted drug sale as well.

On the other hand, the friend does not have the mental state required for attempted sale of cocaine. The *mens rea* for an attempt to commit substantive crime X is the desire to commit acts which, if they were committed, would constitute the commission of crime X. Therefore, the *mens rea* for an attempt to sell drugs is the intent to sell drugs. Since the friend didn't intend to sell drugs, he can't be liable for attempted sale of drugs.

(A), (B), and (C) are not the best responses,

because each is inconsistent with the analysis in D above.

Answer 32

(D) is the best response,

because the woman acted with a reckless indifference and because the man was her accomplice.

Let's first discuss the woman's guilt. The mental state for murder, in a jurisdiction that has abolished the felony murder rule, is any of the following: (1) intent to kill; (2) intent to inflict great bodily harm; or a (3) reckless indifference to an unjustifiably high risk to human life.

Here, a court would probably (though not certainly) hold that a person who (1) brings automatic weapons with her to a bank robbery; and then (2) fires those weapons into the ceiling, with lots of people around, meets the standard for "reckless indifference to an unjustifiably high risk to life." Bear in mind that (1) the woman's conduct is of as little redeeming social utility as it can be (so that a lower degree of risk to others should suffice for "reckless indifference" than if the woman were pursuing some socially-worthwhile goal, e.g., speeding to the hospital with her deathly ill child); and (2) any reasonable person ought to know of the large danger of ricocheting bullets, especially where the bullets are fired in a bank containing stone columns and lots of people. Since the woman has proximately caused a death, while satisfying one of the mental-state requirements for common-law murder, she's guilty of murder.

Now, on to the man: A person who intentionally aids, abets or encourages another to commit substantive crime X is himself guilty of substantive crime X as an accomplice. The accomplice needs, however, to have the (or a) mental state required for crime X. So here, the question is whether the man can be guilty of murder as an accomplice to the woman's commission of murder.

If a court is willing to find that the woman had the "reckless indifference" mental state that will suffice for murder, the court will probably also find that the man had that mental state. (This is not certain—the man might have strongly believed that neither he nor the woman would fire the weapons, in which case it wouldn't be logically inconsistent for the court to conclude that the woman, by not only carrying but firing her automatic weapon, met the reckless-indifference standard, but that the man didn't. *Probably*, however, the court would conclude that one who carries automatic weapons into a bank robbery, and who accompanies a co-felon who he knows is also carrying such weapons, has behaved with the requisite reckless indifference to the great danger of death from the joint conduct. In that event the man would be found to meet the reckless-indifference standard.)

There is the further question of whether the man meets the *actus reus* requirement for reckless-indifference murder. The man has clearly given knowing assistance to the woman's commission of this recklessly-dangerous armed bank robbery. Therefore, his assistance to her, in what we've concluded is murder by her, will also be deemed to be the *actus reus* for accomplice liability in that murder by her. Since he's satisfied both the mental-state requirement for reckless-indifference murder and the *actus-reus* requirement for reckless-indifference murder (knowing assistance to a person who herself commits reckless-indifference murder), the man is guilty of being an accomplice to the substantive crime of reckless-indifference murder. That makes him, too, guilty of the substantive crime of reckless-indifference murder. Whew!

(A), (B), and (C) are not the best responses,

because each of them fails to recognize at least one defendant's guilt of murder.

Answer 33

(A) is the best response,

because the customer is guilty of common-law arson, and is guilty of felony-murder because of the arson.

Arson, as defined by the common law, is the: (1) malicious, (2) burning, (3) of the dwelling, (4) of another. Malice for arson does not require a specific intent, but only that the defendant acted with *either*: (1) the intent or knowledge that the structure would burn, or (2) the reckless disregard of an obvious risk that the structure would burn.

Under this definition, the customer is guilty. Since, as noted, common-law arson does not require that the defendant had a particular desire to burn down the building, only that he acted with a reckless disregard for an obvious risk of burning, the customer's intentional driving into the pump qualifies—a court or jury would be justified in concluding that intentionally driving a car into a gas pump manifests a reckless disregard of the high risk of fire and/or explosion. Once the intent element of malice is satisfied, the other elements of arson are clearly satisfied—there was a burning; the building that burned contained not only the convenience store but the businessman's dwelling on the second floor; and the building was not the customer's but another's (the businessman's).

Now, on to murder: Felony-murder occurs where a defendant commits a killing—even an accidental one—that occurs during the course of, and as a result of, the defendant's commission of any of a series of defined dangerous felonies.

Arson is one of the "dangerous felonies" for common-law felony murder. Since as described above the customer is guilty of arson, and since the death of the businessman occurred during and as the direct result of the arson, the customer is also guilty of felony murder.

(B), (C), and (D) are not the best responses,

because each choice fails to make the customer guilty of both murder and arson.

Answer 34

(D) is the best response,

because on these facts the defendant does not have the mental state for either murder or manslaughter.

Murder is the unlawful killing of another human being with malice aforethought. Malice aforethought is deemed to exist if the defendant has any of the following states of mind: (1) intent to kill, (2) intent to inflict great bodily harm, (3) a reckless indifference to an unjustifiably high risk to human life, or (4) the intent to commit a felony.

Here, since by hypothesis the jury believes that the defendant thought the gun was empty, none of the required states of mind can exist: (1) the defendant clearly didn't intend to kill, (2) the defendant clearly didn't intend to inflict great bodily harm, (3) the defendant wasn't recklessly indifferent to an unjustifiably high risk to human life (since we're told the jury thinks the defendant's mistaken belief that the gun contained blanks was "reasonable"), and (4) the defendant didn't intend to commit any felony.

Involuntary manslaughter is death caused by gross negligence or recklessness. Since we're told to assume that the jury believes both that the defendant thought the gun had blanks and that this belief was reasonable, the defendant has not manifested either gross negligence or recklessness. Therefore, she can't be guilty of involuntary manslaughter.

Nor can the defendant be guilty of voluntary manslaughter, which requires an intent to kill or seriously injure, under partly extenuating circumstances (e.g., extreme provocation). Since there was no intent to kill or seriously injure, voluntary manslaughter can't exist.

(A), (B), and (C) are not the best responses,

because each of them makes the defendant guilty of either murder or manslaughter.

Answer 35

(D) is the best response,

because it most closely fits the classic attributes of a strict liability offense.

Note that the question here asks which crime is *most likely* to be found a strict liability offense. Thus, you must consider the elements of a strict liability crime, and see which choice is the best fit. This requires comparing choices, since all of them will have some elements of a strict liability offense.

The purpose of strict liability crimes is to help the prosecution where the mental element will be difficult to prove, or the harm caused is such that it's worth convicting people who lack "guilty minds." Strict liability crimes generally have the following attributes: (1) they are regulatory in nature; (2) they do not involve serious penalties; (3) they involve serious harm to the public; and (4) it's easy to determine the true facts. In fact, statutes regulating food, drugs and misbranded articles, as well as hunting license requirements and the like, are all common forms of valid strict liability statutes. Furthermore, making such a crime a strict liability crime would not be consistent with the purposes of strict liability: that is, to help the prosecution where the mental element will be difficult to prove, or the harm caused is such that it's worth convicting people who lack "guilty minds." D involves the sale of adulterated milk. The seriousness of the harm to the public, the fact that it's a misdemeanor instead of a felony, and the difficulty of proof of a "guilty mind" all make it a candidate for strict liability. Since D recognizes this, and none of the other choices are as satisfactory, D is the best response.

(A) is not the best response,

because it's highly unlikely shoplifting would be regarded a strict liability crime, even if the statute did not specify which *mens rea* it would require.

Strict liability crimes generally have the following attributes: (1) they are regulatory in nature; (2) they do not involve serious penalties; (3) they involve serious harm to the public; and (4) it's easy to determine the true facts. Here, what would make this statute a less-than-perfect candidate for strict liability is that shoplifting is a type of larceny, and thus a court would likely imply a *mens rea* requirement—that is, the intent to steal. Furthermore, shoplifting is not regulatory in nature (e.g., firearms registration, hunting license requirements, and the like), and so is not a likely strict liability offense. Most importantly, another choice—D—describes a crime that is a classic strict liability offense. As a result, A is not the best response.

(B) is not the best response,

because it's unlikely that possessing heroin, as a felony, would be a strict liability crime, even if the statute did not mention a *mens rea.*

Strict liability crimes generally have the following attributes: (1) they are regulatory in nature; (2) they do not involve serious penalties; (3) they involve serious harm to the public; and (4) it's easy to determine the true facts. Here, the crime is a *felony*, so it's unlikely it would be a strict liability crime.

Furthermore, making such a crime a strict liability crime would not be consistent with the purposes of strict liability: that is, to help the prosecution where the mental element will be difficult to prove, or the harm caused is such that it's worth convicting people who lack "guilty minds." A "possession" statute would be aimed at people who knowingly possess heroin. Thus, the statute in choice B would be an unlikely candidate for strict liability, making B not the best response.

(C) is not the best response,

but it's close.

Strict liability crimes generally have the following attributes: (1) they are regulatory in nature; (2) they do not involve serious penalties; (3) they involve serious harm to the public; and (4) it's easy to determine the true facts. The thing that makes this choice difficult is that firearms registration statutes are classic strict liability offenses. *However,* the wrinkle here is that it's a *felony*—thus, with a stiff penalty, a *mens rea* is likely to be required. Since this makes it a less-than-perfect choice for a strict liability offense, and, more importantly, there's another choice that's more appropriate, C is not the best response.

Answer 36

(B) is the best response,

because it correctly identifies the key factor that will exonerate the law student: His mistake negates the necessary *mens rea* for burglary.

The key here is to remember the elements of burglary, the defenses that apply, and apply them strictly. Common law burglary requires the breaking and entering of the dwelling house of another, at night, with the intent to commit a felony therein. Most states broaden this to include entry at all times in all kinds of structures (thus eliminating the breaking, dwelling house, and nighttime requirements). Here, the law student's mistake—believing that looking at the exam questions is criminal when, in fact, it isn't—negates his *mens rea.* There's no burglary when a defendant breaks and enters to commit a non-felony. The defense that covers these facts is legal impossibility—that is, what he intended to do is not defined as a crime. Since this negates the required intent for burglary, he'll be acquitted.

What this problem points out is how important it is to remember that burglary and larceny are a kind of "inchoate" crime. That is, they are complete once a defendant does something—in burglary, breaking and entering, in larceny, taking and carrying away personal property—with the intent to do something else—in burglary, committing a felony, and in larceny, stealing. However, the crimes are complete once the first act is done, if there's the appropriate mental state—intent.

Since B correctly identifies that legal impossibility means there's no intent under these facts, it's the best response.

(A) is not the best response,

because it does not correctly apply the burglary definition to these facts.

At common law, burglary requires breaking and entering the dwelling house of another, at night, with intent to commit a felony therein. Under most modern statutes, entry at all times in all kinds of structures is covered (thus eliminating the breaking, dwelling house, and nighttime requirements). Thus, the crime is *complete* once the breaking and entering with the appropriate intent has taken place. It's not necessary that the person actually *commit* the felony therein—he need only *intend* to do so. Thus, choice A's language about the law student not completing the crime *cannot* be correct, since if he avoids liability for burglary, it cannot be on that basis.

(C) is not the best response,

because it does not apply to these facts, and arrives at the wrong result.

If the law student *had* the correct mental state, his breaking and entering would make him liable for burglary. At common law, burglary requires breaking and entering the dwelling house of another, at night, with the intent to commit a felony therein (most modern statutes broaden this to include entry at all times in all kinds of structures, thus eliminating the breaking, dwelling house, and nighttime requirements).

Thus, the "mental state" to which C refers is intent. Although it seems as though the law student had the right mental state, his mistaken belief that what he was doing was criminal, when in fact it wasn't, will exonerate him—since his mistake negates his intent to commit a felony. There's no burglary when a defendant breaks and enters for the purpose of carrying out an act that is not itself a felony. Since choice C does not recognize the "mistake" defense, it's not the best response.

(D) is not the best response,

because it misstates the facts—what's involved here is *legal* impossibility, not *factual* impossibility.

Factual impossibility occurs when completion of the crime is impossible due to physical facts not known to the defendant, e.g., a pickpocket picking an empty pocket. As D states, factual impossibility is no defense. However, what's involved here is *legal* impossibility, which arises when what the defendant intends to do is not criminal. It is a valid defense, and applies to these facts. It will exonerate the law student because it negates the intent requirement of burglary. Common law burglary requires the breaking and entering of the dwelling house of another at night with the intent to commit a felony therein. Most states broaden burglary to cover entry at all times in all kinds of structures. Either way, without the intent to commit a felony once inside, a defendant cannot be convicted. Here, the legal impossibility defense removes the intent. Since D does not apply the correct rule to these facts and arrives at an incorrect result, it's not the best response.

Answer 37

(B) is the best response,

for three principal reasons: (1) it arrives at the correct result; (2) it ascribes to the jury its correct role as finder of facts; and (3) it offers reasoning that would, indeed, result in a manslaughter conviction instead of murder.

This is a somewhat tricky question because it's a hybrid: You need to know the procedural rule that the jury decides issues of fact, and the judge decides issues of law.

As a general rule, if the evidence would be sufficient for conviction of a lesser offense (here, manslaughter), the issue should be submitted to the jury. By stating that whether the issue of manslaughter should go to the jury is based on what the jury could find, instead of on what the judge believes the evidence shows, B correctly states this rule. Furthermore, the reasoning in B correctly identifies a basis on which the jury could find the defendant guilty only of manslaughter. Voluntary manslaughter is a murder committed under adequate provocation. Murder is an unlawful killing committed with malice aforethought. Thus, if the jury finds that an act by the other customer sufficiently provoked the defendant, it will find him guilty of voluntary manslaughter instead of murder. Being hit in the face with an umbrella is just the sort of thing that could be considered provocation sufficient to reduce the defendant's liability to manslaughter. A wrinkle in this problem is that the defendant, in a way, incited the provocation by stealing the tip. That's not relevant for the defendant's liability in this question (whereas it would be relevant to the customer's liability in attacking the defendant, since she would have a crime prevention argument). Since B correctly identifies the result, the jury's role, and the basis on which the defendant may be liable for only manslaughter instead of murder, it's the best response.

(A) is not the best response,

because it does not apply the correct rule to voluntary manslaughter.

In order to be found liable for only manslaughter instead of murder, the jury would have to find that the defendant acted under provocation; that is, he committed an unlawful killing with malice aforethought, but was provoked. If you chose A, you probably did so because you confused the rule for voluntary manslaughter with that of depraved heart murder, which is what A states. Thus, if the jury found that the defendant acted recklessly and not with the intent to kill or seriously injure, it would *still* find him guilty of depraved heart murder.

A does however correctly identify two things: (1) that the request should be granted; and (2) that granting the request should be on the basis of how the jury could find, not on the basis of what the evidence shows. Despite this, since A applies the wrong test to these facts, it's not the best response.

(C) is not the best response,

because it arrives at an incorrect result and does not allow the jury to find voluntary manslaughter, which is possible from these facts.

First, choice C states that the request should be denied because of what the evidence shows. In fact, in its role as the finder of *facts,* the jury should have the choice to find a result that is possible on these facts—voluntary manslaughter. The reason the jury *could* find this is because they *could* find adequate provocation to reduce murder to manslaughter. Thus, choice C's statement that the defendant intended to kill or cause serious harm doesn't go far enough, because even if he *did* act with intent, if he did so under adequate provocation he'll only be liable for voluntary manslaughter. Since C denies the jury the opportunity to make a finding that is possible under these facts, it's not the best response.

(D) is not the best response,

for three principal reasons: (1) it arrives at the wrong result; (2) it denies the jury its role as finder of fact; and (3), it does not cite an appropriate reason as to why the request should be denied.

In its role as finder of fact, if the evidence would be sufficient for conviction of a lesser offense (here, manslaughter), the issue should be submitted to the jury. Thus, the test is not what the evidence shows, but how the jury could find. D is also incorrect in the reasoning it provides, because the defendant's provoking the assault on himself would *not* prevent him from being found guilty of manslaughter, but would, instead, go against a defense of self-defense under the "imperfect self-defense doctrine," a modern rule adopted by some states. Under it, when the defendant intentionally kills another, he'll be liable for manslaughter if either he was the aggressor in a fight (and therefore not entitled to a self-defense claim), *or* he honestly but unreasonably believed deadly force was necessary. The reason that the judge would deny the defendant's request would be if the jury could *not* find him liable for manslaughter instead of murder. By offering reasoning that would make the defendant guilty of manslaughter, D does just the opposite: Since it arrives at an incorrect result, preempts the jury, and employs incorrect reasoning, D is not the best response.

Answer 38

(B) is the best response,

because the customer obtained possession of, but not title to, the watch by lying about a present fact.

In order to commit common law larceny, the customer must meet each of the following six elements: (1) the trespassory (2) taking and (3) carrying away of (4) personal property (5) of another (6) with intent to steal. Here all the elements were met by the customer's actions, unlike the other three crimes listed.

(A) is not the best response,

because the customer did not take the watch by force or threat of force.

Robbery is defined as larceny with two additional elements: (1) the property is taken from the person or presence of the owner; and (2) the taking is accomplished by using force or putting the owner in fear. Here, the taking itself was not accomplished by putting the owner in fear, as the customer had already accomplished the theft when he threatened the clerk. Thus, this is a larceny, as the customer obtained possession of, but not title to, the watch by lying about a present fact.

(C) is not the best response,

because the customer did not obtain title to the watch.

In order to commit false pretenses, the customer must meet each of the following six elements: (1) a false representation of a (2) material present or past fact (3) that causes the person to whom it is made (4) to pass title to (5) his property to the misrepresenter, who (6) knows that his representation is false and intends to defraud. While the customer knows that his representation is false and intends to defraud, he does not obtain title to the watch. Thus, this is a larceny, as the customer obtained possession of, but not title to, the watch by lying about a present fact.

(D) is not the best response,

because the customer was never in lawful possession of the watch.

In order to commit embezzlement, the customer must meet each of the following five elements: (1) a fraudulent (2) conversion of (3) the property (4) of another (5) by one who is already in lawful possession of it. Here, there was a trespassory taking, so the customer was never in lawful possession of the watch. Thus, this is a larceny, as the customer obtained possession of, but not title to, the watch by lying about a present fact.

Answer 39

(D) is the best response,

because it most closely applies to these facts, and it provides a valid defense to murder.

Note that the question asks the defendant's "best chance" of being acquitted. That means three of these choices will result in a conviction, and one won't.

The most common test for insanity is the M'Naghten Rule, which requires that the defendant have a diseased mind which caused a defect of reason, such that when the defendant acted he *either* didn't know his act was wrong *or* he didn't understand the nature and quality of his actions (e.g., mistaking someone's head for a baseball and hitting it with a bat). Here, it's not necessary to do a strict analysis under M'Naghten to appreciate the fact that the defendant is off his rocker, and didn't know what he was doing was wrong. Since the facts indicate the defendant has a promising insanity defense, and insanity is a good defense to murder, D is the best response.

(A) is not the best response,

because an intoxication defense would not exonerate the defendant under a murder charge.

Murder requires an unlawful killing with malice aforethought. Malice can take the form of intent to kill or inflict great bodily injury, felony murder, or "depraved heart"—acting in spite of an unjustifiably high risk to human life. Voluntary intoxication, which is involved here, is only a defense to prove a lack of capacity for specific intent crimes—it cannot be used if the *mens rea* requirement is only recklessness or negligence. Since depraved heart does not require intent, voluntary intoxication cannot be a valid defense to garden-variety murder. If you chose this response, it could be because you were thinking of *involuntary* intoxication, which could, theoretically, be a defense to a murder charge. Involuntary intoxication only applies when the defendant is misled about the nature of what he's taking, or where the defendant is physically forced to take the intoxicant, like Cary Grant in the movie *North by Northwest*. Involuntary intoxication is a valid defense if it prevents the defendant from understanding the criminal nature of his conduct. Thus, it resembles an insanity defense.

Under the facts here, this might be a defense, although there would be a problem with causation (since the defendant hallucinates *without* alcohol, as well). In any case, since the intoxication here is voluntary, and thus not be a valid defense, A is not the best response.

(B) is not the best response,

because it misstates the facts here.

It's true that murder requires an unlawful killing with malice aforethought. Malice aforethought can take the form of intent to kill or do great bodily harm, felony murder, or acting in spite of an unjustifiably high risk to human life ("depraved heart"). Under these facts, the last type of malice aforethought would likely be satisfied, since it does not have, in most states, a subjective element—it's only viewed objectively. By strangling the old woman, the defendant clearly acted in spite of an unjustifiably high risk to human life. As a result, a "lack of malice aforethought" defense would be unlikely to succeed, making B not the best response.

(C) is not the best response,

because self-defense would not be a valid defense to murder on these facts.

Self-defense has both an objective and a subjective element: The defendant must *in fact* believe the danger exists (the subjective part), and the defendant must be *reasonable* in this belief (the objective part). Here, the defendant misapprehended the danger: The old woman was only slapping him, and thus deadly force was not required. Since the defendant's perception of danger was not reasonable, self-defense will not be available as a defense, and C will not be the best response.

Answer 40

(A) is the best response,

because it identifies the most serious crime, of these four, for which the defendant can be convicted.

Robbery is a larceny from a person accomplished with violence or intimidation. (Larceny is a trespassory taking and carrying away of personal property of another, with intent to steal it.) The wrinkle here is that the victim, the husband, is not in fear for himself, and the violence is not directed at him. However, the rule is that the threat can be made to relatives or a companion. Since the facts here satisfy robbery—the question tells you that robbery is the most serious crime of the four choices—and the question asks for the most serious crime for which the defendant can be convicted, A is the best response.

(B) is not the best response,

because although the defendant could be convicted of larceny, he could be convicted of a more serious crime—robbery.

Larceny requires a trespassory taking and carrying away of personal property, of another, with intent to steal it. These elements are satisfied by the facts here. Specifically, it would be called "larceny from the person." However, these facts *also* indicate two *additional* elements, which raise the "larceny from the person" to robbery: the use of force or fear. What may have tricked you into choosing this response is that the force was directed at *the wife,* not the victim—the husband. However, the rule is that the threat can be made to relatives or a companion. Since these facts are covered by this, the defendant will be guilty of robbery from the husband. Since he'll be liable for a more serious crime than larceny, and the question asks for the most serious crime for which he can be convicted, B is not the best response.

(C) is not the best response,

because the defendant will be liable for robbery, a more serious crime than assault.

Criminal assault can take one of two forms: either an attempt to commit a battery, or the intentional and physical creation of fear of imminent bodily harm in the mind of the victim. Under these facts, the defendant would be liable for assault on the husband and wife for the period of time when he leaped out of the dark alleyway brandishing a gun. However, he will *also* be liable for *at least* battery on the wife, and robbery from the husband. If you chose this response, you overlooked the robbery. The defendant will be liable for robbery from the husband, because his act satisfies all the elements: a larceny from a person or a person's presence, by either force or fear. Here, the threat against the wife is sufficient for the force or fear element of robbery, since the force or fear *can* be directed at the victim's relative or companion. Since the defendant satisfies the robbery elements—the question tells you that robbery is a more serious crime than assault—and the question asks for the most serious crime for which the defendant can be convicted, C is not the best response.

(D) is not the best response,

because the defendant will be liable for a more serious crime than assault.

Criminal assault can take one of two forms: either an attempt to commit a battery, or the intentional and physical creation of fear of imminent bodily harm in the mind of the victim. Under these facts, the defendant would be liable for assault on the wife for the period of time when he leaped out of the dark alleyway brandishing a gun. However, the defendant will also be liable for more serious crimes, as well: assault on *both* the husband and wife, larceny from the husband, and robbery from the husband. The defendant's act satisfies all the elements of robbery: a larceny from a person or a person's presence, by force or fear. Here, the threat against the wife is sufficient for the force or fear element, since the force or fear can be directed at the victim's relative or companion. Since the defendant satisfies the robbery elements—the question tells you robbery is a more serious crime than assault—and the question asks for the most serious crime for which the defendant can be convicted, D is not the best response.

Answer 41

(C) is the best response,

because the crime of solicitation is completed with the concurrence of act and intent.

Solicitation consists of inciting, inducing, or urging another to commit a felony with the specific intent that the person solicited commit the crime. The offense is complete at the time the solicitation is made, whether the solicitee agrees or not. Therefore, the college student's effort to withdraw a few days before payment was due would not be a defense to the crime of solicitation—the crime was already completed. (Nor does it make any difference that the solicitee was only pretending to agree to commit the underlying crime.)

(A) is not the best response,

because the crime was completed as soon as the college student made his proposal to the police officer.

Nothing that happened after that—including the college student's withdrawal—could undo the crime.

(B) is not the best response,

because the crime was completed once the college student made his proposal to the police officer.

The fact that no "substantial act" was performed by either the college student or the police officer was irrelevant.

(D) is not the best response,

because the college student would be convicted even if the police officer had not agreed.

Solicitation consists of inciting, inducing, or urging another to commit a felony with the specific intent that the person solicited commit the crime. The offense is complete at the time the inciting, inducing, or urging of the other occurs. Even if the solicitee does not agree to do the requested act, the solicitor is guilty. So choice D, insofar as it recites the police officer's agreement as being the reason for the college student's guilt, is the wrong explanation for the correct result.

Answer 42

(D) is the best response,

because the young woman did not have the mental state for burglary or any form of assault.

Let's look first at assault. An assault is either (1) an attempt to commit a battery or (2) an intentional placing of another in apprehension of receiving an immediate battery. (Also, any completed battery contains an assault.) Since the young woman intentionally sprayed the guard with a harmful or offensive substance, she meets the prima facie requirement for type (1) assault (since she was trying to commit a battery—i.e., trying to cause a harmful or offensive contact). The question is whether she has a valid defense.

Here, the young woman has a valid claim of self-defense: She was acting to prevent the attack against her. It's true that the defense of self-defense doesn't apply where the defendant was the aggressor, but neither the fact that the young woman was a trespasser, nor the fact that she cursed at the guard, made her into an aggressor for the purpose of losing the right to defend herself.

Since the young woman acted under the right of self-defense, this will be a complete defense to aggravated assault as well as to simple assault.

Nor is this burglary. Burglary is the breaking and entering of the dwelling of another in the nighttime with intent to commit a felony therein. Here, although the hotel probably qualifies as the "dwelling of another," there is no indication that the young woman intended to commit a felony once she got inside. Therefore, she can't be guilty of burglary.

Consequently, the worst crime she can be convicted of is trespass.

(A), (B), and (C) are not the best responses,

because each of them names a crime that (as shown in the discussion of choice D above) the young woman did not commit.

Answer 43

(A) is the best response,

because it correctly identifies that the defendant satisfies all the elements of *both* burglary and larceny.

The key here is that both burglary and larceny are "inchoate" offenses in the sense that once *one* act is complete with the *intent* to do another, the crimes are satisfied.

The defendant is guilty of burglary because he satisfied all its elements: breaking and entering the dwelling house of another, at night, with the intent to commit a felony therein. Thus, once the defendant *entered* the house the *first* time—even before he actually took the silverware—he had completed the burglary, because burglary requires only the *intent* to commit a felony inside. The defendant is also liable for larceny: the trespassory taking and carrying away of another's personal property, with the intent to steal it. Under these facts, the defendant would be liable for larceny once he took the silverware, because he did so with the intent to steal it. The wrinkle here is that the defendant returned the silverware, thus renouncing his criminal purpose. However, once a criminal act is complete, it's too late to abandon it and escape liability. Thus, subsequent renunciation, or the accompanying forgiveness or condonation by the victim, won't exonerate the defendant. Furthermore, note that the larceny that's involved in these facts requires some different elements than burglary does, so it's not a "lesser included offense" of burglary, and the defendant can be convicted of both crimes. Since A correctly identifies that the defendant will be liable for both burglary *and* larceny, it's the best response.

(B) is not the best response,

because although it correctly identifies that the defendant will be guilty of burglary, it incorrectly states he'll be guilty of attempted larceny (in fact, he'll be liable for larceny as well).

The defendant satisfied all the elements of common-law burglary, because he broke into and entered the dwelling house of another at night, with the intent to commit a felony therein. Thus, once the defendant *entered* the house the *first* time—even before he actually took the silverware—he had completed the burglary, because burglary only requires the *intent* to commit a felony inside. Larceny is the trespassory taking and carrying away of personal property of another, with intent to steal it. Under these facts, the defendant would be liable for larceny once he took the silverware, because he did so with the intent to steal it. If you chose B, it was probably because you focused on the defendant's returning the silverware, and thought it must count somehow. In fact, it doesn't, because the crimes of burglary and larceny were already complete, and subsequent acts of repentance won't change that. Although attempt has several different tests, in general, attempted larceny would require that the defendant only have come sufficiently close to committing the larceny, with the intent to commit the larceny in a specific way.

The defendant completed the crime, so he wouldn't be liable only for attempt. Since B only identifies one of the two crimes for which the defendant will be liable, and another choice identifies them both, B is not the best response.

(C) is not the best response,

because although it correctly identifies that the defendant will be guilty of burglary, it incorrectly acquits the defendant for larceny.

As C states, the defendant will be liable for burglary, because he satisfies all its elements: breaking and entering the dwelling house of another, at night, with the intent to commit a felony therein. Thus, once the defendant *entered* the house the first time—even before he actually took the silverware—he had completed the burglary, because burglary requires only the *intent* to commit a felony inside. However, the defendant is *also* liable for larceny. Larceny requires the trespassory taking and carrying away of personal property of another, with the intent to steal it. Under these facts, the defendant would be liable for larceny once he took the silverware, because he did so with the intent to steal it. If you chose choice C, it's probably because you mistook larceny for a lesser included offense of burglary, and figured the defendant couldn't be liable for both. A lesser included offense is one that requires only proof of some but not all of the elements of another offense, and no other elements. As examples, attempted crimes are included in completed crimes, and voluntary manslaughter is included in murder (provocation is not considered an additional element). You may have confused burglary with robbery, which is a larceny from the person by force or fear. As a result, larceny is a lesser included offense of robbery. But the larceny that's involved in these facts requires some different elements than burglary does, since burglary can involve *any* felony.

Since C mistakenly acquits the defendant of larceny, it's not the best response.

(D) is not the best response,

because the defendant is guilty of both burglary *and* larceny.

The defendant will be liable for burglary because he satisfies all of its elements: breaking and entering the dwelling house of another, at night, with the intent to commit a felony therein. Thus, once the defendant *entered* the house the *first* time—even before he actually took the silverware—he had completed the burglary, because burglary requires only the *intent* to commit a felony inside. The defendant is *also* liable for larceny. Larceny requires the trespassory taking and carrying away of another's personal property, with intent to steal it. Under these facts, the defendant would be liable for larceny once he took the silverware, because he did so with the intent to steal it. If you chose this response, it's probably because you believed that returning the silverware would exonerate him. However, once a crime is *complete,* acts of renunciation, or condonation by the victim, will not erase the criminal liability! Since D does not recognize this, it's not the best response.

Answer 44

(B) is the best response,

because it states the felony, of these four, that's least likely to form a basis for felony murder.

The key here is to identify the felony that is least "independent" from homicide. Note that the question asks for the "least likely" basis for felony murder. This means three *will* be suitable, and one *won't* be. B is the only one that *won't* be.

Felony murder requires an underlying felony that is inherently dangerous to human life, while remaining sufficiently "independent" from homicide. Such crimes traditionally include rape, robbery, arson, burglary, and kidnapping. Here, manslaughter *is* a homicide, so it *cannot* be "independent" from it. The same would go for a crime like aggravated battery. Since the question here asks the least likely basis for felony murder, and B is the *only* choice that would *not* be amenable to felony murder, it's the best response.

(A) is not the best response,

because arson is one of the most likely felonies to form a basis for felony murder.

Felony murder requires an underlying felony that is inherently dangerous to life, which does not require personal violence. The most common such crimes are rape, robbery, arson, burglary, and kidnapping. Arson is considered sufficiently "independent" from homicide to be covered by the felony murder rule. If you chose this response, you may have mistakenly read "least" likely for "most" likely, since most MBE questions ask for the choice "most" likely to do something. However, since the question here asks for the *least* likely basis for felony murder, A isn't the best response.

(C) is not the best response,

because rape is a valid underlying crime for felony murder.

Felony murder requires an underlying felony that is inherently dangerous to human life, while remaining sufficiently "independent" from homicide (including, traditionally, rape, robbery, arson, burglary, and kidnapping). The traditional test is to exclude those crimes requiring personal violence, but it would be a misnomer to say rape doesn't require personal violence. Nonetheless, rape is one of the traditional bases of felony murder, due to its independence from homicide. Note that the fact that only an attempt is involved here does not change the result, since the felony murder rule encompasses attempts. Since the question here asks for the least likely basis for felony murder, C is not the best response.

(D) is not the best response,

because burglary is a likely basis for felony murder.

Felony murder requires an underlying felony that is inherently dangerous to human life, while remaining sufficiently "independent" from homicide, typically because the crime is said not to require personal violence. Such crimes include, traditionally, rape, robbery, arson, burglary, and kidnapping. Since the question here asks for the least likely basis for felony murder, D isn't the best response.

Answer 45

(B) is the best response,

because the gangster's two friends did nothing to assist the gangster's attack.

An accomplice is one who, with the intent that the crime be committed, aids, counsels, or encourages the principal before or during the commission of the crime.

The gangster's friends should be acquitted as accomplices to manslaughter because the facts make clear they did not intend that the gangster murder the woman, nor did they do anything during the gangster's attack to aid, counsel or encourage the gangster. Only after the crime was complete, when the elderly woman fell to the ground, did they urge the gangster to flee.

Nor does the fact that the friends did nothing to help the woman—when assistance to her during the beating could conceivably have prevented the death—make any difference. Except in special circumstances (none of which applies here) a witness to a crime has no affirmative duty to intervene to prevent the crime or aid the victim, even if this could be easily done. Therefore, failing to render such assistance cannot give rise to criminal liability.

(A) is not the best response,

because the gangster's friends could be found guilty of being accomplices even if the gangster was not convicted.

An accomplice is one who, with the intent that the crime be committed, aids, counsels, or encourages the principal before or during the commission of the crime. Under the modern view of accomplice liability, the fact that the principal has not yet been convicted of the substantive crime does not bar trial and conviction of the accomplices. If the principal were actually *acquitted*, this might bar prosecution, but that's not what happened here—a mistrial would not in most jurisdictions bar the prosecution of the alleged accomplices.

(C) is not the best response,

because urging the accomplice to flee was not a form of aid or counsel before or during the crime.

An accomplice is one who, with the intent that the crime be committed, aids, counsels, or encourages the principal *before or during* the commission of the crime.

The gangster's friends should be acquitted because to be accomplices they would, before or during the assault on the victim, have to have aided, counseled, or encouraged the gangster in the attack, with the intent that the attack be committed. By definition, they could not be accomplices merely by urging the gangster to flee after the crime was completed.

(D) is not the best response,

because they had no duty to intervene.

As a general matter no legal duty is imposed on any person to affirmatively act for the benefit of others. Absent one of several types of legal relationships between two parties, no legal duty is imposed on any person to affirmatively act for the benefit of others. None of those legal relationships existed here. Therefore, the gangster's friends had no duty to intervene to prevent the gangster's attack. Consequently, they cannot be made criminally liable for that failure to intervene.

Answer 46

(B) is the best answer,

because a co-conspirator need not be present at the commission of each crime in order to be guilty of a conspiracy.

Furthermore, the arrest of one co-conspirator does not automatically terminate the conspiracy when other co-conspirators continue to carry out the mission of the conspiracy. Accordingly, the jailed defendant may still be guilty of conspiracy, and a judgment of acquittal at the close of the government's case is improper on these facts.

(A) is not the best answer,

because conspirators must agree to the joint pursuit of unlawful ends.

More importantly, it is irrelevant factually, as the defendant is raising a defense based on his failure to be present (i.e., he was in jail), not on his failure to agree to all of the objects of the conspiracy. As a co-conspirator need not be present at the commission of each crime in order to be guilty of a conspiracy, a judgment of acquittal at the close of the government's case is improper on these facts.

(C) is not the best answer,

because even if the defendant had complied with the rule requiring pretrial notice of alibi, a judgment of acquittal will not be entered.

A co-conspirator need not be present at the commission of each crime in order to be guilty of a conspiracy. Furthermore, the arrest of one co-conspirator does not automatically terminate the conspiracy when other co-conspirators continue to carry out the mission of the conspiracy. Accordingly, the jailed defendant may still be guilty of conspiracy, and a judgment of acquittal at the close of the government's case is improper on these facts.

(D) is not the best answer,

because the government is not "bound by exculpatory evidence elicited during its case-in-chief."

The government is free to contest such evidence and is in no way bound by it. Furthermore, even if the government were so bound, a judgment of acquittal will not be entered. A co-conspirator need not be present at the commission of each crime in order to be guilty of a conspiracy. Furthermore, the arrest of one co-conspirator does not automatically terminate the conspiracy when other co-conspirators continue to carry out the mission of the conspiracy. Accordingly, the jailed defendant may still be guilty of conspiracy, and a judgment of acquittal at the close of the government's case is improper on these facts.

Answer 47

(D) is the best response,

because even an unnecessarily suggestive identification procedure will not violate due process if the identification itself was reliable under all the circumstances.

In a series of cases, the Supreme Court has held that an identification procedure may be so "*unnecessarily suggestive*" that allowing the results of that identification into evidence violates the accused's *due process* rights. *See, e.g., Stovall v. Denno*, 388 U.S. 293 (1967). In fact, in extreme cases the unnecessarily suggestive procedure may so irreparably taint the out-of-court identification that the witness is even forbidden to make an *in-court* identification of the accused at trial.

Here, the out-of-court identification was certainly needlessly suggestive, both because it used only a single photograph, and because the officer told the store owner before the identification that the police were pretty sure the person in the photo was the culprit. However, even where an unnecessarily suggestive identification procedure is used, neither the out-of-court identification itself, nor the witness' later in-court identification, will be excluded unless the trial court concludes that there is "a *very substantial likelihood of irreparable misidentification*." *Manson v. Brathwaite,* 432 U.S. 98 (1977). The likelihood of misidentification is to be determined by considering the "totality of the circumstances," including such factors as how good an opportunity the witness had to observe the perpetrator. So, here, as long as the court believes that the in-court identification is reasonably reliable, the fact that it may have been influenced by earlier unnecessarily suggestive out-of-court identification methods will not cause the in-court testimony to be excluded.

(A) is not the best response,

because it falsely states a categorical rule against exclusion of in-court testimony.

The procedure by which a witness makes an out-of-court identification may be so unnecessarily suggestive, and may so taint the identification process, that the court will conclude that even the later in-court identification of the accused by the witness is so unreliable that its admission would violate the defendant's due process rights. So to the extent that this choice asserts that suppression of in-court testimony can *never* be a proper remedy for an improper out-of-court identification, this choice is overly broad and thus incorrect.

(B) is not the best response,

because the out-of-court identification here was improper.

An out-of-court identification is improper if it is "unnecessarily suggestive." The identification here clearly meets that standard, both because it used only a single photograph, and because the officer told the store owner before the identification that the police were pretty sure that the perpetrator was the person shown in the photo. However, this choice is incorrect in asserting that where the out-of-court identification is improper, a later in-court identification by the same witness must automatically be excluded—only if the trial judge believes that, under the totality of circumstances, the in-court identification is very unreliable, will that in-court identification be excluded.

(C) is not the best response,

because the improper out-of-court identification did not necessarily taint the later in-court identification.

There are indeed situations in which the procedure by which a witness makes an out-of-court identification is so unnecessarily suggestive that it irreparably taints the entire identification process, leading the court to exclude even the witness' later in-court identification of the accused as being so unreliable that its admission would violate the defendant's due process rights. But such a taint will not be found to have occurred merely because the original process was needlessly suggestive—the court will look at all the circumstances to determine whether the in-court identification is reasonably reliable, and if so, that identification will be allowed despite the earlier suggestiveness. Since this choice says that the improper out-of-court identification "necessarily tainted" any in-court identification, the choice misstates the decision-making process that the trial court would use.

Answer 48

(C) is the best response,

because double jeopardy does not attach until the trial has begun.

The protection against double jeopardy does not apply until jeopardy has "*attached*." Therefore, if a proceeding is terminated before jeopardy has attached, the Double Jeopardy Clause does not limit the prosecution's right to try the defendant for the same charge in a new proceeding. In a case to be tried before a jury, jeopardy is deemed to attach when the jury has been selected and all its members have taken the oath. *Crist v. Bretz*, 437 U.S. 28 (1978). In a case that is to be tried by a judge sitting without a jury, jeopardy is deemed to attach when the first witness has been sworn in. Here, although we don't know whether the first proceeding would have been a jury trial or a bench trial, we know that the dismissal for lack of probable cause happened before either the jury was impaneled or the first witness was sworn. So jeopardy could not have attached, and the new charges could not violate the Double Jeopardy Clause.

(A) is not the best response,
because the dismissal of the first charges occurred before jeopardy had attached.

As is discussed in choice C, the Double Jeopardy Clause cannot be triggered until jeopardy is deemed to have "attached," which does not happen until the jury has been selected and sworn in, or (in a bench trial) the first witness has been sworn in. This choice, by asserting that dismissal during the preliminary hearing triggered the Clause, is therefore incorrect as a matter of law.

(B) is not the best response,
because it ignores the issue of when jeopardy attaches.

The Double Jeopardy Clause cannot be triggered until jeopardy has "attached," which happens when the jury is chosen and sworn in, or (in a bench trial) when the first witness is sworn in. If jeopardy has not attached, the Clause will not be triggered even if the prosecution does not have any evidence that was not presented in the first case. Since this choice ignores the significance of whether jeopardy has attached, it is not the best response.

(D) is not the best response,
because it incorrectly states the time at which the Double Jeopardy Clause comes into play.

The Double Jeopardy Clause is triggered when jeopardy has "attached," which happens when the jury is chosen and sworn in, or (in a bench trial) when the first witness is sworn in. This choice, by asserting that jeopardy cannot attach until there has been a conviction or an acquittal, is therefore legally incorrect. For instance, if the jury has been chosen and sworn in, and the judge declares a mistrial during the testimony of the first witness, the Double Jeopardy Clause may well bar a re-prosecution (though this is not automatically so—if there was a "manifest necessity" for declaring a mistrial, re-prosecution will be allowed.)

Answer 49

(A) is the best response,
because the man was subjected to a custodial interrogation.

If *Miranda* warnings are required and are not given, any resulting confession is normally not admissible. *Miranda* warnings are required whenever the police engage in a "*custodial interrogation*." There was obviously an "interrogation" here, since we're told that an officer "asked the man if he had committed a particular robbery."

It's a closer question whether this interrogation was a "*custodial*" one. An interrogation is "custodial" if and only if the one being questioned believes he is not free to leave. The prosecution could argue that since the man was in his own house, and had not yet been formally told that he was under arrest, he could reasonably have believed that he was free to leave. But the prosecution is unlikely to prevail with this argument: When police break into a person's house at 6 a.m., and with guns drawn awaken the person in his bed and say "We've got you now," a reasonable person in that person's position would typically not believe that he was free to leave. *See, e.g., Orozco v. Texas*, 394 U.S. 324 (1969) (where police break into D's bedroom at 4 a.m. to question him, this was a custodial interrogation).

Since this was almost certainly a custodial interrogation, the police's failure to give the *Miranda* warnings before asking the question about the robbery will almost certainly require suppression of the response. (In any event, you're asked for the man's "best argument," and of the four choices this is the only one that is even plausible.)

(B) is not the best response,
because an argument based on voluntariness will be harder to succeed with than one based on an absence of *Miranda* warnings.

If the man could establish that his statement was not voluntary this fact would indeed result in suppression of the statement. However, voluntariness depends on the totality of the circumstances, and it's not clear that the man could establish that his statement was involuntary—for instance, there is no evidence that he was threatened with harm if he failed to respond. The test for a *Miranda* violation, by contrast, is much more bright-line: As long as the person is being subjected to custodial interrogation, failure to give the warnings automatically requires suppression. So while the man might succeed with his voluntariness argument, the *Miranda* argument is clearly the easier one for him to establish on these facts.

(C) is not the best response,

because *Miranda* can apply even where the suspect has not been told he is under arrest.

Miranda warnings must be given whenever a person is subjected to custodial interrogation. The test for whether a person is in custody is whether a reasonable person in his position would believe that he was not free to leave. For this test to be satisfied, it is not necessary that the person be formally informed that he is under arrest; even without such a notification, the circumstances may make it clear to the person that he is not free to leave. That's what happened here: When the police burst into his bedroom with guns drawn at 4 a.m. and said "We've got you now," the man could reasonably have believed that he was not free to leave (i.e., that he was in custody), even though he had not yet been formally told that he was under arrest.

(D) is not the best response,

because the arrest warrant sufficed for entry.

If the police had had *neither* an arrest warrant nor a search warrant, the man would have had a plausible chance of successfully arguing that the entry violated his Fourth Amendment rights (since in non-exigent circumstances an arrest warrant is needed for the police to enter private premises to make an arrest, [*U.S. v. Watson*, 423 U.S. 411 (1976)], and the circumstances here might be held non-exigent); in that event, the man's incriminating statement would have to be suppressed as the fruit of that illegal entry. But where the police *have* a validly-issued *arrest* warrant, they may enter a private residence even in non-daylight hours, and without warning, and without exigent circumstances. Since their entry was legal on account of the arrest warrant, the absence of a search warrant didn't matter.

Answer 50

(A) is the best response,

because even if some or all of the evidence heard by the grand jury was inadmissible, that is not grounds for dismissing an indictment.

In a series of decisions, the Supreme Court has held that even if a grand jury relies on inadmissible evidence while issuing an indictment, dismissal of the indictment is not the proper remedy. *See, e.g., U.S. v. Calandra*, 414 U.S. 338 (1974): "[A]n indictment valid on its face is not subject to challenge on the ground that the grand jury acted on the basis of inadequate or incompetent evidence[.]" So even though the agent here violated the defendant's Fourth Amendment rights by entering his house without a warrant and without probable cause, and even if the man's boasting in the bar was held to be the direct fruit of that Fourth Amendment violation (not at all clear), the appropriate remedy would be for the trial judge to exclude the boast from the trial, not to dismiss the indictment.

(B) is not the best response,

because even if hearsay was used, dismissal of the indictment is not the appropriate remedy.

As is discussed further in choice A, even where a grand jury relies on inadmissible evidence (or evidence that taken in its entirety is not sufficient to justify a conviction), dismissal of the indictment is not the proper remedy.

(C) is not the best response,

because even if the evidence stemmed from an unlawful search, dismissal of the indictment is not the appropriate remedy.

It's pretty clear that the agent here violated the defendant's Fourth Amendment rights by entering his house without a warrant and without probable cause. It's also possible (though not certain) that the man's boasting in the bar would be held to be the direct fruit of that Fourth Amendment violation, and thus inadmissible at his trial. But even if both of those issues were resolved in the defendant's favor, the appropriate remedy would be for the trial judge to exclude the boast from the trial, not to dismiss the indictment.

(D) is not the best response,

because even if there was a violation of the right to counsel, this would not justify dismissal of the indictment.

First, there was almost certainly no violation of the man's right to counsel. The Sixth Amendment right to counsel is triggered only following the commencement of formal proceedings against the defendant (e.g., an indictment), so the use of a government agent to have a conversation with the man without counsel present (if counsel for the man even existed) could not have been a Sixth Amendment violation. And the right to presence of counsel that is part of the package of *Miranda* rights (i.e., that derives from the Fifth Amendment privilege against self-incrimination) applies only where the person being interrogated (1) is in custody and (2) knows that he is being interrogated by a government official, neither of which is the case here. Furthermore, even if the boasting was found to be the product of a violation of the right to counsel (highly unlikely), exclusion of the evidence at the man's trial, rather than dismissal of the indictment, would be the appropriate remedy.

Answer 51

(A) is the best response,

because the use of a death-qualified jury does not violate a defendant's constitutional right be tried by a representative jury.

It's true that a criminal defendant has a Sixth Amendment right to be tried by a jury selected from a representative cross-section of the community. But where a prospective juror indicates in voir dire that her opposition to the death penalty is so strong that it may prevent her from voting to impose that penalty, that prospective juror may be removed for cause without violating the defendant's right to a representative jury. *Lockhart v. McCree*, 476 U.S. 162 (1986). And that's true even if the juror is removed before the guilt phase in a bifurcated trial (i.e., one divided into a phase that determines guilt, followed by a separate sentencing phase if the defendant is found guilty).

(B) is not the best response,

because removal of these jurors from both phases of the trial was constitutional.

The Supreme Court has held that jurors whose opposition to the death penalty may prevent them from imposing it may be removed for cause from *both* the guilt and sentencing phases of a capital trial, without violating the defendant's Sixth Amendment right to be tried by a jury chosen from a fair cross-section of the community. (See the discussion of choice A.) Since this choice asserts that the jurors' removal from the sentencing phase was improper, it is not the best choice.

(C) is not the best response,

because removal of these jurors from both phases of the trial was constitutional.

The Supreme Court has held that jurors whose opposition to the death penalty may prevent them from imposing it may be removed for cause from both the guilt and sentencing phases of a capital trial, without violating the defendant's Sixth Amendment right to be tried by a jury chosen from a fair cross-section of the community. (See the discussion of choice A.) This choice, like choice B, asserts that the jurors' removal from the sentencing phase was improper; the two choices differ only as to the remedy for such an improper removal. Since the removal was proper, conversion to a life sentence is not an appropriate remedy, any more than the new sentencing hearing in choice B would have been appropriate.

(D) is not the best response,

because removal of these jurors from both phases of the trial was constitutional.

The Supreme Court has held that jurors whose opposition to the death penalty may prevent them from imposing it may be removed for cause from both the guilt and sentencing phases of a capital trial, without violating the defendant's Sixth Amendment right to be tried by a jury chosen from a fair cross-section of the community. (See the discussion of choice A.) Since this choice asserts that the jurors' removal violated the defendant's fair-cross-section rights in two separate respects (as to the guilt phase and as to the sentencing phase), it is doubly-incorrect.

Answer 52

(B) is the best response,

because the officers had the right to be in the kitchen, but not to open the drawer in the bedroom.

First, let's look at whether the officers had a right to be in the house at all. As a general rule, the police may not enter a private dwelling without either an arrest warrant or a search warrant. But there are various exceptions to the requirement of a warrant. One of the exceptions is where the police are responding to the need to give emergency assistance. As the Supreme Court said in *Brigham City v. Stuart*, 547 U.S. 398 (2006), "law enforcement officers may enter a home without a warrant to render emergency assistance to an injured occupant or to protect an occupant from imminent injury." Since the police had a right to be standing outside the house looking through the window (they were properly responding to a call that shots had been fired inside the house), when they saw the man lying on the floor they had the right to make a warrantless entry in order to give him emergency assistance.

Then, while the police were waiting for the ambulance to come, they had the right to make a "protective sweep" of the house. In a case in which the police had arrested a suspect in his home, the Supreme Court held that the officers could then, incident to that arrest, and without a search warrant or probable cause, check the area for other persons, provided the police possessed "articulable facts which, taken together with the rational inferences from those facts, would warrant a reasonably prudent officer in believing that the area to be swept harbors an individual posing a danger to those on the arrest scene." *Maryland v. Buie*, 494 U.S. 325 (1990).

Here, since the police knew that the man on the floor had recently been shot in the back (which couldn't have been a suicide), the police knew that an armed and dangerous person had recently been in the house, and if still present posed a danger to them. So the police were clearly justified in making a protective sweep of all places in the house where that person might be hiding. That gave them the right to enter the kitchen. Once the officer was in the kitchen, and saw in plain view the bags filled with what looked like cocaine, he was justified in seizing those bags for testing. (When the police see in plain view an item that they have probable cause to believe is contraband or evidence, case law generally allows them to seize the item without a warrant, if they have a right to be in the place where the item is located.)

Now, let's consider what happened in the upstairs bedroom. Under the same "protective sweep" rationale described above, the police were justified in going throughout the house, and looking in every place where a human might be hiding. So the officer who remained at the house was entitled to check in the bedroom. But he was not entitled under the protective-sweep rationale to look in places that were too small to hide a human. The drawer was such a place. Therefore, unless the officer had probable cause to believe that evidence or contraband might be found in the drawer (which he did not), by opening the drawer the officer violated the young woman's Fourth Amendment freedom from unreasonable searches and seizures. *See, e.g., Arizona v. Hicks*, 480 U.S. 321 (1987) (where officer was validly in D's apartment, and saw a stereo turntable in plain view, officer nonetheless violated D's Fourth Amendment rights when, without probable cause, he lifted the turntable to read its serial number). So the marijuana must be suppressed as the fruit of a search and seizure made without probable cause, and not falling within any exception to the probable cause requirement. (Indeed, before the police were entitled to open the drawer they needed not only probable cause but a search warrant as well.)

Choices (A), (C), and (D) are not the best choice,
because each is inconsistent with the above analysis.

Answer 53

(C) is the best response,
because it's theoretically correct, it applies to these facts, and it's the easiest to prove of these choices.

This is a somewhat difficult question because three of the responses are potential answers theoretically, but two of them are difficult to prove. The question asks for the *best* argument, which will be the one that's theoretically correct, applies to the facts, and will be the easiest to prove—and that's choice C.

There are six general exceptions to the requirement of a search warrant: the search is incident to a lawful, custodial arrest; the "automobile" exception (which requires probable cause that vehicle contains evidence of crime, and exigent circumstances); plain view; consent; stop and frisk; and hot pursuit/evanescent evidence. The consent exception applies where one with the authority to consent offers voluntary and intelligent consent to the search. Under the "third-party consent" version of the consent exception, one who surrenders possession of property to another is likely to be found to have surrendered his expectation of privacy in the event that the other might consent to a search of that property. That's the case here: The ex-convict authorized his cellmate to drive his car and, thus, impliedly authorized his cellmate to consent to a search.

(A) is not the best response,
Because it fails to assert a valid exception to the requirement of a search warrant.

There are six general exceptions to the requirement of a search warrant: the search is incident to a lawful, custodial arrest; the "automobile" exception (which requires probable cause that vehicle contains evidence of crime, and exigent circumstances); plain view; consent; stop and frisk; and hot pursuit/evanescent evidence. There is no general exception allowing a warrantless search when such a search is "reasonable under the circumstances," and this choice in effect asserts that there *is* such an exception. Furthermore, although an officer who makes a proper automobile stop and then has probable cause to believe that a search of the passenger compartment will likely turn up evidence of the crime for which the stop occurred will qualify for the "automobile exception" (the second in the above list of six exceptions), the stop here was for speeding, and nothing suggested to the officer that he might find "evidence of speeding" (the crime for which the stop occurred) by searching the trunk. So Choice A does not successfully assert the automobile exception or any other exception to the usual requirement of a search warrant.

(B) is not the best response,
because the facts do not mention a custodial arrest.

A search can be justified as "incident to a valid arrest" only if there is in fact an arrest. Furthermore, the Supreme Court's cases on officers' right to make a warrantless search incident to arrest make it clear that the search-incident-to-arrest exception to the warrant requirement applies only where the "arrest" is a "custodial" one, i.e., the arrestee will be taken into custody rather than merely given a summons. *See, e.g., U.S. v. Robinson*, 414 U.S. 218, 236 (1973), a case upholding the search incident to arrest at issue there, and mentioning that "it is the fact of custodial arrest which gives rise to the authority to search." Here, where the facts say that the cellmate was told he would *not* be put under arrest, but merely issued a summons for the speeding, there was no custodial arrest, and thus no right to make a search incident to arrest. As a result, B is not the best response.

(D) is not the best response,
because the facts here do not trigger the "automobile exception," which is what this choice refers to.

There are six general exceptions to the requirement of a search warrant: the search is incident to a lawful, custodial arrest; the "automobile" exception (which requires probable cause to believe that vehicle contains evidence of crime, and exigent circumstances); plain view; consent; stop and frisk; and hot pursuit/evanescent evidence. The reference in this choice to "exigent circumstances, including the inherent mobility of a car," suggests that the choice is an attempt to qualify for the automobile exception. But the automobile exception, as noted, requires that the officer have probable cause to believe that the vehicle contains evidence of crime. Here, where the crime or offense that led to the stop was speeding (making it almost impossible that a search would produce "evidence" of that crime or offense), and where no factors other than the cellmate's nervousness indicated that the car might contain evidence of some other crime, it's very unlikely that a court would hold that the officer had probable cause to suspect that a search of even the passenger compartment would qualify for the automobile exception. (Furthermore, the actual area searched was the trunk, and the automobile exception usually doesn't apply to allow a search of the trunk -- as opposed to the passenger compartment -- unless there is probable cause that evidence of crime might be found in the trunk itself.) Therefore, Choice D is not the best answer.

Answer 54

(B) is the best response,

because it correctly identifies the ground on which the evidence will be excluded. This is a tricky question because it turns on a "hidden" issue—the freshness of the information serving as a basis for the search warrant.

This is how a search warrant is issued: A police officer submits a written, signed affidavit to a neutral, detached magistrate, who decides if there is probable cause to issue the warrant. The affidavit must set forth the underlying circumstances to a degree sufficient for the magistrate to determine probable cause. If the information is *stale*, it will *defeat* probable cause by diminishing the possibility that the items in question are still at the location. That's the problem here: The information was two months old and, as a result, probably too old to justify a search warrant. This is a tricky question because this is *not* an issue that would jump off the page at you. Nonetheless, it's the central issue here. Since B correctly identifies this as the reason for excluding the evidence, it's the best response.

(A) is not the best response,

because it misstates the rule of law.

An informant's information *can* constitute probable cause for a search or arrest if it meets the "totality of the circumstances" test from *Illinois v. Gates* (1983). Under that test, elements determining the reliability of the informant include: the informant's prior use and reliability; the informant's status as a member of a reliable group (e.g., a minister); clarity of detail in the informant's tip, showing the informant has personal knowledge of where evidence is located; and the tip includes a declaration against the informant's penal interest (e.g., that he bought narcotics from the individual named). Thus, not only is the statement in choice A incorrect, but it's likely that, under these facts, the informant's tip would be sufficient grounds for a search warrant *if the information was fresh* instead of being two months old. The *age* of the information is what makes the search warrant defective, not the *source* of the information, because the two-month gap diminishes the probability that the items in question are still there. Since A misstates the law, even though it arrives at the correct result, it's not the best response.

(C) is not the best response,

because it misstates the law.

In fact, "mere evidence" is what *most* searches involve. Apart from the suspect himself, it's not clear what else a search *could* involve.

In order to obtain a search warrant, there must be probable cause to believe that the items in question are at the location. A search can be conducted *without* a warrant under certain circumstances (e.g., stop and frisk, search incident to a lawful custodial arrest, evanescent evidence). Thus, the blanket statement in C is incorrect, making it not the best response.

(D) is not the best response,

because although it correctly characterizes the informant, it ignores the fact that the information was "stale," and thus cannot form the basis of a valid search warrant.

As D implies, an informant's information *can* constitute probable cause for a search or arrest if it meets the "totality of the circumstances" test from *Illinois v. Gates* (1983). Under that test, elements determining the reliability of the informant include: the informant's prior use and reliability; the informant's status as a member of a reliable group (e.g., a minister); clarity of detail in the informant's tip, showing the informant has personal knowledge of where evidence is located; and the tip includes a declaration against the informant's general interest (e.g., that he bought narcotics from the individual named). Thus, the factors D names—the informant's reliability in the past and the correctness of his information this time—would make his tip a valid basis for a search warrant *but for* one crucial fact: The tip was based on "stale" information—it was two months old. Stale information diminishes the probability that the items in question are still at the location. While "staleness" is a fluid concept, courts take into account whether the crime is ongoing or short-lived. Here, the age of the information would defeat the validity of the warrant. If you missed this one, take heart—it's a *very* close call. Nonetheless, although D correctly states the law, ignoring the "staleness" issue makes it not the best response.

Answer 55

(C) is the best response,

because it correctly identifies the basis on which the heroin will be admissible.

This is a tricky question because it involves a not-so-obvious issue: *standing to object*. A person only has standing to claim a search or seizure violated the Fourth Amendment when the evidence was obtained from a search or seizure that violated that person's *own* "legitimate expectation of privacy." *Rakas v. Illinois* (1978). This means that even if the defendant owns the property in question, or is present when the search takes place, he will have no standing to challenge the search *unless* the search violated his legitimate expectation of privacy as to the place being searched. Under the facts here, the defendant clearly had no legitimate expectation of privacy in the back seat of the addict's car. And by long-standing Supreme Court case law, a criminal defendant is not permitted to assert "third party rights," i.e., the Fourth Amendment rights of someone else, in this case the addict. Therefore, the defendant cannot object to the validity of the search. Since C correctly identifies this standing problem, it's the best response.

(A) is not the best response,

because the "plain view" doctrine would not be determinative under these facts.

The "plain view" doctrine provides one means by which the police can conduct a warrantless search. It states that police can make a warrantless seizure when they are on the premises for lawful purposes, and they inadvertently discover evidence in "plain view." Choice A correctly states the facts, in the sense that, since the heroin was under the rear seat, it was not in "plain view." However, the choice ignores the central reason why the motion to suppress will be denied: The defendant has no standing to object to the search, since it was the addict's car that was searched, and the defendant had no privacy interest in that car. If it were *the addict* who was being tried, the result would likely be different, because the *issues* would be different, since the addict clearly would have standing to object. (And at the moment the officer found the heroin under the rear seat, the officer was not in a place he had the right to be, since no exception to the requirement of a warrant entitled the officer to be inside the car looking under the seat.)

Thus, even though choice A is correct in that the heroin would *not* be covered by the plain view doctrine, it ignores the standing issue, which is central to solving this question. As a result, A is not the best response.

(B) is not the best response,

because it ignores the central issue in the case: The defendant does not have standing to object to the search.

If you chose this response, it's probably because you overlooked the fact that the *defendant* is objecting to a search of *the addict's* car, in which the defendant has no privacy interest.

Let's suppose, though, that it was the addict who was on trial, and was objecting to the introduction of the evidence against him. Then, this choice probably *would* be correct. That's because, according to *Arizona v. Gant*, 556 U.S. 332 (2009), even when a driver is subjected to a full custody arrest, the officer may not search the passenger compartment incident to that arrest unless either (1) the arrestee has access to the passenger compartment at the moment of the search; or (2) the officer reasonably believes that the passenger compartment may contain evidence of the particular offense for which the arrest is being made. Here, by the time one officer began to search the passenger compartment, the addict was already handcuffed and in the patrol car, preventing him from having access to the passenger compartment. And since the arrest was for speeding, the officer who did the search could not have had a reasonable belief that the passenger compartment would contain evidence of that offense (what physical evidence of speeding could there have been in the compartment?). So if the fruits of the search were being introduced against the addict, not the defendant/seller, Choice B's assertion that the scope of the search was excessive (in that it included the car, not just the addict's person) would have been correct.

(D) is not the best response,

because it both ignores the standing issue and would be legally incorrect even apart from that issue.

First, as is explained in the discussion of Choice B, the search here was not properly incident to the arrest, under *Arizona v. Gant*. Second, the court would never even get to the point of considering whether the search was proper as incident to arrest, because as is explained in Choice C, the defendant does not have standing to raise the issue of whether the search was proper under the incident-to-arrest doctrine.

Answer 56

(D) is the best response,

because the homeowner consented to the police entering his house.

An officer of the law can make a warrantless arrest for a felony, such as robbery. The police can then make a warrantless search of an arrestee's person incident to an arrest. So the motion would have to be denied unless, prior to the moment when the police recognized that the defendant matched the description of the drugstore robber, the police's presence violated some constitutional right of the thief.

The owner of a house unquestionably has the right to invite the police in — when they enter in response to such an invitation and move around the house, they are not violating the rights of a guest, as long as they stay within the scope of the owner's invitation. That's what happened here: The police were invited (by the homeowner) into, or to a place near, the kitchen. (If the thief had, say, rented a particular *bedroom* from the owner for the night, then it's conceivable that the owner would be found to have surrendered his right to invite the police into *that bedroom* during the night – but here, of course, the invitation to the police was to enter the kitchen, not the bedroom.) Since the police were authorized to be in or near the kitchen, they were entitled to be in the place from which they recognized the thief. And that recognition triggered their right to arrest and then to search incident to arrest, all without constitutional violation.

(A) is not the best response,
because the homeowner's consent overrides the thief's right to contest entry.

The owner's consent to a search of (or other police entry on) a premises is binding on a non-paying guest, even if the guest refuses consent. So here, the homeowner's right to consent to the police's warrantless entry into the house overrode any expectation of privacy the thief might have had in in kitchen, as is more fully explained in Choice D above.

(B) is not the best response,
because the answer incorrectly mixes two aspects of the law.

The thief's mere presence at the scene of the search may in a sense have given him "standing" to protest the police's entry into the house and the kitchen. But the real question is whether the thief's constitutional rights were violated by the police presence in the kitchen. And, under the analysis in choice D above, the answer to this question is no. So choice B reaches the wrong result, and does so on a completely wrong (or at least irrelevant) theory.

(C) is not the best response,
because the thief's lack of ownership or possessory interest in the premises isn't what caused him to lose—the homeowner's consent is.

An overnight social guest probably has a legitimate expectation of privacy in at least the particular parts of the home where he is staying. (In other words, the guest's lack of ownership or "other possessory interest" in the premises is not automatically fatal to his right to protest a premises search.) However, the owner's consent to a search of the premises will be binding on a non-paying guest, even if the guest refuses consent. So when the homeowner consented, that consent took priority over whatever privacy interest the thief may have had in the premises. Thus choice C reaches the right result for the wrong reason.

Answer 57

(C) is the best response,
because the drug dealer's statement was not in response to any "interrogation," and only the results of interrogations can be barred by a failure to give a *Miranda* warning.

Miranda does not bar all statements made prior to the giving of *Miranda* rights. Statements made without any questions being asked are considered volunteered, and admissible even if the required *Miranda* warning wasn't given.

The drug dealer's statement that "You never would have caught me with the stuff if it hadn't been for that lousy snitch" was volunteered, not made in response to any police questions. Therefore, the statement is not covered by *Miranda*.

(A) is not the best response,
because the police had the right to force the door open.

As a general rule, the officer executing the warrant must announce that he is a law enforcement officer, that he possesses a warrant, and that he is there to execute it. If the officer identifies himself and then is not answered he may use force to break into the premises described.

The facts make clear that the police followed correct procedures for executing the warrant and that their forcing open the door was reasonable. The police met the announcement requirements. They announced that they were law officers when they knocked on the drug dealer's door and called out, "Police." They announced they possessed a warrant. And they made clear that they were there to execute the warrant when they called, "Open up." They then waited a few seconds and when they received no response they broke down the door and entered. Contrary to choice A, this entry was permissible.

(B) is not the best response,
because the drug dealer's statement was volunteered before the police could read him his *Miranda* rights.

Miranda does not bar all statements made prior to the giving of *Miranda* rights. The *Miranda* decision itself says that "volunteered statements of any kind" are not barred by the Fifth Amendment, and thus are not affected by failure to give a *Miranda* warning. (*Miranda* covers only responses that are given in response to "interrogations" by the police.)

It's clear from the facts here that the drug dealer's remark "You never would have caught me with the stuff if it hadn't been for that lousy snitch" was a spontaneous outburst, not a response to interrogation.

(D) is not the best response,
because while the motion should be denied, the reason given is not correct.

The police do indeed have the right to make a "public safety" search while making arrests, and answers to questions that the police ask during such a public safety search don't fall within the *Miranda* rule. *N.Y. v. Quarles* (1984). But the drug dealer's statement was not made in response to questions asked during a public-safety search, so the public-safety exception to *Miranda* doesn't apply here.

Answer 58

(A) is the best response,

because evidence generally will not be suppressed where police reasonably held a good faith belief that their action leading to its discovery was authorized by a valid warrant. *See Arizona v. Evans*, 514 U.S. 1 (1995).

In this case, the computer check on the license number of the driver's car revealed that there was an outstanding warrant for the driver's arrest based on unpaid parking tickets. The police had no reason to believe that the warrant was invalid, so the search of the car was proper as a valid search incident to arrest.

(B) is not the best response,

because absent a custodial arrest or probable cause, a traffic stop does not authorize a full-blown search of the passenger compartment. *See Knowles v. Iowa*, 525 U.S. 113 (1998).

In this case, however, the troopers did arrest the driver of the car pursuant to an arrest warrant that they believed in good faith to be valid. Accordingly, the search was proper and the driver's motion to dismiss will be denied. *See Arizona v. Evans*, 514 U.S. 1 (1995) (applying good faith exception under similar circumstances).

(C) is not the best response,

because evidence generally will not be suppressed where police reasonably held a good faith belief that their actions leading to its discovery were authorized by a valid warrant.

Here, the arrest was made in the good faith belief that there was a valid outstanding warrant, so the court's clerical error would not require suppression. *See Arizona v. Evans*, 514 U.S. 1 (1995) (applying good faith exception under similar circumstances). Thus, this was a valid search incident to an arrest.

(D) is not the best response,

because neither probable cause nor reasonable suspicion was required, as the search was incident to an arrest.

It is true that the arrest warrant turned out to be invalid, but evidence generally will not be suppressed where, as in this case, police reasonably held a good faith belief that their actions leading to its discovery were authorized by a valid warrant. *See Arizona v. Evans*, 514 U.S. 1 (1995) (applying good faith exception under similar circumstances).

Answer 59

(A) is the best response,

because it correctly identifies that the defendant's handwriting sample will be admissible.

The key here is that a handwriting sample is considered *physical*, not communicative, evidence—and the Fifth Amendment only covers communicative evidence. As a result, handwriting samples are not covered by the Fifth Amendment, and will be admissible even if the suspect wasn't given the opportunity to obtain counsel, or told any other *Miranda* warning. Since A recognizes that the handwriting sample will be admissible, it's the best response.

(B) is not the best response,

because it does not correctly characterize the law.

A handwriting sample is considered "physical" evidence. The Fifth Amendment privilege against self-incrimination refers to communicative, not physical, evidence. Thus, the defendant could be required to submit to a handwriting sample without his being given his *Miranda* warning. Since B suggests the defendant *was* entitled to a *Miranda* warning before the handwriting sample was taken, it's not the best response.

(C) is not the best response,

because it misstates the law: The defendant is not entitled to refuse a handwriting sample.

Choice C implies that the defendant is entitled to avoid incriminating himself through a handwriting sample. In fact, a handwriting sample (like a fingerprint or a blood sample) is *not* a Fifth Amendment violation, because the privilege against self-incrimination refers to *communicative,* not *physical,* evidence. Handwriting samples are "physical evidence" and thus not subject to Fifth Amendment constraints. Thus, the defendant would not be entitled to refuse to give a handwriting sample. Since C gives the defendant a right he doesn't, in fact, have, it's not the best response.

(D) is not the best response,

because it misstates the law: The defendant was not entitled to have counsel present for the handwriting sample.

The two sources of the right to counsel are the Fifth Amendment and the Sixth Amendment. Under the Fifth Amendment, the suspect is entitled to counsel for the investigative stage of the prosecution, but only for custodial questioning (under *Miranda*), when a defendant must take part in a lineup or show up after "formal proceedings" have begun, or undercover agents elicit incriminating statements from an already indicted suspect. The Sixth Amendment covers "critical stages" of the trial (e.g., arraignment and trial). Choice D implies that a handwriting sample is the equivalent of questioning. However, the Fifth Amendment only covers *communicative,* not *physical,* evidence. Handwriting samples, like fingerprints and blood samples, are considered physical evidence, and thus are not covered by the Fifth Amendment. Since D implies otherwise, it's not the best response.

Answer 60

(B) is the best response,

because it correctly identifies the reason why the accomplice's testimony will not be admissible against the defendant: It was derived from the defendant's immunized testimony. The defendant was granted immunity for his grand jury testimony. This means that he was immunized from the use of his testimony, or evidence derived from that testimony. (The other type of immunity is transactional immunity, under which, in general, the witness is immunized from prosecution for any crime related to the transaction to which the witness testifies.) When a defendant is given use immunity and then prosecuted, the prosecution bears the "affirmative duty to prove that the evidence it proposes to use is derived from a legitimate source *wholly independent* of the compelled testimony." *Murphy v. Waterfront Commission*, 378 U.S. 52 (1964). Here, the prosecution cannot bear this burden -- indeed, just the opposite is true, since the facts tell us that the *only* clue that the prosecutors had to the accomplice's identity was the defendant's compelled testimony. Therefore, the accomplice's testimony was derived from the defendant's immunized testimony, and thus cannot be used against the defendant. Since B identifies this fact, it's the best response

(A) is not the best response,

because it misstates the law: The prosecutor *can* bargain away the rights of one co-defendant in a deal with another.

In a way, every time a prosecutor makes a deal with one defendant, he's impacting the rights of the other, since a defendant's testimony against his co-defendant will hurt the co-defendant. Furthermore, A ignores the real reason the objection to the accomplice's testimony will be sustained: because it was derived from the defendant's immunized testimony, since the defendant's testimony is the only way the prosecutor discovered the accomplice. Thus, the accomplice's testimony against the defendant derived from the defendant's own immunized testimony, so it cannot be used against the defendant. Since A doesn't recognize this, it's not the best response.

(C) is not the best response,

because it arrives at the wrong result, and does not focus on relevant issues.

The fact that the police suspected the defendant before he testified is not relevant; his *immunized testimony,* in which he identified the accomplice, is the focal point here. The defendant's immunized testimony is the only source of evidence as to the accomplice's identity.

Since the accomplice was discovered through the defendant's testimony, the accomplice's testimony would be considered derived from the immunized testimony, and thus could not be used against the defendant. Thus, the police's notion that the defendant was involved *before* he testified won't be relevant.

If you chose this response, it could be because you were thinking of the other kind of immunity—*transactional* immunity—under which the witness is immunized from prosecution for any crime related to the transaction to which the witness testifies. However, the witness may nonetheless be prosecuted if the prosecution can show an independent source for the evidence—i.e., any source other than the immunized testimony. Under these facts, however, it's *use* immunity, not *transactional* immunity, that's involved—so the "independent source" concept isn't relevant. Since C states otherwise, it's not the best response.

(D) is not the best response,

because it misstates the law, and arrives at the wrong result.

There are many reasons why a witness who is willing to testify may not be able to: if his testimony is cumulative evidence, if he's incompetent to testify, and many others. Thus, as a blanket statement, D is incorrect. Under these facts specifically, D ignores the fact that the accomplice's testimony was derived from the defendant's immunized testimony, and thus cannot be used against the defendant. Since D fails to recognize this, it's not the best response.

Answer 61

(A) is the best response,

because it correctly identifies that the evidence is inadmissible due to an illegal stop.

The stop was illegal because the officer was stopping cars *at random.* This is not permissible because such a system relies on the officer's discretion in determining whom to stop, and the intrusion is great because the driver is likely to be anxious about being stopped at random. *See Delaware v. Prouse*, 440 U.S. 648 (1979) (where the police made random traffic stops to ensure that drivers were licensed, and police did not have probable cause or even reasonable suspicion to believe that any particular driver stopped was unlicensed, the stop of D's car violated his Fourth Amendment right, making drugs noticed by the police through D's window and seized the fruits of an unlawful stop).

There are two ways such a system of traffic stops *can* be made legal: one is by setting up a checkpoint where *every* car is stopped and checked for license and registration (since that eliminates offer discretion). The other is to require a reasonable suspicion of illegal activity before any particular car is stopped. However, the random system here is illegal under *Prouse*, *supra*. Since A correctly identifies this, it's the best response.

(B) is not the best response,

because it misstates the law, and ignores the central issue here.

First, use of a flashlight does not constitute a search, since it only augments the officer's vision.

However, B *does* say that probable cause would be required, and that implies the correct test: In order to stop vehicles, police need a reasonable suspicion of illegal activity. Here, it's the stop *itself* that's deficient, *not* the fact that a flashlight was used to conduct a search. Since B ignores the fact that the stop itself was invalid, it's not the best response.

(C) is not the best response,

because although it correctly states the facts, it ignores the fact that the plan *itself* is invalid.

The key is that the stops were made *at random.* There are two things that could make the system valid: either the police could require a reasonable suspicion of illegal activity for a stop, *or* they could set up a checkpoint, and stop every car to check for license and registration. A system like that would be valid because (1) it does not rely on the officer's discretion in determining whom to stop, and (2) the intrusion is considered less because the driver is not likely to be as anxious as he would be with a random stop. However, on the facts here, the stops are purely random, and thus this plan is not valid (as is further discussed as to Choice A). As a result, compliance with the plan does not make a stop valid. Since C doesn't recognize that the plan itself is deficient, it's not the best response.

(D) is not the best response,

because although the facts it states are true, it ignores the threshold issue that the stop *itself* was invalid.

Had the *stop* been valid, the search would have been justified under plain view, the frisk would have been valid due to a reasonable suspicion of criminal activity and that the suspect was armed, and the discovery of drugs and the gun would have been valid. However, the stop here was *not* valid, and so everything flowing from it would be invalid as well. The stop was invalid because of the plan for random stops. Random stops are impermissible because they rely on the officer's discretion in determining whom to stop, and the intrusion is great because the driver is anxious when he's randomly stopped. Instead, a stop requires either reasonable suspicion of illegal activity, or a fixed check—e.g., a checkpoint where *every* car is checked for license and registration. Since the stop itself was invalid under these facts, and D ignores this, it's not the best response.

Answer 62

(C) is the best response,

because it correctly identifies the central reason why the friend's confession will be admissible.

Certainly the most obvious issue where a confession is concerned is whether the *Miranda* warning was required and given. Here, the *Miranda* warning was *not* required because there was no custodial interrogation. An interrogation is custodial only if the individual questioned is not free to leave. Here, the friend voluntarily went to the police station, and he volunteered his confession.

Under these facts, there was no time up to and including his confession when the friend was *not* free to leave. Thereafter, when the police were no longer willing to allow the friend to leave and wanted to question him further, they properly gave him his *Miranda* warning. Since C correctly identifies that the friend's statement will be admissible because it was voluntarily given and he was not entitled to a *Miranda* warning, it's the best response.

(A) is not the best response,

because it misstates the facts, and arrives at the wrong result.

A *Miranda* warning is only necessary when the police intend to conduct a custodial interrogation.

When a person voluntarily comes to the station house, he is not considered "in custody," and as a result, is not entitled to a *Miranda* warning. *Oregon v. Mathiason* (1977). That's what's happening under these facts. The friend voluntarily came to the station, and apparently realized he was free to leave at any time (which is what distinguishes "custody" from not being in custody). His confession was completely voluntary. As a result, he would not be entitled to a *Miranda* warning. Note that if the police wanted to question him *after* his confession and didn't want him to be free to leave—as they undoubtedly would have done—then they *would* have had to give him his *Miranda* warning. Even then, the volunteered confession given *before* the custodial interrogation would be admissible. Since A mistakenly states that the *Miranda* warning would be required at the beginning of the discussion, it's not the best response.

(B) is not the best response,

because it mischaracterizes the facts and arrives at the wrong result.

The right to counsel and due process were not violated by the interrogation because it was not a custodial interrogation, and as a result the *Miranda* warning was not required. An interrogation is "custodial" if the one being questioned believes he is not free to leave. Here, the friend voluntarily came to the station, and from these facts was free to leave. Since the friend was there voluntarily and *confessed* voluntarily, his right to counsel and due process were not violated. Since B doesn't recognize this, it's not the best response.

(D) is not the best response,

because although it arrives at the correct result, it misidentifies the friend's conduct as a *waiver* of his *Miranda* rights, which it isn't.

The issue of waiving one's *Miranda* rights only comes into being when the warning is required—i.e., the police are going to conduct a custodial interrogation. At *that* point, the suspect can only waive his rights if the waiver is done knowingly, intelligently, and voluntarily—and the burden is on the *prosecution* to prove that the waiver is valid.

Here, there *was* no custodial interrogation, the *Miranda* warning was not required, and so there's no issue of waiver. An interrogation is custodial only if the individual questioned is not free to leave. Here, the friend voluntarily went to the police station, and he volunteered his confession. Under these facts, there was no time when the friend was *not* free to leave. Thus, the *Miranda*-warning requirement was never "triggered." Since D doesn't recognize this, it's not the best response.

Answer 63

(C) is the best response,

because the inspections were allowed pursuant to a statute with reasonable requirements.

Businesses subject to extensive regulation may be subjected to warrantless, unannounced searches, at least where frequent unannounced inspections are the only effective way to enforce the regulatory requirements. *See, e.g., U.S. v. Biswell*, 406 U.S. 311 (1972) (warrantless inspections of weapons dealers are constitutional, because such dealers are subject to heavy regulations, which can only be enforced by "unannounced, even frequent, inspections.")

Of the various ways to achieve the aim of the statute (that is, deterring motor vehicle theft and trafficking in stolen motor vehicles), the state selected a relatively unintrusive means of inspection. All an owner would have to do is permit an inspector who showed up during normal business hours to take a physical inventory of the motor vehicles on the lot. Since the junkyard industry is a heavily regulated one, and the state has chosen a reasonably nonintrusive way of carrying out its regulation, no warrant was required.

(A) is not the best response,

because the statute has a reasonable inspection requirement.

No warrant was required, for the reason stated in the discussion of choice A. If the police had arbitrarily inspected the junkyard owner's business more often than others, or for improper purposes, the warrantless inspection here might nonetheless have been found to be an "unreasonable" Fourth Amendment search. But the facts say that officers periodically visit all junkyards in town, and give no hint that the junkyard owner is being singled out. Therefore, the inspection was reasonable even though warrantless.

(B) is not the best response,

because heavily regulated industries can be inspected without a warrant.

The motion should be denied because there is no indication that the statute was in anyway a pretext. In fact, the Supreme Court has stated that businesses administered by heavy regulations that can only be enforced by unannounced or frequent inspections are subject to warrantless searches.

(D) is not the best response,

because not all commercial establishments are subject to warrantless searches.

"Ordinary" businesses—ones not subject to unusually heavy governmental regulations—are not subject to warrantless inspections, any more than homes are. So this choice is far too broad.

Answer 64

(C) is the best response,

because it correctly identifies the constitutionally required prerequisite for a plea hearing, which is lacking in this case: that the defendant understand his right to a jury trial.

In order to ensure that a defendant's guilty plea is intelligent and voluntary, a judge is constitutionally required to confirm that the defendant understands the following: the nature of the charge, the maximum possible penalty and the mandatory minimum penalty for the offense and that he is waiving his right to a jury trial as a result of pleading guilty. Although the judge did ask the defendant whether he understood that he did not have to plead guilty, he did not specifically ask the defendant whether he was aware that he was waiving his right to a jury trial. Since C identifies that the plea bargain was constitutionally deficient for this reason, it is the best response.

(A) is not the best response,

because it misstates the law.

There is no constitutional requirement that a judge rule on outstanding motions before accepting a plea from a defendant. It may appear odd that the criminal did not wait for an order on the motion before deciding to plead guilty, but there is no constitutional duty on the judge's part requiring him to first decide the motion. Perhaps an argument could be made that the criminal's attorney did not provide him with effective counsel and should have advised him to wait for the ruling before pleading. However, that argument is irrelevant in light of the fact that there was a definite constitutional violation in that the judge did not determine whether the criminal understood that he had a right to a jury trial. Since A does not correctly identify the reason for setting aside the defendant's plea, it is not the best response.

(B) is not the best response,

because it misstates the law.

In order to ensure that a defendant's guilty plea is intelligent and voluntary, a judge is constitutionally required to confirm that the defendant understands the following: the nature of the charge, the maximum possible penalty and the mandatory minimum penalty for the offense, and that he is waiving his right to a jury trial as a result of pleading guilty. Additionally, federal courts and some state courts require that the judge inquire as to the factual basis for the plea in order to determine its accuracy. However, this is not constitutionally required (except in the case where the defendant testifies that he is innocent, but then pleads guilty for some other reason—e.g., to avoid a harsh sentence in case he is convicted). Since B erroneously states that the judge is constitutionally required to determine that the defendant actually committed the acts, it is not the best response.

(D) is not the best response,

because it incorrectly states the law.

The judge is not required to determine whether the prosecutor has failed to disclose any exculpatory material. The disclosure of exculpatory evidence is a constitutional requirement, the purpose of which is to guarantee a defendant a fair trial and which is relevant at the trial stage. Since D incorrectly states that this is a constitutional requirement at the plea bargaining stage, it is not the best response.

Answer 65

(A) is the best response,

because the rival farmer was not told he had the right to be silent.

When an individual is taken into custody by the authorities and is subjected to interrogation, he is entitled to a *Miranda* warning. When one deputy pinned the rival farmer's arms behind his back, the rival farmer was clearly in "custody" (he was not, and knew he was not, free to leave). When the other deputy demanded, "Tell us what you did with the missing farmer . . . " this was interrogation, since it was a demand for information. Therefore, the *Miranda* warning was required. Since it wasn't given, the rival farmer's response is inadmissible. (Had he been given the warning, he might have voluntarily waived his right to remain silent. But where the warning isn't given, the court will not find a waiver no matter how likely the court thinks it is that the subject would have waived his rights had he been told of them.)

(B) is not the best response,

because the entry and search of the farm was not illegal.

Had the entry and search of the farm been illegal, the rival farmer would indeed have had a good argument that his statement was the fruit of that illegality, and thus inadmissible. But the area the deputies entered was "open fields" not within the farmhouse's curtilage, so the rival farmer had no justifiable expectation of privacy in them (and no warrant was therefore required). Consequently, the deputies' entry was not a violation of the Fourth Amendment, and the fruit-of-the-poisonous-tree doctrine had no application.

In any event, the rival farmer's failure to receive a *Miranda* warning is (as described in the discussion of choice A above) the far more direct explanation of why the statement must be suppressed.

(C) is not the best response,

because there is no "hot pursuit" exception to the *Miranda* doctrine.

As the discussion of choice A above shows, the *Miranda* warning was required here. Choice C might be correct if there were a "hot pursuit" exception to the requirement of the *Miranda* warning, but there isn't. (There's a "public safety" exception, but that's not what the choice says, and the situation here didn't fall within that exception anyway).

It's true that there's a "hot pursuit" exception somewhere in criminal procedure, but it's an exception to the requirement of a search warrant. (If the police are chasing a suspect whom they have probable cause to arrest, and the suspect enters a dwelling, even his own, the police may follow and look for him in the premises without a warrant.) The exception has no relevance to the facts here (since you're asked about questioning, not searching).

(D) is not the best response,

because this was not the sort of emergency that triggers the "public safety" exception to the *Miranda* rule.

For the reasons described in the analysis of choice A above, the *Miranda* warning was required here.

It's true that there's a "public safety" exception to *Miranda*, announced in *N.Y. v. Quarles* (1984). But the doctrine applies only where unwarned questioning is dictated by "overriding considerations of public safety" (e.g., an attempt to find a weapon that may have been hidden nearby by the suspect). Here, after arresting the rival farmer, the police had plenty of time to check for the grave based on the tip they'd received (and no danger from delay in doing so), so there was no imminent need or public danger of the sort that triggers the public-safety exception.

Answer 66

(D) is the best response,

because authorities encouraged and offered to reward the second computer search.

Therefore, with regard to the second search, the woman was acting as a government agent and a warrant was required. Lacking a warrant, the second search violated the Fourth Amendment. On the other hand, the woman's first entry of the computer and copying of the file constituted an entirely private search and did not trigger Fourth Amendment protections, as she was not acting as a government agent. Accordingly, only the second set of photographs should be suppressed.

(A) is not the best response,

because authorities encouraged and offered to reward the second computer search.

Therefore, with regard to the second search, the woman was acting as a government agent and a warrant was required. Lacking a warrant, the second search violated the Fourth Amendment.

(B) is not the best response,

because the woman did not need to act with probable cause for the first search.

The first search was an entirely private search (the authorities did not encourage it or offer to reward her), and therefore it did not trigger the Fourth Amendment protections. Accordingly, the first photograph should not be suppressed.

(C) is not the best response,

because a private violation of this statute does not itself require suppression of the evidence. *United States v. Steiger,* 318 F.3d 1039 (11th Cir. 2003).

However, because authorities encouraged and offered to reward the second computer search, the woman was acting as a government agent with regard to that search, which did in fact violate the Fourth Amendment because it was conducted without a warrant. Accordingly, only the second set of photographs should be suppressed.

STRATEGIES AND TACTICS

EVIDENCE

When it comes to Evidence questions on the MBE, there's both good news and bad news. The good news is that these questions virtually always require a mechanical application of the Federal Rules of Evidence (the "FRE"); however, that's the source of the bad news as well—the FRE are intricate, so you have to be ***thoroughly*** familiar with them in order to answer MBE Evidence questions successfully. For all MBEs given in 2016 or later, the test assumes that the FRE as restyled in 2011 are in force.

OUTLINE OF COVERAGE

The following outline of coverage for the Evidence portion of the MBE was adopted by the Bar Examiners for all MBEs given on or after February 2016. It was designed to clarify what's covered on the Evidence portion of the exam. This is the most up-to-date outline of coverage released by the Bar Examiners, and your substantive study for Evidence should focus on it.

Here's what you need to know:

I. Presentation of evidence
   A. Introduction of evidence
      1. Requirement of personal knowledge
      2. Refreshing recollection
      3. Objections and offers of proof
      4. Lay opinions
      5. Competency of witnesses
      6. Judicial notice
      7. Roles of judge and jury
      8. Limited admissibility
   B. Presumptions
   C. Mode and order
      1. Control by court
      2. Scope of examination
      3. Form of questions
      4. Exclusion of witnesses
   D. Impeachment, contradiction, and rehabilitation
      1. Inconsistent statements and conduct
      2. Bias and interest
      3. Conviction of crime
      4. Specific instances of conduct
      5. Character for truthfulness
      6. Ability to observe, remember, or relate accurately
      7. Impeachment of hearsay declarants
      8. Rehabilitation of impeached witnesses
      9. Contradiction
   E. Proceedings to which evidence rules apply

II. Relevancy and reasons for excluding relevant evidence
   A. Probative value
      1. Relevancy
      2. Exclusion for unfair prejudice, confusion, or waste of time
   B. Authentication and identification
   C. Character and related concepts
      1. Admissibility of character
      2. Methods of proving character

        3. Habit and routine practice
        4. Other crimes, acts, transactions, and events
        5. Prior sexual misconduct of a defendant
    D. Expert testimony
        1. Qualifications of witnesses
        2. Bases of testimony
        3. Ultimate issue rule
        4. Reliability and relevancy
        5. Proper subject matter for expert testimony
    E. Real, demonstrative, and experimental evidence
III. Privileges and other policy exclusions
    A. Spousal immunity and marital communications
    B. Attorney-client and work product
    C. Physician/psychotherapist-patient
    D. Other privileges
    E. Insurance coverage
    F. Remedial measures
    G. Compromise, payment of medical expenses, and plea negotiations
    H. Past sexual conduct of a victim
IV. Writings, recordings, and photographs
    A. Requirement of original
    B. Summaries
    C. Completeness rule
V. Hearsay and circumstances of its admissibility
    A. Definition of hearsay
        1. What is hearsay
        2. Prior statements by witness
        3. Statements attributable to party-opponent
        4. Multiple hearsay
    B. Present sense impressions and excited utterances
    C. Statements of mental, emotional, or physical condition
    D. Statements for purposes of medical diagnosis and treatment
    E. Past recollection recorded
    F. Business records
    G. Public records and reports
    H. Learned treatises
    I. Former testimony; depositions
    J. Statements against interest
    K. Other exceptions to the hearsay rule
    L. Right to confront witnesses

WHAT TO EXPECT

You'll face 28 or 29 Evidence questions on the MBE (though only 27 will be scored, and you won't know which ones won't). Of these, approximately one-third will be based on category I (presentation of evidence), one-third on category V (hearsay), and one-third on categories II, III, and IV.

Evidence questions on the MBE virtually always consist of short, focused hypotheticals. Inevitably, the hypothetical will involve a piece of evidence or an item of testimony, and you will be asked to identify the basis on which the evidence will be found admissible or inadmissible.

STUDY STRATEGIES: DETAILS, DETAILS, DETAILS

Naturally, the Bar Examiners could test you on virtually any aspect of Evidence. Because they're interested in determining whether or not you're thoroughly familiar with Evidence law, they tend to test concepts that are particularly difficult—those that are tricky either because the concept tested involves a lot of elements (e.g., some of the hearsay exceptions) or because it has a misleading, seductive name (e.g., prior inconsistent statements, Best Evidence Rule). Although you should be fully prepared on every topic, pay particular attention to the following:

1. Study only the Federal Rules of Evidence.

The Multistate exam follows the Federal Rules of Evidence, ***not the common law.*** You absolutely must keep the differences between the two straight in your mind because this is a very easy area for the Bar Examiners to test. Look out for situations where the result under the FRE and the common law will be different. Here's an example:

> A plaintiff sued a defendant for $100,000 for injuries received in a traffic accident. The defendant charges the plaintiff with contributory negligence and alleges that the plaintiff failed to have his lights on at a time when it was dark enough to require them. The defendant offers to have a bystander testify that he was talking to the bystander's friend just before the crash, and heard the friend say in a matter-of-fact voice, "That car doesn't have any lights on." The friend has since died. The bystander's testimony is
>
> A. admissible as a statement of present sense impression.
> B. admissible, because the friend is not available to testify.
> C. inadmissible as hearsay, not within any exception.
> D. inadmissible, because of the Dead Man's Statute.

Under FRE 803(1), statements of present sense impression are admissible as an exception to the hearsay rule without regard to whether the declarant is available. (Thus, A is the correct response). If you remembered and applied the common law rule—that there's a hearsay exception for *excited utterances*, but that there is no separate exception for present sense impressions (and thus no exception for *un*excited statements of present perception, which is what happened here)—you'd choose choice C, and you'd be wrong.

While we're talking about hearsay, here's a simple rule to remember. If you aren't sure whether something is hearsay or not, ***try to identify the out-of-court declarant.*** Remember, hearsay is an out-of-court statement offered to prove the truth of its assertion. If it's a statement, it must have a declarant. If you can't identify one (e.g., the speaker of a comment, or the writer of a document), then the item can't be hearsay.

2. Know the requirements for the substantive use of prior inconsistent statements, prior consistent statements, and statements of identifications. (FRE 801(d)(1)).

Questions involving these three hearsay exclusions are extremely tricky, both because the exceptions are very technical and because their names may tempt you to apply them incorrectly. Here's an example:

> A defendant is tried for armed robbery of a bank.
>
> At the request of police, the teller who was robbed prepared a sketch bearing a strong likeness to the defendant, but the teller died in an automobile accident before the defendant was arrested. At trial the prosecution offers the sketch. The sketch is
>
> A. admissible as an identification of a person after perceiving him.
> B. admissible as a past recollection recorded.
> C. inadmissible as hearsay not within any exception.
> D. inadmissible as an opinion of the teller.

A is a tempting response, because the item in question is, indeed, what A says it is: an identification of a person after perceiving him. Watch out, though; that's ***not enough*** to make the prior identification admissible: To apply this exception, the declarant must also be a ***currently testifying witness,*** subject to cross-examination. According to the facts, the teller is dead, so this exception can't possibly apply. (The correct response is C.)

The one commonly-encountered factor that makes prior statements of these three types ***inadmissible*** is that ***the facts do not satisfy the "presently testifying witness" requirement,*** as illustrated by the example above; therefore, whenever an answer choice on the MBE mentions a prior identification, prior inconsistent statement, or prior consistent statement, you can eliminate common distractors easily by checking to see if the declarant is currently testifying. If he isn't, that answer can't possibly be correct!

In addition, with prior inconsistent statements, there's something else to keep in mind. Even if a prior inconsistent statement doesn't meet all the requirements for substantive admissibility under FRE 801(d)(1), it will always be available, as non-hearsay, to ***impeach or rehabilitate*** a witness (FRE 613(a)). MBE questions often require you to say whether a given piece of evidence is substantively admissible, admissible for impeachment, both or neither. And this is often true of questions involving prior inconsistent statements of a testifying witness.

For instance, suppose a teller was an eyewitness to a robbery, and gave an informal statement to the police one day later ("The robber had red hair.") At trial, the lawyer for the red-haired accused calls the teller, who testifies, "The robber had brown hair." The prosecution, in cross, asks the teller, "Didn't you tell the police that the robber had red hair?" This prior inconsistent statement is hearsay that is not substantively admissible (i.e., not admissible to prove that the robber actually had red hair), because a prior inconsistent statement is admissible under FRE 801(d)(1)(A)'s hearsay exclusion only if it was made "under *penalty of perjury* at a trial, hearing, or other *proceeding* or in a deposition," and the statement to the police here doesn't qualify. But the statement *is* admissible for the non-substantive purpose of *impeaching* the teller's credibility.

3. **Know the requirements of admissibility on items like authentication and expert testimony.**

You need to be familiar with the ***minimums required*** to admit documents, photographs, expert testimony, and the like. For instance, you should know that expert testimony is ***not*** needed to authenticate a photograph—all that's required is a person who saw the scene in question and can testify that the photograph ***fairly and accurately represents or illustrates*** what it's supposed to depict. (This rule is not explicitly set out in the FRE, but it follows from FRE 901(b)(1)'s general statement authorizing authentication by a "witness with knowledge" who testifies "that an item is what it is claimed to be.")

Likewise, expert testimony isn't required to authenticate a signature—anyone personally familiar with an individual's handwriting can testify as to its authenticity, as long as the familiarity was ***not acquired for the purposes of the litigation.*** FRE 901(b)(2). Of course, a graphologist ***could*** authenticate handwriting by comparing handwriting samples, without ***any*** personal familiarity with the individual's handwriting—but the expert testimony isn't necessary if a lay witness (who meets the above requirements) testifies.

Here's a sample question on authentication:

> In a trial between a plaintiff and defendant, an issue arose about the defendant's ownership of a horse, which had caused damage to the plaintiff's crops.
>
> The plaintiff seeks to introduce in evidence a photograph of his cornfield in order to depict the nature and extent of the damage done. The judge should rule the photograph
>
> A. admissible if the plaintiff testifies that it fairly and accurately portrays the condition of the cornfield after the damage was done.
> B. admissible if the plaintiff testifies that the photograph was taken within a week after the alleged occurrence.
> C. inadmissible if the plaintiff fails to call the photographer to testify concerning the circumstances under which the photograph was taken.
> D. inadmissible if it is possible to describe the damage to the cornfield through direct oral testimony.

The correct response is A. Under FRE 901(b)(1), quoted above, the plaintiff is certainly qualified to authenticate the photograph, because he is a "witness with knowledge," testifying that what is claimed to be an accurate photo of the damage caused to the cornfield is exactly that. The question tries to muddy the waters here, because the plaintiff, as the owner of the property, has reason to make the damage seem more extensive than it actually was; but the possibility of falsified evidence is an entirely unrelated matter, and does not bear on whether the photo has been adequately authenticated. Here, all that counts is that under FRE 901(b)(1), the plaintiff has adequately authenticated the photograph.

4. **Be thoroughly familiar with the Best Evidence Rule.**

It's important to know ***exactly*** what situations are covered by the Best Evidence Rule. Generally, the MBE contains relatively few questions to which the Best Evidence Rule actually applies; it is, however, a popular "distractor," because it ***sounds*** as though it applies to a far broader spectrum of situations than it ***actually*** does. Under the Best Evidence Rule, FRE 1002, ***where the material terms of a writing are at issue, the "original writing" itself*** (which under FRE 1001(e) and 1003 normally includes mechanical "duplicates," such as photocopies) ***must be produced. Non-mechanical copies and oral testimony concerning the writing's contents are permissible only on a showing that the original is unavailable and that its lack of availability is not the result of the proponent's serious misconduct.***

In simpler terms, this means there are really only ***two*** situations in which the Best Evidence Rule requires that the original document, if available, be introduced:

1. The terms of the writing are being proven; or
2. The witness is testifying relying on the writing.

Remember, this rule only applies to ***material terms.*** A common trap on the MBE is to offer a situation in which the witness is, in fact, testifying relying on a writing, but in which the ***subject of the testimony is only a collateral matter*** (so the Best Evidence Rule doesn't apply—see FRE 1004(d), making the BER inapplicable where "the writing . . . is not closely related to a controlling issue.") Here's an example:

> A consumer purchased a suit of thermal underwear manufactured by a defendant corporation from synthetic materials. While he was attempting to stamp out a fire, the consumer's' thermal underwear caught fire and burned in a melting fashion up to his waist. He suffered a heart attack a half hour later. In a suit against the defendant corporation, the consumer alleged that negligence and breach of warranty caused both the burn and the heart attack. The consumer testified to the foregoing.
>
> The consumer testified that his purchase of the underwear occurred on April 17th, a fact of minor importance in the case. He stated that he could identify the date because his secretary had taken the day off to attend the first game of the baseball season and he had checked his company's payroll records to verify the date. The defendant corporation moved to strike the testimony as to the date. The motion should be
>
> A. sustained, because the best evidence of the information contained in the payroll records is the records themselves.
> B. sustained, because the consumer's testimony is based upon hearsay declarations contained in the payroll records.
> C. overruled if the judge has personal knowledge of the date on which the baseball season opened.
> D. overruled, because the payroll records relate to a collateral matter.

A is a tempting choice, because the consumer *is* testifying relying on the payroll records. Note, however, that the Best Evidence Rule only applies when the writing is "closely related to a controlling issue." Here, the only purpose the payroll records served was to ***bolster the consumer's memory on a "fact of minor importance"***; they have no other effect on the case. Therefore, A is not the best choice. The best response is choice D—the payroll records themselves needn't be offered, because they relate to a collateral matter.

EXAM TACTICS

1. Break the question down to its theoretical basis.

On Evidence questions, it is vitally important that you analyze questions both logically and theoretically, because Evidence law is frequently counterintuitive. Your instinct may tell you that a piece of evidence should be inadmissible, whereas in fact, under the Federal Rules, it ***is*** admissible. The reverse is also true—you may believe in your heart that a piece of evidence should be admitted, but, according to the FRE, it's inadmissible hearsay. To avoid being misled, when you read an Evidence question, you should always ask yourself: What in theory is going on here? Here's an example:

> A defendant is tried for armed robbery of a bank.
>
> The defendant testifies on his own behalf. On cross-examination of the defendant, the prosecutor asks the defendant whether he was convicted in the previous year of tax fraud. This question is
>
> A. proper to show that the defendant is inclined to lie.
> B. proper to show that the defendant is inclined to steal money.
> C. improper, because the conviction has insufficient similarity to the crime charged.
> D. improper, because the probative value of the evidence is outweighed by the danger of unfair prejudice.

If you break this question down to what's happening ***theoretically and logically***, you can see that the prosecutor is attempting to impeach a witness with evidence from the witness's own mouth—in other words, "intrinsic" impeachment. He's attempting to do so by using a recent, prior conviction for a crime involving dishonesty.

Your instinct will probably tell you that this evidence should not be admissible, because, regardless of the purpose for which it is ***intended***, we all know what the jury is likely to do with it—they're going to take it as evidence that the defendant is inclined to steal money. Your instinct will be even stronger in this instance, because the witness is the criminal defendant himself. The inference the prosecution is likely hoping for is that these prior, unrelated acts show the defendant's character for stealing money; but if you analyze the facts coldly and theoretically, you should realize that the prosecutor's question is a proper form of intrinsic impeachment of the defendant's character for truthfulness, under FRE 609(a), because the conviction isn't more than ten years old and is for a crime involving dishonesty or false statement (whether a felony or a misdemeanor).

If, therefore, you set aside your emotional reaction and analyze the answer choices logically, you'll find that A is the correct answer, because the prior conviction is being used to impeach the defendant; it's being used to attack his credibility—in other words, to show that he's inclined to lie. That's what choice A says, and it's the correct answer. (By the way, even with a "cold" analysis of the facts, you might still consider D as a potentially correct answer, because the Rule 403 balancing of prejudicial effect against probative value is usually not a choice you can dismiss out of hand. In this question, though, the balancing is not a problem, because the evidence doesn't have the "shocking" quality of evidence normally excluded on this ground: The probative value of a tax fraud conviction is unlikely to be substantially outweighed by the probability of undue prejudice. Issues of legal relevance generally arise in instances of shocking evidence, such as severed limbs, gruesome photos, and the like.)

Here's another example:

> In a tort action, the plaintiff's witness testified against the defendant. The defendant then called a witness, who testified that the plaintiff's witness had a bad reputation for veracity. The defendant then also called a second witness to testify that the plaintiff's witness once perpetrated a hoax on the police.
>
> The testimony of the defendant's second witness is
>
> A. admissible, provided that the hoax involved untruthfulness.
> B. admissible, provided that the hoax resulted in conviction of the plaintiff's witness.
> C. inadmissible, because it is merely cumulative impeachment.
> D. inadmissible, because it is extrinsic evidence of a specific instance of misconduct.

Reading this question, you should first identify what's going on: The plaintiff's witness is being impeached with *extrinsic* evidence (i.e., not from his own mouth) about an unconvicted bad act; such impeachment is *in*admissible—evidence of unconvicted bad acts must be intrinsic in order to be valid. FRE 608(b). So the correct answer is D. This example shows that in impeachment scenarios, if you categorize the method being used before you try to answer, you'll save time and improve your chances of answering correctly.

2. **Eliminate answer choices that don't apply to the facts.**

As with all MBE questions, you should attack questions by eliminating the wrong choices until you're left with only one, the correct choice. In some Evidence questions, the Bar Examiners have made this even easier for you because ***some answer choices don't even apply to the facts.*** Any answer choice that doesn't apply to the facts in the question ***can't*** be the correct response! Here's an example:

> An issue in a plaintiff's action against a defendant for causing the plaintiff's back injury was whether the plaintiff's condition had resulted principally from a similar occurrence five years before, with which the defendant had no connection.
>
> The plaintiff called his treating physician, who offered to testify that when she saw the plaintiff after the latest occurrence, the plaintiff told her that before the accident he had been working full time, without pain or limitation of motion, in a job that required lifting heavy boxes.
>
> The physician's testimony should be
>
> A. admitted, because it is a statement of the plaintiff's then existing physical condition.
> B. admitted, because it is a statement made for purposes of medical diagnosis or treatment.
> C. excluded, because it is hearsay not within any exception.
> D. excluded, because the plaintiff is available as a witness.

A is an example of an answer choice that doesn't apply to the facts. In talking to his physician, the plaintiff was describing his condition ***before*** the latest occurrence, not his condition as it existed at the time of the physical exam, which is what A suggests. Because A ***misstates*** the facts, it cannot be correct! (In fact, the correct response is B.)

Making such a mistake is inexcusable, because the question itself provides you with all the grounds you need to eliminate the incorrect choice. Here's another example:

> A bus passenger sued a bus company for injuries to his back from an accident caused by the bus company's negligence. The bus company denies that the bus passenger received any injury in the accident.
>
> The bus passenger's counsel seeks to introduce an affidavit he obtained in preparation for trial from a doctor who has since died. The affidavit avers that the doctor examined the bus passenger two days after the bus company's accident and found him suffering from a recently incurred back injury. The judge should rule the affidavit
>
> A. admissible as a statement of present bodily condition made to a physician.
> B. admissible as prior recorded testimony.
> C. inadmissible, because it is irrelevant.
> D. inadmissible, because it is hearsay, not within any exception.

Here, choice A can't possibly be correct, because the facts indicate the statement was that of the doctor, not that of the bus passenger, so the statement *can't* be "a statement of present bodily condition made to a physician"! Because A doesn't correctly characterize the facts, it cannot be the correct response, and you should eliminate it immediately. (The best response is D.)

3. Know the doctrine of limited admissibility.

For some MBE questions, it's not enough to know that a piece of evidence is admissible; you must also know ***for what purposes*** it's admissible. A common trap in MBE questions is to make you forget that evidence may be admissible for one purpose (which is given in one of the answers) and not for another (which is given in another answer choice). You may be tricked into choosing a wrong answer if you realize that an answer choice contains a correct rule, and so choose that answer. If the rule ***isn't applicable to the facts,*** you'll be wrong—needlessly wrong.

Here's an example:

> A victim was held up at the point of a gun, an unusual revolver with a red-painted barrel, while she was clerking in a neighborhood grocery store. The defendant is charged with armed robbery of the victim.
>
> The prosecutor calls a witness to testify that, a week after the robbery of the victim, he was robbed by the defendant with a pistol that had red paint on the barrel. The witness's testimony is
>
> A. admissible as establishing an identifying circumstance.
> B. admissible as showing that the defendant was willing to commit robbery.
> C. inadmissible, because it is improper character evidence.
> D. inadmissible, because its probative value is substantially outweighed by the danger of unfair prejudice.

Here, the evidence being offered will establish an identifying circumstance—that makes what would otherwise be inadmissible character evidence into admissible evidence. If it were offered only to show the defendant is willing to commit robbery, it would be inadmissible, but, here, it's offered to help identify the defendant. Thus, applying the doctrine of limited admissibility, A is the correct response—not C.

Here's another example:

> In a plaintiff's negligence action against a defendant arising out of a multiple-car collision, a witness testified for the plaintiff that the defendant went through a red light. On cross-examination, the defendant seeks to question the witness about her statement that the light was yellow, made in a deposition that the witness gave in a separate action between different parties. The transcript of the deposition is self-authenticating. On proper objection, the court should rule the inquiry
>
> A. admissible for impeachment only.
> B. admissible as substantive evidence only.
> C. admissible for impeachment and as substantive evidence.
> D. inadmissible, because it is hearsay not within any exception.

Here, the statement in the witness's deposition will be covered by FRE 801(d)(1)(A), giving a hearsay exclusion for inconsistent prior statements where "The declarant testifies and is subject to cross examination about a prior statement, and the statement: (A) is *inconsistent* with the declarant's testimony and was given under penalty of perjury at a trial, hearing, or other proceeding *or in a deposition*." Because the statement falls within an exclusion from the hearsay rule, it is available ***both*** for impeachment ***and*** as substantive evidence. It wouldn't be enough to know that the deposition will be admissible as a "prior inconsistent statement"; you'd need to know that when such testimony is admissible under FRE 801(d)(1), it's admissible for *both* impeachment purposes and as substantive evidence (to prove that the light really was yellow)!

4. Dealing with common answer choices to Evidence questions.

A. "The testimony is inadmissible due to its self-serving nature."

This is a relatively common distractor (a "distractor" is MBE-lingo for a "wrong choice.") Whenever you see a choice like this, it's ***incorrect,*** regardless of the facts. The self-serving nature of the testimony affects its ***credibility,*** not its ***admissibility.***

B. "Admissible as *res gestae*" or "Inadmissible as testimony on ultimate issues."

These alternatives, especially *res gestae*, are common distractors on the MBE. ***Don't choose old rules like these.*** *Res gestae*, for instance, is a common law concept that dealt with hearsay exceptions that are now covered, under the FRE, by declarations of present bodily condition, declarations of present state of mind, excited utterances, and declarations of present sense impression. The hearsay exceptions under the FRE are far more precise than the old *res gestae* concept. The same goes for testimony on ultimate issues. "Testimony on ultimate issues" is a limitation that is not recognized under the FRE. Remember, the MBE is concerned with the present state of the law. Don't clutter up your already overtaxed memory by learning fine points of outmoded concepts, which will show up only as "distractors."

C. "Inadmissible because the declarant is available to testify."

This is a relatively common answer choice in questions dealing with hearsay. Although it ***can*** be correct, because a few hearsay exceptions do require that the declarant be unavailable, ***for the majority of hearsay exceptions, unavailability is not required.*** The hallmark of the hearsay exceptions under the FRE is ***trustworthiness,*** not unavailability. (The hearsay exceptions that ***do*** require unavailability are found in FRE 804; they include ***prior testimony, dying declarations, declarations against interest,*** and ***statements of pedigree.***)

D. "Inadmissible because the probative value of the evidence is substantially outweighed by the probability of undue prejudice."

FRE 403 indeed gives this as a ground for excluding otherwise-relevant evidence. On the MBE, this 403 balancing-test is a ***wild card***—sometimes it's the best choice, and sometimes it's not. The best thing you can do is to keep in mind the type of evidence typically excluded under FRE 403: ***shocking*** evidence. Imagine yourself as a juror and decide whether or not the evidence would jolt your mind. Here's an example:

> A defendant is tried for armed robbery of a bank.
>
> The prosecution, in its case in chief, offers evidence that when the defendant was arrested one day after the crime, he had a quantity of heroin and a hypodermic needle in his possession. This evidence should be
>
> A. admitted to prove the defendant's motive to commit the crime.
> B. admitted to prove the defendant's propensity to commit crimes.
> C. excluded, because its probative value is substantially outweighed by the danger of unfair prejudice.
> D. excluded, because such evidence may be offered only to rebut evidence of good character offered by defendant.

The correct answer is C—the evidence will be excluded, because it will be given unfairly great weight by the jury. Wouldn't you tend to give it more weight than it deserves, if you were a juror? An important point to remember is that, but for the unfair-prejudice problem, the evidence would be admissible, because it would tend to prove the defendant's motive to commit the crime (choice A). But the evidence is only very weakly probative on the issue of motive for the robbery. However, it's relatively rare on the MBE for FRE 403 unfair prejudice to be the correct answer (as it is in the above example).

E. "Inadmissible because it is hearsay not within any exception."

As with the "legal relevance" answer choice in item D, above, the "inadmissible" choice is one that can go either way. There is a way, however, to increase your chances of answering a question successfully when one of the choices is the "inadmissible" choice:

Overcome your natural instinct to conclude that every piece of evidence is somehow admissible.

What the answer choice is ***really*** saying when it says ***"inadmissible as hearsay not within any exception"*** is "inadmissible under any other answer choice for this question." If you read it this way, it becomes obvious that ***the only way to arrive at the "inadmissible" answer choice is through a process of elimination.*** In fact, questions in which the "inadmissible" choice is the correct one tend to be more "cut and dried" than other Evidence questions, because, for "inadmissible" to be the correct choice, the other three alternatives must be clearly wrong. Here's an example:

> A defendant is tried for armed robbery of a bank.
>
> At the request of police, the teller who was robbed prepared a sketch bearing a strong likeness to the defendant, but the teller died in an automobile accident before the defendant was arrested. At trial the prosecution offers the sketch. The sketch is
>
> A. admissible as an identification of a person after perceiving him.
> B. admissible as past recollection recorded.
> C. inadmissible as hearsay not within any exception.
> D. inadmissible as an opinion of the teller.

The correct answer here is C. This is a good example of an "inadmissible hearsay" question, because your gut reaction on reading these facts is that ***the judge would find a way to admit the sketch.*** Maybe the judge would, but not on any of these grounds. The sketch clearly does not fit any of the answers other than C! It can't be choice A, because, as stated earlier (See "Study Strategies," #2), a prior identification is only admissible when the declarant is testifying. Similarly, choice B, for past recollection recorded, is only applicable if there is a live "sponsoring witness" who testifies about having made the record or supplied the information from which it was made. Choice D is not applicable, because lay testimony by the teller would not necessarily be inadmissible even though it was an opinion (but the teller/preparer would have to be giving live testimony as to that opinion). That leaves only C, which ***must,*** therefore, be the correct response.

F. Avoid any answer choice stating a concept you don't recognize.

If you've prepared sufficiently for the MBE, you will not come across any correct answer choices that mention concepts you don't recognize at all. The Bar Examiners are exceptionally skillful at making nonsense concepts sound like the real thing, and these can prove a tempting trap for the unwary. Here's an example:

A plaintiff was injured when his car was struck by a truck owned by the defendant corporation.

The plaintiff's counsel proffers evidence showing that shortly after the accident the defendant corporation put a speed governor on the truck involved in the accident. The judge should rule the proffered evidence

A. admissible as an admission of a party.
B. admissible as *res gestae.*
C. inadmissible for public policy reasons.
D. inadmissible, because it would lead to the drawing of an inference on an inference.

Choice D here doesn't sound familiar to you, does it? It shouldn't—there's no such legal principle. It ***sounds*** like a legal principle, but it isn't one. The only way you'd choose an answer choice like this was if you weren't sufficiently prepared for the MBE. If you feel you've prepared adequately, there shouldn't be any unfamiliar concepts in correct answer choices. (By the way, the correct response here is C—subsequent remedial measures cannot be admitted to prove negligence or wrongdoing, due to public policy reasons.)

This question also illustrates two of the principles we addressed earlier: One, *res gestae* is never the correct response; two, you need to be familiar with rationales as well as the rules themselves. As to this second point, notice that the correct choice, C, only ***implies*** that the rule excluding evidence of subsequent remedial measures is involved, it doesn't explicitly mention the key words "subsequent remedial measures" (because that would tip you off, and make the problem too easy). So be prepared to recognize that a given doctrine supplies the solution, even if that doctrine isn't expressly mentioned anywhere in the stem or the answer choices.

G. Avoid any answer choice that would exclude testimony because of witness incompetence.

The FRE are extremely liberal concerning competence. In fact, there are only two requirements: The witness must have personal knowledge of the matter on which he will testify (FRE 602), and he must declare that he will testify truthfully, by oath or affirmation (FRE 603). Also, whenever you see "incompetence" as a possibility on the MBE, be careful not to confuse it with ***bias***—that's ***normally*** what's at issue when competence is raised as a possibility. Here's an example:

A defendant was tried for the July 21 murder of a victim. The defendant called a witness to testify to alibi. On cross-examination of the witness, the prosecution asked, "Isn't it a fact that you are the defendant's first cousin?" The question is

A. proper, because it goes to bias.
B. proper, because a relative is not competent to give reputation testimony.
C. improper, because the question goes beyond the scope of direct examination.
D. improper, because the evidence being sought is irrelevant.

Choice B is incorrect, because only the witness's lack of personal knowledge, or his refusal to declare by oath or affirmation that he will testify truthfully, can be sources of incompetence. (The correct answer is A, because the familial relationship tends to show the witness's bias, and is therefore a proper subject of cross-examination.)

H. How to handle any answer choice dealing with expert testimony.

You should remember the liberal bases on which expert testimony can rely. Under FRE 703 and 705, an expert may testify on three types of information: personal observation, facts presented to the expert at trial (e.g., answering a hypothetical question), or facts introduced to the expert outside the courtroom (e.g., by technicians or consultants) of the type upon which experts in his field reasonably rely. An expert may base his opinion on facts not in evidence and even on facts that could not be admitted as evidence because they're inadmissible hearsay. Thus, when you come across a question on expert testimony, look closely before you decide the testimony is inadmissible. Here's an example:

> A defendant was indicted for the murder of a victim by poison. At trial, the prosecutor calls the county coroner who is a board-certified pathologist, to testify that, in accord with good practice in her specialty, she has studied microphotographic slides, made under her supervision by medical assistants, of tissue taken from the victim's corpse and that it is the coroner's opinion, based on that study, that the victim died of poisoning. The slides have not been offered in evidence. The coroner's opinion should be
>
> A. excluded, because the cause of death is a critical issue to be decided by the trier of fact.
> B. excluded, because her opinion is based on facts not in evidence.
> C. admitted, because the coroner followed accepted medical practice in arriving at her opinion.
> D. admitted, because her opinion is based on matters observed pursuant to a duty imposed by law.

Here, C is the best response, because, under the test stated above, C correctly identifies that the expert testimony was based on a suitable source. Any time you face an "expert testimony" question, it pays to keep in mind how broad the realm is on which an expert may rely.

I. How to handle answer choices dealing with admissions in conjunction with offers to settle or offers to pay medical bills.

When you enter the world of admissions in relation to offers to pay medical bills and offers of compromise, you've opened a real can of worms. The FRE and the common law overlap to a small extent, and there are four different possibilities for each. Also, the rationale for excluding some of these admissions and admitting others is not at all obvious. The four possibilities under the FRE are: offers and payment of settlements themselves (FRE 408), admissions in conjunctions with an offer to pay a settlement (also FRE 408), offers and payment of medical bills (FRE 409), and admissions in conjunction with an offer to pay medical bills (not excluded or otherwise mentioned in the FRE).

Of these four, all are *in*admissible ***except*** admissions in conjunction with an offer to pay medical bills. If you remember a simple word picture, you can easily memorize this rule. First, notice that the payment of settlements or of medical bills, as well as offers to pay, are always inadmissible. Thus, it's only the admissions that you have to worry about: Admissions with medical bills are admissible, whereas admissions with settlements are not. Here's a simple way to remember that: Picture, in your mind, a settlement of some sort—an Indian settlement, pilgrims, whatever is easiest for you to picture. Then, picture a big, red plastic "X" laid over the settlement; it's so big the settlers are tripping over it. This should remind you that admissions in conjunction with settlements are not admissible, and, by process of elimination, that admissions in connection with medical bills ***are.*** This distinction is obviously one that does not come up on every MBE, but if it does, you'll be prepared for it!

QUESTIONS

EVIDENCE

QUESTIONS

EVIDENCE

Question 1

A defendant is being tried for the murder of a woman who disappeared 10 years ago and has not been heard from since. Her body has never been found. The prosecutor has presented strong circumstantial evidence that she was murdered by the defendant. To help establish the fact of her death, the prosecutor has requested that the judge give the following instruction, based on a recognized presumption in the jurisdiction: "A person missing and not heard from in the last seven years shall be presumed to be deceased."

Is the instruction proper?

(A) No, because the fact that someone has not been heard from in seven years does not necessarily lead to a conclusion that the person is dead.

(B) No, because mandatory presumptions are not allowed against a criminal defendant on an element of the charged crime.

(C) Yes, because it expresses a rational conclusion that the jury should be required to accept.

(D) Yes, because the defendant has a chance to rebut the presumption by offering evidence that the woman is alive or has been heard from in the last seven years.

Question 2

Several defendants, senior executives of a corporation, were charged with securities fraud. The government called as a witness another executive of the corporation, who had not been charged and who had been given immunity from prosecution, to authenticate handwritten notes that she had made after meetings of the corporation's management team at which the alleged fraud was discussed. The witness testified that she had prepared the notes on her own initiative to help her remember what had happened at the meetings. After this testimony, the government offered the notes into evidence to establish what had happened at the meetings.

Should the witness's notes be admitted?

(A) No, because the notes are hearsay not within any exception.

(B) No, because the witness's immunity agreement with the government makes her notes untrustworthy and thus substantially more prejudicial than probative.

(C) Yes, because they are business records.

(D) Yes, because they are past recollections recorded.

Question 3 

A plaintiff sued a defendant, alleging that she was seriously injured when the defendant ran a red light and struck her while she was walking in a crosswalk. During the defendant's case, a witness testified that the plaintiff had told him that she was "barely touched" by the defendant's car.

On cross-examination, should the court allow the plaintiff to elicit from the witness the fact that he is an adjuster for the defendant's insurance company?

(A) No, because testimony about liability insurance is barred by the rules of evidence.

(B) No, because the reference to insurance raises a collateral issue.

(C) Yes, for both substantive and impeachment purposes.

(D) Yes, for impeachment purposes only.

Question 4

A defendant was charged with the crime of defrauding the federal agency where he worked as an accountant. At trial, the court allowed the defendant to call his supervisor at the large corporation where he had previously worked, who testified about the defendant's good reputation in the community for honesty. Over objection, the defendant then sought to elicit testimony from his former supervisor that on several occasions the corporation had, without incident, entrusted him with large sums of money.

Should the testimony be admitted?

(A) No, because the testimony is extrinsic evidence on a collateral matter.

(B) No, because good character cannot be proved by specific instances of conduct unless character is an essential element of the charge or defense.

(C) Yes, because it is evidence of a pertinent character trait offered by an accused.

(D) Yes, because it is relevant to whether the defendant was likely to have taken money as charged in this case.

Question 5

A plaintiff sued his insurance company for the proceeds of a casualty insurance policy covering his 60-foot yacht, claiming that the yacht was destroyed by an accidental fire. The company denied liability, claiming that the plaintiff hired his friend to set the fire. In the hospital the day after the fire, the friend, who had been badly burned in the fire, said to his wife, in the presence of an attending nurse, "I was paid to set the fire." Two weeks later, the friend died of an infection resulting from the burns. At trial, the insurance company called the wife to testify to the friend's statement.

Is the wife's testimony admissible over the plaintiff's objection?

(A) No, because the marital privilege survives the communicating spouse's death.

(B) No, because the statement was made after the conspiracy ended.

(C) Yes, because it is a statement against interest.

(D) Yes, because it is a statement by a co-conspirator.

Question 6

A defendant was charged with possession of marijuana with intent to distribute. On direct examination, the defendant testified that he worked with disadvantaged children as a drug counselor, that he hated drugs, that he would "never possess or distribute drugs," and that he had never used drugs and would not touch them. The government offered as a rebuttal witness a police officer who would testify that, three years earlier, he saw the defendant buy cocaine from a street dealer. The defendant objected.

Is the testimony of the police officer about the prior drug transaction admissible to impeach the defendant?

(A) No, because the bad act of buying drugs is not sufficiently probative of a witness's character for truthfulness.

(B) No, because it is contradiction on a collateral matter.

(C) Yes, because it is proper contradiction.

(D) Yes, because the bad act shows a disregard for the law and makes it less likely that the defendant would respect the oath of truthfulness.

Question 7

A woman sued her friend for injuries she received as a passenger in the friend's car. On direct examination, the woman testified that the friend had been speeding and ran a red light. On cross-examination, the woman was asked whether she was under the influence of drugs at the time of the accident. The woman invoked the privilege against self-incrimination.

How should the court treat the woman's claim of privilege?

(A) Deny it, because the woman waived the privilege by voluntarily testifying.

(B) Deny it, because evidence of the woman's drug intoxication is essential to assessing the accuracy of her observations.

(C) Uphold it, because the privilege applies in both civil and criminal cases.

(D) Uphold it, because the woman's credibility cannot be impeached by a crime for which she has not been convicted.

Question 8

A consumer has sued the manufacturer of a microwave oven for burn injuries allegedly caused by the manufacturer's negligent failure to warn purchasers of the dangers of heating foods in certain types of containers. The consumer has offered into evidence three letters, all received by the manufacturer before the oven was shipped to the consumer, in which customers had complained of serious burns under circumstances similar to those in the consumer's case. The manufacturer has objected to the letters on the grounds of hearsay and, in the alternative, has asked for a limiting instruction directing that the letters be considered not for the truth of the assertions contained in them but only regarding the issue of notice.

How should the court respond?

(A) The court should sustain the objection and treat the request for a limiting instruction as moot.

(B) The court should overrule the objection and deny the request for a limiting instruction.

(C) The court should overrule the objection and give the limiting instruction.

(D) The court should overrule the objection but allow only that the letters be read to the jury, not received as exhibits.

Question 9

A plaintiff sued for injuries arising from a car accident, claiming a back injury. At trial, she wishes to testify that prior to the accident she had never had any problems with her back.

Is the plaintiff's proposed testimony admissible?

(A) No, because the plaintiff has not been qualified as an expert.

(B) No, because the plaintiff's pain could have been caused by factors arising after the accident, such as an injury at work.

(C) Yes, because it is probative evidence of the plaintiff's injury.

(D) Yes, because the testimony of parties is not subject to the lay opinion rule.

Question 10

A plaintiff, who had been injured in an automobile collision with the defendant, sued the defendant for damages. The defendant denied negligence and denied that the plaintiff's injuries were severe. At trial, the plaintiff has offered in evidence a color photograph of himself made from a videotape taken by a television news crew at the scene of the collision. The plaintiff has demonstrated that the videotape has since been routinely reused by the television station and that the footage of the plaintiff was erased. The photograph shows the plaintiff moments after the collision, with his bloodied head protruding at a grotesque angle through the broken windshield of his car.

Should the photograph be admitted over the defendant's objection?

(A) No, because the plaintiff has failed to establish that a duplicate could not be found.

(B) No, because the plaintiff has failed to produce the original videotape or a duplicate.

(C) Yes, because it tends to prove a controverted fact.

(D) Yes, because a photograph that establishes a disputed fact cannot be excluded as prejudicial.

Question 11

A cyclist sued a defendant corporation for injuries sustained when she was hit by a truck owned by the defendant and driven by its employee, who was making deliveries for the defendant. The day after the accident, the employee visited the cyclist in the hospital and said, "I'm sorry for what I did." At trial, the employee testified that he had exercised due care.

Why is the cyclist's testimony relating what the defendant's employee said at the hospital admissible to prove negligence?

(A) It is a prior inconsistent statement.

(B) It is a statement against interest.

(C) It is a statement by a party-opponent's agent.

(D) It is a statement of then-existing state of mind.

Question 12

A defendant is on trial for bank robbery. Evidence at the trial has included testimony by a bank teller who was present during the robbery. The teller testified for the prosecution after having refreshed her memory by looking at an FBI agent's investigative report that was created shortly after the robbery. The defendant has asked to examine the report.

How should the court respond?

(A) The court may allow the examination if the report was used by the teller to refresh her memory before testifying, and must allow it if she used it during her testimony.

(B) The court must allow the examination, but only to the extent that the report contains the teller's own statement to the FBI agent.

(C) The court should not allow the examination, unless the report was used by the teller to refresh her memory while on the witness stand.

(D) The court should not allow the examination, because the report was not shown to have been read and approved by the teller while the matter was fresh in her mind.

Question 13

A patient sued a hospital for medical negligence, claiming that a nurse employed by the hospital failed to administer critical medication prescribed by the patient's treating physician during the plaintiff's hospitalization. To prove the nurse's failure to administer the prescribed medication, the patient called the medical records librarian, who authenticated the hospital's record of the patient's treatment, which contained no entry showing that the medication in question had been administered.

Is the hospital record admissible?

(A) No, because it is hearsay not within any exception.

(B) No, because the nurse's testimony would be the best evidence of her actions in treating the plaintiff.

(C) Yes, although hearsay, because it is a statement against interest by agents of the hospital.

(D) Yes, because it is within the hearsay exception covering the absence of entries in business records.

Question 14

A college student sued an amusement company for injuries he sustained when the amusement company's roller coaster allegedly malfunctioned so that the student fell out. At trial, after the student presented his case, the amusement company called a witness who testified that just before the accident he heard a bystander say to the bystander's companion, "That crazy fool is standing up in the car."

The student then offered the testimony of another witness who would testify that the day after the accident she was with the same bystander, and that in describing the accident, the bystander told her that the car jerked suddenly and "just threw the guy out of his seat."

How should the court rule with respect to this offered testimony?

(A) Rule it admissible only to impeach the bystander's credibility.

(B) Rule it admissible to impeach the bystander's credibility and to prove the amusement company's negligence.

(C) Rule it inadmissible, because the bystander was given no opportunity to deny or explain her apparently inconsistent statement.

(D) Rule it inadmissible, because the bystander herself was not called as a witness.

Question 15

A defendant was charged with robbery of a savings and loan branch after being arrested near the scene and found with marked bills. An hour after the robbery, the officer investigating the crime videotaped an interview with an eyewitness, in which the eyewitness described the crime and the robber. The officer then arranged for a lineup, at which the teller who was robbed identified the defendant as the robber. The officer later obtained computerized records of that day's deposits and withdrawals at the savings and loan, which allowed the calculation of how much cash was taken in the robbery. A month later, the teller testified before a grand jury, which indicted the defendant. The teller and the eyewitness both died of unrelated causes shortly afterward.

At trial, which of the following evidence, if properly authenticated, may properly be admitted against the defendant over his attorney's objection that its receipt would violate the confrontation clause?

(A) A transcript of the teller's sworn grand jury testimony.
(B) The computerized records from the savings and loan.
(C) The officer's testimony that the teller picked the defendant out of the lineup as the robber.
(D) The videotape of the eyewitness's statement.

Question 16

A defendant is being prosecuted for conspiracy to possess with intent to distribute cocaine. At trial, the government seeks to have its agent testify to a conversation that he overheard between the defendant and a co-conspirator regarding the incoming shipment of a large quantity of cocaine. That conversation was also audiotaped, though critical portions of it are inaudible. The defendant objects to the testimony of the agent on the ground that it is not the best evidence of the conversation.

Is the testimony admissible?

(A) No, because the testimony of the agent is not the best evidence of the conversation.
(B) No, because the testimony of the agent reports hearsay not within any exception.
(C) Yes, because the best evidence rule does not require proof of the conversation through the audiotape.
(D) Yes, because the audiotape is partly inaudible.

Question 17

A plaintiff sued his employer for illegal discrimination, claiming that the employer fired him because of his race. At trial, the plaintiff called a witness, expecting him to testify that the employer had admitted the racial motivation. Instead, the witness testified that the employer said that he had fired the plaintiff because of his frequent absenteeism. While the witness is still on the stand, the plaintiff offers a properly authenticated secret tape recording he had made at a meeting with the witness in which the witness related the employer's admissions of racial motivation.

The tape recording is

(A) admissible as evidence of the employer's racial motivation and to impeach the witness's testimony.
(B) admissible only to impeach the witness's testimony.
(C) inadmissible, because it is hearsay not within any exception.
(D) inadmissible, because a secret recording is an invasion of the witness's right of privacy under the U.S. Constitution.

Question 18

At a defendant's trial for burglary, a witness supported the defendant's alibi that they were fishing together at the time of the crime. On cross-examination, the witness was asked whether his statement on a credit card application that he had worked for his present employer for the last five years was false. The witness denied that the statement was false.

The prosecutor then calls the manager of the company for which the witness works, to testify that although the witness had been first employed five years earlier and is now employed by the company, there had been a three-year period during which he had not been so employed. The testimony of the manager is

(A) admissible, in the judge's discretion, because the witness's credibility is a fact of major consequence to the case.
(B) admissible, as a matter of right, because the witness "opened the door" by his denial on cross-examination.
(C) inadmissible, because whether the witness lied in his application is a matter that cannot be proved by extrinsic evidence.
(D) inadmissible, because the misstatement by the witness could have been caused by misunderstanding of the application form.

Question 19

A defendant was charged with attempted murder of a victim in a sniping incident in which the defendant allegedly shot at the victim from ambush as the victim drove his car along an expressway. The prosecutor offers evidence that seven years earlier the defendant had fired a shotgun into a woman's home and that the defendant had once pointed a handgun at another driver while driving on the street.

This evidence should be

(A) excluded, because such evidence can be elicited only during cross-examination.
(B) excluded, because it is improper character evidence.
(C) admitted as evidence of the defendant's propensity toward violence.
(D) admitted as relevant evidence of the defendant's identity, plan, or motive.

Question 20

In a federal investigation of a defendant for tax fraud, the grand jury seeks to obtain a letter written January 15 by the defendant to her attorney in which she stated: "Please prepare a deed giving my ranch to the local university but, in order to get around the tax law, I want it back-dated to December 15." The attorney refuses to produce the letter on the ground of privilege.

Production of the letter should be

(A) prohibited, because the statement is protected by the attorney-client privilege.
(B) prohibited, because the statement is protected by the client's privilege against self-incrimination.
(C) required, because the statement was in furtherance of crime or fraud.
(D) required, because the attorney-client privilege belongs to the client and can be claimed only by her.

Question 21

A plaintiff sued a defendant auto manufacturer for his wife's death, claiming that a defective steering mechanism on the family car caused it to veer off the road and hit a tree when his wife was driving. The defendant auto manufacturer claims that the steering mechanism was damaged in the collision and offers testimony that the deceased wife was intoxicated at the time of the accident.

Testimony concerning the wife's intoxication is

(A) admissible to provide an alternate explanation of the accident's cause.
(B) admissible as proper evidence of the wife's character.
(C) inadmissible, because it is improper to prove character evidence by specific conduct.
(D) inadmissible, because it is substantially more prejudicial than probative.

Question 22

A defendant and a co-defendant were arrested for holding up a gas station. They were taken to police headquarters and placed in a room for interrogation. As a police officer addressing both started to give them the *Miranda* warnings prior to the questioning, the defendant said, "Look, [the co-defendant] planned the damned thing and I was dumb enough to go along with it. We robbed the place—what else is there to say?" The co-defendant said nothing. The co-defendant was escorted into another room and a full written confession was then obtained from the defendant. If the co-defendant is brought to trial on an indictment charging him with robbery, the fact that the co-defendant failed to object to the defendant's statement and remained silent after the defendant had implicated him in the crime should be ruled

(A) admissible, because his silence was an implied admission by the co-defendant that he had participated in the crime.
(B) admissible, because a statement of a participant in a crime is admissible against another participant.
(C) inadmissible, because, under the circumstances, there was no duty or responsibility on the co-defendant's part to respond.
(D) inadmissible, because whatever the defendant may have said has no probative value in a trial against the co-defendant.

Question 23

A plaintiff's estate sued a defendant store claiming that one of the defendant's security guards wrongfully shot and killed the plaintiff when the plaintiff fled after being accused of shoplifting. The guard was convicted of manslaughter for killing the plaintiff. At his criminal trial, the guard, who was no longer working for the defendant, testified that the defendant's security director had instructed him to stop shoplifters "at all costs." Because the guard's criminal conviction is on appeal, he refuses to testify at the civil trial. The plaintiff's estate then offers an authenticated transcript of the guard's criminal trial testimony concerning the instructions of the defendant's security director.

This evidence is

(A) admissible as a statement of an agent of a party opponent.
(B) admissible, because the instruction from the security director is not hearsay.
(C) admissible, although hearsay, as former testimony.
(D) inadmissible, because it is hearsay not within any exception.

Question 24

A defendant is on trial for participating in a drug sale. The prosecution calls an undercover officer as a witness to testify that when the drug dealer sold the drugs to the witness, the dealer introduced the defendant to the witness as "my partner in this," and that the defendant shook hands with the witness but said nothing.

The witness's testimony is

(A) inadmissible, because there is no evidence that the dealer was authorized to speak for the defendant.
(B) inadmissible, because the statement of the dealer is hearsay not within any exception.
(C) admissible as a statement against the defendant's penal interest.
(D) admissible as the defendant's adoption of the dealer's statement.

Question 25

In a federal civil trial, a plaintiff wishes to establish that, in a state court, the defendant had been convicted of fraud, a fact that the defendant denies.

Which mode of proof of the conviction is LEAST likely to be permitted?

(A) A certified copy of the judgment of conviction, offered as a self-authenticating document.
(B) Testimony of the plaintiff, who was present at the time of the sentence.
(C) Testimony by a witness to whom the defendant made an oral admission that he had been convicted.
(D) Judicial notice of the conviction, based on the court's telephone call to the clerk of the state court, whom the judge knows personally.

Question 26

A widow sued a defendant for shooting her husband from ambush. The widow offers to testify that, the day before her husband was killed, he described to her a chance meeting with the defendant on the street in which the defendant said, "I'm going to blow your head off one of these days."

The widow's testimony concerning her husband's statement is

(A) admissible, to show the defendant's state of mind.
(B) admissible, because the defendant's statement is that of a party-opponent.
(C) inadmissible, because it is improper evidence of a prior bad act.
(D) inadmissible, because it is hearsay not within any exception.

Question 27

A defendant entered a guilty plea to a charge of embezzlement. Her attorney hired a retired probation officer as a consultant to gather information for the preparation of a sentencing plan for the defendant that would avoid jail. For that purpose, the consultant interviewed the defendant for three hours.

Thereafter, the prosecution undertook an investigation of the defendant's possible involvement in other acts of embezzlement. The consultant was subpoenaed to testify before a grand jury. The consultant refused to answer any questions concerning her conversation with the defendant. The prosecution has moved for an order requiring her to answer those questions. The motion should be

(A) denied, on the basis of the attorney-client privilege.
(B) denied, in the absence of probable cause to believe the interview developed evidence relevant to the grand jury's inquiry.
(C) granted, because the consultant is not an attorney.
(D) granted, because exclusionary evidentiary rules do not apply in grand jury proceedings.

Question 28

A defendant is on trial for the murder of his father. The defendant's defense is that he shot his father accidentally. The prosecutor calls a police officer as a witness to testify that on two occasions in the year prior to this incident, he had been called to the defendant's home because of complaints of loud arguments between the defendant and his father, and had found it necessary to stop the defendant from beating his father.

The evidence is

(A) inadmissible, because it is improper character evidence.
(B) inadmissible, because the officer lacks firsthand knowledge of who started the quarrels.
(C) admissible to show that the defendant killed his father intentionally.
(D) admissible to show that the defendant is a violent person.

Question 29

A plaintiff sued a defendant under an age discrimination statute, alleging that the defendant refused to hire the plaintiff because she was over age 65.

The defendant's defense was that he refused to employ the plaintiff because he reasonably believed that she would be unable to perform the job. The defendant seeks to testify that the plaintiff's former employer advised him not to hire the plaintiff because she was unable to perform productively for more than four hours a day. The testimony of the defendant is

(A) inadmissible, because the defendant's opinion of the plaintiff's abilities is not based on personal knowledge.
(B) inadmissible, because plaintiff's former employer's statement is hearsay not within any exception.
(C) admissible as evidence that the plaintiff would be unable to work longer than four hours per day.
(D) admissible as evidence of the defendant's reason for refusing to hire the plaintiff.

Question 30

A plaintiff sued a defendant for personal injuries arising out of an automobile accident.

Which of the following would be an error?

(A) The judge allows the defendant's attorney to ask the defendant questions on cross-examination that go well beyond the scope of direct examination by the plaintiff, who has called the defendant as an adverse witness.
(B) The judge refuses to allow the defendant's attorney to cross-examine the defendant by leading questions.

(C) The judge allows cross-examination about the credibility of a witness even though no question relating to credibility has been asked on direct examination.
(D) The judge, despite the defendant's request for exclusion of witnesses, allows the plaintiff's eyewitness to remain in the courtroom after testifying, even though the eyewitness is expected to be recalled for further cross-examination.

Question 31

In a contract suit between a plaintiff and a defendant, the defendant testifies that he recalls having his first conversation with the plaintiff on January 3. When asked how he remembers the date, he answers, "In the conversation, the plaintiff referred to a story in that day's newspaper announcing my daughter's engagement." The plaintiff's counsel moves to strike the reference to the newspaper story. The judge should

(A) grant the motion on the ground that the best evidence rule requires production of the newspaper itself.
(B) grant the motion, because the reference to the newspaper story does not fit within any established exception to the hearsay rule.
(C) deny the motion on the ground that the court may take judicial notice of local newspapers and their contents.
(D) deny the motion on the ground that a witness may refer to collateral documents without providing the documents themselves.

Question 32

A defendant is on trial for extorting $10,000 from a victim. An issue is the identification of the person who made a telephone call to the victim. The victim is prepared to testify that the caller had a distinctive accent like the defendant's, but that he cannot positively identify the voice as the defendant's. The victim recorded the call but has not brought the tape to court, although its existence is known to the defendant.

The victim's testimony is

(A) inadmissible, because the victim cannot sufficiently identify the caller.
(B) inadmissible, because the tape recording of the conversation is the best evidence.
(C) admissible, because the defendant waived the "best evidence" rule by failing to subpoena the tape.
(D) admissible, because the victim's lack of certainty goes to the weight to be given the victim's testimony, not to its admissibility.

Question 33

A plaintiff construction company sued a defendant development company for money owed on a cost-plus contract that required notice of proposed expenditures beyond original estimates. The defendant asserted that it never received the required notice. At trial the plaintiff calls its general manager as a witness to testify that it is the plaintiff's routine practice to send cost overrun notices as required by the contract. The general manager also offers a photocopy of the cost overrun notice letter to the defendant on which the plaintiff is relying, and which he has taken from the plaintiff's regular business files.

On the issue of giving notice, the letter copy is

(A) admissible, though hearsay, under the business record exception.
(B) admissible, because of the routine practices of the company.
(C) inadmissible, because it is hearsay not within any exception.
(D) inadmissible, because it is not the best evidence of the notice.

Question 34

A defendant has pleaded not guilty to a federal charge of bank robbery. The principal issue at trial is the identity of the robber. The prosecutor calls the defendant's wife to testify to the clothing that the defendant wore as he left their house on the day the bank was robbed, expecting her description to match that of eyewitnesses to the robbery. Both the defendant and his wife object to her testifying against the defendant.

Should the wife be required to testify?

(A) No, because the defendant has a privilege to prevent his wife from testifying against him in a criminal case.
(B) No, because the wife has a privilege not to testify against her husband in a criminal case.
(C) Yes, because the interspousal privilege does not apply in criminal cases.
(D) Yes, because the wife's viewing of the defendant's clothing was not a confidential communication.

Question 35

In a murder trial in which the defendant relied on a theory of self-defense, the defendant called a witness to testify that the victim had a reputation among the people with whom he lived and worked for lawbreaking and frequently engaging in brawls.

The trial judge should rule the testimony

(A) admissible to support the defendant's theory of self-defense, touching on whether the defendant or the victim was the aggressor.
(B) admissible, if the witness testifies further as to specific acts of misconduct on the victim's part of which the witness has personal knowledge.

(C) inadmissible on the question of defendant's guilt, because the defendant, not the victim, is on trial.
(D) inadmissible, because the witness failed to lay a proper foundation.

Question 36

The defendant, a young doctor, is charged with falsely claiming deductions on her federal income tax return. At trial, a witness testified for the defendant that she has a reputation in the community for complete honesty. After a sidebar conference at which the prosecutor gave the judge a record showing that the defendant's medical school had disciplined her for altering her transcript, the prosecutor proposes to ask the witness on cross-examination: "Have you ever heard that the defendant falsified her medical school transcript?"

Is the prosecutor's question proper?

(A) No, because it calls for hearsay not within any exception.
(B) No, because its minimal relevance on the issue of income tax fraud is substantially outweighed by the danger of unfair prejudice.
(C) Yes, because an affirmative answer will be probative of the defendant's bad character for honesty and, therefore, her guilt.
(D) Yes, because an affirmative answer will impeach the witness's credibility.

Question 37

A police officer responded to the scene of a one-car accident and arrested the defendant for driving under the influence of alcohol. The prosecutor wants to have the police officer testify to the following statement made to him by the defendant's passenger, out of the presence of the defendant: "We were returning from a party at which we had all been drinking." The passenger is available to testify at trial.

The trial judge should rule this testimony

(A) admissible as an admission of a party.
(B) admissible as a declaration against interest.
(C) inadmissible as hearsay not within any exception.
(D) inadmissible, because it would lead the court into nonessential side issues.

Question 38

A plaintiff sued a defendant for personal injuries suffered in a train-automobile collision. The plaintiff called an eyewitness, who testified that the train was going 20 miles per hour. The defendant then offers the testimony of an experienced police accident investigator that, based on his training and experience and on his examination of the physical evidence, it is his opinion that the train was going between five and ten miles per hour.

Testimony by the investigator is

(A) improper, because there cannot be both lay and expert opinion on the same issue.
(B) improper, because the investigator is unable to establish the speed with a sufficient degree of scientific certainty.
(C) proper, because a police accident investigator has sufficient expertise to express an opinion on speed.
(D) proper, because the plaintiff first introduced opinion evidence as to speed.

Question 39

A defendant is charged with murder in connection with a carjacking incident during which the defendant allegedly shot a victim while attempting to steal the victim's car. The prosecutor calls the victim's four-year-old son, whose face was horribly disfigured by the same bullet, to testify that the defendant shot his father and him.

The son's testimony should be

(A) admitted, provided the prosecutor first provides evidence that persuades the judge that the son is competent to testify despite his tender age.
(B) admitted, provided there is sufficient basis for believing that the son has personal knowledge and understands his obligation to testify truthfully.
(C) excluded, because it is insufficiently probative in view of the son's tender age.
(D) excluded, because it is more unfairly prejudicial than probative.

Question 40

Cars driven by a victim and a defendant collided, and the defendant was charged with driving while intoxicated in connection with the accident. She pleaded guilty and was merely fined, although under the statute the court could have sentenced her to two years in prison.

Thereafter, the victim, alleging that the defendant's intoxication had caused the collision, sued the defendant for damages. At trial, the victim offers the properly authenticated record of the defendant's conviction. The record should be

(A) admitted as proof of the defendant's character.
(B) admitted as proof of the defendant's intoxication.
(C) excluded, because the conviction was not the result of a trial.
(D) excluded, because it is hearsay not within any exception.

Question 41

A plaintiff sued a defendant for damages for injuries that the plaintiff incurred when a badly rotted limb fell from a curbside tree in front of the defendant's home and hit the plaintiff. The defendant claimed that the tree was on city property and thus was the responsibility of the city. At trial, the plaintiff offered testimony that a week after the accident, the defendant had cut the tree down with a chainsaw. The offered evidence is

(A) inadmissible, because there is a policy to encourage safety precautions.
(B) inadmissible, because it is irrelevant to the condition of the tree at the time of the accident.
(C) admissible to show the tree was on the defendant's property.
(D) admissible to show the tree was in a rotted condition.

Question 42

At a defendant's trial for theft, a witness, called by the prosecutor, testified to the following: (1) that from his apartment window, he saw thieves across the street break the window of a jewelry store, take jewelry, and leave in a car; (2) that the witness's wife telephoned the police and relayed to them the license number of the thieves' car as the witness looked out the window with binoculars and read it to her; (3) that he has no present memory of the number, but that immediately afterward he listened to a playback of the police tape recording giving the license number (which belongs to the defendant's car) and verified that she had relayed the number accurately.

Playing the tape recording for the jury would be

(A) proper, because it is recorded recollection.
(B) proper, because it is a public record or report.
(C) improper, because it is hearsay not within any exception.
(D) improper, because the witness's wife lacked firsthand knowledge of the license number.

Question 43

A plaintiff sued a defendant for battery. At trial, the plaintiff's witness testified that the defendant had made an unprovoked attack on the plaintiff.

On cross-examination, the defendant asks the witness about a false claim that the witness had once filed on an insurance policy. The question is

(A) proper, because the conduct involved untruthfulness.
(B) proper, provided that the conduct resulted in conviction of the witness.
(C) improper, because the impeachment involved a specific instance of misconduct.
(D) improper, because the claim form would be the best evidence.

Question 44

While crossing a street, a plaintiff was hit by a car that she did not see. The plaintiff sued the defendant for her injuries.

At trial, the plaintiff calls a police officer to testify that, ten minutes after the accident, a driver stopped him and said, "Officer, a few minutes ago I saw a hit-and-run accident involving a blue convertible, which I followed to the drive-in restaurant at the nearest intersection," and that a few seconds later the officer saw the defendant sitting alone in a blue convertible in the drive-in restaurant's parking lot. The officer's testimony about the driver's statement should be

(A) admitted as a statement of recent perception.
(B) admitted as a present sense impression.
(C) excluded, because it is hearsay not within any exception.
(D) excluded, because it is more prejudicial than probative.

Question 45

A plaintiff sued a defendant for personal injury alleged to have been caused by the defendant's negligence. A major issue at trial was whether the plaintiff's disability was caused solely by trauma or by a preexisting condition of osteoarthritis.

The plaintiff called his doctor, who testified that the disability was caused by trauma. On cross-examination, the plaintiff's doctor testified that a medical textbook entitled *Diseases of the Joints* was authoritative and that she agreed with the substance of passages from the textbook that she was directed to look at, but that the passages were inapplicable to the plaintiff's condition because they dealt with rheumatoid arthritis rather than with the osteoarthritis that the plaintiff was alleged to have. The defendant then called his expert doctor who testified that, with reference to the issue being litigated, there is no difference between the two kinds of arthritis. The defendant's counsel then asks permission to read to the jury the textbook passages earlier shown to the plaintiff's doctor. The judge should rule the textbook passages

(A) admissible only for the purpose of impeaching the plaintiff's doctor.
(B) admissible as substantive evidence if the judge determines that the passages are relevant.
(C) inadmissible, because they are hearsay not within any exception.
(D) inadmissible, because the plaintiff's doctor contended that they are not relevant to the plaintiff's condition.

Question 46

A plaintiff is suing a doctor for medical malpractice occasioned by allegedly prescribing an incorrect medication, causing the plaintiff to undergo substantial hospitalization. When the doctor learned of the medication problem, she immediately offered to pay the plaintiff's hospital expenses.

At trial, the plaintiff offers evidence of the doctor's offer to pay the costs of his hospitalization.

The evidence of the doctor's offer is

(A) admissible as a nonhearsay statement of a party.
(B) admissible, although hearsay, as a statement against interest.
(C) inadmissible, because it is an offer to pay medical expenses.
(D) inadmissible, because it is an offer to compromise.

Question 47

A defendant was prosecuted for armed robbery. At trial, the defendant testified in his own behalf, denying that he had committed the robbery. On cross-examination, the prosecutor intends to ask the defendant whether he had been convicted of burglary six years earlier.

The question concerning the burglary conviction is

(A) proper, if the court finds that the probative value for impeachment outweighs the prejudice to the defendant.
(B) proper, because the prosecutor is entitled to make this inquiry as a matter of right.
(C) improper, because burglary does not involve dishonesty or false statement.
(D) improper, because the conviction must be proved by court record, not by question on cross-examination.

Question 48

A plaintiff sued a defendant for breach of a commercial contract in which the defendant had agreed to sell the plaintiff all of the plaintiff's requirements for widgets. The plaintiff called an expert witness to testify as to damages. The defendant seeks to show that the expert witness had provided false testimony as a witness in his own divorce proceedings.

This evidence should be

(A) admitted only if elicited from the expert witness on cross-examination.
(B) admitted only if the false testimony is established by clear and convincing extrinsic evidence.
(C) excluded, because it is impeachment on a collateral issue.
(D) excluded, because it is improper character evidence.

Question 49

A defendant and co-defendant are being tried in federal court for criminal conspiracy to violate federal narcotics law. At trial, the prosecutor calls the defendant's new wife and asks her to testify about a meeting between the defendant and co-defendant that she observed before she married the defendant.

Which of the following is the most accurate statement of the applicable rule concerning whether the defendant's wife may testify?

(A) The choice is for the defendant's wife to make.
(B) The choice is for the defendant to make.
(C) The defendant's wife is permitted to testify only if both the defendant and his wife agree.
(D) The defendant's wife is compelled to testify even if both the defendant and his wife object.

Question 50

A plaintiff is suing a defendant for injuries suffered in an automobile collision. At trial, the plaintiff's first witness testified that, although she did not see the accident, she heard her friend say just before the crash, "Look at the crazy way [the defendant] is driving!" The defendant offers evidence to impeach the witness's friend by asking the witness, "Isn't it true that your friend beat up the defendant just the day before the collision?"

The question is

(A) proper, because it tends to show the possible bias of the witness's friend against the defendant.
(B) proper, because it tends to show the character of the witness's friend.
(C) improper, because the witness's friend has no opportunity to explain or deny.
(D) improper, because impeachment cannot properly be by specific instances.

Question 51

A defendant is on trial for nighttime breaking and entering of a warehouse. The warehouse owner had set up a camera to take infrared pictures of any intruders. After an expert establishes the reliability of infrared photography, the prosecutor offers the authenticated infrared picture of the intruder to show the similarities to the defendant.

The photograph is

(A) admissible, provided an expert witness points out to the jury the similarities between the person in the photograph and the defendant.
(B) admissible, allowing the jury to compare the person in the photograph and the defendant.
(C) inadmissible, because there was no eyewitness to the scene available to authenticate the photograph.
(D) inadmissible, because infrared photography deprives a defendant of the right to confront witnesses.

Question 52

A lender sued a debtor for nonpayment of a personal loan to the debtor, as evidenced by the debtor's promissory note to the lender. The lender called a witness to testify that he knows the debtor's handwriting and that the signature on the note is the debtor's. On direct examination, to identify himself, the witness gave his name and address and testified that he had been employed by a roofing company for seven years.

During presentation of the debtor's case, the debtor called the roofing company's manager to testify as to her occupation and that she had determined, by examining the company's employment records, that the witness had worked there only three years. The trial judge should rule that the manager's testimony is

(A) inadmissible, because it is not the best evidence.
(B) inadmissible, because it is impeachment on a collateral question.
(C) admissible as evidence of a regularly conducted activity.
(D) admissible as tending to impeach the witness's credibility.

Question 53

A plaintiff sued a defendant for injuries sustained in an automobile collision. During the plaintiff's hospital stay, a staff physician examined the plaintiff's X rays and said to the plaintiff, "You have a fracture of two vertebrae, C4 and C5." An intern, who was accompanying the physician on her rounds, immediately wrote the diagnosis on the plaintiff's hospital record. At trial, the hospital records custodian testifies that the plaintiff's hospital record was made and kept in the ordinary course of the hospital's business.

The entry reporting the physician's diagnosis is

(A) inadmissible, because no foundation has been laid for the physician's competence as an expert.
(B) inadmissible, because the physician's opinion is based upon data that are not in evidence.
(C) admissible as a statement of then-existing physical condition.
(D) admissible as a record of regularly conducted business activity.

Question 54

At a defendant's trial for sale of drugs, the government called a witness to testify, but the witness refused to answer any questions about the defendant and was held in contempt of court. The government then calls an officer to testify that, when the witness was arrested for possession of drugs and offered leniency if he would identify his source, the witness had named the defendant as his source.

The testimony offered concerning the witness's identification of the defendant is

(A) admissible as a prior inconsistent statement by the witness.
(B) admissible as an identification of the defendant by the witness after having perceived him.
(C) inadmissible, because it is hearsay not within any exception.
(D) inadmissible, because the witness was not confronted with the statement while on the stand.

Question 55

A company sued its former vice president for return of $230,000 that had been embezzled during the previous two years. Called by the company as an adverse witness, the former vice-president testified that his annual salary had been $75,000, and he denied the embezzlement. The company calls a banker to show that, during the two-year period, the former vice-president had deposited $250,000 in his bank account.

The witness's testimony is

(A) admissible as circumstantial evidence of the former vice-president's guilt.
(B) admissible to impeach the former vice-president.
(C) inadmissible, because its prejudicial effect substantially outweighs its probative value.
(D) inadmissible, because the deposits could have come from legitimate sources.

Question 56

A pedestrian died from injuries caused when a car struck him. The pedestrian's executor sued the driver of the car for wrongful death. At trial, the executor calls a nurse to testify that two days after the accident, the pedestrian said to the nurse, "The car that hit me ran the red light." Fifteen minutes thereafter, the pedestrian died.

As a foundation for introducing evidence of the pedestrian's statement, the executor offers to the court the doctor's affidavit that the doctor was the intern on duty the day of the pedestrian's death and that several times that day the pedestrian had said that he knew he was about to die. Is the affidavit properly considered by the court in ruling on the admissibility of the pedestrian's statement?

(A) No, because it is hearsay not within any exception.
(B) No, because it is irrelevant since dying declarations cannot be used except in prosecutions for homicide.
(C) Yes, because, though hearsay, it is a statement of then-existing mental condition.

(D) Yes, because the judge may consider hearsay in ruling on preliminary questions.

Question 57

A defendant is on trial for robbing a bank in State A. She testified that she was in State B at the time of the robbery. The defendant calls her friend, as a witness, to testify that two days before the robbery the defendant told him that she was going to spend the next three days in State B.

The witness's testimony is

(A) admissible, because the statement falls within the present sense impression exception to the hearsay rule.
(B) admissible, because a statement of plans falls within the hearsay exception for then-existing state of mind.
(C) inadmissible, because it is offered to establish an alibi by the defendant's own statement.
(D) inadmissible, because it is hearsay not within any exception.

Question 58

At a defendant's murder trial, the defendant calls first a witness to testify that the defendant has a reputation in their community as a peaceable and truthful person. The prosecutor objects on the ground that the witness's testimony would constitute improper character evidence.

The court should

(A) admit the testimony as to peaceableness, but exclude the testimony as to truthfulness.
(B) admit the testimony as to truthfulness, but exclude the testimony as to peaceableness.
(C) admit the testimony as to both character traits.
(D) exclude the testimony as to both character traits.

ANSWERS

EVIDENCE

Answer Key

Use this Answer Key to quickly identify the correct answer to each question.

(1)	B	(11)	C	(21)	A	(31)	D	(41)	C	(51)	B
(2)	A	(12)	A	(22)	C	(32)	D	(42)	A	(52)	B
(3)	D	(13)	D	(23)	D	(33)	B	(43)	A	(53)	D
(4)	B	(14)	A	(24)	D	(34)	B	(44)	C	(54)	C
(5)	C	(15)	B	(25)	D	(35)	A	(45)	B	(55)	A
(6)	C	(16)	C	(26)	D	(36)	D	(46)	C	(56)	D
(7)	C	(17)	B	(27)	A	(37)	C	(47)	A	(57)	B
(8)	C	(18)	C	(28)	C	(38)	C	(48)	A	(58)	A
(9)	C	(19)	B	(29)	D	(39)	B	(49)	A		
(10)	C	(20)	C	(30)	D	(40)	B	(50)	A		

ANSWERS

EVIDENCE

Answer 1

(B) is the best response,

because a mandatory presumption would conflict with the presumption of innocence.

The U.S. Supreme Court has held that the use of a mandatory presumption with respect to an element of a crime violates the accused's due process right to have the prosecution prove each element beyond a reasonable doubt. *See, e.g., Patterson v. New York*, 432 U.S. 197 (1977): "[A] State must prove every ingredient of an offense beyond a reasonable doubt, and . . . it may not shift the burden of proof to the defendant by presuming that ingredient upon proof of the other elements of the offense." In a murder case, one element of the crime is that the victim has died. Instructing the jury that when a person has been missing for seven years, that person "*shall* be presumed" to be dead would likely cause a reasonable juror to believe that she *must* find the missing person to be dead, i.e., that the presumption is mandatory. And use of a mandatory presumption here would unconstitutionally relieve the prosecution of its burden to prove beyond a reasonable doubt that the person is dead.

(A) is not the best response,

because it reaches the right outcome, but on incorrect legal reasoning.

It's certainly true that the conclusion (that the person in question is dead) does not necessarily follow from the starting fact (that the person has not been heard from in seven years). But as long as a presumption is rational (which the one here is), it would not have been improper for the judge to instruct the jury that the presumption exists, and that because of the presumption the jury *"may infer"* that a person not heard from in seven years is dead. The problem comes from the judge's instruction that the missing person "*shall* be presumed" to be dead—a reasonable juror could conclude from the word "shall" that the presumption was *mandatory*, i.e., that the juror was *required* (not merely permitted) to find that because the victim had been missing for seven years, the person is dead. As is discussed more extensively in choice B, use of a mandatory presumption as to an element of a crime violates the accused's due process right to have the prosecution prove every element beyond a reasonable doubt.

(C) is not the best response,

because even a rational presumption cannot be mandatorily imposed as to an element in a criminal case.

In *civil* cases, juries may be required (not just permitted) to apply an applicable presumption, if the conclusion rationally follows from the presumed fact. But in a *criminal* case, the accused has a constitutional due process right to have the jury find each element of the crime *beyond a reasonable doubt*. When the judge said that the jury "shall presume" that a person missing for seven years is dead, the judge was making the presumption *mandatory* as to an element of the crime (the victim's death). Even if a person's death is a "rational conclusion" from the fact that she has been missing for seven years (which it probably is), telling the jury that it *must* find the woman dead because she has been missing for seven years unfairly eases the prosecution's burden of proving the fact of death beyond a reasonable doubt.

(D) is not the best response,

because the availability of rebuttal evidence is not enough to cure the constitutional problem posed by a mandatory presumption on an element of a criminal charge.

It's true that even under the judge's instructions, the defendant was free to rebut either the basic fact (that the woman had not been heard from in seven years) or the presumed fact (that the woman was alive even though she had not been heard from in seven years). But the defendant in a criminal case has a constitutional due process right to have the prosecution affirmatively prove, beyond a reasonable doubt, every element of the charged offense. The mandatory presumption here relieved the prosecution of that burden, with respect to the element of death—as long as the prosecution showed that the woman had not been heard from in seven years, it was unfairly freed of its obligation to prove beyond a reasonable doubt that the woman was dead. And giving the defense the right to rebut the presumption did not solve this—the burden of proof as to death was still effectively being shifted to the defendant.

Answer 2

(A) is the best response,

because the notes are hearsay, and the business-records and past-recollections-recorded exceptions do not apply.

In a multiple-choice format question, where one of the choices is "hearsay not within any exception," you have to perform a two-step analysis: (1) first, ask whether the proposed use is a hearsay use; and (2) if the answer to (1) is yes, analyze each specific hearsay objection that is referred to in the other choices.

So for the first step, let's figure out whether the notes are hearsay. Hearsay is an out-of-court statement offered to prove the truth of a matter asserted in the statement. The notes were kept by the witness to "help her remember what had happened at the meetings." So we can infer that the notes purport to reflect what happened at the meetings. We're told that the government offered the notes "to establish what had happened at the meetings." So the notes are being offered to prove the truth of the matter asserted therein, namely, what happened at the meetings. That makes them hearsay. Unless some exception to the hearsay rule applies, they are inadmissible.

Now, for step (2), let's look at the possible hearsay exceptions. We only have to worry about ones that are set out in the actual choices (because the question couldn't be structured in such a way that the answer turned on the availability of an exception that isn't mentioned or referred to in any choice). The only hearsay exceptions that are specifically referred to are the business-records and past-recollections-recorded exceptions, so let's consider each.

This use does not qualify for the business records exception, because the witness prepared the notes "on her own initiative," and FRE 803(6)'s implementation of the business record exception requires that it be a "regular practice of that [business] activity" to keep the record. For more about this, see the discussion of choice C below.

Nor does the use qualify for the past-recollections-recorded exception of FRE 803(5), for a number of reasons, including most obviously the fact that that exception allows the writing to be "read into evidence" but does not allow the writing itself to be offered as an exhibit by the proponent, which is what the government is trying to do here. For more about this, see the discussion of choice C below.

Since the notes are hearsay and do not fall within either of the two specifically-mentioned exceptions (nor within any other exception, as it happens), "hearsay not within any exception" is the correct analysis.

(B) is not the best choice,

because it cites a "fact" that is irrelevant to the notes' reliability.

It's true that, under FRE 403, the court may exclude evidence "if its probative value is substantially outweighed by a danger of . . . unfair prejudice[.]" And it's also true that the tendency of a piece of evidence to be unreliable is one form of possible "unfair prejudice," to be considered by the court in analyzing whether 403 applies.

But there is no reason to believe that the grant of immunity here caused any meaningful danger of unreliability. The grant of immunity to the witness was made long after the notes were made. There is no reason to believe that the witness, at the time she made the notes, somehow foresaw that questions of securities fraud might possibly emerge someday, and skewed the notes' content in order to improve her chances of getting immunity should that happen. So there is no reason to question the notes' reliability at all on immunity-related grounds, let alone to say that the reliability issue is so great that it "substantially outweighs" the notes' probative value, which is what FRE 403 requires.

(C) is not the best choice,

because these are not "records of regularly conducted activity."

There is no specific "business records" hearsay exception under the FRE. Instead, FRE 803(6) supplies a broader hearsay exception for "records of a regularly conducted activity." However, that exception requires that the record have been "kept in the course of a regularly conducted activity of a business" or other enterprise, and that "making the record was a *regular practice* of that activity."

Here, we're told that the witness "prepared the notes *on her own initiative*." The fact that the witness acted on her own means that the above-quoted 803(6) requirements fail in two respects to be satisfied. First, the "kept in the course of a regularly conducted activity of a business" language means that *the business itself* (not merely some individual employee) must have made the decision to keep the record on behalf of the business, which didn't happen here. Second, the record must have been kept as a matter of "regular practice"—here, the "one-shot" *ad hoc* nature of these notes (there's no evidence that the executive made handwritten notes about *all* meetings, just the meetings at which this particular transaction was discussed) prevents a finding that the notes were kept as part of a "regular practice."

(D) is not the best choice,

because the foundation requirements for the past-recollections-recorded exception have not been met, and because the exception would in any event not allow for admission of the writing itself.

The FRE's exception for past recollection recorded is given in FRE 803(5). The exception covers a record that:

> "(A) is on a matter the witness once knew about but now cannot recall well enough to testify fully and accurately;
> (B) was made or adopted by the witness when the matter was fresh in the witness's memory; and
> (C) accurately reflects the witness's knowledge."

803(5) concludes by saying that "If admitted, the record may be read into evidence but may be received as an exhibit only if offered by an adverse party."

So there are multiple ways in which the notes here fail to fall within the exception. First, the requisite foundation has not been laid—the witness has not testified that she cannot now recall the underlying facts well enough to testify fully and accurately about them, nor that the notes were made or adopted by her when the matter was "fresh in [her] memory," nor that the notes accurately reflect her knowledge. Furthermore, even if the witness had given all this foundational testimony, the prosecution would merely have been entitled to read the notes aloud to the jury, not to have the written documents "offered . . . into evidence" (as an exhibit), which is what the prosecution is attempting to do.

By the way, it will be quite *rare* on the MBE for a document to fall within the exception for past recollection recorded. The exception imposes so many requirements, and it would take so much language in the fact pattern to specify that all requirements have been met, that the examiners are much more likely to use PRR as a *wrong* choice than as the right one.

Answer 3

(D) is the best response,

because the evidence may be offered to show bias but not to show that the defendant was insured.

Let's look first at whether the witness's status as the adjuster for the defendant's insurance company is "substantively" admissible. In this situation, it is not completely clear what it means to say that the evidence is or is not "substantively" admissible. Presumably, what the examiners are asking is, "May this evidence be offered for the purpose of proving that the defendant has liability insurance, as a means of supporting the further inference that one who knows he has liability insurance is more likely to have driven negligently?" And the answer to that question is clearly "no." Under the first sentence of FRE 411, "Evidence that a person was or was not insured against liability is *not admissible to prove whether the person acted negligently or otherwise wrongfully*."

Now, let's look at whether the evidence may be offered for impeachment. Here, the relevant provision is the second sentence of FRE 411: "But the court may admit this evidence [of liability insurance] for *another purpose*, such as proving a witness's *bias* or prejudice or proving agency, ownership, or control." Since the witness is appearing for the defense, and the witness's employer has an incentive to minimize the amount of damage the defendant may have caused, calling the jury's attention to the witness's adjuster status would tend to show that the witness is biased. And showing that the witness is biased is a classic form of impeaching the witness. So FRE 411 allows this showing of bias for impeachment.

(A) is not the best response,

because it ignores the use of the question for impeachment purposes.

This choice falsely asserts the general proposition that "testimony about liability insurance is barred by the rules of evidence." In reality, such testimony about liability insurance is barred (by FRE 411) only when offered to prove that the insured "acted negligently or otherwise wrongfully." Here, the evidence is being offered for another purpose, namely an impeachment purpose (to show bias), and that's a permissible use.

(B) is not the best response,

because bias is not a "collateral issue."

Certain issues are deemed "collateral," and there are limits on the types of evidence that can be used to prove facts that are relevant only in connection with such a collateral issue. But the issue of whether a witness is biased is deemed so important that proof of the witness's bias (or lack of bias) is *never deemed collateral*, so the types of evidence that may be used on the issue are not specifically limited. Therefore, the question about whether the witness is an adjuster for the defendant's insurer does not concern a collateral issue, and is proper for impeachment purposes.

(C) is not the best response,

because the evidence is not admissible for substantive purposes.

As is discussed more fully in connection with choice D above, FRE 411 forbids the use of this evidence for "substantive" purposes, i.e., to prove that the defendant had liability insurance and thus had a greater incentive to drive carelessly than if he had not had such coverage.

Answer 4

(B) is the best response,

because only reputation or opinion evidence may be used by the defendant to prove his good character, assuming character is not an element of the offense.

Under FRE 404(a)(2)(A), a criminal defendant is always entitled to present evidence of his "pertinent trait" of character. (This is the so-called "mercy rule.") Since the crime charged is fraud, the defendant's honesty is a "pertinent trait" of character, so the court properly allowed him to introduce the supervisor's testimony that the defendant had a good reputation in the community for honesty. But FRE 405(a) says that when evidence of a person's character is admissible, that evidence may take the form of "testimony about the person's *reputation* or . . . testimony in the form of an *opinion*." So by negative implication, the defendant's character evidence may *not* take the form of evidence of *specific instances* of his conduct. Then, FRE 405(b) goes on to give a special, narrow exception to this no-specific-instances rule: "When a person's character or character trait is an *essential element* of a charge, claim, or defense, the character or trait may also be proved by relevant specific instances of the person's conduct." Here, the defendant's honesty or dishonesty is not an essential element of any charge, claim or defense, so choice B correctly and precisely summarizes the relevant principle.

(A) is not the best response,
because the defendant's honesty is not deemed to be a collateral matter.

Depending on the factual setting of the case, certain issues may be deemed to be "collateral," i.e., of marginal importance. When an issue is collateral, various rules (often called collectively the "collateral issue rule") may limit "extrinsic evidence" as to that issue. But in a criminal trial, FRE 404(a)(1) gives the defendant a specific right to present evidence of any character trait that he possesses, assuming the trait is "pertinent" to the case (as the trait of honesty is here). Therefore, the defendant's trait of honesty is not in fact "collateral" in this case. The problem here is that the proposed character evidence takes the form of specific instances of conduct, and FRE 405(a) says that only reputation and opinion evidence may be used.

(C) is not the best response,
because even though the accused may offer evidence of this pertinent character trait, the evidence may not take the form of specific instances of conduct.

This choice is correct in stating that "evidence of a pertinent character trait offered by an accused" is admissible. (*See* FRE 404(a)(2)(A).) But FRE 405(a) then says that when evidence of a person's character is admissible, that evidence may take the form of "testimony about the person's *reputation* or . . . testimony in the form of an *opinion*." So by negative implication, the defendant's character evidence may *not* take the form of evidence of specific instances of his conduct (except in the rare case where the character trait is an essential element of a charge, claim or defense).

(D) is not the best response,
because the evidence, though relevant, takes an impermissible form.

It's true that the evidence here is relevant, in the sense that a person who has been entrusted with money in the past and has proved worthy of that trust is less likely to have been a thief on the present occasion than one who has not shown such trustworthiness. Therefore, the proposed evidence qualifies as being directed to a "pertinent trait" of character of an accused, as allowed by FRE 404(a)(1). The problem is that under FRE 405(a), even evidence that is relevant to an accused's pertinent character trait may not take the form of specific instances, and must instead consist of reputation or opinion testimony.

Answer 5

(C) is the best response,
because the statement could subject the friend to civil or criminal liability, and he is now unavailable.

FRE 804 lists the "declarant unavailable" hearsay exceptions. Since the declarant (the friend) is now dead, he is of course "unavailable," so any of the Rule 804 exceptions might apply. One of those exceptions is given in 804(b)(3), for a "statement against interest," defined as "A statement that: (A) a reasonable person in the declarant's position would have made *only if the person believed it to be true* because, when made, it was *so contrary* to the declarant's *proprietary or pecuniary interest* or had so great a tendency . . . to *expose the declarant to civil or criminal liability*[.]"

By saying that he "was paid to set the fire," the declarant (the friend) was implicitly saying that he set the fire, and did so for pay. So he was confessing to arson, a confession that would surely "expose the declarant to civil or criminal liability." Neither the fact that he made the statement to his wife, nor the fact that a third party (the nurse) was present, nullifies the availability of this exception.

(A) is not the best response,
because the marital privilege never arose in the first place.

There are actually two different marital privileges, but neither applies here. First is the "*adverse testimony*" (a/k/a "spousal immunity") privilege. This privilege fails to apply here for several reasons: (1) it applies only in criminal proceedings; (2) the declarant and the testifying witness must be married at the time of the testimony (here, the friend is dead, and thus no longer married to the witness); and (3) a third party (i.e., one who is neither the testifying spouse nor the declarant) cannot assert the privilege.

The second possible marital privilege is the privilege for "*confidential communications*" between spouses. It's true that unlike the adverse testimony privilege, the confidential communications privilege requires only that the declarant and the testifying spouse have been married at the time of the communication, not that they still be married at the time of the testimony. So the fact that the declarant (the friend) is now dead doesn't matter. But as the name "confidential communications" implies, the communication must have been confidential at the time it was uttered. The presence of a *third person* will generally show that the communication was not intended to be confidential. Here, the examiners have carefully said that the statement was made "in the presence of an attending nurse," a fact which made the communication non-confidential.

(B) is not the best response,

because, although this choice correctly explains why the co-conspirator exception does not apply, it ignores the fact that the statement-against-interest exception applies.

801(d)(2) gives non-hearsay status to a statement where "The statement is offered against an opposing party and: . . . (E) was made by *the party's co-conspirator during and in furtherance of the conspiracy*." So this choice is correct in saying that the co-conspirator exception does not apply on these facts, since the conspiracy had ended before the statement was made. But this choice incorrectly implies that there is no other applicable hearsay exception—in fact, the statement-against-interest exception applies.

(D) is not the best response,

because the co-conspirator exception does not apply to statements that are either made after the conspiracy has ended or are not in furtherance of the conspiracy.

FRE 801(d)(2) groups together several types of "admission[s] by a party-opponent," and defines all of them as non-hearsay. Statements offered against a party, and made by that party's *co-conspirator*, fall within 801(d)(2) in some circumstances. More precisely, 801(d)(2) gives non-hearsay status to a statement where "The statement is offered against an opposing party and: . . . (E) was made by *the party's co-conspirator during and in furtherance of the conspiracy*." The statement itself is to be considered (but is not dispositive) in determining whether the conspiracy actually existed; here, the statement, coupled with the fact that the friend had been badly burned in the fire, would be enough to establish that the conspiracy really existed. The problem for admissibility is the requirement that the statement have been made by the co-conspirator "*during and in furtherance of the conspiracy*." First, the conspiracy was over by the time the friend was in the hospital making the statement. Second, there is no indication that, by making the statement to his wife, the friend was attempting to "further" the conspiracy.

Answer 6

(C) is the best response,

because the officer's testimony directly contradicts the defendant's testimony on a material issue, and is therefore a proper form of impeachment.

When a witness (whether a party or not) testifies, the non-calling party is always entitled to try to *impeach* that witness' credibility. (We'll call the party who is trying to impeach the witness the "attacking party.") There are various methods that the attacking party may use, one of which is impeachment by *contradiction*.

The Federal Rules do not expressly deal with impeachment by contradiction. So that form of impeachment is generally left to common-law principles. There are various forms that evidence designed to impeach by contradiction (what we'll call "counterproof") may take. The type of counterproof at issue here is testimony by another witness (the police officer) that rebuts the factual accuracy of the testimony of the witness who is being impeached (the defendant). As a general matter, testimony by the second witness, to contradict the first witness, is permissible. M&K, § 6.43, pp. 542-543. It's true that there are some limitations on the use of a second witness to contradict the first witness (most importantly, the ban on using the second witness to contradict as to a collateral matter, a ban covered in choice B below), but none of those exceptions applies here. The defendant's testimony that he had not ever, and would not ever, possess or distribute drugs, was testimony on a material issue, since the defendant is charged with doing just that. Since the officer's testimony directly contradicts the defendant's testimony on a material issue, the officer's testimony is properly admissible for impeachment.

(A) is not the best response,

because the testimony is not being offered to impeach the witness's character for truthfulness.

It's true that if the principal witness's credibility is being attacked by showing his poor character for truthfulness, the attacking evidence must be probative of his truthfulness. And it's also true that evidence that the witness once purchased cocaine would not be probative as to his character for truthfulness. But this choice mischaracterizes the nature of the government attack on the defendant's testimony. The government is not trying to impeach the defendant by showing that, as a general matter, he has a poor character for truthfulness. Rather, the government is trying to impeach him by showing that a particular aspect of his testimony on direct was factually false; that is, the government is attempting impeachment by direct *contradiction*. That method of impeachment has nothing to do with the defendant's general character for truthfulness, and is a proper method for the reasons discussed in choice C.

(B) is not the best response,

because the matter to which the contradiction is addressed is not a collateral one.

It's true that *if* the matter as to which the police officer was contradicting the defendant's testimony was a "collateral" matter, the officer's testimony would be excludable under the common-law rule prohibiting use of extrinsic evidence to contradict a witness on a collateral matter. (This rule is one member of the collection of rules loosely referred to as "the collateral issue rule.") But the defendant's testimony at issue is that he had never possessed or distributed drugs, and would never do so. Since the defendant is charged with precisely that—the possession and distribution of drugs—his testimony is highly material, and thus not "collateral." Therefore, it may be contradicted by extrinsic evidence (a second witness's testimony).

(D) is not the best response,

because it reaches the correct result, but does so on a "prior bad acts" rationale that would be barred by FRE 608(b).

This choice, by asserting that the police officer's testimony "makes it less likely that the defendant would respect the oath of truthfulness," seems to be saying that the testimony may be admitted to impeach the principal witness by showing a prior "bad act" that is inconsistent with a character for truthfulness. But there are two problems with this choice: (1) it states a rationale that is expressly forbidden by the Federal Rules; and (2) the rationale stated is not the one that the government is (or should be) using to support the evidence. Let's take these two problems in sequence.

The Federal Rules allow the credibility of a witness (here, the defendant) to be "attacked . . . by testimony about the witness's *reputation* for having a character for . . . untruthfulness, or by testimony in the form of an *opinion* about that character." FRE 608(a). So the government would be entitled to impeach the defendant by putting on a rebuttal witness to testify, for instance, that in that witness's opinion, the defendant is a habitual liar. But notice that the above-quoted portion of FRE 608(a) lists as permissible methods of attack only impeachment evidence taking the form of *opinion or reputation*.

On this same point, FRE 608(b) expressly *disallows* the admission of so-called "prior bad acts" for impeachment, which is what choice D seems to be asserting as a rationale. 608(b) says that "Except for a criminal conviction under Rule 609, extrinsic evidence is *not admissible* to prove *specific instances of a witness's conduct* in order to attack or support the witness's character for truthfulness." (There's an exception allowing inquiry into specific acts during the cross-examination of the witness being impeached, but that's not what's happening here.) So if the prosecution's rationale for the officer's testimony was the one stated in this choice (that the defendant bought illegal drugs, thus showing a disregard for the law, in turn showing a character for untruthfulness), the testimony would violate 608(b)'s ban on specific-acts evidence used for showing the principal witness' character for untruthfulness.

But the prosecution need not rely on the FRE 608 right to impeach by proof of a character for untruthfulness. Rather, the prosecution is using (or at least, is entitled to use) a completely different method of impeachment, namely impeachment by *contradiction*. And where the witness being impeached has testified on direct as to a material fact, there is no ban on the attacking party's use of extrinsic evidence to prove prior bad acts by that witness, as long as the existence of those prior bad acts directly contradicts the witness's testimony. (For more about this, see the discussion of choice C.)

Answer 7

(C) is the best response,

because the woman had a reasonable fear that answering might cause her to incriminate herself.

This choice is correct in stating that the privilege against self-incrimination applies in civil cases as well as criminal cases. A witness may refuse to testify if the witness has a reasonable fear that the testimony may lead to her being criminally prosecuted. It is not necessary that the testimony will *certainly* lead to prosecution; a mere possibility of prosecution (as long as it is more than remote) will suffice. Since the judge cannot say on these facts that an affirmative answer could not plausibly lead to a prosecution, the court must sustain the privilege.

(A) is not the best response,

because the woman did not voluntarily testify about the possibly-incriminating matter.

It's true that if the witness voluntarily testifies about a possibly-incriminating matter, she will be deemed to have "opened the door" to further questions *about that matter*, and to have implicitly waived her privilege against self-incrimination as to that matter. But here, the woman only voluntarily testified about the accident itself, not about her own mental state or possible drug use at the time of the accident. The last sentence of FRE 608 makes it clear that the woman has not, by testifying, waived her privilege regarding matters brought up solely to attack her credibility: "By testifying on another matter, a witness does not waive any privilege against self-incrimination for testimony that relates only to the witness's character for truthfulness."

Therefore, the woman would not be found to have waived her privilege to refuse to answer questions about any illegal drug she may have taken.

(B) is not the best response,

because the woman's privilege against self-incrimination would take precedence over the evidentiary value of her testimony on this point.

Where a witness is testifying as to events she witnessed, her testimony may be impeached by showing a defect in her sensory capacity or her memory. Therefore, at least if the questioner had a good faith basis for believing that the woman may have been under the influence of drugs during the trip, the questioner was entitled as a matter of general evidence principles to raise this issue on cross. But even though the question was proper, and even though an affirmative answer would have been impeaching evidence, these principles of evidence law must yield to the woman's federal constitutional right not to be required to give testimony that might tend to incriminate her.

(D) is not the best response,

because it reaches the correct result on incorrect reasoning, and misapplies the legal principle to which it refers.

This choice semi-accurately refers to a real legal principle regarding impeachment by bad acts not leading to a conviction, but overstates and misapplies that principle. FRE 608(b) says that "Except for a criminal conviction under Rule 609, *extrinsic evidence* is *not admissible* to prove *specific instances of a witness's conduct* in order to attack or support the witness's character for truthfulness." So if the defendant's counsel was attempting to attack the witness's character for truthfulness, and was doing so by "extrinsic evidence," counsel would not be permitted to show specific criminal acts by the witness that did not lead to a criminal conviction.

But for several reasons, this choice does not correctly answer the question posed.

First, FRE 608(b) does not even apply to the issue here. The defense is not making a general attack on "the witness's *character for truthfulness*," which is the only situation with which FRE 608(b) deals. Rather, the defense is attempting to impeach the witness by proving her *lack of sensory capacity* due to drug use, and nothing in FRE 608(b) or anywhere else in the Rules prevents questioning a witness about her past unconvicted bad acts that, if proven, would tend to show that the witness had a relevant sensory defect.

Second, even if FRE 608(b) applied on these facts, it would not necessarily bar the question here. That's because, after the sentence from 608(b) quoted above (the one beginning "Except for a criminal conviction . . . "), 608(b) goes on to say, "But the court may, on *cross-examination*, *allow* [specific instances of the witness's conduct] to be inquired into if they are probative of the character for truthfulness or untruthfulness of . . . the witness[.]" So although the defense would not be permitted to put on *extrinsic evidence* (e.g., another witness) to impeach the woman's general character for truthfulness by showing her past possibly-criminal unconvicted bad acts, the judge would have discretion to allow the question about prior bad acts to be asked on *cross-examination* of the woman herself, which is what the defense was trying to do here.

Finally, the question asks you how the court should "treat the woman's claim of privilege." So a correct choice would have to be responsive to the privilege claim. And choice D does not address that claim.

Answer 8

(C) is the best response,

because the letters are not hearsay if used for the limited purpose of showing that the manufacturer knew of the possible dangers prior to manufacturing the plaintiff's unit.

Hearsay is an out-of-court statement offered in evidence to prove the truth of the matter asserted in the statement. FRE 801(c). The letters all contain essentially the statement, "I was burned when I heated food in a certain type of container in your microwave." So the letters would be hearsay if used by the plaintiff for the purpose of proving that the letter-writers were in fact burned in the manner they describe.

But the letters are also relevant to another issue in the case, that of *notice*: The claim is based on the manufacturer's negligent failure to warn of a danger of burning, and such a claim requires the plaintiff to prove that the manufacturer *knew or should have known of the danger* prior to making and selling the unit in question. Using the letters solely for the purpose of demonstrating that the manufacturer knew of the danger prior to selling the plaintiff's unit, and should have investigated whether a warning was justified, is therefore a non-hearsay use: The letters are being offered not to show that the letter writers were in fact burned, but that the writers put the manufacturer on notice that they may have been burned. So plaintiff is entitled to have the hearsay objection overruled, but defendant is entitled to the requested limiting instruction that the letters be considered only for the non-hearsay purpose of notice.

(A) is not the best response,

because the use of the letters to prove only notice is not a hearsay use.

As is described more fully in choice C, the letters are being offered for a non-hearsay purpose, i.e., to show that the manufacturer was on notice that the units posed a serious problem of burns in certain situations. Therefore, if the court were to sustain a hearsay objection, as this choice advocates, the court would be improperly depriving the plaintiff of the right to have the letters considered for this non-hearsay purpose of proving notice.

(B) is not the best response,

because the defendant is entitled not to have the letters used for the hearsay purpose of establishing that the writers were in fact burned in the way they described.

Hearsay is an out-of-court statement offered in evidence to prove the truth of the matter asserted in the statement. FRE 801(c). These letters all contain essentially the statement, "I was burned when I heated food in a certain type of container in your microwave."

So the letters would be hearsay if allowed into evidence without restriction, since the jury would then be invited to infer the truth of the matters asserted in the letters, i.e., that each letter writer was in fact burned in the manner she describes. Since there is no applicable hearsay exception triggered by that scenario, admission of the letters without restriction would violate the manufacturer's right to be free of hearsay not within any exception.

(D) is not the best response,

because permitting the letters to be read but not received as an exhibit does not solve the potential hearsay problem.

There are situations in which the correct judicial response to an offer of hearsay evidence is to have the item read aloud to the jury, but not received as an exhibit. This is true, for instance, of past recollection recorded under FRE 803(5). But here, the letters would be hearsay if offered to prove that the letter-writers really were burned in the manner that they describe. And reading the letters aloud, as opposed to admitting them as exhibits, does not solve this problem, since the letters would still be being used as the source of hearsay not falling within any exception. Therefore, only the proposed limiting instruction can solve the hearsay problem.

Answer 9

(C) is the best response,

because the testimony makes it more likely than it would otherwise be that the back injury was caused by the accident, and the testimony does not run afoul of the lay opinion rule.

FRE 402 sets out the general principle that "relevant evidence is admissible," unless some specific rule or principle (e.g., a particular Federal Rule of Evidence) makes it inadmissible. Evidence is "relevant," according to FRE 401, "if: (a) it has any tendency to make a fact more or less probable than it would be without the evidence; and (b) the fact is of consequence in determining the action." Here, the factual proposition "the accident caused the plaintiff's back injury" is more likely to be true if the plaintiff had not had back problems prior to the accident than if she had had such prior problems. Furthermore, the cause of the plaintiff's back injury is obviously a fact "of consequence" in the action. So the fact that the plaintiff had no back problems prior to the accident is "relevant" evidence ("relevant" is synonymous with "probative"), and is thus admissible unless some other specific rule of evidence makes it inadmissible.

The only other rule of evidence that might conceivably apply here is FRE 701, limiting opinion testimony by lay witnesses. But as is further discussed in the treatment of choice A, the testimony here is not opinion testimony.

(A) is not the best response,

because the plaintiff does not need to be qualified as an expert.

It's true that witnesses who are not qualified as experts are subjected to a special rule limiting their rights to give opinion testimony. But not all lay opinions are excluded by that rule, and in any event the testimony here is probably not an opinion at all.

FRE 701, entitled "Opinion Testimony by Lay Witnesses," says that where a witness is not testifying as an expert, "testimony in the form of an opinion is limited to one that is: (a) rationally based on the witness's perception; (b) helpful to clearly understanding the witness's testimony or to determining a fact in issue; and (c) not based on scientific, technical, or other specialized knowledge within the scope of Rule 702." So even if the testimony "I never had any back problems prior to the accident" was considered an opinion as opposed to a statement of fact, that opinion would meet the requirements of Rule 701: (a) it's "rationally based on the witness's perception," since the witness is saying that prior to the accident, she never perceived any meaningful back pain; (b) it's helpful to the jury in determining whether the back pain was caused by the accident; and (c) the witness isn't relying on any scientific, technical or other specialized knowledge in reaching the "opinion" that she didn't have back pain pre-accident. In any event, it's likely that the court would conclude that this testimony was not opinion at all (rather than being permissible non-expert opinion testimony).

(B) is not the best response,

because it cites a fact that does not have bearing on the admissibility of the testimony.

It's certainly true that the plaintiff's pain could have been caused by post-accident factors. But that doesn't mean that the testimony regarding the absence of pre-accident factors is not relevant, and thus admissible. "There is no requirement that the evidence make the existence of the fact to be proved more probable than not or that it provide a sufficient basis for sending the issue to the jury." M&K, § 4.2, p. 154. So even though the proposed testimony does not *eliminate* the possibility that some post-accident factor caused the injury, the testimony at least tends to *lessen* that possibility, and that's enough to make the testimony admissible as having "any tendency to make a fact more or less probable than it would be without the evidence" (FRE 401).

(D) is not the best response,

because it is flatly incorrect as a statement of law.

FRE 701's limits on opinion testimony by lay witnesses apply whether the witness is a party or not. But it's quite doubtful that the plaintiff's proposed testimony here constitutes "opinion" testimony at all. And even if it does constitute opinion testimony, it falls easily within 701's requirements (e.g., it's "rationally based on the perception of the witness," etc.)

Answer 10

(C) is the best response,

because the photograph is relevant, and its admission would not violate the Best Evidence Rule or any other prohibition.

All relevant evidence is admissible, unless some particular rule or doctrine makes it inadmissible. FRE 402. Evidence is "relevant" if "(a) it has any tendency to make a fact more or less probable than it would be without the evidence; and (b) the fact is of consequence in determining the action." FRE 401. One disputed fact in the litigation (and thus a "fact . . . of consequence" under FRE 401) is whether the plaintiff's injuries were severe. The photograph makes it more probable that the plaintiff's injuries were severe than would be the case if the photograph were not present. Therefore, the photograph is relevant, and it's admissible unless something specific makes it inadmissible.

The only plausible ground for inadmissibility relates to the Best Evidence Rule (BER). But as the discussion of choices A and B below makes clear, admission of the photograph would not violate the BER.

(A) is not the best answer,

because the photograph is either a duplicate or the original, so there is no reason to require use of some other duplicate.

This choice does not mention the BER, but you should recognize from the reference to "duplicate" (and from the fact that the item is a photograph) that the choice is referring to an issue concerning the BER. (That's typical on the MBE: When the very name of a doctrine tends to draw your attention to a key issue, the examiners will go out of their way to avoid using the name in the fact pattern or in any of the choices. "Best Evidence Rule" is one of those doctrines, so questions turning on it will rarely mention the doctrine by name.)

First, let's look at the text of the BER itself, to see whether the doctrine might possibly apply. That text is given in FRE 1002, entitled "Requirement of the Original": "An original writing, recording, or photograph is required in order to prove its content unless these rules or a federal statute provides otherwise." Since we are dealing with the admissibility of a photograph, the BER. applies, so the "original" of that photo must be offered unless some provision (typically, something in the Federal Rules) specifically says otherwise. So, in the case of a photograph, what is the "original"? The last sentence of FRE 1001(d) says that "An 'original' of a photograph includes the negative or a print from it." Although neither this definition nor anything else in the Federal Rules deals specifically with the problem of whether a photograph that is a print from the negative of a *videotape* qualifies as an "original" of the photograph, there is at least a respectable chance that the answer would be found to be "yes." In that event, if the court found that the photograph was made directly from the negative of the videotape, the photo would be an original, and would automatically qualify as admissible, without the court's ever getting to the question of the admissibility of duplicates.

Now, let's assume that the photo is deemed *not* to have been made from the negative of the videotape (either because the court concludes that there *is* no negative of a videotape, or because the court concludes that there was a negative of the videotape, but that the photo was not made from that negative). In that scenario, the photo would still be a "duplicate" of the original image from the video tape. That's because FRE 1001(e) says that a "duplicate" is "a counterpart produced by a mechanical, *photographic*, *chemical*, *electronic*, or other equivalent process or technique *that accurately reproduces the original.*" We don't know exactly how the photograph was made, but the facts tells us that it was "made from [the] videotape[.]" The phrase "made from" indicates that some automatic method (rather than, say, a human sketch artist) was used to go from the videotape to the photo. Therefore, if the photo isn't an "original," it's a "duplicate" from the videotape. FRE 1003, entitled "Admissibility of Duplicates," says that "A duplicate is admissible to the *same extent as the original* unless a *genuine question* is raised about the original's authenticity or the circumstances make it *unfair* to admit the duplicate." So if what's being offered is deemed to be a duplicate, FRE 1003 requires admission, because there's no indication that any "genuine question" has been raised by the defense about the photograph's authenticity, nor is there any indication that the circumstances would make it unfair to admit the duplicate.

So regardless of whether the photo is deemed to be an original or a duplicate (and it's clearly one or the other), nothing requires that some other duplicate be found and used. In other words, even if there was some other duplicate available to the defense, the present photograph would still be admissible.

(B) is not the best choice,

because the original videotape has been destroyed, and there is no principle requiring use of a duplicate videotape in lieu of the photograph.

FRE 1004 says that "An original is not required and other evidence of the content of a . . . photograph is admissible if: (a) all the originals are lost or destroyed, and not by the proponent acting in bad faith[.]" We're told that the original of the videotape has been destroyed, and that this occurred due to the station's routine reuse. Therefore, the original videotape has been destroyed, and not due to the bad faith of the proponent (the plaintiff). Consequently, FRE 1004 says that the original of the videotape is not required and that "other evidence" of the videotape (or, in this case, the single-photo frame of the videotape) may be used. In other words, even if something that was not a duplicate was the best that was available (e.g., a hand-drawn reconstruction of a frame from the videotape), this "other evidence" of the content of the photograph would be sufficient.

But the plaintiff's lawyer won't even have to carry the analysis out that far. As described in choice A, the photograph would itself be found to be either an original or a duplicate. If the photo was made from the negative of the videotape, the photo would be an "original," and would be automatically admissible. If the photo is a duplicate, then under the present circumstances, FRE 1003 would make the photo-as-duplicate automatically admissible. (There is no requirement that before one duplicate is admitted, other duplicates must be shown to be unavailable.)

(D) is not the best response,

because, although it correctly states the outcome, it bases that outcome on an incorrect statement of law.

This choice asserts that a photograph can never be excluded as prejudicial so long as the photograph "establishes a disputed fact." There is no such legal principle. Indeed, FRE 403 indicates the contrary, by saying that "The court *may exclude relevant evidence* if its *probative value* is *substantially outweighed* by a danger of one or more of the following: *unfair prejudice*[.]" There is no exception in FRE 403 for photos, so a photo that posed a risk of unfair prejudice substantially greater than the photo's probative value could be excluded under FRE 403. (For instance, a photo could be excluded if it was unusually gruesome, and was being offered in addition to other less-gruesome photos showing the same basic scene.) But the photo here is probative on the issue of the severity of the plaintiff's injuries, and there is no reason to believe that it is unfairly prejudicial, so it would be admissible.

Answer 11

(C) is the best response,

because the employee was speaking about a matter that fell within the scope of his employment.

If the employee's statement is to be used to prove that he (and by extension the corporation he worked for) was negligent, the proposed use is a hearsay use. That is, the statement "I'm sorry for what I did" only shows negligence by a chain of inference: "I am sorry for what I did, so what I did must be the kind of thing that is in some way blameworthy." Thus the statement is being offered to prove the truth of the matter asserted in it—the speaker says that he did something wrong, and that statement is offered to prove that he indeed did something wrong. Since this is a hearsay use, it must fall within some hearsay exception or exclusion, or else be inadmissible.

This choice presents the best rationale for excluding the statement from the hearsay rule. FRE 801(d)(2) excludes as non-hearsay any statement that is offered against an "opposing party," and that "(D) was made by the party's *agent or employee* on a matter within the *scope of that relationship* and *while it existed*[.]" This is one of the "adoptive admission" exclusions. Here, we're told that the driver was an employee of the defendant corporation, and that he was working for the defendant ("making deliveries for the defendant") at the time the accident occurred. So the statement about what happened concerned a matter within the speaker's employment relationship with the defendant, and was made while the employment relationship still existed. That's enough to exclude the statement from the hearsay rule under 801(d)(2)(D), if offered against the employer. (Notice, by the way, that this exception, as opposed to 801(d)(2)(C)'s exception for "authorized" statements, applies even if the statement was *unauthorized* by the defendant employer, as long as it concerned a matter within the scope of the employment and was made while the employment continued. So we don't have to worry about whether the employer had a policy prohibiting drivers from commenting on accidents in which they were involved.)

(A) is not the best response,

because it supports a rationale that, even if applicable, would not get the statement admitted for a substantive use.

It's true that the statement could be admitted as a prior inconsistent statement, that is, a statement that is inconsistent with the employee's trial testimony that he exercised due care. The common law allows proof of prior inconsistent statements by a testifying witness, and FRE 613 in fact relaxes the common-law rule by not requiring that the prior inconsistent statement be shown to the witness in advance of the questioning. But when a prior inconsistent statement is used, that is an *impeaching* use, not a substantive use. And the question tells you that the plaintiff is offering the prior statement "to prove negligence." That's a substantive use (the plaintiff is trying to demonstrate the truth of the matter asserted therein—that the employee is sorry for "what I did," thus tending to show that what he did was somehow wrongful, i.e., negligent.) Since the statement's status as a "prior inconsistent statement" could only relate to this impeaching use, this choice cannot be the best method of achieving the substantive goal of proving negligence.

(B) is not the best response,

because the declarant is available to testify.

FRE 804(b)(3) gives a hearsay exception for a "statement against interest," defined as a statement that "(A) a reasonable person in the declarant's position would have made only if the person believed it to be true because, when made, it . . . had [a] great . . . tendency to . . . expose the declarant to civil or criminal liability." Since the statement would tend to expose the employee (not just the corporation) to civil liability for the accident, it seems to meet this definition. But the statement against interest exception, like all the 804(b) exceptions, requires that the declarant be *unavailable* as a witness. We're told that the employee has testified at trial, so we know he is not unavailable.

Notice that to eliminate this choice, you have to know that the statement against interest exception is one of the declarant-unavailable exceptions. The three major declarant-unavailable exceptions are for (1) former testimony; (2) dying declarations; and (3) statements against interest. You simply have to *memorize this short list.*

(D) is not the best response,

because the then-existing state of mind exception is not backward looking.

It's true that FRE 803 gives a hearsay exception for what is popularly called "state of mind." 803(3), entitled "Then-Existing Mental, Emotional, or Physical Condition," gives an exception for "A statement of the declarant's *then-existing state of mind* (such as motive, intent, or plan) or emotional, sensory, or physical condition (such as mental feeling, pain, or bodily health)[.]" The problem is that the language giving this exception ends by excluding from the exception "*a statement of memory or belief to prove the fact remembered or believed* unless it relates to the validity or terms of the declarant's will."

Here, the driver is saying that he is sorry for how he acted on the prior day, so his statement is a "statement of memory or belief to prove the fact remembered or believed." (We're not really interested in the employee's present emotional state; we're interested in the underlying fact that he behaved previously in such a way as to cause him to be regretful now—that's the only sense in which the statement tends to prove that his conduct was negligent.)

Answer 12

(A) is the best response,

because this choice precisely summarizes FRE 612's treatment of writings used to refresh a witness's memory.

FRE 612 gives the adverse party certain options when a witness uses a writing to refresh her memory. Those options vary depending on whether the writing was used while the witness was testifying, or merely before the witness took the stand. If the witness used the writing for memory-refreshment "*while testifying*," then 612(b) gives the adverse party an *absolute* right of inspection: That adverse party "*is entitled* to have the writing produced at the hearing, to *inspect it*, to cross-examine the witness about it, and to introduce in evidence any portion that relates to the witness's testimony."

If, on the other hand, the witness merely consulted the writing *before* taking the stand, 612(a) says that the rights of inspection, cross-examination, etc. quoted above from 612(b), apply only "if the court decides that justice requires the party to have those options." Since choice A distinguishes between the witness's use while testifying (where the opponent has a mandatory right of inspection) and her use before testifying (where the court has discretion about whether to allow the right of inspection), it's the correct choice.

(B) is not the best response,

because it incorrectly states that the right of inspection depends on whether the document contains the witness's statement.

When a witness consults a document to refresh her memory, FRE 612 gives the adversary certain rights of inspection. Those rights do not vary according to whether the document contains the witness's own statement. So here, the adversary has a right to inspect the FBI report (a mandatory right if the witness consulted the report during her testimony, and a right that's in the court's discretion if the consultation was only pre-testimony), and that's true whether or not the report mentions or quotes the teller's own statement to the agent who prepared the report. The idea behind FRE 612 is that *whatever* the contents are of the document that the witness consulted, the adversary should have at least a limited right to inspect that document.

(C) is not the best response,

because it incorrectly states that there is no possible right of inspection if the teller used the document to refresh her recollection before taking the stand.

FRE 612 guarantees the adversary the right to inspect any document that the witness consulted while on the stand. But that rule also gives the adversary a shot at persuading the court to allow inspection of a document that the witness consulted during trial preparation, before taking the stand. FRE 612(a) refers to certain options (inspection, etc.) that 612(b) gives the adversary, and says that if the witness used the document to refresh her memory "before testifying," those options exist only "if the court decides that justice requires the party to have those options." Choice C, by saying that the court should not allow the examination if the witness merely consulted the report before taking the stand, is flatly inconsistent with the discretion given to the court in the just-quoted portion of 612(a).

(D) is not the best response,

because it imposes a reading-and-approval condition that is not present in the relevant rule.

The examiners, in offering this choice, seem to be trying to confuse you into relying on an entirely inapplicable rule, FRE 803(5). That Rule contains a hearsay exception for past recollection recorded, an exception that covers a document created shortly after an event, made by (or approved by) a person with fresh knowledge of the matter, whose memory has since become impaired. Here, the defendant is not trying to get the report admitted for its substantive value (he merely wants to examine it), so no hearsay exception is even relevant. FRE 612, the rule that applies here because it gives an adversary the possible right to inspect a document that the witness has consulted during trial preparation, does not impose any requirement that the witness have read or approved the document while the matter covered by it was fresh in her mind.

Answer 13

(D) is the best response,

because the treatment record is a business record, and there is a hearsay exception allowing proof of the absence of an entry in such a record.

First, you have to decide whether the plaintiff, by trying to show absence of an entry, is proposing to make a hearsay use. Hearsay is an out-of-court statement offered to prove the truth of a matter asserted in the statement. The plaintiff is trying to prove that the prescribed medication was not administered by the nurse. The absence of any entry showing administration tends to prove that no such administration occurred, since the administration would probably have been recorded if it had occurred. So the record is in effect asserting, "The medicine wasn't given." This is therefore a hearsay use—the record is being offered to prove that something asserted in the record (failure to give the medicine) is a truthful assertion.

FRE 803(6) embodies the FRE's version of the business records hearsay exception, allowing admission of records of a "regularly conducted activity of a business [or] organization," if the record was made at or near the time of the event being recorded by someone with knowledge, and it was the "regular practice" of the organization to keep such records. The patient record here qualifies. (The fact pattern doesn't go through each individual element that a record must satisfy, but the pattern tells us that the librarian "authenticated the hospital's record," from which we can infer that the requirements of 803(6) have been satisfied.)

What's being offered, of course, is not an affirmative statement found in the patient record, it's the fact that there *is* no statement in the record showing that the medication was administered. This is precisely the situation covered by FRE 803(7), entitled "Absence of a Record of Regularly Conducted Activity." 803(7) says that once a record is shown to qualify as a business record under 803(6), there is a hearsay exception for:

> "Evidence that a matter is not included in [a business] record . . . if:
>
> (A) the evidence is admitted to prove that the matter did not occur or exist;
>
> (B) a record was regularly kept for a matter of that kind; and
>
> (C) the opponent does not show that the possible source of the information or other cir-cumstances indicate a lack of trustworthiness."

Here, the absence of an entry showing the giving of a medication meets all these requirements: (1) plaintiff is trying to show that the giving of the medication is a "matter [that] did not occur or exist"; (2) the librarian's authentication shows that a record was "regularly kept for a matter of that kind" (i.e., that the patient records captured any treatment given to a patient); and (3) there's no indication that the hospital (the "opponent" of the evidence) has shown, or could show, that the source of the record, or any other circumstance, indicates a lack of trustworthiness. (As to (3), the hospital would have had, if anything, an incentive to falsely record that a prescribed treatment *was* given, not an incentive to falsely record that a prescribed treatment was *not* given). So the absence of an entry showing that the medication was given falls within the absence-of-entry provision of 803(7), making it admissible even though hearsay.

(A) is not the best response,

because although the record is hearsay, it falls within the absence-of-entry exception.

As is discussed more fully in the treatment of choice D, this is indeed a hearsay use (an event implicitly stated in the record as not having occurred is being offered to prove that the event didn't occur). But because the patient record is a business record, the absence of an entry in it showing that the medication was given is admissible under FRE 803(7) to prove that the medication was not given, since if it had been, that fact would have been recorded.

(B) is not the best response,

because even if the nurse's testimony is the "best evidence" of her actions, no principle requires the use of the best evidence here.

First, it's not at all clear as a factual matter that the "best evidence" of the nurse's actions is indeed her testimony about those actions. The contrary is probably true—the nurse has an incentive to testify that she gave the medication, so the record is probably a more accurate source of what really happened.

But in any event, even if we were to stipulate that the nurse's testimony *is* the "best evidence" of whether the treatment was given, there is no principle that requires that the "best evidence" be used here. There is something called the "Best Evidence Rule," and that Rule, when it applies, requires that an original writing or photograph be admitted, instead of, say, evidence about what the contents of the writing or photograph were. But there is no principle running in the opposite direction—live testimony is never required merely because it is arguably a "better" source of evidence than some document. So here, the patient has the option to call the nurse, but the patient is entitled instead (or in addition) to present the treatment record.

(C) is not the best response,

because the nurse has not been shown to be unavailable to testify.

The record is being offered for a hearsay purpose. (See the discussion of choice D). So some exception to the hearsay rule is required. And it's true that one of the standard hearsay exceptions is for statements against interest, given by FRE 804(b)(3). But the statement-against-interest exception is a "*declarant unavailable*" exception, and there is nothing to indicate in our facts that the declarant (the nurse) is not available to testify. (Even if the nurse *were* unavailable to testify, it's not certain that an "absence of statement" can qualify as a "statement against interest.")

Answer 14

(A) is the best response,

because the statement is inadmissible hearsay if offered to prove that the car jerked suddenly, but admissible for impeachment as a prior inconsistent statement of a non-testifying declarant.

Let's look first at the statement's use for *substantive* (as opposed to impeachment) purposes. If the statement is being offered to prove that the car suddenly jerked and threw the student out (so as to suggest negligence by the amusement company), that's a hearsay use—the statement is being offered to prove the truth of the matter asserted therein. And there is no applicable hearsay exception. (For instance, the declarant—the bystander—is making a statement about something the bystander witnessed the day before, so it's not a present sense impression or an excited utterance.)

Now, let's think about the statement's use to *impeach the credibility* of the declarant (the bystander). This is a situation in which an initial statement by the bystander/declarant has already been admitted into evidence under a hearsay exception. (That statement, "That crazy fool is standing up . . . ," was properly admitted as an excited utterance under FRE 803(2).) Once a hearsay statement has been admitted, then even if the declarant never appears as a witness, FRE 806 says that "the declarant's credibility may be attacked . . . by any evidence that would be admissible for those purposes if the declarant had testified as a witness." In other words, under FRE 806 the party who is opposing the statement may impeach the declarant's credibility by any means that would be proper if the declarant had testified as a witness. Since a testifying witness may be impeached by showing that he made a prior inconsistent statement, Rule 806 means that the bystander here may similarly be impeached by showing that he made a prior inconsistent statement.

For purposes of FRE 806, the reference to a "prior" inconsistent statement means merely, in effect, "prior to the in-court repetition of the declarant's out-of-court statement." (*See* Rule 806, second sentence: "The court may admit evidence of the declarant's inconsistent statement or conduct, *regardless of when it occurred*[.]") In other words, the fact that the bystander's statement that the "car jerked suddenly" was made *after* the bystander made the "crazy fool standing up" statement doesn't matter—all that counts is that the "car jerked" statement was made before the "crazy fool" statement was *repeated in court*.

One last matter: The two statements are directly inconsistent, since the first statement implies that the student stood up voluntarily, whereas the second suggests that he was thrown out of his seat while still sitting. So the second statement is properly viewed as a prior inconsistent one.

(B) is not the correct response,

because when offered to prove negligence, the statement is hearsay not within any exception.

The statement is admissible for impeachment since it is a prior inconsistent statement offered against a declarant; see the discussion of choice A for more about this. But the statement is not admissible to prove the amusement company's negligence. If the statement were used to prove negligence, it would be being offered to prove the truth of the matter asserted in it. That is, the student would be offering the statement that the car jerked suddenly and threw the student out, as a way to prove that the amusement company operated the roller coaster negligently (since a properly-operated coaster doesn't jerk so suddenly that people are thrown out of their seats). Use of an out-of-court statement to prove the truth of the matter asserted therein is hearsay, and is inadmissible unless an exception applies. No hearsay exception or exclusion applies here. The exceptions that come closest to working are the present sense impression and excited utterance exceptions, but each of these requires that the statement be essentially contemporaneous with the event being described or felt, and the statement here was made the day after the event in question.

(C) is not the best response,

because impeachment of a declarant by prior inconsistent statement does not require that the declarant be given the opportunity to explain or deny the inconsistency.

Even in the case of a testifying witness, FRE 613(b) would not require the questioner to give the witness an opportunity to explain or deny a prior inconsistent statement except *after-the-fact*: "When examining a witness about the witness's prior statement, a party need not show it or disclose its contents to the witness. But the party must, on request, *show it or disclose its contents* to an adverse party's attorney." (Then, the party who called the witness who's being impeached can re-call the witness to explain or deny the statement.)

When the declarant has *not* testified, and the out-of-court declaration is merely introduced by some other means, the party seeking to use the declarant's prior inconsistent statement does not even have to make this after-the-fact disclosure. FRE 806, after stating the general principle that the declarant's credibility may be attacked by any evidence that would be admissible for those purposes if the declarant had testified as a witness, goes on to say that "The court may admit evidence of the declarant's inconsistent statement or conduct, *regardless of . . . whether the declarant had an opportunity to explain or deny it*."

(D) is not the best response,

because there is no requirement that the bystander be called as a witness before being impeached by means of the prior inconsistent statement.

It's true that the bystander has not been called as a witness, yet is having her credibility attacked by means of a prior inconsistent statement. But this is not a problem—FRE 806 says that when a hearsay statement has been admitted, "the declarant's credibility may be attacked . . . by any evidence that would be admissible for those purposes if the declarant had testified as a witness." Here, the declarant's initial statement ("That crazy fool is standing up . . . ") was properly admitted, even though hearsay, under the exceptions for either present sense impression or excited utterance. Once that happened, the opponent (the student) was entitled to impeach the bystander's credibility by any of the techniques that could have been used to impeach a live witness; one of those techniques was the right to prove a prior inconsistent statement by the witness. The student was not required to call the bystander as a witness before making this effort at impeachment.

Answer 15

(B) is the best response,

because it represents a type of statement that is not "testimonial."

Under the Supreme Court's decision in *Crawford v. Washington*, 541 U.S. 36 (2004), the Confrontation Clause bars the introduction against the defendant at a criminal trial of an out of court "*testimonial*" statement, unless either the declarant is made available for cross-examination at trial, or the defendant had a prior opportunity to cross-examine the declarant about the statement. Under *Crawford* and later cases decided under it, statements by witnesses made during the course of police interrogations, or made to a grand jury, will typically be found to be testimonial and thus inadmissible if the witness is not produced for cross-examination at trial.

So the issue in this question is whether the type of evidence is "testimonial." In this choice, we're dealing with documents that would qualify for the business records hearsay exception. As the Supreme Court said in *Melendez-Diaz v. Mass.*, 557 U.S. 305, 324 (2009), "business and public records" are generally admissible without giving the accused the right to confront the maker of the record "because—having been created for the administration of an entity's affairs and not for the purpose of establishing or proving some fact at trial—[these records] are *not testimonial*." (*See also U.S. v. Mashek*, 606 F.3d 922 (8th Cir. 2010), a methamphetamine prosecution, where the court relied on this language to hold that local pharmacies' consumer-purchase records showing that D purchased ingredients commonly used to manufacture meth could be admitted against him without raising a Confrontation Clause issue, because these purchase records were non-testimonial business records.)

So the computerized deposit records here, being business records that were not created for the purpose of establishing or proving some fact at trial, were non-testimonial and can therefore be admitted without a Confrontation Clause issue.

(A) is not the best response,

because the transcript contains the teller's testimony, which was never subject to cross examination by the defendant.

Crawford says that an out-of-court "testimonial" statement may not be used against an accused unless the declarant (the person who made the statement) is either made available for cross-examination at trial, or was subject to cross-examination by the defendant at the time the statement was made. Grand jury testimony is the classic form of testimonial statement, since its purpose is to establish or prove past events for use in a later prosecution. Because the defendant is never permitted to be present during grand jury proceedings, we know that in this case the defendant had no opportunity to cross-examine the teller during that testimony. Since the teller is now dead, he is unavailable at trial. So the Confrontation Clause blocks the use of the testimony no matter how reliable it might seem to be.

(C) is not the best response,
because the teller's identification of the defendant is a testimonial statement that was never subject to cross-examination.

This choice is incorrect for the same reason that choice A is incorrect: The teller's identification of the defendant at the lineup was a testimonial statement, and was never subject to cross-examination by the defendant. It's true that the *officer* is available to be cross-examined at the trial regarding his testimony that he witnessed the teller make the identification at the lineup. But that cross-examination is not a substitute for cross examination of the *teller*—the defendant has been deprived of the opportunity to ask the teller questions about the basis for the latter's statement of identification (e.g., "Was the robber wearing a mask?" or "How good is your eyesight?")

(D) is not the best response,
because the videotaped statement was testimonial, and is not subject to cross-examination.

Although only an hour had passed after the robbery, that was enough time for the eyewitness's videotaped statement to be of a past-looking "What happened?" nature (and thus testimonial) rather than of an emergency non-testimonial nature (as, say, a 9-1-1 call for assistance might be). Therefore, the videotaped eyewitness statement, like the grand jury testimony and the lineup identification, was "testimonial"—it was made for the purpose of proving past events for use in a later prosecution. Since the eyewitness was not subject to cross-examination at the time of the statement, and since he or she is now dead and thus unavailable for cross-examination at trial, use of the statement would violate the defendant's Confrontation Clause rights.

Answer 16

(C) is the best response,
because what is being proven is not the contents of a recording.

The Best Evidence Rule (BER) is specified in FRE 1002: "An original writing, *recording*, or photograph is required in order to *prove its content*[.]" So if the agent was attempting to "prove the content" of a recording, FRE 1002 would require the government to put the audiotape into evidence. But the BER does not apply to events that have by *happenstance* been recorded—it applies only where the terms of the recording, *per se*, are what are being sought to be proved.

Here, what's being proved is the contents of the conspiratorial conversation, as overheard by the agent. The fact that the government happened to have made a tape of the conversation, therefore, does not mean that the prosecution is attempting to "prove the contents" of this incidentally-created tape. So as long as the agent is testifying only to the conversation that he overheard "live" (not what he later learned by listening to the audiotape), the BER doesn't apply.

(A) is not the best response,
because the BER does not apply.

There is no general principle in the law of evidence that the "best evidence" on some point must be used to prove that point. There is something informally called the "Best Evidence Rule." But the BER is narrow in scope—it applies only where what is being proved are the "contents" of a writing, recording or photograph. Here, the agent actually heard the conversation "live," and he is testifying based on what he heard (not on the contents of the audiotape that happens to have been made). Since the agent is not relying on the audiotape for his testimony, the BER does not apply. (The government would also be free to prove the contents of the conversation by playing the audiotape, but it's not *required* to use that evidence in lieu of the agent's testimony.)

(B) is not the best response,
because the statements fall within the hearsay exclusion for admissions.

FRE 801(d)(2) makes several types of statements non-hearsay because they are "party admissions." Here, any statement made by the *defendant* himself is non-hearsay by virtue of 801(d)(2)(A), which excludes from the hearsay rule a statement offered against an opposing party, if the statement "was made by the party in an individual or representative capacity." What about the statements made by the co-conspirator; are these admissible against the defendant? The answer is yes: 801(d)(2)(E) excludes from hearsay, if offered against a party, a statement that was "made by the party's *coconspirator* during and in furtherance of the conspiracy." Since the conspiracy was still alive when the co-conspirator made the statements in question, and since he was attempting to further the conspiracy by planning for the incoming shipment, the requirements of the co-conspirator exclusion are satisfied. So all statements that the agent is testifying to having heard fall within one or the other of these Rule 801(d)(2) exclusions.

(D) is not the correct response,
because it relies on an irrelevant fact.

The testimony of the agent about what he heard is admissible because, as explained in the discussion of choice B, all of the statements being repeated fall within one or another hearsay exclusion relating to admissions. Even if the audiotape were fully audible, the agent would still be permitted to testify to everything he heard, because there is no principle of evidence that would bar this testimony. In particular, the BER does not require production of the audiotape, because the agent is not proving "the contents" of the audiotape, since he is not relying on the audiotape for his testimony. See the discussion of choice (C) for more about this.

Answer 17

(B) is the best response,

because the tape is admissible as a prior inconsistent statement offered to impeach the witness, but inadmissible substantively because of hearsay.

First, let's consider the recording's admissibility for impeachment. FRE 613(b) implicitly allows use of extrinsic evidence to show that a witness has made a prior inconsistent statement. ("Extrinsic evidence of a witness's prior inconsistent statement is admissible only if the witness is given an opportunity to explain or deny the statement and an adverse party is given an opportunity to examine the witness about it, or if justice so requires.")

So here, once the witness said on the stand that the employer had given a non-racial explanation for the firing, the witness's tape recorded statement that the employer had given a racial explanation was extrinsic evidence tending to show a prior inconsistent statement by the witness. Consequently, the statement was admissible for impeachment under FRE 613(b), since the witness was still on the stand (and thus had a chance to explain or deny the statement).

Now, let's consider substantive admissibility. Here, the tape recording is "hearsay within hearsay." The outer level is that the witness is making a recorded, and thus out-of-court, statement. The inner level is that the witness is repeating an admission made by the employer.

Here, the inner level is not inadmissible hearsay, because it falls within the exception for admissions introduced against the maker. See FRE 801(d)(2) (a statement is not hearsay if "[t]he statement is offered against an opposing party and: (A) was made by the party in an individual or representative capacity[.]") But the outer level is hearsay that is not within any exception—the witness is making an out-of-court statement (the witness's words on the recording) offered to demonstrate the truth of the matter asserted (that the employer made a certain admission to the witness). There is nothing in this statement (e.g., "The employer told me he fired the plaintiff for racial reasons") that falls within any hearsay exception. Thus, the statement can't come in for the substantive purpose of demonstrating that the employer was racially motivated.

(A) is not the best response,

because, as is described in the analysis of choice B, the recording is not admissible as "evidence of the employer's racial motivation," which is a substantive (non-impeachment-of-the-witness) purpose.

(C) is not the best response,

because as is described in choice B, the statement is admissible for impeachment as a prior inconsistent statement of the witness.

(D) is not the best response,

because no violation of the Constitution occurs when a person secretly records a conversation to which he is a party (and in any event, the witness was not a governmental actor, again preventing the recording from possibly being a constitutional violation).

Answer 18

(C) is the best response,

because the witness cannot be impeached on a collateral issue by extrinsic evidence.

The manager's testimony is not relevant to any substantive issue in the case—it bears solely on the witness's credibility. Therefore, the matter is governed by FRE 608(b), which says in part that "[e]xcept for a criminal conviction under Rule 609, extrinsic evidence is not admissible to prove specific instances of a witness's conduct in order to attack or support the witness's character for truthfulness." In other words, once a lawyer has completed cross-examination of a witness, he must be satisfied with whatever he could bring out *on cross-examination* that tends to show that the witness lied on a collateral matter (i.e., a matter not pertaining to the substantive issues in the case)—the lawyer may not introduce another witness, or document, to prove that the first witness lied.

Here, the testimony of the manager is extrinsic evidence of specific conduct by the witness, offered for the purpose of attacking the witness's credibility. Therefore, it is barred by the just-quoted portion of 608(b).

(A) is not the best response,

because the judge has no discretion to admit extrinsic evidence to impeach on a collateral issue.

If the prosecutor had presented the witness with a document tending to show he had lied on his credit card application, that would be admissible in the judge's discretion, because the second sentence of Rule 608(b) says that "[t]he court may, on cross-examination, allow [specific instances of a witness's conduct] to be inquired into if they are probative of the character for truthfulness or untruthfulness of: (1) the witness[.]" But since the testimony here is from the manager about the witness's credibility, it's extrinsic evidence governed by the first sentence of 608(b) (quoted in the discussion of choice C above), not the sentence just quoted; therefore, the judge can't use her discretion to admit it.

(B) is not the best response,

because the witness may have "opened the door" to being asked further questions about his application on cross-examination, but he did not (and could not) open the door to the use of extrinsic evidence to show he was lying.

As the discussion of choice C indicates, once a lawyer has completed cross-examination of a witness, he must be satisfied with whatever he could bring out on cross tending to show that the witness lied on a collateral matter (i.e., a matter not pertaining to the substantive issues in the case). The lawyer may not introduce another witness, or document, to show that the first witness lied. So nothing the witness said could have "opened the door" to this type of extrinsic evidence.

(D) is not the best response,

because whether the witness could have honestly misunderstood the form is irrelevant—the evidence is extrinsic evidence and is barred because it pertains to a collateral matter.

The first sentence of Rule 608(b), quoted in the discussion of choice C above, bars extrinsic evidence to prove a collateral matter. The matter here (whether the witness lied on his credit card application) is a collateral matter, since it pertains only to the witness's credibility, not to any substantive issue in the case. Therefore, even if the witness could *not* reasonably have misunderstood the meaning of the question on the application, the prosecutor was still not entitled to present a second witness (a form of extrinsic evidence) to prove either that the witness was generally untruthful or that his testimony on cross about the application was untruthful.

Answer 19

(B) is the best response,

because evidence of prior bad acts to prove that on the present occasion the defendant acted in conformity with the character indicated by those prior bad acts is inadmissible.

FRE 404(a)(1) states the familiar principle that "[e]vidence of a person's character or character trait is not admissible to prove that on a particular occasion the person acted in accordance with the character or trait" (subject to exceptions not relevant here). The prosecution here is trying to get the evidence in to suggest, in effect, that "[s]ince the defendant is the sort of person who has twice before shot at victims or menaced them with a gun, he is likely to have fired the sniper shot charged here."

If the prior bad acts had been extremely similar to the one charged here (e.g., they both involved the firing of sniper shots at a person, in similar circumstances, and with a similar motive), the prior acts might be admissible under FRE 404(b)'s statement that "[e]vidence of a crime, wrong, or other act is not admissible to prove a person's character . . . (2) [but] may be admissible for *another purpose*, such as proving motive, . . . preparation [or] plan[.]" But the two prior acts here are so different from the crime charged—neither is a hidden sniper-style shot fired directly at a human being, as is charged here—that none of the exceptions in 404(b) can even plausibly apply. (The requisite similarity is clearly not established by the mere fact that all the acts, including the one charged, involve a firearm.)

(A) is not the best response,

because evidence of prior bad acts to prove action in conformity therewith is not admissible either on direct or cross.

For the reasons described in choice B above, this is "prior bad acts" evidence offered to show a propensity to act in conformity therewith. Therefore, it's forbidden by 404(A). And that's true whether the evidence is presented on direct or is elicited on cross.

If you were tempted by this answer, you may have thought that these prior bad acts could be used on cross for impeachment purposes. To understand why this is not so, first notice that there's no indication that the defendant was convicted of a crime for these prior actions. Therefore, their use for impeachment is governed by FRE 608(b) (specific instances of conduct), not 609 (impeachment by evidence of conviction of crime).

Now, 608(b), after banning the use of extrinsic evidence to "prove specific instances of a witness's conduct in order to attack or support the witness's character for truthfulness," goes on to say that "the court may, on cross-examination, allow [such specific instances] to be inquired into *if they are probative of the character for truthfulness or untruthfulness* of: (1) the witness[.]" As you can see by the italicized phrase, this exception applies only to prior bad acts that are probative of the witness's *truthfulness*. Since shootings and menacings aren't probative of truthfulness, they cannot be inquired about even on the cross of the defendant.

(C) is not the best response,

because evidence of a propensity to violence is inadmissible character evidence.

The Federal Rules of Evidence embody the principle that prior crimes may not be introduced to show the defendant's character, thereby justifying the inference that he acted in conformity with that character on the present occasion. This rule is discussed in the discussion of choice B above.

The present choice is literally inconsistent with the no-prior-acts-to-show-conforming-character rule, so it's clearly wrong.

(D) is not the best response,

because the prior acts offered are not sufficiently similar to bear on the defendant's identity, plan, or motive.

It's true that FRE 404(b) says that "[e]vidence of a crime, wrong, or other act . . . may be admissible for another purpose, such as proving motive, . . . plan [or] identity[.]" But there's no indication that motive, plan, or identity was at issue in the case, or was the purpose for which this other-bad-acts evidence was offered.

In any event, to bear on motive, plan, or identity, the prior acts would have to be much more similar to the present attack than they in fact are: Neither of the prior acts was a hidden sniper-style shot fired directly at a human being. (It's clearly not enough that all the acts, including the one charged, involve a firearm, or violence.)

Answer 20

(C) is the best response,

because the defendant was attempting to evade taxes.

The essence of the attorney-client privilege is that a client has the right not to disclose, and the right to prevent her lawyer from disclosing, any confidential communication between the two of them relating to the professional relationship. An exception to this rule—the "crime or fraud" exception—states there is no privilege if the services of the lawyer were sought or obtained to enable or aid anyone to commit or plan to commit what the client knew or reasonably should have known to be a crime or fraud.

Here, the letter constitutes the defendant's attempt to have the attorney conspire with the defendant to commit tax fraud. Therefore, the communication covered by the letter falls within the crime-or-fraud exception, and is therefore not privileged.

(A) is not the best response,

because acts in furtherance of a crime are not covered by attorney-client privilege.

For the reasons described in the analysis of choice B above, the letter fell within the crime-or-fraud exception, and thus was not privileged. Therefore, choice A is wrong.

(B) is not the best response,

because the Fifth Amendment does not normally protect against the compelled disclosure of voluntarily created testimonial documents.

The Fifth Amendment protects against compulsory self-incrimination. The document here was voluntarily created by the defendant. Therefore, it would not be a violation of the Fifth Amendment for either the defendant or the attorney to be forced to produce the document.

(D) is not the best response,

because the attorney-client privilege can be claimed by the attorney on behalf of the client.

Where the privilege exists, both the client and the attorney can claim it, but the attorney can claim the privilege only on behalf of the client. However, in the absence of evidence to the contrary, courts will presume that the attorney who claims the privilege is acting on behalf of the client. A court would certainly make this presumption here. Therefore, this choice reaches the right result (privilege does not apply), but for the wrong reason.

Answer 21

(A) is the best response,

because the defendant auto manufacturer is not attempting to prove a character trait, but is trying to provide an alternate explanation.

An issue in the case (indeed, the core issue) is whether the accident was caused by a defective steering wheel or, instead, by some other cause not associated with the defendant auto manufacturer. If the wife was intoxicated at the time she was driving the car, this fact would obviously make it more likely than it would otherwise be that the intoxication, not a steering-wheel defect, was the cause of the accident. Therefore, the wife's intoxication was directly relevant evidence that does not fall within any exclusion. (As to the argument that the evidence is inadmissible character evidence, see the discussion of choice C).

(B) is not the best response,

because the defendant auto manufacturer is not trying to prove a trait of the plaintiff's deceased wife's character.

If the evidence being offered by the defendant auto manufacturer was evidence that the wife was often drunk, then the evidence would in effect be character evidence. In that event, this choice would still be wrong, because character evidence, offered to prove that the person acted in conformity therewith on a particular occasion, is generally inadmissible. FRE 404(a)(1).

But, here, what's being offered is not character evidence (evidence that the wife was often or generally drunk) but rather direct evidence of behavior *on the particular occasion in question* (i.e., evidence that she was drunk while driving into the fatal accident). This is not character evidence at all.

(C) is not the best response,

because, although it more or less correctly states a rule, that rule does not apply on these facts.

It's true that under FRE 404(a)(1), generally evidence of a person's character or a trait of character "is not admissible to prove that on a particular occasion the person acted in accordance with the character or trait." It's also true that under FRE 404(b), "[e]vidence of a crime, wrong, or other act is not admissible to prove a person's character in order to show that on a particular occasion the person acted in accordance with the character." Therefore, if the defendant auto manufacturer were trying to show that the wife was drunk on particular occasions *other than* the one now in question, that evidence would indeed be excludible under 404(b)'s ban on specific-acts evidence to prove conduct in conformity with character.

But that's not what's being offered here: What's being offered is direct evidence that the wife was drunk *on the particular occasion in issue,* and that's not "character" evidence of any sort.

(D) is not the best response,

because proof of the plaintiff's wife's intoxication would be probative of the defendant auto manufacturer's defense.

It's true that under FRE 403, relevant evidence may be excluded "if its probative value is substantially outweighed by a danger of . . . unfair prejudice[.]" But given that the key issue in the case is "What caused the accident?" and given that the wife's intoxication, if it existed, would have tremendous probative value on the issue of the accident's cause, no court would conclude that there was a danger of "unfair" prejudice, or that that prejudice substantially outweighed the evidence's probative value.

Answer 22

(C) is the best response,

because it correctly characterizes the facts as ones that would not give rise to a duty on the co-defendant to respond.

Under these facts, the prosecutor is attempting to admit the defendant's statement against the co-defendant. If it's admissible at all, it will be admissible as an admission by silent adoption—FRE 801(d)(2)(B) excludes, when used against a party, a statement that "is one the party manifested that it adopted or believed to be true." However, as courts have interpreted the adoption-by-silence aspect of 801(d)(2)(B), an admission by silence is only admissible if the person *heard* the accusatory statement, he was *capable of denying* the statement, and a reasonable person *would have denied the statement were it not true*, under the same circumstances. Here, the fact that the co-defendant was in police custody makes it unlikely that a reasonable person under the same circumstances would have denied the statement, since he could reasonably feel that he didn't want to say anything at all in the presence of police. Since C correctly states this, it's the best response.

(A) is not the best response,

because it does not correctly apply the rule on "tacit admissions."

An admission by silence is only admissible, under judicial interpretations of FRE 801(d)(2)(B), if the person heard the accusatory statement, he was capable of denying the statement, and a reasonable person would have denied the statement were it not true, under the same circumstances. Here, the fact that the co-defendant was in police custody makes it unlikely that a reasonable person under the same circumstances would have denied the statement, since he could reasonably feel that he didn't want to say anything at all in the presence of police. Since this element is missing, the statement will not be admissible against the co-defendant as a tacit admission, and so A is not the best response.

(B) is not the best response,

because it misstates the facts: The admission here was not made during the course and in furtherance of the common plan.

An admission by a co-participant is admissible against the defendant if it was made during the course and in furtherance of the common plan. FRE 801(d)(2)(E).

Here, the defendant and co-defendant are in police custody, and, unless they're mighty unusual robbers, they wouldn't have planned to be caught and arrested by the police. Since the common plan had ended before the time in question here, the defendant's statement, as co-participant, is not admissible against the co-defendant. Since B doesn't recognize this, it is not the best response.

(D) is not the best response,

because the defendant's comment *is* of probative value in the co-defendant's trial.

"Probative value" is another way of wording "logical relevance." That is, a piece of evidence is logically relevant if it tends to prove or disprove a material fact. The comment of the defendant, a co-conspirator of the co-defendant, that the co-defendant planned the hold up, would clearly make it more likely that the co-defendant, in fact, took part in the crime. Thus, the statement may be inadmissible, but it won't be because it's irrelevant. Since D wrongly states that the comment is of no probative value, it is not the best response.

Answer 23

(D) is the best response,

because the trial testimony was a statement within a statement, and the outer level was hearsay not within any exception.

Anytime the evidence in question consists of an out-of-court statement by *A* repeating another out-of-court statement by *B*, you have to analyze both *A*'s statement and *B*'s statement—if *either* statement is hearsay not falling within any exception, the combined statement cannot come in.

Here, it's true that the "inner level," i.e., the security director's statement ("Stop shoplifters at all costs"), is admissible, because it's not hearsay—it doesn't assert the truth of any matter, so it can't now be offered to prove the truth of the matter asserted therein.

But the "outer level"—i.e., the guard's trial testimony about what the security director had previously said—is hearsay not within any exception. First, this testimony is hearsay, because it's being offered to show that the security director really uttered the words, "Stop shoplifters at all costs" (meaning that the shooting falls within the defendant's respondeat superior liability), and is thus offered to show the truth of the matter asserted therein.

Second, this testimony by the guard does not fall within any hearsay exception. For example, the testimony is not an admission by an agent of a party, admissible against the party, because by the time of the criminal trial, the guard was no longer working for the defendant.

Nor is the guard's trial testimony admissible under the "former testimony" exception of FRE 804(b)(1), because that exception only applies if the testimony "is now offered against a party who had—or, in a civil case, whose predecessor in interest had—an *opportunity and similar motive to develop it* by direct, *cross-*, or redirect examination." The defendant obviously had no opportunity or motive to cross-examine the guard at the guard's criminal trial. And of the two parties at the criminal trial (the defendant and the prosecution), neither can be said to have been in any way a "predecessor in interest" to the defendant. So the "opportunity and similar motive to cross-examine" requirement for admission of prior testimony is not satisfied here.

Since there are no other exceptions that might cover the guard's testimony, it's inadmissible hearsay, making the whole "package" inadmissible.

(A) is not the best response,

because the piece representing the guard's own testimony is not a party-admission, since the guard no longer worked for the defendant at the time of the statement.

This is hearsay within hearsay, so it's inadmissible unless both pieces (the guard's trial statement and the security director's statement quoted by the guard) fall within a hearsay exception. As described in the analysis of choice D, the guard's trial statement is not admissible against the defendant as an admission by a party opponent's agent, because at the time of the statement (the guard's criminal trial), the guard was no longer employed by the defendant, and his statement was therefore no longer within the agency relationship.

(B) is not the best response,

because, although the instruction by the security director is not hearsay, it's contained within the guard's inadmissible, hearsay "outer" statement.

This choice is probably correct in concluding that the director's own statement is not hearsay—it's an instruction or command, and it's not being offered to prove the "truth" of any matter asserted therein, because there is no "matter" whose "truth" is being asserted. On the other hand, the director's statement is contained in the guard's trial testimony, which is (inadmissible) hearsay. Therefore, although choice B is literally correct, it does not correctly explain the outcome.

(C) is not the best response,

because the former-testimony exception does not apply.

Former testimony, i.e. testimony given at an earlier proceeding, is an exception to the hearsay rule. Under FRE 804(b)(1), one of the requirements for the prior testimony exception is that the testimony must now be "offered against a party who had—or, in a civil case, whose predecessor in interest had—an *opportunity and similar motive to develop it* by direct, *cross-*, or redirect examination." The defendant had no opportunity or motive to cross-examine the guard at the guard's criminal trial, and the prosecution cannot be said to have been a "predecessor in interest" to the defendant. So the former-testimony exception does not apply.

Answer 24

(D) is the best response,

because the defendant's silence in these circumstances constituted his adoption of the dealer's statement.

FRE 801(2)(B) codifies the common-law notion of an adoptive admission: A statement is not hearsay if it is "offered against an opposing party and . . . (B) is one the party manifested that it adopted or believed to be true[.]" The applicable test for adoption is whether, taking into account all circumstances, *A*'s conduct or silence justifies the conclusion that he knowingly agreed to the accuracy of *B*'s statement.

Here, it's clear that the defendant adopted the dealer's statement. The dealer introduced the defendant to the witness as "my partner." The defendant clearly heard and understood the statement, and it was the sort of statement that would, if untrue, have called for a denial by the defendant rather than a shaking of hands.

(A) is not the best response,

because the defendant adopted the dealer's statement.

The defendant did not need to authorize the dealer to speak for him. It's true that one way *A*'s statement can be used as an admission against *B* is if *B* authorized *A* to speak for him. (*See* FRE 801(d)(2)(C).) But another way for *A*'s statement to be used as an admission against *B* is if *B* has "manifested that [*B*] adopted or believed [the statement] to be true[.]" (FRE 801(d)(2)(B)). That's what happened here, as described more fully in the discussion of Choice (D) above.

(B) is not the best response,

because adoptive admissions are not hearsay.

The statement here was admissible as an admission against the defendant, because the defendant adopted it. (See the discussion in choice D.) Consequently, the statement was rendered non-hearsay by FRE 801(d)(2)(B).

(C) is not the best response,

because the defendant is not the declarant.

A statement against interest is one made by a person (the declarant), now unavailable as a witness, against that person's pecuniary, proprietary, or penal interest when made. FRE 804(b)(3) treats statements against interest as an exception to the hearsay rule.

However, there is no doctrine by which a statement made by *A* against *B*'s interest can be admitted against *B* based on *B*'s adoption of the statement. Since the declarant was *A*, the statement would have to be against *A*'s (not *B*'s) interest for it to fall within the statement-against-interest exception. And that's not what this choice specifies. (Also, even if the statement *were* somehow treated as if it were made or authorized by the defendant, the exception wouldn't apply because the defendant is present at trial and thus not unavailable.)

Answer 25

(D) is the best response,

because the clerk is not a source "whose accuracy cannot reasonably be questioned," as required for judicial notice under the FRE.

(A) is not the best response,

because a certified copy would be permitted under FRE 902(4).

FRE 902 lists a number of categories of documents that are self-authenticating. One of these is 902(4)'s category of "certified copies of public records," defined to include "A copy of an official record . . . if the copy is certified as correct by: (A) the custodian or another person authorized to make the certification." A certified copy of a record of conviction would clearly fall within this definition.

(B) is not the best response,

because testimony of someone who heard the sentence be issued would be a good means of authentication.

FRE 901(b) gives a number of illustrations of acceptable methods of authentication—i.e., in FRE 901(a)'s language, of "evidence sufficient to support a finding that the item is what the proponent claims it is." Since the claim is that there has been a conviction, authentication consists of evidence sufficient to find that the conviction really occurred.

The first illustration given in FRE 901(b) is (1), entitled "Testimony of a Witness with Knowledge"—the text of (1) recognizes authentication by means of "testimony that an item is what it is claimed to be." So here, the plaintiff's testimony, from his own personal knowledge, that a sentence of conviction was pronounced, will qualify.

(C) is not the best response,

because the defendant's statement would be admissible as an admission.

The testimony here is a classic admission by a party-opponent. Under FRE 801(d)(2), an out-of-court statement is admissible (as an exclusion from the hearsay rule) if it is "offered against an opposing party and (A) was made by the party in an individual or representative capacity[.]" Since the "oral admission" by the defendant that he had been convicted is a statement by the defendant being offered against him, the testimony by the witness is admissible.

Answer 26

(D) is the best response,

because the widow's testimony would be hearsay within hearsay, and the "outer level" is not within any exception.

The FRE define hearsay as "a statement that: (1) the declarant does not make while testifying at the current trial or hearing; and (2) a party offers in evidence to prove the truth of the matter asserted in the statement." FRE 801(c). Anytime the evidence in question consists of an out-of-court statement by *A* repeating another out-of-court statement by *B*, you have to analyze *both* *A*'s statement and *B*'s statement—if *either* statement is hearsay not falling within any exception, the combined statement cannot come in.

Here, the "inner" level (the defendant's statement to the widow's husband) is an admission being used against a party-opponent, so it falls within the admissions exception to the hearsay rule.

But the "outer" level (the husband's statement to the widow, "Here's what the defendant told me . . . ") is hearsay not within any exception. First, notice that the statement ("[The defendant] told me he'd blow my head off one day") is being offered to prove the matter asserted: It's being offered to prove that the defendant indeed made the threat. (It's also being offered for the additional not-really-hearsay inference that if the defendant made a threat to kill the husband by shooting, it's more likely than it would otherwise be that the fatal shooting of the husband by someone unknown was done by the defendant. But this "secondary" purpose doesn't detract from the fact that the primary purpose — to prove that the defendant made the threat — is a hearsay purpose.)

Second, let's look at whether the husband's statement falls within any exception. It doesn't. For instance, it doesn't fall within the state-of-mind exception, because the husband wasn't saying, "I'm scared of [the defendant] because he threatened to kill me. . . . " It's offered for the pure purpose of showing that the defendant made the threat, and that purpose doesn't qualify for state-of-mind, excited-utterance, or any other exception.

(A) is not the best response,

because the state-of-mind exception doesn't solve the problem that the husband's statement to the widow is, separately, hearsay.

It's true that the defendant's statement alone might well be admissible as evidence of the defendant's state of mind vis-à-vis the husband, under FRE 803(3) (covering declarant's "then-existing state of mind . . . or emotional, sensory, or physical condition[.]"

But the problem (as further discussed in choice D above) is that what's offered is what the husband said out of court that the defendant told him out of court. So if the husband's statement (the "outer" statement) is hearsay not within an exception, the fact that the defendant's statement (the "inner" statement) falls within a hearsay exception doesn't help.

Here, the statement by the husband is hearsay not within any exception, as shown by the analysis in choice D. Therefore, the combined statements of the husband and the defendant can't come in.

(B) is not the best response,

because the admissibility of statements made by, and offered against, a party-opponent doesn't solve the combined hearsay-within-hearsay problem presented here.

It's true that the defendant's statement, if made directly to the testifying witness (the widow) could be repeated by her on the stand, since then it would be a statement made by a party-opponent admitted against that opponent, a non-hearsay use under FRE 801(2)(A).

But the problem (as further discussed in choice D above) is that what's offered is what the husband said out of court that the defendant told him out of court. So if the husband's statement (the "outer" statement) is hearsay not within an exception, the fact that the defendant's statement (the "inner" statement) is a non-hearsay admission doesn't help.

Here, the statement by the husband is hearsay not within any exception, as shown by the analysis of choice D. Therefore, the combined statements of the husband and the defendant can't come in.

(C) is not the best response,

because it mischaracterizes the evidence, and it also doesn't address the hearsay-within-hearsay issue.

First, the answer choice characterizes the evidence incorrectly, as proof of a prior bad act, when it is being offered as a statement. Second, it does not address the pivotal issue: the admissibility of the husband's statement (the "outer" statement). Since that statement is hearsay not within any exception, as shown by the analysis of choice D, the combined statements of the husband and the defendant would be inadmissible as hearsay within hearsay.

Answer 27

(A) is the best response,

because one who obtains a confidential communication while assisting a lawyer is covered by the attorney-client privilege.

If the interview for sentencing preparation had been between the attorney and the defendant, it's perfectly clear that the attorney-client privilege would apply. The fact that it's a non-attorney third person, not the attorney, who had the conversation with the defendant is what makes the problem interesting.

However, it's well established that the attorney-client privilege also applies to communications between the client and a third-party non-lawyer who has been engaged by the lawyer to aid in the representation. Since the probation officer was engaged by the defendant's lawyer to aid in an aspect of the defense, anything the defendant told the probation officer is treated as if it had been told to the lawyer, and is therefore privileged.

(B) is not the best response,

because the attorney-client privilege's applicability makes the probable-cause issue irrelevant.

As described in the analysis of choice A above, the communication is covered by the attorney-client privilege. Therefore, even if the interview did more probably than not develop evidence relevant to the grand jury's inquiry, the interview would still be privileged.

In any event, this choice misstates the criterion for grand jury questioning: As long as the matter under question has a reasonable chance of being either directly relevant or leading to relevant evidence, the proponent of the questioning need not show by "probable cause" that the questions are directly relevant to the grand jury's inquiry.

(C) is not the best response,

because a non-attorney engaged by an attorney is covered by the attorney-client privilege.

See the further analysis of this legal rule in the discussion of choice A above.

(D) is not the best response,

because the rules of privilege very much apply in grand jury proceedings.

It's true that not all rules of evidence apply in grand jury proceedings (the hearsay rule, for instance), but privileges, such as the attorney-client privilege, do apply.

Answer 28

(C) is the best response,

because the beatings would tend to prove that the killing was not accidental.

Under FRE 404(b), "Evidence of a crime, wrong, or other act is not admissible to prove a person's character in order to show that on a particular occasion the person acted in accordance with the character." So if the prosecution were offering the prior beatings on the theory that "[t]hese beatings showed that the defendant had a violent character, making it more likely that he acted violently on this occasion," the evidence would be barred by the above-quoted portion of 404(b).

However, FRE 404(b) goes on to say that such other crimes-or-wrongs evidence "may be admissible for another purpose, such as proving motive, opportunity, intent, preparation, plan, knowledge, identity, *absence of mistake*, or *lack of accident*." Here, that's exactly what's happening: The defendant has claimed that the shooting was accidental, and the prosecution is offering the prior beatings to show "absence of mistake or lack of accident." So the evidence is admissible.

(A) is not the best response,

because the acts of violence here are not being offered as character evidence.

It's true that if the evidence were offered as pure character evidence, to show that the defendant acted in conformity with his character (character for violence, say) on the present occasion, the evidence would be barred by FRE 404(b). But as described in the analysis of choice C, the evidence here is being offered to show "absence of mistake or lack of accident," not to show "character," so it's admissible.

(B) is not the best response,

because the beatings show lack of accident regardless of who started the fights.

The fact that the officer doesn't know firsthand who started the fights is irrelevant, if the mere existence of the fights would tend to show that the shooting on the present occasion was no mistake. For instance, even if the father started the two prior fights, the fact that the defendant responded by beating his father would make it at least somewhat less likely than it would otherwise be that the shooting now was an accident. So the evidence is relevant, and it's admissible (as described in choice C) as tending to prove absence of accident.

(D) is not the best response,

because evidence of a character for violence is not admissible under these circumstances.

Under FRE 404(b), "Evidence of a crime, wrong, or other act is not admissible to prove a person's character in order to show that on a particular occasion the person acted in accordance with the character." So if the evidence of the prior beatings were really being offered to show that "the defendant has a character for violence, and is thus likely to have acted violently on the present occasion," the quoted sentence would apply to make the evidence inadmissible (not admissible, as this choice posits).

However, "character for violence" is not what the prior-acts evidence is being offered for. Instead (as shown in the analysis of choice C), it's being offered to show absence of accident, and that purpose is admissible under 404(b).

Answer 29

(D) is the best response,

because the testimony is not hearsay, in that it is not offered for the truth of the matter asserted, but rather to show the listener's response to the assertion.

Hearsay is a statement offered to prove "the truth of the matter asserted in the statement." FRE 801(c)(2). The matter being "asserted" in the out-of-court declaration is that "the plaintiff can't work productively more than four hours per day." So if the statement were being offered to prove that the plaintiff couldn't in fact work more than four hours per day, it would be hearsay (and not within any exception).

However, the defendant can properly claim that this is *not* the purpose of introducing the former employer's statement. The defendant can say, "I'm offering this statement not to show that the former employer was speaking truthfully or accurately—I have no idea whether the plaintiff could or couldn't work productively—but rather to explain that at the moment I declined to hire her, my having heard this statement, not my desire to avoid hiring someone over 65, was my motivation." A court would agree—where the out-of-court statement is offered to show its effect on the listener rather than its truth, that's a non-hearsay purpose.

(A) is not the best response,

because the defendant's opinion of the plaintiff's abilities is not rendered inadmissible by the fact that it is not based on personal knowledge.

It's true that there are some types of testimony that are not admissible because they are not based on personal knowledge. But here, the defendant's opinion is not being offered to show that the opinion was "true." Rather, it's being offered to show that the opinion—whether "true" or not—was not based on forbidden age discrimination. Therefore, the fact that the opinion was not based on the defendant's personal experience does not make it inadmissible.

(B) is not the best response,

because the employer's statement is not offered for the truth of the matter asserted in it, and therefore cannot be hearsay.

Hearsay is an out-of-court statement offered in evidence to prove the truth of the matter asserted in the statement.

The matter asserted in the statement is that the plaintiff was incapable of working productively for more than four hours in a day. If the statement was offered to prove that the plaintiff in fact was incapable of working more than this amount, the statement would indeed be inadmissible hearsay. But that's not why it's being offered—it's being offered merely to prove that the defendant's reason for not hiring the plaintiff was this advice from the employer (whether that advice was based on real facts or not) rather than an age-discrimination motive. And, as outlined in the discussion of choice D, that's not hearsay.

(C) is not the best response,

because if the statement was offered for this purpose, it would be inadmissible hearsay.

Hearsay is an out-of-court statement offered to prove the truth of the matter asserted.

The out of court statement includes the substatement "the plaintiff can't work more than four hours productively." (The statement also includes a recommendation, "I advise you not to hire her.") If the statement were offered to prove that the plaintiff indeed couldn't work more than four hours productively, the statement would be being offered to prove the truth of the (or a) matter asserted in it. This would make the statement hearsay. Since there is no exception that applies, the statement would be inadmissible, not admissible as this choice asserts.

Answer 30

(D) is the best response,

because the court shall exclude witnesses at the request of a party.

FRE 615 says that "At a party's request, the court must order witnesses excluded so that they cannot hear other witnesses' testimony." Although the eyewitness has already testified, the fact that he is expected to be recalled for further cross-examination means that he's still to be treated as a witness who has not yet testified. (The purpose of the sequestration rule is to prevent the witness from tailoring his testimony to that of other witnesses. This purpose would be thwarted by letting the eyewitness here be in the courtroom before his re-cross.)

(A) is not the best response,

because the court has the discretion to permit inquiry into additional matters.

FRE 611(b) says that as a general rule cross-examination "should not go beyond the subject matter of the direct examination and matters affecting the witness's credibility." But that section goes on to say, "The court may allow inquiry into additional matters as if on direct examination." The court's discretion would be especially proper in this case, since the defendant is effectively the direct examiner (because the plaintiff called the defendant as an adverse, or "hostile," witness).

(B) is not the best response,

because leading questions are not proper when the "cross-examination" is really a direct examination since the party was originally called as an adverse witness.

Here, if the defendant's lawyer is conducting "cross-examination" of the defendant, it must be because the plaintiff called the defendant as an adverse witness (which is, indeed, what choice A specifies happened). In that scenario, this "cross" is to be treated by the court as if it were a direct examination, since the questioner is sympathetic to the witness. In that instance, the cross should not be allowed to make use of leading questions, any more than a standard direct examination may use leading questions. (See FRE 611(c), stating the general rule that leading questions "should not be used on direct examination except as necessary to develop the witness's testimony."

(C) is not the best response,

because matters of credibility are within the scope of cross-examination.

FRE 611(b), in defining the permissible scope of cross-examination, says that the cross may include, in addition to "the subject matter of the direct examination," "matters affecting the witness's credibility." So the fact that credibility was not placed in issue in the direct does not bar it from being covered on cross.

Answer 31

(D) is the best response,

because it correctly states that a witness may refer to collateral documents without having to produce the documents themselves.

The central issue in these facts is that the defendant is testifying relying on a writing—namely, the newspaper story. Thus, there's a potential Best Evidence Rule (BER) problem. Under the BER, when the terms of a writing are being proven, or the witness is testifying relying on a writing, the writing must be produced, if available. FRE 1002. However, under these facts, the only relevance the writing has is that it reinforces the defendant's memory. The BER doesn't cover collateral matters; see FRE 1004(d) (BER doesn't apply where the item is "not closely related to a controlling issue.") The defendant's memory is not closely related to a material issue in the case, and as such is considered "collateral." As a result, the defendant's testimony will be admissible without producing the newspaper.

(A) is not the best response,

because the BER is not applicable to these facts.

The BER, requiring that the document itself be produced if available, only applies if the terms of a writing are being proven or if the witness is testifying relying on a writing. FRE 1002. However, under these facts, the only relevance the writing has is that it reinforces the defendant's memory. The defendant's memory is not closely related to a material issue in the case and, as such, is considered "collateral." The BER doesn't cover collateral matters (FRE 1004(d)), and, as a result, the defendant's testimony will be admissible without producing the newspaper. Since A doesn't recognize this, it's not the best response.

(B) is not the best response,

because there's no hearsay problem under these facts.

Hearsay is an out-of-court statement offered to prove the truth of its assertion. Here, the out-of-court statement is that of the newspaper. However, it's not being offered to prove that the defendant's daughter actually became engaged on that day; thus, it's not being offered to prove the truth of its assertion, but rather only to prove something *unrelated* to the writing: that the defendant talked with the plaintiff that day. As a result, it's not hearsay.

Instead, what B ignores is the central issue under these facts, which involves the BER. The BER, requiring that the document itself be produced if available, only applies if the terms of a writing are being proven or if the witness is testifying relying on a writing. FRE 1002. However, under these facts, the only relevance the writing has is that it reinforces the defendant's memory. The defendant's memory is not closely related to a material issue in the case, and as such is considered "collateral." The BER doesn't cover collateral matters (FRE 1004(d)), and, as a result, the defendant's testimony will be admissible without producing the newspaper. Since B ignores this issue altogether, it's not the best response.

(C) is not the best response,

because it states an incorrect rule of law.

Judicial notice is appropriate for both notorious facts (subject to common knowledge in the community) and manifest facts (capable of positive verification through readily accessible, undoubtedly accurate sources). FRE 201(b). The contents of local newspapers would not fit either one of these categories, since, apart from anything else, the papers could quite easily have misdated the defendant's daughter's engagement announcement. (Appropriate topics for judicial notice include federal and state laws, the normal human gestation period, information available from almanacs, the validity of ballistics tests, the validity of paternity blood tests, and the like—you get the idea.)

Instead, what C fails to address is the central issue under these facts: the applicability of the BER. In fact, since the article only addresses a collateral issue—the defendant's memory for the date his conversation with the plaintiff took place—the BER does not apply, and the defendant's testimony will be admissible without producing the newspaper report. Since C ignores this issue, and misstates the rule on judicial notice, it's not the best response.

Answer 32

(D) is the best response,

because the victim will testify that the voice on the phone is similar to the defendant's, and because the Best Evidence Rule does not apply.

Authentication, the Federal Rules of Evidence say, is the condition precedent to admissibility that is satisfied by evidence sufficient to support a finding that the matter in question is what its proponent claims. Since the prosecution is trying to establish that the voice on the phone was the defendant's, the victim's testimony that he believes the voice was the victim's will have to be authenticated.

FRE 901(b)(5) gives, as an illustration of proper authentication, "An opinion identifying a person's voice—whether heard firsthand or through mechanical or electronic transmission or recording—based on hearing the voice at any time under circumstances that connect it with the alleged speaker." Since the victim has heard the defendant's voice and knows that that voice has a distinctive accent, his proposed opinion testimony (which states that the voice had a similar distinctive accent) meets this requirement. There is no requirement that the giver of the opinion must be positive in the identification—the witness is permitted to say merely that the voice was similar, for instance having a similar, distinctive accent. At that point, the jury is free to give very little weight to the evidence—the point is that the lack of certainty doesn't make the tentative identification inadmissible.

Nor does the BER apply here—see the explanation of this fact in the discussion of choice B.

(A) is not the best response,

because the victim's testimony is admissible.

For the reasons stated in the discussion of choice D above, the fact that the victim cannot conclusively identify the voice as being the defendant's does not prevent the tentative identification from being admissible.

(B) is not the best response,

because the testimony is admissible and the BER does not apply.

The BER states that if the terms of a writing or a recording are to be proved, the original must be produced. The BER does not apply to events that have by happenstance been recorded—it applies only where the terms of the recording, per se, are what are being sought to be proved.

Here, the extortion happened in a live phone call. The prosecution is proving the contents of that live phone call. The fact that the victim happened to have made a tape of the call, therefore, does not mean that the prosecution is attempting to "prove the contents" of this incidentally created tape. So the BER doesn't apply. (It would be different if the extortion occurred when someone sent a threatening tape to victim—then the recording *would* be subject to the BER, because the prosecution's case would require it to show what the contents of the tape were.)

(C) is not the best response,

because the BER wouldn't be waived by a failure to subpoena, and in any case, the BER is not applicable to these facts.

The BER, like any evidentiary requirement, can be waived by the non-proponent party. But that waiver would have to take the form of a failure to object at trial.

The opponent's mere failure to subpoena the tape would not serve as a waiver. (For example, the opponent—the defendant here—might not have known that the tape even existed.)

In any event, the BER doesn't apply to these facts, because the contents of the recording are not what's being proved. See the discussion of choice B above.

Answer 33

(B) is the best response,

because the general manager's testimony was sufficient to prove that it was the plaintiff's habit to have created and mailed a cost overrun notice in circumstances like the one here.

The issue is whether the copy found in the plaintiff's files is indeed a copy of a letter that was actually sent to the defendant. Therefore, FRE 406 is relevant. That rule says that "Evidence of a person's habit or an organization's routine practice may be admitted to prove that on a particular occasion the person or organization acted in accordance with the habit or routine practice. The court may admit this evidence regardless of whether it is corroborated or whether there was an eyewitness." So here, the general manager's testimony that it was the organization's habit to send such a notice as required by its contracts tends to establish that the photocopy was indeed a photocopy of a letter that was sent, as contemplated by FRE 406.

Nor is the letter here hearsay (whether within an exception or not)—see the discussion below of choice A for an explanation.

(A) is not the best response,

because the letter is not hearsay at all, since it's not offered to prove the truth of any matter asserted therein.

It's true that the letter is an "out of court declaration." But the letter is not being offered to prove the "truth of the matter asserted." The matter asserted is that there was a cost overrun. But the purpose for offering the letter in evidence is merely to show that the contractual requirement of a notice was satisfied. (The letter would be equally relevant on the issue of notice even if the letter was incorrect in its assertion that there was a cost overrun. So it's not offered to prove the truth of the matter asserted therein.)

So even though the letter would probably be admissible under the business records exception if it *were* being offered to prove the truth of the matter asserted, there's no hearsay here to require an exception. To put it another way, the phrase "though hearsay" in this choice is an incorrect conclusion of law.

(C) is not the best response,

because the letter is not hearsay at all. See the discussion above of choice A for why this is so.

(D) is not the best response,

because even though the Best Evidence Rule (BER) applies, the duplicate copy is admissible.

FRE 1002's version of the BER (called "Requirement of Original") says that in proving the terms of a writing, the original writing must ordinarily be produced. So on the face of this rule, since the contents of the letter are being proved, FRE 1002 seems to require use of the original.

But FRE 1003 says that "A *duplicate is admissible* to the same extent as the original unless a genuine question is raised about the original's authenticity or the circumstances make it unfair to admit the duplicate." Since the defendant has not raised a genuine question about the authenticity of the original, and since it would be not be unfair to admit the duplicate (the plaintiff obviously couldn't possess the original any more if its story of having sent it to the defendant is true), FRE 1003 allows use of the copy here.

Answer 34

(B) is the best response,

because under the federal common law, as established by the Supreme Court in *Trammel v. U.S.,*

445 U.S. 40 (1980), if the witness and the criminal defendant are married at the time of trial, the witness cannot be placed in contempt for refusing to testify against the defendant.

The testifying spouse holds the privilege, and, here, the question explicitly states that the wife objects to testifying against her husband, the defendant. The rationale underlying the rule is to preserve marital harmony that would otherwise be damaged by one spouse testifying against the other. That rationale is implicated here, as the wife does not want to testify against her husband and aid in his prosecution.

(A) is not the best response,

because it misstates the rule.

Under federal common law, as established by the Supreme Court in *Trammel v. U.S.*, if the witness and the criminal defendant are married at the time of trial, the witness cannot be placed in contempt for refusing to testify against the defendant. It is the testifying spouse, however, who holds the privilege, not the criminal defendant. The rationale for affording the testifying spouse the privilege is that the privilege is meant to preserve marital harmony, and if a witness wants to testify against his or her spouse, then there is no marital harmony left to preserve. Thus, the criminal defendant does not have a privilege to prevent his wife from testifying against him in a criminal case. A criminal defendant does possess a privilege to prevent confidential martial communications from being disclosed by his wife, but the clothing worn by the husband would not qualify as a confidential communication.

(C) is not the best response,

because it misstates the rule.

Under federal common law, as established by the Supreme Court in *Trammel v. U.S.*, if the witness and the criminal defendant are married at the time of trial, the witness cannot be placed in contempt for refusing to testify against the defendant. The interspousal testimonial privilege applies only in criminal cases and not in civil cases. Here, the testifying spouse in a criminal case specifically objected to testifying, so she is immune.

(D) is not the best response,

because it confuses the interspousal communications privilege, which does not apply here, and the interspousal testimonial privilege, which does apply here.

The interspousal communications privilege protects confidential communications made between the spouses during the marriage. The clothing the defendant wore as he left the house would not qualify as a confidential communication—it is unlikely that his clothing choice was a communication and the fact that he wore it out of the house means it is not confidential. Instead, the interspousal testimonial privilege governs this fact pattern. Under federal common law, as established by the Supreme Court in *Trammel v. U.S.*, if the witness and the criminal defendant are married at the time of trial, the witness cannot be placed in contempt for refusing to testify against the defendant. Here, the testifying witness did object to testifying against her spouse in a criminal matter in which he was the defendant, so she will not be forced to testify.

Answer 35

(A) is the best response,

because it correctly identifies that the reputation evidence on the victim will be admissible to exonerate the defendant.

The problem here is that the evidence about the victim is *character* evidence, and character evidence is, as a *very* general rule, inadmissible. However, choice A correctly recognizes the reason the testimony here will be admissible. The defendant can offer reputation and opinion evidence of the victim's character where, if the victim acted in conformity with his character, the conduct would tend to prove the defendant's innocence (*except* in rape cases, where such evidence is generally inadmissible). Here, the testimony will tend to prove that the victim was the aggressor, and it's in the form of reputation evidence. Since A states the correct rule and it applies to these facts, it's the best response.

(B) is not the best response,

because the admissibility of other evidence is irrelevant to the admissibility of *this* evidence.

The problem here is that the evidence about the victim is *character* evidence, and character evidence is, as a *very* general rule, inadmissible. In fact, the evidence here is admissible on its own, because the defendant can offer reputation and opinion evidence of the victim's character where, if the victim acted in conformity with his character, the conduct would tend to prove the defendant's innocence (*except* in rape cases, where such evidence is generally inadmissible).

Choice B incorrectly states that the evidence is only admissible if it is accompanied by testimony of specific acts of misconduct about which the witness knows. In fact, specific instances are *not* admissible to prove victim's character—only reputation and opinion. If you chose this response, you may have been thinking of evidence of *habit,* which is admissible to show that a person acted in conformity with his habit on a specific occasion. Such evidence *must* be in the form of specific instances of misconduct. However, here, the evidence would not be admissible as habit evidence, because the act here—lawbreaking and frequently engaging in brawls—would be *volitional* on every occasion, and habit evidence must be "semi-automatic" (e.g., always running a certain stop sign). FRE 406. In any case, since B fails to recognize that the evidence is admissible by itself, it's not the best response.

(C) is not the best response,

because the evidence will tend to exonerate the defendant even though it concerns the victim.

What choice C suggests is that the evidence will be inadmissible because it's irrelevant. There are two kinds of relevance: legal relevance and logical relevance. Logical relevance, to which choice C alludes, requires that a piece of evidence must prove or disprove a material fact in order to be admissible. FRE 401. Here, the defendant is claiming that he only assaulted the victim in self-defense. Thus, evidence that the victim had a reputation for brawling would tend to suggest that the victim did, in fact, assault the defendant on the occasion in question, making it more likely that the defendant did act in self-defense. Thus, the evidence is relevant.

What choice C ignores is the *character evidence* problem with this testimony. As a general rule, character evidence is inadmissible. However, the facts here fit an exception to this rule. The defendant *can* offer reputation and opinion evidence of the victim's character where, if the victim acted in conformity with his character, the conduct would tend to prove the defendant's innocence (*except* in rape cases, where such evidence is generally inadmissible). Since C fails to recognize this, it is not the best response.

(D) is not the best response,

because a foundation is not necessary for admission of this testimony.

The problem here is that the evidence about the victim is *character* evidence, and character evidence is, as a *very* general rule, inadmissible. However, the facts here fit an exception to the rule. The defendant *can* offer reputation and opinion evidence of the victim's character where, if the victim acted in conformity with his character, the conduct would tend to prove the defendant's innocence (*except* in rape cases, where such evidence is generally inadmissible). Such evidence does not require a *foundation*; instead, the testimony will be admissible if the witness is competent to testify about the victim's reputation. Under FRE 602, a witness is competent to testify if he has personal knowledge of the matter on which he will testify; under FRE 603, the witness must declare, by oath or affirmation, that he will testify truthfully. Reputation testimony only requires that the witness be familiar with the subject's reputation, and as long as the witness is familiar with the victim's reputation, he'll be competent to testify.

If you chose this response, you were thinking of the common-law rule relating to impeachment with extrinsic evidence of prior inconsistent statements. This clearly doesn't apply here. Since D states, incorrectly, that a foundation will be required for admissibility of this testimony, it is not the best response.

Answer 36

(D) is the best response,

because it correctly notes that the sole use of this evidence is to impeach credibility of the testifying witness.

To understand this question you have to recognize that the witness is serving as a character witness. Once this witness has testified to the defendant's character for truthfulness, the credibility of that character witness may be challenged by showing that the witness's assessment is not credible. Thus, if the witness has not heard about the falsification, he might not be attuned to the community and therefore would be a poor character witness. On the other hand, if the witness did hear of the falsification but nonetheless believes that the defendant's reputation in the community is one of "complete honesty," then either the witness or the community (or both) set a very low threshold for "complete honesty." Either way, the witness's knowledge (or lack of knowledge) of the falsification—assuming the falsification occurred and was generally known—would be probative on the issue of whether the witness's testimony about the defendant's reputation is credible.

One additional point: remember that an impeachment attempt of the "Have you heard . . .?" type requires that the cross-examiner have a "good-faith basis" for the question (here, a good-faith reason to believe that the falsification really occurred). That good-faith requirement is met here by the record-of-discipline evidence produced at the sidebar.

(A) is not the best response,

because the question does not call for a statement that would be used for the truth of the matter asserted.

The intent of this question is to test the witness's knowledge of the defendant's reputation on the one hand, and the quality of the community on the other. Thus, if the witness has not heard about the falsification, he might not be attuned to the community and therefore would be a poor character witness. On the other hand, if the witness did hear of the falsification but nonetheless believes that the defendant's reputation in the community is one of "complete honesty," then either the witness or the community (or both) set a very low threshold for "complete honesty." Either way, the witness's knowledge (or lack of knowledge) of the falsification—assuming the falsification occurred and was generally known—would be probative on the issue of whether the witness's testimony about the defendant's reputation is credible. Therefore, the state of the witness's knowledge is not being offered for the truth of the matter asserted.

(B) is not the best response,

because the question is not being offered to prove the income tax fraud.

Rather, the question is being offered to impeach the character witness. Thus, if the witness has not heard about the falsification, he might not be attuned to the community and therefore would be a poor character witness. On the other hand, if the witness did hear of the falsification but nonetheless believes that the defendant's reputation in the community is one of "complete honesty," then either the witness or the community (or both) set a very low threshold for "complete honesty." Either way, the witness's knowledge (or lack of knowledge) of the falsification—assuming the falsification occurred and was generally known—would be probative on the issue of whether the witness's testimony about the defendant's reputation is credible. Since the examiner's question is being offered to prove the character witness's knowledge, rather than the acts of the defendant, the question is not unfairly prejudicial to the defendant.

(C) is not the best response,

because the prosecutor may not use this evidence to explore the defendant's character for honesty.

FRE 405 prohibits evidence of specific acts indicative of a person's character when that character evidence is offered to prove that a person acted in accordance with the character trait on the occasion in question at trial. But that's not what the prosecutor is trying to do here; rather, the prosecutor is attempting to impeach the character witness who offered an opinion on the defendant's honesty. Thus, if the witness has not heard about the falsification, he might not be attuned to the community and therefore would be a poor character witness. On the other hand, if the witness did hear of the falsification but nonetheless believes that the defendant's reputation in the community is one of "complete honesty," then either the witness or the community (or both) set a very low threshold for "complete honesty." Either way, the witness's knowledge (or lack of knowledge) of the falsification—assuming the falsification occurred and was generally known—would be probative on the issue of whether the witness's testimony about the defendant's reputation is credible. So the alleged falsification is being offered to impeach the character witness, not to prove the defendant's character for honesty.

Answer 37

(C) is the best response,

because it correctly identifies that the testimony will be inadmissible because it doesn't fit within any hearsay exception.

Note that what this really means is that the testimony will not be admissible under any of the other alternatives here. Choice C correctly characterizes the testimony as hearsay. Hearsay is an out-of-court statement offered to prove the truth of its assertion. The out-of-court declarant is the passenger: "We were returning. . . ." It's being offered to prove that the defendant was driving drunk, so it's being offered to prove the truth of its assertion. As a result, it's hearsay, and in order to be admissible, it would have to fit a hearsay exception or exclusion. Since the testimony is not admissible as an admission (choice A) or a declaration against interest (choice B), and choice D does not address the hearsay issue, then C must be the correct answer.

(A) is not the best response,

because the statement here would not qualify as an admission by a party-opponent, since the party-opponent is the defendant, not the passenger.

Choice A correctly implies that there is a hearsay problem under these facts. Hearsay is an out-of-court statement offered to prove the truth of its assertion. The out-of-court declarant is the passenger: "We were returning. . . ." It's being offered to prove that the defendant was driving drunk, so it's being offered to prove the truth of its assertion. As a result, it's hearsay, and in order to be admissible, it would have to fit a hearsay exception or exclusion. Choice A suggests that the statement should be admissible under the "admission" hearsay exclusion. However, the problem is that admissions must be from a party-opponent; here, the party-opponent is the defendant, not the passenger. Furthermore, there's no basis on which the defendant could be bound by the passenger's statement. He didn't indicate his agreement, and, beyond that, there's no principal-agent relationship under which the defendant could be bound by the passenger's statement without specifically adopting it. Note that if the facts were different, and the defendant was the declarant, not the passenger, the statement *would* be admissible as an admission, because it's being offered against the party who made the statement. FRE 801(d)(2). However, since it's the passenger's statement, not the defendant's, the statement won't be an admission, making A not the best response.

(B) is not the best response,

because the statement here would not qualify as a declaration against interest.

Choice B correctly implies that there is a hearsay problem under these facts. Hearsay is an out-of-court statement offered to prove the truth of its assertion. The out-of-court declarant is the passenger: "We were returning. . . ." It's being offered to prove that the defendant was driving drunk, so it's being offered to prove the truth of its assertion. As a result, it's hearsay, and in order to be admissible, it would have to fit a hearsay exception or exclusion.

Choice B suggests that the statement should be admissible under the "declaration against interest" hearsay exception. The statement here is not a declaration against interest, because it does not meet several of the requirements of a declaration against interest. Apart from anything else, it wasn't against the passenger's financial, property, or penal interest to make the statement. The exception also requires that the declarant be unavailable to testify. FRE 804(b)(3). Here, the passenger is available to testify. Since B incorrectly characterizes the statement as a "declaration against interest," it's not the best response.

(D) is not the best response,

because it suggests that the evidence is not relevant, or will lead to irrelevant issues.

Evidence is logically relevant if it tends to prove or disprove a material fact. FRE 401. The testimony here will be relevant, since it suggests that the defendant was drunk, which is one of the issues in the case. If evidence is relevant, the possibility that it will lead to nonessential side issues is not determinative of its admissibility. Rather, the evidence here is inadmissible because it's hearsay that doesn't fit within an exception mentioned here. (It's hearsay because it's an out-of-court statement offered to prove the truth of a matter asserted it in, namely, that the defendant was driving drunk.)

If you chose this response, you *may* have been thinking of the "collateral matter" rule. That is, a witness cannot be extrinsically impeached with evidence that is only relevant to discredit the witness; it must also prove or disprove a substantive issue (unless it proves something considered important, like witness bias). FRE 403. However, there's no impeachment involved in these facts, so the "collateral matter" rule wouldn't come into play.

Since D does not identify the correct reason for the testimony's inadmissibility, it's not the best response.

Answer 38

(C) is the best response,

because the police accident investigator's testimony is admissible as that of an expert witness.

FRE 702 imposes five requirements that expert testimony must meet in order to be admissible: (1) it must be the case that *scientific, technical, or other specialized knowledge* will *help* the trier of fact to *understand the evidence or to determine a fact in issue*; (2) the witness must be qualified as an expert by *knowledge, skill, experience, training, or education*; (3) the testimony must be *based upon sufficient facts or data*; (4) the testimony must be the *product of reliable principles and methods*; and (5) the witness must have *reliably applied these principles and methods to the facts of the case*.

The proposed testimony by the investigator is proper. The investigator would be considered an expert witness and his testimony would be admissible because it satisfies the five requirements: (1) the investigator's testimony about the speed of the train will help the trier of fact to understand the evidence in the case; (2) the facts state that the police accident investigator is experienced and has received training; (3) the investigator's testimony is based on his examination of the physical evidence; (4) the techniques used by the investigator were presumably those he received in his training to become a police accident investigator, so the testimony would be the product of reliable principles and methods; and (5) the investigator made his conclusion about the train's speed after applying his training and experience to the physical evidence of the case. Having satisfied all five requirements, the accident investigator's testimony is proper and admissible.

(A) is not the best response,

because it states a non-existent rule of law.

There is simply no principle that says that "there cannot be both lay and expert opinion on the same issue." (For instance, it is perfectly proper for one side to put on lay eyewitness opinion testimony about the approximate speed of the train, and for the other to put on expert scientific opinion on the same subject.)

(B) is not the best response,

because any uncertainty in the investigator's findings would go to the weight of the testimony not its admissibility.

There is no principle that scientific or other expert testimony must reach its conclusion with any particular degree of "scientific certainty." All that is required is that the conclusion be sufficiently "reliable." For the reasons discussed in choice C, this reliability standard is satisfied here.

To the extent that this choice is referring to the fact that the investigator is testifying merely that the speed falls within a range, instead of giving a single number, the existence of a range does not pose a problem. (Indeed, use of a range is probably more, not less, reliable, since it's less likely to give a false impression of precision.)

(D) is not the best response,

because the testimony would be admissible even if the plaintiff had not first introduced opinion evidence on the issue.

The only requirements for expert testimony are those discussed in the analysis of choice C above. There is no requirement that the other side have first introduced some sort of opinion evidence on the issue.

Answer 39

(B) is the best response,

because it correctly states the two competency requirements.

The Federal Rules of Evidence rules on competency of witnesses state that every person is competent to be a witness except as otherwise provided. The *only* two limitations given require that: (1) the witness have *personal knowledge* of the matter about which he is to testify, and (2) the witness indicates his willingness (by oath or affirmation) to testify truthfully. *See* FRE 602 and 603. Since choice B correctly recites these requirements, it's the correct answer.

(A) is not the best response,

because the prosecutor does not have to persuade the judge of the son's competency to testify.

The FRE rules on competency requirements of witnesses state that every person is competent to be a witness except as otherwise provided. The only two limitations given require that: (1) the witness have personal knowledge of the matter about which he is to testify, and (2) the witness must declare, by oath or affirmation, that he will testify truthfully. FRE 602 and 603. There is no requirement that the proponent of evidence first provide evidence of the witness's competence, even where the witness is underage.

(C) is not the best response,

because the victim's son's age would not affect his ability to identify the defendant.

As noted in the discussion of choice B, there are only two requirements regarding the witness's competence. Tender age does not constitute a failure to meet either of those requirements.

(D) is not the best response,

because the probative value of the testimony outweighs its emotional elements.

It's true that FRE 403 says that "[t]he court may exclude relevant evidence if its probative value is substantially outweighed by a danger of . . . unfair prejudice[.]" But the son is an eyewitness who can testify on the core issue in the case, so it's wildly unlikely that a court would conclude that any "prejudice" from having him testify with his disfiguring injuries would either be "unfair" or would "substantially outweigh" the value of his eyewitness testimony about the crime.

Answer 40

(B) is the best response,

because it correctly characterizes the prior conviction as admissible to prove the defendant's intoxication.

Choice B implicitly identifies that the conviction is hearsay. Hearsay is an out-of-court statement offered to prove the truth of its assertion. Here, the out-of-court declarant is the original court that convicted the defendant. The conviction is being offered to prove that the defendant was intoxicated, so it's hearsay, and it must fit a hearsay exception or exclusion to be admissible.

Choice B correctly identifies that the conviction will be admissible under an exception to the hearsay rule. Under the FRE, a felony conviction is admissible to prove "any fact essential to the judgment." FRE 803(22). 803(22) expressly states that the conviction must be for a crime punishable by death, or imprisonment in excess of one year. The facts here indicate that the defendant could have been sentenced to two years in prison, so the crime is one that qualifies for this exception. The defendant's intoxication was a fact essential to the finding of guilt, since she could not have been convicted of drunk driving without such a finding. As a result, the facts here fit the "prior conviction" hearsay exception. (Note, incidentally, that the defendant's guilty plea could be admissible as an admission, since it's an acknowledgement of her guilt.) In any case, since B recognizes that the conviction will be admissible to prove the defendant's intoxication, it's the best response.

(A) is not the best response,

because it states an impermissible goal of prior convictions.

A prior conviction cannot be admitted to prove the defendant's character, since the defendant's character is not in issue here. Character evidence is only admissible when the issue involves testamentary capacity, sanity, child custody (to prove parents' character), defamation, entrapment, notice, or to impeach a reputation witness.

In fact, the problem with offering evidence to prove character is that the jury is likely to find against the defendant because she's a "bad person," not because she committed the act in question.

This doesn't, however, mean that the prior conviction won't be admissible at all. In fact, it will be admissible to prove any fact essential to sustain the judgment. FRE 803(22). The exception expressly states that the conviction must be for a crime punishable by death, or imprisonment in excess of one year. The facts here indicate that the defendant could have been sentenced to two years in prison, so the crime is one that qualifies for this exception. The defendant's intoxication was a fact essential to the finding of guilt, since she could not have been convicted of drunk driving without such a finding. As a result, the facts here fit the "prior conviction" hearsay exception, and will be admissible to prove intoxication. This is an example of the doctrine of limited admissibility, in that the prior conviction will be admissible to prove the defendant's intoxication, but not her character. Since proving character is an impermissible goal under these facts, A is not the best response.

(C) is not the best response,

because the condition it raises is irrelevant; the admissibility of the conviction does not turn on whether or not it followed a trial.

Under FRE 803(22), a felony conviction is admissible to prove any fact essential to sustain the judgment. The exception expressly states that the conviction must be for a crime punishable by death, or imprisonment in excess of one year. The facts here indicate that the defendant could have been sentenced to two years in prison, so the crime is one that qualifies for this exception. The defendant's intoxication was a fact essential to the finding of guilt, since she could not have been convicted of drunk driving without such a finding. As a result, the evidence of her intoxication will be admissible into evidence, regardless of whether she underwent a trial. Since C incorrectly suggests a trial is necessary for use of the conviction, it is not the best response.

(D) is not the best response,

because while the conviction is hearsay, it *is* admissible under the prior convictions exception to the FRE, which is embodied in choice A.

Choice D is correct in identifying that the conviction is hearsay. Hearsay is an out-of-court statement offered to prove the truth of its assertion. Here, the out-of-court declarant is the original court that convicted the defendant. The conviction is being offered to prove that the defendant was intoxicated, so it's hearsay, and it must fit a hearsay exception or exclusion to be admissible. In fact, it fits FRE 803(22), under which a felony conviction is admissible to prove any fact essential to sustain the judgment. The exception expressly states that the conviction must be for a crime punishable by death, or imprisonment in excess of one year. The facts here indicate that the defendant could have been sentenced to two years in prison, so the crime is one that qualifies for this exception. The defendant's intoxication was a fact essential to the finding of guilt, since she could not have been convicted of drunk driving without such a finding. As a result, the evidence of her intoxication will be admissible into evidence. Since choice D doesn't recognize that this exception will make the evidence admissible, it's not the best response.

Answer 41

(C) is the best response,

because it correctly identifies the purpose for which the evidence will be admissible.

The problem here is that cutting down the tree, after a limb fell on the plaintiff, would be considered a subsequent remedial measure. The general rule is that subsequent remedial measures are not admissible to show negligence or "culpable conduct." FRE 407. However, such evidence *is* admissible for other purposes, e.g., to show ownership or control, or to prove the opponent destroyed evidence. Choice C correctly identifies why the evidence of subsequent remedial measures will be admissible here: to prove ownership. The evidence here will tend to prove that the defendant *did*, in fact, own the tree, which he denies at trial. As a result, the evidence will be admissible. This question is an example of the doctrine of limited admissibility, under which a piece of evidence can be admissible for one purpose, but inadmissible for another. Since C correctly identifies this, it's the best response.

(A) is not the best response,

because it misidentifies the purpose for which the evidence is offered.

The problem here is that cutting down the tree, after a limb fell on the plaintiff, would be considered a subsequent remedial measure. The general rule is that subsequent remedial measures are not admissible to show negligence or "culpable conduct." FRE 407. As choice A points out, the rationale of this rule is a policy of encouraging safety precautions. However, what choice A doesn't recognize is that there is a permissible purpose for this evidence: proving ownership of the tree. Here, the defendant disputes that the tree was *his,* so ownership is an issue. His subsequently cutting down the tree would suggest that it *was* his, after all.

If you chose this response, you did so because you overlooked the fact that subsequent remedial measures *are* admissible to prove *non-wrongdoing-related items,* of which ownership is one. Thus, A is not the best response.

(B) is not the best response,

because it mischaracterizes the evidence as irrelevant, and it fails to recognize a purpose for which the evidence could be admitted.

The problem here is that cutting down the tree, after a limb fell on the plaintiff, would be considered a subsequent remedial measure. The general rule is that subsequent remedial measures are not admissible to show negligence or "culpable conduct." FRE 407. However, under these facts, the defendant is denying he owns the tree; his subsequently cutting it down would prove that he does, and ownership is a permissible purpose of evidence of subsequent remedial measures.

Choice B is incorrect in stating that the evidence is irrelevant to the condition of the tree when the accident occurred. A piece of evidence is logically relevant to an issue if it tends to prove or disprove the issue. Here, it's unlikely that the defendant would cut down his tree if it weren't somehow damaged. His cutting it down within a week of the accident would tend to suggest that it was rotted, and *that* would tend to indicate that he was negligent in failing to care for it or cutting it down earlier. Thus, the defendant's cutting down the tree would be relevant to the condition of the tree at the time of the accident. However, the evidence would not be admissible for the purpose, due to the general rule about inadmissibility of subsequent remedial measures. Since B doesn't recognize a purpose for which the evidence could be admitted, and it mischaracterizes the evidence as irrelevant, it's not the best response.

(D) is not the best response,

because it states an impermissible motive for the evidence.

Under these facts, the defendant cut down the tree within a week after one of its branches fell on the plaintiff. If he allowed the tree to stand once it was rotting, he'd likely be liable in negligence for the plaintiff's damages. However, the problem with the evidence is that cutting down the tree would be considered a subsequent remedial measure.

The general rule is that subsequent remedial measures are inadmissible to prove negligence or wrongdoing. FRE 407. Thus, the evidence *could not* be admitted to prove the tree was in a rotted condition. What choice D ignores is that the evidence *will* be admissible to prove ownership of the tree, since the defendant denies that the tree is his, and ownership is a permissible purpose for evidence of subsequent remedial measures. Since D states an impermissible motive for the evidence, it's not the best response.

Answer 42

(A) is the best response,

because the events satisfy all the requirements of the recorded recollection exception.

FRE 803(5) recognizes a hearsay exception for a past recollection recorded. There are four elements to the exception: (1) the memorandum must relate to something of which the witness once had first-hand knowledge; (2) the record must have been made by, or adopted by, the witness when the matter was fresh in the witness's memory; (3) there must currently be some impairment of the witness's memory of the events; and (4) the record must correctly reflect the witness's original knowledge.

Playing the tape for the jury would be proper under the past recollection recorded hearsay exception because it satisfies all four elements of the exception: (1) the tape relates to something of which the witness once had first-hand knowledge, since the witness personally saw the events, including the license number; (2) the tape was made when the matter was fresh in the witness's memory; (3) there is an impairment of the witness's memory, since he has said that he has no present memory of the license plate number; and (4) at trial, the witness is testifying that immediately after the event he listened to a playback and verified that the witness's wife had relayed the license number correctly.

(B) is not the best response,

because the witness is not a public official who had a duty to make the report.

There is a common-law exception to the hearsay rule for public records and reports. This exception is codified in FRE 803(8), which allows the admission of "A record or statement of a public office if: (A) it sets out . . . (ii) a matter observed while under a legal duty to report, but not including, in a criminal case, a matter observed by law-enforcement personnel[.]"

The public records exception to the hearsay rule does not apply in this case because the witness (the one who "observed" the matter in question) was not a public official, and was thus not acting "while under a legal duty to report." (Even if the witness *was*, say, a police officer, the last clause quoted above would prevent the report from coming in against the defendant in the defendant's criminal trial.)

(C) is not the best response,

because the tape recording of the call to the police falls within the past recollection recorded exception. (See the discussion of choice A to understand why this is so.)

(D) is not the best response,

because the defendant's wife does not have to have firsthand knowledge of the license number in order for the recorded recollection exception to apply.

Playing the tape for the jury would be proper under the past recollection recorded hearsay exception. The requirements of FRE 803(5)'s past recollection recorded exception do not require that the witness be the one who physically made the record. All that 803(5) requires in this respect is that the record be one that is "made or *adopted* by the witness when the matter was fresh in the witness's memory." Here, when the witness immediately listened to the playback and pronounced the relayed number correct, the witness adopted the record.

Answer 43

(A) is the best response,

because it correctly indicates that the witness can be impeached with this evidence.

Here, discrediting testimony is being sought from the witness's own mouth. This is "intrinsic" impeachment. There are five general types of questions that may be used to elicit intrinsic impeachment from a witness. They are questions seeking to show (1) bias or interest; (2) prior inconsistent statements; (3) certain prior convictions; (4) bad character for honesty (including unconvicted bad acts); and (5) sensory deficiencies (e.g., eyesight, memory, mental disability).

As this list indicates, the witness can be intrinsically impeached with evidence of his bad character for honesty. A false claim on an insurance policy would be just such an act.

Incidentally, say the facts were different, and the method of impeachment here were *extrinsic,* not *intrinsic.* The methods of extrinsic impeachment include bias; contradicting facts; inconsistent statements (require a foundation); sensory deficiencies; certain convictions; and bad character for truthfulness. While bad character for truthfulness *can* be addressed with extrinsic impeachment, *when the evidence is extrinsic, only reputation or opinion testimony may be used,* under FRE 608(a). This means that the specific instance here could *not* be used!

In any case, since A correctly states that the evidence will be usable as intrinsic impeachment, it's the best response.

(B) is not the best response,

because the conduct didn't have to result in a conviction in order to be usable for impeachment.

Here, discrediting testimony is being sought from the witness's own mouth. This is "intrinsic" impeachment. There are five general types of questions that may be used to elicit intrinsic impeachment from a witness. They are questions seeking to show (1) bias or interest; (2) prior inconsistent statements; (3) certain prior convictions; (4) bad character for honesty (including unconvicted bad acts); and (5) sensory deficiencies (e.g., eyesight, memory, mental disability).

Thus, while one method of intrinsic impeachment is to ask the witness about a prior conviction that bears on his honesty, intrinsic impeachment can also take the form of a question about the witness's prior "bad act" that did not lead to a conviction, as long as the commission of such a bad act would tend to show dishonesty. A false claim on an insurance policy would be just such an act—and its use to intrinsically impeach the witness would be proper whether there was a conviction or not. Since B incorrectly states that the conduct must have resulted in a conviction to be usable as impeachment, it's not the best response.

(C) is not the best response,

because the impeachment *can* be in the form of a specific instance of misconduct.

Here, discrediting testimony is being sought from the witness's own mouth. This is "intrinsic" impeachment. There are five general types of questions that may be used to elicit intrinsic impeachment from a witness. They are questions seeking to show (1) bias or interest; (2) prior inconsistent statements; (3) certain prior convictions; (4) bad character for honesty (including unconvicted bad acts); and (5) sensory deficiencies (e.g., eyesight, memory, mental disability).

As this list indicates, the witness can be intrinsically impeached with evidence of his bad character for honesty. A false claim on an insurance policy would be just such an act.

If you chose this response, you were thinking of the rule for *extrinsic* impeachment with evidence of bad conduct. The methods of extrinsic impeachment include bias; contradicting facts; inconsistent statements (require a foundation); sensory deficiencies; certain convictions; and bad character for truthfulness.

While bad character for truthfulness *can* be addressed with extrinsic impeachment, *when the evidence is extrinsic, this must be done only by reputation or opinion testimony (as allowed by FRE 608(a)), not by "specific instances" testimony (which is barred by FRE 608(b)). Therefore,* the specific instance here could *not* be introduced by extrinsic evidence (proof by some means other than an inquiry to the witness, such as by introducing into evidence a letter in which the insurer rejected the witness's claim as false). Since the false-claim evidence here is intrinsic rather than extrinsic, choice C's reliance on the rule for extrinsic impeachment makes it not the best response.

(D) is not the best response,

because it erroneously applies the Best Evidence Rule (BER) to these facts.

The BER only applies when the terms of a writing are being proven, or the witness is testifying relying on a writing. Under those circumstances, the document itself must be introduced, if it's available.

The BER does not apply to these facts, because, although the best evidence of a writing is the writing itself, whereas here the issue to which the writing relates is "collateral" (i.e., the claim will only address the witness's character for truthfulness), the BER does not apply. *See* FRE 1004(d) (BER does not apply where the writing "is not closely related to a controlling issue.") So the witness's testimony will be admissible without producing the document.

In fact, the claim form itself would be *inadmissible,* under the common-law "collateral matter rule," which though not expressly mentioned in the FRE is deemed to be part of the common-law principles incorporated in the FRE. Under the common-law rule, "extrinsic" evidence (not from the witness's own mouth) is "collateral" and cannot be admitted if it is relevant only to discredit a witness; but if the evidence also proves or disproves a substantive issue (or it proves something deemed material, like witness bias), the evidence is admissible. Here, the claim form would only show that the witness isn't honest; it wouldn't impact any substantive issue in the case. Thus, not only is D incorrect in stating that the claim form is the only way to admit the evidence of the false claim, but the choice fails to recognize that the claim form wouldn't be admissible at all under the collateral matter rule. As a result, D is not the best response.

Answer 44

(C) is the best response,

because it correctly identifies the statement here as inadmissible hearsay.

Note that what this *really* means is that the evidence is not admissible *under any of the other choices in this question*. Of course, the evidence *could* be admissible under the catch-all exception to the hearsay rule; but it's clearly not admissible under the other choices, A and B, so C must be the correct response.

Note that the statement here *is* hearsay, because it's an out-of-court statement offered to prove the truth of its assertion. The out-of-court declarant is the driver: "Officer, a few minutes ago. . . . " The statement is being offered to prove that the defendant was the culprit, so it's hearsay. However, the statement will not be admissible as either a present sense impression or under the fictitious hearsay exception indicated in choice A, the statement of "recent perception." Since C correctly identifies the evidence as hearsay, and it's not admissible under any choice here, C is the best response.

(A) is not the best response,

because it states a hearsay exception that doesn't exist.

Note that choice A *is* correct in characterizing the evidence as hearsay. Hearsay is an out-of-court statement offered to prove the truth of its assertion. The out-of-court declarant is the driver: "Officer, a few minutes ago. . . ." The statement is being offered to prove that the defendant was the culprit, so it's hearsay, and in order to be admissible, it would have to fit a hearsay exception or exclusion.

The problem with choice A is that it doesn't offer a viable means of admitting the hearsay statement. There is no hearsay exception for "statements of recent perception." The closest real exception would be present sense impressions. The rationale of allowing present sense impressions is that the declarant has not had time to fabricate—he's responding to something that's taking place currently. If the declarant has time to reflect, he has time to fabricate, making his statement less trustworthy. Here, it's been at least a few minutes since the driver saw the hit-and-run accident, so even if you read choice A to refer to the "present sense impression" hearsay exception, the statement here wouldn't qualify. In any case, since A states a hearsay exception that doesn't exist, it's not the best response.

(B) is not the best response,

because the facts here would not fit the present sense impression exception to the hearsay rule.

Note that choice B *is* correct in characterizing the evidence as hearsay. Hearsay is an out-of-court statement offered to prove the truth of its assertion. The out-of-court declarant is the driver: "Officer, a few minutes ago. . . ." The statement is being offered to prove that the defendant was the culprit, so it's hearsay, and in order to be admissible, it would have to fit a hearsay exception or exclusion.

The problem here is that the statement wouldn't fit the present sense impression hearsay exception. Under FRE 803(1), a present sense impression is admissible under a hearsay exception if it was made while the declarant was perceiving an event/condition (or immediately thereafter), and it describes or explains the event/condition. Under these facts, the driver has had, according to his statement, "a few minutes" in order to think. The rationale behind the present sense impression hearsay exception is that, because the statement was made contemporaneously with the event it concerns, it will suffer no defects in memory; and, since it usually would have been made to someone else who was also present, there was an opportunity for at least one other person to correct it. Another rationale for the exception is that since the utterance was made at the time of the event, there's no time for the declarant to fabricate. Under these facts, these parameters are not satisfied, making B not the best response.

(D) is not the best response,

because the legal relevance of the evidence here is not a particular problem.

In order to be admissible, every piece of evidence must be "legally relevant"; that is, its probative value must not be substantially outweighed by the danger of unfair prejudice. This typically applies to inflammatory evidence (e.g., body parts, gruesome photos).

Here, instead, the problem is hearsay. Hearsay is an out-of-court statement offered to prove the truth of its assertion. The out-of-court declarant is the driver: "Officer, a few minutes ago. . . ." The statement is being offered to prove that the defendant was the culprit, so it's hearsay, and in order to be admissible, it would have to fit a hearsay exception or exclusion.

Say the facts were different, and it was the driver himself testifying as to what he saw (*not* what he said to the officer, because it would *still* be hearsay). The evidence still wouldn't have legal relevance problems, because there's nothing particularly prejudicial about it. Furthermore, its tremendous probative value—it's direct evidence of the defendant's guilt—would make it admissible. Since D suggests a legal relevance problem where one does not in fact exist, and it ignores the central issue under these facts, it's not the best response.

Answer 45

(B) is the best response,

because it correctly identifies that the treatise can be read into evidence, and gives one possible source for establishing the treatise as a reliable authority: the judge.

Choice B correctly recognizes that there's a hearsay problem with this evidence. Hearsay is an out-of-court statement offered to prove the truth of its assertion. Here, the out-of-court declarant is the author of the treatise. It's being offered to prove that the plaintiff's injuries may not have been caused by the defendant's negligence. Thus, the treatise is hearsay, and it will have to fit some hearsay exception or exclusion to be admissible.

Choice B correctly recognizes that the learned treatise hearsay exception will make the passages admissible. Under the FRE, a statement in a learned treatise can be "read into evidence" (but *cannot* be admitted as an exhibit) if (1) an expert witness relies on it on direct examination or it's called to his attention on cross-examination; *and* (2) the publication is established as reliable authority by the present witness's testimony or admission by another expert's testimony or by judicial notice. FRE 803(18). Since B recognizes a correct basis for reading the treatise's statements into evidence, and states that the evidence is admissible, it's the best response.

(A) is not the best response,

because it is too restrictive.

While the evidence will be admissible to impeach the plaintiff's doctor, under FRE 803(18) it will *also* be admissible as substantive evidence.

Choice A correctly recognizes that there's a hearsay problem with this evidence. Hearsay is an out-of-court statement offered to prove the truth of its assertion.

Here, the out-of-court declarant is the author of the treatise. It's being offered to prove that the plaintiff's injuries may not have been caused by the defendant's negligence. Thus, the treatise is hearsay, and it will have to fit some hearsay exception or exclusion to be admissible.

However, choice A fails to recognize that the treatise can be read into evidence under the "learned treatise" hearsay exception. If you chose A, it's probably because you confused the common-law rule with the rule under the FRE on the admissibility of learned treatises. At common law, learned treatises are only admissible as relied upon and referred to by an expert witness on direct examination, and to impeach an expert witness's testimony on cross-examination (by pointing out how his opinion differs from the source upon which he states he has relied — no *other* source can be used). However, under the FRE, a statement in a learned treatise can be "read into evidence" (but *cannot* be admitted as an exhibit) if (1) an expert witness relies on it on direct examination or it's called to his attention on cross-examination; *and* (2) the publication is established as reliable authority by the present witness's testimony or admission by another expert's testimony or by judicial notice. FRE 803(18). Thus, the textbook's statements here will be admissible substantively. Since A is too restrictive, stating that the textbook will *only* be admissible to impeach, it's not the best response.

(C) is not the best response,

because the evidence here, although hearsay, *is* admissible under the learned treatises exception to the hearsay rule, FRE 803(18).

Choice C correctly recognizes that there's a hearsay problem with this evidence. Hearsay is an out-of-court statement offered to prove the truth of its assertion. Here, the out-of-court declarant is the author of the treatise. It's being offered to prove that the plaintiff's injuries may not have been caused by the defendant's negligence. Thus, the treatise is hearsay, and it will have to fit some hearsay exception or exclusion to be admissible.

What choice C fails to realize is that the testimony fits the "learned treatise" hearsay exception. Under the FRE, a statement in a learned treatise can be "read into evidence" (but *cannot* be admitted as an exhibit) if (1) an expert witness relies on it on direct examination or it's called to his attention on cross-examination; *and* (2) the publication is established as reliable authority by the present witness's testimony or admission by another expert's testimony or by judicial notice. FRE 803(18). Thus, the textbook's statements here will be admissible substantively. Since C states otherwise, it's not the best response.

(D) is not the best response,

because the plaintiff's doctor's acknowledgement of relevance is not a requirement for admissibility.

Under the FRE, a statement in a learned treatise can be "read into evidence" (but *cannot* be admitted as an exhibit) if (1) an expert witness relies on it on direct examination or it's called to his attention on cross-examination; *and* (2) the publication is established as reliable authority by the present witness's testimony or admission by another expert's testimony or by judicial notice. FRE 803(18). Thus, under these facts, as long as the treatise is established as reliable authority, statements from it can be read into evidence even if the plaintiff's doctor thinks these are pure drivel. Since D erroneously states that the expert himself must acknowledge the applicability of the treatise's statements, it's not the best response.

Answer 46

(C) is the best response,

because an offer to pay medical expenses is inadmissible to prove liability.

Although the facts don't state the purpose for which the plaintiff is offering the fact of the doctor's offer to pay expenses, let's assume that the purpose is the obvious one of trying to show liability or responsibility (on the theory that "[t]he doctor wouldn't have offered to pay my hospital expenses unless she believed that she was or might be the cause of my problem.")

In that event, the case is clearly governed by FRE 409, which says that "Evidence of furnishing, promising to pay, or offering to pay medical, hospital, or similar expenses resulting from an injury is not admissible to prove liability for the injury."

(A) is not the best response,

because offers to pay medical expenses fall under a separate rule.

It's true that the offer to pay expenses would not be hearsay. But there are many reasons other than hearsay for exclusion of statements, and the no-evidence-of-offers-to-pay-for-medical-expenses rule (see choice C above) is one of them.

(B) is not the best response,

because the offer is not hearsay, and in any event is inadmissible for other reasons.

First, the out-of-court statement here is "I'll pay your medical expenses." That statement is being offered to supply an inference of liability ("You wouldn't have made the offer unless you thought you might be responsible or liable for my condition.") A statement is hearsay only if it's offered to prove "the truth of the matter asserted therein." Here, there is no matter whose "truth" is asserted in the out-of-court statement; the statement is merely an offer to do something. Therefore, repeating the statement in court couldn't be hearsay. (If the doctor had said, "I'm sorry my negligence caused your hospitalization," then this *would* be a statement containing an assertion of fact, which could make it hearsay.)

A second problem with this choice is that the declaration-against-interest exception to the hearsay rule applies only where the declarant is not available to testify at trial. The doctor is available to testify here, so far as we're aware. (The appropriate hearsay exception would be the one for admissions by, and offered against, a party-opponent.)

(D) is not the best response,

because the doctor's offer was unilateral and not the product of negotiation.

It's true that the fact that a party has offered to settle a claim may not be admitted on the issue of the claim's validity. *See* FRE 408. But the Rule 408 exclusion only applies to offers, or other statements, made "in compromising or attempting to compromise" a "disputed claim." In other words, the exclusion only applies to statements made *during the course of settlement negotiations, and settlement negotiations can't occur before there has even been a claim.* The offer here was made before there was a "claim" (since it was made "immediately" after the doctor "learned of the medication problem," with no indication that the patient had by then threatened to sue or had otherwise made "a claim" against the doctor). Therefore, the offer doesn't fall within the exclusion.

Answer 47

(A) is the best response,

because it most closely reflects the central issue concerning admissibility on these facts.

Under these facts, the criminal defendant is testifying on his own behalf. The prosecutor is attempting to impeach him, intrinsically, with evidence of a six-year-old felony (burglary is always a felony).

Under FRE 609(a)(1), a witness can be impeached (intrinsically or extrinsically) with conviction of any felony, regardless of whether it involved dishonesty or false statement (a "*crimen falsi* "). However, when the witness is a criminal defendant, and the felony did not involve a *crimen falsi*, the witness gets a slight protection from impeachment that's not present where the conviction is for a *crimen falsi*: impeachment is allowed only if the court determines that the probative value of the evidence outweighs its prejudicial effect on the defendant (in which case the court not only may but *must* admit it). Here, since burglary is not a *crimen falsi*, the court may/must admit the burglary conviction for its impeachment value if the court finds that the conviction's probative impeachment value outweighs (even by a small amount) its prejudicial effect on the defendant. Choice A exactly states this rule.

(B) is not the best response,

because the prosecutor would not necessarily have a *right* to ask such a question.

Under these facts, the criminal defendant is testifying on his own behalf. The prosecutor is attempting to impeach him, intrinsically, with evidence of a six-year-old felony.

Under FRE 609(a)(1), a witness can be intrinsically impeached with conviction of any felony, regardless of whether it involved dishonesty or false statement (a "*crimen falsi* "). However, when the witness is a criminal defendant, and the felony did not involve a *crimen falsi*, the witness gets a slight protection from impeachment that's not present where the conviction is for a *crimen falsi*: impeachment is allowed only if the court determines that the probative value of the evidence outweighs its prejudicial effect on the defendant (in which case the court not only may but *must* admit it). Here, since burglary is not a *crimen falsi*, the court may/must admit the burglary conviction for its impeachment value if—and only if—the court finds that the conviction's probative impeachment value outweighs (even by a small amount) its prejudicial effect on the defendant. Choice B, since it implies that the prosecutor would have the right to ask the question in *all* circumstances (i.e., regardless of whether the court finds that the conviction's probative impeachment value would be outweighed by its prejudicial effect), is not correct.

(C) is not the best response,

because it misstates the standard on which prior convictions are admissible to impeach.

Under these facts, the criminal defendant is testifying on his own behalf. The prosecutor is attempting to impeach him, intrinsically, with evidence of a six-year-old felony.

Under FRE 609(a)(1), a witness can be intrinsically impeached with conviction of any felony, regardless of whether it involved dishonesty or false statement (a "*crimen falsi* "). However, when the witness is a criminal defendant, and the felony did not involve a *crimen falsi*, the witness gets a slight protection from impeachment that's not present where the conviction is for a *crimen falsi*: impeachment is allowed only if the court determines that the probative value of the evidence outweighs its prejudicial effect on the defendant (in which case the court not only may but *must* admit it). Here, since burglary is not a *crimen falsi*, the court may/must admit the burglary conviction for its impeachment value if—and only if—the court finds that the conviction's probative impeachment value outweighs (even by a small amount) its prejudicial effect on the defendant.

Here, burglary indeed does not involve dishonesty or false statement, so this choice is correct on that point. However, even though burglary is not a *crimen falsi*, as described in the prior paragraph, the court must nonetheless admit the burglary conviction for its impeachment value unless the court finds that the conviction's probative impeachment value would be outweighed by its prejudicial effect on the defendant. Since this choice asserts that the question is automatically improper solely because the conviction is not for a *crimen falsi*, it is legally incorrect.

(D) is not the best response,

because the conviction *can* be proven through intrinsic impeachment.

Under these facts, the criminal defendant is testifying on his own behalf. The prosecutor is attempting to impeach him, intrinsically, with evidence of a six-year-old felony. Choice D suggests that such impeachment requires that the original court record of the conviction must be introduced. In fact, that's not the case.

As is discussed in the treatments of Choices A, B and C, the impeachment here is proper under FRE 609 unless the court finds that the conviction's probative impeachment value would be outweighed by its prejudicial effect on the defendant.

When impeachment by means of a prior conviction is proper under FRE 609, that conviction may be proved *either* "from the witness's own mouth," i.e., by a question to the witness (which is called "intrinsic" impeachment), or by "extrinsic" evidence (documents or testimony from a witness other than the witness being impeached). So this choice, by asserting that conviction can only be proved by use of the court record (an "extrinsic" method), is wrong.

Answer 48

(A) is the best response,

because it correctly states the rule on extrinsic evidence.

FRE 608(b) says that "Except for a criminal conviction under Rule 609, extrinsic evidence is not admissible to prove specific instances of a witness's conduct in order to attack or support the witness's character for truthfulness. But the court may, on cross-examination, allow them to be inquired into if they are probative of the character for truthfulness or untruthfulness of . . . the witness[.]"

The present use fits the second sentence of FRE 608(b): The giving of false testimony in a prior trial is obviously "probative of the character for . . . untruthfulness." And choice A's limitation to matters "elicited from the expert witness on cross-examination" brings the situation into the second sentence (cross-examination) rather than the first sentence (extrinsic evidence).

(B) is not the best response,

because prior bad acts can be introduced only on cross-examination, but in that event need not be supported by "clear and convincing" extrinsic evidence.

As described in choice A above, the prior-bad-act evidence here can only be brought out on cross. Therefore, choice B is wrong since it does not include this limitation.

On the other hand, if the evidence *is* brought out on cross, it need not be supported by "clear and convincing" evidence. It's true that as a judge-made rule, the cross-examiner must have a "good-faith basis" for believing that the false-testimony episode actually occurred. But such a good-faith basis, not the possession of clear-and-convincing-evidence, is all that is required for introducing the topic on cross.

(C) is not the best response,

because the defendant's testimony would be admissible if elicited on cross-examination.

If the evidence were being offered "extrinsically" (e.g., by testimony from a different witness who witnessed the false testimony), this choice would be correct—see the first sentence of FRE 608(b), quoted in the discussion of choice A above. But the evidence would be allowed to be brought up ("elicited") on cross of the expert witness himself, even though it relates solely to credibility rather than to a substantive issue in the case (and thus concerns a "collateral matter"). Since choice C overstates the situations in which the evidence would be excluded, it's not the best answer.

(D) is not the best response,

because the evidence would be admissible if elicited on cross-examination.

Evidence of a prior bad act by the witness demonstrating the witness's poor character for truthfulness does not fall within the general ban on proof of character traits to show action-in-conformity-there-with-on-the-present-occasion. Instead, FRE 608(b) imposes specific rules governing when such evidence is admissible—as described in choice A, such prior-acts-of-lying evidence may be brought out only on cross of the witness whose veracity is in question, not by means of "extrinsic evidence." Therefore, choice D is an incorrect statement of both the rule and the outcome.

Answer 49

(A) is the best response,

because it correctly applies the rule on spousal privilege in federal courts.

In federal courts, in criminal cases, the witness-spouse holds the privilege exclusively, and can choose to testify if he or she wants, without the consent of the accused-spouse, except as to confidential communications (on which the accused-spouse can forbid testimony). *Trammel v. U.S.*, 445 U.S. 40 (1980). Here, the defendant's wife's potential testimony involves a conversation between the defendant and co-defendant before the defendant's wife even married the defendant, so it can't involve a confidential marital communication. As a result, the choice to testify is entirely for the defendant's wife to make. Since A correctly states this rule, it's the best response.

(B) is not the best response,

because it misapplies the rule on spousal privilege in federal courts.

In federal courts, in criminal cases, the witness-spouse holds the privilege exclusively, and can choose to testify if he or she wants, without the consent of the accused-spouse, except as to confidential communications (on which the accused-spouse can forbid testimony). *Trammel v. U.S.*, 445 U.S. 40 (1980). Since a confidential marital communication was not involved here, the choice is entirely for the defendant's wife to make, not for the defendant to make, making B not the best response.

(C) is not the best response,

because it misapplies the rule on spousal privilege in federal courts.

In federal courts, in criminal cases, the witness-spouse holds the privilege exclusively, and can choose to testify if he or she wants, without the consent of the accused-spouse, except as to confidential communications (on which the accused-spouse can forbid testimony). *Trammel v. U.S.*, 445 U.S. 40 (1980). Since a confidential marital communication was not involved here, the choice is entirely for the defendant's wife to make, and C is not the best response.

(D) is not the best response,

because it misapplies the rule on spousal privilege in the federal courts.

In federal courts, in criminal cases, the witness-spouse holds the privilege exclusively, and can choose to testify if he or she wants, without the consent of the accused-spouse, except as to confidential communications (on which the accused-spouse can forbid testimony). *Trammel v. U.S.*, 445 U.S. 40 (1980). Since a confidential marital communication was not involved here, the choice is entirely for the defendant's wife to make. If you chose choice D, it could be because you confused the federal court rule with the common law rule in civil cases, in which the witness-spouse can be forced to testify against the party-spouse. This is not the rule in federal courts in criminal trials, so D is not the best response.

Answer 50

(A) is the best response,

because evidence of witness bias is allowed.

All courts, including the federal courts under the FRE, allow impeachment on the basis of bias. Although nothing in the FRE specifically deals with when and how a party can show a witness's bias, it's quite clear that the evidence here—which presents a strong indication that the witness's friend dislikes the defendant and might well therefore try to injure him by false testimony—would be admitted.

(B) is not the best response,

because the witness's friend's character isn't in question, whereas his possible bias is.

As described in choice A above, a party may always show that a witness (including an out-of-court declarant whose statement is serving as testimony) was biased.

(C) is not the best response,

because it isn't necessary that the witness's friend be "given an opportunity to explain or deny."

There are very few instances under the FRE under which a person must be given an opportunity to "explain or deny" (or otherwise respond to) particular evidence. Perhaps the examiners were trying to trick you into thinking that the following FRE provision applies: "Extrinsic evidence of a *witness's prior inconsistent statement* is admissible only if the witness is *given an opportunity to explain or deny the statement* and an adverse party is given an opportunity to examine the witness about it, or if justice so requires." FRE 613(b).

However, this provision clearly doesn't apply here because (1) the witness's friend is not "a witness" for purposes of the provision (he hasn't taken the stand); and (2) showing that the witness's friend had a bias is not the same as showing that he's made a prior statement that's inconsistent with the statement being discussed.

There is no other provision concerning an opportunity to "explain or deny" that might apply here.

(D) is not the best response,

because bias *can* be shown by specific instances.

It's clear that when *A* quotes an out-of-court statement by *B*, *A* may be cross-examined about material—including prior acts by *B*—that tends to show that *B* was biased when he made the statement. See FRE 608(b) (specific credibility-related instances of the conduct of a witness may be brought up on cross of either that witness or some other witness about whom the present witness has testified). So in this scenario, among others, witness bias *can* be shown by specific instances.

Answer 51

(B) is the best response,

because no expert witness is required to point out the similarities between the photo and the defendant—the jury is entitled to make the comparison itself.

When an automatic device takes a picture, only a limited type of authentication is needed. A witness must testify about how the machine works, and that testimony must somehow tie the photo to the issue under question (e.g., "The photo was taken at 2:45 a.m. on Aug. 23rd, the same time a burglar alarm went off indicating that the premises had been broken into.") Since the facts tell us the expert has testified to the "reliability of infrared photography," we can presume that this type of testimony was given.

Once this has happened, no further authentication or other expert testimony is needed. The jury is deemed to be capable of comparing the image with the defendant, so as to make its own determination of whether there are interesting resemblances. (Expert testimony would be admissible—if the judge thought that it would help the jury and be "reliable"—but it's not *required*.)

(A) is not the best response,

because, for the reason explained in choice B above, no expert testimony is required (though such testimony might be admissible).

(C) is not the best response,

because no eyewitness identification is needed for photos taken by automatic devices.

Where a photo is taken by an automatic device, only limited authentication (showing that the machine is reliable, and tying the photo to the episode in question) is required. What's NOT required is any testimony by a human who says, "I saw the photo taken, and I can say it was taken at a certain time [or in a certain circumstance.]" So once the expert here testified about how the machine works (see the example, in the discussion of choice B above, of testimony that would have sufficed), no "eyewitness" testimony about the taking of the photo was needed.

(D) is not the best response,

because the camera and the photos taken by it are not "witnesses" for purpose of the Confrontation Clause.

The Confrontation Clause applies only where a human being gives testimony. Where evidence is produced by an inanimate object—such as the camera here—the Clause is never triggered.

Answer 52

(B) is the best response,

because it correctly recognizes the evidence as inadmissible because it is impeachment on a collateral matter.

Under these facts, the witness is being impeached with extrinsic evidence that contradicts his direct testimony. The evidence is that he worked for his employer for only seven years instead of three, which has no bearing on any issue in the case.

The problem with this is that the impeachment violates the "collateral matters" rule. Under the "collateral matters" rule, extrinsic evidence can only be introduced to impeach a witness if it *also* bears on a *substantive* issue in the case (or if it proves something deemed important, like bias). Here, if the employment records are true, they only prove the witness is lying—they do not make any issue in the case either more or less probable.

Note that what this choice doesn't mention, but implies, is that what makes the impeachment impermissible is that it's *extrinsic* impeachment—the witness *could* be impeached by asking *him* about his employment record (which would be "intrinsic" impeachment, since it's from his own mouth). Since B correctly applies this rule to the facts here, it's the best response.

(A) is not the best response,

because it incorrectly applies the Best Evidence Rule (BER).

The BER only applies when the material terms of a writing are being proven, or the witness is testifying relying on a writing. Neither of these applies to the facts here. The terms of the writing (the employment records) are not relevant to any of the issues in the trial. Instead, the witness is being impeached with extrinsic impeachment that contradicts his direct testimony. The evidence is that he worked for his employer for only seven years instead of three, which has no bearing on any issue in the case. Under the "collateral matters" rule, extrinsic evidence can only be introduced to impeach a witness if it *also* bears on a *substantive* issue in the case (or if it proves something deemed important, like bias). Here, if the records are true, they only prove the witness is lying—they do not make any issue in the case either more or less probable. As a result, the records need not be introduced, and A is not the best response.

(C) is not the best response,

because it wrongly invokes the business records exception to the hearsay rule.

While the employment records here could qualify under that exception (if the entries were made in the regular course of business, in conjunction with a business activity, entered under a duty to record, by one with personal knowledge of matters recorded or transmitted from such a person, entered at or near the time of transaction, and authenticated at trial; FRE 803(6)), choice C is incorrect because the records haven't been offered into evidence.

Instead, what choice C fails to take into account is the "collateral matters" rule. Under that rule, extrinsic evidence (i.e., not from the witness's own mouth) can only be introduced to impeach a witness if it *also* bears on a *substantive* issue in the case (or if it proves something deemed important, like bias). Here, if the records are true, they only prove the witness is lying—they do not make any issue in the case either more or less probable. Since C does not recognize the "collateral matter" involved here, it's not the best response.

(D) is not the best response,

because it fails to take into account the "collateral matters" rule.

Choice D correctly recognizes that the evidence here will impeach the witness, by bringing into question his credibility. However, the fact that the evidence here will impeach the witness's credibility is not enough to make it admissible, because extrinsic evidence (i.e., evidence not from the witness's own mouth) is only admissible to impeach a witness if it *also* bears on a *substantive* issue in the case (or if it proves something deemed important, like bias). Here, if the records are true, they only prove the witness is lying—they do not make any issue in the case either more or less probable. Since D does not recognize the "collateral matter" hitch here, it's not the best response.

Answer 53

(D) is the best response,

because the record here satisfies the records-of-regularly-kept-activities exception, and the statement recorded falls within the statements-for-purposes-of-medical-diagnosis exception.

We have here a statement-within-a-statement problem. That is, we have (1) a written statement by the intern (the hospital record), which is the "outer" level; and (2) an oral statement (the statement spoken by the physician), which is the "inner" level. For the written record to come in, both levels must either be nonhearsay or hearsay within an exception.

Let's take the inner level first: This one falls neatly within FRE 803(4)'s hearsay exception for "A statement that: (A) is made for—and is reasonably pertinent to—medical diagnosis or treatment; and (B) describes medical history; past or present symptoms or sensations; their inception; or their general cause."

Now, the outer level: FRE 803(6) gives the FRE's version of what is commonly called the business records exception. It provides a hearsay exception for "A record of an act, event, condition, opinion, or diagnosis if: (A) the record was made at or near the time by—or from information transmitted by—someone with knowledge; (B) the record was kept in the course of a regularly conducted activity of a business, organization, occupation, or calling, whether or not for profit; (C) making the record was a regular practice of that activity; (D) all these conditions are shown by the testimony of the custodian or another qualified witness, or by a certification . . . and (E) the opponent does not show that the source of information or the method or circumstances of preparation indicate a lack of trustworthiness."

The record here qualifies. Note that the fact that the record wasn't physically made by the person "with knowledge" (the physician) doesn't matter, as long as the record was made "from information transmitted by" a person with knowledge. Since the physician transmitted the information to the intern, the fact that the intern was the one who made the physical record is okay.

(A) is not the best response,

because establishment of the physician's expertise is neither sufficient nor necessary for admissibility of the record.

The physician is not giving testimony here, so he's not an "expert witness," and the foundation required for expert testimony is therefore not required. Furthermore, even if such a foundation had been laid, the record couldn't come in unless the two levels of exceptions to the hearsay rule were established (as they were—see the discussion of choice D above).

(B) is not the best response,

because at issue is the admissibility of the record, not data that is not in evidence.

When a record containing an opinion is admissible as an exception to the hearsay rule, the fact that the data on which the maker of the record relied is not in evidence is irrelevant.

In fact, this choice is a complete red herring. Even if the physician were on the stand repeating his diagnosis, the underlying data wouldn't have to be in evidence, or even admissible—see FRE 703: "An expert may base an opinion on facts or data in the case that the expert has been made aware of or personally observed. If experts in the particular field would reasonably rely on those kinds of facts or data in forming an opinion on the subject, they *need not be admissible* for the opinion to be admitted."

(C) is not the best response,

because the entry records the physician's statements, not the plaintiff's.

Statements *by a patient* regarding the patient's physical condition made to a treating physician in connection with treatment are admissible as exceptions to the hearsay rule. They fall within the much more general exception in FRE 803(3) for "[a] statement of the declarant's then-existing state of mind . . . or emotional, sensory, or physical condition[.]" But the statement here wasn't made by the patient (the plaintiff)—it was made by the treating doctor. And the correct hearsay exception for the doctor's oral statement is (as discussed in choice D above) 803(4)'s exception for "a statement made for—and . . . reasonably pertinent to—medical diagnosis or treatment."

Answer 54

(C) is the best response,

because the statement was made out of court, is offered for the truth of the matter asserted, and does not fall within any exception.

FRE 801(c) defines hearsay as a statement, other than one made by the declarant while testifying at trial, offered in evidence to prove the truth of the matter asserted in the statement. The witness's statement naming the defendant as his source was made by the witness after being arrested by the officer, which is to say it was not made when the witness was testifying at trial. The government seeks to offer the officer's repetition of that statement for the truth of the matter asserted in it, i.e., that the defendant was indeed the source for the drugs he is now charged with selling. So the statement is hearsay and is inadmissible unless some exception applies.

However, no exception applies. For instance, the "prior inconsistent statement" exception doesn't apply for the reason stated in the analysis of choice A below, and the "identification" exception doesn't apply for the reason stated in the analysis of choice B below.

(A) is not the best response,

because the witness has made only one statement.

Certain statements by a person who testifies at a trial or hearing, and is subject to cross-examination about the statements, are not hearsay. FRE 801(d)(1) says that where the declarant "testifies and is subject to cross-examination about a prior statement," the prior statement is non-hearsay (and thus admissible) if it "is inconsistent with the declarant's testimony and was given under penalty of perjury at a trial, hearing, or other proceeding or in a deposition[.]" (801(d)(1)(A)).

This exclusion obviously doesn't apply here: The declarant is the witness, and he is not "testif[ying] . . . subject to cross-examination" at trial. Merely appearing at the trial and refusing to answer doesn't count as "testifying," certainly not when there is a requirement of being "subject to cross-examination." And even if the witness's out-of-court statement after his arrest is viewed as being both "prior" and "inconsistent," it wasn't given "under penalty of perjury at a trial, hearing, or other proceeding or in a deposition[.]"

(B) is not the best response,

because the witness has refused to testify.

Certain statements by a person who testifies at a trial or hearing, and is subject to cross-examination about the statements, are not hearsay. FRE 801(d)(1)(C) says that where the declarant "testifies and is subject to cross-examination about a prior statement," the prior statement is non-hearsay (and thus admissible) if it "identifies a person as someone the declarant perceived earlier."

This exclusion doesn't apply here, because the witness has not "testified" or been "subject to cross-examination" (see the analysis of choice A for more detail about why).

(D) is not the best response,

because the lack of confrontation doesn't have anything to do with the inadmissibility of the statement.

There is no general principle that an out-of-court declaration can't be introduced unless the declarant is "confronted with the statement while on the stand."

It's true that in the case of a prior inconsistent statement from a testifying witness, FRE 613(b) says that extrinsic evidence of the prior statement is inadmissible unless "the witness is given an opportunity to explain or deny the statement and an adverse party is given an opportunity to examine the witness about it, or if justice so requires." But this provision doesn't come close to applying, since the witness is not a testifying witness, and the prior statement is not a "prior inconsistent statement."

It's also true that in some cases, the *defendant's* Confrontation Clause rights will constitutionally prevent an out-of-court declaration from being admitted against him. But choice D refers to the *witness's* right to "confront" the statement while on the stand, not the defendant's right to confront the witness.

In summary, the witness had no right to be "confronted with the statement while on the stand."

Answer 55

(A) is the best response,

because it shows the former vice president deposited more than he made, and is thus circumstantial evidence of guilt the admission of which does not violate any evidentiary rule.

Circumstantial evidence is evidence that, even if it is believed, does not resolve the matter at issue unless additional reasoning is used to reach the proposition to which the evidence is directed. Circumstantial evidence will be admitted only if it has probative value, that is, only if it affects the probability of the existence of a fact consequential to the action.

Evidence that the former vice president deposited nearly twice his salary over a two-year period is circumstantial evidence of the former vice president's embezzlement, because this evidence makes it more likely than it would otherwise be that the former vice president had a major non-salary source of income. There is no evidentiary rule that would bar the admission of this very-relevant evidence.

(B) is not the best response,

because the use of the witness's testimony for impeachment purposes would violate FRE 608(b).

FRE 608(b) says that "[e]xcept for a criminal conviction under Rule 609, *extrinsic evidence is not admissible to prove specific instances* of a witness's conduct in order to *attack or support the witness's character for truthfulness.*" The evidence here consists of "specific instances" of the former vice president's conduct. If the evidence is being offered to "impeach" the former vice president as choice B specifies, it is being offered to "attack the witness's character for truthfulness," and falls within 608(b), given that the specific instances of conduct did not lead to a criminal conviction. Therefore, the specific instances of conduct can't be proved by "extrinsic evidence" (which is what separate testimony from the banker would be). Instead, impeachment could only happen by bringing out the instances while the former vice president was on the stand (e.g., "Isn't it true that according to bank records you deposited almost twice the amount of your salary?").

(C) is not the best response,

because the evidence is highly probative of embezzlement, and there is no "unfair" prejudice.

FRE 403 says that "The court may exclude relevant evidence if its probative value is substantially outweighed by a danger of . . . unfair prejudice[.]" However, this provision wouldn't apply here because: (1) the probative value is quite large (surely a person who deposits almost twice his salary into a bank account is significantly more likely to be an embezzler than one who does not); and (2) there is minimal "unfairness" in showing that a person has made bank deposits, certainly not enough unfairness to "substantially outweigh" the large probative value of the evidence.

(D) is not the best response,

because the fact that the deposits could have been legitimate goes to weight, not admissibility.

A piece of evidence, to be admissible (assuming no special rule of exclusion applies), must merely have "any tendency to make a fact more or less probable than it would be without the evidence," where the fact "is of consequence in determining the action." FRE 401. The evidence doesn't have to conclusively "prove" the ultimate proposition to which it's addressed, or even render that proposition "more likely than not" true. As the idea is sometimes put, "a brick is not a wall."

Here, the fact that a person has made bank deposits of almost twice his salary in a two-year period makes it more likely that he's an embezzler than if he had only deposited the amount of his salary or less. So this evidence satisfies the standard in the prior paragraph, even though there may well be a legitimate explanation for the deposits. As the court might say, the possibility of an innocent explanation here merely "goes to weight, not admissibility."

Answer 56

(D) is the best response,

because a trial judge is allowed to use hearsay when ruling on preliminary questions.

FRE 104(a) says that "[t]he court must decide any preliminary question about whether a witness is qualified, a privilege exists, or evidence is admissible. In so deciding, the court is *not bound by evidence rules*, except those on privilege."

The pedestrian's statement to the nurse is admissible if, and only if, the statement qualified for the dying-declaration exception. That exception applies only in homicide and civil cases (i.e., not in a non-homicide criminal case); the exception requires that the declarant have made the statement "while believing the declarant's death to be imminent," and requires that the statement have been "about [the declarant's death's] cause or circumstances." FRE 804(b)(2).

The affidavit is relevant to the issue of whether the pedestrian's statement to the nurse qualifies for the dying-declaration exception, since it's relevant to whether the pedestrian made the statement while believing his death was imminent. It's true that the affidavit is hearsay (since it's an out-of-court statement offered to prove the truth of the matter asserted, i.e., that the pedestrian really knew or believed he was dying). And this hearsay does not fall within any exception. But under FRE 104(a), the court may consider this inadmissible hearsay in making the court's preliminary ruling on the admissibility of the pedestrian's statement to the nurse.

(A) is not the best response,

because even though the affidavit is hearsay not within any exception, it may still be considered on the preliminary matter of the admissibility of the statement to the nurse.

As described in the discussion of choice D above, the fact that the affidavit is hearsay not within any exception does not prevent the court from using it to resolve a preliminary question about the admissibility of other evidence.

(B) is not the best response,

because (1) dying declarations are admissible in civil cases; and (2) the admissibility of the affidavit is irrelevant to whether it can be considered on the preliminary question here.

First, FRE 804(b)(2) gives a hearsay exception for the following type of statement: "In a prosecution for homicide or in a *civil case*, a statement that the declarant, while believing the declarant's death to be imminent, made about its cause or circumstances." So the proposition asserted in choice B—that dying declarations can't be used except in homicide prosecutions—is simply incorrect as a matter of law. Furthermore, even if the rule of law asserted in this choice were true, the rule would be irrelevant here—as described in the discussion of choice D above, the judge may consider inadmissible material in ruling on an evidentiary question.

(C) is not the best response,

because (1) the affidavit is the "outer level" of a two-level hearsay statement, and that outer level doesn't qualify for the then-existing-state-of-mind exception; and (2) the affidavit's admissibility doesn't matter here anyway.

First, notice that we have hearsay within hearsay. The "outer" level is the doctor's affidavit (a statement made out of court, repeating some other statement). The "inner" level is the pedestrian's statement to the doctor. For the combined statement to be admissible despite containing hearsay, *each* level must satisfy a hearsay exception. It's true that the inner statement arguably qualifies for the then-existing-state-of-mind exception (though even this is far from clear, since under FRE 803(3), "a statement of . . . belief to prove the fact . . . believed" does *not* qualify for the exception).

But the *outer* statement is not a statement about *the declarant's* then existing state of mind—for this purpose, the declarant is the doctor, and he's not summarizing his own then existing state of mind (except insofar as he's making a statement of what he currently remembers the pedestrian to have said, which is inadmissible since FRE 803(3) denies the state-of-mind exception for "a statement of memory . . . to prove the fact remembered").

Since one of the two levels is inadmissible hearsay, the entire statement within a statement is inadmissible. But anyway, as described in the discussion of choice D above, the statement need not be admissible to be considered by the judge in making a preliminary admissibility ruling.

Answer 57

(B) is the best response,

because the witness's testimony does in fact fall within the then-existing–state-of-mind exception.

The out-of-court statement here is, "I'm going to spend the next three days in State B," offered to show that the declarant in fact spent the next three days there. So at least in a loose sense, the declaration is being offered to prove the "truth" of the matter asserted.

FRE 803(3) gives a hearsay exception for "[a] statement of the declarant's then-existing state of mind . . . (such as motive, intent, or *plan*)[.]" So to the extent that the statement here is a statement by the defendant of the fact that she currently plans to do act X, it fits within this exception as a statement of then-existing plan. (Once it comes in, it's allowable for the further inference that if the defendant *planned* to do act X, she probably *did* act X as planned.)

(A) is not the best response,

because the defendant's statement wasn't an effort to describe an event she was perceiving.

FRE 803(1)'s implementation of the present-sense impression exception gives an exception for "[a] statement describing or explaining *an event or condition,* made while or immediately after the declarant perceived it." The defendant's plan to make a trip is not an "event or condition," and she didn't "perceive" it, so the exception doesn't apply.

(C) is not the best response,

because there is no special rule against "establish[ing] an alibi by [a] defendant's own statement."

This is one of those cases where the examiners try to trick you into believing that there is a "rule" on a particular subject when there isn't. There is simply no special rule about when a prior statement by a defendant can be introduced to furnish an alibi.

Actually, a prior statement by a witness (whether she's the defendant or otherwise) qualifies for a hearsay exception if the statement is "consistent with the declarant's testimony and is offered: (i) to rebut an express or implied charge that the declarant recently fabricated it or acted from a recent improper influence or motive in so testifying[.]" FRE 801(d)(1)(B). So to the extent that the prior statement here falls within a special rule for prior statements, the rule is one that confers admissibility, not inadmissibility.

(D) is not the best response,

because the statement falls within the then-existing-state-of-mind hearsay exception. See the analysis of choice B for an explanation of why this is so.

Answer 58

(A) is the best response,

because only the testimony about peaceableness is a "pertinent trait" of the accused.

FRE 404(a), after stating the general rule against evidence of a character trait to prove action in conformity therewith, allows a criminal defendant to offer evidence of "the defendant's pertinent trait." Since peaceability and truthfulness are each alleged character traits of the defendant, the evidence will be admissible if and only if that evidence concerns a trait that is "pertinent" in the case.

What traits are "pertinent" depends on the nature of the crime charged and any defenses raised. Here, what's charged is a crime that involves violence, *but not untruthfulness.*

Therefore, the accused's reputation for peaceableness involves a "pertinent" trait (one who is peaceable is less likely to have committed a crime involving violence). However, the accused's reputation for truthfulness would probably be held *not* to be pertinent (since one who is truthful is not less likely to have committed a murder than one who is untruthful.)

(Note, however, that if the defendant *took the stand* and the prosecution attacked his credibility, then the "reputation for truthfulness" testimony *would* become admissible, because the defendant's truthfulness or untruthfulness would now be in issue and would thus be a "pertinent" trait.)

To the extent that choices B, C, and D each either fails to admit the peaceableness testimony or admits the truthfulness testimony, each one is wrong for the reasons described in the analysis of choice A.

STRATEGIES AND TACTICS

REAL PROPERTY

There's no getting around it—Property questions on the MBE are very tough. Unlike Evidence, where most of the questions can be solved with a mechanical application of the Federal Rules, Property questions frequently require careful analysis based on your general knowledge of the subject.

OUTLINE OF COVERAGE / REAL PROPERTY AND FUTURE INTERESTS

The following outline for the Real Property/Future Interests portion of the MBE was adopted by the Bar Examiners for all MBEs given on or after January 2017. This is the most up-to-date outline of coverage released by the Bar Examiners, and your substantive study for Real Property should be focused on it. If you're taking the July 2016 exam, the topics marked by * apparently won't be on the exam, since the Examiners say these will be added beginning in 2017.

Here's what you need to know:

I. Ownership of real property
   A. Present estates and future interests
      1. Present estates
         a. Fees simple
         b. Defeasible fees simple
         c. Life estates
      2. Future interests
         a. Reversions
         b. Remainders, vested and contingent
         c. Executory interests
         d. Possibilities of reverter, powers of termination
         e. Rules affecting these interests (including survivorship, class gifts, waste, and cy pres)
   B. Cotenancy
      1. Types: tenancy in common and joint tenancy
      2. Rights and obligations of cotenants
         a. Partition
         b. Severance
         c. Relations among cotenants
   C. Landlord-tenant law
      1. Types of tenancies
      2. Possession and rent
      3. Transfers by landlord or tenant
      4. Termination (including surrender, mitigation of damages, anticipatory breach, and security deposits)
      5. Habitability and suitability
   D. Special problems
      1. Rule against perpetuities: common law rule and statutory reforms
      2. Alienability, descendibility, and devisability of present and future interests
      3. Fair housing/discrimination
      4. Conflicts of law related to disputes involving real property *
II. Rights in real property
   A. Restrictive covenants
      1. Nature and type
      2. Creation
      3. Scope

        4. Transfer
        5. Termination
        6. Property owners' associations and common interest ownership communities *
    B. Easements, profits, and licenses
        1. Nature and type
        2. Methods of creation
            a. Express
            b. Implied
            c. Prescription
        3. Scope and apportionment
        4. Transfer
        5. Termination
    C. Fixtures
    D. Zoning (fundamentals other than regulatory taking)
        1. Zoning laws
        2. Protection of pre-existing property rights
        3. Rezoning and other zoning changes
III. Real estate contracts
    A. Real estate brokerage
    B. Creation and construction
        1. Statute of frauds and exceptions
        2. Essential terms
        3. Time for performance
        4. Remedies for breach
    C. Marketability of title
    D. Equitable conversion (including risk of loss)
    E. Options and rights of first refusal
    F. Fitness and suitability
    G. Merger
IV. Mortgages/security devices
    A. Types of security devices
        1. Mortgages (including deeds of trust)
            a. In general
            b. Purchase-money mortgages
            c. Future-advance mortgages
        2. Installment land contracts
        3. Absolute deeds as security
    B. Security relationships
        1. Necessity and nature of obligation
        2. Mortgage theories: title, lien, and intermediate
        3. Rights and duties prior to foreclosure
        4. Right to redeem and clogging equity of redemption
    C. Transfers
        1. By mortgagor
            a. Assumption and transfer subject to
            b. Rights and obligations
            c. Application of subrogation and suretyship principles
            d. Restrictions on transfer (including due-on-sale clauses)
        2. By mortgagee
    D. Discharge of the mortgage
        1. Payment (including prepayment)
        2. Deed in lieu of foreclosure
    E. Foreclosure
        1. Types
        2. Acceleration
        3. Parties to the proceeding
        4. Deficiency and surplus
        5. Redemption after foreclosure

V. Titles
   A. Adverse possession
   B. Transfer by deed
      1. Requirements for deed
      2. Types of deeds (including covenants for title)
      2. Drafting, review, and negotiation of closing documents *
      4. Persons authorized to execute documents *
   C. Transfer by operation of law and by will
      1. In general
      2. Ademption
      3. Exoneration
      4. Lapse
   D. Title assurance systems
      1. Recording acts
         a. Types
         b. Indexes
         c. Chain of title
         d. Hidden risks (e.g., undelivered or forged deed)
      2. Title insurance
   E. Special problems (including estoppel by deed and judgment and tax liens)

There will be about 28 or 29 Real Property questions on the MBE (though only 27 will be scored, and you won't know which ones won't). Approximately one-fifth of the questions will be based on each of the categories I-V in the above outline.

WHAT TO EXPECT

Property questions on the MBE tend to involve relatively long, complicated fact patterns. The most difficult Property questions will probably deal with conveyances and covenants, because those concepts are so complex.

STUDY STRATEGIES

As with every multistate subject, you should be as familiar as possible with the entire subject. There are certain topics, nonetheless, that are more likely than others to trip you up if you aren't careful. Here are some to which you should pay particular attention.

1. Remember that bona fide purchaser status does not matter between the original parties to the transaction.

Status as a bona fide purchaser (BFP)—one who takes for value without notice of prior claims—is relevant primarily when examining protection under ***recording statutes.*** Bona fide purchaser status isn't relevant between the original parties; it's only relevant if ***subsequent purchasers*** are involved! Here's an example:

> A landowner gave his lawyer a power of attorney containing the following provision: "My attorney [name of attorney] is specifically authorized to sell and convey any part or all of my real property." The attorney conveyed part of the landowner's land to a developer by deed in the customary form containing covenants of title. The developer now sues the landowner for breach of a covenant. The outcome of the developer's suit will be governed by whether
>
> A. deeds without covenants are effective to convey realty.
> B. the jurisdiction views the covenants as personal or running with the land.
> C. the developer is a bona fide purchaser.
> D. the power to "sell and convey" is construed to include the power to execute the usual form of deed used to convey realty.

*These topics will be added beginning with the February 2017 exam.

Here, the developer's status as a BFP—one who pays value, in good faith, without notice of any prior conveyance—would be relevant to determine if he would be protected by the recording statutes in a notice or race-notice recording statute jurisdiction. It is not relevant, however, in determining ***whether he could sue for breach of covenants of title***! Answer choice C is wrong, illustrating why it's important to remember that, if a party to the lawsuit is one of the original parties to the conveyance, his status as a BFP is not relevant. (Here, D is the best response.)

2. **Be extremely familiar with the concepts of "marketable title" and the doctrine of merger.**

Marketable title is a popular topic on the MBE, and there's a good reason for it: The existence and conveyance of marketable title are implied in land sale contracts, ***but once the deed takes effect, the terms of the deed control.*** This is important because, if a vendor contracts to sell property and later conveys the property via quitclaim deed, ***there are no covenants associated with the deed! Under the doctrine of merger, the deed, not the contract, controls.***

3. **Know restrictive covenants and easements.**

These subjects make for good Multistate questions, because they involve many tricky requirements. If the requirements are met, a person can be bound by them even if they don't appear in his deed! The one issue with which you should be most familiar is ***notice***, because that's the easiest one to miss. Remember that notice can be *express or implied*—for example, the mere physical appearance of a neighborhood (e.g., it's all single-family homes) can provide notice that a building restriction exists.

4. **Know differences between recording statutes.**

Know the three different kinds of recording statutes: ***"pure race," "pure notice," and "race-notice."*** Pure race statutes are a bit of an anomaly, because they don't require good faith, as the others do; further, pure race statutes are very rare and don't pop up on the MBE too often. They are, however, easy to spot, because, under a pure race statute, the first conveyance recorded wins (the ***"first in time"*** rule.)

The other two types of recording statutes—pure notice and race-notice—are easily distinguishable by ***one point***: whether or not a subsequent BFP is ***protected before*** he records ***his own*** interest. Under a pure notice statute, a subsequent BFP is protected from the moment the conveyance to him takes place. Under a race-notice statute, he's not protected ***until he records his own interest.*** Remember, though, that under ***both*** types of statutes, the purchaser must have ***no actual knowledge*** of a prior conveyance at the moment he takes the conveyance. If he does, he won't be a BFP and the conveyance won't be valid against the prior purchaser.

Race-notice is the most commonly tested type of recording statute on the MBE. To identify this type, watch for language such as: "No unrecorded conveyance or mortgage of real property shall be good against subsequent purchasers for value without notice, who shall first record."

5. **When you study Future Interests, here's what's most important:**

A. Particular interests. ***Focus on these interests:***

1. Reversions;
2. Life estates followed by remainders, including the relative rights and duties of the two types of interests;
2. Executory interests, possibilities of reverter, and powers of termination;
4. The Rule Against Perpetuities, especially in connection with the categories of interests listed in (i)-(iii) above.

B. Recognize the difference, for the purpose of the Rule Against Perpetuities, between *inter vivos* class gifts to grandchildren and gifts in a will.

You need to be familiar with class gifts and the Rule Against Perpetuities (RAP). The one rule you really need to focus on is the difference between a class gift in an *inter vivos* conveyance and a class gift in a will. Here's an example:

> A man owned Hilltop in fee simple. By his will, he devised as follows: "Hilltop to such of my grandchildren who shall reach the age of 21; and by this provision I intend to include all grandchildren whenever born." At the time of his death, the man had three children and two grandchildren.

Which of the following additions to or changes in the facts of the preceding question would produce a violation of the common law Rule Against Perpetuities?

A. A posthumous child was born to the man.
B. The man's will expressed the intention to include all after–born grandchildren in the gift.
C. The instrument was an *inter vivos* conveyance rather than a will.
D. The man had no grandchildren living at the time of his death.

If you're familiar with the Rule Against Perpetuities, you know that there is a world of difference between *inter vivos* conveyances and devises under a will. The Rule Against Perpetuities requires that all interests vest, if at all, within a life in being plus 21 years after the creation of the interest. You're most likely to see problems with class gifts when the class that takes is the grandchildren who turn 21 of an *inter vivos* grantor, rather than the grandchildren who turn 21 of a testator. That's because with the *inter vivos* grant, the grantor might have a child *born after the grant* (call her *A*); the grantor might then die, and then *A* might herself have a child (call her *B*). Since *A* wouldn't be a measuring life (she wasn't alive at the time of the grant), at the moment *B*'s gift would vest as she turned 21, that vesting would occur more than 21 years after all measuring lives, a possibility whose mere existence violates the Rule. So the gift to "all my grandchildren when they turn 21" would be an invalid class gift (even if the grantor ended up not having any more children after the date of the grant). With the same gift taking place in the grantor's *will*, that can't happen—the grantor/testator can't have any more children after his death, so no after–born child can produce a grandchild whose taking upon turning 21 would occur more than 21 years after all lives that were in being at the moment of the testator's death. So the answer to the problem above is choice C.

C. Know the rule on splitting mortgage payments between the remaindermen and life estate holder.

Remember the traditional rule: When there's a mortgage on property that is possessed by a life estate holder, the life estate holder is responsible for the interest payments, and the remainderman is liable for the principal. Here's a simple picture to remember this. Imagine Godzilla sitting at a breakfast table, with a box of "Life" cereal in front of him. He opens the box and tries some of the cereal. He takes an ***interest*** in the cereal, devours it hungrily, and eats the box. What did Godzilla do? He took an ***interest*** in ***life.*** This should help you remember that the life estate holder pays the interest only.

D. Concentrate on *results*.

With Future Interests, it's not enough to know, for instance, that an interest that violates the Rule Against Perpetuities is void; you also have to know ***what happens to the interest if it's voided.*** This trips many people up on the MBE, as it's easy to fall into the trap of studying which interests are void, without paying any attention to how the conveyance/devise will change if an interest is voided. Here's an example:

A landowner conveyed Twinoaks Farm "to my niece, her heirs and assigns, so long as the premises are used for residential and farm purposes, then to my nephew and his heirs and assigns." The jurisdiction in which Twinoaks Farm is located has adopted the common law Rule Against Perpetuities unmodified by statute. As a consequence of the conveyance, the landowner's interest in Twinoaks Farm is

A. nothing.
B. a possibility of reverter.
C. a right of entry for condition broken.
D. a reversion in fee simple absolute.

Here, it's not enough to know that the interest to the son and his heirs violates the Rule Against Perpetuities and is therefore void; you have to figure out the ***results of removing that interest from the conveyance***—and do this by looking at what the grantor/testator ***intended*** to create. Here, the landowner wanted to create in the niece a fee simple determinable subject to an executory interest, and a shifting executory interest in the nephew (which is invalid because it violates the Rule Against Perpetuities—it might vest 200 years from now, after the niece's great-great-great-great-grandchild used the property for commercial purposes). Remember that, when the Rule Against Perpetuities is violated, the entire transaction is not voided; ***only the offending part of it fails.*** Here, removing the nephew's interest from the conveyance doesn't mean that the niece's interest is void as well. She's left with a defeasible fee, because the landowner used the "so long as" wording in the conveyance (a fee simple subject to a condition subsequent would have been worded something like, "to my niece and her heirs; ***but if*** the premises are ever used for any purpose other than as a residence or farm, then to my nephew and his heirs"). Thus, there is an interest remaining—a possibility of reverter. When the condition is broken, if ever, Twinoaks Farm will ***automatically*** revert to the landowner and her heirs. So B is the correct response.

To make things even more complicated—if you haven't already decided to give up on Future Interests—you also need to be careful not to confuse a fee simple determinable with a fee simple subject to a condition subsequent. In this problem, had the wording in the parentheses above been used—the "but if" language instead of the "for so long as" language—then deleting the nephew's interest would have left the niece with a fee simple absolute, and the landowner with nothing. In any case, this problem illustrates why it's important to be familiar with ***results.***

EXAM TACTICS

Many of these suggestions will echo recommendations in the section "How to Attack the MBE" but will show you how the principles already covered apply especially to Property questions.

1. Read carefully!

You may be tired of hearing it, but, in Property questions, it's particularly important to ***read the facts carefully.*** Property questions tend to be complex, and, because they're long, they're hard to read. Nevertheless, become as involved as you can with each fact pattern so that you don't miss anything.

2. Method for eliminating wrong answers.

Because Property questions are hard, you may find it more difficult to apply a process of elimination to the answer choices. This is the order you should take:

1. Eliminate the answers that are wrong on the facts.
2. Eliminate the answers that are wrong on the law. Sometimes, you can do that without even referring to the fact pattern (as in the example below).
3. Eliminate the answers that are irrelevant. As you look through the responses, think to yourself, "Does this address—and overcome—a major obstacle to prevailing in this case?" Alternatively, ask, "Even if this were true—so what?"

Here's an example:

> A brother and sister acquired as joint tenants a 20-acre parcel of land called Greenacre. They contributed equally to the purchase price. Several years later, the brother proposed that they build an apartment development on Greenacre. The sister rejected the proposal but orally agreed with the brother that he could go ahead on his own on the northerly half of Greenacre and she could do what she wished with the southerly half of Greenacre. The brother proceeded to build an apartment development on, and generally developed and improved, the northerly ten acres of Greenacre. The sister orally permitted the southerly ten acres of Greenacre to be used by the Audubon Society as a nature preserve. The brother died, leaving his entire estate to his son. The brother's will named the sister as executrix of his will, but she refused so to serve.
>
> In an appropriate action to determine the respective interests of the sister and the brother's son in Greenacre, if the sister is adjudged to be the owner of all of Greenacre, the most likely reason for the judgment will be that
>
> A. the Statute of Frauds prevents the proof of the sister's oral agreement with the brother.
> B. the brother could not unilaterally sever the joint tenancy.
> C. the sister's nomination as executrix of the brother's estate does not prevent her from asserting her claim against the son.
> D. the recorded title of the joint tenancy in Greenacre can be changed only by a duly recorded instrument.

Here, choice B misstates a rule of law. A joint tenant ***can*** unilaterally sever a joint tenancy by any act that disturbs one of the four unities (time, title, possession, and interest); this includes the act of one of the joint tenants in mortgaging the property (in a "title" jurisdiction), as well as an act of alienation by any tenant (whether voluntary or involuntary). Because B misstates this rule, it can't be correct, regardless of the underlying fact pattern.

Both choices C and D focus on irrelevant facts. C cites a rule that does not support a judgment under these facts, though it may accurately state a general rule of law. As C states, the executrix of an estate can assert a claim against the estate. But the fact that the sister can maintain such an action doesn't address the merits of the case: It's a "threshold" issue. D is also irrelevant, because recording is done for the benefit of subsequent purchasers; it does not affect the two parties originally in title (as joint tenants); their interests could be changed without recording.

Because B misstates the law and C and D are both irrelevant, A is the only possible response. Note that the question asks for the most likely reason for the judgment. It might not be the basis ***you'd*** choose if you were litigating the issue, but, ***of these four answer choices,*** it's the one most likely to succeed. The most critical obstacle to the sister's winning the case is that the sister orally gave the brother permission to "go ahead on his own" with respect to building on the northern portion, an agreement that might be construed to sever the joint tenancy. Choice A is the only choice that confronts, and overcomes, this obstacle: Conveyances of an interest in land (including a severance of a joint tenancy) are covered by the Statute of Frauds, which in turn generally requires a writing to evidence the agreement. Although there are numerous exceptions to the Statute of Frauds, none of the other three responses deals with them. As a result, A is the best response.

3. Watch out for constructive notice.

Constructive notice is based on circumstances that appear in the grantee's "chain of title." Most likely to trip you up is a fact pattern containing evidence that something's amiss in a previously recorded deed when the deed itself doesn't appear in the chain of title. If there isn't any indication of a problem in the chain of title, then ***the grantee doesn't have notice of it.*** (Watch out for inquiry notice, though.)

4. Questions asking for the argument that's "most likely to succeed."

On questions like this, determine ***which answer choice most closely addresses the greatest obstacle to success in the case.*** This will involve ***some*** analysis based on your own knowledge of the subject. However, you do get some help here: Remember that at least one of the answer choices ***must*** address a central issue in order to be the best response!

5. In questions asking for the most important point—determine the fact that's *pivotal.*

The most important point in a case is the one that will determine who will prevail. Here's an example:

> In 2007 a landowner held Blackacre, a tract of land, in fee simple absolute. In that year he executed and delivered to a farmer a quitclaim deed that purported to release and quitclaim to the farmer all of the landowner's rights, title, and interest in Blackacre. The farmer accepted the quitclaim and placed the deed in his safety deposit box.
>
> The landowner was indebted to a lender in the amount of $35,000. In September 2011, the landowner executed and delivered to the lender a warranty deed, purporting to convey the fee simple to Blackacre, in exchange for a full release of the debt he owed to the lender. The lender immediately recorded his deed.
>
> In December 2011, the farmer caused his quitclaim deed to Blackacre to be recorded, and notified the lender that he (the farmer) claimed title.
>
> Assume that there is no evidence of occupancy of Blackacre and assume, further, that the jurisdiction where Blackacre is situated has a recording statute that requires good faith and value as elements of the junior claimant's priority. Which of the following is the best comment concerning the conflicting claims of the farmer and the lender?
>
> A. The farmer cannot succeed, because the quitclaim through which he claims prevents him from being deemed to have acted in good faith.
> B. The outcome will turn on the view taken as to whether the lender paid value within the meaning of the statute requiring this element.
> C. The outcome will turn on whether the farmer paid value.
> D. The farmer's failure to record until December 2011 estops him from asserting title against the lender.

The key fact here is the recording statute. Because it has a good faith element, it must be either a notice or a race-notice statute (pure race statutes do not require good faith). Realizing this leads you to the correct answer—B—because, if the lender is ***not*** considered a BFP (because he did not give "fresh consideration" for the deed), the common law rule of "first in time, first in right" will control, and the farmer will be entitled to Blackacre. If the lender ***is*** a BFP, he'll be entitled to protection under the recording statute. As stated earlier, the statute here must be a race-notice or pure notice statute. If it's a pure notice statute, the lender, as subsequent purchaser, will only prevail if, when the conveyance to him took place, the prior interest (the farmer's) had not been recorded. If it's a race-notice statute, then the lender will only prevail if, in addition to being a BFP, he recorded first. Under these facts, the lender would prevail regardless of which type of statute controls, because he recorded first. Thus, who wins the case turns on whether the lender would be considered a BFP, so B is the best response. Recognizing the key fact here—the type of recording statute involved—is crucial to identifying the best response!

6. Chart the facts.

The facts in property questions can be exceptionally complex. In order to effectively test your knowledge of property law (i.e., of complex concepts such as notice or adverse possession), the facts ***have*** to be complex. This means that it's vitally important that you ***chart facts*** on a piece of scrap paper. Otherwise, it's easy to be overwhelmed, and you can be sure that one of the incorrect responses will be a trap for those who haven't charted the question! Here's an example:

> A landowner had title to a lot in fee simple. Without the landowner's knowledge, a rancher entered the lot in 1990 and constructed an earthen dam across a watercourse. The earthen dam trapped water that the rancher used to water a herd of cattle he owned. After 12 years of possession of the lot, the rancher gave possession of the lot to a buyer.
>
> At the same time, the rancher also purported to transfer his cattle and all his interests in the dam and water to the buyer by a document that was sufficient as a bill of sale to transfer personal property but was insufficient as a deed to transfer real property. One year later, the buyer entered into a lease with the landowner to lease the lot for a period of five years. After the end of the five-year term of the lease, the buyer remained on the lot for an additional three years and then left the lot. At that time the landowner conveyed the lot by a quitclaim deed to a farmer. The period of time to acquire title by adverse possession in the jurisdiction is ten years. After the landowner's conveyance to the farmer, title to the lot was in
>
> A. the rancher.
> B. the landowner.
> C. the buyer.
> D. the farmer.

This question clearly requires that you chart the facts on a piece of scrap paper so that you can keep them straight. Your chart would have entries like this:

> 1990: The rancher moves in, builds dam. Adverse possession begins.
>
> 2000: Title vests in the rancher by adverse possession.
>
> 2002: Rancher gives possession of land to buyer; rancher also purports to convey to the buyer, with ineffective deed. Result: The rancher has title to land; the buyer has cattle.
>
> [and so on . . .]

If you chart the events in this problem, it will become clear that the rancher's title in the lot matured after his ten years of adverse possession, in 2000. Thereafter, the buyer's use was permissive, and, beyond that, he didn't occupy the lot long enough to obtain title via adverse possession. So you'll quickly see from your chart that A is the best response, because the rancher obtained title to the lot by adverse possession, and never did anything after that to give up the title.

7. Beware of answers with constitutional implications.

Keep in mind that, in order for a zoning ordinance or covenant to violate the Constitution, it must be far outside the realm of standard restrictions; therefore, if you encounter a question containing a garden-variety restriction, it's unlikely to be repugnant to the Constitution, so any answer choice voiding the restriction on constitutional grounds is likely to be wrong. Here's an example:

> A landowner holds title in fee simple to a tract of 1,500 acres. He desires to develop the entire tract as a golf course, country club, and residential subdivision. He contemplates forming a corporation to own and to operate a golf course and country club; the stock in the corporation will be distributed to the owners of lots in the residential portions of the subdivision, but no obligation to issue the stock is to ripen until all the residential lots are sold. The price of the lots is intended to return enough money to compensate the landowner for the raw land, development costs (including the building of the golf course and the country club facilities), and developer's profit, if all of the lots are sold.
>
> The landowner's market analyses indicate that he must create a scheme of development that will offer prospective purchasers (and their lawyers) a very high order of assurance that several aspects will be clearly established:
>
> 1. Aside from the country club and golf course, there will be no land use other than for residential use and occupancy of the 1,500 acres.
> 2. The residents of the subdivision must have an unambiguous right of access to the club and golf course facilities.
> 3. Each lot owner must have an unambiguous right to transfer his lot to a purchaser with all original benefits.

4. Each lot owner must be obligated to pay annual dues to a pro rata share (based on the number of lots) of the club's annual operating deficit (whether or not such owner desires to make use of club and course facilities).

Of the following, the greatest difficulty that will be encountered in establishing the scheme is that

A. any judicial recognition will be construed as state action, which, under current doctrines, raises a substantial question whether such action would be in conflict with the Fourteenth Amendment.
B. the scheme, if effective, renders title unmarketable.
C. one or more of the essential aspects outlined by the landowner will result in a restraint on alienation.
D. there is a judicial reluctance to recognize an affirmative burden to pay money in installments and over an indefinite period as a burden that can be affixed to bind future owners of land.

Choice A is a good example of why it's important to be wary of "constitutional" answers to questions that give every indication of being Property questions. Make sure you correctly eliminate every Property law possibility before you consider constitutional implications. Here, the facts just don't give rise to a Fourteenth Amendment violation. Although a judicial recognition of the scheme could be construed as state action, this does not, *per se,* amount to a Fourteenth Amendment problem, mainly because the scheme indicates no due process or equal protection problems. (In fact, the best answer is D.)

QUESTIONS

REAL PROPERTY

QUESTIONS

REAL PROPERTY

NOTE: For ease of study, we've put all **Future Interests** questions together, beginning with question 42.

Question 1

A landlord and a tenant orally agreed to a commercial tenancy for a term of six months beginning on July 1. Rent was to be paid by the first day of each month, and the tenant paid the first month's rent at the time of the agreement.

When the tenant arrived at the leased premises on July 1, the tenant learned that the previous tenant had not vacated the premises at the end of her lease term on May 31 and did not intend to vacate. The tenant then successfully sued the previous tenant for possession. The tenant did not inform the landlord of the eviction action until after the tenant received possession.

The tenant then sued the landlord, claiming damages for that portion of the lease period during which the tenant was not in possession.

If the court finds for the landlord, what will be the most likely explanation?

(A) By suing the previous tenant for possession, the tenant elected that remedy in lieu of a suit against the landlord.

(B) The landlord had delivered the legal right of possession to the tenant.

(C) The tenant failed to timely vacate as required to sue for constructive eviction.

(D) The tenant had not notified the landlord before bringing the eviction action.

Question 2

Six months ago, a man told his cousin that he would give her his farm as a gift on her next birthday. The cousin then entered into a valid written contract to sell the farm to an investor with the closing to take place "one week after [the cousin's] next birthday."

The man failed to convey the farm to the cousin on her birthday. One week after the cousin's birthday, on the intended closing date, the investor first learned of the cousin's inability to convey the farm because the man had breached his promise. The investor considered suing the cousin but realized that she could not compel the cousin to convey the farm because it was still owned by the man.

Two weeks after the cousin's birthday, the man died. Under his valid will, the man devised the farm to the cousin. Within a week, the executor of the man's estate gave the cousin an executor's deed to the farm in compliance with state law. The investor promptly learned of this transfer and demanded that the cousin convey the farm to her. The cousin refused.

The investor sued the cousin for specific performance. Who will likely prevail?

(A) The cousin, because the contract to convey was not signed by the legal owner of the farm as of the date of the contract and was therefore void.

(B) The cousin, because she received title by devise rather than by conveyance.

(C) The investor, because the contract to convey merged into the executor's deed to the cousin.

(D) The investor, because the contract to convey remained enforceable by her within a reasonable period of time after the proposed closing date.

Question 3

A mother who died testate devised her farm to her son and her daughter as "joint tenants with right of survivorship." The language of the will was sufficient to create a common law joint tenancy with right of survivorship, which is unmodified by statute in the jurisdiction. After the mother's death and with the daughter's permission, the son took sole possession of the farm and agreed to pay the daughter a stipulated monthly rent.

Several years later, the son defaulted on a personal loan, and his creditor obtained a judgment against him for $30,000. The creditor promptly and properly filed the judgment.

A statute of the jurisdiction provides: "Any judgment properly filed shall, for 10 years from filing, be a lien on the real property then owned or subsequently acquired by any person against whom the judgment is rendered."

Six months later, the son died.

There are no other applicable statutes.

Is the creditor entitled to enforce its judgment lien against the farm?

(A) No, because the daughter became sole owner of the farm free and clear of the creditor's judgment lien when the son died.

(B) No, because the son's interest was severed from the daughter's interest upon the filing of the lien.

(C) Yes, because a joint tenancy cannot be created by devise, and the son died owning a 50 percent undivided interest in the farm as a tenant in common.

(D) Yes, because the son died owning a 50 percent undivided interest in the farm as a joint tenant with the daughter.

Question 4

A landowner borrowed $100,000 from a lender and executed a valid mortgage on a commercial tract of land to secure the debt. The lender promptly recorded the mortgage.

A year later, the landowner conveyed the same tract to a developer by a deed that expressly stated that the conveyance was subject to the mortgage to the lender and that the grantee expressly assumed and agreed to pay the mortgage obligation as part of the consideration for the purchase. The mortgage was properly described in the deed, and the deed was properly executed by the landowner; however, because there was no provision or place in the deed for the developer to sign, he did not do so. The developer promptly recorded the deed.

The developer made the monthly mortgage payments of principal and interest for six payments but then stopped payments and defaulted on the mortgage obligation. The lender properly instituted foreclosure procedures in accordance with the governing law. After the foreclosure sale, there was a $10,000 deficiency due to the lender. Both the landowner and the developer had sufficient assets to pay the deficiency.

There is no applicable statute in the jurisdiction other than the statute relating to foreclosure proceedings.

At the appropriate stage of the foreclosure action, which party will the court decide is responsible for payment of the deficiency?

(A) The developer, because he accepted delivery of the deed from the landowner and in so doing accepted the terms and conditions of the deed.

(B) The developer, because he is estopped by his having made six monthly payments to the lender.

(C) The landowner, because the developer was not a signatory to the deed.

(D) The landowner, because he was the maker of the note and the mortgage, and at most the developer is liable only as a guarantor of the landowner's obligation.

Question 5

Seven years ago, a man, his sister, and his cousin became equal owners, as tenants in common, of a house. Until a year ago, the man lived in the house alone. The sister and the cousin are longtime residents of another state.

One year ago, the man moved to an apartment and rented the house to a tenant for three years under a lease that the man and the tenant both signed. The tenant has since paid the rent each month to the man.

Recently, the sister and the cousin learned about the rental. They brought an appropriate action against the tenant to have the lease declared void and to have the tenant evicted. The tenant raised all available defenses.

What will the court likely decide?

(A) The lease is void, and the tenant is evicted.

(B) The lease is valid, and the tenant retains exclusive occupancy rights for the balance of the term.

(C) The lease is valid, but the tenant is evicted because one-third of the lease term has expired and the man had only a one-third interest to transfer.

(D) The lease is valid, and the tenant is not evicted but must share possession with the sister and the cousin.

Question 6

A man decided to give his farm to his nephew. The man took a deed to his attorney and told the attorney to deliver the deed to the nephew upon the man's death. The man also told the attorney to return the deed to him if he asked. None of these instructions to the attorney were in writing, and the deed was not recorded. The man then e-mailed the nephew informing him of the arrangement.

Shortly thereafter, the nephew died testate. In his will, he devised the farm to his daughter. Several years later, the man died intestate, survived by two sons. The nephew's daughter immediately claimed ownership of the farm and demanded that the attorney deliver the deed to her.

Must the attorney deliver the deed to the daughter?

(A) No, because a gratuitous death escrow is void unless supported by a written contract.

(B) No, because the man never placed the deed beyond his control.

(C) Yes, because the death of the nephew rendered the gratuitous death escrow irrevocable by the man.

(D) Yes, because the deed to the nephew was legally delivered when the man took it to his attorney.

Question 7

A businesswoman owned two adjoining tracts of land, one that was improved with a commercial rental building and another that was vacant and abutted a river.

Twenty years ago, the businesswoman conveyed the vacant tract to a grantee by a warranty deed that the businesswoman signed but the grantee did not. The deed contained a covenant by the grantee as owner of the vacant tract that neither he nor his heirs or assigns would "erect any building" on the vacant tract, in order to preserve the view of the river from the commercial building on the improved tract. The grantee intended to use the vacant tract as a nature preserve. The grantee promptly and properly recorded the deed.

Last year, the businesswoman conveyed the improved tract to a businessman. A month later, the grantee died, devising all of his property, including the vacant land, to his cousin.

Six weeks ago, the cousin began construction of a building on the vacant tract.

The businessman objected and sued to enjoin construction of the building.

Who is likely to prevail?

(A) The businessman, because the commercial building was constructed before the cousin began his construction project.

(B) The businessman, because the cousin is bound by the covenant made by the grantee.

(C) The cousin, because an equitable servitude does not survive the death of the promisor.

(D) The cousin, because the grantee did not sign the deed.

Question 8

A seller owns a 400-acre tract of land with 5,000 feet of frontage on a county highway. The seller and a buyer entered into a written agreement for the sale of a portion of the tract identified only as "a parcel of land, containing not less than 100 acres and having not less than 1,000 feet of frontage on the county highway, whose exact location and dimensions are to be determined by the parties hereto, at a price of $8,000 per acre."

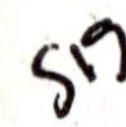

Shortly after the execution of the agreement, the parties met to stake out the parcel of land to be sold, but they could not agree. The disagreement intensified, and the seller repudiated the contract.

The buyer has sued the seller for specific performance. The seller has asserted all available defenses.

Is the buyer entitled to specific performance of the contract?

(A) No, because a contract for the sale of real property that requires further agreement on an essential element cannot be specifically enforced.

(B) No, because the purchase price was not fixed by, nor determinable under, the contract terms.

(C) Yes, because the contract bound the parties to act in good faith and to agree upon the specific land to be conveyed.

(D) Yes, because the equity powers of the court enable the court to appoint a master, or to take other appropriate action, to identify the land to be conveyed.

Question 9

A woman died, devising land that she owned in another state to her daughter, who was then 17 years old.

A neighbor who owned the property immediately adjacent to the land wrongfully began to possess the land at that time. For 24 of the next 25 years, the neighbor planted and harvested crops on the land, hunted on it, and parked cars on it. However, in the sixth year after he first took possession of the land, the neighbor neither planted crops nor hunted nor parked cars on the land because he spent that entire year living in Europe. The neighbor built a small gardening shed on the land, but he never built a residence on it.

When the daughter was 28, she was declared mentally incompetent and had a conservator appointed to oversee her affairs. Since then, she has continuously resided in a care facility.

The applicable statute of limitations provides as follows: "An ejectment action shall be brought within 21 years after the cause of action accrues, but if the person entitled to bring the cause of action is under age 18 or mentally incompetent at the time the cause of action accrues, it may be brought by such person within 10 years after attaining age 18 or after the person becomes competent."

If the daughter's conservator wins an ejectment action against the neighbor, what will be the most likely explanation?

(A) The daughter was age 17 when the neighbor first took possession of the land.

(B) Because the daughter is mentally incompetent, the statute of limitations has been tolled.

(C) The neighbor never built a residence on the land.

(D) The neighbor was not in continuous possession of the land for 21 years.

Question 10

Ten years ago, a seller sold land to a buyer, who financed the purchase price with a loan from a bank that was secured by a mortgage on the land. The buyer purchased a title insurance policy running to both the buyer and the bank, showing no liens on the property other than the buyer's mortgage to the bank. Eight years ago, the buyer paid the mortgage in full.

Seven years ago, the buyer sold the land to an investor by a full covenant and warranty deed without exceptions.

Six years ago, the investor gave the land to a donee by a quitclaim deed.

Last year, the donee discovered an outstanding mortgage on the land that predated all of these conveyances. As a result of a title examiner's negligence, this mortgage was not disclosed in the title insurance policy issued to the buyer and the bank.

Following this discovery, the donee successfully sued the buyer to recover the amount of the outstanding mortgage.

If the buyer sues the title insurance company to recover the amount he paid to the donee, is he likely to prevail?

(A) No, because the buyer conveyed the land to an investor.

(B) No, because the title insurance policy lapsed when the buyer paid off the bank's mortgage.

(C) Yes, because the buyer is protected by the title insurance policy even though he no longer owns the land.

(D) Yes, because the buyer was successfully sued by a donee and not by a bona fide purchaser for value.

Question 11

A woman owned a house on a lot abutting a public street. Six months ago, the city validly revised its zoning ordinances and placed the woman's lot and the surrounding lots abutting the public street from the north in a zone limited to residential use; the lots abutting the public street on the south side were zoned for both residential and light business use.

The woman asked the city's zoning appeals board to approve her proposal to operate a court-reporting service from her house. This type of use would be permitted on the south side of the public street and, in fact, one such business has existed there for several years.

The board approved the woman's proposal.

Why?

(A) A variance was granted.

(B) The doctrine of amortization applied.

(C) The doctrine of change of circumstances applied.

(D) The woman's use of her house was a nonconforming use.

Question 12

A woman acquired title to a four-acre lot. Several years later, she executed a mortgage on the lot to a bank to secure repayment of a $100,000 loan. Subsequently, the woman executed a mortgage on the same four-acre lot to a finance company to secure repayment of a $50,000 loan. Both mortgages were promptly recorded.

The woman recently defaulted on both loans. The bank promptly initiated foreclosure proceedings and sent proper notice to all necessary parties. The current fair market value of the four-acre lot is $250,000.

The finance company has filed a timely motion in the foreclosure proceeding asking the court to require the bank to first foreclose on two of the four acres in the four-acre lot. The bank opposes this motion and insists that it has the right to subject the entire four-acre lot to the foreclosure sale.

Will the court grant the finance company's motion?

(A) No, because the bank holds a purchase-money mortgage.

(B) No, because the entire four-acre lot is subject to the bank's senior mortgage.

(C) Yes, because a pro rata foreclosure of the lot will not prejudice the rights of the bank.

(D) Yes, because of the "two funds" rule of marshalling.

Question 13

Last year, a buyer and a seller entered into a valid contract for the sale of a parcel of real property. The contract contained no contingencies. The seller was killed in a car accident before the parcel was conveyed, but the closing eventually took place with the conveyance by a deed from the personal representative of the seller's estate.

The personal representative of the seller's estate wants to distribute the proceeds of the real property sale. The seller's will was executed many years ago and was duly admitted to probate. Paragraph 5 of his will leaves all of the seller's real property to his son, and Paragraph 6 leaves the residue of the estate to the seller's daughter. No other provisions of the will are pertinent to the question regarding to whom the proceeds of the sale should be distributed.

What will determine who receives the proceeds?

(A) Whether Paragraph 5 refers specifically to the parcel of real property that was sold or simply to "all of my real property."

(B) Whether the closing date originally specified in the contract was a date before or after the seller's death.

(C) Whether the jurisdiction has adopted the doctrine of equitable conversion.

(D) Whether the sale was completed in accordance with a court order.

Question 14

A man conveyed his house to his wife for life, remainder to his only child, a son by a previous marriage. Thereafter, the man died, devising his entire estate to his son.

The wife later removed a light fixture in the dining room of the house and replaced it with a chandelier that was one of her family heirlooms. She then informed her nephew and her late husband's son that after her death, the chandelier should be removed from the dining room and replaced with the former light fixture, which she had stored in the basement.

The wife died and under her will bequeathed her entire estate to her nephew. She also named the nephew as the personal representative of her estate. After the nephew, in his capacity as personal representative, removed the chandelier and replaced it with the original light fixture shortly after the wife's death, the son sued to have the chandelier reinstalled.

Who will likely prevail?

(A) The nephew, because he had the right to remove the chandelier within a reasonable time after the wife's death.

(B) The nephew, because of the doctrine of accession.

(C) The son, because the chandelier could not be legally removed after the death of the wife.

(D) The son, because a personal representative can remove only trade fixtures from real property.

Question 15

A landowner owned a tract of land in fee simple. He executed an instrument in the proper form of a deed, purporting to convey the tract to a purchaser in fee simple. The instrument recited that the conveyance was in consideration of "$5 cash in hand paid and for other good and valuable consideration." The landowner handed the instrument to the purchaser, who promptly and properly recorded it.

Two months later, the landowner brought an appropriate action against the purchaser to cancel the instrument and to quiet title. In support, the landowner proved that no money in fact had been paid by the purchaser, notwithstanding the recitation, and that no other consideration of any kind had been supplied by the purchaser. In such action, the landowner should

(A) lose, because any remedy the landowner might have had was lost when the instrument was recorded.

(B) lose, because the validity of conveyance of land does not depend upon consideration being paid, whether recited or not.

(C) prevail, because the recitation of consideration paid may be contradicted by parol evidence.

(D) prevail, because recordation does not make a void instrument effective.

Question 16

A woman had a season ticket for her home town hockey team's games at a private arena (her ticket was in section B, row 12, seat 16). During the intermission between the first and second periods of a game, the woman solicited signatures for a petition urging that the coach of the home team be fired.

The arena and the home hockey team are owned by a management company, a privately owned entity. As evidenced by many prominently displayed signs, the company prohibits all solicitations anywhere within the arena at any time and in any manner. The company notified the woman to cease her solicitation of signatures. The woman continued to seek signatures on her petition during the team's next three home games at the arena. Each time, the company notified her to cease such solicitation. She announced her intention to seek signatures on her petition again during the next home game at the arena. The management company wrote a letter informing the woman that her season ticket was canceled and tendering a refund for the unused portion. The woman refused the tender and brought an appropriate action to establish the right to attend all home games. In this action, the court will decide for

(A) the management company, because it has a right and obligation to control activities on realty it owns and has invited the public to visit.

(B) the management company, because the woman's ticket to hockey games created only a license.

(C) the woman, because, having paid value for the ticket, her right to be present cannot be revoked.

(D) the woman, because she was not committing a nuisance by her activities.

Question 17

By a writing, an owner leased his house to a tenant for a term of three years, ending December 31 of last year, at the rent of $1,000 per month. The lease provided that the tenant could sublet and assign.

The tenant lived in the house for one year and paid the rent promptly. After one year, the tenant leased the house to his friend for one year at a rent of $1,000 per month. The friend took possession of the house and lived there for six months but, because of her unemployment, paid no rent. After six months, on June 30, the friend abandoned the house, which remained vacant for the balance of that year. The tenant again took possession of the house at the beginning of the third and final year of the term but paid the owner no rent. At the end of the lease term, the owner brought an appropriate action against both the tenant and his friend to recover $24,000, the unpaid rent. In such action the owner is entitled to a judgment

(A) against the tenant individually for $24,000, and no judgment against the friend.

(B) against the tenant individually for $18,000, and against the friend individually for $6,000.

(C) against the tenant for $12,000, and against the tenant and the friend jointly and severally for $12,000.

(D) against the tenant individually for $18,000, and against the tenant and the friend jointly and severally for $6,000.

Question 18

A landowner conveyed a tract of land in fee simple to a lawyer for a recited consideration of "$10 and other valuable consideration." The deed was promptly and properly recorded. One week later, the landowner and the lawyer executed a written document that stated that the conveyance of the tract was for the purpose of establishing a trust for the benefit of the landowner's daughter. The lawyer expressly accepted the trust and signed the document, as did the landowner. This written agreement was not authenticated to be eligible for recordation and there never was an attempt to record it.

The lawyer entered into possession of the tract and distributed the net income from it to the landowner's daughter at appropriate intervals. Five years later, the lawyer conveyed the tract in fee simple to a buyer by warranty deed. The buyer paid fair market value for the tract, had no knowledge of the written agreement between the landowner and the lawyer, and entered into possession of the tract. The landowner's daughter made demand upon the buyer for distribution of income at the next usual time the lawyer would have distributed. The buyer refused. The daughter brought an appropriate action against the buyer for a decree requiring her to perform the trust the lawyer had theretofore recognized. In such action, judgment should be for

(A) the landowner's daughter, because a successor in title to the trustee takes title subject to the grantor's trust.
(B) the landowner's daughter, because equitable interests are not subject to the recording act.
(C) the buyer, because, as a bona fide purchaser, she took free of the trust encumbering the lawyer's title.
(D) the buyer, because no trust was ever created since the landowner had no title at the time of the purported creation.

Question 19

An elderly woman owned the house in which she and her daughter both lived. The daughter always referred to the house as "my property." Two years ago, the daughter, for a valuable consideration, executed and delivered to a buyer an instrument in the proper form of a warranty deed purporting to convey the house to the buyer in fee simple, reserving to herself an estate for two years in the house. The buyer promptly and properly recorded his deed.

One year ago, the woman died and by will, duly admitted to probate, left her entire estate to her daughter. One month ago, the daughter, for a valuable consideration, executed and delivered to her friend an instrument in the proper form of a warranty deed purporting to convey the house to the friend, who promptly and properly recorded the deed. The daughter was then in possession of the house and her friend had no actual knowledge of the deed to the earlier buyer. Immediately thereafter, the daughter gave possession to the friend. The recording act of the jurisdiction provides: "No conveyance or mortgage of real property shall be good against subsequent purchasers for value and without notice unless the same be recorded according to law." Last week, the daughter fled the jurisdiction. Upon learning the facts, her friend brought an appropriate action against the buyer to quiet title to the house. If the daughter's friend wins, it will be because

(A) the daughter had nothing to convey to the buyer two years ago.
(B) the daughter's deed to the buyer was not to take effect until after her deed to her friend.
(C) the friend was first in possession.
(D) the daughter's deed to the buyer was not in her friend's chain of title.

Question 20

A landowner owned several vacant lots in a subdivision. She obtained a $50,000 loan from a bank, and executed and delivered to the bank a promissory note and mortgage describing Lots 1, 2, 3, 4, and 5. The mortgage was promptly and properly recorded.

Upon payment of $10,000, the landowner obtained a release of Lot 2 duly executed by the bank. She altered the instrument of release to include Lot 5 as well as Lot 2 and recorded it. The landowner thereafter sold Lot 5 to a developer, an innocent purchaser, for value. The bank discovered that the instrument of release had been altered and brought an appropriate action against the landowner and the developer to set aside the release as it applied to Lot 5. The landowner did not defend against the action, but the developer did. The recording act of the jurisdiction provides: "No unrecorded conveyance or mortgage of real property shall be good against subsequent purchasers for value without notice, who shall first record." The court should rule for

(A) the developer, because the bank was negligent in failing to check the recordation of the release.
(B) the developer, because she was entitled to rely on the recorded release.
(C) the bank, because the developer could have discovered the alteration by reasonable inquiry.
(D) the bank, because the alteration of the release was ineffective.

Question 21

A farmer owned a farm in fee simple, as the land records showed, when he contracted to sell the farm to a buyer. Two weeks later, the buyer paid the agreed price and received a warranty deed. A week thereafter, when neither the contract nor the deed had been recorded and while the farmer remained in possession of the farm, a creditor properly filed her money judgment against the farmer. She knew nothing of the buyer's interest.

A statute in the jurisdiction provides: "Any judgment properly filed shall, for ten years from filing, be a lien on the real property then owned or subsequently acquired by any person against whom the judgment is rendered." The recording act of the jurisdiction provides: "No conveyance or mortgage of real property shall be good against subsequent purchasers for value and without notice unless the same be recorded according to law." The creditor brought an appropriate action to enforce her lien against the farm in the buyer's hands. If the court decides for the buyer, it will most probably be because

(A) the doctrine of equitable conversion applies.

(B) the jurisdiction's recording act does not protect creditors.

(C) the farmer's possession gave the creditor constructive notice of the buyer's interest.

(D) the buyer was a purchaser without notice.

Question 22

Six years ago, the owner of a parcel in fee simple, executed and delivered to a buyer an instrument in the proper form of a warranty deed, purporting to convey the parcel to the buyer "and his heirs." At that time, the buyer was a widower who had one child, a daughter.

Three years ago, the buyer executed and delivered to a developer an instrument in the proper form of a warranty deed, purporting to convey the parcel to the developer. The buyer's daughter did not join in the deed. The developer was and still is unmarried and childless. The only possibly applicable statute in the jurisdiction states that any deed will be construed to convey the grantor's entire estate, unless expressly limited. Last month, the buyer died, never having remarried. His daughter is his only heir. The parcel is now owned by

(A) the daughter, because the buyer's death ended the developer's life estate *pur autre vie*.

(B) the developer in fee simple pursuant to the buyer's deed.

(C) the daughter and the developer as tenants in common of equal shares.

(D) the daughter and the developer as joint tenants, because both survived the buyer.

Question 23

A landowner owned a lot, which was improved with a dwelling. A developer owned an adjoining, unimproved lot suitable for constructing a dwelling. The developer executed and delivered a deed granting to the landowner an easement over the westerly 15 feet of the unimproved lot for convenient ingress and egress to a public street, although the landowner's lot did abut another public street. The landowner did not then record the developer's deed. After the landowner constructed and started using a driveway within the described 15-foot strip in a clearly visible manner, the developer borrowed $10,000 cash from a bank and gave the bank a mortgage on her lot. The mortgage was promptly and properly recorded. The landowner then recorded the developer's deed granting the easement. The developer subsequently defaulted on her loan payments to the bank.

The recording act of the jurisdiction provides: "No conveyance or mortgage of real property shall be good against subsequent purchasers for value and without notice unless the same be recorded according to law." In an appropriate foreclosure action as to the developer's lot, brought against the landowner and the developer, the bank seeks, among other things, to have the landowner's easement declared subordinate to the bank's mortgage, so that the easement will be terminated by completion of the foreclosure. If the landowner's easement is *not* terminated, it will be because

(A) the recording of the deed granting the easement prior to the foreclosure action protects the landowner's rights.

(B) the easement provides access from a lot to a public street.

(C) the landowner's easement is appurtenant to a lot and thus cannot be separated from a lot.

(D) visible use of the easement by the landowner put the bank on notice of the easement.

Question 24

An hotelier owned a hotel, subject to a mortgage securing a debt the hotelier owed to an investor. The hotelier later acquired a nearby parking garage, financing a part of the purchase price by a loan from a bank, secured by a mortgage on the parking garage. Two years thereafter, the hotelier defaulted on the loan owed to the investor, which caused the full amount of that loan to become immediately due and payable. The investor decided not to foreclose the mortgage on the owner's hotel at that time, but instead brought an action, appropriate under the laws of the jurisdiction and authorized by the mortgage loan documents, for the full amount of the defaulted loan. The investor obtained and properly filed a judgment for that amount.

A statute of the jurisdiction provides: "Any judgment properly filed shall, for ten years from filing, be a lien on the real property then owned or subsequently acquired by any person against whom the judgment is rendered." There is no other applicable statute, except the statute providing for judicial foreclosure of mortgages, which places no restriction on deficiency judgments. The investor later brought an appropriate action for judicial foreclosure of its first mortgage on the hotel and of its judgment lien on the parking garage. The bank was joined as a party defendant, and appropriately counterclaimed for foreclosure of its mortgage on the parking garage, which was also in default. All procedures were properly followed and the confirmed foreclosure sales resulted as follows:

The investor purchased the hotel for $100,000 less than its mortgage balance.

The investor purchased the parking garage for an amount that is $200,000 in excess of the bank's mortgage balance.

The $200,000 surplus arising from the bid paid by the investor for the parking garage should be paid

(A) $100,000 to the investor and $100,000 to the hotelier.
(B) $100,000 to the bank and $100,000 to the hotelier.
(C) $100,000 to the investor and $100,000 to the bank.
(D) $200,000 to the hotelier.

Question 25

A landlord owned a house in fee simple. Three years ago, the landlord and a tenant agreed to a month-to-month tenancy with the tenant paying the landlord rent each month. After six months of the tenant's occupancy, the landlord suggested to the tenant that she could buy the house for a monthly payment of no more than her rent. The landlord and the tenant orally agreed that the tenant would pay $25,000 in cash, the annual real estate taxes, the annual fire insurance premiums, and the costs of maintaining the house, plus the monthly mortgage payments that the landlord owed on the house. They further orally agreed that within six years the tenant could pay whatever mortgage balances were then due and the landlord would give her a warranty deed to the property. The tenant's average monthly payments did turn out to be about the same as her monthly rent.

The tenant fully complied with all of the obligations she had undertaken. She made some structural modifications to the house. The house is now worth 50 percent more than it was when the landlord and the tenant made their oral agreement. The tenant made her financing arrangements and was ready to complete the purchase of the house, but the landlord refused to close. The tenant brought an appropriate action for specific performance against the landlord to enforce the agreement. The court should rule for

(A) the landlord, because the agreements were oral and violated the Statute of Frauds.
(B) the landlord, subject to the return of the $25,000, because the arrangement was still a tenancy.
(C) the tenant, because the doctrine of part performance applies.
(D) the tenant, because the Statute of Frauds does not apply to oral purchase and sale agreements between landlords and tenants in possession.

Question 26

A vendor owned a tract of land in fee simple. He entered into a valid written agreement with a purchaser under which the vendor agreed to sell and the purchaser agreed to buy the tract by installment purchase. The contract stipulated that the vendor would deliver to the purchaser, upon the payment of the last installment due, "a warranty deed sufficient to convey the fee simple." The contract contained no other provision that could be construed as referring to title.

The purchaser entered into possession of the tract. After making 10 of the 300 installment payments obligated under the contract, the purchaser discovered that there was outstanding a valid and enforceable mortgage on the tract, securing the payment of a debt in the amount of 25 percent of the purchase price the purchaser had agreed to pay. There was no evidence that the vendor had ever been late in payments due under the mortgage and there was no evidence of any danger of insolvency of the vendor. The value of the tract now is four times the amount due on the debt secured by the mortgage. The purchaser quit possession of the tract and demanded that the vendor repay the amounts the purchaser had paid under the contract. After the vendor refused the demand, the purchaser brought an appropriate action against the vendor to recover damages for the vendor's alleged breach of the contract. In such action, should damages be awarded to the purchaser?

(A) No, because the time for the vendor to deliver marketable title has not arrived.
(B) No, because the purchaser assumed the risk by taking possession.
(C) Yes, because in the absence of a contrary express agreement, an obligation to convey marketable title is implied.
(D) Yes, because the risk of loss assumed by the purchaser in taking possession relates only to physical loss.

Question 27

An owner held 500 acres in fee simple absolute. In 1960 the owner planned and obtained all required governmental approvals of two subdivisions of 200 acres each, one for commercial use and one for residential use. In 1960 and 1961 commercial buildings and parking facilities were constructed on the commercial subdivision in accordance with the plans disclosed by the plat for each subdivision. The commercial subdivision continues to be used for commercial purposes.

The plat of the residential subdivision showed 250 lots, streets, and utility and drainage easements. All of the lots in the residential subdivision were conveyed during 1960 and 1961. The deeds contained provisions, expressly stated to be binding upon the grantee, his heirs and assigns, requiring the lots to be used only for single-family, residential purposes until 1985. The deeds expressly stated that these provisions were enforceable by the owner of any lot in the residential subdivision. At all times since 1959, the 200 acres of the commercial subdivision have been zoned for shopping center use, and the 200 acres in the residential subdivision have been zoned for residential use in a classification that permits both single-family and multiple-family use. In an appropriate attack upon the limitation to residential use by single families, if the evidence disclosed no fact in addition to those listed above, the most probable judicial resolution would be that

(A) there is no enforceable restriction, because judicial recognition constitutes state action that is in conflict with the Fourteenth Amendment to the U.S. Constitution.
(B) there is no enforceable restriction because of the owner's conflict of interest in that he did not make the restriction applicable to the 100 acres he retains.
(C) the restriction in use set forth in the deeds will be enforced at the suit of any present owner of a lot in the residential subdivision.
(D) any use consistent with zoning will be permitted but that such uses so permitted as are in conflict with the restrictions in the deeds will give rise to a right to damages from owner or the owner's successor.

Question 28

A vacant lot is contiguous to a farm. Thirty years ago the then-record owner of the vacant lot executed and delivered to the owner of the farm an instrument in writing that was denominated "Deed of Conveyance" granting the farmer "and her heirs and assigns a right-of-way for egress and ingress" to the farm. If the quoted provision was sufficient to create an interest in land, the instrument met all other requirements for a valid grant. The farmer held record title in fee simple to the farm.

Twelve years ago, an investor succeeded to the vacant lot owner's title in fee simple in the vacant lot and seven years ago the farmer's daughter succeeded to the farmer's title in fee simple in the farm by a deed that made no mention of a right-of-way or driveway. At the time the farmer's daughter took title, there existed, across the vacant lot, a driveway that showed evidence that it had been used regularly to travel between a highway and the farm. The farm did have frontage on another public road, but this means of access was seldom used because it was not as convenient to the dwelling situated on the farm as was the highway. The driveway originally was established by the farmer. The farmer's daughter has regularly used the driveway since acquiring title. The period of time required to acquire rights by prescription in the jurisdiction is ten years. Six months ago the investor notified the farmer's daughter that he planned to develop a portion of the vacant lot as a residential subdivision and that she should cease any use of the driveway. After some negotiations, the investor offered to pay for this offer on the ground that travel from the lot to the main road would be more circuitous. The farmer's daughter brought an appropriate action against the investor to obtain a definitive adjudication of their respective rights. In such lawsuit the investor relied upon the defense that the location of the easement created by the original grant was governed by reasonableness and that the investor's proposed solution was reasonable. The investor's defense should

(A) fail, because the location had been established by the acts of the original owners of the land.
(B) fail, because the location of the easement had been fixed by prescription.
(C) prevail, because the reasonableness of the investor's proposal was established by the farmer's daughter's refusal to suggest any alternative location.
(D) prevail, because the servient owner is entitled to select the location of a right-of-way if the grant fails to identify its location.

Question 29

A grantor, who owned a parcel in fee simple, conveyed the parcel to a grantee by warranty deed. An adjoining owner asserted title to the parcel and brought an appropriate action against the grantee to quiet title to the parcel. The grantee demanded that the grantor defend her title under the deed's covenant of warranty, but the grantor refused. The grantee then successfully defended at her own expense.

The grantee brought an appropriate action against the grantor to recover her expenses incurred in defending against the adjoining owner's action to quiet title to the parcel. In this action, the court should decide for

(A) the grantee, because in effect it was the grantor's title that was challenged.
(B) the grantee, because the grantor's deed to her included the covenant of warranty.
(C) the grantor, because the title he conveyed was not defective.
(D) the grantor, because the adjoining owner may elect which of the grantor or the grantee to sue.

Question 30

At a time when a landowner held a lot in a subdivision in fee simple, a seller executed a warranty deed that recited that the seller conveyed the lot to a buyer. The deed was promptly and duly recorded.

After the recording of the deed from the seller to the buyer, the landowner conveyed the lot to the seller by a warranty deed that was promptly and duly recorded. Later, the seller conveyed the property to a different buyer by warranty deed and the deed was promptly and duly recorded. The later buyer paid the fair market value of the lot and had no knowledge of any claim of the earlier buyer. In an appropriate action, the two buyers contest title to the lot. In this action, judgment should be for

(A) the earlier buyer, because his deed is senior to the later buyer's.

(B) the later buyer, because he paid value without notice to the earlier buyer's claim.

(C) the earlier buyer or the later buyer, depending on whether a subsequent grantee is bound, at common law, by the doctrine of estoppel by deed.

(D) the earlier buyer or the later buyer, depending on whether the buyer's deed is deemed recorded in the later buyer's chain of title.

Question 31

An owner owned a single-family residence. Fifteen years ago, the owner conveyed a life estate in the house to a landlord.

Fourteen years ago, the landlord, who had taken possession of the house, leased the house to a tenant for a term of 15 years at the monthly rental of $500. Eleven years ago, the landlord died intestate leaving her son as her sole heir. The tenant regularly paid rent to the landlord and, after the landlord's death, to her son until last month. The period in which to acquire title by adverse possession in the jurisdiction is ten years. In an appropriate action, the tenant, the owner, and the landlord's son each asserted ownership of the house. The court should hold that title in fee simple is in

(A) the owner, because the owner held a reversion and the landlord has died.

(B) the landlord's son, because the landlord asserted a claim adverse to the owner when the landlord executed a lease to the tenant.

(C) the landlord's son, because the tenant's occupation was attributable to her son, and the landlord died 11 years ago.

(D) the tenant, because of the tenant's physical occupancy and because the tenant's term ended with the landlord's death.

Question 32

A brother and sister owned a large farm in fee simple as tenants in common, each owning an undivided one-half interest. For five years the brother occupied the farm and conducted farming operations. The brother never accounted to the sister for any income but he did pay all real estate taxes when the taxes were due and kept the buildings located on the farm insured against loss from fire, storm, and flood. His sister lived in a distant city and was interested only in realizing a profit from the sale of the land when market conditions produced the price the sister wanted.

The brother died intestate survived by his grandson, his sole heir. Thereafter the grandson occupied the farm but was inexperienced in farming operations. The result was a financial disaster. The grandson failed to pay real estate taxes for two years. The appropriate governmental authority held a tax sale to recover the taxes due. At such sale the sister was the only bidder and obtained a conveyance from the appropriate governmental authority upon payment of an amount sufficient to discharge the amounts due for taxes, plus interest and penalties, and the costs of holding the tax sale. The amount paid was one-third of the reasonable market value of the farm. Thereafter the sister instituted an appropriate action against the grandson to quiet title in and to recover possession of the farm. The grandson asserted all defenses available to him. Except for the statutes related to real estate taxes and tax sales, there is no applicable statute. In this lawsuit, the sister is entitled to a decree quieting title so that she is the sole owner in fee simple of the farm

(A) because she survived her brother.

(B) because the grandson defaulted in the obligations undertaken by the brother.

(C) unless the grandson pays her one-half of the reasonable market value of the farm.

(D) unless the grandson pays her one-half of the amount she paid for the tax deed.

Question 33

A man and a woman, who were cousins, acquired title in fee simple to a lot, as equal tenants in common, by inheritance from their aunt. During the last 15 years of her lifetime, their aunt allowed the man to occupy an apartment in the house on the lot, to rent the other apartment in the house to various tenants, and to retain the rent. The man made no payments to his aunt; and since her death seven years ago, he has made no payments to the woman. For those 22 years, the man has paid the real estate taxes on the lot, kept the building on the lot insured, and maintained the building. At all times, the woman has lived in a distant city and has never had anything to do with her aunt, her cousin, or the lot.

Recently, the woman needed money for the operation of her business and demanded that the man join her in selling the lot. He refused. The period of time to acquire title by adverse possession in the jurisdiction is ten years. There is no other applicable statute. The woman brought an appropriate action against the man for partition. The man asserted all available defenses and counterclaims. In that action, the court should

(A) deny partition and find that title has vested in the man by adverse possession.
(B) deny partition, confirm the tenancy in common, but require an accounting to determine if either the woman or the man is indebted to the other on account of the rental payment, taxes, insurance premiums, and maintenance costs.
(C) grant partition and require, as an adjustment, an accounting to determine if either the woman or the man is indebted to the other on account of the rental payments, taxes, insurance premiums, and maintenance costs.
(D) grant partition to the woman and the man as equal owners, but without an accounting.

Question 34

A seller agreed to sell and a purchaser agreed to buy a described lot on which a single-family residence had been built. Under the contract, the seller agreed to convey marketable title subject only to conditions, covenants, and restrictions of record and all applicable zoning laws and ordinances. The lot was subject to a 10-foot side-line setback originally set forth in the developer's duly recorded subdivision plot. The applicable zoning ordinance zones the property for single-family units and requires an 8.5-foot side-line setback.

Prior to closing, a survey of the property was made. It revealed that a portion of the seller' house was 8.4 feet from the side line. The purchaser refused to consummate the transaction on the ground that the seller's title is not marketable. In an appropriate action, the seller seeks specific performance. Who will prevail in such an action?

(A) The seller, because any suit against the purchaser concerning the setback would be frivolous.
(B) The seller, because the setback violation falls within the doctrine *de minimis non curat lex.*
(C) The purchaser, because any variation, however small, amounts to a breach of contract.
(D) The purchaser, because the fact that the purchaser may be exposed to litigation is sufficient to make the title unmarketable.

Question 35

A businessman owned in fee simple a lot in a properly approved subdivision, designed and zoned for industrial use. A contractor owned the adjoining lot in the same subdivision. The plat of the subdivision was recorded as authorized by statute.

Twelve years ago, the businessman erected an industrial building wholly situated on his lot but with one wall along the boundary common with the contractor's lot. The construction was done as authorized by a building permit, validly obtained under applicable statutes, ordinances, and regulations. Further, the construction was regularly inspected and passed as being in compliance with all building code requirements. The contractor's lot remained vacant until six months ago, when the contractor began excavation pursuant to a building permit authorizing the erection of an industrial building situated on her lot but with one wall along the boundary common with the businessman's lot. The excavation caused subsidence of a portion of the businessman's lot that resulted in injury to his building. The excavation was not done negligently or with any malicious intent to injure. In the jurisdiction, the time to acquire title by adverse possession or rights by prescription is ten years. The businessman brought an appropriate action against the contractor to recover damages resulting from the injuries to his building. In such lawsuit, judgment should be for

(A) the businessman, if, but only if, the subsidence would have occurred without the weight of the building on his lot.
(B) the businessman, because a right for support, appurtenant to his lot, had been acquired by adverse possession or prescription.
(C) the contractor, because the lots are urban land, as distinguished from rural land and, therefore, under the circumstances the businessman had the duty to protect any improvements on his lot.
(D) the contractor, because the construction and the use to be made of the building were both authorized by the applicable law.

Question 36

A corporation owned a parcel in fee simple, as the real estate records showed. The corporation entered into a valid, written contract to convey the parcel to a buyer, an individual. At closing, the buyer paid the price in full and received an instrument in the proper form of a deed, signed by duly authorized corporate officers on behalf of the corporation, purporting to convey the parcel to the buyer. The buyer did not then record the deed or take possession of the parcel.

Next, a creditor (who had no knowledge of the contract or the deed) obtained a substantial money judgment against the corporation. Then, the buyer recorded the deed from the corporation. Thereafter, the creditor properly filed the judgment against the corporation. A statute of the jurisdiction provides: "Any judgment properly filed shall, for ten years from filing, be a lien on the real property then owned or subsequently acquired by any person against whom the judgment is rendered." Afterward, the buyer entered into a valid written contract to convey the parcel to a developer. The developer objected to the buyer's title and refused to close. The recording act of the jurisdiction provides: "Unless the same be recorded according to law, no conveyance or mortgage of real property shall be good against subsequent purchasers for value and without notice." The buyer brought an appropriate action to require the developer to complete the purchase contract. The court should decide for

(A) the developer, because the creditor's judgment was obtained before the buyer recorded the deed from the corporation.

(B) the developer, because even though the corporation's deed to the buyer prevented the creditor's judgment from being a lien on the parcel, the creditor's filed judgment poses a threat of litigation.

(C) the buyer, because the buyer recorded her deed before the creditor filed his judgment.

(D) the buyer, because the buyer received the deed from the corporation before the creditor filed his judgment.

Question 37

A landowner had title to a lot in fee simple. Without the landowner's knowledge, a rancher entered the lot in 1990 and constructed an earthen dam across a watercourse. The earthen dam trapped water that the rancher used to water a herd of cattle he owned. After 12 years of possession of the lot, the rancher gave possession of the lot to a buyer.

At the same time, the rancher also purported to transfer his cattle and all his interests in the dam and water to the buyer by a document that was sufficient as a bill of sale to transfer personal property but was insufficient as a deed to transfer real property. One year later, the buyer entered into a lease with the landowner to lease the lot for a period of five years. After the end of the five-year term of the lease, the buyer remained on the lot for an additional three years and then left the lot. At that time the landowner conveyed the lot by a quitclaim deed to a farmer. The period of time to acquire title by adverse possession in the jurisdiction is ten years. After the landowner's conveyance to the farmer, title to the lot was in

(A) the rancher.

(B) the landowner.

(C) the buyer.

(D) the farmer.

Question 38

A niece inherited vacant land from her uncle. She lived in a distant state and decided to sell the land to a colleague who was interested in purchasing the land as an investment. They orally agreed upon a price, and, at the colleague's insistence, the niece agreed to provide him with a warranty deed without any exceptions. The price was paid, the warranty deed was delivered, and the deed was promptly and properly recorded. Neither the niece nor the colleague had, at that point, ever seen the land.

After recording the deed, the colleague visited the land for the first time and discovered that it had no access to any public right-of-way and that none of the surrounding lands had ever been held in common ownership with any previous owner of the tract of land. The colleague sued the niece for damages. For whom will the court find?

(A) The colleague, because the lack of access makes title unmarketable.

(B) The colleague, because the covenants of warranty and quiet enjoyment in the deed were breached.

(C) The niece, because no title covenants were breached.

(D) The niece, because the agreement to sell was oral.

Question 39

A little more than five years ago, a man completed construction of a single-family home located on a lot that he owned. Five years ago, the man and a tenant entered into a valid five-year written lease of the lot that included the following language: "This house is rented as is, without certain necessary or useful items. The parties agree that the tenant may acquire and install such items as she wishes at her expense, and that she may remove them if she wishes at the termination of this lease."

The tenant decided that the house needed, and she paid cash to have installed, standard-sized combination screen/storm windows, a freestanding refrigerator to fit a kitchen alcove built for that purpose, a built-in electric stove and oven to fit a kitchen counter opening left for that purpose, and carpeting to cover the plywood living room floor. Last month, by legal description of the land, the man conveyed the lot to a purchaser for $100,000. The purchaser knew of the tenant's soon-expiring tenancy, but did not examine the written lease. As the lease expiration date approached, the purchaser learned that the tenant planned to vacate on schedule, and learned for the first time that the tenant claimed and planned to remove all of the above-listed items that she had installed. The purchaser promptly brought an appropriate action to enjoin the tenant from removing those items. The court should decide that the tenant may remove

(A) none of the items.

(B) only the refrigerator.

(C) all items except the carpet.

(D) all of the items.

Question 40

A landowner owned a tract of land in fee simple. The landowner and a purchaser entered into a written agreement under which the purchaser agreed to buy the tract for $100,000, its fair market value. The agreement contained all the essential terms of a real estate contract to sell and buy, including a date for closing. The required $50,000 down payment was made. The contract provided that in the event of the purchaser's breach, the landowner could retain the $50,000 deposit as liquidated damages.

Before the date set for the closing in the contract, the purchaser died. On the date that the administrator of the purchaser's estate was duly qualified, which was after the closing date, she made demand for return of the $50,000 deposit. The landowner responded by stating that he took such demand to be a declaration that the administrator did not intend to complete the contract and that the landowner considered the contract at an end. The landowner further asserted that the landowner was entitled to retain, as liquidated damages, the $50,000. The reasonable market value of the tract had increased to $110,000 at that time. The administrator brought an appropriate action against the landowner to recover the $50,000. In answer, the landowner made no affirmative claim but asserted that he was entitled to retain the $50,000 as liquidated damages as provided in the contract. In such lawsuit, judgment should be for

(A) the administrator, because the provision relied upon by the landowner is unenforceable.

(B) the administrator, because the death of the purchaser terminated the contract as a matter of law.

(C) the landowner, because the court should enforce the express agreement of the contracting parties.

(D) the landowner, because the doctrine of equitable conversion prevents termination of the contract upon the death of a party.

Question 41

A man owned property that he used as his residence. The man received a loan, secured by a mortgage on the property, from a bank. Later, the man defaulted on the loan. The bank then brought an appropriate action to foreclose the mortgage, was the sole bidder at the judicial sale, and received title to the property as a result of the foreclosure sale.

Shortly after the foreclosure sale, the man received a substantial inheritance. He approached the bank to repurchase the property, but the bank decided to build a branch office on the property and declined to sell.

If the man prevails in an appropriate action to recover title to the property, what is the most likely reason?

(A) He had used the property as his residence.

(B) He timely exercised an equitable right of redemption.

(C) The court applied the doctrine of exoneration.

(D) The jurisdiction provides for a statutory right of redemption.

Question 42

A woman died testate. In her will, she devised a farm she owned to her husband for life, remainder to her niece. Her will did not specify the duties of the husband and the niece with regard to maintenance and expenses related to the farm. The husband took sole possession of the farm, did not farm the land, and did not rent the land to a third person, although the fair rental value was substantial.

For two years in a row after the woman died, the county assessor sent the tax bills to the niece, but the niece did not pay the bills, because she and the husband could not agree on who should pay them. Finally, the niece paid the taxes to avoid a tax foreclosure sale.

The niece then sued the husband for reimbursement for the two years' worth of property taxes.

There is no applicable statute.

Is the niece likely to prevail?

(A) No, because remaindermen are solely responsible for the payment of property taxes.

(B) No, because the county assessor sent the bills to the niece.

(C) No, because the woman's will was silent on responsibility for payment of property taxes.

(D) Yes, because the niece paid an obligation that was the sole responsibility of the husband.

Question 43

Under the terms of his duly probated will, a testator devised his house to his "grandchildren in fee simple" and the residue of his estate to his brother. The testator had had two children, a son and a daughter, but only the daughter survived the testator. At the time of the testator's death, the daughter was 30 years old and had two minor children (grandchildren of the testator) who also survived the testator.

A third grandchild of the testator, who was the child of the testator's predeceased son, had been alive when the testator executed the will, but had predeceased the testator. Under the applicable intestate succession laws, the deceased grandchild's sole heir was his mother.

A statute of the jurisdiction provides as follows: "If a devisee, including a devisee of a class gift, who is a grandparent or a lineal descendant of a grandparent of the testator is dead at the time of execution of the will or fails to survive the testator, the issue of such deceased devisee shall take the deceased's share under the will, unless the will expressly provides that this statute shall not apply. For this purpose, words of survivorship, such as 'if he survives me,' are a sufficient expression that the statute shall not apply."

Who now owns the house?

(A) The testator's brother.
(B) The testator's two surviving grandchildren.
(C) The testator's two surviving grandchildren and all other grandchildren who are born to the testator's daughter.
(D) The testator's two surviving grandchildren and the deceased grandchild's mother.

Question 44

The following facts concern a tract of land in a state that follows general U.S. law. Each instrument is in proper form, recorded, marital property rights were waived when necessary, and each person named was adult and competent at the time of the named transaction.

1. In 1970, the owner of a tract conveyed his interest in fee simple to his "two brothers, their heirs and assigns as joint tenants with right of survivorship."
2. In 1980, the older brother died, devising his interest to his only child "for life, and then to his grandson for life, and then to his grandson's children, their heirs and assigns."
3. In 2000, the younger brother died, devising his interest to "his friend, his heirs and assigns."
4. In 2002, the friend conveyed his quitclaim deed to a purchaser, "his heirs and assigns whatever right, title and interest I own."

The purchaser has never married and has contracted to convey marketable record title in the land. Can the purchaser do so?

(A) Yes, without joinder of any other person in the conveyance.
(B) Yes, if the older brother's son, his grandson, and his grandson's only child (age 25) will join in the conveyance.
(C) No, regardless of who joins in the conveyance, because the older brother's grandson may have additional children whose interests cannot be defeated.
(D) No, regardless of who joins in the conveyance, because a title acquired by quitclaim deed is impliedly unmerchantable.

Question 45

A landowner owned a tract of land in fee simple. He conveyed it to a purchaser, "his heirs and assigns; but if my friend shall be living 30 years from the date of this deed, then to my friend, his heirs and assigns." The limitation "to the friend, his heirs and assigns" is

(A) valid, because the friend's interest is a reversion.
(B) valid, because the interest will vest, if at all, within a life in being.
(C) valid, because the friend's interest is vested subject to divestment.
(D) invalid.

Question 46

The landowner owned in fee simple two lots in an urban subdivision. The lots were vacant and unproductive. They were held as a speculation that their value would increase. The landowner died and, by his duly probated will, devised the residue of his estate (of which the lots were part) to his wife for life with remainder in fee simple to his daughter. The landowner's executor distributed the estate under appropriate court order, and notified the landowner's wife that future real estate taxes on the lots were her responsibility to pay.

Except for the statutes relating to probate and those relating to real estate taxes, there is no applicable statute. The wife failed to pay the real estate taxes due for the two lots. To prevent a tax sale of the fee simple, the daughter paid the taxes and demanded that the wife reimburse her for same. When she refused, the daughter brought an appropriate action against the wife to recover the amount paid. In such action, the daughter should recover

(A) the amount paid, because a life tenant has the duty to pay current charges.
(B) the present value of the interest that the amount paid would earn during the wife's lifetime.
(C) nothing, because the wife's sole possession gave the right to decide whether or not taxes should be paid.
(D) nothing, because the wife never received any income from the lots.

Question 47

A man owned a farm in fee simple. By his will, he devised as follows: "my farm to such of my grandchildren who shall reach the age of 21; and by this provision I intend to include all grandchildren whenever born." At the time of his death, the man had three children and two grandchildren.

Courts hold such a devise valid under the common-law Rule Against Perpetuities. What is the best explanation of that determination?

(A) All of the man's children would be measuring lives.
(B) The Rule of Convenience closes the class of beneficiaries when any grandchild reaches the age of 21.
(C) There is a presumption that the man intended to include only those grandchildren born prior to his death.

(D) There is a subsidiary rule of construction that dispositive instruments are to be interpreted so as to uphold interests rather than to invalidate them under the Rule Against Perpetuities.

Question 48

In 1995, the owner of a tract of land executed and delivered a deed by which he conveyed the tract "[t]o my cousin and his heirs as long as it is used exclusively for residential purposes, but if it is ever used for other than residential purposes, to a charity." In 2000, the owner died leaving a valid will by which he devised all his real estate to his brother. The will had no residuary clause. The owner was survived by his brother and by his daughter, who was the owner's sole heir.

Assume that the common law Rule Against Perpetuities applies in the state where the land is located and that the state also has a statute providing that "[a]ll future estates and interests are alienable, descendible, and devisable in the same manner as possessory estates and interests." In 2005, the owner's cousin and daughter entered into a contract with a purchaser whereby they contracted to sell the tract to the purchaser in fee simple. After examining title, the purchaser refused to perform on the ground that the cousin and the daughter could not give good title. The cousin and the daughter joined in an action against the purchaser for specific performance. Prayer for specific performance will be

(A) granted, because the cousin and the daughter together own a fee simple absolute in the tract.

(B) granted, because the cousin alone owns the entire fee simple in the tract.

(C) denied, because the brother has a valid interest in the tract.

(D) denied, because the charity has a valid interest in the tract.

Question 49

A landowner died, validly devising his land to his wife "for life or until remarriage, then to" their daughter. Shortly after the landowner's death, his daughter executed an instrument in the proper form of a deed, purporting to convey the land to her friend. A year later, the daughter died intestate, with her mother, the original landowner's wife, as her sole heir. The following month, the wife remarried. She then executed an instrument in the proper form of a deed, purporting to convey the land to her new husband as a wedding gift.

Who now owns what interest in the land?

(A) The daughter's friend in fee simple.

(B) The wife owns the fee simple.

(C) The wife's new husband has a life estate in the land for the wife's life, with the remainder to the daughter's friend.

(D) The wife's new husband owns in fee simple.

Question 50

A woman conveyed her one-family residence, to "my son for life, remainder to my daughter, her heirs and assigns, subject, however, to the mortgage thereon." There was an unpaid balance on the mortgage of $10,000, which is payable in $1,000 annual installments plus interest at 6 percent on the unpaid balance, with the next payment due on July 1. The woman's son is now occupying the residence. The reasonable rental value of the property exceeds the sum necessary to meet all current charges. There is no applicable statute.

Under the rules governing contributions between life tenants and remaindermen, how should the burden for payment be allocated?

(A) The daughter must pay the principal payment, but the son must pay the interest.

(B) The daughter must pay both the principal and the interest payments.

(C) The son must pay both the principal and interest payments.

(D) The son must pay the principal payment, but the daughter must pay the interest.

Question 51

A grantor conveyed her only parcel of land to a grantee by a duly executed and delivered warranty deed, which provided: "To have and to hold the described tract of land in fee simple, subject to the understanding that within one year from the date of the instrument said grantee shall construct and thereafter maintain and operate on said premises a public health center."

The grantee constructed a public health center on the tract within the time specified and operated it for five years. At the end of this period, the grantee converted the structure into a senior citizens' recreational facility. It is conceded by all parties in interest that a senior citizens' recreational facility is not a public health center. In an appropriate action, the grantor seeks a declaration that the change in the use of the facility has caused the land and structure to revert to her. In this action, the grantor should

(A) win, because the language of the deed created a determinable fee, which leaves a possibility of reverter in the grantor.

(B) win, because the language of the deed created a fee subject to a condition subsequent, which leaves a right of entry or power of termination in the grantor.

(C) lose, because the language of the deed created only a contractual obligation and did not provide for retention of property interest by the grantor.

(D) lose, because an equitable charge is enforceable only in equity.

Question 52

In 1995, a man executed his will, which in pertinent part provided, "I hereby give, devise, and bequeath my house to my surviving widow for life, remainder to such of my children as shall live to attain the age of 30 years, but if any child dies under the age of 30 years survived by a child or children, such child or children shall take and receive the share which his, her, or their parent would have received had such parent lived to attain the age of 30 years."

At the date of writing his will, the man and his wife had two children, a son and a daughter. The man's wife died in 2000 and he then married his second wife in 2002. At his death in 2010, the man was survived by his second wife and three children, the two from his first marriage, and a son, born in 2004, with his second wife. In a jurisdiction that recognizes the common-law Rule Against Perpetuities unmodified by statute, the result of the application of the rule is that the

(A) remainder to the children and to the grandchildren is void because the man could have subsequently married a person who was unborn at the time he executed his will.

(B) remainder to the children is valid, but the substitutionary gift to the grandchildren is void because the man could have subsequently married a person who was unborn at the time he executed his will.

(C) gift in remainder to the man's children from his first marriage or their children is valid, but the gift to his son from his second marriage or his children is void.

(D) remainder to the children and the substitutionary gift to the grandchildren are valid.

Question 53

For a valuable consideration, a widow who owned a tract of land, signed and gave her niece a duly executed instrument that provided as follows: "The grantor may or may not sell the tract during her lifetime, but at her death, or if she earlier decides to sell, the property will be offered to the grantee at $500 per acre. The grantee shall exercise this right, if at all, within sixty days of receipt of said offer to sell." The friend recorded the instrument. The instrument was not valid as a will. Is the niece's right under the instrument valid?

(A) Yes, because the instrument is recorded.

(B) Yes, because the niece's right to purchase will vest or fail within the period prescribed by the Rule Against Perpetuities.

(C) No, because the niece's right to purchase is a restraint on the owner's power to make a testamentary disposition.

(D) No, because the niece's right to purchase is an unreasonable restraint on alienation.

Question 54

Three years ago a landowner conveyed the tract to a grantee for $50,000 by a deed that provided: "By accepting this deed, the grantee covenants for herself, her heirs and assigns, that the premises herein conveyed shall be used solely for residential purposes and, if the premises are used for nonresidential purposes, the landowner, his heirs and assigns, shall have the right to repurchase the premises for the sum of one thousand dollars ($1,000)." In order to pay the $50,000 purchase price for the tract, the grantee obtained a $35,000 mortgage loan from a bank. The landowner had full knowledge of the mortgage transaction. The deed and mortgage were promptly and properly recorded in proper sequence. The mortgage, however, made no reference to the quoted language in the deed.

Two years ago the grantee converted her use of the tract from residential to commercial without the knowledge or consent of the landowner or of the bank. The grantee's commercial venture failed, and the grantee defaulted on her mortgage payments to the bank. The tract now has a fair market value of $25,000. The bank began appropriate foreclosure proceedings against the grantee. The landowner properly intervened, tendered $1,000, and sought judgment that the grantee and the bank be ordered to convey the tract to the landowner, free and clear of the mortgage. The common-law Rule Against Perpetuities is unmodified by statute. If the court rules against the landowner, it will be because

(A) the provision quoted from the deed violates the Rule Against Perpetuities.

(B) the bank had no actual knowledge of, and did not consent to, the violation of the covenant.

(C) the rights reserved by the landowner were subordinated, by necessary implication, to the rights of the bank as the lender of the purchase money.

(D) the consideration of $1,000 was inadequate.

Question 55

A landowner owned a farm in fee simple and by his will specifically devised the farm as follows: "To my daughter, her heirs and assigns, but if she dies survived by a husband and a child or children, then to her husband during his lifetime with remainder to her children, their heirs and assigns.

Specifically provided, however, that if my daughter dies survived by a husband and no child, the farm is specifically devised to my nephew, his heirs and assigns."

While the landowner's will was in probate, his nephew quitclaimed all interest in the farm to the landowner's daughter's husband. Three years later, the daughter died, survived by her husband but no children. She left a will devising her interest in the farm to her husband. The only applicable statute provides that any interest in land is freely alienable. The landowner's nephew instituted an appropriate action against the husband to establish title to the farm. Judgment should be for

(A) the nephew, because his quitclaim deed did not transfer his after acquired title.
(B) the nephew, because the daughter's husband took nothing under the landowner's will.
(C) the daughter's husband, because the nephew had effectively conveyed his interest in the farm.
(D) the daughter's husband, because the doctrine of after-acquired title applies to a devise by will.

ANSWERS

REAL PROPERTY

Answer Key

Use this Answer Key to quickly identify the correct answer to each question.

(1) B	(11) A	(21) B	(31) C	(41) D	(51) C
(2) D	(12) B	(22) B	(32) D	(42) D	(52) D
(3) A	(13) C	(23) D	(33) C	(43) B	(53) B
(4) A	(14) A	(24) A	(34) D	(44) A	(54) A
(5) D	(15) B	(25) C	(35) A	(45) B	(55) C
(6) B	(16) B	(26) A	(36) D	(46) D	
(7) B	(17) A	(27) C	(37) A	(47) A	
(8) A	(18) C	(28) A	(38) C	(48) C	
(9) D	(19) D	(29) C	(39) D	(49) A	
(10) C	(20) D	(30) D	(40) A	(50) A	

ANSWERS

REAL PROPERTY

Answer 1

(B) is the best response,

because we can infer from the landlord's victory that we are in a jurisdiction that does not require the landlord to put the tenant into actual possession.

It's clear that the landlord has given the new tenant the *legal* right to possess the premises, and that the landlord hasn't given a conflicting legal right to anyone else. (The holdover tenant's term is over, so that tenant cannot be asserting that he has a legal right to possession deriving from the landlord. Furthermore, there's no indication in the facts that the landlord or any third person claiming under him has asserted a legal claim to possession of the premises.) So the new tenant cannot win in his damages suit against the landlord by merely showing that he had a legal right to the premises—the landlord has delivered that to him, free of competing claims. The tenant can win if, and only if, the landlord is found to have had an implied duty to deliver *actual* possession (as opposed to just the legal right to possession) to the tenant.

American courts are split on the issue of whether the landlord owes the tenant an implied duty to put him into actual possession. Most American courts follow the so-called "English rule," under which the landlord has an implied duty to deliver actual possession to the tenant. But a minority follow the so-called "American rule," under which the landlord is merely required to give the tenant legal possession. We're told to assume that the court has found for the landlord. We can infer from this fact that the jurisdiction follows the American rule. That would explain how and why the landlord would win. By contrast, none of the other three explanations would produce a victory for the landlord.

(A) is not the best response,

because the tenant did not in fact, by suing the prior tenant, waive any remedy against the landlord.

The tenant, as the holder of the legal right to the premises, was of course entitled to sue the holdover tenant for possession. There is no principle of law by which the tenant's exercise of that right to sue would be found to be a waiver of his right to later sue the landlord for damages from the delay.

(C) is not the best response,

because the tenant has not been constructively convicted, and his suit against the landlord was not based on a constructive-eviction theory.

Under the constructive-eviction doctrine, if the premises become uninhabitable for the tenant's intended purposes, due to the wrongful act of the landlord, the tenant may stop paying rent and terminate the lease. And it's true that, as this choice implies, the tenant cannot rely on a constructive eviction theory unless he has timely moved out of the premises following the event that made them uninhabitable. But constructive eviction is not the theory on which the tenant here is suing the landlord. One reason we know this is that the tenant is suing for damages, and a constructive eviction suit seeks suspension of rent and/or termination of the lease, not damages. Rather, the tenant is suing the landlord for breach of what the tenant says is the landlord's implied obligation to deliver physical possession.

(D) is not the best response,

because the tenant had no obligation to notify the landlord before bringing the eviction action.

The tenant had the legal right to possession, and the prior tenant was an illegal holdover tenant. Therefore, the tenant had the sole right (and the obligation) to sue the prior tenant to have him evicted. Since the tenant had the absolute right to bring that suit, there was no principle of law that required him to notify the landlord that he was about to do so. Indeed, we can infer from the fact that the landlord prevailed in the damages suit that the landlord had no obligation under state law to deliver actual possession, so there would have been no purpose in requiring the tenant to give the landlord notice that the tenant was about to sue the prior tenant for possession.

Answer 2

(D) is the best response,

because the investor exercised her right to sue for specific performance with reasonable promptness.

The cousin and the investor had a valid contract for the sale of the farm. The fact that the cousin did not have title at the time she signed the contract does not matter. If the investor had "slept on his rights" by delaying the commencement of suit for an unreasonable time after the cousin obtained title, the court might conclude that the investor had intended to abandon the contract. In that event, the court might decline to award specific performance under the doctrine of "laches" (since specific performance is an equitable remedy, requiring that the plaintiff not behave in a way that prejudices the rights of the defendant). But here, the investor acted promptly once she learned that the cousin now had title. Furthermore, the investor's suit was prompt as measured by the fact that only two weeks passed between the scheduled closing date and the cousin's acquisition of title.

(A) is not the best response,
because it states an incorrect rule of law.

This choice asserts that when a person signs a contract to convey property that the person doesn't own as of the signing date, the contract is invalid. This is simply false as a matter of law: It's not uncommon for a person to sign a contract to convey property that she doesn't yet own, and that person takes the risk of not being able to acquire title between the time of signing and the scheduled closing date.

(B) is not the best response,
because the fact that the cousin received title by devise rather than by conveyance does not make any legal difference.

The cousin and the investor had a valid contract requiring the cousin to convey the property to the investor on the scheduled closing date. Once the cousin gained title to the property, the investor was entitled to the remedy of specific performance regardless of the means by which the cousin had gained title. If a long period of time had elapsed between the scheduled closing date and the investor's attempt to get specific performance, this might have been a reason for the court to deny specific performance (a remedy that is equitable and thus highly dependent on whether it would be fair to both parties' expectations), and leave the investor to resort to a claim for money damages. But since the suit followed quickly after the scheduled closing date, specific performance is an appropriate remedy, regardless of the unanticipated sequence by which the cousin gained title.

(C) is not the best response,
because it refers to a doctrine that would not apply on these facts.

In this choice the examiners seem to be trying to trick you into thinking that the doctrine of "estoppel by deed" applies. Under that doctrine, if a grantor under a deed promises a particular title that he does not in fact have, then if the grantor later gets that title, the title automatically passes to the grantee. So let's suppose that on the scheduled closing date, the cousin actually purported to convey to the investor title to the farm (title which the cousin didn't have). Then, when the cousin later got title by means of the executor's deed, estoppel by deed would probably apply, so that the executor's deed would be deemed to automatically vest title in the investor rather than in the cousin. But estoppel by deed operates only when there is a *deed* executed by one who does not own the title being conveyed; the doctrine does not apply where a person merely agrees by *contract* to convey a title that he doesn't yet own, but later acquires. So there was no principle by which the existence of the cousin-investor sale contract caused the executor's deed to automatically convey title (or any other new rights) to the investor.

Answer 3

(A) is the best response,
because the creditor's obtaining of a judgment lien did not cause a severance of the joint tenancy, and the son's death extinguished whatever rights the creditor had with respect to the son's interest.

To solve this problem, you have to answer two separate questions: (1) what, if anything, was the effect of the creditor's getting a lien against the son's real property?; and (2) what was the effect of the son's death on the lien? Let's look at these questions one at a time.

As to question (1): When a creditor gets a judgment lien good against the debtor's real estate interests, the lien *does not cause a severance* of any joint tenancy with right of survivorship to which the debtor is a party. S&W, § 5.4, p. 192. So even after the lien came into existence by virtue of the filing of the judgment, the joint tenancy with right of survivorship continued in place. (In some states, the creditor would have been entitled to enforce the judgment by having the tenancy severed and the debtor's interest sold; but the creditor here didn't do that.)

As to question (2): When the son died, his death automatically caused his interest to be extinguished, with full title vesting in the daughter. At that moment, the creditor's lien disappeared, since that lien attached only to the son's interest in the property, not to the property itself, and the son's interest was extinguished at his death.

(B) is not the best response,
because no severance occurred when the lien was filed.

This choice correctly concludes that the creditor cannot enforce its lien against the farm, but incorrectly states the rationale. As is discussed more fully in the treatment of choice A, the mere creation of a judgment lien good against the real estate interests of the debtor does not act to sever a joint tenancy with right of survivorship to which the debtor is a party. The joint tenancy continued in force after the creation of the judgment lien, but the creditor loses because the son's interest in the joint tenancy (the only thing to which the lien attached) was extinguished at the son's death.

(C) is not the best response,
because it is legally incorrect about whether a joint tenancy can be created by devise, and is therefore factually incorrect about the nature of the son's interest at his death.

A joint tenancy with right of survivorship can be created either by conveyance or devise (will), so long as the creating instrument makes it clear that the grantor intends to create a right of survivorship. Here, the mother's will, by specifying that the farm was to pass by joint tenancy "with right of survivorship," made it adequately clear that the mother intended such a right of survivorship. That joint tenancy continued in force after the creation of the judgment lien, but the creditor loses because the son's interest in the joint tenancy (the only thing to which the lien attached) was extinguished at the son's death.

(If the mother's bequest *had* created a tenancy in common rather than a joint tenancy with right of survivorship, this choice would be a correct explanation of the outcome: The creditor's lien would have attached to the son's 50 percent undivided tenancy-in-common interest in the farm, and the lien would have survived his death, allowing a judicial sale of that interest, with the proceeds going to the creditor.)

(D) is not the best response,

because it misstates the nature of the son's interest at his death.

The phrase "50% undivided interest . . . as a joint tenant" is internally-inconsistent gibberish. The subphrase "joint tenant" *implies* "with right of survivorship" (i.e., the language "right of survivorship" is essentially redundant once we know that the interest is a joint tenancy). Conversely, the phrase "undivided interest" is used only in connection with a *tenancy in common*, not a joint tenancy (so that a "50% undivided interest" means that the holder has a tenancy in common equal to half the value of the property). This is therefore a choice that you could have eliminated without even reading the fact pattern!

Since the mother's will was sufficiently specific to create a joint tenancy with right of survivorship, and since no later event caused the joint tenancy to be severed, this choice is factually incorrect in saying that the son owned a "50% undivided interest" at his death—what in fact happened was that his interest in the joint tenancy was extinguished by his death, and the creditor's lien was extinguished at the same time.

Answer 4

(A) is the best response,

because the developer is deemed to have assumed the mortgage even though he did not sign the deed.

According to the terms of the deed, the developer was assuming the mortgage obligation as part of his consideration for the property. The deed was a "*deed poll*," i.e., a deed signed only by the grantor (here, the landowner). When a grantee accepts a deed poll with knowledge of its contents, he is deemed to have *agreed to all conditions in it*. So the developer will be deemed to have made the promise of assumption recited in the deed.

By assuming the mortgage, the developer became personally liable for paying it. Furthermore, the developer's promise of assumption made him the *primary* obligor, and transformed the landowner into a position of a *surety* or guarantor. So although the landowner is still theoretically liable for the deficiency (since there was no novation, i.e., no agreement by the lender to release the landowner from liability in return for the developer's assumption of liability), the court will require that the deficiency be paid by the developer.

(B) is not the best response,

because the developer's monthly payments did not result in any estoppel, making this choice an incorrect explanation of the correct outcome.

In general, the mere fact that a purchaser of mortgaged property makes payments on the mortgage will not cause the purchaser to become liable for further payments. So if the developer had merely taken the property "subject to" the mortgage, the making of the first six payments would not have obligated him to continue making payments, or to satisfy any deficiency. It's only because the developer took the deed with knowledge that it contained an assumption clause that he became personally liable, as discussed in Choice A.

(C) is not the best response,

because the developer is deemed to have agreed to assume the mortgage even though he did not sign the deed.

As is described more fully in the discussion of choice A, a grantee who accepts a deed poll (a deed signed only by the grantor) is deemed to have agreed to all conditions stated in the document. Therefore, the developer is deemed to have promised to assume payment of the mortgage, even though he did not sign the deed.

(D) is not the best response,

because the developer, having assumed the mortgage, became primarily liable, not just a guarantor.

When the purchaser of property is deemed to have assumed a mortgage on it, the purchaser becomes primarily liable for payment of the mortgage, and it is the original mortgagor who becomes a surety or guarantor. As discussed in choice A, when the developer took the deed poll and recorded it, while knowing that it contained an assumption clause, he became bound by that assumption provision even though he did not sign the deed. That assumption made him primarily liable, a status inconsistent with this choice.

Answer 5

(D) is the best response,

because the tenant's lease was valid, but entitled him only to the transferor's concurrent right of possession.

To solve this problem, you have to answer two questions in sequence: (1) Pre-lease, what were the possessory rights of the man (the original co-tenant with his sister and cousin)?; and (2) What rights, if any, did the lease transfer to the tenant?

As to (1), each tenant in any form of co-tenancy is entitled to possession of all parts of the land at all times. S&W, § 5.8, p. 203. So any tenant in common (such as the man) is entitled to occupy the full premises at all times, so long as he does not interfere with the rights of the other tenants (here, the sister and the cousin) to co-occupy them.

As to (2), each undivided interest in a tenancy in common may be transferred by its holder to a third party. That transfer may be for less than the remainder of the tenancy in common, i.e., for a term of years. So the man's lease to the tenant was proper, and transferred to the tenant whatever rights the man (the transferor) held, for the length of time covered by the lease. As we saw in the answer to (1) above, the rights held by the man did not include the right to exclusive possession, but merely the right to *share* possession with the sister and the cousin. Therefore, this choice correctly states that the tenant may remain in the premises for the rest of the lease term, but that he must share possession with the sister and the cousin (or their transferees) if they want to move in.

(A) is not the best response,

because the lease was valid.

As is discussed more fully in the last paragraph of the discussion of choice D above, the man, as the holder of an undivided interest in a tenancy in common, was entitled to transfer that interest either for the full remainder of the tenancy in common, or for a lesser term of years. Therefore, this choice is incorrect in saying that the lease is void, and also incorrect in saying that the tenant will be evicted.

(B) is not the best response,

because although the lease is valid, the tenant's right of occupancy is not exclusive, and must be shared with the other co-tenants.

As is discussed in point (1) of the treatment of choice D above, each tenant in common is entitled to occupy the full premises at all times, but only so long as he does not interfere with the rights of the other co-tenants to co-occupy the premises. So the man did not have the power to prevent his sister and his cousin from sharing the premises with him whenever they wanted to do so. Consequently, the man could not transfer what he did not have, and thus did not have the power to transfer to the tenant the exclusive right of occupancy.

(C) is not the best response,

because it misstates the effect of the fact that the transferor had only a one-third interest to transfer.

This choice correctly states that the lease is valid. It also correctly states that the man (the transferor) "had only a one-third interest to transfer." But the choice draws a completely wrong conclusion from these two facts. The man's one-third interest (which he was entitled to transfer) was the right to occupy the entire premises for the remainder of the tenancy in common (i.e., forever, unless something happened to extinguish the tenancy in common), subject to a similar right of shared occupancy on the part of the holders of the other two-thirds interest. So the man was entitled to transfer shared occupancy rights for however long he wanted to do so, which in this case was the three years of the lease.

Answer 6

(B) is the best response,

because a death escrow becomes effective only when the grantor places the deed beyond his control.

The man was trying to create a valid gratuitous death escrow. A death escrow is an arrangement in which the grantor hands a deed to a custodian for delivery on the grantor's death. But for a gratuitous death escrow to be valid as a form of delivery, the grantor must place the deed *beyond his control*, by giving up all power to *undo* the arrangement in the future. S&W, § 11.4, pp. 837-38.

Here, the man "told the attorney to return the deed to him if he asked." This explicit power to recall the deed was enough to prevent the man from having placed the deed beyond his control. Therefore, the death escrow was not valid, and the deed was never delivered, either by the unsuccessful escrow or by anything else that happened up until the man's death. (The man's sending of the e-mail to the nephew telling the nephew about the arrangement was also not enough to constitute delivery, since the man still had the power to recall the deed despite having sent the e-mail.)

When the nephew died, the nephew had no property interest in the farm, so his purported devise to his daughter had no effect. When the man died, he was still the owner of the farm, since at no time had he made a successful conveyance of it. Since the attempted death escrow never took effect, the attorney does not have to deliver the deed to the nephew's daughter—the farm passes by intestacy to the man's two sons.

(A) is not the best response,

because it reaches the right conclusion but on incorrect reasoning.

A gratuitous death escrow can certainly be valid despite the lack of a written contract governing the escrow. But to be valid, a death escrow (i.e., a delivery of a deed to a custodian with instructions to deliver it on the grantor's death) must place the deed beyond the grantor's power to revoke the arrangement. Since the man here explicitly retained the right to get the deed back upon request, this "no power to revoke" requirement was not satisfied. So the death escrow was void for this reason, not because of the lack of a written contract between the man and the attorney/escrow agent.

(C) is not the best response,

because the death escrow was never effective, so that the death of the nephew had no consequence.

As is discussed more fully in choice B, to be valid a gratuitous death escrow must place the deed beyond the grantor's control. Because the man retained the power to call the deed back from the escrow arrangement, this "beyond control" requirement was not satisfied. Therefore, the death escrow was never effective, and the man never delivered the deed. That being so, the nephew had no interest in the property at his death, making his death of no consequence to the analysis.

(D) is not the best response,

because it makes an incorrect statement of law.

It is certainly possible to create a valid gratuitous death escrow. And when such an escrow is created, it constitutes a valid delivery of the deed from the grantor to the escrow agent. But for a gratuitous death escrow to be valid, the grantor must place the deed beyond his control. Here, the fact that the man retained the right to reclaim the deed on request meant that he was not putting the deed beyond his control. Therefore, no valid death escrow ever occurred, which meant that no "delivery" occurred when the man handed the deed to his attorney.

Answer 7

(B) is the best response,

because the covenant is a valid equitable servitude, binding on anyone who took with notice.

The deed from the businesswoman created a valid equitable servitude. Let's verify this by reviewing each requirement for creating such a servitude. First, the deed creating the servitude had to satisfy the Statute of Frauds, but it did so: A servitude that is contained in a "deed poll" (i.e., a deed signed by the grantor and accepted by the grantee, but not signed by the latter) is deemed to satisfy the Statute of Frauds as against the grantee. Next, the requirements for creating a servitude (i.e., a restriction whose burden and benefit would both run with the land) were satisfied, because: (1) the building restriction "touches and concerns" both the burdened property and the benefited property (as to the latter, what's being protected is expressly stated to be the river view from the building on the lot retained by the businesswoman); and (2) the fact that the deed placed the no-development obligation on the grantee and "his heirs [and] assigns" makes it clear that both parties to that deed intended that the obligation would be binding on anyone who took from the grantee.

Next, we have to establish whether the servitude, now that we know it exists, is binding on the cousin. An equitable servitude is binding on the burden side only on someone who had, at the time he took, either *actual* or *constructive notice* of the servitude. Since the restriction was contained in the deed to the grantee, and that deed was properly recorded by the grantee, the cousin is deemed to have had constructive notice, of the "*record notice*" variety, at the moment he took. Since nothing has happened to terminate the equitable restriction, that restriction remains binding against the cousin.

One last matter: An equitable servitude may be enforced only *by* a member of a class on whom the original parties who created the servitude *intended* to confer enforcement rights. Where the plaintiff is the present owner of a parcel that was originally intended to be benefitted by the restriction, this requirement is met. So the businessman, as the present owner of the very parcel that was intended to be benefited by that restriction (the parcel with the desirable river view) is entitled to sue for the injunction.

(A) is not the best response,

because, although it correctly states the outcome, it does so on incorrect reasoning.

The businessman is entitled to enforce the equitable servitude created in the deed from the businesswoman to the grantee. The servitude was intended to protect against development of the parcel that abuts the river, and was intended to benefit the other parcel (the one retained by the businesswoman). There is no evidence that the restriction was intended to benefit the retained parcel only because or as long as there was a building on it. So, for instance, if the present owner of the retained parcel had torn down the commercial building on it, that owner would still be entitled to enforce the restriction, on the theory that he (the owner) might someday want to build another structure that would benefit from a comparable river view.

(C) is not the best response,

because an equitable servitude normally *will* survive the death of the promisor.

The deed from the businesswoman to the grantee created a valid equitable servitude, for the reasons discussed in the treatment of choice B. An equitable servitude, by its nature, runs with the land on the "burden" side, so it will not terminate with the death of the promisor (the person who agrees to the restriction). The parties to a deed are always free to specify that the promise contained in it will not run with the land, and is binding only on the promisor (in which case the promise is not a "servitude" at all), but unless they so specify, the burden runs with the land, and is binding on anyone who takes with notice.

(D) is not the best response,

because the grantee accepted the deed and recorded it, thus indicating his willingness to be bound.

As is discussed in choice B, an equitable servitude must satisfy the Statute of Frauds. But where a servitude is contained in a "deed poll" (i.e., a deed signed only by the grantor, not by the grantee), any obligation contained in that deed is binding on the grantee if the latter accepts the deed. And that's even more clearly the case when, as here, the grantee records the deed. So the fact that the grantee didn't sign the deed doesn't prevent the servitude from arising, and burdening the property as against anyone who took with notice of the restriction.

Answer 8

(A) is the best response,

because the contract did not adequately identify the land to be conveyed.

A contract for the sale of an interest in land must satisfy the Statute of Frauds, and must thus be evidenced by a signed writing stating the essential terms of the contract. Courts are usually lenient as to what elements the writing must cover, but all agree that the writing must adequately identify the particular parcel to be sold. Since the writing here indicates that the parties had not yet decided which portion of the seller's larger tract was to be included in the sale, the writing fails to identify the land to be sold with even minimal specificity. Therefore, there is no writing that satisfies the Statute of Frauds, and this fact makes the contract unenforceable, either by specific performance or by an action for damages.

(B) is not the best response,

because it states the correct outcome, but bases it on incorrect reasoning.

The Statute of Frauds applies to contracts for the sale of an interest in land, so a writing was required. The writing was required to state all the essential elements of the deal. Price is certainly an essential element, so the contract could satisfy the Statute of Frauds only if it provided a reasonably certain method for ascertaining the price. But the contract here did so, by quoting the price as a per-acre charge. The problem, as discussed in Choice A, is that the writing does not permit identification of the particular parcel to be sold, so we don't know how many acres will be included. If we had known which acres were to be included, the price would have been fully ascertainable.

(C) is not the best response,

because any requirement that the parties negotiate in good faith would not be sufficient to overcome the Statute of Frauds problem here.

The Statute of Frauds requires that a contract for sale of an interest in land be manifested by a signed writing covering the essential elements of the deal. One of those elements is the particular acreage to be sold. It's true that the parties agreed that they would later determine the precise acreage. And that agreement imposed on each of them the obligation to negotiate in good faith. But that good-faith obligation cannot be a substitute for compliance with the Statute of Frauds. Furthermore, there is no evidence that either party failed to negotiate in good faith, so there is no basis for saying, as this choice does, that the buyer wins. And even if the court believed that the seller had not negotiated in good faith, how would the court decide *which acreage* to require the seller to convey? So even if the buyer could prove the seller's failure to negotiate in good faith, the buyer would be entitled at best to a money-damages recovery, not a decree of specific performance.

(D) is not the best response,

because whatever equity powers the court might have would not authorize the court to ignore the Statute of Frauds.

The Statute of Frauds requires that a contract for the sale of an interest in land be manifested by a signed writing covering the essential elements of the deal. It's true that an action for specific performance is an equitable action, entitling the judge to use his equitable powers. And those powers might include, in an appropriate case, the right to appoint a master. But the existence of those equitable powers would not authorize the court to nullify the Statute of Frauds. Since there is no writing to identify which particular acreage is to be sold, the court's equitable powers are irrelevant.

Answer 9

(D) is the best response,

because the neighbor's year in Europe prevented there from ever being 21 years of continuous adverse possession by him.

An adverse possessor gains title only if he adversely possesses the land *continuously* for the number of years stated in the statute of limitations on ejectment actions. Here, this means that the neighbor would have to have been continuously (and openly and hostilely) in possession for 21 years. The year in Europe meant that the neighbor had one period of five years continuous possession, and another period of 19 years of continuous possession. Neither of these, therefore, met the requirement of 21 continuous years (and they cannot be "tacked together" because of the gap between them). The fact that the neighbor at some point built a gardening shed does not help him—even if the shed was built during the first five years, its existence doesn't constitute ongoing "possession" by him during the year he was in Europe.

(A) is not the best response,

because the fact that the daughter was a minor for some of the relevant period did not extend her time to sue.

This statute does indeed extend the time to sue by one day for each day that the plaintiff is under 18 during the time of adverse possession. But the maximum extension available through this disability-tolling clause is 10 years. So the clause only extended the daughter's time to sue until she turned 28. At the moment she turned 28, she still had 16 years to sue by virtue of the 21 years total given to her in the first part of the statute (she had 21 years from the time she was 23, since she was 23 when the neighbor returned from Europe and started his 21-year clock anew). So the fact that she was under 18 for one year of the adverse possession makes no difference to the analysis.

(B) is not the best response,

because the daughter's mental incompetence did not exist at the time the adverse possession began.

This choice illustrates why you must very carefully read the terms of any statute recited in the question. The statute here gives a 10-year extension of the time to sue "if the person entitled to bring the cause of action is . . . mentally incompetent *at the time the cause of action accrues*[.]" An action for ejectment accrues at the time the would-be adverse possessor first takes open and hostile possession of the property. The relevant possession began when the neighbor returned home from Europe, at which time the daughter was 23. (The first, pre-Europe, five-year possession doesn't matter, since it cannot be tacked to the later post-Europe possession.) Since the daughter was not declared mentally incompetent until the age of 28, she does not meet the requirement of having been incompetent "at the time the cause of action accrue[d]." So the tolling for mental incompetence never applied at all.

(C) is not the best response,

because the lack of a residence did not prevent adverse possession from occurring.

There is no requirement that the possessor build a residence on the land (or, for that matter, "reside" on the land) in order to be deemed in adverse possession of it. Any activity that would bring home to the record owner that the other person is occupying the premises in a continuous, open and hostile way is sufficient to meet the possession requirement. So planting and harvesting crops, hunting, and parking cars on the land are, taken together, more than enough to establish that the neighbor was using the property in an open and hostile manner inconsistent with the rights of the record owner. What causes the adverse possession claim to fail is the fact that there never was any 21-year-period in which these uses were continuously made, due to the neighbor's year in Europe.

Answer 10

(C) is the best response,

because title insurance covers the insured's liability under any warranties of title made when he sold the property.

This question is asking you to anticipate a detail of how title insurance handles the problem of the insured's liability for warranties of title made in the deed by which the insured sells the property. You cannot know for certain how the particular title policy in question handles that issue. But nearly all owner's title policies issued in the United States follow the basic provisions of the standard form of owner policy published by the American Land Title Association (ALTA), the title industry's trade association. That standard policy says that the coverage shall continue in force until the later of various events, one of which is "so long as the insured shall have liability by reason of warranties in any transfer or conveyance of the Title." 2006 ATLA Owner's Policy, Conditions, Par. 2. So no matter how many years elapse between the time when the insured owner makes a warranty of title in connection with his sale of the property, and the time when the owner is successfully sued for damages for breach of the warranty, the standard U.S. title policy covers the owner's liability.

(A) is not the best response,

because the coverage under the buyer's policy continued after the sale, with respect to the buyer's liability for warranties of title.

You have to distinguish between the two title policies involved in this fact pattern. The *lender's* title policy ended when the loan was repaid. But as is more fully described in Choice C above, the standard *owner's* title policy continues to give the owner coverage against liability for warranties of title that the owner makes when he sells the property. So the coverage would not end at the time of the buyer's conveyance to the investor.

(B) is not the best response,

because the coverage under the buyer's policy continued after the buyer paid off the bank mortgage.

As with choice A, you have to distinguish between the two policies in this fact pattern, the lender's policy and the owner's policy. It's true that when the buyer paid off the bank mortgage, the lender's policy terminated. But this payoff had no effect on the owner's policy. You should be able to figure out that this would have to be the case—after paying off the mortgage, the buyer still owned the property, and would still suffer a loss when there turned out to be a prior mortgage not shown on the policy's report of liens, so an owner's title policy wouldn't be much good if it didn't cover this situation. In general, don't check your common sense at the door—as this choice illustrates, you can often anticipate the correct result, or at least eliminate one or more incorrect choices, just by trying to figure out what the answer "ought to be."

(D) is not the best response,
because it reaches the correct conclusion but on incorrect reasoning.

This choice asserts that the BFP status of the person who recovers damages from the owner makes a difference to whether the owner's title policy covers those damages. There is absolutely no reason why there should be such a difference in policy coverage based on the claimant's BFP status, and indeed there is not. As is described more fully in choice C, a standard owner's title policy covers the owner for any loss on a breach of warranty claim brought by one who takes (directly or indirectly) from the owner, regardless of whether the taker is a bona fide purchaser for value or not.

Answer 11

(A) is the best response,
because a variance is the appropriate means of allowing a proposed use that is inconsistent with a parcel's zoning.

A variance is essentially a waiver of some restriction that the applicable zoning act would otherwise impose. S&W, § 9.29, p. 649. To get a variance, the owner must convince the zoning appeals board that without the variance, the owner would suffer an unnecessary hardship in the use of his land. *Id*. On the facts here, it is not at all certain that the board would grant the requested variance—granting or denying variances is within the board's discretion. But the question doesn't ask you whether the woman will win; it tells you to assume that she wins, and asks you to supply the reason. Of the four choices, issuance of a variance is the only one that could possibly explain the decision in the woman's favor.

By the way, an owner is especially likely to be granted a use variance when her property is at the *edge* of one zoning district, and the proposed use would be allowed in the *immediately adjacent* district. Here, where the use would be allowed on the south side of the street (and there is in fact a business of that same type on that side), granting a variance to allow the use on the north side of the street is unlikely to dramatically harm the neighborhood, so the woman's case for a variance is especially strong.

(B) is not the best response,
because the doctrine of amortization could not explain why the use was allowed.

An amortization provision provides that where a particular use was valid under the prior zoning act, but is invalid under a newly-enacted zoning act, the now-non-conforming use may continue, but only for a specified period that will permit the owner to recover, or "amortize," her investment. (For instance, a zoning act might provide that any use that was previously legal but is now illegal in a particular district must be terminated within five years of the adoption of the new act.) So the amortization doctrine is a way to phase out a non-conforming use, not a method of *allowing* a non-conforming use. Therefore, amortization could not explain why the board would approve the woman's proposal.

(C) is not the best response,
because the doctrine of change of circumstances has nothing to do with the zoning process.

In property law, the only "change of circumstances" doctrine is one providing that a party whose land is burdened by an equitable servitude may be relieved of that servitude if the surrounding land-use patterns have changed in a way that makes the restriction no longer appropriate. For instance, a servitude that limits a particular parcel to single-family residence use might be ordered terminated by a court if changes in land-usage patterns have led to the rest of the neighborhood's becoming entirely commercial. Since there is no equitable servitude at issue here, the change-of-circumstances doctrine couldn't be relevant.

(D) is not the best response,
because the woman's use of her house was not a non-conforming use.

A non-conforming use is a use that was permitted under a previous zoning regime, but is not permitted under the new zoning. Typically, the owner is permitted to continue the non-conforming use for a limited period of time, to "amortize" his investment. (See the discussion of the "amortization" doctrine in Choice B.) Here, the woman is not yet using her property to operate a court-reporting service (the now-prohibited use). Rather, she's presently using the house as a residence, a permitted use. So her use is not a non-conforming use, preventing this choice from being a possible explanation of why her proposal was approved.

Answer 12

(B) is the best response,
because a senior lender has the right to foreclose on the entire mortgaged property, regardless of the financial damage that this foreclosure might do to a junior mortgagee.

Both the bank and the finance company have mortgages covering the entire four-acre parcel. When two mortgages cover the same property, priority is determined by which mortgagee recorded first, assuming (as is the case here) that neither mortgage is a purchase-money mortgage. Therefore, since the bank recorded first, it has priority in the foreclosure process, both as to deciding when to foreclose, and as to distribution of proceeds.

This priority means that once the bank's mortgage went into default, the bank had a right to insist that the entire mortgaged property be sold in a single auction. That's true even though the value of the property was much greater than the amount owed on the bank's mortgage, and even though a sale of the entire property rather than of just a part of it might well cause needless financial loss to the holder of the junior mortgage. Therefore, the court will reject the finance company's motion that just two of the four acres be sold—and that's true even if the court is certain that such a sale of two acres would make the bank whole, and would improve the finance company's chances of eventual recovery from the remainder of the acreage.

(A) is not the best response,

because the bank does not hold a purchase-money mortgage, and even if it did, that fact would not change the outcome.

This choice correctly states the outcome (that the bank can foreclose on the entire four acres), but it misstates the reason. A purchase money mortgage is a mortgage given to secure the loan of funds that are used to purchase the mortgaged property. Since the woman already owned the four-acre lot at the time she took out the loan from the bank, the bank's loan was not used by her to purchase the property, a fact that prevents the loan from being a purchase money mortgage.

By the way, the significance of a loan's being a purchase money mortgage is that that loan takes priority over any lien against the property-owner that was filed before the owner bought the property. Restatement (Third) Property, Mortgages, § 7.2(b). So suppose the finance company had lent against the woman's other assets, and filed a mortgage that covered the woman's "after-acquired" property; suppose that the woman had then borrowed from the bank the funds to buy the four-acre parcel. In that scenario, the fact that the bank's mortgage was a purchase money mortgage would have meant that it had priority over the finance company's earlier-filed mortgage, and this choice would be a correct explanation of why the bank would have the right to insist on a foreclosure of the entire parcel. But, of course, that's not the scenario that occurred here.

(C) is not the correct response,

because the senior mortgagee can foreclose on the entire property regardless of what prejudice this might cause to the junior mortgagee.

Since the bank recorded first, and since neither mortgage is a purchase money mortgage, the bank's mortgage has priority in the foreclosure process. This priority means that once the bank's mortgage went into default, the bank had a right to insist that the entire mortgaged property be sold in a single auction. That's true even if selling just the first two acres would have been certain to make the bank whole, and would have improved the chances that the finance company would later recover more on its loan. In other words, equity, fairness, and minimizing overall losses do not enter into the equation at all—the first mortgagee gets to demand a sale of the entire asset regardless of the impact on junior creditors.

In any event, as a factual matter it's not at all clear that a pro rata foreclosure of the lot "will not prejudice the rights of the bank," as this choice asserts. Prices bid at foreclosure sales are often much less than the estimated market value, so a foreclosure on just the first two acres might not in fact make the bank whole, in which case having to wait for a separate foreclosure sale on the second two acres might indeed harm the bank (e.g., because the market deteriorated further, or because the property had more value per acre if sold as a single four-acre parcel).

(D) is not the best response,

because it invokes a doctrine that has no relevance to the present situation.

The "two funds" rule of marshaling applies in a narrow situation where two or more parcels are each subject to at least one mortgage, and one of those parcels is subject to competing mortgages. Let's assume that Parcel 1 is encumbered by two mortgages (held by Senior and Junior, respectively), and that Parcel 2 is encumbered by only one mortgage (held by Senior). Normally, a senior lender's absolute right to foreclose on any mortgage in default would mean that Senior can foreclose on Parcel 1 before Parcel 2, even though that might needlessly damage Junior's ability to recover the full amount of his mortgage on Parcel 1. But the "two funds" rule says that upon request by Junior, and if Senior would not be materially harmed, Senior must first foreclose on Parcel 2 (as to which there are no subordinate interests), before foreclosing on Parcel 1 (as to which there is a subordinate interest, the one held by Junior). That way, if Parcel 1 produces enough cash to pay off Senior's entire loan, Parcel 2 doesn't get subjected to a foreclosure until Junior wants to do so, avoiding unnecessary harm to Junior. *See* Restatement (Third) Property, Mortgages, § 8.6.

Here, there is only a single four-acre parcel subject to two competing mortgages, not two separate parcels one of which has competing mortgages on it and the other of which does not. So the conditions required for use of the "two funds" marshaling rule apply do not exist.

Answer 13

(C) is the best response,

because the daughter will win if and only if equitable conversion applies to give the daughter an equitable interest in the sale proceeds.

To understand why this is the correct choice, you need to compare what the result would be with and without application of the equitable conversion doctrine. Without the doctrine, the analysis is simple: At the moment of the seller's death, the seller still owned the parcel, and the parcel was real estate. Therefore, the parcel, as real estate, would pass to the son under mechanical operation of Paragraph 5 of the will. When the real estate was later sold, the proceeds would belong to the son in return for his having surrendered his interest in the real estate. Apart from equitable conversion, there is no doctrine or rule that would alter this result.

The equitable conversion doctrine, when it applies, supplies special rules for dealing with unexpected events that occur during the "executory period" of a contract for the sale of real estate, that is, the time between when the contract is signed and when the actual conveyance is made. In general, the doctrine holds that "once the parties have entered into a contract that equity would specifically enforce, the buyer's interest in the contract is *converted* into real estate and the *seller's interest to personal property*." S&W, § 10.13, pp. 786-87. Where the seller dies during the gap between contract and closing, application of equitable conversion means that at the moment of death the seller's estate is no longer deemed to hold the real estate, but instead to hold an interest in the eventual sale proceeds, an interest that constitutes personal property. So if the doctrine applies here, then: (1) at the moment of death the estate had no real estate, only personal property in the form of an expectation of proceeds of the to-be-completed sale; and (2) once the personal representative received the proceeds, he was required to treat them as personal property payable to the daughter under Paragraph 6. So the application (or non-application) of the equitable conversion doctrine will be completely determinative of who gets the proceeds.

What's the significance of the statement in the facts that "The contract contains no contingencies"? You can rely on the idea that the examiners seldom if ever tell you a fact that doesn't matter to the analysis of any of the choices. Here's why this fact matters:

Even in states that apply equitable conversion, courts sometimes say that such a conversion occurs only if and when the contract becomes "unconditional." S&W, § 1013, p. 798. So if the contract here had been subject to some contingency not under control of either party (e.g., the buyer's ability to get mortgage financing), then even in an equitable conversion state the court might have held that no conversion had occurred by the moment of the seller's death; and in that event, the son would have won. So the absence of any contingency was required to ensure that if the state has adopted equitable conversion, the doctrine would necessarily apply here and make the daughter victorious.

By the way, most American states *apply* the equitable conversion doctrine in situations in which the vendor or purchaser dies while the contract is in force. So in most states, the daughter would win. But you didn't have to actually know whether most states apply the doctrine or not in order to answer this question—you only had to know that the answer would turn on *whether* the jurisdiction applies the doctrine.

(A) is not the best response,

because the precise phrasing in Paragraph 5 would not affect the outcome.

If equitable conversion did not apply, then the son, as devisee of all real estate, would win whether the Paragraph 5 bequest referred specifically to that parcel, or instead referred generally to "all my real property." And if equitable conversion *did* apply, the son would lose, again without reference to how the parcel was referred to in the Paragraph 5 bequest. So the specificity of the reference would not matter to the outcome—only the use or non-use of equitable conversion would matter.

(B) is not the best response,

because the temporal relationship between the closing date and the seller's death would not affect the outcome.

To see whether this choice is correct, you have to figure out what the outcome would be if the closing date was scheduled for a date that turned out to be *before* the seller's death, and then compare that outcome to the outcome in a scenario where the scheduled closing date was a date that turned out to be *after* the seller's death. If the equitable conversion doctrine did *not* apply, the son would take the proceeds no matter whether the closing was scheduled for before or after the seller's death—in either event, the seller's estate was still the holder of legal title on the date of death, and that fact would be dispositive. Conversely, if equitable conversion *did* apply in the state, the seller's estate would be treated as having a personal-property interest in the proceeds, regardless of whether the contractually-scheduled time for closing had or had not passed as of the moment of the seller's death. So regardless of whether equitable distribution applied, the sequence between scheduled closing date and seller's death could not have affected the outcome.

(D) is not the best response,

because the existence or non-existence of a court order would make no difference to the outcome.

Again, you have to compare how the case would come out if there was a court order and how it would come out if there was not. If equitable conversion did not apply, the proceeds would be deemed to be real estate (making the son victorious) whether the closing occurred under court order or not. Conversely, if equitable conversion did apply, the proceeds would be deemed to be personal property, again regardless of whether the closing occurred under court order. So the applicability of equitable conversion, not the existence of a court order, is the only factor that would have determined who got the proceeds.

Answer 14

(A) is the best response,

because the wife did not intend to make the chandelier a permanent annexation, and the chandelier was removable without seriously damaging the real estate or the chandelier.

When the holder of a life estate (or a tenant for years) annexes a chattel (commonly called a "fixture") to the real estate, and does not intend to make a permanent annexation, the holder or her representative is permitted to *remove* the fixture before or soon after the end of the estate, if removal can be done without causing substantial injury to the real estate or substantial destruction of the fixture itself. S&W, § 4.9, p. 168. These conditions apply here: (1) we know that the wife did not intend to make the chandelier a permanent annexation, since she told her nephew and her stepson that after her death, the chandelier should be removed; and (2) there is no evidence that the removal damaged either the ceiling or the fixture itself. Therefore, the nephew, as the wife's personal representative, had the right to remove the chandelier within a reasonable time after the wife's death.

(B) is not the best response,

because the accession doctrine does not apply where, as here, there is no intent to make a permanent annexation of the chattel to the real estate.

By the doctrine of accession, if a tenant or the holder of a life estate attaches a chattel to the real estate under such circumstances that the law will not permit the chattel to be removed later, ownership of the chattel passes to the owner of the real estate. S&W, § 6.48, p. 353. So if the accession doctrine applied, it would be the son (as owner of the real estate), not the nephew, who would prevail. So whether the accession doctrine applies or not, that doctrine could not be a correct explanation of why the *nephew* would win.

In any event, accession would apply only if, under the circumstances, the woman would not have been entitled to remove the chandelier while she was still alive. As is discussed more extensively in the treatment of choice A, removal was allowed. Therefore, by definition the accession doctrine does not apply.

(C) is not the best response,

because it reaches an incorrect conclusion of law.

As is discussed more extensively in choice A, the fact that the woman never intended to attach the chandelier permanently to the real estate, coupled with the fact that it could be was removed without substantial damage to the real estate or the chandelier itself, means that the chandelier *could* be legally removed after the wife's death.

(D) is not the best response,

because non-trade fixtures can also sometimes be removed from the real estate, and the situation here is one of those times.

A trade fixture is a fixture installed by a tenant for use in her trade or business. At the end of the lease term, the tenant is permitted to remove all trade fixtures, provided that they can be removed without serious damage to the real estate or destruction of the fixture itself. Since the woman was not operating a trade or business, the chandelier was not a trade fixture. But it is not the case, as this choice asserts, that trade fixtures are the *only* type of fixtures that may be removed from real estate. A non-trade fixture may also be removed, as long as the person who attached it did not intend to annex it permanently, and the fixture can be removed without serious damage to the real estate and without destruction of the fixture itself. (See the discussion of choice A.) Here, the chandelier fell into this category of removable non-trade fixtures.

Answer 15

(B) is the best response,

because consideration is not required to make a deed valid.

The valid execution of a deed requires several formalities. The presence of consideration, however, is not one of them. Therefore, even if the landowner was able to prove that no money had in fact been paid by the purchaser, notwithstanding the recitation, and that no other consideration of any kind had been supplied by the purchaser, the landowner would still lose.

(A) is not the best response,

because the purchaser's recording did not end the landowner's right to bring suit.

The principal function of recording acts is to give a subsequent purchaser a way to check the chain of title of a piece of land.

The landowner should lose, but not for the reason given. The purchaser's act of recording would not prevent the landowner from recovering. One of the things that recording does is to create a rebuttable presumption that the recorded instrument is valid. The landowner could still challenge the validity of the deed, i.e., rebut the presumption. However, under these facts, the deed was authentic and validly delivered, notwithstanding the lack of consideration and the false recital about it; therefore, the landowner's attempt to rebut the presumption of validity from recording would fail.

(C) is not the best response,

because whether consideration was paid (and therefore how the existence of consideration can be proved) is irrelevant.

As described in the analysis of choice B above, consideration is not required for a deed to be valid. Consequently, the fact that the parol evidence rule might allow the recitation of consideration to be proved false (a true statement), is irrelevant.

(D) is not the best response,

because the deed was valid, not an ineffective void instrument.

It's true that recordation does not validate an invalid conveyance, such as a forged or undelivered deed. However, that rule does not apply to these facts: The deed the landowner gave to the purchaser is valid, since consideration is not required for the valid execution of a deed. Therefore, the landowner will lose, not prevail as choice D states.

Answer 16

(B) is the best response,

because tickets to a sporting event are licenses.

A ticket to a sporting event or other public function is virtually always considered a license rather than an easement. A license is a right to use the licensor's land that is revocable at the will of the licensor.

The woman's season tickets to the hockey games at the private arena constituted a license granted to her by the management company. Because she held only a license, that interest was revocable at the will of the licensor. (If the revocation had been without proper cause, she would have a claim for damages, but even then a court would not award her the right to attend games. In the actual event, the fact that she violated the announced no solicitation rule would probably prevent her from even getting damages.)

(A) is not the best response,

because the management company's right to revoke the woman's tickets arises under its rights as a licensor, not out of its "right and obligation to control activities. . . ."

A ticket to a sporting event or other public function is nearly always considered a license rather than an easement. A license is a right to use the licensor's land that is revocable at the will of the licensor.

Although the management company may have a right and obligation to control activities on realty it owns, its right to revoke the woman's season tickets arises from the fact that it has issued her only a license.

(C) is not the best response,

because licenses issued for value can be revoked.

A ticket to a sporting event or other public function is nearly always considered a license rather than an easement. A license is a right to use the licensor's land that is revocable at the will of the licensor. The fact that the licensee pays value for the license does not change the license's revocability, at least in cases where (as here) the licensee does not honor the rules governing the license.

(D) is not the best response,

because the terms of the woman's license prohibited solicitation.

The woman would not need to be committing a nuisance for the management company to have the right to revoke her license. The company granted the woman a license in the form of season tickets.

That license expressly prohibited licensees from solicitations anywhere within the arena at any time and in any manner. When the woman violated this prohibition by soliciting signatures for her petition urging that the coach of the team be fired, the management company had the right to revoke her license, whether she was a "nuisance" or not.

Answer 17

(A) is the best response,

because the tenant's sublease to his friend leaves the tenant responsible for all 24 months of unpaid rent.

An "assignment" is the transfer by the lessee of his entire interest in the leased premises. If something less, even a term one day less, is transferred, the transfer is not an assignment, but is a "sublease." A sublease is a lease executed by the lessee of land or premises to a third person, conveying the same interest the lessee enjoys but for a *shorter term* than that for which the lessee holds. With a sublease, there is a relationship between the lessee and the sublessee, but there is no relationship—no privity of estate—between the lessor and sublessee. Since there is no privity of estate between the two, *the lessor cannot sue the sublessee for rent.*

The tenant's lease of the house to his friend was a sublease, because it was for a shorter time (one year) than remained on the original lease (two years).

Because this was a sublease, there was no privity of estate between the owner and the friend. Therefore, the owner cannot sue the friend for the rent not paid during the one year the friend was in possession of the house.

On the other hand, the creation of the sublease did not release the tenant from his original liability to the owner for the full rent (only a release executed by the owner could do that). Therefore, the tenant is responsible to the owner for the full unpaid 24 months.

(B), (C), and (D) are not the best response,

because the tenant subleased the house to his friend, leaving the tenant individually liable for the full amount.

See the discussion of choice A above.

Answer 18

(C) is the best response,

because the buyer had no notice of the lawyer's trust.

One who purchases from the record owner of property is eligible for the protection of the recording act, as against someone else who previously took from that same record owner. Here, the lawyer is the record owner (in fee simple), and the landowner's daughter is a "prior transferee" from the lawyer. (That is, the lawyer created an interest in the landowner's daughter by the trust document, and this interest was created prior to the conveyance to the buyer.) So the buyer is in position to use the recording act to gain protection against the landowner's daughter as prior transferee from the same grantor (the lawyer).

Only bona fide purchasers (BFPs) are entitled to prevail against a prior transferee under recording statutes. To be a BFP, a person must: (1) be a "purchaser" (holder of a fee interest or mortgagee or creditor), (2) take without notice (actual, constructive, or inquiry) of the prior instrument, and (3) pay valuable consideration. Since the buyer (1) holds what purports to be a fee interest, (2) took without either actual or constructive notice (since she couldn't have found anything to indicate the existence of the landowner's daughter's interest by looking in the public records), and (3) paid fair market value, she meets all of these requirements for getting the benefit of the recording act.

Therefore, the failure of the landowner's daughter's interest to be recorded means that as against the landowner's daughter, the buyer's interest takes priority, and the landowner's daughter's interest is null and void.

(A) is not the best response,

because it ignores the effect of the recording act.

It may be true as a general principle that "a successor in title to the trustee takes title subject to the grantor's trust." But this is subject to the rule that a bona fide purchaser (BFP) from the trustee will take free of the unrecorded instrument by which the BFP's grantor created the trust. (If this were not true, no one could ever safely buy property—there would always be the risk that the grantor had secretly created a trust encumbering the property.)

(B) is not the best response,

because trusts creating equitable interests *are* subject to the recording act.

A beneficiary's interest in a trust is indeed, as this choice suggests, an equitable interest. (The trustee has legal title.) But this choice is false in stating that equitable interests are not subject to recording acts. Because no attempt was made to record the instrument creating the trust, the trust was not in the chain of title and the buyer took the tract as a BFP.

(D) is not the best response,

because a trust *was* created, and because this choice ignores the operation of the recording act.

As between the lawyer and the landowner's daughter, the property would be deemed to be held in trust for the landowner's daughter, because the transactions in which the landowner conveyed to the lawyer and the lawyer later signed the trust document were certainly sufficient to create a trust. The problem is that this trust was an unrecorded instrument, and like any unrecorded instrument, *will* be void against a subsequent transferee from the same grantor (the lawyer) who takes without notice and for value. So this choice predicts the correct result, but on incorrect reasoning.

Answer 19

(D) is the best response,

because the deed was indeed not in the friend's chain of title (since it was recorded before the daughter took title), making the friend a BFP who gets the protection of the recording act.

As between the daughter and the buyer, the buyer could rely on the doctrine of "estoppel by deed" (sometimes called "after-acquired title") to establish that he owns the property. Under this doctrine, one who makes a conveyance of property she doesn't own, and who then acquires that property, is estopped from denying the grantee's superior claim to the property. So if the daughter had never made any conveyance of the house to anyone but the buyer, and the buyer sued the daughter to establish that he now owns the property rather than she, the buyer would win.

But most courts hold that the doctrine of estoppel by deed *does not apply as against a subsequent BFP from the original grantor*. That is, most courts would say that as between the friend (the subsequent BFP from the daughter) and the buyer, the buyer cannot rely on the estoppel-by-deed doctrine, even though he recorded his title promptly. The reason is that a contrary rule would mean that the friend would have an immense burden when checking the daughter's title—he would have had to check for conveyances by the daughter dating from *before* the time when, according to the records, the daughter herself got title. For this reason, an *"early recorded document"* (one recorded as a grant by the grantor before the date when the grantor got record title) is in most courts deemed to be *outside the grantor's chain of title.*

There's no guarantee that a court would follow this majority view, but (1) the court would probably do so; and (2) if the court did so, the friend would win.

(A) is not the best response,

because it ignores the possible application of the estoppel-by-deed/after-acquired-title doctrine.

This doctrine (which is summarized in the discussion of choice D above) would mean that the buyer did indeed get title, even though the buyer got nothing at the time of the purported conveyance two years ago. So although choice A is factually correct, it doesn't explain why the friend would win.

(B) is not the best response,

because nothing would delay the buyer's deed from taking effect.

There is nothing under these facts that would make the buyer's deed take effect after the friend's. It's possible that the doctrine of estoppel-by-deed (see the analysis of choice D above) might apply, but even if it did, the doctrine would cause the conveyance from the daughter to the buyer to "relate back" to the date the daughter delivered the instrument to the buyer, not the date the daughter herself got record title. So this choice doesn't explain how things would work. (And in any event, the estoppel-by-deed doctrine probably would apply as against a subsequent purchaser for value like the friend.)

(C) is not the best response,

because the friend's possession would not give him rights greater than the buyer's fee simple.

Priority in possession generally does not affect who wins in a dispute between two people who have received conveyances of the same property. Therefore, if one ignores the possible effect of the estoppel-by-deed doctrine (see the analysis of choice D above), the fact that the buyer recorded before the friend would cause the buyer to win in a dispute between him and the friend even though the friend took possession first. (The fact that the friend was in possession would have put the buyer on inquiry notice of the friend's interest after the time that the friend took possession. So if the friend had received an unrecorded conveyance *before* the buyer did, the buyer might have been deprived of the ability to use the recording act. But here, the buyer, not the friend, has recorded first, so the state of the buyer's knowledge about the friend's interest is irrelevant.)

Answer 20

(D) is the best response,

because the forged release was not effective, and recording this forged document had no effect.

A person who procures record title by forging (and then recording) a deed has nothing to convey. The grantee then gets nothing, despite the apparently perfect record title. (This problem points up a major problem of recording acts: If a person procures title by a forged document that she then records, a prospective grantee from that person has no way to determine from inspection of the records that she is taking nothing. That's one of the risks that title insurance guards against.)

Therefore, the landowner's forged document saying that she had unencumbered title to Lot 5 was of no effect, even when recorded. The developer loses despite the absolutely perfect appearance of the landowner's record title.

(A) is not the best response,

because an owner of an interest has no obligation to check the public records to guard against fraud.

As explained in the analysis of choice D above, the forgery here was not effective. Consequently, the bank was entitled to sit back and ignore the state of the public records. A person who already holds a recorded interest has no "duty to check the records" to guard against a subsequent forgery, and thus cannot be "negligent."

(B) is not the best response,

because the developer was not entitled to rely on the records as protection against a forgery in her grantor's chain of title.

A forged instrument is void. It's void against the forger, of course, but more interestingly it's also void against one who takes from the forger (or even against anyone down the chain from the forger, until the statute of limitations has run). So the developer was not "entitled to rely on the recorded release" as a guarantee that her grantor did not obtain her an unencumbered interest by fraud.

(C) is not the best response,

because even if the developer couldn't have discovered the alteration by reasonable inquiry she would still lose.

It's true that the developer could have seen from the public records that the bank once had a mortgage on the parcel. So the developer could theoretically have asked the bank, "Did you really release your lien on Lot 5?" and the bank might well have answered, "No." But even if a court were to rule that the developer had reason to be suspicious enough to check with the bank, or even if the court were to conclude that the bank wouldn't have answered her inquiry, the developer would still lose. That's because of the general rule (described in the discussion of choice D above) that a forged instrument, even when perfectly recorded, is completely ineffective when relied on by a subsequent grantee.

Answer 21

(B) is the best response,

because creditors are probably not "purchasers for value" as required for protection under the recording act.

Some recording acts have language that specifically protects judgment creditors who file their judgment after the debtor has made an unrecorded conveyance.

But where the language of the recording act is ambiguous about whether judgment creditors are covered (e.g., where, as here, "purchasers for value" are what are covered), most courts have interpreted the statute so as not to cover the judgment creditor. There is no guarantee that a court would interpret the statute in this anti-creditor way, but that's at least a possibility, and of the four choices this is the most likely explanation for an anti-creditor result. (Remember, you're not asked to say how the case will come out—you're merely asked to say what the most likely rationale will be *if* the case is decided for the buyer.)

A second rationale for the creditor's loss, by the way, is that the judgment lien statute here gives a lien on "property then owned or subsequently acquired" by the debtor. A court could very plausibly conclude that this language is limited to "property then *actually* owned," not "property then owned as of record," by the debtor.

(A) is not the best response,

because the doctrine of equitable conversion does not apply to these facts.

The doctrine of equitable conversion applies to conflicts between grantor and grantee arising during the gap between the signing of the contract and the delivery of the deed. (For instance, a structure on the property may be destroyed during the gap, in which case the doctrine would mean that the buyer would be viewed as the equitable owner at the time of destruction, and would be required to close.) Equitable conversion might apply in this scenario if the creditor filed her judgment during the gap (i.e., between the time when the farmer contracted to sell and when he made the conveyance). But once the farmer made the conveyance while the creditor had not yet filed her judgment, the equitable conversion doctrine had no further application.

(C) is not the best response,

because the farmer's possession would not suggest the farmer had sold the farm to the buyer.

Under a recording statute like the one here, a subsequent bona fide purchaser (BFP) (i.e., a person who gives valuable consideration and has no actual or constructive notice of the prior instrument) prevails over a prior grantee who failed to record. If the creditor was trying to become covered by the recording act, and *the buyer* was in possession at the time the creditor filed her lien, the fact that the buyer (not the farmer, the record owner) was in possession at the date of lien filing might have been enough to cause the buyer to lose, since this possession might have put her on inquiry notice that the farmer was perhaps no longer the owner. But the fact that *the farmer* was still in possession didn't put the buyer on notice of anything, so it's irrelevant on these facts.

(D) is not the best response,

because being a purchaser without notice only helps the *subsequent* "purchaser" gain protection of the recording act, and the person seeking protection of the act here is the creditor, not the buyer.

Recording acts protect the second, not the first, purchaser in certain circumstances. Here, it would be the creditor (who can argue that she "purchased" by filing her lien), not the buyer, who is trying to get the protection of the recording act. It is the person seeking the protection of the recording act (the second purchaser), not the person resisting application of the act (the first purchaser) who needs to be "without notice." So here, the notice status of the creditor might well matter (if the recording act otherwise applied to judgment lien creditors). But the notice status of the buyer, the first "purchaser," does not matter at all.

Answer 22

(B) is the best response,

because it recognizes that a grant "to A and his heirs" is a grant of a fee simple interest.

A literal reading of the grant to the buyer "and his heirs" would suggest that the buyer's heirs take something. But a gift "to A and his heirs" has always been interpreted to mean the grant of a fee simple interest to A, with A's heirs taking nothing. Consequently, the buyer had the ability to convey that same fee simple to the developer, which he did, and the fact that the buyer's daughter did not join the deed is irrelevant. (She had no interest to convey or not convey.)

(A), (C), and (D) are not the best response,

because each choice incorrectly suggests that the daughter received an interest as the buyer's "heir."

Answer 23

(D) is the best response,

because the landowner's use of the easement put the bank on notice of her interest, preventing the bank from being a purchaser "without notice" who is entitled to the protection of the recording act.

Under a recording statute like the one here, a subsequent BFP prevails over a prior grantee who failed to record by the time of the subsequent grant. But the statute gives a subsequent purchaser protection only if she had no actual or constructive notice at the time of the conveyance.

The subsequent grantee will be deemed to have notice not only of matters of which he has "actual" notice, and of matters that are shown by the public records ("record notice"), but also of any matter as to which the grantee is (or should be) in possession of facts that would lead the grantee to make an investigation. This is called *"inquiry notice."* One source of inquiry notice is that if the property is in possession of one other than the record owner, the prospective grantee is under a duty to inquire about the facts that put that person into possession (since the reason may be that the possessor has an unrecorded interest).

Here, the bank should have noticed that though the strip was shown as belonging to the developer's parcel, it was "possessed" by the landowner in the form of the driveway. Had the bank made inquiry of the landowner, she would (presumably) have told the bank about her easement. Consequently, the bank is deemed to have been on notice of the landowner's easement, preventing the bank from being the "subsequent purchaser for value and without notice" required for protection under the recording statute. Since the landowner's interest precedes the bank's, the bank could win only with the protection of the recording act, so it loses.

(A) is not the best response,

because the late recording would not have prevented the landowner's rights from being subordinate to the bank's if the bank was a BFP without notice.

Recording the easement deed prior to the foreclosure action would not protect the landowner's rights. If the bank was a BFP without notice of the landowner's interest at the time the bank made the mortgage, the landowner's interest would be subordinate to the bank's recorded mortgage, and the fact that the landowner later (after the mortgage) recorded would not change this. (You can see how this would have to work this way if lenders are to be able to lend in reliance on the records—once the loan is made, the lender needs to be able to be confident that no later-filed interest can take priority over its own interest.)

(B) is not the best response,

because the mere fact that the easement provided access to a public street from the landowner's lot is not sufficient to provide inquiry notice to the bank of the existence of the easement.

The fact pattern indicates that the landowner's property abutted *another* public street, so the public street access afforded by the easement over the developer's lot *would* not by itself impose a duty on a prospective grantee to inquire further. On the other hand, the landowner's visible use of the driveway on the developer's lot would put the bank on notice of the easement, as discussed in choice D above.

(C) is not the best response,

because it ignores the operation of the recording act, and in any event misstates how the assignment of appurtenant easements works.

The easement here is, indeed, "appurtenant" rather than "in gross." (That is, it pertains to a particular benefitted parcel—here, the landowner's lot.) It's true that an easement appurtenant generally passes with the property; so if the landowner sold her lot, the easement would pass with the land, rather than being extinguished.

But here, these mechanics are irrelevant (for one thing, the landowner isn't transferring her interest in her lot). The recording act operates completely separately from the assignment of appurtenant easements. The easement is an interest in the developer's lot, and needed to be recorded if it was not to be subordinated to a BFP of the developer's lot. (In other words, it was only the bank's inquiry notice that prevented the bank from getting protection of the recording statute vis-à-vis the landowner's easement).

Answer 24

(A) is the best response,

because the investor's judgment lien on the garage came ahead of the hotelier's equity.

When the investor filed his judgment for the amount owed on the hotel, that lender got a lien against the garage (as well as against the hotel) for the full amount owed on the garage. So at that moment, the investor was in the position of a second mortgagee on the garage, behind the bank.

Then, when the investor purchased the hotel for \$100,000 less than the mortgage balance, the investor obtained a deficiency judgment for that \$100,000 amount. This became the amount covered by the earlier-filed judgment lien, and was secured by a second position on the garage. (It's irrelevant that the hotel was bought by the investor: The same result, a \$100,000 second-position lien for the investor on the garage, would have come into existence regardless of who bought the hotel at foreclosure, if the price paid was $100,000 less than the balance due.)

When the investor paid $200,000 more than the outstanding mortgage balance for the garage, this $200,000 amount was "excess" and was required to be handled the same way as if the bank had had no mortgage and the total purchase price was $200,000. That is, the investor's lien now moved to first position, and was entitled to be paid in full before anything went to the equity owner (the hotelier). So the investor got the first $100,000 of the excess. The balance, $100,000, went to the equity owner (the hotelier).

(B), (C), and (D), are not the best response,

because they involve computations that are inconsistent with this analysis. (In particular, you should have been able to immediately eliminate choices B and C, since these involved payments to the bank. Like any mortgagee, the bank was not entitled to any money brought in by a foreclosure that was in excess of the money then owed to it on the mortgage.)

Answer 25

(C) is the best response,

because the tenant's actions made the oral contract enforceable.

The Statute of Frauds requires that a promise to transfer or buy any interest in land be in writing. However, even if an oral contract for the transfer of an interest in land is not enforceable at the time it is made due to the lack of a writing, *subsequent acts* by the parties may render it enforceable. Under the "part performance" exception to the Statute of Frauds, a party who takes action in reliance on the oral agreement will be permitted to gain enforcement of it, provided that the acts taken in part performance are "unequivocally referable" to the alleged oral agreement, i.e., are not adequately explained by some other facet of the parties' relationship.

Here, if all that had happened was that after the oral agreement, the tenant had kept making approximately the same monthly payment to the landlord that she had always made, the tenant would have been out of luck—the court would likely have ruled that these payments could simply have been continued rents, and were therefore not "unequivocally referable" to the purchase agreement. But here, the tenant paid the $25,000 in original cash, the taxes, the insurance premiums, and the maintenance costs—all things that she hadn't paid before the oral agreement. So a court would be convinced that these "extra" payments were unequivocally referable to the alleged oral agreement, since they could not be explained by the prior landlord-tenant arrangement.

(A) is not the best response,

because the tenant's actions made the oral promise, which violated the Statute of Frauds, enforceable.

The part performance doctrine, where applicable, furnishes an exception to the Statute of Frauds. See the analysis of choice C above for an explanation of how and why the doctrine applies here.

(B) is not the best response,

because the tenant had an enforceable contract to buy the property.

If the court had ruled that the oral agreement didn't qualify for the part performance doctrine, this might have been a correct answer (since if the court didn't enforce the oral agreement, it's unlikely that the landlord would have been permitted to retain the $25,000). But as described in the analysis of choice C above, the oral agreement did qualify for the part performance doctrine, so the contract was enforceable.

(D) is not the best response,

because the answer incorrectly states the applicable law.

The Statute of Frauds generally applies to contracts for the purchase of land—there's no exception for "purchase and sale agreements between landlords and tenants in possession." Part performance may sometimes take a contract out of the Statute of Frauds, but choice D states a broad principle that's simply incorrect.

Answer 26

(A) is the best response,

because under an installment contract, marketable title need not be delivered until after the last payment.

Ordinarily, the obligation to convey a marketable title is implied. So the vendor has the obligation to convey a marketable title (among other things, a title free from encumbrances such as unsatisfied mortgages) after all installment payments have been made.

There can be circumstances in which the buyer under an installment provision has reasonable grounds for worrying about whether the vendor will be able to convey marketable title when the time comes (e.g., the vendor simply doesn't seem to have record title at all). If the buyer has such grounds for insecurity, most courts say she can demand reasonable assurances that the defect will be cured and, if the assurances are not forthcoming, can rescind or sue for breach.

But here, there are no grounds that would make a reasonable buyer insecure about whether marketable title will ultimately be forthcoming, given that the mortgage is small relative to the value of the property, that the vendor is solvent and pays the mortgage on time each month, and that 97 percent of the purchase price remains to be paid (so that the purchaser will have ample time to see whether the mortgage is continuing to be paid). Consequently, the fact that a very curable encumbrance happens to exist at the moment will not constitute a breach by the vendor.

(B) is not the best response,

because possession did not cause the purchaser to assume the risk that the vendor would end up not being able to convey marketable title.

A vendee who takes under an installment contract—and who (as is usually the case) takes possession before the installments are fully paid—does not "assume the risk" that the vendor won't be able to convey good title. If, for instance, the vendee has reasonable grounds for worrying about whether the vendor will have the ability to convey marketable title down the road, the vendee may be entitled to reasonable assurances that there won't be a problem. (See the discussion of choice A above.)

(C) is not the best response,

because although an obligation to convey marketable title is implied in the absence of an express agreement to the contrary, the vendor hasn't breached that obligation.

Unless the contract of sale otherwise expressly states, courts find an implied duty to convey a marketable title. The reference here to "a warranty deed sufficient to convey the fee simple"—although somewhat vague about just what type of deed has been promised—will not be found to constitute an express provision that marketable title is not required. So, since the promise is ambiguous, the usual presumption in favor of an obligation to convey marketable title will be applied.

The fact that this is an installment contract does not change that presumption. However, for the reasons stated in the discussion of choice A above, the vendor has not breached that obligation, making this choice wrong.

(D) is not the best response,

because risk of loss relating to possession would not be grounds on which the purchaser could recover.

It's true that any "risk of loss" assumed by the purchaser would relate only to physical events (e.g., destruction of a structure on the land). But the fact that "risk of loss" doesn't apply does not by itself mean that the purchaser can recover damages now. Indeed, for the reason given in the discussion of choice A (time to deliver marketable title hasn't yet arrived), the purchaser will lose, not win, so choice D can't be correct.

Answer 27

(C) is the best response,

because it correctly identifies that the restriction will be enforceable by any owner in the residential subdivision.

The basis for this is an implied reciprocal servitude, which is a means by which a subsequent property owner can be bound by a covenant even if it is not present in his own deed, as long as the restriction is in deeds from the same grantor to prior purchasers, typically in the same subdivision. The prior purchasers can enforce the servitudes as long as the restriction in the earlier deeds resulted from a *general plan,* under a covenant that all properties later conveyed would be burdened by the same restriction, and the prior purchasers relied on same. There must also be either actual, constructive, or implied notice of the restriction. This applies to the facts here. There is a general plan for the residential subdivision, and the restrictions in the deeds suggest that all lots in it would be so bound, and would be enforceable by any lot owner in it. Even if the restriction were not present in every deed, there would be, at the very least, implied notice, since a look at the subdivision would indicate that such a restriction exists (because it would be entirely populated by single-family homes). Since the residential subdivision satisfies the requirements of an implied reciprocal servitude, the current owners will be able to enforce the restriction. Since C recognizes this, it's the best response.

(A) is not the best response,

because the restriction here would be constitutional.

Thus, even with judicial recognition, there would not be any conflict with the Fourteenth Amendment to the Constitution. It's when the restriction is *discriminatory* that judicial recognition would be state action in conflict with the Fourteenth Amendment. In these facts, however, there is nothing to suggest that the restriction would be unenforceable; single-family restrictions are fairly common. If you chose this response, you may have been thinking of the Constitutional Law case *Moore v. City of East Cleveland* (1977), in which the Supreme Court held that related people (even if not part of the same "nuclear family") have a fundamental right to live together in a household, and that any zoning ordinance abridging that right would be subject to strict scrutiny (and thus likely be a due process violation). But a zoning regulation requiring a particular area to contain only single-family residences does *not* infringe a fundamental right, involve a suspect classification (as, for instance, a race-conscious zoning classification would), or otherwise trigger heightened scrutiny. So the classification here, based on whether the property is being used by a single family, would be subjected to the easy-to-satisfy "mere rationality" review standard employed in equal protection and substantive due process cases not involving suspect classes or fundamental rights, and would easily survive that review. Since A mistakenly states that the restriction would be unenforceable as a violation of the Fourteenth Amendment, it's not the best response.

(B) is not the best response,

because it's irrelevant.

Whether or not the single-family restriction on the residential subdivision is enforceable depends on whether there is a valid restriction on the use of that land itself; in fact, there is a valid restriction in the form of an implied reciprocal servitude. Contrary to what B states, the owner's non-restricted acreage would not bear on whether or not the restriction on the 100 acres involved here is enforceable, and thus the concept of "conflict of interest" is misapplied. As a result, B is not the best response.

(D) is not the best response,
because it does not correctly apply the law.

Enforcement of the restriction would be through a claim that the restriction was an implied reciprocal servitude. The correct remedy for breach of an implied reciprocal servitude is not damages, but an injunction to enforce the restriction. Choice D is a muddle, because either the restriction is enforceable, in which case the other landowners would be entitled to an injunction against an errant landowner—or it's unenforceable, in which case each landowner need only comply with zoning restrictions. If the restriction *were* unenforceable, then the other landowners would certainly not be entitled to damages from a landowner violating the restriction. Since D states otherwise, it's not the best response.

Answer 28

(A) is the best response,
because the easement was fixed and the investor did not have the right to move it.

There are various ways of creating an easement. One of those ways is by express grant. That is what happened here. Although the investor might argue that the grant of a "right of way" was the grant of a revocable license rather than of an easement, this argument would fail. The reference in the document to the farmer "and her heirs" would convince a court that a permanent interest in land (i.e., an easement), not a revocable personal license, was intended.

The easement by express grant did not, of course, fix the location in the document. However, when the original owner of the vacant lot acquiesced in the farmer's building of the driveway over a particular strip of his property, this acquiescence acted to fix the location of the easement as being the driveway. Once that location was definitively fixed, neither the owner of the vacant lot nor his successor had the right to compel the easement holder (whether the holder was the farmer or her daughter) to move the location, no matter how non-burdensome moving that location would have been for the easement holder.

(B) is not the best response,
because the location of the easement was fixed by grant, not prescription.

Easements can certainly be created by prescription. But that's not what happened here—rather, the easement was created by grant. Then, the original owner of the vacant lot's acquiescence in having the driveway run over particular land acted to fix the location, but this, too, happened by permission, not by prescription. So this choice explains the right result by the wrong reasoning.

(C) is not the best response,
because the farmer's daughter had the right to refuse to move the easement, regardless of the new location's reasonableness.

Once the location of the easement was fixed by the express grant in the document, together with the original owner of the vacant lot's acquiescence to the farmer's choice of location, that route became permanently associated with the easement, and became an interest in land. When an easement has been established over a particular route, the holder cannot be forced to accept a different route, no matter how "reasonable" the suggestion of a different route may be.

(D) is not the best response,
because the easement was defined by the original owner's use.

If an easement is created but not specifically located on the servient tenement, a location of sufficient size to make the intended use reasonably convenient will be implied. The owner of the servient tenement may indeed select the location of the easement so long as her selection is reasonable.

However, once the owner of the servient tenement selects the reasonable route (or acquiesces in the dominant holder's choice, as happened here), that route becomes fixed, and the dominant holder can't later be forced to allow the servient owner to change the route. So the fact that servient owner might have been permitted to select the original location of the right-of-way became irrelevant once the driveway was built and used.

Answer 29

(C) is the best response,
because the covenant of warranty requires defense only against suits that turn out to be meritorious.

The covenant of warranty includes a promise by the covenantor to defend on behalf of the covenantee any lawful or reasonable claims of title by a third party. So if the grantee had lost the suit, she could have recovered her legal costs (and the value of the property) from the grantor.

But ironically, by winning against the adjoining owner, the grantee lost her right to recover from the grantor. When she won versus the neighbor, she established that the adjoining owner's claim was without merit. At that point, the grantor had no obligation to reimburse her for defending this now-known-to-be-valueless claim.

(A) is not the best response,

because although in a sense the grantor's title was challenged, the challenge was without merit.

As discussed in the analysis of choice C above, the grantor was obliged to defend (or cover the costs of defending) only against meritorious challenges to his vendee's title. Because the grantee won against the adjoining owner, this condition was not met. So even though the quality of title that the grantor conveyed to the grantee was being challenged, he had no obligation to defend.

(B) is not the best response,

because the covenant of warranty required the grantor to defend against only meritorious claims.

As described in the discussion of choice C above, the grantor only had an obligation to defend against a meritorious claim. Since the grantee defeated the adjoining owner's claim, that claim is now known not to be meritorious, so the fact that the grantor made a covenant of warranty was irrelevant.

(D) is not the best response,

because the adjoining owner has to sue the holder of title, which at the time was the grantee.

The court should decide for the grantor, but not for the reason given. The adjoining owner cannot elect to sue the grantor. The grantee presently claims to have title to the parcel, so she, not the grantor, is the proper target for the neighbor's suit. In any event, even if the adjoining owner had had a right of election, this would make no difference—the grantor is only obligated to defend meritorious suits against his covenantee, and this suit is now known not to be meritorious. (See the analysis of choice C above).

Answer 30

(D) is the best response,

because it identifies the issue upon which the dispute will be decided.

Note that D does not *resolve* this issue, but states, instead, that the outcome of the case will *turn on how the issue is resolved.* Thus, all you needed to do to answer this question correctly was to identify the central issue. This problem is one in which it's vitally important to chart the facts, to keep track of exactly how each transaction relates to the others.

The "chain of title" refers to the string of recorded instruments reflecting prior ownership and encumbrances of a piece of property. Thus, every grantor should appear as a grantee in the land records to reflect when he received the property, and then as a grantor when he conveys it away. Furthermore, any encumbrance must at least be recited in an instrument in the chain of title in order to bind subsequent grantees. If an interest does not appear in this chain, then it will not be considered recorded and will not give constructive notice to any subsequent purchasers or encumbrancers. Under these facts, the earlier buyer's title would not be considered within the later buyer's chain of title. If the later buyer checked the grantor-grantee index for the jurisdiction, he'd find the seller as a grantee from the landowner, and thus the chain of title wouldn't indicate any gaps or contain any indication that something was amiss. Since the later buyer wouldn't have any indication that there was a problem with title, and since he's a subsequent bona fide purchaser, he'd prevail. Note that this would not be terribly unfair, since if the earlier buyer had checked land records when the seller conveyed to *him*, he'd realize that the seller did not appear in the grantee index in any former instrument. As such, the seller would be an "interloper" and a deed from him would *not* be considered within the chain of title from the landowner to the later buyer. (This problem has an added wrinkle in that title would inure automatically to the earlier buyer when the landowner conveyed to the seller, under the doctrine of "estoppel by deed.") Although it is reasonably clear how this case would be resolved, D is the best answer because it identifies the central issue.

(A) is not the best response,

because the factor it cites is not determinative of who will prevail.

The earlier buyer's deed is senior to the later buyer's because title passed to him first, under the doctrine of estoppel by deed (also known as the "after-acquired title doctrine"). The doctrine of estoppel by deed is applicable where the grantor intends to convey an estate larger than he in fact has, and he later acquires the estate he purportedly conveyed. Under "estoppel by deed," the title inures automatically to the grantee. Here, the seller claimed to own the lot in fee simple when he didn't; once he did, the title would inure automatically to the earlier buyer, the seller's grantee. Here, the earlier buyer obtained title to the lot when the landowner conveyed it to the seller, and recorded it *before* the later buyer recorded his interest.

However, this will not determine if the earlier buyer is entitled to judgment in his favor, because if the later buyer is not bound by the earlier conveyance, then he will prevail. The later buyer will only be bound by the earlier buyer's title if it is deemed recorded in the later buyer's "chain of title." Thus, the mere superiority of the earlier buyer's title will not be determinative, making A not the best response.

(B) is not the best response,

because it cites as a conclusion a fact that is in issue.

If the later buyer did, in fact, pay value without notice of the earlier buyer's claim, he would prevail. However, what's at issue here is whether he actually had notice of the earlier buyer's claim, since it's not clear whether the earlier buyer's deed was recorded in the later buyer's "chain of title." If it *was*, then the earlier buyer will prevail, since the later buyer would have had notice of the earlier buyer's claim; if it *wasn't,* the later buyer will prevail, as a subsequent bona fide purchaser (for value without knowledge of prior conveyances). Since B states this as a conclusion, it's not the best response.

(C) is not the best response,

because the issue it focuses on is not determinative of the result here.

Furthermore, it cites as an issue a fact that is settled at common law, viz., the doctrine of estoppel by deed. The doctrine of estoppel by deed is applicable where the grantor intends to convey an estate larger than he in fact has, and he later acquires the estate he purportedly conveyed. Under "estoppel by deed," the title inures automatically to the grantee. Here, the seller claimed to own the lot in fee simple when he didn't; once he did, the title would inure automatically to the earlier buyer, the seller's grantee. Here, the earlier buyer obtained title to the lot when the landowner conveyed it to the seller, and recorded it *before* the later buyer recorded his interest. Thus, the issue is not whether the doctrine of estoppel by deed applies, but whether the later buyer is bound by the earlier buyer's title. Since C does not address this issue, it's not the best response.

Answer 31

(C) is the best response,

because the tenant's occupancy, as a tenant of the landlord's son, satisfied all the requirements of adverse possession.

Title to real property may be acquired by adverse possession. If all the requirements are fulfilled, at the end of the statutory period title to the property passes from the owner to the possessor, who claims title. The possession must typically meet the following requirements: It must be (1) open, notorious, and visible; (2) hostile; and (3) continuous for the statutory period.

In this case, the owner retained a right of reversion, effective upon the landlord's demise. The landlord died 11 years ago, at which point the owner's reversion became possessory. So at that point, the landlord's son's continued constructive possession of the property (through his tenant) became adverse to the owner's ownership. This started the ten-year statutory period running against the owner.

It's true that the landlord's son did not himself physically occupy the property. But he rented it out to the tenant, by letting the tenant physically occupy it and by collecting rent. So the landlord's son would be deemed to have constructively possessed the property "openly, notoriously and visibly." That is, one in the owner's position who inspected the property would have been able to determine immediately that the tenant was occupying it under a purported grant from the landlord's son, so the owner would have been on notice that the landlord's son was treating the property as if he owned it. Since the landlord's son's possession (through the tenant) was hostile (without the owner's consent), and continuous for more than ten years, the landlord's son gained title by adverse possession.

(A) is not the best response,

because, although the owner had a reversion that became possessory when the landlord died, the owner then lost the property through adverse possession.

Under the analysis discussed in choice C above, the landlord's son gained title from the owner by adverse possession. Therefore, the fact that the owner held a reversion that became possessory when the landlord died is irrelevant.

(B) is not the best response,

because the landlord conveyed an interest less than her life tenancy, so the conveyance was not adverse or hostile to the owner.

A life tenant has a right to convey his interest, such as by a lease. What the life tenant cannot do is convey any estate greater than the life estate he holds.

Since the landlord was entitled to convey the leasehold interest, her doing so was not "adverse" to the owner's reversion. Consequently, that lease is not what started the landlord's son's statutory period of adverse possession running. (Instead, it was the landlord' death, and the landlord's son's collection of rents, that began the period of adverse possession, as discussed in choice C above).

(D) is not the best response,

because the tenant had a leasehold interest, which was not adverse to the landlord's son, while the landlord's son gained title to the house.

It's true that once the landlord died, her estate (or her son, as her heir) no longer had any interest to convey, so the landlord's son's leasehold interest, strictly speaking, ended at the landlord's death. However, the fact that the tenant paid rent to the landlord's son pursuant to what the tenant apparently thought was his leasehold obligation means that the tenant's possession was not "hostile" to the landlord's son. Therefore, the tenant never even began the type of possession required by the statute.

Answer 32

(D) is the best response,

because when the sister bought the tax debt, she will be deemed to have acted on the grandson's behalf.

First, note that the sister and the grandson were tenants in common. (Because the brother and the sister were tenants in common, not joint tenants, the brother's interest passed to his grandson when he died.)

Tenants in common (like joint tenants) owe each other a fiduciary duty of fair dealing and good faith. One aspect of that duty is that when one co-tenant buys an outstanding interest, she holds that interest on behalf of the other co-tenant(s).

So here, when the sister bought the tax deed, she was deemed to have bought on behalf of the grandson as well as herself. Thus the grandson received, in effect, an option to contribute (after the fact) to the tax sale, and the sister got a lien to make sure that if the grandson didn't exercise that option, the sister would own the property free and clear. So now, the grandson can choose either to pay his one-half share of the amount the sister paid at the tax sale (at which point the sister and the grandson would each own one-half of the tax debt and would in effect retire it), or to forfeit his undivided one-half interest. (The grandson is not personally liable for the one-half—the only sanction against him if he doesn't pay is to lose his one-half interest in the property.)

(A) is not the best response,

because there is no right of survivorship with a tenancy in common.

The facts tell us that the brother and the sister held as tenants in common (not joint tenants). There is no right of survivorship under a tenancy in common. Therefore, when the brother died intestate, his undivided one-half interest passed by the statutes of descent and his grandson became a tenant in common with his sister. Consequently, the sister's surviving her brother did not make her sole owner.

(B) is not the best response,

because neither failure to operate the property successfully nor failure to pay taxes ended the grandson's rights as a tenant in common.

Generally, each co-tenant has the right to occupy the entire premises (subject to the other's right to do the same), without accounting to any absent co-tenant(s) for profits made from that occupancy. Nor does the fact that the tenant who is in possession pays more than his share of the taxes or maintenance constitute any kind of an "obligation" or "undertaking" to the other(s) that he will continue to do so, in the absence of an express contract between the two. So there were no "obligations undertaken" by the brother, and no "default" by the grandson.

(C) is not the best response,

because under the duty of fair dealing, the sister's right to purchase is shared by the grandson.

When one co-tenant buys an outstanding interest in the property, the purchaser in a sense buys on behalf of all other co-tenants (see the discussion of choice D above). What the sister bought here was not the whole property, but the government's tax lien on the property. At that point, the sister succeeded to the government's lien position. The grandson had a right to "redeem" his interest in the property from that lien, by paying his share of the tax debt represented by that lien. The grandson was not required to pay the value of his interest in the entire property, because the sister did not own the whole property outright. (In other words, what the grandson had the right to do was analogous to her right to pay off his share of an outstanding mortgage.)

Answer 33

(C) is the best response,

because either co-tenant had the right to demand partition and an accounting.

Either co-tenant has the right, at any time, to demand partition. (Courts will try to physically divide the property where this is feasible; if not, they will order the property sold and the proceeds divided. But in either event, the proceeding is referred to as "partition.")

During the course of partition, the court will order an accounting, to determine whether either party owes the other money for rents collected, taxes paid, etc. It is not clear what substantive rules will govern that analysis—for instance, jurisdictions differ on whether a co-tenant who occupies the premises himself must account for the imputed value of rent received beyond his pro rata share. But the one thing that we can be sure of is that the court will require an accounting, and that's what this choice specifies.

(A) is not the best response,

because the man never occupied the lot in a "hostile" manner.

If the man had occupied the property "hostilely" as against his aunt, he might indeed have obtained title by adverse possession five years before the aunt died. But it's quite clear that the aunt acquiesced in the man's keeping the rent and occupying the house, so his possession was not "hostile" and therefore never started the adverse possession clock running. (Nor did he hostilely possess vis-à-vis the woman, since he never denied her the right to co-occupy the premises.) So the man did not take by adverse possession.

(B) is not the best response,

because the court would grant partition.

As explained in the discussion of choice C above, either co-tenant has the right, at any time, to demand partition. To the extent that this choice indicates that the court would deny partition, it's wrong (though it's correct about requiring an accounting).

(D) is not the best response,

because a court would conduct an accounting to determine if either party has an obligation to pay money to the other.

It's not clear exactly what substantive rules would apply to such questions as whether the man has a duty to pay the woman one-half of the rents he collected from outsiders (probably he does), or whether he has the duty to pay one-half of the imputed value of his own occupancy (probably he doesn't). But the one thing that is certain is that the woman would have the right to have these matters examined in an accounting procedure.

Answer 34

(D) is the best response,

because it correctly identifies that the zoning violation will render the title unmarketable.

Marketable title is title that, viewed objectively, is free from reasonable doubt in both law and fact, and that the reasonable buyer would accept without fear of litigation. Here, the zoning violation would give the purchaser a reasonable fear of litigation, since he could be compelled to make the property comply with the zoning regulation. While there is a possibility he could be granted a variance and thus avoid the restrictions of the setback ordinance, there's no guarantee this would happen, and even if it did, it would still mean that the original title conveyed was not marketable. The seller's supplying marketable title is a condition to the purchaser's performance; without it, the purchaser is excused from performing under the contract. Since D correctly identifies that the setback violation renders the title unmarketable, it's the best response.

(A) is not the best response,

because it misstates the law.

A frivolous lawsuit is one that lacks the purpose of actually determining a controversy. Under these facts, a claim against the purchaser concerning the setback would certainly not be frivolous, since the setback rule has been violated. As a result, the purchaser could be forced to move the house or tear down the offending portion. Since choice A incorrectly states that any suit against the purchaser concerning the setback would be frivolous, it's not the best response.

(B) is not the best response,

because *any* setback violation is sufficient to consider the title unmarketable.

Marketable title is title that, viewed objectively, is free from reasonable doubt in both law and fact, and that the reasonable buyer would accept without fear of litigation. The doctrine *de minimis no curat lex* means that, literally, "the law is not concerned with trifles." While this doctrine generally means that substantial performance is enough for contracts, it does not apply to zoning regulations, which require *strict compliance*. A violation, no matter how small, is actionable. As a result, title to the property would not be "marketable." Since choice B incorrectly states that the violation is not actionable, it's not the best response.

(C) is not the best response,

because it doesn't identify the central reason title here is not "marketable."

Marketable title is title that, viewed objectively, is free from reasonable doubt in both law and fact, and that the reasonable buyer would accept without fear of litigation. While it's true that any variation from a contract amounts to a breach of contract, this in and of itself doesn't address whether the seller will be entitled to specific performance of the contract. The purchaser could only be compelled to perform if the breach was minor, and substantial performance was sufficient to require return performance, and no remedy at law would be adequate. However, the rule with zoning violations is that they require *strict*, not substantial, performance. *Any* violation could subject the purchaser to litigation, which would make the title unmarketable. Since the seller's providing marketable title was a condition to the purchaser's performance, the purchaser will not be forced to perform, as C recognizes. However, it's not due to a breach of contract *alone*, but the fact that the breach *here* relieves the purchaser of his duty to perform. Thus, C is not the best response.

Answer 35

(A) is the best response,

because the contractor is strictly liable if the businessman's building did not contribute to the subsidence, but not liable without negligence if the businessman's building did contribute.

One of the rights incident to land is the right to "lateral support." That is, every landowner is entitled to have his land receive the necessary physical support from adjacent and underlying soil. The right to lateral support is absolute—that is, once support has been withdrawn and injury occurs, the responsible person is liable even if he used utmost care. However, the absolute right to later support exists *only with respect to land in its natural state*. If owner *A* has constructed a building, and the soil under the building subsides in part due to the acts of adjacent owner *B*, but also in part because of the weight of *A*'s building itself, *B* is not liable without negligence. Therefore, this choice accurately states the rule.

(B) is not the best response,

because the businessman's right to lateral support is not gained by adverse possession but is a right incident to his ownership of his own land.

Subject to zoning limits, a landowner is permitted to build right up to the property line. (This happens routinely in large cities.) Therefore, the fact that the businessman put up his building right up against his lot line did not cause him to gain anything by adverse possession. The right to lateral support that he had was an incident of his original ownership of his lot.

(C) is not the best response,

because the businessman has no duty to protect the improvements on his lot against subsidence that would have occurred even had there been no building on that lot.

If the subsidence would not have occurred had there been no building on the businessman's lot, then (C) would essentially be correct—that is, the businessman would lose because in the absence of negligence by the contractor, the risk of damage to the businessman's land would have been borne by him, and it would have been up to him to assure that his building was buttressed in such a way that an excavation on the contractor's lot wouldn't damage his own building.

But this choice also implies that the risk would be borne by the businessman even if the excavation would have caused a cave-in on his lot had there been no building there. And this is not the law—as explained in the analysis of choice A above—a landowner's right to lateral support means that the excavator next door, not the landowner, bears the risk of a cave-in of the landowner's unoccupied land.

(D) is not the best response,

because following the law would not be an excuse or a defense for the contractor.

A's right of lateral support is violated when an adjoining owner, *B*, causes a cave-in that would have occurred even on an unoccupied lot; and that statement is true even if *B* has not only acted non-negligently but also followed all applicable laws.

Answer 36

(D) is the best response,

because by the time the creditor purported to get his lien, the buyer, not the corporation, was the owner of the parcel.

The statute here says that the creditor could get a lien on property "then owned" (or after-acquired) by his judgment debtor. So if the parcel can be viewed as still having been owned by the corporation on the day the creditor filed, the creditor might well win as against the buyer (because the prior unrecorded conveyance would not be good against the creditor's lien, assuming that the creditor was viewed as a "purchaser for value," which he might well be). But the problem for the creditor is that a court would probably conclude that when the creditor filed, the property was not "then owned" by the corporation. That's because this type of statute is generally interpreted to exclude any property that has been properly conveyed by the judgment debtor, even if the conveyance has not been recorded.

Since the creditor's lien isn't valid against the property because it was no longer the corporation's property at the moment of filing, the lien was ineffective, and the buyer has good title.

(A) is not the best response,

because the creditor's judgment did not affect the buyer's title.

It's only the filing of a judgment lien, not the obtaining of a judgment, that causes an encumbrance on the judgment debtor's real estate. So the fact that the creditor got his judgment before the buyer recorded is irrelevant.

(B) is not the best response,

because any suit by the creditor would definitely fail, so that the threat of meritless litigation would not be enough to cloud the buyer's title.

The obligation to convey marketable title does not mean an obligation to convey "perfect title," or title that could not possibly be attacked by anyone. So long as it is quite clear (not merely "barely probable") that the vendor would be found in litigation to have valid unencumbered title, the title is not unmarketable.

For the reasons described in the analysis of choice D above, the buyer would clearly win as against the creditor if the creditor sued. So the mere fact that the creditor might file suit based on his filed judgment would not be enough to render the buyer's title unmarketable.

(C) is not the best response,

because it wasn't the fact that the buyer won the race to record that caused her to prevail.

As explained in the discussion of choice D above, as soon as the unrecorded conveyance to the buyer occurred, the corporation no longer owned the property, and any filing by the creditor of his judgment that occurred after that would have had no effect. So this choice explains the correct outcome by incorrect reasoning—even if the buyer had not recorded until after the creditor filed, the buyer would still have won because the creditor's filing was of no effect.

Answer 37

(A) is the best response,

because the rancher owns the lot.

This is a question where the facts are so complex that it's necessary to chart them in order to be able to arrive at the correct response. Here's basically what happens:

1990: The rancher moves in, builds dam. Adverse possession begins.

2000: Title vests in the rancher by adverse possession.

2002: Rancher gives possession of land to buyer; rancher also purports to convey to the buyer, with ineffective deed. Result: The rancher has title to land; the buyer has cattle.

2003: The buyer leases the lot from the landowner for five years. No lease. The rancher still has title; the buyer is not in adverse possession, because his use isn't adverse as against the rancher, the owner of the lot.

2007: Lease ends—the rancher still has title.

2010: The buyer leaves—the rancher has title. The landowner conveys via quitclaim to the farmer. The farmer gets the landowner's interest, which is nothing. The rancher still has title.

As this chart indicates, the rancher's title in the lot matured after his ten years of adverse possession, in 2000. Thereafter, the buyer's use was permissive, and, beyond that, he didn't occupy the lot long enough to obtain title via adverse possession. When the landowner leased the lot to the buyer in 2003, the landowner went into adverse possession of the lot by treating it as his, but, since the lease lasted only five years, the landowner did not get title to the lot. The buyer's five-year lease would not be tacked on to the buyer's possession, since he possessed the lot for that five-year period under a lease, not a claim of ownership. The three years after the lease were adverse to the rancher's ownership, but a non-permissive period cannot be tacked onto a permissive period for purposes of adverse possession. Thereafter, the landowner's conveyance to the farmer is irrelevant, since the landowner had no interest to convey. Under these facts, once the rancher gained title to the lot, he never surrendered it. Since A correctly identifies the rancher as the owner of the lot, it's the best response.

(B) is not the best response,

because it states an incorrect result.

Under these facts, the last time that the landowner had title was before the rancher's title matured, in 2000. The rancher moved into adverse possession of the lot in 1990, because his use of the lot was open, notorious, continuous, hostile to the landowner's interest, and exclusive. Once the rancher's title matured in 2000, the landowner no longer owned the lot. Granting a lease to the buyer in 2002 would be considered an adverse use of the lot, but the adverse use ended in 2007 for the landowner, when the lease ended, so the use would not satisfy the statutory period of ten years. Even if the landowner had owned the lot after that, his quitclaiming his interest to the farmer would end the landowner's ownership. Since B states that the owner is still owner of the lot, it's not the best response.

(C) is not the best response,

because it states an incorrect result.

Basically, the buyer's use of the lot was only adverse for the three-year period after his lease from the landowner ran out. For the five years of the buyer's ostensible lease from the landowner, it was the landowner whose use was adverse, not the buyer—and, in any case, the use was not long enough to establish title via adverse possession. The rancher had title via adverse possession, and the buyer's use was *permissive*, not adverse; thus title could not mature in the buyer for that period. Since the buyer could not be the owner of the lot, C is not the best response.

(D) is not the best response,

because the farmer is clearly not the owner of the lot.

In order for the farmer to own the lot, he'd have to have received an interest from the landowner. The landowner didn't own the lot, because his title ended when the rancher gained title by adverse possession in 2000. The landowner's leasing the property to the buyer for five years in the 2000s was the type of possession that could be adverse (since it was open, notorious, continuous, exclusive, and hostile), but it did not continue long enough for title to mature in the landowner. Thus, since the landowner did not own the lot, the farmer could not own it either, making D not the best response.

Answer 38

(C) is the best response,

because it is too late for the colleague to challenge the marketability of title.

The warranty of marketable title was likely breached in this situation because the lot lacked access to a public right-of-way. However, the time for a buyer to raise an objection based on failure to convey marketable title is before accepting the deed. In this fact pattern, the colleague did not challenge the conveyance until after the deed was delivered. At this stage, any challenge by the buyer must be based on the title covenant contained in the deed. Since the niece had title to the land she conveyed and there are no encumbrances on the land, the title covenants (which include superiority of title, seisin, right to convey, quiet enjoyment, and the general warranty) have not been breached. Because access to a public right-of-way is not required under any of the title covenants, the colleague has no claim against the niece that can be raised at this point.

(A) is not the best response,

because the colleague cannot raise the issue of lack of access to a public right-of-way after accepting the deed.

While lack of access to a public right-of-way may constitute a breach of the obligation to deliver marketable title, a buyer must raise this issue prior to accepting delivery of the deed. Since the colleague has already accepted the deed, any challenge at this point in time must be based on a breach of one of the title covenants. Since, as discussed in the explanation of choice C above, none of the title covenants has been breached, the colleague has no claim that can be raised at this stage.

(B) is not the best response,

because the covenants have been breached.

The covenants of warranty and quiet enjoyment warrant that the grantor will defend title against other claimants and that the grantor is conveying title that is superior to any other claimant. Since there is no indication that there is any other possible claimant with a superior claim to the niece's, these covenants have been satisfied. The only claim that the colleague has against the niece is that the title may be unmarketable. However, that would be a breach of the obligation to deliver marketable title, which may only be raised prior to acceptance of the deed.

(D) is not the best response,

because the Statute of Frauds may only be raised as a defense if some portion of the contract has yet to be performed.

The Statute of Frauds requires that, in order to be enforceable, a contract for the sale of land must be in writing. However, the colleague is not attempting to avoid the contract, nor could the colleague raise that issue at this point, since both parties have fully performed their duties under the contract of sale. Since no performance is due by either party, the Statute of Frauds cannot be used to rescind the sale. The only claim that the colleague has against the niece is that the title may be unmarketable. However, that would be a breach of the obligation to deliver marketable title, which may only be raised prior to acceptance of the deed.

Answer 39

(D) is the best response,

because none of the items was a fixture.

A tenant may not remove "fixtures" at the end of the lease term. A fixture is a chattel attached to real property so that it ceases being personal property and becomes part of the real property. So the question is which, if any, of the items here is a fixture. The following factors, if present, argue in favor of a finding that the item is a chattel: (1) it is firmly embedded in the real estate; (2) it is peculiarly adapted or fitted to the real estate; (3) removal would destroy the chattel or significantly damage the real estate; and (4) the person who did the annexing (in this case, the tenant) had a substantial and permanent interest in the real estate (with a tenancy of years being the shortest, and a fee simple being the longest).

Here, all of these factors point to none of the chattels being fixtures: (1) none of the items is really "firmly embedded" in the real estate; (2) all were designed and manufactured without reference to the building's particular dimensions and characteristics, so none can be said to be "peculiarly adapted or fitted" to the real estate; (3) removal would be relatively easy and non-damaging in all cases; and (4) the affixer's (the tenant's) interest at the time of affixation was very short and impermanent (a five-year lease). Furthermore, the lease seems to contemplate that all such items can be removed. (Though it's not absolutely certain that these are the items the "may remove" clause was talking about.)

(A), (B), and (C) are not the best responses,

for the same reasons that D is the best choice.

Answer 40

(A) is the best response,

because the liquidated damages clause was not a measure of either the landowner's anticipated or actual losses, and was therefore an unenforceable penalty.

Liquidated damages are agreed to by both parties at the time of the contract. Such liquidated damages clauses, where enforced by the court, determine the measure of damages that the court will award. In order for such a clause to be enforceable, however, it must meet this requirement: The amount fixed must be reasonable relative to either the *anticipated* loss (viewed as of the time the contract was signed) or to the *actual* loss (as determined by the passage of time).

The clause here does not meet this standard. It was not a reasonable forecast viewed as of the time the contract was made, because a loss of $50,000 in value during the contract-closing gap is highly unlikely given that the market value at the outset was $100,000 (i.e., a 50 percent loss of value during a relatively short—two- or three-month—period).

Nor was the amount set in the clause reasonable compared with the actual damages, since we're told that the value of the property had actually increased between the signing and the time for closing. So the clause was not reasonable relative to either the anticipated or actual loss, making it an unenforceable penalty.

(B) is not the best response,

because the purchaser's death does not discharge the contract.

If a contract does not call for significant personal services by a party, that party's death or incapacity generally does not terminate or discharge the contract. The reason is that the dead person's duties can be delegated to some other person and the contract continued.

So here, the purchaser's death did not cause the contract to terminate, since the purchaser's estate could continue to perform its duties under the contract.

(C) is not the best response,

because the court would not enforce an unenforceable term of a contract.

As described in the discussion of choice A above, the liquidated damages clause was an unenforceable penalty. Therefore, the court will not (and should not) enforce it, even though it was the express agreement of the parties. In other words, there are some types of agreements that parties are simply not permitted to make, and a penalty masquerading as a liquidated damages clause is one of those types.

(D) is not the best response,

because, although the doctrine of equitable conversion would indeed prevent the contract from terminating, that doctrine wouldn't make the liquidated damages clause enforceable.

The doctrine of equitable conversion applies to situations that arise during the gap between the signing of the contract and the delivery of the deed. If the purchaser dies while the contract is still executory, the equitable conversion doctrine applies so that (1) the person entitled to receive the decedent's estate is entitled to the land, and (2) the recipients of the personal property not only do not receive the land, but must pay any remaining portion of the purchase price out of their shares of the estate.

So here, the administrator was required to pay the purchase price, so that whoever was entitled to the purchaser's real estate could and would receive the property.

However, this fact did not entitle the landowner to keep the deposit, because (as described in the discussion of choice A above) the liquidated damages clause was an unenforceable penalty. The landowner's remedy was to keep only that portion of the deposit that reflected any damage to him from the breach. Since the property increased in value, there was no damage (except perhaps incidental expenses like having to re-advertise the property). Therefore, the landowner would have to return all or nearly all the deposit.

Answer 41

(D) is the best response,

because it identifies a theory under which the man may be able to repurchase his property.

Some jurisdictions have a statutory right of redemption, which allows an individual to repurchase property sold at a foreclosure sale for a limited amount of time after the sale. This right is not available in all jurisdictions, but it is the only theory among the choices that conceivably would allow the man to recover his property.

(A) is not the best response,

because, absent a specific statute, there is no general right to repurchase one's home after a foreclosure sale.

The only situation in which a landowner can recover property after a foreclosure sale is if the sale took place in a jurisdiction in which there is a statutory right of redemption. Where such statutes exist, they allow the original owner of a property to repurchase the property from the buyer at the sale for a limited time. In jurisdictions that have a statutory right of redemption, the right is not necessarily limited to the owner's residence. However, even if such a limitation were to exist, choice D is still a better response to the question posed because it correctly identifies the basis upon which the man will be able to repurchase his residence after the foreclosure sale.

(B) is not the best response,

because an equitable right of redemption can only be exercised prior to the foreclosure sale.

The equitable right of redemption allows a landowner to prevent a foreclosure sale by paying the amount due on the mortgage. However, the landowner can only exercise this right after foreclosure, but before the foreclosure sale. Since we are told that the foreclosure sale has already occurred, the man will no longer have the option of exercising his right to equitable redemption.

(C) is not the best response,

because the man is alive.

The doctrine of exoneration applies to the situation in which a testator, in his will, has bequeathed land that is subject to a mortgage at the time of his death. The doctrine dictates that the mortgage debt will be paid by the estate, coming from the assets in the residuary estate. However, this doctrine is inapplicable here since the man has not died.

Answer 42

(D) is the best response,

because the husband was obligated to pay all current charges up to the rental value of the land.

Assuming that the document creating the life estate (here, the will) does not say otherwise, a life tenant has the obligation to *pay all current charges*, including property taxes, mortgage interest, and the cost of maintenance. Restatement (First) Property, § 129. This is a personal liability, entitling the holder of the future interest to a damages award. However, the life tenant's obligation to pay current expenses is limited to the income produced by (or that could reasonably have been produced by) the land, such as rents that could have been obtained. *Id.* at § 130. But here, since we are told that "the fair rental value was substantial," we can assume that that rental value was greater than the tax bills; therefore, the limit on the husband's liability to the niece does not come into play. Thus the husband owes the niece reimbursement for the full two years' worth of property taxes, since he was obligated to pay those taxes in the first place.

(A) is not the best response,

because remaindermen have no responsibility for the payment of current charges.

As is more fully described in the answer to choice D, the life tenant, not the remainderman, is responsible for the payment of current charges, including property taxes, up to the level of the income that can be generated from the property. So the statement in choice A is flatly wrong as a matter of law.

(B) is not the best response,

because the assessor's choice of whom to bill is irrelevant on the issue of who is obligated to pay.

Assuming that the instrument creating the life estate (here, the will) is silent on the matter, the issue of which party is required to pay current expenses is to be determined by general legal principles, not by the assessor's choice of whom to bill. Those general principles state that the holder of the life estate has the obligation to pay current charges, at least up to the level of the income that can be generated from the property.

(C) is not the best response,

because when the will was silent on this issue, the holder of the current interest was required to pay all current charges.

This choice is correct in recognizing that if the woman's will had specified which party was to pay the taxes, that provision would be given effect. But where the document creating the present and future interests is silent, it is not the case that the remainderman (the niece) must pay the property taxes. Rather, the rule is exactly the opposite: The holder of the present interest (the husband) is obligated to pay the property taxes and other current charges, at least up to the level of income that could be generated by the property.

Answer 43

(B) is the best response,

because the two surviving grandchildren were covered by the class gift, and the deceased grandchild was not survived by any issue.

The testator made a "class gift" of his house, with the class defined as his "grandchildren." Any grandchild who was alive when the gift took effect (i.e., when the testator died) is obviously covered by the class gift. So the two surviving grandchildren are certainly members of the class. What is the effect of the statute that is quoted? This is an "anti-lapse" statute. The deceased grandchild qualified for protection under the statute, since the grandchild was "a lineal descendant of a grandparent of the testator." So if that grandchild had had "issue" at the time of the testator's death, under the anti-lapse statute the issue would have taken the grandchild's share. But "issue" means "direct descendants," such as children or grandchildren. The deceased grandchild's mother, though she is his "heir" under the intestacy statute, does not qualify as his "issue" because she is not his direct descendant. Therefore, she does not take any share in the house.

What about children who might be born to the testator's daughter after the testator's death? These would be grandchildren of the testator, so it might be argued that once they are born, the class of "grandchildren" should open up to include them. But that is not the way such class gifts are interpreted—the class is deemed to close at the moment the gift takes effect. *See, e.g.,* Amer. Law of Prop., § 22.42: "If a gift of either real or personal property is made by deed or will 'to the children of A,' and A is alive when the instrument takes effect, all children of A born thereafter are excluded."

Thus, the two surviving grandchildren are the only takers.

(A) is not the best response,

because the house never became part of the residue.

If the testator had died without any living grandchildren, and there were no lineal descendants of grandchildren alive either, then the class gift to the "grandchildren" would have failed, and the house would have become part of the residue of the estate. In that event, the brother would have taken the house. But the testator was in fact survived by two grandchildren, which made the class gift effective. Therefore, the house never became part of the residue, and the brother never took any interest in it.

(C) is not the best response,

because the class that received the gift closed at the moment the testator died.

The gift to the grandchildren was a class gift. The class was capable of being increased to include any grandchild who was born between the date the will was executed and the date the testator died. But by general principles of construction, once the testator died (and the gift became effective), the class closed. For more about this, see the last full paragraph of discussion about choice B. So any grandchildren born to the testator's daughter after the testator's death will not gain any interest in the class gift, i.e., the house.

(D) is not the best response,

because the deceased grandchild's mother is not that grandchild's "issue."

The anti-lapse statute would have given a share to any "issue" of the deceased grandchild. But "issue" means "direct descendants." The grandchild's mother was not his descendant, and thus not his issue. So she is not covered by the statute. For more about this, see the first full paragraph of Choice B above.

Answer 44

(A) is the best response,

because it correctly identifies that the purchaser is the owner in fee simple absolute of the land.

You need only have picked up on one key fact to get this answer right: that the older brother was not free to devise his interest in the land, since he owned the land in joint tenancy with the younger brother, and thus the younger brother was entitled to the older brother's interest, on the older brother's death, due to the right of survivorship. The younger brother's right would take precedence over any devise the older brother ostensibly made. Once the older brother dies, the younger brother owns the land in fee simple absolute, and the devises and conveyances thereafter transfer ownership of the land, in fee simple absolute, to his friend, then to the purchaser, then to the purchaser's grantee. Since A correctly identifies that the purchaser need have no one join him in the conveyance, it's the best response.

(B) is not the best response,

because the purchaser can convey the land without joining anyone else in the conveyance.

If you chose this response, it's because you mistakenly found that the older brother could devise his interest in the land to anyone he chose. In fact, the "right of survivorship"—the hallmark of a joint tenancy as opposed to a tenancy in common—means that a co-tenant's devise of the land will be disregarded, and it will automatically go to his co-tenant.

Here, this would mean that the younger brother becomes sole tenant. When the younger brother dies, his devise is valid, since there's no co-tenant with a right of survivorship. That leaves his friend with the property in fee simple absolute. The friend is free to convey the property as he sees fit, so when he conveys it to the purchaser, the purchaser has it in fee simple absolute, and the purchaser is likewise free to dispose of it as he chooses. Since B incorrectly requires that the older brother's son, his grandson, and his grandson's only child join in the conveyance, it's not the best response.

(C) is not the best response,

because no one else needs to join in the conveyance, since the purchaser owns the land in fee simple absolute.

If you chose this response, it's because you didn't realize that the older brother was not free to devise his interest in the land, since the land was held as a joint tenancy that had a right to survivorship—meaning that the younger brother would take the older brother's interest in the land, regardless of any devise by the older brother. Thereafter, *the younger brother* can dispose of the land any way he wants, since he's the sole surviving joint tenant, meaning no one has a right to survivorship as to *the younger brother's interest*. Since C does not recognize this, it's not the best response.

(D) is not the best response,

because it misstates the law, and, beyond that, arrives at the wrong conclusion.

For one thing, the concept of merchantability is not applicable to title; it's *marketable* title that's an implied covenant of land sale contracts. Even if the correct terminology were employed here, it would still be wrong, since title by quitclaim deed means only that the vendor is conveying whatever interest in the property he, in fact, has. Since marketable title is an implied covenant of land sale contracts, if the vendor tries to pass a quitclaim deed at the closing to the vendee, the vendee can refuse to accept it. However, once the deed is passed, the vendee could not claim a breach due to failure to pass a marketable title, since the terms of the deed control under the doctrine of merger, and a quitclaim deed has no covenants associated with it whatsoever. Since D misstates the law, it cannot be the best response.

Answer 45

(B) is the best response,

because it arrives at the correct conclusion, identifies the major obstacle to the interest—the Rule Against Perpetuities—and correctly identifies that the friend's interest will overcome this obstacle.

The key fact here is that, although the friend's interest is a shifting executory interest and thus subject to the Rule Against Perpetuities, it *must* vest within a life in being plus 21 years.

The conveyance here creates a fee simple subject to an executory interest in the purchaser, and a shifting executory interest in the friend (since the friend's interest does not become possessory on the natural termination of the prior estate, and it divests another grantee, not the grantor (making it a "shifting" instead of a "springing" executory interest)). As an executory interest, the most important point about the validity of the friend's interest is whether or not it meets the Rule Against Perpetuities.

In order to do so, it must vest or fail within a life in being plus 21 years. Here, it will vest or fail within a life in being—the friend's. The friend must be alive now, and whether or not he is to take the tract will be determined within a "life in being"—the friend's—since if he's alive 30 years from now, his interest vests and he takes; if he dies, his interest will fail whenever he dies within 30 years. Since the friend's executory interest satisfies the Rule Against Perpetuities, it will be valid, making B the best response.

(A) is not the best response,

because although it arrives at the correct conclusion, it mischaracterizes the facts.

The friend's interest is not a reversion, but a shifting executory interest. A reversion is a future interest arising in the grantor when he conveys an estate of shorter duration than the estate he possesses (e.g., grantor has a fee simple; he conveys a fee tail, life estate or leasehold; grantor's interest is a reversion). Here, the friend's interest cannot be a reversion because, if nothing else, he's not the grantor. Since choice A does not recognize this, it cannot be the best response.

(C) is not the best response,

because although it arrives at the correct conclusion, it does not correctly characterize the facts.

The friend's interest is not a vested remainder subject to divestment, but rather a shifting executory interest. The easiest way to tell if an interest is a remainder or an executory interest is to determine if it takes at the natural termination of the previous interest. Here, the previous estate is the purchaser's. If the friend is to take at all, his interest will divest the purchaser of possession 30 years from now. Since the friend's possession terminates the purchaser's interest at a time other than its natural termination, the friend's interest must be an executory interest, not a remainder. (By the way, the friend's interest is a "shifting" executory interest instead of a "springing" executory interest because he divests another grantee, not the grantor, of possession.) Since C does not correctly characterize the facts, it cannot be the best response.

(D) is not the best response,

because the limitation is valid.

The friend's interest is valid because, although it is a shifting executory interest and thus subject to the Rule Against Perpetuities, it will vest or fail within a life in being plus 21 years. If you chose this response, it could be because mention of the "30 years" threw you off, and made you think that the interest violates the Rule Against Perpetuities. However, the important fact here is that the friend is the life in being, and the interest will vest or fail *in his lifetime*—if he's alive in 30 years' time, it vests, and if he dies before then, the interest fails when he dies. Since D mischaracterizes the friend's interest as invalid, it's not the best response.

Answer 46

(D) is the best response,

because the wife's obligation to pay property tax is limited to the rent she received.

Since a life tenancy is by definition to be followed by another interest, a life tenant has a number of duties vis-à-vis the future interest. One of those duties is to pay all property taxes that come due while the life tenant holds possession of the property. However, a life tenant is liable to the holder of the future interest for property taxes only to the extent of the rents received, or the fair rental value if the life tenant occupies it.

Since the property was vacant, there were no rents, and the wife consequently had no liability to the daughter for failing to pay them. And that's true even though the daughter went into her pocket to pay these taxes.

(A) and (B) are not the best response,

because a life tenant's obligation to pay taxes is limited by the amount received in rent, which in this case is $0; see the discussion of choice D above.

(C) is not the best response,

because had the wife received rental income, her possession would not have given her the right to determine whether or not the taxes should be paid.

In that event, she would have been liable for nonpayment of taxes up to the amount of rent received. In other words, this choice states the correct result, but on wrong reasoning.

Answer 47

(A) is the best response,

because it gives the reason why the class gift will be valid under the Rule Against Perpetuities.

The key fact here is that the class gift was created in a will, and thus the man cannot have more children.

Under the Rule Against Perpetuities, an interest is only valid if it must vest, if at all, no later than 21 years after one or more lives in being at the creation of the interest. "Measuring lives" are the "lives in being" for purposes of the Rule. Here, the man's children will be the measuring lives for determining the validity of the class gift. In fact, the gift here *must* vest or fail within 21 years of the deaths of the man's children, since, once the man's children die, their children can turn 21 after no more than 21 years. In fact, the key to this question is that the man created the class gift *in his will*. Thus, the class gift would not be "created" until the will took effect—that is, upon the man's death. At the man's death, all of his children must be lives in being, since he can't have more children once he's dead. (The law of future interest doesn't recognize things like sperm banks.) Thus, he couldn't have grandchildren who would turn 21 more than 21 years after the "measuring lives"—his children. If there's one rule that you remember for the Multistate concerning class gifts, it should be this: Class gifts (like the one here) that take effect when grandchildren turn 21 are valid if the gift is created in a will, *but not if the gift is created in an inter vivos conveyance*. In the case of a conveyance, the grantor could have children after the conveyance takes place, and those children could have children who would turn 21 *after* the perpetuities period, thus violating the Rule Against Perpetuities. However, since the class gift for the grandchildren was created in a will under these facts, it will be valid. Since A implies this, it's the best response.

(B) is not the best response,

because the Rule of Convenience is not applicable to these facts.

The Rule of Convenience is a rule of construction that applies to class gifts. Where there is no expression of intent that all members of a class should take, the class closes when a member of the class can call for distribution of a share of the class gift. The rule is designed to avoid delaying distribution beyond that period necessary and, at the same time, avoiding rebates in the future. Its primary significance is that, under it, no after-born members can take. However, the rule would not apply here, because the man expressly intended to include "all grandchildren whenever born." Since there is no need to construe this language, the Rule of Convenience will not apply, making B not the best response.

(C) is not the best response,

because there is no basis on which to employ this presumption.

The man could not have intended to include only those grandchildren born prior to his death, because he expressly included "all grandchildren whenever born." This could only be interpreted as including "after-born" children. Note that choice C implies that the Rule of Convenience should apply to these facts. Under the Rule of Convenience, applicable to class gifts, where there is no expression of intent that all members of a class should take, the class closes when a member of the class can call for distribution of a share of the class gift. The rule could have applied if the man had not specifically mentioned "all grandchildren whenever born." Had he merely said, "to all my grandchildren who shall reach the age of 21," children born after his death would not take (while those born before his death, but not 21 by the time he died, could not take a share until and unless they reached age 21). However, since the man was explicit about his wishes and provided for *all* his grandchildren, C cannot be the best response.

(D) is not the best response,

because the Rule Against Perpetuities is interpreted strictly: An interest *must* vest or fail within a life in being plus 21 years in order to be valid.

There isn't room for a Rule of Construction in connection with the Rule Against Perpetuities, because if an interest *may, for whatever remote reason, not vest within the perpetuities period, it's not valid*. Since D states otherwise, it's not the best response.

Answer 48

(C) is the best response,

because it correctly identifies that the owner's brother must join in the conveyance, since he holds a possibility of reverter in the tract.

The key fact here is that the executory interest in the charity is invalid because it violates the Rule Against Perpetuities—and that, as a result, the interest reverts to the owner and his heirs.

The owner tried to convey a fee simple determinable subject to an executory interest to the cousin, and a shifting executory interest to the charity. A "fee simple determinable" is a fee simple estate that automatically terminates on the occurrence of a specified event—it's a type of defeasible fee. An executory interest is an interest, in anyone but the grantor, that *can't* become possessory on the natural termination of the prior estate. (Natural termination meaning, for instance, the death of a life estate holder.) If an executory interest divests another grantee, it's a "shifting" executory interest; if it divests the grantor, it's a "springing" interest.

The problem here is that a future interest can't follow a defeasible fee, since the executory interest may never vest or fail, and thus violates the Rule Against Perpetuities (which requires that an interest vest or fail within a life in being plus 21 years). Since the executory interest must be removed, the cousin is left with a defeasible fee, and the owner and his heirs are left with a possibility of reverter. Since the owner devised all his real estate to his brother, the owner's brother will hold the possibility of reverter.

In order to convey the tract, both the cousin and the owner's brother would have to join to convey a fee simple absolute. (The daughter needn't join in the conveyance at all.) As a result, the prayer for specific performance should be denied. Since C correctly identifies the result and the reasoning behind it, it's the best response.

(A) is not the best response,

because the cousin and the daughter do not own a fee simple absolute in the tract—the owner's brother has a possibility of reverter, and the daughter does not have an interest in the tract.

The owner tried to convey a fee simple determinable subject to an executory interest to the cousin, and a shifting executory interest to the charity. A "fee simple determinable" is a fee simple estate that automatically terminates on the occurrence of a specified event—it's a type of defeasible fee. An executory interest is an interest, in anyone but the grantor, that *can't* become possessory on the natural termination of the prior estate. (Natural termination meaning, for instance, the death of a life estate holder.) If an executory interest divests another grantee, it's a "shifting" executory interest; if it divests the grantor, it's a "springing" interest.

The problem here is that a future interest can't follow a defeasible fee, since the executory interest may never vest or fail, and thus violates the Rule Against Perpetuities (which requires that an interest vest or fail within a life in being plus 21 years). Since the executory interest must be removed, the cousin is left with a defeasible fee, and the owner and his heirs are left with a possibility of reverter. Since the owner devised all his real estate to his brother, the brother will hold the possibility of reverter.

Thus, in order to convey a fee simple absolute in the tract, the cousin and the owner's brother would have to join in the conveyance, since the cousin owns the defeasible fee, and the brother has a possibility of reverter, which "add up" to the entire fee. Since the brother has not been joined in the conveyance and the daughter has, the prayer for specific performance should be denied. Since A states otherwise, it's not the best response.

(B) is not the best response,

because the cousin does not own the whole fee simple in the tract.

The cousin has only a defeasible fee, and so, to convey a fee simple absolute in the tract, the owner's brother, the holder of a possibility of reverter, would have to join in.

The owner tried to convey a fee simple determinable subject to an executory interest to the cousin, and a shifting executory interest to the charity. A "fee simple determinable" is a fee simple estate that automatically terminates on the occurrence of a specified event—it's a type of defeasible fee. An executory interest is an interest, in anyone but the grantor, that *can't* become possessory on the natural termination of the prior estate. (Natural termination meaning, for instance, the death of a life estate holder.) If an executory interest divests another grantee, it's a "shifting" executory interest; if it divests the grantor, it's a "springing" interest.

The problem here is that a future interest can't follow a defeasible fee, since the executory interest may never vest or fail, and thus violates the Rule Against Perpetuities (which requires that an interest vest or fail within a life in being plus 21 years). Since the executory interest must be removed, the cousin is left with a defeasible fee, and the owner and his heirs are left with a possibility of reverter. Since the owner devised all his real estate to his brother, the brother will hold the possibility of reverter. Thus, in order to convey a fee simple absolute in the tract, the cousin and the owner's brother would have to join in the conveyance, since the cousin owns the defeasible fee, and the brother has a possibility of reverter, which "add up" to the entire fee. Since the cousin could not convey the entire fee simple himself, B is not the best response.

(D) is not the best response,

because the charity does not have a valid interest in the tract.

The owner tried to convey a fee simple determinable subject to an executory interest to the cousin, and a shifting executory interest to the charity. A "fee simple determinable" is a fee simple estate that automatically terminates on the occurrence of a specified event—it's a type of defeasible fee. An executory interest is an interest, in anyone but the grantor, that *can't* become possessory on the natural termination of the prior estate. (Natural termination meaning, for instance, the death of a life estate holder.) If an executory interest divests another grantee, it's a "shifting" executory interest; if it divests the grantor, it's a "springing" interest.

The problem here is that a future interest can't follow a defeasible fee, since the executory interest may never vest or fail, and thus violates the Rule Against Perpetuities (which requires that an interest vest or fail within a life in being plus 21 years). Since the executory interest must be removed, the cousin is left with a defeasible fee, and the owner and his heirs are left with a possibility of reverter. Since the owner devised all his real estate to his brother, the brother will hold the possibility of reverter.

If you chose this response, it could be because you mistakenly believed the "charity-to-charity" exception to remote vesting applied to these facts. It doesn't, because for that exception to apply, *both* the cousin *and* the charity would have to be charities; it's not enough if only one of them is a charity. If the cousin had been a charity, the charity would have had a valid shifting executory interest in the tract.

As it is, the cousin and the owner's brother would have to join in a conveyance of the tract. Since D states that the charity would have to join in the conveyance, and not the owner's brother, it's not the best response.

Answer 49

(A) is the best response,

because the daughter validly conveyed her future interest to her friend.

The landowner's will created a determinable life estate in his wife: The words "for life" dictate that her ownership will terminate on her death, while the words "or until remarriage" create a condition upon which her life estate may be cut short. The daughter received a vested remainder (which follows the life estate) as well as an executory interest, which would become possessory in the event that her mother remarried. The owner of a future interest in land may convey that interest, either in their will or *inter vivos*. Thus, when the daughter made the conveyance to her friend, the friend became the holder of both future interests. When the daughter died, the future interests were not in her estate, so they did not pass by intestate succession to her mother. The mother's estate terminated upon her remarriage, and the friend, as holder of the executory interest, gained title in fee simple.

(B) is not the best response,

because the wife's life estate terminated when she remarried.

The landowner's will created a determinable life estate in his wife. Since the condition upon which her estate would end was her remarriage, the land passed to the holder of the executory interest. So, the wife would only own the land if she held the executory interest, which could have only occurred if she acquired it through her daughter's estate. However, the daughter conveyed her future interest to her friend, so the executory interest was not in her estate when she died. Rather, the daughter's friend, as holder of the executory interest, became the owner of the land in fee simple when the landowner's wife remarried.

(C) is not the best response,

because the wife's life estate terminated when she remarried.

The landowner's will created a determinable life estate in his wife. Since the condition upon which her estate would end was her remarriage, the land passed to the holder of the executory interest. When she remarried, the life estate terminated, and the holder of the executory interest owned the land in fee simple. Whoever owns the land at this point (the daughter's friend, as discussed in the explanation for choice A above) owns it in fee simple, rather than a life estate. Since choice C indicates that the new husband holds the land for the life of his wife, it cannot be correct.

(D) is not the best response,

because the daughter's friend owned the executory interest in the land when the wife remarried.

The landowner's will created a determinable life estate in his wife. The daughter received a vested remainder as well as an executory interest, which would become possessory in the event that her mother remarried. The only way that the wife's new husband could own the land in fee simple is if, when the wife's life estate terminated due to her remarriage, she held the executory interest. In that case, she would have acquired title in fee simple and been able to convey title to her new husband. However, the owner of a future interest in land may convey that interest, either in their will or *inter vivos*. Thus, when the daughter made the conveyance to her friend, the friend became the holder of both future interests. When the daughter died, the future interests were not in her estate, so they did not pass by intestate succession to her mother. The mother's estate terminated upon her remarriage, and the friend, as holder of the executory interest, gained title in fee simple. Since the wife had nothing to convey to her new husband, he cannot own the land in fee simple.

Answer 50

(A) is the best response,

because it reflects the traditional rule on splitting mortgage payments between the life estate holder and the remainderman.

That rule is that the life estate holder pays the portion of the mortgage reflecting interest, and the remainderman pays the principal. Since A reflects this rule, it's the best response.

(B) is not the best response,

because the daughter, as remainderman, will be liable only for the portion of the mortgage representing principal.

The traditional rule is that the life estate holder pays interest on any mortgage on the property, whereas the remainderman pays the principal. Under these facts, this would mean that the son pays the interest, and the daughter pays the principal. Since B states otherwise, it's not the best response.

(C) is not the best response,

because the son will be liable only for the portion of the mortgage representing interest.

The traditional rule is that the life estate holder pays interest on any mortgage on the property, whereas the remainderman pays the principal. Under these facts, this would mean that the son pays the interest, and the daughter pays the principal. Since C states that the son should be liable for the entire amount, it's not the best response.

(D) is not the best response,

because while it suggests that the payment should be split between the son and the daughter, it has their liabilities reversed.

The traditional rule is that the life estate holder pays interest on any mortgage on the property, whereas the remainderman pays the principal. Under these facts, this would mean that the son pays the interest, and the daughter pays the principal. Since D has these the other way around, it's not the best response.

Answer 51

(C) is the best response,

because it correctly identifies that the language of the deed created only a contractual obligation for the grantee, not a restriction on the use of the land.

The language here is a bit misleading because it sounds as though it creates a defeasible fee. A "defeasible fee" is a fee simple estate that terminates on the occurrence of a specified event. If the estate automatically terminates when the condition occurs, the estate is known as a "fee simple determinable." If the grantor must reenter and retake the property when the condition occurs, it's a fee simple defeasible subject to a condition subsequent.

What C recognizes is that courts dislike restraints on alienation, so if there is any question as to the interpretation of a conveyance, courts will favor a fee simple absolute over a defeasible fee. As a result, the grantee would be left with a fee simple absolute and a personal, contractual liability to use the property as instructed by the deed. Since C recognizes this, it's the best response.

(A) is not the best response,

because the language of the deed did not create a defeasible fee.

A "defeasible fee" is one that terminates on the occurrence of a specified event. (If it terminates automatically, it's a fee simple determinable; if the grantor must actively reenter and retake the property, it's a fee simple subject to a condition subsequent.)

The "subject to the understanding that" language would not impose restrictions on usage of the estate; instead, it would impose, at most, only a contractual obligation on the grantee's part.

This is somewhat tricky because the language sounds as though it could create a defeasible fee estate. However, courts do not like restraints on alienation, so if there is any question as to the interpretation of a conveyance, courts will favor fee simple absolute over a defeasible fee (either a fee simple determinable or a fee simple subject to a condition subsequent). Thus, the grantor would have to have worded the conveyance something like "to the grantee only so long as the premises are used for a public health center, which the grantee must build within one year," to create a defeasible fee. Since the conveyance did not create a fee simple determinable, A is not the best response.

(B) is not the best response,

because the language of the fee did not create a fee subject to a condition subsequent.

The "subject to the understanding that" would not impose restrictions on the usage of the estate; instead, it would impose, at most, only a contractual obligation on the grantee's part.

This is difficult because the language sounds as though it could create a defeasible fee estate. A "defeasible fee" is one that terminates on the occurrence of a specified event. (If it terminates automatically, it's a fee simple determinable; if the grantor must actively reenter and retake the property, it's a fee simple subject to a condition subsequent.)

However, courts do not like restraints on alienation, so if there is any question as to the interpretation of a conveyance, courts will favor fee simple absolute over a defeasible fee (either a fee simple determinable or a fee simple subject to a condition subsequent). Assuming *arguendo* that the language here had created restrictions on usage, it would not have created a fee simple subject to a condition subsequent anyway, but a fee simple determinable. That's because there's no language here giving the grantor the power to reenter and retake the premises; rather, the property would revert automatically to the grantor. To create a fee simple subject to a condition subsequent, the conveyance would have to have been worded something like "to the grantee as long as he constructs and maintains and operates on said premises a public health center, but if he ever ceases to do so, the grantor or his successors can reenter and retake the premises." Since the conveyance here does not resemble this, B is not the best response.

(D) is not the best response,

because the agreement here would not have to be enforced in equity.

If an obligation was created by the wording of the deed, it will be enforceable at law as a contract, since it would not be sufficient to create a restriction on the use of the estate. Since D would have the obligation enforceable only in equity, it is not the best response.

Answer 52

(D) is the best response,

because it correctly identifies that neither of the gifts created here violates the Rule Against Perpetuities.

The key fact here is that the man created the gift *in his will*, and the day he dies is the date the interests would be considered "created."

Under the Rule Against Perpetuities, an interest must vest or fail within a life in being plus 21 years or the creation of the interest. Both of the classes here—the children and the substitutionary gift to the grandchildren —fulfill this requirement. The key fact here is that the *gift was created in the man's will*. Since the will does not take effect—and the interests are thus not "created"—until he dies, no more members of the class of measuring lives (the children) can be added after the interests are created. Thus, all interests created in it must vest or fail within a life in being plus 21 years. In fact, all the interests will be determined when the youngest of the man's children turns, or would have turned, 30. Since D correctly identifies that the interests created here are valid, it's the best response.

(A) is not the best response,

because the interests were created in a will, not in an *inter vivos* conveyance. As a result, the remainder to the children and the grandchildren is valid.

The Rule Against Perpetuities requires that, to be valid, an interest must vest or fail within a life in being plus 21 years, as of the date of the creation of the interest. Here, the interests would be considered created when the will takes effect, *not* when the man executed the will. Thus, he could not remarry after the instrument takes effect, unless he engages in some Frankensteinian behavior beyond the reach of the Rule Against Perpetuities.

Since the man cannot have any more children once he's dead, all of his children must be "lives in being" when the will takes effect. Thus, his grandchildren cannot take any later than the thirtieth year after the birth of a life in being (namely, the man's children). Since these interests cannot violate the Rule Against Perpetuities, the remainder to the children and grandchildren is valid, making A not the best response.

(B) is not the best response,

for the same reasons as A: Since the interests were created in a will and not in an *inter vivos* conveyance, the remainder to the grandchildren is valid.

The relevant date in these facts is not when the will was executed, but when the man dies, because that's when the interests would be deemed "created." Once the man is dead, he can neither marry again nor have any more children. Thus, his children are all "lives in being" when the interests come into being (the man's death), and the grandchildren's interests either vest (if their parent dies before 30) or fails (if the parent reaches 30) within a life in being, never mind the additional 21 years in the perpetuities period. Since B incorrectly states that the gift to the grandchildren will fail, it's not the best response.

(C) is not the best response,

because the man's will became operative when he died. Thus, it doesn't matter that his youngest son was born after he *executed* his will.

If you chose this response, it's probably because you misapplied the Rule of Convenience. The Rule of Convenience is a rule of construction that applies to class gifts. Where there is no expression of intent that all members of a class should take, the class closes when a member of the class can call for distribution of a share of the class gift. Under the facts here, no member of the "class"—the man's children—can call for distribution until he dies, since the gift is in his will. Thus, all his children will be included, no matter when they are born, since they have to be born before his death (or within nine months of it).

In order to make choice C a correct answer, let's change the facts: Say the man left his house to "my friend Aloysius' children." When the man dies, Aloysius has two children, Allan and Beth, and after the man's death, Aloysius has a child, Carter. With this hypothetical devise, Carter would be excluded, since Allan and Beth could call for distribution of the gift at the man's death. However, under the facts in the problem as given, the operative date is the man's death, when his will takes effect. Since the son from the man's second marriage was a member of the "class" by then, he'll be entitled to a share, making C not the best response.

Answer 53

(B) is the best response,

because it identifies the niece's right as valid.

Under the contract here, the widow has given the niece a valid right of first refusal in the event that she decides to alienate the property, or upon her death. This is an interesting question in that there really isn't a pressing Rule Against Perpetuities issue under these facts; however, it's clear that the other responses are incorrect, leaving B as the best response, even though it doesn't address a central issue. Since B correctly identifies the niece's interest as valid and states correct reasoning, it's the best response.

(A) is not the best response,

because recording an instrument would not make it valid; it only establishes priority.

The question here asks about the validity of the niece's interest, not the priority of it vis-à-vis someone else's interest in the property, and *that's* when priority is an issue. Thus, A cannot be the best response.

(C) is not the best response,

because the widow is restricting only *her own* power to convey or devise the property, by giving her niece a right of first refusal.

Restraints on alienation come into question only when a grantor or testator wants to convey or dispose of property while, *at the same time*, retaining control over its alienation. While it's true that restraints on fee estates are not valid, what the widow has here is not a restraint, but merely a right of first refusal for the niece in the event that the widow *does* decide to unload the property, since she isn't conveying or disposing of property. This will be valid, making C not the best response.

(D) is not the best response,

because there is no transfer of property involved, so there cannot be a restraint on alienation.

Restraints on alienation come into question only when a grantor or testator wants to convey or dispose of property while, *at the same time*, retaining control over its alienation. What the widow has essentially done is to give the niece a right of first refusal in the event she does decide to alienate the property. Since this will be valid, D is not the best response.

Answer 54

(A) is the best response,

because an option to purchase "in gross" is subject to the Rule Against Perpetuities, and this option might be exercised beyond the perpetuities period.

The option to purchase here, although it is contingent, would be held to create an interest in land. (That is, if the holder of the fee refused to convey after using the property for non-residential purposes, the optionee could get an order of specific performance. That's enough to give the optionee a contingent interest in the land.)

The option here is "in gross"—that is, the option is not appurtenant to an interest already held by the optionee in the land. (A purchase option given to a tenant, by contrast, would not be in gross.) Options in gross are generally held to be subject to the Rule Against Perpetuities.

The Rule says that an interest is void if it might vest more than 21 years after some life in being at the time of creation of the interest. Here, the only lives that might qualify as measuring lives are the landowner's and the grantee's. Yet by its terms, the clause might be exercisable in the very distant future—by the landowner's great-great-grandchildren, for instance, as against the grantee's great-great-grandchildren. This exercise would be far after any measuring life mentioned in the document plus 21 years. Consequently, the option would be void if options in gross are subject to the Rule. (It's not absolutely certain that options in gross *would* be subject to the Rule in a particular jurisdiction. But *if* the court rules against the landowner, the only plausible explanation from those given is that the court has found that the Rule applies to options in gross, and that this option violates the Rule.)

(B) is not the best response,

because the bank's rights are subordinate to the option, even though the bank may have been unaware of the option.

A mortgagee's rights are no greater than the rights held by the mortgagor at the moment the mortgage is issued. Therefore, at the moment the bank funded the purchase and took its mortgage, it merely obtained the right, in the event of default, to foreclose on whatever rights the grantee had. Those rights were subject to the option to repurchase. The fact that the bank didn't know this is irrelevant, especially since it had the opportunity to inspect the deed giving the grantee her rights and failed to do so.

(C) is not the best response,

because the landowner's rights were not subordinated to the bank's.

This is simply not a correct statement of how the law works. If there were no perpetuities problem, the landowner's purchase option would be superior to the bank's mortgage, because the purchase option existed in the very deed creating the grantee's interest, and the bank's mortgage merely gave it the right to foreclose on whatever interest the grantee obtained by the deed.

(D) is not the best response,

because courts will not inquire into the adequacy of consideration.

A court will not examine the "adequacy" of the consideration, as long as the court is satisfied that there really was a bargain or exchange. Here, the court would look at the overall transaction, and would undoubtedly conclude that it represented a true bargain, in which the grantee agreed to accept the land with the restriction on it, and to be faced with the chance that if she broke her covenant, the land could be taken away from her (or her heirs) for a less-than-market price. Since there was an actual bargain, the fact that the option standing alone might have been for an "inadequate" (i.e., much-less-than-market) price will be irrelevant.

Answer 55

(C) is the best response,

because it correctly identifies that the conveyance was valid.

Under the will, the nephew took a contingent remainder, contingent on the daughter's dying without children surviving her, but with a husband. The facts state specifically that any interest in land is freely alienable. Thus, the nephew was free to convey his contingent remainder to the daughter's husband.

He did so when he quitclaimed his interest in the farm to the daughter's husband, since a quitclaim deed transfers whatever interest the conveyor has in the property, without any covenants. Since choice C recognizes that the nephew took a valid interest under the will, which he later validly conveyed to the daughter's husband, it's the best response.

(A) is not the best response,

because the after-acquired title doctrine *will not* apply to these facts.

The "after-acquired title doctrine," also known as "estoppel by deed," covers this situation: The grantor purports to convey an estate larger than the one he has; the grantor subsequently acquires the title he's already purportedly conveyed; title *automatically* passes to grantee, by estoppel. Here, the nephew conveyed *whatever interest he had* in the farm. In fact, he had a contingent remainder, contingent on the daughter's dying without children surviving her, but with a husband.

Under the facts here, all interests in land are freely alienable, so the nephew was free to convey his contingent remainder. Thus, once he conveys the contingent remainder to the daughter's husband, the daughter's husband takes whatever interest the nephew had, and it becomes possessory whenever it would have become possessory in the nephew's hands. Thus, the nephew didn't transfer an estate larger than he had; he transferred *exactly* what he had—a contingent remainder. As a result, the after-acquired title doctrine would not apply, and the nephew's quitclaim deed would be sufficient to convey his contingent remainder. Since A states otherwise, it's not the best response.

(B) is not the best response,

because the nephew took a contingent remainder under the landowner's will.

It's a contingent remainder because it's subject to a condition precedent: the daughter's dying with a husband but no children. The facts here state that any interest in land is freely alienable; thus, the nephew was free to quitclaim his interest in the farm to the daughter's husband. If you thought the nephew had no interest in the farm, it could be because his interest hadn't vested when he transferred it. However, that doesn't mean it's not an interest *at all*.

Since B wrongly states that the nephew took no interest in the farm, it's not the best response.

(D) is not the best response,

because the after-acquired title doctrine would not apply to these facts.

The "after-acquired title doctrine," also known as "estoppel by deed," covers this situation: The grantor purports to convey an estate larger than the one he has; the grantor subsequently acquires the title he's already purportedly conveyed; title *automatically* passes to grantee, by estoppel.

Here, the nephew conveyed *whatever interest he had* in the farm. In fact, he had a contingent remainder, contingent on the daughter's dying without children surviving her, but with a husband. Thus, the nephew didn't transfer an estate larger than he had; he transferred *exactly* what he had—a contingent remainder. Since D would wrongly apply the after-acquired title doctrine to these facts, it's not the best response.

STRATEGIES AND TACTICS

TORTS

OUTLINE OF COVERAGE

The following outline for the Torts portion of the MBE was adopted by the Bar Examiners for all MBEs given on or after February 2016.

Important note: You should answer Torts questions according to ***principles of general applicability.*** On the MBE, you must assume that there is no applicable statute unless one is specified. There's one exception: Where a question involves ***survival actions*** and ***wrongful death claims,*** you can assume that a statute is available. In addition, assume that ***joint and several liability,*** with ***pure*** comparative negligence, is the relevant rule, unless you're told otherwise.

Here's what you need to know:

I. Intentional torts
   - A. Harms to the person, such as assault, battery, false imprisonment, and infliction of mental distress; and harms to property interests, such as trespass to land and chattels, and conversion
   - B. Defenses to claims for physical harms
     1. Consent
     2. Privileges and immunities: protection of self and others; protection of property interests; parental discipline; protection of public interests; necessity; incomplete privilege

II. Negligence
   - A. The duty question, including failure to act, unforeseeable plaintiffs, and obligations to control the conduct of third parties
   - B. The standard of care
     1. The reasonably prudent person, including children, physically and mentally impaired individuals, professional people, and other special classes
     2. Rules of conduct derived from statutes and custom
   - C. Problems relating to proof of fault, including res ipsa loquitur
   - D. Problems relating to causation
     1. But for and substantial causes
     2. Harms traceable to multiple causes
     3. Questions of apportionment of responsibility among multiple tortfeasors, including joint and several liability
   - E. Limitations on liability and special rules of liability
     1. Problems relating to "remote" or "unforeseeable" causes, "legal" or "proximate" cause, and "superseding" causes
     2. Claims against owners and occupiers of land
     3. Claims for mental distress not arising from physical harm; other intangible injuries
     4. Claims for pure economic loss
   - F. Liability for acts of others
     1. Employees and other agents
     2. Independent contractors and nondelegable duties
   - G. Defenses
     1. Contributory fault, including common law contributory negligence and last clear chance, and the various forms of comparative negligence
     2. Assumption of risk

III. Strict liability and products liability: common law strict liability, including claims arising from abnormally dangerous activities, and defenses to such claims; claims against manufacturers and other defendants arising out of the manufacture and distribution of products, and defenses to such claims.

IV. Other torts
   A. Claims based on nuisance, and defenses
   B. Claims based on defamation and invasion of privacy, defenses, and constitutional limitations
   C. Claims based on misrepresentations, and defenses
   D. Claims based on intentional interference with business relations, and defenses

WHAT TO EXPECT

You'll face 28 or 29 questions on Torts on the MBE (though only 27 will be scored, and you won't know which ones won't). Approximately ***half*** of those (14 questions) will deal solely with category II—Negligence. The remaining Torts questions will cover the other categories (I, III, and IV).

Accordingly, Torts (and especially negligence) is a subject you can't afford to ignore when you study. The three most common types of Torts questions on the MBE are:

1. Questions asking you the plaintiff's best claim;
2. Questions asking you the defendant's best defense; and
3. Questions asking you whether the plaintiff will prevail.

The most common of these three is the third type; this also represents the most difficult type of question, because you're frequently ***not told the nature of the claim.*** Instead, you're told only that the plaintiff asserted a claim for damages against the defendant, and you're left to figure out what the claim is (e.g., is it based on negligence, or on strict liability?) Handling this kind of question is addressed under "Exam Tactics" below.

STUDY STRATEGIES

1. Memorize this test for negligence.

You may remember the four elements of a negligence claim from your first year of law school: duty, breach, causation, and damages. This simple list is perfectly correct but not terribly helpful on the MBE. You'll find it far easier to analyze negligence questions if you memorize this test:

> A defendant must fail to exercise such care as a reasonable person in his position would have exercised; his conduct must be a breach of the duty to prevent the foreseeable risk of harm to anyone in the plaintiff's position, and this breach must cause the plaintiff's damages.

If you find this a bit cumbersome, keep in mind that ***almost ten percent of the entire*** MBE will cover ***only*** negligence; thus, your grasp of this one definition could mean the difference between passing and failing!

2. Remember the purpose of res ipsa loquitur.

Remember that *res ipsa loquitur* is merely one means of proving a negligence claim: It establishes a *prima facie* case of negligence ***only where direct evidence of the circumstances of the injury is lacking.*** If you have direct evidence of how a result came about, ***res ipsa loquitur will not apply.***

In order for *res ipsa* to establish a *prima facie* case of negligence, these three elements have to exist: (1) the event causing injury would normally not have occurred in the absence of negligence; (2) the defendant was in exclusive control of the instrumentality that likely caused the injury; and (3) the plaintiff must not have voluntarily contributed to the event causing his injury. Perhaps you remember the classic case of the human toe in the sealed can of food, where negligence was established by applying *res ipsa loquitur*. Keep this example in mind when deciding whether *res ipsa exists*.

3. Remember what different causes of action do.

You need to know not only the elements of various torts, but also to which kinds of facts these elements ***apply.*** Because Torts questions frequently don't tell you on what facts the plaintiff is basing her claim, it's important that you be able to determine that from the facts of the question. Although you'll get clues from the answer choices as to what the plaintiff's claim must be, your knowledge of the facts to which various elements apply will help you analyze questions quickly and eliminate incorrect responses.

4. Defamation.

Defamation questions pop up on the MBE a little more often than you might guess—you're likely to face two or three of these. Although much of defamation law is straightforward, here are some elements to keep in mind:

A. Special damages.

There's only one situation where a plaintiff must prove ***special damages*** as part of his defamation claim: when his claim is based on ***slander*** and is for a slanderous statement not falling within any of the following four *slander per se* categories:

1. statements accusing someone of a crime;
2. statements alleging that someone has a foul or loathsome disease;
3. statements adversely reflecting on a person's fitness to conduct her business or trade; and
4. statements imputing serious sexual misconduct to someone (almost always to a woman).

If a plaintiff's claim doesn't fall within one of these four categories, he must prove special damages or his claim will fail. (Special damages are ***pecuniary*** [economic] damages, e.g., a lost job, inheritance, gift, customer). If a plaintiff's claim is for libel, or slander *per se*, she doesn't have to prove special damages. This is a sneaky issue because it's easy to overlook—thus, a perfect basis for an MBE question.

B. Publication.

The Bar Examiners tend to focus a lot on the requirement of ***"publication,"*** i.e., that the defamatory statement be ***communicated*** to someone other than the plaintiff. When you're reading a question involving an allegedly defamatory statement, you should, therefore, look carefully at the facts to see whether the speaker of the statement ***spoke in front of someone else.*** If he didn't make his statement to anyone other than the person claiming defamation, then there's no ***actionable*** defamation.

One aspect of publication that the Bar Examiners like to test is that ***strict liability*** is not permitted; the plaintiff must show that the defendant either ***intended*** to communicate the statement to a third person or ***negligently*** publicized the statement to third persons. Watch out for situations where a third person learns of the statement ***through no fault of the defendant;*** in this situation, the plaintiff ***cannot*** recover damages for the defendant's statement. For instance, suppose that a defendant sends a plaintiff a letter falsely accusing him of molesting the defendant's teenage son. The plaintiff, who receives the letter at work, crumples it up and tosses it in the wastebasket. An hour later, a fellow office worker of the plaintiff, realizing that he threw an important document into the same wastebasket by mistake, goes through the wastebasket looking for his document. In the process, he finds the defendant's letter, reads it, and tells some of his coworkers what it says; as a result, the plaintiff loses his job. If the plaintiff sues the defendant for defamation, ***the plaintiff will lose,*** even though he's been harmed, because the others heard the defamatory statement ***through no fault of the defendant.***

C. No strict liability regarding statement's falsity.

Even if the plaintiff is not a public figure, under prevailing state-law principles ***defamation is never a strict liability offense!*** Instead, the plaintiff will have to prove, at the very least, ***negligence*** with respect to the statement's truth. So if a defendant ***reasonably (but erroneously) believed the statement was true,*** he ***can't*** be liable for negligence, and he therefore can't be liable for defamation, even if the plaintiff is a private figure suing over a private matter.

Of course, if the plaintiff *is* a public figure, and the issue is of public interest, the plaintiff has more to prove; in order to prevail, he has to show that the defendant ***knew*** the statement was false or evidenced a ***reckless disregard*** for its truth or falsity; proving negligence wouldn't be enough. (And even the defendant's ***unreasonable failure to investigate*** won't be enough to prove reckless disregard: only if the defendant in fact ***"entertained serious doubts"*** about the statement's truth will publication constitute reckless disregard of truth or falsity.)

5. Don't confuse defamation and invasion of privacy.

There's an important reason for remembering this: ***Truth*** is not a defense to invasion of privacy, but it's a ***complete*** defense to defamation.

Remember that invasion of privacy is not a tort ***itself,*** but, rather, is an "umbrella" tort covering four separate, distinct claims: (1) appropriation of plaintiff's personality for a defendant's own commercial advantage;

(2) intrusion on a plaintiff's affairs or seclusion; (3) publication of facts that place a plaintiff in a false light; and (4) public disclosure of private facts about a plaintiff. (Here's a mnemonic: **A FLIP** [**A**ppropriation, **F**alse **L**ight, **I**ntrusion, **P**rivate].) Thus, you could say a statement's ***truth*** is the essence of the damage in most invasion-of-privacy claims, and its ***falsity*** is the linchpin of a defamation claim.

6. Remember the sources of strict liability.

Strict liability can be the source of a great deal of frustration on the MBE. You will frequently be tempted to choose it as a response even where it doesn't apply. The easiest way to avoid this trap of thinking strict liability is available when it's not is to remember not just the ***elements*** of strict liability, but also its ***sources.*** If a fact pattern doesn't address those sources, then ***strict liability cannot be the basis of a defendant's liability*****!**

Like negligence, strict liability requires proof of these four elements: duty, breach, causation, and damages. Unlike negligence, strict liability involves an ***absolute*** duty, ***not*** a duty of reasonable care. Again, like negligence, this definition won't help you very much in analyzing MBE questions. What you should keep in mind is that there are ***only three ways*** a defendant can be strictly liable (i.e., liable without regard to fault or intent):

1. by ***keeping a wild animal*****;**
2. by conducting an ***abnormally dangerous activity*****;** or
3. by ***selling a defective product*** (strict ***products liability***).

Strict liability can also be imposed by case law or statute, but, if this arises in an MBE question, the question will have to supply the statute or cases, and you'd just have to recognize and apply what you're given.

The first of the three general sources—animals—is easy to spot. If someone has a skunk, chimpanzee, elephant, or other ***exotic pet*** (and it needn't be one you'd consider ***dangerous*****;** it need only be non-domesticated), and the pet causes damage of the sort that makes the species wild, the owner will be liable, no matter how careful he was about keeping the thing penned up. That's because, with strict liability, it doesn't matter how careful one is—the duty is ***absolute.*** Also, even if a pet is domesticated, if the owner has reason to know it's dangerous (e.g., it's bitten someone before), then the owner will be liable.

The second source, an abnormally dangerous activity, is one to handle carefully. It's easy to mistake any dangerous activity for an abnormally dangerous one. You may find it helpful to remember that abnormally dangerous activities are ones that ***cannot be performed with complete safety no matter how much care is taken – that's why they're a source of strict liability.*** Common abnormally dangerous activities include the use of pesticides, the use of explosives, blasting and excavating. (By contrast, transmission of electricity is not generally considered abnormally dangerous.)

The third source—defective products—is just garden-variety strict products liability (also known simply as "products liability"). Here's our list of all the important things you need to know about strict product liability for the MBE:

1. DEFECT: The product must have been defective;
2. CONTROL: The defective condition must have existed when the product left the defendant's control;
3. CHANGES: The product must not have been expected to undergo significant changes before it got to the user (or, it must not actually undergo significant changes);
4. BUSINESS: The seller must be in the business of selling the product (that is, he can't be a casual seller or a user, even one who uses the product while performing a paid service that does not incorporate a transfer of the product);
5. CAUSATION: Damage must result from the defect (a defendant is liable for any harm to persons or property);
6. NO PRIVITY: The defendant's duty extends to anyone foreseeably endangered by the product (this means there's no ***privity requirement***).

If you take the first letter of each of these elements, and add a vowel, you get a mnemonic: **CCC BoND** (**C**ontrol; **C**hanges; **C**ausation; **B**usiness, **N**o privity; **D**efect). If you can remember the elements without a mnemonic, fine—the point is, if you can remember them, you're unlikely to be fooled by a strict product liability question.

In products liability cases, strict liability can be the ***easiest*** type of claim to prove, because the defendant can be liable for defects created by those who came ***before*** him in the distribution chain, and the plaintiff doesn't have to prove any lack of care. Also remember that, aside from products liability, strict liability is difficult because it applies only to a very limited number of situations.

No matter what type of strict liability question you're examining, don't forget the ***proximate cause*** requirement. Remember what strict liability was designed to do: compensate for damage caused by the extraordinary risks created by certain enterprises. If the consequences are outside the extraordinary risk that ***created*** absolute liability, the defendant won't be liable. For instance, say an animal enthusiast keeps an elephant, Jumbo, as a pet. One day, Jumbo roams over to the neighbor's barn next door, falls through some rotted floorboards, clambers out, and goes home. Later, the neighbor goes to the barn, and, in the darkness, falls through the hole. The neighbor's injuries would be considered sufficiently outside the risk that makes wild elephants a wild species that the owner will not be strictly liable.

7. Products liability.

Remember two things about products liability that you might otherwise overlook:

A. It's not the only basis of liability for harm caused by products.

You must remember that there are actually ***three different ways*** in which someone who makes or sells a product can be held liable for injuries the product causes. They are: (1) ***strict products liability;*** (2) ***breach of warranty;*** and (3) ***negligence.*** Although products liability is by far the most important of the three, you can't completely forget about warranty and negligence on the MBE.

As for warranty, you should remember that it's a ***separate theory*** of recovery for a defective product—it's ***not an element of strict products liability.*** The Bar Examiners sometimes throw a warranty answer choice into a question that assumes you're suing in strict liability. Watch out! It's probably a distractor. Also, remember the two types of warranties: express and implied. Express warranties do show up on the MBE (e.g., a vendor furnishes a sample of the products to be sold; that constitutes an express warranty that the products will match the sample). When an express warranty is present, a commonly tested aspect is that a plaintiff who successfully sues someone for breach of warranty is entitled to the ***benefit of the bargain.***

As for negligence, remember that it's ***always available as an alternative theory*** when a product hurts someone; therefore, in products liability questions, you should be aware that negligence might be the correct answer choice. A defendant can't be liable for product-related negligence, though, unless, at a minimum, the defect was ***discoverable*** by reasonable means.

One common MBE situation occurs when the purchaser of a defective, unreasonably dangerous product ***learns about an available safety device*** but ***fails to install it.*** If the device is cheap, and the danger from not installing the device is great, then the purchaser may be found to be at fault for failing to install the device. But in a comparative-fault jurisdiction (which is what you're told to assume by default on the MBE), that plaintiff-negligence will at most ***reduce, not eliminate,*** the plaintiff's recovery. That's true whether the suit is brought in negligence or strict liability.

B. Privity.

When a product liability claim is based on either negligence or strict liability, ***privity is not an issue,*** because ***anyone*** who could foreseeably be endangered by the product can make a claim.

C. Liability for others' fault.

An important feature of strict products liability, as discussed in #6, above, is that the defendant needn't have created the defect—the defect merely has to be in existence ***when the product leaves his control.*** Thus, a retailer can be liable for a manufacturer-created defect, even if the retailer didn't know about it and couldn't have discovered it. This seems counterintuitive until you remember that the retailer won't necessarily be ***ultimately*** liable; he can seek indemnity from his supplier, who can seek indemnity from his supplier, and so on, until the one originally responsible for creating the defect is held liable. The retailer is, nevertheless, a potential defendant.

Under negligence, by contrast, the defendant himself ***must*** have failed to exercise due care in order to be held liable—he can't be held liable for the negligence of those preceding him in the distribution chain. Be careful, though. A defendant's negligence can take a variety of forms. Watch out for any behavior that is characterized as ***unreasonable.*** Thus, if defendant didn't inspect and a reasonable person would have, or if he ***did*** inspect but didn't find a defect when a ***reasonable*** inspection would have discovered it, he'll be liable, but only because his own conduct has been unreasonable.

EXAM TACTICS

1. Questions asking for a "best argument."

When faced with this type of question, you're likely to look for ***all*** the arguments that will support the choices given you, so you'll fail to look to focus on the only correct answer; instead, look at these questions this way: Only one of the answer choices will provide a successful claim or defense. The other three will ***all*** be flawed in some way, because they either don't apply to the facts or don't correctly apply the law.

2. Questions asking what the plaintiff will need to prove and in which the claim is identified (e.g., nuisance, defamation).

In this kind of question, only one answer choice will supply the correct level of proof. The others will ***overstate*** it or ***understate*** it. An answer choice **overstates** the proof required if, for instance, it overstates the level of fault that the plaintiff must show. An answer choice understates the proof required if, for instance, it's not specific enough, or it's not relevant. ***Whenever*** a claim is mentioned, think of the elements that claim requires, as well as relevant defenses, and keep those in mind as you analyze each choice.

3. Identifying claims when a question doesn't.

As you'll remember from the strategies section, Torts questions frequently don't tell you the basis for the claim (e.g., nuisance, negligence). There are, however, three important categories that are easy to define:

1. intentional tort;
2. negligence; and
3. strict liability.

If you apply the rules on strict liability that we gave you in the "Study Strategies" section, you can easily identify where strict liability applies. Intentional torts are inherently simple to identify. That will leave you in most cases with a negligence claim.

You'll get additional help in identifying the claim if you look at the reasoning of the answer choices, because at least one will contain a material element of the correct claim. Language such as "reason to know" in answer choices is the language of negligence, as that's determined objectively. Also, in the question ***itself,*** the facts will suggest what the plaintiff's claim must be. If there's no intent stated or indicated, you won't base a claim on an intentional tort. If there's no basis for strict liability, you wouldn't claim it. That leaves negligence.

It's important to identify the claim specifically, because incorrect answer choices are often wrong because they are based on something that is ***not relevant to a plaintiff's claim*** but is relevant to ***another,*** similar claim. If you've correctly identified the claim, you can't be fooled this way.

Here's an example of this kind of question:

> When a mother visited a bowling alley to participate in the weekly bowling league competition held there, she brought her two-year-old son along and left him in a nursery provided by the bowling alley for the convenience of its customers. The children in the nursery were normally supervised by three attendants, but at this particular time, as the mother knew, there was only one attendant present to care for about 20 children of assorted ages.
>
> About 30 minutes later, while the attendant was looking the other way, the two-year-old son suddenly started to cry. The attendant found him lying on his back, picked him up, and called his mother. It was later discovered that the son had suffered a skull fracture.
>
> If a claim is asserted against the bowling alley on the son's behalf, will the son prevail?
>
> A. Yes, because the bowling alley owed the child the highest degree of care.
> B. Yes, because a two-year-old is incapable of contributory negligence.
> C. No, unless the bowling alley or its employees failed to exercise reasonable care to assure the son's safety.
> D. No, because the mother assumed the risk by leaving her son in the nursery.

As you can see, you're not told what the claim is for. If you apply the intentional tort/strict liability/negligence analysis to the facts here, you will see that there's no intentional tort; also, babysitting is not a source of strict liability; that leaves only negligence as a basis for a claim. You know that the linchpin of a negligence claim is ***the defendant's unreasonable conduct;*** so, if the defendant behaved reasonably, it can't be liable. This analysis, coupled with the fact that choices B and D rely on defenses that don't correspond with the facts and that Choice A states incorrectly the degree of care owed, should lead you to the best response: C.

4. Where "if" is the modifier in an answer choice.

Analyze these answer choices this way:

1. The reasoning of the answer choice must be ***plausible*** on the facts, i.e., there can't be anything in the facts suggesting that an alternative is true.
2. The answer choice must resolve a significant issue.
3. The result must be consistent with the reasoning.

5. Where "because" is the modifier in an answer choice.

If the corresponding question asks who will prevail, ask yourself: "Would these facts be necessary to make the defendant liable?" Here's an example:

When a fraternal organization came to a town for its convention, its members rented 400 of the 500 rooms in a local hotel, and the hotel opened its convention facilities to them. This fraternal group tends to be rowdy, and during their convention they littered both the inside and the outside of the hotel with debris and bottles. The hotel manager knew that objects were being thrown out of the hotel windows. At his direction, hotel employees patrolled the hallways telling the guests to refrain from such conduct. The owner of the hotel was out of town and was not aware of the problems which were occurring. During the convention, as a pedestrian walked past the hotel on the sidewalk, he was hit and injured by an ashtray thrown out of a window in the hotel. The pedestrian sued the owner for damages for his injuries.

Will the pedestrian prevail in his claim against the owner?

A. Yes, because a property owner is strictly liable for acts on his premises if such acts cause harm to persons using the adjacent public sidewalks.
B. Yes, if the person who threw the ashtray cannot be identified.
C. No, because the owner had no personal knowledge of the conduct of the hotel guests.
D. No, if the trier of fact determines that the hotel employees had taken reasonable precautions to prevent such an injury.

Look at choice C. It uses the modifier "because," so it would have to state an element required to make the defendant liable. Although you're not told the nature of the claim here, using the reasoning from Exam Tactic #3, above, you can determine that the claim must be for negligence. Furthermore, if the owner is to be held liable, it must be due to ***vicarious liability*** for the actions of his employees. In order for the employees to be liable for negligence, they must have failed to exercise the care a reasonable person in their position would have exercised. Could this be true without the owner's having personal knowledge of the conduct of the hotel guests? Sure—employers are constantly held liable for torts of their employees when the employer has no personal knowledge of those torts, or of the underlying situation that required the employees to behave with reasonable care. (That's the nature of *respondeat superior*). Thus, C can't be the best response, because it offers the owner's lack of personal knowledge of the underlying situation as the basis for the pedestrian's failure to prevail.

Because we're talking about modifiers, look at the other three answer choices. Choice A—another answer choice using "because"—is not the best response; if you apply the rules of strict liability from the strategies section, you know that a property owner cannot be held strictly liable for the kind of conduct in this question. Choice B, using the modifier "if," also isn't correct, because, although it is plausible on the facts, it wouldn't result in the owner's being held liable. Last, consider choice D. Remember, an individual can't be held liable for negligence if his conduct was reasonable. Under these facts, it's possible that all employees behaved reasonably, and, if they did, the owner couldn't be held liable (because *respondeat superior* would only kick in if at least one individual employee was the negligent cause of the harm). That makes D the best response.

6. Where "unless" is the modifier in an answer choice.

If an answer choice states that "The plaintiff will not prevail ***unless*** X . . . ," then there must be no ***other*** way than X for the plaintiff to succeed. In other words, if X doesn't exist, the defendant isn't liable.

This reasoning need only be plausible on the facts. As an example, look at the bowling-alley question in Tactics, above, where the correct response, C, uses "unless" as a modifier. If you apply this reasoning to it, you'd ask yourself: If the bowling alley and its employees exercised reasonable care, is there any way the alley could be liable? There isn't, since reasonable behavior precludes liability for negligence. Thus, C must be correct.

7. Negligence questions: a shortcut.

In the "Study Strategies" section, above, we gave you a definition to apply to negligence. Here's a shortcut to the correct response in some circumstances.

Look at the defendant's conduct and see if it was ***reasonable.*** If it was, defendant ***cannot be negligent, because negligence requires unreasonable behavior.*** Here's an example:

> A customer fell and injured himself when he slipped on a banana peel while shopping at a grocer's store. The banana peel was fresh and clean except for a mark made by the heel of the customer's shoe. In an action brought by the customer against the grocer, these are the only facts in evidence.
>
> Should the trial judge permit the case to go to the jury?
>
> (A) No, because the customer had an obligation to watch where he stepped.
> (B) No, because there is not a reasonable basis for inferring that the grocer knew or should have known of the banana peel.
> (C) Yes, because it is more likely than not that the peel came from a banana offered for sale by the grocer.
> (D) Yes, because the grocer could foresee that a customer might slip on a banana peel.

This question is actually designed to test your knowledge of *res ipsa loquitur*. (The correct answer is B, because *res ipsa,* the only plausible basis for liability, doesn't apply since falling on a "fresh and clean" banana peel is not an event that is ordinarily caused by the negligence of someone.) But even if you didn't spot that the question was about *res ipsa*, you should be able to figure out the correct answer by elimination, using our "negligence requires unreasonable behavior" shortcut. The suit would have to be in negligence, since there's no basis for either intentional-tort or strict liability. Nothing in these facts suggests any negligence by any store employee (since the "fresh and clean" state of the banana peel is compatible with the peel's having dropped moments before the customer fell, too soon for it to be negligent of the store's employees not to have removed the peel). So you'd be down to just the choices in which the customer loses, which are A and B. A is pretty clearly wrong (since in the worst case for the plaintiff, his lack of care would not nullify his right to go to the jury; it would just lead to the jury's hearing the case and reducing the plaintiff's recovery by his degree of contributory fault). So you'd get to B by default, even on this superficial "was there unreasonable behavior?" analysis.

8. Handling causation issues.

Causation is one of the trickiest issues on the entire MBE. Here are some pointers to help you analyze causation issues correctly.

The most important thing to remember is not to be intimidated by multiple causes. It's easy to be overwhelmed by fact patterns where there are multiple causes of a plaintiff's damage. Remember:

THERE CAN BE MORE THAN ONE CAUSE IN FACT.

The fact that someone other than the defendant contributed to a plaintiff's damages, ***doesn't, in itself, relieve the defendant of liability*** if the defendant's conduct was a substantial factor in causing a plaintiff's damages. Here's an example:

> Section 1 of the Vehicle Code of a state makes it illegal to cross a street in a central business district other than at a designated crosswalk. Section 2 of the Code prohibits parking any motor vehicle so that it blocks any part of a designated crosswalk. A pedestrian wanted to cross a major street in the central business district of a city located in the state, but a truck parked by a trucker was blocking the designated crosswalk. The pedestrian stepped out into the street and carefully walked around the back of the truck. The pedestrian was struck by a motor vehicle negligently operated by a driver.
>
> If the pedestrian asserts a claim against the trucker, the most likely result is that the pedestrian will
>
> A. prevail, because the trucker's violation of a state statute makes him strictly liable for all injuries caused thereby.
> B. prevail, because the probable purpose of Section 2 of the Vehicle Code of State was to safeguard pedestrians using crosswalks.
> C. not prevail, because the pedestrian assumed the risk of injury when he crossed the street outside the crosswalk.
> D. not prevail, because the driver's conduct was the actual cause of the pedestrian's harm.

Look at choice D: Since it says that the driver's conduct was "the" actual cause of the pedestrian's harm, it's implying that there could only be one cause-in-fact of the harm here, so that the trucker's conduct ***can't*** be considered. This isn't correct, because a defendant's conduct can be a ***substantial factor*** in creating a plaintiff's injuries (which is enough for liability) at the same time as there are additional "actual" causes. So you'd know just from the reference to "the" actual cause that D can't be correct. (B is.)

Another important point:

INTERVENING CAUSES WILL SUPERSEDE ONLY IF THEY WERE UNFORESEEABLE.

Ask yourself this: Were the plaintiff's injuries within the risk created by the defendant's act? Alternatively, if the defendant was negligent, what were the risks his negligence created? This is the ***heart*** of proximate cause. Remember that ***intervening*** causes relieve the original tortfeasor of liability only if the ***results of the intervening causes are unforeseeable.*** Think of intervening causes as insulation, and decide whether they create enough of an insulating barrier to justify the plaintiff's not recovering.

Normally on the MBE, the intervening act *won't* create a sufficient barrier to prevent the plaintiff from recovering against the original tortfeasor. For instance, if D1 puts P in jeopardy, and D2 negligently injures P while trying to *rescue* him, D2's negligence won't get D1 off the hook unless D2 has behaved really bizarrely—"danger invites rescue," so D2's negligent attempt at rescue will likely be viewed as a foreseeable consequence of D1's placing P in danger.

There's one more important point to remember here:

DON'T BE THROWN BY THE FACT THAT THE INTERVENING ACTOR MAY ALSO BE LIABLE.

The negligence of intervening actors won't relieve the original tortfeasor of liability unless the results of that intervening negligence are unforeseeable. Under joint-and-several-liability (which you're told to assume by default), if the negligent acts of the original tortfeasor and of some later tortfeasor combine to produce an individual harm, the plaintiff can pick which tortfeasor to sue, and can recover his *entire damages* from that person. The mere fact that the plaintiff could have sued someone else ***as well*** doesn't exonerate the defendant chosen for suit (whose remedy is a contribution or indemnity claim against the missing tortfeasor).

FINALLY—REMEMBER THAT THERE CAN'T BE PROXIMATE CAUSE WITHOUT CAUSE IN FACT.

If conduct is the proximate cause of damage, it must be a cause in fact as well. If there aren't any intervening acts, proximate cause must exist (as long as the defendant was negligent, of course). In fact, the only time you should be concerned with proximate cause is when ***remote possibilities*** are involved.

QUESTIONS
TORTS

QUESTIONS

TORTS

Question 1

A homeowner was using a six-foot stepladder to clean the furnace in his home. The homeowner broke his arm when he slipped and fell from the ladder. The furnace had no warnings or instructions on how it was to be cleaned.

In a suit by the homeowner against the manufacturer of the furnace to recover for his injury, is the homeowner likely to prevail?

(A) No, because the danger of falling from a ladder is obvious.

(B) No, because the homeowner should have hired a professional to clean the furnace.

(C) Yes, because the furnace did not have a ladder attached to it for cleaning purposes.

(D) Yes, because the lack of warnings or instructions for how to clean the furnace made the furnace defective.

Question 2

A college student was asleep in his bed in a college dormitory when his roommate, in a drunken fury, entered their room intending to attack the student with an ice pick while he slept. Fortunately, the phone rang and awakened the student. The roommate retreated quickly and threw the ice pick under his own bed in the same room. The next day, the student heard from friends about the roommate's murderous plans and later found the ice pick under the roommate's bed. Even though the college expelled his roommate, the student remained extremely upset and afraid to sleep.

In a suit against the roommate for assault, will the student prevail?

(A) No, because the roommate did not touch the student.

(B) No, because the student was not awake when the roommate entered the room and was unaware until later that the roommate was intending to attack him.

(C) Yes, because it was reasonable for the student to feel afraid of sleeping in his room afterward.

(D) Yes, because the roommate intended to inflict serious harm.

Question 3

When a tire of a motorist's car suffered a blowout, the car rolled over and the motorist was badly injured. Vehicles made by the manufacturer of the motorist's car have been found to be negligently designed, making them dangerously prone to rolling over when they suffer blowouts. A truck driver who was driving behind the motorist when the accident occurred stopped to help. Rescue vehicles promptly arrived, and the truck driver walked along the side of the road to return to his truck. As he approached his truck, he was struck and injured by a speeding car. The truck driver has sued the manufacturer of the injured motorist's car.

Is the truck driver likely to prevail in a suit against the car manufacturer?

(A) No, because the car manufacturer's negligence was not the proximate cause of the truck driver's injuries.

(B) No, because the truck driver assumed the risk of injury when he undertook to help the motorist.

(C) Yes, because it is foreseeable that injuries can result from rollovers.

(D) Yes, because the car manufacturer's negligence caused the dangerous situation that invited the rescue by the truck driver.

Question 4

A gas company built a large refining facility that conformed to zoning requirements on land near a landowner's property. The landowner had his own home and a mini-golf business on his property.

In a nuisance action against the gas company, the landowner established that the refinery emitted fumes that made many people feel quite sick when they were outside on his property for longer than a few minutes. The landowner's mini-golf business had greatly declined as a consequence, and the value of his property had gone down markedly.

Is the landowner likely to prevail?

(A) No, because the landowner has offered no evidence demonstrating that the gas company was negligent.

(B) No, because the refinery conforms to the zoning requirements.

(C) Yes, because the refinery has substantially and unreasonably interfered with the landowner's use and enjoyment of his property.

(D) Yes, because the value of the landowner's property has declined.

Question 5

A fire that started in the defendant's warehouse spread to the plaintiff's adjacent warehouse. The defendant did not intentionally start the fire, and the plaintiff can produce no evidence as to how the fire started. However, the defendant had failed to install a sprinkler system, which was required by a criminal statute. The plaintiff can produce evidence that had the sprinkler system been installed, it could have extinguished the fire before it spread.

In an action by the plaintiff against the defendant to recover for the fire damage, is it possible for the plaintiff to prevail?

(A) No, because the statute provides only for criminal penalties.

(B) No, because there is no evidence that the defendant negligently caused the fire to start.

(C) Yes, because a landowner is strictly liable for harm to others caused by the spread of fire from his premises under the doctrine of *Rylands v. Fletcher.*

(D) Yes, because the plaintiff was harmed as a result of the defendant's violation of a statute that was meant to protect against this type of occurrence.

Question 6

A schizophrenic patient who was institutionalized in a psychiatric facility pushed a nurse down a stairwell at the facility. The nurse, a paid employee of the facility who was trained to care for schizophrenic patients, was injured. The patient is an indigent whose care is paid for by the government.

The jurisdiction generally follows the rule that a person with a mental deficiency is held to the standard of a reasonable person. In a negligence action brought by the nurse against the patient, the patient's lawyer will argue that the patient should not be held responsible for the nurse's injury.

Which of the following facts will be LEAST helpful to the patient's lawyer's argument?

(A) The nurse was a professional caregiver.

(B) The nurse was trained to care for patients with schizophrenia.

(C) At the time she pushed the nurse, the patient thought she was being attacked by an elephant.

(D) The patient is an indigent whose care is paid for by the government.

Question 7

A farmer kept antiques in an uninhabited farmhouse on his property. The farmhouse had been broken into several times in the past, and some of the farmer's goods had been stolen. Instead of posting "No Trespassing" signs, the farmer decided to install an alarm system to deter intruders.

While the farmer was in the farmhouse installing the alarm system, he heard a window open in the adjoining room. The farmer crept very quietly to the door of the room, threw the door open, and found an intruder, a young child. The farmer immediately struck the child, a ten-year-old girl, very hard in the face, breaking her nose.

In an action on behalf of the child against the farmer to recover for the injury to her nose, is the child likely to prevail?

(A) No, because the farmer did not use deadly force.

(B) No, because the farmer had probable cause to believe that the child was a thief.

(C) Yes, because the farmer should have posted a "No Trespassing" sign.

(D) Yes, because the farmer used excessive force.

Question 8

A mining company that operated a copper mine in a remote location kept dynamite in a storage facility at the mine. The storage facility was designed and operated in conformity with state-of-the-art safety standards. In the jurisdiction, the storage of dynamite is deemed an abnormally dangerous activity.

Dynamite that was stored in the mining company's storage facility and that had been manufactured by an explosives manufacturer exploded due to an unknown cause. The explosion injured a state employee who was at the mine performing a safety audit. The employee brought an action in strict liability against the mining company.

What would be the mining company's best defense?

(A) The mine was in a remote location.

(B) The mining company did not manufacture the dynamite.

(C) The state employee assumed the risk of injury inherent in the job.

(D) The storage facility conformed to state-of-the-art safety standards.

Question 9

A driver negligently ran into a pedestrian who was walking along a road. The pedestrian sustained an injury to his knee, causing it to buckle from time to time. Several months later, the pedestrian sustained an injury to his shoulder when his knee buckled, causing him to fall down a flight of stairs. The pedestrian then brought an action against the driver for the injuries to his knee and shoulder.

In his action against the driver, for which of his injuries may the pedestrian recover damages?

(A) For the injuries to his knee and shoulder, because the driver takes the victim as he finds him.

(B) For the injuries to his knee and shoulder, if the jury finds that the pedestrian's fall down a flight of stairs was a normal consequence of his original injury.

(C) For the injury to his knee only, because the injury to the pedestrian's shoulder is separable.

(D) For the injury to his knee only, if the jury finds that the driver could not have foreseen that his negligent driving would cause the pedestrian to fall down a flight of stairs.

Question 10

A rancher and his neighbor were involved in a boundary dispute. In order to resolve their differences, each drove his truck to an open pasture area on his land where the two properties were separated by a fence. The rancher was accompanied by four friends, and the neighbor was alone.

The neighbor got out of his truck and walked toward the fence. The rancher got out but simply stood by his truck. When the neighbor came over the fence, the rancher shot him, inflicting serious injury.

In a battery action brought by the neighbor against the rancher, the rancher testified that he actually thought his neighbor was armed, although he could point to nothing that would have reasonably justified this belief.

Is the neighbor likely to prevail?

(A) No, because the rancher was standing on his own property and had no obligation to retreat.

(B) No, because the rancher suspected that the neighbor was armed.

(C) Yes, because deadly force is never appropriate in a property dispute.

(D) Yes, because it was unreasonable for the rancher to consider the use of a gun necessary for self-defense.

Question 11

A driver was traveling along a highway during an unusually heavy rainstorm when the roadway began to flood. To protect his car from water damage, the driver pulled his car up a steep, unmarked driveway abutting the highway that led to a homeowner's residence. The driver left his car parked in the driveway and walked home, intending to return when the floodwater had subsided. Shortly after the driver started to walk home, the homeowner carefully rolled the car back down his driveway and parked it on the highway shoulder. The floodwater continued to rise and caused damage to the driver's car.

If the driver sues the homeowner to recover for damage to the car, is the driver likely to prevail?

(A) Yes, because the driver was privileged to park his car on the homeowner's property.

(B) Yes, because there were no "no trespassing" signs posted.

(C) No, because the driver intentionally drove his car onto the homeowner's property.

(D) No, because the homeowner was privileged to remove the car from his property.

Question 12

A hotel employed a carefully selected independent contractor to rebuild its swimming pool. The hotel continued to operate while the pool was being rebuilt. The contract between the hotel and the contractor required the contractor to indemnify the hotel for any liability arising from the contractor's negligent acts. A guest of the hotel fell into the excavation, which the contractor had negligently left unguarded.

In an action by the guest against the hotel to recover for his injuries, what would be the most likely outcome?

(A) Liability, because the hotel had a nondelegable duty to the guest to keep a safe premises.

(B) Liability, because the contract between the hotel and the contractor required the contractor to indemnify the hotel for any liability arising from the contractor's negligent acts.

(C) No liability, because the contractor was the actively negligent party.

(D) No liability, because the hotel exercised reasonable care in employing the contractor.

Question 13

A newspaper published an editorial in which an editor asserted that a candidate for high political office was a user of illegal drugs. The accusation was untrue. The editor acted unreasonably in not investigating the accusation before publishing it; however, the editor honestly believed that the accusation was true.

The candidate sued the editor for defamation.

Is the candidate entitled to recover?

(A) No, because the accusation appeared in an editorial and was, therefore, merely an opinion.

(B) No, because the editor honestly believed that the accusation was true.

(C) Yes, because calling someone an illegal drug user is defamatory per se.

(D) Yes, because the accusation was false and was injurious to the candidate's reputation.

Question 14

An elderly neighbor hired a 17-year-old boy with a reputation for reckless driving to drive the neighbor on errands once a week. One day the teenager, driving the neighbor's car, took the neighbor to the grocery store. While the neighbor was in the store, the teenager drove out of the parking lot and headed for a party on the other side of town.

While on his way to the party, the teenager negligently turned in front of a moving car and caused a collision. The other driver was injured in the collision.

The injured driver has brought an action for damages against the neighbor, based on negligent entrustment, and against the teenager.

The jury has found that the injured driver's damages were \$100,000, that the injured driver was 10 percent at fault, that the teenager was 60 percent at fault, and that the neighbor was 30 percent at fault for entrusting his car to the teenager.

Based on these damage and responsibility amounts, what is the maximum that the injured driver could recover from the neighbor?

(A) \$100,000.
(B) \$90,000.
(C) \$60,000.
(D) \$30,000.

Question 15

A patient received anesthesia while giving birth. Upon awakening from the anesthesia, she discovered a severe burn on the inner portion of her right knee. The patient has brought a medical malpractice action in which she has joined all of the physicians and nurses who exercised control over her person, the delivery room, the medical procedures, and the equipment used during the period in which she was unconscious.

The defendants have jointly moved for summary judgment. The patient has produced affidavits that establish that the applicable professional standard of care was violated.

What would be the patient's best argument against the motion?

(A) At least one of the defendants had control over whatever agency or instrumentality caused the patient's injury.
(B) The defendants were acting in concert.
(C) The patient has produced affidavits that establish that the applicable professional standard of care was violated.
(D) The patient was in no way responsible for her injury.

Question 16

A customer pledged a stock certificate to a bank as security for a loan. A year later, when the customer fully repaid the loan, the bank refused the customer's demand to return the stock certificate because the officer dealing with the loan had the mistaken belief that there was still a balance due. No one at the bank reviewed the records until two months later, at which time the error was discovered. The bank then offered to return the stock certificate. However, the customer refused to accept it.

At the time the customer pledged the certificate, the shares were worth \$10,000; at the time the customer repaid the loan, the shares were worth \$20,000; and at the time the bank offered to return the certificate, the shares were worth \$5,000.

If the customer brings an action against the bank based on conversion, how much, if anything, should the customer recover?

(A) Nothing, because the bank lawfully came into possession of the certificate.
(B) \$5,000, because that was the value of the shares when the customer refused to accept the certificate back.
(C) \$10,000, because that was the value of the shares when the bank came into possession of the certificate.
(D) \$20,000, because that was the value of the shares when the customer was entitled to the return of the certificate.

Question 17

A man rented a car from a car rental agency. Unbeknownst to the rental agency, the car had a bomb hidden in it at the time of the rental. The bomb exploded an hour later, injuring the man.

Immediately prior to renting the car to the man, the rental agency had carefully inspected the car to be sure it was in sound operating condition. The rental agency did not inspect for hidden explosive devices, but such an inspection for explosives would have revealed the bomb.

There had been no previous incidents of persons hiding bombs in rental cars.

In a negligence action by the man against the car rental agency, is the man likely to prevail?

(A) No, because the rental agency could not have reasonably foreseen the likelihood of someone placing a bomb in the car it was about to rent to the man.
(B) No, because the rental agency did not hide the bomb in the car.
(C) Yes, because an inspection for explosive devices would have revealed the bomb.
(D) Yes, because the bomb made the car abnormally dangerous.

Question 18

In an action by a man against a pharmacy, the man offered only the following evidence:

The man took a clearly written prescription to a pharmacy. The pharmacy's employee filled the prescription by providing pills with 30 milligrams of the active ingredient instead of 20 milligrams, as was prescribed. Shortly after taking the pills as directed, the man, who had no previous history of heart problems, suffered a heart attack. Overdoses of the active ingredient had previously been associated with heart problems.

Does the man have a valid claim against the pharmacy?

(A) No, because pharmacies are not strictly liable for injuries caused by incorrectly filled prescriptions.
(B) No, because the man offered no specific proof as to the pharmacy's negligence.
(C) Yes, because a jury could reasonably conclude that the man would not have suffered a heart attack had the pharmacy provided the correct dosage.
(D) Yes, because by providing the 30-milligram pills rather than the 20-milligram pills, the pharmacy sold the man a defective product.

Question 19

A traveler was flying on a commercial aircraft owned and operated by an airline. The aircraft crashed into a mountain, killing everyone on board. The flying weather was good.

The traveler's legal representative brought a wrongful death action against the airline. At trial, the legal representative offered no expert or other testimony as to the cause of the crash.

On the airline's motion to dismiss at the conclusion of the legal representative's case, the court should

(A) grant the motion, because the legal representative has offered no evidence as to the cause of the crash.
(B) grant the motion, because the legal representative has failed to offer evidence negating the possibility that the crash may have been caused by mechanical failure that the airline could not have prevented.
(C) deny the motion, because the jury may infer that the aircraft crashed due to the airline's negligence.
(D) deny the motion, because in the circumstances common carriers are strictly liable.

Question 20

A sporting goods shop was burglarized by an escaped inmate from a nearby prison. The inmate stole a rifle and bullets from a locked cabinet. The burglar alarm at the sporting goods shop did not go off because the shop owner had negligently forgotten to activate the alarm's motion detector.

Shortly thereafter, the inmate used the rifle and ammunition stolen from the shop in a shooting spree that caused injury to a victim.

If the victim sues the shop owner for the injury she suffered, will the victim prevail?

(A) Yes, if the victim's injury would have been prevented had the motion detector been activated.
(B) Yes, because the owner was negligent in failing to activate the motion detector.
(C) No, because the storage and sale of firearms and ammunition is not an abnormally dangerous activity.
(D) No, unless there is evidence of circumstances suggesting a high risk of theft and criminal use of firearms stocked by the shop owner.

Question 21

Because of a farmer's default on his loan, the bank foreclosed on the farm and equipment that secured the loan. Among the items sold at the resulting auction was a new tractor recently delivered to the farmer by the retailer. Shortly after purchasing the tractor at the auction, the new owner was negligently operating the tractor on a hill when it rolled over due to a defect in the tractor's design. He was injured as a result. The new owner sued the auctioneer, alleging strict liability in tort. The jurisdiction has not adopted a comparative fault rule in strict liability cases.

In this suit, the result should be for the

(A) plaintiff, because the defendant sold a defective product that injured the plaintiff.
(B) plaintiff, if the defendant failed to inspect the tractor for defects prior to sale.
(C) defendant, because he should not be considered a "seller" for purposes of strict liability in tort.
(D) defendant, because the accident was caused in part by the new owner's negligence.

Question 22

A homeowner owns a house on a lake, and a neighbor owns a house across a driveway from the homeowner's property. The neighbor's house sits on a hill and the neighbor can see the lake from his living room window.

The homeowner and the neighbor got into an argument and the homeowner erected a large spotlight on his property that automatically comes on at dusk and goes off at sunrise. The only reason the homeowner installed the light was to annoy the neighbor. The glare from the light severely detracts from the neighbor's view of the lake. In a suit by the neighbor against the homeowner, will the neighbor prevail?

(A) Yes, because the homeowner installed the light solely to annoy the neighbor.
(B) Yes, if, and only if, the neighbor's property value is adversely affected.
(C) No, because the neighbor's view of the lake is not always obstructed.
(D) No, if the spotlight provides added security to the homeowner's property.

Question 23

A driver was driving his car near a house when the homeowner's child darted into the street in front of the driver's car. As the driver swerved and braked his car to avoid hitting the child, the car skidded up into the homeowner's driveway and stopped just short of the homeowner, who was standing in the driveway and had witnessed the entire incident. The homeowner suffered serious emotional distress from witnessing the danger to his child and to himself. Neither the homeowner nor his property was physically harmed.

If the homeowner asserts a claim for damages against the driver, will the homeowner prevail?

(A) Yes, because the driver's entry onto the homeowner's land was unauthorized.
(B) Yes, because the homeowner suffered serious emotional distress by witnessing the danger to his child and to himself.
(C) No, unless the driver was negligent.
(D) No, unless the homeowner's child was exercising reasonable care.

Question 24

A neighbor, who lived next door to another homeowner, went into the homeowner's garage without permission and borrowed the homeowner's chainsaw. The neighbor used the saw to clear broken branches from the trees on the neighbor's own property. After he had finished, the neighbor noticed several broken branches on the homeowner's trees that were in danger of falling on the homeowner's roof. While the neighbor was cutting the homeowner's branches, the saw broke.

In a suit for conversion by the homeowner against the neighbor, will the homeowner recover?

(A) Yes, for the actual damage to the saw.
(B) Yes, for the value of the saw before the neighbor borrowed it.
(C) No, because when the saw broke the neighbor was using it to benefit the homeowner.
(D) No, because the neighbor did not intend to keep the saw.

Question 25

When two parents were told that their child should repeat second grade, they sought to have him evaluated by a psychologist. The psychologist, who charged $300, determined that the son had a learning disability. Based upon the report, the school board placed the son in special classes. At an open meeting of the school board, the parents asked that the $300 they had paid to the psychologist be reimbursed by the school district. A reporter attending the meeting wrote a newspaper article about this request, mentioning the son by name.

In a privacy action brought by the son's legal representative against the newspaper, the plaintiff will

(A) recover, because the story is not newsworthy.
(B) recover, because the son is under the age of consent.
(C) not recover, if the story is a fair and accurate report of what transpired at the meeting.
(D) not recover, if the parents knew that the reporter was present.

Question 26

A city ordinance makes it unlawful to park a motor vehicle on a city street within ten feet of a fire hydrant. At 1:55 p.m. a driver, realizing he must be in his bank before it closed at 2:00 p.m., and finding no other space available, parked his automobile in front of a fire hydrant on a city street. The driver then hurried into the bank, leaving his aged neighbor as a passenger in the rear seat of the car. About five minutes later, and while the driver was still in the bank, a trucker was driving his tractor-trailer down the street. The trucker swerved to avoid what he mistakenly thought was a hole in the street and sideswiped the driver's car. The driver's car was turned over on top of the hydrant, breaking the hydrant and causing a small flood of water. The driver's car was severely damaged and the neighbor was badly injured. There is no applicable guest statute.

If the neighbor asserts a claim against the driver, the most likely result is that the neighbor will

(A) recover, because the driver's action was negligence per se.
(B) recover, because the driver's action was a continuing wrong which contributed to the neighbor's injuries.
(C) not recover, because a reasonably prudent person could not foresee injury to the neighbor as a result of the driver's action.
(D) not recover, because a violation of a city ordinance does not give rise to a civil cause of action.

Question 27

The vintner of a large vineyard offers balloon rides to visitors who wish to tour the grounds from the air. During one of the rides, the vintner was forced to make a crash landing on his own property. Without the vintner's knowledge or consent, a trespasser had entered the vineyard to camp for a couple of days. The trespasser was injured when he was hit by the basket of the descending balloon.

If the trespasser sues the vintner to recover damages for his injuries, will the trespasser prevail?

(A) No, unless the crash landing was made necessary by negligence on the vintner's part.
(B) No, unless the vintner could have prevented the injury to the trespasser after becoming aware of the trespasser's presence.
(C) Yes, because even a trespasser may recover for injuries caused by an abnormally dangerous activity.
(D) Yes, if the accident occurred at a place which the vintner knew was frequented by intruders.

Question 28

A thief was in the act of siphoning gasoline from his neighbor's car in the neighbor's garage and without his consent when the gasoline exploded and a fire followed. A rescuer, seeing the fire, grabbed a fire extinguisher from his car and put out the fire, saving the thief's life and the neighbor's car and garage. In doing so, the rescuer was badly burned. If the rescuer asserts a claim against the neighbor for personal injuries, the rescuer will

(A) prevail, because he saved the neighbor's property.
(B) prevail, because he acted reasonably in an emergency.
(C) not prevail, because the neighbor was not at fault.
(D) not prevail, because the rescuer knowingly assumed the risk.

Question 29

The warden of a state prison prohibits the photographing of the face of any prisoner without the prisoner's consent. A news photographer wanted to photograph a mobster, a notorious organized crime figure incarcerated at the state prison. To circumvent the warden's prohibition, the photographer flew over the prison exercise yard and photographed the mobster. Another prisoner, who was imprisoned for a technical violation of a regulatory statute, happened to be standing next to the mobster when the photograph was taken.

When the picture appeared in the press, the prisoner suffered severe emotional distress because he believed that his business associates and friends would think he was consorting with gangsters. The prisoner suffered no physical harm as the result of his emotional distress. The prisoner brought an action against the photographer for intentional or reckless infliction of emotional distress.

What is the best argument that the photographer can make in support of a motion for summary judgment?

(A) No reasonable person could conclude that the photographer intended to photograph the prisoner.
(B) The prisoner did not suffer any physical injury arising from the emotional distress.
(C) As a news photographer, the photographer was privileged to take photographs that others could not.
(D) No reasonable person could conclude that the photographer's conduct was extreme and outrageous as to the prisoner.

Question 30

A passenger departed on an ocean liner knowing that it would be a rough voyage due to predicted storms. The ocean liner was not equipped with the type of lifeboats required by the applicable statute.

The passenger was swept overboard and drowned in a storm so heavy that even a lifeboat that conformed to the statute could not have been launched. In an action against the operator of the ocean liner brought by the passenger's representative, will the passenger's representative prevail?

(A) Yes, because the ocean liner was not equipped with the statutorily required lifeboats.
(B) Yes, because in these circumstances common carriers are strictly liable.
(C) No, because the storm was so severe that it would have been impossible to launch a statutorily required lifeboat.
(D) No, because the passenger assumed the risk by boarding the ocean liner knowing that it would be a rough voyage.

Question 31

A basketball player suffered a serious injury while participating in an impromptu basketball game at a public park. The injury occurred when the player and his opponent each tried to obtain possession of the ball when it rebounded from the backboard after a missed shot at the basket. During that encounter, the player was struck and injured by the opponent's elbow. The player now seeks compensation from the opponent.

At the trial, evidence was introduced tending to prove that the game had been rough from the beginning, that elbows and knees had frequently been used to discourage interference by opposing players, and that the player had been one of those making liberal use of such tactics. In this action, will the player prevail?

(A) Yes, if the opponent intended to strike the player with his elbow.
(B) Yes, if the opponent intended to cause a harmful or offensive contact with the player.
(C) No, because the player impliedly consented to rough play.
(D) No, unless the opponent intentionally used force that exceeded the player's consent.

Question 32

In a trial to a jury, a restaurateur proved that the power company's negligent maintenance of a transformer caused a fire that destroyed his restaurant. The jury returned a verdict for the restaurateur in the amount of $450,000 for property loss and $500,000 for emotional distress. The trial judge entered judgment in those amounts. The power company appealed that part of the judgment awarding $500,000 for emotional distress.

On appeal, the judgment should be

(A) affirmed, because the power company negligently caused the restaurateur's emotional distress.
(B) affirmed, because harm arising from emotional distress is as real as harm caused by physical impact.

(C) reversed, because the law does not recognize a claim for emotional distress incident to negligently caused property loss.
(D) reversed, unless the jury found that the restaurateur suffered physical harm as a consequence of the emotional distress caused by his property loss.

Question 33

A law student rented a furnished apartment. His landlord began to solicit his advice about her legal affairs, but he refused to provide it. The landlord then demanded that he vacate the apartment immediately. The landlord also engaged in a pattern of harassment, calling the student at home every evening and entering his apartment without his consent during times when he was at school. During these unauthorized visits she removed the handles from the bathroom and kitchen sinks, but did not touch anything belonging to the student. The lease has a year to run, and the student is still living in the apartment. The student has sued the landlord for trespass to land.

Is he likely to prevail?

(A) No, because he has no standing to sue for trespass.
(B) No, because the landlord caused no damage to his property.
(C) Yes, for compensatory damages only.
(D) Yes, for injunctive relief, compensatory damages, and punitive damages.

Question 34

A customer fell and injured himself when he slipped on a banana peel while shopping at a grocer's store. The banana peel was fresh and clean except for a mark made by the heel of the customer's shoe. In an action brought by the customer against the grocer, these are the only facts in evidence.

Should the trial judge permit the case to go to the jury?

(A) No, because the customer had an obligation to watch where he stepped.
(B) No, because there is not a reasonable basis for inferring that the grocer knew or should have known of the banana peel.
(C) Yes, because it is more likely than not that the peel came from a banana offered for sale by the grocer.
(D) Yes, because the grocer could foresee that a customer might slip on a banana peel.

Question 35

An asbestos insulation installer, who worked from 1955 to 1965, contracted asbestosis, a serious lung disorder, as a result of inhaling airborne asbestos particles on the job. The asbestos was manufactured and sold to the installer's employer by an asbestos company. Because neither the asbestos company nor anyone else discovered the risk to asbestos installers until 1966, the asbestos company did not provide any warnings of the risks to installers until after that date.

The insulation installer brought an action against the asbestos company based on strict liability in tort for failure to warn. The case is to be tried before a jury. The jurisdiction has not adopted a comparative fault rule in strict liability cases.

In this action, an issue that is relevant to the case and is a question for the court to decide as a matter of law, rather than for the jury to decide as a question of fact, is whether

(A) a satisfactory, safer, alternative insulation material exists under today's technology.
(B) the defendant should be held to the standard of a prudent manufacturer who knew of the risks, regardless of whether the risks were reasonably discoverable before 1966.
(C) the defendant should reasonably have known of the risks of asbestos insulation materials before 1966, even though no one else had discovered the risks.
(D) the asbestos insulation materials to which the plaintiff was exposed were inherently dangerous.

Question 36

While approaching an intersection with the red light against him, a motorist suffered a heart attack that rendered him unconscious. The motorist's car struck a child, who was crossing the street with the green light in her favor. Under the state motor vehicle code, it is an offense to drive through a red traffic light.

The child sued the motorist to recover for her injuries. At trial it was stipulated that (1) immediately prior to suffering the heart attack, the motorist had been driving within the speed limit, had seen the red light, and had begun to slow his car; (2) the motorist had no history of heart disease and no warning of this attack; (3) while the motorist was unconscious, his car ran the red light.

On cross motions for directed verdicts on the issue of liability at the conclusion of the proofs, the court should

(A) grant the child's motion, because the motorist ran a red light in violation of the motor vehicle code.
(B) grant the child's motion, because, in the circumstances, reasonable persons would infer that the motorist was negligent.
(C) grant the motorist's motion, because he had no history of heart disease or warning of the heart attack.
(D) deny both motions and submit the case to the jury, to determine whether, in the circumstances, the motorist's conduct was that of a reasonably prudent person.

Question 37

A company designed and built a processing plant for the manufacture of an explosive chemical. An engineer was retained by the company to design a filter system for the processing plant. She prepared an application for a permit to build the plant's filter system and submitted it to the state's Department of Environmental Protection (DEP). As required by DEP regulations, the engineer submitted a blueprint to the DEP with the application for permit. The blueprint showed the entire facility and was signed and sealed by her as a licensed professional engineer.

After the project was completed, a portion of the processing plant exploded, injuring the plaintiff. During discovery in an action by the plaintiff against the engineer, it was established that the explosion was caused by a design defect in the processing plant that was unrelated to the filter system designed by the engineer.

In that action, will the plaintiff prevail?

(A) Yes, if the engineer signed, sealed, and submitted a blueprint that showed the design defect.

(B) Yes, because all of the plant's designers are jointly and severally liable for the defect.

(C) No, because the engineer owed no duty to the plaintiff to prevent the particular risk of harm.

(D) No, if the engineer was an independent contractor.

Question 38

A chemical engineer has no interest in or connection with a chemical company. The chemical engineer noticed that the chemical company's most recent, publicly issued financial statement listed, as part of the chemical company's assets, a large inventory of a certain special chemical compound. This asset was listed at a cost of $100,000, but the chemical engineer knew that the ingredients of the compound were in short supply and that the current market value of the inventory was in excess of $1,000,000. There was no current public quotation of the price of the chemical company stock. The book value of the chemical company stock, according to the statement, was $5 a share; its actual value was $30 a share.

Knowing these facts, the chemical engineer offered to purchase from a shareholder at $6 a share the 1,000 shares of the chemical company's stock owned by the shareholder. The shareholder and the chemical engineer had not previously met. The shareholder sold the stock to the chemical engineer for $6 a share.

If the shareholder asserts a claim based on misrepresentation against the chemical engineer, will the shareholder prevail?

(A) Yes, because the chemical engineer knew that the value of the stock was greater than the price she offered.

(B) Yes, if the chemical engineer did not inform the shareholder of the true value of the inventory.

(C) No, unless the chemical engineer told the shareholder that the stock was not worth more than $6 a share.

(D) No, if the chemical company's financial statement was available to the shareholder.

Question 39

A city has an ordinance that makes it an offense, punishable by fine, for the owner of a dog to permit the dog to run unleashed on a public way.

A police officer observed a small dog running loose in the street. As he picked up the dog, an onlooker who was seated in her car lawfully parked at the curb, called out, "Oh, thank you, Officer, for returning Fido." The officer asked the onlooker whether the dog was hers, and when she acknowledged ownership, he asked her to see her driver's license. The onlooker gave her name and address, but she refused to produce a driver's license. The officer then told her to produce her driver's license. The officer then told her to produce her driver's license if she did not want to go to jail. The onlooker responded by saying, "Isn't this ridiculous?" The officer took her by the arm and said, "Let's go. You are under arrest."

The onlooker cried out that the officer was hurting her but he refused to release her arm, and she struck him with her free hand. The officer then dragged the onlooker from her car, forced her into his squad car, and took her to the police station.

The incident took place on the street in front of the apartment where the onlooker and her aged father lived. The officer did not know that the aged father had observed what took place from a window in the apartment.

If the onlooker's aged father asserts a claim against the officer for the intentional infliction of emotional distress, will the aged father prevail?

(A) Yes, if the officer's acts caused the aged father severe emotional distress.

(B) Yes, if it is found that the officer's behavior was extreme and outrageous with respect to the onlooker.

(C) No, because the officer did not know that the aged father was watching.

(D) No, because the aged father was not within the zone of physical danger.

Question 40

A mother rushed her eight-year-old daughter to the emergency room at the local hospital after her daughter fell off her bicycle and hit her head on a sharp rock. The wound caused by the fall was extensive and bloody.

The mother was permitted to remain in the treatment room and held her daughter's hand while the emergency room physician cleaned and sutured the wound. During the procedure, the mother said that she was feeling faint and stood up to leave the room. While leaving the room, the mother fainted and, in falling, struck her head on a metal fixture that protruded from the emergency room wall. She sustained a serious injury as a consequence.

If the mother sues the hospital to recover damages for her injury, will she prevail?

(A) Yes, because the mother was a public invitee of the hospital's.
(B) Yes, unless the fixture was an obvious, commonly used, and essential part of the hospital's equipment.
(C) No, unless the hospital's personnel failed to take reasonable steps to anticipate and prevent the mother's injury.
(D) No, because the hospital's personnel owed the mother no affirmative duty of care.

Question 41

A nurse worked as a private duty nurse and on occasion worked in a hospital. The hospital called the private duty referral agency through which the nurse usually obtained employment and asked that in the future she not be assigned to patients in the hospital. The referral agency asked the hospital why it had made the request. The hospital sent a letter to the referral agency giving as the reason for its request that significant amounts of narcotics had disappeared during the nurse's shift from the nursing stations at which she had worked.

If the nurse asserts a claim based on defamation against the hospital, the nurse will

(A) recover, because the hospital accused the nurse of improper professional conduct.
(B) recover, if the nurse did not take the narcotics.
(C) not recover, if narcotics disappeared during the nurse's shifts.
(D) not recover, if the hospital reasonably believed that the nurse took the narcotics.

Question 42

An electrical engineer designed an electronic game. The electrical engineer entered into a licensing agreement with a toy company under which the toy company agreed to manufacture the electronic game according to the electrical engineer's specifications and to market it and pay a royalty to the electrical engineer.

One girl, whose parents had purchased the electronic game for her, was injured while playing the game. The girl recovered a judgment against the toy company on the basis of a finding that the electronic game was defective because of the electronic engineer's improper design.

In a claim for indemnity against the electrical engineer, will the toy company prevail?

(A) Yes, because as between the electrical engineer and the toy company, the electrical engineer was responsible for the design of the electronic game.
(B) Yes, because the toy company and the electrical engineer were joint tortfeasors.
(C) No, because the toy company, as the manufacturer, was strictly liable to the girl.
(D) No, if the toy company, by a reasonable inspection, could have discovered the defect in the design of the electronic game.

Question 43

For ten years, a vacationer and a neighbor have owned summer vacation homes on adjoining lots. A stream flows through both lots. As a result of a childhood swimming accident, the vacationer is afraid of water and has never gone close to the stream.

The neighbor built a dam on her property that has completely stopped the flow of the stream to the vacationer's property.

In a suit by the vacationer against the neighbor, will the vacationer prevail?

(A) Yes, if the damming unreasonably interferes with the use and enjoyment of the vacationer's property.
(B) Yes, if the neighbor intended to affect the vacationer's property.
(C) No, because the vacationer made no use of the stream.
(D) No, if the dam was built in conformity with all applicable laws.

Question 44

The day after a seller completed the sale of his house and moved out, one of the slates flew off the roof during a windstorm. The slate struck a pedestrian, who was on the public sidewalk. The pedestrian was seriously injured.

The roof is old and has lost several slates in ordinary windstorms on other occasions.

If the pedestrian sues the seller to recover damages for his injuries, will the pedestrian prevail?

(A) Yes, because the roof was defective when the seller sold the house.
(B) Yes, if the seller should have been aware of the condition of the roof and should have realized that it was dangerous to persons outside the premises.

(C) No, because the seller was neither the owner nor the occupier of the house when the pedestrian was injured.
(D) No, if the pedestrian knew that in the past slates had blown off the roof during windstorms.

Question 45

A patient had been under the care of a cardiologist for three years prior to submitting to an elective operation that was performed by a surgeon. Two days thereafter, the patient suffered a stroke, resulting in a coma, caused by a blood clot that lodged in her brain. When it appeared that she had entered a permanent vegetative state, with no hope of recovery, the artificial life-support system that had been provided was withdrawn, and she died a few hours later. The withdrawal of artificial life support had been requested by her family, and duly approved by a court. The surgeon was not involved in that decision, or in its execution.

The administrator of the patient's estate thereafter filed a wrongful death action against the surgeon, claiming that the surgeon was negligent in having failed to consult a cardiologist prior to the operation. At the trial the plaintiff offered evidence that accepted medical practice would require examination of the patient by a cardiologist prior to the type of operation that the surgeon performed.

In this action, the plaintiff should

(A) prevail, if the surgeon was negligent in failing to have the patient examined by a cardiologist prior to the operation.
(B) prevail, if the blood clot that caused the patient's death was caused by the operation which the surgeon performed.
(C) not prevail, absent evidence that a cardiologist, had one examined the patient before the operation, would probably have provided advice that would have changed the outcome.
(D) not prevail, because the surgeon had nothing to do with the withdrawal of artificial life support, which was the cause of the patient's death.

Question 46

The owner of a car left her car at the neighborhood garage to have repair work done. After completing the repairs, the mechanic took the car out for a test drive and was involved in an accident that caused damages to a bystander.

A statute imposes liability on the owner of an automobile for injuries to a third party that are caused by the negligence of any person driving the automobile with the owner's consent. The statute applies to situations of this kind, even if the owner did not specifically authorize the mechanic to test-drive the car.

The bystander sued the car owner and the mechanic jointly for damages arising from the accident. In that action, the car owner cross-claims to recover from the mechanic the amount of any payment the car owner may be required to make to the bystander. The trier of fact has determined that the accident was caused solely by negligent driving on the mechanic's part, and that the bystander's damages were $100,000.

In this action, what would be the proper outcome?

(A) The bystander should have judgment for $50,000 each against the car owner and the mechanic; the car owner should recover nothing from the mechanic.
(B) The bystander should have judgment for $100,000 against the mechanic only.
(C) The bystander should have judgment for $100,000 against the car owner and the mechanic jointly, and the car owner should have judgment against the mechanic for 50 percent of any amount collected from the car owner by the bystander.
(D) The bystander should have judgment for $100,000 against the car owner and the mechanic jointly, and the car owner should have judgment against the mechanic for any amount collected from the car owner by the bystander.

Question 47

A driver drove his car into an intersection and collided with a fire engine that had entered the intersection from the driver's right. The accident was caused by negligence on the driver's part. As a result of the accident, the fire engine was delayed in reaching a homeowner's house, which was entirely consumed by fire. The homeowner's house was located about ten blocks from the scene of the accident.

If the homeowner asserts a claim against the driver, what would the homeowner recover?

(A) The part of his loss that would have been prevented if the collision had not occurred.
(B) The value of his house before the fire.
(C) Nothing, if the driver had nothing to do with causing the fire.
(D) Nothing, because the driver's conduct did not create an apparent danger to the homeowner.

Question 48

A well-known movie star was drinking wine at a nightclub. A bottle of the wine, with its label plainly showing, was on the table in front of the movie star. An amateur photographer asked the movie star if he could take his picture and the movie star said, "Yes." Subsequently, the photographer sold the photo to the wine company, whose wine was pictured in the photo. The wine company, without the movie star's consent, used the photo in a wine advertisement in a nationally circulated magazine. The caption below the photo stated, "This movie star enjoys our wine."

If the movie star sues the wine company to recover damages as a result of the wine company's use of the photograph, will the movie star prevail?

(A) No, because the movie star consented to being photographed.
(B) No, because the movie star is a public figure.
(C) Yes, because the wine company made commercial use of the photograph.
(D) Yes, unless the movie star did, in fact, enjoy that specific wine.

Question 49

A bright nine-year-old child attended a day care center after school. The day care center was located near a man-made duck pond on the property of a corporation. During the winter, the pond was used for ice skating when conditions were suitable. At a time when the pond was only partially frozen, the child sneaked away from the center and walked out onto the ice covering the pond. The ice gave way, and the child fell into the cold water. He suffered shock and would have drowned had he not been rescued by a passerby. At the time of the incident, the pond was clearly marked with signs that stated, "THIN ICE—NO SKATING." When the child left the day care center, the center was staffed with a reasonable number of qualified personnel, and the center's employees were exercising reasonable care to ensure that the children in their charge did not leave the premises. The jurisdiction follows a rule of pure comparative negligence.

In a suit brought on the child's behalf against the day care center, who is likely to prevail?

(A) The child, because he left the center while he was under the center's care.
(B) The child, because the day care center is located near a pond.
(C) The day care center, because it was not negligent.
(D) The day care center, because the child was a trespasser.

Question 50

Chemical company *A* and chemical company *B* both manufacture pesticide *X*. Their plants are located along the same river. During a specific 24-hour period, each plant discharged pesticide into the river. Both plants were operated negligently and such negligence caused the discharge of the pesticide into the river.

A rancher operated a cattle ranch downstream from both plants. The rancher's cattle drank from the river and were poisoned by the pesticide.

The amount of the discharge from either plant alone would not have been sufficient to cause any harm to the rancher's cattle.

If the rancher asserts a claim against chemical company *A* and chemical company *B*, what, if anything, will the rancher recover?

(A) Nothing, because neither company discharged enough pesticide to cause harm to the rancher's cattle.
(B) Nothing, unless the rancher can establish how much pesticide each plant discharged.
(C) One-half of the rancher's damages from each company.
(D) The entire amount of the rancher's damages, jointly and severally, from two companies.

Question 51

A purchaser ordered some merchandise from a store. When the merchandise was delivered, the purchaser decided that it was not what he had ordered, and he returned it for credit. The store refused to credit the purchaser's account, continued to bill him, and, after 90 days, turned the account over to a bill collector for collection.

The bill collector arrived at the purchaser's house at 7 p.m. on a summer evening while many of the purchaser's neighbors were seated on their porches. When the purchaser opened the door, the bill collector, who was standing just outside the door, raised an electrically amplified bullhorn to his mouth. In a voice that could be heard a block away, the bill collector called the purchaser a "deadbeat" and asked him when he intended to pay his bill to the store.

If the purchaser asserts a claim based on defamation against the bill collector, will the purchaser prevail?

(A) Yes, if the bill collector's remarks were heard by any of the purchaser's neighbors.
(B) Yes, because the bill collector's conduct was extreme and outrageous.
(C) No, unless the bill collector knew that the purchaser owed no money to the store.
(D) No, unless the purchaser suffered some special damage.

Question 52

A pedestrian was crossing a street at a crosswalk. A jogger who was on the sidewalk nearby, saw a speeding automobile heading in the pedestrian's direction. The jogger ran into the street and pushed the pedestrian out of the path of the car. The pedestrian fell to the ground and broke her leg.

In an action for battery brought by the pedestrian against the jogger, will the pedestrian prevail?

(A) Yes, because the jogger could have shouted a warning instead of pushing the pedestrian out of the way.
(B) Yes, if the pedestrian was not actually in danger and the jogger should have realized it.

(C) No, because the driver of the car was responsible for the pedestrian's injury.
(D) No, if the jogger's intent was to save the pedestrian, not to harm her.

Question 53

A patron ate a spicy dinner at a restaurant on Sunday night. He enjoyed the food and noticed nothing unusual about the dinner.

Later that evening, the patron had an upset stomach. He slept well through the night, went to work the next day, and ate three meals. His stomach discomfort persisted, and by Tuesday morning he was too ill to go to work.

Eventually, the patron consulted his doctor, who found that the patron was infected with a bacterium that can be contracted from contaminated food. Food can be contaminated when those who prepare it do not adequately wash their hands.

The patron sued the restaurant for damages. He introduced testimony from a health department official that various health code violations had been found at the restaurant both before and after the patron's dinner, but that none of the restaurant's employees had signs of bacterial infection when they were tested one month after the incident.

The restaurant's best argument in response to the patron's suit would be that

(A) No one else who ate at the restaurant on Sunday complained about stomach discomfort.
(B) The restaurant instructs its employees to wash their hands carefully and is not responsible if any employee fails to follow these instructions.
(C) The patron has failed to establish that the restaurant's food caused his illness.
(D) The patron assumed the risk of an upset stomach by choosing to eat spicy food.

Question 54

As an encyclopedia salesman approached the grounds on which a house was situated, he saw a sign that said, "No salesmen. Trespassers will be prosecuted. Proceed at your own risk." Although the salesman had not been invited to enter, he ignored the sign and drove up the driveway toward the house. As he rounded a curve, a powerful explosive charge buried in the driveway exploded, and the salesman was injured.

Can the salesman recover damages from the homeowner for his injuries?

(A) Yes, if the homeowner was responsible for the explosive charge under the driveway.
(B) Yes, unless the homeowner, when he planted the charge, intended only to deter, not to harm, a possible intruder.
(C) No, because the salesman ignored the sign, which warned him against proceeding further.
(D) No, if the homeowner reasonably feared that intruders would come and harm him or his family.

Question 55

A construction company was digging a trench for a new sewer line in a street in a high-crime neighborhood. During the course of the construction, there had been many thefts of tools and equipment from the construction area. One night, the construction company's employees neglected to place warning lights around the trench. A delivery truck drove into the trench and broke an axle. While the delivery driver was looking for a telephone to summon a tow truck, thieves broke into the delivery truck and stole $350,000 worth of goods. The delivery company sued the construction company to recover for the $350,000 loss and for $1,500 worth of damage to its truck. The construction company stipulated that it was negligent in failing to place warning lights around the trench, and admits liability for damage to the truck, but denies liability for the loss of the goods.

On cross-motions for summary judgment, how should the court rule?

(A) Deny both motions, because there is evidence to support a finding that the construction company should have realized that its negligence could create an opportunity for a third party to commit a crime.
(B) Grant the construction company's motion, because no one could have foreseen that the failure to place warning lights could result in the loss of a cargo of valuable goods.
(C) Grant the construction company's motion, because the criminal acts of third persons were a superseding cause of the loss.
(D) Grant the delivery company's motion, because but for the construction company's actions, the goods would not have been stolen.

Question 56

The personnel director of an investment company told a job applicant during an interview that the company was worth millions of dollars and that the company's portfolio would triple in the next several months. The applicant was very excited about the company's prospects and accepted an offer to work for the company. Two days later, the applicant read in the newspaper that the investment company had filed for bankruptcy reorganization. As a result of reading this news, the applicant suffered severe emotional distress but he immediately found another comparable position.

Is the applicant likely to prevail in his action for negligent misrepresentation?

(A) No, because the applicant did not suffer any physical injury or pecuniary loss.
(B) No, because the personnel director's statement was purely speculative.
(C) Yes, because the applicant relied on the personnel director's misrepresentations about the investment company.
(D) Yes, because the personnel director should have foreseen that his misrepresentations would cause the applicant to be upset.

Question 57

A bus passenger was seated next to a woman whom he did not know. The woman stood to exit the bus, leaving a package on the seat. The passenger lightly tapped the woman on the back to get her attention and to inform her that she had forgotten the package. Because the woman had recently had back surgery, the tap was painful and caused her to twist and seriously injure her back.

If the woman sues the passenger to recover for the back injury, will she prevail?

(A) No, because she is presumed to have consented to the ordinary contacts of daily life.
(B) No, because she was not put in apprehension because of the touching.
(C) Yes, because the passenger intentionally touched her.
(D) Yes, because the passenger's intentional touching seriously injured her.

Question 58

A smoker and a nonsmoker were seated at adjoining tables in a small restaurant. The smoker's table was in the smoking section, and the nonsmoker's table was in the nonsmoking section. When the smoker lit a cigarette, the nonsmoker politely requested that he not smoke, explaining that she had a severe allergy to cigarette smoke. The smoker ignored the nonsmoker's request and continued to smoke. As a result, the nonsmoker was hospitalized with a severe allergic reaction to the smoke.

The nonsmoker brought a battery action against the smoker.

Which of the following questions will NOT be an issue in the battery action?

(A) Did the smoker intend to cause the nonsmoker's contact with the cigarette smoke?
(B) Does smoke have the physical properties necessary for making the kind of contact required for battery?
(C) Is contact with cigarette smoke from a lawful smoking section in a restaurant the kind of contact one must endure as a voluntary restaurant patron?
(D) Was the smoker's conduct unreasonable under the circumstances?

Question 59

While driving his open-bed truck with a friend in the open bed, the driver swerved, throwing his friend to the pavement. The friend sustained severe injuries. The friend had often ridden in the open bed of the driver's truck, and on some of those occasions the driver had swerved to frighten his friend. The friend sued the driver to recover both compensatory damages for his injuries and punitive damages.

Which cause of action would NOT permit the friend to recover punitive damages?

(A) Assault.
(B) Battery.
(C) Negligence.
(D) Recklessness.

Question 60

As a shopper was leaving a supermarket, an automatic door that should have opened outward opened inward, striking and breaking the shopper's nose. The owner of the building had installed the automatic door. The lease, pursuant to which the supermarket leased the building, provided that the supermarket was responsible for all maintenance of the premises.

The shopper sued the supermarket. At trial, neither the shopper nor the supermarket offered any testimony, expert or otherwise, as to why the door had opened inward. At the conclusion of the proofs, both the shopper and the supermarket moved for judgment.

How should the trial judge rule?

(A) Grant judgment for the shopper, because it is undisputed that the door malfunctioned.
(B) Grant judgment for the supermarket, because the shopper failed to join the owner of the building as a defendant.
(C) Grant judgment for the supermarket, because the shopper failed to offer proof of the supermarket's negligence.
(D) Submit the case to the jury, because on these facts negligence may be inferred.

Question 61

A dentist was anesthetizing a patient's gum before pulling a tooth. Although the dentist used due care, the hypodermic needle broke off in the patient's gum, causing injury. The needle broke because of a manufacturing defect that the dentist could not have detected.

Is the patient likely to recover damages in an action against the dentist based on strict products liability and malpractice?

(A) No, on neither basis.
(B) Yes, based on malpractice, but not on strict products liability.
(C) Yes, based on strict products liability, but not on malpractice.
(D) Yes, on both bases.

Question 62

Two lawyers are the only members of a law partnership in a small town that has only one other lawyer in it. Both attorneys do a substantial amount of personal injury work. A client was severely and permanently injured in an automobile collision when struck by an automobile driven by a motorist. The client employed the law partnership to represent her in obtaining damages for her injuries. At the time the client employed the partnership, the statute of limitations had six weeks to run on her claim. The complaint was prepared but not filed. Each lawyer thought that the other lawyer would file the complaint. The statute of limitations ran out on the client's claim against the motorist.

The client has filed suit against both lawyers for negligence. That case is on trial with a jury in a court of general jurisdiction.

In order to establish a breach of standard of care owed to her by the two lawyers, the client

(A) must have a legal expert from the same locality testify that the defendants' conduct was a breach.
(B) must have a legal expert from the same state testify that the defendants' conduct was a breach.
(C) can rely on the application of the jurors' common knowledge as to whether there was a breach.
(D) can rely on the judge, as an expert in the law, to advise the jury whether there was a breach.

Question 63

A hiker sustained a head injury when he was struck by a limb that fell from a tree. At the time of his injury, the hiker was walking through a forest on private property without the property owner's knowledge or permission. It was determined that the limb fell because the tree was infested with termites.

In an action by the hiker against the property owner to recover for his head injury, will the hiker prevail?

(A) No, because the property owner could not foresee that anyone would be injured.
(B) No, because the property owner breached no duty to the hiker, who was a trespasser.
(C) Yes, because the property owner had a duty to prevent the trees on his property from becoming dangerous.
(D) Yes, because the property owner is liable for hidden dangers on his property.

Question 64

A homeowner resented the fact that joggers and walkers would sometimes come onto his property just beside the sidewalk in order to enjoy the feel of walking or running on grass. He put up a "No Trespassing" sign, but it did not stop the practice. He then put up a "Beware of Skunk" sign and bought a young skunk. He took the skunk to a vet to have its scent gland removed. Unfortunately, the vet did not perform the operation properly, and the scent gland was not removed. The homeowner was unaware that it had not been removed.

One day a walker was out for a stroll. When she came to the homeowner's property, she walked on the grass alongside the sidewalk on the homeowner's property. The skunk came up behind the walker and sprayed her with its scent. The smell was overpowering, and she fainted. She struck her head on the sidewalk and suffered serious injuries.

The probable result of the walker's claim against the homeowner is that she will

(A) recover, because the skunk was a private nuisance.
(B) recover, because the skunk was not a domesticated animal.
(C) not recover, because the walker was a trespasser.
(D) not recover, because the vet was the cause of the injury.

Question 65

A driver negligently ran over a pedestrian. A bystander witnessed the accident from across the street. The bystander ran to the pedestrian, whom he did not know, and administered first aid, but the pedestrian died in the bystander's arms. The bystander suffered serious emotional distress as a result of his failure to save the pedestrian's life, but he experienced no resulting physical manifestations. The bystander brought a negligence action against the driver.

Is the bystander likely to prevail?

(A) No, because the bystander assumed the risk.
(B) No, because the bystander had no familial or other preexisting relationship with the pedestrian.
(C) Yes, because danger invites rescue.
(D) Yes, because the bystander was in the zone of danger.

Question 66

A motorist was driving his pickup truck along a lonely road on a very cold night. The motorist saw the apparently injured plaintiff lying in a field by the side of the road. The motorist stopped his truck, alighted, and, upon examining the plaintiff, discovered that the plaintiff was intoxicated and in danger of suffering from exposure to the cold. However, the motorist returned to his truck and drove away without making any effort to help the plaintiff. The plaintiff remained lying at the same place and was later injured when struck by a car driven by a traveler, who was drowsy and inattentive and had veered off the road into the field, hitting the plaintiff. The traveler did not see the plaintiff prior to hitting him.

If the plaintiff asserts a claim against the motorist for damages for his injuries, will the plaintiff prevail?

(A) Yes, because by stopping and examining the plaintiff, the motorist assumed a duty to aid him.

(B) Yes, if a reasonably prudent person under the circumstances would have aided the plaintiff.

(C) No, if the motorist did not, in any way, make the plaintiff's situation worse.

(D) No, because the plaintiff himself created the risk of harm by becoming intoxicated.

Question 67

A homeowner owned a large poisonous snake, which had been defanged and was kept in a cage. A storm damaged the homeowner's house and the snake's cage, allowing it to escape. During the cleanup after the storm, a volunteer worker came across the snake. The worker tried to run away from the snake and fell, breaking his arm.

In a suit by the worker against the homeowner based on strict liability in tort to recover for his injury, will the worker prevail?

(A) No, because the snake's escape was caused by a force of nature.

(B) No, because the worker should have anticipated an injury during his volunteer work.

(C) Yes, because the homeowner did not take adequate precautions to secure the snake.

(D) Yes, because the worker's injury was the result of his fear of the escaped snake.

Question 68

A company manufactured metal stamping presses that were usually sold with an installed safety device that made it impossible for a press to close on a worker's hands. The safety device produced a substantially safer machine without affecting the machine's ease of use, and cost the manufacturer little. The company strongly recommended that its presses be purchased with the safety device installed, but would sell a press without the safety device at a slightly reduced price. This alternative model included a warning that the press created a risk of closing on the operator's hand and crushing it.

Rejecting the company's advice, a worker's employer purchased a stamping press without the safety device. The press closed on the worker's hand, crushing it. In an action brought by the worker against the company, will the worker prevail?

(A) Yes, because the company's press was the cause in fact of the worker's injury.

(B) Yes, because the company sold the press to the worker's employer without an installed safety device.

(C) No, because the failure of the worker's employer to purchase the press with a safety device was a superseding intervening cause of the worker's injury.

(D) No, because the company strongly recommended that the worker's employer purchase the press with the safety device.

Question 69

A child was bitten by a dog while playing in a fenced-in common area of an apartment complex owned by a landlord. The child was the guest of a tenant living in the complex, and the dog was owned by another tenant. The owner of the dog knew that the dog had a propensity to bite, but the landlord did not have any notice of the dog's vicious propensities.

In an action by the child against the landlord, will the child prevail?

(A) Yes, because in these circumstances a landlord is strictly liable.

(B) Yes, because a landlord's duty to protect a tenant's guests from dangerous conditions is nondelegable.

(C) No, because the landlord did not have any notice of the dog's vicious propensities.

(D) No, because a landlord owes no duty to a tenant's gratuitous guests.

Question 70

A host pointed an unloaded revolver at her guest, threatening to shoot him. The guest knew that the revolver was not loaded, and that the ammunition for the revolver was stored in a locked basement closet, two stories below where the two were then standing.

In an action brought by the guest against the host for assault, will the guest prevail?

(A) No, because the host did not intend to shoot her guest.
(B) No, because the host did not put her guest in apprehension of an imminent contact.
(C) Yes, because the ammunition was accessible to the host.
(D) Yes, because the host threatened her guest with a revolver.

Question 71

A driver, returning from a long shift at a factory, fell asleep at the wheel and lost control of his car. As a result, his car collided with a police car driven by an officer who was returning to the station after having responded to an emergency. The police officer was injured in the accident. The police officer sued the driver in negligence for her injuries. The driver moved for summary judgment, arguing that the common-law firefighters' rule barred the suit.

Should the court grant the motion?

(A) No, because the firefighters' rule does not apply to police officers.
(B) No, because the police officer's injuries were not related to any special dangers of her job.
(C) Yes, because the accident would not have occurred but for the emergency.
(D) Yes, because the police officer was injured on the job.

ANSWERS

TORTS

Answer Key

Use this Answer Key to quickly identify the correct answer to each question.

(1)	A	(11)	A	(21)	C	(31)	D	(41)	D	(51)	D	(61)	A	(71)	B
(2)	B	(12)	A	(22)	A	(32)	C	(42)	A	(52)	B	(62)	C		
(3)	D	(13)	B	(23)	C	(33)	D	(43)	A	(53)	C	(63)	B		
(4)	C	(14)	B	(24)	B	(34)	B	(44)	B	(54)	A	(64)	B		
(5)	D	(15)	A	(25)	C	(35)	B	(45)	C	(55)	A	(65)	B		
(6)	D	(16)	D	(26)	C	(36)	C	(46)	D	(56)	A	(66)	C		
(7)	D	(17)	A	(27)	B	(37)	C	(47)	A	(57)	A	(67)	D		
(8)	C	(18)	C	(28)	C	(38)	C	(48)	C	(58)	D	(68)	B		
(9)	B	(19)	C	(29)	D	(39)	C	(49)	C	(59)	C	(69)	C		
(10)	D	(20)	D	(30)	C	(40)	C	(50)	D	(60)	D	(70)	B		

ANSWERS

TORTS

Answer 1

(A) is the best response,

because a manufacturer has no obligation to warn against obvious dangers.

In a suit based on strict product liability (as the suit here would likely be), the manufacturer's failure to warn of a danger can itself make the product defective, and trigger strict liability for injuries caused by that defect. Rest. 3d Torts (Prod. Liab.), §§ 1, 2(c). But the seller or manufacturer of a product is generally not liable for failing to warn against a danger that should be *obvious to foreseeable users* of the product. *Id*. at §2, Comment j. That's because "warning of an obvious or generally known risk in most instances will not provide an effective additional measure of safety." *Id*.

Here, the ordinary dangers of working on a ladder are obvious. And there appears to be nothing about using a ladder to clean this furnace that increases the danger of ladder use generally. So the manufacturer's failure to warn about the dangers of ladder use did not make the furnace defective. And nothing else in these facts supplies any other ground for imposing either strict liability or liability for negligence.

(B) is not the best response

because there was no reason for the homeowner to believe that he could not safely maintain the furnace.

There is nothing in these facts to suggest that the homeowner should have hired a professional to clean the furnace. Even if the homeowner's decision to clean the furnace himself rather than hiring an expert was found to be "misuse" of the product, in most courts that misuse would merely *reduce* the homeowner's damages under comparative-fault principles, not *eliminate* his recovery; so misuse would not prevent the homeowner from "prevailing," and the question asks whether he will "prevail." Furthermore, there is no reason to suspect that a "professional" would be less likely to fall from a ladder than the homeowner was—this choice is referring to one who is a professional cleaner of furnaces, not one who is a professional ladder-climber, and there is no reason to believe that a professional furnace-cleaner would be in materially less danger of losing his balance on a ladder than the homeowner would be.

(C) is not the best response,

because the absence of a ladder did not make the product defective.

The manufacturer could be liable only if either the product was defective, or the manufacturer was negligent. There is no reason to believe that the manufacturer's failure to supply a ladder made the furnace defective, because ladders are a readily-available household item, and there is no indication that a special-purpose ladder would have been safer than a standard ladder that the homeowner could have bought at a hardware store. (That is, the homeowner could have fallen just as readily from a manufacturer-supplied ladder as from a standard one bought by the homeowner.)

(D) is not the best response,

because a manufacturer is not required to warn of obvious dangers.

A manufacturer's failure to warn of dangers in using the product may make the product defective, thus triggering strict liability. But a manufacturer is not required to give warnings of *obvious* dangers, as is further described in Choice A. There is no indication from these facts that there was a way to clean the furnace without climbing on a step ladder, so the presence of a warning would not, even if it had been issued and followed, have prevented the homeowner from standing on a ladder tall enough to facilitate the cleaning. The only thing the manufacturer could have warned about was to be careful while standing on top of such a ladder, and that would have been a warning against an obvious danger, something that a manufacturer is not required to give.

Answer 2

(B) is the best response,

because assault requires that the plaintiff become aware of the defendant's attempt to inflict a harmful or offensive contact before the attempt has been terminated.

The defendant is liable to the plaintiff for assault if "(a) [the defendant] acts intending to cause a harmful or offensive contact with the person of the [plaintiff] or a third person, or an imminent apprehension of such a contact, and (b) the [plaintiff] *is thereby put in such imminent apprehension*." Rest. 2d Torts, § 21.

So even if the defendant intends to cause a harmful or offensive contact with the plaintiff, the defendant won't be liable for assault unless the plaintiff is "thereby put in . . . *imminent apprehension*" of such a contact. It's not enough that the plaintiff learns of the threatened contact *after* the threat has passed—"An attempt to inflict a harmful or offensive contact or to cause an apprehension of such contact does not make the actor liable for an assault if the other does *not become aware* of the attempt *before it is terminated*." Rest. 2d Torts, § 22. Since the attempt was over, and the knife was under the bed, by the time the student woke up, there was no moment at which the student feared an imminent (future) contact.

(A) is not the best response,

because assault could have occurred even without any sort of touching.

If you look at the definition of assault in the first full paragraph of the discussion of choice B above, you'll see that no actual touching is required for the tort; the only real-world consequence required is that the plaintiff have been put in imminent *apprehension* of a harmful or offensive touching. So if the student had been awake at the time the roommate approached him with the ice pick, and the student had been afraid of being struck, the student could have recovered for assault even if the roommate changed his mind at the last instant. Therefore, this choice asserts the correct outcome, but gives the wrong reason for it.

(C) is not the best response,

because fear that is felt after the threat of imminent harmful contact has passed does not suffice for assault.

As the discussion of choice B explains, the plaintiff in an assault action must have felt an apprehension of *imminent* harmful or offensive contact. A plaintiff who does not learn of the danger until after the threat has passed does not qualify. So no fear that the plaintiff might feel beginning on the day after the attack could qualify, however reasonable it might be for the plaintiff to feel that fear. And even if the plaintiff reasonably feared that there might be another episode—that the expelled roommate might sneak back into the dorm and conduct another attack against the plaintiff—that fear won't suffice, because it is not fear of an "imminent" attack.

(D) is not the best response,

because it does not address the requirement that the plaintiff suffer an apprehension of imminent contact.

The fact that the roommate intended to inflict serious harm satisfies the first requirement for assault, that the defendant "acts intending to cause a harmful or offensive contact with the person of the [plaintiff] or a third person, or an imminent apprehension of such a contact[.]" Rest. 2d Torts, § 21. But there is a second requirement, that the plaintiff actually be "*put in such imminent apprehension*." *Id*. This choice does not address the second requirement, and, indeed, the second requirement is not satisfied here, because the student was asleep while the threat was imminent, preventing him from "apprehending" that threat until after it had passed.

Answer 3

(D) is the best response,

because it was reasonably foreseeable that negligence by the car's manufacturer might lead to physical harm to a rescuer.

Where the defendant's negligence places one person at physical risk, it is quite foreseeable that another person might come to the rescue, and herself be injured. When this happens, the negligence by the defendant is deemed to be the proximate cause of the injuries to the rescuer. *See* Rest. 3d Torts (Liab. Phys. Harm), § 32, Comment b: "[A]n actor, whose tortious conduct puts the actor or another at risk, is subject to liability to a third person who is injured while attempting to come to the aid of the actor or the other imperiled person."

This choice, by saying that the situation "invited the rescue," is virtually quoting the leading case on the subject, in which Judge Cardozo famously wrote, "*Danger invites rescue*. The cry of distress is the summons to relief." *Wagner v. International Railway Company*, 232 N.Y. 176 (1921).

Here, it was foreseeable to one in the car manufacturer's position that if the car's negligent design made the car unduly liable to roll over after a blowout, a passerby might try to rescue the inhabitants of the rolled-over car and be injured during that attempt. So the manufacturer will be liable to the would-be rescuer. It doesn't matter whether the *particular sequence* by which the truck driver was injured (here, returning to his truck after having ceded the rescue attempts to the professional rescuers) was especially foreseeable; it's enough for proximate cause that car accidents *in general* tend to invoke rescue attempts, and that rescuers are often injured in some way or another during the rescue attempt.

(A) is not the best response,

because the manufacturer's negligence would be considered a proximate cause of the truck driver's injuries.

It's true that the chain of causation here is somewhat lengthy. But as a general principle, it's reasonably foreseeable that where a person is placed in peril, someone else may try to rescue that person, and herself be injured in the attempt. Therefore, courts generally hold that the defendant's negligence towards one person is the proximate cause of injury to someone else who is injured during an attempt to rescue the first person. And that's true even if the particular chain of events by which the rescuer comes to be injured would have been somewhat hard to foresee.

(B) is not the best response,

because the truck driver would not be deemed to have assumed the risk of injury here.

The plaintiff will not be found to have assumed a particular risk of harm unless he "voluntarily" assumed that risk. And where the defendant, through his negligence, has left the plaintiff with no reasonable choice but to encounter the risk, the plaintiff's decision to take the risk is not voluntary. *See* Rest. 2d Torts, § 496 E(2): "The plaintiff's acceptance of a risk is not voluntary if the defendant's tortious conduct has *left him no reasonable alternative course of conduct* in order to (a) avert harm to himself or *another*[.]" *See also id*., Illustr. 3 (D railroad negligently fails to warn that a train is approaching a crossing, and thereby endangers B, a blind man who is about to cross; when C, a bystander, rushes onto the track to push B to safety and is himself struck by the train, C has not assumed the risk).

Here, the truck driver was driving close behind the motorist, and could reasonably have believed that if he didn't stop to help, no one else would help quickly enough. So in the words of the Restatement, the car manufacturer's negligence left the truck driver with "no reasonable alternative course of conduct in order to . . . avert harm to . . . another," thereby preventing the truck driver from being deemed to have voluntarily assumed the risk of danger.

(C) is not the best response,

because it does not deal with the proximate cause issue posed by these facts.

Even a negligent defendant will not be liable for injuries if the defendant's negligent conduct was not the "proximate cause" of the injuries. Here, where the causal sequence between the manufacturer's negligent design of the vehicle and the truck driver's being struck down by a speeding car is somewhat attenuated, an explanation of why the truck driver wins would have to establish why the manufacturer's negligence was the proximate cause of the injury. This choice, by stating merely that "it is foreseeable that injuries can result from rollovers," might be enough to explain why the car manufacturer is liable to an occupant of the rolled-over car. But it does not explain why the manufacturer's liability should extend to a would-be rescuer. The only type of explanation that would successfully deal with this extended proximate-cause issue is one that focuses on the fact that, where a negligent act creates a peril, the act also tends to induce a rescue response. Therefore, this choice, although it correctly predicts the outcome, is much less good an explanation than Choice D's rescue-oriented explanation.

Answer 4

(C) is the best response,

because the decline in both the volume of the business and the value of the property demonstrate that the refinery's interference with the landowner's use and enjoyment of his property was substantial and unreasonable.

One who intentionally causes a substantial and unreasonable interference with another person's use or enjoyment of the latter's property without a valid defense is liable for *private nuisance*. To prevail on such a nuisance claim, the landowner will have to make two major showings: (1) that the interference with his use and enjoyment of his property was "*substantial and unreasonable*"; and (2) that the interference was "*intentional*" (unless he can show that the interference was negligent, reckless, or involved an abnormally dangerous activity). Let's take these requirements one at a time.

The landowner should be able to show that the interference with his use and enjoyment was "substantial and unreasonable" by virtue of the fact that the mini-golf business "greatly declined" as a result of the fumes, and the market value of the property had "markedly" decreased. Even if the gas company is carrying on a socially useful activity, the impact on the landowner will be classified as "unreasonable" if the harm to him is "greater than he ought to be required to bear under the circumstances, at least without compensation." Rest. 2d Torts, § 822, Comment g. Given the objectively-measurable, severe damage to the landowner's economic interests, this test for unreasonableness seems clearly satisfied.

With respect to requirement (2), the landowner will have to prove that the gas company had one of the mental states required for private nuisance liability. The plaintiff in a private nuisance action must show that the defendant's interference with the plaintiff's use and enjoyment was either (a) intentional; (b) negligent; (c) reckless; or (d) stemming from an abnormally dangerous activity. *See* Rest. 2d Torts, § 822(b). Because there is no evidence in these facts of negligence, recklessness, or the conducting of an abnormally dangerous activity, the landowner will, as a practical matter, have to show that the interference was "intentional." In other words, outside of the abnormally-dangerous-activity scenario, there is no nuisance liability for unintentional non-negligent interference with another's use and enjoyment of land.

However, the word "intentional" is defined quite broadly in this context. It's not necessary that the defendant act for the *purpose* of causing the interference. Rather, it's enough that the defendant *knows* that the interference is either occurring, or is substantially certain to occur in the future, as a result of the defendant's conduct. Rest. 2d Torts, § 825(b). So even if the gas company was originally unaware that the fumes it was emitting were making people on the landowner's property sick, once the gas company received complaints that this was happening, and continued with the conduct, the interference became "intentional." (We don't actually know specifically that the landowner complained, but we know he brought a nuisance suit, so at the very least, once the gas company continued emitting the fumes after it received the complaint, it was acting in an "intentional" manner.)

(A) is not the best response,

because negligence by the gas company is not an element that the landowner is required to prove.

It's true that there is no strict liability for private nuisance (outside of the special case of an abnormally dangerous activity). But it does not follow that the plaintiff must establish negligence by the defendant. Other mental states suffice, one of which is that the interference was "intentional." As is described in the last paragraph of Choice C above, as long as the gas company knew that the interference was occurring, that knowledge was enough to meet the requirement of an "intentional" interference, making it unnecessary for the landowner to show that the gas company behaved negligently. So even if the gas company used all plausible measures to reduce fumes, it would still be liable for an intentional interference, simply because it knew that the interference was continuing to occur.

(B) is not the best response,

because the refinery's conformance to zoning requirements is not dispositive.

To establish a case for private nuisance, the plaintiff must show that the defendant's interference with the plaintiff's use and enjoyment is "unreasonable." And the fact that the defendant's use is in conformity with the local zoning rules is certainly a factor tending to show that the interference is not unreasonable. But that factor is not at all dispositive—the court is free to conclude that the activity, despite being permitted by zoning, so greatly interferes with the plaintiff's use and enjoyment that he should not be required to bear it without compensation, making the activity "unreasonable."

(D) is not the best response,

because a mere decline in the value of the property is not enough to establish a nuisance.

The plaintiff in a private nuisance case must show that the defendant's activity has "substantially and unreasonably" interfered with the plaintiff's use and enjoyment of his land. The mere fact that there was some decline in the value of the property would not be enough to establish either that the interference was "substantial" or that it was "unreasonable." The additional facts that many people are being sickened while being on the property for more than a few minutes, and that far fewer people are playing mini-golf as a result, help establish that the interference was substantial and unreasonable. So this choice, although it states the correct outcome, is not the best explanation of why the plaintiff will prevail.

Answer 5

(D) is the best response,

because the statutory violation will cause the court to apply the doctrine of negligence *per se*.

Under the doctrine of negligence *per se*, if the defendant, without excuse, violated a criminal statute that was designed to protect against the type of accident that occurred, then the violation automatically constitutes negligence. *See* Rest. 3d Torts (Liab. Phys. Harm), § 14 ("An actor is negligent if, without excuse, the actor violates a statute that is designed to protect against the type of accident the actor's conduct causes, and if the accident victim is within the class of persons the statute is designed to protect.")

Here, it's pretty obvious that the purpose of the criminal statute is to prevent fires, once they've started, from spreading. So the statute was designed to protect against the type of accident that occurred here—spreading of a fire, regardless of how the fire originated. Therefore, even though there is no evidence that the defendant's acts or omissions contributed to the *start* of the fire, the violation of the statute is enough to permit a jury to conclude that the defendant was negligent in not trying to *stop* the fire once it began.

Notice that you're not required to say whether the plaintiff will in fact win; you're only asked to say whether it is "possible" for him to prevail. Since the negligence *per se* doctrine will entitle him to meet the negligence element of his prima facie case, and thus get to the jury, this choice correctly explains why it is "possible" that the plaintiff will win.

Notice, by the way, that neither this choice nor any other part of the question mentions the magic phrase "negligence *per se*." Where an MBE fact pattern turns on a doctrine with an unusual and evocative name, examiners typically go out of their way to avoid explicitly mentioning that doctrine, so as not to tip you off. ("*Res ipsa loquitur*" is another good example of such a doctrine.) So it's up to you to notice that the doctrine applies, and to figure out which choice represents use of the doctrine. Here, the phrase "violation of a statute that was meant to protect against this type of occurrence" is the sort of formulation that should immediately cause you to be thinking about negligence *per se*.

(A) is not the best response,

because even a statute setting only criminal penalties can establish the standard of care in a negligence case, by use of the negligence *per se* doctrine.

Under the doctrine of negligence *per se*, if the defendant, without excuse, violated a criminal statute that was designed to protect against the type of accident that occurred, then the violation automatically constitutes negligence. (See the discussion of

Choice D.) This choice, by asserting that a statute that provides "only for criminal penalties" cannot be relevant in this civil action, is flatly inconsistent with the negligence *per se* doctrine.

(B) is not the best response,

because the statute imposed a duty on the defendant to install sprinklers in order to stop the spread of any fire, even one that the defendant did not negligently start.

This choice is factually true: There is no evidence that the defendant negligently (or in any other way) caused the fire to start. But the criminal statute imposed on him a duty to install sprinklers, so as to have at least a chance of stopping any fire, regardless of how it was caused. Then, the doctrine of negligence *per se* applies to transform the defendant's failure to obey the statute into a negligent failure to attempt to stop the fire.

(C) is not the best response,

because the doctrine of *Rylands v. Fletcher* would not apply to these facts, since there was no abnormally dangerous activity.

When *Rylands v. Fletcher* was first decided in the 19th century, some American courts interpreted it to make a landowner strictly liable for the spread of fire from his premises. But today, the case stands for the more limited proposition that one who carries on an *abnormally dangerous activity* is strictly liable for any harm caused by that activity. Here, there is no evidence that defendant was carrying on an abnormally dangerous activity in his warehouse. Therefore, strict liability under the *Rylands v. Fletcher* doctrine would not apply.

Answer 6

(D) is the best response,

because even if the patient is indigent, she can still be held liable for negligence.

The key to this question is to recognize that the patient's best defense is *assumption of risk*. As it turns out, all of the choices except D support this defense, whereas D is not relevant either to that defense or to any other disputed fact in the case.

At this stage of the litigation, the patient's lawyer's job is to avoid a judgment against the patient. The fact that the patient is indigent has no bearing on whether the patient has behaved negligently, or on any other issue in the liability or damages portions of the case. The patient's indigent status might well prevent any eventual judgment from being satisfied, but the lawyer is not at this point trying to avoid satisfaction of a judgment, merely to avoid the entry of a judgment in the first instance.

(A) is not the best response,

because the nurse's status as a professional caregiver would be relevant to a defense based on assumption of risk.

The patient might succeed with a defense of assumption of risk. "A plaintiff who voluntarily assumes the risk of harm arising from the negligent or reckless conduct of the defendant cannot recover for such." Rest. 2d Torts, § 496 A. Here, if assumption of risk applies, it would be "implied" rather than "express" assumption. Implied assumption applies where a plaintiff (1) "fully understands a risk of harm . . . caused by the defendant's conduct," and (2) voluntarily chooses to encounter the risk, "under circumstances that manifest [the plaintiff's] willingness to accept [that risk]." Rest. 2d Torts, § 496 C(1). The fact that the nurse was a professional caregiver would be circumstantial evidence that she understood the risk posed by possibly-violent patients, and that by choosing to work in the psychiatric facility, she voluntarily manifested her willingness to accept that type of risk.

(B) is not the best response,

because the nurse's specialized training would support the defense of assumption of risk.

B is not the best response for the same reason as Choice A: The fact that the nurse was trained to care for schizophrenic patients would be relevant evidence in support of an assumption-of-risk defense. Implied assumption of risk would apply if and only if the nurse "fully understood" the risk of harm from the patient's conduct. The fact that the nurse was trained in the care of schizophrenic patients would be circumstantial evidence that she fully understood the risk that such patients are sometimes violent.

(C) is not the best response,

because the patient's mental state bears on whether the risk was one the nurse assumed.

This choice, like choices A and B, refers to a fact that would be relevant on the issue of whether the nurse assumed the risk of the type of attack that occurred. Even if the nurse was found to have impliedly assumed the risk of an attack caused by the patient's schizophrenia, the nurse would not necessarily be found to have assumed the risk of harm from some non-schizophrenia-related cause (e.g., the risk that the patient, while in a completely normal frame of mind, might trip and bump into the nurse, knocking her down the stairs). The fact that the patient thought she was being attacked by an elephant is strong evidence that the patient's conduct was a product of her schizophrenia, bringing the injury within the scope of the risk that the nurse arguably assumed by taking a position in the psychiatric facility that required her to care for schizophrenic patients.

Answer 7

(D) is the best response,

because the farmer should have realized that the child's entry could have been repelled by lesser force.

A property owner is privileged to use reasonable force to prevent or end a trespasser's intrusion on his land. So the farmer was permitted to use some degree of force to escort the child off the premises. But a landowner exercising the privilege to defend his property is not permitted to use a level of force that is "intended or likely to cause bodily harm . . . in *excess* of that which the [owner] correctly or reasonably believes to be *necessary to prevent or terminate the other's intrusion.*" Rest. 2d Torts, § 81(1). The farmer could not reasonably have believed that striking a ten-year-old girl in the face, hard enough to break her nose, was necessary to end her intrusion on the property; grabbing her by the arm and removing her from the property, for instance, would almost certainly have sufficed. Therefore, the farmer is liable for "so much of the force . . . as is excessive." Rest. 2d Torts, § 82(a). Consequently, the farmer is liable for the broken nose, which would not have occurred had he used an appropriate level of force.

(A) is not the best response,

because the farmer was not privileged even to use the level of non-deadly force employed here.

As is discussed in greater detail in Choice D, a person defending his property is only permitted to use the level of force reasonably needed to repel the intrusion. Since the farmer should have realized that a lesser degree of force would suffice to remove the child from the premises (e.g., grabbing her by the arm and marching her off the premises), the farmer has exceeded the level of permissive force even though the force he used was probably not deadly (i.e., was probably not likely to cause death or serious bodily harm).

(B) is not the best response,

because even though the farmer had probable cause to believe that the child was a thief, he was not entitled to use a greater level of force than was reasonably required to repel the intrusion.

It's true that a property owner may use reasonable force to repel an intruder, and certainly that is so when the owner has probable cause to believe that the intruder is a thief. So the farmer was entitled to use *some degree* of force against the child. But as is discussed in greater detail in Choice D, a person defending his property is only permitted to use the level of force *reasonably needed* to repel the intrusion. Since the farmer should have realized that a lesser degree of force would suffice to remove the child from the premises (e.g., grabbing her by the arm and marching her off the premises), the farmer has exceeded the level of permissive force. So the farmer is liable for the excess, despite his having had probable cause to believe that the child was a thief.

(C) is not the best response,

because the farmer had the right to use reasonable force even without having posted a "No Trespassing" sign.

A property owner has a privilege to use reasonable force to protect his property from trespass. And that's true even if the owner has not posted a "No Trespassing" sign. (The presence or absence of such a sign might be a *factor* in deciding whether the owner's overall reaction to the danger of trespass was reasonable or not, but there is no absolute requirement that the owner post a sign—it is up to the third person to know that he is intruding on another person's property, and to presume that the intrusion is without permission.) So although this choice correctly states that the farmer will lose, it misstates the reason—the real reason the farmer will lose is that he used a greater level of force than was reasonably needed to repel the intrusion (as discussed in Choice D).

Answer 8

(C) is the best response,

because assumption of risk can be a defense to a strict liability action, and the employee here assumed the risk of an accident like the one that occurred.

The particular type of strict liability that the employee would be claiming here is strict liability for the conducting of an abnormally dangerous activity. Assumption of risk is a defense to an action brought on abnormally-dangerous-activity grounds. *See* Rest. 2d Torts, § 523: "The plaintiff's assumption of the risk of harm from an abnormally dangerous activity bars his recovery for the harm." Since the employee knew that he was auditing the safety of a mine, a potentially dangerous activity, he will be held to have knowingly and willingly assumed the risk of the type of accidents that make mining possibly abnormally dangerous. A reasonable jury could certainly find that dynamite is often stored at mines, and that explosion of stored dynamite is one of the risks that a person who chooses to perform audits of mine safety knows about and assumes the risk of. (Notice that you're not asked to say whether the mining company would succeed with the defense—you're just asked to determine which the "best" defense is. The assumption of risk defense has a plausible chance of success here, unlike the defenses listed in the other three choices.)

(A) is not the best defense,

because the facts tell us that the storage of explosives is considered to be an abnormally dangerous activity in the jurisdiction.

If you were called upon to say whether the storage of explosives here was an abnormally dangerous activity, the fact that mine was in a remote location would indeed cut against a finding that the activity was abnormally dangerous. But the facts *tell* you that in the jurisdiction, the storage of dynamite is automatically deemed abnormally dangerous—so implicitly, there is no exception given for remote locations. Therefore, the mining company's position won't be improved by citing the remoteness of the mine. (In any event, even if the status of storage of explosives as ultrahazardous was at issue, many courts would hold that such storage *is* ultrahazardous even when it occurs in a remote location.)

(B) is not the best response,

because the suit is premised on carrying out an abnormally dangerous activity, and the defendant does not have to have manufactured the dangerous item in order to be liable.

If the action were based on strict *products* liability, then the fact that the defendant did not manufacture the dynamite (or sell it) would be a defense. But the suit here, though it seeks to impose strict liability, is based upon the conducting of an abnormally dangerous *activity*, not the sale of a dangerous product. Therefore, since the dynamite was part of the activity that the mining company was carrying on, the fact that the company did not manufacture the dynamite is irrelevant.

(D) is not the best response,

because liability for conducting an abnormally dangerous activity is not negated by the fact that the defendant used all possible care.

If this were a suit based on *negligence*, the fact that the defendant used state-of-the-art methods to store the dynamite would strongly indicate that it did not behave negligently. But the action here is based on the conducting of an abnormally dangerous activity. One of the requirements for classifying an activity as abnormally dangerous is that the activity cannot be carried out with perfect safety no matter how carefully the defendant behaved. So by definition, the fact that the defendant used state-of-the-art methods cannot be a defense.

Answer 9

(B) is the best response,

because one who negligently causes an initial injury to another is also liable for a second injury to the other that is a normal consequence of the initial injury.

It's clear that the driver's negligence was the proximate cause of the pedestrian's knee injury. The challenging part of this question is that it requires you to say whether the driver is also liable for the "second" injury, the shoulder injury. This choice correctly states that the answer is "yes" if and only if the second injury is a "normal consequence" of the first injury. Rest. 2d Torts, § 460, covers precisely this situation, and applies the "normal consequence" test: "If the negligent actor is liable for an injury which impairs the physical condition of another's body, the actor is also liable for harm sustained in a *subsequent accident* which would *not have occurred had the other's condition not been impaired*, and which is a *normal consequence* of such impairment."

Notice that it does not matter whether the driver should reasonably have foreseen that his negligent driving would or might ultimately cause this "second injury." We evaluate the second injury by looking at the facts as they existed *after* the first injury, and the defendant is liable if the second injury is a "normal consequence" of the first injury, no matter how unlikely the second injury may have seemed viewed as of the moment of the defendant's initial negligence.

(A) is not the best response,

because it cites a principle that does not apply on these facts.

The saying that the defendant "takes his victim as he finds him" is a famous, and true, statement. But it refers to a different situation than the one here. The phrase refers to the principle that a negligent defendant is responsible for the full extent of the plaintiff's initial injuries, even injuries that stem from the plaintiff's unusual *preexisting vulnerability*. That is, "takes his victim as he finds him" refers to the so-called "*thin skull*" type of problem, exemplified by a plaintiff who receives a blow to the head caused by the defendant's negligence and suffers unusually bad injuries due to the plaintiff's preexisting thin skull. Here, the injury to the plaintiff's shoulder is not due to his preexisting susceptibility to such injuries, but is rather due to the earlier injury at issue in the case. So the saying "takes his victim as he finds him" does not explain why the defendant would be liable for the shoulder injury.

(C) is not the best response,

because separability of injuries matters only when there are multiple defendants.

The separability of injuries (also known as the "divisibility" of injuries) becomes significant only when there are not only multiple injuries, but also *multiple defendants*—if the injuries can be allocated among the multiple defendants (i.e., the injuries are separable), then each defendant is liable only for those injuries that can be specifically attributed to that defendant's fault. Here, both injuries were caused by a single defendant (the driver), so the separability of the injuries never becomes an issue.

(D) is not the best response,

because the driver will be liable for the shoulder injury if it was a "natural consequence" of the knee injury, even if it was not reasonably foreseeable at the time of the negligent driving.

These facts involve the problem of the "second injury," i.e., the situation in which the defendant's negligence causes an initial injury to plaintiff, and the plaintiff then sustains a second injury of which the initial injury was the but-for cause. In this scenario, the defendant who caused the first injury will be *liable for the second injury no matter how unforeseeable that second injury might have been* as of the time of the defendant's negligence, so long as we can say after the fact that the second injury was a "normal consequence" of the first injury. (For more about this, see the discussion of Choice B.) Since this choice asserts that the driver is off the hook so long as the second injury (the fall down the stairs) was not foreseeable at the time of the driver's negligence, it understates the scope of the driver's liability.

Answer 10

(D) is the best response,

because the rancher's belief that the neighbor was armed was unreasonable.

A landowner can be privileged to use even deadly force to prevent an intrusion on his land. However, such a use of deadly force is privileged "if, but only if, the [owner] *reasonably believes* that the intruder, unless expelled or excluded, is *likely to cause death or serious bodily harm* to the [owner] or to a third person whom the [owner] is privileged to protect." Rest. 2d Torts, § 79. So the fact that the rancher genuinely believed that the neighbor had a gun and might well use it was *not enough* to permit the rancher to use deadly force of his own: The rancher's belief had to be *reasonable*, not just genuine. This was not the case here, since the rancher "could point to nothing that would have reasonably justified" his belief that the neighbor was armed.

(A) is not the best response,

because the no-retreat rule, even if adopted by the jurisdiction, would not apply here, since the attack was not in the rancher's *dwelling place*.

Most states (and the Second Restatement) apply the "stand your ground" rule, under which the defendant may sometimes defend himself from harm, even by the use of deadly force, and even if he could avoid injury by retreating. But in states that apply this rule, the rule applies only to an attack that takes place within the defendant's *dwelling place* (which must not also be the dwelling place of the attacker). Rest. 2d Torts, § 65(2)(a). For this purpose, "dwelling place" means a home, i.e., a building in which the defendant resides. Here, the rancher was standing outside on his land, not in his house, so the attack was not in his dwelling place. Therefore, even in a stand-your-ground state the rancher was not permitted to stand his ground by using deadly force, if he could have retreated safely (as it appears he could have).

Furthermore, even if the attack *had* taken place in the rancher's dwelling, he still would have been permitted to use deadly force only if he had a reasonable belief that he was himself being threatened with deadly force; here, the rancher's belief that the neighbor was armed may have been genuine, but it was not reasonable.

(B) is not the best response,

because the rancher's belief that the neighbor was not armed was not a reasonable one.

A landowner's privilege to use deadly force to defend his property against intrusion applies only where the owner *reasonably* believes that the intruder, if not repelled, will himself use deadly force. (See Rest. 2d Torts, § 79, quoted in the discussion of Choice D above.) Here, the rancher's belief that the neighbor was armed (and thus threatening to use deadly force) may have been genuine, but it was not reasonable. So that belief did not justify the rancher's use of deadly force.

(C) is not the best response,

because it is overly broad, and fails to take account of the possibility that a "property dispute" may escalate into an encounter that threatens death or serious injury.

It is true that if the dispute concerns *only* possession of property, neither side may use deadly force in connection with the dispute. But disputes that are initially about property may escalate to a point at which one party is threatening the other with death or serious bodily harm. When that happens, the threatened person may use deadly force in self-defense or defense of property, if he reasonably believes that a lesser degree of force would not suffice.

So here, even though the dispute started as a "property dispute," if the rancher had had a reasonable belief that the neighbor was armed and might shoot him after he came over the fence, the rancher would have prevailed if he could convince the court that no lesser amount of force would likely have sufficed. The problem for the rancher is that his belief that the neighbor was threatening the use of deadly force (i.e., was armed) was not supported by objective circumstances, and was thus not reasonable. So this choice explains the correct outcome (the rancher loses), but does so by incorrectly stating that deadly force is "never appropriate" if the dispute is about property.

Answer 11

(A) is the best response,

because the driver had the privilege of necessity, making the homeowner's removal of the car wrongful.

First, a person has the privilege of "*private necessity*" to enter another's land, if that entry is or reasonably appears to be necessary to prevent serious harm to the person or his chattels. Rest. 2d Torts, § 197(1). So the driver had a privilege to park his car in the owner's driveway since that seemed to be the only way for him to avoid water damage to the car. (If the driver, by parking, had damaged the owner's land, the driver would have been responsible for the damage; that's why the private necessity privilege is called an "incomplete privilege.") Once the driver properly exercised his privilege to enter the driveway, the owner was under a duty to *allow the entry to continue* until the danger had passed. *See* Rest. 2d, § 197, Comment k: "The important difference between the status of one who is a trespasser on land and one who is on the land pursuant to an incomplete privilege is that the latter is *entitled to be on the land* and therefore the possessor of the land is under a *duty to permit him to come and remain there and hence is not privileged to resist his entry.*" So the homeowner, by rolling the car back down the driveway, violated this duty to let the driver remain, and is responsible for the damages caused by that violation.

(B) is not the best response,

because the absence of "no trespassing" signs was irrelevant.

The driver committed what normally would have been a trespassory entry on the owner's land, and that entry would have been a trespass regardless of whether the land was posted with "no trespassing" signs. What made the driver's entry lawful was his privilege of necessity, as discussed in choice A. So this choice, although it correctly predicts the outcome, does so on an incorrect theory.

(C) is not the best response,

because the driver had a privilege to enter, even though his entry was intentional.

As is discussed in choice A, the driver, when he entered the owner's land, was acting pursuant to a privilege of private necessity. That privilege applies even though the entry is "intentional." Since the entry was privileged, the owner had a duty to let the driver's car remain for the duration of the emergency, making the owner responsible to pay for damages caused by his violation of that duty.

(D) is not the best response,

because the homeowner was not in fact privileged to remove the car from his property.

The driver was entitled to enter the homeowner's land by virtue of the privilege of private necessity, since that entry was reasonably necessary to avoid water damage to the car. Because the entry was privileged, the homeowner had a duty to allow the entry to continue until the danger was over. So it is not accurate to say, as this choice does, that the homeowner had a privilege to remove the car. Rather, the homeowner must pay damages for violation of his duty to allow the driver to exercise the driver's privilege of entry.

Answer 12

(A) is the best response,

because a possessor of land open to the public owes the public a duty to keep the premises reasonably safe, and this duty may not be delegated to an independent contractor.

First, all courts agree that when a business or other land-possessor holds its land open to the public, the land-possessor owes the public a duty to use reasonable care to keep the property in a safe condition. *See, e.g.,* Rest. 3d Torts (Liab. Phys. Harm), § 40(b)(3). Second, most courts now agree that where a possessor of land owes such a duty of care, that duty *cannot be delegated to an independent contractor who will do repairs*, at least if the possessor *retains possession* of the premises during the repair activity. *See, e.g.,* Rest. 3d Torts (Liab. Phys. Harm), § 62(a)(2), (the duty of care cannot be delegated to an independent contractor if "the harm occurs while the possessor retains possession of the premises during the [repair] activity").

So here, since the hotel premises were held open to the public, the hotel owed to any member of the public who was properly on the premises a duty to use reasonable care to keep the premises safe. When the hotel assigned the pool-rebuilding job to the contractor, the hotel "retained possession." (We know this because the facts tell us that "the hotel continued to operate while the pool was being rebuilt.") Since the hotel retained possession, its duty to use reasonable care was not delegable to the contractor. Therefore, any negligence by the contractor will be treated as if it was the negligence of the hotel. Since we know that the accident was caused by the contractor's negligence in leaving the pool unguarded, the hotel will be treated as the negligent cause of the accident. The fact that the hotel used all possible care in selecting that particular contractor is irrelevant—that's the significance of deeming the hotel's duty of care to be non-delegable.

(B) is not the best response,

because the indemnification agreement, even though effective, did not relieve the hotel of liability to the guest.

For the reasons discussed in choice A, the hotel owed its guests a duty to use reasonable care to keep its premises safe, and that duty was not delegable to the independent contractor. The fact that the contractor agreed to indemnify the hotel for any negligence by the contractor has no effect on the hotel's duty to its guests. If the hotel is required to pay damages to the guest (as will almost certainly be the case), the indemnification agreement means that the hotel can recover from the independent contractor any damages it has to pay. But that's between the hotel and the contractor—the hotel still has to answer to the guest in the first instance.

(C) is not the best response,

because the hotel's duty of care was non-delegable, even though the contractor was the "actively negligent" party.

For the reasons discussed in choice A, the hotel owed its guests a duty to use reasonable care to keep its premises safe, and that duty was not delegable to the independent contractor. That non-delegability applies regardless of whether the contractor's negligence is classified as "active" or "passive." Therefore, the contractor's negligence will be imputed to the hotel. (Distinctions between active and passive negligence may once have been significant, but such distinctions are now outmoded.)

Answer 13

(B) is the best response,

because the plaintiff was required to show that the defendant either knew the statement was false or had serious doubts about whether it was true.

The Supreme Court has held that the First Amendment requires that a public figure, in order to recover for defamation, must prove that the defendant acted with more than mere negligence with regard to the truth or falsity of the defamatory statement. The public figure plaintiff (a category that includes a "candidate for high political office," as we have here) must show that the defendant made his statement with "*actual malice*." That term was originally defined in *New York Times v. Sullivan*, 376 U.S. 254 (1964), to require that the defendant acted either "with *knowledge* that [the statement] was false or with *reckless disregard* of whether it was false or not."

The candidate would like to be able to argue that the editor's unreasonable failure to investigate the accusation before publishing it constituted "reckless disregard" of whether the accusation was false. But this argument is expressly foreclosed by the post-*Sullivan* case of *St. Amant v. Thompson*, 390 U.S. 727 (1968). There, the Court said that "reckless conduct is *not* measured by whether a reasonably prudent man would have published, or would have *investigated* before publishing." Rather, the Court said, for recklessness "there must be sufficient evidence to permit the conclusion that the defendant *in fact entertained serious doubts* as to the truth of his publication." Since we're told that the editor honestly believed that the accusation was true, he did not "entertain[] serious doubts as to the truth," and therefore did not act recklessly. Thus, he did not act with "actual malice," and cannot be liable.

(A) is not the best response,

because the statement was a statement of alleged fact, even though it appeared in an editorial.

It's true that a *pure statement of opinion* may not be the basis for a defamation action. Rather, the First Amendment requires that only statements that purport to be statements of fact may be made actionable. But the mere fact that a statement is contained within something labeled as an "editorial" does not establish that the statement is a pure opinion rather than a statement of fact. Here, a reasonable reader of the editorial would understand that the editor, during the course of expressing his opinion about whether the candidate should be elected, was stating as a fact that the candidate used illegal drugs. So the fact-versus-opinion distinction does not supply the correct reason the candidate will lose. Instead, he will lose because, as a public figure, he was required to prove that the editor acted with "actual malice," and he has not met that burden of proof, as explained in Choice B.

(C) is not the best response,

because even a statement that is defamatory per se must, if made about a public figure, be made with "actual malice."

First, the fact that a statement is "defamatory per se" matters only in the case of slander actions, not actions for libel. (In a slander action, the plaintiff must prove pecuniary damages, unless the statement falls into one of the "defamatory per se" categories, which include an accusation of serious criminal behavior.) Since the suit here is based upon a written statement, it is an action for libel, not slander, so the statement's status as "defamatory per se" couldn't make any difference to the outcome.

Second, even if this *were* one of the situations in which the statement's status as defamation per se mattered, the candidate would still lose, because, as a public figure, he was required to prove that the editor acted with "actual malice," and he has not met that burden of proof. (See the further explanation in Choice B.)

(D) is not the best response,

because the candidate is required to prove "actual malice," in addition to the elements recited in this choice.

It's true that the candidate was required to prove both that the accusation was false and that it was injurious to his reputation. The candidate succeeded in proving these elements. But these were not the only elements he was required to prove. As a public figure, he was also required to prove that the editor acted with "actual malice," and he has not met that burden of proof. (See the further explanation in Choice B.)

Answer 14

(B) is the best response,

because the neighbor can be held responsible for all damage other than that attributable to the plaintiff.

The instructions for the MBE tell you to assume that "joint and several liability, with pure comparative negligence, is the relevant rule unless otherwise indicated." This fact pattern does not indicate otherwise. So the key is to figure out how to apply to these facts (1) joint and several liability; and (2) pure comparative negligence. Let's take these doctrines one at a time, but in reverse order.

When we say that "pure comparative negligence" applies, we mean that the plaintiff's recovery will be reduced "in proportion to the share of responsibility the factfinder assigns to the plaintiff." Rest. 3d (Apport.), § 7. Since the plaintiff was found to be 10 percent at fault, his total recovery will be reduced by 10 percent, compared with what it would have been had he not been at fault at all. So his $100,000 total "damages pot" becomes $90,000.

Next, when we say that there is "joint and several liability," we mean that "the injured person may sue for and recover the *full amount* of recoverable damages from *any* jointly and severally liable person." Rest. 3d (Apport.), § 10. So the question becomes, given that this is a joint-and-several jurisdiction, are the two defendants here jointly and severally liable? The answer is "yes": "[I]f the independent tortious conduct of *two or more persons* is a *legal cause* [i.e., proximate cause] of an indivisible injury, *each person is jointly and severally liable* for the recoverable damages caused by the tortious conduct." Rest. 3d Torts (Apport.), § A18. Here, the jury found that the neighbor had negligently entrusted his car to the teenager, and that independently, the teenager acted negligently. Since there was only one indivisible harm (a single set of injuries to the driver), the neighbor's negligence and the teenager's negligence were each a "legal cause of [the] indivisible injury," making the two jointly and severally liable. Therefore, the driver may recover the *full amount* of his "recoverable damages" (i.e., the full sum of $90,000) from either defendant. If he chooses to recover all $90,000 from the neighbor, the neighbor will then have the right to recover "contribution" from the teenager, i.e., the teenager's $60,000 share of the $90,000.

Neither Choice A, C, or D is the best response, because each is in some way inconsistent with the above analysis. Choice A wrongly fails to deduct the plaintiff's share of the fault. Choice C wrongly fails to apply joint and several liability—it (correctly) makes the neighbor responsible for the teenager's share of the fault, but omits to make the neighbor responsible for his own share. Choice D has the opposite problem from C—it (correctly) makes the neighbor responsible for his own share of the fault, but fails to make the neighbor responsible for his co-defendant's share (i.e., fails to apply joint and several liability).

Answer 15

(A) is the best response,

because *res ipsa loquitur* would apply, and the court would be likely to shift onto the defendants the burden of coming forward with some evidence about which defendant(s) behaved negligently.

This fact pattern virtually mirrors the facts of one of the most famous cases in Torts, *Ybarra v. Spangard*, 154 P.2d 687 (Cal. 1944), in which a surgical patient who was injured while under anesthesia was able to show that his injuries would not have happened without negligence by some member of the surgical team, but could not show *which* member was likely negligent. In *Ybarra*, the court placed on every defendant who had at any point had control of an instrumentality that could have been responsible for the injury the burden of coming forward with at least an initial explanation of who was negligent. Most modern courts follow the approach of *Ybarra*, at least in the narrow surgery-under-anesthesia context.

Here, the plaintiff would begin by using the basic doctrine of *res ipsa loquitur*, under which the jury "may infer that the defendant has been negligent when the accident causing the plaintiff's harm is a *type of accident* that ordinarily happens as a result of the *negligence of a class of actors* of which the defendant is the relevant member." Rest. 3d Torts (Liab. Phys. Harm), § 17. A reasonable jury could infer that a severe burn during otherwise-normal childbirth is the type of accident that does not ordinarily happen except as a result of negligence by someone on the surgical team.

The trickier aspect, of course, is that there are many defendants, and the plaintiff has not produced any evidence tending to show that any particular defendant was especially likely to have been negligent in a way that caused the burn. But in *Ybarra*, the court held that because each of the many defendants had had control of the patient's care at one point or another during the operation, it was fair to place on the defendants collectively, rather than on the unconscious plaintiff, the burden of coming forward with an explanation of which defendant was negligent. A modern court would likely agree, mainly as a way of preventing the defendants from erecting a "wall of silence" under which no medical professional would be willing to testify against his colleagues. See Rest. 3d Torts (Liab. Phys. Harm), § 17, Comment f, approving of the *Ybarra* approach in surgical cases.

(B) is not the best response,

because there is no evidence that the defendants jointly engaged in negligent activity.

"Acting in concert" refers to "jointly engaging" in the negligent activity. Here, there is no evidence that two or more defendants jointly acted negligently—the burn could easily have occurred due solely to the negligent action of a single defendant. So although this choice is on the right general wavelength, it relies on the existence of a factor—acting in concert—that has not been shown to be present in the facts. (The best argument for requiring all defendants to stand trial is the one made in choice A, which implicitly relies on the idea that fairness requires shifting the burden of explanation to the defendants, regardless of whether they acted jointly.)

(C) is not the best response,

because it does not deal with the lack of evidence pointing to any particular defendant(s) as the cause of the harm.

The affidavits help the plaintiff establish that someone on the surgical team likely was negligent. (But the plaintiff could probably have established that fact even *without* the affidavits, based on the common-sense notion that serious burns do not occur during the course of otherwise-normal anesthesia-assisted childbirth.) The key issue in the case is that the plaintiff has not shown any evidence pointing to *which* particular defendant(s) negligently caused the burn. The affidavits do not help the plaintiff with this central problem, so an argument based on them can't be the best argument.

(D) is not the best response,

because it does not deal with the need for the plaintiff to identify the particular defendant(s) who caused the injury.

It's certainly true that the plaintiff can benefit from the doctrine of *res ipsa loquitur*, and that a plaintiff who wants to use *res ipsa* must normally show that her own conduct was not the cause of the harm. So the fact that the patient was unconscious helps her *res ipsa* argument. But the key issue in the case is that the plaintiff has not shown any evidence pointing to *which* particular defendant(s) negligently caused the burn. The fact that the plaintiff can show that she herself was not one of the responsible persons doesn't help with this key issue, so this argument can't be the best one.

Answer 16

(D) is the best response,

because the conversion occurred at the time the bank wrongfully refused to return the certificate.

Conversion is "an *intentional exercise of dominion or control* over a chattel which so seriously interferes with the right of another to control it that the actor may justly be required to *pay the other the full value* of the chattel." Rest. 2d Torts § 222A. One form of conversion occurs when a person is initially legitimately in possession of the chattel, but then unjustifiably *refuses to return it* upon rightful demand by the owner. *Id*. at § 237. That's what happened here—the bank was initially entitled to hold the certificate as security, but was required to return it as soon as the customer repaid the loan and demanded the return. A brief delay in return—while, say, the bank made reasonable efforts to figure out whether any money was still owed—might have been sufficiently unserious that it would have constituted either no tort at all, or merely trespass to chattels.

But a delay of two full months, and the collateral's extreme loss of value during the delay, were, taken together, serious enough that it's fair to treat the delay as a forced sale (i.e., a conversion).

The conversion will be deemed to have occurred at the time the bank wrongfully refused the customer's demand that the stock be returned. Therefore, the "forced sale" will be deemed to have occurred at that moment of refusal. So the bank will be deemed to have "bought" the stock for its market value as of that moment, $20,000. (The bank then "owned" the stock, so the bank then had the right to keep it and sell it for whatever it was worth.)

(A) is not the best response,

because it states a fact that, while true, is legally irrelevant.

Conversion sometimes occurs when the defendant initially and wrongfully takes dominion over a chattel. But the tort can also occur when the defendant initially comes into rightful possession of a chattel, and later wrongfully refuses to surrender it. (See the discussion of choice D for more about this.) That's what happened here. So the fact that the bank's possession of the certificate was originally lawful doesn't give it a defense for having later refused to return the certificate as soon as the loan was repaid.

(B) is not the best response,

because it calculates the damages as of a time later than when the tort occurred.

The tort of conversion occurred at the moment the customer first rightfully demanded return of the certificate and the bank refused the demand. So that was the moment at which the "forced sale" of the item—which is the essence of conversion—occurred. Therefore, that's the moment as of which the market value of the certificate is to be computed (and the moment as of which the bank became the equitable owner of the certificate). The value as of the later moment at which the bank changed its mind and offered to return the certificate is legally irrelevant.

(C) is not the best response,

because it calculates the damages as of a time before the tort occurred.

The bank's initial possession of the certificate was lawful, since the possession was with the customer's consent. So the value of the certificate at the time of the bank's first possession cannot be the time for valuing the "forced sale" of the item. It was not until the bank later rejected the customer's rightful request for return of the certificate that the bank committed conversion (and involuntarily "bought" the item), so that's the time as of which the certificate's market value must be computed.

Answer 17

(A) is the best response,

because the rental agency could only be liable for harm proximately caused by its negligence, and failing to check for a bomb whose presence was not reasonably foreseeable was not negligent.

You are told that the action was brought on a negligence theory. (And, indeed, on these facts that's the only plausible theory—there's no basis for any sort of strict liability.) So the agency can be liable only if the plaintiff proves two things: (1) that the agency was negligent; and (2) that that negligence was a proximate cause of the plaintiff's injuries. The plaintiff will not be able to show the first of these things, negligence.

There's a good chance that a court would hold that a car rental agency, before renting a car, has a general duty to inspect the car to ensure that it is safe. But even if the court imposed such a general duty, the duty would require only an inspection addressed to *reasonably-foreseeable dangers*. Since there had been no reported incidents of bombs being hidden in rental cars, the danger of such a bomb was not one of the dangers that even a broadly-defined duty of inspection would cover. Therefore, the agency's failure to perform an inspection addressed to that danger was not negligence at all.

(B) is not the best response,

because the agency might have been liable for failing to discover that someone else had hidden the bomb.

An agency that rents cars probably has an affirmative duty to make a reasonable inspection to ensure that the car is safe to drive. And the fact that a safety risk stemmed from the intentional action of a third party would not by itself immunize the defendant from negligence liability for failing to reasonably inspect, find and correct the risk. So, for instance, if there had been recent reports that terrorists had hidden bombs in rental cars, it would likely be negligence for the agency not to check for bombs before each rental. So although this choice correctly predicts the outcome—no liability—it does not give a legally correct explanation for that outcome.

(C) is not the best response,

because the agency had no duty to conduct such an inspection, since the risk in question was not foreseeable.

This action was brought in negligence, so the defendant can be liable only if it failed to use reasonable care. The reasonable care that the agency was required to use probably included a duty to inspect for reasonably-foreseeable dangers. But the fact that no cases had been reported in which terrorists hid bombs in rental cars means that the danger of such a bomb was not reasonably foreseeable. Therefore, the agency had no duty to inspect for that unforeseeable danger, even though such an inspection, had it been conducted, would have exposed the danger.

(D) is not the best response,

because the agency did not intentionally conduct an abnormally dangerous activity.

It's true that one who intentionally or knowingly carries on an abnormally dangerous activity is strictly liable for harms that occur due to the type of risk that made the activity abnormally dangerous. But there are two reasons why this choice does not correctly explain the outcome.

First, the facts tell us that the action is a "negligence action." The fact that an activity is abnormally dangerous is only relevant to an action based on the special, narrow, doctrine imposing *strict liability* (not negligence liability) for conducting such abnormally dangerous activities. Second, even if we were not told that the suit was brought in negligence, the agency would still not be liable based on the abnormally dangerousness of the car, because this form of strict liability applies only where the defendant *intentionally carries out* an activity known to be abnormally dangerous. Since the agency didn't know of the hidden bomb, it didn't know it was carrying out (nor did it intend to be carrying out) an abnormally dangerous activity.

Answer 18

(C) is the best response,

because it is the only response that establishes how the plaintiff would satisfy his burden of proving that the pharmacy's error was the cause-in-fact of his heart attack.

Notice that the facts do not specify the theory on which the man brings his claim—all you're asked is whether the man has a "valid" (but unspecified) claim. So it's up to you to figure out under what theory of liability there could be a recovery. Although there is some possibility of recovery under a strict product liability theory, the much more straightforward theory on these facts is one based on negligence. But no matter which of these two theories was used, the plaintiff would bear the burden of proving that the pharmacy's error was the *cause in fact* of the heart attack. (If the man would probably have had a heart attack anyway, even without the error, then no matter how negligent the error was, and/or no matter how "defective" the product was under a strict liability theory, there could be no recovery.)

This choice is the only one that deals head-on with the causation issue, by asserting that the jury could reasonably conclude that the pharmacy's failure to provide the correct dosage was the but-for cause (i.e., cause in fact) of the heart attack. Not only does this choice deal with the causation issue, but it does so in a legally-accurate way: Given that the man had had no previous history of heart problems, and given that overdoses of the active ingredient had been previously associated with heart problems in other cases, a jury could reasonably find that, more likely than not, the man would not have suffered a heart attack except for the overdose.

For the plaintiff to win on a negligence theory, he would of course also have to establish that, more probably than not, someone at the pharmacy *behaved negligently*. It's true that the facts here don't say anything at all about how this error came about, so there is no direct proof of negligence. But proof of negligence does not always require proof of exactly how the accident came about, and can be based on circumstantial evidence. On this point, the plaintiff can benefit from the doctrine of *res ipsa loquitur*, which permits the jury to "*infer* that the defendant has been negligent when the accident causing the plaintiff's harm is a *type of accident* that ordinarily happens as a result of the *negligence of a class of actors* of which the defendant is the relevant member." Rest. 3d Torts (Liab. Phys. Harm), § 17. A reasonable jury could certainly infer that when a pharmacy employee fills a prescription by giving the wrong dosage, there has been negligence because such a prescription-filling error is the "type of accident that ordinarily happens as a result of the negligence of a class of actors" (pharmacy workers) of which the employee is a member. Then, by the doctrine of *respondeat superior*, the pharmacy would be vicariously liable for the negligence inferred (via *res ipsa*) to have been committed by the employee.

(A) is not the best response,

because the suit could be successfully based on a negligence theory.

Plaintiff might or might not be able to win on a strict product liability theory. (For instance, if plaintiff were somehow able to show that the pills had been mislabeled by the factory as having 20 mg of active ingredients instead of the 30 mg they actually had, the pharmacy would probably be strictly liable for selling a dangerously-mislabeled product.) But plaintiff's suit certainly doesn't have to be based on strict liability, and would be much easier to prove on a negligence theory. In that event, the unavailability of strict liability would be completely irrelevant.

(B) is not the best response,

because *res ipsa loquitur* could be used to justify an inference of negligence.

It's true that the man doesn't seem to be able to show exactly how the error came about, and therefore can't provide "direct" proof of anyone's negligence. But what's undisputed is that the prescription was for 20 mg tablets, and the employee dispensed 30 mg tablets. That's the sort of "accident" that doesn't normally happen without the negligence of someone at the pharmacy, so *res ipsa* justifies the jury in inferring that more likely than not, the employee who dispensed the pills was negligent; that employee's negligence would be attributable to be pharmacy under *respondeat superior*. For more about *res ipsa* on these facts, see the discussion of Choice C.

(D) is not the best response,

because there is no evidence that the pills were a defective product, and in any event a negligence claim would not require such a showing.

As is discussed more fully in Choice C, the most plausible theory for the plaintiff's claim is on a negligence theory, not a strict product liability theory. If the claim is for negligence, it would not be necessary (or even helpful) for the plaintiff to prove that the pills were "defective." Furthermore, there is little if any evidence in these facts to support the assertion that the pills were "defective," which would have to be proved if the suit was based on strict product liability. (Perhaps the bottle was mislabeled, which might be held to make the pills defective.) So at best, this explanation is a much more speculative explanation than Choice C about why the plaintiff would win. An additional problem is that this choice completely fails to address the vital causation-in-fact element, which Choice C deals with directly and accurately.

Answer 19

(C) is the best response,

because the traveler's legal representative has met the requirements for *res ipsa loquitur*.

The doctrine of *res ipsa loquitur* ("the thing speaks for itself") permits the plaintiff to create an inference of the defendant's negligence without any direct evidence showing negligence. There are four requirements: (1) there must be no direct evidence of how the defendant behaved in connection with the event; (2) the event must be of a kind which ordinarily does not occur except through the negligence (or other fault) of someone; (3) the instrument that caused the injury must have been, at the relevant time, in the exclusive control of the defendant; and (4) the injury must not have been due to the plaintiff's own actions.

Here, the four requirements of the doctrine are satisfied: (1) there is no direct evidence of how the defendant airline behaved, only that the airplane carrying the traveler crashed; (2) airplanes do not ordinarily crash except through the negligence or fault of someone (the jury would probably be entitled to take judicial notice of this, even if the traveler's side didn't present formal proof on the subject); (3) a jury could reasonably find that the plane was in the exclusive control of the airline and its pilots (since there is no evidence of, say, hijacking); and (4) the injury suffered by the traveler was not due to his own action. Since all the requirements for *res ipsa loquitur* are met, the jury must be permitted to draw the inference that the plane crashed because of the airline's negligence.

(A) is not the best response,

because the *res ipsa loquitur* doctrine does not require a showing of evidence of the cause of the crash; indeed, the purpose of the doctrine is to eliminate the need for a plaintiff to provide direct evidence of why or how the accident or injury occurred.

(B) is not the best response,

because the doctrine of *res ipsa loquitur* does not require the plaintiff to negate the possibility that the defendant might not have been negligent.

The second requirement for *res ipsa loquitur* (see the discussion of choice C) is that the plaintiff show that the event was of a kind that "ordinarily" does not occur except through the fault of someone. But the plaintiff is *not* required to show that the event couldn't possibly have been due to a cause not involving the defendant's fault (as the phrase "negating the possibility" implies).

(D) is not the best response,

because common carriers are not strictly liable.

Common carriers (including airlines) are required to exercise a very high degree of care toward their passengers and guests, which is to say they are liable for even slight negligence. But they do not have strict liability.

Answer 20

(D) is the best response,

because the shop owner took reasonable care by storing the rifle and bullets in a locked cabinet.

An action in tort for negligence has four elements: (1) the existence of a duty on the part of the defendant to conform to a specific standard of conduct for the protection of the plaintiff against an unreasonable risk of injury; (2) breach of that duty by the defendant; (3) proof that the breach was the actual and proximate cause of the plaintiff's injury; and (4) damage to the plaintiff's person or property.

For the victim to make a case in negligence against the shop owner for the harm she suffered, she would have to show that he did not exercise reasonable care to protect her against injury. The facts state that the inmate escaped from a nearby prison, and then entered the shop owner's store by breaking and entering. Once inside, the inmate had to break into a locked cabinet to get the rifle and bullets. Unless it was foreseeable that someone would succeed in breaking and entering the shop owner's store and the locked cabinet, steal firearms, and then use them in crime, the shop owner would not be held liable, whether or not he negligently failed to activate the store's motion detector. Only with evidence suggesting a high risk of theft and criminal use of his firearms could the victim show that the shop owner failed to exercise reasonable care.

(A) is not the best response,

because the shop owner took reasonable care by storing the rifle and bullets in a locked cabinet.

Of the four elements for negligence (listed in the discussion of choice D above), the second is breach of a duty on the part of the defendant to conform to a specific standard of conduct for the protection of the plaintiff against an unreasonable risk of injury (loosely, D's failure to behave with reasonable care). The mere fact that there was some other act that the shop owner could have taken—activation of the motion detector—that would have prevented the injury is insufficient to make the shop owner liable. That is, other acts taken by the shop owner (e.g., keeping the guns in a locked cabinet inside a locked building) may have already been enough to make the shop owner's conduct non-negligent. So choice A is not a good explanation of the outcome.

(B) is not the best response,

because the shop owner had probably already met the standard of reasonable care when he locked the store and the cabinet.

For the victim to make a case in negligence against the shop owner for the harm she suffered, she would have to show that he did not exercise reasonable care to protect her against injury. The shop owner likely met that requirement when he locked his store and the gun cabinet, even if he was negligent in failing to activate the motion detector. Since choice B asserts that the victim wins automatically because of the shop owner's negligent failure to activate the detector—and ignores the possibility that the shop owner's other protections met the overall standard of due care—choice B is wrong.

(C) is not the best response,

because the shop owner might be liable even under ordinary negligence principles

As the discussion of choice D explains, the presence of a high risk of theft of firearms might be enough to make the shop owner liable under ordinary negligence principles, in which case the fact that there was no abnormally dangerous activity would be irrelevant.

By the way, choice C is probably correct in stating that the storage and sale of firearms and ammunition is not an abnormally dangerous activity (*a.d.a.*)—one of the major factors in determining whether something is an a.d.a. is an "inability to eliminate the risk by the exercise of reasonable care." Locking the material up securely is a way to eliminate at least the risk of theft and subsequent use in crime, so this factor seems not to be satisfied. Thus, were it not for the possibility that the shop owner was liable under ordinary negligence principles, choice C might well be correct.

Answer 21

(C) is the best response,

because the auctioneer was not a seller or distributor of the tractor the new owner purchased.

Strict liability, as usually imposed, applies only against one who is "engaged in the business of selling" the type of product involved. A court would almost certainly conclude that an auctioneer acting at the behest of a creditor to sell various mortgaged items, one of which happens to be a tractor, is not "engaged in the business of selling" tractors.

(A) is not the best response,

because it incorrectly assumes that the auctioneer is a seller as defined in strict liability.

If the auctioneer was "engaged in the business of selling" tractors, choice A would be correct, because it essentially correctly states the principle of strict liability (though it neglects to state that the defect must have caused the injury). But since the auctioneer is not so engaged—as covered in choice C—choice A is wrong.

(B) is not the best response,

because the auctioneer's alleged negligence would not be an element of the new owner's strict liability suit.

Since the new owner is suing in strict liability, the fact that the defendant did or did not behave in a negligent manner is irrelevant. The defendant's failure to make an inspection might be evidence of negligence, but it has no bearing on whether there is strict liability.

(D) is not the best response,

because the new owner's contributory negligence would not bar his strict liability recovery, if the requirements for such liability were otherwise met.

In states that have not adopted comparative fault principles (as the facts state is the case here), a plaintiff's contributory negligence is not a defense to strict liability, because strict liability is independent of general negligence principles. (Indeed, avoiding the total bar from contributory negligence was one of the reasons many jurisdictions initially adopted strict liability.)

Answer 22

(A) is the best response,

because the interference outweighs the utility of the light.

The neighbor's suit here would be based on private nuisance. A private nuisance is a substantial, unreasonable interference with another individual's use or enjoyment of his property. Since the interference with plaintiff's use of his land must be "unreasonable," the severity of the inflicted injury must outweigh the utility of the defendant's conduct. Because choice A specifies that the homeowner put in the light only to annoy the neighbor, we know that there was no socially accepted "benefit" to the homeowner from the conduct. Consequently, even a small burden to the neighbor (such as detracting from his view of the lake) would outweigh the non-existent benefits to the homeowner. Since choice A is the only choice that focuses on the lack of utility of the homeowner's conduct—a necessary part of the cost-benefit analysis—it is the only correct choice.

(B) is not the best response,

because a plaintiff need only show an unreasonable interference with the use of his land, not loss of market value.

Plaintiffs can win a nuisance suit by showing that the interference with their use and enjoyment of their property was substantial. There is no requirement that the value of the property have been reduced. (For instance, suppose that the plaintiff made a special use of the property that the defendant interfered with, and that most buyers of the property wouldn't have made that use—the plaintiff can still win, even though the specialness of his use means that the defendant's conduct didn't reduce the market value of the property.)

(C) is not the best response,

because a plaintiff need only show an unreasonable interference with the use of his land.

An occasional interference with a plaintiff's enjoyment of her property suffices, if the interference is substantial and unreasonable. There is no requirement that the interference be constant.

(D) is not the best response,

because the spotlight's purpose was not to add security.

If the homeowner had installed the light for the *purpose* of adding security, this choice might well be correct, since the existence of an "unreasonable" interference with the plaintiff's enjoyment and use of her property is dependent in part on the utility of the defendant's conduct. But since the facts stipulate that the only reason the homeowner put in the light was to annoy the neighbor, the court won't consider any benefits from the homeowner's actions that didn't in fact motivate the homeowner's conduct. Consequently, this side benefit is irrelevant in weighing the costs against the benefits from the light.

Answer 23

(C) is the best response,

because the driver's unauthorized entry onto the homeowner's land was not an intentional act, thus preventing trespass from occurring.

If the driver was negligent, then a suit based on ordinary negligence could succeed, since the driver's negligence would have placed the homeowner and the homeowner's child in the zone of danger, and then caused emotional distress. So if the driver was negligent, the homeowner would prevail, making this aspect of choice C correct.

If the driver was not negligent, the homeowner's suit could of course not successfully be based on negligence. In that event, the suit would have to be based on trespass. However, trespass requires an intentional entry onto the plaintiff's property. Here, where the driver came onto the homeowner's property only as the result of a skid, the required "intentional entry" would not be found. (By the way, even if the driver intentionally chose to enter on the homeowner's property to avoid hitting the child, the doctrine of private necessity would supply a defense to trespass.)

So this choice is the only one that correctly turns on the culpability of the driver's conduct.

(A) is not the best response,

because the fact that the driver entered the homeowner's land by necessity means that the driver did not need the homeowner's authorization.

First, assume that the homeowner's suit was based on trespass. If so, the suit would fail for two reasons, as detailed in the discussion of choice C: (1) the entry was not "intentional" and (2) the doctrine of private necessity would apply. The fact that the entry was "unauthorized" would be irrelevant.

Now, assume that the homeowner's suit was based on negligence. If so, the suit obviously could not succeed if the driver did not behave negligently, a factor that choice A ignores. (If there were no negligence, the "unauthorized" nature of the entry would be irrelevant.)

(B) is not the best response,

because the presence of serious emotional distress is irrelevant if the driver violated no duty.

The mere fact that the plaintiff suffered serious emotional distress does not make the defendant liable—the defendant must have violated some independent duty to the plaintiff. So the homeowner would have to establish either that: (1) the driver committed the tort of negligence (in which case severe emotional distress in the absence of physical injury would not be a barrier to recovery, given that the homeowner was in the "zone of danger"); or (2) the driver committed trespass. Since, as detailed in the discussion of choice C, neither of these torts is necessarily established by the facts, choice B's focus on the distress cannot be a complete answer to why or whether the homeowner would win.

(D) is not the best response,

because the child's exercise of reasonable care is irrelevant to the outcome.

First, let's assume the homeowner's suit is brought in negligence. If so, the fact that the child was or wasn't careful is irrelevant. If the child *was* careful, the driver still may or may not have behaved with reasonable care. If the child *wasn't* careful, the same is true—the driver might have been, or might have not been, careful. If the driver wasn't careful, the child's negligence would not prevent the driver's conduct from giving rise to liability—one of the common ways for a driver to be negligent is to fail to be attentive to other people's, especially children's, negligence. (Nor would the child's lack of care be imputed to the homeowner.)

Now, let's assume that the homeowner's suit is brought in trespass. Again, the fact that the child was or wasn't careful would be irrelevant. Either way, the driver's conduct was not an intentional and unprivileged entry onto the homeowner's premises (as described in choice C). So choice D's focus on the carefulness of the child is completely irrelevant, no matter what the legal theory of the homeowner's suit.

Answer 24

(B) is the best response,

because it correctly states the damages available for the tort of conversion.

The tort of conversion is the interference with a person's possessory rights in a chattel that is so serious as to warrant that defendant pay full value for the chattel.

Under these facts, the neighbor borrowed the homeowner's chainsaw without permission, thereby interfering with the homeowner's possessory rights. The facts state that the saw broke (as opposed to becoming slightly damaged or in need of minor repair), so we can take this as a serious interference as opposed to a minor one.

Under the law governing conversion, the neighbor is responsible for the full value of the saw (but can keep it). In other words, the law of conversion applies the rule, familiar from retailing, that "you break it, you own it."

The fact that the neighbor was doing something ostensibly to benefit the homeowner would be deemed irrelevant—the homeowner certainly didn't consent to this use, and indeed, the neighbor's entry onto the homeowner's land to borrow the saw without permission, and his consequent uses of it for his own purposes, would certainly be enough to outweigh any possible defense based on a desire to help the neighbor.

(A) is not the best response,

because it incorrectly states the damages for the tort of conversion.

Here "actual damages" would amount to less than the full value of the homeowner's chattel, the chainsaw. The essence of conversion is that it is a "forced sale" of the chattel to the defendant. In other words, the homeowner is entitled to the full value of the saw before it was taken, not just the actual damage amount needed to return it to the condition it was in before the neighbor took it.

(C) is not the best response,

because it incorrectly suggests a defense to the tort of conversion.

The tort of conversion is the interference with a person's possessory rights in a chattel that is so serious as to warrant that defendant pay full value for the chattel.

The homeowner is entitled to the exclusive possession of his chattel. It is not a defense that the neighbor was acting for the homeowner's benefit. (Had the neighbor been using the chain saw to, say, save the homeowner's life in an emergency, the defense of necessity might apply. But here, where the neighbor was initially acting to further his own interests, and then "helping" the homeowner in a non-emergency situation, the defense would not apply.)

(D) is not the best response,

because an intent to keep the chattel is not a necessary element in conversion.

Conversion is the intentional interference with a person's possessory rights in a chattel that is so serious as to warrant that defendant pay full value for the chattel. A person who makes a temporary but serious interference with another's chattel, in a way that causes substantial damage to the chattel, has committed conversion despite his intended return (or indeed his actual return) of the chattel soon after the taking. (For instance, if D takes P's car for a joy ride and smashes it up, the fact that D promptly returns the wrecked car to P is no defense.)

Answer 25

(C) is the best response,

because the reporter has the privilege of making a fair and accurate report of the events of a public proceeding.

The tort of invasion of privacy includes public disclosures of private facts about the plaintiff by the defendant. A plaintiff must show two elements: (1) that defendant published private information about defendant, and (2) that the matter made public is one that a reasonable person would object to having made public.

A qualified privilege exists for accurate reports of public hearings, meetings, or events of sufficient public interest. Under these facts, the parents' disclosure came at a public meeting. Since the news story was a fair and accurate publication of the facts, the qualified privilege for reports of a public meeting applies, shielding the newspaper.

(A) is not the best response,

because the fact that the statements were made at a public hearing makes the issue one of whether the facts were fairly and accurately reported, not whether they were newsworthy. To put it another way, a fact disclosed at a public meeting is, *ipso facto*, deemed newsworthy.

(B) is not the best response,

because (1) the son's parents would probably be held to have implicitly consented to publication when they raised the issue at a public meeting; and, in any event, (2) the privilege to give a truthful report of matters discussed at a public meeting exists independently of whether the speaker (or the person on whose behalf the speaker spoke) consented.

(D) is not the best response,

because whether the parents knew a reporter was present or not is irrelevant to the invasion-of-privacy tort.

A privilege exists to give a truthful accounting of facts disclosed at a public meeting (as discussed in the discussion of choice C). This privilege exists whether or not a speaker at that public meeting knows of the reporter's presence.

Answer 26

(C) is the best response,

because it correctly identifies that the driver did not violate a duty of reasonability as toward the neighbor.

There are really two prongs to analyzing this problem: one is to determine if the driver will be negligent per se due to the statute, and, failing that, another is to determine whether the driver was negligent otherwise.

The standard of care in a city ordinance *can* be the basis for a claim of negligence per se if the following four elements are met:

1. The statute provides for a criminal penalty;
2. The statute was formulated to prevent the kind of harm suffered by the plaintiff;
3. The plaintiff is a member of the class the legislature intended to protect with the statute; and
4. The statute is clear as to the standard of conduct expected, and from whom and when.

The situation here does not satisfy the above elements for negligence per se, because #3 is not satisfied (i.e., the neighbor is not one of the class intended to be protected by the statute). While the question doesn't spell it out, you know from experience that the reason you're not allowed to park near a fire hydrant is to ensure that fire trucks can reach the hydrant in an emergency. Since the neighbor couldn't rely on the statute to establish negligence per se, he'll have to establish that the driver behaved unreasonably under a traditional negligence analysis. (By the way, negligence per se only means that the defendant cannot argue that his conduct was reasonable.)

Under regular negligence analysis, you'd have to find that the driver failed to exercise such care as a reasonable person in his position would have exercised, that this was a breach of the duty to prevent the foreseeable risk of injury to anyone in the plaintiff's position, and this breach must have caused the plaintiff's damages.

Here, parking by a fire hydrant couldn't possibly have created the foreseeable risk that the car would flip over onto the hydrant. Thus, the lack of foreseeability means the driver was not negligent toward the neighbor. Since C correctly identifies this, it's the best response.

(A) is not the best response,

because negligence per se will not apply under these facts.

Violation of a statutory standard is negligence per se, as long as there is a criminal penalty, violation of the statute caused the harm, the plaintiff was a member of the class intended to be protected, and the statute is clear in the standard of conduct expected. The problem here is that the neighbor is not the one the statute is intended to protect; instead, the purpose of such a statute is to enable fire trucks to reach the hydrant in the event of a fire. As a result, the driver will not be liable for negligence per se.

(Note that this doesn't mean the driver couldn't be found negligent *at all*. Instead, what negligence per se does is to stop the defendant from arguing that his conduct was reasonable. Thus, the driver could still be found liable for ordinary negligence.) Since choice A misapplies negligence per se to these facts, it's not the best response.

(B) is not the best response,

because it understates the requirements for the neighbor to prevail on a negligence claim.

In order for the driver to be liable in negligence, he would have to have failed to exercise such care as a reasonable person in his position would have exercised; this must have been a breach of the duty to prevent the foreseeable risk of harm to anyone in the plaintiff's position; and this breach must have caused the plaintiff's damages. As to causation, where there are multiple causes, the defendant can be liable if his act was a "substantial factor" in causing the plaintiff's damages. Thus, while a continuing wrong that contributed to the neighbor's injuries could be the basis of a negligence claim where there are multiple causes, choice B ignores the fact that the neighbor's injury was not a reasonably foreseeable result of the driver's negligence, so the driver did not violate a duty toward the neighbor, and can't be liable as a result. Thus, B isn't the best response.

(D) is not the best response,

because it misstates the law.

In fact, the standard of care in a city ordinance can be the basis of a claim of negligence per se if the following four elements are met:

1. The statute provides for a criminal penalty;
2. The statute was formulated to prevent the kind of harm suffered by the plaintiff;
3. The plaintiff is a member of the class the legislature intended to protect with the statute; and
4. The statute is clear as to the standard of conduct expected, and from whom and when.

If these elements are satisfied, the defendant is said to be negligent per se, meaning that he cannot argue his conduct was reasonable. Thus, D's blanket statement that violation of a city ordinance does not give rise to a civil cause of action is not correct. Under these specific facts the statute won't apply because the neighbor was not intended to be protected by the statute, which was intended to keep the hydrant clear for fire trucks. However, since D offers incorrect reasoning, it's not the best response.

Answer 27

(B) is the best response,

because it recognizes the most important exception to the rule of non-liability to trespassers.

The general rule is that a landowner owes no duty to a trespasser to make his land safe, to warn of dangers on it, to avoid carrying on dangerous activities on it, or to protect the trespasser in any other way. The most important exception to the general rule of non-liability to trespassers is that once the owner has *knowledge* that a particular person is trespassing on his property, he is then under a duty to exercise reasonable care for the latter's safety.

Under these facts the vintner owed no duty to the trespasser while the trespasser remained undiscovered. However, if the vintner became aware of the trespasser before the descending balloon hit him, then the vintner would be required to exercise reasonable care to protect the trespasser's safety.

(A) is not the best response,

because the vintner does not owe the trespasser a duty to protect the trespasser from harm.

The general rule is that a landowner owes no duty to a trespasser to make his land safe, to warn of dangers on it, to avoid carrying on dangerous activities on it, or to protect the trespasser in any other way.

Here, if the trespasser brought suit under a negligence theory, he'd have to show that the vintner owed him a duty to protect the trespasser from injury. However, as just stated a landowner does not owe an undiscovered trespasser a duty to protect the trespasser in any way. Therefore, even if the balloon's crash landing was caused by the vintner's negligence, the trespasser will not be able to make a *prima facie* case for negligence if (as may have been the case) the vintner was unaware of the trespasser's presence.

(C) is not the best response,

because landowners have the right to engage in dangerous activities on their own land if (as may have been the case) the owner doesn't know of the trespasser's presence.

The general rule is that a landowner owes no duty to a trespasser to avoid carrying on dangerous activities on it that might injure the trespasser. (There is an exception if the owner knows of the trespasser's presence.) So even if the trespasser could prove that balloon rides are abnormally dangerous (which is doubtful), the vintner would not be liable to him for the injury, assuming the vintner was not aware that the trespasser was present. Since choice C doesn't mention the vintner's knowledge as a factor, it is not the best choice.

(D) is not the best response,

because the vintner's knowledge of frequent intruders would not make the vintner's conduct negligent.

The general rule is that a landowner owes no duty to a trespasser to make his land safe, to warn of dangers on it, to avoid carrying on dangerous activities on it, or to protect the trespasser in any other way. An exception to the general rule is that if a landowner knows a limited portion of his land is frequently used by trespassers, he must use reasonable care to make the premises safe.

However, even if an owner knows of such frequent use by trespassers, the owner will not be liable unless he behaves without due care (e.g., by failing to warn of a known danger). On the facts here, nothing suggests that the crash-landing was due to the vintner's negligence. Since choice D does not factor any issue of negligence into the analysis, it is not the best choice.

Answer 28

(C) is the best response,

because it addresses the central issue here and resolves it: The neighbor won't be liable because he wasn't negligent.

Here, there are only two ways the neighbor could possibly be liable: (1) his own acts or (2) vicarious liability for the thief's wrongful acts. There's no preexisting relationship justifying the neighbor's liability for the thief's acts, so there's no basis for vicarious liability. As to his own behavior, the neighbor did nothing unreasonable. The only contribution he made to the whole series of events here was to leave his car in his garage, which, without more, is not unreasonable. Without unreasonableness, there's no negligence. The thing that makes this question a little tricky is that your gut feeling is that the neighbor should be liable to the rescuer, because, after all, the rescuer did save the neighbor's property. However, this creates perhaps a moral duty on the neighbor's part, but not a legal one.

Since C correctly identifies that the neighbor won't be liable because he wasn't negligent, C is the best response.

(A) is not the best response,

because the *result* of the rescuer's action is not relevant to whether or not he'll prevail.

If the neighbor is to be liable to the rescuer at all, it must be because the neighbor breached some duty toward the rescuer. Under these facts, the neighbor did nothing wrong. The genesis of the situation here is that the thief was siphoning gas out of the neighbor's car in the neighbor's garage. The neighbor did nothing unreasonable, because leaving one's car in one's garage is, barring some unusual additional facts, not unreasonable. Thus, the rescuer's coincidentally saving the neighbor's property in his effort to save the thief does not create liability for the neighbor in the absence of a breach of duty (or some basis for the neighbor to be liable for the thief's act). Since A focuses incorrectly on the results of the rescuer's acts and not the neighbor's responsibility toward him, it's not the best response.

(B) is not the best response,

because it doesn't address an element that will determine the neighbor's liability.

In order for the neighbor to be liable to the rescuer, he would have to have either breached a duty toward the rescuer, or there must be some basis for holding the neighbor vicariously liable for the thief's acts.

First, there's no basis for vicarious liability for the thief's wrongful act, because there's no preexisting relationship justifying it. Second, under these facts, the neighbor did nothing unreasonable. He merely left his car in his own garage, and this, barring some unusual additional facts, is not unreasonable. What the rescuer's acting reasonably in an emergency would do is ensure he can recover from the thief, as wrongdoer, under the rescuer doctrine (since a negligent defendant is liable to anyone who attempts to help his victim, since rescue is considered "foreseeable"). Even if the rescuer had been negligent, he'd *still* be able to recover under the doctrine, from the thief. Thus, the rescuer's reasonability is relevant in a claim against the thief, but not against the neighbor. Since B doesn't recognize this, it's not the best response.

(D) is not the best response,
because it ignores the central issue and misstates the facts.

D misstates the facts because assumption of the risk would not apply to the rescuer. When a rescuer reasonably believes help is necessary, he can undertake to help without assuming any risk (as long as his acts are reasonable). However, this isn't relevant in the rescuer's claim against the neighbor, but in his claim against the thief, since the thief, as the tortfeasor, would be the one who couldn't use assumption of the risk against the rescuer.

But there's a world of difference between the thief and the neighbor: The thief breached a duty of reasonability by placing himself in peril, thus inviting rescue. The neighbor didn't breach a duty toward the rescuer. All he did was leave his car in his garage, which, barring other facts, is perfectly reasonable. Since D fails to recognize this, it's not the best response.

Answer 29

(D) is the best response,
because this argument correctly states a requirement for the tort of intentional infliction of emotional distress and shows that the requirement is not met.

To establish a *prima facie* case for intentional/reckless infliction of emotional distress, the plaintiff must prove the following elements:

(1) an act by the defendant amounting to extreme and outrageous conduct;
(2) intent on the part of the defendant to cause the plaintiff to suffer severe emotional distress, or recklessness as to the effect of the defendant's conduct;
(3) causation; and
(4) damages.

Here, the photographer is probably correct in arguing that no reasonable person could conclude that the conduct here satisfied requirement (1)'s "extreme and outrageous conduct" standard. As the Second Restatement puts it, the conduct must be "beyond all possible bounds of decency . . . " Rest. 2d Torts, § 46, cmt. d. The conduct here—which, after all, involved pursuit of a newsworthy story by use of the public airspace—does not seem to meet this standard. (In any event, none of the other arguments has any real chance of prevailing, so choice D is the "best" answer even though it is not certain to prevail.)

(A) is not the best response,
because whether the photographer had the intent to photograph the prisoner or not is irrelevant, given the possibility of reckless infliction of distress.

The facts say that the prisoner is suing for "intentional or *reckless*" infliction of distress. Therefore, if the prisoner can show that the photographer recklessly disregarded both the possibility that he was including the prisoner in the photo, and the possibility that this inclusion might well cause the prisoner distress, the prisoner could win (if the "extreme and outrageous" standard were met, which it isn't). So the fact that the photographer didn't specifically intend to photograph the prisoner (even if proven) would be irrelevant. (Also, a court would probably disagree with the proposition that no reasonable person could conclude that the photographer intended to include the prisoner in the shot.)

(B) is not the best response,
because physical injury suffered by a plaintiff is not an element of the *prima facie* case for intentional or reckless infliction of emotional distress.

To establish a *prima facie* case for intentional infliction of emotional distress, the plaintiff must prove the following elements:

(1) an act by the defendant amounting to extreme and outrageous conduct;
(2) intent on the part of the defendant to cause the plaintiff to suffer severe emotional distress, or recklessness as to the effect of the defendant's conduct;
(3) causation; and
(4) damages.

Because physical injury is *not,* according to the above list, one of the required elements of intentional or reckless infliction of emotional distress, choice B is wrong.

(C) is not the best response,
because no "extra" privilege exists for news photographers to take photographs.

News photographers do not have a special privilege exempting them from tortious conduct. In other words, if the taking and publication of a particular photo would be "extreme and outrageous" (which the photo here wouldn't, as discussed with regard to choice A above), this would be true whether the photo was taken by a professional news photographer or by an amateur with a disposable camera.

Answer 30

(C) is the best response,

because the storm was so severe that the absence of lifeboats made no difference.

On these facts, the doctrine of "negligence per se" might have applied. This doctrine states that when a safety rule has sufficiently close application to the facts of the case at hand, an unexcused violation of that statute is "negligence per se." So here, the liner's failure to have the statutorily required lifeboats would automatically be deemed to constitute negligence.

But the negligence per se doctrine doesn't excuse the plaintiff from showing *causation*. In particular, if compliance with the statute wouldn't have prevented the harm from occurring, then the absence of compliance couldn't have been the cause in fact of the injury, and the plaintiff loses.

Here, that's what happened—the absence of the required lifeboat made no factual difference, because such a boat couldn't have been used, and thus couldn't have prevented the harm.

(A) is not the best response,

because not having the lifeboats required by the statute was not the cause of the passenger's drowning.

The "negligence per se" doctrine states that when a safety rule has sufficiently close application to the facts of the case at hand, an unexcused violation of that statute is "negligence per se." However, even where the statute is applicable to the facts of the case, the "negligence per se" does not make the defendant liable unless the plaintiff shows that there is a causal link between the act constituting the violation and the resulting injury. Here, since the presence of the boats would have made no difference, this causal relationship is lacking.

(B) is not the best response,

because common carriers such as ocean liners are not held to the strict liability standard.

It is true that common carriers are required to exercise a very high degree of care toward their passengers and guests, which is to say they are liable for even slight negligence. But this is not the same as "strict liability." So choice B, insofar as it asserts that strict liability applies, is simply wrong.

(D) is not the best response,

because the passenger did not knowingly assume the risk of not having lifeboats.

The assumption-of-risk doctrine states that a plaintiff has assumed the risk of a certain harm if she voluntarily consented to take her chances that the harm would occur. Where such an assumption of risk is shown, the plaintiff is completely barred from recovery.

Here, the passenger may well have assumed the general risk of a "rough voyage." But the passenger would not be held to have assumed the risk that the liner would fail to install statutorily required lifeboats. Indeed, where (as here) a statutory safety requirement is intended to protect a particular class of people who can't protect themselves, courts are very hesitant to find that a member of that class assumed the risk of non-compliance. In any event, here there is no evidence at all that the passenger knowingly assumed the risk of failure to have lifeboats, so assumption of risk could not apply.

Answer 31

(D) is the best response,

because intentional force that exceeded the basketball player's consent would be an offensive contact constituting a battery.

An action for battery has three elements:

(1) the defendant's act bringing about a harmful or offensive contact with the plaintiff's person;
(2) the defendant's intent to bring about such contact or to create the apprehension of immediate contact; and
(3) causation.

For the player to prevail in an action for battery he'd have to prove an offensive contact. Roughness up to the level to which the player impliedly consented would not be deemed harmful or offensive. But consent would not be a defense if the opponent intentionally used more than the consented-to level of force.

(A) is not the best response,

because what is at issue is not the contact, but the level of contact consented to by the players in the game.

Apparent consent is that which a reasonable person would infer from plaintiff's conduct. For example, somebody who voluntarily engages in a body contact sport impliedly consents to the normal contacts inherent in playing it.

If the opponent intended to strike the player, but in a way that was consistent with the play of the game, then the player's consent would be found to be implied by his participation in the game and his use of the same tactics.

(B) is not the best response,

because it ignores the significance of the plaintiff's consent.

What would otherwise be a harmful or offensive contact will not be actionable if it was consented to.

Because the player's participation in the rough game, and his use of the same tactics, would be found to constitute implied consent to a certain level of roughness, the mere fact that the opponent intended to cause, say, an offensive contact that was consistent with the general game-play would not expose him to liability.

(C) is not the best response,

because it ignores the possibility that the opponent may have exceeded the scope of the implied consent.

It's true that if the opponent acted merely with the same level of roughness as previously manifested by various players in the game (including the player), the player would be deemed to have consented to it. But the opponent may have used more than the level of force to which the player would be found to have consented. In that event, the implied consent doctrine wouldn't apply, and the opponent could be liable.

Answer 32

(C) is the best response,

because the law does not recognize a claim for damages for emotional distress incident to negligently caused property loss.

Where due to the defendant's negligence the plaintiff either suffers physical injury or narrowly avoids it, the plaintiff can recover for emotional distress, at least if it is accompanied by physical symptoms. But where the only injury or physical damage from the defendant's negligence is property damage, courts are unwilling to allow the plaintiff to recover for emotional distress at the property damage. (Courts fear inflated claims and liability without a natural stopping point.) Since the restaurateur's distress is due to the property damage (not, say, due to the restaurateur's nearly being burned in the negligently caused fire), this rule applies here to deprive the restaurateur of recovery for the distress.

(A) is not the best response,

because the law does not recognize a claim for damages for emotional distress incident to negligently caused property loss, for the reasons discussed in choice C above.

(B) is not the best response,

because the law does not recognize a claim for damages for emotional distress incident to negligently caused property loss.

Emotional distress harm may be "as real" as physical harm, but courts fear that false claims of emotional harm are far easier to make, and harder to disprove, than those of physical harm. Therefore, in cases of pure property damage, they do not allow recovery of emotional distress incident to that property damage.

(D) is not the best response,

because even a showing of physical harm from the distress would not suffice.

If the restaurateur had been threatened with imminent bodily injury from the fire, then the fact that the restaurateur suffered physical harm from emotional distress at his near escape probably would make the difference (i.e., the restaurateur could recover for distress because he suffered physical symptoms, and couldn't recover if he didn't have physical symptoms.) But where, as here, there was no danger to the plaintiff of bodily injury, and his emotional distress is due solely to his being upset at the property damage, courts do not allow recovery (for the reasons discussed in choice C above) even if there are physical symptoms from the distress.

Answer 33

(D) is the best response,

because the elements of trespass are met here, and the damages are appropriate.

A trespass occurs when the defendant enters the plaintiff's land, and, when the trespass is intentional, no harm is required. Here, a valid lease was in effect, and therefore the law student is entitled to exclusive possession of the apartment. Injunctive relief is appropriate, as the trespasses are ongoing. Compensatory damages are appropriate, as the landlord damaged the property by removing the handles from the bathroom and kitchen sinks. Punitive damages are appropriate, as the repeated pattern of the trespasses, combined with the "pattern of harassment," demonstrates malicious intent and ill will.

(A) is not the best response,

because standing is met here.

The student possesses a leasehold, which is an interest in land that entitles him to exclusive possession. His interest in the property is sufficient to give him standing.

(B) is not the best response,

because damage is not required for intentional trespass, and, in any event, the landlord's actions did in fact damage the law student's leased property.

A trespass occurs when the defendant enters the plaintiff's land, and, when the trespass is intentional, no harm is required. Here, removing handles from sinks likely makes them inoperable, thereby damaging the property.

(C) is not the best response,

because, while compensatory damages are likely to be awarded, injunctive relief and punitive damages are likely to be awarded as well.

A trespass occurs when the defendant enters the plaintiff's land, and, when the trespass is intentional, no harm is required. Here, a valid lease was in effect, and therefore the law student is entitled to exclusive possession of the apartment. Injunctive relief is appropriate, as the trespasses are ongoing. Compensatory damages are appropriate, as the landlord damaged the property by removing the handles from the bathroom and kitchen sinks. Punitive damages are appropriate, as the repeated pattern of the trespasses, combined with the "pattern of harassment," demonstrates malicious intent and ill will.

Answer 34

(B) is the best response,

because *res ipsa loquitur* does not apply to these facts, and this answer choice correctly notes that there is no evidence that the defendant knew or should have known of the banana peel.

Res ipsa loquitur allows a plaintiff to create an *inference* that the defendant behaved negligently, even though there's no direct evidence that the defendant was negligent, if the plaintiff can prove that:

(1) there is no direct evidence of the defendant's conduct;

(2) the type of event in question ordinarily does not occur except through the negligence of someone;

(3) the instrument that caused injury was in exclusive control of the defendant; and

(4) the injury was probably not due to the plaintiff's own action.

Here, the banana peel was "fresh and clean except for a mark made by the heel of a customer's shoe," indicating that the banana peel had not been on the floor for a long period of time. Therefore, there is not a reasonable basis for concluding that the store employees were negligent in not removing the banana peel from the floor. The second element of *res ipsa loquitur* is not met, as the banana may have fallen to the floor seconds before the customer's fall, which is not negligent behavior on the part of the store.

(A) is not the best response,

because even if it were true, the case could still go to the jury.

Under pure comparative negligence, even if a plaintiff is negligent the case may go to the jury, who will reduce any award based on the plaintiff's negligence. As the call of this question asks whether the case should go to the jury, this answer is incorrect.

(C) is not the best response,

because even if it were true, the case will still not go to the jury as there is not a reasonable basis for inferring that the grocer knew or should have known of the banana peel.

This answer incorrectly implies that strict liability applies, but it does not because the banana was not defective. Furthermore, *res ipsa loquitur* does not apply. *Res ipsa loquitur* allows a plaintiff to create an *inference* that the defendant behaved negligently, even though there's no direct evidence that the defendant was negligent, if the plaintiff can prove that:

(1) there is no direct evidence of the defendant's conduct;

(2) the type of event in question ordinarily does not occur except through the negligence of someone;

(3) the instrument that caused injury was in exclusive control of the defendant; and

(4) the injury was probably not due to the plaintiff's own action.

Here, the second element in the above list of *res ipsa loquitur* requirements—that the type of event in question ordinarily does not occur without someone's negligence—is not satisfied. We know that the banana peel was "fresh and clean except for a mark made by the heel of a customer's shoe," indicating that the banana peel had not been on the floor for a long period of time. Therefore, it can't be said that this type of event (slipping on a fresh and clean banana peel) ordinarily does not occur except through someone's negligence: The banana may have fallen to the floor seconds before the customer's fall, meaning that it was not negligence by anyone (especially the store's employees) not to have picked up the peel in time.

(D) is not the best response,

because the plaintiff will need to prove more than foreseeability.

In addition to proving foreseeability, the plaintiff must also prove that the grocer fell below the standard of care by not behaving as a reasonably prudent person. Here, the banana peel was "fresh and clean except for a mark made by the heel of a customer's shoe," indicating that the banana peel had not been on the floor for a long period of time. Therefore, there is not a reasonable basis for concluding that the store employees were not behaving like a reasonably prudent person in not removing the banana peel from the floor. Indeed, the banana peel may have fallen to the floor seconds before the customer's fall, which is not negligent behavior on the part of the store.

Answer 35

(B) is the best response,

because it is the only choice that involves setting the standard of care, rather than determining whether the defendant satisfied the appropriate standard of care.

The suit has been brought on a failure-to-warn theory. The facts stipulate that the dangers that the insulation installer says should have been warned of were not known or knowable at the time of the installer's exposure. Therefore, the judge must at the outset answer a pure question of law: Does a defendant who is selling dangerous substances have a duty to warn of their dangerousness if that dangerousness is unknown at the time? Choice B encapsulates this issue, since if (and only if) the asbestos company is held to have a duty to warn of these not-yet-known dangers can a reasonable jury possibly find that the asbestos company is liable for failing to warn.

(A) is not the best response,

because (1) the issue is irrelevant to the plaintiff's failure-to-warn theory, and (2) in any event, this is a question of fact, to be left to the jury.

The plaintiff has sued on a failure-to-warn theory. Therefore, even if no satisfactory, safe alternative exists even today, there could still be a duty (even today) to warn of these unavoidable dangers. (One in plaintiff's position would be entitled to conclude that in view of the dangers, he should take a different job.) Consequently, the existence of a satisfactory alternative is simply not relevant to the claim.

In any event, even if this issue were relevant, the answer would be a pure question of fact, not law.

(C) is not the best response,

because (1) the issue posed may not even be a relevant issue, and (2) the issue is in any event a question of fact.

As to (1), the judge could quite plausibly decide (as a matter of law, and as described in choice B above), that the installer should be held to have had a duty to warn of not-yet-discoverable risks. If the judge so held, then the issue here (whether D in fact knew of the risks) would be legally irrelevant.

As to (2), in any event, what any defendant should reasonably have known at a particular moment is inevitably a factual issue, properly left to the jury.

(D) is not the best response,

because (1) "inherent dangerousness" is probably not an issue; and (2) even if it were, this would be a factual issue to be left to the jury.

The concept of "inherent dangerousness," to the extent that it's relevant in a product-liability suit, generally refers to the issue of "unavoidable danger." That is, if a product has some social utility, and is "unavoidably dangerous" (or as it is sometimes put, "inherently dangerous"), the defendant may be able to argue that the product is not "defective." (That's because the idea of a "defect" involves something that is "wrong" and needlessly dangerous, and something that is unavoidably hazardous does not meet this standard.)

Here, the case has been brought on a failure-to-warn theory. Even if asbestos is "inherently dangerous" (and thus not defective), this fact would not spare the defendant from having a duty to warn of its inherent dangers (assuming there is a duty to warn of not-yet-knowable dangers). So the inherent dangerousness of the product would be irrelevant.

In any event, even if inherent dangerousness were a relevant issue, this would be a matter of fact, not law, and thus properly left to the jury.

Answer 36

(C) is the best response,

because it was not foreseeable to the motorist that he would suffer a heart attack, and any violation of the red-light statute was not the result of an intentional act.

There is no direct evidence that the motorist failed to exercise due care. Therefore, under ordinary negligence principles, the court would clearly have to find, as a matter of law, that no reasonable jury could find the motorist liable for negligence (the only plausible basis on which the child could recover).

(Had the motorist driven in the face of knowledge that he was especially vulnerable to a heart attack, then this might be enough indication of negligence to permit the case to go to the jury. But the facts carefully make it clear that this was not the case.)

The only interesting question is whether the fact that the motorist's car drove through the red light, in violation of a statute, can give rise to an inference of negligence through operation of the doctrine of negligence per se.

Here, the court could not properly apply the negligence per se doctrine. Since the motorist was unconscious during the violation, the motorist did not even "commit" a violation, since an unconscious act cannot be the basis for a statutory violation. Furthermore, even treating this as a statutory violation, negligence per se would not apply because the court would conclude that any statutory violation was "excused" due to the medical emergency.

(A) is not the best response,

because violation of the motor code is not proof of the motorist's negligence per se.

As is described in the treatment of choice C above, the motorist would not be deemed to have committed a voluntary violation of the statute at all, and even if he did, any violation would be excused. Therefore, the negligence per se doctrine would not be applied.

(B) is not the best response,

because the requirements of proof by inference, otherwise known as "*res ipsa loquitur,*" are not met.

For the judge to issue a directed verdict for the child, the court would have to conclude that no reasonable jury could deny that the motorist was negligent. It is a very rare fact pattern that would cause the judge to find negligence as a matter of law.

The choice's reference to an "inference" of negligence is probably intended to suggest that the doctrine of *res ipsa loquitur* may apply. But there are at least two impediments to applying *res ipsa* here: (1) it cannot be said that car accidents generally don't happen in the absence of negligence by someone (which is why *res ipsa* is rarely applied in car accident cases); and (2) even if *res ipsa* did apply, the doctrine would merely entitle the child to get to the jury (i.e., supply enough evidence of negligence that a jury *could* properly find negligence), not entitle the child to a directed verdict on negligence (i.e., supply such incontrovertible evidence of negligence that the judge would conclude that no reasonable jury could find that there *wasn't* negligence).

(D) is not the best response,

because there is no evidence of the motorist's negligence.

As discussed in choice C above, there is no evidence at all of the motorist's negligence. Therefore, the standard for issuing a directed verdict against the child (that there is at least one element of plaintiff's *prima facie* case that no reasonable jury could find to have been proved) is satisfied.

Answer 37

(C) is the best response,

because the explosion was caused by a design defect in a part of the plant unrelated to the filter system designed by the engineer.

The only plausible basis for the suit here would have to be negligence. (Although the making of explosive chemicals may have been an "abnormally dangerous activity"—triggering strict liability—the engineer was not herself carrying out that manufacturing activity, and only the person carrying out the ultrahazardous activity has strict liability for it).

To be liable in negligence, the engineer would have to have had a duty to avoid a particular type of harm, and then to have failed to use reasonable care in carrying out that duty. If the engineer had worked on the design that contained the defect, she certainly could have been held liable in negligence. But since the engineer dealt only with the filtering system, she never undertook any duty to ascertain the safety of the other aspects of the plant design. Consequently, nothing she did (or didn't do) could possibly have constituted a failure to use reasonable care in the discharging of a duty.

(A) is not the best response,

because the engineer does not become liable for a design defect merely by including that defect in her blueprints.

The facts state that the engineer was retained to design a filter system. Her duty was to protect people from unreasonable risk of injury arising from her design.

The only way to show the design for the filter system was to include the rest of the plant in which the filter system was to be installed. Showing the rest of the plant, including the design defect, does not make her liable for all injuries arising for all design defects in the plant, absent an affirmative requirement to review or inspect those other parts of the blueprints. There is no principle that would impose on an engineer such an affirmative duty to review the safety of parts of blueprints for which the engineer has had no responsibility.

(B) is not the best response,

because joint and several liability does not apply on these facts.

Where two or more tortious acts combine to proximately cause an indivisible injury to a plaintiff, each tortfeasor is jointly and severally liable for that injury.

Under these facts the engineer committed no tort. Merely including a part of the defectively designed plant in her drawings absent a requirement that she knew or should have known of the defect does not make her liable in tort for the defect. Without the engineer's having committed a tort leading to the plaintiff's injury, there can be no joint and several liability.

(D) is not the best response,

because the fact that the plaintiff brought suit against the engineer personally means that it doesn't matter whether the engineer was an independent contractor or not.

Had the plaintiff brought suit against *the company*, then perhaps the engineer's status with the company—that is, whether she was an employee or an independent contractor—might be relevant to the company's liability.

However, the facts state that the plaintiff brought the action against the engineer individually. The engineer's liability will depend solely on whether the engineer behaved negligently, and that would be so (or not so) regardless of whether the company employed her or merely engaged her.

Answer 38

(C) is the best response,

because it adds an element that would create liability in the chemical engineer.

The central problem with these facts is that they don't indicate an active misrepresentation by the chemical engineer, and the chemical engineer had no duty to make an affirmative disclosure of the true value of the stock. Such a duty of disclosure only arises where, for instance, there is a specific query about the matter, a special (e.g., fiduciary) relationship exists, or there are other circumstances requiring disclosure (e.g., a half-truth, subsequent information that makes prior statement misleading, or knowledge of undisclosed facts basic to a transaction). None of these apply to these facts; thus, for there to be liability, an option would have to add facts *creating* liability. That's what C does, by adding a misrepresentation—that the stock is not worth more than $6. This qualifies because it satisfies all the requirements of a misrepresentation:

1. Defendant's misrepresentation of a material past or present fact;
2. Defendant's knowledge of falsity or reckless disregard for falsity;
3. Defendant's intent to induce plaintiff's reliance;
4. Plaintiff's actual, justifiable reliance; and
5. Damages.

Here, the chemical engineer would know the true value, where the shareholder, who presumably doesn't share the chemical engineer's expertise, would be justified in relying on the chemical engineer's statement. The shareholder's reliance would be justifiable because the chemical company's own statements show that the stock's worth $5. Furthermore, the chemical engineer would clearly intend to induce the shareholder's reliance so she could get the stock at a bargain price.

Choice C is thus clever in adding facts that create liability where none existed. Since C accurately assesses the chemical engineer's liability in the light of additional facts, it's the best response.

(A) is not the best response,

because it understates what the shareholder must prove in order to recover for misrepresentation due to nondisclosure.

Choice A suggests that the chemical engineer didn't tell the shareholder that the stock was worth more than $6 a share, but should be liable for *not* telling because the chemical engineer knew the stock was worth more. In fact, this misstates the requirements for misrepresentation based on nondisclosure.

The general rule is that misrepresentation requires some form of active concealment beyond mere silence. Exceptions to this rule include:

1. An affirmative duty to disclose (due to a half-truth, subsequent information making the prior statement misleading, or knowledge of undisclosed facts basic to a transaction);
2. The plaintiff's specific query about the matter; or
3. Existence of a special (e.g., fiduciary) relationship between the parties.

Under these facts, there's nothing to impose a duty of disclosure on the chemical engineer. In point of fact, the chemical engineer got a bargain, with nothing illegal about it. Since A suggests the chemical engineer had a duty to disclose the value of the stock when in fact she didn't, A can't be the best response.

(B) is not the best response,

because the chemical engineer's failure to disclose the true value of the inventory would not make her liable for misrepresentation.

The general rule is that misrepresentation requires some form of active concealment beyond mere silence. Exceptions to this rule include:

1. An affirmative duty to disclose (due to a half-truth, subsequent information making the prior statement misleading, or knowledge of undisclosed facts basic to a transaction);
2. The plaintiff's specific query about the matter; or
3. Existence of a special (e.g., fiduciary) relationship between the parties.

Under these facts, there's nothing to trigger a duty of disclosure, so the chemical engineer cannot be liable for misrepresentation even if she didn't tell the shareholder the true value of the inventory. Since B states otherwise, it's not the best response.

(D) is not the best response,

because the availability of the financial statement would not be relevant to the shareholder's claim.

Furthermore, as a public company, the chemical company's statements *would* be available to the shareholder, as they would be to anyone.

In any case, the statement says that the stock is worth $5, so it's not the value as stated in the statement that would furnish the basis of a misrepresentation claim, but the chemical engineer's knowledge that the statement did not reflect the true value of the stock.

Instead, the chemical engineer would only be liable if she misrepresented the value of the stock (since there's no duty to disclose under these facts). Since D does not address an element that will determine the chemical engineer's liability, it's not the best response.

Answer 39

(C) is the best response,

because it focuses on the missing element of the aged father's claim, and thus, as C states, would result in the officer's prevailing.

Third parties can recover for emotional distress, where someone else is intentionally physically harmed, if:

1. They are present for the physical harm;
2. They are closely related to the injured person; and
3. The actor knows of the third party's presence, and must be able to reasonably anticipate the

third party's distress that will result from the actor's conduct.

The element that's missing here is the officer's knowledge of the aged father's presence. Had the officer known about it, it's quite possible the aged father would prevail—even though the officer's conduct is not extreme and outrageous vis-à-vis the aged father! Since C correctly identifies a central element missing on these facts, and correctly determines the outcome, C is the best response.

(A) is not the best response,

because it understates what the aged father will have to prove in order to recover, and ignores a missing element in the claim.

Third parties can recover for emotional distress, where someone else is intentionally physically harmed, if:

1. They are present for the physical harm;
2. They are closely related to the injured person; and
3. The actor knows of the third party's presence, and must be able to reasonably anticipate the third party's distress that will result from the actor's conduct.

Thus, it wouldn't be enough that the officer's acts caused the aged father's severe emotional distress; what's missing under these facts is that the officer didn't know about the aged father's presence. Since A doesn't recognize this, it's not the best response.

(B) is not the best response,

because it states an element that the aged father need *not* prove in order to recover, and ignores a missing element to the claim the aged father *will* actually have to prove.

Third parties can recover for emotional distress, where someone else is intentionally physically harmed, if:

1. They are present for the physical harm;
2. They are closely related to the injured person; and
3. The actor knows of the third party's presence, and must be able to reasonably anticipate the third party's distress that will result from the actor's conduct.

Thus, it's not necessary that the actor's conduct be extreme and outrageous with respect to the third party, even though, under these facts, the onlooker would have to prove this as part of *her* emotional distress claim against the officer. Instead, what choice B ignores is that the officer can't be liable because he didn't realize the aged father was present. As a result, B can't be the best response.

(D) is not the best response,

because it focuses on an irrelevant point, and ignores a missing element of the aged father's claim.

Third parties can recover for emotional distress, where someone else is intentionally physically harmed, if:

1. They are present for the physical harm;
2. They are closely related to the injured person; and
3. The actor knows of the third party's presence, and must be able to reasonably anticipate the third party's distress that will result from the actor's conduct.

Thus, it's not necessary that the aged father be within the zone of physical danger. (If you chose this response, it's probably because you recognize the "zone of danger" language from an outdated emotional distress claim.) In fact, it's not the third party's fear for his own safety that determines liability, but his reaction to the harm inflicted on the victim. Thus, while his *presence* will be necessary, he needn't be in the "zone of physical danger" to recover.

Instead, what's missing under these facts is the officer's knowledge of the aged father's presence. Since D overlooks this, it can't be the best response.

Answer 40

(C) is the best response,

because it most completely states the duty owed to the mom as an invitee.

An invitee is a person who enters onto the premises in response to an express or implied invitation of the landowner. The landowner owes the invitee a general duty to use reasonable and ordinary care in keeping the property safe for the benefit of the invitee. That duty includes the duty to inspect for and correct hidden dangers and defects.

Under these facts, the mother accompanied her daughter, a minor patient. That makes the mother an invitee, since she entered the premises under the hospital's implied invitation. At issue then is whether the hospital used reasonable and ordinary care to keep the property safe.

The mere fact that the mother injured herself on a protruding fixture does not establish that the hospital failed to use due care to protect one in the mother's position. (For instance, the fixture may have been necessary to the functioning of the emergency room, and there may have been nothing that could reasonably have been done to make it safer for one who happened to faint near it). On the other hand, it's certainly possible that inspection of the fixture would have shown that its shape and or size posed an unreasonable risk to passersby, one which could have been easily corrected by, say, the use of padding.

This choice is the only one, therefore, that turns on the relevant issue: whether the hospital's personnel took, or failed to take, reasonable steps to safeguard invitees like the mother from dangers posed by the fixture.

(A) is not the best response,

because as an invitee the hospital only owed the mother a general duty of reasonable and ordinary care.

The only way the hospital would be liable for damages suffered by the mother was if it did not exercise ordinary care. To the extent that this choice suggests that the mother automatically wins because she was an invitee, it's simply wrong as a matter of law.

(B) is not the best response,

because whether the fixture on which the mother injured herself in her fall was obvious, commonly used, and an essential part of the hospital's equipment does not go to the level of care the hospital owed the mother, or to whether the hospital failed to exercise that level of care.

For example, suppose that the fixture was *non-obvious* and was rarely used. As long as the device did not pose an unreasonable danger to those around it, the hospital would still not be liable, because the hospital would not have failed to use reasonable care in connection with the device. Conversely, even if the fixture *was* obvious, commonly used, and essential, the hospital may have negligently failed to protect passersby from it (e.g., by putting padding around it, if this could be done without interfering with the device's function).

(D) is not the best response,

because the hospital owed the mother the duty of care owed to an invitee, which includes affirmative aspects.

An invitee is a person who enters onto the premises in response to an express or implied invitation of the landowner. The landowner owes the invitee a general duty to use reasonable and ordinary care in keeping the property safe for the benefit of the invitee. For instance, the owner owes invitees the duty to *inspect* the property so as to identify and correct hidden dangers.

Since the mother was an invitee (see the discussion of choice C above), the hospital owed her the whole package of duties that landowners owe to invitees. That includes the affirmative duty to inspect and safeguard the property—for instance, if an inspection would have showed that the fixture's shape or location posed an unreasonable risk of injury to passersby, the hospital owed the mother the affirmative duty of finding and correcting the condition (e.g., by installing protective padding).

Answer 41

(D) is the best response,

because it offers a defense that is plausible under these facts and states a result consistent with the reasoning.

A common law claim for defamation must satisfy four requirements:

1. The defendant's defamatory statement,
2. Of and concerning plaintiff,
3. Negligently or intentionally communicated to at least one third person,
4. Thereby damaged the plaintiff's reputation.

In addition, some degree of fault will have to be proven, and this, under these facts, turns on whether the defendant hospital is entitled to a qualified privilege. Without it, as a non-media defamer, the hospital would still have to be at least negligent. With a qualified privilege, the plaintiff would have to prove malice to recover. No matter how you decide this issue—whether malice or only negligence is required—choice D would be correct, because under its reasoning the defendant hospital wouldn't even be negligent, and so, without fault at all, it *couldn't* be liable for defamation.

A qualified privilege applies when the statement bears some relationship to a public or private interest, of either the publisher, the reader/listener, or both, or of the general public. If the statement is in furtherance of the interest, it's protected, and it can only be destroyed by malice.

A common example of a statement covered by qualified privilege is a past employer telling a prospective future employer of an employee's thieving tendencies. Under the facts in this question, the statement by the defendant hospital would clearly be covered by the privilege, so the defendant hospital could only be liable if it knew the plaintiff hadn't taken the narcotics, or recklessly failed to determine whether or not she had. Thus, if the defendant hospital reasonably believed the plaintiff took the narcotics, it wouldn't even be negligent, let alone reckless, so it *couldn't* be liable.

Note that choice D uses the modifier "if." That means that the reasoning must be plausible on the facts, it must resolve a significant issue, and the result must be consistent with the reasoning. Here, there's nothing to suggest that the defendant hospital's belief was unreasonable. Thus, choice D is plausible on the facts. This resolves a significant issue, because it means the defendant hospital acted without fault, and thus can't be liable for defamation. Finally, the result in D mirrors this. As a result, it's the best response.

(A) is not the best response,

because although it correctly reflects the facts, it does not address the possibility that the claim was true, or the existence of a qualified privilege.

A common law claim for defamation must satisfy four requirements:

1. The defendant's defamatory statement,
2. Of and concerning plaintiff,
3. Negligently or intentionally communicated to at least one third person,
4. Thereby damaged the plaintiff's reputation.

In addition, some degree of fault will have to be proven. That's where qualified privilege comes into play. As a non-media defamer, *without* a qualified privilege, the defendant hospital would have to be *negligent* for the plaintiff to recover. With a qualified privilege, the plaintiff would have to prove *malice*—knowledge of falsity or reckless disregard for the truth.

A "qualified privilege" applies when the statement bears some relationship to a public or private interest, of either the publisher, the reader/listener, or both, or of the general public. If the statement is in furtherance of the interest, it's protected. A common example is a past employer warning a prospective future employer of an employee's thieving tendencies. A qualified privilege can only be destroyed by malice, or by publishing a defamatory statement for a reason other than the protection of the interest involved.

Here, the defendant hospital's statement would certainly be entitled to a qualified privilege, so the plaintiff would have to prove malice—a knowing falsehood or reckless disregard for the truth. Thus, merely proving that the statement was *false* would be insufficient: The plaintiff would have to prove the defendant hospital *knew* it was false or recklessly failed to determine if it was true or false. Since choice B ignores the fault requirement, it's not the best response.

(B) is not the best response,

because the reasoning it states is not determinative of the outcome.

The plaintiff *still* may not recover even if she did not take the narcotics, due to the existence of the defendant hospital's qualified privilege to defame.

A common law claim for defamation must satisfy four requirements:

1. The defendant's defamatory statement,
2. Of and concerning plaintiff,
3. Negligently or intentionally communicated to at least one third person,
4. Thereby damaged the plaintiff's reputation.

In addition, some degree of fault will have to be proven. That's where qualified privilege comes into play. As a non-media defamer, *without* a qualified privilege, the defendant hospital would have to be *negligent* in order for the plaintiff to recover. With a qualified privilege, the plaintiff would have to prove *malice*—knowledge of falsity or reckless disregard for the truth.

A "qualified privilege" applies when the statement bears some relationship to a public or private interest, of either the publisher, the reader/listener, or both, or of the general public. If the statement is in furtherance of the interest, it's protected. A common example is a past employer warning a prospective future employer of an employee's thieving tendencies. A qualified privilege can only be destroyed by malice, or by publishing a defamatory statement for a reason other than the protection of the interest involved.

Here, the defendant hospital's statement would certainly be entitled to qualified privilege, so the plaintiff would have to prove malice—a knowing falsehood or reckless disregard for the truth. Thus, merely proving that the statement was *false* would be insufficient: The plaintiff would have to prove the defendant hospital *knew* it was false or recklessly failed to determine if it was true or false. Since choice B ignores the fault requirement, it's not the best response.

(C) is not the best response,

because although its reasoning is true, it doesn't address the defamatory "sting" of the statement, and thus would not exonerate the defendant hospital.

This is an extremely sneaky issue, so don't be terribly disappointed if you missed it.

A common law claim for defamation must satisfy four requirements:

1. The defendant's defamatory statement,
2. Of and concerning plaintiff,
3. Negligently or intentionally communicated to at least one third person,
4. Thereby damaged the plaintiff's reputation.

In addition, some degree of fault will have to be proven. That's where qualified privilege comes into play. As a non-media defamer, *without* a qualified privilege, the defendant hospital would have to be *negligent* for the plaintiff to recover. With a qualified privilege, the plaintiff would have to prove *malice*—knowledge of falsity or reckless disregard for the truth.

As a general matter, truth is an absolute defense to defamation. However, the truth must refer to the defamatory "sting" of the statement. Here, it's not the fact that the narcotics were missing after the plaintiff's shift that is *itself* defamatory, because if the hospital had been robbed by an outsider during the plaintiff's shift, there would obviously be no adverse reflection on the plaintiff. Instead, it's the implication that the plaintiff *stole* the narcotics that is the defamatory "sting" of the statement, and *that's* what would have to be proven true in order for a defense based on truth to succeed.

What will actually determine the defendant hospital's liability is the degree of fault required. Because the statement related to an interest of both the defendant hospital and the referral agency, as well as any other hospitals where the plaintiff might work, the statement would be protected by a "qualified privilege," which can only be abrogated by malice. Thus, the defendant hospital would have to know the plaintiff hadn't taken the narcotics or been reckless in determining whether she had or hadn't. Since C doesn't recognize that the defendant hospital's liability turns on this, and instead offers an incomplete truth defense, it's not the best response.

Answer 42

(A) is the best response,

because it correctly identifies that the electrical engineer will be responsible for indemnifying the toy company because he created the defect.

While the facts here don't state it explicitly, the girl's claim was likely for strict liability, since she recovered from the toy company for the electrical engineer's improper design—and under strict liability, the toy company could be liable as long as the product was dangerously defective when it left the toy company's control, the toy company was in the business of selling the product, and the product didn't substantially change between the toy company and the girl. In a negligence claim, on the other hand, the toy company could only be held liable for its *own* negligence. Since the facts here say the toy company was held liable for the electrical engineer's defective design, that means the claim must be for strict liability.

Indemnity applies to strict liability in such a way that subsequent suppliers can seek indemnity from those before them in the supply chain, so that whoever was responsible for the defect is ultimately liable for it. This is how indemnity operates: The secondary tortfeasor (here, the toy company) pays a judgment due to the tort of the primary tortfeasor (here, the electrical engineer). The secondary tortfeasor can seek "indemnity" from the primary tortfeasor. (A common example of this is an employer recovering from a tortfeasor employee for judgments the employer paid in vicarious liability). Here, this would mean that the toy company can recover from the electrical engineer. Since A recognizes this, it's the best response.

(B) is not the best response,

because it mischaracterizes the facts.

Joint tortfeasors are tortfeasors who act "in concert" (with an express or implied agreement) to produce a result. The damages must be indivisible between tortfeasors. Under joint liability, traditionally, each defendant is liable for all the damages. (However, many states modify joint liability so that a *negligent* joint tortfeasor who pays a judgment can recover pro rata shares from other joint tortfeasors.)

Under these facts, the electrical engineer and the toy company didn't act in concert; it was the electrical engineer's improper design that created the risk. As a result, they weren't joint tortfeasors. Even if they *were*, this *wouldn't* mean that the toy company would prevail against the electrical engineer—at most, in some states, he could get the electrical engineer's pro rata share of the damages. In any case, this ignores the fact that under these facts, the toy company's claim is based on *indemnity*. In indemnity claims, there is a preexisting relationship between the two parties whereby the burden of a judgment will be shifted from a secondary to a primary tortfeasor (e.g., where an employer is held vicariously liable for an employee's torts, he can seek indemnity from the employee). Since B mischaracterizes the facts, it can't be the best response.

(C) is not the best response,

because its reasoning doesn't agree with its result.

If the toy company was held strictly liable to the girl for a defect created by the electrical engineer, then the electrical engineer *would* have to indemnify the toy company. C states just the opposite.

While the facts don't state it explicitly, it's likely the girl's claim was for strict liability, because the girl recovered against the toy company for the electrical engineer's improper design and under strict liability the toy company *could* be liable as long as the product was defective when it left the toy company's control. (In a negligence claim, the toy company could only be liable for its own negligence, including a negligent failure to inspect.)

Having established that the toy company was held liable for a defect created by the electrical engineer, it follows that the toy company could seek indemnity from the electrical engineer. Where strict liability is involved, all subsequent suppliers can seek indemnity from those before them in the supply chain, so that the one responsible for the defect is ultimately liable. *Normally* that will be the manufacturer, but here, the defect is traceable even further back, to the designer (the electrical engineer). Thus, C is incorrect in stating that the toy company will be unable to seek indemnity, making it not the best response.

(D) is not the best response,

because the original claim here was for strict liability, not negligence. As such, the toy company will be able to recover in indemnity from the electrical engineer, because the toy company was held liable for a defect the electrical engineer created.

While the facts don't state it expressly, it's likely the girl's claim was for strict liability, since she recovered from the toy company for the electrical engineer's improper design—and under strict liability, the toy company *could* be liable as long as the product was defective when it left the toy company's control. In a negligence claim, on the other hand, the toy company could only be liable for its own negligence. This could include a negligent failure to inspect, but for *that* to exist, you'd first have to establish that the toy company was negligent in failing to inspect for defects in the design. In that case, the toy company could be liable for its own negligence, and could not recover from the electrical engineer. However, under these facts, you're told the toy company was held liable for the electrical engineer's improper design. Since D fails to recognize this, it's not the best response.

Answer 43

(A) is the best response,

because if the defendant neighbor's dam unreasonably interfered with the plaintiff's use and enjoyment of his property, the plaintiff would have a valid claim for private nuisance.

A landowner who causes a substantial, unreasonable interference with a neighbor's use or enjoyment of his property without a valid defense is liable for private nuisance.

Most courts apply this rule in the case of watercourses, holding that an upstream owner may not completely block the flow of water if this would unreasonably interfere with a downstream owner's use and enjoyment of the latter's property. So choice A best states the applicable rules of nuisance.

(B) is not the best response,

because the defendant's desire to affect the plaintiff's property is not an element of the tort of private nuisance.

As described in the treatment of choice A above, private nuisance is the unreasonable interference with another's use and enjoyment of the latter's property.

Choice B is wrong mostly because it fails to factor in whether there has been an unreasonable interference with the plaintiff's use and enjoyment of his property. For instance, if the damming was the only way to avoid flooding of the defendant's property, and the harm it posed to the plaintiff's use and enjoyment was very small, a court would conclude that the damning was not "unreasonable," and the plaintiff would lose, even though the defendant "intended" (in the sense of knowing with substantial certainty) that the plaintiff's property would be "affected" (in the sense that water would no longer flow through it).

(C) is not the best response,

because the tort of nuisance covers use and *enjoyment*, not just use.

A landowner who causes a substantial, unreasonable interference with a neighbor's use or enjoyment of his property without a valid defense is liable for private nuisance.

The fact that the plaintiff never goes "close" to the stream is not inconsistent with her having sustained an unreasonable interference with her "use and *enjoyment*" of her property. For instance, it's very possible that the plaintiff used to like to view, from an upstairs window, the stream running through her property, and that she now has much less pleasure from the waterless view. Consequently, her "use and enjoyment" have been substantially impaired, even though in a narrow sense she never "made use" of the stream.

(D) is not the best response,

because compliance with this type of statute would not preclude liability for nuisance.

A landowner who causes a substantial, unreasonable interference with a neighbor's use or enjoyment of his property without a valid defense is liable for private nuisance. Many nuisances are not in violation of any particular law, since "positive law" (statutes, ordinances, and the like) do not purport to be the sole source of legal obligations. (For instance, a factory might get all required local permits, but might still be a private nuisance because it's unreasonably loud and noisy).

Therefore, the fact that the dam satisfied the relevant affirmative laws when it was built does not foreclose the possibility of a successful nuisance suit.

Answer 44

(B) is the best response,

because the seller should have fixed the roof and doesn't escape liability just because he sold the house.

A landowner is required to use reasonable care to ensure that the property does not pose an unreasonable danger to persons outside the property. For example, it's completely clear that if the seller still owned the house when the accident occurred, he would be liable if he should have realized that the roof posed an unreasonable danger to passersby.

The interesting question is whether the fact that the seller sold and vacated the property changes the analysis. The answer is that, at least in most jurisdictions, it does not. *See* Rest. 2d Torts, § 373(1) ("A vendor of land who has created or negligently permitted to remain on the land a structure or other artificial condition which involves an unreasonable risk of harm to others outside of the land . . . is subject to liability to such persons for physical harm caused by the condition after his vendee has taken possession of the land." Under § 373(2), except in the case where the vendor knowingly conceals the defect, the vendor's liability under § 373(1) continues "only until the vendee has had reasonable opportunity to discover the condition and to take . . . precautions.") Since one day was not enough for the buyer to discover and fix the defect, the seller remained on the hook for the defect under this rule, if (as choice B hypothesizes) he was aware of the condition and the danger.

(A) is not the best response,

because the seller wouldn't be strictly liable for a defective roof.

This choice turns only on whether the roof was "defective," not on whether the seller was negligent in any way. Therefore, the choice could be the correct answer only if some type of strict liability applied.

Strict liability does not apply to landowners. It applies only in the case of ultrahazardous activities and sales of "products." When landowners sell real estate, courts normally do not apply strict product liability, even though the structure on the real estate could be thought of as being in some sense a "product." The refusal to apply strict product liability is especially likely where, as here, the seller is an "amateur" seller (i.e., one not in the business of selling real estate).

(C) is not the best response,

because as described in the discussion of choice B above, the fact that the seller no longer owned or occupied the property would not be a defense, if the seller negligently failed to notice and correct the danger to persons outside the property, and the buyer hadn't yet had a chance to discover and fix the problem.

(D) is not the best response,

because the state of the pedestrian's knowledge is irrelevant on these facts.

This choice is pointing you towards the doctrine of assumption of risk—the theory is that if the pedestrian knew that slates had blown off in past storms, the pedestrian assumed the risk that this might happen here.

However, the assumption-of-risk doctrine applies only where the pedestrian's exposure to the risk is "voluntary." Where, as here, the pedestrian is using the public right of way, it's extremely unlikely that a court would conclude that the pedestrian's mere knowledge that slates had fallen in past windstorms amounted to a "voluntary" assumption of the risk that this might happen here, especially where the pedestrian might have believed that only negligently maintained roofs were likely to have this problem. (If the pedestrian knew that speeding cars had sometimes skidded over the curb during past rainstorms, would his use of the curb constitute assumption of the risk that a speeding car would strike him? Obviously not.)

Answer 45

(C) is the best response,

because it is the only answer that correctly requires a causal link between the surgeon's asserted negligence and the injury to the patient.

A plaintiff can prevail in a negligence claim only if she proves that the defendant's negligence was the cause in fact, as well as the proximate cause, of the plaintiff's injury. Since the asserted negligence here consists of failure to consult a cardiologist, the patient's administrator must show that that failure to consult was, more probably than not, the cause in fact ("but-for cause") of the blood clot. The only way this could be true is if the plaintiff shows that such a consultation would, more likely than not, have led to advice to the surgeon that if followed would have prevented the clot from occurring. Since choice C correctly asserts this requirement of a causal link between the asserted negligence and the bad outcome, it is the correct answer.

(A) is not the best response,

because the surgeon would not be liable if his negligence failed to contribute to the bad outcome.

As explained more fully in the discussion of choice C above, even if the surgeon was negligent in not consulting a cardiologist, he cannot be liable unless that negligence was a cause-in-fact of the bad outcome. The only way the lack of a consultation could be the cause-in-fact of the bad outcome is if the consultation would probably have led to a successful outcome. Since choice A does not reflect this requirement of a causal link, it is not correct.

(B) is not the best response,

because it, too, incorrectly eliminates any requirement of a causal link between the negligence and the injury.

The facts tell us enough to know that the patient has made a *prima facie* case of negligence (this was done by the testimony that accepted medical practice would require consultation with a cardiologist). But nothing in the facts indicates that the lack of a consultation changed the outcome, i.e., that had there been a consultation, the outcome would likely have been different. The mere fact that the *operation* caused the blot clot would not be the type of causal link required, because the doing of the operation was not itself an act of negligence; only the doing of it without a consultation constituted negligence. Since choice B does not correctly reflect this requirement of a causal link between the negligent omission and the bad outcome, it is incorrect.

(D) is not the best response,

because it incorrectly assumes that there can only be one cause of the bad outcome.

If the surgeon's failure to make the consultation was *a* cause-in-fact ("but-for cause"), as well as *a* proximate cause, of the patient's death, the surgeon would be liable even though there was also another cause-in-fact/proximate cause of the death, namely the disconnecting of the life support. One bad outcome can have multiple proximate causes/causes-in-fact, so the fact that the defendant was responsible for only one of the causes is no defense at all. Here, if a consultation would probably have led to use of a different procedure that would have eliminated the blot clot, the lack of a consultation would have been a cause in fact of the death (the clot would not have happened without the omission of a consultation) and a proximate cause of it (it led reasonably directly and foreseeably to the clot), which is all that is required causally.

Answer 46

(D) is the best response,

because it correctly identifies what the result will be.

Under the statute in these facts, the car owner could be held liable for damage negligently caused by the mechanic, since he was driving her car when the accident occurred. Thus, the bystander *could* win a judgment against the car owner, or the car owner and the mechanic jointly.

Here, you're told that the bystander sued them both, and that the bystander could recover $100,000 solely due to the mechanic's negligence. The key is that the car owner wasn't negligent *at all*. Since the car owner and the mechanic didn't act in concert, they couldn't be jointly liable; and the mechanic caused *all* the damages, the damages aren't divisible, and several liability won't apply. Instead, indemnity will apply. Under indemnity, the secondary tortfeasor, who is without *any* fault, can seek payment for any judgment he pays due to the tort of the primary tortfeasor. The most common example of this is an employer who pays a judgment, under vicarious liability, due to the tort of an employee.

Due to operation of the statute in this problem, it would also apply here (since the statute only makes available a potential defendant; it doesn't assess fault for loaning a car). Since the mechanic was solely responsible for the accident, he's the only one who will ultimately be liable, and because D correctly identifies the result, it's the best response.

(A) is not the best response,

because it mistakenly pins the car owner, ultimately, with half of the damages.

Contrary to what A states, the car owner would recover from the mechanic anything she actually pays, on grounds of indemnity. Under indemnity, the burden of a judgment is fully shifted from a secondary tortfeasor to a primary tortfeasor. As it applies here, the car owner could recover from the mechanic anything she pays to the bystander, since it was solely the mechanic's negligence that caused the accident. In fact, the car owner is only a defendant because of the statute that makes her liable for any negligence by anyone driving her car. However, since the mechanic was solely responsible for the accident, he's the only one who will ultimately be liable.

If you chose this response, you were probably thinking of "several" liability, where damages are divisible on a logical basis between tortfeasors, based on the damages each one caused—and each one must pay his share of the damages. However, under these facts the car owner wasn't negligent *at all*, so she should be able to recover entirely from the one who was—the mechanic. Since A doesn't recognize this, it's not the best response.

(B) is not the best response,

because it does not take into account operation of the statute.

Under the statute in these facts, the car owner *can* be liable for damage negligently caused by the mechanic, since he was driving her car when the accident occurred. Thus, the bystander *could* win a judgment against the car owner, which choice B fails to recognize.

B *does* recognize, however, what will ultimately happen, because the mechanic will indemnify the car owner. Indemnity applies where a secondary tortfeasor pays a judgment due to the tort of a primary tortfeasor. That's the case here, so the car owner could recover from the mechanic. Since B ignores the intermediate step—that the car owner could initially be held liable for some or all of the damages—it's not the best response.

(C) is not the best response,

because it understates what the car owner will be able to recover from the mechanic.

Under the statute in these facts, the car owner could be held liable for damage negligently caused by the mechanic, since he was driving her car when the accident occurred. Thus, the bystander *could* win a judgment against the car owner, or the car owner and the mechanic jointly.

However, where C goes off the track is in determining how much the car owner could recover from the mechanic, under the doctrine of indemnity. Indemnity applies where a secondary tortfeasor pays a judgment due to the tort of a primary tortfeasor. That's the case here, so the car owner could recover from the mechanic the *entire amount* the bystander recovers from the car owner, not just 50 percent of it, as C suggests.

If you chose this response, you were either thinking of the rule of contribution under *joint* liability, or of several liability.

In joint liability, two or more tortfeasors act "in concert" (with an express or implied agreement) to produce a result. The damages must be indivisible between tortfeasors (here, the damages are completely *divisible*, since the mechanic caused all the damage). While under traditional joint liability each defendant is liable for *all* the damages, many states modify this with the rule of "contribution," whereby a negligent joint tortfeasor who pays a judgment can recover *pro rata* shares from other joint tortfeasors.

Under *several* liability, damages are divisible on a logical basis between tortfeasors, based on the damages each caused. Here, the damages aren't divisible—the mechanic caused them *all*.

As a result, *indemnity* is the correct doctrine, not joint or several liability. Since C doesn't recognize this, it's not the best response.

Answer 47

(A) is the best response,

because it correctly states exactly what damages the defendant will be responsible for.

You're told under these facts that the defendant was negligent. Thus, he'll be liable for any damages flowing from that negligence. Here, the plaintiff's' house was already on fire when the accident occurred; thus, that portion of the damage is not attributable to the defendant. By negligently hitting a fire truck on its way to a fire, the defendant created the foreseeable risk of loss to whoever's house the fire truck was heading. Here, the damages the defendant caused—for which he'll be liable—are the part of the loss that would have been prevented had the accident not occurred. Since A correctly states this, it's the best response.

(B) is not the best response,

because it overstates the damages the plaintiff will be able to recover from the defendant.

The facts here tell you that the defendant was negligent. As a result, he'll be liable for those damages caused by his negligence. Here, the plaintiff's' house was already on fire *before* the defendant's negligence occurred, so the defendant *couldn't* be responsible for the whole house. Even if the defendant hadn't been negligent at all, the firefighters would only have been able to salvage part of the house, and it's only that portion for which the defendant would be liable. Since B ignores this, it's not the best response.

(C) is not the best response,

because the defendant will be liable for damages even if he had no hand in starting the fire.

By negligently hitting a fire truck on its way to a fire, the defendant created the foreseeable risk of loss to whoever's house the fire truck was heading. Here, the damages the defendant caused—for which he'll be liable—is the part of the loss that would have been prevented had the accident not occurred.

Of course, whoever *started* the fire will be liable *as well*, and the defendant's negligence would not exonerate the arsonist (since the defendant's negligence would be considered a foreseeable intervening cause of the plaintiff's damages). However, what's at issue here is *the defendant's* liability, and not having started the fire would not exonerate the defendant. Since C states otherwise, it's not the best response.

(D) is not the best response,

because it doesn't correctly analyze the issue of causation on these facts.

Due to his negligence, the defendant will be liable for all damages flowing from his act. Here, the defendant's negligence prevented the fire truck from reaching the fire.

Thus, the part of the plaintiff's loss that would have been prevented had the accident not occurred is a direct result of the defendant's negligence, since it would not have occurred "but for" the defendant's negligence. Thus, it's not necessary that the defendant's negligence created an "apparent danger" to the plaintiff. Since D states otherwise, it's not the best response.

Answer 48

(C) is the best response,

because this choice correctly states the standard for the misappropriation-of-identity type of invasion of privacy.

To establish a *prima facie* case for invasion of privacy by appropriation of a plaintiff's picture or name, only one element needs to be proved: that there was an unauthorized use by defendant of plaintiff's picture or name for commercial advantage.

Under these facts the movie star consented to an amateur photographer taking his picture as he sat drinking the wine company's wine at a nightclub. He did not consent to the wine company's using his photo for commercial purposes. The wine company's advertisement in a nationally circulated magazine was intended for the wine company's commercial advantage. Since choice C focuses on the key element of the wine company's liability, it's the best response.

(A) is not the best response,

because the movie star's consent was to the amateur photographer, not to the wine company's commercial use.

To establish a *prima facie* case for invasion of privacy by appropriation of a plaintiff's picture or name, only one element needs to be proved: that there was an unauthorized use by a defendant of a plaintiff's picture or name for commercial advantage.

Here, the movie star's consent was specifically to an amateur photographer. The scope of the movie star's consent was to a single amateur photograph. He did not consent to the wine company using that photograph for its commercial advantage. Therefore, his "consent" would not excuse the wine company from liability.

(B) is not the best response,

because public figures retain the right not to have their image utilized for commercial advantage.

To establish a *prima facie* case for invasion of privacy by appropriation of a plaintiff's picture or name, only one element needs to be proved: that there was an unauthorized use by a defendant of a plaintiff's picture or name for commercial advantage.

Here, the movie star was well known and so would be considered a public figure. While this fact might conceivably be relevant in other kinds of invasion of privacy claims, or in some defamation claims, it is irrelevant to the claim here. Therefore, the movie star's status as a public figure does not exonerate the wine company.

(D) is not the best response,

because enjoyment of a product does not convey the rights to commercial use of an image.

To establish a *prima facie* case for invasion of privacy by appropriation of a plaintiff's picture or name, only one element needs to be proved: that there was an unauthorized use by a defendant of a plaintiff's picture or name for commercial advantage.

Falsity is not relevant to the appropriation form of invasion of privacy. Therefore, although the wine company was accurate in its statement that the movie star enjoyed the wine company's wine, that did not give the wine company the right to make commercial use of the movie star's image.

Answer 49

(C) is the best response,

because all the facts point to the conclusion that the day care center exercised reasonable care.

We know that a "bright nine-year old child" chose to "sneak[]" away from his day care center. Furthermore, we know there were a "reasonable number of qualified personnel" at the day care center who exercised "reasonable care" to ensure the safety of the children. In this context, the day care center did not violate its duty of care, even though the child was injured.

(A) is not the best response,

because it incorrectly implies that the day care center can be strictly liable.

Day care centers are held to a negligence standard for injuries to children under their care. Here, we know that a "bright nine-year old child" chose to "sneak[]" away from his day care center. Furthermore, we know there were a "reasonable number of qualified personnel" at the day care center who exercised "reasonable care" to ensure the safety of the children. In this context, the day care center did not violate its duty of care, even though the child was injured in a nearby pond.

(B) is not the best response,

because the location near a pond is not sufficient to establish liability on the part of the day care center.

Day care centers are held to a negligence standard for injuries to children under their care, and the location of the pond by itself is not evidence of negligence. Here, we know that a "bright nine-year old child" chose to "sneak[]" away from his day care center. Furthermore, we know there were a "reasonable number of qualified personnel" at the day care center who exercised "reasonable care" to ensure the safety of the children. In this context, the day care center did not violate its duty of care, even though the child was injured.

(D) is not the best response,

because the day care center was not the owner or possessor of the land on which the child trespassed and, thus, the child's status as a trespasser is irrelevant to a lawsuit against the day care center.

Here, we know that a "bright nine-year old child" chose to "sneak[]" away from his day care center. Furthermore, we know there were a "reasonable number of qualified personnel" at the day care center who exercised "reasonable care" to ensure the safety of the children. In this context, the day care center did not violate its duty of care, even though the child was injured.

Answer 50

(D) is the best response,

because it correctly analyzes how damages will be determined.

Here, both chemical company *A* and chemical company *B* will be liable for *some* part of the rancher's damages, since each one's act was a "substantial factor" in causing the rancher's damages.

Joint and several liability addresses the divisibility of damages between multiple tortfeasors. Joint liability applies where the damages are *not* divisible between tortfeasors, making each defendant liable for all the damages (some states apply the rule of contribution to negligent joint tortfeasors, such that a negligent joint tortfeasor who pays a judgment can recover pro rata shares from the other tortfeasors).

Several liability applies where the damages *are* divisible, making each defendant liable only for the damages he caused.

You can remember the difference between the two this way: Say two people are fighting over a gun and it goes off, injuring a plaintiff. This is joint liability, because there's no way to apportion liability. If two people, each of whom has a gun, shoot a plaintiff, causing two separate injuries, then the damages can be apportioned, and there's several liability.

Here, the percentage of the rancher's liability each defendant caused hasn't been determined, so they'll be jointly and severally liable. (In fact, the damages are not likely to be considered divisible, so each defendant would be liable under joint liability for the entire judgment.) Since D correctly identifies this, it's the best response.

(A) is not the best response,

because it does not correctly apply principles of causation to these facts.

A negligence claim requires proof that a defendant failed to exercise such care as a reasonable person in his position would have exercised; this failure must have been a breach of the duty to prevent the foreseeable risk of injury to anyone in the plaintiff's position; and this breach must have caused the plaintiff's damages. The rule used to determine causation depends on how many causes there are: A single cause involves the "but for" test, and multiple causes involve the "substantial factor" test. Here, with chemical company *A* and chemical company *B* each being a cause of the rancher's damages, each one will be liable as long as its act was a "substantial factor" in creating the rancher's damages.

Under these facts, they were. Since choice A would exonerate each one because it wasn't enough *alone* to cause the damages, it's not the best response.

(B) is not the best response,

because the rancher's recovery would not depend on his ability to precisely apportion damages.

In order to prevail on a negligence claim, a defendant must have failed to exercise such care as a reasonable person in his position would have exercised; this failure must have been a breach of the duty to prevent the foreseeable risk of injury to anyone in the plaintiff's position; and this breach must have caused the plaintiff's damages.

Where there are multiple factual causes, as here, the plaintiff need only prove that an individual defendant's act was a "substantial factor" in causing the plaintiff's damages. Under these facts, this is true of *both* chemical companies. Thus, they'll each be liable, regardless of whether the rancher can assess how much pesticide each discharged.

What the ability to apportion determines is whether chemical company *A* and chemical company *B* will be jointly or severally liable. If the damages are indivisible between the tortfeasors, each defendant will be liable for all the damages (although many states modify joint liability with the rule of "contribution," whereby a negligent joint tortfeasor who pays a judgment can recover *pro rata* shares from other joint tortfeasors). If the damages are divisible on a logical basis between tortfeasors, based on the damage each one caused, then each will only pay its share of the defendant's damages.

Remember the difference this way: Say two people are fighting over a gun, and it goes off, injuring a plaintiff. This is joint liability, because there's no way to apportion liability. If two people with a gun each shoot a plaintiff, causing two separate injuries, then the damages can be apportioned, and each will only be *severally* liable. Thus, while divisibility of damages will determine how much each defendant can be liable for, it doesn't determine if the defendants will be liable. Since choice B states otherwise, it's not the best response.

(C) is not the best response,

because it presupposes that the damages are divisible equally.

While it *may be* that chemical company *A* and chemical company *B* will each be liable for only one-half of the damages, this could not be determined conclusively on these facts.

Since each company's negligence was a "substantial factor" in causing the rancher's damages, they'll each be liable. The central issue under these facts is: for how much? This will turn on whether or not the damages are *divisible* between them. If they are *not* divisible, joint liability will apply, and each defendant could be liable for the entire judgment. If the damages are divisible on a logical basis between them, based on the damage each one caused, they'll be severally liable, and will only have to pay a fair share of the plaintiff's damages. Here, if the damages are considered severable *and* each one is responsible for exactly one-half of the rancher's damages, C would be correct. However, on these facts, it's not clear that the damages are divisible (it depends on whether the amount of pesticide each dumped was calculable), and thus the share of the rancher's damages that each must pay is not determinable. Since C presupposes settlement of an issue which is unsettled on these facts, it's not the best response.

Answer 51

(D) is the best response,

because it identifies the central issue.

Common law defamation has four elements:

1. The defendant's defamatory statement,
2. Of and concerning the plaintiff,
3. Negligently or intentionally "published" to at least one third person,
4. Thereby damaged the plaintiff's reputation.

In addition, the plaintiff will have to prove some level of fault, depending on his and the defendant's status (e.g., media, public figure); furthermore, if the statement was slander and not within a "per se" category, the plaintiff must prove "special" (pecuniary) damages.

As D correctly points out, the issue here is whether the purchaser suffered special damages. That's because the statement doesn't fit any of the slander per se categories (reflecting adversely on business/profession, or imputing a foul and loathsome disease, moral turpitude crime, or lack of chastity in a woman), and it's not obvious from these facts that the purchaser actually suffered any pecuniary loss. Such damages include things like a lost job, inheritance, gift, customers, and the like. (General damages, on the other hand, cover things like damage to reputation or personal relationships, and mental anguish.)

Note that D says the purchaser won't recover unless he can prove special damages. That means that proving special damages must be crucial to the purchaser's success in order for D to be correct. In fact, if the purchaser fails to prove special damages, he'll lose the case entirely. Since D correctly identifies this, it's the best response.

(A) is not the best response,

because it ignores a central issue in the case.

It's true that the remark would have to have been heard by any of the purchaser's neighbors, in order to satisfy the "publication" requirement of defamation. (The other elements are the defamatory statement itself, of and concerning the plaintiff, the plaintiff's reputation damaged, and some level of fault.) However, this isn't really at issue under these facts—after all, you're told that many of the neighbors were out on their porches, and that the statement could be heard a block away.

Instead, the issue here is damages, because the purchaser will have to prove "special" (pecuniary) damages in order to prevail at all. That's because the bill collector's statement was slander, not libel, and it wasn't in one of the four slander per se categories (reflecting adversely on business/profession, or imputing a foul and loathsome disease, moral turpitude crime, or lack of chastity in a woman). Slander not within the four "per se" categories is the only type of defamation requiring proof of special damages. Under these facts, there's no indication the bill collector's statement resulted in any special damages for the purchaser, so the best response would have to address this issue. Since A doesn't, it's not the best response.

(B) is not the best response,

because it offers an element which is not, in fact, an element of the defamation claim.

Common law defamation has four elements:

1. The defendant's defamatory statement,
2. Of and concerning the plaintiff,
3. Negligently or intentionally "published" to at least one third person,
4. Thereby damaged the plaintiff's reputation.

In addition, a plaintiff will have to prove some level of fault depending on his and the defendant's status (e.g., media, public figure); furthermore, if the statement was slander and not within a "per se" category, a plaintiff must prove "special" (pecuniary) damages.

Thus, a statement can be defamatory without having to be the result of extreme and outrageous conduct, and the conduct can be extreme and outrageous without satisfying the elements of defamation. If you chose this response, you were probably thinking of an intentional infliction of emotional distress claim, which does require extreme and outrageous conduct. However, the claim here is for defamation, which does not require such conduct, so B isn't the best response.

(C) is not the best response,

because it overstates the level of fault the purchaser would have to prove in order to prevail.

By using the modifier "unless," C suggests that the only way the bill collector could be liable is if he knowingly defamed the purchaser. In fact, in order to recover from the bill collector, the purchaser will have to satisfy these elements: a defamatory statement, of and concerning the plaintiff, negligently or intentionally published to at least one third person, and the plaintiff's reputation damaged thereby. In addition, because the statement here is slander not within one of the slander per se categories (reflecting adversely on business/profession, or imputing foul and loathsome disease, moral turpitude crime, lack of chastity in a woman), the purchaser will have to prove "special" (pecuniary) damages.

On the fault issue, it's likely the purchaser need only prove that the bill collector was negligent in not determining the truth, not that he acted knowingly. Normally, non-media defamers can only be liable if they're negligent (as opposed to media defamers, where malice must be proven, or where a qualified privilege exists due to a special interest of the defamer, the defamed, or the general public). Even if the purchaser had to prove malice, reckless disregard for the truth would suffice; he still wouldn't have to prove the bill collector acted knowingly. Since choice C overstates the level of fault the purchaser will have to prove, it's not the best response.

Answer 52

(B) is the best response,

because the defense of "defense of others" would be negated if the jogger's belief about the danger was unreasonable.

Since the jogger has intentionally caused a harmful or offensive contact with another, he's liable for battery unless he has a defense. The only defense that plausibly applies here is "defense of others." That is, just as a person has the right to use self-defense to save himself from harm, he has that right with respect to another person who is threatened with harm (even a stranger, under the modern view).

However, the defense-of-others defense, like the right of self-defense, requires that both the actor's belief that danger exists, and his belief that the proposed conduct is a good way to deal with the danger, be reasonable. If the jogger should have realized that the pedestrian was not in fact in danger, this requirement for the defense-of-others defense would not exist.

(A) is not the best response,

because the fact that an alternative method of dealing with the danger might have solved the problem does not automatically mean that the jogger's method was unreasonable.

As described in the analysis of choice B above, the jogger was entitled to the defense of defense of others unless either his choice of methods, or his belief in the pedestrian's peril, was unreasonable. The mere fact that the alternative method of shouting a warning might have solved the problem doesn't mean that the jogger's approach was unreasonable. (For one thing, pushing the pedestrian to the ground merely threatened minor injury, whereas if she were hit she might well be killed or seriously injured. For another, the jogger could reasonably have believed that the pedestrian wouldn't hear his shout, that she wouldn't know that she was the one being shouted at, or that there wasn't time for her to react if she did hear.)

(C) is not the best response,

because the jogger might be jointly and severally liable with the driver.

The speeding driver would clearly be *a* cause of the injury, and would therefore likely be jointly and severally liable with the jogger if the jogger was liable. But this fact wouldn't save the jogger from liability, if the jogger's choice of methods (or his belief in the danger) were unreasonable. Always remember that a given injury can have multiple causes, and can thus lead to multiple tortfeasors (even if they did not act in concert) being held jointly liable.

Here, the jogger's liability would (as discussed in the analysis of choice B above) turn on the reasonableness of his belief in the danger, not on the existence of some other jointly acting cause.

(D) is not the best response,

because the jogger's intent to save the pedestrian wouldn't immunize him if his belief in the danger was unreasonable.

As is discussed in the analysis of choice B above, the jogger only qualifies for the defense of defense of others if his belief in the existence of the danger, and his choice of methods, were reasonable. Since choice D ignores this fact, and focuses only on the genuineness of the jogger's desire to save the pedestrian it is incorrect.

Answer 53

(C) is the best response,

because the plaintiff cannot prove the defendant restaurant actually caused him to get sick.

A plaintiff bears the burden of proving by a preponderance of the evidence that a defendant actually caused his injury, just as he must bear the burden of proving the other parts of his *prima facie* case.

Under these facts, the plaintiff cannot produce any real evidence that the defendant restaurant caused him to become sick. At best the plaintiff can introduce facts that raise a mere suspicion that the defendant restaurant was the cause. All the plaintiff can show is that he had an upset stomach later in the evening and that various health code violations had been found at the restaurant. What he cannot show is that the meal was the but-for cause of his becoming ill; that is, but for the defendant restaurant's actions the plaintiff would not have become ill. In response to the plaintiff's facts, the defendant restaurant can show that the plaintiff had three meals after eating in their restaurant, any of which could have caused his infection. The defendant restaurant could also argue that the bacterium causing the plaintiff's illness could have come from the plaintiff's own hands. While this "no causation" defense might not work, it is the defendant restaurant's best chance of those defenses listed.

(A) is not the best response,

because the fact that no one else became ill creates only an inference that the defendant restaurant was not the cause.

The fact that no one else got sick certainly doesn't prove that the defendant restaurant wasn't the cause—perhaps one employee failed to wash his hands, prepared the one dish eaten by the plaintiff, then washed them. In any event, the defendant restaurant is better off making the much more general argument (listed in choice C) that the plaintiff is required to make an affirmative showing that the defendant restaurant's negligence caused the illness, and that he has failed to carry this burden by a preponderance of the evidence.

(B) is not the best response,

because the defendant restaurant is responsible for the acts of its employees while in the course of their duties, even if they disregard instructions.

Under the doctrine of *respondeat superior*, an employer is vicariously liable for the negligent acts of its employees, done within the scope of the employment. The fact that the employee has disobeyed rules formulated by the employer is not a defense. Thus, as long as there was evidence that an employee failed to wash her hands and then prepared a dish eaten by the plaintiff, the fact that this happened in violation of the defendant restaurant's instructions would not prevent *respondeat superior* from applying against it.

(D) is not the best response,

because the plaintiff brought suit for an illness caused by bacterium, not an upset stomach caused by spicy food.

The assumption of the risk doctrine bars a plaintiff from recovery if he voluntarily consented to take the chance that the harm will occur.

Here the plaintiff may have assumed the risk of an upset stomach caused by spicy food, but he did not assume the risk of becoming ill because of a bacterium in contaminated food. Without voluntary consent, there can be no assumption of the risk.

Answer 54

(A) is the best response,

because a landowner may not use deadly force to defend property.

Defense of property is a defense to an intentional tort—one may use *reasonable* force to prevent trespass, or other interference with one's land or chattels. However, deadly force (i.e., force that is likely to cause death or serious bodily harm) cannot be used except to prevent an intrusion that is likely to cause death or serious injury to the inhabitants. When a property owner uses force indirectly, by means of an automatic mechanical device like the one here, the case is judged by the same standards as if the owner were acting directly. Consequently, if a live person in the owner's position would not reasonably have believed that the intruder posed a serious risk of death or serious injury to the inhabitants, use of the deadly force mechanical device would not be privileged.

By this standard, even though the salesman was an outright trespasser, because he did not pose a threat of death or serious bodily harm the homeowner was only entitled to use reasonable, non-deadly force to deter him.

(B) is not the best response,

because even if the intent is only to deter, deadly force cannot be used against trespassers who do not pose a threat of death or serious injury to the inhabitants, as is more fully explained in the analysis of choice A above.

(C) is not the best response,

because deadly force cannot be used against non-dangerous trespassers, even if a warning is given.

As is described more fully in the discussion of choice A above, deadly force cannot be used against trespassers who do not pose a threat of death or serious injury to the inhabitants. This rule is true even if the owner gives a warning against entry. (In any event, the warning here did not even specify that serious force, posing the risk of bodily injury or death, would be used, so it's doubly unlikely to immunize the homeowner from liability.)

(D) is not the best response,

because even if the homeowner did reasonably fear that intruders would come to harm him or his family, the salesman himself did not pose such a danger.

When an owner uses an automatic mechanical device to protect against intruders, the situation is judged by the same standards as if the owner were personally applying the force. Therefore, the mechanical device can supply deadly force (force likely to cause death or serious bodily injury) only if the owner could do so personally on the particular occasion in question. An owner could use such deadly force only if the owner reasonably feared, in that particular situation, that the intruder posed a risk of death or serious bodily harm to the owner or other inhabitants.

Here, one in the homeowner's position would have realized that the salesman was unlikely to pose such harm. Since the homeowner would not have been entitled to use deadly force "by hand" against the salesman (e.g., by shooting him), he is not protected when his automatic device applied deadly force.

Answer 55

(A) is the best response,

because this response recognizes the exception for when a negligent tortfeasor may be liable for the criminal acts of a third party.

When a tortfeasor should have realized the likelihood of the crime at the time of his negligence, he may be liable for the criminal acts of a third party. The issue of foreseeability is generally a question for the jury, so we must look closely at the facts of this question. Here, we are informed that this was a "high-crime neighborhood" and "there had been many thefts of tools and equipment from the construction area." Thus, there is enough evidence of foreseeability that this issue should go to the jury. Also note that the evidence must be overwhelming for the judge to take the issue away from the jury by granting summary judgment for the defendant. Here, the evidence was not overwhelming based on the criminal activity at the construction site.

(B) is not the best response,

because enough facts of criminality in the neighborhood exist such that it might have been foreseeable that a damaged vehicle would be vulnerable to theft.

While normally a negligent tortfeasor will not be liable for the criminal acts of a third party, an exception exists. When a tortfeasor should have realized the likelihood of the crime at the time of his negligence, he may be liable for the criminal acts of a third party. The issue of foreseeability is generally a question for the jury, so we must look closely at the facts of this question. Here, we are informed that this was a "high-crime neighborhood" and "there had been many thefts of tools and equipment from the construction area." Thus, there is enough evidence of foreseeability that this issue should go to the jury. Also note that the evidence must be overwhelming for the judge to take the issue away from the jury by granting summary judgment for the defendant. Here, the evidence was not overwhelming based on the criminal activity at the construction site.

(C) is not the best response,

because this response states the general rule, but the exception to the rule applies here.

While normally a negligent tortfeasor will not be liable for the criminal acts of a third party, an exception exists. When a tortfeasor should have realized the likelihood of the crime at the time of his negligence, he may be liable for the criminal acts of a third party. The issue of foreseeability is generally a question for the jury, so we must look closely at the facts of this question. Here, we are informed that this was a "high-crime neighborhood" and "there had been many thefts of tools and equipment from the construction area." Thus, there is enough evidence of foreseeability that this issue should go to the jury. Also note that the evidence must be overwhelming for the judge to take the issue away from the jury by granting summary judgment for the defendant. Here, the evidence was not overwhelming based on the criminal activity at the construction site.

(D) is not the best response,

because whether the theft by a third party was foreseeable is a jury question.

While normally a negligent tortfeasor will not be liable for the criminal acts of a third party, an exception exists. When a tortfeasor should have realized the likelihood of the crime at the time of his negligence, he may be liable for the criminal acts of a third party. The issue of foreseeability is generally a question for the jury, so we must look closely at the facts of this question. While we are informed that this was a "high-crime neighborhood" and "there had been many thefts of tools and equipment from the construction area," this is not enough evidence for a judge to conclude, as matter of law, that if a vehicle was left unattended a third party would commit a theft. This is a factual dispute that would be resolved by the jury, thus mandating that the motion be denied.

Answer 56

(A) is the best response,

because the plaintiff did not suffer the appropriate damages.

For a claim of negligent misrepresentation, the defendant's mental state must be negligent, the defendant must have made the statement during the course of his business and with a pecuniary interest in the transaction, and the plaintiff must be a person or member of a limited group that the defendant intended to reach or who the defendant knows a recipient of the information intended to reach. Even if these elements are met, recovery for negligent misrepresentation is usually limited to pecuniary loss unless it involves a risk of physical harm. Here, the applicant did not face any risk of physical harm, and he "immediately found another comparable position." His emotional distress, standing alone, is not sufficient to assert a claim for negligent misrepresentation.

(B) is not the best response,

because the statement was not "purely" speculative, as specific facts were mentioned.

It is true that if the defendant predicts something will happen it will almost always be held to be merely an unactionable opinion, but, here, some of information conveyed to the job applicant was factual (e.g., that the company was worth millions). This factual information was intended to assure the applicant that the company was in fact economically strong and to induce reliance by the applicant. Thus, the better choice would be to focus on the fact that plaintiff did not suffer the appropriate damages, as in answer choice A.

(C) is not the best response,

because this response states a necessary, but not sufficient, condition.

A plaintiff must show that he relied on the misrepresentation and that his reliance was justifiable. But, another element, namely the appropriate damages, is not met here. Recovery for negligent misrepresentation is usually limited to pecuniary loss unless it involves a risk of physical harm. Here, the applicant did not face any risk of physical harm, and he "immediately found another comparable position." His emotional distress, standing alone, is not sufficient to assert a claim for negligent misrepresentation.

(D) is not the best response,

because recovery for negligent misrepresentation does not extend to all foreseeable damages, such as emotional distress.

Recovery for negligent misrepresentation is usually limited to pecuniary loss unless it involves a risk of physical harm. Here, the applicant did not face any risk of physical harm, and he "immediately found another comparable position." His emotional distress, standing alone, is not sufficient to assert a claim for negligent misrepresentation, even if it was foreseeable.

Answer 57

(A) is the best response,

because the passenger's touch was neither unreasonable nor inconsistent with ordinary social norms privileging such contacts.

Here, the woman gave no indication that she did not want to be subjected to the ordinary touches that are part of life in crowded society. In the absence of such an indication from her, the passenger was entitled to believe that she implicitly consented to a light tap to get her attention.

(B) is not the best response,

because, while this would prohibit a claim for assault, it would not prohibit a successful claim for battery or negligence.

An assault is the intentional causing of an apprehension of harmful or offensive contact. Here, the woman would not be able to prove that she thought that she was about to be touched, as she was tapped on the back and likely did not see the passenger as he reached to tap her on the back. But, the call of this question states that "the woman sues the passenger to recover for the back injury" and thus does not state the cause of action upon which she will rely. As the elements of negligence or battery could be established without any reference to whether she had an apprehension of being touched, the reasoning of this choice is incorrect.

(C) is not the best response,

because, even if the passenger did intentionally touch her, he may still effectively rely on the defense of consent.

In this case, the passenger's touch was neither unreasonable nor inconsistent with ordinary social norms privileging such contacts. Here, the woman gave no indication that she did not want to be subjected to the ordinary touches that are part of life in crowded society. In the absence of such an indication from her, the passenger was entitled to believe that she implicitly consented to a light tap to get her attention.

(D) is not the best response,

because serious injury is neither necessary nor sufficient to support either battery or negligence.

Here, even though she was seriously injured, the passenger may still effectively rely on the defense of consent. In this case, the passenger's touch was neither unreasonable nor inconsistent with ordinary social norms privileging such contacts. Here, the woman gave no indication that she did not want to be subjected to the ordinary touches that are part of life in crowded society. In the absence of such an indication from her, the passenger was entitled to believe that she implicitly consented to a light tap to get her attention.

Answer 58

(D) is the best response,

because the reasonableness of the defendant's conduct is irrelevant.

Battery is the intentional infliction of a harmful or offensive bodily contact. Consequently, whether the defendant's conduct was reasonable under the circumstances is irrelevant if in fact the defendant intended to make a harmful or offensive contact with the plaintiff. Thus, it would be relevant in a negligence action but not in a battery action.

(A) is not the best response,

because the smoker's intent is an issue in a battery action.

Battery is the intentional infliction of a harmful or offensive bodily contact. Consequently, the plaintiff must establish the smoker's intent to cause contact with the plaintiff.

(B) is not the best response,

because whether the smoke is bodily contact is an issue in a battery action.

Battery is the intentional infliction of a harmful or offensive bodily contact. Consequently, the plaintiff must prove that some sort of bodily contact occurred.

(C) is not the best response,

because the plaintiff must establish that the contact was offensive.

Battery is the intentional infliction of a harmful or offensive bodily contact. Consequently, the legislative determination that to allow restaurants to retain some space where patrons may smoke is, arguably, evidence that this type of touching is not offensive in this context. As the plaintiff must establish offensive contact, this will be an issue in a battery action.

Answer 59

(C) is the best response,

because punitive damages are not available in ordinary negligence cases. As this is the only cause of action listed that would NOT allow punitive damages, it is the best response.

(A) is not the best response,

because punitive damages are available to victims of intentional torts. Ordinary negligence cases, however, do not allow for punitive damages.

(B) is not the best response,

because punitive damages are available to victims of intentional torts. Ordinary negligence cases, however, do not allow for punitive damages.

(D) is not the best response,

because punitive damages may be available to victims of reckless conduct. Ordinary negligence cases, however, do not allow for punitive damages.

Answer 60

(D) is the best response,

because the theory of *res ipsa loquitur* will allow the jury to infer negligence.

Res ipsa loquitur allows a plaintiff to create an *inference* that the defendant behaved negligently, even if there's no direct evidence of that the defendant was negligent, if the plaintiff can prove that:

(1) There is no direct evidence of the defendant's conduct;
(2) The type of event in question ordinarily does not occur except through the negligence of someone;
(3) The instrument that caused injury was in exclusive control of the defendant; and
(4) The injury was probably not due to the plaintiff's own action.

Here, the elements are met, as no direct evidence was offered by the plaintiff of defendant's conduct, the automatic door would normally not open in the wrong direction absent someone's negligence, the supermarket had exclusive control of its maintenance, and the plaintiff did not cause or contribute to his injury. Accordingly, negligence may be inferred even without testimony as to why the door opened inward, so the supermarket's motion should be denied. The shopper's motion should also be denied, because a reasonable jury could decide that the supermarket was not negligent, if, for example, the injury was caused by the owner's installation. Furthermore, the plaintiff cannot rely on a strict liability theory, as there is neither a sale of a product nor an abnormally dangerous activity.

(A) is not the best response,

because a reasonable jury could conclude that the supermarket was not negligent.

Granting judgment for the shopper is only permissible when a reasonable jury could only conclude that the defendant is negligent. Here, based on the facts provided, a reasonable jury may conclude that the supermarket was not negligent (e.g., the jury may determine that the owner was negligent when he installed the door). Furthermore, the plaintiff cannot rely on a strict liability theory, as there is neither a sale of a product nor an abnormally dangerous activity.

(B) is not the best response,

because the plaintiff is not required to sue all negligent persons.

The defendant supermarket may join the building owner as a third-party defendant, if it chooses to do so. Accordingly, the failure to join the owner of the building as a defendant is not a sufficient reason that plaintiff would triumph.

(C) is not the best response,

because the theory of *res ipsa loquitur* will allow the jury to infer negligence.

Res ipsa loquitur allows a plaintiff to create an *inference* that the defendant behaved negligently, even though there's no direct evidence that the defendant was negligent, if the plaintiff can prove that:

(1) There is no direct evidence of the defendant's conduct;
(2) The type of event in question ordinarily does not occur except through the negligence of someone;
(3) The instrument that caused injury was in exclusive control of the defendant; and
(4) The injury was probably not due to the plaintiff's own action.

Here, the elements are met, as no direct evidence was offered by the plaintiff of defendant's conduct, the automatic door would normally not open in the wrong direction absent someone's negligence, the supermarket had exclusive control of its maintenance, and the plaintiff did not cause or contribute to his injury. Accordingly, negligence may be inferred even without testimony as to why the door opened inward, and the supermarket's motion should be denied.

Answer 61

(A) is the best response,

because the plaintiff cannot satisfy his *prima facie* case for either cause of action.

To succeed in a strict products liability claim in this context, plaintiff would need to prove that a product was sold in a defective condition that is unreasonably dangerous to the user or consumer. As the dentist was not in the business of selling the product, the plaintiff cannot succeed against the dentist (although the plaintiff could sue the product's manufacturer). To succeed in a malpractice claim in this context, the plaintiff must prove that the dentist did not act with the level of skill and learning commonly possessed by members of the profession in good standing. Here, the dentist used "due care," so the plaintiff cannot satisfy this burden.

(B) is not the best response,

because the dentist did not depart from a professional standard of care.

To succeed in a malpractice claim in this context, the plaintiff must prove that the dentist did not act with the level of skill and learning commonly possessed by members of the profession in good standing. Here, the dentist used "due care," so the plaintiff cannot satisfy this burden.

(C) is not the best response,

because the dentist is not in the business of selling this product.

To succeed in a strict products liability claim in this context, the plaintiff would need to prove that a product was sold in a defective condition that is unreasonably dangerous to the user or consumer. As the dentist was not in the business of selling the product, the plaintiff cannot succeed against the dentist (although the plaintiff could sue the product's manufacturer).

(D) is not the best response,

because the plaintiff cannot satisfy his *prima facie* case for either cause of action.

To succeed in a strict products liability claim in this context, the plaintiff would need to prove that a product was sold in a defective condition that is unreasonably dangerous to the user or consumer. As the dentist was not in the business of selling the product, the plaintiff cannot succeed against the dentist (although the plaintiff could sue the product's manufacturer). To succeed in a malpractice claim in this context, the plaintiff must prove that the dentist did not act with the level of skill and learning commonly possessed by members of the profession in good standing. Here, the dentist used "due care," so the plaintiff cannot satisfy this burden.

Answer 62

(C) is the best response,

because it correctly states that expert testimony will not be necessary to determine whether the two attorneys breached their standard of care.

This is a bit of a tricky question, because to answer it correctly, you must be able to eliminate some distractors dealing with tort law on standards of care for professionals.

Under these facts, all the jury must do is determine whether the two attorneys filed the suit within the period authorized by the statute of limitations. Although this is not an Evidence question, the law of evidence bears on whether expert testimony was required on this matter. According to Federal Rule of Evidence 702, expert testimony is used where the court determines that "scientific, technical, or other *specialized knowledge* will assist the trier of fact to understand the evidence or to determine a fact in issue." The timeliness issue here is not a matter that would require the kind of sophistication that would trigger the need for expert testimony; all an expert would do, really, is point to a deadline on a calendar. Since the jury can "understand" and "determine" the issue of timeliness of filing without "specialized knowledge," expert testimony was not needed, making C the best response.

(A) is not the best response,

because it erroneously suggests that expert testimony is necessary to determine breach of the standard of care, and, beyond that, it misstates the standard by which the two attorneys would be judged.

Under FRE 702, expert testimony is only necessary where the court determines that "scientific, technical, or other specialized knowledge will assist the trier of fact to understand the evidence or to determine a fact in issue." Determining whether the two attorneys missed their deadline would not be the kind of matter necessarily meriting expert testimony. Furthermore, the standard against which lawyers are judged is the minimum common skill of members in good standing in their profession. The "locality" requirement that choice A mentions is an old concept, which is only one factor for juries to consider in modern cases determining if the actor behaved reasonably in the circumstances; and even when this rule was applied, it was applied generally to general medical practitioners. Since A does not state the correct result or the correct standard, it's not the best response.

(B) is not the best response,

because it erroneously suggests that expert testimony is necessary to determine breach of the standard of care, and, beyond that, it misstates the standard by which the two attorneys would be judged.

Under FRE 702, expert testimony is only necessary where the court determines that "scientific, technical, or other specialized knowledge will assist the trier of fact to understand the evidence or to determine a fact in issue." Determining whether the two attorneys missed their deadline would not be the kind of matter necessarily meriting expert testimony, because all that needs to be determined is if the two attorneys made the deadline. Furthermore, the standard against which lawyers are judged is the minimum common skill of members in good standing in their profession. Thus, the "statewide" standard B suggests would not be appropriate for the two attorneys. Since B misses both of these points, it's not the best response.

(D) is not the best response,

because the judge is not competent as a witness in a case, and even if he were, expert testimony is not appropriate here.

Even though the judge is (hopefully) an expert on the law, he cannot testify as to whether the two attorneys breached their duty, since that is a matter of fact, not law, and thus it's a matter for the jury to decide. The judge cannot offer expert testimony, because judges are not competent witnesses. FRE 605.

Even if the judge could offer expert testimony, it's not merited here. Under FRE 702, expert testimony is only necessary where the court determines that "scientific, technical, or other specialized knowledge will assist the trier of fact to understand the evidence or to determine a fact in issue." Determining whether the two attorneys missed their deadline would not be the kind of matter meriting expert testimony, because all that needs to be determined is whether the two attorneys complied with the deadline. Since D mistakenly states that the judge can testify as an expert witness, and it states the expert testimony is needed on a matter where it's not, D is not the best response.

Answer 63

(B) is the best response,

because the trespasser was owed no duty.

The general rule is that the landowner owes no duty to a trespasser to make her land safe, to warn of dangers on it, to avoid carrying on dangerous activities on it, or to protect the trespasser in any way. Although an exception carves out a duty to discovered trespassers, that exception would not apply here, as the hiker was on the property "without the property owner's knowledge or permission."

(A) is not the best response,

because nothing in the fact situation suggests that the weakness of the limb could not have been discovered by the exercise of reasonable care.

If the property owner had owed a duty to take reasonable care to protect the hiker, he might have been required to make regular inspections of the conditions on his land. But, this trespasser was not owed such a duty. The general rule is that the landowner owes no duty to a trespasser to make her land safe, to warn of dangers on it, to avoid carrying on dangerous activities on it, or to protect the trespasser in any way.

(C) is not the best response,

because the property owner did not have such a duty to trespassers.

The general rule is that the landowner owes no duty to a trespasser to make her land safe, to warn of dangers on it, to avoid carrying on dangerous activities on it, or to protect the trespasser in any way. Although an exception carves out a duty to discovered trespassers, that exception would not apply here, as the hiker was on the property "without the property owner's knowledge or permission."

(D) is not the best response,

because the property owner is not liable to trespassers for hidden dangers on his property.

The general rule is that the landowner owes no duty to a trespasser to make her land safe, to warn of dangers on it, to avoid carrying on dangerous activities on it, or to protect the trespasser in any way. Although an exception carves out a duty to discovered trespassers, that exception would not apply here, as the hiker was on the property "without the property owner's knowledge or permission." Furthermore, any duty owed to a discovered trespasser would make the landowner liable only for artificial conditions highly dangerous to trespassers, and the tree in this instance would not qualify.

Answer 64

(B) is the best response,

because it identifies the key reason the homeowner will be liable.

The rule is that the owner of a wild animal is strictly liable for the animal's conduct creating damage. Thus, the point that B raises—that a skunk is not domesticated—is the lynchpin of the homeowner's liability. The wrinkle here is that you don't typically consider a skunk "wild," in the sense of a lion or tiger or Tasmanian devil or other animals of that ilk. Nonetheless, a skunk isn't domesticated, so it can be a source of strict liability for the homeowner. Since it caused the walker's damages, and the walker's damages were within the scope of the extraordinary risk created by maintaining a skunk, the homeowner will be strictly liable. Since B correctly identifies the basis of the homeowner's liability, it's the best response.

(A) is not the best response,

because the private nuisance tort would not apply to these facts.

A private nuisance is an act by a defendant that creates an unreasonable, substantial interference with the plaintiff's use or enjoyment of property. The interest protected is the right to use and enjoy one's land. Here, the walker *has* no right to use and enjoy the land she was on when she was injured; she's a trespasser. Thus, private nuisance *cannot* apply to these facts. Although A arrives at the right response, it ignores the real basis of liability: A person is strictly liable for the torts of his pets if the pets are "wild animals," of which a skunk would be one. As a result, A is not the best response.

(C) is not the best response,

because although the walker's status will determine the duty the homeowner owes to the walker as an entrant on the land, it will not determine the homeowner's liability on these facts.

At common law, the landowner's duty to trespassers depended on whether they were "discovered" or "undiscovered." The landowner owes no duty to undiscovered trespassers; whereas a discovered trespasser (i.e., one whom the landowner anticipates, as here, due to the homeowner's knowledge the grass is used as a footpath) is owed a duty of reasonable care, generally satisfied by a warning of man-made dangers known to the landowner and unlikely to be discovered by the trespasser. The modern trend is to consolidate the duties owed to various levels of entrants into a "reasonable person" standard.

In any case, these are not relevant here because they all address levels of *fault* that will be necessary for landowner liability. Instead, here the homeowner will be *liable without any fault at all* because the skunk will be considered a wild animal, making the homeowner strictly liable for damage it creates. As a result, the walker's status as a trespasser will not relieve the homeowner of liability.

This is a somewhat tricky choice in that your gut feeling is that the walker *shouldn't* recover because she's a trespasser. However, as many MBE questions show, you can't react instinctively to the facts. A mechanical application of the law indicates that the homeowner will be strictly liable to the walker, so C is not the best response.

(D) is not the best response,

because the reasoning it states would not relieve the homeowner of liability.

The general rule is that owners are strictly liable for the torts of wild animals they keep as pets. Thus, even if the pet is caged, has its teeth removed, is declawed, or any other type of precaution has been taken, the owner will *still* be liable, because strict liability requires no proof of fault—merely keeping a wild animal as a pet will be sufficient to impose liability if the pet causes harm, and that harm is within the extraordinary risk that merited imposing strict liability in the first place. Admittedly, the vet was negligent under these facts, and the homeowner could recover against him for any damages paid to the walker. Nonetheless, this does not erase the fact that the homeowner's skunk injured the walker, and this *alone* makes the homeowner liable. Since D doesn't recognize this, it's not the best response.

Answer 65

(B) is the best response,

because even states that allow witnesses who are not in the zone of danger to recover for the emotional distress of observing an accident limit recovery to witnesses who are closely related to the injured person.

These states typically mandate that, to recover, a plaintiff who was outside the zone of danger must

(1) be closely related to the injury victim;
(2) be present at the scene of the injury-producing event and have been aware that the event was causing an injury to the victim; and
(3) have suffered serious emotional distress as a result of his or her presence at the scene.

While the plaintiff in this problem clearly satisfies the latter two requirements, he does not satisfy the first, and therefore his claim will fail. The requirement of close relation to the injury victim is meant as a limitation of liability. Otherwise, in every car accident there could be a hundred potential bystanders who witnessed the accident and suffered compensable severe emotional distress.

(A) is not the best response,

because one who negligently injures another is liable to rescuers even when the rescuer voluntarily comes to the aid of the injured person.

Accordingly, an assumption of the risk defense will not work in this scenario. Instead, this suit will fail because the bystander had no familial or other preexisting relationship to the pedestrian, which is required by most states that allow witnesses who are not in the zone of danger to recover for the emotional distress of observing an accident.

(C) is not the best response,

because, while it is true that one who negligently injures another is liable to rescuers who are physically injured in the course of the rescue, the bystander was not physically injured.

The bystander was across the street when the accident happened and only suffered emotional injuries. Lacking either physical harm or a close relationship with the injured person, the bystander cannot recover in negligence for his emotional distress, as discussed in the analysis of choice B above. Thus, this suit will fail because the bystander had no familial or other preexisting relationship to the pedestrian, which is required by most states that allow witnesses who are not in the zone of danger to recover for the emotional distress of observing an accident.

(D) is not the best response,

because it is not supported by the facts.

Here, the bystander "witnessed the accident from across the street." As such, he was not in the path of the car and therefore was not in the zone of danger. Instead, this suit will fail because the bystander had no familial or other preexisting relationship to the pedestrian, which is required by most states that allow witnesses who are not in the zone of danger to recover for the emotional distress of observing an accident.

Answer 66

(C) is the best response,

because it most closely identifies the reason why the motorist will not be liable to the plaintiff. The key here is duty to aid, since the motorist came upon the plaintiff, who was obviously in need of help, and didn't aid him.

This is one of those questions on the MBE that is made difficult because your *instinct* is that the motorist should be liable. You may feel, and rightly so, that the motorist had a moral duty to stop and help the plaintiff. This, however, doesn't equate with a legal duty, and since the motorist had no legal duty to help, his merely *not* helping wouldn't render him liable.

The general rule is that there is no duty to aid unless one of these elements exist: the defendant's negligence created the peril, a "special relationship" mandates affirmative acts (e.g., parent-child), or the defendant had previously undertaken to act for the plaintiff's benefit. Thus, unless the motorist made the plaintiff's situation worse, he was not under a duty to help, and thus couldn't be liable. Note that C says the motorist will not be liable *if* he didn't make the plaintiff's situation worse. Where "if" is the modifier, the reasoning must be plausible on the facts, it must resolve a central issue in the question, and the result must be consistent with the reasoning. Here, it's possible that the motorist didn't exacerbate the plaintiff's condition; this resolves the motorist's duty to aid, which is the central issue here. As a result, C is the best response.

(A) is not the best response,

because the facts it cites—stopping and examining the plaintiff—would not create liability in the motorist.

The central issue here is the duty to aid. As a general rule, there is no duty to aid unless one of these elements exist: a defendant's negligence created the peril, a "special relationship" mandates affirmative acts (e.g., common carrier-patron), or a defendant has previously undertaken to act for a plaintiff's benefit. Here, although the motorist stopped and examined the plaintiff, he did not make his condition worse, and it couldn't be said that he'd undertaken to act for the plaintiff's benefit. True, it's morally repugnant that the motorist left the plaintiff in the field, but this doesn't make him legally liable. Since A states otherwise, it's not the best response.

(B) is not the best response,

because it does not state a basis on which the motorist can be held liable.

What a reasonably prudent person would do under the circumstances doesn't make the motorist's doing *something else* tortious; that is, it isn't what the reasonable person would do, but whether the behavior the motorist undertook was *unreasonable*. This is the standard for negligence, which requires that a defendant must have failed to exercise such care as a reasonable person in his position would have exercised. This failure to exercise care must have been a breach of the duty to prevent the foreseeable risk of harm to anyone in the plaintiff's position, and this breach must have caused the plaintiff's damages.

The problem here is duty: the motorist didn't have one. As a general rule, there is no affirmative duty to aid, unless one of these elements exist: a defendant's negligence created the peril, a "special relationship" mandates affirmative acts (e.g., parent-child), or the defendant has previously undertaken to act for the plaintiff's benefit. None of these exist under these facts, so the motorist had no duty to aid the plaintiff. As a result, he could not be held liable for *not* aiding the plaintiff. Since B states otherwise, it's not the best response.

(D) is not the best response,

because it does not address the motorist's liability.

If the motorist was under a duty to aid the plaintiff and didn't do so, he'd be liable, even if the plaintiff had created the risk of harm to himself. As a general rule, one is under no affirmative duty to aid, unless one of these elements exist: a defendant's negligence created the peril, a "special relationship" mandates affirmative acts (e.g., guardian-ward), or a defendant has previously undertaken to act for the plaintiff's benefit. None of these exist under these facts, so the motorist had no duty to aid the stranger. What D *implies* is that the plaintiff was contributorily negligent, which would be a defense to the motorist's negligence.

However, negligence requires breach of a duty, and here, there was no breach. Thus, even though D correctly recognizes that the motorist will not be liable, it does not identify the reason why, so it cannot be the best response.

Answer 67

(D) is the best response,

because an owner of a wild animal or an abnormally dangerous animal is strictly liable for harm caused by that animal's dangerous nature.

Part of what makes wild animals dangerous is that third persons who encounter the animal may well experience acute fear, whether that fear is well-founded or not as to the particular animal. Rest. 2d Torts, § 507, cmt. g and illus. 1. Here, even though the snake was defanged, the worker had no reason to know this. Therefore, his injury was caused by a foreseeable aspect of the animal's wild and dangerous nature, namely, its tendency to cause fear of being bitten.

(A) is not the best response,

because owners of dangerous animals are strictly liable even when the harm would not have occurred but for the operation of a force of nature. Thus, the fact that a storm caused the snake to be released, rather than any action on the part of the homeowner, does not limit the homeowner's liability.

(B) is not the best response,

because an owner of a wild animal or an abnormally dangerous animal is strictly liable for harm caused by that animal's dangerous nature.

The contributory negligence of the worker would not be a defense to strict liability, and in any case there is nothing in the facts to indicate that the worker would have reason to foresee the risk of a poisonous snake.

(C) is not the best response,

because, while this answer correctly states that the worker will prevail, it misstates the legal basis for this conclusion.

There is probably not enough evidence here to support a finding of negligence. In any event, whether the owner did or did not take precautions that would be "adequate" (i.e., that would constitute reasonable care), this won't matter—the whole point of strict liability for keeping wild animals is that if the wild animal causes harm in a way that is related to its wildness, the plaintiff does not have to show negligence by the owner. Nor does it matter that the snake was defanged; the worker had no reason to know this, and his injury falls within the risk run by the homeowner because it was caused by the worker's foreseeable reaction to seeing an escaped snake.

Answer 68

(B) is the best response,

because a product is defective if it fails to include a feasible safety device that would prevent injuries foreseeably incurred in ordinary use.

If a plaintiff is injured by a product with a defective design, the manufacturer of the product is strictly liable. A plaintiff can prove that a product's design is defective by pointing out a reasonable alternative design that offers a better balance of costs and benefits. Usually this better balance means that the alternative design is safer without being significantly more expensive or less useful than the design the defendant used. *See* Rest. 3d Torts (Prod. Liab.), § 2, cmt. f. In this case, the plaintiff can make that showing easily enough: The manufacturer itself had designed an alternative model that we are told was considerably safer, only slightly more expensive, and equally useful. The existence of that safer model makes the model sold here unreasonably dangerous. Note that if a product is unreasonably dangerous, its maker is not saved from liability either by a warning or by the consumer's free choice in selecting the product—a manufacturer is obliged to take all reasonable, cost-effective steps to make the product safe.

(A) is not the best response,

because a plaintiff cannot win a claim based on a design defect simply by showing that the defendant's product was a cause in fact of his injury.

As explained in the discussion of choice B above, the plaintiff also must show that the product was defective. In a case involving a product's design, this means showing that a safer "reasonable alternative design" was available. *See* Rest. 3d (Prod. Liab.), § 2(b); Dobbs, § 361.

(C) is not the best response,

because the manufacturer of a defective product is strictly liable for harm that it causes.

A consumer's decision to buy the product, and not to buy a safer one, does not cut off the manufacturer's liability. Moreover, a "superseding intervening cause" of an accident generally has to be some event that could not be foreseen by the party who committed the initial tortious act—here, the manufacturer. But in this case the supposed "intervening cause" was simply the employer's decision to buy a cheaper press. This was foreseeable, and indeed was foreseen: The manufacturer produced a model just for that purpose. The foreseeability of the buyer's decision to buy the less-safe model is one of the reasons why the manufacturer should not have sold the less-safe model at all.

(D) is not the best response,

because, as explained in the discussion of choice B above, a manufacturer cannot insulate itself from liability for its defective products by warning about the defects.

The manufacturer is obliged to produce a reasonably safe product—in other words, a product that can easily be made safer. If the manufacturer fails to do that, its liability is clear regardless of whatever warnings it may give. *See* Dobbs, § 363.

Answer 69

(C) is the best response,

because, due to his lack of notice of the dog's propensities, the landlord acted reasonably.

Any duty that the landlord may have in this context is at most a duty to act reasonably. If the landlord had no reason to know that the dog posed a risk to those on his property, his failure to take precautions against that risk was not negligent.

(A) is not the best response,

because the landlord is not the possessor of the dog.

The possessor of a vicious dog may be strictly liable to those injured by the dog, but the landlord here is not in possession of the dog. Moreover, the liability, where it exists, is limited to cases in which the possessor has reason to know the dog is unusually dangerous. Thus, while the owner may be strictly liable, the landlord is not.

(B) is not the best response,

because a dog does not qualify as a dangerous condition.

A landlord may have a non-delegable duty to protect persons who come upon the land from dangerous conditions of the property, such as cracked walks and broken stairs, but the presence of the dog is not such a condition. Furthermore, the landlord's duty is only a duty to act reasonably, and there is no evidence here that the landlord acted unreasonably, as he "did not have any notice of the dog's vicious propensities."

(D) is not the best response,
because a landlord does owe a duty to those who are foreseeably on the land, including guests of his tenants.

As this is a business venture of the landlord, guests of his tenants would be the landlord's invitees. However, any duty that the landlord may have is at most a duty to act reasonably. If the landlord had no reason to know that the dog posed a risk to those on his property, his failure to take precautions against that risk was not negligent.

Answer 70

(B) is the best response,
because the plaintiff did not have apprehension of imminent bodily contact.

Assault is the intentional causing of an imminent apprehension of harmful or offensive contact. Thus, assault requires an *effect*: The plaintiff must either actually undergo a harmful or offensive contact or be put in immediate apprehension of such a contact. Here, the apprehension of harm is missing, as the guest knew that the revolver was not loaded and that the ammunition was in "a locked basement closet, two stories below where the two were then standing."

(A) is not the best response,
because it chooses the wrong legal basis for the conclusion.

Assault is the intentional causing of an imminent apprehension of harmful or offensive contact. Here, the host may have intended to cause the guest apprehension of getting shot, even if the host did not intend to shoot the guest. The better choice here focuses on the guest's missing apprehension of harm, as the guest knew that the revolver was not loaded and that the ammunition was in "a locked basement closet, two stories below where the two were then standing."

(C) is not the best answer,
because the harm was not imminent.

Assault is the intentional causing of an imminent apprehension of harmful or offensive contact. Here, the host could not quickly retrieve ammunition from a "locked basement closet, two stories below where the two were standing." The better choice here focuses on the guest's missing apprehension of harm, as the guest knew that the revolver was not loaded and the ammunition was far away.

(D) is not the best answer,
because a threat alone is not enough to cause an assault unless the apprehension of bodily contact is imminent.

Thus, assault requires an *effect*: The plaintiff must either actually undergo a harmful or offensive contact or be put in immediate apprehension of such a contact. Here, the apprehension of harm is missing, as the guest knew that the revolver was not loaded and that the ammunition was in "a locked basement closet, two stories below where the two were then standing."

Answer 71

(B) is the best response,
because this answer choice correctly applies the firefighters' rule to the facts.

The common-law "firefighters' rule" says that when firefighters or police officers are injured during the course of the job, they normally have no claim against the person whose conduct created the peril. Dobbs, § 285. Not all states follow the firefighters' rule. But even among those that do, the doctrine is generally limited to risks that are inherent in, and special to, that particular occupation. Dobbs, § 286. This limit means that the doctrine will not apply here because being struck by a car in normal traffic is not one of the special risks inherent to dangerous police work. So the driver can be held liable under ordinary negligence principles. (Also, many courts say that the firefighters' rule applies only where the negligently created peril was *responsible for the officer's presence at the scene*, and that approach, too, would cause the rule not to apply here, since the officer was not responding to the risk caused by the driver and was instead present at the scene by coincidence.)

(A) is not the best response,
because, although this answer correctly states that the driver's motion should be denied, it misstates the legal basis for this conclusion.

The firefighters' rule, although named with reference to firefighters, also covers police officers. They, too, are public servants at risk of injury by the perils that they have been employed to confront.

(C) is not the best response,
because but-for causation is not sufficient to support the firefighters' rule defense here.

As further described in the analysis of choice B above, the firefighters' rule applies to bar liability only when the risk that materialized was one of the unique risks inherent to the officer's dangerous work. Here, the fact that the officer was returning from an emergency when she was struck was just a coincidence.

So the driver could still be held liable for his negligence because being struck by a car in normal traffic is not one of the special risks inherent in dangerous police work.

(D) is not the best response,

because it overstates the scope of the firefighters' rule.

The firefighters' rule only bars claims for injuries that result from risks that are unique or special to the plaintiff's inherently dangerous work. Thus where, as here, the officer is injured on the job, but by a risk that was not part of what makes the officer's job inherently dangerous, the firefighters' rule will not apply, and the driver can be held liable under garden-variety negligence principles.

QUESTIONS

PRACTICE MBE — A.M. EXAM

Directions: Each of the questions or incomplete statements below is followed by four suggested answers or completions. You are to choose the *best* of the stated alternatives. Answer all questions according to the generally accepted view, except where otherwise noted.

For the purposes of this test, you are to assume that Articles 1 and 2 of the Uniform Commercial Code have been adopted. You are also to assume relevant application of Article 9 of the UCC concerning fixtures. The Federal Rules of Evidence are deemed to control. The terms "Constitution," "constitutional," and "unconstitutional" refer to the federal Constitution unless indicated to the contrary. You are to assume that there is no applicable statute unless otherwise specified; however, survival actions and claims for wrongful death should be assumed to be available where applicable. You should assume that joint and several liability, with pure comparative negligence, is the relevant rule unless otherwise indicated.

QUESTIONS

PRACTICE MBE — A.M. EXAM

Question 1

The owner of a three-acre tract of land with a small residence rented it to a tenant at a monthly rental of $200. After the tenant had been in possession of the tract for several years, the tenant and the owner orally agreed that the tenant would purchase the tract from the owner for the sum of $24,000, payable at the rate of $200 a month for ten years and also would pay the real estate taxes and the expenses of insuring and maintaining the tract. The owner agreed to give the tenant a deed to the tract after five years had passed and $12,000 had been paid on account and to accept from the tenant a note secured by a mortgage for the balance. The tenant continued in possession of the tract and performed his obligations as orally agreed. The tenant, without consulting the owner, made improvements for which he paid $1,000. When the tenant had paid $12,000, he tendered a proper note and mortgage to the owner and demanded delivery of the deed as agreed. The owner did not deny the oral agreement but told the tenant that she had changed her mind, and she refused to complete the transaction. The tenant then brought an action for specific performance. The owner pleaded the Statute of Frauds as her defense. If the owner wins, it will be because

(A) nothing the tenant could have done would have overcome the original absence of a written agreement.

(B) the actions and payments of the tenant are as consistent with his being a tenant as with an oral contract.

(C) the tenant did not secure the owner's approval for the improvements that he made.

(D) the owner has not received any unconscionable benefit, and, therefore, the tenant is not entitled to equitable relief.

Question 2

During 2010, a series of arsons occurred in a city. In early 2011, the city council adopted this resolution:

The city will pay $10,000 for the arrest and conviction of anyone guilty of any of the 2010 arsons committed here.

The foregoing was telecast by the city's sole television station once daily for one week.

In which of the following ways could the city's reward offer be effectively accepted?

(A) Only by an offeree's return promise to make a reasonable effort to bring about the arrest and conviction of an arsonist within the scope of the offer.

(B) Only by an offeree's making the arrest and assisting in the successful conviction of an arsonist within the scope of the offer.

(C) By an offeree's supplying information leading to arrest and conviction of an arsonist within the scope of the offer.

(D) By an offeree's communication of assent through the same medium (television) used by the city in making its offer.

Question 3

A cigarette maker created and published a magazine advertisement that featured a model dressed as a race-car driver standing in front of a distinctive race car. In fact, the car looked almost exactly like the very unusually marked one driven by a famous and popular driver. The driver in the ad was not identified, and his face was not shown in the advertisement. The cigarette maker published the advertisement without obtaining the famous driver's permission. The race-car driver sued the cigarette maker for economic loss only, based on common-law misappropriation of the right of publicity. The cigarette maker moved to dismiss the complaint.

Will the cigarette maker's motion to dismiss the complaint be granted?

(A) No, because there are sufficient indicia of the driver's identity to support a verdict of liability.

(B) Yes, because the driver is a public figure.

(C) Yes, because there was no mention of the driver's name in the ad.

(D) Yes, because the driver did not claim any emotional or dignitary loss.

Question 4

A man was the illegitimate, unacknowledged child of his father, who died intestate, leaving neither spouse nor any children other than the man. The state's law of intestate succession provides that an unacknowledged illegitimate child may not inherit his father's property. The spouse, all other blood relations, and the state are preferred as heirs over the unacknowledged illegitimate child. The man filed suit in an appropriate court alleging that the state statute barring an illegitimate child from sharing in a parent's estate is invalid, and that he should be declared lawful heir to his father's estate.

In challenging the validity of the state statute, the man's strongest argument would be that

(A) there is no rational basis for preferring as heirs collateral relatives and even the state over unacknowledged children, and, therefore, the law violates the Equal Protection Clause.

(B) he has been deprived of property without due process because his fundamental right to inherit has been compromised without a compelling state need.

(C) it violates the Privileges and Immunities Clause of the Fourteenth Amendment.

(D) it is a denial of procedural due process because it does not give the unacknowledged illegitimate child an opportunity to prove paternity.

Question 5

In which of the following situations is the defendant most likely to be **not guilty** of the charge made?

(A) The police arrested a thief and recovered goods he had stolen. At the direction of the police, the thief took the goods to the defendant. The defendant, believing the goods to be stolen, purchased them. The defendant is charged with attempting to receive stolen property.

(B) The defendant misrepresented his identity to secure a loan from a bank. The banker was not deceived and refused to grant the loan. The defendant is charged with attempting to obtain property by false pretenses.

(C) Believing that state law made it a crime to purchase codeine without a prescription, the defendant purchased, without a prescription, cough syrup containing codeine. Unknown to the defendant, the statute had been repealed and codeine could be legally purchased without a prescription. The defendant is charged with attempting to purchase codeine without a prescription.

(D) The defendant, intending to kill a woman, shot at the woman. Unknown to the defendant, the woman had died of a heart attack minutes before the defendant shot at her. The defendant is charged with attempted murder.

Question 6

A farm was conveyed to a man and a woman by a deed that, in the jurisdiction in which the farm is situated, created a cotenancy in equal shares and with the right of survivorship. The jurisdiction has no statute directly applicable to any of the problems posed.

The woman, by deed, conveyed "my undivided one-half interest" in the farm to a purchaser. The woman has since died. In an appropriate action between the purchaser and the man in which title to the farm is at issue, the man will

(A) prevail, because he is the sole owner of the farm.

(B) prevail if, but only if, the cotenancy created in the man and the woman was a tenancy by the entirety.

(C) not prevail if he had knowledge of the conveyance prior to the woman's death.

(D) not prevail, because the purchaser and the man own the farm as tenants in common.

Question 7

A storekeeper of a large hardware store sells power saws for both personal and commercial use. He often takes old power saws as trade-ins on new ones. The old power saws are then completely disassembled and rebuilt with new bearings by the storekeeper's employees and sold by the storekeeper as "reconditioned saws." A purchaser, the owner and operator of a cabinetmaking shop, informed the storekeeper that he wanted to buy a reconditioned circular saw for use in his cabinetmaking business. However, the blade that was on the saw he picked out had very coarse teeth for cutting rough lumber. The purchaser told the storekeeper that he wanted a saw blade that would cut plywood. The storekeeper exchanged the coarse blade for a new one with finer teeth that would cut plywood smoothly. The new blade was manufactured by a saw-blade company and contained defects. The reconditioned saw had been manufactured by a power-saw company.

The week after the saw was purchased, the employee, who works for the purchaser in the purchaser's cabinetmaking shop, was injured while using the saw. The employee's arm was severely cut. As a result, the cabinetmaking shop was shut down for a week until a replacement for the employee could be found. The jurisdiction has adopted a pure comparative fault rule in strict liability cases.

If the employee was injured while cutting plywood when the shaft holding the saw blade came loose when a bearing gave way and the shaft and blade flew off the saw, and if the employee asserts a claim based on strict liability in tort against the power saw company, the employee will probably

(A) recover if the shaft that came loose was a part of the saw when it was new.

(B) recover, because the power saw company was in the business of manufacturing dangerous machines.

(C) not recover, because the employee was not the buyer of the power saw.

(D) not recover, because the saw had been rebuilt by the storekeeper.

Question 8

Plaintiff, a State A corporation, has sued Defendant, an individual, in State B state court. Defendant was served at his home in State B. The suit, based on State E law, sought money damages. The suit contended that Defendant breached a contract to convey a piece of State E real estate to Plaintiff, thereby depriving Plaintiff of the benefit of his bargain. The terms of the contract were negotiated face-to-face in State C by Plaintiff's CEO and by Defendant; the next day, after a final document had been created, the document was signed by Defendant while he was in State D. No activities connected with the contract occurred in State B.

Defendant has timely moved to dismiss the suit for lack of personal jurisdiction over him. State B's statute governing jurisdiction permits the exercise of jurisdiction "to the full extent allowed under the United States Constitution." Should the State B court grant Defendant's motion?

(A) Yes, because the cause of action does not arise out of or relate to Defendant's contacts within State B, the forum state.

(B) Yes, because when a claim arises out of breach of a contract to convey real estate, only the state in which the real estate is located has jurisdiction.

(C) No, because the state in which a defendant resides may exercise general jurisdiction regardless of the nature of the cause of action.

(D) No, because the plaintiff and defendant are citizens of different states, permitting the court to exercise diversity jurisdiction over the suit.

Question 9

At a civil trial for slander, the plaintiff showed that the defendant had called the plaintiff a thief. In defense, the defendant called a witness to testify, "I have been the plaintiff's neighbor for many years, and people in our community generally have said that he is a thief."

Is the testimony concerning the plaintiff's reputation in the community admissible?

(A) No, because character is an essential element of the defense, and proof must be made by specific instances of conduct.

(B) Yes, to prove that the plaintiff is a thief, and to reduce or refute the damages claimed.

(C) Yes, to prove that the plaintiff is a thief, but not on the issue of damages.

(D) Yes, to reduce or refute the damages claimed, but not to prove that the plaintiff is a thief.

Question 10

An insurer is incorporated in State A, and has had its principal place of business there for many years. Ten years ago, the insurer sold a disability insurance policy to a surgeon. At the time the surgeon purchased the policy, the surgeon was a resident of State A, and all communications and activities regarding the purchase occurred in State A. Last year, the surgeon moved to State B. The insurer has had for some time a small office in State B, from which it markets insurance policies to State B residents; these policies account for about 10 percent of the insurer's worldwide revenues. When the insurer's website (run from State A) receives an inquiry from a State B resident, the insurer refers the inquiry to the company's State B office.

The surgeon now claims that for the last six months he has been disabled and is entitled to disability benefits from the insurer. The insurer has refused to pay, on the grounds that the policy lapsed eight months ago for non-payment. Prior to the surgeon's demand for disability payments, the insurer took no actions in State B concerning the policy, except to send the surgeon bills for premiums at his new State B address once it received a change-of-address notice from him. Last month, the surgeon filed suit against the insurer in State B court, alleging that the insurer's failure to make the disability payments was a breach of their contract. Under the State B long-arm statute, a State B resident bringing a contract action in the State B courts may make service on an out-of-state corporate defendant by causing a summons and complaint to be personally served upon the CEO or other officer of the defendant wherever in the United States that officer can be found. (The State B courts will exercise personal jurisdiction over an out-of-state corporate defendant in such a suit brought so long as such jurisdiction would not violate the U.S. Constitution.) The process server hired by the surgeon handed the summons and complaint to the insurer's CEO at the CEO's home in State A; the suit named only the insurer, not the CEO.

One week after the insurer's CEO received the summons on behalf of the insurer, the CEO happened to travel to State B for a one-day conference on an unrelated matter. While he was in State B, he was handed a summons and complaint in a divorce action brought against him in the State B courts by his long-estranged wife. The two had been married decades ago in State A, and the wife had moved to State B a few years ago. Until the one-day conference, the CEO had not visited—or done any activity connected to—State B at any time in the last ten years. By coincidence, the divorce suit was assigned to the same State B judge as the surgeon's suit against the insurer.

The CEO and the insurer, in their respective suits, have each made timely motions in State B court to have the suit against each dismissed for lack of personal jurisdiction; each defendant argues that the court's exercise of such jurisdiction over that defendant would violate the Due Process Clause of the Fourteenth Amendment. How should the court rule on the two motions?

(A) Grant the motion as to both suits.

(B) Deny the motion as to both suits.

(C) Grant the motion as to the suit against the insurer, but deny the motion as to the suit against the CEO.

(D) Grant the motion as to the suit against the CEO, but grant the motion as to the suit against the insurer.

Question 11

The childhood home of a former U.S. president is part of a national park located in a city. The National Park Service entered into a contract with an independent antiques collector to acquire items owned by residents of the city during the president's lifetime. According to the contract, the collector purchases items and then sells them to the Park Service at a price equal to the collector's cost plus a 10 percent commission. Purchases by antiques collectors are ordinarily subject to the sales tax of the state in which the city is located. The collector files suit in state court to enjoin collection of the tax on these purchases, claiming that the sales tax is unconstitutional as applied to them.

Should the state court issue the injunction?

(A) No, because as the purchaser of these antiques, the collector, rather than the federal government is liable for the tax.

(B) No, because the suit is within the exclusive jurisdiction of the federal courts.

(C) Yes, because the federal government is contractually obligated to pay the amount of the sales tax when it covers the collector's cost of these antiques.

(D) Yes, because under the Supremacy Clause, the federal program to acquire these antiques preempts the state sales tax on the purchase of these items.

Question 12

In a civil trial for professional malpractice, the plaintiff sought to show that the defendant, an engineer, had designed the plaintiff's flour mill with inadequate power. The plaintiff called an expert witness who based his testimony solely on his own professional experience but also asserted, when asked, that the book *Smith on Milling Systems* was a reliable treatise in the field and consistent with his views. On cross-examination, the defendant asked the witness whether he and Smith were ever wrong. The witness answered, "Nobody's perfect." The defendant asked no further questions. The defendant called a second expert witness and asked, "Do you accept the Smith book as reliable?" The second witness said, "It once was, but it is now badly out of date." The plaintiff requested that the jury be allowed to examine the book and judge for itself the book's reliability.

Should the court allow the jury to examine the book?

(A) No, because the jury may consider only passages read to it by counsel or witness.

(B) No, because the plaintiff's expert in testifying did not rely on the treatise but on his own experience.

(C) Yes, because an expert has testified that the treatise is reliable.

(D) Yes, because the jury is the judge of the weight and credibility to be accorded both written and oral evidence.

Question 13

A car owner washed her car while it was parked on a public street, in violation of a statute that prohibits the washing of vehicles on public streets during rush hours. The statute was enacted only to expedite the flow of automobile traffic. Due to a sudden and unexpected cold snap, the car owner's waste water formed a puddle that froze. A pedestrian slipped on the frozen puddle and broke her leg. The pedestrian sued the car owner to recover for her injury. At trial, the only evidence the pedestrian offered as to negligence was the car owner's admission that she had violated the statute. At the conclusion of the proofs, both parties moved for a directed verdict.

How should the trial judge proceed?

(A) Deny both motions and submit the case to the jury, because, on the facts, the jury may infer that the car owner was negligent.

(B) Deny both motions and submit the case to the jury, because the jury may consider the statutory violation as evidence that the car owner was negligent.

(C) Grant the car owner's motion, because the pedestrian has failed to offer adequate evidence that the car owner was negligent.

(D) Grant the pedestrian's motion, because of the car owner's admitted statutory violation.

Question 14

Plaintiff owns and operates a restaurant located in State A. Defendant, a citizen of State B, works as a freelance restaurant reviewer for a website. After eating at Plaintiff's restaurant, Defendant published a highly critical online review of it. On July 1, Plaintiff filed an action for libel in federal district court for State C (the state in which Plaintiff resides) based on diversity jurisdiction. On August 1, Defendant served an answer, in which he made a general denial. On October 1, Defendant suddenly realized the State C district court was not a proper venue for the action under the appropriate federal statute. Which of the following choices describes Defendant's best opportunity to raise the venue objection on October 2 and the court's appropriate response to that objection?

(A) Defendant can move to amend his answer to include the venue defense, at which point the court will have discretion whether to dismiss the action if the court agrees that venue was improper.

(B) Defendant can make a motion to dismiss based on the venue objection, at which point the court will have discretion whether to dismiss the action if the court agrees that venue was improper.

(C) Defendant can make a motion to dismiss based on the venue objection, at which point the court must as a jurisdictional matter dismiss the action if the court agrees that venue was improper.

(D) Defendant has waived the venue objection and therefore cannot raise that objection by any method.

Question 15

A buyer entered into a written contract to purchase from a seller 1,000 sets of specially manufactured ball bearings of a non-standard dimension for a price of $10 per set. The seller correctly calculated that it would cost $8 to manufacture each set. Delivery was scheduled for 60 days later. Fifty-five days later, after the seller had completed production of the 1,000 sets, the buyer abandoned the project requiring use of the specially manufactured ball bearings and repudiated the contract with the seller. After notifying the buyer of his intention to resell, the seller sold the 1,000 sets of ball bearings to a salvage company for $2 per set. The seller sued the buyer for damages.

What damages should the court award to the seller?

(A) $2 per set, representing the difference between the cost of production and the price the buyer agreed to pay.

(B) $6 per set, representing the difference between the cost of manufacture and the salvage price.

(C) $8 per set, representing the lost profits plus the unrecovered cost of production.

(D) Nominal damages, as the seller failed to resell the goods by public auction.

Question 16

A defendant decided to kill his neighbor. He set out for his neighbor's house. Before he got there, he saw his neighbor's brother, who resembled the defendant's neighbor. Thinking the neighbor's brother was the neighbor, the defendant shot at the neighbor's brother. The shot missed the neighbor's brother but wounded a bystander, who was some distance away. The defendant had not seen the bystander.

In a prosecution under a statute that proscribes attempt to commit murder, the district attorney should indicate that the intended victim(s) was (were)

(A) the neighbor only.

(B) the neighbor's brother only.

(C) the bystander only.

(D) the neighbor and the neighbor's brother.

Question 17

At the defendant's trial for a gang-related murder, the prosecution introduced, as former testimony, a statement by a gang member who testified against the defendant at a preliminary hearing and has now invoked his privilege against self-incrimination.

If the defendant now seeks to impeach the credibility of the gang member, which of the following is the court most likely to admit?

(A) Evidence that the gang member had three misdemeanor convictions for assault.

(B) Testimony by a psychologist that persons with the gang member's background have a tendency to fabricate.

(C) Testimony by a witness that at the time the gang member testified, he was challenging the defendant's leadership role in the gang.

(D) Testimony by a witness that the gang member is a cocaine dealer.

Question 18

While negligently driving his father's uninsured automobile, a 25-year-old student crashed into an automobile driven by a woman. Both the student and the woman were injured. The student's father, erroneously believing that he was liable because he owned the automobile, said to the woman: "I will see to it that you are reimbursed for any losses you incur as a result of the accident."

In an action by the woman against the student's father for wages lost while she was incapacitated as a result of the accident, which of the following would be the father's best defense?

(A) Lack of consideration

(B) Mistake of fact as to basic assumption

(C) Statute of Frauds

(D) Indefiniteness of father's promise

Question 19

A farmer borrowed $100,000 from a bank and gave the bank a promissory note secured by a mortgage on the farm that she owned. The bank promptly and properly recorded the mortgage, which contained a due-on-sale provision.

A few years later, the farmer borrowed $5,000 from a second bank and gave it a promissory note secured by a mortgage on her farm. The bank promptly and properly recorded the mortgage.

Subsequently, the farmer defaulted on her obligation to the first bank, which then validly accelerated the debt and instituted nonjudicial foreclosure proceedings as permitted by the jurisdiction. The second bank received notice of the foreclosure sale but did not send a representative to the sale. At the foreclosure sale, a buyer who was not acting in collusion with the farmer outbid all other bidders and received a deed to the farm.

Several months later, the original farmer repurchased her farm from the buyer, who executed a warranty deed transferring the farm to her. After the farmer promptly and properly recorded that deed, the second bank commenced foreclosure proceedings on the farm. The farmer denied the validity of the second bank's mortgage.

Does the second bank continue to have a valid mortgage on the farm?

(A) Yes, because of the doctrine of estoppel by deed.

(B) Yes, because the original owner reacquired title to the farm.

(C) No, because the purchase at the foreclosure sale by the buyer under these facts eliminated the second bank's junior mortgage lien.

(D) No, because of the due-on-sale provision in the farmer's mortgage to the first bank.

Question 20

A woman offered to pay her friend one-third of the stolen proceeds if the friend would drive the getaway car to be used in a bank robbery. The friend agreed but made the woman promise not to hurt anyone during the robbery.

The woman then drove to a sporting goods store, where she explained to the store owner that she needed a small firearm for use in a bank robbery. The store owner responded that he would charge extra because the woman was so unwise as to confide her unlawful plans for using the weapon, and he sold her a handgun at four times the regular price.

During the robbery, the woman used the gun to threaten a bank teller into handing over the money. The gun discharged by accident and killed a bank customer.

At common law, who in addition to the woman could properly be convicted of murder in the death of the customer?

(A) Both the friend and the store owner.

(B) Neither the friend nor the store owner.

(C) Only the friend.

(D) Only the store owner.

Question 21

Plaintiff, a citizen of State A, purchased a used car from Defendant, a corporation that is a citizen of State B, in a transaction that occurred in State B. At the time of the sale, Plaintiff did not know that the car had defective brakes. While driving the car in State A, Plaintiff crashed into a taxi, owned and driven by Taxi Driver (a citizen of State B), which was going faster than the speed limit. Plaintiff brought a diversity action against Defendant in federal district court for the Eastern District of State B for personal injuries and property damage suffered by Plaintiff in the crash; Plaintiff's theory was that Defendant committed fraud on her (as defined under State B common-law principles) by knowingly concealing the brakes, and that the fraud was the proximate cause of Plaintiff's damages. A jury awarded Plaintiff the full $100,000 she sought, but Plaintiff was unable to collect because Defendant went bankrupt.

Plaintiff then sued Taxi Driver in a separate diversity action in federal district court for the Southern District of State A, again for $100,000, for the same personal injury and property damage sustained by Plaintiff in the crash. Taxi Driver raised the affirmative defense of claim preclusion, arguing that any claim Plaintiff might have had against Taxi Driver should have been asserted as part of the State B action since Plaintiff's claim against Defendant and her claim against Taxi Driver arose out of a single episode. Since Plaintiff failed to assert the claim against Taxi Driver, Taxi Driver argued, that claim became merged into Plaintiff's successful judgment against Defendant, and may no longer be asserted. Taxi Driver has therefore moved for summary judgment on the basis of this claim-preclusion theory.

Which statement provides the best explanation of how the State A federal court should resolve Taxi Driver's motion?

(A) The federal court should grant the motion because once Plaintiff chose to bring any suit in State B concerning the accident, Plaintiff was required to sue all parties involved in the accident in that first action.

(B) The federal court should grant the motion under the transactional test for claim preclusion.

(C) The court should deny the motion because Taxi Driver was not a party to the State B action.

(D) The court should deny the motion because the judgment of the State B court will not be final until all appeals have been concluded.

Question 22

In a civil action for misrepresentation in the sale of real estate, the parties contested whether the defendant was licensed by the State Board of Realtors, a public agency established by statute to license real estate brokers. The defendant testified she was licensed. On rebuttal, the plaintiff offers a certification, bearing the seal of the secretary of the State Board of Realtors. The certification states that the secretary conducted a thorough search of the agency's records and all relevant databases, and that this search uncovered no record of a license ever having been issued to the defendant. The certification is signed by the secretary.

Is the certification that there was no record of a license issuance admissible?

(A) No, because it is hearsay not within any exception.

(B) No, because the writing was not properly authenticated.

(C) Yes, for the limited purpose of impeaching the defendant.

(D) Yes, to prove the nonexistence of a public record.

Question 23

A federal statute imposes an excise tax of $100 on each new computer sold in the United States. It also appropriates the entire proceeds of that tax to a special fund, which is required to be used to purchase licenses for computer software that will be made available for use, free of charge, to any resident of the United States.

Is this statute constitutional?

(A) No, because the federal government may not impose any direct taxes on citizens of the United States.

(B) No, because this statute takes without just compensation the property of persons who hold patents or copyrights on computer software.

(C) Yes, because it is a reasonable exercise of the power of Congress to tax and spend for the general welfare.

(D) Yes, because the patent power authorizes Congress to impose reasonable charges on the sale of technology and to spend the proceeds of those charges to advance the use of technology in the United States.

Question 24

A jogger was stopped by a police officer, who thought the jogger matched the description of a burglar being sought by the police. The officer arrested the jogger, handcuffed her, and brought her to the police station, where the charges were dismissed as a case of mistaken identity. The jogger, a citizen of State A, brought a civil suit against the officer (also a citizen of State A) in State A federal court. The suit contained two claims: (1) a common-law claim for false arrest based on State A tort law; and (2) a claim that the officer's stop of the jogger and his excessive force against her was a denial of her federal civil rights made under color of law, thereby entitling her to recover damages under a federal statute known as "§1983." The State A statute of limitation for the false-arrest claim is two years from the arrest; the federal statute of limitations on the §1983 claim is four years.

The officer asserted various defenses, one of which (asserted solely in response to the §1983 claim) was the defense of qualified immunity. By the time the parties completed discovery, nearly three years had elapsed since the arrest. At the close of discovery, the officer moved for summary judgment on the §1983 claim based on his immunity defense. The judge granted the motion, and therefore dismissed the §1983 claim with prejudice. The officer then moved to have the false-arrest claim dismissed on the grounds that the court now lacked subject-matter jurisdiction over that claim due to the dismissal of the §1983 claim. The jogger opposed the dismissal, pointing out (correctly) that discovery was complete, and that the court and litigants had devoted significant time to the issues raised by the false-arrest claim. The jogger also expressed the fear that if the court dismissed the claim, she might be time-barred from refiling it in State A court. Which of the following best summarizes how the federal court should rule on the officer's motion to dismiss the false-arrest claim?

(A) The court must dismiss the false-arrest claim regardless of whether the claim could be refiled in State A, because the court's dismissal of the §1983 claim deprived that court of subject-matter jurisdiction to hear the false-arrest claim.

(B) The court must try the false-arrest claim, because supplemental jurisdiction applies to that claim, and the court does not have discretion to decline to exercise that jurisdiction.

(C) The court has discretion whether to dismiss the false-arrest claim or try it, and if it dismisses, federal law guarantees the jogger 30 days to refile the claim in State A court.

(D) The court must dismiss the false-arrest claim, but federal law guarantees the jogger 30 days to re-file the claim in State A court.

Question 25

A plaintiff sued her employer, alleging that poor working conditions had caused her to develop a stomach ulcer. At trial, the plaintiff's medical expert testified to the cause of the plaintiff's ulcer and stated that his opinion was based in part on information in a letter the plaintiff's personal physician had written to the plaintiff's employer, explaining why the plaintiff had missed work.

When offered to prove the cause of the plaintiff's condition, is the letter from the plaintiff's doctor admissible?

(A) No, because it is hearsay not within any exception.

(B) No, because the plaintiff's physician is not shown to be unavailable.

(C) Yes, because it was relied upon by the plaintiff's medical expert.

(D) Yes, under the business records exception to the hearsay rule.

Question 26

A customer wanted to purchase a used motor vehicle. The used car company's lot, in a remote section away from town, was enclosed by a ten-foot chain link fence. While the customer and a sales representative, an employee of the used car company, were in the used car lot looking at cars, a security guard locked the gate at 1:30 p.m., because it was Saturday and the lot was supposed to be closed after 1:00 p.m. Saturday until Monday morning. At 1:45 p.m., the customer and the sales representative discovered they were locked in.

There was no traffic in the vicinity and no way in which help could be summoned. After two hours, the customer began to panic at the prospect of remaining undiscovered and without food and water until Monday morning. The sales representative decided to wait in a car until help came. The customer tried to climb over the fence and, in doing so, fell, and was injured. The customer asserts a claim against the used car company for damages for his injuries.

If the customer's claim is based on false imprisonment, will the customer prevail?

(A) Yes, because he was confined against his will.

(B) Yes, because he was harmed as a result of his confinement.

(C) No, unless the security guard was negligent in locking the gate.

(D) No, unless the security guard knew that someone was in the lot at the time the guard locked the gate.

Question 27

An investor offered a landowner $200 for a 30-day option to buy the landowner's land for $10,000. As the landowner knew, the investor, if granted the option, intended to resell the land at a profit. The landowner declined, believing that she could find a desirable purchaser herself. The investor thereupon said to the landowner, "Make me a written, 30-day offer, revocable at your pleasure, to sell me your land at a sale price of $10,000, and tomorrow I will pay you $200 for so doing." The landowner agreed and gave the investor the following signed document:

"For 30 days I offer my land to the investor for $10,000, this offer to be revocable at my pleasure at any time before acceptance."

Which of the following would best describe the basis of any duty or duties created by the investor's oral promise and the landowner's writing?

(A) Firm option

(B) Precontractual liability by promissory estoppel

(C) Unilateral contract

(D) Quasi-contractual liability

Question 28

Twenty-five years ago, a man who owned a 45-acre tract of land conveyed 40 of the 45 acres to a developer by warranty deed. The man retained the rear five-acre portion of the land and continues to live there in a large farmhouse.

The deed to the 40-acre tract was promptly and properly recorded. It contained the following language:

"It is a term and condition of this deed, which shall be a covenant running with the land and binding on all owners, their heirs and assigns, that no use shall be made of the 40-acre tract of land except for residential purposes."

Subsequently, the developer fully developed the 40-acre tract into a residential subdivision consisting of 40 lots with a single-family residence on each lot.

Although there have been multiple transfers of ownership of each of the 40 lots within the subdivision, none of them included a reference to the quoted provision in the deed from the man to the developer, nor did any deed to a subdivision lot create any new covenants restricting use.

Last year, a major new medical center was constructed adjacent to the subdivision. A doctor who owns a house in the subdivision wishes to relocate her medical offices to her house. For the first time, the doctor learned of the restrictive covenant in the deed from the man to the developer. The applicable zoning ordinance permits the doctor's intended use. The man, as owner of the five-acre tract, however, objects to the doctor's proposed use of her property.

There are no governing statutes other than the zoning code. The common-law Rule Against Perpetuities is unmodified in the jurisdiction.

Can the doctor convert her house in the subdivision into a medical office?

(A) No, because the owners of lots in the subdivision own property benefitted by the original residential covenant and have the sole right to enforce it.

(B) No, because the man owns property benefitted by the original restrictive covenant and has a right to enforce it.

(C) Yes, because the original restrictive covenant violates the Rule Against Perpetuities.

(D) Yes, because the zoning ordinance allows the doctor's proposed use and preempts the restrictive covenant.

Question 29

With the advice and consent of the Senate, the President entered into a self-executing treaty with a foreign country. The treaty provided that citizens of both nations were required to pay whatever torts damages were awarded against them by a court of either nation.

A man and a woman who were U.S. citizens and residents of the same state were traveling separately in the foreign country when their cars collided. The foreign court awarded the woman a judgment for $500,000 in damages for her injuries from the accident.

In federal district court in their home state, the woman filed suit against the man to enforce the judgment. The man filed a motion to dismiss for lack of jurisdiction.

Should the court grant the motion to dismiss?

(A) Yes, because the citizenship of the parties is not diverse.

(B) Yes, because the traffic accident was a noncommercial transaction outside interstate commerce.

(C) No, because the case falls within the federal question jurisdiction of the court.

(D) No, because the treaty power is plenary and not subject to judicial review.

Question 30

Section 1 of the Vehicle Code of a state makes it illegal to cross a street in a central business district other than at a designated crosswalk. Section 2 of the Code prohibits parking any motor vehicle so that it blocks any part of a designated crosswalk.

A pedestrian wanted to cross Main Street in the central business district of a city, located in the state at issue, but a truck parked by a trucker was blocking the designated crosswalk. The pedestrian stepped out into Main Street and carefully walked around the back of the truck. The pedestrian was struck by a motor vehicle negligently operated by a driver.

If the pedestrian asserts a claim against the driver, the pedestrian's failure to be in the crosswalk will have which of the following effects?

(A) It is not relevant in determining the right of the pedestrian.

(B) It may be considered by the trier of facts on the issue of the driver's liability.

(C) It will bar the pedestrian's recovery unless the driver saw the pedestrian in time to avoid the impact.

(D) It will bar the pedestrian's recovery as a matter of law.

Question 31

Plaintiff is an individual who lives in State A. While on holiday in State B, he bought an antique map from Defendant, a corporation that deals in art, and whose principal place of business is in State B. The map turned out to be a counterfeit, and Plaintiff filed a diversity suit against Defendant in federal district court for the Northern District of State A. The action alleged breach of contract, misrepresentation, and fraud, and sought $100,000 in damages. Before filing suit, Plaintiff learned from the Internet that Defendant advertised the fact that "We frequently visit the West Coast, including State A, to show our inventory." Plaintiff also learned that Defendant owned a storage facility in State A valued at $95,000. A State A long-arm statute ("Statute 1") authorizes service in a State A state court action by registered mail to any person found in the U.S. outside of State A, if such service would be consistent with the Due Process Clause of the Fourteenth Amendment. Another State A statute ("Statute 2") provides: "The courts of this state have authority, consistent with the Due Process Clause of the Fourteenth Amendment, to exercise *quasi in rem* jurisdiction based on attachment of the defendant's tangible or intangible property located within this state." No federal statute bears on the use of quasi in rem jurisdiction on facts such as those presented in Plaintiff's suit.

Plaintiff did not attempt to obtain personal jurisdiction over Defendant by using Statute 1, because he was not aware of that statute's existence. Instead, he served Defendant by attaching the storage facility, and asserting *quasi in rem* jurisdiction under authority of Statute 2. (He was willing to take the risk that he might get a judgment for the full $100,000 sought, but be able to realize only $95,000 by having the storage facility seized and sold to satisfy the judgment.)

Defendant has now moved to dismiss the action for lack of personal jurisdiction over it. How should the district court resolve the motion?

(A) The court should grant the motion because Plaintiff has not made reasonable efforts to use the service-by-registered-mail provisions of Statute 1 to establish in personam jurisdiction.

(B) The court should deny the motion because Plaintiff was entitled to use Statute 2 to establish *quasi in rem* jurisdiction and met the requirements of that statute.

(C) The court should grant the motion because no federal statute or rule authorizes *quasi in rem* jurisdiction in lawsuits filed in federal court.

(D) The court should grant the motion because the attached assets are not related to Plaintiff's claim against Defendant.

Question 32

FBI agents, without a warrant and without permission of Mexican law enforcement or judicial officers, entered Mexico, kidnapped an American citizen wanted in the United States for drug smuggling violations, and forcibly drove him back to Texas. Thereafter, the agents, again without a warrant, broke into the Texas home of the accomplice of the kidnapped citizen, and arrested her.

The kidnapped citizen and his accomplice were both indicted for narcotics violations. Both moved to dismiss the indictment on the ground that their arrests violated the Fourth Amendment.

The court should

(A) grant the motions of both the kidnapped citizen and his accomplice.

(B) grant the motion of the kidnapped citizen and deny the motion of his accomplice.

(C) grant the motion of the accomplice and deny the motion of the kidnapped citizen.

(D) deny the motions of both the kidnapped citizen and his accomplice.

Question 33

A victim was held up at the point of a gun, an unusual revolver with a red-painted barrel, while she was clerking in a neighborhood grocery store. The defendant is charged with armed robbery of the victim.

The prosecutor calls a witness to testify that, a week after the robbery of the victim, he was robbed by the defendant with a pistol that had red paint on the barrel. The witness's testimony is

(A) admissible as establishing an identifying circumstance.
(B) admissible as showing that the defendant was willing to commit robbery.
(C) inadmissible, because it is improper character evidence.
(D) inadmissible, because its probative value is substantially outweighed by the danger of unfair prejudice.

Question 34

An act of Congress provides that "no federal court shall order the implementation of a public school desegregation plan that would require the transportation of any student to a school other than the school closest or next closest to his place of residence."

Which of the following is the strongest argument for the constitutionality of the act?

(A) The Fourteenth Amendment authorizes Congress to define governmental conduct that violates the Equal Protection Clause.
(B) Under Article III, Congress may restrict the jurisdiction of the federal courts.
(C) Transportation of students is subject to regulation by Congress because commerce is involved.
(D) Congress provides partial support for public education and is therefore entitled to establish conditions upon the expenditure of federal grants.

Question 35

Five homeowners who took out mortgage loans from a large bank filed a putative class action in federal court against the bank in which the five served as named plaintiffs. Each of the five was either black or Hispanic, and they claimed that the bank had engaged in a pattern of charging black and Hispanic mortgage borrowers higher fees than Caucasian borrowers, in violation of a federal statute prohibiting such discrimination. The suit sought certification of a plaintiff class consisting of many thousands of black and Hispanic homeowners who had taken out mortgages from the bank. In response to the bank's objection to certification of this class, the district court denied certification, ruling that the proposed class action did not satisfy FRCP 23(a)(2)'s requirement that there be "questions of law or fact common to the class." The judge indicated that she was, however, willing to allow the five named members to proceed to trial on their individual claims.

Because the plaintiffs' lawyer took the case only on the assumption that certification of a class would permit the lawyer to receive adequate fees upon success, the lawyer is unwilling to go forward with the individual claims without a large retainer, which the five named claimants are unable or unwilling to advance. The five, and their lawyer, would like to make an immediate appeal of the district court's denial of certification. Which of the following best describes the named plaintiffs' right to make such an immediate appeal?

(A) The court of appeals does not have jurisdiction to hear the immediate appeal, so the denial cannot be appealed until a final judgment has been entered on the individual plaintiffs' claims after a trial.
(B) The court of appeals has discretion whether to allow the immediate appeal, provided that promptly following the trial court's denial of certification, the named plaintiffs file a petition for permission to appeal.
(C) The named plaintiffs have a right to take the immediate appeal, provided that promptly after the trial court's denial of certification, they file a notice of appeal.
(D) The district court has discretion to allow the immediate appeal if the judge believes that without such an appeal, the denial of certification will effectively sound the "death-knell" of the suit because the small size of the five individual claims would make a non-class trial financially unfeasible.

Question 36

A seller and a buyer have dealt with each other in hundreds of separate grain contracts over the last five years. In performing each contract, the seller delivered the grain to the buyer and, upon delivery, the buyer signed an invoice that showed an agreed-upon price for that delivery. Each invoice was silent in regard to any discount from the price in exchange for prompt payment. The custom of the grain trade is to allow a 2 percent discount from the invoice price for payment within ten days of delivery. In all of their prior transactions and without objection from the seller, the buyer took 15 days to pay and deducted 5 percent from the invoice price. The same delivery procedure and invoice were used in the present contract as had been used previously. The present contract called for a single delivery of wheat at a price of $300,000. The seller delivered the wheat and the buyer then signed the invoice. On the third day after delivery, the buyer received the following note from the seller: "Payment in full in accordance with signed invoice is due immediately. No discounts permitted." s/Seller.

Which of the following statements concerning these facts is most accurate?

(A) The custom of the trade controls, and the buyer is entitled to take a 2 percent discount if he pays within ten days.

(B) The parties' course of dealing controls, and the buyer is entitled to take a 5 percent discount if he pays within 15 days.
(C) The seller's retraction of his prior waiver controls, and the buyer is entitled to no discount.
(D) The written contract controls, and the buyer is entitled to no discount because of the parol evidence rule.

Question 37

In which of the following situations is the defendant most likely to be guilty of common-law murder?

(A) Angered because his neighbor is having a noisy party, the defendant fires a rifle into the neighbor's house. The bullet strikes and kills a guest at the party.
(B) During an argument, the defendant's cousin slaps the defendant. Angered, the defendant responds by shooting and killing his cousin.
(C) The defendant drives his car through a red light and strikes and kills a pedestrian who is crossing the street.
(D) Using his fist, the defendant punches a victim in the face. As a result of the blow, the victim falls and hits his head on a concrete curb, suffers a concussion, and dies.

Question 38

A defendant is tried for armed robbery of a bank. The prosecution, in its case in chief, offers evidence that when the defendant was arrested one day after the crime, he had a quantity of heroin and a hypodermic needle in his possession.

This evidence should be

(A) admitted to prove the defendant's motive to commit the crime.
(B) admitted to prove the defendant's propensity to commit crimes.
(C) excluded, because its probative value is substantially outweighed by the danger of unfair prejudice.
(D) excluded, because such evidence may be offered only to rebut evidence of good character offered by the defendant.

Question 39

A man contacted his lawyer regarding his right to use a path on his neighbor's vacant land.

Fifteen years ago, after a part of the path located on his land and connecting his cabin to the public highway washed out, the man cleared a small part of his neighbor's land and rerouted a section of the path through the neighbor's land.

Twelve years ago, the neighbor leased her land to some hunters. For the next 12 years, the hunters and the man who had rerouted the path used the path for access to the highway.

A month ago, the neighbor discovered that part of the path was on her land. The neighbor told the man that she had not given him permission to cross her land and that she would be closing the rerouted path after 90 days.

The man's land and the neighbor's land have never been in common ownership.

The period of time necessary to acquire rights by prescription in the jurisdiction is ten years. The period of time necessary to acquire title by adverse possession in the jurisdiction is ten years.

What should the lawyer tell the man concerning his right to use the rerouted path on the neighbor's land?

(A) The man has fee title by adverse possession of the land included in the path.
(B) The man has an easement by necessity to use the path.
(C) The man has an easement by prescription to use the path.
(D) The man has no right to use the path.

Question 40

A debtor owed a lender $1,500. The statute of limitations barred recovery on the claim. The debtor wrote to the lender, stating, "I promise to pay you $500 if you will extinguish the debt." The lender agreed.

Is the debtor's promise to pay the lender $500 enforceable?

(A) No, because the debtor made no promise not to plead the statute of limitations as a defense.
(B) No, because there was no consideration for the debtor's promise.
(C) Yes, because the debtor's promise provided a benefit to the lender.
(D) Yes, because the debtor's promise to pay part of the barred antecedent debt is enforceable.

Question 41

In one state, certain kinds of advanced diagnostic medical technology were located only in hospitals, where they provided a major source of revenue. In many other states, such technology was also available at "diagnostic centers" that were not affiliated with hospitals.

A group of physicians announced its plan to immediately open in the state a diagnostic center that would not be affiliated with a hospital. The state hospital association argued to the state legislature that only hospitals could reliably handle advanced medical technologies. The legislature then enacted a law prohibiting the operation in the state of diagnostic centers that were not affiliated with hospitals.

The group of physicians filed suit challenging the constitutionality of the state law.

What action should the court take?

(A) Uphold the law, because the provision of medical services is traditionally a matter of legitimate local concern that states have unreviewable authority to regulate.
(B) Uphold the law, because the legislature could rationally believe that diagnostic centers not affiliated with hospitals would be less reliable than hospitals.
(C) Invalidate the law, because it imposes an undue burden on access to medical services in the state.
(D) Dismiss the suit without reaching the merits, because the suit is not ripe.

Question 42

Plaintiff, a corporation incorporated and headquartered in State A that manufactures office supplies, purchased wood pulp from Defendant, a corporation incorporated in State B and headquartered in State C. The sales contract required Defendant to deliver the pulp to Plaintiff's factory in State A on or before May 1 and was silent about which state's law should govern in case of a dispute between the parties. Defendant delivered the pulp 45 days late, after which Plaintiff sued Defendant in federal district court in State B, invoking diversity jurisdiction. The complaint alleged breach of contract and sought damages in excess of $75,000. Defendant moved to dismiss the complaint for failure to state a claim. Defendant argued that the judge was required to apply State B law to the case and pointed out (correctly) that a State 2 statute, the Grace Period for Deliveries Act (GPDA), provides that "Every supply contract is deemed to permit the vendor to deliver goods up to 60 days after the date specified in the contract." Plaintiff opposed the motion and argued that the court should apply generally federal common-law principles. Assume that federal common law principles—such as those applicable to contracts involving the federal government—do not provide for a grace period analogous to that of the GPDA.

Is the federal district court required to apply the GPDA to the dispute?

(A) No, because a federal court sitting in diversity is required to apply federal common-law principles to this dispute.
(B) Yes, because State B is the state of Defendant's incorporation, so its law governs the interpretation of any contract to which the company is a party.
(C) Yes, so long as the highest court of State B has held that the GPDA applies to a supply contract of the sort involved in this dispute.
(D) Yes, so long as a State B state court would apply the GPDA to this contract dispute if the case were being heard in that court.

Question 43

In a civil trial for fraud arising from a real estate transaction, the defendant claimed not to have been involved in the transaction. The plaintiff called a witness to testify concerning the defendant's involvement in the fraudulent scheme, but to the plaintiff's surprise the witness testified that the defendant was not involved, and denied making any statement to the contrary. The plaintiff now calls a second witness to testify that the first witness had stated, while the two were having a dinner conversation, that the defendant was involved in the fraudulent transaction.

Is the testimony of the second witness admissible?

(A) No, because a party cannot impeach the party's own witness.
(B) No, because it is hearsay not within any exception.
(C) Yes, but only to impeach the first witness.
(D) Yes, to impeach the first witness and to prove the defendant's involvement.

Question 44

By a valid written contract, a seller agreed to sell land to a buyer. The contract stated, "The parties agree that closing will occur on next May 1 at 10 a.m." There was no other reference to closing. The contract was silent as to quality of title.

On April 27, the seller notified the buyer that she had discovered that the land was subject to a longstanding easement in favor of a corporation for a towpath for a canal, should the corporation ever want to build a canal.

The buyer thought it so unlikely that a canal would be built that the closing should occur notwithstanding this outstanding easement. Therefore, the buyer notified the seller on April 28 that he would expect to close on May 1.

When the seller refused to close, the buyer sued for specific performance.

Will the buyer prevail?

(A) No, because the easement renders the seller's title unmarketable.
(B) No, because rights of third parties are unresolved.
(C) Yes, because the decision to terminate the contract for title not being marketable belongs only to the buyer.
(D) Yes, because the seller did not give notice of the easement a reasonable time before the closing date.

Question 45

In a civil action, the plaintiff sued a decedent's estate to recover damages for the injuries she suffered in a collision between her car and one driven by the decedent. At trial, the plaintiff introduced undisputed evidence that the decedent's car swerved across the median of the highway, where it collided with an oncoming car driven by the plaintiff. The decedent's estate introduced undisputed evidence that, prior to the car's crossing the median, the decedent suffered a fatal heart attack, which she had no reason to foresee, and that, prior to the heart attack, the decedent had been driving at a reasonable speed and in a reasonable manner. A statute makes it a traffic offense to cross the median of a highway.

In this case, for whom should the court render judgment?

(A) The decedent's estate, because its evidence is undisputed.
(B) The decedent's estate, because the plaintiff has not established a *prima facie* case of liability.
(C) The plaintiff, because the accident was of a type that does not ordinarily happen in the absence of negligence on the actor's part.
(D) The plaintiff, because the decedent crossed the median in violation of the statute.

Question 46

Plaintiff, a black woman, has long worked as a data-entry clerk for Defendant, a sizable corporation with many small corporate offices spread throughout the United States When Plaintiff applied for a promotion and was denied it, she concluded that she had been passed over based on a combination of her gender and race, and that such discrimination against black women was widespread throughout the company. She filed a class action lawsuit in federal court for the district of State A, in which her particular office of Defendant was located. The suit alleged that Defendant's hiring and promotion policies violated Title I of a federal anti-employment-discrimination statute. Title I prohibits an employer from disfavoring an applicant in the hiring or promotion process, as a matter of intentional corporate policy, on account of the applicant's gender or race. The suit defined the class as consisting of every black woman who was denied an initial clerical job or a promotion to such a job, on account of her gender and race, by Defendant, over a ten-year period. The suit alleged that Defendant, at any given time, has nearly 100 low-level managers (few of whom are black women), that each such manager is given substantial discretion in hiring or promoting clerks who would report to that manager, and that many of the managers have intentionally discriminated against black women. Plaintiff framed the suit as a Rule 23(b)(3) class action and sought compensatory damages and back pay for each of what she estimated as 100 class members. The suit listed Plaintiff as the sole named class member. The suit estimated that individual class members' claims would each have a value ranging from $40,000 to $200,000 and would in the aggregate total at least $4 Million in value.

Discovery has been completed, and Defendant now wishes to oppose certification of the class. Each of the following choices represents a legal objection that Defendant is considering making to class certification, based upon a factual assertion. For each objection, assume that the federal judge concludes that the factual assertion on which the objection is based is true. Which of the objections is most likely to lead the court to grant Defendant's motion to deny the requested class certification?

(A) The class as defined includes only 100 clerical workers or applicants, a number so small that a class action is not clearly superior to individual actions.
(B) Because the mental states of nearly 100 managers who made individual hiring and promotion decisions are in issue, there are no questions of law or fact common to all class members that predominate over questions involving only individual class members.
(C) The overall amount claimed to be in controversy does not exceed $5 million.
(D) Nearly all of the 100 putative class members other than Plaintiff live outside State A, the state in which the federal court hearing the dispute is located, causing the court to lack personal jurisdiction over these absent class members.

Question 47

A woman told a man to go into her friend's unlocked barn and retrieve an expensive black saddle that she said she had loaned to the friend. The man went to the friend's barn, opened the door, found a black saddle, and took it back to the woman's house. The friend had in fact not borrowed a saddle from the woman, and when the friend discovered her black saddle missing, she suspected that the woman was the thief. The friend used a screwdriver to break into the woman's house to find the saddle. Upon discovering the saddle on the woman's table, the friend took it back and called the police.

The jurisdiction follows the common law, except that burglary covers structures in addition to dwellings and the nighttime element has been eliminated.

Which, if any, of these individuals is guilty of burglary?

(A) All of them.
(B) Only the friend.
(C) Only the man.
(D) Only the woman.

Question 48

Plaintiff is a construction company. Plaintiff is incorporated in State A and operates in that state as well as in State B. Defendant is an Internet-based company that is incorporated in State C. Plaintiff's complaint alleged that

Defendant defrauded Plaintiff in violation of a federal statute called the Internet Commercial Fraud Act (ICFA). Section 1 of the ICFA creates a federal private right of action for anyone defrauded in a commercial transaction conducted over the Internet. Section 2 of the statute authorizes suit to be brought in the federal court located anywhere in plaintiff's state of principal residence (which in the case of a corporate plaintiff includes the plaintiff's state of incorporation); Section 3 allows service in an ICFA action "on the defendant in any U.S. state in which the defendant may be found"; and Section 4 says that in ICFA suits the court will be deemed to have personal jurisdiction over the defendant regardless of the nature of the defendant's contacts with the plaintiff's state of principal residence. Plaintiff's complaint, filed in federal district court in State A, asserted that an employee of Plaintiff working out of Plaintiff's State A office purchased a computer online from Defendant; that Defendant knew the order came from that State A office; that Defendant knew the computer was defective; and that Defendant shipped the computer as requested to Plaintiff's State B office. The State B long-arm statute allows nationwide service of process upon, and personal jurisdiction over, any defendant who "voluntarily and knowingly ships any item of tangible personal property into this state." After Plaintiff filed the suit, Plaintiff's sole effort to make service on the Defendant was to have the summons and complaint handed to the CEO of Defendant while the CEO was visiting State D to attend a technology conference. Defendant has never sold a computer to a State D resident.

Has Plaintiff established personal jurisdiction over Defendant for purposes of this ICFA claim?

(A) Yes, because the ICFA statute and the Federal Rules of Civil Procedure, taken together, authorize the service that occurred here, and the State A federal court's exercise of jurisdiction would not offend due process.

(B) Yes, because service in federal-question suits may be made anywhere in the United States where the defendant may be found, and in this case the Defendant could be found wherever the CEO was at the moment of service.

(C) Yes, because a federal court will exercise personal jurisdiction where service and personal jurisdiction would be allowed by the long-arm of the state where the federal court sits, and the State B long-arm would apply to these facts.

(D) No, because the Defendant does not have minimum contacts with State A and the exercise of personal jurisdiction over the Defendant in the State A federal courts would therefore violate the Defendant's due process rights.

Question 49

An insurance company issued an insurance policy to a homeowner. The policy failed to contain certain coverage terms required by a state insurance statute. When the homeowner suffered a loss due to a theft that was within the policy's terms, the insurance company refused to pay, claiming that the contract was unenforceable because it violated the statute.

Will the homeowner succeed in an action against the insurance company to recover for the loss?

(A) No, because the insurance policy is not a divisible contract.

(B) No, because the insurance policy violated the statute.

(C) Yes, because the homeowner belongs to the class of persons intended to be protected by the statute.

(D) Yes, because the insurance policy would be strictly construed against the insurance company as the drafter.

Question 50

On a foggy night, a victim was clubbed from behind by a man wielding a blackjack. The defendant was arrested in the vicinity shortly thereafter. As they were booking the defendant, the police took his photograph. They promptly showed that photograph, along with the photographs of seven people who had the same general features as the defendant, to the victim. The victim identified the defendant as the culprit.

At trial, the defendant objects to the introduction into evidence of his out-of-court identification. His objection should be

(A) sustained, because the victim did not have a good opportunity to observe the culprit.

(B) sustained, because the defendant was not represented by counsel at the showing of the photographs to the victim.

(C) sustained, because the action of the police in showing the photographs to the victim was unnecessarily suggestive.

(D) denied.

Question 51

Husband, Wife, and Child, all citizens of State A, ate a can of soup that turned out to be contaminated. Each suffered food poisoning that resulted in permanent neurological damage. Defendant, a food company in State B, processed and distributed the can of soup. Husband, Wife, and Child sued Defendant in a federal district court in State A. Defendant has moved to dismiss the complaint for lack of subject-matter jurisdiction. He concedes that the parties are citizens of diverse states, but argues that the complaint does not meet the amount-in-controversy test. Assume that all allegations in the choices below regarding the amount of plaintiffs' damages are made in good faith, and that it is not "legally certain" that any plaintiff has suffered smaller damages than he or she alleges. Assume also that as to each choice, there are no allegations regarding the amount of damages other than those mentioned in the choice.

How should the court resolve the motion?

(A) The court should grant the motion if the complaint alleges that: (i) Husband suffered $60,000 in personal damages; (ii) Wife suffered $50,000 in personal damages; and (iii) Child suffered $40,000 in personal damages.

(B) The court should deny the motion if the complaint alleges that each family member suffered $40,000 in personal damages, because supplementary jurisdiction applies.

(C) The court should grant the motion if the complaint alleges that (i) Husband suffered $40,000 in personal damages and $40,000 for loss of consortium; and (ii) Wife and Child each suffered $40,000 in personal damages.

(D) The court should deny the motion if the complaint alleges that Husband and Wife each suffered $40,000 in personal damages, because their claims are based on a common and undivided interest.

Question 52

On a parcel of land immediately adjacent to a woman's 50-acre farm, a public school district built a large consolidated high school that included a 5,000-seat lighted athletic stadium. The woman had objected to the district's plans for the stadium and was particularly upset about nighttime athletic events that attracted large crowds and that, at times, resulted in significant noise and light intensity levels. On nights of athletic events, the woman and her family members wore earplugs and could not sleep or enjoy a quiet evening until after 10 p.m. In addition, light from the stadium on those nights was bright enough to allow reading a newspaper in the woman's yard.

Which of the following doctrines would best support the woman's claim for damages?

(A) Constructive eviction

(B) Private nuisance

(C) Public nuisance

(D) Waste

Question 53

On March 1, an excavator entered into a contract with a contractor to perform excavation work on a large project. The contract expressly required that the excavator begin work on June 1 to enable other subcontractors to install utilities. On May 15, the excavator requested a 30-day delay in the start date for the excavation work because he was seriously behind schedule on another project. When the contractor refused to grant the delay, the excavator stated that he would try to begin the work for the contractor on June 1.

Does the contractor have valid legal grounds to cancel the contract with the excavator and hire a replacement?

(A) Yes, because the excavator committed an anticipatory repudiation of the contract by causing the contractor to feel insecure about the performance.

(B) Yes, because the excavator breached the implied covenant of good faith and fair dealing.

(C) No, because the excavator would be entitled to specific performance of the contract if he could begin by June 1.

(D) No, because the excavator did not state unequivocally that he would delay the beginning of his work.

Question 54

Ten years ago, a labor leader divorced his wife. Both he and his first wife have since married other persons. Recently, a newspaper in another city ran a feature article on improper influences it asserted had been used by labor officials to secure favorable rulings from government officials. The story said that in 1980 the labor leader's first wife, with his knowledge and concurrence, gave sexual favors to the mayor of the labor leader's hometown and then persuaded the mayor to grant concessions to the labor leader's union.

The story named the labor leader and identified his first wife by her former and current surnames. The reporter for the newspaper believed the story to be true, since it had been related to him by two very reliable sources.

The labor leader's first wife suffered emotional distress and became very depressed. If she asserts a claim based on defamation against the newspaper, she will

(A) prevail, because the story concerned her personal, private life.

(B) prevail if the story was false.

(C) not prevail, because the newspaper did not print the story with knowledge of its falsity or with reckless disregard for its truth or falsity.

(D) not prevail if the newspaper exercised ordinary care in determining if the story was true or false.

Question 55

The owner in fee simple of a small farm consisting of 30 acres of land improved with a house and several outbuildings, leased the same to a farmer for a ten-year period. After two years had expired, the government condemned 20 acres of the property and allocated the compensation award to the owner and the farmer according to their respective interest so taken. It so happened, however, that the 20 acres taken embraced all of the farm's tillable land, leaving only the house, outbuildings, and a small wooded lot. There is no applicable statute in the jurisdiction where the property is located nor any provision in the lease relating to condemnation. The farmer quit possession, and the owner brought suit against him to recover rent. The owner will

(A) lose, because there has been a frustration of purpose that excuses the farmer from further performance of his contract to pay rent.
(B) lose, because there has been a breach of the implied covenant of quiet enjoyment by the owner's inability to provide the farmer with possession of the whole of the property for the entire term.
(C) win, because of the implied warranty on the part of the tenant to return the demised premises in the same condition at the end of the term as they were at the beginning.
(D) win, because the relationship of landlord and tenant was unaffected by the condemnation, thus leaving the farmer still obligated to pay rent.

Question 56

Statutes in the jurisdiction define criminal assault as "an attempt to commit a criminal battery" and criminal battery as "causing an offensive touching."

As a defendant was walking down the street, a gust of wind blew off his hat. The defendant reached out, trying to grab his hat, and narrowly missed striking the plaintiff in the face with his hand.

If charged with criminal assault, the defendant should be found

(A) guilty, because he caused the plaintiff to be in apprehension of an offensive touching.
(B) guilty, because he should have realized he might strike someone by reaching out.
(C) not guilty, because he did not intend to hit the plaintiff.
(D) not guilty, because he did not hit the plaintiff.

Question 57

Residents of a city complained that brightly colored signs detracted from the character of the city's historic district and distracted motorists trying to navigate its narrow streets. In response, the city council enacted an ordinance requiring any "sign or visual display" visible on the streets of the historic district to be black and white and to be no more than four feet long or wide.

A political party wanted to hang a six-foot-long, red, white, and blue political banner in front of a building in the historic district. The party filed suit to challenge the constitutionality of the sign ordinance as applied to the display of its banner.

Which of the following would be the most useful argument for the political party?

(A) The ordinance is not the least restrictive means of promoting a compelling government interest.
(B) The ordinance is not narrowly tailored to an important government interest, nor does it leave open alternative channels of communication.
(C) The ordinance imposes a prior restraint on political expression.
(D) The ordinance effectively favors some categories of speech over others.

Question 58

A car dealer owed a bank $10,000, due on June 1. The car dealer subsequently sold an automobile to a buyer at a price of $10,000, payable at $1,000 per month beginning on June 1. The car dealer then asked the bank whether the bank would accept payments of $1,000 per month for ten months beginning June 1, without interest, in payment of the debt. The bank agreed to that arrangement and the car dealer then directed the buyer to make the payments to the bank. When the buyer tendered the first payment to the bank, the bank refused the payment, asserting that it would accept payment only from the car dealer. On June 2, the bank demanded that the car dealer pay the debt in full immediately. The car dealer refused to pay and the bank sued the car dealer to recover the $10,000.

In this suit, which of the following arguments best supports the bank's claim for immediate payment?

(A) The agreement to extend the time for payment was not in writing.
(B) The car dealer could not delegate its duty to pay to the buyer.
(C) The car dealer gave no consideration for the agreement to extend the time of payment.
(D) The car dealer's conduct was an attempted novation that the bank could reject.

Question 59

A landowner owned a vacant lot. He entered into a written contract with a contractor to build a house of stated specifications on the lot and to sell the house and lot to the contractor. The contract provided for an "inside date" of April 1, 2010, and an "outside date" of May 1, 2010, for completion of the house and delivery of a deed. Neither party tendered performance on the dates stated. On May 3, 2010, the contractor notified the landowner in writing of the contractor's election to cancel the contract because of the landowner's failure to deliver title by May 1. On May 12, the landowner notified the contractor that some unanticipated construction difficulties had been encountered but that the landowner was entitled to a reasonable time to complete in any event. The notification also included a promise that the landowner would be ready to perform by May 29 and that he was setting that date as an adjourned closing date. The landowner obtained a certificate of occupancy and appropriate documents of title, and he tendered performance on May 29. The contractor refused. The landowner brought an action to recover damages for breach of contract. The decision in the case will most likely be determined by whether

(A) the landowner acted with due diligence in completing the house.
(B) the contractor can prove actual "undue hardship" caused by the delay.
(C) the expressions "inside date" and "outside date" are construed to make time of the essence.
(D) there is a showing of good faith in the contractor's efforts to terminate the contract.

Question 60

A man owned a much-loved cat, worth about $25, that frequently trespassed on a neighbor's property. The neighbor repeatedly asked the man to keep the cat on his own property, but the trespasses did not diminish. Aware of the man's attachment to the cat, the neighbor killed the cat with a shotgun in full view of the man. As a consequence, the man suffered great emotional distress.

In an action by the man against the neighbor, which of the following claims would be likely to result in the greatest monetary recovery?

(A) Battery
(B) Intentional infliction of mental suffering
(C) Trespass to chattel
(D) Conversion

Question 61

A plaintiff sued a defendant for injuries allegedly suffered when he slipped and fell on the defendant's business property. Without asking that the defendant's property manager be declared a hostile witness, the plaintiff called him solely to establish that the defendant was the owner of the property where the plaintiff fell. On cross-examination of the manager, the defendant's attorney sought to establish that the defendant had taken reasonable precautions to make the property safe for business invitees.

Should the defendant's cross-examination of the manager be permitted over the plaintiff's objection?

(A) No, because cross-examination should be limited to the subject matter of the direct examination and matters affecting the credibility of the witness.
(B) No, because the court has not declared the manager hostile.
(C) Yes, because the cross-examiner is entitled to explore matters relevant to any issue in the case, including credibility.
(D) Yes, because the manager is the agent of a party, as to whom the scope of cross-examination is unlimited.

Question 62

In order to combat terrorism, Congress enacted a statute authorizing the President to construct surveillance facilities on privately owned property if the President determined that the construction of such facilities was "necessary to safeguard the security of the United States." The statute provided no compensation for the owner of the land on which such facilities were constructed and provided that the surveillance facilities were to be owned and operated by the U.S. government.

Pursuant to this statute, the President has determined that the construction of a surveillance facility on a very small, unused portion of an owner's large tract of land is necessary to safeguard the security of the United States. The construction and operation of the facility will not affect any of the uses that the owner is currently making of the entire tract of land.

The owner has filed suit to challenge the constitutionality of the construction of a surveillance facility on the parcel of land at issue without compensation.

How should the court rule?

(A) It would be a taking of the owner's property for which the owner must be compensated.
(B) It would single out the owner for adverse treatment in violation of the equal protection component of the Fifth Amendment.
(C) It would not interfere with any use the owner is currently making of the entire tract of land and, therefore, would not entitle the owner to any compensation.
(D) It would be valid without any compensation, because it has been determined to be necessary to protect a compelling government interest in national security.

Question 63

A landowner executed an instrument in the proper form of a deed, purporting to convey his land to a friend. The landowner handed the instrument to the friend, saying, "This is yours, but please do not record it until after I am dead. Otherwise, it will cause me no end of trouble with my relatives." Two days later, the landowner asked the friend to return the deed to him because he had decided that he should devise the land to the friend by will rather than by deed. The friend said that he would destroy the deed and a day or so later falsely told the landowner that the deed had been destroyed. Six months ago, the landowner, who had never executed a will, died intestate, survived by a daughter as his sole heir at law. The day after the landowner's death, the friend recorded the deed from him. As soon as the daughter discovered this recording and the friend's claim to the land, she brought an appropriate action against the friend to quiet title to the land.

For whom should the court hold?

(A) The daughter, because the death of the landowner deprived the subsequent recordation of any effect.
(B) The daughter, because the friend was dishonest in reporting that he had destroyed the deed.
(C) The friend, because the deed was delivered to him.
(D) The friend, because the deed was recorded by him.

Question 64

Plaintiff owns and resides in a house in State A and has no plans to move. He ordered a garden hose for $100 by telephone from a catalogue distributed by Defendant, a garden-supply company that is incorporated in State A and has its principal place of business there. The garden hose turned out to have a defective nozzle, and while Plaintiff was watering his garden a flood developed, ruining his garden. Plaintiff was angry, and therefore posted disparaging comments about Defendant on an online discussion board. Plaintiff also sued Defendant in State A state court on a breach-of-warranty theory to recover the purchase price plus consequential damages for his lost garden, for a total of $5,000. Defendant filed a counterclaim alleging violation of a federal statute entitled the "Federal Trade Libel Law" (the FTLL), which provides: "Any false or disparaging online statement made about a business that conducts online sales or sales by mail shall be per se actionable in state or federal court, and the disparaged business shall be entitled to recover from the maker of the statement, without proof of pecuniary harm, statutory damages of $10,000 for each day in which said statement is publicly accessible online." Defendant's counterclaim alleged that Plaintiff's disparaging statement appeared online for ten days, and the company therefore sought $100,000 in damages. Defendant then removed the action to federal court for the district of State A. Plaintiff now seeks to have the case remanded to State A state court.

Should the federal district court remand the action or any part of it?

(A) No, because the federal court has power to hear Defendant's counterclaim.
(B) No, because the federal court may exercise federal-question jurisdiction over the counterclaim, and supplemental jurisdiction extends to cover Plaintiff's claim.
(C) Yes as to the entire action, because the removal was not proper.
(D) Yes as to Plaintiff's state-law claim, but the court may and should retain jurisdiction over Defendant's federal counterclaim.

Question 65

After a liquor store was robbed, the police received an anonymous telephone call naming a store employee as the perpetrator of the robbery. Honestly believing that their actions were permitted by the U.S. Constitution, the police talked one of the employee's neighbors into going to the employee's home with a hidden tape recorder to engage him in a conversation about the crime. During the conversation, the employee admitted committing the robbery. The employee was charged in state court with the robbery. He moved to suppress the recording on the grounds that the method of obtaining it violated his constitutional rights under both the state and federal constitutions. Assume that a clear precedent from the state supreme court holds that the conduct of the police in making the recording violated the employee's rights under the state constitution, and that the exclusionary rule is the proper remedy for this violation.

Should the court grant the employee's motion?

(A) No, because the employee's federal constitutional rights were not violated, and this circumstance overrides any state constitutional provisions.
(B) No, because the police were acting in the good-faith belief that their actions were permitted by the federal Constitution.
(C) Yes, because the making of the recording violated the state constitution.
(D) Yes, because use of the recording would violate the neighbor's federal constitutional rights.

Question 66

A man who had become very drunk left a bar and started to walk home. Another patron of the bar, who had observed the man's condition, followed him. The patron saw the man stumble and fall to the ground near an alley. The patron then began to pull out a gun but saw that the man had passed out asleep in the gutter. The patron reached into the man's pocket, grabbed his wallet, and started to walk away. When the patron heard police officers approaching, he dropped the wallet and ran off.

The crimes below are listed in descending order of seriousness.

What is the most serious crime for which the patron properly could be convicted?

(A) Robbery
(B) Larceny

(C) Attempted robbery
(D) Attempted larceny

Question 67

A pedestrian, while crossing the street, was seriously injured when she was hit by a car driven by a messenger. The day after the accident, she started a lengthy period of medical treatment. Shortly after the accident, she sued the messenger for negligence in a federal diversity action in State A. As a part of automatic disclosure, the pedestrian provided the name and contact information of both the doctor who examined her in the emergency room and of the physician who treated her during her long period of recuperation. During discovery, the messenger requested that the pedestrian produce all medical records kept by any doctor or hospital relating to any injuries allegedly suffered by the pedestrian as a consequence of the accident. The pedestrian's counsel produced certain records, but these did not include any handwritten notes taken by the treating physician over the 18-month treatment period. At trial, the treating physician was called as part of the pedestrian's direct case; the pedestrian's lawyer authenticated 70 pages of handwritten notes he had made during the various treatment sessions, and the lawyer offered these into evidence under an appropriate exception to the hearsay rule.

The messenger's lawyer then objected to the admission of the notes; the lawyer pointed out that detailed analysis of the notes would be needed for the lawyer to adequately cross-examine the physician and argued that the court should exclude the notes from evidence because they were not produced during discovery. In a sidebar conference, the pedestrian testified in response that she had not learned of the existence of the treatment notes until the prior week. The trial judge will most likely

(A) rule that the notes may not be excluded without the defendant's first making a motion for sanctions.
(B) rule that the notes should not be excluded unless the messenger shows that his case will be prejudiced if the pedestrian is permitted to use the notes as evidence without her having made timely disclosure of them.
(C) rule that the notes should not be excluded if the judge believes that the pedestrian had learned about the notes only the prior week, since in that event the failure to produce the notes would be substantially justified.
(D) rule that the notes must be excluded unless the judge believes that the failure to produce them is now harmless.

Question 68

The Federal Automobile Safety Act establishes certain safety and performance standards for all automobiles manufactured in the United States. The Act creates a five-member "Automobile Commission" to investigate automobile safety, to make recommendations to Congress for new laws, to make further rules establishing safety and performance standards, and to prosecute violations of the Act. The chairman is appointed by the President, two members are selected by the president pro tempore of the Senate, and two by the speaker of the House of Representatives.

A minor U.S. car manufacturer seeks to enjoin enforcement of the Commission's rules.

The best argument that the manufacturer can make is that

(A) legislative power may not be delegated by Congress to an agency in the absence of clear guidelines.
(B) the commerce power does not extend to the manufacture of automobiles not used in interstate commerce.
(C) the manufacturer is denied due process of law because it is not represented on the Commission.
(D) the Commission lacks authority to enforce its standards because not all of its members were appointed by the President of the United States.

Question 69

An uncle was the record title holder of a vacant tract of land. He often told friends that he would leave the land to his nephew in his will. The nephew knew of these conversations. Prior to the uncle's death, the nephew conveyed the land by warranty deed to a woman for $10,000. She did not conduct a title search of the land before she accepted the deed from the nephew. She promptly and properly recorded her deed. Last month, the uncle died, leaving the land to the nephew in his duly probated will. Both the nephew and the woman now claim ownership of the land. The nephew has offered to return the $10,000 to the woman.

Who has title to the land?

(A) The nephew, because at the time of the deed to the woman, the uncle was the owner of record.
(B) The nephew, because the woman did not conduct a title search.
(C) The woman, because of the doctrine of estoppel by deed.
(D) The woman, because she recorded her deed prior to the uncle's death.

Question 70

A mother, whose adult son was a law school graduate, contracted with a tutor to give the son a bar exam preparation course. "If my son passes the bar exam," the mother explained to the tutor, "he has been promised a job with a law firm that will pay $55,000 a year." The tutor agreed to do the work for $5,000, although the going rate is $6,000.

Before the instruction was to begin, the tutor repudiated the contract. Although the mother or the son reasonably could have employed, for $6,000, an equally qualified instructor to replace the tutor, neither did so. The son failed the bar exam and the law firm refused to employ him. It can be shown that had the son received the instruction, he would have passed the bar exam.

If the mother and the son join as parties plaintiff and sue the tutor for breach of contract, how much, if anything, are they entitled to recover?

(A) $1,000, because all other damages could have been avoided by employing another equally qualified instructor.

(B) $55,000, because damages of that amount were within the contemplation of the parties at the time they contracted.

(C) Nominal damages only, because the mother was not injured by the breach and the tutor made no promise to the son.

(D) Nothing, because neither the mother nor the son took steps to avoid the consequences of the tutor's breach.

Question 71

A defendant became intoxicated at a bar. He got into his car and drove away. Within a few blocks, craving another drink, he stopped his car in the middle of the street, picked up a brick, and broke the display window of a liquor store. As he was reaching for a bottle, the night watchman arrived. Startled, the defendant turned, and struck the watchman on the head with the bottle, killing him. Only vaguely aware of what was happening, the defendant returned to his car, consumed more liquor, and then drove off at a high speed.

Relevant statutes define burglary to include "breaking and entering a building not used as a dwelling with the intent to commit a crime therein." Manslaughter is defined as the "killing of a human being in a criminally reckless manner." Criminal recklessness is "consciously disregarding a substantial and unjustifiable risk resulting from the actor's conduct." Murder is defined as "the premeditated and intentional killing of another or the killing of another in the commission of committing rape, robbery, burglary, or arson." Another statute provides that intoxication is not a defense to crime unless it negates an element of the offense.

The defendant was charged with the murder of the watchman and manslaughter in the death of the pedestrian. Assume that he is tried separately on each charge.

At a defendant's trial for the murder of the watchman, the court should in substance charge the jury on the issue of the defense of intoxication that

(A) intoxication is a defense to the underlying crime of burglary if the defendant, due to drunkenness, did not form an intent to commit a crime within the building, in which case there can be no conviction for murder unless the defendant intentionally and with premeditation killed the watchman.

(B) voluntary intoxication is not a defense to the crime of murder.

(C) the defendant is guilty of murder despite his intoxication only if the state proves beyond a reasonable doubt that the killing of the watchman was premeditated and intentional.

(D) voluntary intoxication is a defense to the crime of murder if the defendant would not have killed the watchman but for his intoxication.

Question 72

A defendant was charged with assault and battery in a jurisdiction that followed the "retreat" doctrine, and he pleaded self-defense. At his trial, the evidence established the following: a man and his wife were enjoying a drink at a tavern when the defendant entered and stood near the door. The wife whispered to her husband that the defendant was the man who had insulted her on the street the day before. The husband approached the defendant and said, "Get out of here, or I'll break your nose." The defendant said, "Don't come any closer, or I'll hurt you." When the husband raised his fists menacingly, the defendant pulled a can of pepper spray from his pocket, aimed it at the husband's face, and sprayed. The husband fell to the floor, writhing in pain.

Should the defendant be convicted?

(A) No, because he had no obligation to retreat before resorting to non-deadly force.

(B) No, because there is no obligation to retreat when one is in an occupied structure.

(C) Yes, because he failed to retreat even though there was an opportunity available.

(D) Yes, because the husband did not threaten to use deadly force against him.

Question 73

A defendant was charged with aggravated assault. At trial, the victim testified that the defendant beat her savagely, but she was not asked about anything said during the incident. The prosecutor then called a witness to testify that when the beating stopped, the victim screamed: "I'm dying—don't let [the defendant] get away with it!"

Is the testimony of the witness concerning the victim's statement admissible?

(A) No, because it is hearsay not within any exception.

(B) No, because the victim was not asked about the statement.

(C) Yes, as a statement under belief of impending death, even though the victim did not die.
(D) Yes, as an excited utterance.

Question 74

A developer was the owner of a large subdivision. A buyer became interested in purchasing a lot but could not decide between Lot 40 and Lot 41. The price and fair market value of each of these two lots was $5,000. The buyer paid the developer $5,000, which the developer accepted, and the developer delivered to the buyer a deed that was properly executed, complete, and ready for recording in every detail except that the space in the deed for the lot number was left blank. The developer told the buyer to fill in either Lot 40 or Lot 41 according to his decision and then record the deed. The buyer visited the development the next day and completely changed his mind, selecting Lot 25. He filled in Lot 25 and duly recorded the deed. The price of Lot 25 and its fair market value was $7,500.

Immediately upon learning what the buyer had done, the developer brought an appropriate action against the buyer to rescind the transaction. If the developer loses, the most likely basis for the judgment is that

(A) the developer's casual business practices created his loss.
(B) the need for certainty in land title records controls.
(C) the agency implied to complete the deed cannot be restricted by the oral understanding.
(D) the recording of the deed precludes any questioning of its provisions in its recorded form.

Question 75

An accountant and a bookkeeper, as part of a contract dissolving their accounting business, agreed that each would contribute $100,000 to fund an annuity for a clerk who was a longtime employee of the business. The clerk's position would be terminated due to the dissolution, and he did not have a retirement plan. The accountant and the bookkeeper informed the clerk of their plan to fund an annuity for him. The clerk, confident about his financial future because of the promised annuity, purchased a retirement home. The accountant later contributed his $100,000 to fund the annuity, but the bookkeeper stated that he could afford to contribute only $50,000. The accountant agreed that the bookkeeper should contribute only $50,000.

Does the clerk have a valid basis for an action against the bookkeeper for the unpaid $50,000?

(A) No, because the clerk was bound by the modification of the agreement made by the accountant and the bookkeeper.
(B) No, because the clerk was only a donee beneficiary of the agreement between the accountant and the bookkeeper, and had no vested rights.
(C) Yes, because the clerk's reliance on the promised retirement fund prevented the parties from changing the terms.
(D) Yes, because the promises to establish the fund were made binding by consideration from the clerk's many years of employment.

Question 76

A report released by a Senate investigating committee named three U.S. citizens as helping to organize support for terrorist activities. All three were employed by the U.S. government as park rangers.

Congress enacted a statute naming the three individuals identified in the report and providing that they could not hold any position of employment with the federal government.

Which of the following constitutional provisions provides the best means for challenging the constitutionality of the statute?

(A) The Bill of Attainder Clause
(B) The Due Process Clause
(C) The Ex Post Facto Clause
(D) The Takings Clause

Question 77

Under the Federal Tort Claims Act, with certain exceptions not relevant here, the federal government is liable only for negligence. A federally owned and operated nuclear reactor emitted substantial quantities of radioactive matter that settled on a nearby dairy farm, killing the dairy herd and contaminating the soil. At the trial of an action brought against the federal government by the farm's owner, the trier of fact found that the nuclear plant had a sound design, but that a valve made by the Acme Engineering Company had malfunctioned and allowed the radioactive matter to escape, that Acme Engineering Company is universally regarded as a quality manufacturer of components for nuclear plants, and that there was no way the federal government could have anticipated or prevented the emission of the radioactive matter.

If there is no other applicable statute, for whom should the trial judge enter judgment?

(A) The plaintiff, on the ground that the doctrine of *res ipsa loquitur* applies.
(B) The plaintiff, on the ground that one who allows dangerous material to escape to the property of another is liable for the damage done.
(C) The defendant, on the ground that a case under the Federal Tort Claims Act has not been proved.

(D) The defendant, on the ground that the Acme Engineering Company is the proximate cause of the owner's damage.

Question 78

Driving down a dark road, a defendant accidentally ran over a man. The defendant stopped and found that the victim was dead. The defendant, fearing that he might be held responsible, took the victim's wallet, which contained a substantial amount of money. He removed the identification papers and put the wallet and money back into the victim's pocket. The defendant is not guilty of

(A) larceny, because he took the papers only to prevent identification and not for his own use.

(B) larceny, because he did not take anything from a living victim.

(C) robbery, because he did not take the papers by means of force or putting in fear.

(D) robbery, because he did not take anything of monetary value.

Question 79

In a civil trial arising from a car accident at an intersection, the plaintiff testified on direct examination that he came to a full stop at the intersection. On cross-examination, the defendant's lawyer asked whether the plaintiff claimed that he was exercising due care at the time, and the plaintiff replied that he was driving carefully. At a sidebar conference, the defendant's lawyer sought permission to ask the plaintiff about two prior intersection accidents in the last 12 months where he received traffic citations for failing to stop at stop signs. The plaintiff's lawyer objected.

Should the court allow defense counsel to ask the plaintiff about the two prior incidents?

(A) No, because improperly failing to stop on the recent occasions does not bear on the plaintiff's veracity and does not contradict his testimony in this case.

(B) No, because there is no indication that failing to stop on the recent occasions led to convictions.

(C) Yes, because improperly failing to stop on the recent occasions bears on the plaintiff's credibility, since he claims to have stopped in this case.

(D) Yes, because improperly failing to stop on the recent occasions tends to contradict the plaintiff's claim that he was driving carefully at the time he collided with the defendant.

Question 80

A developer, the owner of a large, undeveloped parcel of land, prepared a development plan creating 200 house lots in the development with the necessary streets and public areas. The plan was fully approved by all necessary governmental agencies and duly recorded. However, construction of the streets, utilities, and other aspects of the development of the parcel has not yet begun, and none of the streets can be opened as public ways until they are completed in accordance with the applicable ordinances in the municipality in which the parcel is located.

One of the streets laid out as part of the development plan is a border road that abuts an adjacent one-acre parcel owned by a widower. The widower's land has no access to any public way except an old, poorly developed road, which is inconvenient and cannot be used without great expense. The widower sold his plot to a buyer. The description used in the deed from the widower to the buyer was the same as that used in prior deeds except that the portion of the description that formerly said, "thence by land of the developer, north-easterly a distance of 200 feet, more or less," was changed to "thence by the border road as laid out on the development plan North 46 degrees East 201.6 feet," with full reference to the plan and its recording data.

The buyer now seeks a building permit that will show that he intends to use the border road for access to his land. The developer objects to the granting of a building permit on the grounds that he has never granted any right to the widower or the buyer to use the border road. There are no governing statutes or ordinances relating to the problem. The developer brings an appropriate action in which the right of the buyer to use the border road without an express grant from the developer is at issue.

The best argument for the developer in this action is that

(A) the buyer's right must await the action of appropriate public authorities to open the border road as a public street, since no private easements arose by implication.

(B) the Statute of Frauds prevents the introduction of evidence that might prove the necessity for the buyer to use the border road.

(C) the buyer's right to use the border road is restricted to the assertion of a way by necessity and the facts preclude the success of such a claim.

(D) the buyer would be unjustly enriched if he were permitted to use the border road.

Question 81

A landowner entered into a single contract with a builder to have three different structures built on separate pieces of property owned by the landowner. Each structure was distinct from the other two and the parties agreed on a specific price for each. After completing the first structure in accordance with the terms of the contract, the builder demanded payment of the specified price for that structure. At the same time, the builder told the landowner that the builder was "tired of the construction business" and would not even begin the other two structures. The landowner refused to pay anything to the builder.

Is the builder likely to prevail in a suit for the agreed price of the first structure?

(A) No, because substantial performance is a constructive condition to the landowner's duty to pay at the contract rate.

(B) No, because the builder's cessation of performance without legal excuse is a willful breach of the contract.

(C) Yes, because the contract is divisible, and the landowner will be required to bring a separate claim for the builder's failure to complete the other two structures.

(D) Yes, because the contract is divisible, but the landowner will be able to deduct any recoverable damages caused by the builder's failure to complete the contract.

Question 82

A city owned and operated a municipal bus system. The city sold space on its buses for the posting of placards. Decisions on the type of placards that could be posted on the buses were left wholly to the discretion of the administrator of the bus system. Although most of the placards that appeared on city buses were commercial advertisements, the administrator had often sold space on the buses for placards promoting various political, charitable, and religious causes.

A circus bought space on the city buses for placards advertising its forthcoming performances. An animal rights organization asked the administrator to sell it space for a placard with photographs showing the mistreatment of animals in circus shows.

The administrator denied the organization's request. She said that the display of this placard would be offensive to the circus, which had paid a substantial sum to place its placards on the buses, and that she had been told by a circus employee that none of the photographs on the organization's placard depicted an animal belonging to this particular circus. Under the relevant city ordinance, the administrator's decision was final.

The organization sued the administrator in an appropriate court for a declaration that she could not, consistent with the First Amendment as made applicable to the states by the Fourteenth Amendment, refuse to sell the organization space for its placard for the reasons she gave.

Will the organization prevail?

(A) No, because the administrator's denial of space to the organization was a reasonable time, manner, and place restriction of speech.

(B) No, because a public official may not allow the use of public facilities for the propagation of a message that he or she believes may create a false or misleading impression.

(C) Yes, because a public official may not refuse to permit the dissemination of a message in a public forum wholly on the basis of its content unless that denial is necessary to serve a compelling government interest.

(D) Yes, because a public official may not refuse to allow the use of any public facility to publish a message dealing with an issue of public concern.

Question 83

A homeowner and a purchaser entered into a valid, enforceable, written contract by which the homeowner agreed to sell and the purchaser agreed to purchase the homeowner's residence. One of the contract provisions was that after closing, the homeowner had the right to remain in the residence for up to 30 days before delivering possession to the purchaser. The closing took place as scheduled. Title passed to the purchaser and the homeowner remained in possession. Within a few days after the closing, the new house next door, which was being constructed for the homeowner, burned to the ground, and at the end of the 30-day period after closing the homeowner refused to move out of his old house; instead, the homeowner proposed to pay the purchaser a monthly rental payment in excess of its fair rental value. The purchaser rejected the proposal and that day brought an appropriate action to gain immediate possession of the residence. The contract was silent as to the consequences of the homeowner's failure to give up possession within the 30-day period, and the jurisdiction in which the property is located has no statute dealing directly with this situation, although the landlord-tenant law of the jurisdiction requires a landlord to give a tenant 30 days' notice before a tenant may be evicted. The purchaser did not give the homeowner any such 30-day statutory notice. The purchaser's best legal argument in support of his action to gain immediate possession is that the homeowner is a

(A) trespasser *ab initio*.

(B) licensee.

(C) tenant at sufferance.

(D) tenant from month to month.

Question 84

A producer engaged an inexperienced actress to do a small role in a new Broadway play for a period of six months at a salary of $200 a week. The actress turned down another role in order to accept this engagement. On the third day of the run, the actress was hospitalized with influenza and a replacement was hired to do the part. A week later, the actress recovered, but the producer refused to accept her services for the remainder of the contract period. The actress then brought an action against the producer for breach of contract.

Which of the following is the actress's best legal theory?

(A) Her acting contract with the producer was legally severable into weekly units.

(B) Her performance of the literal terms of the contract was physically impossible.

(C) Her reliance on the engagement with the producer by declining another acting role created an estoppel against the producer.

(D) Her failure to perform for one week was not a material failure so as to discharge the producer's duty to perform.

Question 85

A defendant was arrested moments after a forcible rape and was prosecuted for it. The victim testified she tore the assailant's shirt. The defendant did not testify. In jury argument, the defendant's counsel urged that the state's failure to offer in evidence the shirt the defendant was wearing when arrested indicated that the evidence would be unfavorable to the state's case. In his closing argument, the prosecutor said, "If the defense had thought the clothing would show anything, they could have brought it in as evidence themselves." The prosecutor's argument is

(A) proper as rebuttal to the inference that the evidence would be unfavorable to the prosecution.

(B) proper as a comment on the defendant's failure to testify.

(C) improper as an argument going beyond the evidence in the case.

(D) improper as a comment on the defendant's failure to testify.

Question 86

A professor, in a lecture in her psychology course at a private university, described an experiment in which a group of college students in a neighboring city rushed out and washed cars stopped at traffic lights during the rush hour. She described how people reacted differently—with shock, joy, and surprise. At the conclusion of her report, she said, "You understand, of course, that you are not to undertake this or any other experiment unless you first clear it with me." Four of the professor's students decided to try the same experiment but did not clear it with the professor.

One motorist who was a subject of their experiment said, "I was shocked. There were two people on each side of the car. At first I thought negatively. I thought they were going to attack me and thought of driving away. Then I quieted down and decided there were too many dirty cars in the city anyway."

Charitable immunity has been abolished in the jurisdiction. If the motorist has a valid claim against the students, will he also prevail against the university?

(A) Yes, if the students would not have performed the experiment but for the professor's lecture.

(B) Yes, if the motorist's claim against the students is based on negligence.

(C) No, because the students were not the professor's employees.

(D) No, because the professor did not authorize the car washing experiment as a class project.

Question 87

Nine gang members were indicted for the murder of a tenth gang member who had become an informant. The gang leader pleaded guilty. At the trial of the other eight, the state's evidence showed the following: The gang leader announced a party to celebrate the recent release of a gang member from jail. But the party was not what it seemed. The gang leader had learned that the recently released gang member had earned his freedom by informing the authorities about the gang's criminal activities. The gang leader decided to use the party to let the other gang members see what happened to a snitch. He told no one about his plan. At the party, after all present had consumed large amounts of liquor, the gang leader announced that the released gang member was an informant and stabbed him with a knife in front of the others. The eight other gang members watched and did nothing while the informant slowly bled to death. The jury found the eight gang members guilty of murder and they appealed.

Should the appellate court uphold the convictions?

(A) No, because mere presence at the scene of a crime is insufficient to make one an accomplice.

(B) No, because murder is a specific intent crime, and there is insufficient evidence to show that they intended to kill.

(C) Yes, because the gang members made no effort to save the informant after he had been stabbed.

(D) Yes, because voluntary intoxication does not negate criminal responsibility.

Question 88

A recently established law school constructed its building in a quiet residential neighborhood. The law school had obtained all of the necessary municipal permits for the construction of the building, which included a large clock tower whose clock chimed every hour. The chimes disturbed only one homeowner in the neighborhood, who had purchased her house prior to the construction of the building. The homeowner was abnormally sensitive to ringing sounds, such as bells and sirens, and found the chimes to be extremely annoying.

In a nuisance action by the homeowner against the law school, will the homeowner prevail?

(A) Yes, because the chimes interfere with the homeowner's use and enjoyment of her property.

(B) Yes, because the homeowner purchased her house prior to the construction of the building.

(C) No, because the chimes do not disturb the other residents of the neighborhood.

(D) No, because the law school had the requisite municipal permits to erect the clock tower.

Question 89

A defendant is on trial for attempted fraud. The state charges that the defendant switched a price tag from a cloth coat to a more expensive fur-trimmed coat and then presented the latter for purchase at the cash register. The defendant testified in her own behalf that the tag must have been switched by someone else. On cross-examination, the prosecutor asks whether the defendant was convicted on two prior occasions of misdemeanor fraud in the defrauding of a retailer by the same means of switching the price tag on a fur-trimmed coat.

Is the question about the convictions for the earlier crimes proper?

(A) It is not proper either to impeach the defendant or to prove that the defendant committed the crime.

(B) It is proper both to prove that the defendant committed the crime and to impeach the defendant.

(C) It is proper to impeach the defendant, but not to prove that the defendant committed the crime.

(D) It is proper to prove the defendant committed the crime, but not to impeach the defendant.

Question 90

On March 1, a mechanic contracted to repair a textile manufacturer's knitting machine and to complete the job by March 6. On March 2, the manufacturer contracted to produce and deliver on March 15 specified cloth to a clothing designer. The manufacturer knew that it would have to use the machine then under repair to perform this contract. Because the designer's order was for a rush job, the designer and the manufacturer included in their contract a liquidated damages clause, providing that the manufacturer would pay $5,000 for each day's delay in delivery after March 15.

The mechanic was inexcusably five days late in repairing the machine, and, as a result, the manufacturer was five days late in delivering the cloth to the designer. The manufacturer paid $25,000 to the designer as liquidated damages and now sues the mechanic for $25,000. Both the mechanic and the manufacturer knew when making their contract on March 1 that under ordinary circumstances the manufacturer would sustain little or no damages of any kind as a result of a five-day delay in the machine repair.

Assuming that the $5,000 liquidated damages clause in the designer-manufacturer contract is valid, which of the following arguments will serve as the mechanic's best defense to the manufacturer's action?

(A) Time was not of the essence in the mechanic-manufacturer contract.

(B) The mechanic had no reason to foresee on March 1 that the designer would suffer consequential damages in the amount of $25,000.

(C) By entering into the contract with the designer while knowing that its knitting machine was being repaired, the manufacturer assumed the risk of any delay loss to the designer.

(D) In all probability, the liquidated damages paid by the manufacturer to the designer are not the same amount as the actual damages sustained by the designer in consequence of the manufacturer's late delivery of the cloth.

Question 91

In response to the need for additional toxic waste landfills in a state, the state's legislature enacted a law authorizing a state agency to establish five new state-owned and state-operated toxic waste landfills. The law provided that the agency would decide the locations and sizes of the landfills after an investigation of all potential sites and a determination that the particular sites chosen would not endanger public health and would be consistent with the public welfare.

A community in the state was scheduled for inspection by the agency as a potential toxic waste landfill site. Because the community's residents obtained most of their drinking water from an aquifer that ran under the entire community, a citizens' group, made up of residents of that community, sued the appropriate officials of the agency in federal court. The group sought a declaratory judgment that the selection of the community as the site of a toxic waste landfill would be unconstitutional and an injunction preventing the agency from selecting the community as a site for such a landfill. The agency officials moved to dismiss.

Which of the following is the most appropriate basis for the court to dismiss this suit?

(A) The case presents a non-justiciable political question.

(B) The interest of the state in obtaining suitable sites for toxic waste landfills is sufficiently compelling to justify the selection of the community as a location for such a facility.

(C) The Eleventh Amendment bars suits of this kind in the federal courts.

(D) The case is not ripe for a decision on the merits.

Question 92

The Rapido is a sports car manufactured by a car company. The Rapido has an excellent reputation for mechanical reliability with one exception: the motor may stall if the engine has not had an extended warm-up. The plaintiff had just begun to drive her Rapido in city traffic without a warm-up when the engine suddenly stalled. A car driven by a truck driver rear-ended the plaintiff's car. The plaintiff suffered no external physical injuries as a result of the collision. However, the shock of the crash caused her to suffer a severe heart attack.

The plaintiff brought an action against the car company based on strict liability in tort. During the trial, the plaintiff presented evidence of an alternative engine design of equal cost that would eliminate the stalling problem without impairing the functions of the engine in any way. The car company moves for a directed verdict at the close of the evidence.

This motion should be

(A) denied, because the jury could find that an unreasonably dangerous defect in the engine was a proximate cause of the collision.

(B) denied, if the jury could find that the Rapido was not crashworthy.

(C) granted, because the truck driver's failure to stop within an assured clear distance was a superseding cause of the collision.

(D) granted, if a person of normal sensitivity would not have suffered a heart attack under these circumstances.

Question 93

Suspecting that students in a dormitory were using narcotics, the president of a private college arranged for local police to place concealed microphones in several suites of the dormitory. Using these microphones, the college security officers recorded a conversation in which a student offered to sell marijuana to a school employee. The tape was turned over to the local police, who played it for a local judge. The judge issued a warrant to search the student's room. The room was searched by police, and marijuana was discovered.

The student is charged with unlawful possession of narcotics. At trial, the student's motion to prevent the introduction of the marijuana into evidence will most probably be

(A) denied, because the college president, *in loco parentis*, had the responsibility of preventing unlawful activity by students under the president's supervision.

(B) denied, because there was probable cause to make the search and police obtained a warrant before commencing the search.

(C) granted, because the student's privacy was unreasonably invaded.

(D) granted, because the electronic surveillance was "fundamentally unfair".

Question 94

A hospital patient had a heart ailment so serious that his doctors had concluded that only a heart transplant could save his life. They therefore arranged to have him flown to a bigger hospital to have the operation performed.

The patient's nephew, who stood to inherit from him, poisoned him. The poison produced a reaction that required postponing the journey. The plane on which the patient was to have flown crashed, and all aboard were killed. By the following day, the patient's heart was so weakened by the effects of the poison that he suffered a heart attack and died. If charged with criminal homicide, the nephew should be found

(A) guilty.

(B) not guilty, because his act did not hasten the deceased's death, but instead prolonged it by one day.

(C) not guilty, because the deceased was already suffering from a fatal illness.

(D) not guilty, because the poison was not the sole cause of death.

Question 95

A seller, the owner of a tract of land, entered into an enforceable written agreement with a buyer providing that the seller would sell the tract to the buyer for an agreed price. At the place and time designated for the closing, the seller tendered an appropriate deed, but the buyer responded that he had discovered a mortgage on the tract and would not complete the transaction, because the seller's title was not free of encumbrances, as the contract required. The seller said that it was his intent to pay the mortgage from the proceeds of the sale, and he offered to put the proceeds in escrow for that purpose with any agreeable, responsible escrowee. The balance due on the mortgage was substantially less than the contract purchase price. The buyer refused the seller's proposal. The seller began an appropriate legal action against the buyer for specific performance. There is no applicable statute in the jurisdiction where the tract is located. The seller's best legal argument in support of his claim for relief is that

(A) as the seller of real estate, he had an implied right to use the contract proceeds to clear the title being conveyed.

(B) the lien of the mortgage shifts from the tract to the contract proceeds.
(C) under the doctrine of equitable conversion, title has already passed to the buyer and the only issue is how the purchase price is to be allocated.
(D) no provision of the contract has been breached by the seller.

Question 96

Plaintiff, an environmental activist in State A, was concerned that extensive lakeshore development would destroy vegetation that fish need in order to spawn. Defendant was a wealthy individual who owned a 3-acre parcel of undeveloped shoreline in State A, which she had started to develop into a single-family residence for herself. The plans Defendant filed with the local municipality showed that she intended to plant a lawn to a point within five feet of the shoreline. A federal statute, the Fish Protection Act (or "FPA"), provides, "Because overdeveloped shorelines are harmful to fish, owners of shoreline property are strongly encouraged to maintain a 30-foot strip of natural vegetation between the shoreline and the part of their grass or lawn nearest the shoreline." Plaintiff sued Defendant in federal court for State A on a claim based on the FPA; the lawsuit asked the court to permanently enjoin Defendant from planting a lawn within the 30 feet of her property nearest the shoreline. Plaintiff also made a motion for a preliminary injunction against such planting until the case could be tried on the merits. Defendant has now opposed the motion for preliminary injunction.

Which statement best expresses how the federal court should decide Plaintiff's motion?

(A) The court should grant the motion, because damages will never be able to repair the injury that the environment will suffer if the fish cannot spawn due to Defendant's illegal development of her property.
(B) The court should grant the motion, because otherwise Defendant will develop the land without the necessary buffer and the public interest will be hurt.
(C) The court should deny the motion, because money damages will be sufficient to remedy a violation of the Fish Protection Act.
(D) The court should deny the motion because Plaintiff is unlikely to succeed on the merits.

Question 97

A manufacturing plant located near a busy highway uses and stores highly volatile explosives. The owner of the plant has imposed strict safety measures to prevent an explosion at the plant. During an unusually heavy windstorm, a large tile was blown off the roof of the plant and crashed into the windshield of a passing car, damaging it. The driver of the car brought a strict liability action against the owner of the plant to recover for the damage to the car's windshield.

Is the driver likely to prevail?

(A) No, because the damage to the windshield did not result from the abnormally dangerous aspect of the plant's activity.
(B) No, because the severity of the windstorm was unusual.
(C) Yes, because the plant's activity was abnormally dangerous.
(D) Yes, because the plant's location near a busy highway was abnormally dangerous.

Question 98

On January 5, a creditor lent $1,000 to a debtor under a contract calling for the debtor to repay the loan at the rate of $100 per month payable on the first day of each month. On February 1, at the debtor's request, the creditor agreed to permit payment on February 5. On March 1, the debtor requested a similar time extension and the creditor replied, "Don't bother me each month. Just change the date of payment to the fifth of the month. But you must now make the payments by cashier's check." The debtor said, "Okay," and made payments on March 5 and April 5. On April 6, the creditor sold the loan contract to a bank, but did not tell the bank about the agreement permitting payments on the fifth of the month. On April 6, the bank wrote to the debtor: "Your debt to [the creditor] has been assigned to us. We hereby inform you that all payments must be made on the first day of the month."

Can the debtor justifiably insist that the payment date for the rest of the installments is the fifth of each month?

(A) No, because a contract modification is not binding on an assignee who had no knowledge of the modification.
(B) No, because although the creditor waived the condition of payment on the first of the month, the bank reinstated it.
(C) Yes, because although the creditor waived the condition of payment on the first of the month, the creditor could not assign to the bank his right to reinstate that condition.
(D) Yes, because the creditor could assign to the bank only those rights the creditor had in the contract at the time of the assignment.

Question 99

Al and Bill are identical twins. Al, angry at his neighbor, said, "You'd better stay out of my way. The next time I find you around here, I'll beat you up." Two days later, while in the neighborhood, the neighbor saw Bill coming toward him. As Bill came up to the neighbor, Bill raised his hand. Thinking Bill was Al and fearing bodily harm, the neighbor struck Bill.

If Bill asserts a claim against the neighbor and the neighbor relies on the privilege of self-defense, the neighbor will

(A) not prevail, because Bill was not an aggressor.

(B) not prevail unless Bill intended his gesture as a threat.

(C) prevail if the neighbor honestly believed that Bill would attack him.

(D) prevail only if a reasonable person under the circumstances would have believed that Bill would attack him

Question 100

Re-direct examination of a witness must be permitted in which of the following circumstances?

(A) To reply to any matter raised in cross-examination.

(B) Only to reply to significant new matter raised in cross-examination.

(C) Only to reiterate the essential elements of the case.

(D) Only to supply significant information inadvertently omitted on direct examination.

QUESTIONS

PRACTICE MBE— P.M. EXAM

Directions: Each of the questions or incomplete statements below is followed by four suggested answers or completions. You are to choose the *best* of the stated alternatives. Answer all questions according to the generally accepted view, except where otherwise noted.

For the purposes of this test, you are to assume that Articles 1 and 2 of the Uniform Commercial Code have been adopted. You are also to assume relevant application of Article 9 of the UCC concerning fixtures. The Federal Rules of Evidence are deemed to control. The terms "Constitution," "constitutional," and "unconstitutional" refer to the federal Constitution unless indicated to the contrary. You are to assume that there is no applicable statute unless otherwise specified; however, survival actions and claims for wrongful death should be assumed to be available where applicable. You should assume that joint and several liability, with pure comparative negligence, is the relevant rule unless otherwise indicated.

QUESTIONS

PRACTICE MBE—P.M. EXAM

Question 101

A four-year-old child sustained serious injuries when a playmate pushed him from between two parked cars into the street, where he was struck by a car. The child, by his representative, sued the driver of the car, the playmate's parents, and his own parents. At trial, the child's total injuries were determined to be $100,000. The playmate's parents were determined to be 20 percent at fault because they had failed to adequately supervise her. The driver was found to be 50 percent at fault. The child's own parents were determined to be 30 percent at fault for failure to adequately supervise him. The court has adopted the pure comparative negligence doctrine, with joint and several liability, in place of the common-law rules relating to plaintiff's fault. In addition, the common-law doctrines relating to intra-family liability have been abrogated.

How much, if anything, is the child's representative entitled to recover from the driver?

(A) $30,000
(B) $50,000
(C) $100,000
(D) $0

Question 102

In 2004, the owner of a 100-acre tract, prepared and duly recorded a subdivision plan that called for the development of the tract. The plan showed 90 one-acre lots and a ten-acre tract in the center that was designated "Future Public School." The owner published and distributed a brochure promoting the development that emphasized the proximity of the lots to the school property and indicated potential tax savings "because the school district will not have to expend tax money to acquire this property." There is no specific statute concerning the dedication of school sites.

The owner sold 50 of the lots to individual purchasers. Each deed referred to the recorded plan and also contained the following clause: "No mobile homes shall be erected on any lot within the development." A dentist was one of the original purchasers from the owner.

In 2010, the owner sold the remaining 40 lots and the ten-acre tract to a real estate speculator by a deed that referred to the plan and contained the restriction relating to mobile homes. The speculator sold the 40 lots to individual purchasers and the ten-acre tract to a purchaser. None of the deeds from the speculator referred to the plan or contained any reference to mobile homes.

The purchaser has announced his intention of erecting a fast food restaurant on the ten-acre tract and the dentist has filed an action to enjoin him. If the dentist wins, it will be because

(A) the dentist has an equitable servitude concerning the use of the tract.
(B) the dentist, as a taxpayer, has legal interest in the use of the tract.
(C) the dentist is a creditor beneficiary of the owner's promise with respect to the tract.
(D) the purchaser is not a bona fide purchaser.

Question 103

A husband and wife took their 12-year-old son to a political rally to hear a controversial U.S. senator speak. The speaker was late, and the wife stepped outside to smoke a cigarette. While there, she saw a man placing what she believed to be a bomb against a wall at the back of the building. She went back inside and told her husband what she had seen. Without alerting anyone, they took their son and left. Some 20 minutes later, the bomb exploded, killing 8 persons and injuring 50. In the jurisdiction, murder in the first degree is defined as an intentional homicide committed with premeditation and deliberation; murder in the second degree is defined as all other murder at common law; and manslaughter is defined as either a homicide in the heat of passion arising from adequate provocation or a homicide caused by gross negligence or reckless indifference to consequence.

As to the deaths of the eight persons, what crime, if any, did the wife commit?

(A) Manslaughter
(B) Murder in the first degree
(C) Murder in the second degree
(D) No crime

Question 104

A lender met a borrower on the street, demanded that the borrower pay a debt owed to the lender, and threatened to punch the borrower in the nose. A fight ensued between them. A passerby came upon the scene just as the lender was about to kick the borrower in the head. Noting that the lender was getting the better of the fight, the passerby pointed a gun at the lender and said, "Stop, or I'll shoot." If the lender asserts a claim against the passerby based on assault, will the lender prevail?

(A) Yes, because the passerby threatened to use deadly force.
(B) Yes, unless the passerby was related to the borrower.
(C) No, if it was apparent that the lender was about to inflict serious bodily harm upon the borrower.
(D) No, because the lender was the original aggressor by threatening the borrower with a battery.

Question 105

In January, a teacher contracted with a summer camp to serve as its head counselor at a salary of $10,000 for ten weeks of service from the first of June to the middle of August. In March, the camp notified the teacher that it had hired someone else to act as head counselor and that the teacher's services would not be needed. In April, the teacher spent $200 traveling to interview at the only other nearby summer camp for a position as its head counselor. The teacher was not chosen for that job. The teacher then took a position teaching in a local summer school at a salary of $6,000 for the same ten-week period as the summer camp.

In a breach-of-contract action against the camp, to which of the following amounts, as damages, is the teacher entitled?

(A) $4,000
(B) $4,200
(C) $10,000
(D) $10,200

Question 106

A state legislature received complaints from accident victims who, in the days immediately following their accidents, had received unwelcome and occasionally misleading telephone calls on behalf of medical care providers. The callers warned of the risks of not obtaining prompt medical evaluation to detect injuries resulting from accidents and offered free examinations to determine whether the victims had suffered any injuries.

In response to these complaints, the legislature enacted a law prohibiting medical care providers from soliciting any accident victim by telephone within 30 days of his or her accident.

Which of the following is the most useful argument for the state to use in defending the constitutionality of the law?

(A) Because the commercial speech that is the subject of this law includes some speech that is misleading, the First Amendment does not limit the power of the state to regulate that speech.
(B) Because the law regulates only commercial speech, the state need only demonstrate that the restriction is rationally related to achieving the state's legitimate interests in protecting the privacy of accident victims and in regulating the medical profession.
(C) The state has substantial interests in protecting the privacy of accident victims and in regulating the practice of medical care providers, and the law is narrowly tailored to achieve the state's objectives.
(D) The law is a reasonable time, place, and manner regulation.

Question 107

A plaintiff sues a bar for injuries suffered in an automobile accident caused by a drunk motorist, who had been a patron of that bar. The plaintiff claims that the motorist was permitted to drink too much liquor at the bar before the accident.

A witness who was in the bar before the accident testified that, on the night of the accident, the motorist was drunk. The witness then proposed to testify that he remarked to his companion, "He [the motorist] is so drunk he can't even stand up."

The witness's remark to his companion is

(A) admissible as an excited utterance.
(B) admissible as a prior consistent statement.
(C) admissible as a statement by the witness regarding a condition he observed, made while he was observing it.
(D) inadmissible if there was no evidence that the witness had expertise in determining drunkenness.

Question 108

A sand company operated an installation for distributing sand and gravel. The installation was adjacent to a residential area. On the company grounds there was a chute with polished metal sides for loading sand and gravel into trucks. The trucks being loaded stopped on the public street below the chute.

After closing hours, a plywood screen was placed in the chute and the ladder used for inspection was removed to another section of the installation. For several months, however, a number of children, eight to ten years of age, had been playing on company property and the adjoining street after closing hours. The children found the ladder and also discovered that they could remove the plywood screen from the chute and slide down to the street below. The company knew of this activity.

One evening, the children were using the chute as a play device. As an automobile driven by a commuter approached the chute, an eight-year-old boy slid down just in front of the automobile. The commuter applied her brakes, but they suddenly failed, and she hit and injured the boy. The commuter saw the child in time to have avoided hitting him if her brakes had worked properly. Two days previously, the commuter had taken her car to a garage to have her brakes inspected. The garage inspected the brakes and told her that the brakes were in perfect working order. Claims were asserted on behalf of the boy by his proper legal representative against the company, the commuter, and the garage.

On the boy's claim against the company, will the boy prevail?

(A) Yes, if the company could have effectively secured the chute at moderate cost.

(B) Yes, because the company is strictly liable for harm resulting from an artificial condition on its property.

(C) No, if the commuter had the last clear chance to avoid the injury.

(D) No, because the boy was a trespasser.

Question 109

A rectangular parcel of undeveloped land contained three acres and had 150 feet of frontage on a public street. The applicable zoning ordinance required that a buildable lot contain at least two acres and have frontage of not less than 100 feet on a public street.

A brother and sister owned the land as tenants in common, the brother owning a one-third interest and the sister owning a two-thirds interest. Neither of them owned any other real property.

The sister brought an appropriate action to partition the land and proposed that a two-acre rectangular lot with 100 feet of frontage be set off to her and that a one-acre rectangular lot with 50 feet of frontage be set off to the brother. The brother's defense included a demand that the land be sold and its proceeds be divided one-third to the brother and two-thirds to the sister.

Who will prevail?

(A) The brother, because partition by sale is the preferred remedy, unless a fair price is not the likely result of a sale.

(B) The brother, because the zoning ordinance makes it impossible to divide the land fairly.

(C) The sister, because partition by sale is not appropriate if the subject property can be physically divided.

(D) The sister, because the ratio of the two lots that would result from her proposal conforms exactly to the ownership ratio.

Question 110

Plaintiff is an insurance company that is incorporated in State A and has its principal place of business in State B. It provides liability insurance coverage for automobile accidents. Plaintiff wrote a liability policy on Driver, a State C resident, the face value of which was $1 million. (This was the maximum amount Plaintiff would be committed to pay for claims against Driver arising out of multiple accidents in any single 6-month policy period.) Plaintiff then received claims filed by seven different individuals against Driver, all of whom were involved in different car accidents in which the other driver was Driver during a single 6-month policy period. Four of the claimants are citizens of State C; two of the claimants are citizens of State D; and the seventh is a citizen of State B. All had brought suits in various state courts against Driver (who was and is insolvent) and received default judgments that total $2 million. Under relevant state-law insurance principles, Plaintiff is responsible to pay the full amount of these judgments, subject to the $1 million aggregate policy limit.

Plaintiff has filed a statutory interpleader action in State C federal district court to determine which of the claimants, if any, should receive payment under Driver's insurance policy and how much each should receive. Plaintiff has caused service to be made on each of the seven claimants. One claimant, a citizen of State C, has moved to have the interpleader action dismissed for lack of subject-matter jurisdiction.

Should the court grant the motion to dismiss the interpleader action for lack of subject-matter jurisdiction?

(A) Yes, because complete diversity does not exist between Plaintiff and the seven claimants.

(B) No, because two or more claimants are citizens of different states and the amount in controversy exceeds the statutory amount.

(C) Yes, because although diversity-of-citizenship is present, the amount in controversy is less than $5 million, the statutory amount for high-stakes, multi-state disputes.

(D) Yes, because the competing claims do not have a common origin and do not arise out of the same transaction.

Question 111

A father was fired from his job. Too proud to apply for unemployment benefits, he used his savings to feed his family. When one of his children became ill, he did not seek medical attention for the child at a state clinic because he did not want to accept what he regarded as charity. Eventually, weakened by malnutrition, the child died as a result of the illness. The father has committed

(A) murder.

(B) involuntary manslaughter.

(C) voluntary manslaughter.

(D) no form of criminal homicide.

Question 112

In a personal injury case, the plaintiff sued a retail store for injuries she sustained from a fall in the store. The plaintiff alleged that the store negligently allowed its entryway to become slippery due to snow tracked in from the sidewalk. When the plaintiff threatened to sue, the store's manager said, "I know that there was slush on that marble entry, but I think your four-inch-high heels were the real cause of your fall. So let's agree that we'll pay your medical bills, and you release us from any claims you might have." The plaintiff refused the offer. At trial, the plaintiff seeks to testify to the manager's statement that "there was slush on that marble entry."

Is the statement about the slush on the floor admissible?

(A) No, because it is a statement made in the course of compromise negotiations.

(B) No, because the manager denied that the slippery condition was the cause of the plaintiff's fall.

(C) Yes, as an admission by an agent about a matter within the scope of his authority.

(D) Yes, because the rule excluding offers of compromise does not protect statements of fact made during compromise negotiations.

Question 113

A driver was injured when her Model X car suddenly swerved off the road and hit a tree. The driver sued the car's manufacturer in federal district court based on diversity; the suit claimed that the steering wheel failed on account of a manufacturing defect, causing the swerve. At an appropriate time, the driver's lawyer submitted a Rule 34 request that the manufacturer produce in hard copy form all accident reports submitted to the manufacturer during the prior 15 years by any owner of any make or model car manufactured by the company, if the owner alleged that the accident may have been due to a product defect, whether of the steering wheel or any other part of the vehicle. Within the time allowed for a response, the manufacturer submitted a written response to the request: (1) stating that it would make available for inspection all accident reports in which the owner mentioned a possibility that the accident was caused by a steering-wheel defect; but (2) objecting to the request as it related to reports of possible defects of components other than the steering wheel, on the grounds that the burden and expense of identifying and producing such documents was not proportional to the needs of the case, and vastly outweighed the document's relevance to the driver's claim.

After the driver's lawyer received this response, she made no attempt to contact the manufacturer's lawyer. Instead, the driver's lawyer made a motion in the court where the action was pending, seeking an order to compel the manufacturer to produce the accident reports as to which the manufacturer had made its objection. The court gave both sides the opportunity to be heard both with respect to the merits of the driver's motion, as well as with respect to any sanctions against the losing party (whichever party that turned out to be) that might be appropriate in the circumstances. Which of the following is the most legally accurate statement about what sanctions the court may, must, or may not issue after it decides the motion on the merits?

(A) If the court wholly denies the motion, the court must order the driver (and/or her lawyer) to pay the manufacturer's attorney's fees incurred in opposing the motion, if the court believes that the motion was not substantially justified and that such a fee award would not be unjust.

(B) If the court wholly denies the motion, the court has discretion whether or not to order the driver (and/or her lawyer) to pay the manufacturer's attorney's fees incurred in opposing the motion, except that the court may not order such a fee award if the court believes that the motion was substantially justified or that such a fee award would not be unjust.

(C) If the court wholly denies the motion, the court may not order the driver (and/or her lawyer) to pay the manufacturer's attorney's fees incurred in opposing the motion, regardless of whether the motion was substantially justified, because the manufacturer did not move for a protective order before the driver made her motion to compel discovery.

(D) If the court wholly grants the motion, the court has discretion whether or not to order the manufacturer (and/or its lawyer) to pay the driver's attorney's fees, if the court concludes that the manufacturer's objection was not substantially justified.

Question 114

A man intensely disliked his neighbors, who were of a different race. One night, intending to frighten his neighbors, he spray-painted their house with racial epithets and threats that they would be lynched. The man was arrested and prosecuted under a state law providing that "any person who threatens violence against another person with the intent to cause that person to fear for his or her life or safety may be imprisoned for up to five years." In defense, the man claimed that he did not intend to lynch his neighbors, but only to scare them so that they would move away.

Can the man constitutionally be convicted under this law?

(A) No, because he was only communicating his views and had not commenced any overt action against the neighbors.

(B) Yes, because he was engaged in trespass when he painted the words on his neighbors' house.
(C) Yes, because his communication was a threat by which he intended to intimidate his neighbors.
(D) Yes, because his communication was racially motivated and thus violated the protections of the Thirteenth Amendment.

Question 115

A debtor's liquidated and undisputed $1,000 debt to a creditor was due on March 1. On March 15, the creditor told the debtor that if the debtor promised to pay the $1,000 on or before December 1, then the creditor wouldn't sue to collect the debt. The debtor orally agreed. On April 1, the creditor sued the debtor to collect the debt that had become due on March 1. The debtor moved to dismiss the creditor's complaint.

Should the court grant the debtor's motion?

(A) No, because there was no consideration to support the creditor's promise not to sue.
(B) No, because there was no consideration to support the debtor's promise to pay $1,000 on December 1.
(C) Yes, because a promise to allow a debtor to delay payment on a past debt is enforceable without consideration.
(D) Yes, because the debtor was bargaining for the creditor's forbearance.

Question 116

During a comprehensive evaluation of an adult patient's psychiatric condition, the psychiatrist failed to diagnose the patient's suicidal state. One day after the misdiagnosis, the patient committed suicide. The patient's father, immediately after having been told of his son's suicide, suffered severe emotional distress, which resulted in a stroke. The patient's father was not present at his son's appointment with the psychiatrist and did not witness the suicide. The father brought an action against the psychiatrist to recover for his severe emotional distress and the resulting stroke.

Will the father prevail?

(A) No, because the father did not sustain a physical impact.
(B) No, because the psychiatrist's professional duty did not extend to the harms suffered by the patient's father.
(C) Yes, because the father was a member of the patient's immediate family.
(D) Yes, because the psychiatrist reasonably could have foreseen that a misdiagnosis would result in the patient's suicide and the resulting emotional distress of the patient's father.

Question 117

In 1995, the owner in fee simple absolute of a five-acre tract of land conveyed his land. The relevant, operative words of the deed conveyed to "my church [a duly organized religious body having power to hold property] for the life of my son [who was named in the deed], and from and after the death of my said son, to all of my grandchildren and their heirs and assigns in equal shares: provided, my church shall use the premises for church purposes only."

In an existing building on the tract, the church immediately began to conduct religious services and other activities normally associated with a church.

In 2010, the church granted to a landscaper a right to remove sand and gravel from a one-half acre portion of the tract upon the payment of royalty. The landscaper has regularly removed sand and gravel since 2010 and paid a royalty to the church. The church has continued to conduct religious services and other church activities on the tract.

All four of the living grandchildren of the owner, joined by a guardian ad litem to represent unborn grandchildren, instituted suit against the church and the landscaper seeking damages for the removal of sand and gravel and an injunction preventing further acts of removal. There is no applicable statute. Which of the following best describes the likely disposition of this lawsuit?

(A) The plaintiffs will succeed, because the interest of the church terminated with the first removal of sand and gravel.
(B) The church and the landscaper will be enjoined, and damages will be recovered but impounded for future distribution.
(C) The injunction will be granted, but damages will be denied, because the owner and his son are not parties to the action.
(D) Damage will be awarded, but the injunction will be denied.

Question 118

In which of the following cases is a conviction of the named defendant for robbery LEAST likely to be upheld?

(A) The defendant forced his way into a woman's home, bound her, and compelled her to tell him that her jewelry was in an adjoining room. The defendant went into the room, took the jewelry, and fled.
(B) A confederate of the defendant pushed a man in order to cause him to lose his balance and drop his briefcase. The defendant picked up the briefcase and ran off with it.
(C) Having induced a woman to enter his hotel room, the defendant forced her to telephone her maid to tell the maid to bring certain jewelry to the hotel. The defendant locked the woman in the bathroom while he accepted the jewelry from the maid when she arrived.
(D) The defendant unbuttoned the vest of a man too drunk to notice and removed his wallet. A minute later, the victim missed his wallet and accused the defendant

of taking it. The defendant pretended to be insulted, slapped the victim, and went off with the wallet.

Question 119

A six-year-old child, while playing on the sidewalk in front of his parents' home, was run over by a motorcyclist. The motorcyclist, a recent college graduate, was visiting his aunt and uncle, who lived next door to the child and his family. The motorcycle was owned by the aunt and uncle, and the motorcyclist had borrowed it without their permission or knowledge. The child's family intends to file a federal lawsuit based on diversity, seeking recovery for the child's injuries on account of the motorcyclist's negligence. Which of the following statements is correct about the parties to the action?

(A) The child must be listed as the plaintiff, because he is the real party in interest.
(B) A guardian or parent of the child may be listed as the plaintiff, without the need to include the child as a plaintiff.
(C) The motorcyclist's insurance carrier must be joined as a defendant because it is the real party in interest on the defense side.
(D) The motorcyclist's aunt and uncle must be joined as co-defendants because they will be either primarily or secondarily liable.

Question 120

A creditor received a valid judgment against a debtor and promptly and properly filed the judgment in the county. Two years later, the debtor purchased land in the county and promptly and properly recorded the warranty deed to it. Subsequently, the debtor borrowed $30,000 from his aunt, signing a promissory note for that amount, which note was secured by a mortgage on the land. The mortgage was promptly and properly recorded. The aunt failed to make a title search before making the loan. The debtor made no payment to the creditor and defaulted on the mortgage loan from his aunt. A valid judicial foreclosure proceeding was held, in which the creditor, the aunt, and the debtor were named parties. A dispute arose as to which lien has priority. A statute of the jurisdiction provides: "Any judgment properly filed shall, for ten years from filing, be a lien on the real property then owned or subsequently acquired by any person against whom the judgment is rendered." A second statute of the jurisdiction provides: "No unrecorded conveyance or mortgage of real property shall be good against subsequent purchasers for value without notice, who shall first record."

Who has the prior lien?

(A) The aunt, because a judgment lien is subordinate to a mortgage lien.
(B) The aunt, because she is a mortgagee under a purchase money mortgage.
(C) The creditor, because its judgment was filed first.
(D) The creditor, because the aunt had a duty to make a title search of the property.

Question 121

At a trial of a contract dispute, the plaintiff offered to testify to what the defendant said in a private conversation between the two of them, which the plaintiff had secretly recorded on an audiotape that she did not offer in evidence.

Is the plaintiff's testimony admissible?

(A) Yes, because the plaintiff has personal knowledge of the statement of a party-opponent.
(B) Yes, because the original document rule does not apply to audiotapes.
(C) No, because the statement must be proved by introduction of the audiotape itself.
(D) No, because of the plaintiff's deception, even if the recording was not illegal.

Question 122

A student published a highly critical written online review of a college course she attended taught by a professor; the review claimed that the professor delivered false information and handed out written materials that she had plagiarized. The professor filed a complaint for defamation against the student in federal court based on diversity; the complaint described in detail the student's statements and how they were false. The suit sought $100,000 in damages for "intangible injury to the plaintiff's professional reputation," and also sought "reasonable attorney's fees." The professor's lawyer arranged for proper personal service of the summons and complaint, but the student never answered the complaint or took any other action regarding the suit. After several months passed, the clerk of the court noted on the court's docket that the student had defaulted and sent a letter to the student's last known address warning that a default judgment would be entered against her if she did not object within 30 days. After the 30-day period passed without an objection, the professor's lawyer applied in writing to have the clerk enter a default judgment for $110,000 against the student; the application was accompanied by an affidavit from the professor saying that she had suffered $100,000 in loss as claimed in the complaint, plus had incurred legal fees (documented in the affidavit) of $10,000.

Is the clerk authorized to enter the requested $110,000 judgment against the student?

(A) No, because only the judge may enter such a judgment, and only after having made an independent determination of what would constitute a reasonable amount of damages and attorney's fees in the circumstances.

(B) No, unless the clerk conducts an evidentiary hearing, as the result of which the clerk concludes that $100,000 is a reasonable estimate of the damages actually suffered by the professor from the defamation and that $10,000 was actually and reasonably spent by her on legal fees.

(C) Yes, because once the professor requested the entry of the judgment and submitted an affidavit stating that the sum due was $110,000, the clerk was required to enter judgment for that amount without further notice to the student.

(D) Yes, but only if the professor's lawyer or the clerk serves the student with at least seven days advance written notice that the clerk will conduct an evidentiary hearing as to the amount of damages and the clerk then conducts such a hearing based on which the clerk concludes that the $110,000 is a reasonable estimate of the professor's damages and attorney's fees.

Question 123

A freelance photographer took a picture of a sports player in front of a shoe store. The player was a nationally known amateur basketball star, who had received much publicity in the press. At the time, the window display in the shoe store featured "Jumpers," a well-known make of basketball shoes. The photographer sold the picture, greatly enlarged, to the shoe store and told the shoe store that the photographer had the player's approval to do so and that the player had consented to the shoe store's showing the enlarged picture in the window. The shoe store made no effort to ascertain whether the player had given his consent to the photographer. In fact, the player did not even know that the photographer had taken the picture. The shoe store put the enlarged picture in the window with the display of "Jumpers" shoes. The college that the player attended believed that the player had intentionally endorsed the shoe store and "Jumpers" shoes, and the college cancelled his athletic scholarship.

If the player asserts a claim based on invasion of privacy against the shoe store, will the player prevail?

(A) Yes, because the photographer had no right to take the player's picture.

(B) Yes, because the shoe store, without the player's permission, used the player's picture for profit.

(C) No, because the player was already a basketball star who had received much publicity in the press.

(D) No, because the shoe store believed it had permission to put the picture in its window.

Question 124

Plaintiff, a State A partnership, filed suit in federal district court in State B against Defendant, a State C corporation. The complaint alleged that Defendant violated a federal antitrust statute. The antitrust statute allows a private party to bring a civil damage suit against violators of the statute. The statute also provides that in any such suit, nationwide service-of-process may be made against, and personal jurisdiction exercised over, any defendant found within the United States.

Defendant has asserted that the court's exercise of *in personam* jurisdiction against Defendant would violate Defendant's constitutional right to due process. When the court decides whether Defendant is correct, the primary issue will be whether:

(A) Defendant has minimum contacts with State A, as required by the Due Process Clause of the Fifth Amendment to the United States Constitution.

(B) Defendant has minimum contacts with the United States, as required by the Fifth Amendment to the United States Constitution.

(C) Defendant has minimum contacts with State A, as required by the Due Process Clause of the Fourteenth Amendment to the United States Constitution.

(D) Defendant has minimum contacts with the United States, as required by the Due Process Clause of the Fourteenth Amendment to the United States Constitution.

Question 125

A plaintiff sued a defendant on a product liability claim. A witness testified for the plaintiff. On cross-examination, which of the following questions is the trial judge most likely to rule **improper**?

(A) "Isn't it a fact that you are the witness's close friend?"

(B) "Isn't it true that you are known in the community as a lush because of your addiction to alcohol?"

(C) "Didn't you fail to report some income on your tax return last year?"

(D) "Weren't you convicted, seven years ago in this court, of obtaining money under false pretenses?"

Question 126

In an action to recover for personal injuries arising out of an automobile accident, a plaintiff calls a bystander to testify. Claiming the privilege against self-incrimination, the bystander refuses to answer a question as to whether she was at the scene of the accident. The plaintiff moves that the bystander be ordered to answer the question. The judge should allow the bystander to remain silent only if

(A) the judge is convinced that she will incriminate herself.
(B) there is clear and convincing evidence that she will incriminate herself.
(C) there is a preponderance of evidence that she will incriminate herself.
(D) the judge believes that there is some reasonable possibility that she will incriminate herself.

Question 127

The owner of a house and lot leased the same to a tenant for a term of five years. In addition to the house, there was also an unattached, two-car brick garage located on the lot. The tenant earned his living as an employee in a local grocery store, but his hobby consisted of wood carving and the making of small furniture. The tenant installed a work bench, electric lights, and a radiator in the garage. He also laid pipes connecting the radiator with the heating plant inside the house. Thereafter the owner mortgaged the premises to a bank to secure a loan. The tenant was not given notice of the mortgage, but the mortgage was recorded. Still later, the owner defaulted on the mortgage payments, and the bank began foreclosure proceedings, as it was entitled to do under the terms of the mortgage. By this time the tenant's lease was almost ended. The tenant began the removal of the equipment he had installed in the garage. The bank brought an action to enjoin the removal of the equipment mentioned above. Both the tenant and the owner were named as defendants.

If the court refuses the injunction, it will be because

(A) the tenant was without notice of the mortgage.
(B) the circumstances reveal that the equipment was installed for the tenant's exclusive benefit.
(C) in the absence of a contrary agreement, a residential tenant is entitled to remove any personal property he voluntarily brings upon the premises.
(D) the Statute of Frauds precludes the bank from claiming any interest in the equipment.

Question 128

A bottling company sent a purchase order to a wholesaler that stated, "Ship 100,000 empty plastic bottles at the posted price." Two days after receipt of this purchase order, the wholesaler shipped the bottles and the bottling company accepted delivery of them. A week after the bottles were delivered, the bottling company received the wholesaler's acknowledgment form, which included a provision disclaiming consequential damages. After using the bottles for two months, the bottling company discovered a defect in the bottles that caused its product to leak from them. The bottling company recalled 10,000 of the bottles containing its product, incurring lost profits of $40,000.

Assuming all appropriate defenses are seasonably raised, will the bottling company succeed in recovering $40,000 in consequential damages from the wholesaler?

(A) No, because buyers are generally not entitled to recover consequential damages.
(B) No, because the bottling company's acceptance of the goods also constituted an acceptance of the terms included in the wholesaler's acknowledgement.
(C) Yes, because the disclaimer of consequential damages is unconscionable.
(D) Yes, because the wholesaler's acknowledgment did not alter the terms of an existing contract between the parties.

Question 129

The owner of a milk container manufacturing firm sought to focus public attention on the milk packaging law of a state in order to have it repealed. On a weekday at 12:00 p.m., he delivered an excited, animated, and loud harangue on the steps of the state capitol building in front of the main entryway. An audience of 200 onlookers, who gathered on the steps, heckled him and laughed as he delivered his tirade. The owner repeatedly stated, gesturing expressively and making faces, that "the damned milk packaging law is stupid," and that "I will strangle every one of those damned legislators I can get hold of because this law they created proves they are all too dumb to live." After about 15 minutes, he stopped speaking, and the amused crowd dispersed.

There are three relevant statutes of the state. The first statute prohibits "all speech making, picketing, and public gatherings of every sort on the Capitol steps in front of the main entryway between 7:45 a.m.-8:15 a.m., 11:45 a.m.-12:15 p.m., 12:45 p.m.-1:15 p.m., and 4:45 p.m.-5:15 p.m., on Capitol working days."

If the owner is prosecuted under the "Capitol steps" statute and defends on constitutional grounds, which of the following best describes the proper burden of proof?

(A) He would have to prove that the state did not have a rational basis for enacting this statute.
(B) He would have to prove that the state did not have a compelling need for this statute or that it had less restrictive means by which it could satisfy that need.
(C) The state would have to prove that it had a rational basis for enacting this statute.
(D) The state would have to prove that it had a compelling need for this statute and that there were no less restrictive means by which it could satisfy that need.

Question 130

A motorist arranged to borrow his friend's car to drive for one day while the motorist's car was being repaired. The friend knew that the brakes on his car were faulty and might fail in an emergency. The friend forgot to tell the motorist about the brakes when the motorist picked up the car, but the friend did telephone the motorist's wife, and told her about them. The wife, however, forgot to tell the motorist.

The motorist was driving his friend's car at a reasonable rate of speed and within the posted speed limit, with his wife as a passenger. Another car, driven by a sightseer, crossed in front of the motorist at an intersection and in violation of the traffic signal. The motorist tried to stop, but the brakes failed, and the two cars collided. If the brakes had been in proper working order, the motorist could have stopped in time to avoid the collision. The motorist and his wife were injured.

If the motorist asserts a claim against the friend, will the motorist prevail?

(A) Yes, in negligence, because the friend knew the brakes were faulty and failed to tell the motorist.
(B) Yes, in strict liability in tort, because the car was defective and the friend lent it to the motorist.
(C) No, because the friend was a gratuitous lender, and thus his duty of care was slight.
(D) No, because the failure of the wife to tell the motorist about the brakes was the cause in fact of the motorist's harm.

Question 131

In which of the following situations is the defendant most likely to be guilty of larceny?

(A) The defendant took the victim's television set, with the intention of returning it the next day. However, he dropped it and damaged it beyond repair.
(B) The defendant went into a victim's house and took $100 in the belief that the victim had damaged the defendant's car to that amount.
(C) Mistakenly believing that larceny does not include taking a dog, the defendant took his neighbor's dog and sold it.
(D) Unreasonably mistaking his neighbor's car for his own, the defendant got into his neighbor's car in a parking lot and drove it home.

Question 132

A member of a state legislature is prosecuted in federal court for a violation of the Federal Securities Act arising out of the activities of a state-owned corporation. The legislator's defense includes a claim that the alleged wrongful acts were committed in the course of legislative business and are immune from scrutiny.

Which of the following is the strongest constitutional argument supporting the legislator?

(A) Because of doctrines of federalism, federal law generally cannot be applied to state legislators acting in the course of their official duties.
(B) State legislators enjoy the protection of the Speech and Debate Clause of the U.S. Constitution.
(C) A federal court must follow state law respecting the scope of legislative immunity.
(D) To apply the Federal Securities Act to state legislators would violate the Due Process Clause.

Question 133

A defendant was charged in federal court with selling a controlled substance (heroin) in interstate commerce. At trial, the prosecutor introduced evidence that the defendant obtained the substance from a supplier in Kansas City and delivered it in Chicago. The defendant denied that the substance in question was heroin, but he introduced no contrary evidence on the issue of transportation.

Which of the following instructions regarding judicial notice may the judge legitimately give the jury?

(A) "If you find that the defendant obtained the drugs in Kansas City and delivered them to Chicago, I instruct you to find that the substance was sold in an interstate transaction."
(B) "If you find that the defendant obtained the drugs in Kansas City and delivered them to Chicago, then the burden of persuasion is on the defendant to establish that the transaction was not interstate."
(C) "If you find that the defendant obtained the drugs in Kansas City and delivered them to Chicago, then you may, but you are not required to, find that the transaction was interstate in nature."
(D) "I instruct you that there is a presumption that the substance was sold in an interstate transaction, but the burden of persuasion on that issue is still on the government."

Question 134

An associate professor in the pediatrics department of a local medical school was denied tenure. He asked a national education lobbying organization to represent him in his efforts to have the tenure decision reversed. In response to a letter from the organization on the professor's behalf, the dean of the medical school wrote to the organization explaining truthfully that the professor had been denied tenure because of reports that he had abused two of his former patients. Several months later, after a thorough investigation, the allegations were proven false and the professor was granted tenure. He had remained working at the medical school at full pay during the tenure decision review process and thus suffered no pecuniary harm.

In a suit for libel by the professor against the dean of the medical school, will the professor prevail?

(A) No, because the professor invited the libel.
(B) No, because the professor suffered no pecuniary loss.
(C) Yes, because the dean had a duty to investigate the rumor before repeating it.
(D) Yes, because the dean's defamatory statement was in the form of a writing.

Question 135

Plaintiff, an individual who lives and works in State A, was visiting State B. While crossing the street, he was struck by a car driven by Defendant, a citizen of State B. Plaintiff was seriously injured and brought a diversity suit for negligence against Defendant in federal court for the district of State B for $200,000. Plaintiff would like to obtain, during the discovery process, as much information as possible about any liability insurance coverage that Defendant may have that would cover a judgment that Plaintiff receives in the suit. Also, Plaintiff would like to obtain that information with as little effort as possible. The following statements about what information Plaintiff is entitled to, and under what procedure, are arranged in descending order of their desirability from Plaintiff's perspective. Which one represents the MOST DESIRABLE (and thus earliest-listed) outcome to which Plaintiff is entitled? Plaintiff is entitled to . . .

(A) A copy of the policy, without Plaintiff's being required to make any discovery request for it.
(B) A copy of the policy, upon Plaintiff's submission of a proper request for document production.
(C) The name of the insurance company and the policy limits, upon Plaintiff's submission of an interrogatory to Defendant asking for this information.
(D) No information about any such policy, unless Plaintiff establishes good cause for believing that the information would be relevant to a claim or defense in the case.

Question 136

Plaintiff owns and operates a retail store in State A. It licenses security software from Defendant, a corporation specializing in security technology with its principal place of business in State B and incorporated in State C. Despite the software, hackers broke into Plaintiff's financial system. Plaintiff sued Defendant in a state court in State C for breach of contract, choosing that forum because of the three plausible fora, State C had the longest statute of limitations. After a trial, Plaintiff lost on the merits; the state court held that Plaintiff's own faulty installation of the software was the sole proximate cause of the vulnerability to hackers. Plaintiff then filed a second lawsuit against Defendant, this time in federal court for the district of State C, and based on diversity jurisdiction. (Other than filing the pair of lawsuits, Plaintiff has had no contacts with State C.) This second suit essentially repeated the breach-of-contract claim that was held invalid in the first suit. Defendant in its answer raised the affirmative defense of claim preclusion. Defendant also asserted a counterclaim alleging that Plaintiff's filing of multiple lawsuits constituted the tort of wrongful use of civil proceedings; the counterclaim alleged that this tort had caused Defendant to suffer pecuniary loss (in the form of lost business profits) in excess of $75,000.

Plaintiff therefore moved to dismiss the counterclaim for (1) lack of personal jurisdiction over him; and (2) failure to properly serve him, in that no summons was served with the counterclaim (a factually-correct allegation). The court should

(A) deny the motion because a compulsory counterclaim does not require an independent basis for personal jurisdiction over the plaintiff.
(B) grant the motion because a permissive counterclaim requires an independent basis for personal jurisdiction over the plaintiff.
(C) grant the motion on the grounds that Defendant failed to properly serve Plaintiff.
(D) deny the motion because Plaintiff has effectively consented to the court's exercise of personal jurisdiction over him.

Question 137

Several sites on a mountain within federal public lands are regarded as sacred to a group that for years has gathered there to perform religious ceremonies. The U.S. Forest Service recently issued a permit to a private developer to construct a ski facility in an area that includes the sites that are sacred to the group.

The group filed suit in federal district court against the Forest Service to force cancellation of the permit. The group claimed solely that the permit violated its First Amendment right to the free exercise of religion. The Forest Service conceded that the group's religious beliefs were sincere and that the ski facility would adversely affect the group's religious practices.

In order to prevail in its First Amendment claim, what must the group show?

(A) Construction of the ski facility will have a discriminatory impact on the group's religious practices in relation to the practices of other religious groups.
(B) The burden on the group's religious practices imposed by construction of the ski facility outweighs the government's interest in allowing the facility.

(C) The Forest Service can achieve its legitimate interest in allowing the ski facility by issuing a permit that is less burdensome on the group's religious practices.
(D) The permit issued by the Forest Service is aimed at suppressing the religious practices of the group.

Question 138

In order to reduce the federal deficit, Congress enacted a statute imposing a 5 percent national retail sales tax. The tax was levied upon all retail sales in the United States and applied equally to the sales of all kinds of goods.

Is this tax constitutional as applied to retail sales of newspapers?

(A) Yes, because it is within Congress's power to tax.
(B) Yes, because the tax is necessary to serve the compelling interest of balancing the federal budget.
(C) No, because retail sales taxes are within the taxing power of the states.
(D) No, because the imposition of a tax on the sale of newspapers violates the freedom of the press.

Question 139

A bakery offered a chef a permanent full-time job as a pastry chef at a salary of $2,000 per month. The chef agreed to take the position and to begin work in two weeks. In her employment application, the chef had indicated that she was seeking a permanent job. One week after the chef was hired by the bakery, a hotel offered the chef a position as a restaurant manager at a salary of $2,500 a month. The chef accepted and promptly notified the bakery that she would not report for work at the bakery.

Is the bakery likely to prevail in a lawsuit against the chef for breach of contract?

(A) No, because a contract for permanent employment would be interpreted to mean the chef could leave at any time.
(B) No, because the position the chef took with the hotel was not substantially comparable to the one she had agreed to take with the bakery.
(C) Yes, because the chef's acceptance of a permanent position meant that she agreed to leave the bakery only after a reasonable time.
(D) Yes, because the chef's failure to give the bakery a chance to match the salary offered by the hotel breached the implied right of first refusal.

Question 140

A defendant was charged with battery for allegedly attacking a man as they left a local bar together. No one else witnessed the fight. At trial, each testified that he had acted only in self-defense. The defendant called his next-door neighbor as a witness to testify as to the defendant's reputation both for truthfulness and for peacefulness. The government objected to the testimony in its entirety.

How should the court proceed?

(A) Admit the evidence in its entirety.
(B) Admit the evidence regarding the defendant's reputation for peacefulness, but exclude the evidence regarding his truthfulness.
(C) Exclude the evidence regarding the defendant's reputation for peacefulness, but admit the evidence regarding his truthfulness.
(D) Exclude the evidence in its entirety.

Question 141

Plaintiff is a privately held money-management company that is incorporated in State A and has its headquarters in State B. Defendant is an investment bank incorporated in State C and with its headquarters in State D. Plaintiff bought from Defendant certain mortgage-backed securities issued by Defendant. Five-and-a-half years after the purchase, Plaintiff sued Defendant in federal district court for the district of State C, invoking diversity jurisdiction and asserting that under State C contracts law Defendant was liable to Plaintiff for having fraudulently induced the sale by misrepresenting the securities as a triple-A rated investment when in fact they were of an inferior grade. Defendant has recently moved to dismiss the action as time-barred, on the assumption that State C's five-year statute of limitations controls; the federal court has not yet ruled on this motion. (The statute of limitations in States A, B, and D is six years.) For unknown reasons, Plaintiff has now moved to transfer the action from the State C federal district court to the federal district court for State D (which has only one judicial district). In support of this motion, Plaintiff argues (you should assume that the argument is factually correct) that the convenience of witnesses and counsel will be better served by having the action tried in State D than in State C. Defendant refuses to consent to the transfer, though its position stems from considerations not of convenience but of tactics (it would like to have the case heard by the particular State C federal judge who has been assigned it).

Which of the following statements best describes the effect the Plaintiff's transfer motion will have on the choice of which state's statute of limitations should control?

(A) If transfer is granted on Plaintiff's motion, the transferee court will apply the statute-of-limitations law of the state in which it sits (State D) to determine whether the action is time-barred, because the federal transfer-of-venue statute so requires.
(B) If transfer is granted on Plaintiff's motion, the transferee court will apply whichever state's statute-of-limitations law a State C state court would apply had the action

been brought in that court, because *Erie* principles so require.

(C) If transfer is granted on Plaintiff's motion, the transferee court will apply the law of whichever state's statute-of-limitations law a State D state court would apply had the action been brought in that court, because the federal transfer-of-venue statute requires treating the case as if it had originally been filed in the transferee court.

(D) Transfer will not be granted because, since Plaintiff chose the original forum (State C federal court) and venue properly lies in that forum, Plaintiff is not permitted to transfer the action; therefore, the State C federal court will apply whichever state's statute-of-limitations law a State C state court would apply had the action been brought in that court.

Question 142

A defendant was charged with murder. His principal defense was that he had killed in "hot blood" and should be guilty only of manslaughter. The judge instructed the jury that the state must prove guilt beyond a reasonable doubt, that the killing was presumed to be murder, and that the charge could be reduced to manslaughter, and the defendant accordingly found guilty of this lesser offense, if the defendant showed by a fair preponderance of the evidence that the killing was committed in the heat of passion on sudden provocation. The defendant was convicted of murder. On appeal, he now seeks a new trial and claims error in the judge's instructions to the jury.

The defendant's conviction will most probably be

(A) affirmed, because the judge carefully advised the jury of the state's obligation to prove guilt beyond a reasonable doubt.

(B) affirmed, because the defendant's burden to show hot blood was not one of ultimate persuasion but only one of producing evidence to rebut a legitimate presumption.

(C) reversed, because the instruction put a burden on the defendant, which denied him due process of law.

(D) reversed, because presumptions have a highly prejudicial effect and thus cannot be used on behalf of the state in a criminal case.

Question 143

Husband and Wife, American citizens, were married in State A and then moved, together with their two children, to State B. After a number of years, Husband relocated to State C, where he now works, insures his car, and votes. He decided to end his marriage and sued Wife for divorce in federal district court for the district of State B. In addition to a divorce decree, he sought joint custody of the children and a court order that each parent would contribute $25,000 per year for the next ten years to support the children.

Wife has now moved to dismiss the State B federal-court action for lack of subject-matter jurisdiction. The court should

(A) deny the motion because diversity jurisdiction is present.

(B) remand the action to a state court in State B, since that is where Husband should have brought it.

(C) transfer the action to the state courts of State A, where the marriage took place.

(D) decline to exercise jurisdiction even if the case meets the requirements for diversity jurisdiction.

Question 144

National statistics revealed a dramatic increase in the number of elementary and secondary school students bringing controlled substances to school for sale. In response, Congress enacted a statute requiring each state legislature to enact a state law making it a crime for any person to sell, within 1,000 feet of any elementary or secondary school, any controlled substance that had previously been transported in interstate commerce.

Is the federal statute constitutional?

(A) No, because Congress has no authority to require a state legislature to enact any specified legislation.

(B) No, because the sale of a controlled substance in close proximity to a school does not have a sufficiently close nexus to interstate commerce to justify its regulation by Congress.

(C) Yes, because it contains a jurisdictional provision that will ensure, on a case-by-case basis, that any particular controlled substance subject to the terms of this statute will, in fact, affect interstate commerce.

(D) Yes, because Congress possesses broad authority under both the General Welfare Clause and the Commerce Clause to regulate any activities affecting education that also have, in inseverable aggregates, a substantial effect on interstate commerce.

Question 145

On a camping trip in a state park, a hiker discovered metal signs near a rubbish heap stating, "Natural Wildlife Area No Hunting." She took two of the signs and used them to decorate her room at home. She is charged with violation of a state statute, which provides, "Any person who appropriates to his own use property owned by the state shall be guilty of a crime and shall be punished by a fine of not more than $1,000, or by imprisonment for not more than five years, or by both such fine and imprisonment."

At trial, the hiker admits taking the signs but says she believed they had been thrown away. In fact, the signs had not been abandoned.

The hiker should be found

(A) guilty, because this is a public welfare offense.
(B) guilty, because she should have inquired whether the signs were abandoned.
(C) not guilty if the jury finds she honestly believed the signs had been abandoned.
(D) not guilty unless the jury finds that the state had taken adequate steps to inform the public that the signs had not been abandoned.

Question 146

In 1965, the owner in fee simple of a large, undeveloped tract of land granted an easement to the Water District "to install, inspect, repair, maintain, and replace pipes" within a properly delineated strip of land 20 feet wide across the tract. The easement permitted the Water District to enter the tract for only the stated purposes. The Water District promptly and properly recorded the deed. In 1966, the Water District installed a water main that crossed the tract within the described strip; the Water District has not since entered the tract.

In 1970, the owner sold the tract to a purchaser, but the deed, which was promptly and properly recorded, failed to refer to the Water District easement. The purchaser built his home on the tract in 1970, and since that time he has planted and maintained, at great expense in money, time, and effort, a formal garden area that covers, among other areas, the surface of the 20-foot easement strip.

In 2011, the Water District proposed to excavate the entire length of its main in order to inspect, repair, and replace the main, to the extent necessary. At a public meeting, at which the purchaser was present, the Water District announced its plans and declared its intent to do as little damage as possible to any property involved. The purchaser objected to the Water District plans.

The purchaser asked his attorney to secure an injunction against the Water District and its proposed entry upon his property. The best advice that the attorney can give is that the purchaser's attempt to secure injunctive relief will be likely to

(A) succeed, because the purchaser's deed from the owner did not mention the easement.
(B) succeed, because more than 40 years have passed since the Water District last entered the tract.
(C) fail, because the Water District's plan is within its rights.
(D) fail, because the Water District's plan is fair and equitable.

Question 147

A woman is cited for contempt of the House of Representatives after she refused to answer certain questions posed by a House Committee concerning her acts while serving as a U.S. ambassador. A federal statute authorizes the attorney general to prosecute contempts of Congress. Pursuant to this law, the House directs the attorney general to begin criminal proceedings against the woman. A federal grand jury indicts the woman, but the attorney general refuses to sign the indictment.

Which of the following best describes the constitutionality of the attorney general's action?

(A) Illegal, because the attorney general must prosecute if the House of Representatives so directs.
(B) Illegal, because the attorney general must prosecute those who violate federal law.
(C) Legal, because ambassadors are immune from prosecution for acts committed in the course of their duties.
(D) Legal, because the decision to prosecute is an exclusively executive act.

Question 148

A home improvement store telegraphed an appliances manufacturer on June 1, "At what price will you sell 100 of your QT-Model garbage-disposal units for delivery around June 10?" Thereafter, the following communications were exchanged:

1. Telegram from the manufacturer received by the store on June 2: "You're in luck. We have only 100 QT's, all on clearance at 50 percent off usual wholesale of $120 per unit, for delivery at our shipping platform on June 12."
2. Letter from the store received in U.S. mail by the manufacturer on June 5: "I accept. Would prefer to pay in full 30 days after invoice."
3. Telegram from the manufacturer received by the store on June 6: "You must pick up at our platform and pay C.O.D."
4. Letter from the store received in U.S. mail by the manufacturer on June 9: "I don't deal with people who can't accommodate our simple requests."
5. Telegram from the store received by the manufacturer on June 10, after the manufacturer had sold and delivered all 100 of the QT's to another buyer earlier that day: "Okay. I'm over a barrel and will pick up the goods on your terms June 12." The store now sues the manufacturer for breach of contract.

Which of the following arguments will best serve the manufacturer's defense?

(A) The manufacturer's telegram received on June 2 was merely a price quotation, not an offer.
(B) The store's letter received on June 5 was not an acceptance because it varied the terms of the manufacturer's initial telegram.

(C) The store's use of the mails in response to the manufacturer's initial telegram was an ineffective method of acceptance.

(D) The store's letter received on June 9 was an unequivocal refusal to perform that excused the manufacturer even if the parties had previously formed a contract.

Question 149

A man died testate. The man's estate consisted of a residence as well as significant personal property. By his duly probated will, the man devised the residence to a friend who was specifically identified in the will. The residue of the estate was given to a stated charity.

The man's friend, although alive at the time the man executed the will, predeceased the man. The friend's wife and their child, who has a disability, survived the man.

The value of the residence has increased significantly because of recent zoning changes. There is credible extrinsic evidence that the man wanted his friend to own the residence after the man's death so that the friend and his wife could care for their child there.

There is no applicable statute.

If both the charity and the child claim the residence, to whom should the estate distribute the residence?

(A) The charity, because the devise to the friend adeemed.

(B) The charity, because the devise to the friend lapsed.

(C) The child, because extrinsic evidence exists that the man's intent was to benefit the child.

(D) The child, because no conditions of survivorship were noted in the will.

Question 150

On the lawn in front of a homeowner's home and within five feet of the public sidewalk there was a large tree. The roots of the tree caused the sidewalk to buckle severely and become dangerous. An ordinance of the city in which the homeowner lives requires adjacent landowners to keep sidewalks in safe condition. The homeowner engaged a contractor to repair the sidewalk, leaving it to the contractor to decide how the repair should be made.

The contractor dug up the sidewalk, cut back the roots of the tree, and laid a new sidewalk. Two days after the homeowner had paid the contractor the agreed price of the repair, the tree fell over onto the street and damaged a parked car.

The driver of the damaged car has asserted claims against the homeowner and the contractor, and both defendants admit that cutting the roots caused the tree to fall.

The theory on which the car driver is most likely to prevail against the homeowner is that the homeowner is

(A) strictly liable, because the tree was on his property.

(B) liable for the contractor's negligence if, to the homeowner's knowledge, the contractor was engaged in a hazardous activity.

(C) liable, because he assumed responsibility when he paid the contractor for the repair.

(D) liable on the basis of *respondeat superior.*

Question 151

On March 1, a seller orally agreed to sell his land to a buyer for $46,000 to be paid on March 31. The buyer orally agreed to pay $25,000 of the purchase price to a creditor in satisfaction of a debt that the seller said he had promised to pay the creditor.

On March 10, the buyer dictated the agreement to his secretary but omitted all reference to the payment of the $25,000 to the creditor. In typing the agreement, the secretary mistakenly typed in $45,000 rather than $46,000 as the purchase price. Neither the buyer nor the seller carefully read the writing before signing it on March 15. Neither noticed the error in price and neither raised any question concerning omission of the payment to the creditor.

Which of the following would be most important in deciding an action by the creditor against the buyer for $25,000?

(A) Whether the buyer-seller agreement was completely integrated.

(B) Whether the buyer was negligent in not having carefully read the written agreement.

(C) Whether the seller was negligent in not having carefully read the written agreement.

(D) Whether the creditor was a party to the contract.

Question 152

A seller who owned land in fee simple entered into a valid written agreement to sell the land to a buyer by installment purchase. The contract stipulated that the seller would deliver to the buyer, upon the payment of the last installment due, "a warranty deed sufficient to convey a fee simple title." The contract contained no other provision that could be construed as referring to title.

The buyer entered into possession of the land. After making 10 of the 300 installment payments obligated under the contract, the buyer discovered that there was outstanding a valid and enforceable mortgage on the land, securing the payment of a debt in the amount of 25 percent of the purchase price that the buyer had agreed to pay. There was no evidence that the seller had ever been late in payments due under the mortgage and there was no evidence of any danger of insolvency of the seller. The value of the land was then four times the amount due on the debt secured by the mortgage.

The buyer quit possession of the land, stopped making payments on the contract, and demanded that the seller repay the amounts that the buyer had paid under the contract. After the seller refused the demand, the buyer sued the seller to recover damages for the seller's alleged breach of the contract.

In such action, should damages be awarded to the buyer?

(A) Yes, because in the absence of a contrary express agreement, an obligation to convey marketable title is implied.

(B) Yes, because an installment purchase contract is treated as a mortgage and the outstanding mortgage impairs the buyer's equity of redemption.

(C) No, because an installment purchase contract is treated as a security device.

(D) No, because the time for the seller to deliver marketable title has not arrived.

Question 153

A state statute divides murder into degrees. First degree murder is defined as murder with premeditation and deliberation or a homicide in the commission of arson, rape, robbery, burglary or kidnapping. Second degree murder is all other murder at common law.

In which of the following situations is a defendant most likely to be guilty of first degree murder?

(A) Immediately after being insulted by an acquaintance, the defendant takes a knife and stabs and kills the acquaintance.

(B) Angered over having been struck by a bicyclist, the defendant buys rat poison and puts it in the bicyclist's coffee. The bicyclist drinks the coffee and dies as a result.

(C) Intending to injure his co-worker, the defendant lies in wait and, as the co-worker comes by, the defendant strikes him with a broom handle. As a result of the blow, the co-worker dies.

(D) The defendant, highly intoxicated, discovers a revolver on a table. He picks it up, points it at the babysitter, and pulls the trigger. The gun discharges, and the babysitter is killed.

Question 154

In 2010, a utility constructed a new plant for the generation of electricity. The plant burns lignite, a low-grade fuel, which is available in large quantities. Although the plant was constructed in accordance with the best practicable technology, the plant emits a substantial quantity of invisible fumes. The only way the utility can reduce the fumes is by the use of scrubbing equipment that would cost $50 million to install and would increase the retail price of generated electricity by 50 percent while reducing the volume of fumes by only 20 percent. Because of the expense of such equipment and its relative ineffectiveness, no other generating plants burning lignite use such equipment.

The plant is located in a sparsely settled rural area, remote from the large city served by the utility. A farmer owned a farm adjacent to the plant. He had farmed the land for 40 years and lived on the premises. The prevailing winds carried fumes from the new plant over the farmer's land. His 2010 crop was less than half the average size of his crop in each of the five years immediately preceding the construction of the plant. It can be established that the fumes caused the crop reduction.

The farmer's hay fever, from which he had long suffered, became worse in 2011. Physicians advised him that the lignite fumes were affecting it and that serious lung disease would soon result unless he moved away from the plant. He did so, selling his farm at its reasonable market value, which was then $10,000 less than before the construction of the plant.

If the farmer asserts a claim based on nuisance against the utility for damages for personal injuries, will the farmer prevail?

(A) No, because there is no practicable way for the utility to reduce the fumes.

(B) No, because the utility's acts constituted a public nuisance.

(C) Yes, because the farmer's personal injuries were within the scope of the liability imposed on the utility.

(D) Yes, because the generation of electricity is an ultrahazardous activity.

Question 155

A collector bought from a gallery a painting correctly described in the parties' signed contract as a "one-of-a-kind self-portrait" by a famous artist who had recently died. The contract price was $100,000 in cash, payable one month after a truck carrier delivered the painting to the collector.

The painting was damaged in transit. The collector timely rejected it after inspection and immediately notified the gallery of the rejection. The gallery then sold the painting to a third party. It informed the collector that it would pick up the painting within a couple of weeks. Two weeks later, before the gallery picked up the painting, the collector sold the painting to an art admirer for $120,000 cash, after notifying her about the damage.

If the collector's sale of the painting was NOT an acceptance of the goods, what is the maximum amount that the gallery is entitled to recover from the collector?

(A) $120,000 (damages for conversion).
(B) $100,000 (the collector-gallery contract price).
(C) $20,000 (the excess of the market price over the contract price).
(D) Only the allowance of lost profit to the gallery as a volume dealer.

Question 156

A plaintiff sues a defendant for a libelous letter received by an investigator. The authenticity and contents of the letter are disputed.

The plaintiff's attorney asks the investigator to testify that, a week before receiving the libelous letter, he had written to the defendant inquiring about the plaintiff.

The testimony is

(A) admissible, provided this inquiry was made in the regular course of the investigator's business.
(B) admissible, without production of the inquiry letter or the showing of its unavailability.
(C) inadmissible, unless the plaintiff's attorney has given the defendant notice of the investigator's intended testimony.
(D) inadmissible, unless the inquiry letter itself is shown to be unavailable.

Question 157

A realty company acquired a large tract of land upon which it developed a mobile home subdivision. The tract was divided into 60 lots, appropriate utilities were installed, and a plat of the entire tract, including a Declaration of Restrictions, was properly drawn and recorded. The Declaration of Restrictions included the following: "3. Ownership and/or occupancy are restricted to persons 21 years of age or over; one family per lot." As the separate lots were sold, the deed to each lot included the following provision: "As shown on recorded plat [properly identified by page and plat book reference] and subject to the restrictions therein contained." One of the lots was purchased by a carpenter, who now resides in a mobile home on the lot together with his wife and two children, aged 11 and 13. Other lot owners in the subdivision brought action against the carpenter to enjoin further occupancy by the children under 21 years of age. If judgment is for the carpenter, the issue that most likely will determine the case will be whether

(A) the mobile home is treated as personalty or realty.
(B) the restriction constitutes an unlawful restraint on alienation.
(C) enforcement of the restriction is considered a violation of the Equal Protection Clause of the Fourteenth Amendment of the U.S. Constitution.
(D) the terms of the restriction are expressly repeated verbatim in the carpenter's deed.

Question 158

In the application for a life insurance policy, a woman answered in the negative the question, "Have you ever had any heart disease?" Both the application and the insurance policy that was issued provided: "Applicant warrants the truthfulness of the statements made in the application and they are made conditions to the contract of insurance." Unknown to the woman, she had had a heart disease at a very early age.

If the question is raised in an action against the insurance company, how is the court likely to construe the clause dealing with the truthfulness of statements in the application?

(A) The clause is a condition, and because the condition was not met, the company will not be liable.
(B) The clause is a condition, but it will be interpreted to mean, "truthfulness to the best of my knowledge."
(C) The clause is not a condition, and therefore the company may be liable even though the woman's statement was not true.
(D) The clause is not a condition but is a promise, and therefore the company will have a cause of action against the woman's estate for any losses it suffered because of her misstatement.

Question 159

Plaintiff owns a luncheonette called the Healthy Home. Defendant runs a company that sells baked goods that it labels as "organic." Plaintiff entered into a contract with Defendant for the weekly delivery of organic oatmeal cookies. After several such deliveries, Plaintiff learned that the "organic" cookies were really repackaged highly-processed cookies that Defendant bought in bulk from a foreign wholesale company. Plaintiff sued Defendant in federal court, alleging diversity jurisdiction. The complaint included a proper jurisdictional statement and alleged that (1) Defendant entered into a contract with Plaintiff to weekly deliver thirty pounds of organic oatmeal cookies; and (2) Defendant instead knowingly delivered non-organic cookies; (3) Defendant consequently engaged in fraud. The complaint made no other statements regarding Defendant's conduct or state of mind.

Before answering, Defendant moved to dismiss the complaint for failing to state a claim. The court will most likely

(A) grant the motion because the complaint fails to plead Defendant's alleged special matters.
(B) deny the motion because Defendant has not shown that Plaintiff can prove no set of facts in support of the fraud claim.
(C) deny the motion because Defendant was required to move for judgment on the pleadings.

(D) grant the motion because the complaint improperly joins a contract claim with a tort claim.

Question 160

A defendant was tried for the murder of a victim. The alleged killing followed a barroom argument. The prosecution, in its case in chief, offered evidence that the defendant acted without having been threatened by the victim. In his case in chief, the defendant called, as his first witness, a friend of the defendant to testify to the defendant's reputation in his community as "a peaceable man."

The testimony is

(A) admissible as tending to prove the defendant is believable.
(B) admissible as tending to prove the defendant is innocent.
(C) inadmissible, because the defendant has not testified.
(D) inadmissible, because reputation is not a proper way to prove character.

Question 161

In 2003, a man was appointed to a tribunal established pursuant to a congressional act. The tribunal's duties were to review claims made by veterans and to make recommendations to the Veterans Administration on their merits. Congress later abolished the tribunal and established a different format for review of such claims. The man was offered a federal administrative position in the same bureau at a lesser salary. He thereupon sued the government on the ground that Congress may not remove a federal judge from office during good behavior nor diminish his compensation during continuance in office. Government attorneys filed a motion to dismiss the action.

The court should

(A) deny the motion because of the independence of the federal judiciary constitutionally guaranteed by Article III.
(B) deny the motion, because the man has established a property right to his federal employment of the tribunal.
(C) grant the motion, because the man lacked standing to raise the question.
(D) grant the motion, because the man was not a judge under Article III and is not entitled to life tenure.

Question 162

In 1975, a cattle company paid $30,000 for a 150-acre tract of agricultural land well suited for a cattle feed lot. The tract was ten miles from the city, which was then a community of 50,000 people, and five miles from the nearest home. By 2011, the city limits extended to the cattle company's feed lot, and the city had a population of 350,000. About 10,000 people lived within three miles of the cattle feeding operation. The cattle company land is outside the city limits and no zoning ordinance applies. The cattle company land is now worth $300,000, and $25,000 has been invested in buildings and pens.

The cattle company, conscious of its obligations to its neighbors, uses the best and most sanitary feed lot procedures, including chemical sprays, to keep down flies and odors, and frequently removes manure. Despite these measures, residents of the city complain of flies and odors. An action has been filed by five individual homeowners who live within half a mile of the cattle company feed lot. The plaintiffs' homes are valued currently at $25,000 to $40,000 each. Flies in the area are five to ten times more numerous than in other parts of the city, and extremely obnoxious odors are frequently carried by the wind to the plaintiffs' homes. The flies and odors are a substantial health hazard.

If plaintiffs assert a claim based on public nuisance, the plaintiffs will

(A) prevail if the plaintiffs sustained harm different from that suffered by the public at large.
(B) prevail if the cattle company's acts interfered with any person's enjoyment of his property.
(C) not prevail, because only the state may bring an action based on public nuisance.
(D) not prevail, because the plaintiffs came to the nuisance.

Question 163

A drug dealer agreed with another individual to purchase heroin from the individual in order to sell it on a city street corner. Unknown to the drug dealer, the other individual was an undercover police officer whose only purpose was to arrest distributors of drugs. The drug dealer made a down payment for the heroin and agreed to pay the remainder after he sold it on the street. As soon as the undercover officer handed over the heroin, other officers moved in and arrested the dealer.

The jurisdiction follows the common-law approach to conspiracy.

Could the dealer properly be convicted of conspiring to distribute drugs?

(A) No, because there was no overt act.
(B) No, because there was no plurality of agreement.
(C) Yes, because neither an overt act nor plurality of agreement is required under common law.
(D) Yes, because the dealer believed all the elements of conspiracy were present and cannot take advantage of a mistake of fact or law.

Question 164

A mother, the owner in fee simple of a parcel of land, by quitclaim deed conveyed the parcel to her daughter, who paid no consideration for the conveyance. The deed was never recorded. About a year after the delivery of the deed, the mother decided that this gift had been ill-advised. She requested that her daughter destroy the deed, which her daughter dutifully and voluntarily did. Within the month following the destruction of the deed, both the mother and daughter were killed in a common disaster. Each of the successors in interest claimed title to the parcel. In an appropriate action to determine the title to the parcel, the probable outcome will be that

(A) the mother was the owner of the parcel, because her daughter was a donee and therefore could not acquire title by quitclaim deed.
(B) the mother was the owner of the parcel, because title to the parcel reverted to her upon the voluntary destruction of the deed by her daughter.
(C) the daughter was the owner of the parcel, because her destruction of the deed to the parcel was under the undue influence of her mother.
(D) the daughter was the owner of the parcel, because the deed was merely evidence of her title, and its destruction was insufficient to cause title to pass back to her mother.

Question 165

Under the terms of a written contract, a builder agreed to construct a garage for a homeowner for $10,000. Nothing was stated in the parties' negotiations or in the contract about progress payments during the course of the work.

After completing 25 percent of the garage according to the homeowner's specifications, the builder demanded $2,000 as a reasonable progress payment. The homeowner refused, and the builder abandoned the job.

If each party sues the other for breach of contract, which of the following will the court decide?

(A) Both parties are in breach, and each is entitled to damages, if any, from the other.
(B) Only the builder is in breach and is liable for the homeowner's damages, if any.
(C) Only the homeowner is in breach and is liable for the builder's damages, if any.
(D) Both parties took reasonable positions, and neither is in breach.

Question 166

Plaintiff heads a company that sells photography equipment. Defendant, an individual who owns a film school, bought five hundred cameras from Plaintiff. Defendant received the cameras but refused to pay, insisting that the goods did not meet industry standards. Plaintiff sued Defendant in federal district court for breach of contract, invoking the court's diversity jurisdiction. Plaintiff knows from publicly available sources that Defendant has purchased studio lighting from a particular lighting company. Plaintiff wants to find out, through discovery, whether Defendant also defaulted on that contract.

Which statement best describes whether Plaintiff may get discovery about any contract between Defendant and the lighting company?

(A) Plaintiff may, during a deposition of Defendant, ask about the lighting contract so long as the information is not privileged, is relevant to a claim or defense in the case, and is proportional to the needs of the case.
(B) Plaintiff may not, during a deposition of Defendant, ask about the lighting contract if the answer would not be admissible at trial.
(C) Plaintiff may propound interrogatories to the lighting company asking about the company's contracts with Defendant, if that information would be relevant to a claim or defense in the case.
(D) Plaintiff is entitled to receive a copy of the lighting contract as a part of automatic initial disclosure from Defendant.

Question 167

A pedestrian sued a driver for injuries suffered in a hit-and-run accident. At trial, the pedestrian called a witness who testified that he saw the accident and that as the car sped off he accurately dictated the license number into his properly operating pocket dictating machine. The witness stated that he no longer remembered the number.

May the tape recording be played?

(A) Yes, as a present sense impression only.
(B) Yes, as a recorded recollection only.
(C) Yes, as a present sense impression and as a past recollection recorded.
(D) No, because it is hearsay not within any exception.

Question 168

Acting on an anonymous telephone call, police went to a defendant's apartment, knocked on the door, and demanded to search it for narcotics. When the defendant refused, the police forced the door open and placed him under arrest. As they were removing him from the apartment, the defendant offered to give the officers "valuable information" in exchange for his release. Before he could say anything else, the defendant was given *Miranda* warnings by the police. Thereafter, he told the police that he had stored some heroin in his friend's apartment and that he and his friend had been going to sell it. The heroin was recovered, and the defendant was prosecuted for conspiracy to sell narcotics and for possession of narcotics. At his trial, the defendant moved to suppress his statements. Which of the following is the defendant's best argument in support of the motion to suppress?

(A) The defendant is entitled to know the identity of his accuser, and the state cannot supply this information.

(B) The police should have given the defendant *Miranda* warnings prior to entry into the apartment, and the warnings were ineffectual once the defendant offered to give the police information.

(C) The defendant was intimidated by the forced entry into the apartment, and since the statements were involuntary and coerced, their use against him would violate due process of law.

(D) The statements were fruits of an unlawful arrest, and though the *Miranda* warnings may have been sufficient to protect his right against self-incrimination, they were not sufficient to purge the taint of the illegal arrest.

Question 169

A woman occupied an apartment in a building owned by a landlord. She paid rent of $125 in advance each month. During the second month of occupancy, the woman organized the tenants in the building as a tenants' association and the association made demands of the landlord concerning certain repairs and improvements the tenants wanted. When the woman tendered rent for the third month, the landlord notified her that rent for the fourth and subsequent months would be $200 per month. The woman protested and pointed out that all other tenants paid rent of $125 per month. Thereupon, the landlord gave the required statutory notice that the tenancy was being terminated at the end of the third month.

By an appropriate proceeding, the woman contests the landlord's right to terminate. If the woman succeeds, it will be because

(A) a periodic tenancy was created by implication.

(B) the doctrine prohibiting retaliatory eviction is part of the law of the jurisdiction.

(C) the $200 rent demanded violates the agreement implied by the rate charged to other tenants.

(D) the law implies a term of one year in the absence of any express agreement.

Question 170

Congressional committees heard testimony from present and former holders of licenses issued by state vocational licensing boards. According to the testimony, the boards had unfairly manipulated their disciplinary proceedings in order to revoke the licenses of some license holders as a means of protecting favored licensees from competition.

In response, Congress enacted a statute prescribing detailed procedural requirements for the disciplinary proceedings of all state vocational licensing boards. For example, the statute required the state boards to provide licensees with adequate notice and opportunity for an adjudicatory hearing in all disciplinary proceedings. The statute also prescribed criteria for the membership of all state vocational licensing boards that were designed to ensure that the boards were likely to be neutral.

Which of the following provides the best source of authority for this federal statute?

(A) Section 5 of the Fourteenth Amendment.

(B) The General Welfare Clause of Article I, § 8.

(C) The Privileges and Immunities Clause of Article IV, § 2.

(D) The Takings Clause of the Fifth Amendment.

Question 171

A photographer lent 200 of his photographic prints to a museum to be featured in an upcoming exhibit. The museum agreed to return all prints in the same condition as it received them. Due to staff error, the museum instead sent the prints to a recycling bin, where they were compressed beyond recognition. The photographer sued the museum in federal court for breach of contract, alleging diversity jurisdiction, and sought to recover the market value of the 200 prints. The evidence presented to the jury showed that none of the photographer's photo prints throughout his career had ever sold for more than $500 a print. No motions were made by either side before the case went to the jury. The jury returned a verdict of $1 million. The judge mentally agreed with the jury that the museum ought to be held liable but believed that the jury's award reflected an arithmetic error and that the jurors had intended to issue a verdict of $100,000 in damages rather than $1 million.

After judgment was entered on the jury's verdict for the photographer, the museum made a motion for judgment as a matter of law, by which it asked the judge to set the judgment at $100,000 rather than $1 million. What action can the judge take, if any, that is procedurally proper, is not wasteful of judicial resources, and will correct the judgment to or near the $100,000 that the judge believes the jury intended?

(A) The judge should grant the museum's motion and enter judgment for $100,000.

(B) The judge on her own initiative should conditionally order a new trial unless the photographer agrees to a reduction of the damages to $100,000, an amount set by the court.

(C) The judge on her own initiative should order a new jury trial solely on the issue of damages.

(D) The judge must deny the museum's motion because the Seventh Amendment requires that the judge accept the jury's damage award without adjustment.

Question 172

A plaintiff purchased a suit of thermal underwear made of synthetic materials and manufactured by a company. While attempting to stamp out a fire, the plaintiff's thermal underwear caught fire and burned in a melting fashion up to his waist. He suffered a heart attack a half hour later. In a suit against the company, the plaintiff alleged that negligence and breach of warranty caused both the burn and the heart attack.

The plaintiff testified that his purchase of the underwear occurred on April 17th, a fact of minor importance in the case. He stated that he could identify the date because his secretary had taken the day off to attend the first game of the baseball season and he had checked his company's payroll records to verify the date. The clothing company moves to strike the testimony as to the date. The motion should be

(A) sustained, because the best evidence of the information contained in the payroll records is the records themselves.
(B) sustained, because the plaintiff's testimony is based upon hearsay declarations contained in the payroll records.
(C) overruled if the judge has personal knowledge of the date on which the baseball season opened.
(D) overruled, because the payroll records relate to a collateral matter.

Question 173

On March 1, a programmer orally agreed with a department store to write a set of programs for the store's computer and to coordinate the programs with its billing methods. A subsequent memo, signed by both parties, provided in its entirety:

"The store will pay the programmer $20,000 in two equal installments within one month of completion if the programmer is successful in shortening by one-half the processing time for the financial transactions now handled on the store's computer system; the programmer is to complete by July 1. This agreement may be amended only by a signed writing."

On June 6, the programmer demanded $10,000, saying the job was one-half done. After the store denied liability, the parties orally agreed that the store should deposit $20,000 in escrow, pending completion to the satisfaction of the store's computer systems manager. The escrow deposit was thereupon made. On July 5, the programmer completed the programs, having used an amount of time in which it could have earned $18,000 had it devoted that time to other jobs. Tests by the programmer and the store's computer systems manager then showed that the computer programs, not being perfectly coordinated with the store's billing methods, cut processing time by only 47 percent. They would, however, save the store $12,000 a year. Further, if the store would spend $5,000 to change its invoice preparation methods, as recommended by the programmer, the programs would cut processing time by a total of 58 percent, saving the store another $8,000 a year.

The store's computer systems manager refused in good faith to certify satisfactory completion. The store requested the escrow agent to return the $20,000 and asserted that nothing was owed to the programmer even though it has continued to use the programs.

If the store denies liability on the ground that the programmer had orally agreed to coordinate with the store's methods of accounting, and the programmer seeks in litigation to bar introduction of that agreement because of the Parol Evidence Rule, the store's most effective argument is that

(A) the Parol Evidence Rule does not bar the introduction of evidence for the purpose of interpreting a written agreement.
(B) the memorandum was not a completely integrated agreement.
(C) the store detrimentally relied on the oral promise of coordination in signing the memorandum.
(D) the memorandum was not a partially integrated agreement.

Question 174

A federal statute required that any individual or entity owning more than 100 cars had to ensure that at least 10 percent of those cars were electric powered.

A city filed suit in federal district court against the federal official who enforced this requirement. The city sought an injunction prohibiting enforcement of the statute on the ground that it was unconstitutional.

Should the court grant the injunction?

(A) No, because the statute is valid under the Commerce Clause and does not violate the Tenth Amendment.
(B) No, because the federal government has sovereign immunity and cannot be sued without its explicit consent.
(C) Yes, because the statute violates the reserved rights of the states under the Tenth Amendment.
(D) Yes, because as applied to state and local governments, the statute exceeds Congress's power under the Commerce Clause.

Question 175

A lumber supplier agreed to sell and a furniture manufacturer agreed to buy all of the lumber that the manufacturer required over a two-year period. The sales contract provided that payment was due 60 days after delivery, but that a 3 percent discount would be allowed if the manufacturer paid within ten days of delivery. During the first year of the contract, the manufacturer regularly paid within the ten-day period and received the 3 percent discount. Fifteen days after the supplier made its most recent lumber delivery to the manufacturer, the supplier had received no payment from the manufacturer. At this time, the supplier became aware of rumors from a credible source that the manufacturer's financial condition was precarious. The supplier wrote the manufacturer, demanding assurances regarding the manufacturer's financial status. The manufacturer immediately mailed its latest audited financial statements to the supplier, as well as a satisfactory credit report prepared by the manufacturer's banker. The rumors proved to be false. Nevertheless, the supplier refused to resume deliveries. The manufacturer sued the lumber supplier for breach of contract.

Will the manufacturer prevail?

(A) No, because the contract was unenforceable, since the manufacturer had not committed to purchase a definite quantity of lumber.

(B) No, because the supplier had reasonable grounds for insecurity and was therefore entitled to cancel the contract and refuse to make any future deliveries.

(C) Yes, because the credit report and audited financial statements provided adequate assurance of due performance under the contract.

(D) Yes, because the supplier was not entitled to condition resumption of deliveries on the receipt of financial status information.

Question 176

A state legislature passed a statute providing that juries in criminal trials were to consist of 6 rather than 12 jurors, and providing that jury verdicts did not have to be unanimous but could be based on 5 votes out of 6 jurors. A defendant was tried for murder. Over his objection, he was tried by a jury composed of 6 jurors. The jurors found him guilty by a vote of 5 to 1 and, over the defendant's objection, the court entered a judgment of conviction, which was affirmed on appeal by the state supreme court. The defendant seeks to overturn his conviction in a *habeas corpus* action in federal court, claiming his constitutional rights were violated by allowing a jury verdict that was not unanimous and by allowing a jury composed of fewer than 12 members.

How is the federal court likely to rule in this action?

(A) It will set aside the conviction, because the jury was composed of fewer than 12 members.

(B) It will set aside the conviction, because the 6-person jury verdict was not unanimous.

(C) It will set aside the conviction for both reasons.

(D) It will uphold the conviction.

Question 177

National regulation of predatory wild animals on federal lands is most likely

(A) constitutional, because the protection of wild animals is important to the general welfare.

(B) constitutional, because Congress has authority to make regulations respecting federal property.

(C) unconstitutional, because wild animals as defined by state common law are not federal property.

(D) unconstitutional, because regulation and control of wild animals is retained by the states under the Tenth Amendment.

Question 178

By her validly executed will, a woman devised a certain tract of land to her son for his life with remainder to such of his children as should be living at his death, "Provided, however, that no such child of my son shall mortgage or sell, or attempt to mortgage or sell, his or her interest in the property prior to attaining 25 years of age: and, if any such child of my son shall violate this provision, then upon such violation his or her interest shall pass to and become the property of the remaining children of my son then living, share and share alike."

The woman's will included an identical provision for each of her four other children concerning four other tracts of land. The residuary clause of the will gave the residuary estate to the woman's five children equally. The woman died and was survived by the five children named in her will and by 11 grandchildren. Several additional grandchildren have since been born.

In an action for a declaration of rights, it was claimed that the attempted gifts to the woman's grandchildren were entirely void and that the interests following the life estates to her children passed to the children absolutely by the residuary clause. Assuming that the action was properly brought with all necessary parties and with a guardian ad litem appointed to represent the interests of unborn and infant grandchildren, the decision should be that

(A) the attempted gifts to grandchildren are void under the Rule Against Perpetuities.

(B) the attempted gifts to grandchildren are void as unlawful restraints on alienation.

(C) the provisions concerning grandchildren are valid and will be upheld according to their terms.
(D) even if the provisions against sale or mortgage by the grandchildren are void, the remainders to grandchildren are otherwise valid and will be given effect.

Question 179

A landowner who owned a large tract of land in the mountains sought to protect a herd of wild deer that frequented the area. Although the landowner had posted signs that said, "No Hunting—No Trespassing," hunters frequently intruded to kill the deer. Recently, the landowner built an eight-foot chain-link fence, topped by three strands of barbed wire, across a gully on her land that provided the only access to the area frequented by the deer.

A wildlife photographer asked the landowner for permission to enter the property to photograph the deer. Because the landowner feared that any publicity would encourage further intrusions, she denied the photographer's request. Frustrated, the photographer attempted to climb the fence. He became entangled in the barbed wire and suffered extensive lacerations. The wounds became infected and ultimately caused his death. The photographer's personal representative brought an action against the landowner.

Will the plaintiff prevail?

(A) Yes, because the landowner may not use deadly force to protect her land from intrusion.
(B) Yes, because the landowner had no property interest in the deer that entitled her to use force to protect them.
(C) No, because the photographer entered the landowner's land after the landowner had refused him permission to do so.
(D) No, because the potential for harm created by the presence of the barbed wire was apparent.

Question 180

A homeowner sued a plumber for damages resulting from the plumber's allegedly faulty installation of water pipes in her basement, causing flooding. At trial, the homeowner was prepared to testify that when she first detected the flooding, she turned off the water and called the plumber at his emergency number for help. The plumber responded, "I'll come by tomorrow and will redo the installation for free."

Is the plumber's response admissible?

(A) No, because it is an offer in compromise.
(B) No, because it is hearsay not within any exception.
(C) Yes, as a subsequent remedial measure.
(D) Yes, as evidence of the plumber's fault.

Question 181

A driver, returning from a long shift at a factory, fell asleep at the wheel and lost control of his car. As a result, his car collided with a police car driven by an officer who was returning to the station after having responded to an emergency. The police officer was injured in the accident. The police officer sued the driver in negligence for her injuries. The driver moved for summary judgment, arguing that the common-law firefighters' rule barred the suit.

Should the court grant the motion?

(A) No, because the firefighters' rule does not apply to police officers.
(B) No, because the police officer's injuries were not related to any special dangers of her job.
(C) Yes, because the accident would not have occurred but for the emergency.
(D) Yes, because the police officer was injured on the job.

Question 182

An owner owned a tract of land in fee simple. At a time when the tract was in the adverse possession of a squatter, a neighbor obtained the oral permission of the owner to use as a road or driveway a portion of the tract to reach adjoining land which the neighbor owned in fee simple. Thereafter, during all times relevant to this problem, the neighbor used this road regularly for ingress and egress between his land and a public highway.

The squatter quit possession of the tract before acquiring title by adverse possession. Without communicating further with the owner, the neighbor continued to use the road for a total period, from the time he first began to use it, sufficient to acquire an easement by prescription. The owner then blocked the road and refused to permit its continued use. The neighbor brought suit to determine his right to continue use of the road. The neighbor should

(A) win, because his use was adverse to the squatter and once adverse it continued adverse until some affirmative showing of a change.
(B) win, because the neighbor made no attempt to renew permission after the squatter quit possession of the tract.
(C) lose, because his use was with permission.
(D) lose, because there is no evidence that he continued adverse use for the required period after the squatter quit possession.

Question 183

A state requires licenses of persons "who are engaged in the trade of barbering." It will grant such licenses only to those who are graduates of barber schools located in the state, who have resided in the state for two years, and who are citizens of the United States.

The requirement that candidates for license must be graduates of barber schools in the state is probably

(A) unconstitutional, as an undue burden on interstate commerce.
(B) unconstitutional, as a violation of the Privileges and Immunities Clause of the Fourteenth Amendment.
(C) constitutional, because the state does not know the quality of out-of-state barber schools.
(D) constitutional, because barbering is a privilege and not a right.

Question 184

Plaintiff, a black woman, worked for a bookstore owned by Defendant, a large corporation with stores in many states. The bookstore where Plaintiff worked was in State A. Plaintiff's supervisor, the store manager, passed her over for a promotion. Believing she had been passed over because of her race and/or gender, Plaintiff sued Defendant in federal district court for State A, alleging discrimination in violation of federal employment-discrimination statutes. The complaint has survived a motion to dismiss. Plaintiff's lawyer now wants to depose a man who was her colleague at the store, where he served as a cashier; the lawyer believes the colleague has knowledge of the circumstances under which Plaintiff was passed over for the promotion. The colleague, who has since left the employ of Defendant, now works and lives in State B, at a location 200 miles from the federal courthouse in State A where the suit is pending; he rarely travels more than 50 miles from his present home and place of business. Plaintiff's lawyer wishes to depose the colleague in person at the lawyer's office, which is next door to the State A federal courthouse. Can the lawyer require the colleague to attend the deposition at this office, assuming the lawyer will choose a date when the colleague has no conflicting appointments and assuming that the lawyer pays the colleague's reasonable expenses of travelling to the deposition?

(A) Yes, but only if the lawyer issues a subpoena.
(B) Yes, and the lawyer may do so by means of a notice of deposition.
(C) Yes, so long as the lawyer demonstrates good cause for not holding the deposition in State B at a location within 100 miles of the colleague's home or place of business.
(D) No, because the colleague is not a party or an officer of a party.

Question 185

In financial straits and needing $4,000 immediately, a nephew orally asked his uncle for a $4,000 loan. The uncle replied that he would lend the money to the nephew only if the nephew's mother "guaranteed" the loan. At the nephew's suggestion, the uncle then telephoned the nephew's mother, told her about the loan, and asked if she would "guarantee" it. She replied, "Surely. Lend my son the $4,000 and I'll repay it if he doesn't." The uncle then lent $4,000 to the nephew, an amount the nephew orally agreed to repay in six weeks. The next day, the nephew's mother wrote to him and concluded her letter with the words, "Son, I was happy to do you a favor by promising your uncle I would repay your six-week $4,000 loan if you don't. /s/ Mother." Neither the nephew nor his mother repaid the loan when it came due and the uncle sued the mother for breach of contract. In that action, the mother raised the Statute of Frauds as her only defense.

Will the mother's Statute Frauds defense be successful?

(A) No, because the amount of the loan was less than $5,000.
(B) No, because the mother's letter satisfies the Statute-of-Frauds requirement.
(C) Yes, because the mother's promise to the uncle was oral.
(D) Yes, because the nephew's promise to the uncle was oral.

Question 186

A husband and wife, walking on a country road, were frightened by a bull running loose on the road. They climbed over a fence to get onto the adjacent property, owned by a grower. After climbing over the fence, the husband and wife damaged some of the grower's plants, which were near the fence. The fence was posted with a large sign that said, "No Trespassing."

The grower saw the husband and wife and came toward them with his large watchdog on a long leash. The dog rushed at the wife. The grower had intended only to frighten the husband and the wife, but the leash broke, and before the grower could restrain the dog, the dog bit the wife.

If the wife asserts a claim based on battery against the grower, will the wife prevail?

(A) Yes, because the grower intended that the dog frighten the wife.
(B) Yes, because the breaking of the leash establishes liability under *res ipsa loquitur*.
(C) No, because the wife made an unauthorized entry onto the grower's land.
(D) No, because the grower did not intend to cause any harmful contact with the wife.

Question 187

In a civil action for breach of an oral contract, the defendant admits that there had been discussions, but denies that he ever entered into an agreement with the plaintiff.

Which of the following standards of admissibility should be applied by the court to evidence proffered as relevant to prove whether a contract was formed?

(A) Whether a reasonable juror would find the evidence determinative of whether the contract was or was not formed.

(B) Whether the evidence has any tendency to make the fact of contract formation more or less probable than without the evidence.

(C) Whether the evidence is sufficient to prove, absent contrary evidence, that the contract was or was not formed.

(D) Whether the evidence makes it more likely than not that a contract was or was not formed.

Question 188

A defendant was arrested and taken to police headquarters, where she was given her *Miranda* warnings. The defendant indicated that she wished to telephone her lawyer and was told that she could do so after her fingerprints had been taken. While being fingerprinted, however, the defendant blurted out, "Paying a lawyer is a waste of money because I know you have me."

At trial, the defendant's motion to prevent the introduction of the statement she made while being fingerprinted will most probably be

(A) granted, because the defendant's request to contact her attorney by telephone was reasonable and should have been granted immediately.

(B) granted, because of the "fruit of the poisonous tree" doctrine.

(C) denied, because the statements were volunteered and not the result of interrogation.

(D) denied, because fingerprinting is not a critical stage of the proceeding requiring the assistance of counsel.

Question 189

The owner of a shopping mall hired a construction company to design and construct the entryway to the mall. The construction company negligently selected an unusually slippery material for the floor covering. A customer at the mall slipped on the floor of the entryway, sustaining injuries. The customer sued the mall owner for the construction company's negligent design of the mall's entryway.

Will the injured customer recover damages?

(A) No, if the construction company was an independent contractor.

(B) No, if no customers had previously slipped on the floor.

(C) Yes, if the customer intended to make a purchase at the mall.

(D) Yes, if the mall's duty to maintain safe conditions was nondelegable.

Question 190

A brother and sister acquired as joint tenants a 20-acre parcel of land. They contributed equally to the purchase price. Several years later, the brother proposed that they build an apartment development on the parcel. His sister rejected the proposal but orally agreed with her brother that he could go ahead on his own on the northerly half of the parcel and she could do what she wished with the southerly half. The brother proceeded to build an apartment development on, and generally developed and improved, the northerly ten acres of the parcel. The sister orally permitted the southerly ten acres of the parcel to be used by a conservation group as a nature preserve. The brother died, leaving his entire estate to his son. The brother's will named his sister as executrix of his will, but she refused to so serve.

In an appropriate action to determine the respective interests of the sister and the brother's son in the parcel, if the son is adjudged to be the owner of the northerly ten acres of the parcel, the most likely reason for the judgment will be that

(A) the close blood relationship between brother and sister removes the necessity to comply with the Statute of Frauds.

(B) the sister's conduct during her brother's lifetime estops her from asserting title to the northerly half of the parcel.

(C) the joint tenancy was terminated by the oral agreement of the brother and sister at the time it was made.

(D) the sister has a fiduciary obligation to her nephew by reason of her being named executrix of her brother's will.

Question 191

A seller and a buyer entered into a written agreement providing that the seller was to deliver 1,000 cases of candy bars to the buyer during the months of May and June. Under the agreement, the buyer was obligated to make a selection by March 1 of the quantities of the various candy bars to be delivered under the contract. The buyer did not make the selection by March 1, and on March 2 the seller notified the buyer that because of the buyer's failure to select, the seller would not deliver the candy bars. The seller had all of the necessary candy bars on hand on March 1 and made no additional sales or purchases on March 1 or March 2.

On March 2, after receiving the seller's notice that it would not perform, the buyer notified the seller of its selection and insisted that the seller perform. The seller refused.

If the buyer sues the seller for breach of contract, is the buyer likely to prevail?

(A) No, because a contract did not exist until selection of the specific candy bars, and the seller withdrew its offer before selection.
(B) No, because selection of the candy bars by March 1 was an express condition to the seller's duty to perform.
(C) Yes, because a delay of one day in making the selection did not have a material effect on the seller.
(D) Yes, because upon the buyer's failure to make a selection by March 1, the seller had a duty to make a reasonable selection.

Question 192

A consumer became physically ill after drinking part of a bottle of soda that contained a large decomposed snail. The consumer sued the store from which she bought the soda to recover damages for her injuries. The parties agreed that the snail was put into the bottle during the bottling process, over which the store had no control. The parties also agreed that the snail would have been visible in the bottle before the consumer opened it.

Will the consumer prevail in her action against the store?

(A) No, because the consumer could have seen the snail in the bottle.
(B) No, because the store was not responsible for the bottling process.
(C) Yes, because the consumer was injured by a defective product sold to her by the store.
(D) Yes, because the store had exclusive control over the bottle before selling it to the consumer.

Question 193

A painter had painted a homeowner's house under a contract that called for payment of $2,000. The homeowner, contending in good faith that the porch had not been painted properly, refused to pay anything.

The homeowner's refusal to pay anything to the painter when he finished painting was a

(A) partial breach of contract only if the painter had properly or substantially painted the porch.
(B) partial breach of contract whether or not the painter had properly or substantially painted the porch.
(C) total breach of contract only if the painter had properly or substantially painted the porch.
(D) total breach of contract whether or not the painter had properly or substantially painted the porch.

Question 194

The strongest constitutional basis for the enactment of a federal statute requiring colleges and universities receiving federal funds to offer student aid solely on the basis of need is the

(A) police power.
(B) war and defense power.
(C) power to tax and spend for the general welfare.
(D) power to enforce the Privileges and Immunities Clause of the Fourteenth Amendment.

Question 195

A defendant was charged with manslaughter. At the preliminary hearing, the magistrate dismissed the charge on the grounds that the evidence was insufficient. The prosecutor then brought the case before a grand jury. After hearing the evidence presented by the prosecutor, the grand jury refused to return an indictment. The prosecutor waited a few months until a new grand jury had been impaneled and brought the case before that grand jury, which returned an indictment charging the defendant with manslaughter. The defendant moves to dismiss the indictment on double jeopardy grounds.

Should the motion be granted?

(A) No, because jeopardy had not attached.
(B) No, because there has been no conviction or acquittal.
(C) Yes, because any proceeding after the preliminary hearing would violate double jeopardy.
(D) Yes, because bringing the case before the second grand jury was a violation of double jeopardy.

Question 196

Thirty years ago, a landowner conveyed land by warranty deed to a church (a charity) "so long as the land herein conveyed is used as the site for the principal religious edifice maintained by said church."

Twenty years ago, the landowner died intestate, survived by a single heir.

One year ago, the church dissolved and its church building situated on the land was demolished.

There is no applicable statute. The common law Rule Against Perpetuities is unmodified in the jurisdiction.

In an appropriate action, the landowner's heir and the attorney general, who is the appropriate official to assert public interests in charitable trusts, contest the right to the land.

In such action, who will prevail?

(A) The landowner's heir, as successor to the landowner's possibility of reverter.
(B) The landowner's heir, because a charity cannot convey assets donated to it.

(C) The attorney general, because *cy pres* should be applied to devote the land to religious purposes to carry out the charitable intent of the landowner.
(D) The attorney general, because the landowner's attempt to restrict the church's fee simple violated the Rule Against Perpetuities.

Question 197

A physician called as a witness by the defendant was asked to testify to statements made by her patient, for the purpose of obtaining treatment from the physician. Which of the following is the best basis for excluding evidence of the patient's statements in a jurisdiction with a doctor-patient privilege?

(A) An objection by the physician asserting her privilege against disclosure of confidential communications made by a patient.
(B) An objection by the plaintiff's attorney on the grounds of the doctor-patient privilege.
(C) A finding by the trial judge that the patient had left the office without actually receiving treatment.
(D) The assertion of a privilege by the patient's attorney, present at the trial as a spectator at the patient's request, and allowed by the trial judge to speak.

Question 198

A roofer entered into a written contract with a homeowner to repair the roof of her home, the repairs to be done "in a workmanlike manner." The roofer completed the repairs and took all of his equipment away, with the exception of a 20 foot extension ladder, which was left against the side of the house. He intended to come back and get the ladder the next morning. At that time, the homeowner and her family were away on a trip. During the night, a thief, using the ladder to gain access to an upstairs window, entered the house and stole some valuable jewels. The homeowner has asserted a claim against the roofer for damages for the loss of the jewels.

In her claim against the roofer, the homeowner will

(A) prevail, because by leaving the ladder the roofer became a trespasser on the homeowner's property.
(B) prevail, because by leaving the ladder, the roofer created the risk that a person might unlawfully enter the house.
(C) not prevail, because the act of the thief was a superseding cause.
(D) not prevail, because the homeowner's claim is limited to damages for breach of contract.

Question 199

Congress decides that the application of the Uniform Consumer Credit Code (UCCC) should be the same throughout the United States. To that end, it enacts the UCCC as a federal law directly applicable to all consumer credit, small loans, and retail installment sales. The law is intended to protect borrowers and buyers against unfair practices by suppliers of consumer credit.

Which of the following constitutional provisions may be most easily used to justify federal enactment of this statute?

(A) The Obligation of Contracts Clause
(B) The Privileges and Immunities Clause of the Fourteenth Amendment
(C) The Commerce Clause
(D) The Equal Protection Clause of the Fourteenth Amendment

Question 200

On March 1, a homeowner contacted a builder about constructing an addition to the homeowner's house. The builder orally offered to perform the work for $200,000 if his pending bid on another project was rejected. The homeowner accepted the builder's terms and the builder then prepared a written contract that both parties signed. The contract did not refer to the builder's pending bid. One week later, upon learning that his pending bid on the other project had been accepted, the builder refused to perform any work for the homeowner.

Can the homeowner recover for the builder's nonperformance?

(A) No, because efficiency principles justify the builder's services being directed to a higher-valued use.
(B) No, because the builder's duty to perform was subject to a condition.
(C) Yes, because the builder's attempt to condition his duty to perform rendered the contract illusory.
(D) Yes, because the parol evidence rule would bar the builder from presenting evidence of oral understandings not included in the final writing.

SUBJECT-MATTER BREAKDOWN

PRACTICE MBE

SUBJECT-MATTER BREAKDOWN

PRACTICE MBE

The following are lists of Practice MBE questions by subject matter.

CIVIL PROCEDURE

8, 10, 14, 21, 24, 31, 35, 42, 46, 48, 51, 64, 67, 96, 110, 113, 119, 122, 124, 135, 136, 141, 143, 159, 166, 171, 184

CONSTITUTIONAL LAW

11, 23, 29, 34, 68, 76, 91, 132, 138, 144, 147, 161, 170, 174, 177, 183, 194, 199

Individual rights: 4, 41, 57, 62, 82, 106, 114, 129, 137, 157

CONTRACTS

2, 18, 27, 40, 49, 53, 58, 59, 70, 75, 81, 84, 90, 98, 105, 115, 139, 151, 155, 158, 165, 173, 185, 193, 200

Sales (UCC): 15, 36, 128, 148, 175, 191

CRIMINAL LAW

16, 56, 71, 72, 87, 145,

Criminal procedure: 32, 65, 93, 126, 142, 168, 176, 188, 195

Common-law crimes: 5, 20, 37, 47, 66, 78, 94, 103, 111, 118, 131, 153, 163

EVIDENCE

9, 17, 33, 38, 61, 79, 85, 89, 100, 112, 125, 133, 140, 156, 160, 172, 187, 197

Hearsay: 12, 22, 25, 43, 50, 73, 107, 121, 167, 180

REAL PROPERTY

1, 6, 19, 28, 39, 44, 52, 55, 63, 69, 74, 80, 83, 95, 102, 109, 117, 120, 127, 146, 149, 152, 164, 169, 178, 182, 190, 196

TORTS

3, 7, 26, 54, 60, 88, 92, 97, 99, 104, 116, 123, 134, 154, 162, 179, 186, 192

Negligence: 13, 30, 45, 77, 86, 101, 108, 130, 150, 181, 189, 198

ANSWERS

PRACTICE MBE—A.M. EXAM

Answer Key

Use this Answer Key to quickly identify the correct answer to each question.

(1) B	(11) A	(21) C	(31) A	(41) B	(51) A	(61) A	(71) A	(81) D	(91) D
(2) C	(12) A	(22) D	(32) D	(42) D	(52) B	(62) A	(72) A	(82) C	(92) A
(3) A	(13) C	(23) C	(33) A	(43) C	(53) D	(63) C	(73) D	(83) B	(93) C
(4) A	(14) D	(24) C	(34) B	(44) C	(54) D	(64) C	(74) C	(84) D	(94) A
(5) C	(15) C	(25) A	(35) B	(45) A	(55) D	(65) C	(75) C	(85) A	(95) A
(6) B	(16) B	(26) D	(36) B	(46) B	(56) C	(66) B	(76) A	(86) D	(96) D
(7) D	(17) C	(27) C	(37) A	(47) D	(57) B	(67) D	(77) C	(87) A	(97) A
(8) C	(18) A	(28) B	(38) C	(48) A	(58) C	(68) D	(78) C	(88) C	(98) D
(9) B	(19) C	(29) C	(39) C	(49) C	(59) C	(69) C	(79) A	(89) B	(99) D
(10) C	(20) A	(30) B	(40) D	(50) D	(60) B	(70) A	(80) A	(90) B	(100) B

ANSWERS

PRACTICE MBE—A.M. EXAM

Answer 1

(B) is the best response,

because it identifies the central issue under these facts and resolves it in the owner's favor.

The genesis of the conflict here was the *oral* agreement for the sale of an interest in land. Such a contract falls within the Statute of Frauds, and thus must be in writing to be enforceable. However, there are circumstances under which the writing requirement will be excused, and one of them appears to be a major obstacle for the owner under these facts: part performance. In a contract for the sale of land, if the buyer pays all or part of the purchase price AND performs some act explainable only by the contract's existence, the contract will be enforceable even without a writing. Thus, the owner would *have* to explain away the tenant's $1,000 in improvements in order to prevail, since people as a rule don't spend money improving what they believe is someone else's property. One way she could overcome this is suggested by choice B: she could argue that spending $1,000 on improvements is as consistent with the tenant's being a long-term tenant as with the oral contract. That's because the buyer's act must be *unequivocally referable* to an oral contract to be excused from the writing requirement. If the action is attributable to anything else, it won't suffice.

This is an interesting problem because your gut reaction is that the tenant will *prevail,* due to part performance. Then, the question throws you for a loop by stating that *the owner* prevailed, and asking you why. In a way, the element that most made you believe the tenant should win—the $1,000 in improvements—leads you to the correct response, because it tells you the *central issue* that the owner must address in order to prevail. Since the argument in choice B represents a plausible way for the owner to overcome the central obstacle in these facts, it's the best response.

(A) is not the best response,

because it misstates the law.

Choice A has a *kernel* of truth in it, in that contracts for the sale of land are within the Statute of Frauds and, thus, must be in writing to be enforceable. However, even *without* a writing, under *some* circumstances, a land sale contract will be enforced. In general, the Statute of Frauds writing requirement will be excused when to do otherwise would result in fraud or undue hardship. The traditional rule is that, when the buyer pays all or part of the purchase price *and* performs some act "unequivocally referable" to the existence of the contract, the writing requirement will be *excused.* An act is "unequivocally referable" if it's explainable only by the contract's existence. Thus, it's not correct to say that there's no way to overcome a lack of a writing. Since A says this, it can't be the best response.

(C) is not the best response,

because although it addresses the central issue, it makes an argument that would benefit the tenant, not the owner.

The source of the conflict here is that contracts for the sale of land are within the Statute of Frauds and thus must be in writing to be enforceable. However, the Statute of Frauds writing requirement will be excused when to do otherwise would result in fraud or undue hardship. In a traditional rule relevant to these facts, when the buyer in a land sale contract pays all or part of the purchase price *and* performs some act "unequivocally referable" to the agreement, the writing will be *excused.* An act is "unequivocally referable" if it's explainable only by the contract's existence. Thus, the major obstacle the owner had to overcome is the tenant's $1,000 worth of improvements, which would tend to suggest that the contract existed since the tenant would be unlikely to improve someone *else's* land at their own expense. In fact, the argument C makes would support *the tenant's* position, since he wouldn't ask permission to undertake improvements on his own land. Since C addresses a factor that would not help resolve the case in the owner's favor, it's not the best response.

(D) is not the best response,

because it does not address completely the basis on which the tenant would be denied specific performance.

Specific performance is an equitable remedy, appropriate only where there's no adequate legal remedy (e.g., money damages). It's appropriate where the subject is unique (e.g., a piece of land or an antique), and/or the money value is not ascertainable. As an equitable remedy, specific performance is granted to avoid injustice. However, this would be determined primarily by the unjust *harm* to the tenant, *not* unjust enrichment to the owner. Since choice D focuses on the unjust benefit to the owner and not the unjust harm to the tenant, it's not the best response.

Answer 2

(C) is the best response,

because it identifies the correct means of accepting the offer, and also the appropriate interpretation of the performance requested.

An offer for a bilateral contract seeks a return promise; an offer for a unilateral contract seeks performance. In cases where the offer is ambiguous as to whether it's seeking performance or a promise, an offeree has his choice of performing or promising to perform. There are very few situations where an offer *clearly* seeks performance instead of a return promise. However, a reward offer is just such an offer. The city clearly doesn't want someone to promise to find the arsonist—it only wants *action.* Thus, only performance would constitute acceptance.

As to the interpretation of the offer, it would be unreasonable to interpret the offer as literally requiring a private citizen to arrest and convict the arsonist. Instead, the offer would be interpreted as only requiring information *leading* to the arrest and conviction. To interpret the offer literally would confine the scope of offerees to the police (since they are generally the only ones who can conduct an arrest), and the city council clearly didn't intend to so restrict the offer. (Apart from anything else, a police officer likely couldn't accept the reward offer due to problems of consideration underlying the contract: catching the arsonist would be considered a police officer's preexisting legal duty.) Since C correctly addresses the means and medium of acceptance, it's the best response.

(A) is not the best response,

because the offer here was for a *unilateral* contract, and thus it could only be accepted by performance, not a return promise.

An offer for a bilateral contract seeks a return promise; an offer for a unilateral contract seeks performance. In cases where the offer is ambiguous, as to whether it's seeking a unilateral or bilateral contract, an offeree has his choice of performing or promising to perform. There are very few situations where an offer *clearly* seeks performance instead of a return promise. An offer of a reward, as in these facts, is one of them; another is where the offeror specifically limits the acceptance to performance. Here, the city was looking for someone to aid in finding an arsonist, not for a promise to look for the arsonist. Thus, the only way to accept the city's offer would be by offering information leading to the arsonist's arrest. Since A ignores this, it's not the best response.

(B) is not the best response,

because it overstates what an offeree would need to do in order to accept the reward offer.

Here, because a reward is offered, the offer is seeking a *unilateral* contract. That is, the *only* way a person could accept would be through the requested performance. What B addresses is exactly what form that performance must take. This requires interpretation of the "for the arrest and conviction" language. Since the offer is being broadcast to the general public, the city council couldn't have meant to limit the reward to any citizen who actually arrested the arsonist, since this would effectively cut out any offeree except a police officer (who would probably be precluded from accepting since finding the arsonist would probably fulfill a preexisting legal duty, meaning that consideration would be lacking). Instead, a reasonable interpretation would require an offeree only to offer information leading to the arrest and conviction of the arsonist. Since choice B interprets the offer too literally, it's not the best response.

(D) is not the best response,

because an offeree could only accept the reward offer via performance, not a return promise; and even if a promise *were* required, it wouldn't require using the same medium as the offer.

An offer for a bilateral contract seeks a return promise; an offer for a unilateral contract seeks performance. In cases where the offer is ambiguous as to whether it's seeking performance or a promise, an offeree has his choice of performing or promising to perform. There are very few situations where an offer *clearly* seeks performance instead of a return promise. However, a reward offer is just such an offer. The city obviously doesn't want a promise to perform; it wants *action* only—information about the arsonist. Thus, the communication of assent by an offeree, contrary to what D suggests, would not suffice.

Even if the offer were for a bilateral contract, an offeree *could* perform instead of promising to perform, and D ignores this. In fact, even if an offeree *did* have to promise to perform in return, he wouldn't have to use the same medium as the offer. Under modern rules, an acceptance may be made via any medium that is reasonable in the circumstances, as long as the offeror did not expressly limit acceptance to a particular medium. Thus, while using the same medium as the offer would generally be appropriate, it wouldn't be reasonable to expect an acceptance via television, as choice D suggests. (Apart from anything else, buying the TV time alone would wipe out the reward money!) Since choice D misstates the means and medium required for acceptance, it's not the best response.

Answer 3

(A) is the best response,

because the advertisement leaves little doubt that the ad is intended to depict a specific celebrity who has not consented to the use of his identity.

The plaintiff can sue if his name or picture has been appropriated by the defendant for the defendant's own financial benefit. A common-law right of publicity can be violated when an advertisement causes the reader to think that the celebrity is being referred to for the advertiser's benefit. That is what happened here, as an unidentified driver whose face is not visible is standing in front of a distinctive race car. By linking the person depicted to a "distinctive" and "very unusually marked" race car, the advertisement intended to depict a specific celebrity who has not consented to the use of his identity, so the motion to dismiss should not be granted.

(B) is not the best response,

because, in the context of misappropriation of the right to publicity, the driver being a public figure is irrelevant.

The plaintiff can sue if his name or picture has been appropriated by the defendant for the defendant's own financial benefit, and being a public figure does not allow the defendant to profit from his image. In fact, the plaintiff's celebrity may increase the value of the identity that has been misappropriated.

(C) is not the best response,

because the person whose identity has been misappropriated need not be identified by name so long as it is clear that the ad is meant to depict that person.

The plaintiff can sue if his name or picture has been appropriated by the defendant for the defendant's own financial benefit. A common-law right of publicity can be violated when an advertisement causes the reader to think that the celebrity is being referred to for the advertiser's benefit. That is what happened here, as an unidentified driver whose face is not visible is standing in front of a distinctive race car. The advertisement intended to depict a specific celebrity who has not consented to the use of his identity, so the motion to dismiss should not be granted.

(D) is not the best response,

because proof of emotional or dignitary loss is not required.

The plaintiff can sue if his name or picture has been appropriated by the defendant for the defendant's own financial benefit. The injury in a right of publicity case is based on the commercial exploitation of someone's name or likeness, not on the subject's emotional or dignitary loss. As the plaintiff's likeness was commercially exploited by the defendant, the motion to dismiss should not be granted.

Answer 4

(A) is the best response,

because it correctly identifies the problem here as being one of equal protection, and it applies the correct standard to it.

Where a classification is involved that determines people's rights, the issue is most likely one of equal protection. Here, there is a classification: legitimate versus illegitimate children. The test to apply in determining whether the statute is valid depends on the basis of the classification. For instance, a classification relating to who may exercise a fundamental right, or based on a suspect classification (race or alienage), requires that the classification must be necessary to promote a compelling governmental interest. If, on the other hand, economic and social legislation is concerned, the rational basis test is used. That is, if there is a set of facts imaginable that would make the law a reasonable one to achieve a legitimate governmental purpose, the law is valid. Classifications based on "sensitive" classifications, like gender and legitimacy, require application of "intermediate scrutiny." That is, the law must be substantially related to an important state interest in order to be valid. Thus, if the man could prove that this substantial relation does not exist, he will have a valid equal protection claim.

Note that this question asks for the man's best argument, and since choice A is the only choice that recognizes that these facts involve an equal protection problem, it's his best argument. Of course, that doesn't mean he'll prevail, and, in fact, he probably won't. Under *Lalli v. Lalli* (1978), the state's interest in the just and expeditious disposition of property makes a law denying intestate succession to intestate children valid, where the paternity of the father hasn't formally been proven sometime before his death. However, the fact that the man won't win doesn't mean A isn't his best argument. Because it's the only choice addressing the central issue, it's the best response.

(B) is not the best response,

because the man has not been deprived of property, and there is no fundamental right to inherit, and, more importantly, the issue here is equal protection, not due process.

First, as to the property issue: it's true that due process is an issue when the effect of a state's activity amounts to a deprivation of a property interest or right (or life or liberty). Property in its most literal sense means ownership of property. However, under these facts, the man isn't being deprived of property he owns; rather, he's seeking the right to his father's property.

Second, the fundamental right issue: When a law limits a fundamental right, it must be necessary to promote a compelling governmental interest, or else it's a due process violation. The fundamental rights are limited to these: the First Amendment rights, interstate travel, voting, and privacy. Thus, the right to inherit is not a fundamental right, but, rather, any law limiting the right need only rationally relate to any possible legitimate end of government. Choice B thus mischaracterizes the right to inherit as a fundamental right.

Finally, choice B mischaracterizes the whole issue itself. This is how you tell the difference between a due process issue and an equal protection issue: Look to see if there's a classification involved. If there is, it's most likely an equal protection problem. If there's no classification, but the effect of the state's activity amounts to a deprivation of a property interest or right, it's a due process problem.

Here, there's quite clearly a classification involved: legitimate versus illegitimate children. Thus, any argument on which the man would prevail would *have* to address equal protection, not due process. Since B doesn't recognize this, it's not the best response.

(C) is not the best response,

because the law here does not violate the Privileges and Immunities Clause of the Fourteenth Amendment.

The Privileges and Immunities Clause voids those state enactments that clearly infringe privileges enjoyed by U.S. citizens. It is construed narrowly, typically being restricted to fundamental rights that are shared in common by all citizens, namely the right to:

1. Travel freely from state to state;
2. Petition Congress for redress of grievances;
3. Vote for national officers;
4. Assemble peaceably; and
5. Discuss matters of national legislation.

Thus, the right to inherit is not a privilege enjoyed by all U.S. citizens, and as a result it does not violate the Privileges and Immunities Clause. As a result, an argument by the man centering on the Privileges and Immunities Clause would not be a strong one. Since choice C states otherwise, it's not the best response.

(D) is not the best response,

because it mischaracterizes the issue here as one of procedural due process instead of equal protection.

Under these facts, there's a classification involved: legitimate versus illegitimate children. Thus, the problem is one of equal protection. A due process problem is one where there's no classification, but the effect of a state's activity amounts to a deprivation of a property interest or right. Procedural due process (as opposed to substantive due process) involves the situation where a property right (or life or liberty) is taken by government; some fair process or procedure is required.

The problem with applying this here is that due process only applies to presently enjoyed rights. Here, the man wants the right to inherit—it's not as though that he currently has it and it's being taken away from him. Thus, due process would not apply. Since D states otherwise, it's not the best response.

Answer 5

The key here is distinguishing between legal and factual impossibility. Choices A, B, and D are all examples of factual impossibility, which is *not* a valid defense to a crime. Choice C describes *legal* impossibility, which *is* a valid defense. What could key you in to which of these is the correct response is the fact that A, B, and D each describe the *same behavior* by the defendant—mistaking the facts. Thus, *none* of them can be the best response.

(C) is the best response,

because it represents the *only* choice of these four under which the defendant is likely to be acquitted.

That's because the defendant has a valid *legal impossibility* defense: What he intended to do was not criminal. Here, the defendant did everything he intended to do—purchase codeine without a prescription—but his actions do not constitute a crime. This should be contrasted with factual impossibility, which arises when completion of the crime is impossible due to physical facts not known to the defendant. Factual impossibility, unlike legal impossibility, is *not* a valid defense. Even if you had forgotten which of legal and factual impossibility was a valid defense, a clue here is that the three incorrect choices are all similar: the defendant makes a *factual* mistake. The nature of the defendant's misperception is fundamentally different in C, which would key you in to the likelihood that it's the best response.

(A) is not the best response,

because it depicts factual impossibility, which is not a valid defense to an attempt charge.

Factual impossibility arises when completion of the crime is impossible due to physical facts not known to the defendant. (Don't confuse this with *legal* impossibility, where what a defendant intends to do is not criminal. Legal impossibility *is* a valid defense to attempt.) Under choice A, the defendant did not know the physical fact that the police had intercepted the stolen goods. Had this fact not been true, the defendant would be liable for receiving stolen goods. Since factual impossibility is not a valid defense to an attempt charge, the defendant will likely be guilty, and since the question asks for the choice where the defendant is most likely to be *not* guilty, A is not the best response.

(B) is not the best response,

because it depicts factual impossibility, which is not a valid defense to an attempt charge.

Factual impossibility arises when completion of the crime is impossible due to physical facts not known to the defendant. (Don't confuse this with *legal* impossibility, where what a defendant *intends* to do is not criminal. Legal impossibility *is* a valid defense to attempt.) Under choice B, the defendant did not know that the banker realized his true identity. Where the victim is not deceived by the wrongdoer's lies, the defendant will be liable for attempted false pretenses. Since the question asks for the choice where the defendant is most likely to be acquitted, B is not the best response.

(D) is not the best response,

because it depicts factual impossibility, which is not a valid defense to an attempt charge.

Factual impossibility arises when completion of the crime is impossible due to physical facts not known to the defendant. (Don't confuse this with *legal* impossibility, where what a defendant *intends* to do is not criminal. Legal impossibility *is* a valid defense to attempt.) Under choice D, the defendant did not know the woman was dead. Thus, his attempt to kill her was thwarted by a physical fact he didn't know—i.e., that she was already dead. As a result, the defendant will be liable for attempted murder. Since the question asks for the choice under which the defendant is most likely to be acquitted, D isn't the best response.

Answer 6

(B) is the best response,

because it states the correct response *if* the condition it supplies is satisfied.

The key fact here is the characterization of the tenancy. If you're familiar with cotenancies, you know that the only two that have the right to survivorship are joint tenancies and tenancies by the entirety.

B says that the man will win *if* he and the woman were tenants by the entirety in the farm. Under the facts here, this is possible. A tenancy by the entirety is a tenancy that exists between husband and wife, with the right of survivorship, and it cannot be destroyed by severance. It requires the same "four unities" as a joint tenancy: in other words, the tenancy for each tenant must be created by the same instrument; the tenancy must be of the same duration; all tenants must hold an equal, undivided interest in the whole; and there must be a simultaneous vesting of interests. All of these conditions are satisfied by the facts here. However, the *if* makes B correct, because if the woman and the man were *not* married at the time of the conveyance, a joint tenancy would result. A joint tenancy is similar to a tenancy by the entirety in most respects but differs significantly in one respect that is crucial here: a joint tenant *can* convey his interest away, and, in doing so, leaves a tenancy in common between the conveyee and the other tenants. Since B conditions the man's prevailing on the existence of a tenancy by the entirety, it's the best response.

(A) is not the best response,

because the conclusion it states *may not* be correct.

The facts here indicate two possibilities: the woman and the man were *either* joint tenants or tenants by the entirety, since those are the only two cotenancies that feature a right to survivorship. (The other cotenancy, a tenancy in common, does not.) If they were married when the farm was conveyed to them, the tenancy is a tenancy by the entirety, which *cannot be destroyed by severance*. In other words, the woman's conveyance would have no effect, and, when she died, her interest would go to the man due to the right to survivorship. However, what makes A an incorrect response is that it states that the man is *necessarily* the sole owner of the farm, and he's not. It's equally likely that the cotenancy created by these facts was a joint tenancy, if the woman and the man *weren't* married. A joint tenancy, unlike a tenancy by the entirety, *can* be destroyed by severance—i.e., one of the tenants conveying his interest in the property. (In that case the joint tenancy is only destroyed as to that tenant; however, where there are only two tenants, the joint tenancy is totally destroyed.) This would leave the man and the purchaser as tenants in common—a cotenancy without the right to survivorship. Choice A states merely that the man *is* the sole owner of the farm, without taking into account that he and the purchaser may be tenants in common. As a result, A is not the best response.

(C) is not the best response,

because the man's knowledge of the conveyance before the woman died does not control resolution of the issue here.

If the original conveyance created a joint tenancy, the woman's conveyance to the purchaser destroyed it, and the man's knowledge of the conveyance to the purchaser is irrelevant; and if the original conveyance created a tenancy by the entirety, because the man and the woman were married, then the woman's conveyance was meaningless. That's because a tenancy by the entirety cannot be destroyed by one tenant's conveying away his/her interest. Since C focuses on a fact that is not relevant to resolving this issue, it's not the best response.

(D) is not the best response,

because it states as a *certainty* something that is only a *possibility.*

If the woman and the man were not married when the conveyance to them took place, then the tenancy created was a joint tenancy. When the woman conveyed her interest to the purchaser, a tenancy in common would result between the man and the purchaser (since conveyance by one of the co-tenants destroys a joint tenancy, leaving a tenancy in common). If this were the *only* possibility, D would be the best response. However, if the man and the woman were married when the conveyance to them took place, the resulting tenancy would be a tenancy by the entirety. A tenancy by the entirety cannot be severed by one spouse attempting to convey his interest. If a spouse does so, the conveyance is meaningless;

the tenancy by the entirety remains intact, and, when either spouse dies, the other is left as a sole owner (due to the right to survivorship). Thus, there exists at least one possibility, under these facts, that would make D incorrect. As a result, D cannot be the best response.

Answer 7

(D) is the best response,

because it identifies the central reason the power saw company will not be strictly liable.

A defendant can only be liable if

1. The product was defective;
2. When it left the defendant's control (meaning the defendant can be liable even if he didn't cause the defect);
3. Product must not be expected to undergo significant changes before it gets to the user/consumer (or not actually undergo such changes);
4. The seller must be in the business of selling the product (thus, the defendant can't be a casual seller);
5. Damage must result from the defect (the defendant is liable for any harm to persons or property);
6. And the duty extends to anyone foreseeably endangered by the product (meaning, there's no privity requirement).

Choice D correctly identifies the reason the power-saw company won't be strictly liable under these facts: The storekeeper disassembled and rebuilt the saw after it left the power saw company's control. Since D correctly identifies this, it's the best response.

(A) is not the best response,

because it is not relevant to determining the power-saw company's liability.

A alludes to the issue of *change* in the product between the time it left the power-saw company and when it reached the employee. A defendant can only be liable if

1. The product was defective;
2. When it left the defendant's control (meaning the defendant can be liable even if he didn't cause the defect);
3. Product must not be expected to undergo significant changes before it gets to the user/consumer (or not actually undergo such changes);
4. The seller must be in the business of selling the product (thus, the defendant can't be a casual seller);
5. Damage must result from the defect (the defendant is liable for any harm to persons or property);
6. And the duty extends to anyone foreseeably endangered by the product (meaning, there's no privity requirement).

You're told that the storekeeper completely disassembles and rebuilds the saws after they leave the power-saw company's contol. This is enough to remove the power-saw company from strict liability *regardless* of whether the specific shaft was replaced. Since A focuses on an element that will not determine the power-saw company's liability, it's not relevant.

(B) is not the best response,

because the element it cites, although true, is not sufficient to hold the power-saw company liable.

A defendant can only be liable if

1. The product was defective;
2. When it left the defendant's control (meaning the defendant can be liable even if he didn't cause the defect);
3. Product must not be expected to undergo significant changes before it gets to the user/consumer (or not actually undergo such changes);
4. The seller must be in the business of selling the product (thus, the defendant can't be a casual seller);
5. Damage must result from the defect (the defendant is liable for any harm to persons or property);
6. And the duty extends to anyone foreseeably endangered by the product (meaning, there's no privity requirement).

As a result, it's not the power-saw company's manufacturing dangerous machines that would make it liable, but selling machines that are *defective.* Merely manufacturing power saws itself is not a basis for strict liability. In any case, choice B ignores the reason the power-saw company will avoid strict liability: because the saw was *overhauled* before it reached the employee. Since B doesn't recognize this, it's not the best response.

(C) is not the best response,

because it's irrelevant.

Strict product liability extends to anyone endangered by the defective product. According to most courts, this even includes bystanders, as well as users and consumers. The employee would fit well within this scope, since he's the intended user.

In fact, choice C ignores the reason the power-saw company will escape strict liability: the saw was *overhauled* by the storekeeper after it left the power-saw company. As a result, C is not the best response.

Answer 8

(C) is the best response,

because in-state residence is a recognized basis for the exercise of general jurisdiction, and its use is constitutional under the federal Due Process Clause.

The Supreme Court has long held that it does not violate due process for a state to exercise personal jurisdiction over any cause of action against a ***resident of that state***, whether or not the claim is related to the defendant's in-state activities. (That is, "general jurisdiction"—jurisdiction for all claims, whether related to in-state activities or not—is allowed against residents of the forum state.) *See Goodyear Dunlop Tires Operations, SA v. Brown*, 131 S. Ct. 2846 (2011). It is true that personal jurisdiction may only be exercised by a state court if a state statute permits such jurisdiction in the type of situation in question. But you're told that State B's jurisdiction statute does so (since it extends the state's personal jurisdiction as far as the U.S. Constitution allows). Indeed, this statute is typical of many state jurisdictional statutes.

(A) is not the best response,

because it is based on a rule of law about the exercise of personal jurisdiction that is legally incorrect.

A state court can exercise "specific jurisdiction"—that is, jurisdiction over a plaintiff's claim that arises out of or relates to defendant's in-state contacts—even if the defendant is *not* a resident of the forum state. However, *the converse is not true*; that is, the fact that the suit does *not* relate to any in-forum-state activities does not automatically mean that jurisdiction is improper. Rather, a court can always exercise "general jurisdiction" (i.e., "all-purpose" jurisdiction over suits that do not involve in-state activities) in some circumstances. And one of those circumstances where general jurisdiction is always allowed is where the defendant is ***domiciled in the forum state***, as is the situation here. *See Goodyear Dunlop Tires Operations, SA v. Brown*, 131 S. Ct. 2846 (2011).

(B) is not correct,

because it contains an incorrect statement of law.

It's true that only a court in the state in which property is located can exercise *"in rem"* jurisdiction regarding that property. But here Plaintiff is seeking money damages for breach of contract, so the court is being asked to act *"in personam,"* not *"in rem."* (Only a suit to determine the property's *status*, such as who properly holds title, would be *"in rem."*) And the court will have *in personam* jurisdiction—assuming defendant does not consent to jurisdiction or waive any defect—only if the exercise of jurisdiction satisfies the tests of ***minimum contacts and reasonableness*** articulated in such decisions as *World-Wide Volkswagen v. Woodson*, 444 U.S. 286 (1980). It's true that the location of the property here would be *one* of the factors to be considered on the issue of reasonableness. But the fact that the property is located outside the forum state would ***not by itself automatically make exercise of jurisdiction unreasonable***, as this choice suggests it would. (Indeed, the fact that Defendant ***resides*** in the forum state would automatically have the opposite effect, i.e., suffice to make the exercise of jurisdiction automatically ***reasonable***).

(D) is not correct,

because diversity of citizenship is an irrelevant concept on these facts.

Diversity of citizenship is a condition of ***subject-matter jurisdiction*** for actions brought in ***federal*** court, as authorized by 28 U.S.C. § 1332. So the existence (or non-existence) of diversity of citizenship is irrelevant here for two reasons: (1) the concept never applies to a ***state*** court suit; and (2) even in a federal court, diversity jurisdiction would not be relevant to a motion to dismiss based on lack of "personal jurisdiction." *See* FRCP 12(b)(2). (For diversity to be relevant, the plaintiff's complaint would have to be based solely upon diversity—not the existence of a federal question—and the motion would have to be one asserting lack of "subject matter jurisdiction," not lack of "personal jurisdiction.")

Answer 9

(B) is the best response,

because in this type of slander case, character is considered "in issue."

In slander cases where the defendant makes a statement that the plaintiff has an unsavory character, the plaintiff's character is considered "in issue" (i.e., an essential element of the claim or defense under the substantive law) in two respects. First, the plaintiff's actual character will determine whether the defendant was incorrect in his assessment, and thus liable for slander, because truth is a defense. Second, the plaintiff will allege that he is damaged by the statement, which is another way of saying that his true character has been besmirched; but if the plaintiff actually has a bad reputation anyway, then damages are limited. Thus, in slander cases like the one in this question, character evidence is relevant both to whether the plaintiff has a certain character and to the extent of damages. Under Federal Rule of Evidence 405, when character is "in issue" it can be proved by evidence of reputation, opinion, or specific acts.

(A) is not the best response,

because when character is "in issue" it can be proved by evidence of reputation, opinion, or specific acts.

In slander cases where the defendant makes a statement that the plaintiff has an unsavory character, the plaintiff's character is considered "in issue" (i.e., an essential element of the claim or defense under the substantive law) in two respects. First, the plaintiff's actual character will determine whether the defendant was incorrect in his assessment, and thus liable for slander, because truth is a defense. Second, the plaintiff will allege that he is damaged by the statement, which is another way of saying that his true character has been besmirched; but if the plaintiff actually has a bad reputation anyway, then damages are limited. Thus, in slander cases like the one in this question, character evidence is relevant both to whether the plaintiff has a certain character and to the extent of damages. Under Federal Rule of Evidence 405, when character is "in issue" it can be proved by evidence of reputation, opinion, or specific acts.

(C) is not the best response,

because if plaintiff possessed a bad reputation, it would affect his damages, and, therefore, the evidence may be admissible on the issue of damages.

In slander cases where the defendant makes a statement that the plaintiff has an unsavory character, the plaintiff's character is considered "in issue" (i.e., an essential element of the claim or defense under the substantive law) in two respects: First, the plaintiff's actual character will determine whether the defendant was incorrect in his assessment, and thus liable for slander, because truth is a defense. Second, the plaintiff will allege that he is damaged by the statement, which is another way of saying that his true character has been besmirched; but if the plaintiff actually has a bad reputation anyway, then damages are limited. Thus, in slander cases like the one in this question, character evidence is relevant both to whether the plaintiff has a certain character and to the extent of damages. Under Federal Rule of Evidence 405, when character is "in issue" it can be proved by evidence of reputation, opinion, or specific acts.

(D) is not the best response,

because the defendant may use truth as a defense, which makes the evidence admissible to prove that the plaintiff is a thief.

In slander cases where the defendant makes a statement that the plaintiff has an unsavory character, the plaintiff's character is considered "in issue" (i.e., an essential element of the claim or defense under the substantive law) in two respects. First, the plaintiff's actual character will determine whether the defendant was incorrect in his assessment, and thus liable for slander, because truth is a defense. Second, the plaintiff will allege that he is damaged by the statement, which is another way of saying that his true character has been besmirched; but if the plaintiff actually has a bad reputation anyway, then damages are limited. Thus, in slander cases like the one in this question, character evidence is relevant both to whether the plaintiff has a certain character and to the extent of damages. Under Federal Rule of Evidence 405, when character is "in issue" it can be proved by evidence of reputation, opinion, or specific acts.

Answer 10

(C) is the best response,

because the CEO's in-state presence at the time of service sufficed for personal jurisdiction over him, but the insurer's contacts with the state were not sufficient to allow for "general jurisdiction" over it.

Let's take the two suits one at a time. Suit against the insurer: The first thing to notice is that the suit against the insurer involves a particular policy sold by it, and that all activities connected with that sale occurred in State A, during the time the surgeon/insured was a State A resident. Furthermore, in the years since the policy has been in force, no activities by the insurer in connection with the policy have occurred in State B, beyond the fact that the insurer has corresponded with the surgeon at his State B address and has received premiums sent by him from that address. Therefore, the suit brought by the surgeon against the insurer in State B—since the suit does not arise out of the insurer's State B activities or contacts—will have to be based on ***"general"*** jurisdiction rather than "specific" jurisdiction.

When a suit is brought against an out-of-state corporation and is based on general jurisdiction, it's been clear since a 2011 Supreme Court decision that the corporation must have contacts with the forum state that are so "'continuous and systematic' as to render [the corporation and its affiliates] ***essentially at home*** in the forum State." *Goodyear Dunlop Tires Operations, S.A. v. Brown*, 131 S. Ct. 2846 (2011). Then, in the later case of *Daimler AG v. Bauman*, 134 S.Ct. 746 (2014), the Court said that in determining whether a corporation is "essentially at home" in the forum state, the corporation must (except in an "exceptional case") either (1) have its ***principal place of business*** in the forum state or (2) be ***incorporated*** in that state. Here, the insurer is neither incorporated in State B nor has its principal place of business there. And there is nothing in the case that would dictate treating any connection between the insurer and State B as sufficiently "extraordinary" to merit deviating from this rule requiring either in-forum-state incorporation or in-forum-state principal place of business. So under *Goodyear* and *Daimler*, it would violate the insurer's federal due process rights to be required to defend in State B a suit that has no real connection with that state beyond the fact that the plaintiff now lives there (i.e., a suit based on general jurisdiction). The State B judge will therefore dismiss the suit for lack of personal jurisdiction.

Divorce suit: Now, let's turn to the divorce suit against the CEO. Ever since *Pennoyer v. Neff*, 95 U.S. 714 (1877), the Supreme Court has recognized that if an individual who doesn't reside in the forum state voluntarily enters the state and is ***served with process there***, the state may exercise personal jurisdiction over him without violating his due process rights, even if the defendant has absolutely no other contacts with the forum state. And more recently, in *Burnham v. Superior Court*, 495 U.S. 604 (1990), the Supreme Court decided a case involving precisely the issue here: Because D had voluntarily visited the forum state and been served with process in a divorce suit brought there by his estranged wife, the forum state had personal jurisdiction over him regardless of whether he had any connection whatsoever with the forum state beyond this one visit. So in light of *Burnham*, there is no due process impediment to the State B court's exercising personal jurisdiction over the CEO for purposes of issuing a divorce decree (or, indeed, for any other purpose that would require the court to exercise personal jurisdiction over him).

(A), (B), and (D) are not the best responses, because each of them reaches the wrong conclusion as to at least one of the two motions.

Answer 11

(A) is the best response,

because the collector is not the federal government, and is therefore not exempt from state taxation.

The federal government and its agencies are immune from state taxation. For example, in this problem, the state could not collect sales tax on the sales made by the collector to the National Park Service. However, a state may tax a private contractor who does work for the federal government under a cost-plus contract, since the "legal incidence" of the tax does not fall on the federal government. (*James v. Dravo Contracting* (1937).) Here, the collector is not an employee of the National Park Service, but rather an independent contractor. Further, he is selling what he has acquired to the Park Service for 10 percent more than he paid (a cost-plus contract). Therefore, the collector is not immune from state taxation and the state court should not issue the injunction.

(B) is not the best response,

because this case is not within the exclusive jurisdiction of the federal courts.

Generally, state courts have concurrent jurisdiction over claims arising under federal statutes or the Constitution. The exceptions are in areas where the Constitution or a federal statute specifically limits jurisdiction to the federal courts. These include cases relating to intellectual property, antitrust, bankruptcy, federal crimes, and suits against the federal government. A case concerning the constitutionality of a state's imposition of sales tax is within the concurrent jurisdiction of the federal and state courts, and may be heard in either forum.

(C) is not the best response,

because the "legal incidence" of the tax does not fall on the federal government, but rather on the collector.

The federal government and its agencies are immune from state taxation. Under the rule of *James v. Dravo Contracting* (1937), a state may tax a private contractor who does work for the federal government under a cost-plus contract. Here, the collector is not an employee of the National Park Service, but rather an independent contractor. Further, he is selling what he has acquired to the Park Service for 10 percent more than he paid (a cost-plus contract). Therefore, the collector is not immune from state taxation, and the court should not issue the injunction.

(D) is not the best response,

because the state sales tax does not conflict with any federal law.

The Supremacy Clause of Article VI of the Constitution dictates that when a state statute and a federal law are inconsistent, the state law is invalid. However, that is not the case in this problem. Although the state sales tax may cause an increase in the amount that the National Park Service will have to pay the collector, it does not conflict with any federal law. In order for the Supremacy Clause to apply to this situation, there would have to be a federal statute stating that no sales tax may be levied on sales made to contractors working for the National Park Service. Since no such federal statute exists, the Supremacy Clause is not brought into play.

Answer 12

(A) is the best response,

because, pursuant to FRE 803(18), statements from the learned treatise may only be read to the jury.

FRE 803(18), the learned treatise exception, provides that if the court finds a publication to be a reliable authority, then if a statement in the publication is "called to the attention of an expert witness on cross-examination or relied on by the expert on direct examination," the statement "may be read into evidence *but not received as an exhibit*." Thus, the jury is not allowed to bring learned treatises into the jury room. (There is a concern that if juries were allowed unrestricted access to the whole publication, they may rely on parts of the publication that are not germane to the case. Moreover, the intent of the rule is that juries need to be guided through the pertinent parts of the publication by the testifying experts.)

(B) is not the best response,

because FRE 803(18) does not require that the witness rely on the treatise.

FRE 803(18), the learned treatise exception, allows a statement from a treatise to be read into evidence where the court finds the treatise to be a reliable authority, and the statement is "called to the attention of an expert witness on cross-examination or relied on by the expert on direct examination." In this case, the publication was called to the attention of the defendant's expert.

(C) is not the best response,

because the decision on reliability is for the court, and the entire publication may not be submitted to the jury for this or any purpose.

FRE 803(18), the learned treatise exception, allows a statement from a publication to be read into evidence when "the statement is called to the attention of an expert witness on cross-examination or relied on by the expert on direct examination," provided that the "publication is established as a reliable authority by the expert's admission or testimony, by another expert's testimony, or by judicial notice." The plaintiff's expert's testimony probably suffices to establish reliability under this standard. But even so, this would not permit the entire treatise to be submitted to the jury, since 803(18) does not allow the publication to be received as an exhibit, and the jury is not the arbiter of whether the publication is reliable.

(D) is not the best response,

because, pursuant to FRE 803(18), only statements from the learned treatise may be read to the jury.

The statement is true so far as it goes, but it does not mean that the jury gets to consider any evidence that the parties wish to present. FRE 803(18), the learned treatise exception, requires the judge to determine that the publication is reliable before it can be considered by the jury. In addition, the rule allows "statements" from a learned treatise to be read into evidence, but does not allow the publication to be received as an exhibit.

Answer 13

(C) is the best response,

because the pedestrian offered no evidence supporting the claim of negligence other than the violation of a statute that does not protect against the same type of accident that materialized in this case.

Under certain circumstances, the violation of a statute may be determined to be negligence per se. The three requirements for negligence per se are that (1) a defendant violated a statute, (2) the statute was designed to protect against the same type of accident that defendant's conduct caused, and (3) the accident victim falls within the class of persons the statute was designed to protect. Here, the statute was enacted "only" to expedite "automobile" traffic. As the statute was not designed to prevent a pedestrian's slip and fall, negligence per se will not apply. Accordingly, the pedestrian failed to offer adequate evidence that the car owner was negligent.

(A) is not the best response,

because the doctrine of negligence per se does not apply, and the facts do not support a reasonable inference of negligence.

Under certain circumstances, the violation of a statute may be determined to be negligence per se. The three requirements for negligence per se are that (1) a defendant violated a statute, (2) the statute was designed to protect against the same type of accident that defendant's conduct caused, and (3) the accident victim falls within the class of persons the statute was designed to protect. Here, the statute was enacted "only" to expedite "automobile" traffic. As the statute was not designed to prevent a pedestrian's slip and fall, negligence per se will not apply. Furthermore, because the cold weather was "sudden and unexpected," the inference of negligence is tenuous. On the facts presented, the car owner's motion should be granted, as the pedestrian has failed to offer adequate evidence that the car owner was negligent.

(B) is not the best response,

because the statutory violation will not be considered as evidence that the car owner was negligent.

Under certain circumstances, the violation of a statute may be determined to be negligence per se. The three requirements for negligence per se are that (1) a defendant violated a statute, (2) the statute was designed to protect against the same type of accident that defendant's conduct caused, and (3) the accident victim falls within the class of persons the statute was designed to protect. Here, the statute was enacted "only" to expedite "automobile" traffic. As the statute was not designed to prevent a pedestrian's slip and fall, negligence per se will not apply. Accordingly, the pedestrian failed to offer adequate evidence that the car owner was negligent.

(D) is not the best response,

because the statutory violation will not be considered as evidence that the car owner was negligent.

Under certain circumstances, the violation of a statute may be determined to be negligence per se. The three requirements for negligence per se are that (1) a defendant violated a statute, (2) the statute was designed to protect against the same type of accident that defendant's conduct caused, and (3) the accident victim falls within the class of persons the statute was designed to protect. Here, the statute was enacted "only" to expedite "automobile" traffic. As the statute was not designed to prevent a pedestrian's slip and fall, negligence per se will not apply. Accordingly, the pedestrian failed to offer adequate evidence that the car owner was negligent.

Answer 14

(D) is the correct answer,

because it recognizes that Defendant has ***waived*** the defense of improper venue by failing to include it when he filed a responsive pleading.

Rule 12(b) lists seven special defenses that may be asserted by motion; one of these is "improper venue," listed in Rule 12(b)(3). Rule 12(h) then says that each of these seven defenses is waived by a party's "failing to either (i) make [the defense] by motion under [Rule 12]; or (ii) include it in a responsive pleading or in an amendment allowed by Rule 15(a)(1) as a matter of course." We know by negative implication from the facts that Defendant did not raise the venue defense by a Rule 12 motion. Therefore, Defendant will be deemed to have waived the defense unless he included it either in "a responsive pleading" or in "an amendment allowed by Rule 15(a)(1) as a matter of course." As to raising it in a responsive pleading, Defendant's only "responsive pleading" so far has been his answer, and the facts tell us that he did not include the venue defense in that answer. So Defendant's only hope for avoiding losing the defense by waiver is if the Rules permit him to include it in "an amendment allowed by Rule 15(a)(1) as a matter of course." But Rule 15(a)(1)(A) says that where the pleading to be amended will not require a responsive pleading (which is the situation here), the pleader's time to amend as a matter of course expires 21 days after the pleader served the pleading. So on August 21, Defendant's time to amend his answer as a matter of course expired. Thus by now (October 2), he has no way to avoid the waiver that Rule 12(h) says has occurred.

(A) is not the best response,

because Defendant can no longer amend his answer.

As this choice suggests, under some circumstances a defendant who has answered without including a venue defense might be able to amend the answer to include that defense. But as is discussed more fully in the treatment of Choice (D), for the amendment to include the addition of a venue defense, the amendment must be one that is allowed "as a matter of course" (rather than by leave of court), and Defendant's power to amend as a matter of course ended on August 21, 21 days after he served his original answer. Therefore, Defendant does not have the power to place the issue of whether the action should be dismissed for lack of venue in front of the court.

(B) is not the best response,

because Defendant can no longer make a motion to dismiss based on the venue objection.

When Defendant was first served with the complaint, a motion by him to dismiss for improper venue would have been proper: Under FRCP 12(b), a party may assert various defenses by motion, including a motion under 12(b)(3) to dismiss for improper venue. However, as is discussed more fully in the explanation of Choice (D), once defendant served his answer without including the venue defense, he waived his right to assert the defense by motion. *See* Rule 12(h)(i). So the court will not have discretion to dismiss the action for improper venue even if the court concludes that venue was improper.

(C) is not correct,

because defendant has waived his right to make a motion based on the venue objection.

As is described in the explanation to both Choice (D) and Choice (B), when Defendant filed an answer that did not include the venue defense, he waived his right to assert that defense by motion. Therefore, the court is not authorized to dismiss the action for lack of venue, even if the judge is satisfied that venue was improper. Unlike a lack of subject matter jurisdiction, a lack of venue is not deemed "jurisdictional," so the federal court has power to hear the case even though the case was brought in a district where venue did not lie.

Answer 15

(C) is the best response,

because it correctly calculates the expectation damages recoverable by the seller.

First we should note that Article 2 of the Uniform Commercial Code applies since the contract is for a sale of goods. When a buyer breaches, UCC 2-708(2) allows the seller to recover the profit that would have been made had the buyer not breached, plus the costs incurred in manufacturing the goods minus any proceeds that the seller received from selling the goods to a third party. Here, the seller expected to make a profit of $2 per set under the contract—the seller expected to be paid $10 per set, while spending $8 to manufacture each. Each set cost the seller $8 to produce, and was sold to a third party (the salvage company) for $2. Thus, the damages recoverable by the seller are $2 (the expected profit under the contract) + $8 (the cost incurred in producing each set of bearings) - $2 (the amount received from the salvage company) = $8 per set.

Another way of thinking about expectation damages is that the seller expected to make a profit of $2 per set, but, because of the buyer's breach, the seller actually *lost* $6 per set (since it cost $8 to produce each set that eventually sold for $2 each). To put the seller in the same position as he would have been had the buyer performed, the seller will have to recover the $8 difference between the expected $2 profit and the actual $6 loss.

(A) is incorrect,

because it only allows the seller to recover the profit he expected under the contract, but not the costs he incurred in performing.

When a buyer breaches, UCC 2-708(2) allows a seller to recover *both* the expected profit *and* the net costs incurred in manufacturing the goods. By only awarding $2 per set, choice A does not compensate the seller for the $6 per set loss ($8 to manufacture–$2 salvage sale) that he suffered as a result of the buyer's breach.

(B) is incorrect,

because it does not provide the seller the expected benefit of his bargain.

While choice B correctly allows the seller to recover the $6 per set he lost as a result of the buyer's breach, it does not make him whole. Under UCC 2-708(2), the non-breaching seller may recover *both* the loss incurred in the production of the goods for sale *and* the profit expected as a result of the contract. Here, the seller expected to realize a $2 profit on each set of bearings sold ($10 sale price–$8 cost of manufacturing). This $2 expected profit per set must be added to the $6 loss per set in order to come up with the total expectation damages due to the seller.

(D) is incorrect,

because there is no requirement that the seller attempt to sell the bearings at public auction.

While it is true that the seller, upon the buyer's anticipatory repudiation of the contract, is under a duty to mitigate damages, there is no provision in the UCC that requires any particular method of doing so. If the seller mitigates damages by selling the goods to a third party, UCC 2-706 allows either a public sale (an auction) or a private sale. The only restriction is that the sale must be made in good faith and in a commercially reasonable manner. Therefore, the fact that the seller chose to sell the bearings privately to a salvage company will not bar the seller from recovering full expectation damages unless the buyer can show that the sale was conducted in bad faith or in an unreasonable manner. Further, even if the seller didn't attempt to resell the bearings, the failure to mitigate damages would only reduce the damages he could recover, not eliminate them. The seller would still be entitled to recover his expected profits under the contract, which in this case would be $2 per set ($10 per set contract price–$8 per set cost of production).

Answer 16

(B) is the best response,

because it correctly identifies that the defendant intended to kill the neighbor's brother and the neighbor's brother alone. The key here is distinguishing between intent and mistake.

One is said to intend a result when he desires that result or, alternatively, he knows the result is substantially certain to be caused by his conduct. Here, when the defendant raised his gun to fire, he intended to kill the neighbor's brother. Admittedly, he was mistaken about the neighbor's brother's identity, but he nonetheless intended to kill the neighbor's brother. He did not intend to kill the bystander, but his intent to kill the neighbor's brother will be "transferred" to the bystander. Since B correctly identifies that the defendant intended to kill the neighbor's brother, B is the best response.

(A) is not the best response,

because the defendant set out to kill the neighbor, but the intent that actuated the actual killing was the defendant's raising the gun and aiming at the neighbor's brother.

Under these facts, although the defendant wanted to kill the neighbor, he didn't perform an act toward that end that would qualify as an attempt, since an attempt to commit a crime requires the intent to commit the crime coupled with acts that come dangerously close to accomplishing the criminal goal. There would not be enough on these facts to constitute an attempt to kill the neighbor. Here, the defendant was *mistaken* about the neighbor's brother's identity, but he did intend to kill the neighbor's brother. Since A states that the defendant intended to kill the neighbor, it's not the best response.

(C) is not the best response,

because the defendant didn't intend to kill the bystander at all.

In fact, he'll be guilty of attempt to commit murder for the bystander's wound, because his intent to kill the neighbor's brother will be "transferred" to the bystander, and otherwise the defendant would satisfy the requirements for attempt to commit murder (since he had the intent to commit murder, and came dangerously close to achieving his goal). Transferred intent comes about when a person intending to commit one crime accidentally commits another; the intent will be "transferred" from the person he intended to harm to the person he actually harmed. Here, when the defendant raised his gun to fire, he intended to kill the neighbor's brother, not the bystander. Since the defendant did not intend to kill the bystander, C is not the best response.

(D) is not the best response,
because the defendant intended to kill the neighbor's brother, not the neighbor.

Intent here refers to what actuated the defendant's raising the gun and firing. He was *mistaken* as to the neighbor's brother's identity, and although he *wanted* to kill the neighbor, he *intended* to kill the neighbor's brother only. Since D incorrectly states that the defendant also intended to kill the neighbor, it's not the best response.

Answer 17

(C) is the best answer,
because it proves bias.

Under the FRE, bias is liberally admitted to prove such things as hostility, self-interest, or a personal relationship that may affect the truthfulness of a witness's testimony. Here, the facts indicate both self-interest and hostility from the witness to the defendant, and these facts would be admissible to prove bias. Additionally, the witness may still be impeached under FRE 806 even though he is a hearsay declarant. FRE 806 allows all modes of impeachment that can occur to a live witness to apply to a hearsay declarant.

(A) is not the best answer,
because these misdemeanors do not involve dishonesty.

Under FRE 609(a)(1), in order to impeach with a conviction, the conviction must be a felony. Under FRE 609(a)(2), misdemeanors may be used to impeach, but only if they involve dishonesty or false statement. Here, the misdemeanor assault convictions do not involve dishonesty or false statement, and therefore cannot be used to impeach the witness.

(B) is not the best answer,
because experts generally may not testify as to credibility.

Credibility is an issue for the jury, who must not abdicate their role of critical assessment to an expert. Although, on occasion, courts have allowed experts latitude in discussing credibility, the general rule is that such testimony is not allowed. As this question sought the "most likely" admitted evidence, bias is the better answer. Here, the facts indicate both self-interest and hostility from the witness to the defendant, and these facts would be admissible to prove bias. Additionally, the witness may still be impeached under FRE 806 even though he is a hearsay declarant. FRE 806 allows all modes of impeachment that can occur to a live witness to apply to a hearsay declarant.

(D) is not the best answer,
because the prior bad act is a "specific instance of conduct," and does not relate to truthfulness.

As this is not a conviction, FRE 608(b) will govern this prior bad act evidence. What we have here is testimony by Witness 2 (the "witness") that Witness 1 (the gang member) is a cocaine dealer. So what Witness 2 has to say about Witness 1 is "extrinsic evidence" about Witness 1's credibility (since the evidence is not from the "mouth" of Witness 1). FRE 608(b) says that "Except for a criminal conviction under Rule 609, extrinsic evidence is not admissible to prove *specific instances of a witness's conduct* in order to attack or support the witness's character for truthfulness." The testimony here would probably be considered "specific instances of a witness's conduct" (as opposed to admissible reputation or opinion testimony), thus making it inadmissible extrinsic evidence. Furthermore, being a cocaine dealer has little if any probative value on the gang member's character for truthfulness, which is the only subject on which the witness might be permitted to testify under FRE 608.

Answer 18

(A) is the best response,
because it offers a defense that is likely to prevail on these facts.

A contract has three basic elements: offer, acceptance, and consideration or some substitute for consideration (e.g., promissory estoppel). Consideration requires a bargained-for exchange and either detriment to the promisee or benefit to the promisor, and typically both. Here, the student's father had no legal obligation to reimburse the woman for her expenses. His promise to do so didn't create any benefit to him, and the woman didn't suffer any detriment as a result of it, either. As such, the promise would be considered *gratuitous,* and thus not enforceable.

Say instead that the woman agreed not to claim against the student's estate in return for his father's promise. Then she would suffer a detriment in the form of surrendering a valid legal claim. As a result, there would be consideration. Under the facts as they exist, however, there is no consideration. Without consideration, or some substitute for it, the father's promise is an unenforceable gratuitous promise. Since A recognizes this, it's the best response.

(B) is not the best response,
because unilateral mistake is, in general, not a good defense to breach of contract.

The rule on unilateral mistake is that where the other party (here, the woman) reasonably did not know of the mistake, the mistaken party must perform. It's only if the other party knew or should have known of the mistake, that the mistaken party's performance will be excused.

Here, the woman had no reason to know that the student's father believed he was liable for the accident simply because he owned the car. Thus, mistake would not excuse his performance.

If you chose this response, you were probably thinking of *mutual* mistake. As a general rule, when both parties are mistaken as to a basic assumption of fact on which the contract was created, the contract is voidable. However, what's involved here is *unilateral* mistake. Since the father's mistake won't relieve him of his duty to perform under the contract, mistake is not his best defense, making B not the best response.

(C) is not the best response,

because the agreement here would not fall within the Statute of Frauds.

Under the Statute of Frauds, a writing is generally required for certain contracts, including those for the sale of an interest in land, incapable of performance in less than one year, to answer for another's debt, and the like. Here, the student's father's promise to the woman is a direct promise to pay her expenses. Such an agreement is not covered by the Statute of Frauds, so no writing is required to make it enforceable.

If you chose this response, you were probably thinking that the student's father was covering his son's obligation to the woman and so the agreement was designed to answer for another's debt, and would thus be covered by the Statute of Frauds. However, the student's father wasn't promising to pay his son's debt, but rather to cover the woman's expenses, so the Statute wouldn't apply. Since the father's agreement with the woman falls outside the Statute of Frauds, a writing would not be required to make the agreement enforceable, so a Statute of Frauds defense would fail. Since C states otherwise, it's not the best response.

(D) is not the best response,

because it misstates the facts.

While it's true that a promise must be sufficiently definite to be enforceable, under these facts, the student's father's promise *is* definite. He offered to pay the woman for any losses the accident caused. While the exact *amount* of the damages wouldn't be predictable, this itself wouldn't make the promise unduly vague, since the damages are defined by the woman's good-faith expenses. Since D mischaracterizes the father's promise, it can't be the best response.

Answer 19

(C) is the best response,

because the second bank's rights were eliminated at the foreclosure sale.

The second bank's lien was junior to the first bank's, so the first bank had priority. Although the second bank was a necessary party to the sale, and was given notice of the sale, it did not participate or take any other action. At the conclusion of the sale, the senior lien was removed, and the buyer received the interest that the farmer had at the time she took out the mortgage with the first bank. The buyer held title to the land free of any liens, and was able to convey clear title to the farmer. As a result, the second bank's interest was extinguished, and it has no claim against the farmer. Note that it is important that the buyer was not in collusion with the farmer at the time of the sale. If he were, the second bank could make the argument that the foreclosure sale was a fraud designed to eliminate its interest in the farm.

(A) is not the best response,

because the farmer owned the farm when she executed the mortgages.

The doctrine of estoppel by deed applies in situations where a person purports to convey property that he or she does not own. If that person later acquires title to that property, it will automatically pass to the grantee in the earlier conveyance. This doctrine is clearly inapplicable to this situation because each time the farmer conveyed an interest in the farm (the mortgages), she held title to the farm.

(B) is not the best response,

because the original owner reacquired the land free of the second bank's mortgage.

The second bank's lien was junior to the first bank's, so the first bank had priority. Although the second bank was a necessary party to the sale, and was given notice of the sale, it did not participate or take any other action. At the conclusion of the sale, the senior lien was removed, and the buyer received the interest that the farmer had at the time she took out the mortgage with the first bank. The buyer held title to the land free of any liens, and was able to convey clear title to the farmer. As a result, the second bank's interest was extinguished, and it has no claim against the farmer. Note that it is important that the buyer was not in collusion with the farmer at the time of the sale. If he were, the second bank could make the argument that the foreclosure sale was a fraud designed to eliminate its interest in the farm.

(D) is not the best response,

because the farmer never sold the farm.

A due-on-sale clause requires that if the owner of mortgaged land conveys the land, the balance of the mortgage will immediately become due. These clauses are included to protect banks from default by individuals who no longer possess the land. However, the clause was never implicated in this situation since the farmer never sold the land—she only lost title to the farm because it was sold at a foreclosure sale.

Answer 20

(A) is the best response,

because both parties bear responsibility for the murder.

Let's look at the friend's liability first. The friend is both a conspirator to bank robbery and an accomplice to bank robbery. It's easiest to speak of the friend as being an accomplice. The issue is therefore whether and when an accomplice becomes liable for additional crimes committed by his principal, beyond the basic crime that the accomplice intended to aid and abet. "The established rule . . . is that accomplice liability extends to acts of the principal . . . which were a 'natural and probable consequence' of the criminal scheme the accomplice encouraged or aided." LaFave, Criminal Law, § 6.8(b). Courts that apply this "natural and probable consequences" rule vary as to exactly how likely the consequences have to be, but the basic idea is that if the consequences are unintended but *reasonably foreseeable*, they're "natural and probable." This test would probably, but not certainly, make the friend substantively liable for the killing. The prosecution has a decent argument that the friend was aiding and abetting what he knew was an armed robbery, and that an accidental death due to the discharging of the weapon used in an armed robbery is a reasonably foreseeable (or "natural and probable") consequence of that armed robbery.

But the prosecution is not certain to win with this argument—a judge or jury might reach a contrary result on either of two theories: (1) that the woman's promise not to "hurt anyone" during the robbery made the accidental firing of the gun too unlikely to be considered a natural-and-probable-consequence of the supposedly non-violent robbery scheme that the friend thought he was facilitating; or (2) that the friend did not have any reason to believe that the woman would even acquire or use a gun (she may have hidden it in her purse, so that the friend didn't know about it until after the robbery), again making the shooting not a natural-and-probable-consequence of the scheme as the friend understood it. Furthermore, not all courts purporting to apply common-law principles even accept the "natural and probable consequence" rule. But the friend's liability becomes dramatically clearer once we recognize that by saying that the problem is to be answered "at common law," we must take account of the *felony murder doctrine.* Although jurisdictions purporting to apply common-law doctrines vary in exactly how they apply the felony murder rule, some form of that rule is almost universal at common law. *See* LaFave, Criminal Law, § 7.5(a) and (b). (Most often, the rule is held to apply only to deaths that occur as the proximate result of one of a few specified dangerous felonies.) Under even a narrow version of the felony murder doctrine, where a death occurs directly on account of dangerous and violent conduct by the principal during the course of a robbery, that death is automatically murder. And that's true even if the death was clearly an unintended accident. Furthermore, if the felony murder rule applies, it automatically makes the *friend* guilty of murder just as surely as it makes the woman guilty. Since the friend is substantively guilty of robbery by virtue of his being an accomplice to robbery, he becomes guilty of felony murder even if the death was not a "natural and probable consequence" of the robbery. *See* LaFave, Criminal Law, § 7.5(c).

Now, let's consider the store owner's liability. Most courts say that it's not enough for either accomplice liability or conspiracy liability that a person merely supplied goods with the knowledge that his supplies might enable others to pursue a particular criminal objective. But other factors beyond the mere supplying of goods to the venture *are* enough to justify the inference that the supplier desired to further the criminal objective, making him liable as both a conspirator and accomplice. Two of those special factors are present here: (1) the fact that the supplier charges a dramatically inflated price for the item helps justify the inference that the supplier is in some sense becoming part of the underlying criminal venture; and (2) the more serious the underlying crime as the supplier understands it, the more likely a court is to find that the act of supplying a necessary item demonstrates an intent to further the crime. So the store owner will be held to be both a conspirator to the robbery and an accomplice to it. Then, the felony murder doctrine makes the store owner a murderer, on the same reasoning by which the doctrine makes the woman and the friend murderers.

(B), (C), and (D) are not the best response,

because each is in some way inconsistent with the analysis of choice A above.

Answer 21

(C) is the best response,

because it accurately states and applies the rule that only parties to the first action (or their "privies") may receive the benefit of claim preclusion in a second action.

Claim preclusion is a judicially-created doctrine that bars the relitigation of a claim raised in a prior suit. The basic rule of claim preclusion is that a person will receive both the benefit and the burden of a valid and final judgment from one suit ("Suit 1"), for purposes of another suit ("Suit 2"), ***if only if that person was a party to Suit 1.*** In other words, both federal and state courts universally follow the rule that ***neither the benefit nor the burden of claim preclusion applies to a "stranger" to the first action.*** Since Taxi Driver was not a party to Plaintiff's initial suit against Defendant, Plaintiff's potential claim against Taxi Driver was not "merged into" Plaintiff's judgment against Defendant, just as that claim wouldn't have been "barred" had the judgment in the first suit gone in favor of Defendant rather than Plaintiff.

Note that in some rare cases, there may be a such a ***close pre-existing legal relationship*** between a party to Suit 1 (call him X) and a person who is absent from Suit 1 but present in Suit 2 (call him Y) that it's fair to give Y the benefit (and charge him with the burden) of the result in Suit 1. (In this situation, X and Y might be called "proxies" or "privies" for each other.) But no such close pre-existing relationship exists here between Defendant and Taxi Driver, so the court will not find that Plaintiff's failure to join Taxi Driver in the suit against Defendant caused Plaintiff to lose her right to bring the separate suit against Taxi Driver. (Or, to put it another way, there was no principle that required Plaintiff to join Defendant and Taxi Driver as co-defendants in a single action arising out of the same episode, even if it was the case that no jurisdictional or other procedural reasons would have prevented such a joinder.)

(A) is not the best response,

because the rule that it states does not apply to the problem.

Taxi Driver was not a "party to be joined if feasible" in the State B action as that term is defined in FRCP 19 (entitled "Required Joinder of Parties"); therefore, he was not required to be joined in the lawsuit. Aside from situations in which Rule 19 requires joinder, ***the rules of claim preclusion do not*** (with very few exceptions, none applicable here) ***require a claimant to join in one lawsuit all parties to the transaction***. Thus, Plaintiff was not required to join Taxi Driver in his original lawsuit. As is described further in the discussion of Choice (C), Taxi Driver was a stranger to the lawsuit between Plaintiff and Defendant and therefore cannot invoke the benefits and is not bound by the burdens of the judgment in that earlier lawsuit.

(B) is not the best response,

because the rule that it mentions does not apply on these facts.

If Plaintiff had had two different claims ***against Defendant*** arising out of the same transaction, and Plaintiff had asserted only one of those claims against Defendant in the first action, Plaintiff would indeed probably now be precluded from bringing a separate suit against Defendant on the second claim (assuming that no procedural rule would have prevented Plaintiff from bringing both claims in a single proceeding). And this choice would be correct in asserting that whether Plaintiff was required to join both claims against Defendant in a single suit would be determined based on a "transactional test," i.e., on whether both claims arose out of the same transaction. But the transactional test has no relevance to a situation in which a plaintiff brings one claim against one defendant in Suit 1 and a different claim against ***a different defendant*** in Suit 2—the mere fact that different defendants are involved is enough to prevent the transactional test from applying (and the plaintiff won't be precluded from bringing the second suit against the second defendant, as further described in Choice (C)).

(D) is not the best response,

because the rule it states is not pertinent.

Whether or not the State B judgment is final, it cannot be raised as a bar by Taxi Driver because he is not a party to that judgment. It's true that *as between the same parties*, a judgment must be valid and final to have claim preclusive effect. But the finality of the judgment in the first action is irrelevant on the issue of whether that judgment is binding in favor of, or against, a ***stranger*** to the first action who is now a party to the second action. So although this choice correctly states that the court will deny the motion, the choice is incorrect in citing the possible lack of finality of the first judgment as the reason for the denial.

Answer 22

(D) is the best response,

because, although the certification is hearsay, it qualifies under FRE 803(10), the hearsay exception for a certification offered to prove the absence of a public record.

FRE 803(10) gives a hearsay exception for "[A] certification under Rule 902 . . . that a diligent search *failed to disclose a public record or statement* if the . . . certification is admitted to prove that: (A) *the record or statement does not exist*[.]" The certification here meets the requirements of FRE 902, since it was prepared and signed by a state public official and indicates that a diligent search of the records was conducted. So the certificate is self-authenticating.

The certification is offered for the proper inference that if a license had been issued, it would have been recorded in the public record. Thus, the fact that there was no record found is probative (and admissible) evidence that a license was never issued.

(A) is not the best response,

because the certification qualifies under FRE 803(10), the hearsay exception for a certification offered to prove the absence of a public record.

To be admissible, the certification must be prepared by a public official and must on its face indicate that a diligent search of the records was conducted. This certification satisfies the requirements of the exception.

(B) is not the best response,

because no extrinsic evidence of authenticity is required to admit a domestic public document bearing a government seal under FRE 902(1).

Here, the certification is from a public agency of a U.S. state, and bears the agency's seal. Therefore, it is self-authenticating under Rule 902(1), and is admissible under FRE 803(10), the hearsay exception for a certification offered to prove the absence of a public record.

(C) is not the best response,
because the certification qualifies under FRE 803(10), the hearsay exception for a certification offered to prove the absence of a public record.

The certification can be offered for its truth (i.e., that there was no record of any issuance of a license to the defendant). Therefore its admissibility is not limited to impeachment; it can be used both for impeachment and as substantive proof of the disputed fact.

Answer 23

(C) is the best response,
because Congress has the authority to tax and spend for the general welfare.

Congress can only act within the scope of its powers as enumerated in Article I of the Constitution. Thus, whenever a problem asks whether a statute passed by Congress is constitutional, the first step is to locate the enumerated power under which the statute could have been passed. In this case, the statute (1) imposes a tax on the sale of computers, and (2) uses the resulting funds to purchase software for U.S. residents to use. Article I, § 8, gives Congress the power to tax and spend for the general welfare. Since this statute is a taxing and spending law, our only concern is whether it is for the general welfare. Courts review taxing and spending statutes with great deference to congressional judgment—a challenged statute will be upheld so long as the statute is reasonably related to furthering the general welfare. The statute in this problem clearly meets the test. The purpose of the tax is to provide a useful product to the public free of charge. Since this would enhance the public welfare, the statute is constitutional.

(A) is not the best response,
because Congress may impose direct taxes on U.S. citizens.

Article I, § 9, of the Constitution allows Congress to impose direct taxes so long as the tax is "apportioned among the several States which may be included within this Union, according to their respective Numbers[.]" So, a direct tax is constitutional as long as the revenue raised from each state is proportional to that state's share of the national population. Most taxes imposed by Congress (e.g., income tax) are "indirect." The most common "direct" tax to look out for is a tax on real property.

(B) is not the best response,
because no taking will occur as a result of the statute.

The Fifth Amendment to the Constitution prohibits the government from taking private property without just compensation. However, under this statute, copies of the software will be purchased, not taken. Further, the sale of the software is (presumably) voluntary on the part of the patent or copyright holders. The Takings Clause applies only to situations where the government forces a person to relinquish possession of his or her property. Since there is no element of compulsion evident in this situation, the Takings Clause is not relevant to the problem.

(D) is not the best response,
because the patent power does not relate to taxing and spending.

Article I, § 8, of the Constitution gives Congress the power to "promote the progress of science and the useful arts" by granting patents to inventors. The clause makes no mention of imposing a fee on patents. Congress's authority to tax the sale of new computers arises under its taxing power, which is independent of the patent power.

Answer 24

(C) is the best response,
because supplemental jurisdiction applies, but the court has discretion to decline to exercise that jurisdiction because all claims over which the court had original jurisdiction have been dismissed.

The key to this question is to recognize that whether the court may (or indeed must) decide the state-law false-arrest claim depends entirely on whether and how the doctrine ***of supplemental jurisdiction*** applies. The mechanics of supplemental jurisdiction are laid out in great detail in 28 U.S.C. §1367, and everything you need in order to answer this question can be found somewhere in sub-sections (a) through (d) of §1367. First, let's look at sub-section (a), which contains the main language granting the federal courts supplemental jurisdiction over a claim that could be sued on if it were the only claim in the suit:

"(a) Except as provided in subsections (b) and (c) or as expressly provided otherwise by Federal statute, in any civil action of which the district courts have ***original jurisdiction***, the district courts shall have ***supplemental jurisdiction*** over ***all other claims that are so related to claims in the action within such original jurisdiction that they form part of the same case or controversy*** under Article III of the United States Constitution. Such supplemental jurisdiction shall include claims that involve the joinder or intervention of additional parties."

Here, the federal court has (or, more accurately, it *had*, at the time the suit was filed) "original jurisdiction" over the §1983 claim, since that is a federal question claim (i.e., it arises under a federal statute). So the above-quoted language means that the court also has "supplemental jurisdiction" over "all other claims that are so related to" the §1983 claim that the other claims "form part of the same case or controversy" as the §1983 claim. Where the "anchor claim" (here, the §1983 federal-question claim) shares the same ***"common nucleus of operative facts"*** as the "other claim" in question (here, the state-law false-arrest claim), that's clearly a sufficiently close relationship to make the two claims part of the "same case or controversy." Here, both claims arise out of a single episode or transaction (the arrest and handcuffing of the plaintiff by the defendant), so the two claims share a "common nucleus of operative facts," and the false-arrest claim therefore satisfies §1367(a) and triggers supplemental jurisdiction unless something in §1367(b) or (c) changes this result.

Sub-section (b) (i.e., 28 U.S.C. §1367(b)) doesn't apply here—that sub-section applies only to cases where the only reason the "anchor claim" falls within the court's "original jurisdiction" is because of ***diversity***; here, the §1983 claim is a federal-question claim, so we can ignore §1367(b) entirely. Sub-section (c), however, not only applies, but is key to solving our question; here's what that section provides:

"(c) The district courts may ***decline to exercise supplemental jurisdiction*** over a claim under subsection (a) if—

(1) the claim raises a novel or complex issue of State law,

(2) the claim substantially predominates over the claim or claims over which the district court has original jurisdiction,

(3) ***the district court has dismissed all claims over which it has original jurisdiction***, or

(4) in exceptional circumstances, there are other compelling reasons for declining jurisdiction."

As you can see, (3) above—"the district court has ***dismissed all claims*** over which it has original jurisdiction" – fits our situation exactly, since the only claim over which the court ever had original jurisdiction was the §1983 claim, and that claim has now been dismissed. Therefore, §1367(b)(3) says that the judge "may decline to exercise supplemental jurisdiction" over any remaining claim. And Choice C correctly indicates that the court has such discretion.

But what about the last phrase of Choice C, that "federal law guarantees the jogger 30 days to refile the claim in State A court"? Well, sub-section (d) of §1367 says that:

"The period of limitations for any claim asserted under subsection (a), and for any other claim in the same action that is voluntarily dismissed at the same time as or after the dismissal of the claim under subsection (a), ***shall be tolled while the claim is pending and for a period of 30 days after it is dismissed unless State law provides for a longer tolling period."***

The state-law false-arrest claim is a "claim asserted under subsection (a)" (i.e., it's a claim that triggers subsection (a)'s grant of supplemental jurisdiction). Therefore sub-section (d) provides that the statute of limitations for that state claim will be "tolled" not only for the whole time the claim was "pending" (i.e., while the federal action was pending), but also for a minimum of 30 days after the federal court dismisses the claim, to give the jogger this period in which to refile in State A court. (If State A would grant a ***longer*** tolling period, the jogger would get that longer time—but §1367(d) guarantees her *at least* the 30 days.) Normally, federal law wouldn't lengthen the statute of limitations for a state-law claim asserted in state court, but under the Supremacy Clause and the Necessary and Proper Clause, Congress has the power to do so in the exercise of Congress' power over the federal judiciary, and it has chosen to use that power to guarantee, to any claimant whose claim has been dismissed from the federal action based on the court's discretion, the time to refile in state court. Therefore, Choice C correctly indicates that the judge has discretion whether or not to hear the now standalone false arrest claim, and that the jogger will have at least 30 days to refile in state court if the judge declines to exercise that discretion. (By the way, on these facts, the judge could plausibly go either way on the dismissal decision: Generally, federal courts will dismiss the remaining state claim if all federal claims have been dismissed before the start of trial; but if the judge believes that both sides have expended significant resources in getting the surviving state-court claim(s) ready for trial, and one party affirmatively desires to have the federal court try the surviving claim, the court may well accede to that request in the interest of judicial efficiency.)

(A) is not the best response,

because the federal court has supplemental jurisdiction over the surviving state-law claim and may choose to exercise that discretion.

As is described in detail in the discussion of choice (C) above, the fact that the federal court had original jurisdiction over the federal-question §1983 claim at the time the suit was filed was enough to give the court supplemental jurisdiction over the transactionally related state-law false arrest claim; and that remained true even after the §1983 claim was dismissed. This choice, by saying that the federal court "must" (rather than "may") dismiss the state-law claim, is thus legally incorrect.

(B) is not the best response,

because the federal court *does* have discretion to decline to exercise supplemental jurisdiction over the state-law claim.

This choice correctly states that supplemental jurisdiction applies to the state-law false-arrest claim; the reason this is true is extensively discussed in the treatment of choice (C). But this choice is exactly wrong in asserting that the court lacks discretion *to decline to exercise* that jurisdiction. As the discussion of choice (C) indicates, §1367(b)(3) gives the court discretion to dismiss the supplemental-jurisdiction claim(s) once all claims falling within the court's original jurisdiction (here, the §1983 claim) have been dismissed.

(D) is not the best response,

because the court has discretion about whether to dismiss, or instead try, the false-arrest claim.

As is described in the treatment of choice (C) above, the federal court has discretion either to try the false-arrest claim or dismiss it. Therefore, this choice is legally incorrect in saying that the court "must" dismiss the false-arrest claim. However, the second clause in this choice is exactly correct; if the court *does* dismiss the claim, §1367(d) guarantees the jogger at least 30 days after dismissal to refile that claim in State A court (and the jogger would have a longer period in which to refile if State A law would grant her such a longer period under the circumstances).

Answer 25

(A) is the best response,

because the doctor's letter is not a business record, and the expert's reliance on the letter is not enough to make it admissible.

The doctor's letter is not a business record under FRE 803(6) because it was not prepared in the ordinary course of regularly conducted activity. A letter from the plaintiff's doctor to his employer is not the type of routine business transaction contemplated by FRE 803(6), as it is a specific diagnostic evaluation of a patient who may have an eye toward litigation.

In addition, it cannot be admitted simply because an expert relies upon it. FRE 703 does allow an expert to rely on hearsay in reaching a conclusion, so long as other experts in the field would reasonably rely on such information. But the rule distinguishes between expert *reliance* on the hearsay and *admitting* the hearsay at trial for the jury to consider. As to admitting the hearsay itself, Rule 703 says "But if the facts or data [relied on by the expert] would otherwise be inadmissible, the proponent of the opinion may disclose them to the jury *only if their probative value in helping the jury evaluate the opinion substantially outweighs their prejudicial effect.*" That strict balancing test is not met in this case due to the danger that the jury will misuse the evidence for substantive purposes (i.e., the truth of the medical diagnosis in the letter) rather than the permissible purpose (i.e., assisting the jury in evaluating the expert's opinion). There is no other exception that appears even close to being applicable (and none listed in the possible answers), so the letter is inadmissible hearsay.

(B) is not the best response,

because unavailability is relevant only to the FRE 804 exceptions, and none of them apply here.

The letter does not fit under FRE 804 exceptions such as statement against interest or statement of personal or family history. Furthermore, if the hearsay qualified as a hearsay exception under FRE 803 (e.g., if it were a business record), then the doctor's availability would be completely irrelevant, because unavailability need not be shown for those exceptions.

(C) is not the best response,

because, under these facts, the expert's reliance on the hearsay will not justify admission of the hearsay.

The letter cannot be admitted simply because an expert relies upon it. FRE 703 does allow an expert to rely on hearsay in reaching a conclusion, so long as other experts in the field would reasonably rely on such information. But the rule distinguishes between expert *reliance* on the hearsay and *admitting* the hearsay at trial for the jury to consider. Otherwise-inadmissible items relied on by the expert are admissible "*only if their probative value in helping the jury evaluate the opinion substantially outweighs their prejudicial effect*," so it's not correct to say, as this choice does, that the mere fact that the expert relied on the letter is enough to guarantee the letter's admission.

(D) is not the best response,

because the doctor's letter is not a business record.

The doctor's letter is not a business record under FRE 803(6) because it was not prepared in the ordinary course of regularly conducted activity. A letter from the plaintiff's doctor to his employer is not the type of routine business transaction contemplated by FRE 803(6), as it is a specific diagnostic evaluation of a patient who may have an eye toward litigation.

Answer 26

(D) is the best response,

because it addresses the central issue under these facts, and resolves it satisfactorily.

A *prima facie* case for false imprisonment has three elements: the defendant's act/omission that confines or restrains the plaintiff to a bounded area (the plaintiff must believe there's no reasonable means of escape), the defendant's intent to so confine or restrain the plaintiff, and causation. If the guard knew someone was in the lot, you could infer that the guard intended to lock that person inside. (It wouldn't be necessary to prove he intended to lock up *the customer* specifically.) Without that knowledge, it wouldn't be possible to prove the guard *intended* to falsely imprison someone. Since D focuses on the issue most in doubt on these facts—intent—and resolves it satisfactorily, it's the best response.

(A) is not the best response,

because it is insufficient to support a false imprisonment claim.

While confinement is an element of false imprisonment, there are other elements, one of which is a central issue under these facts. A *prima facie* claim for false imprisonment requires proof of the defendant's act/omission that confines or restrains the plaintiff to a bounded area (such that the plaintiff believes there's no reasonable means of escape), the defendant's intent to so confine or restrain the plaintiff, and causation. Thus, along with the confinement, the customer would have to prove that the used car company (through its agent) *intended* to confine him. Since A doesn't recognize that this is the missing element, it's not the best response.

(B) is not the best response,

because it relies on an element that need not be proven for false imprisonment.

A *prima facie* case of false imprisonment has three elements: the defendant's act/omission that confines or restrains the plaintiff to a bounded area (the plaintiff must believe there's no reasonable means of escape), the defendant's intent to so confine or restrain the plaintiff, and causation. Thus, the fact that the customer was harmed will impact his damages, but will not determine if his claim will prevail. Since B ignores the elements of a *prima facie* case for false imprisonment, it's not the best response.

(C) is not the best response,

because the mental element it states would be insufficient for a false imprisonment claim.

Choice C suggests that negligence is all that such a claim requires. In fact, the plaintiff must prove the defendant *intended* to confine or restrain the plaintiff. Thus, if the guard was only negligent, the used car company wouldn't be liable. Since C suggests otherwise, it's not the best response.

Answer 27

(C) is the best response,

because it correctly characterizes the contract here as a unilateral contract.

An offer for a unilateral contract is one that requests performance in return (unlike a bilateral contract, which requests a return promise). Here, the investor asked the landowner to "make me a written, 30-day offer . . ." in return for which he would pay $200. Thus, he *didn't* want a return promise, and the landowner's performing the requested act—making the written offer—constitutes consideration for the contract, making the contract enforceable. Thus, the combination of the investor's oral promise and the landowner's writing creates a unilateral contract. Since C recognizes this, it's the best response.

(A) is not the best response,

because consideration is missing, so there cannot be a firm option.

An "option" is a means by which a non-merchant can make an irrevocable offer. The option must be supported by consideration. Typically, the offeree pays the offeror to keep the offer open for a given period of time.

Without the irrevocability, an option is *illusory,* because the *offeror* has an unrestricted right to revoke the offer (and it's the restriction of this right that forms part of the consideration for the option). Here, the landowner's right to revoke at any time defeats the option. Since choice A doesn't recognize this, it's not the best response.

(B) is not the best response,

because promissory estoppel only applies when consideration is lacking, and there's consideration here.

Promissory estoppel is designed to avoid injustice where consideration is lacking for a contract. It comes into being when there is a gratuitous promise that is likely to, and does, induce the promisee's reliance. As choice B suggests, in theory there can be justifiable reliance on a promise before a contract is created, such as where the promisee must perform before the offer can be accepted (e.g., a businessman selling his business before he can buy a franchise). Thus, there *can* be pre-contractual promissory estoppel, which can make an offer irrevocable or enforce a promise made during preliminary negotiations. However, it doesn't apply to these facts, because the investor bargained for, and got, a revocable offer. In promissory estoppel, the bargaining element is missing. Since promissory estoppel doesn't apply to these facts, B isn't the best response.

(D) is not the best response,

because quasi-contract only applies, to prevent unjust enrichment, where no contract exists.

Under quasi-contract, a plaintiff is entitled to recovery where he conferred a benefit on the defendant with the expectation he would be paid, defendant knew or should have known plaintiff expected to be paid, and defendant would be unjustly enriched if he got to keep the benefit without paying for it. Thus, quasi-contract only applies when a person receives benefits in the absence of an enforceable promise to pay.

This doesn't apply here because there is a contract, and thus there's no reason to turn to quasi-contractual recovery. The investor requested that the landowner perform—i.e., make a written, revocable offer—in return for $200. Once she did so, an enforceable unilateral contract was formed, and quasi-contract isn't relevant. Since D doesn't recognize this, it's not the best response.

Answer 28

(B) is the best response,

because the restrictive covenant is enforceable by the man.

The language in the deed conveying the 40-acre tract to the developer, which restricted the use of that tract to residential purposes, is a restrictive covenant. A restrictive covenant will be binding against a later purchaser of the promisor's land and will be enforceable by later purchasers of the promisee's land. In order for the benefit and burden of the restrictive covenant to bind successive purchasers, the purchaser must have notice, either actual or constructive, of the covenant. Although the doctor in this problem did not have actual notice of the restrictive covenant, she was on constructive notice of it because it was recorded in her chain of title. As a result, the doctor will be bound by the restrictive covenant, and the man, who still owns the five-acre tract, will be able to enforce it against her.

(A) is not the best response,

because the restrictive covenant was intended to benefit the man.

The language in the deed conveying the 40-acre tract to the developer, which restricted the use of that tract to residential purposes, is a restrictive covenant. A restrictive covenant will be binding against a later purchaser of the promisor's land and will be enforceable by later purchasers of the promisee's land. In order for the benefit and burden of the restrictive covenant to bind successive purchasers, the purchaser must have notice, either actual or constructive, of the covenant. Although the doctor in this problem did not have actual notice of the restrictive covenant, she was on constructive notice of it because it was recorded in her chain of title. Any landowner who was intended to be the beneficiary of the obligations contained in a restrictive covenant may enforce the covenant. As a result, the doctor will be bound by the restrictive covenant, and the man, who still owns the five-acre tract, will be able to enforce it against her.

(C) is not the best response,

because restrictive covenants are unaffected by the Rule Against Perpetuities.

The Rule Against Perpetuities requires that interests in land must vest, if at all, within 21 years of a life in being at the time the interest was created. However, a restrictive covenant is unaffected by the Rule Against Perpetuities since there is no question as to whether or not the right to enforce the restrictive covenant will vest: so long as there is notice, the benefit and burden of the restrictive covenant will run with the land and will be binding on successive purchasers.

(D) is not the best response,

because the zoning ordinance does not override the restrictive covenant.

While it may be the case that the local zoning ordinance would allow the doctor's proposed use, it has no effect on the enforceability of the restrictive covenant. The man may enforce this restrictive covenant against the doctor, because the doctor was on constructive notice of the restrictive covenant, since it was in her chain of title. There is no rule stating that a zoning ordinance that allows certain uses of land will preempt a restrictive covenant that disallows those uses. Such a rule would not make sense, since it would render all restrictive covenants ineffective, as they could not constrain what is allowed by zoning, nor could they allow users what zoning does not.

Answer 29

(C) is the best response,

because the district court has jurisdiction over claims arising under treaties.

In order to fall within the subject matter jurisdiction of the federal district courts, there must be either diversity jurisdiction or federal question jurisdiction. Since we are told that the man and woman in this problem were residents of the same state, there is no diversity jurisdiction. However, there is federal question jurisdiction, since Article III, § 2, of the Constitution provides that "[t]he judicial power shall extend to all cases, in law and equity, arising under this Constitution, the laws of the United States, *and treaties made*, or which shall be made, under their authority." Since the basis for the woman's suit is the treaty that requires citizens to pay tort judgments awarded by the foreign court, the suit involves a "federal question" and is within the district court's jurisdiction.

(A) is not the best response,

because the suit raises a federal question.

In order to fall within the subject matter jurisdiction of the federal district courts, there must be either diversity jurisdiction or federal question jurisdiction. Since we are told that the man and woman in this problem were residents of the same state, there is no diversity jurisdiction. However, there is federal question jurisdiction, since Article III, § 2, of the Constitution provides that "[t]he judicial power shall extend to all cases, in law and equity, arising under this Constitution, the laws of the United States, *and treaties made*, or which shall be made, under their authority." (Emphasis added.) Since the basis for the woman's suit is the treaty that requires citizens to pay tort judgments awarded by the foreign court, the suit involves a "federal question" and is within the district court's jurisdiction.

(B) is not the best response,

because the Commerce Power applies to Congress, not the federal judiciary.

The federal district court will have jurisdiction over the woman's suit because the suit arises under a treaty of the United States, and thus raises a "federal question." If you selected this choice, you are probably thinking that since the traffic accident was not a commercial transaction, Congress could not pass a law governing the accident because the Commerce Power does not reach it. This line of reasoning makes two errors. First, whether or not Congress could legislate an issue is an entirely distinct question from whether the federal courts have jurisdiction over a suit, which requires only that either diversity or federal jurisdiction applies. Second, it erroneously implies that the Commerce Power is the only power under which Congress may legislate. This is not the case, as Article I, § 8, provides several other enumerated powers of the legislative branch. (Although none of these other powers would allow Congress to legislate in this arena, that fact does not make choice B any more correct.)

(D) is not the best response,

because it is irrelevant.

The scope of the President's power to enter into treaties (with the advice and consent of the Senate) is very broad. However, that information does not inform the question asked, which is whether the federal district court has subject matter jurisdiction to hear the woman's claim. In this case, the district court will have subject matter jurisdiction because the woman's claim involves a federal question. Article III, § 2, of the Constitution provides that "[t]he judicial power shall extend to all cases, in law and equity, arising under this Constitution, the laws of the United States, *and treaties made*, or which shall be made, under their authority." (Emphasis added.) Since the basis for the woman's suit is the treaty that requires citizens to pay tort judgments awarded by the foreign court, the suit involves a "federal question" and is within the district court's jurisdiction.

Answer 30

(B) is the best response,

because it identifies the correct use of the evidence.

If the pedestrian did not exercise due care for his own safety, his contributory negligence will bar his recovery, even if the driver was negligent. The statute will be relevant in determining the pedestrian's negligence; so will the trucker's blocking the crosswalk, since it may indicate that the pedestrian's violating the statute was excusable. Thus, the trier of fact should be able to examine the facts determining the pedestrian's negligence, to see if the driver will have a valid contributory negligence defense. Since B recognizes this, it's the best response.

(A) is not the best response,

because the pedestrian's failure to cross at the crosswalk *is* relevant to determining the pedestrian's rights.

If failing to cross at the crosswalk were considered contributorily negligent, it would bar the pedestrian from recovering at all. (Note that you're told in the instructions that contributory, not comparative, negligence is recognized.) Since A mistakenly considers the evidence irrelevant, it's not the best response.

(C) is not the best response,

because it assumes that the pedestrian was contributorily negligent. Why? Because C suggests that the driver's liability depends on the Last Clear Chance doctrine ("in time to avoid the impact" language).

Last Clear Chance is used by plaintiffs to rebut a claim of contributory negligence. It allows that a defendant with the last clear chance to avoid a negligent act, but who fails to do so, is liable. However, as this definition indicates, Last Clear Chance presupposes contributory negligence. Here, the pedestrian was only contributorily negligent if stepping off the crosswalk and around the truck amounted to a failure to exercise due care for his own safety. If anything, these facts would suggest the pedestrian was *not* negligent; they certainly don't suggest for sure that he *was.* While the driver's seeing the pedestrian in time to avoid the impact will be relevant to the driver's negligence, it won't be contingent on the pedestrian's contributory negligence. Since C states otherwise, it's not the best response.

(D) is not the best response,

because negligence per se would not apply to these facts.

Negligence per se occurs when a court decides violation of a statute will amount to negligence as a matter of law. However, this only occurs in a small number of statutes, and generally only when a court finds the legislature intended for violation of the statute to amount to negligence per se. There's no evidence here that that's the case. As such, D cannot be the best response.

Answer 31

(A) is the best response,

because it explains why Plaintiff has not met the requirements for use of federal *quasi in rem* jurisdiction.

FRCP 4(n) allows the use of *quasi in rem* jurisdiction in a federal lawsuit, but only in special circumstances where personal jurisdiction over the defendant cannot readily be obtained in the district where the plaintiff plans to bring the action. Rule 4(n)(2) says that "On a ***showing that personal jurisdiction over a defendant cannot be obtained in the district where the action is brought by reasonable efforts to serve a summons*** under this rule, the court may assert jurisdiction over the defendant's ***assets found in the district***." (The reference to "this rule" refers to the entirety of FRCP 4, which includes 4(e) and 4(k)(1); those two sub-sections, when taken together, would allow service in the U.S. outside of State A on any defendant if State A's long-arm would allow the exercise of personal jurisdiction.)

So if Plaintiff had been able to "show[] that personal jurisdiction over [Defendant] cannot be obtained in [N.D. State A] by reasonable efforts to serve a summons under [FRCP 4]," Plaintiff would indeed have been entitled to assert *quasi in rem* jurisdiction based on attachment of "defendant's assets found in the district" (the storage facility). But the facts, by citing Defendant's Internet statement that its personnel often visit State A to solicit business, indicate that Defendant has the "minimum contacts" with State A that would suffice for the state to exercise personal jurisdiction over Defendant. (And Statute 1 is a long-arm that would suffice to let State A exercise that jurisdiction.) In other words, it is clearly *not* the case that "personal jurisdiction over [Defendant] cannot be obtained in [N.D. State A] by reasonable efforts to serve a summons," and indeed Plaintiff has not even tried to make the showing that it is the case. So FRCP 4(n)(2) doesn't apply, and there is no other provision allowing *quasi in rem* jurisdiction in this type of case either. (If there *were* a federal statute that authorized *quasi in rem* jurisdiction for the type of case in question, FRCP 4(n)(1) would allow that statute to serve as the basis for *quasi in rem* jurisdiction; but the facts tell you that there is no such federal statute.)

(B) is not the best response,

because compliance with Statute 2 is not sufficient to establish a basis for the federal court's exercise of *quasi in rem* jurisdiction.

As explained in Choice (A), Plaintiff must show that personal jurisdiction cannot be obtained over Defendant "in the district where the action is brought by reasonable efforts to serve a summons." FRCP 4(n)(2). And Plaintiff has not even tried to make this showing, nor could he do so successfully, given Defendant's more-than-minimum contacts with State A.

(C) is not the best response,

because it misstates the rules governing when a federal court can exercise *quasi in rem* jurisdiction.

As explained in Choice (A), a federal court *is* permitted to exercise *quasi in rem* jurisdiction over property located in the district upon a showing that due process is satisfied and that the requirements of FRCP 4(n)—mainly the unavailability of *in personam* jurisdiction—are satisfied. This choice, by asserting that no federal statute or rule *ever* authorizes *quasi in rem* jurisdiction in federal lawsuits, states a rule that is incorrectly broad (even though the choice reaches the correct conclusion).

(D) is not the best response,

because it misstates the constitutional principles governing the exercise of *quasi in rem* jurisdiction.

An action *quasi in rem* seeks to impose a monetary judgment on the defendant. Property is attached as a basis for the court's power and as a means to secure any eventual judgment that the plaintiff obtains. One use of *quasi in rem* jurisdiction is to adjudicate the rights of ownership of particular persons to the attached property. The other use is to obtain a basis for jurisdiction. In the latter use, the property that is attached is ***unrelated to the subject matter*** of the lawsuit. Here, Plaintiff is using *quasi in rem* jurisdiction for that latter purpose, to secure jurisdiction. So the fact that the storage facility is unrelated to his contract and other claims against Defendant does not matter. (Notice, by the way, that if Defendant does not make a general appearance in the suit, the very nature of *quasi in rem* jurisdiction means that Defendant's exposure to liability will be capped at the value of the property that is attached—in this case, $95,000.)

Answer 32

(D) is the best response,

because Supreme Court precedents do not furnish a defense on either grounds.

With respect to the kidnapped citizen, the Supreme Court held in *Ker v. Illinois* (1886) that "forcible abduction is no sufficient reason why the party should not answer when brought within the jurisdiction of the court which has the right to try him for such an offence." *Ker* was a case in which agents abducted an American citizen from a foreign country, so it's on all fours with the facts here (and it's never been overruled).

As to the accomplice, the analysis is somewhat different. The warrantless entry into the accomplice's home to arrest her violated her Fourth Amendment rights. *See Payton v. New York* (1980) (warrant required for entry into private dwelling to arrest the inhabitant, if there are no exigent circumstances). This violation would have entitled the accomplice to suppress any evidence found incident to the arrest. *Id*. But the violation does *not* entitle the accomplice to have the indictment dismissed, because the indictment preceded the arrest, and was not in any way the product of the later illegality. (The mere fact that the prosecution had the ability to try the accomplice because it had her in custody through an illegal arrest does not make a difference. "Illegal arrest does not void a subsequent prosecution." *Gerstein v. Pugh* (1975).) In summary, neither defense works.

(A), (B), and (C) are not the best response,
because each answer incorrectly asserts that at least one of the defenses will be successful.

Answer 33

What's going on here? The prosecutor is attempting to enter evidence of an unrelated instance of misconduct—the other robbery. As such, it will require independent relevance in order to be admissible.

(A) is the best response,
because it correctly states that evidence of the other robbery will be admissible to establish an identifying circumstance.

Here, the prosecutor is attempting to enter evidence of an unrelated instance of misconduct—the other robbery. The danger of this is that the jury is likely to convict the defendant because he's a "bad man," not because he's guilty in this instance. Nonetheless, under FRE 404(b), evidence of other, specific instances of misconduct will be admissible when they have independent relevance. These include knowledge, absence of mistake or accident, preparation, plan, opportunity, motive, intent, and identity. Here, the evidence will do more than just identify the defendant as a habitual armed robber; it helps establish that the defendant committed the robbery by identifying an unusual circumstance, known to have occurred at the victim's robbery, which happened at another robbery the defendant committed.

The common identity will provide the "independent relevance" necessary to make the evidence admissible, and since A recognizes this, it is the best response.

(B) is not the best answer,
because it misstates the purpose for which the evidence will be admissible.

Under the doctrine of "limited admissibility," evidence may be admissible for one purpose and against one party, but not admissible for some other purpose or against some other party. For instance, insurance can be admitted to show ownership but not the ability to pay. Here, evidence of other instances of misconduct is *never* admissible to show the defendant's propensity to commit crimes, because the jury would be likely to convict the defendant because of his general criminal propensities—"since he did it before, he probably did it again"—not because he's guilty in this instance.

Instead, under FRE 404(b), evidence of other, specific instances of misconduct will only be admissible when they have relevance to some contested issue other than character. Under 404(b)(2), these include knowledge, absence of mistake or accident, preparation, plan, opportunity, motive, intent, and identity. Here, the evidence will establish that the defendant committed the robbery by identifying an unusual circumstance, known to have occurred at the victim's robbery, which happened at another robbery that the defendant has already been proven to have committed. Of course, it will also prove that the defendant is a habitual robber, which is going to be the most likely thing the jury will remember. (Wouldn't you?) But since the evidence fits the requirements of FRE 404(b)(2) on independent relevance, it will be admissible. Since B states otherwise, it is not the best answer.

(C) is not the best answer,
because although it correctly characterizes the evidence here as character evidence, and character evidence as a general rule is inadmissible, it fails to recognize that the character evidence here is admissible because it has *independent relevance*; it's not being offered for the impermissible purpose of showing the defendant's criminal propensities.

Here, the prosecutor is offering evidence of another, specific act of misconduct: the defendant's holding up the witness with a pistol painted red. Specific acts of misconduct *are* admissible against criminal defendants when the instances have independent relevance under FRE 404(b)(2). These include knowledge, absence of mistake or accident, preparation, plan, opportunity, motive, intent, and identity. Here, the evidence will do more than just identify the defendant as a habitual armed robber; it helps establish that the defendant committed the robbery by identifying an unusual circumstance, known to have occurred at the victim's robbery, which happened at another robbery the defendant committed. The common identity will provide the "independent relevance" necessary to make the evidence admissible. Since C does not recognize this, it is not the best response.

(D) is not the best response,
because although it's not a bad response, it does not correctly characterize the facts. In fact, this is a reasonably tough question, because you have to do some balancing and make a judgment call.

D suggests that the evidence will not be admissible because it is not legally relevant: if the probative value of a piece of evidence is substantially outweighed by the danger of unfair prejudice it will engender, then it is not admissible, even if it satisfies every other obstacle of admissibility.

The danger here is that the jury will place too much weight on the witness's testimony, and convict the defendant because he's a habitual criminal, not because he committed the crime for which he's being tried—holding up the victim. However, this is a balancing test, and the fact is that the witness's testimony has a great deal of probative value. It was evidence of a similar robbery, only a week after the victim's alleged robbery, committed with a gun with a very unusual characteristic—a barrel painted red. While of course the jury will be prejudiced by this evidence, legal relevance addresses *unfair* prejudice, and the prejudice here would not likely be considered unfair. Instead, the witness's testimony is character evidence that fits the "independent relevance" requirements of FRE 404(b)(2): It is evidence of a common plan and identity. Since it will not unfairly prejudice the defendant, it will be admitted. Since D doesn't recognize this, it's not the best response.

Answer 34

(B) is the best response,

because it represents a valid means by which the statute could be considered constitutional.

The main problem with the statute here has to do with equal protection. Public school desegregation plans are addressed at curing problems of equal protection; thus, by forbidding federal courts from enforcing desegregation plans, Congress seems to be acting in derogation of the constitution.

By forbidding the federal courts from ordering the implementation of such plans, the law in these facts does an "end run" around the constitutionality issue.

Under Article III, § 2, of the Constitution, Congress is given the power to regulate the appellate (but not original) jurisdiction of federal courts. Thus, Congress could, for instance, stop federal courts from hearing appeals in cases involving abortion, and it could likewise stop the courts from hearing cases like the one under these facts. Since B offers a basis on which the congressional act could be found constitutional, it's the best response.

(A) is not the best response,

because it misstates the law: Congress doesn't have the power to define equal protection violations—that's a judicial function.

The judiciary has the power to declare unconstitutional the acts of other branches of government. *Marbury v. Madison* (1803). Congress is the exclusive holder of the legislative power, and the judiciary has the power to determine the constitutionality of Congress's actions. Thus, Congress could not determine whether its own conduct violates the Equal Protection Clause. Since A states otherwise, it's not the best response.

(C) is not the best response,

because there's no evidence here that transportation of students would affect interstate commerce.

Congress has power to regulate interstate commerce, under Article I, § 8, cl. 3, of the Constitution. Under the "affectation doctrine," Congress can regulate any activity that has any appreciable direct or indirect effect on interstate commerce (states may regulate commerce when Congress intended that the states be able to regulate the activity in question). While the commerce power is admittedly broad, it would be unlikely that the power could be interpreted broadly enough to encompass the facts here. Public school desegregation would only concern local transportation, not interstate transportation, and it wouldn't have any appreciable effect on any interstate activity. As a result, the commerce power would not be a good basis for the constitutionality of the act. Since C doesn't recognize this, it's not the best response.

(D) is not the best response,

because although Congress can attach "strings" to federal grants, it couldn't do so under these facts.

Public school desegregation plans are designed to promote equal protection of the law. Presumably, failure to implement such a plan in the face of an equal protection violation would be unconstitutional. Thus, if Congress were to insist that federal courts not order desegregation, it would be promoting an equal protection violation. While Congress can attach "strings" to federal grants to encourage permissible goals, like general welfare objectives, it can't act in derogation of those goals—and that's what the argument in choice D would do. As a result, D is not the best response.

Answer 35

(B) is the best response,

because FRCP 23(f) gives the court of appeals discretion to allow the appeal if the plaintiffs petition for permission to appeal within 14 days after the trial judge entered her order denying certification.

This question, like most MBE Civil Procedure questions, can be reliably answered solely by looking at the text of the relevant rule or statute. In this case, the relevant provision is FRCP 23(f). (Remember that Rule 23 sets out most details regarding how and when federal class actions are permitted.) The first sentence of 23(f) says that "A court of appeals ***may permit an appeal from an order granting or denying class-action certification*** under this rule if a petition for permission to appeal is filed with the circuit clerk within 14 days after the order is entered." The Advisory Committee's Notes to Rule 23(f) make it clear that this provision gives ***full discretion*** to the Court of Appeals—the court can hear, or reject, the immediate appeal for any reason or no reason.

(A) is not the best response,

because it incorrectly asserts that the court of appeals does not have jurisdiction to hear the immediate appeal even if it wishes to do so.

As the discussion of Choice (B) makes clear, FRCP 23(f) gives the court of appeals complete discretion to hear the immediate appeal, so long as the named plaintiffs file their petition to appeal with that court within 14 days of the entry of the trial court's denial of certification. In other words, the court of appeals has jurisdiction to hear the appeal if it wishes to do so; this choice, by asserting that the court does not have jurisdiction, is flatly incorrect.

(C) is not the best response,

because it incorrectly asserts that the plaintiffs may immediately appeal as of right.

As the discussion of Choice (B) shows, FRCP 23(f) leaves it to the court of appeals to decide, in its discretion, whether to hear the immediate appeal. Choice (C), by asserting that the named plaintiffs have a "right" to take the appeal if they file promptly, is inconsistent with Rule 23(f). (To look at it another way, federal appeals are generally allowed as of right only after the entry of a "final judgment" in the case. Here, where the trial judge is willing to have the case go forward to trial on the five named plaintiffs' individual claims, no final judgment has yet been entered; the order denying certification is not viewed as a "final judgment" for this purpose.)

(D) is not the best response,

because the trial judge does not have the power to allow the immediate appeal, at least for the reasons stated in the choice.

In limited circumstances, a federal district judge has the power to in effect *urge* the court of appeals to hear an interlocutory appeal. 28 U.S.C. §1292(b) says:

> "When a district judge, in making in a civil action an order not otherwise appealable . . . , shall be of the opinion that such order involves a ***controlling question of law*** as to which there is ***substantial ground for difference of opinion*** and that an immediate appeal from the order may materially advance the ultimate termination of the litigation, he shall ***so state in writing*** in such order. The Court of Appeals which would have jurisdiction of an appeal of such action may thereupon, in its discretion, permit an appeal to be taken from such order, if application is made to it within ten days after the entry of the order[.]"

But there are at least two reasons why Choice (D) is not correct despite §1292(b): (1) that section applies only where the district judge believes that her order (in this case, the denial of class certification) involves a "controlling question of law as to which there is substantial ground for difference of opinion," and there's nothing in the facts to indicate that the judge believes that this "ground for difference of opinion" requirement is satisfied (and the fact that denial will sound the "death knell" of the suit is not at all the same concept); and (2) even if the district judge *does* invoke §1292(b) in a written order, this fact doesn't automatically bring about an interrogatory appeal—it's still within the complete *discretion* of the Court of Appeals to hear or not hear the appeal. (But as a practical matter, if the named plaintiffs here were able to convince the trial judge to include a §1292(b) statement in the order, that statement would materially increase the odds that the Court of Appeals would exercise its discretion to hear the immediate appeal.) Therefore, Choice (D) is not the best response.

Answer 36

(B) is the best response,

because the parties' course of dealing will control the terms of the discount.

Generally, when there is a final written agreement between parties, the parol evidence rule bars introduction of evidence of prior writings or discussions that contradict the writing. However, where the writing is ambiguous or the contract is silent on an issue, extrinsic evidence may be used to interpret the contract. Since this contract is for the sale of goods, the Uniform Commercial Code is applicable. UCC 2-202(1) specifically addresses the forms of extrinsic evidence that may be used to aid in interpreting a contract. Three forms of evidence may be used: course of dealing, usage of trade, and course of performance. When more than one of these types of evidence is available, the most specific controls. In this problem, the usage of trade is to allow a 2 percent discount for payment within ten days. Additionally, there is a course of dealing that has arisen from the buyer and seller's hundreds of previous transactions with each other, which allows a 5 percent deduction if payment is received within 15 days. The seller's note is not a course of performance because it does not describe how this particular transaction has been proceeding. Rather, it is an additional demand that has been made after the seller's performance is complete. Since both a usage of trade and a course of dealing are available, the latter will control, since it is more specifically related to the parties in this contract. As a result, the buyer is entitled to continue with the prior understanding and take a 5 percent discount if payment is made within 15 days.

(A) is not the best response,

because it applies the usage of trade when evidence of the course of dealing between the two parties is available.

When choosing between usage of trade, course of dealing, and course of performance evidence, the most specific pattern will control. Since the prior transactions between buyer and seller are more specific than the general custom in the grain trade, the course of dealing will control.

(C) is not the best response,

because there has been no waiver.

A waiver is the intentional foregoing of the right to enforce a condition. While it may seem that, by allowing the buyer to take a discount on prompt payments in the past, the seller has waived the right to be paid the full contract price, there is no indication in this problem that it was ever the intention of the parties that prompt payments not be given a discount. The seller could only waive a condition if he originally had the right to enforce it. In this case, the evidence provided by the course of dealing between the buyer and seller indicates that they always intended there to be a discount for prompt payments, even if they never put the discount in writing. A court interpreting this contract would read it as if the discount allowance was included in the writing. As a result, the seller never had the right to demand full payment if the buyer paid within 15 days. Since the seller never had the benefit of a condition, he had nothing to waive.

(D) is not the best response,

because, as discussed above in the explanation of choice B, UCC 2-202 allows consideration of certain extrinsic evidence that would otherwise be barred by the parol evidence rule when the meaning of a term in a written contract is ambiguous.

Since there is a latent ambiguity in the price term of this contract, a court may consider extrinsic evidence, in the form of usage of trade, course of dealing, or course of performance, in its determination of the meaning of the term.

Answer 37

(A) is the best response,

because the risk the defendant created was high enough to justify a murder conviction.

Common-law murder is the unlawful killing of a human being with malice aforethought. While murder does not require *intent,* the type that does *not* require it—depraved heart murder—requires that the defendant engage in extremely negligent conduct, which a reasonable person would realize creates a very high degree of risk to human life, and which results in death. Here, the defendant's conduct—shooting a gun into a crowded party—creates just such a risk. A wrinkle in this choice is that you're told the defendant was "angered." While this might trigger thoughts of provocation—and thus voluntary manslaughter, not murder—keep in mind that the provocation must be of the type that would provoke a *reasonable person,* not just the defendant. While a reasonable person might be provoked sufficiently to call the police under these circumstances, whipping out a gun and shooting the partying crowd would certainly be three standard deviations away from what a reasonable person would do under the circumstances. Since A provides the facts most likely to result in a murder conviction, of these four choices, it's the best response.

(B) is not the best response,

because the defendant would likely be liable for only voluntary manslaughter, not murder.

Voluntary manslaughter is murder committed under the "heat of passion." Thus, it's an unlawful killing with malice aforethought (either intent to kill or do serious bodily injury, depraved heart, or felony murder), where the act was provoked. The provocation must be one that would provoke a reasonable person and in fact provoked the defendant; and the defendant must not have calmed down since the provocation, and a reasonable person would similarly not have calmed down in time for the killing. Here, you're only told that the defendant's cousin slapped the defendant during an argument, and the defendant shot him in response. Without more, it's not crystal clear that the defendant would only be liable for voluntary manslaughter instead of murder, but what facts there are suggests it's a strong possibility. As a result, B is not the best response.

(C) is not the best response,

because it's unlikely that the risk the defendant created would be great enough to convict him of murder.

Common-law murder requires an unlawful killing with malice aforethought. While malice can take several forms, the one that does not require intent—depraved heart murder—does require extremely negligent conduct, which a reasonable person would realize creates a very high degree of risk to human life. If the risk is *not* that high, but still criminally negligent, the defendant will be liable for criminal negligence-type involuntary manslaughter, which is probably the case here. While running a red light does create *some* danger to human life, without other facts, the risk would not be high enough to justify a common law conviction. As a result, C is not the best response.

(D) is not the best response,

because it's unlikely that the risk the defendant created would be great enough to justify a murder conviction.

Common-law murder requires an unlawful killing with malice aforethought. While malice has several forms, the one that does not require intent—depraved heart murder—does require extremely negligent conduct, which a reasonable person would realize creates a very high degree of risk to human life. Creating a *lower* level of risk, which is still criminally negligent, would result in liability for involuntary manslaughter of the criminal negligence type. That's probably the result here.

Punching the victim in the face is an act, in and of itself, that a reasonable person would not anticipate resulting in a very high degree of risk to human life. Thus, D is not the best response.

Answer 38

(C) is the best response,

because it correctly identifies the reason for inadmissibility as the fact that the evidence is not legally relevant.

A piece of evidence, apart from meeting every other hurdle of admissibility, must be legally relevant—in other words, its probative value cannot be substantially outweighed by the probability of undue prejudice. FRE 403. This happens most frequently with "inflammatory" evidence in criminal cases—graphic and gruesome photos, body parts, etc. However, its applicability here is reasonably straightforward, since the jury is likely to be unduly influenced by its reaction to the defendant's heroin addiction. This is, of course, a judgment call, but legal relevance should always come to your mind when the evidence is particularly shocking. Since C correctly identifies the evidence here as being inadmissible due to the probability of undue prejudice it will invoke, it's the best response.

(A) is not the best response,

because it ignores the issue of legal relevance.

Here, the prosecution is offering evidence of another instance of misconduct in order to prove the defendant's guilt. The problem with such evidence is its logical *relevance.* Under FRE 404(b), such evidence can only be admissible when it has independent relevance, such as to show:

1. Knowledge;
2. Absence of mistake or accident;
3. Preparation;
4. Plan;
5. Opportunity;
6. Motive;
7. Intent; or
8. Identity.

As you can see, motive is one of these. However, what this ignores is the fact that the evidence must still meet the legal relevance requirement of FRE 403. That is, the probative value of the evidence must not be substantially outweighed by the probability of undue prejudice. While this happens most frequently with "inflammatory" evidence in criminal cases (graphic and gruesome photos, body parts, etc.), the jury here is likely to be unduly influenced by the heroin evidence. Since A does not take this into account, it is not the best response.

(B) is not the best response,

because it states a clearly impermissible goal for the evidence.

Here, the prosecution is offering evidence of another instance of misconduct in order to prove the defendant's guilt. The problem with such evidence is its logical *relevance.* Under FRE 404(b), such evidence can only be admissible when it has independent relevance, such as to show:

1. Knowledge;
2. Absence of mistake or accident;
3. Preparation;
4. Plan;
5. Opportunity;
6. Motive;
7. Intent; or
8. Identity.

Evidence is never admissible to prove the defendant's propensity to commit crimes, because if a person's character is shown through such evidence, the jury is likely to be unduly influenced by its reaction to the person, not by his actions under the circumstances in question. As a result, B is not the best response.

(D) is not the best response,

because it incorrectly applies the "Mercy Rule" to these facts.

Under the Mercy Rule of FRE 404(a)(2)(A), the defendant can introduce evidence of his own good character to show he did not commit the crime in question. Once a defendant has done so, the prosecutor can rebut. FRE 405(a) limits both the defendant and the prosecutor to reputation and opinion evidence. Here, the evidence is in the form of a specific act—the defendant's possession of heroin and a hypodermic needle on one occasion—not reputation or opinion, so it could not be admitted under the Mercy Rule even if the defendant had already offered evidence of his good character. Since D misstates the rule, it's not the best response.

Answer 39

(C) is the best response,

because the man has used the path for the statutory period without the neighbor's consent.

An easement by prescription can be obtained by the use of the easement, without permission of the servient landowner, openly and continuously for the statutory period. Here, the man never had the permission of his neighbor to use the path on the neighbor's land, and he used the path for 15 years—a period that exceeds the statute's ten-year requirement for acquiring an easement by prescription. The man has used the land continuously and without interruption. As a result, the man has acquired an easement by prescription. Note that the fact that the man's use was not exclusive does not defeat his claim; there is no general rule that easements must interfere with the servient landowner's use of his land.

(A) is not the best response,

because the requirements for adverse possession have not been met.

In order to acquire title by adverse possession, a party must continuously possess the property in a manner that is "open, notorious, and visible" and hostile to the title owner's interest for the statutory period. While the man's use of the path satisfies most of these criteria, he failed to "possess" the land, since his use was not exclusive. Since the hallmark of ownership of property is the right to exclude others, and the man never attempted to do so, he never manifested ownership of the land, as required to acquire title by adverse possession.

(B) is not the best response,

because there was no common ownership of the two parcels.

A court will find an easement by necessity if two parcels are situated such that the easement is strictly necessary for the enjoyment of one parcel (for example, if the only access to the dominant parcel involves crossing the servient parcel). In addition to the above requirement, an easement by necessity will only arise when, at one time, the two parcels were under common ownership. Neither requirement has been met in this case. We do not know that it would be impossible for the man to construct a path on his own land to reach the highway, and there is no indication that the two parcels were ever under common ownership. Accordingly, there is no easement by necessity.

(D) is not the best response,

because the man has acquired an easement by prescription.

An easement by prescription can be obtained by the use of the easement, without permission of the servient landowner, openly and continuously for the statutory period. Here, the man never had the permission of his neighbor to use the path on the neighbor's land, and he used the path for 15 years—a period that exceeds the statute's ten-year requirement for acquiring an easement by prescription. The man has used the land continuously and without interruption. As a result, the man has acquired an easement by prescription. Note that the fact that the man's use was not exclusive does not defeat his claim: there is no general rule that easements must interfere with the servient landowner's use of his land.

Answer 40

(D) is the best response,

because a promise to pay a debt after the statute of limitations has run is enforceable without consideration.

Generally, consideration is required for a contract to be enforceable. However, there are several exceptions to this rule. One such exception is a promise to pay a debt that would be otherwise unenforceable because it is barred by the statute of limitations. In order for this exception to be applicable, most states require that the promise be made in writing. In addition, if the promisor only promises to pay a part of the debt, the promise will only be enforceable up to the amount of the new promise, not the full amount of the debt. Since the debtor made his promise to pay $500 in writing, his comments will be enforceable up to that amount, even without consideration.

(A) is not the best response,

because it is irrelevant.

The question asked whether the debtor's new promise to pay $500 is enforceable, not whether he will plead the statute of limitations in a suit seeking to recover the original $1,500 debt. As discussed in the explanation of choice D above, the debtor's promise to pay $500 of the otherwise time-barred debt will be enforceable even absent consideration. Therefore, the lender will be able to enforce this new promise, but, should the lender seek to recover the full amount of the debt, the debtor will be able to plead the statute of limitations as a defense.

(B) is not the best response,

because no consideration is needed to support a promise to pay a debt otherwise unenforceable due to the statute of limitations.

Generally, consideration is required for a contract to be enforceable. However, there are several exceptions to this rule. One such exception is a promise to pay a debt that would otherwise be unenforceable because it is barred by the statute of limitations. In order for this exception to be applicable, most states require that the promise he made in writing. In addition, if the promisor only promises to pay a part of the debt, the promise will only be enforceable up to the amount of the new promise, not the full amount of the debt. Since the debtor made his promise to pay $500 in writing, his comments will be enforceable up to that amount, even without consideration.

(C) is not the best response,

because it does not address the issue of whether the lender has provided consideration.

Generally, consideration is required for a contract to be enforceable. However, there are several exceptions to this rule. One such exception is a promise to pay a debt that would be otherwise unenforceable because it is barred by the statute of limitations. In order for this exception to be applicable, most states require that the promise be made in writing. In addition, if the promisor only promises to pay a part of the debt, the promise will only be enforceable up to the amount of the new promise, not the full amount of the debt. Since the debtor made his promise to pay $500 in writing, his comments will be enforceable up to that amount, even without consideration. It is clear in this case that the debtor is providing consideration (the promise to pay $500 on his debt). What seems to be missing is consideration on the part of the lender, who is not giving up anything because, even absent the new agreement, he would be unable to enforce the debtor's debt in court.

Answer 41

(B) is the best response,

because the law will be judged using rational basis review.

Unless a law falls into one of the limited categories which require a heightened level of review, a court will assess the constitutionality of the law using rational basis review. The law prohibiting the operation of diagnostic centers unaffiliated with the hospital does not fall into one of these categories. Heightened levels of scrutiny are generally reserved for cases that implicate Equal Protection or First Amendment concerns. Since this law is neither, it will be upheld if it is rationally related to a legitimate state interest. Since it is possible that the state legislature rationally believed that the law would be in the best interest of the population's health (a legitimate state interest) to have this restriction, the law will be upheld.

(A) is not the best response,

because it is too broad.

While it is true that the provision of medical services is a traditional matter of local concern, it is not the case that a state's ability to regulate in the arena is beyond judicial review. All laws passed by a state legislature must fall within constitutional limitations. For example, a law that prohibited members of a certain minority group from being admitted to state hospitals would clearly violate Equal Protection, and a court would properly strike such legislation. However, in this case no such class-based determinations are being made, so the law will be upheld as it survives rational basis review. Remember that there is a difference between a law being constitutional and the law being unreviewable. Even though the law in this problem will be upheld, a court may still review it for constitutionality.

(C) is not the best response,

because it raises an irrelevant concern.

Whether the law imposes an undue burden on access to medical services is only a concern if such access is a fundamental right. The Supreme Court has not held that access to medical services is a fundamental right, so no heightened level of judicial scrutiny is appropriate. As a result, the law will be judged under rational basis review, and will likely be upheld since the state legislature could rationally believe that the law would promote the general welfare of its citizenry (which is a legitimate state interest).

(D) is not the best response,

because the suit is ripe.

In order for a suit to be heard in federal court, it must be ripe for adjudication. A controversy is ripe when harm to the plaintiff either has occurred or is reasonably likely to occur imminently. The latter condition is satisfied here. The physicians group presently has plans to open a diagnostic center, unaffiliated with a hospital, in the state. The state statute prohibiting such centers is an imminent threat to their plan. Since the harm threatened to the physicians group is not merely theoretical, but is reasonably likely to occur in the near future, the case is ripe, and may be heard on its merits.

Answer 42

(D) is the best response,

because a federal district court sitting in diversity in a particular state is required to apply the ***same rule of decision*** as a state court sitting in that same state would apply.

This means that if the State B ***conflict-of-law rule*** requires a State B state court to apply the GPDA to the dispute, a federal court sitting in State B is required to as well. This result follows indirectly from *Erie Railroad Co. v. Tompkins*, 304 U.S. 64 (1938), in which the Supreme Court held that in the absence of federal statutory law on point, a federal district court sitting in diversity must follow the common-law decisions as well as state statutes and state constitutional rules of the state where the federal court sits. More directly, the Court held post-*Erie* in *Klaxon Co. v. Stentor Electric Mfg. Co.*, 313 U.S. 487 (1941) that the *Erie* doctrine requires a federal district court sitting in diversity to apply not only the substantive rules of decision of the state in which it sits but ***also that state's choice-of-law (i.e., conflicts) rules***. (The *Klaxon* rule has the advantage that it ***discourages the parties from forum shopping***. Thus a plaintiff will not get the benefit of a different substantive rule by filing in a federal court for State X rather than in a State X state court; likewise, a defendant will not get the benefit of a different substantive rule by removing the action from a state court to a federal court in that same state.)

Choice (D), by making the federal court's decision on whether to apply the State B statute turn on whether the State B courts would apply the statute to this same dispute, correctly expresses the *Klaxon* choice-of-law-based rule. Under that rule, for instance, if the State B courts would apply State A rather than State B substantive contracts principles to this dispute because delivery was to occur in State A and/or because the Plaintiff was a citizen of State A, then the federal court would also be free to disregard the State B statute.

(A) is not the best response,

because this choice ascribes to the federal court a power it does not have.

Under a long-standing federal statute called the Rules of Decision Act, 28 U.S.C. § 1652, a federal court is required, in the absence of a contrary federal statute or rule, to apply "the laws of the several states," which are to be treated as "rules of decisions" in federal civil actions. The phrase "the laws of the several states" has long been interpreted to include a state's statutes. (*Erie v. Tompkins* expanded the meaning of the phrase to include a state's *judicial* decisions in the category of "laws of [a] state." But even pre-*Erie*, a state's statutes were always treated as being part of that state's laws.) Here, there is no federal statute or rule governing the issue. So even if the federal court thinks that federal "common law" (the body of non-statutorily-focused decisions by federal judges on analogous issues) would supply a good rule for deciding the issue of whether Defendant's delay constituted a material breach, the Rules of Decision Act requires the court to defer to any State B statute on point, if the State B courts would apply that statute to the case at hand in a state-court suit. Since choice (A) ignores the effect of the Rules of Decision Act, it is not the correct answer.

(B) is not the best response,

because the rule it states does not apply to the facts.

The state of incorporation is relevant to determining the ***citizenship of a corporation*** for purposes of determining whether diversity jurisdiction exists under 28 U.S.C. § 1332. But the citizenship of the defendant corporation here is not directly relevant to the issue of what body of law should control on the substantive issue of whether the Defendant has materially breached the contract. In determining whether to apply state law to a dispute, the federal diversity court in the first instance must look to the ***choice-of-law rule*** of the state in which the federal court sits—whichever state's substantive law would be applied by the state where the federal court sits, the federal court must apply that state's law. So here, the question is, "Under State B's choice-of-law rules, which state's substantive contracts law—State A or State B—would be applied by the State B courts, if the State B courts were hearing this case?" State B's choice of law rules might or might not give weight to the Defendant's state of incorporation; and if State B *wouldn't* consider that state of incorporation as part of the state's choice-of-law analysis, the federal court may not do so either. So Choice (B), by implying that the federal court must use the substantive law of the Defendant's state of incorporation, makes an incorrect statement of law.

(C) is not the best response,

because it incorrectly imposes a condition on the federal court's duty to apply the State B statute.

Under the federal Rules of Decision Act, 28 U.S.C. § 1652, a federal court, assuming no federal statute or rule applies, is required to apply state law to resolve the dispute before it. So the federal court here, where no federal statute or rule applies, must apply the relevant State B law—first, the State B choice-of-law rule (State B's method of deciding which state's substantive law should apply), and then, the substantive law of State B if that's the body of law the State B courts would apply on these facts. When the federal court carries out this task of ascertaining state law, it of course looks to any decisions by the state's highest court, so the federal court here would indeed look to see what State B's highest court has to say about the choice-of-law issue and thus about whether the GPDA would apply to this suit. But ***whether or not the highest state court has ruled***, the federal court is not free to disregard the GPDA if it believes State B's trial courts would choose to apply that statute to the dispute before it. Since choice (C) suggests that the federal court must apply the GPDA *only* if the highest court of State B has held that the statute applies to this sort of dispute, the choice places an incorrect limit on the federal court's duty to apply the GPDA.

Answer 43

(C) is the best response,

because this statement impeaches the witness's credibility, but it does not fall under a hearsay exception.

Here, the witness's prior statement is plainly inconsistent with his current testimony, as he "denied making any statements to the contrary." Therefore, the prior inconsistent statement can be used to impeach the witness's credibility and demonstrate that his trial testimony is not believable.

In order for the statement to be admissible to prove the defendant's involvement (a substantive rather than impeaching use), it must be offered for the truth of the matter asserted and therefore must satisfy a hearsay exception. The closest possible exception for an inconsistent prior statement of a witness is FRE 801(d)(1)(A), but that exception mandates that the prior statement be given under oath at a trial, hearing, or other proceeding. As this prior statement was not under oath, that exception will not apply. Since no other hearsay exception is satisfied under the facts, the statement will come in only to impeach the witness and not for its truth.

(A) is not the best response,

because it is wrong legally.

Pursuant to FRE 607, the credibility of a witness may be attacked by any party, including the party calling the witness. Here, the witness's prior statement is plainly inconsistent with his current testimony, as he "denied making any statements to the contrary." Therefore, the prior inconsistent statement can be used to impeach the witness's credibility and demonstrate that his trial testimony is not believable. The fact that the party calling the witness impeaches the witness is irrelevant.

(B) is not the best response,

because, while it is inadmissible hearsay if offered for the truth of the matter asserted, it is still admissible to impeach.

As the call of the question asked if this testimony is admissible, all grounds for admissibility must be explored, including impeachment. The witness's prior statement is plainly inconsistent with his current testimony, as he "denied making any statements to the contrary." Therefore, the prior inconsistent statement can be used to impeach the witness's credibility and demonstrate that his trial testimony is not believable.

(D) is not the best response,

because, while it is admissible to impeach, it is inadmissible hearsay if offered to prove the truth of the matter asserted.

Here, the witness's prior statement is plainly inconsistent with his current testimony, as he "denied making any statements to the contrary." Therefore, the prior inconsistent statement can be used to impeach the witness's credibility and demonstrate that his trial testimony is not believable. But in order for the statement to be admissible to prove the defendant's involvement, it must be offered for the truth of the matter asserted and therefore must satisfy a hearsay exception. The closest possible exception for an inconsistent prior statement of a witness is FRE 801(d)(1)(A), but that exception mandates that the prior statement be given under oath at a trial, hearing, or other proceeding. As this prior statement was not under oath, that exception will not apply. Since no other hearsay exception is satisfied under the facts, the statement will come in only to impeach the witness and not for its truth.

Answer 44

(C) is the best response,

because the seller's obligation to convey title clear of encumbrances benefits only the buyer.

The contract is silent as to the quality of title that the seller must convey. When the contract for sale is silent on this issue, a duty to convey marketable title will be implied. Because of the corporation's easement, the seller will not be able to do so. However, the condition requiring the delivery of marketable title, which is read into the contract, is designed only to benefit the buyer. Consequently, the buyer is free to waive that condition and insist that the seller go through with the sale. Here, the buyer was aware of the corporation's easement, but elected to go forward anyway. As a result, the seller will be obligated to sell the land, but the buyer will be unable to claim that the seller breached her duty to deliver marketable title in any later action.

(A) is not the best response,

because the buyer waived the requirement that the seller convey marketable title.

The contract is silent as to the quality of title that the seller must convey. When the contract for sale is silent on this issue, a duty to convey marketable title will be implied. Because of the corporation's easement, the seller will not be able to do so. However, the condition requiring the delivery of marketable title, which is read into the contract, is designed only to benefit the buyer. Consequently, the buyer is free to waive that condition and insist that the seller go through with the sale. Here, the buyer was aware of the corporation's easement, but elected to go forward anyway. As a result, the seller will be obligated to sell the land, but the buyer will be unable to claim that the seller breached her duty to deliver marketable title in any later action.

(B) is not the best response,

because the buyer waived the requirement that the seller convey marketable title.

The contract is silent as to the quality of title that the seller must convey. When the contract for sale is silent on this issue, a duty to convey marketable title will be implied. Because of the corporation's easement, the seller will not be able to do so. However, the condition requiring the delivery of marketable title, which is read into the contract, is designed only to benefit the buyer. Consequently, the buyer is free to waive that condition and insist that the seller go through with the sale. Here, the buyer was aware of the corporation's easement, but elected to go forward anyway. As a result, the seller will be obligated to sell the land, but the buyer will be unable to claim that the seller breached her duty to deliver marketable title in any later action.

(D) is not the best response,

because the buyer waived the requirement that the seller convey marketable title.

The contract is silent as to the quality of title that the seller must convey. When the contract for sale is silent on this issue, a duty to convey marketable title will be implied. Because of the corporation's easement, the seller will not be able to do so. However, the condition requiring the delivery of marketable title, which is read into the contract, is designed only to benefit the buyer. Consequently, the buyer is free to waive that condition and insist that the seller go through with the sale. In this case, the seller did not discover the corporation's easement until after the contract date. She was therefore under an obligation to promptly disclose this information to the buyer, which she did. The buyer's willingness to go forward with the deal, even though he only learned of the corporation's easement four days before the closing date, is clear evidence that the buyer did not consider the notification untimely. As a result, the seller will be obligated to sell the land, but the buyer will be unable to claim that the seller breached her duty to deliver marketable title in any later action.

Answer 45

(A) is the best response,

because in this battle of dueling undisputed evidence, the defendant (i.e., the decedent's estate) has rebutted the plaintiff's *prima facie* case.

Under the doctrine of "negligence per se," where a legislature has enacted a statute that is intended to prescribe the standard of conduct of a reasonable person in a particular situation, an excused violation of that standard that leads to the harm will constitute a *prima facie* showing of negligence if certain requirements are met (e.g., that the statute was intended to guard against the type of harm and to protect the class of persons at issue in the present case). So if the statutory violation were the only evidence regarding negligence that had been presented on either side, the plaintiff would win. But notice that the above formulation refers to an *unexcused* violation of the statute.

Here, the decedent's estate, by demonstrating that the decedent had an unforeseeable heart attack while otherwise driving reasonably, has established that the statutory violation was excused. *See, e.g.,* Rest. 2d Torts, § 288A(2)(a) (giving an excuse for a statutory violation where "the violation is reasonable because of the actor's incapacity"). Since this evidence of excuse is undisputed, and since there is no other evidence of negligence, the decedent's estate wins.

(B) is not the best response,

because, while this answer correctly states that the decedent's estate will prevail, it misstates the legal basis for this conclusion.

The plaintiff's evidence that the decedent violated the statute by crossing over into her lane of traffic *does* establish a *prima facie* case of negligence. (That is, if it were the only evidence of negligence in the case, plaintiff would be entitled to go to the jury.) Nevertheless, the decedent's estate successfully rebutted the plaintiff's evidence by providing an uncontested explanation of how the accident happened that is inconsistent with a finding of negligence (that the decedent's unforeseeable heart attack made her unable to comply with the statute, or indeed with any standard of care). Keep in mind that when a statement says that the plaintiff has or has not "established a *prima facie* case for liability," the statement is referring merely to the facts presented by the plaintiff in the plaintiff's case, not to the overall set of proven facts after both sides have rested. So it can happen—as it did here—that the plaintiff establishes a *prima facie* case in her own case, but that the defendant then produces counterproof to rebut that *prima facie* case, entitling the defendant to a verdict (perhaps even a directed verdict that takes the case away from the jury).

(C) is not the best response,

because while it may or may not be true that accidents of this type do not ordinarily happen in the absence of negligence, that is beside the point. This choice is suggesting the applicability of *res ipsa loquitur,* one requirement for which is that the accident be of a type that ordinarily does not happen in the absence of negligence.

There are two problems with the use of *res ipsa* here: (1) it is far from clear that median-crossing accidents "do not ordinarily happen in the absence of negligence" (there are a lot of heart attack, seizure, and other involuntary median-crossing scenarios, perhaps amounting to a majority); and (2) even where the "does not usually happen without negligence" requirement is met, the doctrine will not be applied where there is direct and unrebutted evidence that something other than the defendant's negligence was the cause. (Here, that evidence exists in the form of the heart attack evidence.)

(D) is not the best response,

because the plaintiff's evidence that the decedent violated the statute and crossed over into her lane of traffic establishes only a *prima facie* case of negligence.

The decedent's estate successfully rebutted the plaintiff's evidence—and thus made the "negligence per se" doctrine inapplicable—by providing an undisputed explanation of how the accident happened that is inconsistent with a finding of negligence.

Answer 46

(B) is the best answer,

because for a 23(b)(3) class action, common issues of law or fact must predominate.

The facts tell you that the case has been brought as a (b)(3) action, which is both the most common kind of class action and the only type whose principal object can be the award of compensatory damages. (In other words, where the plaintiff representing the class is mainly interested in obtaining compensation for the members, a (b)(3) action is usually the only realistic alternative.) But as 23(b)(3) says in its initial words, a (b)(3) is suitable where (and only where), among other factors, "the court finds that the ***questions of law or fact common to class members predominate*** over any questions affecting only individual members."

Here, the facts tell you that Title I only prohibits *intentional* race or gender discrimination. The facts also tell you that there are nearly 100 low-level managers who each made his or her own decision about whether to hire or promote a particular class member. Therefore, for the fact-finder to decide which of the plaintiffs had her Title I rights violated by Defendant (and even ignoring the further issue of damages), the fact-finder would have to consider the relevant manager's mental state concerning ***separately*** as to each hiring decision, in order to determine whether the class member was indeed intentionally discriminated against by her manager. Therefore, it's unlikely that the trial judge can or will conclude that questions of law or fact ***"common to class members"*** will indeed ***predominate*** over these intent-focused issues that will have to be resolved on a per-claimant basis. *See, e.g., Wal-Mart Stores, Inc. v. Dukes*, 131 S. Ct. 2541, 2561 (2011), noting that in the employment-discrimination class suit there, the corporate defendant would have to be given the chance to "demonstrate that [each] *individual applicant* was denied an employment opportunity for lawful reasons," thereby preventing common issues from predominating over individual issues. In any event, the question asks you to choose the objection that is *most likely* to succeed for Defendant, and while the argument here might not succeed, it is the only one that offers even a decent possibility of success.

(A) is not correct,
because it's not likely that the 100 potential class members will be found insufficiently non-numerous.

It's true that according to Rule 23(a)(1), no class action (i.e., regardless of whether the action is brought under 23(b)(1), (b)(2), or (b)(3)) may be certified unless the court concludes that "the class is so numerous that joinder of all members is impracticable[.]" There is no hard and fast rule on how large the class must be to meet this requirement. Classes as small as 14 members have been found sufficient to meet the numerosity requirement, although generally the class must include at least forty members. *See Consolidated Rail Corp. v. Town of Hyde Park*, 47 F.3d 473, 483 (2d Cir. 1995). Here, where there are about 100 potential class members, it's unlikely that the court would find that the number of members is so small as to be disqualifying. In any event, the common-question objection cited in Choice (B) is far more likely to succeed than the numerosity objection here.

(C) is not correct,
because it states a rule that is irrelevant to these facts.

It's of course true that class actions, like all actions filed in federal court, must satisfy subject-matter jurisdiction requirements. But here, the complaint alleges a violation of a federal statute, making this a "federal question" class action rather than a class action based solely on diversity. And in federal question suits, jurisdiction does not require the showing of any amount in controversy (*see* 28 U.S.C. §1331), and that's just as true with respect to class actions as in individual actions. If you were attracted to this choice, you might have been thinking of the one situation in which the availability of a class action *does* depend on at least $5 million being at stake: Under the Class Action Fairness Act or CAFA (embodied in 28 U.S.C. §1332(c)(2) and (3)), a state-law-based class action in which at least one class member is of citizenship diverse to at least one defendant, the amount in controversy is satisfied if at least $5 million is at stake in the aggregate, even if no single claim would meet the ordinary $75,000 amount-in-controversy requirement. But since the suit here is based on a federal question, CAFA never comes into play, and there is no amount in controversy requirement at all.

(D) is not correct,
because the rule that it recites is not correct.

In a class action, the court must be able to exercise personal jurisdiction over *defendant*. However, there is ***no requirement that the court determine whether it could exercise personal jurisdiction over the class members.*** *See Phillips Petroleum Co. v. Shutts*, 472 U.S. 797 (1985). Thus, even if the class members have no connection to the state in which the district court sits, the court is not thereby prevented from hearing the case. (There might be some due process problems if the absent class members who had no contacts with the forum state were nonetheless bound by a negative outcome in the suit, after those members were denied a chance to opt out from the suit. But in a (b)(3) action, such as the one here, absentees are always given the right to opt out, so there would be no problem in binding a class member who did not opt out, even if that member had never had any contacts with State A, where the class suit is proceeding.)

Answer 47

(D) is the best response,

because the friend and the man lacked the intent for a burglary.

The slight modifications to common-law burglary in this jurisdiction mean that the crime is defined as the breaking and entering of the dwelling or other structure of another with intent to commit a felony therein. Let's see how each of the three potential defendants stacks up against this definition.

The woman: The woman meets all the requirements for burglary. She broke into and entered the dwelling or other structure of another (by means of an innocent agent—more about this below). She intended to cause a felony to be committed therein: larceny of the saddle. What she intended to bring about after the breaking and entering was indeed larceny, because larceny is the trespassory taking and carrying away of personal property of another with intent to steal. Since the woman knew that the saddle belonged to the friend, and since she intended to steal it, she intended to commit larceny (and, incidentally, succeeded, though this isn't a requirement for the completed crime of burglary).

What about the fact that the woman didn't do the breaking and entering, or taking, herself, but instead used the man to do it for her? One who successfully recruits an "innocent agent" to carry out criminal acts is guilty as a principal, if the person doing the recruiting has the intent required for the crime. So the woman is guilty of burglary as a principal (and we do not need to resort to the theory of accomplice liability to have her be guilty).

The man: The man is not guilty of burglary, because he lacked the required intent. Burglary requires breaking and entering with intent to commit a felony. Even if the man is guilty of breaking and entering (which he probably is), he can be guilty of burglary only if he intended to commit a felony once inside the structure, and the only plausible felony here is larceny. But larceny requires intent to steal the property of another. A person who takes what he honestly (whether reasonably or not) believes to be his own property, or the property of someone who has authorized him to do the taking, lacks the required intent to "steal the property of another." Since the man did not intend to do acts, which, if carried out, would have constituted a felony, he cannot be guilty of burglary even though he unwittingly enabled the woman to commit burglary.

The friend: The friend is not guilty of burglary, because she lacked the required intent. As with the man, the friend could be guilty of burglary only if she intended to commit a felony once she broke and entered a structure, and the only plausible felony is larceny. But larceny requires intent to steal the property of another, and the friend's honest belief (in this case, a correct belief—but the correctness of the belief is irrelevant) that what she would be taking was her own property negates the requisite "intent to steal another's property."

(A), (B), and (C) are not the best response,

because each is inconsistent in some way with the analysis in D above.

Answer 48

(A) is the best response,

because nationwide service of process was permissible in this situation.

FRCP 4(k)(1) lists several situations in which serving a summons "establishes personal jurisdiction over a defendant" for a federal-court suit. Rule 4(k)(1)(C) covers one of these situations by saying that service of the summons will establish personal jurisdiction "when ***authorized by a federal statute***." The purpose of FRCP 4(k)(1)(C) is to allow Congress to add special rules of service, and special rules for ascertaining whether the federal court has personal jurisdiction over the defendant, for particular statutes. This allows a defendant to be served and subject to the federal court's personal jurisdiction without regard to whether the defendant has minimum contacts with the state where the federal court sits; so Congress can even provide for ***"nationwide service of process"*** for a particular category of federal suits. That's what Congress has done here in Section 2 of the IFCA—Congress has said that even if the defendant has no connection with the state where the federal court hearing the IFCA claim is located (in this case, State A), personal service on the defendant that occurs anywhere within the United States will suffice to establish personal jurisdiction.

Keep in mind that even when Congress uses its power to authorize nationwide service for a particular type of federal claim, the exercise of that power in the case at hand must still ***comport with constitutional due process***. *See, e.g., Hogue v. Milodon Eng'g, Inc.*, 736 F.2d 989, 991 (4th Cir. 1984) ("Where . . . Congress has authorized nationwide service of process . . . so long as the assertion of jurisdiction over the defendant is **compatible with due process**, the service of process is sufficient to establish the jurisdiction of the federal court over the person of the defendant."). Notice that the final clause of choice (A) correctly refers to this requirement. But is this choice also correct in asserting that the due process requirement is satisfied on these facts? Consider these points: (1) Congress has the express power under the Constitution's Commerce Clause to regulate interstate transactions; (2) Congress has a strong interest in providing a local forum for anyone who is harmed by the sort of interstate Internet-based fraud that the IFCA is directed against (rather than, say, requiring the person harmed to sue in the fraudster's home state); and (3) as Defendant knew when it took Plaintiff's order, the order by the Plaintiff originated from Plaintiff's State A office. Therefore, it does not seem especially unfair to Defendant to require it to defend in State A a suit arising out of an order that as Defendant knew originated in State A. In any event, it's unlikely that a court would hold that any unfairness is great enough to constitute a violation of Defendant's due process rights. And that's true even though Defendant shipped the computer to a non-forum state (State B).

(B) is not the best response,

because it incorrectly states applicable law.

It is *not* true that in all federal-question suits, service may be made anywhere in the U.S. where the defendant may be found. Rather, on our present facts, nationwide service is permissible *only* because Congress took the trouble to specify for ICFA suits in particular that service may be made nationwide. If Congress had merely drafted the ICFA to create a federal civil cause of action, and had not said anything about where suit on such a claim could be brought, nationwide service—as conditionally allowed by FRCP 4(1)(k)(C)—would *not* apply. (Service might still be valid under some *other* provision of the federal rules, but this choice specifically, and incorrectly, relies on the availability of nationwide service.)

(C) is not correct,

because the rule that it recites does not apply to these facts.

It's true that a federal court will exercise personal jurisdiction where service and personal jurisdiction would be allowed by the long-arm ***of the state where the federal court sits***. *See* FRCP 4(k)(1)(A), so stating. But Choice (C) is a trick; the state whose long-arm is quoted is State B (and the computer was indeed shipped into State B), but the state where the federal court is sitting is *State A*, not State B, so it's State A's long-arm, assuming one existed, that would apply. (If the suit were pending in State B federal court, this choice would be correct—Rule 4(k)(1)(A) allows the plaintiff to rely on the local state long-arm even if the suit is based on a federal question rather than on diversity.)

(D) is not correct,

because it relies on an incorrect legal premise.

It's true that in a case based solely on *diversity*, the defendants' lack of minimum contacts with the state where the federal court is based might well prevent the federal court from hearing the case, because it may well be a due process violation to force the defendant to defend a state-law-based action if it has no minimum contacts with the state where the federal court sits. (It's possible that Congress could constitutionally authorize the exercise of personal jurisdiction by a federal court sitting in diversity even in this circumstance of no-contacts-with-the-forum-state, but that issue has never been decided by the Supreme Court. In any event, it's clear that as a matter of *practice*, federal courts won't hear diversity actions where the long-arm of the state where the federal court sits wouldn't allow a state-court suit on analogous facts.) But the Supreme Court has never held that minimum contacts with the state where the federal court sits are necessary if the suit is based in part on ***a federally-created right of action*** (i.e., the suit is a "federal question suit"). And, in fact, in those instances where Congress has authorized ***nationwide service of process*** for a particular type of federally-created claim (as it not infrequently does), it's *often* the case that the defendant does not have minimum contacts with the state where the federal court is hearing the case. Since Choice (D) says that the defendant's lack of minimum contacts with State A makes it an automatic due process violation for the State A federal court to hear this federal-question case, it's wrong as a matter of law.

Answer 49

(C) is the best response,

because the state insurance statute was designed to protect homeowners.

In many cases, a contract that violates the law will be unenforceable based on public policy grounds. However, if the violation is of a policy that is intended to protect only the party seeking to enforce the contract, a court may enforce the contract so as to avoid frustrating the objectives of the legislature in enacting the statute. In this case, the requirement that insurance policies have certain coverage terms is clearly intended to benefit homeowners rather than insurance companies. It would be inconsistent with the legislative intent to allow insurance companies to escape liability under a policy based on their own violation of the statue. Accordingly, a court will protect the homeowner by enforcing the contract even though it does not meet all statutorily mandated requirements.

(A) is not the best response,

because divisibility is irrelevant to the situation.

A contract is divisible if it calls for a party to perform discrete tasks, each of which may be completed independently of the others. Under a divisible contract, a party that has only completed some, but not all, of the discrete tasks may sue the other party for non-performance even though his own performance is not complete. However, the divisibility of an insurance contract is not at issue here, since it doesn't address the key issue of whether the contract is enforceable despite its failure to comply with statutory requirements.

(B) is not the best response,

because the state insurance statute was designed to protect homeowners.

In many cases, a contract that violates the law will be unenforceable based on public policy grounds. However, if the violation is of a policy that is intended to protect only the party seeking to enforce the contract, a court may enforce the contract so as to avoid frustrating the objectives of the legislature in enacting the statute. In this case, the requirement that insurance policies have certain coverage terms is clearly intended to benefit homeowners rather than insurance companies. It would be inconsistent with the legislative intent to allow insurance companies to escape liability under a policy based on their own violation of the statue. Accordingly, a court will protect the homeowner by enforcing the contract even though it does not meet all statutorily mandated requirements.

(D) is not the best response,

because it raises issues of interpretation rather than enforceability.

In most cases, it is true that ambiguous terms in a contract will be interpreted against the drafter of the contract. It is also very likely that the insurance company drafted the homeowner's policy. However, the fact that ambiguities will be resolved against the insurance company is not the issue here. We are concerned with whether the contract is enforceable, not how it should be interpreted. Accordingly, issues pertaining to how the contract will be construed are irrelevant.

Answer 50

(D) is the best response,

because it correctly identifies that the photo identification will be admissible.

There are two separate issues here: first, whether the identification itself comports with the defendant's constitutional rights, which is a criminal procedure issue; and second, whether the victim's in-court testimony is admissible, which is an evidence issue.

First, the criminal procedure problem: what's involved here is a pre-trial identification. A pre-trial identification procedure only violates due process if two elements are satisfied:

1. The identification must be unnecessarily suggestive.
2. There must be a substantial likelihood of irreparable mistaken identification.

This is a difficult standard to meet, and is clearly not met by the facts here. Furthermore, there's no right to counsel for photo identifications, so the evidence here won't be excludable on that basis.

Second, the evidence issue—more specifically, the problem is one of hearsay: hearsay is an out-of-court statement offered to prove the truth of its assertion. Here, it's the victim's fingering of the defendant as the culprit, out of court, which amounts to an assertion, since she's in effect saying, "He did it!" However, as a prior identification of a person made by a presently testifying witness, the statement will be excluded from hearsay, under FRE 801(d)(1).

There may be another evidence issue that nagged at you here, and that is that the victim didn't actually see the defendant—she was clubbed from behind. However, this is an issue of credibility, and since the victim is testifying, the defendant's lawyer could attack her on this issue on cross-examination. Perry Mason would certainly make mincemeat out of her. However, the victim's not having actually seen the defendant doesn't make her testimony inadmissible, as D identifies. In fact, since D is the only choice that correctly identifies that the photo identification will be admissible, it's the best response.

(A) is not the best response,

because it does not represent a sound basis on which to exclude the victim's pre-trial identification, and it arrives at the wrong result.

A prior identification of a person, made by a presently testifying witness, is admissible as an exclusion from the hearsay rule. FRE 801(d)(1). That's what's going on here. The victim identified the defendant from the photographs. The quality of the declarant's opportunity to see the person can be attacked on cross-examination. If she didn't get a chance to see the defendant, the opposing attorney will draw this out and destroy her credibility. This alone doesn't provide a sound basis on which to exclude her testimony. This is actually quite a difficult call, because an underlying issue here is the fact that the victim didn't, apparently, see the defendant at all, and so you could question whether she's a competent witness as to his identity (since a witness must have personal knowledge of the matter on which she testifies, under FRE 602). However, choice A gives you a hint that it's not the best response by adding the word "good" to the victim's opportunity to see the defendant. *Any* opportunity, no matter how insignificant, would give her a basis for testifying; choice A overstates what would be required by stating that the opportunity to observe must be "good." Since A doesn't recognize that the identification will be admissible, it is not the best response.

(B) is not the best response,

because it misstates the law, and arrives at the wrong result.

The correct rule is that the suspect does not have a right of counsel at a photographic identification. *U.S. v. Ash* (1973). In a photo identification, the suspect is not even *present,* so the rationale of the right to counsel in line-up situations—to prevent the suspect from suffering for his inability to identify and object to prejudicial conditions—does not exist.

In fact, the prior identification will be admissible as an exclusion from the hearsay rule, since it fits all the requirements of the exclusion: the victim is a presently testifying witness who can be cross-examined, and the identification was made after perceiving the one identified. FRE 801(d)(1). (If the identification weren't expressly excluded from the hearsay rule, it would be considered hearsay, because it was an out-of-court statement, in the form of assertive conduct, offered to prove the truth of its assertion—that the defendant was the culprit. By identifying him, the victim was effectively saying: "That's him!") Although it's not clear from these facts *when* exactly the victim snuck a peak at the defendant, the defendant's lawyer will be able to attack her credibility on cross-examination. Since B ignores the fact that the identification will be admissible, and states a criminal procedure problem where in fact none exists, it's not the best response.

(C) is not the best response,

because although it states a potential theoretical basis on which to exclude the evidence, it does not apply to these facts.

A photo identification can be "unnecessarily suggestive" where, for instance, the other photos are of people who look significantly different than the suspect (e.g., of a different race). Since this focuses attention on the suspect, it's considered a due process violation. *Foster v. California* (1969). However, this doesn't apply to these facts, which state that the other seven people photographed "have the same general features as the defendant." As a result, the photo identification would not be unnecessarily suggestive. Since choice C states an inappropriate basis on which to exclude the pre-trial identification, and in fact the evidence is admissible as a prior identification made by a presently testifying witness, C is not the best response.

Answer 51

(A) is the correct answer,

because it correctly applies the rule that aggregation is ordinarily not allowed where no single plaintiff meets the jurisdictional amount.

When no single plaintiff's claim independently meets the amount-in-controversy requirement for diversity jurisdiction, ***multiple plaintiffs may not meet the amount-in-controversy requirement by aggregating the value of their claims unless their claims are "common and indivisible,"*** which the tort claims of the plaintiffs are not. Article III of the U.S. Constitution does not impose any amount-in-controversy requirement on the grant of diversity jurisdiction (*see* Article III, § 2), but Congress has always imposed such a minimum-dollar requirement in the federal statute that authorizes diversity jurisdiction. The current statute requires that the amount exceed "the sum or value of ***$75,000***, exclusive of interest and costs." 28 U.S.C. § 1332(a). When a lawsuit involves multiple plaintiffs, and each plaintiff's claims are separate and distinct from the claims of the others (not "common and indivisible"), ***at least one plaintiff must by him/herself have claims that meet the statutory requirement.*** (If one plaintiff's claims *do* meet the statutory requirement, the claims of the other plaintiffs can be heard under the discretionary doctrine of supplemental jurisdiction, assuming the other requirements of the statute are met. *See* 28 U.S.C. § 1367; *Exxon Mobil Corp. v. Allapattah Services, Inc.*, 545 U.S. 546 (2005).) Here, since no plaintiff independently has claims aggregating $75,000 or more, and since each plaintiff's claims are separate and distinct from the others' claims, aggregation is not allowed and the entire case must be dismissed.

Be attentive as to *why* plaintiffs' claims here would ***not*** be considered ***"common and indivisible."*** Claims are considered to be common and indivisible ***only where, "if one plaintiff were to fail to collect his share, the remaining plaintiffs would collect a larger share."*** *Durant v. Servicemaster Co. Trugreen, Inc.*, 147 F. Supp. 2d 744, 749 (E.D. Mich. 2001). Such claims typically involve a ***shared interest in a property title*** or in a status of entitlement. A series of individual torts, even when arising from the same contaminated product, do not come within this definition; in torts, each plaintiff is suing for the harm he or she individually suffered—the co-plaintiffs are not suing to recover part of a shared interest.

(B) is not the best response,

because it incorrectly applies the amount-in-controversy requirement for diversity jurisdiction.

Under the federal statute, a court may exercise diversity jurisdiction only if the claim exceeds the value of $75,000. *See* 28 U.S.C. § 1332(a). Here, no individual plaintiff meets that requirement, because each party's claim is valued only at $40,000. Moreover, the plaintiffs may not aggregate their claims to meet the amount-in-controversy requirement because their claims are not common and indivisible; as discussed in the second paragraph of Choice (A) above, each plaintiff's claims are considered to be separate and distinct from the claims of the other plaintiffs, even though all claims arise out of the same transaction or occurrence. And supplementary jurisdiction does not apply, because that doctrine applies only where at least one plaintiff's claim(s) independently meet subject-matter-jurisdictional requirements (in which case other claims by other parties may often be added even though they don't independently meet jurisdictional requirements); here, there is no plaintiff whose claim(s) independently meet subject-matter-jurisdictional requirements.

(C) is not the best response,

because it incorrectly applies the amount-in-controversy requirement for diversity jurisdiction.

As explained with respect to Choices (A) and (B), the diversity statute permits the exercise of jurisdiction only "where the matter in controversy exceeds the sum or value of $75,000, exclusive of interest and costs." 28 U.S.C. § 1332. ***An individual plaintiff may aggregate all claims against a single defendant, whether or not the claims are transactionally related.*** Here, Husband's two claims against Defendant together aggregate $75,000 or more, so he is deemed to meet the amount-in-controversy requirement. Once that happens, supplemental jurisdiction permits the other two plaintiffs to remain in the action, since their claims and Husband's are all "so related" (since they arise out of the same basic occurrence, joint consumption of a single can of soup) as to form one "case or controversy," the standard for triggering the availability of supplemental jurisdiction under 28 U.S.C. §1367(a). Since this Choice grants a dismissal to Defendant, it's wrong.

(D) is not the best response,

because it's wrong as a factual matter.

If Husband's and Wife's claims were in fact all based on a "common and undivided interest," this choice would be correct, as is explained in Choice (A): When multiple plaintiffs have claims based on a common and undivided interest, all claims by all plaintiffs based on that interest may be aggregated together for amount-in-controversy purposes. But as explained in the second paragraph of the discussion of Choice (A), the claims of Husband and Wife are not based on such a common and undivided interest.

Answer 52

(B) is the best response,

because the lights interfered with the woman's right to the use and enjoyment of her land.

A private nuisance is an unreasonable and substantial interference with a landowner's use and enjoyment of his or her land. If the private nuisance has already occurred, the plaintiff can recover compensatory damages. In this case, as a result of the noise and excess light from the stadium, the woman and her family were unable to use their farm as they would absent the stadium: they could not sleep a normal schedule or enjoy a quiet evening. These facts strongly indicate that there was a substantial interference with her right to enjoy her land. In addition to showing that there was a disruption, in order to succeed the woman will have to show that the school district's actions were negligent or intentional (with knowledge of the substantial certainty of causing the interference) and that the district's actions were unreasonable. The first requirement is clearly met, since the woman had made known her objections to the district's plans before the stadium was built. It is unclear from the facts we are given whether the placement of the stadium was unreasonable. Despite that uncertainty in the woman's case, private nuisance is still a superior basis for her claim than any of the other choices presented.

(A) is not the best response,

because the school district was not the woman's landlord.

Constructive eviction occurs when a landlord breaches an obligation to the tenant in a manner that makes the premises virtually uninhabitable for its intended use. For example, if a landlord prevents a residential tenant from having running water, constructive eviction has occurred. However, the doctrine of constructive eviction has no application outside the landlord-tenant relationship, so it does not provide the woman with a good basis for a claim for damages against the school district, which is not her landlord.

(C) is not the best response,

because the woman's damages are not shared by other members of the community.

A public nuisance is an interference with a right that is common to the general public. The plaintiff in a public nuisance suit must have suffered damage that is different in kind from that suffered by the general public. The facts we are given indicate that only one landowner is being disturbed by the presence of the stadium. As a result, the woman's suit will be more properly grounded in private nuisance (see the explanation for choice B above), rather than public nuisance.

(D) is not the best response,

because the woman does not possess an interest in the land on which the stadium was built.

Waste occurs when a party in possession of land makes use of the land in a manner that impacts the rights of other interest holders in the land. As an example, if the party in possession holds a life estate and sells all of the topsoil from the land, the remaindermen will be able to sue the life tenant for waste. In this problem, the woman and the school district do not both have interests in the same parcel of land, so the doctrine of waste is inapplicable.

Answer 53

(D) is the best response,

because there has been no anticipatory repudiation.

Generally, a plaintiff must wait until the date that performance is due before he can sue a non-performing defendant for breach. However, when a party, before performance is due, unequivocally indicates that he will not perform his obligations under the contract, he has anticipatorily repudiated, and the other party to the contract may treat that repudiation as a breach. In this case, there has been no unequivocal statement of the excavator's intent not to perform. The excavator only requested a 30-day delay. When the contractor didn't grant the delay, the excavator indicated that he would try to perform as scheduled. As a result, the contractor cannot treat the excavator's statements as an anticipatory repudiation and cannot cancel the contract. Note that the contractor, if he is reasonably concerned about the excavator's ability to perform, can lawfully request that the contractor provide adequate assurance that he will be able to meet his obligations under the contract.

(A) is not the best response,

because the excavator has not unequivocally stated that he will not perform.

Generally, a plaintiff must wait until the date that performance is due before he can sue a non-performing defendant for breach. However, when a party, before performance is due, unequivocally indicates that he will not perform his obligations under the contract, he has anticipatorily repudiated, and the other party to the contract may treat that repudiation as a breach. In this case there has been no unequivocal statement of the excavator's intent not to perform. The excavator only requested a 30-day delay. When the contractor didn't grant the delay, the excavator indicated that he would try to perform as scheduled. As a result, the contractor cannot treat the excavator's statements as an anticipatory repudiation and cannot cancel the contract. Note that the contractor, if he is reasonably concerned about the excavator's ability to perform, can lawfully request that the contractor provide adequate assurance that he will be able to meet his obligations under the contract.

(B) is not the best response,

because the excavator has not breached the covenant of good faith and fair dealing.

The implied covenant of good faith and fair dealing is read into all contracts. It requires all parties to a contract to refrain from acting in a deceitful or unfair manner with each other. There is no indication that the excavator has done anything of the sort. Absent any indication that his request for more time to perform was part of some fraud directed at the contractor, the excavator has not breached the covenant of good faith and fair dealing.

(C) is not the best response,

because money damages would be adequate.

In general, the appropriate remedy in contract cases is monetary damages. A court will only award specific performance if monetary damages are inadequate to make the plaintiff whole (for example, where the contract calls for the sale of a unique or irreplaceable item). The excavator-contractor contract is a typical commercial agreement. The contractor's primary obligation under the agreement is to pay the excavator for his services. Accordingly, should the contractor breach in any way, the excavator could gain the benefit of his bargain through the award of monetary damages. To put it another way, there is no indication that the excavator considers this a special job that he absolutely has to do. He'd be perfectly happy to make a profit *without* having to do the job, which is what would result from the contractor's breach followed by a court's monetary award.

Answer 54

(D) is the best response,

because it correctly identifies the issue that will determine *the newspaper's* liability. Understanding why requires a fairly detailed knowledge of the basic hierarchy of defamation claims against media defendants:

1. If a plaintiff is a public figure and the issue is "public," the plaintiff must prove malice (i.e., knowing falsehood or reckless disregard for the truth);
2. If a plaintiff is a public figure, but the issue involves his personal, private life, the plaintiff need only prove negligence, not malice;
3. If a plaintiff is a private figure, the plaintiff need only prove negligence, not malice; and
4. Regardless of the status of the plaintiff, if the item is "newsworthy," malice must be proven.

Thus, under these facts, arriving at the correct response requires that you (1) correctly characterize the leader's first wife as a private individual (since she lacks the "notoriety" a public figure requires), and (2) apply the negligence standard to it. The "ordinary care" language in D is referring to a negligence standard, since if one uses ordinary care he *cannot* be negligent. Note that D scrupulously avoids *concluding* whether *the newspaper* was negligent or not; it uses the modifier "if" instead of "because." As with any choice using "if," you have to determine whether the reasoning plausibly applies to the facts, whether it resolves a central issue, and whether the result is consistent with the reasoning. These are all satisfied here. While *the newspaper* could always have done more to check the facts, the reporter did rely on two "very reliable" sources. Thus, it's possible he used reasonable care in verifying the truth of the story, and as a result wouldn't be liable for negligence. As a rule of thumb, negligence could be shown, for instance, by a *failure* to check sources. (On a related note, malice would require more: whether the reporter entertained serious doubts about the truth of what he was printing.) Since D correctly identifies the standard that will determine if *the newspaper* is liable, and the result it offers is consistent with the reasoning, it's the best response.

(A) is not the best response,

because it only addresses *part* of what the leader's first wife would have to prove, on these facts, to prevail.

Realizing why A isn't sufficient requires a quick refresher on the "hierarchy" of defamation claims against media defendants:

1. If a plaintiff is a public figure and the issue is "public," the plaintiff must prove malice (i.e., knowing falsehood or reckless disregard for the truth);
2. If a plaintiff is a public figure, but the issue involves his personal, private life, the plaintiff need only prove negligence, not malice;
3. If a plaintiff is a private figure, the plaintiff need only prove negligence, not malice; and
4. Regardless of the status of the plaintiff, if the item is "newsworthy," malice must be proven.

Here, there's no real question but that the leader's first wife is a private individual, not a public figure, so the observation in A—that the issue involves her personal, private life—is not relevant. (She probably couldn't be considered a public figure in relation to her husband, especially since they are long divorced and the incident alleged occurred over 30 years ago.) What *is* relevant is whether or not *the newspaper* was negligent in its fact-checking. If it was, it will be liable; if it wasn't, it won't. Since A focuses on a fact that in and of itself will not determine who will prevail, it's not the best response.

(B) is not the best response,

because it understates the standard necessary for holding *the newspaper* liable for defamation.

A statement must be false to be defamatory. However, some level of fault will also have to be proven. With a private individual as a plaintiff, the defendant would have to have been at least *negligent* in failing to determine that what it reported was false. If you chose this response, you probably had in mind the common-law rule, which made defamation a strict liability offense. Since modern courts require fault, and B doesn't recognize this, it's not the best response.

(C) is not the best response,

because even without the element it offers, the newspaper could *still* be liable.

The reasoning in C states the definition of malice. However, malice isn't required here. Where a media defendant and a private individual plaintiff are concerned, the rule is this: no recovery for defamation is allowed unless the defendant was at least negligent. If the defendant was negligent but without malice, the plaintiff will prevail in the action (but won't be able to claim punitives without proof of malice).

If you chose this response, it's probably because you confused the rule for public figure plaintiffs with the rule for private figures. Public figures suing for defamatory statements about public matters must prove malice in order to recover. However, since the leader's first wife will be considered a private individual—being married years ago to a local labor leader would not give her the notoriety necessary to be considered a public figure—she need only prove negligence. Note that choice C *does* correctly characterize the facts (since *the newspaper* did not have malice), since malice would require, at the very least, that the reporter entertained serious doubts about the truth of what he was printing. However, since C states a standard that is stricter than the one that will apply, it's not the best response.

Answer 55

(D) is the best response,

because it correctly identifies that, under these facts, the farmer will still be liable to the owner for the rent on the remaining portion of the farm.

There are a couple of facts that are key to arriving at the correct result. First, the farmer has already been compensated for his portion of the condemnation.

When property is condemned, the tenant is entitled to a share representing the current value of the unexpired term of the lease, less future rents payable (which will not have to be paid). Presumably, the farmer's recovery represented the unexpired term for the 20 acres of farmland. In general, when the condemnation is only *partial,* the relationship of landlord and tenant will be unaffected. As a result, the tenant will still be liable for rent to reflect the amount of the property not condemned. Since D states this correctly, it's the best response.

(A) is not the best response,

because the facts here do not satisfy the doctrine of frustrated purpose.

In order to discharge a contractual duty due to frustration of purpose, four requirements must be met. First, the frustration must be caused by a supervening act or event. Second, the supervening act or event must have been unforeseeable when the parties entered into the contract. Third, the act or event must destroy or almost destroy the purpose of the contract. Finally, both parties must have realized this purpose when the contract was formed. You should also keep in mind that courts dislike discharging contracts due to frustration of purpose. Under the facts here, there are two facts that argue against applying the frustration of purpose doctrine. First, there are still ten acres that were *not* taken by the government. Frustration of purpose requires that the frustration be complete or almost complete. Taking two-thirds of the land probably would not qualify. Second, the farmer has already been compensated for his interest in the property. As a result, it's unlikely that the frustration of purpose doctrine would apply, making A not the best response.

(B) is not the best response,

because it misstates the facts: there has been *no* breach of the implied covenant of quiet enjoyment.

The implied covenant of quiet enjoyment is a covenant implied in every lease, which provides, first, that the tenant will not be ousted by any third party with "paramount title" (superior title to the landlord), and, second, that the landlord and his representatives will not interfere with the tenant's use and enjoyment of the premises. Furthermore, the tenant must leave the premises within a reasonable time after the breach in order to preserve his claim, otherwise it will be waived.

What makes this argument inapplicable here is that it's not the landlord or a third party with paramount title who has interfered with the farmer's use and enjoyment, but the government.

Apart from that, the farmer hasn't really been ousted from the premises—only part of the land has been taken by the government. Since there hasn't been a breach of the implied covenant of quiet enjoyment, and that's what B says, B cannot be the best response.

(C) is not the best response,

because it mistakenly characterizes condemnation of the property as the tenant's responsibility.

The tenant is only liable not to commit waste on the property. He will have no responsibility for acts outside his responsibility and control. Condemnation of the property by the government is just such an act. Since choice C incorrectly blames the condemnation on the farmer, it's not the best response.

Answer 56

(C) is the best response,

because it arrives at the correct result, and focuses on the reason why the defendant won't be guilty—because he didn't intend to cause an offensive touching.

The criminal assault statute in this problem requires an attempt to commit a criminal battery. Attempt has two elements: Intent, and an overt act done in furtherance of the intent, beyond mere preparation. Here, the defendant had no intent to touch the plaintiff in any way; he was trying to retrieve his hat. Since he didn't intend to touch the plaintiff, he couldn't be liable for any crime that explicitly or implicitly requires intent. Since intent is an element of attempt, he can't be liable. Since C correctly identifies that this is the element that will exonerate the defendant, it's the best response.

(A) is not the best response,

because it ignores the intent element of the crime, and it reaches the wrong result.

The statute under which the defendant was charged, the criminal assault statute, would require that the defendant attempted to cause an offensive touching. Attempt has two elements: intent, and an overt act done in furtherance of the intent, beyond mere preparation. Under these facts, this would mean that the defendant would have to have intended to cause an offensive touching. However, the facts indicate the only thing the defendant intended to touch was his hat, not the plaintiff. Since he didn't intend to touch the plaintiff, he couldn't be found guilty of a crime involving attempt, which is what the criminal assault statute requires. Since A stops short of what would be required to convict the defendant, it's not the best response.

(B) is not the best response,

because it arrives at the wrong result, and offers a standard of culpability that is *lower* than the standard in the statute given.

The statute under which the defendant was charged, the criminal assault statute, would require that the defendant attempted to cause an offensive touching. Attempt has two elements: intent, and an overt act done in furtherance of the intent, beyond mere preparation. Choice B suggests that the defendant should be culpable for merely *negligent* behavior—because he *should have realized* harm might result from his act. This is not sufficient for attempt, since attempt requires intent. Since B would hold the defendant liable for assault without intent, it's not the best response.

(D) is not the best response,

because although it offers the right result, it requires *more* than the actual statute requires.

The criminal assault statute only requires *an attempt* to cause an offensive touching. D suggests that an *actual* touching is required. If you chose this response, it could be because you mistakenly believed the defendant was charged with criminal battery—if he *had* been charged with criminal battery, a touching would have been required. As it is, a criminal assault only requires an attempt to commit a criminal battery, and so D is not the best response.

Answer 57

(B) is the best response,

because it correctly identifies the level of scrutiny a court will apply to the ordinance.

The city ordinance is a content-neutral restriction. Since it only restricts the physical characteristics of visual displays, and not their content, the ordinance will be reviewed using intermediate scrutiny. Intermediate scrutiny requires that the defendant show that the ordinance is narrowly tailored to achieve an important governmental interest, and that it leaves open the alternate channels of communication where the plaintiff may disseminate their message. Choice B therefore lays out exactly the argument that the party must make in order to succeed. Note that this does not mean that the party will win, but only that it is their best argument. When an MBE question asks for a party's "best argument," it is not required that the correct answer be the winning argument, but only that it be superior to the other choices presented.

(A) is not the best response,

because strict scrutiny is inapplicable to the ordinance.

This choice lays out the elements for arguing that an ordinance does not satisfy strict scrutiny: i.e., that the ordinance is not the least restrictive means of achieving a compelling governmental interest. Strict scrutiny will be applied to *content-based* restrictions on free speech. Since the city ordinance does not attempt to regulate speech based on the content of the message, but only on the format in which it is presented, a court will assess the constitutionality of the ordinance using intermediate scrutiny rather than strict scrutiny.

(C) is not the best response,

because the ordinance does not impose a prior restraint.

A prior restraint is an ordinance that requires governmental permission before an individual or group may exercise its right to publish particular information. The city ordinance does not attempt to institute a system under which prior permission is needed, but rather only to regulate the format in which material is presented. This is a content-neutral restriction. As a result, a court assessing the constitutionality of the ordinance will apply intermediate scrutiny, and uphold the ordinance if the city can show that it is narrowly tailored to important government interest.

(D) is not the best response,

because the ordinance is content-neutral.

The ordinance, as written, does not seek to favor some categories of speech over others, but rather to regulate the format in which the speech is conveyed when posted along the roadside. So long as the ordinance is applied equally to all those who seek to post signs in the city's historic district, it is a content-neutral restriction on speech, and will be analyzed under intermediate scrutiny. Therefore, so long as the ordinance is narrowly tailored to achieve an important government interest and leaves alternate channels for the party to speak, it will be upheld.

Answer 58

(C) is the best response,

because the car dealer was already obligated to pay in full by June 1.

When the car dealer asked the bank to accept ten monthly payments, rather than a lump-sum payment due by June 1, the dealer was requesting that a modification be made to the existing dealer-bank contract. In order for a modification to be effective, there must be consideration given for the modification. Here, the bank offered consideration in the form of allowing the car dealer to pay over time. However, the car dealer's offer to provide monthly payments for ten months was not a legal detriment to it, because the dealer was already under the pre-existing duty to pay the full sum within that time. As a result, the car dealer has not offered consideration for the bank's promise, and the modification to their existing agreement is ineffective. Accordingly, the bank will be able to succeed in its suit, since the car dealer breached their contract by not paying on June 1. Note that this would not be the case if the dealer had promised that the buyer would be responsible for making the payments, since the bank would then get the additional consideration of having another obligor on the debt.

(A) is not the best response,

because the Statute of Frauds does not apply.

An agreement only needs to be in writing if it is within the Statute of Frauds. The Statute of Frauds applies only in limited circumstances: suretyship, promises in consideration of marriage, land sales, sales of goods valued over $500, and promises not possible to complete within one year. If a contract, as modified, would fall within the Statute of Frauds, then the modification must be in writing. However, an agreement to extend the time in which a debtor must repay a loan falls into none of the categories covered by the Statute of Frauds. As a result, it is irrelevant whether the agreement was in writing or not.

(B) is not the best response,

because the dealer has not attempted to delegate its duty to pay.

The agreement made between the car dealer and the bank only pertains to the timing of payment, not to who is obligated to pay the debt. The bank has only promised to allow the dealer to make periodic payments, not to substitute the buyer as an obligor on the debt. Moreover, there is no reason why the dealer could not delegate its duty to pay to the buyer, since the obligation to pay a debt is not a non-delegable duty. Remember that, even if the dealer delegates its duty to pay to the buyer, the dealer will remain liable on the debt to the bank.

(D) is not the best response,

because there was no attempted novation.

A novation is an agreement between the parties to a contract and a third-party to substitute the third-party for one of the original parties to the contract, releasing the original party from his obligations. There is no indication in the facts we are given that the dealer attempted to substitute the buyer's obligation to pay the bank for its own. The mere direction to the buyer to make his payments to the bank is insufficient to release the dealer from its own obligation, and it will remain liable on the debt. The car dealer is not claiming that it is not liable on the debt, but rather that it should have the right to pay the debt back at a rate of $1,000 per month, beginning on June 1. The issue is thus *when* payment is due, not *who* is responsible for making the payments.

Answer 59

(C) is the best response,

because it identifies that interpretation of the delay is the central issue in the case.

In non-UCC cases, a reasonable delay is generally *not* considered a material breach. Here, since there's no transaction in goods involved, the common law will control. Thus, absent extraordinary circumstances, known to the landowner when the contract was created, that would make the May 1 deadline essential, the landowner's delay would only be a minor breach, requiring that the contractor perform and sue for damages. If time *was* of the essence, *any* delay would be a material breach. Thus, this is a key issue in determining if the contractor was entitled to cancel the contract.

If time was *not* of the essence, the contractor's undue hardship could become important in determining whether the landowner substantially performed under the contract (thus meriting return performance). However, since choice B ignores the central issue, it's not the best response.

Keep in mind that the UCC treats delays somewhat differently, due to the "perfect tender" rule under § 2-601. That is, the presumption in contracts for the sale of goods is that time is of the essence. However, this isn't as strict as it sounds, due to the seller's right to cure defective performance. §2-508. Where performance is late, the seller can *still* cure, if he notifies the buyer of his intent to cure, and he had reason to believe that the buyer would accept the delay (the delay making the goods, in effect, non-conforming).

Since C identifies the central issue on these facts, it's the best response.

(A) is not the best response,

because it ignores the central issue where there is a delay in performance: whether time was of the essence.

In non-UCC cases, a reasonable delay is generally *not* considered a material breach. Here, since there's no transaction in goods involved, the common law will control. Thus, absent extraordinary circumstances, known to the landowner when the contract was created, that would make the May 1 deadline essential, the landowner's delay would only be a minor breach, requiring that the contractor perform and sue for damages.

If time *was* of the essence, *any* delay would be a material breach. Thus, this is a key issue in determining if the contractor was entitled to cancel the contract.

The landowner's due diligence is, at best, of minor importance in the case. If time *was* of the essence, the landowner's diligence is entirely irrelevant; if it *wasn't,* then the landowner's diligence would be relevant in determining if the landowner substantially performed under the contract. However, since the significance of the delay is the central issue, and A ignores this, it's not the best response.

(B) is not the best response,

because it ignores the central issue where there is a delay in performance: whether time was of the essence.

In non-UCC cases, a reasonable delay is generally *not* considered a material breach. Here, since there's no transaction in goods involved, the common law will control. Thus, absent extraordinary circumstances, known to the landowner when the contract was created, that would make the May 1 deadline essential, the landowner's delay would only be a minor breach, requiring that the contractor perform and sue for damages.

(D) is not the best response,

because it ignores a central issue in the case: whether time was of the essence.

In non-UCC cases, a reasonable delay is generally *not* considered a material breach. Here, since there's no transaction in goods involved, the common law will control. Thus, absent extraordinary circumstances, known to the landowner when the contract was created, that would make the May 1 deadline essential, the landowner's delay would only be a minor breach, requiring that the contractor perform and sue for damages.

If time *was* of the essence, *any* delay would be a material breach. Thus, this is a key issue in determining if the contractor was entitled to cancel the contract.

If time was *not* of the essence, and the four-week delay was considered a minor breach, then the contractor's good faith in cancelling the contract would be an issue. However, if the delay was not a material breach, the contractor would probably have to perform under the contract and sue for any damages the delay cost him. Since the contractor's good faith is a secondary issue at best under these facts, D is not the best response.

Answer 60

(B) is the best response,

because under the tort of intentional infliction of mental suffering (also called intentional infliction of emotional distress) the plaintiff can be compensated for his emotional suffering in addition to the value of the cat.

The tort of intentional infliction of mental suffering is an intentional or reckless infliction, by extreme and outrageous conduct, of severe emotional distress, even in the absence of physical harm. If the plaintiff can establish this claim (and the facts support that he can, as the neighbor was aware that the plaintiff was fond of his cat and shot the cat in full view of the plaintiff), he can be compensated for his own emotional suffering as well as the value of the cat. As the other responses are either not supported on the facts or could only lead to compensation for the value of the cat, B is the best response,

(A) is not the best response,

because the neighbor did not touch the man, so the neighbor is not liable for battery.

Battery is the intentional infliction of a harmful or offensive bodily contact. As there was not a bodily contact to the plaintiff here, the plaintiff could not establish a battery. If the plaintiff had been holding the cat when it was struck, he could conceivably argue that an item closely identified with his body was struck, thereby creating a battery. Here, however, the facts do not support the inference that he was holding the cat at the time.

(C) is not the best response,

because, if established, trespass to chattel would only award the plaintiff the value of his cat.

A trespass to chattel is an intentional interference with a person's use or possession of the chattel. While a trespass to chattel is established by these facts, the plaintiff could recover only $25, the value of the cat. As the call of the question asks what claim would result in the greatest monetary recovery, trespass to chattel is inferior to intentional infliction of mental suffering, which would allow the plaintiff to recover damages based on his emotional suffering in addition to the value of the cat.

(D) is not the best response,

because, if established, conversion would only award the plaintiff the value of his cat.

The tort of conversion occurs when the defendant so substantially interferes with the plaintiff's possession or ownership of property that it is fair to require the defendant to pay the property's full value. While a conversion is established by these facts, the plaintiff could recover only $25, the value of the cat. As the call of the question asks what claim would result in the greatest monetary recovery, conversion is inferior to intentional infliction of mental suffering, which would allow the plaintiff to recover damages based on his emotional suffering in addition to the value of the cat.

Answer 61

(A) is the best response,

because this choice is a precise and accurate statement of the scope of cross-examination set forth by FRE 611(b).

Rule 611(b) states that cross-examination "should not go beyond the subject matter of the direct examination and matters affecting the witness's credibility." Since the property manager was asked on direct "solely" whether the defendant was the owner of the property, the question on cross-examination, concerning the precautions taken by the defendant, fell far outside the limited scope of direct examination. While the second sentence of 611(b) gives the trial judge discretion to allow questions going beyond the scope of direct examination, there is no reason for the judge to exercise that discretion to allow the question here.

(B) is not the best response,

because denominating someone as a hostile witness has no bearing on the permissible scope of cross-examination.

Categorizing a witness as hostile means only that such a witness can be examined through the use of leading questions; it does not relate to the scope of cross-examination. FRE 611(b), which restricts cross-examination to the scope of the direct examination and to witness-credibility issues, applies equally to hostile and non-hostile witnesses. Thus, the fact that the witness is hostile does not permit cross-examination to extend beyond the scope of direct examination in matters unrelated to credibility of the witness.

(C) is not the best response,

because under FRE 611(b), cross-examination should be limited to the subject matter of the direct examination and matters affecting credibility.

Although the second sentence of FRE 611(b) gives the trial court *discretion* to permit inquiry into additional matters, this choice states that the defendant is "entitled" to a wider scope of cross-examination, and that statement is incorrect.

(D) is not the best response,

because there is no such rule permitting cross-examination of unlimited scope of an agent of a party.

The scope of cross-examination for all witnesses is controlled by FRE 611(b), which limits it to the scope of direct examination and credibility.

Answer 62

(A) is the best response,

because the government permanently occupied a portion of the owner's land.

The Fifth Amendment contains the Taking Clause: "nor shall private property be taken for public use, without just compensation." Under the rule of *Loretto v. Teleprompter* (1982), *any* permanent physical occupation of any portion of an individual's land, no matter how small or unobtrusive, constitutes a taking, and compensation will be due to the landowner. (In cases where the occupation is minimal, the amount of compensation may be negligible.) Here, the government has constructed a surveillance facility on the owner's land, and is therefore occupying a portion of it. The fact that the government's use does not interfere with the owner's current use of the land is irrelevant.

(B) is not the best response,

because safeguarding the nation's security is a legitimate governmental interest.

The test for determining if a governmental action comports with the requirement of the Equal Protection Clause is whether the action is rationally related to a legitimate governmental interest. Here, safeguarding national security is certainly a legitimate objective of the federal government. In addition, the construction of the surveillance facility appears to be a rational way to pursue that goal. Therefore, the government's construction of the surveillance facility will not constitute an Equal Protection violation.

(C) is not the best response,

because the physical occupation of the owner's land is a taking even if it does not interfere with the owner's use of the land.

The Fifth Amendment contains the Taking Clause: "nor shall private property be taken for public use, without just compensation." Under the rule of *Loretto v. Teleprompter* (1982), *any* permanent physical occupation of any portion of an individual's land, no matter how small or unobtrusive, constitutes a taking, and compensation will be due to the landowner. (In cases where the occupation is minimal, the amount of compensation may be negligible.) Here, the government has constructed a surveillance facility on the owner's land, and is therefore occupying a portion of it. The fact that the government's use does not interfere with the owner's current use of the land is irrelevant.

(D) is not the best response,

because the government's need is irrelevant to the issue of whether there has been a taking.

The Fifth Amendment contains the Taking Clause: "nor shall private property be taken for public use, without just compensation." Under the rule of *Loretto v. Teleprompter* (1982), *any* permanent physical occupation of any portion of an individual's land, no matter how small or unobtrusive, constitutes a taking, and compensation will be due to the landowner. (In cases where the occupation is minimal, the amount of compensation may be negligible.) Here, the government has constructed a surveillance facility on the owner's land, and is therefore occupying a portion of it. The fact that the government's use does not interfere with the owner's current use of the land is irrelevant.

Answer 63

(C) is the best response,

because the delivery of the deed completed the conveyance.

In order for a conveyance to be effective, certain formalities must be observed. The deed must describe the property, be signed by the grantor, and identify the parties to the conveyance. The deed must then be "delivered," completing the conveyance. Delivery requires that there be a physical transfer of the deed and that the grantor use words or conduct evidencing his intent to make the deed presently operative. The recording of a deed is not necessary for an effective conveyance. In this problem, the deed was in proper form and was physically delivered to the friend. Although the landowner expressed his desire that the deed not be recorded until after his death, the statement "this is yours" indicated his intention that the land described in the deed should belong to his friend. Title to the land passed to the friend upon delivery, and the landowner no longer had any control over the parcel. As a result, the land was not in the landowner's estate when he died and will not pass to his intestate heirs.

(A) is not the best response,

because recording a deed is not necessary for a conveyance of land to be effective.

The only formal requirement necessary to transfer real property is that a deed, proper in form, be delivered from the grantor to the grantee. Delivery requires that there be a physical transfer of the deed and that the grantor use words or conduct evidencing his intent to make the deed presently operative. In this problem, the deed was in proper form and was physically delivered to the friend. Although the landowner expressed his desire that the deed not be recorded until after his death, the statement "this is yours" indicated his intention that the land described in the deed should belong to his friend. Title to the land passed to the friend upon delivery, and the landowner no longer had any control over the parcel. As a result, the land was not in the landowner's estate when he died and will not pass to his intestate heirs.

(B) is not the best response,

because the friend's dishonesty regarding the destruction of the deed is irrelevant.

Destroying a deed does not operate to rescind a conveyance. In order for a conveyance to be effective, certain formalities must be observed. The deed must describe the property, be signed by the grantor, and identify the parties to the conveyance. The deed must then be "delivered," completing the conveyance. Delivery requires that there be a physical transfer of the deed and that the grantor use words or conduct evidencing his intent to make the deed presently operative. The recording of a deed is not necessary for an effective conveyance. In this problem, the deed was in proper form and was physically delivered to the friend. Although the landowner expressed his desire that the deed not be recorded until after his death, the statement "this is yours" indicated his intention that the land described in the deed should belong to his friend. Title to the land passed to the friend upon delivery, and the landowner no longer had any control over the parcel. Since the friend then owned the land, in order for it to pass back to the landowner, the formalities would have to be followed. Destroying the deed is ineffective; for the land to pass back to the landowner, a new deed would have to be written and delivered to the landowner.

(D) is not the best response,

because title to the land passed to the friend immediately upon delivery.

The subsequent recording of the deed was not necessary to vest title to the land in the friend. In order for a conveyance to be effective, certain formalities must be observed. The deed must describe the property, be signed by the grantor, and identify the parties to the conveyance. The deed must then be "delivered," completing the conveyance. Delivery requires that there be a physical transfer of the deed and that the grantor use words or conduct evidencing his intent to make the deed presently operative. The recording of a deed is not necessary for an effective conveyance. In this problem, the deed was in proper form and was physically delivered to the friend. Although the landowner expressed his desire that the deed not be recorded until after his death, the statement "this is yours" indicated his intention that the land described in the deed should belong to his friend. Title to the land passed to the friend upon delivery, and the landowner no longer had any control over the parcel. The friend's recording of the deed serves to provide notice to future takers of the land, but is not needed for the friend to take title.

Answer 64

(C) is the correct answer,

because it recognizes that the removal here was improper.

The removal was improper for two reasons. First, ***when the federal court would have lacked original jurisdiction over the plaintiff's claim, removal is not proper.*** Second, even if original subject-matter jurisdiction (based on diversity) over the plaintiff's original claim *had* existed, **an in-state defendant cannot remove when jurisdiction is based solely on diversity**. And as to each of these two reasons, the presence of Defendant's counterclaim does not change the analysis. Let's take each of these steps in turn.

First, an action can be removed to federal court only if, as an original matter, the plaintiff could have initially filed the suit in federal court for the district where the plaintiff in fact brought the state-court suit. A plaintiff can file suit in a federal court if either (i) there are grounds for federal-question jurisdiction (*see* 28 U.S.C. § 1331), or (ii) diversity jurisdiction is present (*see* 28 U.S.C. § 1332) (as well as if there is some other jurisdictional basis that is not relevant to this problem). Here, there are no grounds for federal-question jurisdiction because plaintiff has asserted solely a ***state-law*** breach-of-warranty claim and has not asserted any claim arising under federal law. Therefore, the suit could have been filed in federal court only if diversity jurisdiction would have been available for that warranty claim. Diversity jurisdiction requires both complete diversity of citizenship as between all plaintiffs and all defendants, plus satisfaction of the amount-in-controversy requirement. (*See* 28 U.S.C. § 1332(a).) Neither condition is met here. The citizenship requirement is not met because both the Plaintiff and the Defendant are citizens of State A. (The Plaintiff, who owns a home in State A, would be considered a citizen of that state based on his domicile plus his intent to remain. Defendant is incorporated in, and has its principal place of business in, State A, and therefore is considered to be a citizen of that state. *See* 28 U.S.C. § 1332(c); *Hertz Corp. v. Friend*, 559 U.S. 77 (2010).) Moreover, the amount-in-controversy requirement for suits based solely on diversity is met only by a claim that exceeds $75,000, and Plaintiff's claim is for less than that amount. Therefore, the federal district court could not have exercised original subject-matter jurisdiction over Plaintiff's claim, making removal improper, and requiring that the court remand the case to state court.

Second, even if diversity jurisdiction *were* present, the federal removal statute ***bars a defendant who is a citizen of the state where the action is pending from removing if diversity is the sole basis for subject-matter jurisdiction***. (*See* 28 U.S.C. § 1441(b)(2).) Here, Defendant is a citizen of State A, the state in which the state-court action is pending, and so Defendant is automatically barred from removing the litigation to federal court.

Finally, does the analysis change if Defendant's counterclaim arises under federal law (i.e., would qualify for "federal question jurisdiction" if it were sued on alone)? The answer is ***"no."*** Federal-question jurisdiction over a claim is available only if (i) an issue of federal law appears on the face of the well-pleaded complaint, (ii) the federal issue is actually disputed and substantial, and (iii) that issue's resolution by the federal court would not disturb the allocation of judicial business as between the federal and state courts. *See Gunn v. Minton*, 133 S. Ct. 1059 (2013). So Defendant's counterclaim would indeed fall within the federal court's federal-question jurisdiction ***if it were brought as a separate federal action***. However, the fact that federal-question jurisdiction would exist over the *counterclaim* had it been filed in an independent lawsuit is irrelevant to the removal issue—the case is removable only if the ***plaintiff's complaint*** independently meets the requirements for removal. *See, e.g., Mortgage Electronic Registration Systems, Inc. v. Malugen*, 2012 WL 1382265, *8 (M.D. Fl. 2012) ("[t]he law is well settled that federal claims raised in a counterclaim may not serve as a basis for removal jurisdiction").

(A) is not the best response,

because it makes an incorrect assertion of law.

As explained with respect to Choice (C), removal jurisdiction exists only if the district court could have exercised subject-matter jurisdiction over the suit had it been filed as an original matter in the federal, rather than the state, court. (*See* 28 U.S.C. § 1441.) In determining whether subject-matter jurisdiction as an original matter exists, the district court is required to look ***solely at the complaint***, and not to the answer or the notice of removal. The Plaintiff's well-pleaded complaint did not raise any federal question. Furthermore, two factors prevent the requirements for diversity jurisdiction from being met (no diversity between Plaintiff and Defendant, and lack of amount-in-controversy). Thus, regardless of whether the district court could have exercised subject-matter jurisdiction over Defendant's federal-law counterclaim, jurisdiction would not exist over the suit as an original matter, and this fact means that the federal court must remand the case to the state court from which it was (improperly) removed.

(B) is not the best response,

because it misapplies the rules for diversity jurisdiction and for removal jurisdiction.

As is explained with respect to Choice (C), removability is judged by whether the main complaint (the Plaintiff's original claim) could have been brought originally in federal court. And the complaint here could not have been brought, because it is not supported by either complete diversity or federal-question jurisdiction. And even if the Plaintiff's claim could have been brought in federal court, a defendant who is a citizen of the state where the action is pending may not remove, according to 28 U.S.C. § 1441(b).

(D) is not the best response,

because it misapplies the rule governing removal of a non-removable state-law claim and a removable federal claim.

Under 28 U.S.C. §§ 1441(c)(1) and 1441(c)(2), if a civil action includes both a claim arising under federal law (a "removable federal claim") and "a claim not within the original or supplemental jurisdiction of the district court" (a "non-removable claim," usually one based on state law), then the entire matter may be removed to district court, but the district court shall ***sever*** the non-removable state law claims and remand them "to the State court from which the action was removed." *Id.* While this might appear to match the circumstances of the problem here, it doesn't. That's because Plaintiff's complaint did ***not*** include both a non-removable state-law claim and a removable federal claim, as required under 28 U.S.C. § 1441(c)(1)-(2). Rather, Plaintiff's complaint contained *only* a state-law claim that could not have qualified for diversity jurisdiction (because the citizenship and amount-in-controversy requirements were not met), and that was therefore not removable. (Defendant's assertion of a removable federal claim in the form of a counterclaim is irrelevant, because that claim was not part of the original civil action. As discussed at the start of this paragraph, even partial removal is allowed solely when there is at least one claim *by the plaintiff* as to which the federal courts would have had original jurisdiction.) As a result, the district court must remand the entire action.

Answer 65

(C) is the best response,

because a state may grant broader rights under its own constitution than are granted by the federal Constitution.

Thus, even though the secret recording of a conversation by a government informant does not violate the Fourth Amendment, the state may extend their rule beyond the federal guarantee. As the "clear" precedent here held "that the conduct of the police in making the recording violated the employee's rights under the state constitution, and that the exclusionary rule is the proper remedy for this violation," then the court should grant the employee's motion.

(A) is not the best response,

because, although the initial premise is correct (the employee's federal constitutional rights were not violated), the latter premise is not, as a state may grant broader rights under its own constitution than are granted by the federal Constitution.

Thus, even though the secret recording of a conversation by a government informant does not violate the Fourth Amendment, the state may extend their rule beyond the federal guarantee. As the "clear" precedent here held "that the conduct of the police in making the recording violated the employee's rights under the state constitution, and that the exclusionary rule is the proper remedy for this violation," then the court should grant the employee's motion.

(B) is not the best response,
because it is irrelevant.

Regardless of the belief of the police officers regarding the legality of their action under the federal Constitution, the precedent under the state constitution will control here. A state may grant broader rights under its own constitution than are granted by the federal Constitution. Thus, even though the secret recording of a conversation by a government informant does not violate the Fourth Amendment, the state may extend their rule beyond the federal guarantee. As the "clear" precedent here held "that the conduct of the police in making the recording violated the employee's rights under the state constitution, and that the exclusionary rule is the proper remedy for this violation," then the court should grant the employee's motion.

(D) is not the best answer,
because it is incorrect legally.

The secret recording of a conversation by a government informant does not violate the Fourth Amendment. Furthermore, the precedent under the state constitution will control here. A state may grant broader rights under its own constitution than are granted by the federal Constitution. As the "clear" precedent here held "that the conduct of the police in making the recording violated the employee's rights under the state constitution, and that the exclusionary rule is the proper remedy for this violation," then the court should grant the employee's motion.

Answer 66

(B) is the best response,
because, even though he possessed the wallet briefly, all the elements of larceny are met.

Larceny is (i) the trespassory (ii) taking and (iii) carrying away of (iv) personal property (v) of another with (vi) intent to steal. All the elements are satisfied here. The taking away element requires movement of only a slight distance, so it was satisfied even though the patron discarded the wallet shortly after taking it.

(A) is not the best response,
because the taking was not accomplished by using force or putting the owner in fear.

Robbery is defined as larceny committed with two additional elements: (i) the property is taken from the person or presence of the owner and (ii) the taking is accomplished by using force or putting the owner in fear. As the victim here was passed out, the taking was not accomplished by using force or putting the owner in fear. Thus, while all the elements of larceny are met, it is not a robbery.

(C) is not the best response,
because the patron could be convicted of the more serious crime of larceny.

Thus, even assuming the patron could be convicted of attempted robbery, this offense is not the most serious possible crime of conviction, so this response is incorrect.

(D) is not the best response,
because the patron could be convicted of the more serious crime of larceny.

Thus, even assuming the patron could be convicted of attempted larceny, this offense is not the most serious possible crime of conviction, so this response is incorrect.

Answer 67

(D) is the correct answer,
because the plaintiff was under an obligation to correct and supplement her disclosure, and the sanction for the failure to do so is exclusion of the evidence.

First, the treatment notes were documents that the pedestrian was required to provide at the beginning of the case, without a request for them, according to the automatic-disclosure provisions of Rule 26(a)(1)(A). That's because 26(a)(1)(A)(ii) requires a party to provide "a copy . . . of ***all documents*** . . . that the ***disclosing party has in its possession, custody, or control*** and ***may use to support its claims*** or defenses, unless the use would be solely for impeachment[.]" It's true that most if not all of these notes did not yet exist at the moment the pedestrian was required to make initial disclosures (since the 18-month treatment period probably continued past the time of this disclosure). However, Rule 26(e) says that a party who has made a Rule 26(a) automatic disclosure "***must supplement or correct its disclosure*** or response: (A) in a timely manner if the party learns that in some material respect the disclosure or response is incomplete or correct . . ." And the facts tell you that the pedestrian is now "using" these notes as evidence in support of her claim, making the notes fall within this duty-to-supplement-automatic-disclosure category. So the pedestrian was required to supplement her prior disclosure by furnishing the notes once they came into existence. (As is discussed more fully in Choice (C), it's very unlikely that the court will find that the pedestrian's ignorance of the notes was reasonable on these facts, and therefore unlikely that the court will conclude that her failure to supplement was excusable.)

Since the pedestrian and her lawyer were required to furnish the notes in a timely way, the only question is whether the remedy for the non-disclosure should include excluding the notes as evidence in support of the pedestrian's case. The issue is dealt with directly by Rule 37(c)(1): "If a party ***fails to provide information*** or identify a witness as required by Rule 26(a) or (e), the party is ***not allowed to use that information*** or witness to ***supply evidence*** on a motion, at a hearing, or ***at a trial***, unless the failure was ***substantially justified or is harmless***." Since what the pedestrian is trying to do is precisely what Rule 37(c)(1) is talking about—to use as evidence at a trial material that she was required to produce by the combination of Rule 26(a)'s automatic-disclosure requirements and Rule 26(e)'s requirement to supplement prior Rule 26(a) disclosures—the judge is not only permitted, but required, to exclude the evidence unless the judge makes an affirmative determination that the failure was "substantially justified or is harmless." As to the "harmless" possibility, Choice (D) already covers this possibility by adding the escape hatch that exclusion won't be required if the judge believes the failure to be harmless (which is an unlikely outcome, since the messenger's lawyer will be entitled to cross-examine the maker of the notes, and it's unlikely that, say, a brief continuance will be enough to undo that lawyer's inability to make up for the loss of an adequate time to study 70 pages of detailed notes). And although this choice does not refer to the possibility that the judge might conclude that the failure was "substantially justified," it's very unlikely that where a patient/litigant undergoes many treatment sessions for injuries that are the subject of the litigation, that patient and her lawyer are "substantially justified" in not bothering to inquire whether the treating physician has taken notes during the course of the treatments.

(A) is not correct,

because it inaccurately states the procedure for sanctioning a party who has failed to supplement prior disclosures. The federal discovery rules provide that a sanction is ***automatic*** if a party fails to provide information (or to identify a witness) as required by the combination of the Rule 26(a) initial duty to make disclosure and the Rule 26(e) duty to supplement such disclosures as time passes; the wronged party is not required to make a prior motion for sanctions in this situation. See the text of FRCP 37(c)(1), quoted in the final paragraph of the discussion of Choice (D) above, which sets exclusion as the sanction while making no reference to the need for a motion by the wronged party.

(B) is not correct,

because it incorrectly imposes a requirement that prejudice be shown.

FRCP 37(c)(1) says that a party who fails to correct or supplement its prior disclosures as required under Rule 26(e) may not use that evidence at trial "unless the failure was substantially justified or is harmless." This language does not require the wronged party to show that he or she would be prejudiced if the non-disclosed materials were permitted to be used as evidence. Courts have, rather, concluded that under Rule 37(c)(1) **the burden is on the party facing the sanction** "to demonstrate that the failure to comply ... is substantially justified or harmless." *Torres v. City of Los Angeles*, 548 F.3d 1197, 1213 (9th Cir. 2008).

(C) is not correct,

because the pedestrian's ignorance of the notes' existence would not "substantially justify" the lack of disclosure.

It's true that the automatic sanction imposed by Rule 37(c)(1) for non-disclosure—exclusion of the material from use as evidence by the wrongdoer—does not apply where the lack of disclosure "was substantially justified or is harmless." But here, the pedestrian's contention that she did not know about the notes of the treating physician will almost certainly be found not meet to this standard. Courts interpreting this 37(c)(1) language have concluded that a party who does not actually know of the existence of the material, but who *should* reasonably have been aware of it, is not "substantially justified" in failing to disclose it. *See, e.g., Arthur v. Atkinson Freight Lines, Corp.*, 164 F.R.D. 19, 20 (S.D.N.Y. 1995), a similar case in which plaintiff and her counsel claimed to have been unaware until the eve of trial of the existence of a medical report in plaintiff's doctor's possession: "[Rule 26(e)] place[s] a duty on a party to turn over not only proper materials of which he is aware, but also those of which he reasonably *ought* to have been aware."

Answer 68

(D) is the best response,

because it correctly identifies that the Commission lacks enforcement powers.

Under the Constitution, Congress has the power to legislate, and the President has the executive power, including the power to enforce laws. The problem under these facts is that the Commission has the power to prosecute, which is an enforcement power exclusively possessed by the President. As such, all members of the Commission would have to be appointed by the President and approved by the Senate, under Article II, § 2 of the Constitution. *Buckley v. Valeo* (1976). Since the Commission wouldn't have the power of enforcement, choice D represents the manufacturer's best argument, making D the best response.

(A) is not the best response,

because it overstates the actual standard, it probably misstates the facts, and it ignores the central issue here.

Congress may delegate its legislative power, as long as three requirements are met: (1) Congress must actually have the power it's ostensibly delegating; (2) the power must be of a kind capable of delegation; and (3) Congress must set adequate standards to govern the exercise of the power delegated.

Choice A addresses the third requirement—the adequacy of standards. In fact, this requirement is interpreted liberally by the courts. In one case, standards phrased in terms of "public interest, convenience or necessity" were upheld. Thus, the standards delineated in these facts—to investigate automobile safety, to make recommendations to Congress for new laws, to make further rules establishing safety and performance standards, and to prosecute violations of the Federal Automobile Safety Act—would more than suffice. Also, note that choice A suggests the standards must be clear; in fact, they need only be "adequate." As a result, this would not be a good argument for the manufacturer.

All of this ignores the central issue here, which is that the power involved in these facts was not Congress's to delegate. Congress has legislative power, which includes the power to investigate. However, the power enjoyed by the Automobile Commission is the power to *enforce,* which is an executive power enjoyed exclusively by the executive branch, not Congress. The first requirement of valid delegation of power by Congress is that Congress must hold the power delegated. Here, it doesn't. Since choice A ignores this, it's not the best response.

(B) is not the best response,

because it misstates the law, and ignores the central issue on these facts.

Congress has broad powers over interstate commerce under Article I, § 3, cl. 3 of the Constitution. In fact, under the "affectation doctrine," Congress can regulate any activity that has any appreciable direct or indirect effect on interstate commerce. Clearly automobiles would qualify, since they are capable of, and do, undertake interstate travel. Thus, Congress would have the power to regulate automobiles, and a claim by the manufacturer that Congress overstepped its commerce power would not be a good argument.

Instead, choice B ignores the fact that the power Congress delegated here was not its to delegate. Congress may delegate its legislative power, as long as three requirements are met: (1) Congress must actually have the power it's ostensibly delegating; (2) the power must be of a kind capable of delegation; and (3) Congress must set adequate standards to govern the exercise of the power delegated. Congress has legislative power, which includes the power to investigate. The power enjoyed by the Automobile Commission is the power to *enforce,* which is an executive power enjoyed exclusively by the executive branch, not Congress. Thus, Congress was incapable of delegating power to the Automobile Commission, making the Commission invalid. This is the manufacturer's best argument. Since choice B ignores this, it's not the best response.

(C) is not the best response,

because the Commission would not represent a denial of due process.

Due process is triggered by a governmental activity that amounts to a deprivation of a property interest or right. A property interest at the very least requires interests already acquired in specific benefits. Then, if that right or interest is "fundamental," the strict scrutiny test is used to determine the validity of the enactment. For economic issues, the "rational relation" test is used.

However, due process would not apply to the facts here, because due process doesn't require that a private individual or organization receive representation on a congressional, investigative agency (as long as the workings of the agency weren't conducted in a discriminatory fashion). If the Commission itself were able to enforce laws, and it prosecuted the manufacturer, *then* it would be entitled to due process. Under these facts, it's not. Since C doesn't recognize this, it's not the best response.

Answer 69

(C) is the best response,

because the doctrine of estoppels by deed protects her interest in the land.

The doctrine of estoppels by deed states that when a grantor delivers a warranty deed, describing property the grantor does not own, to a grantee and later acquires title to the property in question, as soon as the grantor acquires title, title immediately passes to the grantee. The grantor is estopped from defending himself on the basis of his non-ownership of the land at the time of the conveyance. In this problem, the nephew delivered a warranty deed to the woman. Therefore, once the nephew acquired title to the land, which he did upon probate of the uncle's will, title immediately passed to the woman.

(A) is not the best response,

because the doctrine of estoppels by deed protects the interest of the woman even though the nephew did not own the tract at the time of the conveyance.

The doctrine of estoppels by deed states that when a grantor delivers a warranty deed, describing property the grantor does not own, to a grantee and later acquires title to the property in question, as soon as the grantor acquires title, title immediately passes to the grantee. The grantor is estopped from defending himself on the basis of his non-ownership of the land at the time of the conveyance. In this problem, the nephew delivered a warranty deed to the woman. Therefore, once the nephew acquired title to the land, which he did upon probate of the uncle's will, title immediately passed to the woman.

(B) is not the best response,
because the notice provided by a title search would only be relevant to a dispute between the woman and the uncle.

Had the woman conducted a title search, she would have discovered that the uncle was the owner of the tract of land. However, this fact is irrelevant to a suit between the nephew and the woman. The doctrine of estoppels by deed states that when a grantor delivers a warranty deed, describing property the grantor does not own, to a grantee and later acquires title to the property in question, as soon as the grantor acquires title, title immediately passes to the grantee. The grantor is estopped from defending himself on the basis of his non-ownership of the land at the time of the conveyance. In this problem, the nephew delivered a warranty deed to the woman. Therefore, once the nephew acquired title to the land, which he did upon probate of the uncle's will, title immediately passed to the woman.

(D) is not the best response,
because the woman's recording of her deed is irrelevant to the issue of who holds title to the tract of land.

Recording serves to provide notice to future purchasers that the woman claimed an interest in the land. It does not have any effect on the validity of her claim to the tract in a dispute between her and her grantor (the nephew). However, the woman's interest in the tract of land is protected by the doctrine of estoppel by deed, which states that when a grantor delivers a warranty deed, describing property the grantor does not own, to a grantee and later acquires title to the property in question, as soon as the grantor acquires title, title immediately passes to the grantee.

Answer 70

(A) is the best response,
because the mother and son failed to mitigate damages.

When the tutor repudiated the contract, the mother and son were under a duty to take reasonable steps to minimize the amount of damage that the tutor's breach would cause. They could have satisfied this duty to mitigate damages by hiring a substitute tutor for $6,000. Had they done so, they would have been able to recover the $1,000 price difference in a suit against the tutor. Their failure to do so bars them from recovering consequential damages that arose from the tutor's breach, but not market price differential damages. As a result, the only damages available to them is the price differential between the $6,000 market price and the $5,000 contract price. Note that they are able to recover this damage whether or not they actually hired the substitute tutor.

(B) is not the best response,
because the consequential damages were avoidable.

When the tutor repudiated the contract, the mother and son were under a duty to take reasonable steps to minimize the amount of damage that the tutor's breach would cause. They could have satisfied this duty to mitigate damages by hiring a substitute tutor for $6,000. Had they done so, they would have been able to recover the $1,000 price difference in a suit against the tutor. Their failure to do so bars them from recovering consequential damages that arose from the tutor's breach, but not market price differential damages. Although this choice correctly states that the son's lost salary was a consequence foreseeable by the parties at the time the contract was made, it is incorrect to categorize this harm is a consequential damage, because the lost opportunity was not caused by the tutor's breach, but rather by the failure of the plaintiffs to hire a substitute teacher.

(C) is not the best response,
because the son was an intended beneficiary of the mother-tutor contract.

When the parties to a contract intend, at the time of the contract's formation, that a third party receive benefits from the contract's performance, that third party is an intended third-party beneficiary of the contract. Intended third-party beneficiaries are entitled to sue in the event that the contract is breached. Here the mother-tutor contract was made in contemplation of benefiting the son, who would be receiving the tutoring. As a result, he was an intended beneficiary of the contract, and may sue the tutor for damages.

(D) is not the best response,
because they can still recover the market price differential.

When the tutor repudiated the contract, the mother and son were under a duty to take reasonable steps to minimize the amount of damage that the tutor's breach would cause. They could have satisfied this duty to mitigate damages by hiring a substitute tutor for $6,000. Had they done so, they would have been able to recover the $1,000 price difference in a suit against the tutor. Their failure to do so bars them from recovering consequential damages that arose from the tutor's breach, but not market price differential damages. As a result, the only damages available to them is the price differential between the $6,000 market price and the $5,000 contract price. Note that they are able to recover this damage whether or not they actually hired the substitute tutor.

Answer 71

You have an advantage with a problem like this one, because it's fully integrated—everything you need to solve it is given to you. Thus, with this type of problem, it's particularly important to *read each statute carefully*.

(A) is the best response,

because it addresses both types of murder under the statute, and correctly applies them to the facts.

The murder statute here provides two possibilities: either premeditated and intentional murder, OR felony murder. The intoxication statute exonerates the defendant only if his drunkenness negates an element of the crime. Choice A correctly identifies that the defendant cannot be guilty of felony murder *if* he was unable to form an intent to commit a felony; it further correctly states that he could only be guilty of the first type of murder in the statute if he intentionally and with premeditation killed the watchman. Since A addresses both parts of the murder statutes and analyzes them correctly, it's the best response.

(B) is not the best response,

because voluntary intoxication is *potentially* a good defense to the crime of murder, since it could negate an element of the offense—namely, intent.

There are two possibilities for murder in the statute given in these facts—either premeditated and intentional killing, or killing in the commission of the named crimes, the relevant one here being burglary. However, burglary requires intent as well—the intent to commit a crime in the building broken into. Either way, if the jury found that the voluntary intoxication negated the defendant's ability to form an intent, he would be acquitted. Since choice B does not comport with the statutes stated in the facts, it's not the best response.

(C) is not the best response,

because it incorrectly eliminates a possibility for the defendant being found guilty.

The murder statute in the question offers *two* possible bases on which the defendant could be found guilty: either premeditated and intentional killing, OR a "felony murder"-type provision—a killing in the commission of the named crimes. Thus, the defendant could be found guilty of murder if he's found to have committed a killing in the commission of a burglary. Note that choice C *limits* the defendant's being found guilty to the *first* type of murder in the statute by stating that the defendant can be found guilty "only if" he premeditated and intended the killing. Here, it's possible that the court could find the defendant guilty of a killing in the commission of a burglary, without finding him guilty of premeditated, intentional killing. (Note that the defendant's intoxication couldn't exonerate him from the second type of murder without exonerating him from the first type. If the defendant was drunk enough not to form an intent, it would exonerate him from both types of murder.) Since C incorrectly limits the potential for the defendant's guilt, it's not the best response.

(D) is not the best response,

because it misapplies the intoxication defense.

The statute here clearly states that intoxication is only a defense if it negates an element of the offense. Thus, the "but for" reasoning in choice D is incorrect, because it's not a question of whether the defendant *wouldn't* have killed the watchman if he was sober, but rather whether his intoxication negated an element of the offense. It's possible for the defendant to have been intoxicated *without* having his intoxication negate an element of the offense. Thus, choice D applies the intoxication defense too broadly, making it not the best response.

Answer 72

(A) is the best response,

because he did not intend to use deadly force.

The defendant may utilize the defense of self-defense when he (i) is resisting unlawful force, (ii) does not use excessive force, (iii) does not use deadly force unless the danger being resisted was also deadly force, (iv) is not the aggressor (unless he was a non-deadly aggressor confronted with the unexpected use of deadly force), and (v) must not have been in a position from which he could retreat with complete safety (unless the attack takes place in the defendant's dwelling or the defendant uses only non-deadly force). Here, all the elements are met. The husband, through both his physical and verbal action, threatened unlawful force. The defendant did use excessive force or deadly force and was not the aggressor. Furthermore, because the defendant did not intend to use deadly force (i.e., pepper spray), he was not under the obligation to retreat.

(B) is not the best response,

because it misstates the retreat rule.

The defendant may utilize the defense of self-defense when he (i) is resisting unlawful force, (ii) does not use excessive force, (iii) does not use deadly force unless the danger being resisted was also deadly force, (iv) is not the aggressor (unless he was a non-deadly aggressor confronted with the unexpected use of deadly force), and (v) must not have been in a position from which he could retreat with complete safety (unless the attack takes place in the defendant's dwelling or the defendant uses only non-deadly force). Here, the defendant was not in his dwelling, and stating that an exception exists for all "occupied structures" is too broad. Instead, the reason that the defendant did not have to retreat is that the defendant did not intend to use deadly force (i.e., pepper spray).

(C) is not the best response,

because it misstates the retreat rule.

The defendant may utilize the defense of self-defense when he (i) is resisting unlawful force, (ii) does not use excessive force, (iii) does not use deadly force unless the danger being resisted was also deadly force, (iv) is not the aggressor (unless he was a non-deadly aggressor confronted with the unexpected use of deadly force), and (v) must not have been in a position from which he could retreat with complete safety (unless the attack takes place in the defendant's dwelling or the defendant uses only non-deadly force). Here, the answer choice is too broad: a person utilizing self-defense does not have to retreat whenever an opportunity is available if he is using non-deadly force. Thus, the reason that the defendant did not have to retreat is that the defendant did not intend to use deadly force (i.e., pepper spray).

(D) is not the best response,

because a response of non-deadly force is justified where the defender reasonably believes the other is about to inflict unlawful bodily harm, which need not be deadly harm.

The defendant may utilize the defense of self-defense when he (i) is resisting unlawful force, (ii) does not use excessive force, (iii) does not use deadly force unless the danger being resisted was also deadly force, (iv) is not the aggressor (unless he was a non-deadly aggressor confronted with the unexpected use of deadly force), and (v) must not have been in a position from which he could retreat with complete safety (unless the attack takes place in the defendant's dwelling or the defendant uses only non-deadly force). Here, the husband threatened unlawful force, so the defendant was entitled to defend himself using reasonable force. The defendant responded to the threat of a punch with non-deadly force (i.e., pepper spray), so his use of force was justified. As this answer choice implies either that self-defense may only be used in response to deadly force or that this defendant used deadly force, it is wrong.

Answer 73

(D) is the best answer,

because it fits all the elements of an excited utterance.

FRE 803(2), entitled "Excited Utterance," gives a hearsay exception for "A statement relating to a startling event or condition, made while the declarant was under the stress of excitement that it caused." So the utterance must relate to a startling event and must be uttered while still under the influence of the startling event. Here, an assault qualifies as a startling event, and the victim "screamed" (indicating her excited state) a statement immediately after the beating stopped.

(A) is not the best answer,

because the statement fits all the elements of an excited utterance.

An excited utterance must relate to a startling event and must be uttered while still under the influence of the startling event. Here, an assault qualifies as a startling event, and the victim "screamed" (indicating her excited state) a statement immediately after the beating stopped.

(B) is not the best answer,

because it states an unnecessary requirement.

This statement is an excited utterance, and, under FRE 803, the statement is admissible even if the witness is unavailable. So there is no requirement that the declarant (if available) be "asked about the statement."

(C) is not the best answer,

because this statement does not satisfy the dying declaration exception (FRE 804(b)(2)).

Under the dying declaration exception, an *unavailable* declarant's statement, while believing that his or her death is imminent, concerning the cause or circumstances of his or her impending death, is admissible in either a civil case or a homicide prosecution concerning that death. So, while it is true that the victim does not need to die, this exception is not met here for two reasons. First, the declarant is not unavailable, as she testified earlier in the trial. Second, this is a criminal case for aggravated assault, not a civil case or a homicide prosecution.

Answer 74

(C) is the best response,

because it correctly identifies the strongest basis on which a judgment for the buyer could be based—the Parol Evidence Rule.

There are two key facts here: first, that the prior oral agreement contradicts the writing, thus invoking the Parol Evidence Rule; and second, that recording transactions is for the benefit of subsequent bona fide purchasers, not one of the parties to the transaction.

In order to prevail based on his requirement that the buyer only fill in Lots 40 or 41, the developer would have to rely on his prior, oral understanding with the buyer. Under the Parol Evidence Rule, a writing that is "completely integrated" cannot be contradicted or supplemented with prior written or oral agreements, or contemporaneous oral agreements. A "completely integrated" agreement is one that the parties intended to be a final and complete statement of their agreement. The deed here would likely qualify, so that oral restrictions on the lot number to be included would contradict the document itself, and would not be provable.

Of course, the Parol Evidence Rule does not bar evidence of defects in contract formation, like lack of consideration, fraud, and duress, but there are no such facts evident here. For instance, there is no evidence that the buyer *fraudulently* put in the number of a more expensive lot; the facts merely indicate that he changed his mind, apparently ignorant of the difference in cost, so the Parol Evidence Rule could not be avoided on grounds of fraud.

In fact, a more appropriate remedy would be *reformation,* where the court rewords the contract to reflect the parties' true intent. However, under these facts, the developer is attempting to say that a contract never existed, because the buyer was in breach of the "Lot 40 or Lot 41" agreement. As such, the developer is seeking a rescission, and, due to operation of the Parol Evidence Rule, he's unlikely to succeed. Since C recognizes this as the most likely basis for the buyer's prevailing, it's the best response.

(A) is not the best response,

because it does not form as strong a basis for the judgment as does choice C.

An estoppel occurs, in facts like these, when one has done or omitted to do something and is, as a result, forbidden from pleading or proving an otherwise important fact. Here, the developer's carelessness in allowing the buyer to fill in the deed would lead to his being bound by the resultant deed—he'd be "estopped" from denying its validity.

However, what choice A fails to take into account is the existence of the deed, which would constitute a written contract between the buyer and the developer, embodying their agreement. The buyer's most likely means of prevailing is enforcing the written agreement, without resorting to estoppel. He can do so if his argument focuses on the Parol Evidence Rule. Under the Parol Evidence Rule, a writing that is "completely integrated" cannot be contradicted or supplemented with prior written or oral agreements, or contemporaneous oral agreements. A "completely integrated" agreement is one that the parties intended to be a final and complete statement of their agreement. The deed here would likely qualify, so that oral restrictions on the lot number to be included would contradict the document itself, and would not be provable.

While there are exceptions to the Parol Evidence Rule, these facts do not neatly fit into any of them. Thus, a choice focusing on the Parol Evidence Rule, choice C, provides a stronger basis for a judgment in the buyer's favor than the estoppel argument in A, making A not the best response.

(B) is not the best response,

because although it states a correct rule, it would not apply to these facts.

Choice B suggests that the fact that the land title records show the buyer owning Lot 25 means that the buyer should prevail. In fact, recording conveyances is required for the benefit of subsequent, bona fide purchasers, *not* parties to transactions themselves, so the buyer could not prevail on this basis. Instead, the buyer's prevailing depends on the oral agreement, restricting the purchase to Lots 40 or 41, being *inadmissible*. Since the land title records will not be a basis on which the buyer could prevail, B is not the best response.

(D) is not the best response,

because, although it states a correct rule, the developer—as a party to the transaction—cannot rely on it.

Recording conveyances is required for the benefit of subsequent, bona fide purchasers, *not* parties to transactions themselves. Thus, had the action been between the developer and a subsequent purchaser, choice D could form the basis of a judgment in the purchaser's favor—even if the deed were, in fact, void! Here, since the dispute is between the parties to the transaction, the recording of the deed is irrelevant. Instead, the buyer's prevailing depends on the oral agreement, restricting the purchase to Lots 40 or 41, being *inadmissible*. Since D doesn't recognize this, it's not the best response.

Answer 75

(C) is the best response,

because the clerk's rights vested when he purchased the retirement home.

When two parties enter into a contract that benefits someone else, that person is considered a third-party beneficiary of the contract. If the contracting parties intended to create the benefit, then the individual is an intended third-party beneficiary. An intended beneficiary has the right to sue on the contract in the event of breach even though he is not a party to the contract. More important to this situation is that when a third-party beneficiary's rights "vest," the contracting parties can no longer modify their agreement to the detriment of the beneficiary. The third-party rights vest in several circumstances, the most common being when the beneficiary acts in detrimental reliance on the promise. That is precisely what has happened here. The contract was intended to create an annuity for the clerk so that he could be secure in his retirement. The clerk knew of the agreement and its amount, and made the decision to purchase a retirement home in reliance on the agreement being performed. This caused his rights to vest. When the bookkeeper subsequently attempted to change the agreement by reducing the amount he would contribute, he was attempting to modify the contract in a manner that adversely affected the vested rights of the clerk. The bookkeeper could therefore not change his obligation without the clerk's permission. As a result, the bookkeeper is liable to the clerk for the unpaid $50,000.

(A) is not the best response,

because the accountant and bookkeeper could not modify their agreement without the clerk's permission.

When two parties enter into a contract that benefits someone else, that person is considered a third-party beneficiary of the contract. If the contracting parties intended to create the benefit, then the individual is an intended third-party beneficiary. An intended beneficiary has the right to sue on the contract in the event of breach even though he is not a party to the contract. More important to this situation is that when a third-party beneficiary's rights "vest," the contracting parties can no longer modify their agreement to the detriment of the beneficiary. The third-party rights vest in several circumstances, the most common being when the beneficiary acts in detrimental reliance on the promise. That is precisely what has happened here. The contract was intended to create an annuity for the clerk so that he could be secure in his retirement. The clerk knew of the agreement and its amount, and made the decision to purchase a retirement home in reliance on the agreement being performed. This caused his rights to vest. When the bookkeeper subsequently attempted to change the agreement by reducing the amount he would contribute, he was attempting to modify the contract in a manner that adversely affected the vested rights of the clerk. The bookkeeper could therefore not change his obligation without the clerk's permission. As a result, the bookkeeper is liable to the clerk for the unpaid $50,000.

(B) is not the best response,

because the clerk's rights had vested.

When two parties enter into a contract that benefits someone else, that person is considered a third-party beneficiary of the contract. If the contracting parties intended to create the benefit, then the individual is an intended third-party beneficiary. Whether the intent was to satisfy a debt to the third party or merely to make a gift is immaterial. An intended beneficiary has the right to sue on the contract in the event of breach even though he is not a party to the contract. More important to this situation is that when a third-party beneficiary's rights "vest," the contracting parties can no longer modify their agreement to the detriment of the beneficiary. The third-party rights vest in several circumstances, the most common being when the beneficiary acts in detrimental reliance on the promise. That is precisely what has happened here. The contract was intended to create an annuity for the clerk so that he could be secure in his retirement. The clerk knew of the agreement and its amount, and made the decision to purchase a retirement home in reliance on the agreement being performed. This caused his rights to vest. When the bookkeeper subsequently attempted to change the agreement by reducing the amount he would contribute, he was attempting to modify the contract in a manner that adversely affected the vested rights of the clerk. The bookkeeper could therefore not change his obligation without the clerk's permission. As a result, the bookkeeper is liable to the clerk for the unpaid $50,000. If you chose this response, you were probably thinking of the distinction between a "creditor" beneficiary and a "donee" beneficiary. However, under the modern view, that distinction is not the relevant inquiry. Rather, a court will assess whether the third party was an "intended" beneficiary, or merely an "incidental" beneficiary, with only the former having enforceable rights under the contract.

(D) is not the best response,

because past consideration is not consideration.

In order to be enforceable, a contract must be supported by consideration. Choice D indicates that the clerk's prior employment would satisfy this requirement. However, under the bargained-for-exchange test for consideration, this is not the case. The relevant question is whether, when the clerk agreed to do his work, he did so with the expectation that the annuity would be set up for him upon the firm's dissolution. Since the answer to that question is clearly no (the accountant and bookkeeper only came up with the idea recently), the clerk's prior work is insufficient on its own to be consideration for the accountant and bookkeeper's promise.

Answer 76

(A) is the best response,

because the statute singled out the three park rangers.

A bill of attainder, which is explicitly prohibited by the Constitution, is a law that identifies particular individuals for punishment. The Supreme Court has held that punishment includes not only imprisonment, but an array of other conditions, including the prohibition of government employment. Since the law in this problem both named the specific individuals who were to be targeted and punished them by prohibiting them from obtaining government employment, it is an unconstitutional bill of attainder.

(B) is not the best response,

because the Due Process Clause does not apply to laws passed by the legislature.

The Due Process Clause requires that an individual who is to be deprived of a property or liberty interest be given a hearing before the deprivation takes place. So, for example, if the park rangers were each fined under a different, valid, federal statute for their actions, they would have the right to a hearing before their property was taken. The Due Process Clause operates in situations where an individual determination must be made, and is therefore inapplicable to valid statutes enacted by Congress.

(C) is not the best response,

because the park rangers were not charged with a crime under the statute.

The Ex Post Facto Clause prohibits punishing individuals for past conduct by applying laws that were enacted after the conduct took place. If, for example, after the park rangers had ceased their activities in support of terrorism, Congress passed a law criminalizing such acts, the rangers could not be convicted under the statute, since their acts were not prohibited at the time they were done. However, the Ex Post Facto Clause only applies to criminal punishment. It is inapplicable to situations that only involve civil punishment, such as the prohibition of federal employment at issue in this problem.

(D) is not the best response,

because no property has been taken from the park rangers.

The Takings Clause prohibits the government from taking an individual's property without paying just compensation. The park rangers were punished by prohibiting them from obtaining government employment, not by taking their property. The Takings Clause is only applicable to governmental appropriation of property, and is therefore not at issue here.

Answer 77

(C) is the best response,

because the trier of fact has found no evidence of negligence on the part of the defendant.

More specifically, the nuclear power plant did not breach any duty owed to the plaintiff as the plant had a sound design, had chosen a quality manufacturer for the component part, and had "no way" of anticipating or preventing the emission of the radioactive matter. The plaintiff is limited to a negligence cause of action under the Federal Torts Claim Act, so his claim will fail for lack of proof of a breach of duty.

(A) is not the best response,

because the doctrine of *res ipsa loquitur* cannot be established here.

Res ipsa loquitur is established when (i) there is no direct evidence of defendant's conduct; (ii) the event ordinarily does not occur except through the negligence of someone; (iii) the instrument that caused the injury was, at the relevant time, in the exclusive control of the defendant; and (iv) the injury was not due to plaintiff's own action. Here, the trier of fact could not find that the event ordinarily does not occur except through the negligence of someone, as we are dealing with complex machinery in the context of nuclear engineering. Furthermore, another potential defendant is involved, and the findings of the jury are inconsistent with a conclusion that this is the sort of accident that would not ordinarily occur in the absence of the government's negligence.

(B) is not the best response,

because, pursuant to the Federal Tort Claims Act, the plaintiff may not rely on a strict liability theory.

This answer choice articulates the reasoning of *Rylands v. Fletcher* (1868), a case based on a strict liability theory. As the plaintiff is limited to a cause of action in negligence, this strict liability theory will not allow the plaintiff to be successful in his suit.

(D) is not the best response,

because, while proximate cause is necessary to establish liability in negligence, it is not sufficient.

This answer choice understates the reason that the defendant will win, as it does not focus on all the elements of a negligence claim. As answer choice C encompasses a broader answer, incorporating the precise reason the plaintiff will lose (i.e., the defendant did not breach a duty owed to the plaintiff), it is the superior answer.

Answer 78

(C) is the best response,

because it correctly states that the defendant will not be liable for robbery, and states the correct reason why.

Robbery is a larceny either from a person or a person's presence, by either force or fear. A dead person is incapable of being put in fear, or being subject to force. As a result, robbery from a dead person is impossible. Since C correctly identifies this, it's the best response.

(A) is not the best response,

because it does not state a reason that would exonerate the defendant from liability for larceny.

Common-law larceny requires only a trespassory taking and carrying away of another's personal property, with intent to steal it. Choice A misstates the facts because the defendant satisfies the elements of larceny—preventing identification *is* the defendant's "own use," and would not provide a valid defense to larceny. Since A states a defense that would not exonerate the defendant, it's not the best response.

(B) is not the best response,

because it states an element that is not, in fact, a requirement of larceny.

Common-law larceny requires only a trespassory taking and carrying away of another's personal property, with intent to steal it. It does not require a living victim.

If you chose this response, you may have been thinking of *robbery,* which requires a living victim since it's larceny from a person with the use of force or fear, and only a living person is susceptible to force or fear. Since B adds an element that is not a requirement of larceny, it's not the best response.

(D) is not the best response,

because although it arrives at the correct conclusion—that the defendant is not guilty of robbery—it does not offer the correct reasoning.

Choice D states an element that is not, in fact, a requirement of robbery. Robbery is a larceny either from a person or a person's presence, by either force or fear. The larceny element only requires that one take another's personal property—it does not require that the personal property have monetary value. While it's true that the defendant is not guilty of robbery, it's not because he took something lacking monetary value, but rather because the victim was dead, thus preventing the use of force or fear. Since D offers incorrect reasoning, it's not the best response.

Answer 79

(A) is the best answer,

because the prior bad acts have no bearing on truthfulness and do not contradict his earlier testimony.

Under FRE 608(b), a prior bad act must bear on the witness's truthfulness, and driving carelessly does not qualify under that standard. Additionally, a prior bad act may be admissible if it contradicts a witness's testimony on an issue in dispute, but this evidence does not contradict the witness. The witness testified that he "was exercising due care **at the time** [of the accident.]" Introducing a prior instance when he did not exercise due care has no bearing on whether he was exercising due care **at the time** of the accident. As such, it does not contradict his earlier testimony and is inadmissible.

(B) is not the best answer,

because it confuses the requirements of FRE 609 and FRE 608.

FRE 608 does not require a conviction. Rather, under FRE 608(b), a prior bad act must bear on the witness's truthfulness, and driving carelessly does not qualify under that standard. Additionally, a prior bad act may be admissible if it contradicts a witness's testimony on an issue in dispute, but this evidence does not contradict the witness. The witness testified that he "was exercising due care **at the time** [of the accident.]" Introducing a prior instance when he did not exercise due care has no bearing on whether he was exercising due care **at the time** of the accident. As such, it does not contradict his earlier testimony and is inadmissible.

(C) is not the best answer,

because "improperly failing to stop on the recent occasions" does **not** bear on plaintiff's credibility in this case.

In this case, the plaintiff specifically testified that he "was exercising due care **at the time** [of the accident.]" Introducing a prior instance when he did not exercise due care has no bearing on whether he was exercising due care **at the time** of the accident. As such, it does not affect the credibility of his earlier testimony and is inadmissible under FRE 608(b).

(D) is not the best answer,

because "improperly failing to stop on the recent occasions" does **not** contradict plaintiff's claim in this case.

In this case, plaintiff specifically testified that he "was exercising due care **at the time** [of the accident.]" Introducing a prior instance when he did not exercise due care has no bearing on whether he was exercising due care **at the time** of the accident. As such, it does not contradict his earlier testimony and is inadmissible under FRE 608(b).

Answer 80

(A) is the best response,

because it correctly identifies that the buyer does not have an easement by implication, and thus his rights should wait until the border road opens as a public street.

While the border road is still private, the buyer's right to use it depends on whether he has an interest in the border road that would allow him use of it. The developer, as owner of the border road, didn't expressly grant the buyer the right to use it, so, if the buyer has any easement at all, it's implied. The two most likely easements, an implied easement and an easement by necessity, both have the same stumbling block for the buyer: They each require that the two parcels of land have been under common ownership in the past. The facts here do not indicate that the widower's plot and the developer's tract were ever under common ownership, so there can be no implied easement or easement by necessity. Since A correctly identifies that there is no private easement by implication, and suggests a plausible alternative, it's the best response.

(B) is not the best response,

because the Statute of Frauds would not bar evidence proving an implied easement.

This is so because implied easements are created by operation of law, *not* expression of the parties, so they *cannot* be in writing! An implied easement arises when a tract of land under one owner is divided, and one part of the land had been used for the benefit of the other part. A related easement, an "easement by necessity," arises where enjoyment of one parcel of land strictly requires use of another. These are the two most likely easements here, and, since neither one of them requires a writing, the Statute of Frauds would not apply to them. As a result, B cannot be the best response.

(C) is not the best response,

because although it is internally consistent (in that the facts preclude the success of a claim based on a way of necessity), this is *not* the only claim that the buyer could make.

It's likely that the buyer would claim a way by necessity because the facts here make such a claim attractive, in every way but one: there is no indication here that the two parcels of land involved were *ever* under common ownership, and this is a requirement of a way by necessity. However, it's likely that the buyer would also claim that there is an implied easement, which is an easement created by operation of law. An implied easement arises when a tract of land under one owner is divided, and one part of the land had been used for the benefit of the other part. Thus, the stumbling block with the buyer's proving an implied easement is the same as for an easement by necessity: there never was common ownership of the two parcels, under these facts. Nonetheless, it's as likely that the buyer would claim an implied easement as it is that he would claim an easement by necessity, and so his *assertion* would not be limited to a way by necessity, as C claims. Thus, C is not the best response.

(D) is not the best response,

because unjust enrichment need not be addressed in order to deny the buyer the right of way.

Under the doctrine of unjust enrichment, one has received and retained property, money, or benefits that justifiably and equitably belong to another. While the buyer's use of the border road *could* constitute unjust enrichment, it is not necessary to go as far as proving unjust enrichment, since, if the developer can prove that the buyer wouldn't be within his legal rights to use the border road, he needn't prove any more. In other words, in order to recover for unjust enrichment, the developer would be implying that the buyer was within his legal rights to use the border road, but it would be inequitable for him to do so. Here, there is no indication that the buyer is within his legal rights to use the border road at all, and since choice A recognizes this, D is not the best response.

Answer 81

(D) is the best response,

because the contract is divisible.

A divisible contracts is one in which the performance is divided into discrete units. The construction contract in this problem is divisible because it called for three distinct buildings to be constructed, and called for a separate price for each building. A divisible contract is, for all practical purposes, treated as a series of separate contracts. As a result, the builder will be able to recover from the landowner the contract price for the structure that he had completed.

(A) is not the best response,

because the builder completed the first structure.

The substantial performance doctrine is applicable here because the contract was divisible. The substantial performance doctrine generally states that as a constructive condition of one party's duty of performance, the other party substantially perform his duties under the contract. If this contract were not divisible, the landowner would argue that completion of only one of three buildings was not substantial performance of a contract that called for the construction of three. As a result of the divisibility of this contract, a court would treat the landowner-builder contract as if it were three separate contracts. Since the builder has completed the first of these "contracts," he may recover the contract price on the structure that he has completed. The landowner will have a claim against the builder for his failure to complete the other two structures.

(B) is not the best response,

because the builder completed the first structure.

Although the builder's voluntary cessation of work before completing the second and third structures was a breach of the contract, it will not prevent him from recovering against the landowner for the contract price of the first structure. Since this contract called for three separate buildings to be constructed at three separate prices, it is divisible, and the court will treat it as if it were a series of three separate contracts. Because the builder has already completed the first structure, he will only be found to have breached the contract for the construction of the second and third structures. The builder will still be able to recover the contract price on the structure he has completed.

(C) is not the best response,

because the landowner will be able to bring his claim for breach in the builder's action.

The first half of choice C is correct: this contract is divisible, and the builder will be able to recover the contract price for the first structure, which he has completed. (See the explanation of choice D above.) However, the second half of this choice is incorrect: There is no requirement that the landowner bring his claims against the builder in a separate action, since they arise from the same contract that the builder is suing under. In fact, it would further the goal of judicial economy for the landowner to bring his claims in the same suit, since this would allow a single action to dispose of these closely related claims.

Answer 82

(C) is the best response,

because the city buses are a designated public forum.

Because the city sells space on the side of its buses for the placement of placards, that space is considered a public forum. For a designated public forum, the city cannot prevent a group from using the forum in a manner consistent with the city's rules for its use unless the reason for denying access passes strict scrutiny. A governmental regulation or decision that discriminates based on the content of speech will only survive First Amendment scrutiny if it is necessary to serve a compelling governmental interest (i.e., pass the "strict scrutiny" test). Here, the administrator's reason for not allowing the anti-animal-cruelty ads on the buses was that the city did not wish to offend the circus, which was another advertiser on the buses. Although this may be a valid concern for the city, since the circus may decide to pull its advertisements, it does not rise to the level of a "compelling" governmental interest.

(A) is not the best response,

because it applies the incorrect level of scrutiny.

Content-based restrictions on speech are analyzed under strict scrutiny, which requires that the restriction be necessary to achieve a compelling governmental interest. Here, the rationale for the administrator's decision to exclude the anti-animal-cruelty group's advertisements was based entirely on the content of the group's message. Accordingly, it was a content-based restriction, rather than a time, place, or manner restriction. The administrator's decision will not pass strict scrutiny because avoiding offending the circus is not a compelling governmental need.

(B) is not the best response,

because it raises irrelevant considerations.

The truth or falsity of a statement is only relevant to the speaker's access to a public forum if the statement is either defamation or commercial speech. The anti-animal-cruelty group's message is neither, even if some people viewing their ad would mistakenly believe that the circus in town also treated its animals in a cruel fashion. Since the decision not to allow the group's ad to be placed on the buses, which were a public forum, was based entirely on the content of the ads, the administrator's decision will be subject to strict scrutiny, which requires that the decision be necessary to achieve a compelling governmental interest. The administrator's decision will not pass strict scrutiny because avoiding offending the circus is not a compelling governmental need.

(D) is not the best response,

because it is too broad.

While the First Amendment does provide broad protections for individuals and groups seeking to avail themselves of public forums, choice D goes too far in two respects. First, it attempts to provide public-forum-level protection to all public facilities, rather than only to public forums. While in this case, the sides of the city buses are a designated public forum, it is not the case that all public facilities are so categorized. Second, choice D implies that a public official may never refuse to allow a message discussing a matter of public concern to be distributed in a public forum. This is not true even if the decision is based entirely on the content of the speech (which is not required by choice D). Although such content-based restrictions trigger strict scrutiny analysis, they do not always fail, as it is possible, although not the case here, that a content-based restriction is in fact necessary to achieve a compelling governmental interest.

Answer 83

(B) is the best response,

because it removes the situation from coverage by the statute mentioned in the facts.

Getting this problem correct requires a careful analysis of the facts, not merely a mechanical application of a rule of law. The key fact here is the statute, requiring 30 days' notice for eviction. What this should tell you is that the purchaser's best legal argument will involve *characterizing the homeowner as something other than a tenant!*

Under the facts, if the homeowner is characterized as a tenant, it's at least possible that he would be protected by the 30 days' notice provision. Thus, the purchaser's best argument would be to characterize the homeowner as something *other than* a tenant, if such an argument is possible on these facts. Such an argument is possible here, since the homeowner could be characterized as a licensee. A licensee is one with a personal privilege to enter upon the licensor's land. A license is not considered an interest in land, and it is, with exceptions that don't apply here, revocable. Here, the homeowner's right, created under the contract, could be construed as a license, because it could be said that the contract creates in the homeowner a personal privilege to enter the purchaser's land. Since the homeowner's possession could be characterized as a license, and doing so removes the *single greatest obstacle to the purchaser's winning the case*—the statutory 30 days' notice provision—B is the best response.

(A) is not the best response,

because it does not correctly characterize the facts.

A trespasser *ab initio* is a trespasser "from the beginning." Here, the homeowner initially validly possessed the home under a provision in the contract between him and the purchaser. While his residence after the 30-day period ended might be characterized as a trespass, certainly the period *before* that could not be considered a trespass. Thus, the homeowner was not a trespasser "from the beginning," making A not the best response.

(C) is not the best response,

because it does not avoid the statutory 30 days' notice provision for tenants.

Otherwise, C would be an attractive response, because a tenancy at sufferance is created when a tenant wrongfully maintains possession of the premises ("holds over") after the expiration of the lease. Doing so makes him liable as a trespasser, unless the lessor holds the tenant to a new tenancy (e.g., by accepting rent). However, C does not take into account the operation of the statute here, and if you chose this response, you probably overlooked the statute, too. Since characterizing the homeowner as a tenant would likely invoke the 30 days' notice provision, which is *unfavorable* to the purchaser, C is not the best response.

(D) is not the best response,

because it does not avoid the statutory 30 days' notice provision for tenants. Furthermore, D misstates the facts, since, regardless of the statute, the homeowner could not be characterized as a tenant from month to month.

When a tenant wrongfully maintains possession of the premises ("holds over") after the expiration of the lease, he is liable as a trespasser, unless the lessor holds the tenant to a new tenancy (e.g., by accepting rent). If the lessor does allow a new tenancy, the resulting tenancy is a tenancy from period-to-period (a/k/a "month to month"). However, the facts here indicate that the purchaser *did not* accept the rent, and instead sued immediately to gain immediate possession of the home. Thus, the homeowner could not be considered a tenant from month to month. Furthermore, D does not take into account the operation of the statute. The purchaser's best legal argument would involve avoiding invocation of the 30 days' notice statute for tenants. Characterizing the homeowner as a tenant would *invite* invocation of the statute, not *avoid* it. Since D does not recognize this, it's not the best response.

Answer 84

(D) is the best response,

because it represents an argument on which the actress can prevail.

First, you have to classify the actress's duty to perform in the play. It's a constructive condition precedent to the producer's duty to pay. As a constructive condition, the actress need only substantially perform her duties (unlike express conditions, which require strict performance). Thus, if the actress's illness is considered a minor breach, she's substantially performed, and so the producer's duties under the contract were not relieved, and he couldn't cancel the contract (although he could recover any damages due to the breach). If, on the other hand, the actress's absence was a *major* breach (due to a *lack* of substantial performance), then the producer *would* be able to terminate the contract. Under these facts, it's certainly arguable that the actress's one week absence, in light of a six month contract, would not be major. If this is true, the producer's cancellation of the contract would be a major breach of contract, and the actress would prevail. Since D recognizes this, it's the best response.

(A) is not the best response,

because such an argument could only hurt the actress, not help her.

In order to recover from the producer, the actress will have to prove that she did not commit a material breach of contract, and the producer did. That's because the actress's acting in the play would be a constructive condition precedent to the producer's duty to pay her. If her illness were only a partial breach of contract, the producer could recover damages from her, but he couldn't cancel the entire contract; and in cancelling the contract as he did, he'd be liable for the entire remaining term of the six-month contract.

If, on the other hand, the actress argues that the contract is severable into *weeks,* the producer would only be liable for the weeks or portions thereof when he refused to perform. Thus, it's advantageous for *the producer* to make this argument, not the actress. Since A doesn't recognize this, it's not the best response.

(B) is not the best response,

because such an argument would be of no benefit to the actress.

In order to recover from the producer, the actress must establish that she substantially performed a constructive condition precedent of the contract—by performing in the play. This would mean that the producer wasn't entitled to cancel the contract, and he'd be liable for the rest of the six-month contract.

By claiming impossibility, the actress would be admitting that she didn't substantially perform her duties under the contract, which would relieve the producer of *his* duty to perform, enabling him to cancel the contract.

If the tables were turned and the producer were suing the actress for breach, impossibility would be a good defense, since her illness would excuse her from her duties under the contract. However, a plaintiff's failure to perform a constructive condition precedent to defendant's duty is virtually never excusable due to impossibility.

Thus, it wouldn't be a good argument for the actress, making B not the best response.

(C) is not the best response,

because the actress has a *contract* to rely on; she needn't resort to promissory estoppel.

What the actress *wants* to establish is that she substantially performed a constructive condition precedent to the producer's duty to pay (that is, that she performed in the play) and that the producer's cancellation of the contract thus constituted a major breach of contract.

If in fact her illness caused only a *partial* breach of contract, then she'll be entitled to the contract price less damages her absence caused. If, on the other hand, her absence is considered a *major* breach, then she'd only get damages due to her reliance, but these would be determined by the contract—that is, her two days' of work—not on the basis of other jobs she passed up before the contract existed.

Instead, promissory estoppel is triggered by a gratuitous promise that is likely to, and does, induce the promisee's reliance. It is a substitute for consideration to avoid injustice; it differs from consideration in that there's no bargain. The lack of an enforceable contract is a prerequisite for promissory estoppel; here, there is an enforceable contract, so promissory estoppel cannot apply. Since C doesn't recognize this, it's not the best response.

Answer 85

(A) is the best response,

because it correctly identifies the central reason the argument will be admissible: it rebuts the defendant's argument that the shirt would have been damaging to the prosecutor's case.

As a general rule, where it would be natural for a party to introduce a certain piece of available evidence, and he doesn't do so, the other party can use this failure so as to invoke an adverse inference. Here, the prosecutor didn't offer the torn shirt as evidence, when it would seem to have been advantageous for him to do so. That's why the defendant's lawyer commented on it. However, the rest of the rule holds that once such an inference has been invoked, the other party can rebut the inference. Under normal circumstances, the other party would rebut by explaining why the evidence in question wasn't introduced. By suggesting that the shirt wouldn't have benefitted the defendant either, the prosecutor rebutted the inference that the shirt was advantageous to the defendant. Since A recognizes that this is the basis of admitting the prosecutor's argument, it's the best response.

(B) is not the best response,

because it misstates the facts, and even if it correctly stated the facts, such an argument would violate the defendant's right against self-incrimination.

Here, the prosecutor isn't commenting on the defendant's failure to testify; he's rebutting the inference that the shirt would have hurt his case by suggesting it wouldn't have been helpful to either party. This doesn't address the defendant's failure to testify at all, and in stating that it does, B misstates the facts.

Assuming *arguendo* that the prosecutor did comment on the defendant's failure to testify, B is incorrect in stating that this would be proper. Any comment by the prosecutor as to the defendant's failure to testify is a violation of the Fifth Amendment privilege against self-incrimination. *Griffin v. California* (1965). Thus, the prosecutor's comment would not be proper. (Incidentally, such a comment may, however, only constitute harmless error, where the prosecutor notes the defendant's failure to produce evidence rebutting testimony of the victim, where there is overwhelming evidence of the defendant's guilt, and what scant evidence the defendant has is inconsistent. *U.S. v. Hasting* (1983).) Since B mischaracterizes the facts and misstates the law, it can't be the best response.

(C) is not the best response,

because it misstates the facts.

While it's true that a closing argument cannot go beyond the evidence in the case, that's not what's going on here; instead, the prosecutor is rebutting an inference invoked by the defendant's counsel.

As a general rule, where it would be natural for a party to introduce a certain piece of available evidence, and he doesn't do so, the other party can use this failure so as to invoke an adverse inference. Here, the prosecutor didn't offer the torn shirt as evidence, when it would seem to have been advantageous for him to do so. That's why the defendant's lawyer commented on it.

However, the rest of the rule holds that once such an inference has been invoked, the other party can rebut the inference. Under normal circumstances, the other party would rebut by explaining why the evidence in question wasn't introduced. By suggesting that the shirt wouldn't have benefitted the defendant either, the prosecutor rebutted the inference that the shirt was advantageous to the defendant. Thus, the prosecutor didn't go beyond the evidence in the case. Since C doesn't recognize this, it's not the best response.

(D) is not the best response,

because it mischaracterizes the facts.

It's true that a comment by the prosecutor as to the defendant's failure to testify is improper, as a violation of the defendant's Fifth Amendment privilege against self-incrimination. However, under these facts, the prosecutor hasn't said anything about the defendant's failure to testify. Instead, he's rebutting the inference that the shirt would have hurt his case by suggesting it wouldn't have been helpful to either party. Thus, any correct response would have to address whether the rebuttal was proper. Since D instead discusses the defendant's failure to testify, it's not the best response.

Answer 86

(D) is the best response,

because it identifies the most likely basis on which the university could be liable—vicarious liability—and cites correct reasoning as to why the university will avoid liability.

Under vicarious liability, one is liable for another's wrongful conduct due to a "special relationship" between them (e.g., employer-employee). To be liable, the wrongful conduct must be authorized by the master, performed under his control, or the servant must seek to advance the interests of the master. However, under these facts, it's clear the professor did not intend the students to carry out the experiment, they were not under her control, and in fact she encouraged them not to carry out the experiment. From the facts here the professor's behavior was not unreasonable, so the university could not be liable on that basis.

Since D correctly identifies the most likely result under these facts, it's the best response.

(A) is not the best response,

because it does not identify a sound basis on which the university will be liable.

If the university is to be liable for the professor's actions, it must be due to the professor's own negligence or vicarious liability. Since the professor's behavior seems reasonable, it could not be grounds for negligence. Since the students were neither subject to the professor's control nor acting on her behalf, the university could not be liable on grounds of vicarious liability. What choice A's "but/for" language addresses is not the basis of liability, but causation where there is only one cause of damage. While causation must exist for there to be tort liability, alone it's not enough. Since A fails to recognize this, it's not the best response.

(B) is not the best response,

because it does not provide a source of liability for the university.

Merely pressing a negligence claim against the students for negligence would be insufficient to pin liability on the university. Instead, the professor's behavior itself must have been unreasonable, or there must be some basis to hold her vicariously liable for the acts of the students. From the facts here the professor's behavior was not unreasonable, so the university could not be liable on that basis. As to vicarious liability, there's no liability either, since the students were neither subject to the professor's control, nor were they acting on her behalf. Since B does not provide a basis on which the university could be held liable, it's not the best response.

(C) is not the best response,

because the professor could be liable even if the students were not her employees (and, by the same token, even if they were her employees, she may not be vicariously liable).

Choice C is referring to the most common form of vicarious liability: the employer-employee relationship, under which the employer is liable when the employee performs a tortious act within the scope of the employment relationship. However, the concept of vicarious liability is not *confined* to the employer-employee relationship—the university *could* be liable for the students' act if the students had acted under the professor's direction, within her control, or to serve her interests. Under these facts, they acted *in spite* of her warning not to do so without her permission.

Even if there *had* been a preexisting relationship justifying vicarious liability, it's unlikely it would apply here, since the professor specifically told the students not to undertake the experiment. While a servant's doing what he is told not to do is not *determinative* on the issue of vicarious liability, it's strong evidence that he's acting outside the scope of his duties, and thus the master should not be liable.

Since C wrongly confines the vicarious liability concept to the employer-employee relationship, which is both too broad and too narrow, it's not the best response.

Answer 87

(A) is the best answer,

because the eight defendants took no affirmative act and had no legal duty requiring them to act.

The eight defendants did not take part in the stabbing and therefore undertook no affirmative act. Additionally, a special legal duty to act may exist when there is a special relationship between the defendant and victim, when there is a duty based on contract, when the danger was caused by the defendant, and/or when the defendant attempts to give assistance.

Based on these facts, no special legal duty to act existed, as the eight defendants had no idea about the leader's plan, and therefore did not cause the danger to the victim. Likewise, the eight defendants had no relationship with the victim requiring that they aid him and did not attempt to give assistance to the victim. Accordingly, the eight defendants did not have a duty to act as the victim "slowly bled to death."

(B) is not the best answer,

because it is legally wrong.

Murder does not **require** specific intent to kill, as it may occur in other circumstances, such as depraved heart murder or felony murder. Rather, the eight defendants are not guilty because the eight defendants took no affirmative act and had no legal duty requiring them to act. The eight defendants did not take part in the stabbing and therefore undertook no affirmative act. Additionally, a special legal duty to act may exist when there is a special relationship between the defendant and victim, when there is a duty based on contract, when the danger was caused by the defendant, and/or when the defendant attempts to give assistance. Based on these facts, no special legal duty to act existed, as the eight defendants had no idea about the leader's plan, and therefore did not cause the danger to the victim. Likewise, the eight defendants had no relationship with the victim requiring that they aid him and did not attempt to give assistance to the victim. Accordingly, the eight defendants did not have a duty to act as the victim "slowly bled to death."

(C) is not the best answer,

because the eight defendants did not have a legal duty requiring them to act.

A special legal duty to act may exist when there is a special relationship between the defendant and victim, when there is a duty based on contract, when the danger was caused by the defendant, and/or when the defendant attempts to give assistance. Based on these facts, no special legal duty to act existed, as the eight defendants had no idea about the leader's plan, and therefore did not cause the danger to the victim. Likewise, the eight defendants had no relationship with the victim requiring that they aid him and did not attempt to give assistance to the victim. Accordingly, the eight defendants did not have a duty to act as the victim "slowly bled to death."

(D) is not the best answer,

because it is irrelevant under the facts presented.

The reasons the eight defendants are not guilty have nothing to do with their level of intoxication. Rather, the eight defendants are not guilty because the eight defendants took no affirmative act and had no legal duty requiring them to act. The eight defendants did not take part in the stabbing and therefore undertook no affirmative act. Additionally, a special legal duty to act may exist when there is a special relationship between the defendant and victim, when there is a duty based on contract, when the danger was caused by the defendant, and/or when the defendant attempts to give assistance. Based on these facts, no special legal duty to act existed, as the eight defendants had no idea about the leader's plan, and therefore did not cause the danger to the victim. Likewise, the eight defendants had no relationship with the victim requiring that they aid him and did not attempt to give assistance to the victim. Accordingly, the eight defendants did not have a duty to act as the victim "slowly bled to death."

Answer 88

(C) is the best response,

because a hypersensitive plaintiff will not be able to recover for nuisance unless the harm would affect the use and enjoyment of the land by a normal member of the community.

To prove a private nuisance, the plaintiff must prove (i) that his use and enjoyment of his land was interfered with in a substantial way and (ii) that the defendant's conduct was negligent, abnormally dangerous, or intentional. In determining the interference with the plaintiff's use of his property, the significant harm must be of a kind that would be suffered by a normal member of the community. Here, that is not the case, as the chimes "disturbed only one homeowner" who was "abnormally sensitive to ringing sounds[.]"

(A) is not the best response,

because interference with the homeowner's use and enjoyment is not sufficient to win a claim for private nuisance.

To prove a private nuisance, the plaintiff must prove (i) that his use and enjoyment of his land was interfered with in a substantial way and (ii) that the defendant's conduct was negligent, abnormally dangerous, or intentional. The interference with plaintiff's use of his property must be substantial and unreasonable. Thus, this answer choice understates what must be proven by ignoring the substantial and unreasonable nature of the interference. Furthermore, in this problem the interference was not unreasonable, as the chimes "disturbed only one homeowner" who was "abnormally sensitive to ringing sounds[.]"

(B) is not the best response,

because priority is not dispositive in a private nuisance action.

To prove a private nuisance, the plaintiff must prove (i) that his use and enjoyment of his land was interfered with in a substantial way and (ii) that the defendant's conduct was negligent, abnormally dangerous, or intentional. What constitutes a substantial interference will generally depend in part on the neighborhood, and priority in time may be *a* factor in determining the character of the neighborhood. Priority in time is not *determinative* of whether an invasion is a nuisance. Here, the better response is one that is determinative: a hypersensitive plaintiff (like the one here) will not be able to recover for nuisance unless the harm would affect the use and enjoyment of the land by a normal member of the community.

(D) is not the best response,

because compliance with government requirements is not a defense to a claim of private nuisance.

To prove a private nuisance, the plaintiff must prove (i) that his use and enjoyment of his land was interfered with in a substantial way and (ii) that the defendant's conduct was negligent, abnormally dangerous, or intentional. In determining the interference with the plaintiff's use of his property, the significant harm must be of a kind that would be suffered by a normal member of the community. If the plaintiff could prove this type of significant harm (which she cannot, as discussed in answer choice C above), any compliance with government requirements would not be a defense for the law school.

Answer 89

(B) is the best response,

because the evidence may be admitted to prove "plan," and, additionally, may be used to impeach her character for truthfulness.

First, as to substantive use: Under FRE 404(b)(2), prior bad acts can be admitted to prove the defendant's conduct if offered for some purpose other than to show that the defendant acted in conformity with a character trait. The rule mentions "*plan*, knowledge, identity, absence of mistake, or lack of accident" as a non-exclusive list of "other purposes." In this case, the defendant denies switching the price tags and is then confronted by two prior instances of switching a price tag. The prior bad acts are very similar to the acts in dispute and demonstrate the defendant's plan or *modus operandi*. Therefore, they are not being offered to prove that because defendant is a person of criminal character she probably committed the crime with which she is now charged. This use to prove plan or *modus operandi* is a substantive use (i.e., the prior acts are offered to prove that this time, the defendant really did commit the tag-switching that's charged).

As to impeachment use: FRE 609(a)(2) provides that evidence of a past conviction "must be admitted" to impeach the credibility of a witness if "establishing the elements of the [prior] crime required proving—or the witness's admitting—a *dishonest act or false statement.*" In this case, the fraud convictions clearly involved dishonesty, and they are therefore properly admitted to impeach the credibility of the witness/defendant.

Accordingly, the convictions are admissible *both* to prove that the defendant committed the crime and to impeach the defendant.

(A) is not the best response,

because the evidence may be admitted to prove "plan," and, additionally, may be used to impeach her character for truthfulness.

Under FRE 404(b)(2), prior bad acts can be admitted to prove the defendant's conduct if offered for some purpose other than to show that the defendant acted in conformity with a character trait. In this case, the defendant denies switching the price tags and is then confronted by two prior instances of switching a price tag. The prior bad acts are very similar to the acts in dispute and demonstrate the defendant's plan or *modus operandi*. Therefore, they are not being offered to prove that because defendant is a person of criminal character she probably committed the crime with which she is now charged. In addition, FRE 609(a)(2) provides that evidence of a past conviction "must be admitted" to impeach the credibility of a witness if "establishing the elements of the [prior] crime required proving—or the witness's admitting—a dishonest act or false statement."

Accordingly, the convictions are admissible *both* to prove that the defendant committed the crime and to impeach the defendant.

(C) is not the best response,

because, while it is true that the evidence is admissible to impeach the defendant, it also may be admitted to demonstrate plan.

As is more fully explained in Choice (B), under FRE 404(b)(2), prior bad acts can be admitted to prove the defendant's conduct if offered for some purpose other than to show that the defendant acted in conformity with a character trait. The prior bad acts are very similar to the acts in dispute and demonstrate the defendant's plan or *modus operandi*. This use to prove plan or *modus operandi* is a substantive use (i.e., the prior acts are offered to prove that this time, the defendant really did commit the tag-switching that's charged).

(D) is not the best response,

because, while it is true that the evidence is admissible to prove that the defendant committed the crime, it is also admissible to impeach the defendant as a conviction involving dishonesty.

FRE 609(a)(2) provides that evidence of a past conviction "must be admitted" to impeach the credibility of a witness if "establishing the elements of the [prior] crime required proving—or the witness's admitting—a dishonest act or false statement." In this case, the fraud convictions clearly involved dishonesty, and they are therefore properly admitted to impeach the credibility of the witness/defendant.

Answer 90

(B) is the best response,

because consequential damages are limited to those that are reasonably foreseeable by the defendant.

The rule of *Hadley v. Baxendale* (1854) states that courts will not award consequential damages for breach unless the damages either arise naturally from the breach or the defendant had notice of the possibility of unusual consequences of the breach. In this problem, the mechanic had no such notice. The mechanic knew that under usual circumstances, a five-day delay in his performance would have caused negligible damage to the manufacturer (the damages do not "arise naturally") and had no notice of the liquidated damages provision. Therefore, the mechanic should not be liable for the $25,000 in liquidated damages that the manufacturer paid to the designer as a result of the mechanic's delay.

(A) is not the best response,

because even if time were of the essence in the mechanic-manufacturer contract, the mechanic would not be liable for the liquidated damages.

A "time is of the essence" clause causes a significant delay in performance to constitute a material breach of the contract. So, if the mechanic-manufacturer contract included such a clause, and five days was considered significant delay, then the mechanic would have materially breached the contract. However, he would still not be liable for the liquidated damages since they were not foreseeable to him. The rule of *Hadley v. Baxendale* (1854) states that courts will not award consequential damages for breach unless the damages either arise naturally from the breach or the defendant had notice of the possibility of unusual consequences of the breach. In this problem, the mechanic had no such notice. The mechanic knew that under usual circumstances, a five-day delay in his performance would have caused negligible damage to the manufacturer (the damages do not "arise naturally") and had no notice of the liquidated damages provision. Therefore, the mechanic should not be liable for the $25,000 in liquidated damages that the manufacturer paid to the designer as a result of the mechanic's delay.

(C) is not the best response,

because, apart from any assumption of risk taken by the manufacturer, the mechanic could not reasonably foresee the liquidated damages that would accrue as a result of his delay.

The rule of *Hadley v. Baxendale* (1854) states that courts will not award consequential damages for breach unless the damages either arise naturally from the breach or the defendant had notice of the possibility of unusual consequences of the breach. In this problem, the mechanic had no such notice. The mechanic knew that under usual circumstances, a five-day delay in his performance would have caused negligible damage to the manufacturer (the damages do not "arise naturally") and had no notice of the liquidated damages provision. Therefore, the mechanic should not be liable for the $25,000 in liquidated damages that the manufacturer paid to the designer as a result of the mechanic's delay.

(D) is not the best response,

because liquidated damages do not have to be identical to actual damages suffered by a non-breaching party.

Liquidated damages are permissible when actual damages are difficult to predict and the amount of liquidated damages are a reasonable forecast of actual damages. There is no requirement that the amount fixed as liquidated damages is identical to actual damages (since that would require a calculation of actual damages, making the liquidated damages clause useless), only that the amount be reasonable relative to the anticipated or actual loss from the breach. Even if the mechanic were to make an argument that the amount fixed as liquidated damages was excessive, that would only reduce the amount that the manufacturer would be able to recover from him. In contrast, arguing that the damages were unforeseeable, as discussed in the explanation for choice B above, would relieve the mechanic of having to pay any portion of the liquidated damages.

Answer 91

(D) is the best response,

because the state has not yet selected the community as a site.

In order for a federal court to hear a case, it must be ripe for adjudication. In order to be ripe, it is not necessary that the plaintiff has already suffered harm, but it is required that there is at least a reasonable probability of harm to the plaintiff. The harm alleged by the plaintiff must be specific as to the type of harm and when and how it will occur. This requirement is not met in this problem because harm will only come to the citizens of this community if the state chooses their site for a landfill. It is entirely possible, and in fact likely given the facts we are told, that the state will not choose to locate a toxic dump near the community's aquifer. Until the site is chosen, the potential harm from the state's action is not yet likely enough to occur to consider the case ripe for adjudication. The court will not hear the case because there is still a substantial probability that no harm will come to the residents of the community.

(A) is not the best response,

because the agency's decision is not a political question.

The "political question" doctrine prohibits courts from deciding questions that are properly designated to the other branches of government. In order to determine whether a case presents a non-justiciable political question, a court will assess whether the case presents an issue that the Constitution commits to another branch of the federal government and if there are no manageable standards by which a court can decide the case. No such issues are raised in the community's suit. In particular, the act that the community seeks to enjoin would be carried out by the state government, not another branch of the federal government.

(B) is not the best response,

because the court will not hear the case on the merits.

Choice B indicates that the court would apply strict scrutiny to the state's decision to locate the toxic waste dump in the community. This is wrong for several reasons. First, it is not responsive to the question posed. The question asked on what basis the court would dismiss the suit, not what the disposition of the case would be if heard on the merits. Second, there are no facts in this case that indicate that strict scrutiny would be the appropriate level of judicial review of the agency's decision. Finally, the court will not decide this case on the merits because it will dismiss the suit as unripe. As discussed in the explanation of choice D above, the fact that the agency has not yet decided to locate a dump in the community causes this case to be not yet ripe for adjudication, as there is a significant probability that, even without judicial intervention, no harm will come to the residents of the community.

(C) is not the best response,

because the plaintiffs are not suing the state.

The Eleventh Amendment bars federal suits "against any one of the states by citizens of another state, or by citizens or subjects of any foreign state." In particular, it bars suits by individuals seeking damages against a state from being a brought in federal court. The Eleventh Amendment is inapplicable in this situation for two reasons. First, the community's suit does not seek damages, but rather an injunction. Suits seeking injunctive relief under federal rights are not barred by the Eleventh Amendment. Second, the community is not suing the states, but rather the officials of the agency making the decision. The Eleventh Amendment only applies to suits against states, not their officers.

Answer 92

(A) is the best response,

because the plaintiff can make a *prima facie* case for Rapido's strict liability.

If one engaged in a business of selling or otherwise distributing products proceeds to sell or distribute a defective product, then liability attaches if the product contains a manufacturing defect, is defective in design, or is defective because of inadequate instructions or warnings. Here, a reasonable jury could find that (1) the car company was engaged in the business of selling or distributing cars; (2) the fact that Rapido's motor may stall if the engine has not had an extended warm-up is a design defect since an alternative design was feasible; and (3) the stalling motor and ensuing accident caused the plaintiff's shock, which resulted in a heart attack. Thus, the plaintiff can make her *prima facie* case, so the car company's motion should be denied.

(B) is not the best response,

because the crashworthiness of the car was not at issue on these facts.

Crashworthiness in a vehicle is the attribute of being able to withstand a collision without posing an unacceptably large risk of injury to the passengers. Non-crashworthiness can certainly be a type of defect. Here, the injury to the plaintiff occurred from the "shock of the crash," not from any failure of the vehicle to appropriately withstand the collision. In other words, the facts indicate that even in a perfectly crashworthy vehicle, the plaintiff would probably have had the same shock and thus the same heart attack. Consequently, even if a reasonable jury could find that the vehicle was "defective" because it was non-crashworthy (something not at all clear on these facts), the jury would probably not be entitled to find that the defect of non-crashworthiness was the legal cause of the injury. In that event, the car company would still win on its motion. So, although the conclusion (the car company loses on the motion) is correct, the explanation for why it loses is not correct.

(C) is not the best response,

because it was foreseeable that cars with engines that stall could be in accidents, so the truck driver's failure to stop was not superseding.

An intervening cause is a force that takes effect after the defendant's negligence and contributes to that negligence in producing the plaintiff's injury. Some, but not all, intervening causes are sufficient to prevent the defendant's negligence from being considered the proximate cause of the injury. Intervening causes of this kind are usually called "superseding causes" because they supersede or cancel the defendant's liability. An intervening cause that was foreseeable as something that might combine with a defect to cause an injury will generally not be deemed to be a superseding cause. Here, it was perfectly foreseeable that a car that stalled due to a defect would be more likely to be hit from the rear. Therefore, being hit from the rear was a foreseeable (and thus non-superseding) intervening cause given a "defective because likely to stall" engine.

(D) is not the best response,

because the defendant "takes the plaintiff as he finds him."

Where the defendant's negligence causes an aggravation of plaintiff's existing physical or mental illness, the defendant is liable for the damages caused by the aggravation. Here, the car company cannot escape liability by arguing that a person of normal sensitivity would not have suffered a heart attack under these circumstances.

Answer 93

(C) is the best response,

because it correctly identifies the central reason why the evidence will be excluded: the student's actual and reasonable expectation of privacy was violated.

While it's possible for the police to conduct electronic surveillance under a warrant, the warrant requirements are very strict, and clearly have not been satisfied under these facts. A wrinkle in this problem is that the college president "arranged" for the local police to bug the student's room. This implies *private* action, which is *not* circumscribed by the Fourth Amendment (only *governmental* action is covered, or those acting under police direction). Thus, the college president's acts will not make the surveillance valid. Note that *after* the surveillance, the search warrant and subsequent search are not obviously flawed; since the tape provided probable cause for a warrant, and it was apparently given by a neutral, detached magistrate. Nonetheless, the original illegal surveillance requires that the evidence be excluded at trial. Since C recognizes this, it's the best response.

(A) is not the best response,

because it does not focus on the central fact: that the police unreasonably invaded the student's privacy.

In fact, the reasoning A states would not make the evidence admissible even if the college president's acts were determinative, because his acting "in loco parentis" would not in and of itself give him the duty to make sure the students are law abiding. Rather, it's the police activity that will determine the admissibility of the evidence. A wrinkle in these facts is that the college president called in the police. If you chose response A, you may have been thinking of the rule that the Fourth Amendment does not address *private* conduct, only *official* conduct (unless the private person is closely related to the state, e.g., operating at the direction of the police). That isn't the case here. Since A does not focus on the central issue, and arrives at an incorrect result, it's not the best response.

(B) is not the best response,

because although it's correct as far as it goes, it ignores the fact that the police *initially* unreasonably invaded the student's privacy.

By placing microphones in the student's room, they violated the student's reasonable expectation of privacy, and they had no warrant to place any kind of electronic surveillance. The requirements for doing so are strict: for a start, there must be probable cause to believe specific criminal activity has taken place or is taking place, the warrant must describe with particularity the conversations that will be heard, etc. Here, these requirements are clearly not met, which is why the evidence will not be admissible. This aside, the latter part of the police conduct—the search warrant and the search itself—are satisfactory, as B suggests. However, since B does not recognize that the foundation for the search warrant was faulty, it's not the best response.

(D) is not the best response,

because although it arrives at the correct result, it doesn't cite the correct reasoning.

"Fundamental fairness" is not the test for determining if the electronic surveillance is unfair; rather, it's whether the person's reasonable expectation of privacy has been violated. (While electronic surveillance can be conducted under a warrant, the warrant requirements are very strict, and clearly not satisfied here).

Since D does not apply the correct test to these facts, it's not the best response.

Answer 94

(A) is the best response,

because it recognizes that the nephew will be guilty. The key factor here is causation—the nephew did, in fact, cause the patient's death.

Criminal homicide requires causing the death of a living human being, where death occurs within a year and a day. The fortuitous plane crash would not change this result; nor would the patient's preexisting heart condition. The nephew's conduct was the cause in fact and legal cause of the patient's death. Since A correctly identifies that the nephew will be guilty of criminal homicide, it's the best response.

(B) is not the best response,

because the reason it gives does not negate the nephew's liability for homicide.

The plane crash was a fortuitous coincidence, but does not alter the fact that the nephew is culpable. Criminal homicide is causing the death of a living human being, where death occurs within a year and a day. Here, the nephew deliberately poisoned the patient, intending to kill him, and the poison did in fact kill the patient. It doesn't matter that the patient would have died without the poisoning—the key fact is that the poison did, in fact, kill him. The fortuity of saving the patient from dying in the plane crash would not exonerate the nephew, so B is not the best response.

(C) is not the best response,

because its reasoning is irrelevant.

The important fact is that the nephew caused the patient's death, which is what criminal homicide requires. The fact that the patient would have died anyway is not an issue. The classic example of this is the person who kills a person who is scheduled to be executed the following day. The inevitability of the result from other causes is not a defense (since, taken to an extreme, there could be no such thing as homicide—since everyone will *eventually* die). Since C states incorrect reasoning, it's not the best response.

(D) is not the best response,

because it misstates the rule on causation.

In order to be a legal cause, the conduct or omission must be a substantial factor in bringing about the result. Under the facts here, although the patient's heart was already weakened, the poison was a substantial factor in bringing on the fatal heart attack. Beyond that, criminal homicide only requires causing a death of a living human being. Here, the nephew did far more than what's necessary for homicide—he intended to kill the patient, and administered a fatal dose of poison. The fact that the patient's preexisting heart condition contributed to his death would not exonerate the nephew. Thus, D is not the best response.

Answer 95

(A) is the best response,

because it correctly identifies that the seller can use the sale proceeds to pay off the mortgage, and thus force the buyer to honor the contract.

Under these facts, you're told that the seller and the buyer had an "enforceable written agreement" for the sale of the tract. The agreement, as a land sale contract, would carry with it the implied covenant of marketable title. This means that the seller, at the closing, must convey title that, viewed objectively, is free from reasonable doubt in both law and fact, and that a reasonable buyer would accept without fear of litigation. Liens, mortgages, taxes, and other encumbrances render title "unmarketable," and allow the buyer to avoid the sale. Thus, for the seller to obtain specific performance of the contract, he'd have to get around the "marketable title" problem, since on the date of the closing, there's a mortgage on the tract, which theoretically renders title unmarketable (and renders the seller in breach of contract).

Choice A suggests a viable way to avoid the "marketable title" problem. Here, you're told that the proceeds will cover the mortgage. When that's the case, the seller has an implied right to use the proceeds of the sale to pay off the mortgage. By arguing this, the seller not only avoids being in breach of the contract, but he can enforce the contract against the buyer, since this means that the buyer won't have the right to cancel the contract. When you think about it, this rule comports with what you'd expect to happen, since many homeowners, in real life, couldn't buy a new home if this weren't the case. Since choice A recognizes a means by which the seller can enforce the contract, it's the best response.

(B) is not the best response,

because it misstates the law.

Under these facts, you're told that the seller and the buyer had an "enforceable written agreement" for the sale of the tract. The agreement, as a land sale contract, would carry with it the implied covenant of marketable title. This means that the seller, at the closing, must convey title that, viewed objectively, is free from reasonable doubt in both law and fact, and that a reasonable buyer would accept without fear of litigation. Liens, morgages, taxes, and other encumbrances render title "unmarketable," and allow the buyer to avoid the sale. Thus, for the seller to obtain specific performance of the contract, he'd have to get around the "marketable title" problem, since on the date of the closing, there's a mortgage on the tract, which theoretically renders title unmarketable (and renders the seller in breach of contract). Choice B doesn't offer a viable means of avoiding the "marketable title" problem. Although it's possible that the law of the jurisdiction may make the mortgage payable from the proceeds, and the mortgage agreement itself may insist on payoff if the property is conveyed, this doesn't remove the mortgage from the tract—and that's the central problem here. A strong argument for the seller would have to address how the mortgage is removed from the tract, since that's what prevents the seller from enforcing the contract. Since B doesn't recognize this, it's not the best response.

(C) is not the best response,

because the doctrine of equitable conversion would not apply to these facts.

The doctrine of equitable conversion addresses the period between the signing of the land sale contract, and the closing. Under the doctrine, the vendor has a personal property interest in the property, between the signing of the contract and the closing, in the form of the balance of the purchase price owed to him; the vendee is considered the beneficial owner of the property.

What this doctrine does, as an equitable doctrine, is to allocate risks the parties didn't address. However, under these facts, marketable title *was* addressed, since the conveyance of marketable title is an implied covenant in land sale contracts. As a result, the seller impliedly assumed the risk that the title might not be marketable, and that the buyer could avoid the contract on this basis. Any encumbrance on property, like the mortgage here, would render it unmarketable. Since conveying marketable title is a duty allocated to the seller under the land sale contract, the seller cannot turn to equity to avoid providing it, and the doctrine of equitable conversion won't help him. Since C doesn't recognize this, it's not the best response.

(D) is not the best response,

because it states an insufficient ground on which the seller could prevail. Of course, his underlying argument must be that he hasn't breached the contract, because if he had, he wouldn't be entitled to specific performance. However, choice D, in and of itself, doesn't provide a rule allowing the seller to use the proceeds to pay off the mortgage, and enforce the contract.

Under these facts, you're told that the seller and the buyer had an "enforceable written agreement" for the sale of the tract. The agreement, as a land sale contract, would carry with it the implied covenant of marketable title. This means that the seller, at the closing, must convey title that, viewed objectively, is free from reasonable doubt in both law and fact, and that a reasonable buyer would accept without fear of litigation. Liens, morgages, taxes, and other encumbrances render title "unmarketable," and allow the buyer to avoid the sale. Thus, for the seller to obtain specific performance of the contract, he'd have to get around the "marketable title" problem, since on the date of the closing, there's a mortgage on the tract, which theoretically renders title unmarketable (and renders the seller in breach of contract).

Simply saying that the seller hasn't breached the contract doesn't provide an argument for enforcing the contract. In fact, the seller has an implied right to use the proceeds of the sale to pay off the mortgage, assuming the proceeds cover the mortgage (which is true, under these facts)—and it's this implied right that makes the contract enforceable. Thus, what choice D does is fail to take the extra step taken by choice A, addressing the implied right and forcing the buyer to honor the contract. As a result, D isn't the best response.

Answer 96

(D) is the correct answer,

because it correctly recognizes that Plaintiff's motion for preliminary injunctive relief will not succeed due to the fact that the federal statute upon which it is based is advisory, not mandatory.

A court will issue a preliminary injunction only if the person seeking it shows that she is ***likely to succeed on the merits*** and can also demonstrate three additional factors: (1) the likelihood of irreparable injury if provisional relief is not granted; (2) a balance of hardships in favor of the movant; and (3) a showing that the requested relief is in the public interest. *See Winter v. Natural Resources Defense Council, Inc.*, 555 U.S. 7, 20 (2008). A preliminary injunction is never awarded as of right; it is an equitable order and viewed as "an extraordinary remedy that may only be awarded upon a clear showing that the plaintiff is entitled to such relief." *Id*.

Plaintiff cannot show that she will succeed on the merits, because the FPA does not create a mandatory duty on waterfront homeowners to refrain from lawn-planting in the buffer zone—it merely recommends that they do so. Because Plaintiff's likely success on the merits is a necessary condition for a preliminary injunction, her failure to prove likely success on the merits ends the analysis. (The other three conditions would only become relevant if Plaintiff showed a likelihood that she would succeed on the merits.)

(A) is not the best response,

because the rule it states, while accurate, is insufficient to support the granting of preliminary relief.

It is true that preliminary injunctive relief is available only on a showing of *irreparable* harm, meaning harm that cannot be remedied through the payment of money damages. And this choice plausibly suggests that during the pendency of the suit, Defendant may well over-develop her land, impede spawning, and cause damage that cannot be remedied through the payment of money. However, the likelihood of irreparable harm means merely that *one* of the four requirements for an injunction has been met. Given the fact that Plaintiff can't meet the other three requirements (because she can't show she's likely to succeed on the merits, as described in the treatment of Choice (D) above), the court must deny the injunction.

(B) is not the best response,

because as with Choice (A), the rule that it states is insufficient to support the granting of preliminary relief.

The possibility that an injunction may be in the public interest is only one of the four necessary conditions before a preliminary injunction may be granted. So while it's true that the district court, before *granting* preliminary relief, would be required to consider whether the order will serve the public interest, the fact that Plaintiff is unlikely to succeed on the merits (as described in Choice (D)) means that the four conditions can't all be satisfied and that the motion must be denied.

(C) is not the best response,

because although the answer correctly states the expected outcome of the request for the preliminary injunction, it misidentifies the most likely reason for the denial.

It's true that, as this choice indicates, a preliminary injunction is an equitable form of relief and is available only when money damages will not be able to compensate for the harm (making the harm irreparable). But it's far from clear on these facts that an award of money will indeed be sufficient to remedy the harm—perhaps an award of damages would be enough to adequately remediate the harm prospectively, in that the award could pay for removal of the lawn, so that any interim damage to fish would be minor and temporary. In any event, this choice refers to a "violation" of the FPA, and the advisory nature of the FPA means that planting by Defendant would not be a "violation." A far more compelling reason for the court to deny the motion is Plaintiff's failure to show likely success on the merits, for the reason described in the analysis of Choice (D).

Answer 97

(A) is the best response,

because the damage for abnormally dangerous activities is limited to the kind of harm that makes the activity abnormally dangerous.

A natural first thing to notice is that the defendant was engaged in an "abnormally dangerous activity": storing explosives. But the second thing to notice—even more important than the first—is that the accident was *unrelated to the abnormally dangerous aspects* of the defendant's conduct. There is strict liability for injuries caused by an abnormally dangerous activity, but only when the harm that occurs is the kind that causes the activity to be considered abnormally dangerous in the first place. *See* Rest. 2d Torts, § 519(2). Here the loose roof tile had nothing to do with the explosives that made the defendant's plant abnormally dangerous—a tile could just as easily have come loose if the building had been used to store grain or some other safe product. It's possible that the defendant was negligent in failing to more carefully secure the tile, but the facts tell us that the plaintiff brought a claim for strict liability, not negligence. There is no strict liability for loose roof tiles.

(B) is not the best response,

because the strength of the windstorm is not relevant to the defendant's liability.

If the owner of the plant were strictly liable for the accident, the high winds would not excuse him. (So if the unexpected winds had somehow caused the defendant's dynamite to explode, he would be liable for the results—because there is strict liability for the storage of dynamite.) The defendant avoids strict liability not because the winds were unusual, but because the accident was not related to the abnormally dangerous features of the defendant's conduct. Notice that the unexpected nature of the winds might have helped the owner defeat a claim that he wasn't careful enough in securing the roof tile—he could claim that he did a careful enough job to protect against normal winds, just not against these very unusual winds. But that would be a defense to a negligence claim, which the plaintiff did not bring.

(C) is not the best response,

because, as noted in the discussion of choice A above, to win a strict liability claim it is not enough to show that the defendant was engaged in an abnormally dangerous activity (which storing explosives certainly is). The plaintiff also has to show that he suffered the very sort of harm that caused the activity to be considered abnormally dangerous. Here the loose roof tiles had nothing to do with the risks that make storing explosives an abnormally dangerous activity.

(D) is not the best response,

because strict liability applies to activities, not to the *location* of an activity.

If a dangerous activity is carried out in an unsuitable location, that fact may help a court conclude that strict liability should apply to the harm the activity causes. But that strict liability will still be limited to the kinds of harms that arise from the activity's special dangers. Since the harm caused by the loose roof tile was unrelated to the special dangers of the defendant's plant, he cannot be held strictly liability for the damage the tile caused when it fell, regardless of the location of the plant.

Answer 98

(D) is the best response,

because the creditor could not have insisted on payment on the first day of each month.

When a party assigns their rights under a contract, they may only assign rights that they could enforce themselves. The bank could therefore only insist on prompt payment if the creditor could have done so, since the bank is the creditor's assignee. However, the creditor and the debtor had modified their contract to allow the debtor to pay on the fifth of each month. It is important to note that this modification was effective since it was supported by consideration on both sides: the creditor agreed to accept later payment, while the debtor took on the additional obligation of paying by cashier's check. Since this modification was effective, the contract, as modified, called for payment on the fifth of each month. Upon the assignment, the bank "stepped into the shoes" of the creditor, and could only enforce the contract as it existed at the time of the assignment.

(A) is not the best response,

because the bank's knowledge of the modification is irrelevant.

When a party assigns their rights under a contract, they may only assign rights that they could enforce themselves. The bank could therefore only insist on prompt payment if the creditor could have done so, since the bank is the creditor's assignee. Since the contract between the debtor and the creditor had been modified (see the explanation for choice D above), the bank could only enforce the agreement as modified. To allow the bank to ignore the debtor's bargained-for modification simply because it was unaware of it would be unfair to the debtor (and would essentially re-modify the contract without additional consideration). If the bank is harmed by the modification, its sole source of remedy would be an action against the creditor for failing to disclose a material term of the contract that was being assigned.

(B) is not the best response,

because the contract was modified.

Choice B correctly states the rule that a party that waives a condition may at any time reinstate the condition for future performance. However, the creditor has not waived the condition in the contract calling for payment on the first of each month. Instead, there has been a modification of the contract, with each party providing consideration for the alteration (the creditor agreeing to take payment four days later and the debtor agreeing to pay by cashier's check). A modification cannot be unilaterally reinstated by one party, so the creditor would not be able to require the debtor to pay on the first of each month. Since the bank, as the assignee of the creditor's rights under the contract, "steps into the shoes" of the creditor, it could only exercise the rights available to the creditor. Therefore, the bank has to accept the debtor's payment by cashier's check, even if it comes in after the first of each month.

(C) is not the best response,

because the contract was modified.

The reason that the debtor has the right to delay payment to the fifth of each month is that the contract was modified to allow later payment, not that a waived condition could not be reinstated. A waiver is the voluntary agreement not to enforce a condition of a contract. Generally, a party may reinstate waived conditions as to future performance. However, the creditor has not waived the condition in the contract calling for payment on the first of each month. Instead, there has been a modification of the contract, with each party providing consideration for the alteration (the creditor agreeing to take payment four days later and the debtor agreeing to pay by cashier's check). A modification cannot be unilaterally reinstated by one party, so the creditor would not be able to require the debtor to pay on the first of each month. Since the bank, as the assignee of the creditor's rights under the contract, "steps into the shoes" of the creditor, it could only exercise the rights available to the creditor. Therefore, the bank has to accept the debtor's payment by cashier's check, even if it comes in after the first of each month.

Answer 99

(D) is the best response,

because it correctly characterizes a valid self-defense claim, and plausibly fits these facts.

All a self-defense claim requires is a reasonable belief in the existence of danger, with immediate force being the only way to avoid it. Thus, choice D, by invoking the "reasonable person" standard, recognizes this. Note that choice D uses the modifier "if" instead of "because." That means that the facts need only plausibly fit the reasoning. That's the case here. It's possible on these facts that a reasonable person would, indeed, view the gesture as threatening. Since D correctly identifies the test for self-defense, and it's consistent with these facts, it's the best response.

(A) is not the best response,

because it does not address an element that will determine the validity of the neighbor's claim of privilege

It's not whether Bill was *actually* an aggressor that counts, but whether the neighbor could *reasonably believe* in the existence of danger, with immediate force being the only way to avoid it. Thus, a valid self-defense claim focuses on the belief of the one claiming the privilege. Since A doesn't recognize this, it's not the best response.

(B) is not the best response,

because it does not address an element that will determine the validity of the neighbor's claim of privilege.

It's not how Bill intended his gesture that's relevant, but whether the gesture created in the neighbor a *reasonable belief* as to the existence of danger, with immediate force being the only way to avoid it. Thus, a valid self-defense claim focuses on the belief of the one *claiming* the privilege. Since B ignores this, it's not the best response.

(C) is not the best response,

because an honest belief is not sufficient for a self-defense claim—it must be a *reasonable* belief, as well.

Thus, if the neighbor's perception of danger was a result of his hallucinating, even if his belief was honest, he would *still* be liable because his belief wasn't reasonable. Since C ignores the objective element of the self-defense claim, it's not the best response.

Answer 100

(B) is the best response,

because it's the only choice that addresses the correct scope of re-direct examination.

This is an unusual MBE question, in that it's purely theoretical: Either you know the answer, or you don't. There's no factual analysis required. In fact, the rule is just what B says it is: Only new, *material* matters addressed on cross-examination may be covered on re-direct, as a general rule. This is not a matter specifically addressed in the text of the FRE—it's left to common-law principles. Under those principles, the judge *may,* in his discretion, allow counsel to address on re-direct a matter overlooked on direct due to an oversight, but this isn't relevant here, because the question asks you for the circumstances under which a judge *must* allow re-direct examination, not where he *may* allow it. Since B cites the correct rule, it's the best response.

(A) is not the best response,

because it overstates the scope of re-direct examination.

The judge is only required to allow re-direct examination to address new, material matters addressed on cross-examination. He needn't allow it for insignificant matters addressed on cross, and thus A overstates the scope of re-direct examination, by stating that the judge must allow re-direct to reply to *any* matter raised on cross. As a result, A is not the best response.

(C) is not the best response,

because it misstates the rule.

The judge is required to allow re-direct examination to address new, material matters addressed on cross-examination. In fact, allowing a party to reiterate the essential elements of the case on re-direct would contradict FRE 403, which authorizes the judge to exclude evidence if admitting it would constitute a waste of time. Since C does not recognize the correct rule on re-direct examination, it is not the best response.

(D) is not the best response,

because it misstates the rule.

Here, the question asks you when a judge *must* allow re-direct examination of a witness. The judge is only *required* to allow re-direct examination to address new, material matters addressed on cross-examination. The material D addresses is allowable in the judge's discretion—he *may,* if he sees fit, allow re-direct on matters overlooked on direct due to an oversight. However, this is not mandatory. This answer indicates the level of precision necessary to correctly answer MBE questions! Since D does not state the rule correctly, it is not the best response.

ANSWERS

PRACTICE MBE — P.M. EXAM

Answer Key

Use this Answer Key to quickly identify the correct answer to each question.

(101) C	(111) B	(121) A	(131) C	(141) B	(151) A	(161) D	(171) B	(181) B	(191) C
(102) A	(112) A	(122) A	(132) A	(142) B	(152) D	(162) A	(172) D	(182) C	(192) C
(103) D	(113) A	(123) B	(133) C	(143) D	(153) B	(163) B	(173) B	(183) A	(193) C
(104) C	(114) C	(124) B	(134) A	(144) A	(154) C	(164) D	(174) A	(184) D	(194) C
(105) B	(115) A	(125) B	(135) A	(145) C	(155) A	(165) B	(175) C	(185) B	(195) A
(106) C	(116) B	(126) D	(136) D	(146) C	(156) B	(166) A	(176) B	(186) A	(196) A
(107) C	(117) B	(127) B	(137) D	(147) D	(157) C	(167) C	(177) B	(187) B	(197) D
(108) A	(118) D	(128) D	(138) A	(148) D	(158) B	(168) D	(178) D	(188) C	(198) B
(109) B	(119) B	(129) D	(139) A	(149) B	(159) A	(169) B	(179) D	(189) D	(199) C
(110) B	(120) C	(130) A	(140) B	(150) B	(160) B	(170) A	(180) D	(190) B	(200) B

ANSWERS

PRACTICE MBE — P.M. EXAM

Answer 101

(C) is the best response,

because under joint and several liability the entire amount can be collected from any one of the defendants.

Here, there are three defendants, all of whom were a proximate cause of the plaintiff's harm. In this situation, the plaintiff may recover his full damages from one defendant. That defendant can seek to recover a proportional share of the damages from other defendants. Furthermore, because the plaintiff was not found to be at fault, he may recover the full amount of his damages under pure comparative negligence.

(A) is not the best response,

because it applies a pro rata allocation of damages rather than applying joint and several liability.

Under joint and several liability the entire amount can be collected from any one of the defendants. Here, there are three defendants, all of whom were a proximate cause of the plaintiff's harm. In this situation, the plaintiff may recover his full damages from one defendant. That defendant can seek to recover a proportional share of the damages from other defendants. Furthermore, because the plaintiff was not found to be at fault, he may recover the full amount of his damages under pure comparative negligence.

(B) is not the best response,

because it applies several liability, rather than joint and several liability, to the fact pattern.

Under joint and several liability the entire amount can be collected from any one of the defendants. Here, there are three defendants, all of whom were a proximate cause of the plaintiff's harm. In this situation, the plaintiff may recover his full damages from one defendant. That defendant can seek to recover a proportional share of the damages from other defendants. Furthermore, because the plaintiff was not found to be at fault, he may recover the full amount of his damages under pure comparative negligence.

(D) is not the best response,

because it applies contributory negligence, rather than comparative negligence, to the fact pattern.

As the plaintiff was not found to be at fault, he may recover the full amount of his damages in a pure comparative negligence jurisdiction where the negligence of the parents is not imputed to the child. Furthermore, under joint and several liability the entire amount can be collected from any one of the defendants. Here, there are three defendants, all of whom were a proximate cause of the plaintiff's harm. In this situation, the plaintiff may recover his full damages from one defendant. That defendant can seek to recover a proportional share of the damages from other defendants.

Answer 102

(A) is the best response,

because it applies to these facts, it would be relatively easy to prove, and it overcomes a central obstacle in the case.

This problem indicates a pattern found in many MBE property questions: you have to be familiar with several areas of law in order to answer correctly. Here, you need to know contract law, to eliminate the creditor beneficiary choice in C, and constitutional law, to eliminate the taxpayer choice in B.

In order to bind a subsequent purchaser, an equitable servitude must meet the following requirements: there must be notice, whether actual, constructive, or inquiry (here, there is constructive notice); there must be an intent that it bind subsequent purchasers; and the benefit and burden both must touch and concern the land.

(Note that under the modern rule, as represented by § 3.2 of the Restatement (Third) of Property, the touch and concern requirements are entirely eliminated.) The notice requirement is satisfied, because although the purchaser's deed did not refer to the restriction on use of the ten-acre tract, the restriction is present in a prior recording in the chain of title, thus satisfying "constructive notice." The intent to bind subsequent purchasers exists, because such a restriction in the deed would be meaningless otherwise. The "benefit and burden" requirement is satisfied because, according to most courts, the benefit attaches to the properties of owners of other tracts in the development, as long as the common scheme is in existence for lots sold both before and after the one in question. The restriction itself constitutes a burden. As a result, the facts here fit the requirements of an equitable servitude relatively easily, and, in doing so, would bind the purchaser, as a subsequent purchaser—and this is exactly what the dentist wants to do. Since A applies to the facts here, is not difficult to prove, and addresses a central issue in the case, it's the best response.

(B) is not the best response,

because, while it is factually correct, it does not provide a strong basis for the dentist's prevailing in the action.

In general, the dentist's status as a state or municipal taxpayer would not give her a status sufficient to merit her recovery. Her status as a taxpayer gives her, at best, an indirect interest in the use of the ten-acre tract; it's her position as one of the surrounding landowners that gives her an opportunity for relief. Since B does not recognize this, it's not the best response.

(C) is not the best response,

because, while it could be factually correct, it does not provide a strong basis for the dentist's prevailing in the action.

In order to be a creditor beneficiary to the owner/purchaser contract, the owner would have to owe the dentist a preexisting duty, which the purchaser's performance will fulfill, and the dentist would have to prove that the owner specifically intended that the purchaser's performance benefit *her.* Under these facts, it's unlikely that the owner intended the owner/purchaser contract to benefit the dentist in any significant way, and, beyond that, it would be difficult to characterize her as a creditor of the owner's, since she only purchased a lot from him. While the dentist could, *in theory,* prevail on a third-party beneficiary theory, these factors indicate that it would be a very difficult case to prove. As a result, C is not the best answer.

(D) is not the best response,

because, although it is factually correct, it does not offer a strong basis for the dentist's prevailing in the action.

A bona fide purchaser is a subsequent purchaser, who pays value, without notice of any prior conveyance, and is of good faith. Here, the purchaser has *at least* constructive notice of the owner's intent to use the ten-acre tract for a school, since the owner's plan was *recorded.* As a result, the purchaser is not a bona fide purchaser. However, the purchaser's non-bona-fide-purchaser status would only deal with his being bound by the recorded notice; it would not have a significant impact on a dispute between the purchaser and the dentist. Since it does not impact a major issue in the dispute, D is not the best response, even though it is factually correct.

Answer 103

(D) is the best response,

because there was no legal duty requiring the wife to act.

A special legal duty to act may exist when there is a special relationship between the defendant and victim, when there is a duty based on contract, when the danger was caused by the defendant, and/or when the defendant attempts to give assistance. Based on these facts, no special legal duty to act existed, as the wife had no relationship with the crowd, did not cause the danger, and did not attempt to give assistance. Accordingly, the defendant did not commit a crime.

(A) is not the best response,

because there was no legal duty requiring the wife to act.

While the facts may arguably demonstrate a "reckless indifference to consequence," a special legal duty to act must still exist in order for criminal liability to attach. A special legal duty to act may exist when there is a special relationship between the defendant and victim, when there is a duty based on contract, when the danger was caused by the defendant, and/or when the defendant attempts to give assistance. Based on these facts, no special legal duty to act existed, as the wife had no relationship with the crowd, did not cause the danger, and did not attempt to give assistance. Accordingly, the defendant did not commit a crime.

(B) is not the best response,

because it is not legally or factually supported.

Legally, there was no duty for the wife to act. A special legal duty to act may exist when there is a special relationship between the defendant and victim, when there is a duty based on contract, when the danger was caused by the defendant, and/or when the defendant attempts to give assistance. Based on these facts, no special legal duty to act existed, as the wife had no relationship with the crowd, did not cause the danger, and did not attempt to give assistance. Accordingly, the defendant did not commit a crime. Additionally, the facts do not support that the defendant intentionally committed a homicide with premeditation and deliberation, as the defendant did not actively seek the death of the victims or even know if they would occur.

(C) is not the best response,

because there was no legal duty requiring the wife to act.

While the facts may arguably demonstrate second degree murder through a "depraved heart" theory, a special legal duty to act must still exist in order for criminal liability to attach. A special legal duty to act may exist when there is a special relationship between the defendant and victim, when there is a duty based on contract, when the danger was caused by the defendant, and/or when the defendant attempts to give assistance. Based on these facts, no special legal duty to act existed, as the wife had no relationship with the crowd, did not cause the danger, and did not attempt to give assistance. Accordingly, the defendant did not commit a crime.

Answer 104

(C) is the best response,

because it correctly identifies the central issue that will determine the passerby's liability.

A tricky "twist" to this question is that you aren't told who threw the first punch. If the borrower did, he wouldn't be privileged to defend himself (unless the fight "escalated"), so that would call into question whether the passerby could use force to protect him. The courts are split on this issue, that is, whether a third party can defend a person who wouldn't be privileged to defend himself. This question prudently avoids this issue altogether.

Note that since C uses the qualifier "if" instead of "because," you needn't determine if the facts represent the proposition in C—that the lender was about to inflict serious bodily harm on the borrower. Instead, you need only determine that it's possible this could be true under these facts, that this determines an issue central to the passerby's liability, and that the result is consistent with the reasoning.

This is the rule on privilege to defend others: anyone can go to the defense of another threatened with serious bodily injury. The third party may use any force reasonably necessary for such defense (thus, unnecessary force will be subject to liability). The threat of harm to the other person must be immediate (so past attacks or future threats won't be sufficient). The courts are split as to whether mistake—as to belief that intervention is required or that the one being attacked would be privileged to use self-defense (i.e., he was the "aggressor"), or that the force applied is called for—will be a defense.

Thus, whether the lender appeared to be about to inflict serious bodily harm on the borrower will be the central issue determining the passerby's liability. Since C correctly identifies this, and resolves it satisfactorily, it's the best response.

(A) is not the best response,

because under these facts the passerby *might* be privileged to use deadly force.

The rule is that anyone can go to the defense of another threatened with serious bodily injury. The third party may use any force reasonably necessary for such defense (thus, unnecessary force will be a source of liability). The threat of harm to the other person must be immediate (so past attacks or future threats won't be sufficient). The courts are split as to whether mistake—either as to belief that intervention is required, or that the one being attacked would be privileged to use self-defense (i.e., he was the "aggressor"), or that the force applied is called for—will be a defense.

Here, choice A says the passerby will be liable *because* he threatened to use deadly force. However, this is not necessarily true. The facts say the lender was about to kick the borrower in the head. This could well be justification for threatening deadly force. Even if the passerby were *mistaken* as to the need for deadly force, in some jurisdictions he'd avoid liability anyway. Since A states as a concrete proposition that threatening deadly force will make the passerby liable, and there are at least some circumstances under these facts under which it *won't*, A is not the best response.

(B) is not the best response,

because it cites a fact that is irrelevant. The passerby's right to use force depends on whether he'd fit the privilege to defend another.

Note that choice B uses the modifier "unless." This means that, if the passerby was related to the borrower, there's no way under these facts that he could be liable. In fact, that's not true: The passerby's liability does not depend on whether he's related to the borrower.

The rule is that anyone can go to the defense of another threatened with serious bodily injury. The third party may use any force reasonably necessary for such defense (thus, unnecessary force will be subject to liability). The threat of harm to the other person must be immediate (so past attacks or future threats won't be sufficient). The courts are split as to whether mistake—either as to belief that intervention is required, or that the one being attacked would be privileged to use self-defense (i.e., he was the "aggressor"), or that the force applied is called for—will be a defense.

Thus, the issue of *relationship* between the defender and the one being defended is not relevant. If the defender fits the rule, he'll avoid liability due to the defense of privilege; if he *doesn't*, he'll be liable even if he's related to the victim.

If you chose this response, you may have been thinking of the *old* rule that provided members of the same family with the privilege to defend each other. However, this rule has given way completely to the modern rule, as stated above. Since B focuses on an irrelevant issue, it's not the best response.

(D) is not the best response,

because it implies an incorrect rule of law, and in any case focuses on an irrelevant point.

The passerby's liability will turn on whether he was privileged to defend the borrower with the amount of force he used. The rule is that anyone can go to the defense of another threatened with serious bodily injury. The third party may use any force reasonably necessary for such defense (thus, unnecessary force will create liability). The threat of harm to the other person must be immediate (so past attacks or future threats won't be sufficient). The courts are split as to whether mistake—either as to belief that intervention is required or that the one being attacked would be privileged to use self-defense (i.e., he was the "aggressor"), or that the force applied is called for—will be a defense.

As a result, the fact that D cites that the lender initially threatened the borrower will not determine the passerby's liability. In most cases, a mere threat does not *generally* justify an apprehension of immediate harm, and thus wouldn't merit the use of force. Even if the lender *were* considered the "aggressor," if deadly force were not reasonably required, the passerby would be liable for using unnecessary force. Since D focuses on a point that would not determine the passerby's liability, it's not the best response.

Answer 105

(B) is the best response,

because the teacher is entitled to expectation damages as a result of the summer camp's breach.

When an employer breaches an employment contract, the employee may recover expectation damages, which are designed to put the employee in the same position as he or she would have been had the employer not breached. The formula for expectation damages is the contract price minus whatever benefit the non-breaching party has gained by not having to perform, plus reasonable incidental costs incurred in mitigating damages. Here, the teacher expected to work for ten weeks and be paid $10,000 (the contract price). As a result of the camp's breach, he had to accept substitute employment paying $6,000 for the same period (which is a benefit he would not have received had he worked for the summer camp instead). Additionally, he had to spend $200 in his search for alternate employment (an incidental cost). Thus, his expectation damages are $10,000 – $6,000 + $200 = $4,200. Put another way, the teacher expected to have $10,000 at the end of the summer, but because of the breach he only has $5,800 (the $6,000 he was paid less the $200 he had to spend). In order to put him in the same position as he would have been without the breach, he has to recover $10,000 – $5,800 = $4,200.

(A) is not the best response,

because it does not account for the incidental expense the teacher incurred searching for a different job.

If you chose this response, you took the difference between the contract salary and the salary that the teacher was able to get from the summer school. However, this response neglects to compensate the teacher for the $200 he spent traveling to the other summer camp in his attempt to get a job there. This additional, incidental expense was incurred in the teacher's attempt to mitigate damages by seeking alternate employment for the summer. Since $200 to travel to the only other summer camp in the area for an interview is a reasonable cost related to mitigating the teacher's loss, he will be able to recover it in an action against the summer camp.

(C) is not the best response,

because it ignores the teacher's duty to mitigate damages and does not award reasonable incidental expenses to the teacher.

When one party to a contract anticipatorily repudiates a contract, the non-breaching party has a duty to mitigate damages. In the case of an employment contract, the non-breaching employee does this by attempting to find alternate employment elsewhere. In this problem, the teacher successfully found another job teaching at a local summer school. The $6,000 he was paid for this work he would not have received had he worked for the summer camp, and therefore needs to be subtracted from the contract price when calculating the teacher's expectation damages. In addition, the teacher's expectation damages include the $200 he spent traveling to the other camp for an interview, since he did so in a reasonable attempt to find another job as a camp counselor.

(D) is not the best response,

because it ignores the teacher's duty to mitigate damages and does not award reasonable incidental expenses to the teacher.

When one party to a contract anticipatorily repudiates a contract, the non-breaching party has a duty to mitigate damages. In the case of an employment contract, the non-breaching employee does this by attempting to find alternate employment elsewhere. In this problem, the teacher successfully found another job teaching at a local summer school. The $6,000 he was paid for this work is money he would not have received had he worked for the summer camp, and therefore needs to be subtracted from the contract price when calculating the teacher's expectation damages.

Answer 106

(C) is the best response,

because the statute regulates commercial speech.

Since the statute is only applicable to medical care providers, it is a regulation of commercial speech, which does not receive the same level of protection under the First Amendment as do other forms of speech. In particular, a statute that restricts commercial speech that is not false, deceptive, or illegal is only valid if it directly advances a substantial government interest and is reasonably tailored to achieve the government's objective. Choice C correctly identifies this test as the one the state must pass in order to defend the constitutionality of the statute. Note that this answer does not guarantee that the state will win, but only identifies their best argument in defense of the statute, as the question asked.

(A) is not the best response,

because the statute regulates speech that is not misleading.

While we are told that the telephone calls were occasionally misleading, the statute seeks to prohibit all such calls, not just the misleading ones. While, factually, this choice is inaccurate, the rule of law identified is correct. A state may validly prohibit commercial speech that is false or deceptive. So, if the statue were instead written to prohibit medical care providers from making misleading statements in their solicitations to victims within 30 days of the victim's accident, it would be constitutional as a restriction on deceptive commercial speech.

(B) is not the best response,

because it incorrectly identifies the level of scrutiny used to assess the constitutionality of a restriction on commercial speech.

Since the statute is only applicable to medical care providers, it is a regulation of commercial speech, which does not receive the same level of protection under the First Amendment as do other forms of speech. In particular, a statute that restricts commercial speech that is not false, deceptive, or illegal is only valid if it directly advances a substantial government interest and is reasonably tailored to achieve the government's objective. Thus, the correct level of scrutiny for non-deceptive commercial speech is an intermediate level of scrutiny, rather than rational basis review, as identified by choice B.

(D) is not the best response,

because the statute is not a time, place, and manner restriction.

A time, place, and manner restriction regulates speech based on where and when the speaking takes place, without regard to the content of the speech. That is not the case in this law, which only regulates a particular type of speech (solicitation by medical service providers) based on its content. Since this is a regulation pertaining to non-deceptive commercial speech, the proper inquiry is whether the law directly advances a substantial government interest and is reasonably tailored to achieve its objective.

Answer 107

(C) is the best response,

because it correctly infers that the witness's remark will be admissible under the "present sense impression" hearsay exception.

FRE 803(1), entitled "Present Sense Impression," gives a hearsay exception for "A statement *describing or explaining an event or condition*, made *while or immediately after* the *declarant perceived it*." That's what the witness's statement does. Such statements are considered trustworthy—the hallmark of hearsay exceptions—because they are made contemporaneously with the event they concern, and thus the statement suffers no defects in memory. Furthermore, since such a statement usually would have been made to someone else who was also present, there was an opportunity for at least one other person to correct the statement.

Note that the witness's statement is hearsay even though he's repeating it himself. A hearsay statement is an out-of-court statement offered to prove the truth of its assertion. Here, the witness's statement says that the witness is drunk, and it's offered to prove that the motorist was indeed drunk, so it's hearsay. However, since it fits the present sense impression hearsay exception, it will be admissible. Since C recognizes this, it's the best response.

(A) is not the best response,

because the facts here do not fit that the witness was excited when he made the comment.

In order to be admissible under the "excited utterance" exception to the hearsay rule, an out-of-court statement must meet the requirements in FRE 803(2). It must have been made while a declarant was under the stress of excitement, it must have been due to a startling event or condition, and it must relate to the event or condition. Such statements are considered trustworthy because the "stress of excitement" generated by the event minimizes the possibility of fabrication, since the declarant doesn't have time to consciously reflect on the event.

Under these facts, the key word is "remarked." An excited utterance would require some evidence that the declarant was under stress of excitement when the statement was made; simply "remarking" would not qualify.

Instead, the witness's statement would most likely be admissible under the present sense impression hearsay exception, FRE 803(1), as further described in Choice C.

(B) is not the best response,

because the statement here does not satisfy the prior consistent statement hearsay exclusion under the FRE.

Under FRE 801(d)(1)(B), a prior consistent statement of a currently testifying declarant is admissible only if it is "offered to *rebut an express or implied charge* that the declarant *recently fabricated it or acted from a recent improper influence or motive* in so testifying." There's no indication here that the party not sponsoring the witness (the defendant) has made any express or implied charge of recent fabrication or recent improper influence or motive.

If you chose B, it's probably because you were seduced by the words themselves—"prior consistent statement" *sounds* as though it should be correct. Keep in mind that the prior statements hearsay exclusion for testifying witnesses, FRE 801(d)(1)(B), is both extremely narrow *and* a popular MBE distractor.

Instead, the witness's statement would most likely be admissible under the present sense impression hearsay exception, FRE 803(1), as discussed in Choice C.

(D) is not the best response,

because the appearance of drunkenness is a subject that is appropriate for lay opinion testimony.

As a general rule—and "general" is the operative word here, since there are many exceptions—lay witnesses cannot offer opinion testimony. However, under FRE 701, where a lay opinion would be helpful to understanding the witness's testimony or determining a fact in issue, and is rationally based on the witness's firsthand knowledge, such opinion testimony will be admissible. Testimony is often admitted on this basis when it is a kind of shorthand for various factors that the witness has observed and processed. Here, the witness has presumably observed various aspects of the motorist's behavior (including his inability to stand up), so his conclusion that the witness was "so drunk he can't even stand up" would be admissible as a helpful summary of the witness's observations and conclusion, based on firsthand knowledge.

Beyond that, another problem with choice D is that it does not address the fact that the witness's statement is hearsay. Here, the witness's statement is being offered to prove that the motorist was crocked; thus, it's hearsay, and any correct response would have to address this issue. Since D doesn't do this, and it doesn't recognize that lay opinion testimony would be appropriate here, it's not the best response.

Answer 108

(A) is the best response,

because it addresses the central issue and resolves it satisfactorily.

There are two alternative sources for the company's liability, under these facts: attractive nuisance and landowner's duty to "discovered" trespassers. Under the attractive nuisance doctrine, landowners must use ordinary care to avoid harm to children (those too young to appreciate risk), which is due to a reasonably foreseeable risk, caused by artificial conditions on the land. Also, the risk of injury must outweigh the cost of remedying the dangerous condition. Note that choice A states that the company will only be liable *if* securing the chute could be accomplished at moderate cost. That means that this must be plausibly applicable to the facts, and it must resolve a central issue in the case. That's exactly what A does, since if securing the chute could be done at moderate expense, the company would not be exercising ordinary care by failing to do so, and would be liable due to an "attractive nuisance."

Another alternative is garden-variety landowner liability. The modern trend is to impose a duty of reasonable care on the landowner as to *all* entrants. At common law, the duty depends on the status of the entrant (e.g., licensee, invitee). A discovered trespasser (of whose presence the landowner has reason to know) is owed the duty of reasonable care for the trespasser's safety, as to artificial conditions on the property. Thus, even under standard landowner liability analysis, choice A would be a good choice, since it requires reasonability. As a result, A is the best response.

(B) is not the best response,

because it misstates the standard for determining the company's liability.

There are three general sources of strict liability: animals, ultra-hazardous activities, and defective products (strict liability can also be imposed by case law or statute). There is no strict liability just because an injury occurs on one's property or an unsafe condition exists thereon; fault, at least *negligence*, must be proven.

Since B would make the company strictly liable for the boy's injuries just because of an artificial condition on its property, it's not the best response.

(C) is not the best response,

because the doctrine of Last Clear Chance does not apply to these facts.

Last Clear Chance is used by plaintiffs to rebut a claim of contributory negligence; it states that a person with the last clear chance to avoid an act, who fails to do so, is liable. It is used to avoid the harsh results of contributory negligence.

Choice C would use Last Clear Chance as a defense by the company, not as a rebuttal by the boy to a contributory negligence defense. Unless the commuter's conduct is considered a superseding force between the company's negligence and the boy's injuries, it's the company's own negligence that will determine its liability. Since choice C fails to recognize this, it's not the best response.

(D) is not the best response,

because it does not determine the company's liability.

The duty a landowner owes to various entrants onto his land is traditionally determined by a hierarchy of duties, depending on whether the entrant is an undiscovered trespasser, a discovered trespasser, a licensee, or an invitee. A discovered trespasser is one whose presence should be known to defendant—here, you know the boy is a discovered trespasser because the facts state that the company knew children were using the slide. A discovered trespasser is owed the duty of reasonable care for the trespasser's safety as to artificial conditions on the land. Thus, even as a *trespasser,* the company would owe the boy a duty of reasonable care. This, coupled with the attractive nuisance doctrine, would require that the company take reasonable steps for the safety of the children. Since D ignores this, it's not the best response.

Answer 109

(B) is the best response,

because it is impossible for both siblings to obtain usable lots.

There are two different schemes when a tenant in common brings an action to partition property. The first, and preferred, method is "partition in kind," in which the court will physically divide the property between the tenants in common. The second is "partition by sale," in which the property is sold, with the proceeds going to the tenants in common in proportion to their share in ownership of the property. Partition by sale will only be ordered when it is impossible to come up with a fair and equitable partition in kind. In this example, it is impossible to come up with an equitable physical division of the lot since it is not large enough to divide into two buildable lots. As a result, the court will order a partition by sale and will rule in favor of the brother.

(A) is not the best response,

because partition in kind is the preferred remedy.

There are two different schemes when a tenant in common brings an action to partition property. The first, and preferred, method is "partition in kind," in which the court will physically divide the property between the tenants in common. The second is "partition by sale," in which the property is sold, with the proceeds going to the tenants in common in proportion to their share in ownership of the property. Partition by sale will only be ordered when it is impossible to come up with a fair and equitable partition in kind. In this example, it is impossible to come up with an equitable physical division of the lot since it is not large enough to divide into two buildable lots. As a result, the court will order a partition by sale, and rule in favor of the brother.

(C) is not the best response,

because the parcel cannot be partitioned equitably.

There are two different schemes when a tenant in common brings an action to partition property. The first, and preferred, method is "partition in kind," in which the court will physically divide the property between the tenants in common. The second is "partition by sale," in which the property is sold, with the proceeds going to the tenants in common in proportion to their share in ownership of the property. Partition by sale will only be ordered when it is impossible to come up with a fair and equitable partition in kind. In this example, it is impossible to come up with an equitable physical division of the lot since it is not large enough to divide into two buildable lots. As a result, the court will order a partition by sale, and rule in favor of the brother.

(D) is not the best response,

because it ignores the zoning ordinance.

Choice D's statement is factually true. If the lot were to be partitioned in kind, it would be appropriate to give her two-thirds of the area since she is the owner of a two-thirds interest in the land. However, the result of such a partition would be that the brother would get a lot that is too small and lacking sufficient frontage to build upon, rendering the brother's parcel worthless. Consequently, the only equitable solution would be to order the sale of the land (partition by sale) and distribute the proceeds to the siblings: two-thirds to the sister and one-third to the brother.

Answer 110

(B) is the best response,

because it states the correct rule and applies it properly to the facts.

Interpleader is a joinder device that allows a person who faces multiple and possibly conflicting claims to property to resolve all claims in one proceeding. Interpleader can be used when the property is a "common fund," making it a very useful procedural device in the insurance context. In the federal system a stakeholder can use one of two different interpleader mechanisms: ***statutory*** interpleader, under 28 U.S.C. § 1335, or ***rule*** interpleader, under FRCP 22. Statutory interpleader eases the subject-matter jurisdictional requirements in a way that Rule interpleader does not. The question tells you that the stakeholder has commenced a statutory interpleader action. The statute, 28 U.S.C. § 1335(a), applies when ***"[t]wo or more adverse claimants, of diverse citizenship*** . . . , are claiming or may claim to be entitled to . . . ***money or property"*** that the stakeholder has in its "custody or possession . . . of the value of ***$500*** or more." The action that Plaintiff has commenced here easily meets the requirements of statutory interpleader. First, statutory interpleader's watered-down diversity requirements are met; the statute requires only "minimal" diversity, i.e., requires only that two or more of the adverse claimants be citizens of different states (versus the usual requirement of complete diversity as between all plaintiffs and all defendants). Since there are at least two "adverse claimants" that are of different citizenship from each other (e.g., a State B claimant and a State C claimant), that's enough to create minimal diversity. (In other words, it's irrelevant that Plaintiff, the stakeholder, is a citizen of State B given that its principal place of business is there and that one claimant is also a citizen of State B.) Second, the watered-down amount-in-controversy requirement is also met, because the value of the fund (here, $1 million) ***exceeds $500***.

(A) is not the best response,

because the rule of diversity that it applies does not apply to federal statutory interpleader.

The federal statutory interpleader mechanism provides an exception to the usual rule of complete diversity. That is, as long as there is diversity between two or more of the adverse claimants, diversity under the federal interpleader statute is met. (See the language of 28 U.S.C. § 1335(a), quoted in the discussion of Choice (B) above.) The fact that the individual commencing the interpleader action—the stakeholder who is in custody of the property, here, Plaintiff—is not diverse from all the claimants is irrelevant. *See State Farm Fire & Casualty Co. v. Tashire*, 386 U.S. 523, 530-531 (1967).

(C) is not the best response,

because the amount-in-controversy requirement that it mentions is irrelevant.

There *is* a context in which the amount in controversy must be $5 million or more, but that context involves ***class actions***; under the Class Action Fairness Act (CAFA), embodied in 28 U.S.C. § 1332(d), any class action in which at least $5 million is in controversy meets the jurisdictional amount, and the requirement of diversity is satisfied as long as at least one member of the plaintiff class is diverse with at least one defendant. But here, since the action is not a class action, this Choice is not correct.

(D) is not the best response,

because the rule of joinder that it applies is irrelevant to federal statutory interpleader actions.

It is true that many federal joinder rules limit joinder to claims that share common facts or law and that are therefore likely to arise from a common origin or from the same transaction. *See, e.g.*, Fed. R. Civ. P. 24(b)(A)(B) (permitting permissive intervention by "anyone . . . who . . . has a claim or defense that shares with the main action a common question of law or fact"). But statutory interpleader is not one of the joinder devices that requires that the claims have a common origin or arise out of a single transaction. In fact, statutory interpleader specifically authorizes the court to maintain the action "although the titles or claims of the conflicting claimants ***do not have a common origin, or are not identical***." 28 U.S.C. § 1335(b). What is critical is the fact that the claims to be resolved "are ***adverse to and independent of one another***." *Id.* And when the stakeholder is confronted by competing demands for payment by beneficiaries under insurance policies, the "adverse and independent claims" requirement is satisfied.

Answer 111

(B) is the best response,

because it correctly identifies that the father will be guilty of involuntary manslaughter.

Remember the process of elimination you should go through when you encounter a homicide problem. First, look at murder as a possibility. A murder is an unlawful killing (neither justifiable nor excusable) with malice aforethought. While malice doesn't require intent, it can be satisfied by "depraved heart," that is, the actor disregards an unreasonably high risk of harm to human life. Here, the father's omission would not rise to this level of negligence (since depraved heart is generally viewed objectively). Since he won't be guilty of murder, the next possibility is involuntary manslaughter, of which the father *will* be guilty.

Specifically, the father will be guilty of criminal negligence manslaughter (the other type, unlawful act manslaughter, is a manslaughter that occurs as a result of or during a *malum in se* misdemeanor or a felony that is not sufficient for felony murder). Predictably, criminal negligence manslaughter is manslaughter that occurs through gross or criminal negligence (either by act or omission). Criminal negligence is a somewhat stricter standard than tortious negligence, which requires a higher degree of unreasonability. (However, criminal negligence, like tortious negligence, is generally judged objectively.) Under the facts here, the father knew the child was ill, but refused to seek help at a state clinic solely because of his pride. This kind of conduct could easily be considered a criminally negligent omission, especially in view of the father's fiduciary relationship with his children. Since B best characterizes the facts here, it's the best response.

(A) is not the best response,

because the father's conduct would not qualify as murder.

Common-law murder is an unlawful killing (neither justifiable nor excusable) with malice aforethought. While malice aforethought does not require ill-will, it would require either intent to kill, knowledge that death or unreasonably high risk of injury will result, or intent to commit a felony. While the father will be culpable for failing to get medical attention for his child, this would not rise to the level of intent or knowledge of an unreasonably high risk of injury. As a result, A is not the best response.

(C) is not the best response,

because the father's conduct would not qualify as voluntary manslaughter.

Voluntary manslaughter is essentially murder except it is committed under adequate provocation (e.g., heat of passion). Under the facts here, the father didn't commit a murder. Common-law murder is an unlawful killing (neither justifiable nor excusable) with malice aforethought. While malice aforethought does not require ill-will, it would require either intent to kill, knowledge that death or unreasonably high risk of injury will result, or intent to commit a felony. While the father will be culpable for failing to get medical attention for his child, this would not rise to the level of intent or knowledge of an unreasonably high risk of injury.

In any case, even if the father's conduct did rise to the level of murder, he wasn't provoked, so he couldn't be guilty of voluntary manslaughter. As a result, C is not the best response.

(D) is not the best response,

because the father *will* be guilty of involuntary manslaughter.

In fact, the father will be guilty of involuntary manslaughter of the criminal negligence type. Criminal negligence manslaughter is manslaughter that occurs through gross or criminal negligence (either by act or omission). Under the facts here, the father knew the child was ill, but refused to seek help at a state clinic solely because of his pride. This kind of conduct could easily be considered a criminally negligent omission, especially in view of the father's fiduciary relationship with his children.

If you chose this response, it could be because you placed too much importance on the fact that the child died as a result of the illness. *However,* a "killing" takes place whenever a death is hastened by any time at all (e.g., killing someone who was to be executed in five minutes could still be murder, if the requisite *mens rea* existed). The facts here state that the child's death was hastened because he was weakened by malnutrition. Thus, the father is guilty of some form of homicide, making D not the best response.

Answer 112

(A) is the best response,

because the statement falls within FRE 408's blanket prohibition of settlement statements offered to prove liability for a disputed claim.

FRE 408 covers not only statements that relate to the proposed settlement itself, but also collateral statements (what the rule calls "conduct or a statement made during compromise negotiations about the claim[.]") Here, the statement about slush was made during the course of settlement negotiations, since the plaintiff "threatened to sue" and the manager sought a "release . . . from any claims" of the plaintiff. So the statement, though arguably collateral, is covered. (The fact that the conversation also concerned payment of medical bills—as to which collateral statements are not excluded, under FRE 409—doesn't matter, because the statement at issue must survive *both* the bans in FRE 408 and 409 in order to be admissible.)

(B) is not the best response,

because although the statement may be an admission by a party opponent, it still falls within FRE 408's blanket prohibition of settlement statements offered to prove liability for a disputed claim.

As the defendant's statement is being offered by a party opponent, it would not be considered hearsay under FRE 801(d)(2)(A), but it still must survive an objection under FRE 408. Here, they were in settlement negotiations, as the plaintiff "threatened to sue" and the manager sought a "release . . . from any claims" of the plaintiff. Introducing the statement of slush on the entry is an attempt to prove liability through a statement made during the course of settlement negotiations and will be excluded.

(C) is not the best response,

because although the statement may be an admission by an agent about a matter within the scope of his authority, it still falls within FRE 408's blanket prohibition of settlement statements offered to prove liability for a disputed claim.

As the defendant's statement is being offered by a party opponent, and the manager was discussing matters within a manager's scope of authority, it would not be considered hearsay under FRE 801(d)(2)(D), but it still must survive an objection under FRE 408. Here, the parties were in settlement negotiations, as the plaintiff "threatened to sue" and the manager sought a "release . . . from any claims" of the plaintiff. Introducing the statement of slush on the entry is an attempt to prove liability through a statement made during the course of settlement negotiations and will be excluded.

(D) is not the best response,

because any "conduct or a statement made during compromise negotiations about the claim" is excluded by FRE 408. In other words, even statements that are somewhat collateral to the discussion of settlement itself are excluded, if the statements were part of the general settlement discussion.

Here, the parties were in settlement negotiations, as the plaintiff "threatened to sue" and the manager sought a "release . . . from any claims" of the plaintiff. Introducing the statement of slush on the entry is an attempt to prove liability through a statement made during the course of settlement negotiations and will be excluded.

Answer 113

(A) is the best response,

because if the court denies the motion under the circumstances described in this choice, Rule 37(a)(5)

(B) leaves the court no choice but to make the attorney's fee award.

Before we look at the attorney's-fees-as-sanctions issue, it's worth examining the procedural correctness of the *manufacturer's* conduct: Notice that the manufacturer raised its objection to the document-production request but then took no other affirmative acts to shield itself from the request. The manufacturer *could* have taken the affirmative step of seeking a "protective order" from the trial court, as authorized by Rule 26(c)(1). But the manufacturer was not *required* to take this step, and did not expose itself to any serious "extra" sanctions by not seeking the order and instead waiting for the driver to move to compel discovery (since the manufacturer faced the same risk of sanctions if its refusal to produce was held to be wrongful whether the court's holding came in response to the manufacturer's motion to protect or in response to the driver's motion to compel).

Once the driver moved for an order compelling the document production, the motion was governed by Rule 37. More specifically, Rule 37(a)(3)(B) says that

> "A party seeking discovery may move for an order compelling an answer [or] production[.] This motion may be made if: . . . (iv) a party ***fails to produce documents*** . . . as requested under Rule 34."

But Choice (A) tells you to assume that the court "wholly denies" the motion. (Such a denial is a very plausible holding for the court to make on these facts: Rule 26(b)(1) says that "Parties may obtain discovery regarding any nonprivileged matter that is relevant to any party's claim or defense and ***proportional to the needs of the case***, considering the importance of the issues at stake in the action, the amount in controversy, the parties' relative access to relevant information, the parties' resources, the importance of the discovery in resolving the issues, and ***whether the burden or expense of the proposed discovery outweighs its likely benefit.***" Requiring the manufacturer to supply documents about accidents having no apparent connection to steering wheel problems is just the sort of large-scale and time-consuming request that a court might well decide was wholly disproportional to the "needs of the case.")

So we need to know how Rule 37 deals with sanctions in the event the court denies the motion to compel. That issue is dealt with by Rule 37(a)(5)(B), which says:

> "If the motion [to compel discovery] is denied, the court ***may*** issue any protective order authorized under Rule 26(c) and ***must***, after giving an opportunity to be heard, ***require the movant, the attorney filing the motion, or both to pay the party or deponent who opposed the motion its reasonable expenses incurred in opposing the motion, including attorney's fees***. But the court must not order this payment if the motion was substantially justified or other circumstances make an award of expenses unjust."

The key word in the above-quoted passage is the word "must" in the middle of the first sentence -- that word means that if the court wholly denies the motion, the court has ***no choice*** but to "require the movant [and/or her lawyer] to pay the party . . . who opposed the motion its reasonable expenses incurred in opposing the motion, including ***attorney's fees***[,]" unless the special circumstances spelled out in the second sentence are present. But here, Choice (A) tells you to assume that the court "believes that the motion was not substantially justified and that such a fee award would not be unjust," thus making it clear that none of the special conditions that would relieve the court of its obligation (and even its authority) to order payment of the expenses as a sanction exist here. So Choice (A), by emphasizing that an order that the driver pay the manufacturer's attorney's fees incurred in opposing the motion to compel is not discretionary but mandatory on the part of the court, is legally correct.

(B) is not the best response,

because it incorrectly says that the court has discretion to order or not order the driver to reimburse the attorney's fees.

As is discussed more fully in the treatment of Choice (A) above, if the court wholly denies the motion to compel, and neither of the special circumstances in the second sentence of Rule 37(a)(5)(B) (e.g., "the motion was substantially justified") is present, the court "must" (not "may") order that the motion's opponent be reimbursed for its reasonable expenses, including attorney's fees, incurred in opposing the motion. So Choice (B), by indicating that even where the special circumstances are not present, a reimbursement order is only discretionary, is legally incorrect.

(C) is not the best response,

because the sanction of expense-reimbursement was not dependent on the manufacturer's having made a motion for a protective order.

It's true that the manufacturer had the *right* to seek a protective order against being required to produce the objected-to documents. (For more about this right, see the first paragraph in the discussion of Choice (A) above.) But such a motion for a protective order was ***optional*** on the manufacturer's part—the manufacturer was free to instead do nothing (beyond noting its objection, and its reasons for making that objection, in a timely response to the production request), and wait for the requesting party (the driver) to make her own motion to compel. And nothing in Rule 37(a)(5)(B)'s procedures regarding sanctions in the event the motion to compel is wholly denied makes those sanctions weaker or less available because the opponent of the motion never sought a protective order. (The overall approach of Rule 37—applicable whether the motion to compel succeeds or fails—is that "the loser pays" the winner's litigation expenses in making or opposing the motion.) So Choice (C), by asserting that the manufacturer's failure to seek a protective order prevents the court from awarding sanctions to that party, relies on a wholly-irrelevant fact, and is flatly incorrect.

(D) is not the best response,

because the driver's failure to try to resolve the dispute without court action would eliminate any right the driver might otherwise have to recover sanctions if she prevailed on the motion.

This choice is a bit tricky, because its wrongness stems from the non-occurrence of an event the significance of which would be apparent only if you knew a particular detail about how Rule 37 limits the award of sanctions to a successful movant. First, notice that of the four choices this is the only one that assumes that the driver has *succeeded* in her motion. Therefore, sanctions are governed by Rule 37(a)(5)(A), which says that

> ***"If the motion is granted—or if the disclosure or requested discovery is provided after*** the motion was filed -- the court must, after giving an opportunity to be heard, require the party or deponent whose conduct necessitated the motion, the party or attorney advising that conduct, or both to ***pay the movant's reasonable expenses incurred in making the motion, including attorney's fees***. But the court must not order this payment if:
>
> (i) ***the movant filed the motion before attempting in good faith to obtain the disclosure or discovery without court action***;
> (ii) the opposing party's nondisclosure, response, or objection was substantially justified; or
> (iii) other circumstances make an award of expenses unjust."

In analyzing Choice (D), the key provision in the above language is subsection (i): the court not only *isn't required* to award sanctions to the victorious movant, but is *forbidden* to award her sanctions, if "the movant filed the motion ***before attempting in good faith to obtain the disclosure or discovery without court action[.]"*** The facts tell us that "After the driver's lawyer received this response, she made no attempt to contact the manufacturer's lawyer. Instead, the driver's lawyer made a motion. . . . " If the driver's lawyer brought the motion without even trying to contact her adversary, she couldn't have "attempt[ed] in good faith to obtain the . . . discovery without court action." And by failing to try to resolve the matter without court intervention, she deprived the judge of even the power—let alone the obligation—to award her any expense reimbursement as a sanction in the event she prevailed on the motion to compel. Therefore, Choice (D)—by asserting that the court would have power to award the driver attorney's fees assuming the manufacturer's objection was not "substantially justified"—is legally incorrect.

Answer 114

(C) is the best response,

because intimidation is not protected free speech.

To be valid, restrictions on the content of speech must be narrowly tailored to promote a compelling government interest. As a result, there are several narrow categories of speech where such a restriction is justified and that do not receive protection from the First Amendment. Speech within these categories can be validly prohibited based on the content of the speech. One such category is words intended to intimidate the person who is the target of the speech. It is permissible to prohibit such speech whether or not the speaker actually intends to carry out the threats. An example of such a statute is the one at issue in *Virginia v. Black* (2003), in which the Supreme Court upheld a statute that prohibited cross burning with the intent to intimidate. Although the burning of a cross could be considered a form of symbolic speech, the intent to intimidate another renders it a "true threat," even if the individual burning the cross does not actually intend to harm the person they are intimidating.

(A) is not the best response,

because the man intended to intimidate his neighbor.

To be valid, restrictions on the content of speech must be narrowly tailored to promote a compelling government interest. As a result, there are several narrow categories of speech where such a restriction is justified and that do not receive protection from the First Amendment. Speech within these categories can be validly prohibited based on the content of the speech. One such category is words intended to intimidate the person who is the target of the speech. It is permissible to prohibit such speech whether or not the speaker actually intends to carry out the threats. An example of such a statute is the one at issue in *Virginia v. Black* (2003), in which the Supreme Court upheld a statute that prohibited cross burning with the intent to intimidate. Although the burning of a cross could be considered a form of symbolic speech, the intent to intimidate another renders it a "true threat," even if the individual burning the cross does not actually intend to harm the person they are intimidating.

(B) is not the best response,

because it is irrelevant whether or not he was trespassing.

It is not permissible for a state to punish an individual for speaking simply because at the time they were also engaged in another criminal act. This answer choice correctly comes to the conclusion that the man may be convicted under the statute, but arrives at that conclusion for the wrong reason. The statute is constitutional because it is permissible to prohibit speech that constitutes a "true threat." (See the explanation for choice C above.) Here, the man intended to intimidate his neighbor, in violation of the statute, and may be convicted without regard to whether or not he was trespassing at the time.

(D) is not the best response,

because the Thirteenth Amendment is inapplicable to the situation.

The Thirteenth Amendment prohibits involuntary servitude (slavery). It has no application to whether or not racially motivated threats may be prohibited by law. The reason that the statute under which the man is being prosecuted is constitutional is that it prohibits speech that constitutes a "true threat." Content-based restrictions on speech are only valid if they are narrowly tailored to achieve a compelling state interest, so the statute would not be constitutional if it criminalized all racially motivated speech, since, absent the intent to intimidate another, there is no compelling interest served by restricting the right of an individual to make such statements.

Answer 115

(A) is the best response,

because there was no consideration for the creditor's promise not to sue.

In order to be enforceable, a contract must be supported by consideration. Here, the creditor promised not to sue on the debt (a right he had since the debtor was late repaying the debt). Foregoing this legal right furnishes consideration on the creditor's side. However, the debtor has supplied no consideration. His only promise under the contract was to pay the liquidated debt by December 1st. However, the debtor was already under that obligation—in fact, he was already late in paying. In essence, he has only promised to do something he was already legally obligated to do. The preexisting duty rule states that the promise to do something one is already obligated to do is not consideration. The lack of consideration embodied in the debtor's promise makes the contract fail for lack of consideration. Accordingly, the creditor's promise is not binding.

(B) is not the best response,

because the creditor has provided consideration.

In order to be enforceable, a contract must be supported by consideration. Here, the creditor promised not to sue on the debt (a right he had since the debtor was late repaying the debt). Foregoing this legal right furnishes consideration on the creditor's side. This contract will fail because of the *debtor's* promise failing to constitute consideration, not the creditor's. The preexisting duty rule, discussed in the explanation for choice A above, dictates that the debtor's promise to pay an already-owed liquidated debt cannot furnish consideration for the creditor's promise to refrain from suing, which is consideration, since the creditor is foregoing a legal right.

(C) is not the best response,

because it misstates the law.

The promise to allow a debtor to delay payment on a past debt is only enforceable if consideration is provided by the debtor because of the preexisting duty rule. The preexisting duty rule states that the promise to do something one is already obligated to do is not consideration. Thus, for the promise to allow additional time for a debtor to pay a liquidated sum, the debtor must promise to provide additional consideration (i.e., not simply to pay the sum already owed).

(D) is not the best response,

because the promise to allow more time to pay is only enforceable if the debtor provides additional consideration.

In order to be enforceable, a contract must be supported by consideration. Here, the creditor promised not to sue on the debt (a right he had since the debtor was late repaying the debt). Foregoing this legal right furnishes consideration on the creditor's side. However, the debtor has supplied no consideration. His only promise under the contract was to pay the liquidated debt by December 1st. However, the debtor was already under that obligation—in fact, he was already late in paying. In essence, he has only promised to do something he was already legally obligated to do. The preexisting duty rule states that the promise to do something one is already obligated to do is not consideration. The lack of consideration embodied in the debtor's promise means that there was no bargained-for exchange. As a result, the contract will fail for lack of consideration, and the creditor's promise is not binding.

Answer 116

(B) is the correct response,

because none of the exceptions to the general rule that a medical professional's duty of care extends only to his or her patient apply in this instance.

One exception to this rule is found in *Tarasoff v. The Regents of California* (1976), which states that a medical professional does have a duty of care to others when the patient poses a threat to others. But this scenario was not presented by these facts. As the patient was only a threat to himself, and was an adult, the doctor did not owe a duty of care to non-patients. Additional facts in the problem further support that no duty of care was owed, as the father was not present at his son's appointment and did not witness his son's suicide.

(A) is not the best response,

because physical impact is not required for the father to prevail.

Virtually all jurisdictions have rejected the impact rule in cases involving negligent infliction of emotional distress. Thus, this response states the right result for the wrong reason. The correct reason is that, in general, a medical professional's duty of care extends only to his or her patients, and thus no duty of care is owed to the father of the patient. As the patient was only a threat to himself, and was an adult, the doctor did not owe a duty of care to non-patients. Additional facts in the problem further support that no duty of care was owed, as the father was not present at his son's appointment and did not witness his son's suicide.

(C) is not the best response,

because being a member of the patient's immediate family is irrelevant in this kind of emotional distress case.

In a *bystander* case, a family member who suffers emotional distress upon witnessing a negligently caused injury to a family member may recover. In this case, however, the facts do not support a bystander case, as the father was not present at his son's appointment and did not witness his son's suicide. This fact pattern instead focuses on the duty of care owed by a medical professional. The general rule is that a medical professional's duty of care extends only to his or her patients, so the plaintiff here cannot recover.

(D) is not the best response,

because foreseeability is ordinarily not sufficient to create a duty to a non-patient of a medical professional.

In general, a medical professional's duty of care extends only to his or her patients, and thus no duty of care is owed to the father of the patient. As the patient was only a threat to himself, and was an adult, the doctor did not owe a duty of care to non-patients. Additional facts in the problem further support that no duty of care was owed, as the father was not present at his son's appointment and did not witness his son's suicide.

Answer 117

(B) is the best response,

because it correctly indicates that both an injunction and damages are appropriate remedies in this action.

The grant here created a life estate determinable *pur autre vie* in the church, and a vested remainder in the grandchildren as a class. As life tenant, the church is obliged not to unreasonably impair the value of the property. Since the church allowed the sand and gravel to be removed, it will have to cease doing so and it will be liable for the damage already done. The added wrinkle here is that the vested remaindermen may not all exist yet, since there may yet be other grandchildren born to the "class." Thus, the appropriate remedy is to impound the damages until no more members can be added to the class of grandchildren—that is, until all of the owner's children die, because only then can the class of grandchildren be established. Since B states the appropriate result, it's the best response.

(A) is not the best response,

because while it correctly recognizes that the plaintiffs will succeed, it does not give the correct reason.

The estates created in the conveyance here were a life estate determinable *pur autre vie* in the church, and a vested remainder in the grandchildren in the form of a class gift (the class being the owner's grandchildren). As a life estate holder, the church is obliged not to unreasonably impair the value of the property. If the life estate holder does so, his estate does not cease; however, he will be liable to the vested remainderman for the diminution in value. Since A incorrectly states that committing waste terminates the life estate, it's not the best response.

(C) is not the best response,

because it incorrectly states that damages will not be awarded because the owner and his son are not parties to the action.

In fact, the relevant parties here are the church and the vested remaindermen—the grandchildren and a representative for the as-yet unborn grandchildren, as a class. The church, because it is allowing waste to be committed on the premises, is liable to the vested remaindermen. It is liable for the damages done so far, and can be enjoined from continuing to remove the sand and gravel. Choice C incorrectly states that damages will not be available because the owner and his son are not parties to the action. They aren't necessary, and so C is not the best response.

(D) is not the best response,

because it incorrectly states that the injunction will be denied.

A life estate holder, as the church is here, is obliged not to unreasonably impair the value of the property. Allowing sand and gravel to be removed would constitute waste. As a result, the church will be liable to the vested remaindermen for the diminution in value, and will be required to stop the waste from occurring. Thus, the vested remaindermen should recover damages *and* the injunction should be granted. Since D is only half right, it is not the best response.

Answer 118

(D) is the best response,

because the element of force or fear was missing, and thus the defendant would not be liable for robbery.

The key here is simply to know the elements of robbery. Robbery is a larceny from either a person or in the presence of a person, by either force or fear. Here, the defendant's victim was not cognizant of the fact his wallet was being taken, so he wasn't in fear, and since the defendant merely removed his wallet, there wasn't force, either.

The subsequent slap wouldn't be considered force for purposes of determining the defendant's guilt, because the force did not relate to the crime. While the use of force encompasses the period immediately after the taking, this only controls if the wrongdoer uses force to stop the victim from catching him or regaining the property.

Under facts like the ones in choice D, the force would be considered separate from the taking. Since the defendant would not satisfy the elements of robbery, he won't be guilty, making D the best response.

(A) is not the best response,

because the defendant likely would be guilty of robbery.

Robbery is a larceny from either a person or in the presence of a person, by either force or fear. The element that's most in question under the facts in choice A is the larceny from the person or in the presence of a person. However, the crime would be considered in the woman's presence, since it involved the area she would control if not for the force or fear used by the defendant. Since the defendant would likely be guilty of robbery, A is not the best response.

(B) is not the best response,

because the defendant would likely be guilty of robbery under these facts.

Robbery is a larceny from either a person or in the presence of a person, by either force or fear. Here, although the defendant did not employ force, his confederate did, and so together they would be liable for robbery, since their conduct would fit all the elements of robbery. Since the defendant would likely be guilty of robbery, B is not the best response.

(C) is not the best response,

because the defendant likely would be guilty of robbery.

Robbery is a larceny from either a person or in the presence of a person, by either force or fear. Here, the force was involved in compelling the woman to make the phone call. When the defendant later took the jewels, he satisfied the remaining element of robbery. Since the defendant would likely be guilty of robbery, C is not the best response.

Answer 119

(B) is correct,

because a suit may be brought on behalf of a minor by a parent or guardian.

Federal Rule of Civil Procedure 17(c)(1) says that "The following representatives may sue or defend on behalf of a ***minor*** or an incompetent person: (A) a ***general guardian*** . . . or (D) a like fiduciary." Rule 17(c)(2) then says that "A minor or an incompetent person ***who does not have a duly appointed representative*** may sue ***by a next friend or by a guardian ad litem***." So in this case, assuming that neither parent has been appoi nted to be a "general guardian" for the child (i.e., his guardian for all legal purposes), either parent can file suit as a "next friend" of the child, as authorized by 17(c)(2). "A next friend is one who, without being [a] regularly-appointed guardian, represents an infant plaintiff." *Till v. Hartford Acc. & Indem. Co.*, 124 F.2d 405, 408 (10th Cir. 1941). So the suit would be captioned "[Parent] as next friend of [Child] v. Motorcyclist."

Not only is the parent *permitted* to appear as the named plaintiff/next friend, but under the Federal Rules there *must* be some competent adult who is given responsibility for protecting the interests of the minor if the suit is brought solely in the name of the minor. That's because the final sentence of Rule 17(c)(2) (which follows the sentence quoted above) says that "The court ***must appoint a guardian ad litem—or issue another appropriate order***—to protect a minor or incompetent person who is unrepresented in an action." So it's very likely that the court will either require that the child's parent be the named plaintiff as a "next friend" or insist that the parent or someone else with the child's welfare at heart be named as a guardian *ad litem* (i.e., guardian for the limited purposes of protecting the child's interest in the litigation).

(A) is not the best choice,

because the rule that it asserts—that the plaintiff in a lawsuit must be the real party in interest—is correct in most situations, but not correct in the special situation where the party in interest is a minor.

Federal Rule 17 (which is in fact entitled "Real Party in Interest") begins by announcing the general rule that "An action must be prosecuted in the name of the real party in interest." But Rule 17 then goes on to list various exceptions to this rule. One exception is that a "guardian" is among several types of people all of whom "may sue in their own names without joining the person for whose benefit the action is brought." Rule 17(a)(1)(C). So if the child's parent or some other adult had been appointed as the child's guardian for all purposes, the guardian *would* be allowed to bring suit in his own name. Furthermore, Rule 17(c)(1) says that "A minor or an incompetent person who does not have a duly appointed representative may sue by a next friend or by a guardian ad litem." So even if, say, no one had been appointed a general guardian for the child, the child's parent could in effect appoint himself or herself "next friend," and bring suit in his/her name as authorized by 17(c)(1). So Choice (A), by saying that the child must be named as plaintiff because he is the real party in interest, is simply wrong.

(C) is not the best choice,

because the insurance carrier is not in fact a "real party in interest."

First, as a matter of nomenclature, under the FRCP, the phrase "real party in interest" refers *only* to people on the ***plaintiff*** side of the action, not those on the defense side. So even if there were some rule requiring that the insurance carrier be made a defendant, that result would not be correctly explained by saying that the carrier was a "real party in interest."

More substantively, there simply is no procedural rule in the federal system that would require the joinder of the insurer as a party at all. It's true that in some circumstances, a party must be joined—whether as a plaintiff or as a defendant—because that party's presence in the action is required in order for the court to do justice in the action. *See* FRCP 19. But a party is a required party only if one of several quite specific fact patterns exists: either (1) in that party's absence, the court cannot accord complete relief among the existing parties, or (2) the person alleged to be required to be joined claims an interest related to the action's subject and that person is so situated that not joining the person may "impair or impede the person's ability to protect the interest" or "leave an existing party subject to a substantial risk of incurring double, multiple, or otherwise inconsistent obligations because of the interest." FRCP 19(a)(1)(B). Here, the motorcyclist's insurance carrier does not fit into any of these categories: First, the carrier's absence does not prevent complete relief among the existing parties. Second, the carrier does not have an interest that needs to be protected in the current lawsuit, because the motorcyclist's liability can be determined without assessing his insurance situation. Finally, there is no person already a party (and the only plausible "already present" party would be the motorcyclist) who would be subjected to double, multiple, or otherwise inconsistent obligations—the motorcyclist will be entitled to have the insurer pay any judgment and/or legal expense up to the policy limits, even if the carrier is not joined.

(D) is not the best choice,

because the underlying rule of liability that it asserts is not legally correct.

Whether a party must be joined in a lawsuit is governed by the rules determining who is a required party, and those rules are set out in FRCP 19. Even if the aunt and uncle were joint tortfeasors with the motorcyclist, "[i]t has long been the rule that it *is **not necessary for all joint tortfeasors to be named as defendants in a single lawsuit.***" *Temple v. Synthes Corp., Ltd.*, 498 U.S. 5, at 7 (1990). The Advisory Committee Notes to the 1966 amendments to Rule 19(a) state that "a tortfeasor with the usual 'joint-and-several' liability is merely a ***permissive*** party to an action against another with like liability." Therefore, it is up to the child (or his lawyer or guardian) to decide whether to make permissive joinder of the aunt and uncle.

Furthermore, as a matter of substantive tort law, it's not at all clear that the aunt and uncle would indeed be primarily or secondarily liable as this choice asserts. Since they didn't give the motorcyclist permission to use the cycle or even know that he was planning to do so, they can't be primarily liable for, say, negligent entrustment. And unless there existed a somewhat unusual state statute making them strictly or vicariously liable for damage done by a vehicle or instrument they owned, they would not have secondary liability.

Answer 120

(C) is the best response,

because the recording statute protects the creditor's interest.

Under the race-notice statute applicable in this jurisdiction, a second-in-time transferee is only protected if she *both* takes for value without notice of the prior interest *and* records her conveyance first. Here, the aunt meets neither of these requirements. Although the aunt had no actual knowledge of the judgment lien on the debtor's land, she will be charged with constructive notice because the creditor's interest had been recorded and would have been located easily had the aunt conducted a title search before making the loan. Additionally, the aunt did not record the mortgage until after the creditor's lien was recorded. Although the creditor never filed a lien on the debtor's subsequently acquired land, the judgment lien statute makes the already-recorded judgment a lien on not only the land owned by the debtor at the time of the judgment, but also any property acquired within ten years of the filing of the judgment. Since the debtor purchased the mortgaged land only two years after the judgment was filed, a lien will be placed on the land by operation of the statute. Because the creditor was first in time and the recording statute does not protect the aunt, the creditor's lien will be prior to that of the aunt.

(A) is not the best response,

because the creditor recorded first.

As discussed in the explanation for choice C above, the jurisdiction's race-notice statute does not protect the aunt's mortgage. While in many circumstances a judgment lien will be subordinate to a mortgage lien, this is not the case when the judgment lien creditor takes first and records first. The general reason why a judgment lien is not protected under a recording statute is that most jurisdictions do not treat judgment creditors as bona fide purchasers for value. However, the protection of a recording statute is only necessary for subsequent purchasers. In this case, the judgment lien is first in time and was recorded before the mortgage, so it has priority over the mortgage lien without need for the protection of the recording statute.

(B) is not the best response,

because the aunt was not a purchase money mortgagee.

As discussed in the explanation for choice C, above, the jurisdiction's race-notice statute does not protect the aunt's mortgage. Additionally, choice B incorrectly states that the aunt's mortgage is a purchase money mortgage. A purchase money mortgage is a mortgage on property that is given as security for a loan used to purchase that property. In this problem, the debtor already owned the land when he got the loan from his aunt.

(D) is not the best response,

because the creditor's judgment lien will have priority whether or not the aunt conducted a title search of the property.

As discussed in the explanation for choice C above, the jurisdiction's race-notice statute can only protect a subsequent conveyance if both the subsequent interest-holder takes for value and without notice and records first. Since the creditor's interest was first recorded, it will be the prior lien on the debtor's property whether or not the aunt conducted a title search. There is no requirement that a purchaser of an interest in land conduct a title search, but it is generally wise to do so in order to avoid being in the aunt's position in this problem.

Answer 121

(A) is the best response,

because this is a statement of a party opponent, and the best evidence rule does not apply to this particular audiotape.

What the defendant said to the plaintiff, even in a private conversation, is an admission of a party. It can therefore be introduced against that party, under FRE 801(d)(2)(A)'s hearsay exclusion for a statement that "is offered against an opposing party and (A) was made by the party in an individual or representative capacity." The plaintiff has personal knowledge of what the defendant said and can testify about it.

The fact that the audiotape might be better evidence of what the defendant actually said makes no difference. The Best Evidence Rule (FRE 1002) applies only where a party is trying to "prove [the] content" of a writing, recording or photograph. Here, because the plaintiff did not obtain all her knowledge of the conversation from the audiotape, she is not "proving the content" of the audiotape—she's proving the content of a live discussion, and the fact that the statements happen to have been captured on audiotape is just a coincidence. So the Best Evidence Rule doesn't apply.

(B) is not the best response,

because, even though the original document rule (also called the Best Evidence Rule) does apply to audiotapes, the plaintiff is not proving the contents of the recording.

The original document rule, FRE Rule 1002, applies to writings, *recordings*, and photographs. Nonetheless, in this case, the original document rule does not apply. As noted in the analysis of choice A above, the testimony is admissible because the plaintiff will testify to what she heard directly from the defendant, not about what she heard on the audiotape. Therefore, she would not be attempting to prove the content of the audiotape and there would be no violation of the original document rule.

(C) is not the best response,

because FRE Rule 1002 (the Best Evidence Rule or the "original document rule") requires a recording to be introduced only when its contents are being proved, which is not the case in this problem.

Here the plaintiff is offering to testify about what she heard directly from the defendant, not about what she heard on the audiotape. The fact that an audiotape was contemporaneously made does not mean that the tape has to be produced, since the plaintiff has independent knowledge of what the defendant said. If the problem were changed so that the plaintiff only learned of the defendant's statements by listening to an audiotape, then the audiotape would have to be produced.

(D) is not the best response,

because there is no rule automatically barring evidence obtained by deception.

Moreover, the evidence obtained by deception (the secretly recorded audiotape) was not in fact offered. Some state and federal statutes do regulate secret recordings of conversations, and violation of such statutes sometimes means that recordings obtained in violation thereof must be excluded. But the recording was not offered in evidence in this problem. As noted in the discuss of choice A above, only the statements made by the defendant were offered, and they would be admissible whether or not a contemporaneous recording was made.

Answer 122

(A) is the best response,

because under the federal rules, only the court can enter a default judgment if plaintiff's claim is not "for a sum certain or a sum that can be made certain by computation."

One key factor that determines how and when a default judgment may be entered is whether the claim can be considered for a "sum certain"—when the claim meets this definition, entry of a default judgment for that amount is essentially ministerial, whereas if the sum is not certain, the procedure is far more complex and a judge's participation is required. The entry of default judgments is governed by FRCP 55. Rule 55(b)(1) (entitled "By the Clerk"), says that "If the plaintiff's claim ***is for a sum certain or a sum that can be made certain by computation***, the clerk—on the plaintiff's request, with an affidavit showing the amount due—***must enter judgment for that amount*** and costs against a defendant who has been defaulted for not appearing and who is neither a minor nor an incompetent person." So at least where the defendant never answers or otherwise "appears" in the suit, if the claim is for a "sum certain" (or for a sum that "by computation" can be made certain), ***no involvement by the judge*** is necessary, and the clerk of the court not only may but "must" enter judgment for that amount at the plaintiff's request, as long as the plaintiff submits an affidavit showing the amount due. So if, on our facts here, the professor's claim met the requirements for a "sum certain," the answer to the question would be yes, the clerk could enter judgment without further action by anyone (making Choice (C) correct).

However, the professor's claim here is definitely ***not*** one "for a sum certain or a sum that can be made certain by computation." A claim is not for a sum certain "unless there ***is no doubt as to the amount*** to which a plaintiff is entitled as a result of the defendant's default." *KPS & Assocs. v. Designs by FMC, Inc.*, 318 F.3d 1, 19-20 (1st Cir. 2003). Or, as the idea is sometimes put, the claim must be for some sort of ***"liquidated amount."*** Examples of sums certain include a suit to enforce another court's money judgment and a suit on a promissory note—in those situations, the damages can be "determined without resort to extrinsic proof[.]" *Id*. Here, the professor is claiming damages for "intangible harm" to her reputation, and it cannot be said that there is "no doubt" about what the proper amount is (even assuming liability), or that the amount can be determined without resort to proof other than that contained in the complaint or the professor's affidavit. Furthermore, where the plaintiff seeks attorney's fees, those fees are virtually never deemed to constitute an "amount certain," even if the claim being sued on *is* for such an amount.

Once it's clear that the claim is not for "a sum certain or a sum that can be made certain by computation," the method for entering a default judgment is completely different than the clerk-administered method mentioned above for sum-certain claims. Now, the situation is governed by Rule 55(b)(2) (entitled "By the Court"). Under that section, "the party must ***apply to the court*** for a default judgment." If the defendant has "appeared" in the action (which the student here did not do), seven days advance notice has to be given to the defendant before the court (i.e., the judge) can conduct any hearing. The judge then determines the appropriate amount for the judgment. In doing so the court "may" (but is not required to) "conduct hearings" in order to "determine the amount of damages." Even when the judge decides that the hearing is not necessary, the judge will typically make a careful review of the pleadings, affidavits, documentary evidence submitted by the plaintiff, etc., to make a reasonable estimate of the actual damages. In other words, the judge does not simply reason that since the complaint was not answered, the allegations in it about damages must be taken at face value. So Choice (A) is an accurate statement about the steps that the judge will have to go through before entering a default judgment on the professor's claim.

(B) is not the best response,

because it is not within the clerk's authority to conduct the type of evidentiary hearing described.

If the claim here were for a "sum certain," then as described in the explanation of Choice (A), the clerk could, indeed would be required to, enter judgment—but that would happen without any evidentiary hearing or even examination of evidence. But the claim here is *not* for a sum certain, so the job of fixing the amount of the judgment must be handled by the judge, not the clerk. And when the judge does this, the judge is permitted—though not required—to conduct an evidentiary hearing of the sort described in this choice.

(C) is not the best response,

because the claim was not for a sum certain.

Under Rule 55(b)(1), if the claim was "for a sum certain or a sum that can be made certain by computation," then the clerk could indeed enter judgment automatically and without notice to the student, as suggested in this choice (at least assuming that the student was neither a minor nor an "incompetent person," and that she had never appeared in the action). But as discussed in the analysis of Choice (A), the claim here does not meet the definition of "sum certain." Therefore, the ministerial procedure carried out by the clerk, as described in this choice, is not available.

(D) is not the best response,

because it incorrectly gives a role to the clerk as hearing officer and incorrectly requires notice to the student.

This choice is correct in suggesting that there are some scenarios in which a seven-day notice has to be given to the defendant in advance of a hearing at which the amount of damages will be set, but the present fact pattern is not such a scenario. Rule 55(b)(2) says that in cases in which the claim is not for a sum certain (so that the judge will have to determine the appropriate judgment amount), seven days advance notice of any hearing by the judge must be given to the defendant if the defendant "has appeared personally or by a representative" previously in the action. But there are two reasons why this advance-notice provision does not apply in the way suggested by this choice: First, the facts tell you that the student never appeared in the action (so she is not entitled to any notice at all) and second, this choice refers to an evidentiary hearing that will be conducted by the clerk, but in reality if an evidentiary hearing is to be conducted (which will happen only where the claim is not for a sum certain) the hearing is conducted by the *judge*, not the clerk. So as is correctly stated in Choice (A), any evidentiary hearing will be conducted by the judge (and it will be in the judge's discretion whether to conduct a true hearing or to simply review documentary evidence), and no advance notice to the student will need to be given if there *is* going to be a hearing.

Answer 123

(B) is the best response,

because it identifies the basis on which the shoe store will be liable.

Invasion of privacy is an "umbrella" tort encompassing four individual torts: the defendant's appropriation of the plaintiff's picture or name for the defendant's own commercial advantage; the defendant's intrusion on the plaintiff's affairs or seclusion; the defendant's publication of facts that place the plaintiff in a false light; and the defendant's public disclosure of private facts about the plaintiff.

The first type (appropriation) is applicable to these facts, since it describes—as does choice B—that the shoe store used the player's picture for profit. While "consent" would be a defense, the shoe store did not have permission under these facts. While the shoe store believed it had permission, this fact is irrelevant – even a reasonable (but mistaken) belief that it had permission would not be a defense, unless the mistake was brought about by the plaintiff's own speech or conduct. In any event, here the store's mistake was unreasonable, given the store's failure to even attempt to verify the photographer's self-interested claim that the player had consented. Since B accurately describes the tort, it's applicable to these facts, and since no other choice is satisfactory, B is the best response.

(A) is not the best response,

because it misstates the law, and does not focus on a central issue.

It isn't the photographer's *taking* the picture that the player finds objectionable, but the shoe store's *use* of the photo, falsely suggesting the player endorsed the shoes. In fact, merely taking one's picture, in public, is not actionable; if you're out in public, you're pretty much fair game for photographers. (Just ask Madonna.) Since A states otherwise and ignores a central issue in the case, it's not the best response.

(C) is not the best response,

because it's irrelevant.

The player's status as a celebrity would not subject him to unauthorized use of his name. In fact, it's the player's fame that *prompted* the shoe store to misappropriate his picture for its commercial advantage; simply being famous doesn't mean the player has waived his right to sue for invasion of privacy. Instead, under these facts, the player will have a valid claim for invasion of privacy in the form of appropriating the plaintiff's name or picture for commercial advantage. As long as he proves this, his status is irrelevant. Since C states otherwise, it's not the best response.

(D) is not the best response,

because it incorrectly suggests that the store's mistake as to consent is a defense.

D suggests that if the shoe store *believed* it had the player's permission, it will not be liable. However, in an invasion of privacy claim based on misappropriation, the defendant's mistaken belief that the plaintiff has consented is fatal—even a *reasonable* mistake as to consent (as long as it is not induced by the plaintiff's own ambiguous conduct or speech) would not be a valid defense. Here, the store's mistaken belief that the player had consented was not even reasonable (given the store's complete lack of effort to verify the photographer's claim of consent), so the mistake is certainly not a defense, as D suggests it is. So D is not the best response.

Answer 124

(B) is correct because,

it correctly recognizes that what's at issue is the Fifth Amendment's impact ***on the federal government***.

The federal government operates the federal courts, and the Fifth Amendment's Due Process Clause, binding on the federal government, applies to the federal judiciary. Therefore, when Congress enacts a statute creating a federal cause of action and includes a nationwide service-of-process provision, the question is whether the federal court's exercise of power to hear a suit comports with the Fifth Amendment standard of due process. Answering that question in turn requires the court to decide whether the defendant has the requisite minimum contacts ***with the entire nation***, not merely with the state where the federal court hearing the suit is located. *See, e.g.,* F,K&M (4th), § 3.18, pp. 172-73, approving of the suggestion that "[i]n applying the minimum-contacts standard to actions under some federal statutes, such as antitrust, or in suits against alien defendants, the court may consider the ***aggregate contacts*** of the defendants ***with the nation as a whole***, rather than simply contacts with the forum state." So even if Defendant has no contacts whatsoever with State B, personal jurisdiction over Defendant will likely be constitutional if the *sum* of its contacts with *all* U.S. states and/or territories satisfies the requirement of Fifth Amendment due process.

(A) is not the best response,

because it incorrectly recites the entity with which the Defendant must have the required minimum contacts.

When Congress enacts a statute creating a federal cause of action and includes a nationwide service-of-process provision in the statute, the test for determining whether service establishes personal jurisdiction is to look to at the defendant's minimum contacts ***with the entire nation***, not merely contacts with the state in which the federal court sits. See the further discussion in Choice (B).

(C) is not the best response,

because it refers to the wrong constitutional amendment and the wrong sort of contacts.

First, when Congress enacts a statute and includes a nationwide service-of-process provision, the sufficiency of Defendant's contacts is determined by reference to the Due Process Clause of the *Fifth Amendment* (not of the Fourteenth Amendment) to the U.S. Constitution. As explained in Choice (A), the federal government operates the federal courts. Therefore, it's the Fifth Amendment's Due Process Clause—binding on the federal government—that applies to this federally-run operation. Since the Due Process Clause of the Fourteenth Amendment applies only to the *states*, and since no state action is involved here, that Amendment is irrelevant. Second, what is determinative is Defendant's contacts with the *entire nation*, not just with State B.

(D) is not the best response,

because it refers to the wrong constitutional Amendment.

When Congress enacts a statute and includes a nationwide service-of-process provision, the court assesses the sufficiency of Defendant's contacts with the nation under the Fifth Amendment to the United States Constitution, and not the Fourteenth Amendment, which applies only to the states. See the further discussion in Choice (C).

Answer 125

(B) is the best response,

because it is irrelevant.

Impeachment is the means of casting doubt on the credibility of the witness. It can be accomplished via either reputation or opinion testimony, under FRE 608(a). The problem here is that the witness's alcoholism would not reflect on his character for truthfulness, which is what "credibility" is all about. Since the evidence isn't relevant to the witness's credibility, it's not admissible under FRE 608(a) (or any other provision).

(A) is not the best response,

because it is a question seeking to show bias or interest, which is a proper basis for intrinsic impeachment under the FRE.

If it's true that the witness is the plaintiff's close friend, this indicates bias, since it's possible that he would lie on the plaintiff's behalf. Thus, the evidence will be relevant to the witness's credibility. Since A fails to recognize that the evidence here will be a proper form of intrinsic impeachment, it's not the best response.

(C) is not the best response,

because it is a question seeking to show a bad character for honesty via unconvicted bad acts, which can be a proper basis for intrinsic impeachment under the FRE.

Impeachment is the means of casting doubt on the credibility of the witness. FRE 608(b) says that "Except for a criminal conviction under Rule 609, *extrinsic evidence* is *not* admissible to prove *specific instances of a witness's conduct* in order to attack or support the witness's character for truthfulness. But the court *may*, on *cross-examination*, allow them [i.e., unconvicted specific instances] to be inquired into if they are probative of the character for truthfulness or untruthfulness of (1) the witness[.]" Failure to report income is a specific instance of bad conduct, and there's no indication that the witness was convicted. But since the matter is probative of the witness's character for truthfulness, the judge has discretion to allow it to be inquired into on cross (which is what's happening here). While it's not certain that the court will allow the question, that's a much more likely outcome than that the court will allow the question about alcoholism (Choice B), which is not probative of truthfulness at all.

(D) is not the best response,

because it is a question seeking to show a prior conviction, which because of the nature of the crime is a proper basis for impeachment under the FRE.

Under FRE 609(a)(2), a witness can be impeached by proof of a conviction "for any crime regardless of the punishment . . . if the court can readily determine that establishing the elements of the crime required proving—or the witness's admitting—a *dishonest act or false statement*." So assuming the questioner had a good-faith basis for believing that the conviction occurred, the question is proper for impeachment whether the crime involved a felony or a misdemeanor, because it necessarily involved dishonesty or false statement. Furthermore, the choice indicates that the conviction is only seven years old, so it meets the 10-year time limit of FRE 609(a).

Answer 126

(D) is the best response,

because it correctly states the standard.

In both federal and state courts, a witness's proper invocation of the privilege against self-incrimination is judged under the "reasonable possibilities" test. Under it, the court must find reasonable grounds for believing the witness is subject to criminal liability (not civil liability or public disgrace), and that his answer will at least provide a link to evidence which may incriminate him, in order to allow him to remain silent. *Hoffman v. U.S.* (1951). Since D correctly states this rule, it's the best response.

(A) is not the best response,

because it overstates the actual standard.

In both federal and state courts, a witness's proper invocation of the privilege against self-incrimination is judged under the "reasonable possibilities" test. Under it, the court must find reasonable grounds for believing the witness is subject to criminal liability (not civil liability or public disgrace), and that his answer will at least provide a link to evidence which may incriminate him, in order to allow him to remain silent. Choice A states a standard that is much stricter than the actual standard. As a result, it's not the best response.

(B) is not the best response,

because it overstates the standard.

In both federal and state courts, a witness's proper invocation of the privilege against self-incrimination is judged under the "reasonable possibilities" test. Under it, the court must find reasonable grounds for believing the witness is subject to criminal liability (not civil liability or public disgrace), and that his answer will at least provide a link to evidence that may incriminate him, in order to allow him to remain silent. B states a standard that is much stricter than the real standard. As a result, it's not the best response.

(C) is not the best response,

because it overstates the standard.

In both federal and state courts, a witness's proper invocation of the privilege against self-incrimination is judged under the "reasonable possibilities" test. Under it, the court must find reasonable grounds for believing the witness is subject to criminal liability (not civil liability or public disgrace), and that his answer will at least provide a link to evidence that may incriminate him, in order to allow him to remain silent. C states a standard that is slightly more strict than the real standard. As a result, it's not the best response.

Answer 127

(B) is the best response,

because it addresses the central issue of the case: whether or not the equipment will be characterized as a fixture.

The factor B discusses—intent—is the single most important factor in determining whether a chattel has become a fixture. If the intent is that the chattel *not* be considered annexed to realty and thus not a fixture, this will be a strong indication that the chattel will be considered personalty by a court. If, as B suggests, the equipment was installed for the tenant's exclusive benefit, it would manifest an *intent* on his part that the equipment not be considered part of the realty. Under these facts, this would mean a judgment in the tenant's favor, refusing the injunction. As a result, B is the best response.

(A) is not the best response,

because it's irrelevant.

The tenant's ability to remove the equipment turns on whether it will be characterized as a fixture or not. If the equipment is not a fixture, then he will be able to remove it. If it *is* considered a fixture, it becomes part of the realty, and he cannot remove it (at which point notice to him *may* become important). Factors that will be taken into account in determining status as a fixture will include the annexation of the chattel to realty, the appropriateness to the use of the realty to which the chattel is connected, and the intent to make a permanent accession. Thus, the existence of the landlord's mortgage will not enter into this determination, making A not the best response.

(C) is not the best response,

because, although it states a correct rule, the rule does not address the central issue here: whether the equipment can be characterized as "personal property" *at all.*

The major issue here is whether or not the equipment could be characterized as a "fixture." If it *is,* it will be regarded as *real* property, and the tenant cannot remove it. If it is *not,* it will retain its character as personalty, and he can remove it. The status as a fixture is determined by analyzing these factors: The item's annexation to realty (e.g., heating system installed = fixture); appropriateness to the use of the realty to which it is connected (the more appropriate, the more likely it's a fixture); and, most importantly, the intent to make a permanent accession, viewed objectively (look at, e.g., any agreement, and annexor's estate in the land). Since C fails to recognize the central issue in the case, it's not the best response.

(D) is not the best response,

because, like C, it fails to address the central issue in the case: the characterization of the equipment as real or personal property.

D implies that the equipment *is* real property, since, if that's true, then the Statute of Frauds would apply (since the Statute of Frauds requires that any conveyance of real property must be in writing). However, on the facts here, it's not at all clear that the equipment would be considered part of the real property, as a "fixture." If the equipment *isn't* a fixture, the Statute of Frauds would not be relevant. A fixture is a chattel, which has been annexed to land in such a way as to be regarded as real property. The status as a fixture is determined by analyzing these factors: the item's annexation to realty (e.g., heating system installed = fixture); appropriateness to the use of the realty to which it is connected (the more appropriate, the more likely it's a fixture); and, most importantly, the intent to make a permanent accession, viewed objectively (look at, e.g., any agreement, and annexor's estate in the land). Since D does not recognize that this is the central issue, it's not the best response.

Answer 128

(D) is the best response,

because the acknowledgment letter was sent after the bottles were shipped.

UCC 2-206 provides that an offer to buy goods for immediate shipment may be accepted either by promising to ship or by shipping the goods. As a result, the contract was formed at the moment the wholesaler shipped the bottles to the bottling company. The terms that will govern the contract are those that the two parties had agreed upon at that time. Because the acknowledgment letter was not sent until a week following delivery, its terms cannot constitute an effective modification of the contract. Since, by default, consequential damages are allowed in a contract action, and the wholesaler's disclaimer of those damages was ineffective, the bottling company will succeed in its suit to recover the $40,000 in lost profits, which were a consequence of the wholesaler's breach.

(A) is not the best response,

because it misstates the law.

Article 2 of the UCC provides that, absent a contractual provision to the contrary, buyers are generally allowed to recover consequential damages in suits for breach, so long as the damages were foreseeable at the time the contract was made. (This is the rule of *Hadley v. Baxendale* (1854).) When a contract for the sale of goods is silent on an issue, the UCC gap-fillers will augment the contract as written. Since the UCC default provision allows consequential damages, and the wholesaler's disclaimer of such damages was ineffective because it was delivered too late, consequential damages will be recoverable by the bottling company in its action.

(B) is not the best response,

because the wholesaler's acknowledgement was sent after the contract was formed, and thus could not affect the terms of that contract.

UCC 2-206 provides that an offer to buy goods for immediate shipment may be accepted either by promising to ship or by shipping the goods. As a result, the contract was formed at the moment the wholesaler shipped the bottles to the bottling company. The terms that will govern the contract are those that the two parties had agreed upon at that time. Because the acknowledgment letter was not sent until a week following delivery, its terms cannot constitute an effective modification of the contract. If you chose this response, you were probably thinking of the "battle of the forms," which governs sales contracts made between merchants. Under certain conditions, additional terms in an offeree's acceptance may become part of the contract if not objected to by the offeror. This was inapplicable to this situation because the additional term was not included in the wholesaler's acceptance but, rather, was sent a week after the contract had been formed. The additional term in the acknowledgement was at most a request for a modification of the contract, but even if it was, that request was never accepted by the bottler, so no modification occurred.

(C) is not the best response,

because disclaimers of consequential damages are sometimes permissible.

This choice reaches the correct conclusion (that the buyer will win), but for the wrong reason. The bottling company will win because the wholesaler's acknowledgment letter, which contained the disclaimer of consequential damages, was not sent until a week after the contract had been formed, and thus was not part of the contract. (See the discussion of choice D above.) While it is true that under certain conditions, a disclaimer of consequential damages is unconscionable, there are situations where such disclaimers are permissible. Therefore, the better reason for the bottling company's ability to recover consequential damages is that the disclaimer was never part of the agreement, not that the courts should strike the disclaimer based upon its unconscionability.

Answer 129

(D) is the best response.

because it correctly identifies both the level of the burden of proof, and the party on which it is placed.

Here, the law limits the First Amendment, the fundamental right to free speech in a public place—the capitol steps. The right to such speech is not absolute; it can be limited, for instance, by valid "time, place, and manner" regulations. In order to be valid as such a regulation:

1. The law must be neutral as to the content of the speech;
2. It must further a significant government interest that is not capable of accomplishment by less restrictive means; and
3. There must be alternative media of communication available.

Thus, the law must promote a significant governmental interest; choice D correctly recognizes this. Furthermore, it places the burden on the correct party. Once a law is shown to adversely impact a First Amendment right, the burden is on the state to prove that the statute is valid. Since choice D correctly identifies the burden and the party on which it will be placed, it's the best response.

(A) is not the best response,

because it both places the burden on the wrong party, and it misstates the level of scrutiny the statute will undergo.

Here, the law limits the First Amendment, the fundamental right to free speech in a public place—the capitol steps. The right to such speech is not absolute; it can be limited, for instance, by valid "time, place, and manner" regulations. In order to be valid as such a regulation:

1. The law must be neutral as to the content of the speech;
2. It must further a significant government interest that is not capable of accomplishment by less restrictive means; and
3. There must be alternative media of communication available.

Thus, the law must promote a significant governmental interest; choice A understates the interest required by stating that the law need only meet the rational basis test. The rational basis test is used for economic and social legislation, not laws limiting First Amendment rights (among others).

Furthermore, choice A misplaces the burden of proof. Once a law is shown to adversely impact a First Amendment right, the burden is on the state to prove that the statute is valid. Since A puts the burden on the wrong party, and misstates that burden, it's not the best response.

(B) is not the best response,

because although it correctly states the burden of proof, it places it on the wrong party.

Here, the law limits the First Amendment, the fundamental right to free speech in a public place—the capitol steps. The right to such speech is not absolute; it can be limited, for instance, by valid "time, place, and manner" regulations. In order to be valid as such a regulation:

1. The law must be neutral as to the content of the speech;
2. It must further a significant government interest that is not capable of accomplishment by less restrictive means; and
3. There must be alternative media of communication available.

Here, choice B correctly identifies this burden—it just places that burden on the wrong party. All the owner needs to prove is that his First Amendment rights were adversely impacted by the law. Then, it's up to the state to prove that the statute is valid. Since B misplaces this burden, it's not the best response.

(C) is not the best response,

because although it correctly identifies that the state bears the burden of proof, it understates that burden.

Here, the law limits the First Amendment, the fundamental right to free speech in a public place—the capitol steps. The right to such speech is not absolute; it can be limited, for instance, by valid "time, place, and manner" regulations. In order to be valid as such a regulation:

1. The law must be neutral as to the content of the speech;
2. It must further a significant government interest that is not capable of accomplishment by less restrictive means; and
3. There must be alternative media of communication available.

Thus, the law must promote a significant governmental interest; choice C understates the interest required by stating that the law need only meet the rational basis test. The rational basis test is used for economic and social legislation, not laws limiting First Amendment rights (among others).

Although choice C understates the burden, it does place it on the correct party. Once a law is shown to adversely impact a First Amendment right, the burden is on the state to prove that the statute is valid. However, since choice C understates the state's burden, it's not the best response.

Answer 130

(A) is the best response,

because it correctly identifies a basis on which the friend will be liable to the motorist.

Negligence requires that the defendant failed to exercise such care as a reasonable person in his position would have exercised, this must have been a breach of the duty to prevent the foreseeable risk of harm to anyone in the plaintiff's position, and this breach must have caused the plaintiff's damages.

Here, the friend's failure to warn the motorist would be considered a breach of duty, since he didn't exercise the care a reasonable person in his position would have exercised. So much for duty and breach.

Damages are not an issue under these facts, so that leaves causation. While the wife's failure to warn the motorist was a substantial factor in causing his damages, the friend was negligent in failing to warn the motorist directly, since he had no right to rely on the wife to pass along the message, and the warning to the wife could not be imputed to the motorist. While it's true that you'd *expect* the wife to pass along the message, there's no legal basis for relieving the friend of his duty. Thus, as long as the friend's failure to warn the motorist was a substantial factor in causing his damages, the causation element is satisfied. Since A summarizes the elements of negligence as they apply to these facts, and arrives at the correct conclusion, A is the best response.

(B) is not the best response,

because the reasoning does not support a finding of strict liability, and, beyond that, it's unlikely strict liability would apply to these facts.

In general, strict liability has four elements: an absolute duty of care; breach of duty, which proximately causes the plaintiff's injury; and damages. There are three, general sources of strict liability: animals, abnormally dangerous activities, and defective products. (In addition, strict liability can be imposed by case law or statutes.) Thus, it wouldn't be enough, as B suggests, merely for there to be a defect: There would also need to be an absolute duty. The friend wouldn't be liable for strict product liability, because, apart from anything else, he's not a commercial supplier of cars. Lending a defective car would not be considered an abnormally dangerous activity. Since the animal basis wouldn't apply, and there's no statutory or case law source for strict liability on these facts, the friend wouldn't be strictly liable in tort.

Remember that this doesn't mean the friend will escape liability altogether; it's just that the motorist will have to prove *some* fault, at least negligence, in order to recover (which wouldn't be difficult to prove on these facts). Since B would impose liability on the friend without proof of fault, and fault would in fact need to be proven, B isn't the best response.

(C) isn't the best response,

because no matter how slight the friend's duty was, he breached it.

In fact, where a bailment is for the exclusive benefit of the bailee, the bailor's duty will, as C states, be slight. This, however, doesn't mean that the bailor can run roughshod over the bailee's rights. Here, the friend's failing to tell the motorist about the faulty brakes would satisfy *any* standard of negligence, no matter how slight.

Since C fails to recognize this, it's not the best response.

(D) is not the best response,

because it incorrectly states that the wife's negligence was the sole cause of the motorist's damages.

While it's true that the wife was negligent in failing to pass along the friend's warning, this doesn't mean that the friend is relieved of liability for failing to warn the motorist directly. Unless the friend's warning to the wife could be imputed to the motorist (for which there is *no* basis), then the friend would be required to inform the motorist directly; that is, he had no right to rely on the wife. Thus, while the wife's failure to warn contributed to the motorist's damages, the friend's negligent failure to warn was also a substantial factor in causing the motorist's injuries, making him liable in negligence. Since D would improperly shift the friend's liability to the wife, it's not the best response.

Answer 131

(C) is the best response,

because the defendant satisfies all the elements of larceny.

A larceny requires a trespassory taking and carrying away of another's personal property, with intent to steal it. Here, the defendant is laboring under a mistake of law: he mistakenly believes that larceny doesn't include taking a dog. However, mistake of law, as a general principle, is not a valid defense. Thus, his act fulfills all the requirements of larceny, and as a result he'd likely be convicted. Since choice C presents the facts, of these four choices, in which the defendant is most likely to be found guilty of larceny, it's the best response.

(A) is not the best response,

because one of the elements of larceny—the intent to steal—is missing.

A larceny requires a trespassory taking and carrying away of personal property of another, with intent to steal it. Since the defendant intended to return the TV set the following day, his intent was to borrow, not steal. As a result, he cannot be liable for larceny—*even though* the upshot of his act was the same—the plaintiff never got her TV back intact. Since the defendant under the facts in choice

A would not be liable for larceny, A cannot be the best response.

(B) is not the best response,

because the defendant's belief that he had a right to the money negated his intent to steal it.

Since larceny requires intent, the defendant could not be convicted on these facts. A larceny requires a trespassory taking and carrying away of personal property of another, with intent to steal it. Here, the defendant's "claim of right" is a valid defense to larceny, since it is not larcenous to take another's property in repayment of a debt, *as long as* it is done openly and with full explanation of why the property is being taken. The theory is that because the taking is being done to repay a debt, the element of intending to deprive another of his property is missing. Although the facts here do not describe the attendant circumstances—i.e., whether the taking was done openly—and although the defendant would certainly be liable for *some* crime, it's likely that the defendant would not be liable for larceny on these facts. As a result, B is not the best response.

(D) is not the best response,

because the neighbor's mistake negated one of the elements of larceny—intent to steal.

Larceny requires the taking and carrying away of another's personal property, with the intent to steal. Even an unreasonable mistake as to ownership negates the "intent to steal" requirement, as long as the belief is honest. (Of course, the more unreasonable the belief, the less likely it is that the jury will believe the mistake was "honest.") Choice D is an attractive response, because your gut reaction is that an unreasonable mistake cannot be a defense to a crime. However, as noted above, it negates the intent to steal. As a result, D is not the best response.

Answer 132

(A) is the best response,

because it recognizes that federalism is the basis of the legislator's strongest argument.

Under the Tenth Amendment, the states and the people retain all rights not delegated to the United States by the Constitution. Here, the Federal Securities Act would have been passed pursuant to Congress's broad commerce power. While that power is broad, it's not absolute. The concept of state sovereignty under the Tenth Amendment would mean that *some* state functions are outside the scope of Congress's commerce power. The state's legislative functions could well be outside the ambit of federal regulation. While this isn't an airtight argument, it's the best of the four possibilities, making A the best response.

(B) is not the best response,

because the Speech and Debate Clause does not apply to state legislators.

Under Article I, § 6, of the Constitution, members of Congress enjoy immunity "for any Speech or Debate in either House." The immunity covers only "legislative acts," which include those matters that form "an integral part of the deliberative and communicating processes" of Congress. This provision does not apply to the states, and thus the legislator could not use it as an argument. Even if he *were* a federal legislator, it's unlikely that the source of the prosecution—a Federal Securities Act violation—could be considered "legislative business." In any case, the central reason this argument is not good for the legislator is that he isn't covered by speech and debate immunity as a state legislator. Since B doesn't recognize this, it's not the best response.

(C) is not the best response,

due to operation of the Supremacy Clause.

Under the Supremacy Clause, found in Article VI, § 2, of the Constitution, federal law takes precedence over inconsistent state laws. That's the essence of the issue here. Congress would have power to legislate concerning securities under its commerce power, thus making the Federal Securities Act valid. Thus, any state law contradicting the federal act would be invalid. In fact, under these facts there is no indication of any state law concerning legislative immunity. Under the Supremacy Clause, it doesn't matter—as long as Congress has the power to legislate in an area, even if a state has the power to legislate in that area as well, the federal law will control. (Note that this is only true where the power is *concurrent* – that is, held by both the federal and state governments). Since choice C ignores the application of the Supremacy Clause, it's not the best response.

(D) is not the best response,

because such an application would not constitute a due process violation.

When the effect of a governmental activity amounts to the deprivation of a property interest or right, there's a potential due process problem. However, that's not what the legislator's immunity argument is about. Due process has nothing to do with immunity; it has to do with fair process when a right or privilege is limited. Thus, what's at issue here is not whether the legislator's rights or privileges were fairly limited, but whether he's immune from prosecution altogether; as a result, there's no due process issue. Since D doesn't recognize this, it's not the best response.

Answer 133

(C) is the best response,

because, in a criminal case, a judge may only instruct that it *may* accept a judicially noticed fact as conclusive.

FRE 201(f) provides that "In a criminal case, the court must instruct the jury that it may or may not accept the noticed fact as conclusive." Therefore, this instruction correctly states that the interstate nature of the transaction is a permissible inference rather than a mandate the jury must follow.

(A) is not the best response,

because a judge may not instruct a jury to find a fact in a criminal case, even if it is a fact that is subject to judicial notice.

FRE 201(f) provides that "In a criminal case, the court must instruct the jury that it may or may not accept the noticed fact as conclusive." Accordingly, this instruction would violate 201(f) (as well as the accused's Sixth Amendment right to a trial by jury on all elements of the crime). A proper instruction would inform the jury that it *may* accept a judicially noticed fact as conclusive.

(B) is not the best response,

because the government has the burden of proving all elements of a crime beyond a reasonable doubt.

FRE 201(f) provides that "In a criminal case, the court must instruct the jury that it may or may not accept the noticed fact as conclusive." So a judicially noticed fact in a criminal case cannot shift the constitutionally mandated burden of proof on all issues from the prosecution to the defendant. Here, the court may instruct on a permissible inference the jury may make, but nothing more.

(D) is not the best response,

because a judicially notice fact in a criminal case does not create a presumption.

There is a chance that this instruction would be interpreted by a reasonable jury to establish a "mandatory" presumption. Mandatory presumptions are not permitted in criminal cases, because they would violate the accused's Sixth Amendment right to have the prosecution bear the full burden of proof (including the burden of production) on all elements of the crime.

Answer 134

(A) is the best response,

because the dean has a valid defense.

The professor can state a *prima facie* case of defamation. (To establish a *prima facie* case for either libel or slander, the plaintiff must prove a defamatory statement concerning him, publication of the statement to a person other than the plaintiff, fault on the part of the defendant, and harm.) But the professor cannot prevail because the dean has a valid defense based on his reasonable belief that the professor invited him to speak. *See* Rest. 2d Torts, § 583 ("The consent of another to the publication of defamatory matter concerning him is a complete defense to his action for defamation.") By authorizing his agents to investigate his case, the professor apparently consented to limited publication in response to their inquiries. By the way, ill will on the part of the dean, even if it existed, would be irrelevant to this defense.

(B) is not the best response,

because, while this answer correctly states that the professor will lose, it misstates the legal basis for this conclusion.

Some jurisdictions may require evidence of pecuniary loss for oral statements that are not slander per se, but this is a written statement. Under the common law applicable to libel (written defamations), damages to the professor's reputation would be presumed, allowing him to recover even if he sustained no provable pecuniary loss.

(C) is not the best response,

because the tort of defamation does not turn on whether an investigation, reasonable or not, has been conducted.

It is true that defamation is not a strict liability tort, and requires at least negligence by the defendant (and indeed requires knowledge of falsity or reckless disregard of the truth if the plaintiff is a public figure). So the dean's failure to investigate might constitute negligence, thereby supplying the requisite mental state. But even with the mental-state requirement satisfied, the professor would lose on the grounds of consent, as further detailed in the discussion of choice A above.

(D) is not the best response,

because the fact that the statement was in writing does not affect the outcome here.

Even if the statement were oral, the professor could recover for slander if the dean were shown to have behaved negligently (e.g., by not investigating the rumor) and if no defense applied. But a defense does apply, namely the defense of consent, as further detailed in choice A above.

Answer 135

(A) is the best response,

because the federal discovery rules make the disclosure of insurance agreements a subject of mandatory initial disclosure without a discovery request.

Under Rule 26(a)(1)(A)'s provisions governing "initial disclosure," a party must, ***"without awaiting a discovery request***, provide to the other parties" various items. One of those items (specified in 26(a)(1)(A) (iv)) is "for inspection and copying . . . ***any insurance agreement*** under which ***an insurance business may be liable to satisfy all or part of a possible judgment*** in the action or to indemnify or reimburse for payments made to satisfy the judgment." As with the other mandatory initial disclosures, the copy of the insurance policy must normally be provided by the insured early in the case, at or within 14 days after the parties hold a Rule 26(f) mandatory conference in which they plan for discovery and discuss settlement.

(B) is not correct,

because Plaintiff need not make the request.

As is discussed more fully in the treatment of Choice (A) above, Defendant must furnish Plaintiff with a copy of the policy "without awaiting a discovery request[.]" Rule 26(a)(1)(A), including 26(a)(1)(A)(iv).

(C) is not correct,

because Plaintiff is entitled to receive a copy of the full insurance policy.

The question asks you to select the choice that represents the largest amount of relevant information to which Defendant is entitled and specifies that the choices are in descending order of the amount of information covered. Since Choice (A) correctly says that Plaintiff is automatically entitled to a copy of the full policy, and that's more information than just the name of the insurer and the policy limits, Choice (A) is correct and Choice (C) is not.

(D) is not correct,

because Plaintiff is entitled to the full policy, and without any showing of relevance.

This choice hints at a correct statement about the scope of discovery in federal suits: that as a normal matter, a party may obtain discovery only of information that is "relevant to any party's claim or defense and proportional to the needs of the case[.]" (Rule 26(b)(1). And, it will often be the case that liability insurance is not relevant to any claim or defense in the case (and will usually not be admissible as evidence, in part for that reason). But the federal rules reflect a policy decision that the existence and terms of a defendant's liability insurance coverage have such large practical implications for the plaintiff that the former should be compelled to disclose the full details of that coverage early in the case, and even without a request.

Answer 136

(D) is the correct answer,

because Plaintiff consented to personal jurisdiction by filing the counterclaim.

A plaintiff's ***filing of a lawsuit*** is treated as ***consent by the plaintiff*** to personal jurisdiction in the forum for any counterclaim. *Adam v. Saenger*, 303 U.S. 59, 67-68 (1938). As the Supreme Court has explained, deeming the plaintiff to have consented to personal jurisdiction in the forum in which he has elected to sue "is the price which the state may exact as the condition of opening its courts to the plaintiff" and is consistent with the requirements of the Due Process Clause. *Id.* Therefore, when Plaintiff chose to bring the second suit in federal district court for State C, he availed himself of the benefits of litigating in State C. By doing that, Plaintiff effectively waived any objection to personal jurisdiction over him by the courts in State C (whether state or federal courts) with respect to the counterclaim. And that waiver is effective even though Plaintiff might have successfully asserted lack of personal jurisdiction had Defendant brought a separate and independent suit against him in the state or federal courts of State C for the same wrongful-civil-proceedings claim that Defendant is now asserting via the counterclaim.

(A) is not the best response,

because it relies on an irrelevant legal rule.

A compulsory counterclaim is a claim made by any party against an opposing party that "arises out of the transaction or occurrence that is the subject matter of the opposing party's claim." FRCP 13(a)(1)(A). And where a federal court has jurisdiction of an "anchor" claim by the plaintiff against the defendant, the court will also have "supplemental jurisdiction" over closely-related claims; a compulsory counterclaim (since by hypothesis it arises out of the same transaction or occurrence as the main claim) will *always* be sufficiently closely related to the main claim as to fall within the court's supplemental jurisdiction. But supplemental jurisdiction is relevant only as a means of curing a problem with *subject-matter jurisdiction* (e.g., lack of complete diversity in a case founded solely on diversity, or failure to meet the amount-in-controversy requirement). Supplemental jurisdiction ***cannot cure a lack of personal jurisdiction over the defendant to the counterclaim***. Since this choice says that the presence of a compulsory counterclaim can cure what would otherwise be a lack of personal jurisdiction over the Plaintiff, the choice is incorrect as a matter of law—the cure comes not from the fact that a compulsory counterclaim is involved, but from the fact that Plaintiff, by suing, is deemed to consent to the court's personal jurisdiction over him for *any* counterclaim, compulsory or permissive (as discussed in the treatment of Choice (D) above.)

(B) is not the best response,

because it relies on an irrelevant legal rule.

A permissive counterclaim is defined as a counterclaim that does not arise out of the same transaction or occurrence as the opposing party's claim. *See* FRCP 13(b). Unlike a compulsory counterclaim,

a permissive counterclaim requires an independent basis of subject-matter jurisdiction. And most (though not all) federal courts have held that the doctrine of supplemental jurisdiction, now codified in 28 U.S.C. § 1367, doesn't change this rule. *See* W&K (7th Ed.), § 79, p. 573. But the entire issue of whether the counterclaim here is permissive or compulsory is irrelevant to whether there is *personal* jurisdiction over the defendant to the counterclaim (i.e., over the original plaintiff)—even if the counterclaim here were compulsory, that fact would have no bearing on the existence of personal jurisdiction. (See the discussion of Choice (A) above.) Therefore, since this choice says that the presence of a permissive counterclaim is what creates—or at least fails to cure—a lack of personal jurisdiction over the Plaintiff, the choice is incorrect. (The cure to the lack of personal jurisdiction comes from the fact that Plaintiff, by suing, is deemed to consent to the court's personal jurisdiction over him for *any* counterclaim, as discussed in the treatment of Choice (D) above.)

(C) is not the best response,

because it misstates the procedure for asserting a counterclaim.

A party asserts a counterclaim either by ***pleading the counterclaim in an answer*** or by ***raising it as a reply to a prior-asserted counterclaim.*** In either scenario, no summons is required. *See Schnabel v. Lui*, 302 F.3d 1023, 1036 (9th Cir. 2002) ("Because the Third Amended Complaint stated claims in the nature of compulsory counterclaims, no service of summons was necessary to effect personal jurisdiction.").

Answer 137

(D) is the best response,

because it correctly identifies the standard by which the validity of the permit will be analyzed.

In determining whether a government action that impinges on a group's religious practices violates the Free Exercise Clause of the First Amendment, courts will uphold a facially neutral act unless it was intended to target the practices of a particular religious group. If the action is found to have been aimed at suppressing a particular religion, then the court will apply strict scrutiny to the action, upholding it only if the government can show the action necessary to achieve a compelling governmental interest. In most cases, the application of strict scrutiny will result in the government action being invalidated.

(A) is not the best response,

because discriminatory impact is insufficient to invalidate a governmental action.

Discriminatory impact on a particular religious group is insufficient by itself to invalidate a government action. In determining whether a government action that impinges on a group's religious practices violates the Free Exercise Clause of the First Amendment, courts will uphold a facially neutral act unless it was intended to target the practices of a particular religious group. If the action is found to have been aimed at suppressing a particular religion, then the court will apply strict scrutiny to the action, upholding it only if the government can show the action necessary to achieve a compelling governmental interest.

(B) is not the best response,

because it misstates the level of scrutiny that will be applied to the Forest Service's decision.

Choice B implies that the utility of the government's act will be weighed against its discriminatory impact. This is not the case. In determining whether a government action that impinges on a group's religious practices violates the Free Exercise Clause of the First Amendment, courts will uphold a facially neutral act unless it was intended to target the practices of a particular religious group. If the action is found to have been aimed at suppressing a particular religion, then the court will apply strict scrutiny to the action, upholding it only if the government can show the action necessary to achieve a compelling governmental interest.

(C) is not the best response,

because strict scrutiny will only be applied if the group can show intentional discrimination.

In determining whether a government action that impinges on a group's religious practices violates the Free Exercise Clause of the First Amendment, courts will uphold a facially neutral act unless it was intended to target the practices of a particular religious group. If the action is found to have been aimed at suppressing a particular religion, then the court will apply strict scrutiny to the action, upholding it only if the government can show the action necessary to achieve a compelling governmental interest. If the group can show that the permit was issued in an attempt to impinge on their freedom to practice their religion *and* the court finds that the ski facility is a compelling governmental objective (which is extremely unlikely), only then will it become relevant if a less restrictive alternative was available to the Forest Service.

Answer 138

(A) is the best response,

because Congress has plenary power to raise revenue through taxes.

Article 1, § 8, of the Constitution provides that Congress may levy taxes for the purpose of raising revenue. In general, the only limitation on a generally applicable tax is that it must be designed to raise revenue. Whether or not the tax has incidental effects on a particular industry is an irrelevant consideration.

Since a 5 percent national retail sales tax would certainly raise funds, and the freedom of the press is not being curtailed because the tax is generally applied to all sales, the tax is constitutional, both as written, and as applied to the newspapers.

(B) is not the best response,

because strict scrutiny does not apply to the taxing and spending powers.

Congress's power under the Constitution to raise funds through taxes is limited only by the concern of whether the tax is designed to raise revenue, rather than to affect an otherwise unconstitutional goal. Here, it is obvious that a national retail sales tax would raise funds. There is no indication in the law that seeks to target newspapers, nor is there disproportionate impact since the tax is levied on all retail sales. If you chose this response, you were probably thinking that strict scrutiny applies to certain types of decisions that restrict free speech. However, since this tax in no way targets the newspapers, or any other form of speech, First Amendment analysis is not needed.

(C) is not the best response,

because it mistakes the law.

The Constitution permits Congress to enact this national sales tax since doing so would be an exercise of the taxing and spending power in Article one, § 8. The Constitution does not prohibit states from enacting their own sales taxes, but it also does not prohibit Congress from doing so as well. In general, the only limitation on a generally applicable tax is that it must be designed to raise revenue. Whether or not the tax has incidental effects on a particular industry is an irrelevant consideration. Since a 5 percent national retail sales tax would certainly raise funds, and the freedom of the press is not being curtailed because the tax is generally applied to all sales, the tax is constitutional, both as written, and as applied to the newspapers.

(D) is not the best response,

because the tax is not targeting newspapers.

Article 1, § 8, of the Constitution provides that Congress may levy taxes for the purpose of raising revenue. In general, the only limitation on a generally applicable tax is that it must be designed to raise revenue. Since this tax in no way targets the newspapers, or any other form of speech, First Amendment analysis is not needed. Since a 5 percent national retail sales tax would certainly raise funds, and the freedom of the press is not being curtailed because the tax is generally applied to all sales, the tax is constitutional, both as written, and as applied to the newspapers.

Answer 139

(A) is the best response,

because the chef was an at-will employee.

Even if a position is characterized as "permanent," the position will be considered at will, absent any defined duration in the employment contract. Therefore, the chef was an at-will employee, and was free to leave the job at any time and for any reason without breaching her employment contract. As a result, the chef's leaving, even though it occurred very soon after she was hired, does not constitute a breach of contract.

(B) is not the best response,

because the chef left by her own choice.

The chef has not breached her employment contract since she was an at-will employee and free to cease working for the bakery at any time. (See the explanation for choice A above.) If you chose this response, you were probably thinking of the limitations on a wrongfully terminated employee's obligation to mitigate damages by seeking alternate employment. When an employer breaches an employment contract, the employee must mitigate damages by seeking work elsewhere. The employee's duty only extends to comparable positions in the same geographic area. This is not at issue in this problem, however, since the bakery has not breached its contract with the chef.

(C) is not the best response,

because an at-will employee may leave his or her position at any time, including soon after being hired.

Even if a position is characterized as "permanent," the position will be considered at will, absent any defined duration in the employment contract. Therefore, the chef was an at-will employee, and was free to leave the job at any time and for any reason without breaching her employment contract. As a result, the chef's leaving, even though it occurred very soon after she was hired, does not constitute a breach of contract.

(D) is not the best response,

because the bakery did not have a right of first refusal.

The holder of a right of first refusal is given the opportunity to match the price offered by any other party. For example, if a developer holds a right of first refusal on a plot of land, and the landowner offers the land for sale to a buyer, the developer must be given the opportunity to match the buyer's bid and purchase the land for the agreed price. Rights of first refusal are never implied—they must be explicitly included in a contract. Additionally, due to the public policy consideration of not forcing an individual to work in a particular position against their will, they are not applicable to employment contracts. Since there was no right of refusal to enforce, choice D is incorrect.

Answer 140

(B) is the best response,

because the defendant's character for peacefulness is a pertinent trait of character under FRE 404(a)(2)(A).

Under FRE 404(a)(2)(A), evidence of the character of the defendant in a criminal case is admissible when it is offered by the defendant and it relates to a "pertinent" character trait. Plus, under FRE 405(a), such evidence of character is admissible only when it comes in the form of opinion or reputation testimony. The defendant's character for *peacefulness* is a pertinent character trait, since the defendant is charged with battery, a crime of violence. And since character was proven here through reputation evidence, it meets the requirements of FRE 405(a). So the evidence of the defendant's peaceful reputation is admissible.

However, the evidence of the defendant's *truthfulness* is *not* admissible under FRE 404(a)(2)(A), because it is not pertinent to the charge of battery. It is also true, however, that the defendant was a witness. And evidence of a pertinent trait of character of a testifying witness is admissible under the combination of FRE 404(a)(3) and 608(a). But under FRE 608(a), evidence of a witness's truthful character is admissible "only after the witness's character for truthfulness has been attacked." There is no indication that the defendant's character for truthfulness has been attacked. (The victim's claim that contrary to the defendant's testimony, the defendant, not the victim, was the aggressor, would constitute impeachment by contradiction, but would not be considered to be an attack on the defendant's overall "character for truthfulness.") Thus, the evidence of the defendant/witness's truthful character must be excluded.

(A), (C), and (D) are not the best responses,

because, to the extent these choices each fail to admit the peacefulness testimony or admit the truthfulness testimony, each is wrong for the reasons described in the analysis of choice B above.

Answer 141

(B) is the best choice,

because a transfer does not change which state's substantive law should apply, and under *Erie* the choice-of-law rule of the forum state controls.

This is a quite subtle problem—solving it requires you to combine a knowledge of *Erie* principles and knowledge of how the Supreme Court has interpreted the federal transfer-of-venue statute. Let's take these one at a time. First, let's figure out what state's substantive statute-of-limitation rule would have applied if the suit had been filed in State C federal court (as indeed it was) and neither party had ever tried to have it transferred elsewhere. In this situation the Supreme Court has always held—ever since the immediately-post-*Erie* case of *Klaxon Co. v. Stentor Manufacturing Co.*, 313 U.S. 487 (1941)—that where *Erie* principles require following state law, the issue of *which state's* law should be followed is to be decided by using the ***conflicts*** (i.e., ***"choice of law"***) rule of the ***state where the federal court sits***. (That's the only way to ensure that a litigant cannot "forum shop" by choosing, say, the federal court for State X instead of the State X state courts; requiring the federal court to apply whatever choice-of-law rule would be used by the State X courts ensures that the ***same underlying state substantive rule will apply*** regardless of whether the action is heard in State X federal court or State X state court.) So here, since the suit was brought in State C federal court, in a no-transfer-requested scenario the federal court would have to use whichever state's statute-of-limitations rule would be applied to this controversy by the State C state courts had the action been brought there.

Next, we have to figure out whether the fact that a transfer based on *forum non conveniens*—if it's granted by the federal court for State C—would change the above result; is there something about the active transfer that would cause the transferee federal court (here, the federal court for State D) to use a different conflict rule than the conflict rule that would have been applied by the transferor court (the federal court for State C)? The answer is "no," because the Supreme Court has so held in a pair of cases squarely posing the issue. But before we get to those cases, let's take a quick look at the federal statute that would govern the request for transfer here. Assuming that the case is brought in a federal district where venue is proper (and that's the situation here), a change of venue is governed by 28 U.S.C. § 1404. The main provision is § 1404(a), which says that "For the ***convenience of parties and witnesses***, in the ***interest of justice***, a district court ***may transfer any civil action to any other district or division where it might have been brought*** or to any district or division to which all parties have consented." The case could have been brought originally in State D federal court. (That's because one of the places in which venue is proper under 28 U.S.C. § 1391(b) and (c) is a judicial district in which the sole defendant resides, and a corporate defendant is deemed to reside in a district in which it is headquartered, so Defendant is a resident of the sole district covering State D in view of its headquarters location there.) Since the case could originally have been brought in the district of State D, the State C federal judge is authorized by 28 U.S.C. § 1404(a) to transfer it the district of State D for convenience of the parties, even if Defendant refuses to consent.

This leads us to the ultimate question: Once there has been a transfer to the State D federal court, how should that federal court decide ***which state's statute of limitations*** should be applied? The answer is that the State D federal court should apply the limitations law of whichever state the federal judge in State C (where the action was ***originally*** brought) would have applied—and we know from the first major paragraph above (the one that cites *Klaxon*) that the federal judge for the district of State C would have to select the limitations law that would be selected by the State C courts when the latter applied their own conflict-of-laws principles. Why is this the answer? Because the Supreme Court has held that "[a] change of venue under § 1404(a) generally should be, with respect to state law, but a change of court-rooms." *Van Dusen v. Barrack*, 376 U.S. 612 (1964). In other words, once the plaintiff (or the defendant in a case in which the defendant has removed a case filed in state court) has chosen an original forum in a diversity case, the fortuitous fact that a federal statute allows a transfer for the convenience of the parties ***should not result in a change of the underlying substantive law***. *Van Dusen* involved a transfer by request of the defendant, but the Supreme Court has reached the same conclusion in the case of a transfer made by request of the *plaintiff*, which is what we have here. *See Ferens v. John Deere Co.*, 494 U.S. 516 (1990) (the transferee court must "apply the law of the transferor court, regardless of who initiates the transfer. A transfer under Section 1404(a), in other words, does not change the law applicable to a diversity case.").

(A) is not the best response,

because it incorrectly states how the federal transfer-of-venue statute works.

As is explained with respect to Choice (B), the *Van Dusen* rule—that the law of the transferor court applies to a transfer effected under 28 U.S.C. § 1404(a)—governs whether it is the plaintiff or the defendant who moves to transfer the action. *See Ferens v. John Deere Co.*, 494 U.S. 516, 521 (1990) (the transferee court must "apply the law of the transferor court, regardless of who initiates the transfer."). So no aspect of the substantive law of the state in which the transferee court sits (State D)—whether we're talking about the statute-of-limitations law of that state or the state's conflicts principles—would have any role when the case was transferred to State D federal court.

(C) is not the best response,

because it incorrectly states how the federal transfer-of-venue statute works.

As with Choice (A), this choice incorrectly starts with the proposition that some body of law that would be applied by the State D state court is relevant, merely because the action has been transferred to the federal court sitting in that state. But the *Van Dusen* and *Ferens* cases (discussed *supra*, Choices (B) and (A)) make it clear that when a case is transferred under 28 U.S.C. § 1404(a), whatever decision-making rules would have been used to pick the state whose statute of limitations should apply had the case not been transferred, also apply post-transfer, so that no aspect of the law of the state where the transferee court sits (here, State D) plays any role.

(D) is not the best response,

because it is based on an incorrect substantive rule.

This choice asserts that because Plaintiff originally elected to bring suit in State C federal court, Plaintiff lost the right to request a transfer to a more convenient venue under 28 U.S.C. § 1404(a). But this assertion is false: As you can see by reading the excerpt from 28 U.S.C. § 1404(a) quoted in the discussion of Choice (B) above (see the paragraph starting with "Next, we have to figure out . . . "), nothing in § 1404(a) bars the transfer from occurring in response to a request by the plaintiff. And, in fact, in the one of the two key Supreme Court cases establishing the principle that a § 1404(a) transfer of a diversity case doesn't result in a change of substantive law, *Ferens v. John Deere Co.*, 494 U.S. 516 (1990) (discussed in connection with Choice (B)), the request for transfer was successfully made by the plaintiff, even though it was the plaintiff who had originally selected the transferor forum before changing his mind.

Answer 142

(B) is the best response,

because it correctly identifies precisely why the instructions were correct: The burden of ultimate persuasion remained with the prosecution, and the defendant only bore the burden of rebutting a presumption of murder.

First, take a close look at what's going on here. The defendant was charged with murder—that is, the killing of another, with malice aforethought. The burden of persuasion is on the prosecution to prove every element of the crime beyond a reasonable doubt. This burden does not shift throughout the trial. The burden of production, or "going forward," requires only that a party introduce enough evidence on an issue such that a reasonable jury could infer the fact alleged. If the defendant wants to claim an affirmative defense—like self defense or provocation—he will have the burden of going forward.

The judge's instructions create a rebuttable presumption that a killing is murder; he lays the burden of ultimate persuasion on the prosecution, to prove every element of the crime beyond a reasonable doubt; and he establishes that the defendant can rebut the presumption of murder by producing evidence that shows, by a fair preponderance, that the killing was committed under adequate provocation. Note that this doesn't shift the burden of persuasion from the prosecution to the defendant, because that would violate the defendant's due process rights. Instead, it requires only that, once the state has borne its burden of proving every element beyond a reasonable doubt, the defendant has the burden of producing evidence on his affirmative defense; he must show it was more likely than not that he was adequately provoked.

(A) is not the best response,

because it does not address with sufficient precision, unlike response (B), exactly why the defendant's conviction will be upheld.

Choice A ignores entirely the defendant's burden of going forward, which is significant, due to the potential due process violation placing a burden on a criminal defendant could create. As a result, A is not the best response.

The judge's instructions create a rebuttable presumption that a killing is murder; he lays the burden of ultimate persuasion on the prosecution, to prove every element of the crime beyond a reasonable doubt; and he establishes that the defendant can rebut the presumption of murder by producing evidence that shows, by a fair preponderance, that the killing was committed under adequate provocation. Note that this doesn't shift the burden of persuasion from the prosecution to the defendant, because that would violate the defendant's due process rights. Instead, it requires only that, once the state has borne its burden of proving every element beyond a reasonable doubt, the defendant has the burden of producing evidence on his affirmative defense; he must show it was more likely than not that he was adequately provoked. This reflects a fair distribution of the burden between the prosecution and the defendant, and so the defendant's conviction will be upheld.

What choice A does is to address only the state's burden of ultimate persuasion. It does not address the defendant's burden of production at all.

(C) is not the best response,

because the defendant was not denied due process of law, and, because the judge correctly identified the burdens of proof for both the state and the defendant, the conviction will be upheld.

Due process requires fairness of process in circumstances when one is being deprived of life, liberty, or property. Here, if the defendant were required to prove his *innocence,* he'd be denied due process. However, he's only required to introduce enough evidence to create a reasonable doubt in the minds of the jury that he was adequately provoked. This is only a burden of going forward, and is thus considered fair.

The burden of persuasion is on the prosecution, to prove every element of the crime beyond a reasonable doubt. This burden does not shift throughout the trial. The burden of production, or "going forward," requires only that a party introduce enough evidence on an issue such that a reasonable jury could infer the fact alleged. If the defendant wants to claim an affirmative defense—like self defense or provocation—he will have the burden of going forward.

The judge's instructions create a rebuttable presumption that a killing is murder; he lays the burden of ultimate persuasion on the prosecution, to prove every element of the crime beyond a reasonable doubt; and he establishes that the defendant can rebut the presumption of murder by producing evidence that shows, by a fair preponderance, that the killing was committed under adequate provocation. Note that this doesn't shift the burden of persuasion from the prosecution to the defendant, because that would violate the defendant's due process rights. Instead, it requires only that, once the state has borne its burden of proving every element beyond a reasonable doubt, the defendant has the burden of producing evidence on his affirmative defense; he must show it was more likely than not that he was adequately provoked. Since C mistakenly states that the defendant's due process rights were violated by the jury instructions, it's not the best response.

(D) is not the best response,

because it misstates the law: presumptions *can,* in fact, be used by the state in a criminal case.

First, a little background. There are two types of burdens of proof: the burden of persuasion and the burden of going forward. The burden of persuasion is on the prosecution, to prove every element of the crime beyond a reasonable doubt. This burden does not shift throughout the trial. The burden of production, or "going forward," requires only that a party introduce enough evidence on an issue such that a reasonable jury could infer the fact alleged. If the defendant wants to claim an affirmative defense—like self defense or provocation—he will have the burden of going forward.

A rebuttable presumption has the effect of shifting the burden of "going forward" to the party adversely effected by the presumption. It does not shift the burden of persuasion, which cannot shift throughout the trial.

Contrary to what D states, there are many, rebuttable presumptions that operate validly on behalf of the state in a criminal case. For instance, as a general rule, people who commit crimes are sane, conscious, sober, and not operating under duress. These are, as a general rule, presumptions that operate in favor of the state, such that it need not prove in a criminal case *any* of these elements—that is, unless the defendant introduces evidence on any of these elements, or in fact any justification or excuse or affirmative defense. Thus, if the defendant introduces no evidence on any presumed fact, the jury can, but doesn't have to, find that those facts exist. However, if the defendant meets the burden of going forward—that is, introduces enough evidence to create a reasonable doubt about a presumed fact in the minds of the trier of fact—then the state must prove the challenged fact beyond a reasonable doubt. There's nothing legally repugnant about any of this; the only presumptions that couldn't operate in the state's favor are those that address the ultimate issue of proof of a crime's elements. As a result, C's statement, that presumptions cannot operate in favor of a state in a criminal case, is incorrect, making C not the best response.

Answer 143

(D) is the best response,

because even though the case probably falls within the court's diversity jurisdiction, federal courts will ***abstain*** from exercising such power when the lawsuit pertains solely to divorce and child custody.

Usually, a federal court is required to exercise subject-matter jurisdiction over a state-law claim if the individual parties are citizens of different states and the amount in controversy is satisfied. However, the U.S. Supreme Court has long recognized an exception as a matter of policy in diversity actions for suits that ***seek a divorce decree, an alimony award, or a child-custody determination.*** "The rationale for this limitation is that family relations are uniquely a matter of state policy and state interest, with which the federal courts should not interfere." F,K&M (5th Ed.), § 2.5, p. 29. See also *Ankenbrandt v. Richards*, 504 U.S. 689 (1992). The Constitution does not mandate this limitation; rather, the Court has based the limitation on the history and statutory language of the grant of diversity jurisdiction. Since what Husband is seeking is precisely these three types of domestic-relations orders, the district court must obey the Supreme Court's policy determination by declining to exercise diversity jurisdiction even if it is present.

(A) is not the best response,

because the court won't hear the case regardless of whether diversity exists.

As explained with respect to Choice (D), the Supreme Court has decided that federal courts should decline to exercise their diversity jurisdiction in cases that seek a divorce decree, an alimony award, or a child-custody determination. So whether or not the requirements of diversity are met here (which they probably are), this choice, by implying that the court should hear the case, is not correct.

(B) is not the best response,

because it incorrectly assumes that a federal court can remand an action when a party moves to dismiss the action for lack of subject-matter jurisdiction.

Remand is a procedure that applies only in removal situations; the procedure requires the federal court to transfer an action back to state court when defendant has improperly removed an action from state court to federal court. *See* 28 U.S.C. § 1441. Since the case here was never filed in state court and was never "removed," the federal court cannot "remand" it to that (or any) court.

(C) is not the best response,

because a federal court can't "transfer" a case to a state court.

Although it is true that the district court will exercise discretion and decline to exercise diversity jurisdiction in a suit that pertains to divorce, alimony, or child custody, a federal court does not have power to "transfer" a federal lawsuit to the court of a different system, including the court of a state system in the United States. The transfer rules that apply in federal district court allow a district court to change the venue of an action, including by transferring the suit to another federal court that sits in a state different from the one in which the transferor court sits. *See* 28 U.S.C. § 1404. However, apart from the special case of a remand to the original court of an improperly-removed action (see choice (B) above), a federal court may not transfer a federal suit to a state court, whether it is a court of the state where the federal court sits or a court of some other state.

Answer 144

(A) is the best response,

because Congress cannot force states to enact laws.

Principles of federalism, embodied in the Tenth Amendment, create a system of dual sovereignty. Congress may legislate within the scope of its enumerated powers, and the states may legislate in any manner not inconsistent with federal law. However, Congress, even if it is acting within the scope of its powers, cannot dictate what laws are passed by a state legislature. (*See New York v. U.S.* (1992).) Here, although it is arguably the case that Congress could pass a law making it a crime for any person to sell, within 1,000 feet of any elementary or secondary school, any controlled substance that had previously been transported in interstate commerce under its Commerce Power, it cannot force the state legislatures to enact such a law.

(B) is not the best response,

because these sales, in aggregate, have a substantial effect on interstate commerce.

The Commerce Clause allows Congress to regulate economic or commercial activity that involves the transportation of goods across state or international boundaries. Here, the statute specifically addresses only controlled substances that have been transported in interstate commerce. However, the question remains whether there is a substantial effect on interstate commerce rather than a negligible one. While choice B correctly states that a single sale of a controlled substance in proximity to a school is unlikely to have a substantial effect on interstate commerce, it ignores the aggregation principle. When taken as a whole, if the aggregation of numerous transactions has a substantial effect on interstate commerce, then it is within Congress's power to legislate each individual transaction. In this problem, we are told that "national statistics revealed a dramatic increase in the number of elementary and secondary school students bringing controlled substances to school for sale." This indicates that there has been a significant amount of commerce affected, rather than a minimal amount. This data, combined with the jurisdictional requirement in the statute, provides a sufficient nexus with interstate commerce to allow Congress to regulate in this area. However, as noted in the explanation for choice A above, Congress may not force states legislatures to enact this legislation.

(C) is not the best response,

because Congress cannot force states to enact laws.

Principles of federalism, embodied in the Tenth Amendment, create a system of dual sovereignty. Congress may legislate within the scope of its enumerated powers, and the states may legislate in any manner not inconsistent with federal law. However, Congress, even if it is acting within the scope of its powers, cannot dictate what laws are passed by a state legislature. (*See New York v. U.S.* (1992).) Here, although it is arguably the case that Congress could pass a law making it a crime for any person to sell, within 1,000 feet of any elementary or secondary school, any controlled substance that had previously been transported in interstate commerce under its Commerce Power, it cannot force the state legislatures to enact such a law.

(D) is not the best response,

because it mistakes the law.

Congress does not have the power to legislate for the general welfare; the police power is reserved to the states. This is a common trap on the MBE. Congress has the power to *tax and spend* for the general welfare, but may not legislate for it. So, for example, Congress could conceivably refuse to provide federal education funding to states that do not criminalize the sale of controlled substances in close proximity to a school. (*See South Dakota v. Dole* (1987).) However, this choice can also be eliminated because it comes to the wrong conclusion. As discussed in the explanation for choice A above, the means used here by Congress—forcing states to enact legislation—is impermissible under the rule of *New York v. U.S.* (1992).

Answer 145

(C) is the best response,

because it focuses on the central issue, and, based, on the condition it provides, arrives at the correct result.

The key fact here is that, while it is not expressly mentioned in the statute, the requirement of criminal intent will be implied. That's because the statute here would not be considered to create a strict liability offense, since those generally involve regulatory offenses or serious potential harm to the public.

As a result, the hiker cannot be found guilty of any crime if she is found to lack criminal intent. An honest belief that the signs were abandoned would preclude her guilt, since she would lack the intent to appropriate public property. Note that C focuses on an element *it provides itself*. Choice C states that she won't be guilty *if* the jury believes her. The use of the modifier "if" means that the reasoning must be plausible on the facts, it must address a central issue, and the result must be consistent with the reasoning. Here, it's possible that the jury could believe the hiker. If the jury *does* believe her, it will believe that she did not have the requisite criminal intent, and as a result she will be found not guilty. Since C correctly identifies the central issue and resolves it satisfactorily, and its result is consistent with its reasoning, it's the best response.

(A) is not the best response,

because regardless of whether the offense is a public welfare offense, the hiker would still have to have a criminal intent in order to be convicted under the statute.

That's because the statute here would not be considered to create a strict liability offense, since those generally involve regulatory offenses or serious potential harm to the public. Thus, it would have to be proven that the hiker intended to appropriate government property in order to be convicted. Since choice A suggests the hiker would be guilty even without the requisite intent, it's not the best response.

(B) is not the best response,

because it does not focus on the central issue.

The central issue under these facts is whether the hiker had the requisite intent to be convicted. That's because the statute here would not be considered to create a strict liability offense, since those generally involve regulatory offenses or serious potential harm to the public.

If the hiker believed the signs were abandoned, then she would not have the duty to inquire, since the two are mutually exclusive. Inquiring about whether the signs were abandoned would call into question her honesty about believing they were abandoned.

Not asking about whether the signs were abandoned would thus not establish her intent to steal the signs. As a result, B is not the best response.

(D) is not the best response,

because whether the state had adequately informed the public that the signs were public property is not a central issue, and, by using the modifier "unless," choice D suggests that the state's lack of notice is a prerequisite to the hiker's conviction.

The central issue instead is the hiker's criminal intent, since intent will have to be proven in order to find her guilty under the statute. That's because the statute here would not be considered to create a strict liability offense, since those generally involve regulatory offenses or serious potential harm to the public. If the hiker lacked criminal intent, then it wouldn't matter whether the state had adequately notified the public that the signs weren't abandoned. Since D focuses on an issue that is not controlling, it's not the best response.

Answer 146

(C) is the best response,

because it correctly identifies the basis on which the Water District will prevail.

The Water District has a valid easement as to the tract. While there are several bases on which an easement can be terminated, the only ones that apply to an easement in gross under these circumstances are:

1. a release, in writing
2. abandonment
3. adverse use by servient tenement holder, for statutory period
4. estoppel

The facts here indicate that none of these have been satisfied, so the easement is still in force. The general rule is that the dominant tenement holder has both the right and the duty to maintain the easement. That's what the Water District is doing.

Since the Water District's proposed acts will do no more than maintain the easement, the adverse impact on the purchaser's property will not change the result. Since C correctly identifies the basis on which the Water District will prevail, it's the best response.

(A) is not the best response,

because it does not state a basis on which the purchaser can prevail.

While the deed itself does not mention the easement, the purchaser is on constructive notice of the easement, since it appears in his "chain of title." The facts here state that the easement was properly and timely recorded, and, as such, in most states the purchaser would take subject to the easement, since an easement is considered an interest in property. Since constructive notice is sufficient to give the purchaser notice of the easement, the fact that the easement did not appear on his deed *itself* is not enough for him to succeed. Note that this is yet another example of how popular a topic "constructive notice" is on the MBE. Since A does not take into account the fact that the purchaser would have constructive notice of the easement, it's not the best response.

(B) is not the best response,

because it does not suggest a proper basis on which the purchaser could prevail.

The Water District has a valid easement as to the tract. While there are several bases on which an easement can be terminated, the only ones that apply to an easement in gross under these circumstances are:

1. a release, in writing
2. abandonment
3. adverse use by servient tenement holder, for statutory period
4. estoppel

The facts here indicate that none of these have been satisfied, so the easement is still in force. The general rule is that the dominant tenement holder has both the right and the duty to maintain the easement. That's what the Water District is doing.

In fact, it couldn't accurately be said that the Water District hadn't entered the tract for 40 years, because its entry has been continuous—the water pipes have been there the whole time. Nonetheless, if you chose this response you might have done so due to a notion that the equitable doctrine of laches should apply to these facts, since "40 years" indicates a length of time that that doctrine would cover. However, the doctrine of laches only applies where one has not enforced his rights for an unreasonable period of time, and another party has relied on this failure. As noted earlier, the doctrine of laches would not apply to easements, since it does not constitute a basis on which an easement could be terminated. The "abandonment" required for an easement requires more than mere non-use—there must be acts indicating a clear intent to abandon. Here, that could entail, for instance, digging up and removing the pipes, filling in the space, and not replacing them. However, the facts here indicate that the Water District still has full rights to the easement, so B is not the best response.

(D) is not the best response,

because it's irrelevant.

Assuming D were true, it wouldn't make a difference to the outcome here, since, even if the plan were fair and equitable, if it wasn't within the Water District's rights, it would be impermissible. In fact, the dominant estate holder (here, the Water District) has both the right and the duty to maintain the easement, and *this* is the basis of its right to excavate the pipe. As long as the Water District is within its rights in doing so, any damage done to the property would not be actionable.

Since D would mistakenly pin the Water District's right to excavate on whether the plan is fair and equitable, it's not the best response.

Answer 147

(D) is the best response,

because it recognizes that the attorney general is not subject to direction from Congress as to whom to prosecute.

Law enforcement is an exclusively executive power. The President is the only source of executive power, under Article II, § 1, of the Constitution. He can, of course, delegate those executive functions to others in the executive branch. The attorney general is the chief law enforcement official. He can prosecute criminal activity as he sees fit, and in his discretion, he can choose not to do so, as a general rule. Since choice D recognizes this, it's the best response.

(A) is not the best response,

because the attorney general is not subject to any orders from the legislative branch.

The President is the only source of executive power, under Article II, § 1, of the Constitution. Many of his duties are delegated to others within the executive branch, including the attorney general, the chief law enforcement official. The law enforcement function is an *exclusively* executive branch power. Thus, Congress enjoys *no* law enforcement powers, and could not direct the attorney general to prosecute anyone. Since A doesn't recognize this, it's not the best response.

(B) is not the best response,

because it misstates the law.

Law enforcement is an exclusively executive power. The President is the only source of executive power, under Article II, § 1, of the Constitution. He can, of course, delegate those executive functions to others in the executive branch. The attorney general is the chief law enforcement official. He can prosecute criminal activity as he sees fit, and in his discretion, he can choose not to do so, as a general rule. Since B states that the attorney general *must* prosecute all federal law violators when, in fact, prosecution is generally discretionary, B is not the best response.

(C) is not the best response,

because the woman's immunity from prosecution for acts committed in office would be *irrelevant* as to whether the attorney general must prosecute her for contempt.

When someone does not comply with a congressional investigation, contempt is the appropriate punishment. Here, the woman's contempt charge is due to her failure to answer questions posed during a congressional investigation, *not* due to any wrongdoing in the course of her duties.

Instead, the reason the attorney general needn't prosecute is that law enforcement is exclusively an *executive* function, and thus the House of Representatives, as part of the *legislative* branch, can't order the attorney general to prosecute. Since C doesn't recognize this, it's not the best response.

Answer 148

(D) is the best response,

because it correctly makes the case that the store's June 9 letter was either a rejection or a breach.

The manufacturer's June 2 telegram was probably specific enough to be an offer, since it included price, quantity, and delivery terms. The fact that it did not include a time-for-payment term would not prevent the telegram from functioning as an offer, because time-for-payment terms are not so important that their absence indicates that no offer is present, and because the UCC stands by with an appropriate gap-filler (§ 2-310(a): "Unless otherwise agreed (a) payment is due at the time and place at which the buyer is to receive the goods even though the place of shipment is the place of delivery.")

The store's June 5 letter was probably an acceptance, even though the store said that he'd "prefer to pay in full 30 days after invoice." This is probably an acceptance because § 2-207(1) says that "[a] definite and seasonable expression of acceptance . . . operates as an acceptance even though it states terms additional to or different from those offered or agreed upon, unless acceptance is expressly made conditional on assent to the additional or different terms." Here, the store is not saying in effect, "I'm only accepting if you agree that I can pay in 30 days"; it's saying something more like "I'm accepting. I hope that the contract we're making will include 30 days to pay." So its response is not "expressly made conditional on assent to the different [30-days-to-pay] terms," and is thus a "definite and seasonable expression of acceptance [that] operates as an acceptance even though it states terms additional to or different from those offered or agreed upon."

If the June 5 letter was an acceptance, the 30-days credit request was, under § 2-207(2), an "additional term [that is] to be construed as [a] proposal for addition to the contract." Section 2-207(2)(b) then says that "[b]etween merchants[, which is what both the store and the manufacturer are] such [additional] terms become part of the contract unless: . . . (b) [the additional term] materially alter[s] [the contract]." A court would almost certainly conclude that when the offer demands C.O.D. payment, a proposal for credit constitutes a "material alteration." In that event, the contract that, by hypothesis, was formed on June 5 did not include the 30-days credit term, since a proposal in the acceptance for a "different" term doesn't enter the contract if it "materially alters" the contract. So the contract that was formed required C.O.D. payment.

If the store's June 5 letter indeed formed a contract, then its June 9 "I don't deal with people who can't accommodate our simple requests" letter was a repudiation (and thus a breach). That's because the June 9 letter unequivocally stated that the store wouldn't be performing ("deal[ing] with" the manufacturer) on account of the manufacturer's refusal to give him credit, and no credit was required under the contract. A refusal to perform unless the other party gives up a right under the contract is a repudiation and a breach. So by the "unequivocal refusal to perform" defense asserted in choice D, the manufacturer wins even if the "parties had previously formed a contract."

Now, what happens if the store's June 5 letter *didn't* form a contract? In that event, this letter was probably a counteroffer. If it was a counteroffer, then either: (a) the manufacturer's June 6 "[y]ou must pay C.O.D." telegram was a rejection, causing the counteroffer to terminate; or (b) the counteroffer survived the manufacturer's June 6 telegram, in which case the store's June 9 "I don't deal" letter was a revocation of the counteroffer. In either scenario, there was no offer open to accept by the time the store owner changed his mind and purported to accept on June 10.

So in summary, (1) if there was a contract formed prior to June 9, the store's June 9 "I don't deal" letter was a repudiatory breach, the store loses because it materially breached; and (2) if there wasn't a contract formed prior to June 9, no offer was open by the store's June 10 purported acceptance, so the store loses because there was never a contract.

(A) is not the best response,

because a court could find that the June 2 letter was an offer.

It is true that this argument *might* work—the court might conclude that the June 2 letter was indeed only a price quote and not an offer. If the court reached this conclusion, the manufacturer would probably win, because nothing else that happened later would be likely to be found to constitute an offer and acceptance.

However, the court probably will not agree with the manufacturer's contention that the June 2 letter was not an offer, for several reasons. First, the store's June 1 telegram was pretty clearly an attempt to solicit an offer (not just to solicit a quote), since it specified precise quantity and delivery-time terms—a court would probably presume that the response to this solicitation-of-offer was in fact an offer. Second, the quote mentioned the exact quantity the seller had for sale, and when the quantity in stock is mentioned a court is likely to find an offer rather than merely a quote. If the court did find that the June 2 letter was an offer, then it would probably find that the store accepted on June 5, and that the manufacturer breached by selling the units to someone else.

So this "quote not an offer" approach is merely one that *possibly* succeeds, whereas choice D almost definitely succeeds.

(B) is not the best response,

because it misstates how the UCC operates.

UCC 2-207(1) provides that any timely and definite "expression of acceptance" operates as an acceptance, "even though it states terms additional to or different from those offered . . . unless acceptance is expressly made conditional on assent to the additional or different terms." Here, the store's June 5 letter was clearly timely and definite, and didn't say that the acceptance was "expressly . . . conditional on [the manufacturer's] assent to" any additional or different terms. So the fact that the June 5 letter included an "additional" term (request for 30 days' credit) did not prevent the letter from being an acceptance. (Whether the credit request became part of the contract is a different story—that would depend on whether this was a "material alteration," which it probably was. In that event, the credit term would not have become part of the contract.)

Notice that this answer is wrong because it (incorrectly) assumes that the common-law "mirror image" rule (in which a not-perfectly-matching response cannot be an offer) applies in a UCC context. As the above analysis shows, the UCC rejects this common-law approach.

(C) is not the best response,

because use of the mails would have been a valid method of acceptance.

It's true that an offer (which we can assume, for the purpose of this discussion, was what the manufacturer's June 2 telegram was) can state the method by which acceptance is to be made. But the manufacturer did not do this. The mere fact that the manufacturer used a telegram doesn't mean that the manufacturer was in effect saying, "you must accept, if at all, by a telegram." So the store was free to accept by any method that was reasonable under the circumstances. (*See* § 2-206(1): "Unless otherwise unambiguously indicated by the language or circumstances (a) an offer to make a contract shall be construed as inviting acceptance in any manner and by any medium reasonable in the circumstances[.]") And given that there was no indication that the market price was changing rapidly or the items were perishable, acceptance by letter was reasonable here.

Answer 149

(B) is the best response,

because the friend predeceased the man.

When the recipient of a specific bequest in a will predeceases the testator, his gift will lapse, and the bequeathed property will fall into the residuary estate. An exception to this rule occurs when a state anti-lapse statute provides for a substitute taker of the bequest. However, the problem states that there is no anti-lapse statute. (Even if there were, most anti-lapse statutes do not save gifts to non-family members.) As a result, the gift will lapse, and the residence will pass to the charity, which will take the residuary of the estate.

(A) is not the best response,

because the residence was in the man's estate when he died.

Ademption occurs when the object of a specific bequest is no longer in the testator's estate when he dies. For example, if the man's will directed that his Cadillac should be given to his wife, but he sold the Cadillac two years before he died, then the gift will have adeemed. This is not the situation here, since the man still owned the residence at the time of his death. Choice A comes to the right conclusion, but for the wrong reason. The charity will take the residence because the gift to the friend, who had predeceased the man, will have lapsed, causing the residence to fall into the residuary of the man's estate.

(C) is not the best response,

because the will was clear on who should take the residence.

The man's will was unambiguous as to who should take the residence upon his death (his friend). Although there may be credible extrinsic evidence that the he wanted his child to take, a court will not consider that evidence. Had the man wished to bequeath his residence to his child, the proper course of action would have been to revise his will. Although the gift to his friend lapsed (see the explanation for choice B above), the law dictates that the residence fall into his residuary estate. The court will not rewrite the man's will based on extrinsic evidence absent significant ambiguities.

(D) is not the best response,

because the charity takes the residuary of the man's estate.

When the recipient of a specific bequest in a will predeceases the testator, his gift will lapse, and the bequeathed property will fall into the residuary estate. An exception to this rule occurs when a state anti-lapse statute provides for a substitute taker of the bequest. However, the problem states that there is no anti-lapse statute. (Even if there were, most anti-lapse statutes do not save gifts to non-family members.) As a result, the gift will lapse, and the residence will pass to the charity, which will take the residuary of the estate. Had the man wanted to leave his residence to his friend, but, in the event that the friend pre-deceased him, to his child, he could have done so by including the child as an alternate taker of the residence: "I leave my residence to my friend, but should he pre-decease me, then to my child."

Answer 150

(B) is the best response,

because it addresses the central issue under these facts, and resolves it in the car driver's favor. The real problem here is pinning the contractor's conduct on the homeowner, since it's likely the contractor would be considered an independent contractor, which, as a general rule, would exonerate the homeowner from liability for the contractor's conduct.

An independent contractor is distinguished from an employee in that, traditionally, his physical conduct in performing services is not subject to a right of control by the employer; a servant's is. The clue under these facts is that you're told that the homeowner engaged the contractor to repair the sidewalk, "leaving it to the contractor to decide how the repair should be made." This simply suggests the contractor is an independent contractor, not an employee.

As a result, in order to prevail, the driver would have to address some basis on which *either* the contractor could be considered an employee, *or* a basis on which the homeowner could be liable for the contractor's acts as an independent contractor. There are two general grounds on which employers will be liable for the conduct of independent contractors: first, where ultra-hazardous activities are involved (e.g., demolition); or, second, the duty is non-delegable due to public policy considerations (e.g., duty of railroad to fence in tracks). Under these facts, it would be *possible* to characterize the contractor's acts as hazardous, and if they *were*, the homeowner would be liable.

Note that B is stated *conditionally* that is, *if* the contractor was engaged in hazardous activity, the homeowner will be liable. Thus, all that's required is that it be plausible on these facts that the conduct could be considered hazardous. Had B used the word "because" instead of "if," the facts would have to show conclusively that the activity *was* hazardous. As it is, B addresses the central issue and offers a plausible ground on which to resolve it in the driver's favor. As a result, it's the driver's best theory of these four choices, making B the best response.

(A) is not the best response,

because it's unlikely a claim for strict liability would succeed on these facts.

There are two principal problems with strict liability as it applies here: one, it's not clear that the concept of strict liability would apply to a sidewalk maintenance statute; and two, it's not clear that the homeowner would be responsible for the contractor's conduct (since the contractor created the risk).

There are three general sources of strict liability: animals, abnormally dangerous activities, and defective products (strict liability can also be imposed under statute or case law). With these, there is said to be an absolute duty of care, such that where there is a breach of that duty that causes a plaintiff's damages, a plaintiff can recover without proving fault.

Without more, it's not clear that the facts here would merit strict liability, and even if they did, it wouldn't be due to mere ownership of the land, as choice A suggests.

Furthermore, choice A does not address the contractor's status as either an employee or an independent contractor. This is critical because, in general, an employer is vicariously liable for the torts of his employees, within the scope of employment, but *not* for torts of independent contractors (unless the activity is ultra-hazardous, or non-delegable due to public policy). The two are distinguishable in that, traditionally, an independent contractor's physical conduct in performing services is not subject to a right of control by the employer, and an employee's is. Under these facts, if the contractor is considered an independent contractor and the activity is non-hazardous, the homeowner will not be strictly liable even though the tree is on his property.

In fact, the best argument for the driver is to claim that the activity was hazardous and, as a result, the homeowner could be liable even if the contractor is considered an independent contractor. Since A ignores this, it's not the best response.

(C) is not the best response,

because merely paying for a repair would not, in and of itself, make the homeowner liable.

Instead, there would have to be some basis on which the homeowner himself should be held liable due to his own conduct, or a means by which he would be vicariously liable for the contractor's conduct. Paying for services would not be sufficient to assume liability nor to relieve the contractor of liability. Since C fails to recognize this, it's not the best response.

(D) is not the best response,

because it's unlikely that the homeowner would be liable for the contractor's conduct on grounds of *respondeat superior*.

Under *respondeat superior*, an employer is liable for the torts of his employees if the tort occurred within the scope of the employment. The problem here is that the contractor is unlikely to be considered an employee; rather, he'd be considered an independent contractor, in which case the doctrine of *respondeat superior* would not result in liability for the homeowner. An independent contractor is distinguished from an employee in that, traditionally, his physical conduct in performing services is not subject to a right of control by the employer; a servant's is. The tip-off under these facts is that you're told that the homeowner engaged the contractor to decide how the repair should be made. This suggests a lack of control associated with independent contractors.

Thus, in order to be correct, D would have to address some basis for the homeowner to be liable even though the contractor is likely to be an independent contractor. Since D doesn't do this, it's not the best response.

Answer 151

(A) is the best response,

because it would seriously impair the creditor's ability to prevail.

The most significant thing to remember here is that if the buyer owes the creditor as an intended beneficiary under the agreement, there is no need for this provision to be in writing, because it doesn't fall within the Statute of Frauds. Thus, in order for the written contract to be relevant, there must be *some* significance attached to the fact that the provision *wasn't* in the written contract. That's what choice A provides.

The concept of "complete integration" is relevant to the Parol Evidence Rule. That rule provides that a writing that is "completely integrated" cannot be contradicted or supplemented with prior written or oral agreements, or contemporaneous oral agreements. A "completely integrated" agreement is one which the parties intended to be a final and complete statement of their agreement.

If the buyer was to pay $25,000 to the creditor instead of the seller, this would vary the written term under which the buyer would pay the entire amount to the seller. Thus, if the agreement is fully integrated, it may prevent the creditor from proving the existence of his claim *at all.* If the written contract *isn't* fully integrated, meaning that it doesn't embody the entire agreement, then the creditor *will* be able to prove his claim, since the Parol Evidence Rule doesn't bar evidence of consistent additional terms where the contract is only partially integrated.

Thus, whether or not the agreement is completely integrated will have a significant impact on the case. Since A recognizes this, it's the best response.

(B) is not the best response,

because the buyer's negligence in reading the agreement would have no bearing on the creditor's claim against him.

If the buyer is to be liable to the creditor, he can be liable even without a writing, since the agreement to pay the creditor falls *outside* the Statute of Frauds. Thus, in order to impact the creditor's claim against the buyer, there must be some relevance to the provision's not appearing in the contract (which would be present, for instance, if the contract were considered fully integrated, since the creditor provision would not be provable *at all* under the Parol Evidence Rule). The buyer's negligence in failing to include the provision would not be relevant to the creditor's claim except that if it were written, the creditor's claim would be easier to prove. Thus, the buyer's negligence alone isn't actionable because there's no causation: the buyer is liable even without the writing. Since B attaches significance to the buyer's negligence where none actually exists, B isn't the best response.

(C) is not the best response,

because *the seller's* negligence couldn't be asserted by *either* party.

The existence of the buyer's duty to pay the creditor depends on whether the creditor's rights as a third party beneficiary under the contract "vested." Since the provision for paying the creditor is not covered by the Statute of Frauds, it's not necessary that the agreement appear in writing. Thus, a negligence claim centering on the failure to put the agreement in writing would not succeed, because there's no *causation*. The creditor *could* recover even without a writing; a writing would only make the claim easier to prove.

Even if negligence were relevant to the claim, neither the buyer nor the creditor could assert *the seller's* negligence. Since C fails to recognize this, it's not the best response.

(D) is not the best response,

because the creditor can recover without being a party to the contract, and, beyond that, the creditor clearly *isn't* a party to the contract under these facts.

A third party *can* recover under a contract if he was an *intended beneficiary* (or, alternatively, if he was an assignee). Thus, if the creditor proves that it was the promisee's (the seller's) intent that the creditor receive the payment from the promisor (the buyer), he'd have enforceable rights under the contract. Since the creditor could recover regardless of whether he's a party or not, D, which conditions the creditor's recovery on whether he's a party to the contract, cannot be the best response.

Answer 152

(D) is the best response,

because the seller does not have to convey marketable title until after all of the installment payments have been made.

The contract calls for the seller to convey "a warranty deed sufficient to convey a fee simple title." Therefore, the seller will have to be able to convey title free of any encumbrances at the time of delivery. In this case, delivery is not due until the buyer has paid 290 more installment payments to the seller. Although the land is currently encumbered by a mortgage, there is no reason to believe that the seller will be unable to provide clear title when the time comes to convey the property. The seller has never been late in making the mortgage payments, the debt is much less than the purchase price, and the seller has a significant amount of time to pay off the mortgage. Further, the seller can use the proceeds from the remaining installment payments to pay down the mortgage. These factors combine to give an adequate assurance that the seller will be able to convey fee simple at closing. The buyer may not sue for damages at this time, because the seller has not breached the contract.

(A) is not the best response,

because there is no reason to believe the seller will be unable to convey marketable title.

Choice A's statement of law is correct: unless the parties agree otherwise, the seller of land is under an implied duty to convey marketable title when delivery of the deed is due. In this case, delivery is not due until the buyer has paid 290 more installment payments to the seller. Although the land is currently encumbered by a mortgage, there is no reason to believe that the seller will be unable to provide clear title when the time comes to convey the property. The seller has never been late in making the mortgage payments, the debt is much less than the purchase price, and the seller has a significant amount of time to pay off the mortgage. Further, the seller can use the proceeds from the remaining installment payments to pay down the mortgage. These factors combine to give an adequate assurance that the seller will be able to convey fee simple at closing. The buyer may not sue for damages at this time, because the seller has not breached the contract.

(B) is not the best response,

because the seller has not attempted to redeem the property.

In many cases, an installment contract for the purchase of land will be treated as a mortgage. Nonpayment by the buyer may be treated as defaulting on the mortgage, which would allow the seller to enforce the contract by ordering the sale of the buyer's interest in the property. However, this is a right that must be exercised by the seller, not the buyer. Since it is the buyer who is seeking damages, the possible treatment of the installment purchase contract as a mortgage is irrelevant.

(C) is not the best response,

because the use of an installment contract as a security device is designed to protect the seller.

An installment purchase contract protects the seller by not conveying the property to the buyer until the full amount of the purchase price is paid in full. Although it may act as a mortgage (see the explanation for choice B above), the seller is not obligated to convey clear title to the property until after the last installment payment has been made. Although the land is currently encumbered by a mortgage, there is no reason to believe that the seller will be unable to provide clear title when the time comes to convey the property. The seller has never been late in making the mortgage payments, the debt is much less than the purchase price, and the seller has a significant amount of time to pay off the mortgage. Further, the seller can use the proceeds from the remaining installment payments to pay down the mortgage. These factors combine to give an adequate assurance that the seller will be able to convey fee simple at closing. The buyer may not sue for damages at this time, because the seller has not breached the contract.

Answer 153

(B) is the best response,

because it identifies the situation, of these four, that most likely satisfies the first degree murder statute in the problem.

The key here is to realize that the defendant's merely being angered by the bicyclist's conduct would not be enough to reduce murder to voluntary manslaughter, since voluntary manslaughter requires that the provocation be recent enough that the actor was still in the "heat of passion" when the killing took place, and that a reasonable person would still have been in the "heat of passion," as well. The act of having to buy rat poison and put it in the bicyclist's coffee indicates that the defendant had time to cool off, and, by the same token, premeditate and deliberate the killing. Furthermore, the use of poison would be clear evidence of the intent to kill, thus satisfying the "malice aforethought" requirement of common law murder (which is what's missing from choice C). Since choice B satisfies the statute in the problem, and the use of poison would supply the "malice aforethought" requirement of common law murder, B is the best response.

(A) is not the best response,

because it would not satisfy the "premeditation and deliberation" element of the statute given in the problem.

At common law, murder requires an unlawful killing (neither justifiable nor excusable) committed with malice aforethought. Voluntary manslaughter is murder committed in the "heat of passion." In fact, under these facts, the defendant would most likely be guilty of voluntary manslaughter. The key word here is *immediately*. If the defendant was responding immediately to an insult, there's a strong possibility that he killed the acquaintance in the *heat of passion*. That would make the killing voluntary manslaughter, not murder. Even if he were guilty of murder, he wouldn't be guilty of first degree murder, since there was no time to premeditate and deliberate, and there was no other crime being committed. As a result, A is not the best response.

(C) is not the best response,

but it's an appealing one.

The "lying in wait" in choice C would certainly satisfy the premeditation and deliberation requirement of first degree murder, as given in the statute; however, the problem here is whether there was a murder at all. While murder does not require intent, it does require malice aforethought. Malice aforethought can take the form of intending to inflict great bodily injury (short of an intent to kill), or acting in spite of an unjustifiably high risk to human life. Under choice C, the defendant did intend to injure the co-worker however, striking the co-worker with a broom handle could not be considered evidence of an intent to inflict great bodily injury, since great injury would typically not result from a whack with a broom handle. As a result, C is not the best response.

(D) is not the best response,

because it would probably not satisfy the premeditation and deliberation element of the statute in the problem.

As a prerequisite, you have to remember what common law murder requires: an unlawful killing (neither justifiable nor excusable) committed with malice aforethought. At common law, voluntary intoxication can only be used to prove a lack of capacity for specific intent crimes, and it can only be used if the defendant was intoxicated before he formulated the intent to commit the crime. Some courts restrict the use of voluntary intoxication as a defense to first degree murder. Here, the defendant's drunkenness apparently stopped him from forming the necessary *mens rea* for murder. As a result, he may not be guilty of murder at all, making D not the best response.

Answer 154

(C) is the best response,

because it identifies the central reason why the utility will be liable for the farmer's injuries.

A private nuisance—which is probably the type involved here, due to the small scope of injury—is an act by a defendant that creates an unreasonable, substantial interference with a plaintiff's use and enjoyment of property. Here, the utility deliberately created the fumes, and they harmed the farmer. The creator of a private nuisance is liable for all harm resulting proximately from the nuisance, both personal (including diseases like the farmer's) and property. That's all there is to it. What's important to note here is that it doesn't matter how feasible alternatives are, like the scrubbing equipment. Once the nuisance is created, there's liability. Since C correctly identifies the central reason the utility will be liable, it's the best response.

(A) is not the best response,

because it focuses on a fact that is irrelevant.

All a private nuisance requires is an act by a defendant creating an unreasonable, substantial interference with a plaintiff's use or enjoyment of property. Thus, the ease with which the defendant could prevent the nuisance is *irrelevant*. As a result, in nuisance, it's important to focus on the damage to the plaintiff, *not* the fault of the defendant. Since A ignores this, it's not the best response.

(B) is not the best response,

because it's not clear that it appropriately characterizes the facts, and even if it *does*, it would not prevent the farmer from recovering for nuisance.

The distinction between a public and a private nuisance is the scope of the injury. A public nuisance affects the community at large through an act or condition that unreasonably interferes with the health, safety, or convenience of the general public (e.g., blocking a public highway, operating a brothel). A private nuisance, on the other hand, requires an act by a defendant creating an unreasonable, substantial interference with a plaintiff's use or enjoyment of property. While the fumes here might affect the community in general, the facts here tell you the farmer's land is adjacent to, and downwind from, the plant, and there's no mention of others being affected. Assuming *arguendo* that the nuisance is public and not private, the farmer will be able to recover damages nonetheless. Normally, public nuisance suits are brought by the state. In order for a private person to recover for public nuisance, he has to prove that he suffered special damages above and beyond the ordinary damage the public incurred. Here, the farmer's proximity to the fumes, and the damages he suffered, suggest he would probably be able to recover under a public nuisance claim. Thus, since B probably does not correctly characterize the facts, and the fact it cites is irrelevant, it's not the best response.

(D) is not the best response,

because there's no causation between the ultra-hazardous activity and the farmer's damages.

Private nuisance is an act by a defendant that creates an unreasonable, substantial interference with a plaintiff's use or enjoyment of property. Here, it's not the electricity that creates the interference, but the fumes emitted by the plant, which is *not* an ultrahazardous activity. Had the farmer been electrocuted by downed power lines, say, there *would* be causation. In fact, the utility will be liable in nuisance for the interference created by the fumes. Thus, the ultrahazardous nature of electricity is not a central concern in this problem, making D not the best response.

Answer 155

(A) is the best response,

because the gallery had resold the painting in reliance on the collector's rejection.

When the collector rightfully rejected the painting, the gallery justifiably attempted to, and succeeded at, finding a substitute buyer for the painting. It then informed the collector that it would be reclaiming the painting within a couple of weeks. At this point, the gallery has changed its position based on the collector's rejection, and the collector cannot treat the painting as his property. However, the collector did so when he sold the painting to the art admirer. Since the gallery was the owner of the painting at the time the collector sold it, the collector has wrongfully converted the gallery's property. The remedy for conversion is the fair market value of the item at the time of the conversion. The seller's ability to get $120,000 for the painting is strong evidence that the market value of the painting was at least that much.

(B) is not the best response,

because it does not maximize the amount that the gallery may recover from the collector.

When the collector rightfully rejected the painting, the gallery justifiably attempted to, and succeeded at, finding a substitute buyer for the painting. It then informed the collector that it would be reclaiming the painting within a couple of weeks. At this point, the gallery has changed its position based on the collector's rejection, and the collector cannot treat the painting as his property. However, the collector did so when he sold the painting to the art admirer. Since the gallery was the owner of the painting at the time the collector sold it, the collector has wrongfully converted the gallery's property. The remedy for conversion is the fair market value of the item at the time of the conversion. The seller's ability to get $120,000 for the painting is strong evidence that the market value of the painting was at least that much. Alternatively, the gallery can sue the collector for the contract price. However, since the market price of the painting is greater than the contract price, the gallery can obtain a greater recovery by suing for the market price.

(C) is not the best response,

because it does not maximize the amount that the gallery may recover from the collector.

While a seller may recover the market/contract price differential after a buyer's breach, the $20,000 that would provide in this case is far less than would be obtained by suing for the market price, which the gallery is able to do. When the collector rightfully rejected the painting, the gallery justifiably attempted to, and succeeded at, finding a substitute buyer for the painting. It then informed the collector that it would be reclaiming the painting within a couple of weeks. At this point, the gallery has changed its position based on the collector's rejection, and the collector cannot treat the painting as his property. However, the collector did so when he sold the painting to the art admirer. Since the gallery was the owner of the painting at the time the collector sold it, the collector has wrongfully converted the gallery's property. The remedy for conversion is the fair market value of the item at the time of the conversion. The seller's ability to get $120,000 for the painting is strong evidence that the market value of the painting was at least that much.

(D) is not the best response,

because it does not maximize the amount that the gallery may recover from the collector.

While a volume seller may recover its lost profits on a sale after a buyer's breach in certain circumstances, the damages doing so would provide in this case are less than would be obtained by suing for the market price, which the gallery is able to do. (Even if the gallery got the painting for free, they would only make $100,000 on the sale.) When the collector rightfully rejected the painting, the gallery justifiably attempted to, and succeeded at, finding a substitute buyer for the painting. It then informed the collector that it would be reclaiming the painting within a couple of weeks. At this point, the gallery has changed its position based on the collector's rejection, and the collector cannot treat the painting as his property. However, the collector did so when he sold the painting to the art admirer. Since the gallery was the owner of the painting at the time the collector sold it, the collector has wrongfully converted the gallery's property. The remedy for conversion is the fair market value of the item at the time of the conversion. The seller's ability to get $120,000 for the painting is strong evidence that the market value of the painting was at least that much.

Answer 156

(B) is the best response,

because it correctly applies the appropriate rule to these facts.

In this question, the contents of a letter are involved—the investigator's letter to the defendant inquiring about the plaintiff. Thus, there's at least facially a Best Evidence Rule issue. The Best Evidence Rule is triggered when a party wants to prove the material terms of a writing (or a witness is testifying relying on a writing). Then, the "original writing" (which includes photocopies) must be produced, and copies and oral testimony about the writing's contents will only be admissible if the original is shown to be unavailable for some other reason than the proponent's misconduct. FRE 1002.

The thing that makes the Best Evidence Rule inadmissible here is that no one is seeking to *prove the contents* of the inquiry letter. It doesn't particularly matter how the request was worded, and there's nothing for the jury to interpret. Furthermore, it is not clear that the investigator is relying on the letter for his testimony, since he wrote the letter and could remember the contents. All that matters is that the investigator asked the defendant about the plaintiff, and the investigator's testimony will suffice for this. Since the terms of the letter are not material to the case, the investigator's testimony will be admissible without accounting for the unavailability of the letter.

Note that once you've removed any Best Evidence Rule problem, you've also taken care of a potential hearsay problem, as well. Had the contents of the investigator's letter been at issue, there would be a hearsay issue as well as a Best Evidence Rule problem, because the testimony would be repeating the out-of-court statements found in the letter. Since the investigator is merely being asked if he wrote to the defendant inquiring about the plaintiff—and this doesn't require that he repeat any out-of-court statements—there's no hearsay problem.

Since B recognizes and confronts the central, Best Evidence Rule issue, and satisfactorily resolves it, it is the best response.

(A) is not the best response,

because it is irrelevant.

The admissibility of the investigator's testimony is not dependent on whether or not the inquiry was made in the regular course of business; rather, all that's necessary is that the investigator have personal knowledge of the substance of his testimony—that is, whether an inquiry was made.

What choice B implies is that the testimony is hearsay, and will only be admissible if it fits the business records exception to the hearsay rule. The reason this doesn't apply is that the investigator's testimony isn't hearsay. Hearsay is an out-of-court statement offered to prove the truth of its assertion. Here, the contents of the investigator's letter aren't being offered to prove that anything in the letter was true. Rather, the only thing that's important about his out-of-court statement is that it was made—i.e., to prove that he inquired about the plaintiff at all. As a result, it's not hearsay, and there's no need for it to fit in any exception, let alone the business records exception. Since A doesn't recognize this, it's not the best response.

(C) is not the best response,

because the admissibility of the investigator's testimony would not depend on the defendant's prior notification.

The "prior notification" language addresses the issue of surprise. At common law, even though a piece of evidence is relevant, it can be excluded under some circumstances if there are factors that outweigh the probative value of the evidence. One such circumstance is unfair surprise to the opponent. The theory is that, with no reasonable grounds for anticipating such proof, the opponent would be unprepared to meet it. This is addressed in the Federal Rules, in the Advisory Committee's Notes to Rule 403, where it's suggested that it's more appropriate for the affected party to seek a continuance, rather than having the evidence rejected outright, in cases of surprise.

In any case, under these facts, there'd be no basis for excluding the investigator's testimony about the inquiry even if the plaintiff's attorney didn't specifically know about it beforehand. The entire basis of this lawsuit was a defamatory letter. Here, the investigator's inquiry would provide the reason the defamatory letter was sent. This is close enough to a central issue that the plaintiff's attorney should reasonably have anticipated it, thus negating the possibility of unfair surprise. Since C doesn't recognize this, it's not the best response.

(D) is not the best response,

because it incorrectly implies that the Best Evidence Rule applies to the investigator's testimony, since the Best Evidence Rule requires proof that a document is unavailable before testimony about its contents will be admissible.

The Best Evidence Rule only applies when the terms of a writing are being proven, or the witness is testifying relying on a writing. Then, the "original writing" (which includes photocopies) must be produced, and copies and oral testimony about the writing's contents will only be admissible if the original is shown to be unavailable for some other reason than the proponent's misconduct. FRE 1002.

The thing that makes the Best Evidence Rule inadmissible here is that no one is seeking to prove the contents of the inquiry letter. It doesn't particularly matter how the request was worded, and there's nothing for the jury to interpret. Furthermore, it is not clear that the investigator is relying on the letter for his testimony, since he wrote the letter and could remember the contents. All that matters is that the investigator asked the defendant about the plaintiff, and the investigator's testimony will suffice for this. Since the terms of the letter are not material to the case, and the investigator isn't relying on the letter for his testimony, the investigator's testimony will be admissible without accounting for the unavailability of the letter. Note that the *defendant's* letter is an entirely different matter, since that's the letter that allegedly contains the defamatory matter. Since the terms of that letter would be material to the case, it *would* be covered by the Best Evidence Rule. However, what's at issue in this question is the investigator's inquiry letter, not the defendant's response. Since testimony about the inquiry letter will be admissible without proving the unavailability of the letter itself, and D doesn't recognize this, D isn't the best response.

Answer 157

(C) is the best response,

because the equal protection issue will determine the validity of the restriction under these facts.

Restrictions on the use of land are valid as long as they aren't repugnant to law or public policy. The restriction here creates a classification: people aged 21 and over versus those under 21. A classification that determines people's rights—here, the right to occupy land—is the hallmark of an equal protection problem.

However, this question involves one further step, because the restriction here is a private agreement between owners of land in the subdivision, and the Constitution doesn't ban purely private acts of discrimination; some state action is required. What makes this an equal protection issue is that the other lot owners are seeking to have the restriction enforced in court, and such enforcement constitutes state action. Thus, if the restriction is an equal protection violation, the court could not enforce it. You might argue that the classification here addresses who can exercise the fundamental right of procreation, since those living in the subdivision could not have children. In that case, the restriction would be subject to strict scrutiny, and would thus almost certainly be invalid. What this shows is that an analysis of the restriction under the Equal Protection Clause would determine its validity, and this is the only argument of these four that will determine the lawfulness of the restriction. Thus, choice C is the best response.

(A) is not the best response,

because the distinction between realty and personalty would be irrelevant here.

The restriction here addresses who may own or occupy the land. Thus, it doesn't matter how the land is occupied, whether it's realty, personalty, a gingerbread house, or a giant shoe, as long as the restriction is lawful. The distinction of realty versus personalty would be relevant, say, to whether or not the mobile home were considered a fixture, or, alternatively, for probate purposes in determining who is entitled to the mobile home (if the decedent has willed personalty to one person and realty to someone else). The distinction isn't relevant to this restriction; the only distinction involved here is between people aged 21 and over, and those under 21. Thus, the realty versus personalty distinction won't be the issue deciding the case, making A not the best response.

(B) is not the best response,

because the restriction here wouldn't be unlawful because it's a restraint on alienation.

A deed restriction is only an invalid restraint on alienation if landowners could not sell their lots as restricted. Otherwise, property is frequently sold with restraints, like easements and restrictions on use. Here, the property owners could clearly sell their lots to adults without children. Thus, it's not the restriction's impact on alienation that would make it unlawful. As a result, it's not the alienation issue that would decide this case. Since B states otherwise, it's not the best response.

(D) is not the best response,

because if the restriction were valid, it needn't be expressly repeated verbatim in the carpenter's deed in order to bind him.

As long as the property holder has, at the very least, constructive notice of the restriction, it doesn't matter that it doesn't appear in his own deed. For instance, real covenants and equitable servitudes are binding as long as they appear somewhere in the chain of title, even if they are completely absent from the current owner's deed. Here, the carpenter's deed specifically references the plat for the subdivision; thus, he had notice of the restriction, and, if the restriction were lawful, it would be binding on the carpenter even without its being repeated verbatim in his deed. Since choice D discusses an issue that will not be determinative under these facts, it's not the best response.

Answer 158

(B) is the best response,

because it correctly characterizes the clause as a condition, not a promise, and addresses and resolves a central issue.

A condition is the occurrence or non-occurrence of an event that triggers, limits, or extinguishes an absolute duty to perform. While it *can* be difficult to distinguish a condition from a promise, courts consider primarily the language used (i.e., how the parties characterize the clause). Furthermore, Rest. 2d of Contracts § 206 provides this guideline: If the contractual provision purports to be the words of the party of whom performance is required, the provision is a promise; if it's supposed to be the words of the other party, it's a condition. Here, taken together, these suggest that the clause is a condition. B correctly characterizes this.

More importantly, B addresses the *specific* question asked, which is how the court will construe the truthfulness warranty. What the truthfulness provision would be reasonably interpreted to do is prevent fraud by requiring truthfulness to the best of the applicant's knowledge. This requires that you address the rules of contract interpretation. As a general rule, contract terms are interpreted objectively, by determining what interpretation a reasonable person (knowing all that the parties know) would place on the terms. Here, it wouldn't be reasonable to require an *absolute* guarantee. The truthfulness provision would be designed to let the insurance company determine the risks it is undertaking. Thus, the reasonable interpretation in choice B will suffice. As a result, B is the best response.

(A) is not the best response,

because although it correctly characterizes the clause as a condition, it does not interpret it correctly.

A condition is the occurrence or non-occurrence of an event that triggers, limits, or extinguishes an absolute duty to perform. Here, the company's duty to pay is expressly made dependent on the truth of the woman's statements in the application, so it's an *express condition*. As an express condition, it requires strict compliance and any deviation would be considered a major breach, relieving the other party (the company) of its duty to perform.

As a result, it's easy to see why you might choose this response. However, even a condition is subject to the rules of contract interpretation. As a general rule, contract terms are interpreted objectively, by determining what interpretation a reasonable person, knowing all that the parties know, would place on the terms.

Here, the insurance company could only expect applicants to warrant their statements to the extent of their knowledge. It would be unreasonable to, in effect, make applicants strictly liable for their statements. Since choice A places an unreasonable interpretation on the clause, even though it correctly states the theoretical law, it's not the best response.

(C) is not the best response,

because it mischaracterizes the clause, and does not address an element relevant to determining the company's liability.

A condition is the occurrence or non-occurrence of an event that triggers, limits, or extinguishes an absolute duty to perform. While it *can* be difficult to distinguish a condition from a promise, courts consider primarily the language used (i.e., how the parties characterize the clause). Furthermore, Rest. 2d of Contracts § 206 provides this guideline: If the contractual provision purports to be the words of the party of whom performance is required, the provision is a promise; if it's supposed to be the words of the other party, it's a condition. Here, taken together, these suggest that the clause is a condition, not a promise.

Even if the clause is *not* a condition, contrary to what choice C states, this does not determine the company's liability. If the clause is a promise, and the woman breached it, the company would be entitled to positive relief, e.g., damages. Thus, the mere characterization of the clause as a promise would not make the company liable.

Instead, the company's liability will turn on the interpretation of the clause, *given* that it's a condition. The fact is that the woman warranted the truthfulness of the statements in her application, and the statement about heart disease was not true. Thus, if the condition is interpreted strictly, the company won't be liable. However, the rule is that contract provisions are interpreted *reasonably*, meaning that the statements need only be true to the best of the woman's knowledge. Since choice C mischaracterizes the clause and ignores the central issue, it's not the best response.

(D) is the best response,

because it mischaracterizes the clause as a promise instead of a condition, and ignores the central issue, namely, the interpretation of the "truthfulness" warranty.

A condition is the occurrence or non-occurrence of an event that triggers, limits, or extinguishes an absolute duty to perform. While it *can* be difficult to distinguish a condition from a promise, courts consider primarily the language used (i.e., how the parties characterize the clause). Furthermore, Rest. 2d of Contracts § 206 provides this guideline: If the contractual provision purports to be the words of the party of whom performance is required, the provision is a promise; if it's supposed to be the words of the other party, it's a condition. Here, taken together, these suggest that the clause is a condition, not a promise. Thus, D mischaracterizes the clause.

Beyond that, D ignores the central issue here: interpretation of the warranty clause. Regardless of whether the clause is a condition or a promise, you *still* need to determine if it was breached. If the truthfulness warranty is interpreted strictly, the woman's estate would be liable whether it's a condition or a promise. However, that doesn't reflect the rule on contract interpretation, which is that provisions must be interpreted *reasonably*. Here, it's reasonable to interpret the warranty as requiring truth to the best of the applicant's knowledge. Thus, characterizing the clause as a promise doesn't determine the company's liability—instead, that turns on interpretation of the warranty language. Since D doesn't recognize this, it's not the best response.

Answer 159

(A) is correct,

because the complaint alleges fraud and so is required to plead the particulars of the fraud.

FRCP 9(b) requires that, "[i]n ***alleging fraud*** or mistake, a party must ***state with particularity the circumstances constituting fraud*** or mistake." Here the complaint includes only the conclusory allegation that Defendant, by delivering non-organic cookies, engaged in fraud. Courts interpret the special pleading rules for fraud to require that the complaint allege the relatively-precise misconduct that constitutes the fraud. Generally this heightened pleading requirement is met when the complaint alleges the "who, what, when, where, and how" of the fraudulent representation. *See, e.g., Lerner v. Fleet Bank, N.A.*, 459 F.3d 273 (2d Cir. 2006) (to meet the requirements of FRCP 9(b) when fraud is alleged, "the complaint must: (1) specify the statements that the plaintiff contends were fraudulent, (2) identify the speaker, (3) state where and when the statements were made, and (4) explain why the statements were fraudulent"). Here, the allegations of the complaint do not meet this standard because they do not specify when and where Defendant made the fraudulent statements, how Plaintiff knows that the statements were untrue, or how Plaintiff knows that any falsity was intentional (i.e., how/why Plaintiff believes that Defendant knew of the falsity when it made the statement, or at least when it shipped the merchandise). Moreover, most courts say the allegations of fraud must include specific facts giving rise to a "strong inference" of fraud, whereas the complaint here contains only a bare assertion that fraud occurred.

(B) is not correct,

because it relies on a pleading standard that the Supreme Court no longer applies.

Prior to 2007, the Court held that a complaint should not be dismissed for failure to state a claim "unless it appears beyond doubt that the plaintiff can prove no set of facts in support of his claim which could entitle him to relief." *Conley v. Gibson*, 355 U.S. 41, 45-46 (1957). But in *Bell Atlantic Corp. v. Twombly*, 550 U.S. 544, 554-563 (2007), the Court "retired" the *Conley* formulation, and announced a new ***"plausibility"*** standard for when to dismiss a federal-court complaint for failing to state a claim; *Twombly* "require[s] that the allegations in the complaint must allege facts showing that recovery [is] not merely 'conceivable' but that it [is] 'plausible.' " F,K&M (5th Ed.), s. 5.9. See also the post-*Twombly* decision in *Ashcroft v. Iqbal,* 556 U.S. 662, 684 (2009) (held, a federal complaint must state a "plausible" claim, and "threadbare ***recitals of the elements*** of a cause of action, supported by ***mere conclusory statements***, do not suffice" to meet the requirement of plausibility.) Choice (B), by asserting that the motion must be denied unless defendant has shown that there is "no set of facts" that plaintiff could prove that would be sufficient to show fraud, adheres to the now-abandoned *Conley* standard rather than to the current standard by which the motion will be granted if the court determines that plaintiff's allegations are "conclusory" and not "plausible."

(C) is not correct,

because a party is never required to move for a judgment on the pleadings and, in any event, such a motion is available only after the pleadings are "closed." FRCP 12(c). In contrast, a motion to dismiss for failure to state a claim is filed prior to any responsive pleading, and thus prior to any motion for judgment on the pleadings. *See* FRCP 12(b) ("A motion asserting any of these defenses [including a motion under 12(b)(6) for "failure to state a claim upon which relief can be granted"] must be made before pleading if a responsive pleading is allowed.") The pleadings are closed only after an answer has been filed. *See* FRCP 7(a). Here, since the facts say that Defendant has not yet answered, it's clear that Defendant was not required to move for judgment on the pleadings.

(D) is not correct,

because under federal pleading rules, a plaintiff *may* join a tort and a contract claim in one lawsuit and, indeed, may join "as many claims as it has against an opposing party." FRCP 18(a). The federal joinder rules are broad and do not restrict the joinder of claims even if they relate to different transactions or depend on different legal theories.

Answer 160

What's going on here? The facts, and a quick glance at the answers, suggest that the question concerns the Mercy Rule—a criminal defendant's right to introduce evidence of his pertinent trait of good character.

(B) is the best response,

because it correctly states that the testimony will be admissible to prove that the defendant is innocent.

First, you have to disassemble these facts, and determine what's going on here. The criminal defendant, who has not testified, is calling a witness to testify to his good character. This should trigger the Mercy Rule in your mind. The FRE's version of the Mercy Rule is given in 404(a)(2). FRE 404(a)(1) states the general rule that "Evidence of a person's character or character trait is not admissible to prove that on a particular occasion the person acted in accordance with the character or trait." But 404(a)(2) lists some exceptions, one of which is that "in a criminal case: (A) a defendant may offer evidence of the *defendant's pertinent trait*." Here, evidence that the defendant is a "peaceable man" would contradict the prosecutor's contention that the defendant murdered the victim without having been attacked or threatened. Therefore, the "peaceable man" evidence would tend to show that the defendant was innocent (e.g., by making it more likely than it would otherwise be that he was attacked).

Note, incidentally, that once the defendant has offered such character evidence, 404(a)(2)(A) lets the prosecutor rebut the defendant's evidence with reputation and opinion testimony as to the defendant's bad character for the trait in question (which the prosecutor couldn't otherwise do). Since B correctly states the law and applies it to the facts here, B is the best response.

(A) is not the best response,

because it's not logically relevant.

If you chose this response, you realized that the Mercy Rule is at issue in this question, but you didn't apply it properly. Under the Mercy Rule, the defendant in a criminal case may offer pertinent character evidence to prove his innocence. The mistake A makes is to suggest that the witness's testimony is admissible on the issue of the defendant's *credibility* (since that's what believability addresses). The defendant's honesty is not in issue *because these facts tell you that the witness is the defendant's first witness,* which means that the defendant himself has not yet testified, and thus his credibility hasn't yet been attacked, and so is not "pertinent."

(C) is not the best response,

because it's irrelevant.

Under the Mercy Rule of FRE 404(a)(2)(A), the defendant in a criminal case may offer pertinent character evidence to prove his innocence. That's exactly what the witness's testimony does; evidence that the defendant is a "peaceable man" would contradict the prosecutor's contention that the defendant murdered the victim, which makes it pertinent.

It's not necessary that the defendant testify in order to offer evidence of his good character under the Mercy Rule. Of course, if he did choose to testify, then the prosecutor could impeach him with evidence reflecting on his credibility; and, in fact, even if the defendant doesn't testify, if he invokes the Mercy Rule, the prosecutor can rebut the defendant's evidence with reputation and opinion testimony as to the defendant's bad character.

Since C creates a prerequisite to admitting the evidence here that does not, in fact, exist, it is not the best response.

(D) is not the best response,

because it misstates the rule on how a character trait may be proven.

As is discussed in Choice B, FRE 404(a)(2) allows a criminal defendant to offer "evidence of the *defendant's pertinent trait*" of character. FRE 405(a) then says that "When evidence of a person's character or character trait is admissible, it may be proved by testimony about the person's *reputation* or by testimony in the form of an opinion." So given that the defendant was entitled to prove his character trait for peaceableness, he was entitled to do so by testimony about his reputation.

Answer 161

(D) is the best response.

D is the best response, because it correctly identifies the central reason why the motion to dismiss should be granted: the man was not a federal judge, and thus was not entitled to life tenure.

As these facts state, federal judges, serving on federal courts created pursuant to Article III of the Constitution, are entitled to lifetime tenure and undiminished pay. Had the man been a federal judge, he would have been entitled to both these benefits. However, the man wasn't a federal judge; instead, you're told he served on a tribunal created by Congress. Problematically, Congress can create tribunals under Article I of the Constitution, and can create lower federal courts under Article III.

The difference between a tribunal and a court depends on the functions served; a tribunal is legislative in nature, and a court is adjudicative. Here, the functions of the tribunal were legislative, and as a result the man wouldn't enjoy the Article III privileges of a federal judge. Instead, he'd serve at the pleasure of Congress.

Thus, the motion to dismiss should be granted, because the man could prove no set of facts under which he'd be entitled to life tenure, an Article III privilege. Sine choice D recognizes this, it's the best response.

(A) is not the best response,

because the man is not an Article III judge, and thus there's no issue under Article III; and even if there were an Article III issue, A misstates the law.

Congress in fact has considerable power with regard to Article III courts. Under Article III, § 1, of the Constitution, the federal judicial power is "vested in one Supreme Court, and in such inferior Courts as the Congress may from time to time . . . establish." Congress can not only create new, inferior courts, but it can regulate the appellate jurisdiction of federal courts under Article III, § 2. Thus, the federal judiciary could hardly be characterized as "independent," contrary to what choice A states.

In any case, the man was not an Article III judge. Instead, he was a member of a legislative tribunal created by Congress. While it's true that federal judges cannot be removed from office during good behavior, nor can their pay be cut, this would not apply to the man. Instead, he was appointed by Congress and Congress could remove him as it sees fit. Since A doesn't recognize that the man wasn't a judge, it's not the best response.

(B) is not the best response,

because the man had no property right in his federal employment.

With the words "property right," choice B suggests that the man's removal, without some form of fair hearing, constitutes a due process violation. When the effect of a governmental activity amounts to a deprivation of a property interest or right, there's a potential due process problem. While "property" needn't necessarily be actual, tangible land or chattels, it requires at least interests already acquired in specific benefits. As far as governmental employment is concerned, the existence of a "property" interest in continued employment is determined under applicable federal, state, or municipal law. Thus, the statute creating the job, or the employment contract, or a clear understanding must provide for termination only "for cause." Here, there's no indication that the man's employment was anything other than at the pleasure of Congress. He served only as a member of a tribunal, not as a federal judge, so the lifetime employment and prohibition of salary diminution applicable to federal judges wouldn't apply to him.

Even if the man *had* a property right in his employment, this wouldn't determine that his dismissal involved a due process violation. Instead, he'd have to establish that he wasn't granted a fair hearing pursuant to his dismissal. Here again, there are no facts under this question to indicate this. Since B incorrectly focuses on a due process issue when none are indicated under these facts, it's not the best response.

(C) is not the best response,

because the man *did* have the standing to challenge his dismissal.

In order to press a claim, a party must have standing. Standing requires that the governmental action challenged must have caused or is imminently likely to cause, an injury to the party seeking review. Here, the man was removed from his job, so he clearly suffered an injury. While his claim isn't *valid,* since he wasn't a federal judge, this doesn't address the threshold question of whether or not he has standing. Since C doesn't recognize this, it's not the best response.

Answer 162

(A) is the best response,

because it offers the cornerstone of a public nuisance claim by private individuals.

A public nuisance is an act that unreasonably interferes with the health, safety, or convenience of the public in general. Such claims are typically brought by the state. However, a private individual *can* recover for public nuisance if he suffered special damages above and beyond the ordinary damage the public incurred. Since A recognizes this, it's the best response.

(B) is not the best response,

because its reasoning is an insufficient basis for a public nuisance claim brought by private individuals.

In order for a private claim of public nuisance to succeed, the plaintiff must prove that he suffered special damages above and beyond the ordinary damage the public incurred, both in kind and degree. Thus, merely proving an interference with the use or enjoyment of property would be insufficient. If you chose this response, it's probably because you were thinking of a *private* nuisance claim, which is what the reasoning in B would support. However, a public nuisance claim is stricter, and since B fails to recognize this, it's not the best response.

(C) is not the best response,

because it misstates the law.

While the state typically *is* the plaintiff in public nuisance actions, a private individual *may* recover for public nuisance if he suffered special damages above and beyond the ordinary damage the public incurred. Thus, the state is *not* the only potential plaintiff. Since C incorrectly restricts the claim to the state, it's not the best response.

(D) is not the best response,

because "coming to the nuisance" does not, in and of itself, defeat a nuisance claim.

Even if one moves into a neighborhood knowing about a nuisance, he is *still* entitled to the reasonable use and enjoyment of his land. Only if one moves in lacking good faith, or for the sole purpose of launching a lawsuit will "coming to the nuisance" defeat a nuisance claim. (The Restatement of Torts views "coming to the nuisance" as a factor to be considered in determining liability.) Instead, as private individuals pressing a public nuisance suit, plaintiffs will have to prove they suffered damages above and beyond the damage the public incurred. A public nuisance itself is an act that unreasonably interferes with the health, safety, or convenience of the public in general. Since the mere fact of "coming to the nuisance" alone won't determine who prevails, D is not the best response.

Answer 163

(B) is the best response,

because the officer feigned agreement, which means that no conspiracy formed in a common-law jurisdiction.

A conspiracy is defined as an agreement between two or more persons to do either an unlawful act or a lawful act by unlawful means. The agreement between two or more persons is called the "plurality" requirement, and, under the common law, if only one party really means to agree, and the other(s) is/are merely feigning agreement, the plurality requirement is not met. On the other hand, under the modern (and Model Penal Code) approach, regardless of one party's lack of subjective intent to carry out the object crime, the other party may nonetheless be convicted of conspiracy. In this problem, the common-law rule governs, and therefore the dealer cannot be convicted, as the dealer was the only person who agreed to commit the crime.

(A) is not the best response,

because the common law does not require an overt act for conspiracy.

A conspiracy is defined as an agreement between two or more persons to do either an unlawful act or a lawful act by unlawful means. An overt act is not required, and, even if it were, in this instance payment for the drugs likely would qualify as an overt act in jurisdictions imposing such a requirement.

(C) is not the best response,

because, while the common law does not require an overt act, it does require plurality of agreement, and therefore no agreement was formed here.

A conspiracy is defined as an agreement between two or more persons to do either an unlawful act or a lawful act by unlawful means. The agreement between two or more persons is called the "plurality" requirement, and, under the common law, if only one party really means to agree, and the other(s) is/are merely feigning agreement, the plurality requirement is not met. On the other hand, under the modern (and Model Penal Code) approach, regardless of one party's lack of subjective intent to carry out the object crime, the other party may nonetheless be convicted of conspiracy. In this problem, the common-law rule governs, and therefore the dealer cannot be convicted, as the dealer was the only person who agreed to commit the crime.

(D) is not the best response,

because the officer feigned agreement, which means that no conspiracy formed in a common law jurisdiction; any alleged mistake of fact or law is irrelevant, as the elements of conspiracy are not met.

A conspiracy is defined as an agreement between two or more persons to do either an unlawful act or a lawful act by unlawful means. The agreement between two or more persons is called the "plurality" requirement, and, under the common law, if only one party really means to agree, and the other(s) is/are merely feigning agreement, the plurality requirement is not met. On the other hand, under the modern (and Model Penal Code) approach, regardless of one party's lack of subjective intent to carry out the object crime, the other party may nonetheless be convicted of conspiracy. In this problem, the common law rule governs, and therefore the dealer cannot be convicted, as the dealer was the only person who agreed to commit the crime.

Answer 164

(D) is the best response,

because it focuses on the central issue and analyzes it correctly: the daughter's destruction of the deed would probably be insufficient to convey title back to the mother.

In order to make a valid gift of real property, there must be the intent to bestow a gift, coupled with delivery of the deed. Under these facts, the mother made a valid gift to the daughter. However, the daughter's mere destruction of the deed, *even though it was at the mother's request,* would probably not constitute either an intent to make a gift *or* delivery of the deed, with the most obvious shortfall being in delivery of the deed. The thing that makes these facts a bit more difficult to analyze is that the mother is the original grantor. However, this wouldn't change the rule, and indicates why it's so important on MBE questions just to *mechanically apply rules.* In this case, doing so reveals that title to the parcel was still in the daughter, making D the best response.

(A) is not the best response,

because the factor it relies on is irrelevant, and its conclusion is incorrect.

Even though the daughter did not pay for the parcel, she can still be the owner of it. A grantor may make a gift of real property by delivering a deed, with the intent to make a gift. These requirements are satisfied here. (A "quitclaim deed" is merely a deed that conveys whatever interest the grantor had in the property; it has no warranties associated with it.) Since the conveyance was valid, the daughter acquired valid title to the parcel via quitclaim deed, making A not the best response.

(B) is not the best response,

because it misstates the law.

While the conveyance from the mother to the daughter was valid, the parcel was never conveyed back to the mother, because mere destruction of a deed is not sufficient for a conveyance. In order to make a gift of real property, there are two elements required: intent to make a gift, and delivery of a deed. Here, the daughter's destruction of the deed would probably not constitute delivery of the deed. Furthermore, there is no evidence that the daughter intended to make a gift of the property back to the mother, since voluntarily destroying the deed would probably not suffice. As a result, the parcel would remain the daughter's, making B not the best response.

(C) is not the best response,

because it wrongly applies undue influence to these facts, and does not focus on the central issue involved.

First, the facts do not suggest undue influence. Undue influence is a kind of constructive fraud, under which a person is deprived of his free will by another.

This type of thing typically turns up in wills cases, where a schemer in the family of the testator exerts moral coercion on the testator. (The kind of thing Bette Davis did to Joan Crawford in "Whatever Happened to Baby Jane?"—you know.) The facts here just don't measure up. Second, choice C does not focus on the central issue, which is whether, in fact, the daughter's destroying the deed would constitute a valid conveyance back to the mother. In fact, it probably would *not,* since a valid gift of real property requires an intent to bestow a gift coupled with delivery of the deed. Neither of these is apparently present here. As a result, C is not the best response.

Answer 165

(B) is the best response,

because the contract did not specify that progress payments should be made.

In general, when one party promises to perform a task and the other party promises only to pay, the party performing the task must complete its performance before the obligation to pay will arise. In this problem, the builder has agreed to construct a garage for the homeowner and the homeowner has promised to pay the builder $10,000. Absent a provision in the contract providing for progress payments, the homeowner will not be obligated to pay anything to the builder until the job has been completed. Therefore the homeowner is not in breach. On the other hand, the builder has wrongfully abandoned his obligations under the contract (i.e., he has repudiated the contract). Since the homeowner has not committed a material breach of the contract, the builder's obligation to construct the garage has not been relieved. Thus, when the builder abandoned work on the garage, he breached the contract. Since the builder has breached and the homeowner has not, the builder will be liable for whatever damages the homeowner sustains as a result of the breach, while the homeowner will not be liable to the builder for anything.

(A), (C), and (D) are not the best response,
because they are inconsistent with the analysis above.

Answer 166

(A) is the best response,
because it correctly reflects the general scope of discovery.

Here is the FRCP's basic statement about what information may be obtained in discovery: "Unless otherwise limited by court order, the scope of discovery is as follows: Parties may obtain discovery regarding any nonprivileged matter that is ***relevant to any party's claim or defense and proportional to the needs of the case***[.]" Rule 26(b)(1), first sentence. (Notice, by the way, that the material has to be relevant to a "claim or defense in the case"—it's not enough that the material, though not directly relevant to any claim or issue, might reasonably *lead* to discovery of information that *is* relevant to a claim or issue.) So unless Plaintiff can show that the contract between Defendant and the lighting company somehow has bearing on Plaintiff's own claim (e.g., by helping to establish a pattern in which defendant intentionally orders goods and then refuses to pay), Plaintiff won't be entitled to the information, since it relates to a contract between different parties than does the contract presently in dispute.

(B) is not the best response,
because it states a requirement that does not in fact exist.

The last sentence of Rule 26(b)(1) says that "Information within this scope of discovery [defined in the prior sentence of the Rule] ***need not be admissible in evidence to be discoverable***." So as long as Defendant's answer would somehow be relevant to a claim or defense—relevant in the sense of making some proposition of fact or law more or less likely to be true then without the answer—the fact that the answer would not be directly admissible (e.g., because of some technical evidence rule like hearsay) is irrelevant.

(C) is not the best response,
because ***an interrogatory may not be used to obtain information from a nonparty***.

The "only to parties" limitation on the use of the interrogatory is clear from the language of the Federal Rule on interrogatories. The Rule is actually entitled "Interrogatories ***to Parties***," and says that "[a] party may serve ***on any other party*** no more than 25 written interrogatories" FRCP 33(a)(1). There is no analogous provision allowing for interrogatories to non-parties. Court decisions confirm that interrogatories may not be directed at a nonparty. *See, e.g.*, *Lehman v. Kornblau*, 206 F.R.D. 345, 346 (E.D.N.Y. 2001) ("any interrogatories . . . served on non-parties are a nullity."). Since the choice refers to interrogatories "to the lighting company," and since there's no indication that the lighting company is a party to Plaintiff's case, the choice is incorrect.

(D) is not the best response,
because it misapplies the standard that governs automatic initial discovery under FRCP 26(a)(1)(ii).

Disclosure without a request or court order is required under the federal discovery rules as to all documents "that the disclosing party has in its possession, custody, or control and ***may use to support its claims or defenses***, unless the use would be solely for impeachment." FRCP 26(a)(1)(ii). So unless the document is one that the disclosing party (here, Defendant) thinks it may use in motions or at trial during the case, that party has no duty to make automatic disclosure of the document. Here, it is highly unlikely that Defendant will rely in any way on its contract with the lighting company to support its defenses in the present case—how would that contract plausibly help Defendant (though it could conceivably *hurt* Defendant, by showing a pattern of fraud)? Therefore, Defendant has no obligation to furnish a copy of the contract (or even to allude to its existence) as part of automatic initial disclosure. (Then, if Defendant later were to change its mind and try to use the contract as part of its case, that use would be prohibited unless Defendant could show that its earlier failure to disclose was "substantially justified or was harmless." FRCP 37(c)(1).)

Answer 167

(C) is the best response,
Because the elements of both hearsay exceptions are met.

This testimony consists of the repeating of an out-of-court statement (dictation of the license plate number) that is offered to prove the truth of its content, i.e., that the car in question had that license number. Thus, it meets the hearsay definition of FRE 801(c). However, it also fits into two exceptions to the hearsay rule. Let's examine each in turn.

First, the statement is admissible as a present sense impression under FRE 803(1). That exception applies to a statement that (1) describes or explains an event, and (2) was made while the declarant observed the event or immediately thereafter. Both of these requirements are met here. First, the witness dictated what he saw, i.e., the number on the license plate of the car; this is certainly a partial "description" of the event. Second, the facts tell us that the witness dictated the license number "as the car sped off"; this certainly qualifies as done while the event occurred or immediately thereafter.

The recording also fits with the past recollection recorded exception to the hearsay rule codified at FRE 803(5). That exception applies when the record (here, a recording) (1) concerns "a matter the witness once knew about"; (2) as to which the witness "now cannot recall well enough to testify fully and accurately"; (3) which was made "when the matter was fresh in the witness's memory," and (4) which "accurately reflects the witness's knowledge." All of these four requirements are met in this case. First, the witness dictated his observation as he was viewing the car, so he had knowledge of the license number. Second, the witness testified that "he no longer remembered the number." Third, he dictated the information just as he was observing the license plate, so the matter was fresh in his memory. Fourth, the witness testified that "he accurately dictated the license number." Consequently, the testimony fits under this exception, too.

(A) and (B) are not the best response

because each of these choices incorrectly indicates that one of the named hearsay exceptions discussed in choice C does not apply.

(D) is not the best choice,

because it incorrectly suggests that neither the present-sense-impression nor the past-recollection-recorded exception applies.

Answer 168

(D) is the best response,

because it is theoretically correct, and it will result in suppression of the defendant's confession under these facts.

The fruit of the poisonous tree doctrine holds that any evidence derived from unlawfully obtained evidence is inadmissible. Such "derivative" evidence is called the tainted fruit of the poisonous tree. Under these facts, the "poisonous tree" is the illegal arrest. The *Miranda* warnings, as D notes, are not enough, in and of themselves, to "purge the taint" of the illegal arrest (although they are a factor in favor of admissibility). However, courts also consider the wrongful intent of the police, intervening acts, and the proximity in time between the illegality and the confession in determining the admissibility of the confession. Here, although there was no wrongful intent, the police were only acting on an anonymous telephone call, which is insufficient to provide probable cause for arrest. Otherwise, there are no facts in favor of admissibility—the interrogation took place soon after the illegal arrest, and there were no intervening acts. As a result, the confession is likely to be excluded on the basis of this argument. Since the argument is theoretically correct, it applies to these facts, and it would result in suppression of the evidence, it's the defendant's best argument—and as a result D is the best response.

(A) is not the best response,

because it misstates the rule of law, and does not correctly identify the facts it implies.

First, criminal defendants, in general, are not entitled to know the identity of their accusers, because informants are generally entitled to a privilege of anonymity at common law. (There are two principal exceptions to this rule: one, when the identity has already been found out by those with cause to resent the communication (e.g., the disclosure was made to other law enforcement agencies), and two, where the identity is important to establishing a defense.) The rationale of this rule is to encourage informants to come forward with information about crimes.

Thus, the rule choice A states is wrong. In any case, what choice A implies is not the identity of the accuser, since that's not what's involved in these facts, but rather the use by the police of an anonymous tip. An anonymous tip *can* be the basis for an arrest or search warrant as long as it meets the "totality of the circumstances" test from *Illinois v. Gates* (1983). Under that test, these elements will be weighed to determine the reliability of the informant: the informant's prior use and reliability, his status as a member of a reliable group (e.g., a minister), clarity of detail in the tip, showing that informant has personal knowledge of where evidence is located, and whether the tip includes a declaration against the informant's penal interest (e.g., that he bought narcotics from the individual named). Furthermore, courts will be less strict in determining the reliability of noncriminal informants than criminal informants. Under the facts here, the tip, without more facts, wouldn't be sufficient for a warrant since it wouldn't meet this test (at least certainly not for an *arrest*). What A ignores is the central flaw in the police behavior here: the arrest was unlawful, making the confession inadmissible as the tainted fruit of the poisonous tree, the poisonous tree being the unlawful arrest. Since A misstates the law and ignores the central flaw, it's not the best response.

(B) is not the best response,

because it misstates the law, and ignores the central flaw in the behavior of the police.

The *Miranda* warnings requirement is triggered by the police's intent to *interrogate* in custody, not by arrest. If the arrest here were otherwise valid, the police behaved correctly by stopping the defendant and reading him his rights *before* they asked him any questions. What choice B *does* is to ignore the central flaw in the police behavior: The arrest was unlawful and the confession will be considered the tainted fruit of the poisonous tree (the poisonous tree being the unlawful arrest). Since B ignores this, and misstates the law, it cannot be the best response.

(C) is not the best response,

because although it states the law correctly and it *may* be true under these facts, it does not apply to these facts as closely as choice D.

If the defendant's statements were, in fact, involuntary and coerced, they would not be admissible *even though* he was given his *Miranda* warnings first. A confession *must* be voluntary in order to be admissible. Here, it's possible that the defendant was intimidated by the way the arrest took place, making his confession involuntary and coerced. The problem is, the facts really don't indicate that the defendant's confession was involuntary; rather, it seems more like he was ratting on his friend to secure his own release. Thus, although C correctly states the law, it does not apply to these facts with any certainty, and so is not the best response.

Answer 169

(B) is the best response,

because it supplies a condition that would apply to these facts, and, assuming the condition is satisfied, it reaches the correct response.

If the law of the jurisdiction prohibited evictions intended to punish the tenant for some act, the facts here would likely fit such a statute, since it would be easily provable that the landlord is punishing the woman for organizing the tenants. If the woman proved such facts, she would prevail. Since B recognizes this, it's the best response.

(A) is not the best response,

because although the lease here is a periodic tenancy created by implication, this does not provide a ground for the woman to succeed—since the landlord gave adequate notice to terminate the lease.

A periodic tenancy is a tenancy that is renewed *automatically* at the end of each "period" (e.g., week, month, quarter) unless either lessor or lessee terminates it. A periodic tenancy by implication is one where the lease is silent as to duration. The amount of notice required to terminate a periodic tenancy is the same as the length of the period. That is, if the tenancy is month-to-month, as here, a month's notice is required. The landlord gave just that amount of notice. Since the landlord complied with the requirements for terminating the lease, the fact that the lease is a periodic lease by implication does not provide a ground for the woman to prevail in a wrongful termination suit. Thus, A is not the best response.

(C) is not the best response,

because it is a misstatement of law.

The amount of rent charged to the other tenants does not create an implied agreement between the woman and the landlord for the woman's apartment. After all, apartment buildings frequently contain apartments of different sizes, for which different rents are charged. If the same rent is charged for every apartment, this is mere coincidence—no implied agreement would spring from it as between the landlord and the woman. Since C states otherwise, it's not the best response.

(D) is not the best response,

because it is a misstatement of the law.

The amount of notice required to terminate a periodic tenancy, like the one here, depends on the length of the period. At common law, the amount of notice required is the same as the period. That is, if the tenancy is week-to-week, a week's notice is required; if it's month-to-month, a month's notice is necessary. For periods of a year or more, six months' notice is required. According to modern statutes in many states, 30 days' notice is required regardless of the period involved. Thus, it is not correct to say that the law implies a term of one year without an express agreement otherwise. Thus, D is not the best response.

Answer 170

(A) is the best response,

because the state vocational licensing boards were violating the provisions of the Fourteenth Amendment.

Section 5 of the Fourteenth Amendment allows Congress to pass appropriate legislation to enforce the other provisions of the Amendment. Such legislation is appropriate if it seeks to remedy Fourteenth Amendment violations by state or local governments and is proportional to the violations it seeks to remedy. Here, it appears that the state vocational licensing boards are violating the Fourteenth Amendment Due Process Clause by instituting unfair practices in their disciplinary proceedings. Proportionality is satisfied because the congressional statute simply requires that such proceedings comport with procedural due process and that the disciplinary boards be neutral so as to ensure fair hearings.

(B) is not the best response,

because the statute is not a taxing or spending measure.

The only "General Welfare" Clause contained in Article I, § 8, does not grant Congress the authority to legislate for the general welfare—the police power is reserved to the states. Instead, it only allows Congress *to tax and spend* for the general welfare. Since this statute does not involve spending federal funds, the taxing and spending power is inapplicable.

(C) is not the best response,

because the Privileges and Immunities Clause of Article IV, § 2, is not a source of congressional power.

Article IV's Privileges and Immunities Clause prohibits states from discriminating against citizens of other states. This is an incorrect response to this question for two reasons. First, the Privileges and Immunities Clause is not applicable to the federal government. Second, it is not an independent source of congressional power to legislate. For a congressional statute to be valid, it must be enacted pursuant to an enumerated power in the Constitution. Most of these powers are found in Article I, § 8. However, in this case, the proper source of congressional authority is § 5 of the Fourteenth Amendment. (See the discussion of choice A above.)

(D) is not the best response,

because the statute does not involve a taking.

The Takings Clause of the Fifth Amendment prohibits the government from taking an individual's property without paying just compensation. The Takings Clause is inapplicable to this situation because the statute only details procedures that must be followed in operating a state vocational licensing board—it does not authorize the appropriation of any individual's property. We should also note that the Takings Clause is not a source of congressional power, but rather a limitation on it. For a congressional statute to be valid, it must be enacted pursuant to an enumerated power in the Constitution. Most of these powers are found in Article I, § 8. However, in this case, the proper source of congressional authority is § 5 of the Fourteenth Amendment. (See the discussion of choice A above.)

Answer 171

(B) is the best response,

because the district judge has discretion to use this "remittitur" device.

The museum has not moved for a new trial (which is what it probably should have done). But even without a motion by one of the parties, Rule 69(d) gives the trial judge the right to order a new trial on her own: "No later than 28 days after the entry of judgment, the court, ***on its own***, may ***order a new trial for any reason that would justify granting one on a party's motion***." So we have to determine whether the excessiveness of the verdict here is a "reason that would justify granting [a new trial] on a party's motion." Rule 59(a)(1) gives the answer, by saying that "The court may, on motion, grant a new trial on all or some of the issues—and to any party—as follows: (A) after a jury trial, for ***any reason for which a new trial has heretofore been granted in an action at law in federal court***[.]" This reference to reasons for which new trials have "heretofore been granted in an action at law in federal court" means that if the reason for a new trial is one that the common-law courts would have recognized as valid before the 1938 enactment of the FRCP, the reason will suffice for a new trial under Rule 59.

One of the best-established reasons for granting a new trial is that the verdict is ***greatly excessive***—sometimes the phrase used to described such a verdict is that it is so large that it "shocks the conscience." Since there is good reason to believe that a verdict calculated by valuing each of the photographer's 200 prints at ten times the highest amount ($500) that he had ever sold a print for during his career is greatly excessive, the judge would be entitled to avoid this excess award by ordering either an entirely new trial on liability and damages or a new trial just on the issue of damages. But by long-standing federal practice, federal trial judges are permitted, instead of unconditionally ordering a new trial, to issue a "conditional new trial order," which is what we have here; that is, the trial judge orders a new trial (either on all issues or just damages) but agrees that the new trial need not take place if the plaintiff is willing to consent to a reduction of the verdict to a lesser amount that the judge believes is justified by the evidence. (This "conditional new trial order" device is often called a "***remittitur.***") *See, e.g., Kirsch v. Fleet Street, Ltd.*, 148 F.3d 149, 165 (2d Cir. 1998) (district judge may enter a conditional order of remittitur, "compelling a plaintiff to choose between reduction of an excessive verdict and a new trial.")

(A) is not the best choice,

because the museum's motion does not meet the procedural requirements for a motion for a judgment as a matter of law.

The facts tell you that the nature of the motion made by the museum post-verdict is that it is a motion for "judgment as a matter of law" (a/k/a a "JML" motion). The procedures governing JML motions are set out in FRCP 50. Of critical importance, Rule 50(a)(2) says that "A motion for judgment as a matter of law may be made at any time ***before the case is submitted to the jury.***" Then, if the court does not grant the motion before submitting the case to the jury, and the jury comes back with a verdict that the movant views as unfavorable, the movant may "file a ***renewed motion*** for judgment as a matter of law[.]" Courts have interpreted this language as meaning, by negative implication, that if the would-be movant does not make any JML motion before the case is submitted to the jury, the movant has ***waived his right to do so after the verdict.*** Here, the facts tell you that "No motions were made by either side before the case went to the jury," so you know the museum waived its right to make a JML motion. (Indeed, you should have interpreted the very fact that the statement of facts bothered to specify the lack of any pre-verdict motions as a signal that a post-verdict JML motion might be coming, and if made, would be found to have been made too late.) So due to the absence of a pre-verdict version of the motion, the JML motion referred to in this choice is one that the judge may not grant, no matter how much the judge thinks that justice would be well served if it could be granted. (By the way, Rule 50 does not give the trial judge the right to issue judgment as a matter of law *sua sponte*, i.e., without a motion having been made for it.) But as is discussed in the treatment of Choice (B), the judge can achieve much the same result as a grant of JML at a reduced amount by using the remittitur or "conditional new trial" order mentioned in that choice.

(C) is not the best response,

because it is wasteful of judicial resources and therefore not the "best" alternative.

What's proposed by this choice is that the judge grant a partial new trial. FRCP 59(a)(1) indeed allows the judge to do this, by giving her the right to grant, on motion, "a new trial on all ***or some*** of the issues[.]" But the question asks you to choose the procedurally-available alternative that will avoid being "wasteful of judicial resources," and the partial new trial will waste resources by requiring the impaneling of a whole new jury to decide the damages issue from scratch. The device of remittitur, i.e., conditional grant of new trial, mentioned in Choice (B), is a better approach because it will avoid such waste if the photographer accepts the reduction—and if he doesn't accept, the consequent new trial on damages won't be any more wasteful than if such a new trial had been unconditionally ordered as mentioned in this Choice (C).

(D) is not the best response,

because it misstates the current state of Seventh Amendment jurisprudence.

The Seventh Amendment guarantees the litigants in federal trials brought "at law" (as opposed to "in equity") the right to a jury trial. Part of the Seventh Amendment is the so-called ***"re-examination clause,"*** which says that "no fact tried by a jury, shall be otherwise re-examined in any Court of the United States, than according to the rules of the common law." The re-examination clause would be violated by the court's overturning of a jury verdict for reasons that would not have been permitted "at common law" as that law existed in 1789, when the Seventh Amendment was enacted. But the Supreme Court has held that a grant of a new trial on grounds of the excessiveness of the verdict (as well as the use of a conditional new trial order or remittitur) were permitted at common law, and therefore do not normally violate the Seventh Amendment. So this choice, by saying that the museum's motion for judgment as a matter of law would violate the Seventh Amendment, is legally incorrect. (The court is indeed not permitted to grant the motion—but as is discussed in the analysis of choice (A), the reason is that the museum didn't make the motion before the case was submitted to the jury, not that the granting of the motion would violate the Seventh Amendment.)

Answer 172

(D) is the best response,

because it correctly identifies that the reason for admitting the testimony is that the payroll records relate to a collateral matter, and thus the payroll records themselves are not required in order to admit the testimony.

The central issue here is applicability of the Best Evidence Rule. The Best Evidence Rule is triggered when a party wants to prove the material terms of a writing, or a witness is testifying relying on a writing. Under those circumstances, the original writing (which includes photocopies) must normally be produced. FRE 1002. The rationale for this rule is that errors or gaps in memory, as well as fraud, can be avoided by allowing the trier of fact to see the writing itself, if the writing is available.

But the Best Evidence Rule does not apply where "the writing, recording, or photograph is *not closely related to a controlling issue*." FRE 1004(d). Here, the payroll records relate to the date of purchase, which the facts specifically tell you is "a fact of minor importance in the case." As a result, the records are "not closely related to a controlling issue," and the 1004(d) exception applies.

(A) is not the best response,

because it mistakenly invokes the Best Evidence Rule.

If the contents of the payroll records were a material issue in the case, then any attempt to prove those contents would require production of the records themselves, rather than testimony about the contents, under the Best Evidence Rule. But, as is further explained in choice D, the Best Evidence Rule does not apply where "the writing, recording, or photograph is not closely related to a controlling issue." FRE 1004(d).

(B) is not the best response,

because it fails to recognize that the payroll records would be admissible under the business records exception to the hearsay rule.

The plaintiff's testimony is arguably subject to the hearsay rule. The payroll records here would likely be considered hearsay (since they are out-of-court statements offered to prove the truth of their assertion, namely, the date of opening day). However, the records would probably be admissible under the business records hearsay exception, FRE 803(6). Under that exception, such records are admissible if the entries are made in the regular course of business, in conjunction with a business activity, entered under a duty to record, entered by one with personal knowledge of the matters recorded or transmitted from such a person, entered at or near the time of the transaction (and the records must be authenticated at trial). While there's a possibility that the records here wouldn't satisfy all these requirements, they probably would, and B states unequivocally that such records would be inadmissible hearsay. As a result, B is not the best response.

(C) is not the best response,

because it states a factor that is irrelevant to whether or not a fact is subject to judicial notice.

The judge's personal knowledge is not sufficient to establish judicial notice. The only two ways a fact can be subject to judicial notice are when the fact is subject to common knowledge in the community OR is capable of positive verification through readily accessible, undeniably accurate sources. FRE 201(b).

Answer 173

(B) is the best response,

because it represents the most likely basis on which the store could get the prior oral agreement admitted into evidence.

In order to be the store's best argument, the reasoning must be both legally correct and applicable to these facts. Determining this requires analysis of the facts under the Parol Evidence Rule. Under that rule, a written agreement which is "completely integrated" may not be contradicted or supplemented with evidence of prior written or oral agreements, or contemporaneous oral agreements. A "completely integrated" agreement is one that the parties intended to be a final and complete statement of their agreement. A "partially integrated" agreement, on the other hand, is one that is final, but not complete. As a result, unlike a completely integrated agreement, it *may* be supplemented by consistent additional terms.

Determining whether a written agreement is partially or completely integrated is subject to a wide variety of tests, but the presumption typically is that the writing is only a partial integration barring clear evidence to the contrary. Under these facts, the very fact that there was no mention of coordination in the written agreement suggests that the writing was *not* complete even though it was final as to the terms it stated. Thus, the store could successfully argue on these facts that the agreement was only partially integrated, and legally this would result in the store's being able to introduce evidence of the coordination provision as a consistent additional term. Since B represents the store's best argument both factually and legally, it's the best response.

(A) is not the best response,

because although it states a correct legal theory, it doesn't apply to the facts here.

Under the Parol Evidence Rule, a writing that is "completely integrated" cannot be contradicted or supplemented with prior written or oral agreements, or contemporaneous oral agreements. A "completely integrated" agreement is one that the parties intended to be a final and complete statement of their agreement.

While it's true that evidence may be admitted to *interpret* the agreement, the oral agreement on coordinating with the store's methods of accounting wouldn't do that, since this isn't addressed in the written agreement *at all.* At common law, additional evidence would be admitted to interpret a term only if the contract contains an ambiguity. (Under the UCC, no ambiguity is required, but the UCC wouldn't apply here since this is likely a *service* contract, not a transaction in goods.)

In fact, the fact that this issue doesn't appear in the written contract would suggest that the written agreement didn't embody the entire agreement between the parties and thus was not completely integrated. When a writing is a *partial* integration, it may not be contradicted but it *may* be supplemented by additional, consistent terms. That's the store's best argument for admitting evidence of the oral agreement. Since A doesn't recognize this, it's not the best response.

(C) is not the best response,

because although it implies a rule that is correct in theory, it would not apply to these facts.

Under the Parol Evidence Rule, a writing that is "completely integrated" cannot be contradicted or supplemented with prior written or oral agreements, or contemporaneous oral agreements. A "completely integrated" agreement is one that the parties intended to be a final and complete statement of their agreement.

The Parol Evidence Rule does *not* bar evidence of defects in contract formation, like lack of consideration, fraud, and duress. However, mere detrimental reliance on an oral promise would not, in and of itself, rise to the level of fraud.

Instead, the store should argue that the written agreement was only partially integrated—that is, that it didn't represent the *complete* agreement. A partially integrated agreement *may* be supplemented by consistent additional terms. The oral "coordination" clause would likely be a consistent additional term, and this is, as a result, the store's best chance of having it admitted. Since the store's detrimental reliance would be insufficient by itself to allow admission of the coordination term, and C fails to recognize this, C isn't the best response.

(D) is not the best response,

because it's exactly the opposite of what the store *would* want to argue.

A partially integrated agreement is a written agreement that does not reflect the *complete* agreement of the parties. It's final as to the terms it states, but it may be supplemented by consistent additional terms. In fact, arguing that the memo here is a partial integration is the store's best chance of getting the coordination term admitted into evidence, since there's nothing in the contract to contradict it.

If the written contract isn't a partial integration, it's either not integrated at all or is fully integrated. The store couldn't argue that it's not integrated because this wouldn't comport with the facts, which show that the parties intended the writing to be final as to the terms it includes. The store wouldn't want to argue that it's completely integrated, because that would preclude admission of a prior oral agreement supplementing the written agreement, which is what the "coordination" provision would do. Since D represents an argument that would not be advantageous to the store, it's not the best response.

Answer 174

(A) is the best response,

because the purchase of cars is a commercial activity.

For a congressional statute to be constitutional, it must be enacted pursuant to one of Congress's enumerated powers under Article I of the Constitution. Choice A identifies the Commerce Clause as the source of the power to enact this statute. Under the Commerce Clause (Article I, § 8, cl. 3), Congress has the power to "regulate commerce with foreign nations, and among the several states." Congress's powers under the Commerce Clause are read quite broadly by courts, and on the MBE it should always be the first of the enumerated powers you consider when approaching a problem. Here, the statute falls within the commerce power because the large-scale purchase of cars has a significant effect on interstate commerce. The Tenth Amendment prohibits the federal government from commandeering the lawmaking power of state or local legislatures. So, for example, Congress could not pass an act requiring all of the states to pass laws mandating the purchase of electric cars. However, the directive in this statute is generally applicable since it applies to all owners of large fleets of cars, not only to governmental owners. Since it is a direct regulation that is generally applicable, and does not commandeer the legislative function of the local government, it does not violate the Tenth Amendment.

(B) is not the best response,

because the city is seeking an injunction.

The federal government has sovereign immunity from suits seeking compensatory damages. However, there is no bar against a plaintiff seeking injunctive relief against the federal government or its officers. Here, we are told that the city "sought an *injunction* prohibiting enforcement of the statute." Since the city is not seeking monetary relief, its suit is not barred by the federal government's sovereign immunity.

(C) is not the best response,

because the statute is applicable to both private and governmental entities.

The Tenth Amendment prohibits the federal government from commandeering the lawmaking power of state or local legislatures. So, for example, Congress could not pass an act requiring all of the states to pass laws mandating the purchase of electric cars. However, the directive in this statute is generally applicable since it applies to all owners of large fleets of cars, not only to governmental owners. Since it is a direct regulation that is generally applicable, and does not commandeer the legislative function of the local government, it does not violate the Tenth Amendment.

(D) is not the best response,

because this exercise of commerce power is not in violation of the Tenth Amendment.

The Tenth Amendment reserves to the states all legislative power not specifically provided to the federal government in the Constitution. However, the commerce power is a specifically enumerated power of Congress (Article I, § 8, cl. 3). The Tenth Amendment prohibits the federal government from commandeering the lawmaking power of state or local legislatures, but that has not occurred in this situation. The directive in this statute is generally applicable since it applies to all owners of large fleets of cars, not only to governmental owners. Since it is a direct regulation that is generally applicable, and does not commandeer the legislative function of the local government, it does not violate the Tenth Amendment.

Answer 175

(C) is the best response,

because the manufacturer supplied adequate assurances of its ability to pay.

If a party to a sale of goods contract is genuinely concerned that the other party will be unable to perform its obligations under the contract, UCC 2-609 allows the concerned party to request reasonable assurances of the other party's ability to perform and to suspend its own performance if adequate assurances are not given. The lumber supplier exercised this right, and the furniture manufacturer provided information that should have convinced the lumber supplier that its concerns were unfounded. As a result, the lumber supplier was not allowed to suspend its own performance, and its election to do so was a breach of the contract.

(A) is not the best response,

because requirements contracts are enforceable.

Quantity is considered a material term that must be agreed to in a contract for the sale of goods. However, it is not true that one can only specify a quantity by stating a definite amount. UCC 2-306 provides that output and requirements contracts are enforceable. The lumber supplier-furniture manufacturer contract was a requirements contract: the specified quantity being "all the lumber that the manufacturer required." Pursuant to UCC 2-306, the contract is thus sufficiently definite to be enforceable.

(B) is not the best response,

because the furniture manufacturer provided adequate assurances of its ability to pay.

If a party to a sale of goods contract is genuinely concerned that the other party will be unable to perform its obligations under the contract, UCC 2-609 allows the concerned party to request reasonable assurances of the other party's ability to perform and to suspend its own performance if adequate assurances are not given. The lumber supplier exercised this right, and the furniture manufacturer provided information that should have convinced the lumber supplier that its concerns were unfounded. As a result, the lumber supplier was not allowed to suspend its own performance, and its election to do so was a breach of the contract.

(D) is not the best response,

because the UCC provides this right to the lumber supplier.

If a party to a sale of goods contract is genuinely concerned that the other party will be unable to perform its obligations under the contract, UCC 2-609 allows the concerned party to request reasonable assurances of the other party's ability to perform and to suspend its own performance if adequate assurances are not given. The lumber supplier exercised this right, and the furniture manufacturer provided information that should have convinced the lumber supplier that its concerns were unfounded. As a result, the lumber supplier was not allowed to suspend its own performance, and its election to do so was a breach of the contract.

Answer 176

(B) is the best answer,

because the Sixth Amendment allows juries of 6, but decisions by 6-member juries must be unanimous. Note, however, that non-unanimous juries are apparently permissible if they contain 7 to 11 jurors.

(A) is not the best answer,

because it chooses the correct result, but for the wrong reason. The Sixth Amendment allows juries of 6, but decisions by 6-member juries must be unanimous.

(C) is not the best answer,

because it misstates the legal basis for the conclusion. The Sixth Amendment allows juries of 6, but decisions by 6-member juries must be unanimous.

(D) is not the best answer,

because the Sixth Amendment allows juries of 6, but decisions by 6-member juries must be unanimous.

Answer 177

(B) is the best response,

because it identifies the reason why the regulation will be valid.

The regulation here involves congressional regulation of federally owned lands. Under Article IV, § 3, cl. 2, of the Constitution, Congress has the power "to dispose of and make all needful rules and regulations respecting" lands of the United States. States only have power to the extent that they reserved jurisdiction when ceding the land to the federal government (or, alternatively, to the extent that Congress has, via legislation, granted jurisdiction to the state). Under these facts, there's no indication of any basis for state jurisdiction over the federally owned lands. Thus, Congress would have the authority to pass regulations protecting wild animals on those lands. Since choice B recognizes this, it's the best response.

(A) is not the best response,

because the Welfare Clause would not empower the federal government to enact this type of legislation.

The Welfare Clause, found in Article 1, § 8, of the Constitution, empowers Congress to levy and collect taxes and to provide for the general welfare, and to make all laws that are necessary and proper to implement those powers. Thus, the Welfare Clause only addresses Congress's power to collect taxes and spend money. That's not what's involved in these facts; here, protecting predatory wild animals is the aim of the legislation. As a result, the Welfare Clause could not be the source of the regulation's validity. Since A states otherwise, it's not the best response.

(C) is not the best response,

because it skirts the central issue. It's not the wild animals themselves that are the focus of the legislation, but wild animals *on federal lands,* and federal lands are the exclusive domain of the federal government.

Under Article IV, § 3, cl. 2, of the Constitution, Congress has the power "to dispose of and make all needful rules and regulations respecting" lands of the United States. States only have power to the extent that they reserved jurisdiction when ceding the land to the federal government (or, alternatively, to the extent that Congress has, via legislation, granted jurisdiction to the state). Under these facts, there's no indication of any basis for state jurisdiction over the federally owned lands. Thus, the state common-law definition of wild animals would not be relevant. Since choice C doesn't recognize this, it's not the best response.

(D) is not the best response,

because the Tenth Amendment would not provide a source of power for the states under these facts.

Under these facts, the regulation is a federal regulation concerning federally owned lands. While it's theoretically true that the states reserve the powers not delegated to the federal government in the Constitution, this ignores application of Article IV, § 3, cl. 2, of the Constitution, which expressly grants the federal government control over federally owned lands. Since this power is expressly delegated to the Congress in the Constitution, it can't be reserved by the states under the Tenth Amendment. Since choice D doesn't recognize this, it's not the best response.

Answer 178

(D) is the best response,

because it correctly recognizes that the gift to the grandchildren itself is valid, regardless of whether the restraint on alienation is invalid. (In fact, the restraint is invalid as a *disabling* restraint on alienation, and as a result it will be removed.)

The gift does not violate the Rule Against Perpetuities because the members of the class will be determined within a life in being plus 21 years. In fact, it will be determined at the son's death, and since he's a life in being at the time the will takes effect, the Rule Against Perpetuities is satisfied. (The same goes for all of the woman's other children and grandchildren, since their gifts are identically worded.) Since choice D recognizes this, it's the best response.

(A) is not the best response,

because it does not correctly apply the Rule Against Perpetuities to these facts.

The class gift to the grandchildren does not violate the Rule Against Perpetuities, because it will vest or fail within a life in being plus 21 years. In fact, it will be determined at the son's death, and since he's a life in being at the time the will takes effect, the Rule Against Perpetuities is satisfied. (The same goes for all of the woman's other children and grandchildren, since their gifts are identically worded.)

If you chose this response, it's probably because you didn't realize that the no-sale-or-mortgage-until-age-25 provision was a disabling restraint on alienation, and figured that it wasn't until all the children were 25 that the members of the class could be determined. If this were true, the grandchildren's gift wouldn't vest or fail until a life in being (the son's and his siblings') plus *25* years, which is outside the perpetuities period. However, the sale or mortgage provision will be removed, because disabling restraints on alienation are always *invalid* on legal interests, like the class gift here. (A disabling restraint makes any attempted transfer invalid, which in effect makes the interest granted inalienable.) As such, the gift to the grandchildren does not violate the Rule Against Perpetuities, making A not the best response.

(B) is not the best response,

because while it correctly characterizes the restraint on alienation here as invalid, it does not correctly state the *result* of this invalidity.

The restraint on alienation here is not valid because it's a *disabling* restraint on alienation. A disabling restraint makes any attempted transfer invalid, which in effect makes the interest granted inalienable. A disabling restraint is *always* invalid on a legal interest, like the gift here. However, the result is *not* to make the gift itself invalid, but to remove the restraint. This would leave a valid gift to the grandchildren, primarily because the gift would satisfy the Rule Against Perpetuities, since the interests of the grandchildren would vest or fail at the son's death. (The same goes for all of the woman's other children and grandchildren, since their gifts are identically worded.) The son is a life in being, and the Rule Against Perpetuities only requires that interests vest or fail within a life in being *plus* 21 years. Since choice B does not correctly state the result of the invalidity of the restraint on alienation, it's not the best response.

(C) is not the best response,

because the provisions are not enforceable in their entirety.

There are two principle issues under these facts: whether the class gift is valid under the Rule Against Perpetuities, and whether the restraint on alienation is valid.

As to the Rule Against Perpetuities, it requires that, to be valid, any interest must vest or fail within a life in being plus 21 years. Here, the gifts to the grandchildren will be determined when the son dies (the same goes for all of the woman's other children and grandchildren, since their gifts are identically worded). The son was a life in being when the interest was created, as were his siblings. Thus, the gift satisfies the Rule Against Perpetuities, and C is correct in recognizing that this provision will be upheld.

However, C fails to recognize that the restraint on alienation will not be upheld. In fact, the sale-or-mortgage provision is a disabling restraint on alienation. A disabling restraint makes any attempted transfer invalid, which in effect makes the interest granted inalienable. This kind of restraint is always invalid on legal interests. As a result, it will be removed, leaving a valid class gift to the grandchildren. Since the gift to the grandchildren will be upheld but the restraint on alienation won't be upheld, C is not the best response.

Answer 179

(D) is the best response,

because the landowner was privileged to protect her property.

The general rule is that the landowner owes no duty to a trespasser to make her land safe, to warn of dangers on it, to avoid carrying on dangerous activities on it, or to protect the trespasser in any way. A landowner is privileged to protect her property from intrusion by a means not intended or likely to cause death or serious bodily injury. Here, the barbed wire presented its own warning and was not a hidden trap, and therefore it is a reasonable device for discouraging trespassers that was not likely to cause death or serious bodily injury.

(A) is not the best response,

because, while this statement is legally correct, it is inapplicable to these facts.

The landowner did not use deadly force, as the barbed wire presented its own warning and was not a hidden trap. A landowner is privileged to protect her property from intrusion by a means not intended or likely to cause death or serious bodily injury, which is what the landowner did here. The barbed wire was a reasonable device for discouraging trespassers that was not likely to cause death or serious bodily injury.

(B) is not the best response,

because the property interest in the deer is irrelevant; here, the landowner had a property interest in the land.

The general rule is that the landowner owes no duty to a trespasser to make her land safe, to warn of dangers on it, to avoid carrying on dangerous activities on it, or to protect the trespasser in any way. Here, the landowner was entitled to take reasonable precautions to protect against intrusion on her land, even if her main purpose in doing so was to protect the deer on the land.

(C) is not the best response,

because the photographer would still be a trespasser.

The general rule is that the landowner owes no duty to a trespasser to make her land safe, to warn of dangers on it, to avoid carrying on dangerous activities on it, or to protect the trespasser in any way. Here, the photographer would have been a trespasser whether or not the landowner had specifically told him not to enter, as posted signs warned of no trespassing on the property. The landowner was entitled to make reasonable precautions to protect against intrusion on her land from the trespassing photographer, which is what she did here.

Answer 180

(D) is the best response,

because this is a party admission under FRE 801(d)(2)(A).

Here, the statement is being offered against the plumber and is the plumber's own statement. This statement is also relevant, as offering to redo the installation for free is indicative that the installation was faulty.

(A) is not the best response,

because there was no claim here that was disputed as to validity or amount.

While FRE 408 makes offers to compromise inadmissible, it does so only when the parties are seeking to compromise a "disputed claim." Here, there was no pending dispute at the time the statement was made. The homeowner was calling for help and had not complained about the plumber's work or in any other way indicated that there was a dispute between the parties. As the plumber did not make the statement in order to effectuate a compromise, it does not fall under FRE 408.

(B) is not the best response,

because this statement is a party admission under FRE 801(d)(2)(A).

Here, the statement is being offered against the plumber and is the plumber's own statement. This statement is also relevant, as offering to redo the installation for free is indicative that the installation was faulty.

(C) is not the best response,

because no subsequent remedial measure was undertaken.

FRE 407 excludes evidence of measures taken that, had they been taken prior to the event that caused the injury, would have made the injury or harm less likely to occur. Here, the homeowner wants to introduce a statement, not an action taken by the plumber that would have made the injury or harm less likely to occur. Accordingly, FRE 407 is inapplicable.

Answer 181

(B) is the best response,

because this answer choice correctly applies the firefighters' rule to the facts.

The common-law "firefighters' rule" says that when firefighters or police officers are injured during the course of the job, they normally have no claim against the person whose conduct created the peril. Dobbs, § 285. Not all states follow the firefighters' rule. But even among those that do, the doctrine is generally limited to risks that are inherent in, and special to, that particular occupation. Dobbs, § 286. This limit means that the doctrine will not apply here because being struck by a car in normal traffic is not one of the special risks inherent to dangerous police work. So the driver can be held liable under ordinary negligence principles. (Also, many courts say that the firefighters' rule applies only where the negligently created peril was *responsible for the officer's presence at the scene*, and that approach, too, would cause the rule not to apply here, since the officer was not responding to the risk caused by the driver and was instead present at the scene by coincidence.)

(A) is not the best response,

because, although this answer correctly states that the driver's motion should be denied, it misstates the legal basis for this conclusion.

The firefighters' rule, although named with reference to firefighters, also covers police officers. They, too, are public servants at risk of injury by the perils that they have been employed to confront.

(C) is not the best response,

because but-for causation is not sufficient to support the firefighters' rule defense here.

As further described in the analysis of choice B above, the firefighters' rule applies to bar liability only when the risk that materialized was one of the unique risks inherent to the officer's dangerous work. Here, the fact that the officer was returning from an emergency when she was struck was just a coincidence. So the driver could still be held liable for his negligence because being struck by a car in normal traffic is not one of the special risks inherent in dangerous police work.

(D) is not the best response,

because it overstates the scope of the firefighters' rule.

The firefighters' rule only bars claims for injuries that result from risks that are unique or special to the plaintiff's inherently dangerous work. Thus where, as here, the officer is injured on the job, but by a risk that was not part of what makes the officer's job inherently dangerous, the firefighters' rule will not apply, and the driver can be held liable under garden-variety negligence principles.

Answer 182

(C) is the best response,

because it correctly identifies the reason the neighbor will lose: His use of the tract was not "adverse," i.e., non-permissive.

The key facts here are that the neighbor had oral permission from the owner *originally* to use the road across the tract, and the squatter quit possession of the tract before acquiring title by adverse possession. What does this mean? That the neighbor's use of the tract was never adverse to the interests of the landowner, and that the squatter never had any enforceable rights to the tract.

In order to gain an easement by prescription, one's use of another's property must be actual, open and notorious, continuous for the statutory period, exclusive, and hostile and adverse (non-permissive). Here, the facts specifically state that the neighbor had the owner's oral permission to use the road across the tract. The red herring here is the presence of the squatter. However, the squatter is merely in possession of the tract. The facts state that he quit possession before he acquired title to it.

Thus, the elements of an easement by prescription would apply to the neighbor and the owner, *not* the neighbor and the squatter. Since C correctly identifies this, it's the best response.

(A) is not the best response,

because it focuses on the wrong fact.

Here, it doesn't matter if the neighbor's use is adverse to the squatter, because the squatter is not the landowner—*the owner* is. The neighbor's use is not adverse to the owner, because the facts state that the owner granted the neighbor oral permission to use the road across the tract. An easement by prescription requires use of another's property that is actual, open and notorious, continuous for the statutory period, exclusive, and hostile and adverse. "Hostile and adverse" means non-permissive in this context.

Here, since the neighbor's use was with the permission of the landowner the entire time, his use was *never* adverse. Since A does not recognize this, it's not the best response.

(B) is not the best response,

because of two principal faults.

First, B states that the neighbor will prevail in part because he made no attempt to renew permission when possession of the tract changed hands. In order to gain an easement by prescription, the use of another's property must be adverse—that is, *non*-permissive. B correctly identifies that the neighbor's use was permissive, but by doing so eliminates the possibility of gaining an easement by prescription based on that time. In other words, it misstates the law.

The second fault is that B suggests that the squatter's quitting possession of the tract is relevant. It is not, because an easement by prescription is gained by adverse use against the *landowner,* not the *possessor.* The neighbor could only gain an easement by prescription if his use of the tract *as against the owner* was actual, open and notorious, continuous for the statutory period, exclusive, and non-permissive. Since B incorrectly states the rule of law, it's not the best response.

(D) is not the best response,

because it fails to recognize that it's not the adverse use as against *the squatter* that's at issue, because the squatter is not the landowner at any time under these facts.

In order for one to gain an easement by prescription, his use of another's property must be actual, open and notorious, continuous for the statutory period, exclusive, and non-permissive. Here, *another's* property means another *landowner's* property. Here, the squatter was simply in possession of the tract; he was not the owner of the tract at any time (since he quit possession before his adverse use ripened into ownership). As a result, D is not the best response.

Answer 183

(A) is the best response,

because it correctly characterizes the facts, and arrives at the correct result.

In order to be valid, a state law must pass a three-part test:

1. It must be enacted within the state's powers (e.g., police powers);
2. It must not violate any person's constitutional rights; and
3. It must not improperly burden interstate commerce.

Choice A addresses the third element. In order to determine if a state statute unduly burdens interstate commerce, you need to ask two questions:

1. Does it burden interstate commerce? If it has an effect on interstate commerce, it does.
2. Is the burden outweighed by legitimate interests of the state in protecting its citizens? Consider less burdensome alternatives.

Here, as to the first element, the statute clearly affects interstate commerce—it prevents out-of-state trained hairdressers from plying their trade in the state.

Second, the burden on interstate commerce is not outweighed by a legitimate state interest in protecting its citizens, considering available, less burdensome alternatives, like a state licensing exam. Since choice A correctly recognizes that the statute will be unconstitutional due to its impact on interstate commerce, it's the best response.

(B) is not the best response,

because the Privileges and Immunities Clause of the Fourteenth Amendment wouldn't apply to make this statute unconstitutional.

In order to be valid, a state law must pass a three-part test:

1. It must be enacted within the state's powers (e.g., police powers);
2. It must not violate any person's constitutional rights; and
3. It must not improperly burden interstate commerce.

Choice B addresses the second element. The Privileges and Immunities Clause of the Fourteenth Amendment voids those state enactments that clearly infringe privileges enjoyed by U.S. citizens. It is construed narrowly, typically being restricted to fundamental rights that are shared in common by all citizens, namely:

1. The right to travel freely from state to state;
2. The right to petition Congress for redress of grievances;
3. The right to vote for national officers;
4. The right to assemble peaceably; and
5. The right to discuss matters of national legislation.

Twining v. New Jersey (1908). In fact, the Privileges and Immunities Clause of the Fourteenth Amendment has virtually no practical effect, although, the Court "breathe[d] new life" into the Clause with its decision in 1999 of *Saenz v. Roe.* There the Court held that the Clause protects an aspect of the right to travel—a person who has moved into and recently become a citizen of a state has the right to the same privileges enjoyed by longer-resident citizens of the state. The Clause, though, would not affect this particular requirement—that candidates for license be graduates of barber schools in the state.

If you chose this response, you may have been thinking of the *Interstate* Privileges and Immunities Clause, found in Article IV, § 2, of the Constitution. That Clause prevents states from discriminating against out-of-state citizens and residents (not aliens), as regards "essential activities" (e.g., pursuing one's livelihood, owning property) and "basic rights" (e.g., medical care, court access), except where the discrimination is closely related to a substantial state purpose (e.g., protecting natural resources by the state), keeping in mind less restrictive means. Since plying one's trade would be considered an "essential activity," the statute here would be a violation of the Interstate Privileges and Immunities Clause. However, that's not the clause that choice B addresses. Since the statute wouldn't be unconstitutional on the basis of violating the Privileges and Immunities Clause of the Fourteenth Amendment, B is not the best response.

(C) is not the best response,

because while it provides a rationale for a licensing law, it doesn't make such a law valid.

In order to be valid, a state law must pass a three-part test:

1. It must be enacted within the state's powers (e.g., police powers);
2. It must not violate any person's constitutional rights; and
3. It must not improperly burden interstate commerce.

Choice C addresses the second element. While addressing a valid concern of the state, choice C doesn't address any of the elements that would make the statute constitutional.

The central problem with this statute is its impact on interstate commerce. Where interstate commerce is an issue, there are two questions to ask:

1. Does the statute burden interstate commerce? If it has an effect on interstate commerce, it does.
2. Is the burden outweighed by a legitimate interest of the state in protecting its citizens? Consider less burdensome alternatives.

Here, the licensing statute impacts interstate commerce by preventing out-of-state barber school graduates from plying their trade in the state. While the state has a legitimate interest in protecting its residents from a "Sweeney Todd"-type barber, it could accomplish the same goal by far less burdensome means, e.g., a licensing exam of some sort. Thus, even though the state admittedly doesn't know the quality of out-of-state barber schools, this in and of itself would not make the licensing exam constitutional. Since C doesn't recognize this, it's not the best response.

(D) is not the best response,

because characterizing barbering as a privilege and not a right would not determine if the statute is constitutional.

In order to be valid, a state law must pass a three-part test:

1. It must be enacted within the state's powers (e.g., police powers);
2. It must not violate any person's constitutional rights; and
3. It must not improperly burden interstate commerce.

If the statute here meets this test, it doesn't matter if barbering is classified as a privilege or a right. If barbering were considered an "essential activity," the statute would violate the Interstate Privileges and Immunities Clause. Alternatively, if barbering were a fundamental right, the statute would probably fail as a violation of equal protection. Thus, classifying barbering as a privilege and not a right does not, in and of itself, determine the constitutionality of the statute.

Since D attaches undue significance to this classification, it's not the best response.

Answer 184

(D) is the best response,

because one who is not a party or an officer of a party cannot be required to travel to be deposed if the deposition is more than 100 miles from the deponent's residence, place of business, or where he regularly transacts business.

First, non-parties may be deposed only if they are first subpoenaed. Second, the places to which the non-party may be required to travel for a deposition are strictly limited by FRCP 45(c)(1), which provides that

"A subpoena may command a person to attend a trial, hearing, or deposition only as follows:

(A) ***within 100 miles*** of where the person resides, is employed, or regularly transacts business in person; or

(B) within the state where the person resides, is employed, or regularly transacts business in person, if the person

(i) is a ***party or a party's officer***; or

(ii) is commanded to attend a ***trial*** and would not incur substantial expense."

So under Rule 45(c)(1)(A) and (B), if the person to be deposed is not a "party or a party's officer," that person may only be required to attend the deposition in a place covered by sub-paragraph (A), not one covered by sub-paragraph (B). That is, the person can be required only to travel "within 100 miles of where the person resides, is employed, or regularly transacts business in person[.]" The facts tell you that the colleague (the person to be deposed) no longer works for Defendant, so the colleague cannot be an "officer" of the only party that is an entity rather than an individual (Defendant). And the facts also tell you that the colleague lives and works 200 miles away from the State A federal courthouse (and thus 200 miles from the deposing lawyer's office, since the office is next door to that courthouse). Lastly, the facts (laboriously) tell you that the colleague rarely travels more than 50 miles from his home and business, so you can infer that the lawyer's office is not within the 100-mile radius of any place the colleague "regularly transacts business in person." In sum, you can be confident that the deposing lawyer's office is not a place covered by Rule 45(c)(1)(A), and is therefore not a place to which this non-party can be compelled to travel.

(A) is not the best response,

because the colleague's attendance at the specified place for deposition cannot be compelled even by a subpoena.

As is more fully discussed in the analysis of choice (D) above, the deponent is a non-party and therefore cannot be required to take the more-than-100-mile trip to the lawyer's office. (But this choice is partially correct in the sense that it accurately implies that even if the specified deposition site *were* within the 100-mile-radius of the deponent's home or workplace, a subpoena, not a mere notice of the deposition, would be required since the deponent is a non-party, and a notice of deposition may be used only as to a party. *See* the Advisory Committee Note to 2013 Amendments to Rule 45: "Depositions of parties, and officers, directors, and managing agents of parties, need not involve use of a subpoena.")

(B) is not the best response,

because the colleague can't be required to make the trip at all, let alone be required to do so by means of a notice of deposition rather than subpoena.

First, as is discussed in the analysis of Choice (D), the place of deposition is beyond the 100-mile-radius of the deponent's home or office, which represents the limit of the distance a deponent can be required to travel if the deponent is neither a party nor the officer of a party. Second, as is described in the parenthetical portion of the discussion of Choice (A), where the deponent is a non-party, attendance to a proper place for deposition must be compelled by a subpoena, not a mere notice of deposition.

(C) is not the best response,

because not even "good cause" would support requiring the colleague to travel more than 100 miles to the lawyer's office.

As is explained more fully in the analysis of Choice (D), if the deponent is neither a party nor the officer of a party, the deponent cannot be required to travel more than 100 miles from his residence, workplace, or place where he routinely transacts business. And that's true no matter how much "good cause" there is for holding the deposition outside the 100-mile radius. Furthermore, the fact that the deposition will be in state in which the deponent resides, works, or routinely does business in person, is ***irrelevant*** if the deponent is not a party or the officer of a party. (Where the deponent *is* a party or the officer of a party, then according to Rule 45(c)(1)(B), the deponent *may* be compelled to attend a deposition anywhere in the state in which he resides, works, or routinely transacts business, even if this would require a more-than-100-mile trip.)

Answer 185

(B) is the best response,

because the mother's writing was sufficient.

The Statute of Frauds renders certain types of contracts unenforceable unless they are in writing. One such category is a suretyship, which is a promise to pay the debts of another. Here, the mother's promise is to pay the debt of her son should he not repay his uncle, so her promise falls within the Statute of Frauds. The Statute of Frauds "writing" requirement is satisfied by a memorandum if the memorandum reasonably identifies the subject matter, indicates the contract has been made, states the essential terms of the contract, and is signed "by or on behalf of the party to be charged." Here, the mother's letter to her son satisfies all of these requirements. It is signed by the mother, indicates that she promises to repay the loan, and states the amount of the debt. The fact that the letter was not addressed the uncle is irrelevant. There is no need that the memorandum that satisfies the Statute of Frauds be addressed to or sent to the obligee (in this case, the uncle).

(A) is not the best response,

because the amount of the loan is irrelevant.

The Statute of Frauds renders certain types of contracts unenforceable unless they are in writing. One such category is a suretyship, which is a promise to pay the debts of another. Here, the mother's promise is to pay the debt of her son should he not repay his uncle, so her promise falls within the Statute of Frauds. If you chose response A, you are probably thinking of the UCC Statute of Frauds, which requires that contracts for sales of goods over a certain value be in writing. However, Article 2 of the UCC is inapplicable here, since this contract was a suretyship, not a sale of goods.

(C) is not the best response,

because the mother's letter satisfied the Statute of Frauds.

The Statute of Frauds renders certain types of contracts unenforceable unless they are in writing. One such category is a suretyship, which is a promise to pay the debts of another. Here, the mother's promise is to pay the debt of her son should he not repay his uncle, so her promise falls within the Statute of Frauds. The Statute of Frauds "writing" requirement is satisfied by a memorandum if the memorandum reasonably identifies the subject matter, indicates the contract has been made, states the essential terms of the contract, and is signed "by or on behalf of the party to be charged." Here, the mother's letter to her son satisfies all of these requirements. It is signed by the mother, indicates that she promises to repay the loan, and states the amount of the debt.

(D) is not the best response,

because it is irrelevant.

Whether or not the nephew's promise to his uncle to repay his debt is enforceable is irrelevant to the question asked, which was whether the mother's Statute of Frauds defense will be successful. As discussed in the analysis of choice B above, the mother's letter to her nephew was a sufficient memorandum to satisfy the Statute of Frauds. If you chose response D, you were probably thinking that the mother had a defense based on the unenforceability of the nephew's underlying promise. This is an error for two reasons. First, it does not address the question that was asked, which focused solely on one defense that the mother might raise. Second, the nephew's promise to repay the loan he received from his uncle is enforceable even though it was oral, since the promise to repay one's own debt is not within the Statute of Frauds.

Answer 186

(A) is the best response,

because it identifies the central issue under these facts, resolves it, and arrives at the correct result.

The main problem with a battery claim on these facts is that the grower didn't intend that the dog bite the wife. In fact, the intent battery requires can be satisfied by the intent assault requires—that is, the intent to create the apprehension of harmful or offensive contact, followed by actual conduct. Thus, the grower's intent to frighten the wife with the threat of contact is sufficient intent for battery. Since A identifies the central element and resolves it satisfactorily, it's the best response.

(B) is not the best response,

because it's irrelevant: *res ipsa loquitur* is a doctrine of circumstantial evidence of *negligence.* Here, the grower is charged with an *intentional* tort—battery.

Battery requires an intentional act resulting in harmful or offensive contact with plaintiff's person. Even if the claim had been in negligence, it's not obvious that *res ipsa loquitur* would apply. *Res ipsa loquitur* establishes a *prima facie* claim for negligence where the following elements are shown: The event would not normally have occurred in the absence of negligence, the defendant was in exclusive control of the instrumentality causing injury, and the plaintiff did not voluntarily contribute to the event causing his injury. Here, a leash could break in the absence of negligence, so it's not likely *res ipsa loquitur* would attach. In any case, since the claim here is for battery, *res ipsa loquitur* will be irrelevant, making B not the best response.

(C) is not the best response,

because the wife's unauthorized entry was justified by *necessity*.

Under the privilege of necessity, one must be apparently facing threatened injury from a source not connected with the other party, and the invasion committed must be substantially less serious than the injury faced. Here, the wife and husband technically were trespassers; however, they entered the property to avoid a charging bull, and since they only trampled a few plants, their entry would be privileged.

Assuming *arguendo* that the wife *had* been a trespasser with no necessity defense, the grower *still* would not have been entitled to attack the wife with his dog, since it would be considered unreasonable force under the circumstances, even if he was acting in defense of his property (especially since the grower had no reasonable fear for his own safety). Since the wife had a privilege of necessity in entering the property, and even without the privilege the grower's use of force was excessive, C is not the best response.

(D) is not the best response,

because it states an element that is not required for battery.

It's true that battery requires an intentional act resulting in harmful or offensive contact with a plaintiff's person; however, the "intent" requirement can be satisfied by the intent to create the apprehension of harmful or offensive contact, followed by such contact, even if the contact *itself* is completely unintentional. That's the case here: The grower's intent to create the fear that he was about to "sic" his dog on the wife was enough to satisfy the intent for battery, even though the grower couldn't have intended for the leash to break (and undoubtedly didn't want it to). Since D misstates the intent requirement of battery, it's not the best response.

Answer 187

(B) is the best response,

because this is the proper standard under FRE 401.

FRE 401 provides the standard of admissibility for relevant evidence. Under FRE 401, evidence is relevant if "(a) it has any tendency to make a fact more or less probable than it would be without the evidence; and (b) the fact is of consequence in determining the action." Since whether the contract was formed is a fact of consequence in the litigation, choice B correctly states how FRE 401 would be applied to determine the admissibility of the evidence.

(A) is not the best response,

because, pursuant to FRE 104(a), the test for admissibility is whether the judge believes that the evidence is probative, not whether a reasonable jury could believe it to be so.

Under FRE 401, evidence is relevant if "(a) it has any tendency to make a fact more or less probable than it would be without the evidence; and (b) the fact is of consequence in determining the action."

(C) is not the best response,

because the judge determines admissibility and the jury determines sufficiency.

The correct standard is found in FRE 401: Evidence is relevant if "(a) it has any tendency to make a fact more or less probable than it would be without the evidence; and (b) the fact is of consequence in determining the action."

(D) is not the best response,

because this response is the standard of proof used by a jury, not the standard of admissibility used by the judge.

Under FRE 401, evidence is relevant if "(a) it has any tendency to make a fact more or less probable than it would be without the evidence; and (b) the fact is of consequence in determining the action."

Answer 188

(C) is the best response,

because it correctly states the central reason the defendant's confession will be admissible: it was volunteered.

The right to counsel under *Miranda* is only triggered by an *interrogation*. Here, the police showed no intention of interrogating the defendant; until they did, or until there was a "critical stage" in the inquiry, they needn't have responded to her request. The mere taking of fingerprints would not in and of itself trigger the right to counsel; and volunteered confessions are admissible. Since C correctly identifies the reason why the defendant's confession will be admissible, it's the best response.

(A) is not the best response,

because the police were not under a duty to grant the defendant's request *immediately.*

There are only two theories on which the defendant would be entitled to counsel: Under the Sixth Amendment, for "critical stages" of the inquiry (e.g., trial); and under the Fifth Amendment, for "investigative" stages of the inquiry (e.g., custodial interrogations). Here, since the police did not intend to interrogate her, she wouldn't be entitled to counsel on Fifth Amendment grounds. Furthermore, since fingerprinting is not a "critical stage" of the inquiry, the defendant wouldn't be entitled to counsel under the Sixth Amendment. Thus, her mere request to speak to a lawyer doesn't mean the request must be granted immediately, in and of itself. What choice A fails to realize is that the defendant volunteered her statement, and so it can be validly offered against her. Since A doesn't recognize this, it's not the best response.

(B) is not the best response,

because the "fruit of the poisonous tree" doctrine does not apply to these facts, and B arrives at the wrong result.

The "fruit of the poisonous tree" doctrine holds that evidence derived from unlawfully obtained evidence is inadmissible. Such "derivative" evidence is called the "tainted fruit of the poisonous tree." The reason this doesn't apply here is that there *is* no unlawfully obtained evidence, and even if the defendant's confession *were* illegally obtained, it would be the direct result of the illegality—that is, the "poisonous tree" itself—not the *fruit* of it.

There was no illegality in terms of the defendant's confession since she *volunteered* it, and, in any case, she wasn't entitled to counsel under the Sixth Amendment because fingerprinting is not a "critical stage" of the inquiry. Since B misapplies the "fruit of the poisonous tree" doctrine to these facts, it's not the best response.

(D) is not the best response,

because although it states the correct result, it does not offer appropriate reasoning.

Although, as D states, fingerprinting is not a critical stage of the proceeding requiring the assistance of counsel, it ignores the fact that the defendant's statement is a confession. Thus, while choice D recognizes that there's no problem with the *Sixth* Amendment right to counsel, it doesn't address the Fifth Amendment. In fact, the reason it will be admissible is that it was *volunteered,* and thus there can't be a Fifth Amendment, "interrogation" problem. If the police had, in fact, interrogated the defendant without honoring her request to see her lawyer, her confession would be *inadmissible.* Thus, the central reason that the defendant's confession is admissible is because it was volunteered. Since D doesn't recognize this, it's not the best response.

Answer 189

(D) is the best response,

because if the duty was non-delegable, then the defendant will be liable for the slippery material that was negligently selected.

This question involves the doctrine of *respondeat superior.* That doctrine governs cases where one person (the "principal" or "master") hires another (an "agent" or "servant"), who then commits an act of negligence. The question is, when is the principal liable for the agent's negligence? The general rule is that the principal, such as the shopping mall in this case, is liable for the negligence of anyone it hires as an employee, but not liable for the negligence of someone it hires as an independent contractor. The construction firm here is likely an independent contractor, since the mall probably didn't have much control over the details of how the firm did its job. But there are some situations where a principal is responsible for the negligence even of an independent contractor. Those are called non-delegable duties. A common "non-delegable duty" involves work done in public places. *See* Dobbs, § 337. So if the mall's duty was "nondelegable," as this answer choice says, then the mall will be held liable for the accident even though the mall did not behave negligently.

(A) is not the best response,

because even if the construction company was an independent contractor, the shopping mall is still liable for the negligence of anyone hired to perform a "non-delegable duty."

As noted in the discussion of choice D above, this could be such a case: If you hire someone to do work for you in a public place, you typically will be liable for any negligence the worker commits—even if the worker is an independent contractor whose behavior you did not control (rather than an employee).

(B) is not the best response,

because it is not necessary for the plaintiff to prove that anyone else had slipped on the floor.

Proof of previous accidents might be helpful to the plaintiff, but there are many other ways to prove negligence on the part of the construction company or the shopping mall. It is especially clear that a prior slip is not necessary to the plaintiff's case here, because the facts tell you that the construction company was negligent in its choice of flooring. By itself that is enough to show that the construction company breached its duty—and enough to support a claim against the shopping mall, too, if the construction company was performing a non-delegable duty.

(C) is not the best response,

because it doesn't matter whether the plaintiff was planning to buy anything.

If the construction company was performing a non-delegable duty, then the shopping mall is potentially liable to anyone hurt by the company's negligence—whether the victim is a customer planning to buy something, a customer not planning to buy anything, or just a random passerby. The intention to buy something might sound relevant to whether the customer was an invitee (that is, a business guest of the mall). But one can be an invitee without buying anything—just being in the store for business purposes is enough. Again, however, this really is beside the point because the plaintiff doesn't need to be an invitee to win. Having "invitee" status helps a plaintiff who wants to claim that the defendant failed to inspect the premises. Here the plaintiff's theory is different: it is that the shopping mall is responsible for a negligent decision made by the company it hired, because the duty to make the decision carefully was not delegable—and the plaintiff's status as an invitee is irrelevant to that theory.

Answer 190

(B) is the best response,

because it states that it would be principally due to estoppel.

The biggest obstacle here is getting around the fact that the agreement between the brother and sister, concerning partitioning the parcel, was not in writing. This partitioning would be considered the conveyance of an interest in land, and would therefore be covered by the Statute of Frauds. If the partitioning is not considered valid, then the sister takes the land when the brother dies, because a joint tenant enjoys the right to survivorship.

However, you're told here that the partitioning was valid, because the brother's son inherited the land from his father. Thus, there must be something that *overrides* the writing requirement. B identifies a factor that does just that: promissory estoppel.

Estoppel prevents one from denying something in the future due to his conduct in the past. Promissory estoppel is triggered by a gratuitous promise that is likely to, and does, induce the promisee's reliance. Here, when the sister orally agreed to the partitioning, she should have recognized that her brother would rely on this. He in fact did so by erecting an apartment development on the northerly ten acres of the parcel. This would relieve the writing requirement for the Statute of Frauds, and would leave the brother as the sole owner of the northerly ten acres of the parcel, with his sister as the owner of the rest. Thus, when the brother died, his son would be entitled to the northerly ten acres of the parcel. Since choice B recognizes the Statute of Frauds problem with these facts, and suggests a viable means of getting around it, it's the best response.

(A) is not the best response,

because it misstates the rule of law.

The conveyance here would be covered by the Statute of Frauds, because it involves an interest in land. In effect, the brother and sister are partitioning the parcel. This generally requires a writing, as A recognizes; however, the familial relationship of the parties does not remove the contract from the Statute of Frauds. Since A states otherwise, it's not the best response.

(C) is not the best response,

because it misstates the rule of law.

The conveyance here (partitioning the parcel) involves an interest in land. As such, it is covered by the Statute of Frauds, and must be in writing (or otherwise removed from it) in order to be valid. If the agreement was valid, then the joint tenancy would be terminated, and the brother would be the sole owner of the northerly ten acres, with his sister being the sole owner of the rest. Since the facts tell you that the brother's son is adjudged to be the owner of the northerly ten acres of the parcel, you know that the partitioning must be valid, and thus *something* must have removed it from the Statute of Frauds. However, C doesn't identify a viable means of doing so. While there are circumstances which *may* remove conveyances from the Statute of Frauds, C is wrong in saying that the oral agreement *necessarily* terminated the joint tenancy. Thus, C is not the best response.

(D) is not the best response,

for three reasons; two involve misstating the correct rule of law, and one involves misstating the facts.

For one thing, the sister's appointment as executrix would not, in and of itself, stop her from watching out for her own interests (since executors of estates are frequently interested in the distribution of those estates). Second, even if she had *accepted* the appointment (which she didn't), she would be obligated to represent the interests of the *estate,* not the beneficiaries thereof. Finally, and most conclusively, the sister didn't accept the appointment—the facts state that she turned it down. The fact that she is not executrix of the estate is the easiest, and most obvious, way to determine that D is not the best response.

Answer 191

(C) is the best response,

because the buyer's delay was not material.

UCC 2-311(3) provides that when the specification of the assortment of goods to be purchased "would materially affect the other party's performance but is not seasonably made or where one party's cooperation is necessary to the agreed performance of the other but is not seasonably forthcoming," the seller is excused from damages relating to a delay in his own performance. Here, the buyer's specification was only one day late, and was received before the seller had changed its position based on the non-receipt of the buyer's specification. As a result, the buyer's delay was not a material breach, and will not allow the seller to suspend his own performance. The seller will, however, be able to sue the buyer for any damages the seller incurred as a result of the delay (although there appear to be none) and will not be liable to the buyer for any damages that resulted from the buyer's delay.

(A) is not the best response,

because the contract was sufficiently definite to be enforceable.

UCC 2-311(1) provides that an "agreement for sale which is otherwise sufficiently definite to be a contract is not made invalid by the fact that it leaves particulars of performance to be specified by one of the parties." Since all of the terms of this contract (price, quantity, time for delivery) other than the selection of particular candy bars are sufficiently definite, UCC 2-311 dictates that the contract was binding even before the buyer specified the assortment of candy to be delivered.

(B) is not the best response,

because the requirement of selection by March 1 was a constructive, rather than an express, condition.

Courts will generally enforce express conditions strictly, so if the March 1 deadline was an express condition, the buyer will have breached the contract. However, UCC 2-311(3) provides that a delay in making a selection of goods is not a material breach of a contract, but rather only insures the seller against a suit for damage that were caused by the buyer's delay. Absent a material breach by the buyer, the seller will not be allowed to suspend its own performance under the contract.

(D) is not the best response,

because the seller has the option, but not the duty, to make such a selection.

Under UCC 2-311(3), when a seller does not timely make a selection of goods for delivery and "such specification would materially affect the [seller's] performance but is not seasonably made," the seller may "perform in any reasonable manner," including making a reasonable selection for the buyer. However, this is only one among a number of options available to the seller, and is therefore not compulsory. Other options include waiting for the buyer to select the goods or waiting for the time performance is due and suing for breach. Since the seller did not change his position based on the buyer's one-day delay, the delay had no material effect on the seller's performance, and cannot be treated as a material breach. Accordingly, the seller was not permitted to suspend his own performance.

Answer 192

(C) is the best response,

because the seller would be strictly liable for the product it sold.

A person who is engaged in the business of selling products, and who sells a defective product, is subject to liability for harm to persons or property caused by the defect. Rest. 3d Torts (Prod. Liab.), § 1. One type of defect is a manufacturing defect, which occurs when the product "departs from its intended design even though all possible care was exercised in the preparation and marketing of the product." *Id.*, § 2. The store is liable under these facts since: (1) the store was "engaged in the business of selling products," and sold the product in question; and (2) the product had a manufacturing defect (the design didn't include snails). The fact that the store did not cause the defect, and could not have spotted or avoided it even with the exercise of utmost care, is irrelevant.

(A) is not the best response,

because the seller of a product containing a manufacturing defect is strictly liable for the injuries it causes.

In this case, there is nothing to indicate that the consumer actually saw the snail; the facts tell you merely that the consumer "could have seen" it. Even if the consumer might have seen the snail had she been paying a reasonable level of attention, this would not save the store from liability, because (1) the default rule on the MBE (applicable here, since the facts don't tell us otherwise) is that pure comparative negligence rather than contributory negligence applies, and (2) pure comparative negligence might reduce the consumer's recovery but would not totally negate it. (*See* Rest. 3d Torts (Apport.), § 17.) The question asks you whether the consumer would "prevail," so even a recovery reduced but not eliminated on account of comparative negligence would still mean that the consumer "prevailed," under an everyday reading of what "prevailed" means.

(B) is not the best response,

because the seller of a product with a manufacturing defect is strictly liable for the injuries it causes.

Because the store sold the bottle in a defective condition to the consumer, it can be held strictly liable even though it did not bottle the soda.

(D) is not the best response,

because, while this answer correctly states that the consumer will prevail, it misstates the legal basis for this conclusion.

Strict product liability, applicable here, is not based on exclusive control but on the sale to the consumer. In any event, the store did not have exclusive control over the bottle at the time the defect was introduced, the manufacturer/bottler did. And anyway, *res ipsa loquitur*—which is the only doctrine to which the concept of exclusive control is relevant—is neither necessary nor appropriate here: if anyone was negligent, it was the bottler. Nevertheless, the store will be liable because the seller of a product with a manufacturing defect is strictly liable for the injuries it causes.

Answer 193

(C) is the best response,

because it correctly identifies that the homeowner's duty to pay is only triggered by the painter's substantial performance.

The painter's performance under the contract would be considered a constructive condition precedent to the homeowner's performance. Constructive conditions require only *substantial* performance to trigger the other party's duty to perform (unlike *express* conditions, which require *complete* performance). Thus, if the painter didn't substantially perform, the homeowner's duty to pay would not exist. If the painter *did* substantially perform, the homeowner's failure to pay would be, as C points out, a total breach of contract (since he failed to pay anything).

Since C correctly analyzes the effect of the painter's performance on the homeowner's duty to pay, it's the best response.

(A) is not the best response,

because its result and its reasoning don't agree. If in fact the painter had properly or substantially painted the porch, the homeowner's refusal to pay anything would be a total breach of contract, not a partial one.

As a preliminary matter, note that A uses the modifier "if"; that means that the reasoning must be plausible on the facts, the reasoning must address a central issue, and the result must be consistent with the reasoning.

First, it's plausible that the painter substantially performed his duty under the contract. The difference between a material (or total) breach and minor (or partial) breach is, naturally, one of degree. The distinction is an important one, because a *major* breach relieves the non-breaching party of his duty to perform under the contract; a *minor* breach means the non-breaching party must perform, but can sue for damages.

The Rest. 2d of Contracts § 241 looks to six factors to determine if a breach is material, weighing them according to what's critical in each case:

1. To what extent has the injured party received benefits?
2. Can the injured party be adequately compensated in damages?
3. Is the breaching party "close" to full performance?
4. Will the breaching party face great hardship if termination is permitted?
5. How willful is the breach?
6. How great is the certainty of completion?

Here, if the painter substantially performed, the homeowner's refusal to pay would be a total breach.

Second, this reasoning addresses a central issue, because the homeowner's duty to pay is only triggered by the painter's substantially performing his duty under the contract, since the painter's performance will be a constructive condition precedent to the homeowner's performance. Under these facts it's possible that the painter substantially performed, and if he did, the homeowner's refusal to pay would be a total breach of contract. Since A doesn't arrive at the correct result, it's not the best response.

(B) is not the best response,

because if the painter didn't substantially perform, the homeowner's refusal to pay wouldn't be a breach *at all*.

The painter's performance under the contract would be considered a constructive condition precedent to the homeowner's performance. Constructive conditions require only *substantial* performance to trigger the other party's duty to perform (express conditions require *complete* performance). Thus, if the painter didn't substantially perform, the homeowner's duty to pay would not exist. If the painter *did* substantially perform, the homeowner's breach would be *total,* not partial, since he refused to perform his entire duty.

Note that this could be analyzed in terms of breach: a failure to substantially perform would be a major breach, relieving the other party of a duty to perform; substantial performance, which is defective in some way, involves a *minor* breach, and requires the other party to perform and sue for damages. Since B would impose the homeowner's duty to pay even if the painter's breach was major, it's not the best response.

(D) is not the best response,

because the homeowner's failure to pay is only a total breach if the painter substantially performed his duty under the contract.

The painter's performance under the contract would be considered a constructive condition precedent to the homeowner's performance. Constructive conditions require only *substantial* performance to trigger the other party's duty to perform (unlike *express* conditions, which require *complete* performance). Thus, if the painter didn't substantially perform, the homeowner's duty to pay would not exist. If the painter *did* substantially perform, the homeowner's failure to pay would be, as D points out, a total breach of contract (since he failed to pay anything).

Note that this could be analyzed in terms of breach: a failure to substantially perform would be a major breach, relieving the other party of a duty to perform; substantial performance, which is defective in some way, involves a *minor* breach, and requires the other party to perform and sue for damages.

Since D would impose the homeowner's duty to pay even if the painter's breach was major, it's not the best response.

Answer 194

(C) is the best response,

because it offers a federal power to which a need-based student aid program is rationally related.

The welfare power addresses the federal government's power to collect taxes and spend money for all matters of national concern. In implementing this power, Congress *can* impose any reasonable conditions on the states as a prerequisite to participating in federal spending programs. Here, student aid will have a general beneficial effect on the welfare of the country. Requiring that the aid be distributed on the basis of need is a reasonable condition to place on such a program. As such, the welfare power provides a strong constitutional basis for the statute.

Incidentally, the reason that this problem requires some thought is that education is traditionally a *state* function. Congress can only pass laws rationally related to its enumerated powers (e.g., defense, interstate commerce, etc.). As this question indicates, Congress can use its spending power to indirectly achieve objectives it couldn't achieve directly pursuant to its regulatory powers (as long as it doesn't violate any independent constitutional limitations, like due process). By relying on the Welfare Clause, choice C overcomes the problem that education is a state function, making it the best response.

(A) is not the best response,

because there is no federal police power, and the question here addresses a federal statute.

Under the police power, a state enactment is a valid means of achieving a legitimate state interest where the public health, safety, welfare, and morals is involved. There is no federal equivalent of the police power, although Congress can achieve many of the same ends through valid use of its powers. (For instance, Congress can use its commerce power to regulate the use of interstate channels, thus prohibiting interstate transport of stolen property, misbranded goods, lottery tickets, and the like.) Since choice A doesn't recognize this, it's not the best response.

(B) is not the best response,

because the war and defense power would not provide a basis for a statute of this sort.

Congress gets its war and defense power from Article I, § 8, of the Constitution, under which it can declare war, raise and support armed forces, and, in general, administer those forces. The types of regulations Congress could pass under the war power include conducting a draft, instituting economic controls in wartime, excluding people from sensitive areas, and confiscating the property of enemies. In order to be upheld under an enumerated power, a statute must be rationally related to the power, or a necessary and proper means of effectuating that power. A need-based student aid program has no obvious connection with the war power, and as such the war power wouldn't provide a strong constitutional basis for the legislation. Since B states otherwise, it's not the best response.

(D) is not the best response,

because the Privileges and Immunities Clause of the Fourteenth Amendment is not a source of constitutional power for the federal government.

The Privileges and Immunities Clause of the Fourteenth Amendment voids those state enactments that clearly infringe privileges enjoyed by U.S. citizens. It is construed narrowly, typically being restricted to fundamental rights that are shared in common by all U.S. citizens, namely:

1. The right to travel freely from state to state;
2. The right to petition Congress for redress of grievances;
3. The right to vote for national officers;
4. The right to assemble peaceably; and

5. The right to discuss matters of national legislation.

Thus, the Clause would not provide a means by which to *support* the constitutionality of a need-based student aid program. The Clause *limits* the power of the *states*, but is not a source of power for the *federal* government.

Since D doesn't recognize this, it's not the best response.

Answer 195

(A) is the best answer,

because jeopardy does not attach at either a preliminary hearing or at grand jury proceedings.

Instead, jeopardy attaches in a jury trial when the jury is sworn in and in a bench trial when the court begins to hear evidence. Thus, neither the preliminary hearing nor the initial grand jury will prevent the prosecutor from bringing charges against the defendant.

(B) is not the best answer,

as neither conviction nor acquittal is required for jeopardy to attach.

Instead, jeopardy attaches in a jury trial when the jury is sworn in and in a bench trial when the court begins to hear evidence. Thus, neither the preliminary hearing nor the initial grand jury will prevent the prosecutor from bringing charges against the defendant.

(C) is not the best answer,

because jeopardy does not attach to "any" proceeding after the preliminary hearing.

Jeopardy does not attach at either a preliminary hearing or at grand jury proceedings. Instead, jeopardy attaches in a jury trial when the jury is sworn in and in a bench trial when the court begins to hear evidence. Thus, neither the preliminary hearing nor the initial grand jury will prevent the prosecutor from bringing charges against the defendant.

(D) is not the best answer,

because the double jeopardy clause does not bar a grand jury from returning an indictment when a prior grand jury refused to do so.

Jeopardy does not attach at either a preliminary hearing or at grand jury proceedings. Instead, jeopardy attaches in a jury trial when the jury is sworn in and in a bench trial when the court begins to hear evidence. Thus, neither the preliminary hearing nor the initial grand jury will prevent the prosecutor from bringing charges against the defendant.

Answer 196

(A) is the best response,

because the landowner's possibility of reverter passed to his heir when he died.

When approaching a future interests problem, it is crucial to identify the interests created by each conveyance. Here, the landowner conveyed the land to a church "so long as the land herein conveyed is used as the site for the principal religious edifice maintained by said church." The language of duration ("so long as") indicates that the church received a fee simple determinable. A fee simple determinable is conveyable *inter vivos*, is devisable by will, and, absent a will, can pass by intestate succession. The landowner retained a possibility of reverter, which would become possessory if and when the land was no longer used as the site of the church. When the landowner died, his possibility of reverter passed to his heir. The church's estate ended when it ceased to maintain a church building on the land, and the land automatically reverted to the landowner's heir.

(B) is not the best response,

because it misstates the law.

There is no general restriction against a charity conveying assets that are donated to it. In this case, however, should the church convey the land it received from the landowner, its estate would terminate, because the land will revert to the holder of the possibility of reverter as soon as the church ceased to use the land as the site of its primary church. Since the church could not convey a greater interest in the land than it possessed, whoever took the land from the church would get nothing. Thus, the reason the landowner's heir will hold title to the land is that the church's estate would terminate, not that the church, as a charity, was barred from conveying the land.

(C) is not the best response,

because *cy pres* is inapplicable to this situation.

Cy pres will be applied to approximate the wishes of the grantor when the charity to which he transferred assets no longer can use the assets. However, it is inapplicable in cases where the grantor has explicitly stated what should happen to the donated land in the event that the charity is no longer using it, since there is no need to approximate the grantor's intent. Here, we know that the landowner wanted the land to revert to him, or his heirs and assigns, in the event that the church ceased to use the premises as the site of its principal religious edifice. As a result, there is no need to apply the *cy pres* doctrine.

(D) is not the best response,

because possibilities of reverter are not subject to the Rule Against Perpetuities.

The Rule Against Perpetuities states that an interest in land must vest, if at all, within 21 years of a life in being at the time the interest was created. It is inapplicable to possibilities of reverter because they are vested at the moment they are created. As a result, the fact that it may be an arbitrarily long period of time before the possibility of reverter becomes possessory does not cause it to fail as a violation of the Rule Against Perpetuities. Since the possibility of reverter passed through the landowner's estate by intestate succession to his heir, at the moment the church ceased to use the land for its primary church building, ownership immediately passed to the landowner's heir.

Answer 197

(D) is the best response,

because the privilege belongs to the patient, who has designated the attorney to appear on behalf of the patient.

The basic fact to remember here is that the privilege belongs to the *patient,* not the *doctor.*

There are seven, basic requirements for the application of a privilege:

1. Appropriate *relationship* between communicants (e.g., attorney-client, doctor-patient);
2. *Relationship existed at the time* of communication;
3. *Appropriate person is claiming* the privilege (i.e., client or patient holds privilege, not attorney or doctor);
4. There was a *communication* (i.e., verbal or communicative act);
5. The communication was made *in confidence* (presence of third parties normally destroys privilege);
6. Privilege has not been *waived* (via contract or in court); and
7. There is no reason privilege should not control (e.g., legal advice sought for future wrongdoing; medical advice not in course of treatment).

Under choice D, the person asserting the privilege on the patient's behalf is one closely associated with him: his attorney. His attorney has been designated to act on the patient's behalf to assert the privilege.

(A) is not the best response,

because it states an erroneous rule.

Asserting a privilege has seven requirements:

1. Appropriate *relationship* between communicants (e.g., attorney-client, doctor-patient);
2. *Relationship existed at the time* of communication;
3. *Appropriate person is claiming* the privilege (i.e., client or patient holds privilege, not attorney or doctor);
4. There was a *communication* (i.e., verbal or communicative act);
5. The communication was made *in confidence* (presence of third parties normally destroys privilege);
6. Privilege has not been *waived* (via contract or in court); and
7. There is no reason privilege should not control (e.g., legal advice sought for future wrongdoing; medical advice not in course of treatment).

The problem here is with the third element. A doctor simply does not have a privilege against disclosure of confidential communications made by a patient. The doctor-patient privilege rests exclusively with the patient. The problem here is that the patient cannot object to disclosure himself. In such cases, the doctor normally asserts it on the patient's behalf. Thus, the physician could theoretically assert the privilege on the patient's behalf. However, the physician could not assert the privilege on the ground suggested here—an ostensible privilege against disclosing confidential communications made by a patient. Since A states a rule that is wrong, it is not the best response.

(B) is not the best response,

because a third party is not entitled to assert the doctor-patient privilege.

Asserting a privilege has seven requirements:

1. Appropriate *relationship* between communicants (e.g., attorney-client, doctor-patient);
2. *Relationship existed at the time* of communication;
3. *Appropriate person is claiming* the privilege (i.e., client or patient holds privilege, not attorney or doctor);
4. There was a *communication* (i.e., verbal or communicative act);
5. The communication was made *in confidence* (presence of third parties normally destroys privilege);
6. Privilege has not been *waived* (via contract or in court); and
7. There is no reason privilege should not control (e.g., legal advice sought for future wrongdoing; medical advice not in course of treatment).

The problem here is the third requirement. It's someone other than the privilege holder, the patient, who's asserting the privilege. The privilege exists for the patient's benefit. Since the plaintiff is not concerned with the patient's best interests, he is clearly not the appropriate person to invoke the privilege. Thus, B is not the best response.

(C) is not the best response,

because it relies on facts irrelevant to the determination of invoking the privilege.

Asserting a privilege has seven requirements:

1. Appropriate *relationship* between communicants (e.g., attorney-client, doctor-patient);
2. *Relationship existed at the time* of communication;

3. *Appropriate person is claiming* the privilege (i.e., client or patient holds privilege, not attorney or doctor);
4. There was a *communication* (i.e., verbal or communicative act);
5. The communication was made *in confidence* (presence of third parties normally destroys privilege);
6. Privilege has not been *waived* (via contract or in court); and
7. There is no reason privilege should not control (e.g., legal advice sought for future wrongdoing; medical advice not in course of treatment).

Choice C addresses the second element—the existence of an appropriate relationship at the time of the communication. However, C's incorrect in that the relationship requirement was satisfied here. The applicability of the doctor-patient privilege does not depend on whether the patient *actually* received treatment, but whether the doctor-patient relationship existed at the time the confidential communication was made. This can exist in the absence of receiving actual treatment. In any case, the judge's finding that the patient left without receiving treatment would, if anything, vie for *admitting* the evidence, not *excluding* it. This, apart from anything else, should have tipped you off to the fact that C is not the best response.

Answer 198

(B) is the best response,

because it impliedly identifies the basis on which the roofer will be liable: negligence.

One is negligent if he fails to exercise such care as a reasonable person in his position would have exercised, this must have been a breach of the duty to prevent the foreseeable risk of harm to anyone in plaintiff's position, and this breach must have caused plaintiff's damages. Here, by leaving the ladder in place, the roofer behaved unreasonably in creating a risk that the home could be burglarized. He left a ladder against the house, leading to a second story window, which a burglar could not otherwise have reached. Coupled with the fact that no one was at home at the time, this creates a risk of unlawful entry, which the roofer's exercise of due care could have avoided. Since the roofer's negligence caused the homeowner's damages and his due care would have avoided those damages, the homeowner will prevail. Since B recognizes this, it's the best response.

(A) is not the best response,

because it's highly unlikely the roofer would be considered a trespasser.

Trespass requires proof of three elements: defendant's physical invasion of plaintiff's exclusive possessory interest in real property without plaintiff's consent; defendant's intent to bring about such invasion; and causation. Under these facts, it's unlikely the roofer's presence on the property would be considered non-permissive. Naturally, while he was *performing* his work, his presence would be considered permissive, and as a result he would be a licensee, not a trespasser. His leaving a ladder on the property overnight would not be sufficient to change his status to trespasser. Instead, what the roofer will be liable for is *negligence,* since he failed to exercise such care as a reasonable person in his position would have exercised, this was a breach of the duty to prevent the foreseeable risk of harm to anyone in the homeowner's position, and this breach caused the homeowner's damages. Leaving the ladder in place created the risk that a thief would take advantage of the ladder to enter the house. Since A doesn't recognize this, it's not the best response.

(C) is not the best response,

because although it correctly states the *general* rule of law, it does not apply to facts like these.

The intentional misconduct of others *only* relieves the original actor of liability *when the misconduct is unforeseeable.* Here, theft is exactly the outcome of the roofer's negligence—in leaving the ladder propped up to a second story window of an unoccupied house—is likely to produce, and as such it will be considered "within the risk" the roofer's negligence created. Thus, intervening misconduct only relieves the original actor of liability when it's *not foreseeable*. Since C fails to recognize that the facts here do not fit the general rule, it's not the best response.

(D) is not the best response,

because it misstates the law: the homeowner's claim is *not* limited to damages for breach of contract, and, in any case it's unlikely the homeowner would be able to claim for breach of contract under these facts.

The homeowner would be able to claim under the contract only if the roofer's repairs on the roof were not done "in a workmanlike manner." There is no indication of any deficiency in the repairs under these facts. Even if there *had* been, this would not have prohibited a tort claim by the homeowner for the roofer's negligence in leaving the ladder against the house, since a claim under the contract and a claim in tort are not mutually exclusive. Since D states otherwise, it's not the best response.

Answer 199

(C) is the best response,

because it's the only response that offers a source of power for the federal government.

In order to be valid, a congressional enactment must be rationally related to one of Congress's enumerated powers, or it must be necessary and proper to effectuate such a power. Congress's power to regulate interstate commerce is found in Article I, § 8, cl. 3, of the Constitution. The power is exceptionally broad. Under the "affectation doctrine," Congress can regulate any activity that has any appreciable direct or indirect effect on interstate commerce. Consumer credit affects interstate commerce, so Congress will be able to enact a law governing it. Since C offers a plausible source of support for the legislation, and no other response does, it's the best response.

(A) is not the best response,

because the Contracts Clause limits *state* power; it's not a source of power for the federal government.

As a general rule, the Contracts Clause, Article I, § 10, of the Constitution, prohibits states from passing laws that impair the obligations of existing contracts. Here, the law was enacted by the *federal* government, not a state; furthermore, the Contracts Clause is a *limitation* on power, not a *source* of it, and this question is looking for a source of power to justify the law. Since A doesn't recognize this, it's not the best response.

(B) is not the best response,

because the Privileges and Immunities Clause of the Fourteenth Amendment *limits* the power of the *states,* it's not a source of power for the federal government.

The Privileges and Immunities Clause of the Fourteenth Amendment voids those state enactments that clearly infringe privileges enjoyed by U.S. citizens. It is construed narrowly, typically being restricted to fundamental rights that are shared in common by all citizens, namely:

1. The right to travel freely from state to state;
2. The right to petition Congress for redress of grievances;
3. The right to vote for national officers;
4. The right to assemble peaceably; and
5. The right to discuss matters of national legislation.

The Privileges and Immunities Clause of the Fourteenth Amendment wouldn't apply here. Consumer credit is not a fundamental right, the law here isn't a state law but a federal one, and this clause is a limit on power, where the question here asks for the source of the power to enact the UCCC. Since B doesn't recognize this, it's not the best response.

(D) is not the best response,

because the Equal Protection Clause is triggered by a classification that determines people's rights. It *prohibits* enactments; it doesn't provide a source of power for the federal government.

Here, the law addresses fair credit practices; it doesn't create a classification. Furthermore, the question asks for the source of the federal power to enact the UCCC, not a limitation on power, which the Equal Protection Clause is. Finally, the Equal Protection Clause only addresses *state* action; it's not applicable to the federal government. Since D doesn't offer a source of power to support the law, it's not the best response.

Answer 200

(B) is the best response,

because the condition will be enforced even though it was not included in the writing.

Generally, the Parol Evidence Rule prohibits the introduction of statements made prior to a signed written contract from being considered by a court interpreting the contract. However, there are several important exceptions to the Parol Evidence Rule, one of which is the "condition exception." This exception allows the introduction of a prior oral agreement that imposes a condition on the enforceability of a contract. Here, the homeowner and the builder had orally agreed that their agreement would be enforceable only if the builder's other pending bid was rejected. Since this was a condition on the enforceability of the contract, a court will read the condition into the written contract.

(A) is not the best response,

because efficiency principles will not relieve the builder from being liable for damages that result from his breach.

The general rule is that a breaching party is liable for damages resulting from his breach. Even if the builder's excuse for breaching his obligation to the homeowner was to make a higher-value use of his time, it will not result in the builder not being liable to the homeowner in a suit on the contract. If you chose this response, you were probably thinking of an "efficient breach." An efficient breach is an intentional breach of a contract by a party who would take a greater loss by performing the contract than by breaching it. The efficiency principle at work is that a party should be allowed to breach *and pay damages* if doing so would be more economically efficient than performing under the contract.

(C) is not the best response,

because the builder's promise was definite.

The condition on enforceability (that the contract would only be enforceable if the builder's other bid fell through) provides for a situation in which the builder would not have to perform. However, if the condition fails to occur, then the builder would be bound to construct the addition to the homeowner's house. Since the condition is outside the builder's control, it is a conditional promise, rather than an illusory one. A promise is illusory if the promisor is free to choose not to perform if he does not wish to. For example, if the builder had promised to build the addition, but had retained the right to cancel the contract at no notice and with no penalty, then his promise would have been illusory, since he would be entirely in control of whether or not he was bound to perform.

(D) is not the best response,

because the oral condition on enforceability is within an exception to the Parol Evidence Rule.

Generally, the Parol Evidence Rule prohibits the introduction of statements made prior to a signed written contract from being considered by a court interpreting the contract. However, there are several important exceptions to the Parol Evidence Rule, one of which is the "condition exception." This exception allows the introduction of a prior oral agreement that imposes a condition on the enforceability of a contract. Here, the homeowner and the builder had orally agreed that their agreement would be enforceable only if the builder's other pending bid was rejected. Since this was a condition on the enforceability of the contract, a court will read the condition into the written contract.

ANSWER SHEETS

The following pages of answer sheets have been provided for your use. The A.M. and P.M. Practice Exam sheets are replicas of those you will see on the Bar Exam. The individual-subject answer sheet has been modified to provide you with space for your own notes, etc. Feel free to remove the individual-subject answer sheet from this book and make as many copies of it as you need while working through the questions in each section. Please note that the subjects are not scored separately on the exam and that the individual-subject answer sheet is provided for your convenience only.

For each section, fill in the corresponding oval for each answer. As you answer each question, make a note of the answers that were only good guesses and not firmly based on your knowledge of the law so you can check the answers to those questions more carefully.

SIDE 1

JURISDICTION CODE

Jurisdiction	Code
Ala.	01
Alaska	02
Ariz.	03
Ark.	04
Calif.	05
Colo.	06
Conn.	07
Del.	08
D.C.	09
Fla.	10
Ga.	11
Hawaii	12
Idaho	13
Ill.	14
Ind.	15
Iowa	16
Kans.	17
Ky.	18
La.	19
Maine	20
Md.	21
Mass.	22
Mich.	23
Minn.	24
Miss.	25
Mo.	26
Mont.	27
Nebr.	28
Nev.	29
N.H.	30
N.J.	31
N. Mex.	32
N.Y.	33
N.C.	34
N. Dak.	35
Ohio	36
Okla.	37
Oreg.	38
Pa.	39
R.I.	40
S.C.	41
S. Dak.	42
Tenn.	43
Tex.	44
Utah	45
Vt.	46
Va.	47
Wash.	48
W.Va.	49
Wisc.	50
Wyo.	51
Guam	52
Northern Marana Islands/ Saipan	53
Virgin Islands	55
All Others	56

NOTES

STRATEGIES AND TACTICS FOR THE MBE
Score Sheet

CONSTITUTIONAL LAW

TEST FORM: 78526

BE SURE EACH MARK IS DARK AND COMPLETELY FILLLS THE INTENDED OVAL, AS SHOWN IN THE ILLUSTRATION AT THE RIGHT. COMPLETELY ERASE ANY MISTAKES OR STRAY MARKS. (A) ● (C) (D)

1 (A) (B) (C) (D)	21 (A) (B) (C) (D)	41 (A) (B) (C) (D)	61 (A) (B) (C) (D)	81 (A) (B) (C) (D)
2 (A) (B) (C) (D)	22 (A) (B) (C) (D)	42 (A) (B) (C) (D)	62 (A) (B) (C) (D)	82 (A) (B) (C) (D)
3 (A) (B) (C) (D)	23 (A) (B) (C) (D)	43 (A) (B) (C) (D)	63 (A) (B) (C) (D)	83 (A) (B) (C) (D)
4 (A) (B) (C) (D)	24 (A) (B) (C) (D)	44 (A) (B) (C) (D)	64 (A) (B) (C) (D)	84 (A) (B) (C) (D)
5 (A) (B) (C) (D)	25 (A) (B) (C) (D)	45 (A) (B) (C) (D)	65 (A) (B) (C) (D)	85 (A) (B) (C) (D)
6 (A) (B) (C) (D)	26 (A) (B) (C) (D)	46 (A) (B) (C) (D)	66 (A) (B) (C) (D)	86 (A) (B) (C) (D)
7 (A) (B) (C) (D)	27 (A) (B) (C) (D)	47 (A) (B) (C) (D)	76 (A) (B) (C) (D)	87 (A) (B) (C) (D)
8 (A) (B) (C) (D)	28 (A) (B) (C) (D)	48 (A) (B) (C) (D)	68 (A) (B) (C) (D)	88 (A) (B) (C) (D)
9 (A) (B) (C) (D)	29 (A) (B) (C) (D)	49 (A) (B) (C) (D)	69 (A) (B) (C) (D)	89 (A) (B) (C) (D)
10 (A) (B) (C) (D)	30 (A) (B) (C) (D)	50 (A) (B) (C) (D)	70 (A) (B) (C) (D)	90 (A) (B) (C) (D)
11 (A) (B) (C) (D)	31 (A) (B) (C) (D)	51 (A) (B) (C) (D)	71 (A) (B) (C) (D)	91 (A) (B) (C) (D)
12 (A) (B) (C) (D)	32 (A) (B) (C) (D)	52 (A) (B) (C) (D)	72 (A) (B) (C) (D)	92 (A) (B) (C) (D)
13 (A) (B) (C) (D)	33 (A) (B) (C) (D)	53 (A) (B) (C) (D)	73 (A) (B) (C) (D)	93 (A) (B) (C) (D)
14 (A) (B) (C) (D)	34 (A) (B) (C) (D)	54 (A) (B) (C) (D)	74 (A) (B) (C) (D)	94 (A) (B) (C) (D)
15 (A) (B) (C) (D)	35 (A) (B) (C) (D)	55 (A) (B) (C) (D)	75 (A) (B) (C) (D)	95 (A) (B) (C) (D)
16 (A) (B) (C) (D)	36 (A) (B) (C) (D)	56 (A) (B) (C) (D)	76 (A) (B) (C) (D)	96 (A) (B) (C) (D)
17 (A) (B) (C) (D)	37 (A) (B) (C) (D)	57 (A) (B) (C) (D)	76 (A) (B) (C) (D)	97 (A) (B) (C) (D)
18 (A) (B) (C) (D)	38 (A) (B) (C) (D)	58 (A) (B) (C) (D)	78 (A) (B) (C) (D)	98 (A) (B) (C) (D)
19 (A) (B) (C) (D)	39 (A) (B) (C) (D)	59 (A) (B) (C) (D)	79 (A) (B) (C) (D)	99 (A) (B) (C) (D)
20 (A) (B) (C) (D)	40 (A) (B) (C) (D)	60 (A) (B) (C) (D)	70 (A) (B) (C) (D)	100 (A) (B) (C) (D)

SIDE 1

JURISDICTION	CODE
Ala.	01
Alaska	02
Ariz.	03
Ark.	04
Calif.	05
Colo.	06
Conn.	07
Del.	08
D.C.	09
Fla.	10
Ga.	11
Hawaii	12
Idaho	13
Ill.	14
Ind.	15
Iowa	16
Kans.	17
Ky.	18
La.	19
Maine	20
Md.	21
Mass.	22
Mich.	23
Minn.	24
Miss.	25
Mo.	26
Mont.	27
Nebr.	28
Nev.	29
N.H.	30
N.J.	31
N. Mex.	32
N.Y.	33
N.C.	34
N. Dak.	35
Ohio	36
Okla.	37
Oreg.	38
Pa.	39
R.I.	40
S.C.	41
S. Dak.	42
Tenn.	43
Tex.	44
Utah	45
Vt.	46
Va.	47
Wash.	48
W.Va.	49
Wisc.	50
Wyo.	51
Guam	52
Northern Mariana Islands/ Saipan	53
Virgin Islands	55
All Others	56

A JURISDICTION CODE

(1) (1)
(2) (2)
(3) (3)
(4) (4)
(5) (5)
(6)
(7)
(8)
(9)
(0) (0)

B APPLICANT NUMBER

(1) (1) (1) (1) (1)
(2) (2) (2) (2) (2)
(3) (3) (3) (3) (3)
(4) (4) (4) (4) (4)
(5) (5) (5) (5) (5)
(6) (6) (6) (6) (6)
(7) (7) (7) (7) (7)
(8) (8) (8) (8) (8)
(9) (9) (9) (9) (9)
(0) (0) (0) (0) (0)

C DATE OF BIRTH

Month		
○ Jan.		
○ Feb.	(1)	(1)
○ March	(2)	(2)
○ April	(3)	(3)
○ May		(4)
○ June		(5)
○ July		(6)
○ August		(7)
○ Sept.		(8)
○ Oct.		(9)
○ Nov.	(0)	(0)
○ Dec.		

USE A SOFT LEAD PENCIL ONLY

DO NOT FOLD, STAPLE, OR ATTACH TAPE TO THIS SHEET

NATIONAL CONFERENCE OF BAR EXAMINERS
Multistate Bar Examination

A.M. EXAM

TEST FORM: 78526

BE SURE EACH MARK IS DARK AND COMPLETELY FILLLS THE INTENDED OVAL, AS SHOWN IN THE ILLUSTRATION AT THE RIGHT. COMPLETELY ERASE ANY MISTAKES OR STRAY MARKS. Ⓐ ● Ⓒ Ⓓ

1 Ⓐ Ⓑ Ⓒ Ⓓ	21 Ⓐ Ⓑ Ⓒ Ⓓ	41 Ⓐ Ⓑ Ⓒ Ⓓ	61 Ⓐ Ⓑ Ⓒ Ⓓ	81 Ⓐ Ⓑ Ⓒ Ⓓ
2 Ⓐ Ⓑ Ⓒ Ⓓ	22 Ⓐ Ⓑ Ⓒ Ⓓ	42 Ⓐ Ⓑ Ⓒ Ⓓ	62 Ⓐ Ⓑ Ⓒ Ⓓ	82 Ⓐ Ⓑ Ⓒ Ⓓ
3 Ⓐ Ⓑ Ⓒ Ⓓ	23 Ⓐ Ⓑ Ⓒ Ⓓ	43 Ⓐ Ⓑ Ⓒ Ⓓ	63 Ⓐ Ⓑ Ⓒ Ⓓ	83 Ⓐ Ⓑ Ⓒ Ⓓ
4 Ⓐ Ⓑ Ⓒ Ⓓ	24 Ⓐ Ⓑ Ⓒ Ⓓ	44 Ⓐ Ⓑ Ⓒ Ⓓ	64 Ⓐ Ⓑ Ⓒ Ⓓ	84 Ⓐ Ⓑ Ⓒ Ⓓ
5 Ⓐ Ⓑ Ⓒ Ⓓ	25 Ⓐ Ⓑ Ⓒ Ⓓ	45 Ⓐ Ⓑ Ⓒ Ⓓ	65 Ⓐ Ⓑ Ⓒ Ⓓ	85 Ⓐ Ⓑ Ⓒ Ⓓ
6 Ⓐ Ⓑ Ⓒ Ⓓ	26 Ⓐ Ⓑ Ⓒ Ⓓ	46 Ⓐ Ⓑ Ⓒ Ⓓ	66 Ⓐ Ⓑ Ⓒ Ⓓ	86 Ⓐ Ⓑ Ⓒ Ⓓ
7 Ⓐ Ⓑ Ⓒ Ⓓ	27 Ⓐ Ⓑ Ⓒ Ⓓ	47 Ⓐ Ⓑ Ⓒ Ⓓ	76 Ⓐ Ⓑ Ⓒ Ⓓ	87 Ⓐ Ⓑ Ⓒ Ⓓ
8 Ⓐ Ⓑ Ⓒ Ⓓ	28 Ⓐ Ⓑ Ⓒ Ⓓ	48 Ⓐ Ⓑ Ⓒ Ⓓ	68 Ⓐ Ⓑ Ⓒ Ⓓ	88 Ⓐ Ⓑ Ⓒ Ⓓ
9 Ⓐ Ⓑ Ⓒ Ⓓ	29 Ⓐ Ⓑ Ⓒ Ⓓ	49 Ⓐ Ⓑ Ⓒ Ⓓ	69 Ⓐ Ⓑ Ⓒ Ⓓ	89 Ⓐ Ⓑ Ⓒ Ⓓ
10 Ⓐ Ⓑ Ⓒ Ⓓ	30 Ⓐ Ⓑ Ⓒ Ⓓ	50 Ⓐ Ⓑ Ⓒ Ⓓ	70 Ⓐ Ⓑ Ⓒ Ⓓ	90 Ⓐ Ⓑ Ⓒ Ⓓ
11 Ⓐ Ⓑ Ⓒ Ⓓ	31 Ⓐ Ⓑ Ⓒ Ⓓ	51 Ⓐ Ⓑ Ⓒ Ⓓ	71 Ⓐ Ⓑ Ⓒ Ⓓ	91 Ⓐ Ⓑ Ⓒ Ⓓ
12 Ⓐ Ⓑ Ⓒ Ⓓ	32 Ⓐ Ⓑ Ⓒ Ⓓ	52 Ⓐ Ⓑ Ⓒ Ⓓ	72 Ⓐ Ⓑ Ⓒ Ⓓ	92 Ⓐ Ⓑ Ⓒ Ⓓ
13 Ⓐ Ⓑ Ⓒ Ⓓ	33 Ⓐ Ⓑ Ⓒ Ⓓ	53 Ⓐ Ⓑ Ⓒ Ⓓ	73 Ⓐ Ⓑ Ⓒ Ⓓ	93 Ⓐ Ⓑ Ⓒ Ⓓ
14 Ⓐ Ⓑ Ⓒ Ⓓ	34 Ⓐ Ⓑ Ⓒ Ⓓ	54 Ⓐ Ⓑ Ⓒ Ⓓ	74 Ⓐ Ⓑ Ⓒ Ⓓ	94 Ⓐ Ⓑ Ⓒ Ⓓ
15 Ⓐ Ⓑ Ⓒ Ⓓ	35 Ⓐ Ⓑ Ⓒ Ⓓ	55 Ⓐ Ⓑ Ⓒ Ⓓ	75 Ⓐ Ⓑ Ⓒ Ⓓ	95 Ⓐ Ⓑ Ⓒ Ⓓ
16 Ⓐ Ⓑ Ⓒ Ⓓ	36 Ⓐ Ⓑ Ⓒ Ⓓ	56 Ⓐ Ⓑ Ⓒ Ⓓ	76 Ⓐ Ⓑ Ⓒ Ⓓ	96 Ⓐ Ⓑ Ⓒ Ⓓ
17 Ⓐ Ⓑ Ⓒ Ⓓ	37 Ⓐ Ⓑ Ⓒ Ⓓ	57 Ⓐ Ⓑ Ⓒ Ⓓ	76 Ⓐ Ⓑ Ⓒ Ⓓ	97 Ⓐ Ⓑ Ⓒ Ⓓ
18 Ⓐ Ⓑ Ⓒ Ⓓ	38 Ⓐ Ⓑ Ⓒ Ⓓ	58 Ⓐ Ⓑ Ⓒ Ⓓ	78 Ⓐ Ⓑ Ⓒ Ⓓ	98 Ⓐ Ⓑ Ⓒ Ⓓ
19 Ⓐ Ⓑ Ⓒ Ⓓ	39 Ⓐ Ⓑ Ⓒ Ⓓ	59 Ⓐ Ⓑ Ⓒ Ⓓ	79 Ⓐ Ⓑ Ⓒ Ⓓ	99 Ⓐ Ⓑ Ⓒ Ⓓ
20 Ⓐ Ⓑ Ⓒ Ⓓ	40 Ⓐ Ⓑ Ⓒ Ⓓ	60 Ⓐ Ⓑ Ⓒ Ⓓ	70 Ⓐ Ⓑ Ⓒ Ⓓ	100 Ⓐ Ⓑ Ⓒ Ⓓ

SIDE 1

JURISDICTION	CODE
Ala.	01
Alaska	02
Ariz.	03
Ark.	04
Calif.	05
Colo.	06
Conn.	07
Del.	08
D.C.	09
Fla.	10
Ga.	11
Hawaii	12
Idaho	13
Ill.	14
Ind.	15
Iowa	16
Kans.	17
Ky.	18
La.	19
Maine	20
Md.	21
Mass.	22
Mich.	23
Minn.	24
Miss.	25
Mo.	26
Mont.	27
Nebr.	28
Nev.	29
N.H.	30
N.J.	31
N. Mex.	32
N.Y.	33
N.C.	34
N. Dak.	35
Ohio	36
Okla.	37
Oreg.	38
Pa.	39
R.I.	40
S.C.	41
S. Dak.	42
Tenn.	43
Tex.	44
Utah	45
Vt.	46
Va.	47
Wash.	48
W.Va.	49
Wisc.	50
Wyo.	51
Guam	52
Northern Marana Islands/ Saipan	53
Virgin Islands	55
All Others	56

A JURISDICTION CODE

(1) (1)
(2) (2)
(3) (3)
(4) (4)
(5) (5)
(6)
(7)
(8)
(9)
(0) (0)

B APPLICANT NUMBER

(1) (1) (1) (1) (1)
(2) (2) (2) (2) (2)
(3) (3) (3) (3) (3)
(4) (4) (4) (4) (4)
(5) (5) (5) (5) (5)
(6) (6) (6) (6) (6)
(7) (7) (7) (7) (7)
(8) (8) (8) (8) (8)
(9) (9) (9) (9) (9)
(0) (0) (0) (0) (0)

C DATE OF BIRTH

Month		
◯ Jan.		
◯ Feb.	(1)	(1)
◯ March	(2)	(2)
◯ April	(3)	(3)
◯ May		(4)
◯ June		(5)
◯ July		(6)
◯ August		(7)
◯ Sept.		(8)
◯ Oct.		(9)
◯ Nov.	(0)	(0)
◯ Dec.		

USE A SOFT LEAD PENCIL ONLY

DO NOT FOLD, STAPLE, OR ATTACH TAPE TO THIS SHEET

NATIONAL CONFERENCE OF BAR EXAMINERS

Multistate Bar Examination

P.M. EXAM

TEST FORM: 78526

BE SURE EACH MARK IS DARK AND COMPLETELY FILLLS THE INTENDED OVAL, AS SHOWN IN THE ILLUSTRATION AT THE RIGHT. <u>COMPLETELY ERASE ANY MISTAKES OR STRAY MARKS.</u> (A) ● (C) (D)

1 (A) (B) (C) (D)	21 (A) (B) (C) (D)	41 (A) (B) (C) (D)	61 (A) (B) (C) (D)	81 (A) (B) (C) (D)
2 (A) (B) (C) (D)	22 (A) (B) (C) (D)	42 (A) (B) (C) (D)	62 (A) (B) (C) (D)	82 (A) (B) (C) (D)
3 (A) (B) (C) (D)	23 (A) (B) (C) (D)	43 (A) (B) (C) (D)	63 (A) (B) (C) (D)	83 (A) (B) (C) (D)
4 (A) (B) (C) (D)	24 (A) (B) (C) (D)	44 (A) (B) (C) (D)	64 (A) (B) (C) (D)	84 (A) (B) (C) (D)
5 (A) (B) (C) (D)	25 (A) (B) (C) (D)	45 (A) (B) (C) (D)	65 (A) (B) (C) (D)	85 (A) (B) (C) (D)
6 (A) (B) (C) (D)	26 (A) (B) (C) (D)	46 (A) (B) (C) (D)	66 (A) (B) (C) (D)	86 (A) (B) (C) (D)
7 (A) (B) (C) (D)	27 (A) (B) (C) (D)	47 (A) (B) (C) (D)	76 (A) (B) (C) (D)	87 (A) (B) (C) (D)
8 (A) (B) (C) (D)	28 (A) (B) (C) (D)	48 (A) (B) (C) (D)	68 (A) (B) (C) (D)	88 (A) (B) (C) (D)
9 (A) (B) (C) (D)	29 (A) (B) (C) (D)	49 (A) (B) (C) (D)	69 (A) (B) (C) (D)	89 (A) (B) (C) (D)
10 (A) (B) (C) (D)	30 (A) (B) (C) (D)	50 (A) (B) (C) (D)	70 (A) (B) (C) (D)	90 (A) (B) (C) (D)
11 (A) (B) (C) (D)	31 (A) (B) (C) (D)	51 (A) (B) (C) (D)	71 (A) (B) (C) (D)	91 (A) (B) (C) (D)
12 (A) (B) (C) (D)	32 (A) (B) (C) (D)	52 (A) (B) (C) (D)	72 (A) (B) (C) (D)	92 (A) (B) (C) (D)
13 (A) (B) (C) (D)	33 (A) (B) (C) (D)	53 (A) (B) (C) (D)	73 (A) (B) (C) (D)	93 (A) (B) (C) (D)
14 (A) (B) (C) (D)	34 (A) (B) (C) (D)	54 (A) (B) (C) (D)	74 (A) (B) (C) (D)	94 (A) (B) (C) (D)
15 (A) (B) (C) (D)	35 (A) (B) (C) (D)	55 (A) (B) (C) (D)	75 (A) (B) (C) (D)	95 (A) (B) (C) (D)
16 (A) (B) (C) (D)	36 (A) (B) (C) (D)	56 (A) (B) (C) (D)	78 (A) (B) (C) (D)	96 (A) (B) (C) (D)
17 (A) (B) (C) (D)	37 (A) (B) (C) (D)	57 (A) (B) (C) (D)	76 (A) (B) (C) (D)	97 (A) (B) (C) (D)
18 (A) (B) (C) (D)	38 (A) (B) (C) (D)	58 (A) (B) (C) (D)	78 (A) (B) (C) (D)	98 (A) (B) (C) (D)
19 (A) (B) (C) (D)	39 (A) (B) (C) (D)	59 (A) (B) (C) (D)	79 (A) (B) (C) (D)	99 (A) (B) (C) (D)
20 (A) (B) (C) (D)	40 (A) (B) (C) (D)	60 (A) (B) (C) (D)	70 (A) (B) (C) (D)	100 (A) (B) (C) (D)

NCBE PRACTICE EXAM

OPE-4

Editor's Note: The following is a 100-question set of actual past MBE questions, which has previously been released by the NCBE only as an on line practice exam. We did not receive NCBE clearance to reprint the exam until just before we went to press with this edition. Therefore, the brief explanations of each answer choice (written by the NCBE, and not altered by us) are interspersed with the choices, as we received the exam from the NCBE.

Question # 1 - Constitutional Law

A federal civil statute prohibited fishing in any body of water that was located within a national park and contained a particular endangered species of fish. The statute authorized federal district courts to enjoin knowing violators of the statute from the use of all national park facilities for up to two years. After a vacationer was found by a federal district court to have knowingly violated the statute, the court issued an injunction against his use of all national park facilities for two years. The vacationer appealed.

Before the appeals court heard the vacationer's case, Congress repealed the statute by a law that expressly made the repeal effective retroactive to a date one month before the vacationer's violation of the statute. The law also directly cited the vacationer's case and stated that it was intended to "repeal all the statutory prohibitions that formed the basis for decisions" such as that rendered against the vacationer.

On the basis of this law, the vacationer has asked the appeals court to vacate the injunction issued against him. Counsel for the United States has objected, contending that, as applied to the specific case pending in the appeals court, the law is unconstitutional.

How should the appeals court rule?

(A) For the United States, because Congress defied the constitutional prohibition against ex post facto laws by retroactively changing the consequences for violating the statute after the violation was proved in a trial court.

Incorrect. The constitutional prohibition against ex post facto laws applies only to retroactive changes in statutes that result in the punishment of individuals for conduct that was legal before the changes. Congress's retroactive repeal of the statute in this case had the opposite effect. The appeals court should rule for the vacationer, because the vacationer's appeal of the district court's injunction was pending when Congress repealed the statute that authorized the injunction. Congress may change federal civil statutes and may direct federal courts to apply those changes in all actions in which a final judgment has not been rendered.

(B) For the United States, because the law's citation to the vacationer's case demonstrates that Congress intended to compel the appeals court to reach a particular result and, therefore, sought to exercise judicial powers vested exclusively in the courts by Article III.

Incorrect. Congress may not direct the outcome of a particular case under existing law, but Congress may effect a change in the law with retroactive application to pending actions. The appeals court should rule for the vacationer, because the vacationer's appeal of the district court's injunction was pending when Congress repealed the statute that authorized the injunction. Congress may change federal civil statutes and may direct federal courts to apply those changes in all actions in which a final judgment has not been rendered.

(C) For the vacationer, because Congress has the power to determine the laws to be applied by the federal courts and to require retroactive application of those laws to any specifically identified case that it chooses.

Incorrect. Although Congress may change the laws to be applied in federal courts, Congress may not direct federal courts to apply the new laws to reverse final judgments in already-decided actions. While it is correct that the appeals court should rule for the vacationer, it should do so because the vacationer's appeal of the district court's injunction was pending when Congress repealed the statute that authorized the injunction. Congress may change federal civil statutes and may direct federal courts to apply those changes to all actions in which a final judgment has not been rendered.

(D) For the vacationer, because Congress is authorized to make substantive changes to federal civil statutes and to direct that those changes be applied by the courts to all actions in which a final judgment has not yet been rendered.

Correct. The appeals court should rule for the vacationer, because the vacationer's appeal of the district court's injunction was pending when Congress repealed the statute that authorized the injunction. Congress may change federal civil statutes and may direct federal courts to apply those changes in all actions in which a final judgment has not been rendered.

Question # 2 - Real Property

A man obtained a bank loan secured by a mortgage on an office building that he owned. After several years, the man conveyed the office building to a woman, who took title subject to the mortgage. The deed to the woman was not recorded. The woman took immediate possession of the building and made the mortgage payments for several years.

Subsequently, the woman stopped making payments on the mortgage loan, and the bank eventually commenced foreclosure proceedings in which the man and the woman were both named parties. At the foreclosure sale, a third party purchased the building for less than the outstanding balance on the mortgage loan. The bank then sought to collect the deficiency from the woman.

Is the bank entitled to collect the deficiency from the woman?

(A) No, because the woman did not record the deed from the man.

Incorrect. The woman took title to the office building subject to the mortgage debt, which means that the debt was to be satisfied out of the building. The building is the principal, and the man, as transferor, is the only party liable for any deficiency. This situation can be contrasted with one in which a buyer expressly assumes the mortgage debt. In that case, the buyer would be primarily liable for any deficiency and the seller, absent a release by the mortgagee, would be secondarily liable. Recording the deed would give the bank constructive notice of the transfer but would have no effect on the collection of the deficiency.

(B) No, because the woman is not personally liable on the loan.

Correct. The woman took title to the office building subject to the mortgage but did not assume the mortgage debt. The debt is to be satisfied out of the building. The building is the principal, and the man, as transferor, is the only party liable for any deficiency. This situation can be contrasted with one in which a buyer expressly assumes the mortgage debt. In that case, the buyer would be primarily liable for any deficiency and the seller, absent a release by the mortgagee, would be secondarily liable.

(C) Yes, because the woman took immediate possession of the building when she bought it from the man.

Incorrect. The woman took title to the building subject to the mortgage. Her title to the building allowed her to take possession of the building, but her possession has no effect on the payment of any deficiency judgment. Taking title to the building subject to the mortgage means that the debt is to be satisfied out of the building. The building is the principal, and the man, as transferor, is the only party liable for any deficiency. This situation can be contrasted with one in which a buyer expressly assumes the mortgage debt. In that case, the buyer would be primarily liable for any deficiency and the seller, absent a release by the mortgagee, would be secondarily liable.

(D) Yes, because the woman was a party to the foreclosure proceeding.

Incorrect. Because the woman took title to the building subject to the mortgage debt, she was a necessary party to the foreclosure proceeding. However, the fact that she took title to the building subject to the mortgage means that the debt is to be satisfied out of the building. The building is the principal, and the man, as transferor, is the only party liable for any deficiency. This situation can be contrasted with one in which a buyer expressly assumes the mortgage debt. In that case, the buyer would be primarily liable for any deficiency and the seller, absent a release by the mortgagee, would be secondarily liable.

Question # 3 - Criminal Law and Procedure

A state statute provides: "The sale of an alcoholic beverage to any person under the age of 21 is a misdemeanor."

A woman who was 20 years old, but who looked older and who had a very convincing fake driver's license indicating that she was 24, entered a convenience store, picked up a six-pack of beer, and placed the beer on the counter. The store clerk, after examining the driver's license, rang up the purchase.

Both the clerk and the store owner have been charged with violating the state statute.

If the court finds both the clerk and the store owner guilty, what standard of liability must the court have interpreted the statute to impose?

(A) Strict liability only.

Incorrect. The court must have applied strict liability to convict the clerk (who did not act knowingly, and arguably not even negligently), but must have applied vicarious liability to convict the store owner for the sale by the clerk.

(B) Vicarious liability only.

Incorrect. The court must have applied vicarious liability to convict the store owner for the sale by the clerk, but must have applied strict liability to convict the clerk (who did not act knowingly, and arguably not even negligently).

(C) Both strict and vicarious liability.

Correct. The court must have applied strict liability to convict the clerk (who did not act knowingly, and arguably not even negligently) and vicarious liability to convict the store owner for the sale by the clerk.

(D) Either strict or vicarious liability.

Incorrect. The court must have applied strict liability to convict the clerk (who did not act knowingly, and arguably not even negligently) and vicarious liability to convict the store owner for the sale by the clerk.

Question # 4 - Evidence

A businessman was the target of a grand jury investigation into the alleged bribery of American and foreign officials in connection with an international construction project. The businessman had stated at a press conference that no bribes had been offered or taken and that no laws of any kind had been broken. The grand jury issued a subpoena requiring the businessman to testify before it. The businessman moved to quash the subpoena on the ground that his testimony could tend to incriminate him. The prosecutor responded with a grant of use immunity (under which the businessman's compelled statements before the grand jury could not be used against him in any state or federal prosecution). The businessman responded that the grant of use immunity was not sufficient to protect his Fifth Amendment rights.

Should the businessman be compelled to testify?

(A) No, because the businessman remains subject to the risk of foreign prosecution.

Incorrect. While the businessman does face the possibility of foreign prosecution, the U.S. Supreme Court has squarely held that the Fifth Amendment does not protect against the risk of foreign prosecution. Because the businessman has been protected against the use of his statements in a domestic prosecution, his statements cannot tend to incriminate him in any sense protected by the Fifth Amendment. He should therefore be compelled to testify.

(B) No, because use immunity does not prevent the government from prosecuting the businessman on the bribery scheme.

Incorrect. It is true that the grant of use immunity does not protect the businessman from being prosecuted. Instead, it protects against the businessman's compelled statements--or any fruits of those statements--being used against him in any domestic prosecution. The U.S. Supreme Court has long held that the Fifth Amendment right is satisfied by a grant of use immunity. The Fifth Amendment does not require a grant of immunity from prosecution ("transactional immunity"). The businessman should therefore be compelled to testify.

(C) Yes, because the businessman has denied any criminal liability and therefore his Fifth Amendment rights are not at stake.

Incorrect. The fact that the businessman has denied liability does not mean that any statement he makes could never tend to incriminate him. Even an innocent person might say something that would tend to incriminate himself, and a tendency to incriminate is all that is required to trigger Fifth Amendment protection. However, because the grant of use immunity is coextensive with the businessman's Fifth Amendment rights, he should be compelled to testify.

(D) Yes, because the grant of use immunity is coextensive with the businessman's Fifth Amendment rights.

Correct. The U.S. Supreme Court has held that if a person is guaranteed, through a grant of use immunity, that neither his statements nor the fruits of those statements can be used against him in a domestic prosecution, then he loses his right to refuse to testify because his statements cannot tend to incriminate him. Because the businessman has been protected against the use of his statements in a domestic prosecution, his statements cannot tend to incriminate him in any sense protected by the Fifth Amendment.

Question # 5 - Constitutional Law

The United States had long recognized the ruling faction in a foreign country as that country's government, despite an ongoing civil war. Throughout the civil war, the ruling faction controlled the majority of the country's territory, and the United States afforded diplomatic immunity to the ambassador representing the ruling faction.

A newly elected President of the United States decided to recognize a rebel group as the government of the foreign country and notified the ambassador from the ruling faction that she must leave the United States within 10 days. The ambassador filed an action in federal district court for a declaration that the ruling faction was the true government of the foreign country and for an injunction against enforcement of the President's order that she leave the United States. The United States has moved to dismiss the action.

If the court dismisses the action, what will be the most likely reason?

(A) The action involves a nonjusticiable political question.
Correct. The action likely satisfies the political question doctrine and therefore should be dismissed as nonjusticiable. The President's Article II power to receive

foreign ambassadors is likely a textually demonstrable commitment by the Constitution of exclusive authority to recognize foreign governments. Moreover, Article II provides no judicially manageable standards by which a court could review the constitutionality of a President's decision on whether to recognize a foreign government. Finally, because the action involves the President's administration of foreign affairs, the prudential elements of the political question doctrine also indicate that the court should dismiss the action as nonjusticiable.

(B) The action is not ripe.

Incorrect. The action is ripe for adjudication even though the ambassador may remain in the United States for 10 days. The ambassador has suffered immediate harm because she no longer represents the foreign country in the United States, she has lost her diplomatic immunity, and she is facing expulsion within a very short period of time. Also, the constitutional issues are fit for review without waiting for the ambassador's expulsion.

The reason the action should be dismissed is that it likely is nonjusticiable under the political question doctrine. The President's Article II power to receive foreign ambassadors is likely a textually demonstrable commitment by the Constitution of exclusive authority to recognize foreign governments. Moreover, Article II provides no judicially manageable standards by which a court could review the constitutionality of a President's decision on whether to recognize a foreign government. Finally, because the action involves the President's administration of foreign affairs, the prudential elements of the political question doctrine also indicate that the court should dismiss the action as nonjusticiable.

(C) The action is within the original jurisdiction of the U.S. Supreme Court.

Incorrect. Although Article III of the Constitution provides that the Supreme Court has original jurisdiction over actions involving ambassadors, federal district courts also may exercise original jurisdiction over actions within the Supreme Court's original jurisdiction.

The reason the action should be dismissed is that it likely is nonjusticiable under the political question doctrine. The President's Article II power to receive foreign ambassadors is likely a textually demonstrable commitment by the Constitution of exclusive authority to recognize foreign governments. Moreover, Article II provides no judicially manageable standards by which a court could review the constitutionality of a President's decision on whether to recognize a foreign government. Finally, because the action involves the President's administration of foreign affairs, the prudential elements of the political question doctrine also indicate that the court should dismiss the action as nonjusticiable.

(D) The ambassador does not have standing.

Incorrect. The ambassador has standing, because she has been injured by the President's decision that her faction is no longer the government of her country, her injury is fairly traceable to this decision, and the injury is likely redressable by a court order invalidating the decision.

The reason the action should be dismissed is that it likely is nonjusticiable under the political question doctrine. The President's Article II power to receive foreign ambassadors is likely a textually demonstrable commitment by the Constitution of exclusive authority to recognize foreign governments. Moreover, Article II provides no judicially manageable standards by which a court could review the constitutionality of a President's decision on whether to recognize a foreign government. Finally, because the action involves the President's administration of foreign affairs, the prudential elements of the political question doctrine also indicate that the court should dismiss the action as nonjusticiable.

Question # 6 - Torts

An assistant to a famous writer surreptitiously observed the writer as the writer typed her private password into her personal computer in order to access her email. On several subsequent occasions in the writer's absence, the assistant read the writer's email messages and printed out selections from them.

The assistant later quit his job and earned a considerable amount of money by leaking information to the media that he had learned from reading the writer's email messages. All of the information published about the writer as a result of the assistant's conduct was true and concerned matters of public interest.

The writer's secretary had seen the assistant reading the writer's emails and printing out selections, and she has told the writer what she saw. The writer now wishes to sue the assistant for damages. At trial, the writer can show that the media leaks could have come only from someone reading her email on her personal computer.

Can the writer recover damages from the assistant?

(A) No, because the assistant was an invitee on the premises.

Incorrect. The assistant exceeded the scope of any invitation, whether through his employment as an assistant or through the invitation to work on the premises. The writer did not leave the emails exposed so that others might see them. An invitation to enter premises does not normally include permission to access personal email, especially when the email is password-protected.

(B) No, because the published information resulting from the assistant's conduct was true and concerned matters of public interest.

Incorrect. Truth is a common law defense to defamation but not to invasion of privacy. In some circumstances, the First Amendment or a common law defense based on the public interest in the material disclosed can provide a defense to an action for disclosure of private matters. However, even if these defenses were applicable to the disclosure aspect of this case, they would not provide a defense to the privacy action based on intrusion. News-gathering does not provide general immunity from tort law.

(C) Yes, because the assistant invaded the writer's privacy.

Correct. By accessing the writer's email, the assistant was intruding upon her privacy. "Intrusion upon seclusion" is one category of the tort of invasion of privacy that is recognized in many states. The assistant did not have permission to access the emails, and the writer did not leave the emails exposed so that others might see them.

(D) Yes, because the published information resulting from the assistant's conduct constituted publication of private facts concerning the writer.

Incorrect. The appropriate privacy action here would be for "intrusion" rather than for "public disclosure of embarrassing private facts." Publication is irrelevant to whether a cause of action for intrusion has been established. By accessing the writer's email, the assistant was intruding upon her privacy. "Intrusion upon seclusion" is one category of the tort of invasion of privacy that is recognized in many states. The assistant did not have permission to access the emails, and the writer did not leave the emails exposed so that others might see them.

Question # 7 - Evidence

A defendant is on trial for knowing possession of a stolen television. The defendant claims that the television was a gift from a friend, who has disappeared. The defendant seeks to testify that he was present when the friend told her neighbor that the television had been given to the friend by her mother.

Is the defendant's testimony about the friend's statement to the neighbor admissible?

(A) No, because the friend's statement is hearsay not within any exception.

Incorrect. The statement would be hearsay if it were offered to prove that the friend actually owned the television. But the defendant is offering the friend's statement as evidence that the defendant thought that the friend owned the television (i.e., that it had not been stolen). Because the defendant is charged with knowing possession of a stolen television, his state of mind is relevant. If the defendant had heard the friend say that the television was hers, that evidence would be relevant to the defendant's state of mind regardless of the truth of the statement. Therefore, the friend's out-of-court statement is not hearsay and is admissible.

(B) No, because the defendant has not presented evidence of circumstances that clearly corroborate the statement.

Incorrect. There is no requirement that a statement offered to prove its effect on the person who heard it must be corroborated. In this case, the defendant is offering the friend's statement as evidence that the defendant thought that the friend owned the television (i.e., that it had not been stolen). Because the defendant is charged with knowing possession of a stolen television, his state of mind is relevant. If the defendant had heard the friend say that the television was hers, that evidence would be relevant to the defendant's state of mind regardless of whether it was corroborated. Because the statement is not being offered for its truth, it is not hearsay and is admissible.

(C) Yes, as nonhearsay evidence of the defendant's belief that the friend owned the television.

Correct. The defendant is offering the friend's statement as evidence that the defendant thought that the friend owned the television (i.e., that it had not been stolen). Because the defendant is charged with knowing possession of a stolen television, his state of mind is relevant. If the defendant had heard the friend say that the television was hers, that evidence would be relevant to the defendant's state of mind regardless of the truth of the statement. Therefore, the friend's out-of-court statement is not hearsay.

(D) Yes, under the hearsay exception for statements affecting an interest in property.

Incorrect. The statement is offered for a nonhearsay purpose, so there is no need to find an applicable hearsay exception. The defendant is offering the friend's statement as evidence that the defendant thought that the friend owned the television (i.e., that it had not been stolen). Because the defendant is charged with knowing possession of a stolen television, his state of mind is relevant. If the defendant had heard the friend say that the television was hers, that evidence would be relevant to the defendant's state of mind regardless of the truth of the statement. Therefore, the friend's out-of-court statement is not hearsay.

Moreover, if an exception were required, the exception for statements affecting an interest in property would not be applicable, because that exception requires that the statement be contained in a document. Here the statement was oral.

Question # 8 - Contracts

A restaurant supplier sent a letter to a regular customer offering to sell the customer an industrial freezer for $10,000. Two days later, the customer responded with a letter that stated: "I accept your offer on the condition that you provide me with a warranty that the freezer is merchantable." In response to the customer's letter, the supplier called the customer and stated that the offer was no longer open. The supplier promptly sold the freezer to another buyer for $11,000.

If the customer sues the supplier for breach of contract, is the customer likely to prevail?

(A) No, because the customer's letter added a term, making it a counteroffer.

Incorrect. It is true that a purported acceptance that is conditioned on an offeror's assent to a term additional to or different from the terms contained in an offer is a counteroffer. In this case, however, the customer's letter constituted an acceptance rather than a counteroffer. Under UCC § 2-314, a warranty of merchantability is implied in every contract for the sale of a good by a seller who is a merchant with respect to goods of that kind. Therefore, the condition contained in the customer's letter merely stated a term that was already implied in the sale. A contract arose when the customer mailed its letter accepting the offer. Accordingly, the supplier's attempted revocation of its offer was ineffective, and its sale of the freezer to the third party breached its contract with the customer.

(B) No, because the subsequent sale to a bona fide purchaser for value cut off the claims of the customer.

Incorrect. Under some circumstances, the sale of goods to a bona fide purchaser may cut off the claims of other parties. In this case, however, the dispositive issue is whether the customer's letter in response to the supplier's offer constituted an acceptance or a counteroffer. Under UCC § 2-314, a warranty of merchantability is implied in every contract for the sale of a good by a seller who is a merchant with respect to goods of that kind. Therefore, the condition contained in the customer's letter merely stated a term that was already implied in the sale. A contract arose when the customer mailed its letter accepting the offer. Accordingly, the supplier's attempted revocation of its offer was ineffective, and its sale of the freezer to the third party breached its contract with the customer.

(C) Yes, because the customer's letter was an acceptance of the supplier's offer, since the warranty of merchantability was already implied in the sale.

Correct. It is true that a purported acceptance that is conditioned on an offeror's assent to a term additional to or different from the terms contained in an offer is a counteroffer. In this case, however, the customer's letter constituted an acceptance rather than a counteroffer. Under UCC § 2-314, a warranty of merchantability is implied in every contract for the sale of a good by a seller who is a merchant with respect to goods of that kind. Therefore, the condition contained in the customer's letter merely stated a term that was already implied in the sale. A contract arose when the customer mailed its letter accepting the offer. Accordingly, the supplier's attempted revocation of its offer was ineffective, and its sale of the freezer to the third party breached its contract with the customer.

(D) Yes, because the supplier's letter was a firm offer that could not be revoked for a reasonable time.

Incorrect. The supplier's letter did not create a firm offer because it failed to give assurance that the offer would be held open, a principal requirement of a firm offer under UCC § 2-205. The dispositive issue here is whether the customer's response to the supplier's offer constituted an acceptance or a counteroffer. Under UCC § 2-314, a warranty of merchantability is implied in every contract for the sale of a good by a seller who is a merchant with respect to goods of that kind. Therefore, the condition contained in the customer's letter merely stated a term that was already implied in the sale. A contract arose when the customer mailed its letter accepting the offer. Accordingly, the supplier's attempted revocation of its offer was ineffective, and its sale of the freezer to the third party breached its contract with the customer.

Question # 9 - Real Property

A credit card company obtained and properly filed a judgment against a man after he failed to pay a $10,000 debt. A statute in the jurisdiction provides as follows: "Any judgment properly filed shall, for 10 years from filing, be a lien on the real property then owned or subsequently acquired by any person against whom the judgment is rendered."

Two years later, the man purchased land for $200,000. He made a down payment of $20,000 and borrowed the remaining $180,000 from a bank. The bank loan was secured by a mortgage on the land. Immediately after the closing, the deed to the man was recorded first, and the bank's mortgage was recorded second.

Five months later, the man defaulted on the mortgage loan and the bank initiated judicial foreclosure proceedings. After receiving notice of the proceedings, the credit card company filed a motion to have its judgment lien declared to be the first lien on the land.

Is the credit card company's motion likely to be granted?

(A) No, because the bank's mortgage secured a loan used to purchase the land.

Correct. The bank's mortgage is a purchase-money mortgage, meaning that the funds the bank advanced were used to purchase the land. A purchase-money mortgage executed at the same time as the purchase of the real property encumbered takes precedence over any other claim or lien, including a previously filed judgment lien. Therefore, the bank's purchase-money mortgage takes precedence over the credit card company's judgment lien.

(B) No, because the man's down payment exceeded the amount of his debt to the credit card company.

Incorrect. The relative amounts of the down payment and the credit card debt are irrelevant. The bank's mortgage is a purchase-money mortgage, meaning that the funds the bank advanced were used to purchase the land. A purchase-money mortgage executed at the same time as the purchase of the real property encumbered takes precedence over any other claim or lien, including a previously filed judgment lien.

(C) Yes, because the bank had constructive notice of the judgment lien.

Incorrect. It is true that the judgment lien was properly filed and thus provided the bank with constructive notice of the lien. The bank's mortgage, however, is a purchase-money mortgage, meaning that the funds the bank advanced were used to purchase the land. A purchase-money mortgage executed at the same time as the purchase of the real property encumbered takes precedence over any other claim, including a previously filed judgment lien.

(D) Yes, because the bank is a third-party lender and not the seller of the land.

Incorrect. The bank's mortgage is a purchase-money mortgage, meaning that the funds the bank advanced were used to purchase the land. A purchase-money mortgage may be granted by a seller, by a third party, or both. A purchase-money mortgage executed at the same time as the purchase of the real property encumbered takes precedence over any other claim, including a previously filed judgment lien. Therefore, the bank's purchase-money mortgage takes precedence over the credit card company's judgment lien.

Question # 10 - Criminal Law and Procedure

A woman charged with murder has entered a plea of not guilty by reason of insanity. At her trial, in which the questions of guilt and sanity are being tried together, the evidence shows that the woman stalked the victim for several hours before following him to an isolated hiking trail where she shot and killed him. Expert witnesses for the defense have testified that the woman knew that killing was illegal and wrong, but that she suffered from a serious mental illness that left her in the grip of a powerful and irresistible compulsion to kill the victim.

If the jury believes the testimony of the defense experts, under what circumstances could the jury properly acquit the woman of murder?

(A) Only if the jurisdiction follows the M'Naghten test for insanity.

Incorrect. The jury could not find the woman to be legally insane under the M'Naghten test, which requires either that she did not know the nature and quality of the act she was committing or that she did not know the difference between right and wrong.

(B) Only if the jurisdiction follows the ALI Model Penal Code test for insanity.

Correct. The jury could find the woman to be legally insane under the ALI Model Penal Code test, because she could not conform her conduct to the requirements of the law.

(C) If the jurisdiction follows either the M'Naghten or the ALI Model Penal Code test for insanity.

Incorrect. The jury could not find the woman to be legally insane under the M'Naghten test, which requires either that she did not know the nature and quality of the act she was committing or that she did not know the difference between right and wrong. The jury could find the woman to be legally insane under the ALI Model Penal Code test, because she could not conform her conduct to the requirements of the law.

(D) Even if the jurisdiction has abolished the insanity defense.

Incorrect. The woman committed all the elements of murder and can be excused from responsibility only if she meets a recognized defense of insanity.

Question # 11 - Evidence

A plaintiff has brought a civil suit against a defendant for injuries arising out of a fistfight between them. The day after the fight, a police officer talked to the plaintiff, the defendant, and an eyewitness, and made an official police report. At trial, the plaintiff seeks to introduce from the properly authenticated police report a statement attributed to the eyewitness, who is unavailable to testify at trial, that "[the defendant] started the fight."

Should the court admit the statement from the report?

(A) No, unless the entire report is introduced.

Incorrect. The statement is inadmissible hearsay even if the entire report is introduced; the eyewitness's statement is hearsay within the hearsay report. The report itself could be admissible as a business or public record, but the hearsay within it is admissible only if it satisfies a separate hearsay exception or if it can be shown that the eyewitness had a business or public duty to report the information accurately. The eyewitness had no such duty, and no other hearsay exception applies.

(B) No, because it is hearsay not within any exception.

Correct. The eyewitness's statement is hearsay within the hearsay report. The report itself could be admissible as a business or public record, but the hearsay within it is admissible only if it satisfies a separate hearsay exception or if it can be shown that the eyewitness had a business or public duty to report the information accurately. The eyewitness had no such duty. The eyewitness's statement is also not a present sense impression, because it was made the day after the fight, and no other hearsay exception applies.

(C) Yes, because it was based on the eyewitness's first-hand knowledge.

Incorrect. The fact that the eyewitness purports to have personal knowledge does not solve the hearsay problem, which arises because the eyewitness might not have told the truth about the event he purportedly saw and is not subject to cross-examination about it. The eyewitness's statement is hearsay within the hearsay report. The report itself could be admissible as a business or public record, but the hearsay within it is admissible only if it satisfies a separate hearsay exception or if it can be shown that the eyewitness had a business or public duty to report the information accurately. The eyewitness had no such duty, and no other hearsay exception applies.

(D) Yes, because it is an excerpt from a public record offered in a civil case.

Incorrect. The eyewitness's statement is hearsay within the hearsay report. The report itself could be admissible as a business or public record, but the hearsay within it is admissible only if it satisfies a separate hearsay exception or if it can be shown that the eyewitness had a business or public duty to report the information accurately. The eyewitness had no such duty, and no other hearsay exception applies.

Question # 12 - Torts

A man sued his neighbor for defamation based on the following facts:

The neighbor told a friend that the man had set fire to a house in the neighborhood. The friend, who knew the man well, did not believe the neighbor's allegation, which was in fact false. The friend told the man about the neighbor's allegation. The man was very upset by the allegation, but neither the man nor the neighbor nor the friend communicated the allegation to anyone else.

Should the man prevail in his lawsuit?

(A) No, because the friend did not believe what the neighbor had said.

Incorrect. A successful defamation action does not depend on whether a third party actually believed the defamatory statement. It is enough that the defamatory statement was communicated to a third party.

(B) No, because the man cannot prove that he suffered pecuniary loss.

Incorrect. The statement was spoken rather than written, so the rules of slander apply. Often an action in slander requires that pecuniary loss be shown, but there is no such requirement where the statement accuses the plaintiff of engaging in serious criminal conduct. Arson is a crime of moral turpitude, so the neighbor's statement falls within the exception.

(C) Yes, because the man was very upset at hearing what the neighbor had said.

Incorrect. Proof of emotional distress is not required to establish a cause of action for defamation, whether the action is in libel or slander. The man should prevail, but it is because the defamatory statement was communicated to a third party. Here, the statement was spoken rather than written, so the rules of slander apply. Often an action in slander requires that pecuniary loss be shown, but there is no such requirement where the statement accuses the plaintiff of engaging in serious criminal conduct. Arson is a crime of moral turpitude, so the neighbor's statement falls within the exception, and special harm need not be shown.

(D) Yes, because the neighbor communicated to the friend the false accusation that the man had committed a serious crime.

Correct. The core of a defamation action is the communication of a defamatory statement about the plaintiff to a third party. Here, the statement was spoken rather than written, so the rules of slander apply. Often an action in slander requires that pecuniary loss be shown, but there is no such requirement where the statement accuses the plaintiff of engaging in serious criminal conduct. Arson is a crime of moral turpitude, so the neighbor's statement falls within the exception, and special harm need not be shown.

Question # 13 - Contracts

A seller sent an email to a potential buyer, offering to sell his house to her for $150,000. The buyer immediately responded via email, asking whether the offer included the house's front porch swing. The seller emailed back: "No, it doesn't." The buyer then ordered a front porch swing and emailed back to the seller: "I accept your offer." The seller refused to sell the house to the buyer, claiming that the offer was no longer open.

Is there a contract for the sale of the house?

(A) No, because the buyer's initial email was a counteroffer.

Incorrect. A reply to an offer that merely requests information regarding the offer constitutes an inquiry rather than a counteroffer. The buyer's response asking whether the seller intended to include the front porch swing in his offer was an inquiry rather than a counteroffer. The buyer's subsequent email stating "I accept your offer" was an acceptance that created a contract between the parties. Therefore, the seller's attempted revocation of his offer was ineffective.

(B) No, because the offer lapsed before the buyer accepted.

Incorrect. An offeree's power of acceptance may terminate due to a lapse of time when the offeree fails to accept the offer within the time stated in the offer or within a reasonable time. In this case, the offer did not include an express time limitation. Therefore, the buyer could accept within a reasonable period of time. The email exchanges between the buyer and the seller demonstrate that the buyer accepted the seller's offer within a reasonable time period. The dispositive issue here is whether the buyer's reply to the seller's offer constituted an acceptance or a counteroffer.

A reply to an offer that merely requests information regarding the offer constitutes an inquiry rather than a counteroffer. The buyer's response asking whether the seller intended to include the front porch swing in his offer was an inquiry rather than a counteroffer. The buyer's subsequent email stating "I accept your offer" was an acceptance that created a contract between the parties. Therefore, the seller's attempted revocation of his offer was ineffective.

(C) Yes, because the buyer relied on the offer by ordering the swing.

Incorrect. An offeree's reliance on an offer can create a binding option contract that precludes an offeror from revoking its offer. In this case, however, there is no indication that the buyer's purchase of the swing was the type of act performed in substantial reliance on the offer that the seller reasonably could have expected at the time he communicated his offer. The dispositive issue here is whether the buyer's reply to the seller's offer constituted an acceptance or a counteroffer.

A reply to an offer that merely requests information regarding the offer constitutes an inquiry rather than a counteroffer. The buyer's response asking whether the seller intended to include the front porch swing in his offer was an inquiry rather than a counteroffer. The buyer's subsequent email stating "I accept your offer" was an acceptance that created a contract between the parties. Therefore, the seller's attempted revocation of his offer was ineffective.

(D) Yes, because the buyer's initial email merely asked for information.

Correct. A reply to an offer that merely requests information regarding the offer constitutes an inquiry rather than a counteroffer. The buyer's response asking whether the seller intended to include the front porch swing in his offer was an inquiry rather than a counteroffer. The buyer's subsequent email stating "I accept your offer" was an acceptance that created a contract between the parties. Therefore, the seller's attempted revocation of his offer was ineffective.

Question # 14 - Criminal Law and Procedure

A valid warrant was issued for a woman's arrest. The police learned that a person with the woman's name and physical description lived at a particular address. When police officers went to that address, the house appeared to be unoccupied: the windows and doors were boarded up with plywood, and the lawn had not been mowed for a long time. A neighbor confirmed that the house belonged to the woman but said that the woman had not been there for several months.

The officers knocked repeatedly on the front door and shouted, "Police! Open up!" Receiving no response, they tore the plywood off the door, smashed through the door with a sledgehammer, and entered the house. They found no one inside, but they did find an illegal sawed-off shotgun. Upon her return to the house a few weeks later, the woman was charged with unlawful possession of the shotgun.

The woman has moved to suppress the use of the shotgun as evidence at her trial. Should the court grant the motion?

(A) No, because the officers acted in good faith under the authority of a valid warrant.

Incorrect. Under the Fourth Amendment, the arrest warrant would have authorized forcible entry only if the officers had reason to believe that the woman was at home at the time of the entry. Here, the officers knew that the woman was not at home.

(B) No, because the officers did not violate any legitimate expectation of privacy in the house since the woman had abandoned it.

Incorrect. The facts here are legally insufficient to suggest that the woman had abandoned any reasonable expectation of privacy in the house.

(C) Yes, because the officers entered the house by means of excessive force.

Incorrect. Under the Fourth Amendment, the arrest warrant would have authorized forcible entry if the officers had reason to believe that the woman was at home at the time of the entry. Here, however, the officers knew that the woman was not at home.

(D) Yes, because the officers had no reason to believe that the woman was in the house.

Correct. Under the Fourth Amendment, the arrest warrant would have authorized forcible entry only if the officers had reason to believe that the woman was at home at the time of the entry. Here, the officers knew that the woman was not at home.

Question # 15 - Constitutional Law

An employer owed an employee $200 in unpaid wages. A law of the state in which the employer and the employee reside and in which the employee works provides that the courts of that state must decide claims for unpaid wages within 10 days of filing.

After the employee filed a claim in state court pursuant to this law, the employer filed a voluntary bankruptcy petition in federal bankruptcy court. In the bankruptcy proceeding, the employer sought to stay further proceedings in the unpaid wages claim on the basis of a federal statute which provides that a person who files a federal bankruptcy petition receives an automatic stay of all proceedings against him or her in all federal and state courts. No other federal laws apply.

In addition to the supremacy clause of Article VI, what is the most obvious constitutional basis for the imposition of a stay of the unpaid wages claim in the state court?

(A) Congress's power to provide for the general welfare.

Incorrect. Congress's power to provide for the general welfare authorizes only taxing and spending laws. Because the statute requiring the imposition of a stay of the unpaid wages claim concerns neither taxing nor spending, it is not authorized by the general welfare clause.

Congress's power to provide uniform rules of bankruptcy offers the most obvious constitutional basis for a federal statute requiring a stay of court proceedings against a person who has filed a federal bankruptcy petition.

(B) Congress's power to provide uniform rules of bankruptcy.

Correct. Congress's power to provide uniform rules of bankruptcy offers the most obvious constitutional basis for a federal statute requiring a stay of court proceedings against a person who has filed a federal bankruptcy petition.

(C) Congress's power to regulate the jurisdiction and procedures of the courts.

Incorrect. The constitutional provisions that give Congress the power to regulate the jurisdiction and procedures of federal courts do not authorize Congress to regulate state courts.

Congress's power to provide uniform rules of bankruptcy offers the most obvious constitutional basis for a federal statute requiring a stay of court proceedings against a person who has filed a federal bankruptcy petition.

(D) Congress's power to regulate commerce among the states.

Incorrect. A federal statute providing for a stay of court proceedings against a person who has filed a federal bankruptcy petition is not authorized by the commerce clause, because it is not a regulation of the channels or instrumentalities of interstate commerce, nor does it regulate an economic or commercial activity.

Congress's power to provide uniform rules of bankruptcy offers the most obvious constitutional basis for a federal statute requiring a stay of court proceedings against a person who has filed a federal bankruptcy petition.

Question # 16 - Real Property

A husband and wife acquired land as common law joint tenants with right of survivorship. One year later, without his wife's knowledge, the husband executed a will devising the land to his best friend. The husband subsequently died.

Is the wife now the sole owner of the land?

(A) No, because a joint tenant has the unilateral right to end a joint tenancy without the consent of the other joint tenant.

Incorrect. As a general rule, a joint tenant's interest is freely alienable during his or her lifetime without the consent of the other joint tenant. However, a joint tenant's interest cannot be devised in a will. In this case, on the death of the husband, the wife's interest in the joint tenancy immediately swelled and she became the sole owner of the land as the surviving joint tenant.

(B) No, because the wife's interest in the husband's undivided 50% ownership in the land adeemed.

Incorrect. The doctrine of ademption applies only when an individual dies testate and attempts to devise land that the testator no longer owns. Although as a general rule a joint tenant's interest is freely alienable during his or her lifetime without the consent of the other joint tenant, that interest cannot be devised in a will. In this case, on the death of the husband, the wife's interest in the joint tenancy immediately swelled and she became the sole owner of the land as the surviving joint tenant.

(C) Yes, because of the doctrine of after-acquired title.

Incorrect. The doctrine of after-acquired title applies when an individual attempts to convey title (usually by warranty deed) at a time when the individual does not have title to the land but later acquires title to the land. Although as a general rule a joint tenant's interest is freely alienable during his or her lifetime without the consent of the other joint tenant, that interest cannot be devised in a will. In this case, on the death of the husband, the wife's interest in the joint tenancy immediately swelled and she became the sole owner of the land as the surviving joint tenant.

(D) Yes, because the devise to the friend did not sever the joint tenancy.

Correct. Although as a general rule a joint tenant's interest is freely alienable during his or her lifetime without the consent of the other joint tenant, that interest cannot be devised in a will. In this case, on the death of the husband, the wife's interest in the joint tenancy immediately swelled and she became the sole owner of the land as the surviving joint tenant.

Question # 17 - Evidence

A plaintiff has sued a defendant, alleging that she was run over by a speeding car driven by the defendant. The plaintiff was unconscious after her injury and, accompanied by her husband, was brought to the hospital in an ambulance.

At trial, the plaintiff calls an emergency room physician to testify that when the physician asked the plaintiff's husband if he knew what had happened, the husband, who was upset, replied, "I saw my wife get run over two hours ago by a driver who went right through the intersection without looking."

Is the physician's testimony about the husband's statement admissible?

(A) No, because it relates an opinion.

Incorrect. An out-of-court statement is not inadmissible simply because it contains an opinion. Statements of opinion by out-of-court declarants may be admitted if they qualify under a hearsay exception and otherwise satisfy the rules governing opinion testimony of in-court witnesses. This statement, however, is hearsay not within any exception and is inadmissible.

(B) No, because it is hearsay not within any exception.

Correct. The statement is offered to prove liability for the accident. As such, it is not a statement made for purposes of diagnosis or treatment. Moreover, the statement was made two hours after the accident, so it is very unlikely that the husband (who was not himself an accident victim) was under a continuous state of excitement between the time of the accident and the time he made the statement. Therefore, the statement is not admissible as an excited utterance, and no other hearsay exception applies.

(C) Yes, as a statement made for purposes of diagnosis or treatment.

Incorrect. The husband's statement is making an accusation of fault for the accident. Such a statement is not pertinent to the diagnosis or treatment of the plaintiff, as is required by the hearsay exception. No other hearsay exception applies, so the statement is inadmissible.

(D) Yes, as an excited utterance.

Incorrect. In order for this statement to be admissible as an excited utterance, the declarant must have been under a continuous state of excitement between the time of the event and the time of the statement. Here, the husband made the statement two hours after the accident, so it is very unlikely that the husband (who was not himself an accident victim) was under a continuous state of excitement between the time of the accident and the time he made the statement. Therefore, the statement is not admissible as an excited utterance, and no other hearsay exception applies, so the statement is inadmissible.

Question # 18 - Contracts

In a telephone conversation, a jewelry maker offered to buy 100 ounces of gold from a precious metals company if delivery could be made within 10 days. The jewelry maker did not specify a price, but the market price for 100 ounces of gold at the time of the conversation was approximately $65,000. Without otherwise responding, the company delivered the gold six days later.

In the meantime, the project for which the jewelry maker planned to use the gold was canceled. The jewelry maker therefore refused to accept delivery of the gold or to pay the $65,000 demanded by the company.

Is there an enforceable contract between the jewelry maker and the company?

(A) No, because the parties did not agree on a price term.

Incorrect. Under UCC § 2-305, a contract may be enforceable in the absence of a price term so long as the parties otherwise intended to enter into a contract. In this case, the dispositive issue is whether the parties' oral agreement is enforceable. Under UCC § 2-201(1), a contract for the sale of goods for a price of $500 or more is not enforceable unless there is a writing indicating the contract that is signed by the party against whom enforcement is sought. In this case, the absence of such a writing signed by the jewelry maker renders the parties' oral agreement unenforceable. An exception to the writing requirement arises when a seller delivers goods that are accepted by the buyer, but in this case, the jewelry maker did not accept the gold.

(B) No, because the parties did not put their agreement in writing.

Correct. The parties failed to comply with the writing requirement of UCC § 2-201(1). Under that section, a contract for the sale of goods for a price of $500 or more is not enforceable unless there is a writing indicating a contract of sale that is signed by the party against whom enforcement is sought. In this case, the absence of such a writing signed by the jewelry maker renders the parties' oral agreement unenforceable. An exception to the writing requirement arises when a seller delivers goods that are accepted by the buyer, but in this case, the jewelry maker did not accept the gold.

(C) Yes, because the absence of a price term does not defeat the formation of a valid contract for the sale of goods where the parties otherwise intended to form a contract.

Incorrect. Under UCC § 2-305, a contract may be enforceable in the absence of a price term so long as the parties otherwise intended to enter into a contract. In this case, however, the dispositive issue is whether the parties' oral agreement is enforceable. Under UCC § 2-201(1), a contract for the sale of goods for a price of $500 or more is not enforceable unless there is a writing indicating the contract that is signed by the party against whom enforcement is sought. The absence of such a writing signed by the jewelry maker renders the parties' oral agreement unenforceable. An exception to the writing requirement arises when a seller delivers goods that are accepted by the buyer. In this case, however, the jewelry maker did not accept the gold.

(D) Yes, because the company relied on an implied promise to pay when it delivered the gold.

Incorrect. The dispositive issue in this case is whether the parties' oral agreement is enforceable. Under UCC § 2-201(1), a contract for the sale of goods for a price of $500 or more is not enforceable unless there is a writing indicating the contract that is signed by the party against whom enforcement is sought. The absence of such a writing signed by the jewelry maker renders the parties' oral agreement unenforceable. An exception to the writing requirement arises when a seller delivers goods that are accepted by the buyer. In this case, however, the jewelry maker did not accept the gold.

Question # 19 - Real Property

A landlord leased a building to a tenant for a 10-year term. Two years after the term began, the tenant subleased the building to a sublessee for a 5-year term. Under the terms of the sublease, the sublessee agreed to make monthly rent payments to the tenant.

Although the sublessee made timely rent payments to the tenant, the tenant did not forward four of those payments to the landlord. The tenant has left the jurisdiction and cannot be found. The landlord has sued the sublessee for the unpaid rent.

There is no applicable statute.

If the court rules that the sublessee is not liable to the landlord for the unpaid rent, what will be the most likely reason?

(A) A sublessee is responsible to the landlord only as a surety for unpaid rent owed by the tenant.

Incorrect. In a sublease, the tenant transfers a right of possession for a time shorter than the balance of the leasehold. Therefore, the sublessee and the tenant are in privity of estate with each other, but only the tenant remains in privity of estate with the landlord. There also is no privity of contract between the sublessee and the landlord, because the sublessee made no promise, either to the landlord or to the tenant, to pay rent to the landlord. Lacking privity, the sublessee is not liable to the landlord for the rent and also is not a surety for the tenant.

(B) The sublease constitutes a novation of the original lease.

Incorrect. A novation occurs when a tenant seeks to avoid future liability for rent after an assignment and the landlord agrees to release the tenant from such liability. An assignment occurs when the tenant transfers the entire period of time remaining on the lease agreement. Here, the tenant only transferred a portion of the remaining time on the lease agreement, and the tenant did not seek a release or novation from the landlord.

(C) The sublessee is not in privity of estate or contract with the landlord.

Correct. In a sublease, the tenant transfers a right of possession for a time shorter than the balance of the leasehold. Therefore, the sublessee and the tenant are in privity of estate with each other, but only the tenant remains in privity of estate with the landlord. There also is no privity of contract between the sublessee and the landlord, because the sublessee made no promise, either to the landlord or to the tenant, to pay rent to the landlord. Lacking privity, the sublessee is not liable to the landlord for the rent. Although privity may not be required under an equitable servitude theory, a finding for the sublessee would mean that the court did not use such a theory.

(D) The sublessee's rent payments to the tenant fully discharged the sublessee's obligation to pay rent to the landlord.

Incorrect. The sublessee had no obligation to pay rent to the landlord. In a sublease, the tenant transfers a right of possession for a time shorter than the balance of the leasehold. Therefore, the sublessee and the tenant are in privity of estate with each other, but only the tenant remains in privity of estate with the landlord. There also is no privity of contract between the sublessee and the landlord, because the sublessee made no promise, either to the landlord or to the tenant, to pay rent to the landlord. Lacking privity, a sublessee is not liable to the landlord for the rent. Although privity may not be required under an equitable servitude theory, a finding for the sublessee would mean that the court did not use such a theory.

Question # 20 - Torts

A manufacturing plant emitted a faint noise even though the owner had installed state-of-the-art sound dampeners. The plant operated only on weekdays and only during daylight hours. A homeowner who lived near the plant worked a night shift and could not sleep when he arrived home because of the noise from the plant. The other residents in the area did not notice the noise.

Does the homeowner have a viable nuisance claim against the owner of the plant?

(A) No, because the homeowner is unusually sensitive to noise during the day.

Correct. A landowner is liable for nuisance only when his invasion of another's use and enjoyment is both substantial and unreasonable. Under the norms of the area, the plant owner is not imposing an unreasonable degree of noise upon his neighbors. An unusually noise-sensitive neighbor will not be permitted to block the plant owner's use of his own land.

(B) No, because the plant operates only during the day.

Incorrect. If the noise were too loud given the normal expectations of residents in the area, it could still constitute a nuisance even if limited to daylight hours. The homeowner does not have a valid nuisance claim, but it is because he is unusually sensitive to noise during the day.

(C) Yes, because the noise is heard beyond the boundaries of the plant.

Incorrect. Recovery in nuisance requires evidence of substantial and unreasonable interference with the plaintiff's use and enjoyment of his own land. Merely showing that a noise can be heard beyond the boundaries of the defendant's land is not enough to establish a nuisance, especially when the noise can be heard only by an unusually noise-sensitive person.

(D) Yes, because the operation of the plant interferes with the homeowner's quiet use and enjoyment of his property.

Incorrect. It is not enough to demonstrate interference with quiet use and enjoyment. The interference also must be shown to be both substantial and unreasonable. The noise emitted by the plant interferes only with one unusually noise-sensitive neighbor, so it is unlikely to be found to be unreasonable.

Question # 21 - Criminal Law and Procedure

A woman was subpoenaed to appear before a grand jury. When she arrived, she was taken into the grand jury room to be questioned. She answered preliminary questions about her name and address. She was then asked where she had been at a certain time on a specified night when a murder had occurred. Before answering the question, the woman said that she wanted to consult her attorney, who was waiting outside the grand jury room, and she was allowed to do so. When she returned to the grand jury room, she stated that she refused to answer the question because the answer might incriminate her.

The prosecutor believes that the woman's nephew committed the murder. The nephew has said that he was with the woman at the time of the murder, and the prosecutor believes that this alibi is false. The prosecutor does not believe that the woman is guilty of the murder, either as a principal or as an accomplice, although he does believe that the woman may be guilty of other crimes. The prosecutor wants to compel the woman to answer the question by whatever means will result in the least harm to the prosecution's case.

Which of the following steps should the prosecutor take to get the woman to answer the question?

(A) Request the grand jury to order the woman to answer the question.

Incorrect. The woman cannot be compelled to provide potentially incriminating testimony unless she is granted use and derivative-use immunity.

(B) Ask the woman's attorney to explain to the woman that the rules of evidence do not apply in grand jury proceedings, and to advise her that she cannot refuse to testify.

Incorrect. While the rules of evidence do not apply before grand juries, a witness cannot be compelled to provide potentially incriminating testimony unless the witness is granted use and derivative-use immunity.

(C) Prepare the documents necessary to grant the woman immunity from any future use against her of her grand jury testimony or any evidence derived from it.

Correct. A witness cannot be compelled to provide potentially incriminating testimony unless the witness is granted use and derivative-use immunity.

(D) Prepare the documents necessary to grant the woman immunity from any future prosecution for any crime she might disclose in the course of her testimony.

Incorrect. A witness cannot be compelled to provide potentially incriminating testimony unless the witness is granted use and derivative-use immunity, but the witness need not be granted transactional immunity.

Question # 22 - Constitutional Law

Congress enacted a statute directing U.S. ambassadors to send formal letters to the governments of their host countries, protesting any violations by those governments of international treaties on weapons sales. The President prefers to handle violations by certain countries in a less formal manner and has directed ambassadors not to comply with the statute.

Is the President's action constitutional?

(A) No, because Congress has the power to implement treaties, and therefore the statute is binding on the President.

Incorrect. Although Congress has the power, under the necessary and proper clause, to enact legislation in support of treaties, the President's action is constitutional, because the U.S. Supreme Court has ruled that the President alone has the authority to represent the United States in foreign affairs. Because the statute intrudes on that authority, it is unconstitutional and has no effect.

(B) No, because Congress has the power to regulate commerce with foreign nations, and therefore the statute is binding on the President.

Incorrect. Congress has the power to regulate commerce with foreign nations, but this statute does not concern commercial relationships between the United States and foreign nations. The President's action is constitutional, because the U.S. Supreme Court has ruled that the President alone has the authority to represent the United States in foreign affairs. Because the statute intrudes on that authority, it is unconstitutional and has no effect.

(C) Yes, because Congress has no jurisdiction over matters outside the U.S. borders.

Incorrect. Article I of the Constitution gives Congress several powers concerning matters outside the U.S. borders, including the power to declare war and the power to regulate commerce with foreign nations. However, because the U.S. Supreme Court has ruled that the President alone has the authority to represent the United States in foreign affairs, the President's action is constitutional. Because the statute intrudes on the President's authority, it is unconstitutional and has no effect.

(D) Yes, because the President and his subordinates are the exclusive official representatives of the United States in foreign affairs.

Correct. The President's action is constitutional, because the U.S. Supreme Court has ruled that the President alone has the authority to represent the United States in foreign affairs. Because the statute intrudes on the President's authority, it is unconstitutional and has no effect.

Question # 23 - Real Property

A woman who owned a house executed a deed purporting to convey the house to her son and his wife. The language of the deed was sufficient to create a common law joint tenancy with right of survivorship, which is unmodified by statute in the jurisdiction. The woman mailed the deed to the son with a letter saying: "Because I intend you and your wife to have my house after my death, I am enclosing a deed to the house. However, I intend to live in the house for the rest of my life, so don't record the deed until I die. The deed will be effective at my death."

The son put the deed in his desk. The wife discovered the deed and recorded it without the son's knowledge. Subsequently, the son and the wife separated, and the wife, without telling anyone, conveyed her interest in the house to a friend who immediately reconveyed it to the wife.

The woman learned that the son and the wife had separated and also learned what had happened to the deed to the house. The woman then brought an appropriate action against the son and the wife to obtain a declaration that the woman was still the owner of the house and an order canceling of record the woman's deed and the subsequent deeds.

If the court determines that the woman owns the house in fee simple, what will be the likely explanation?

(A) The deed was not delivered.

Correct. To be valid, a deed must be properly executed and delivered. Delivery is a question of the grantor's intent. In this case, the woman did not intend the deed to be effective until her death. An intent to have a transfer be effective at the grantor's death is valid in a will but not in a deed unless the deed expressly reserves a life estate, which this deed did not do. The woman remained in possession of the house and intended to retain title to the house until her death. The deed was not delivered, so she owns the house in fee simple.

(B) The wife's conduct entitles the woman to equitable relief.

Incorrect. The wife's conduct may have been inappropriate, but it is not relevant to whether the woman properly delivered the deed to the son and the wife. To be valid, a deed must be properly executed and delivered. Delivery is a question of the grantor's intent. In this case, the woman did not intend the deed to be effective until her death. An intent to have a transfer be effective at the grantor's death is valid in a will but not in a deed unless the deed expressly reserves a life estate, which this deed did not do. The woman remained in possession of the house and intended to retain title to the house until her death. The deed was not delivered, so she owns the house in fee simple.

(C) The woman expressly reserved a life estate.

Incorrect. The woman did not expressly reserve a life estate, and she remained in possession of the house. To be valid, a deed must be properly executed and delivered. Delivery is a question of the grantor's intent. In this case, the woman did not intend the deed to be effective until her death. An intent to have a transfer be effective at the grantor's death is valid in a will but not in a deed unless the deed expressly reserves a life estate, which this deed did not do. The woman remained in possession of the house and intended to retain title to the house until her death. The deed was not delivered, so she owns the house in fee simple.

(D) The woman received no consideration for her deed.

Incorrect. A grantor may convey property for no consideration. To be valid, however, a deed must be properly executed and delivered. Delivery is a question of the grantor's intent. In this case, the woman did not intend the deed to be effective until her death. An intent to have a transfer be effective at the grantor's death is valid in a will but not in a deed unless the deed expressly reserves a life estate, which this deed did not do. The woman remained in possession of the house, and the deed was not delivered, so she owns the house in fee simple.

Question # 24 - Contracts

A man sent an email to a friend that stated: "Because you have been a great friend to me, I am going to give you a rare book that I own." The friend replied by an email that said: "Thanks for the rare book. I am going to give you my butterfly collection." The rare book was worth $10,000; the butterfly collection was worth $100. The friend delivered the butterfly collection to the man, but the man refused to deliver the book.

If the friend sues the man to recover the value of the book, how should the court rule?

(A) For the man, because there was no bargained-for exchange to support his promise.

Correct. To constitute consideration, a return promise must be bargained for. A return promise is bargained for when it is sought by the promisor in exchange for his promise and is given by the promisee in exchange for that promise. Because the man's promise to give the rare book to the friend did not seek a return promise or performance, the friend's promise to give the man her butterfly collection did not constitute consideration for the man's promise. Accordingly, no contract arose between the parties, and the court should rule in favor of the man.

(B) For the man, because the consideration given for his promise was inadequate.

Incorrect. Instead of giving inadequate consideration, the friend gave no consideration at all. To constitute consideration, a return promise must be bargained for. A return promise is bargained for when it is sought by the promisor in exchange for his promise and is given by the promisee in exchange for that promise. Because the man's promise to give the rare book to the friend did not seek a return promise or performance, the friend's promise to give the man her butterfly collection did not constitute consideration for the man's promise. Accordingly, no contract arose between the parties, and the court should rule in favor of the man.

(C) For the friend, because she gave the butterfly collection to the man in reliance on receiving the book.

Incorrect. Although it is true that a promisee's reliance may provide the basis for the enforcement of a promise in the absence of consideration, that principle is inapplicable here. The man's promise failed to induce reliance by the friend of the type that the man reasonably might have expected when he promised to give her the rare book. In addition, this is not a case in which injustice could only be avoided by the enforcement of the man's promise. The dispositive issue here is whether the friend's promise to give her butterfly collection to the man constituted consideration for the man's promise. Because the man's promise to give the rare book to the friend did not seek a return promise or performance, the friend's promise did not constitute consideration for the man's promise. Accordingly, no contract arose between the parties, and the court should rule in favor of the man.

(D) For the friend, because she conferred a benefit on the man by delivering the butterfly collection.

Incorrect. The fact that a promisee confers a benefit on a promisor does not create an enforceable obligation on the part of the promisor. The dispositive issue here is whether the friend's promise to give her butterfly collection to the man constituted consideration for the man's promise. Because the man's promise to give the rare book to the friend did not seek a return promise or performance, the friend's promise did not constitute consideration for the man's promise. Accordingly, no contract arose between the parties, and the court should rule in favor of the man.

Question # 25 - Torts

Toxic materials being transported by truck from a manufacturer's plant to a warehouse leaked from the truck onto the street a few miles from the plant. A driver lost control of his car when he hit the puddle of spilled toxic materials on the street, and he was injured when his car hit a stop sign.

In an action for damages by the driver against the manufacturer based on strict liability, is the driver likely to prevail?

(A) No, because the driver's loss of control was an intervening cause.

Incorrect. The driver's loss of control was not intentional, nor was it either unforeseeable or unusual. For that reason, it should raise no proximate cause problem.

(B) No, because the driver's injury did not result from the toxicity of the materials.

Correct. Strict liability in this situation would be based on the abnormally dangerous nature of the toxic materials. But a successful strict liability action requires that the risk that materializes be the same risk that led courts to label the activity "abnormally dangerous" in the first place. Here, the toxicity of the materials did not contribute to the driver's injury, so his only cause of action would be in negligence.

(C) Yes, because the manufacturer is strictly liable for leaks of its toxic materials.

Incorrect. Strict liability in this situation would be based on the abnormally dangerous nature of the toxic materials. But a successful strict liability action requires that the risk that materializes be the same risk that led courts to label the activity "abnormally dangerous" in the first place. Here, the toxicity of the materials did not contribute to the driver's injury, so his only cause of action would be in negligence.

(D) Yes, because the leak occurred near the manufacturer's plant.

Incorrect. The manufacturer would be strictly liable for injuries caused by its toxic materials regardless of where the leak occurred, so long as the manufacturer could be said to be responsible for the leak. However, in this situation the toxicity of the materials did not contribute to the driver's injury, so his only cause of action would be in negligence.

Question # 26 - Constitutional Law

Congress enacted a statute that authorized the construction of a monument commemorating the role of the United States in liberating a particular foreign nation during World War II. Another statute appropriated $3 million for the construction. When the United States became involved in a bitter trade dispute with the foreign nation, the President announced that he was canceling the monument's construction and that he would not spend the appropriated funds. Although the actual reason for the President's decision was the trade dispute, the announcement stated that the reason was an unexpected rise in the federal deficit.

Assume that no other statutes apply.

Is the President's decision constitutional?

(A) No, because the President failed to invoke his foreign affairs powers in his announcement.

Incorrect. The constitutionality of the President's decision does not depend on whether he invoked a constitutional power to support the decision. While it is correct that the decision is unconstitutional, it is so because Article II of the Constitution obligates the President to take care that the laws are faithfully executed. Because the appropriations statute is a valid exercise of Congress's spending power, the President must abide by the requirements of the statute.

(B) No, because the President is obligated to spend funds in accordance with congressional directions.

Correct. The President's decision is unconstitutional, because Article II of the Constitution obligates the

President to take care that the laws are faithfully executed. Because the appropriations statute is a valid exercise of Congress's spending power, the President must abide by the requirements of the statute.

(C) Yes, because the President is vested with inherent executive power to control federal expenditures.

Incorrect. The Constitution does not give the President power to control federal expenditures by refusing to authorize spending directed by Congress. The President's decision is unconstitutional, because Article II of the Constitution obligates the President to take care that the laws are faithfully executed. Because the appropriations statute is a valid exercise of Congress's spending power, the President must abide by the requirements of the statute.

(D) Yes, because the President's decision is a valid exercise of his foreign affairs powers.

Incorrect. The President's foreign affairs powers do not justify his refusal to authorize spending directed by Congress. The President's decision is unconstitutional, because Article II of the Constitution obligates the President to take care that the laws are faithfully executed. Because the appropriations statute is a valid exercise of Congress's spending power, the President must abide by the requirements of the statute.

Question # 27 - Real Property

A woman borrowed $100,000 from a bank and executed a promissory note to the bank in that amount. As security for repayment of the loan, the woman's brother gave the bank a mortgage on a tract of land solely owned by him. The brother did not sign the promissory note.

The woman subsequently defaulted on the loan, and after acceleration, the bank instituted foreclosure proceedings on the brother's land. The brother filed a timely objection to the foreclosure.

Will the bank succeed in foreclosing on the tract of land?

(A) No, because the bank has an equitable mortgage rather than a legal mortgage.

Incorrect. A mortgage is security for the performance of an act. The performance may be by the mortgagor or by some other person. Therefore, the mortgage granted by the brother to secure the debt of the woman is valid, and the bank may foreclose on it.

(B) No, because a mortgage from the brother is invalid without a mortgage debt owed by him.

Incorrect. A mortgage is security for the performance of an act. The performance may be by the mortgagor or by some other person. Therefore, the mortgage granted by the brother to secure the debt of the woman is valid, and the bank may foreclose on it.

(C) Yes, because the bank has a valid mortgage.

Correct. A mortgage is security for the performance of an act. The performance may be by the mortgagor or by some other person. The mortgage granted by the brother to secure the debt of the woman is valid even though the woman also has personal liability on the debt.

(D) Yes, because the bank is a surety for the brother's mortgage.

Incorrect. The bank is the mortgagee under the mortgage and not a surety. The bank may foreclose on the mortgage, however, because the mortgage is valid and the debt is in default. A mortgage is security for the performance of an act. The performance may be by the mortgagor or by some other person.

Question # 28 - Criminal Law and Procedure

A defendant was validly arrested for the murder of a store clerk and was taken to a police station where he was given Miranda warnings. When an interrogator asked the defendant, "Do you understand your Miranda rights, and are you willing to give up those rights and talk to us?" the defendant replied, "Yes." When asked, "Did you kill the clerk?" the defendant replied, "No." When asked, "Where were you on the day the clerk was killed?" the defendant replied, "Maybe I should talk to a lawyer." The interrogator asked, "Are you sure?" and the defendant replied, "I'm not sure." The interrogator then asked, "Why would you want to talk with a lawyer?" and the defendant replied, "Because I killed the clerk. It was an accident, and I think I need a lawyer to defend me." At that point all interrogation ceased. Later, the defendant was formally charged with murdering the clerk.

The defendant has moved to suppress evidence of his statement "I killed the clerk" on the ground that this statement was elicited in violation of his Miranda rights.

Should the defendant's motion be granted?

(A) No, because although the defendant effectively asserted the right to counsel, the question "Why would you want to talk with a lawyer?" did not constitute custodial interrogation.

Incorrect. The defendant did not effectively assert his right to counsel, because such an assertion must be unambiguous. The defendant's statement "Maybe I should talk to a lawyer" is not an unambiguous request for counsel.

(B) No, because the defendant did not effectively assert the right to counsel, and his conduct prior to making the statement constituted a valid waiver of his Miranda rights.

Correct. The defendant did not effectively assert his right to counsel, because such an assertion must be unambiguous. The defendant's statement "Maybe I should talk to a lawyer" is not an unambiguous request for counsel. In addition, the defendant had unequivocally waived his Miranda rights prior to making this statement.

(C) Yes, because although the defendant did not effectively assert the right to counsel, his conduct prior to making the statement did not constitute a valid waiver of his Miranda rights.

Incorrect. The defendant unequivocally waived his Miranda rights, and his statement "Maybe I should talk to a lawyer" did not affect the validity of that waiver.

(D) Yes, because the defendant effectively asserted the right to counsel, and the question "Why would you want to talk with a lawyer?" constituted custodial interrogation.

Incorrect. The defendant did not effectively assert his right to counsel, because such an assertion must be unambiguous. The defendant's statement "Maybe I should talk to a lawyer" is not an unambiguous request for counsel.

Question # 29 - Evidence

A plaintiff has sued a defendant for personal injuries the plaintiff suffered when she was bitten as she was trying to feed a rat that was part of the defendant's caged-rat experiment at a science fair. At trial, the plaintiff offers evidence that immediately after the incident the defendant said to her, "I'd like to give you this $100 bill, because I feel so bad about this."

Is the defendant's statement admissible?

(A) No, because it is not relevant to the issue of liability.

Incorrect. The defendant's statement of contrition and offer of compensation clearly have a tendency to prove that he is liable, and a tendency is all that is required for the evidence to be relevant under Rule 401. The statement is admissible as the statement of a party-opponent.

(B) No, because it was an offer of compromise.

Incorrect. The statement would not be excluded under Rule 408, which excludes statements that are made to settle a claim, because that rule applies only when the statement is made as a compromise to a disputed claim. Here, at the time the defendant made the statement, he was not contesting that he was at fault. Therefore, there was no disputed claim, and the statement is admissible as the statement of a party-opponent.

(C) Yes, as a present sense impression.

Incorrect. The exception to the hearsay rule for present sense impressions covers a statement describing or explaining an event or condition made during or immediately after the event or condition. The defendant's statement is just an expression of contrition and not an attempt to explain any event or condition. However, the statement is admissible as the statement of a party-opponent.

(D) Yes, as the statement of a party-opponent.

Correct. An out-of-court statement by a party that is relevant to his or her liability is admissible under the exception to the hearsay rule for statements of a party-opponent. One might think that the statement would be excluded because of Rule 408, which excludes statements that are made to settle a claim. But that rule is inapplicable, because it applies only when the statement is made to compromise a disputed claim. Here, at the time the defendant made the statement, he was not contesting that he was at fault. Therefore, there was no disputed claim.

Question # 30 - Contracts

A farmer who wanted to sell her land received a letter from a developer that stated, "I will pay you $1,100 an acre for your land." The farmer's letter of reply stated, "I accept your offer." Unbeknownst to the farmer, the developer had intended to offer only $1,000 per acre but had mistakenly typed "$1,100." As both parties knew, comparable land in the vicinity had been selling at prices between $1,000 and $1,200 per acre.

Which of the following states the probable legal consequences of the correspondence between the parties?

(A) There is no contract, because the parties attached materially different meanings to the price term.

Incorrect. There is a general rule that contract formation may be defeated, under some circumstances, where parties attach materially different meanings to a material term. That rule, however, is inapplicable here where the critical issue relates to the developer's intent, as manifested by his conduct, and the impact of the farmer's lack of knowledge of the developer's mistake. An enforceable contract requires mutual assent as determined by the parties' objective, rather than subjective, manifestations of that assent. Here, given the parties' knowledge of the price of comparable land, the developer's offer created a reasonable understanding that the developer would purchase the land for $1,100 per acre. Moreover, because the farmer neither knew nor had reason to know that the developer intended to purchase the land for only $1,000 per acre, the developer will be bound to purchase it for $1,100 per acre. Accordingly, the parties' conduct gave rise to a contract formed at $1,100 per acre when the farmer accepted the developer's offer.

(B) There is no enforceable contract, because the developer is entitled to rescission due to a mutual mistake as to a basic assumption of the contract.

Incorrect. While a mutual mistake may give rise to an action for rescission, there was no mutual mistake in this case. The critical issue here relates to the developer's intent as manifested by his conduct, and the impact of the farmer's lack of knowledge of the developer's mistake. An enforceable contract requires mutual assent as determined by the parties' objective, rather than subjective, manifestations of assent. Given the parties' knowledge of the price of comparable land, the developer's offer created a reasonable understanding that the developer would purchase the land for $1,100 per acre. Moreover, because the farmer neither knew nor had reason to know that the developer intended to purchase the land for only $1,000 per acre, the developer will be bound to purchase it for $1,100 per acre. Accordingly, the parties' conduct gave rise to a contract formed at $1,100 per acre when the farmer accepted the developer's offer.

(C) There is a contract formed at a price of $1,000 per acre.

Incorrect. An enforceable contract requires mutual assent as determined by the parties' objective, rather than subjective, manifestations of assent. Given the parties' knowledge of the price of comparable land, the developer's offer created a reasonable understanding that the developer would purchase the land for $1,100 per acre. Moreover, because the farmer neither knew nor had reason to know that the developer intended to purchase the land for only $1,000 per acre, the developer will be bound to purchase it for $1,100 per acre. Accordingly, the parties' conduct gave rise to a contract formed at $1,100 per acre when the farmer accepted the developer's offer.

(D) There is a contract formed at a price of $1,100 per acre.

Correct. An enforceable contract requires mutual assent as determined by the parties' objective, rather than subjective, manifestations of assent. Given the parties' knowledge of the price of comparable land, the developer's offer created a reasonable understanding that the developer would purchase the land for $1,100 per acre. Moreover, because the farmer neither knew nor had reason to know that the developer intended to purchase the land for only $1,000 per acre, the developer will be bound to purchase it for $1,100 per acre. Accordingly, the parties' conduct gave rise to a contract formed at $1,100 per acre when the farmer accepted the developer's offer.

Question # 31 - Criminal Law and Procedure

Two defendants were being tried together in federal court for bank robbery. The prosecutor sought to introduce testimony from the first defendant's prison cellmate. The cellmate would testify that the first defendant had admitted to the cellmate that he and the second defendant had robbed the bank. The prosecutor asked the court to instruct the jury that the cellmate's testimony could be considered only against the first defendant.

Can the cellmate's testimony be admitted in a joint trial over the second defendant's objection?

(A) No, because the first defendant made the statement without Miranda warnings.

Incorrect. Miranda warnings were not required, because the first defendant was not compelled by a known law enforcement agent to make the statement, and in any event the second defendant could not assert Miranda rights belonging to the first defendant.

(B) No, because the limiting instruction cannot ensure that the jury will not consider the testimony in its deliberations regarding the second defendant.

Correct. The limiting instruction is constitutionally insufficient to avoid the risk that the jury will consider the incriminating statement against the second defendant, who has no opportunity at trial to confront the first defendant.

(C) Yes, because the first defendant's statement was a declaration against penal interest.

Incorrect. The first defendant's statement incriminating the second defendant could not, under the Sixth Amendment confrontation clause, be considered against the second defendant on a theory that it constitutes a declaration against penal interest.

(D) Yes, because the limiting instruction sufficiently protects the second defendant.

Incorrect. The limiting instruction is constitutionally insufficient to avoid the risk that the jury will consider the incriminating statement against the second defendant, who has no opportunity at trial to confront the first defendant.

Question # 32 - Torts

A man and his friend, who were both adults, went to a party. The man and the friend had many drinks at the party and became legally intoxicated. They decided to play a game of chance called "Russian roulette" using a gun loaded with one bullet. As part of the game, the man pointed the gun at the friend and, on her command, pulled the trigger. The man shot the friend in the shoulder.

The friend has brought a negligence action against the man. Traditional defenses based on plaintiff's conduct apply. What is likely to be the dispositive issue in this case?

(A) Whether the game constituted a joint venture.

Incorrect. The fact that the man and the friend might have been engaged in a joint venture would be relevant if the action were being brought by a third party who was not part of the venture but who had been injured as a consequence of their activities. It is irrelevant to a suit among participants in a joint venture unless it indicates an assumption of risk.

(B) Whether the friend could validly consent to the game.

Incorrect. It is likely that consent to this activity would be routinely found to be against public policy, although the consequences of such a determination would vary from state to state. But consent is a defense more appropriately raised in an intentional tort case, not a case for negligence. There is no indication that the friend consented to any negligence, and in any case she was too intoxicated to give a valid consent.

(C) Whether the friend was also negligent.

Correct. Contributory negligence is an appropriate defense to a negligence action, and here both parties seem to have been acting unreasonably in exactly the same way. Whether the argument is put in the form of the friend's carelessness in engaging in the activity or in her unreasonable assumption of risk, many states would now evaluate the defense under comparative negligence principles.

(D) Whether the man was legally intoxicated when he began playing the game.

Incorrect. The man's intoxication would not insulate him from liability to those he injured while in that state. He would still be held to the "reasonably prudent person" standard.

Question # 33 - Real Property

A mother executed a will devising vacant land to her son. The mother showed the will to her son.

Thereafter, the son purported to convey the land to a friend by a warranty deed that contained no exceptions. The friend paid value for the land and promptly recorded the deed without having first conducted any title search. The friend never took possession of the land.

The mother later died, and the will devising the land to her son was duly admitted to probate.

Thereafter, the friend conducted a title search for the land and asked the son for a new deed. The son refused, because the value of the land had doubled, but he offered to refund the purchase price to the friend.

The friend has sued to quiet title to the land. Is the friend likely to prevail?

(A) No, because the friend failed to conduct a title search before purchasing the land.

Incorrect. A buyer may want to search the title before purchasing land to determine if title is as called for in the contract, but such a search is not required. The doctrine of estoppel by deed (sometimes referred to as after-acquired title) provides that even if the grantor has no title to the land at the time the deed is delivered, title automatically passes to the grantee when title is so acquired, provided that the grantor asserts the quality of title conveyed in the deed. In this case, the son conveyed to the friend by a warranty deed with no exceptions.

(B) No, because the son had no interest in the land at the time of conveyance.

Incorrect. It is true that the son had no interest in the land at the time of conveyance. The doctrine of estoppel by deed (sometimes referred to as after-acquired title), however, provides that in such a case title automatically passes to the grantee when the title is so acquired, provided that the grantor asserts the quality of title conveyed in the deed. In this case, the son conveyed to the friend by a warranty deed with no exceptions.

(C) Yes, because of the doctrine of estoppel by deed.

Correct. The doctrine of estoppel by deed (sometimes referred to as after-acquired title) provides that even if the grantor has no title to the land at the time the deed is delivered, the title automatically passes to the grantee when title is so acquired, provided that the grantor asserts the quality of title conveyed in the deed. In this case, the son conveyed to the friend by a warranty deed with no exceptions.

(D) Yes, because the deed was recorded.

Incorrect. Recording has no effect on title in this case. The doctrine of estoppel by deed (sometimes referred to as after-acquired title) provides that even if the grantor has no title to the land at the time the deed is delivered, the title automatically passes to the grantee when title is so acquired, provided that the grantor asserts the quality of title conveyed in the deed. In this case, the son conveyed to the friend by a warranty deed with no exceptions. It is irrelevant to the doctrine of estoppel by deed whether the deed was recorded or not.

Question # 34 - Criminal Law and Procedure

A prosecutor presented to a federal grand jury the testimony of a witness in order to secure a defendant's indictment for theft of government property. The prosecutor did not disclose to the grand jury that the witness had been convicted four years earlier of perjury. The grand jury returned an indictment, and the defendant pleaded not guilty.

Shortly thereafter, the prosecutor took the case to trial, calling the witness to testify before the jury. The prosecutor did not disclose the witness's prior perjury conviction until the defense was preparing to rest. Defense counsel immediately moved for a mistrial, which the court denied. Instead, the court allowed the defense to recall the witness for the purpose of impeaching him with this conviction, but the witness could not be located. The court then allowed the defense to introduce documentary evidence of the witness's criminal record to the jury before resting its case. The jury convicted the defendant.

The defendant has moved for a new trial, arguing that the prosecutor's failure to disclose the witness's prior conviction in a timely manner violated the defendant's right to due process of law.

If the court grants the defendant's motion, what will be the most likely reason?

(A) The defendant was unable to cross-examine the witness about the conviction.

Incorrect. The court did not limit the defendant's right to cross-examine the witness. Rather, the constitutional violation, if any, was the prosecutor's untimely disclosure of impeachment information that would have created a reasonable probability of a different outcome had it been disclosed earlier.

(B) The prosecutor failed to inform the grand jury of the witness's conviction.

Incorrect. The prosecutor is not required to present a grand jury with evidence favorable to a defendant. Rather, the constitutional violation, if any, was the prosecutor's untimely disclosure of impeachment information that would have created a reasonable probability of a different outcome had it been disclosed earlier.

(C) The court found it reasonably probable that the defendant would have been acquitted had the defense had timely access to the information about the witness's conviction.

Correct. The untimely disclosure of evidence favorable to the defense (including impeachment information) violates the Constitution if the evidence would have created a reasonable probability of a different outcome had it been disclosed earlier.

(D) The court found that the prosecutor had deliberately delayed disclosing the witness's conviction to obtain a strategic advantage.

Incorrect. The prosecutor's motive is not an element of a constitutional claim involving untimely disclosure of evidence favorable to the defense (including impeachment information). Rather, such untimely disclosure would violate the Constitution only if the evidence would have created a reasonable probability of a different outcome had it been disclosed earlier.

Question # 35 - Constitutional Law

A motorist who resided in State A was severely injured in a traffic accident that occurred in State B. The other vehicle involved in the accident was a truck owned by a furniture manufacturer and driven by one of its employees. The manufacturer's headquarters are in State B. Its products are sold by retailers in State A, but it has no office, plant, or agent for service of process there.

The motorist brought an action against the manufacturer in a state court in State A. The manufacturer appeared specially to contest that court's jurisdiction over it. The court ruled that it had jurisdiction over the manufacturer by virtue of State A's long-arm statute.

At trial, the court instructed the jury to apply State A law, under which a plaintiff's contributory negligence is a basis for reducing an award of damages but not for denying recovery altogether. Under State B law, contributory negligence is a complete defense. The jury found that the manufacturer was negligent and that its negligence was a cause of the motorist's injuries. It also found that the motorist was negligent, though to a lesser degree than the manufacturer, and that the motorist's negligence contributed to the accident. It returned a verdict in favor of the motorist and awarded her $1 million in damages.

The manufacturer appealed the judgment entered on this verdict, asserting error in the court's ruling on jurisdiction and in its application of State A law instead of State B law. The manufacturer raised all federal constitutional claims pertinent to these claims of error. The highest court in State A affirmed the trial court's judgment, and the U.S. Supreme Court denied the manufacturer's petition for a writ of certiorari.

The motorist has brought an action against the manufacturer in a state court in State B to collect on the judgment. The manufacturer has defended on all relevant federal constitutional grounds.

How should the State B court rule?

(A) For the manufacturer, because a judgment entered by a court that lacks jurisdiction over one of the parties is not entitled to full faith and credit, and the State A court could not constitutionally assert jurisdiction over the manufacturer because of the manufacturer's lack of a presence in that state.

Incorrect. The jurisdiction of the State A court was litigated in the State A court, and the ruling by that court in favor of jurisdiction is final and must be recognized by the State B court. The State B court should rule for the motorist, because the full faith and credit clause of the Constitution obligates the courts of each state to recognize the final judgments of the courts of every other state. Because the judgment of the State A court is final, it is entitled to full faith and credit in the State B court.

(B) For the manufacturer, because the State A court was bound by the full faith and credit clause to apply State B law to an accident that occurred in State B and in which a State B company was involved.

Incorrect. The full faith and credit clause of the Constitution obligates states to recognize laws enacted by other states, but it does not obligate a state court to apply the laws of another state in cases before it. The State B court should rule for the motorist, because the full faith and credit clause of the Constitution obligates the courts of each state to recognize the final judgments of the courts of every other state. Because the judgment of the State A court is final, it is entitled to full faith and credit in the State B court.

(C) For the motorist, because the manufacturer litigated the issues of jurisdiction and choice of law in the State A court, and the final judgment of that court is entitled to full faith and credit in the State B court.

Correct. The State B court should rule for the motorist, because the full faith and credit clause of the Constitution obligates the courts of each state to recognize the final judgments of the courts of every other state. Because the judgment of the State A court is final, it is entitled to full faith and credit in the State B court.

(D) For the motorist, because the Supreme Court's denial of certiorari to review the judgment of the highest court in State A conclusively establishes that the manufacturer's federal constitutional claims are invalid.

Incorrect. The Supreme Court's denial of certiorari is not a ruling on the merits of the case; it is simply a decision not to review the case. The State B court should rule for the motorist, however, because the full faith and credit clause of the Constitution obligates the courts of each state to recognize the final judgments of the courts of every other state. Because the judgment of the State A court is final, it is entitled to full faith and credit in the State B court.

Question # 36 - Contracts

A buyer and a seller entered into a written contract for the sale of a copy machine, using the same form contract that they had used a number of times in the past. The contract stated that payment was due 30 days after delivery and provided that the writing contained the complete and exclusive statement of the parties' agreement.

On several past occasions, the buyer had taken a 5% discount from the contract price when paying within 10 days of delivery, and the seller had not objected. On this occasion, when the buyer took a 5% discount for paying within 10 days, the seller objected because his profit margin on this particular machine was smaller than on his other machines.

If the seller sues the buyer for breach of contract, may the buyer introduce evidence that the 5% discount was a term of the agreement?

(A) No, because the seller timely objected to the buyer's proposal for different terms.

Incorrect. Under UCC § 1-303(b), course of dealing is defined as "a sequence of conduct concerning previous transactions between the parties to a particular transaction. . . ." In this case, on several past occasions the buyer had taken a 5% discount without objection from the seller, thus establishing a course of dealing. Given the course of dealing between the parties, the seller's objection to the 5% discount, after the buyer had acted in accordance with the course of dealing, was ineffective. Under the UCC's parol evidence rule, course-of-dealing evidence is admissible to explain or supplement a final written agreement.

(B) No, because the writing contained the complete and exclusive agreement of the parties.

Incorrect. Under UCC § 1-303(b), course of dealing is defined as "a sequence of conduct concerning previous transactions between the parties to a particular transaction. . . ." In this case, on several past occasions the buyer had taken a 5% discount without objection from the seller, thus establishing a course of dealing. Under the UCC's parol evidence rule, course-of-dealing evidence is admissible to explain or supplement a final written agreement even if the parties intended the agreement to be complete and exclusive. Accordingly, the course-of-dealing evidence is admissible.

(C) Yes, because a modification made in good faith does not require consideration.

Incorrect. UCC Article 2 contains a general rule that a good- faith modification does not require consideration to be enforceable. However, the enforceability of a modification is not at issue here. The issue here is whether the UCC's parol evidence rule will preclude the admissibility of evidence of course of dealing. The facts indicate that in the parties' previous contracts the buyer had taken a 5% discount without objection from the seller. This conduct amounted to a course of dealing that is defined under UCC § 1-303(b) as "a sequence of conduct concerning previous transactions between the parties to a particular transaction. . . ." Because the UCC's parol evidence rule explicitly allows for the admission of course-of-dealing evidence to explain or supplement a final written agreement, the evidence is admissible.

(D) Yes, because evidence of course of dealing is admissible even if the writing contains the complete and exclusive agreement of the parties.

Correct. Under UCC § 1-303(b), course of dealing is defined as "a sequence of conduct concerning previous transactions between the parties to a particular transaction. . . ." In this case, on several past occasions the buyer had taken a 5% discount without objection from the seller, thus establishing a course of dealing. Under the UCC's parol evidence rule, course-of-dealing evidence is admissible to explain or supplement a final written agreement even if the parties intended the agreement to be complete and exclusive. Accordingly, the course-of-dealing evidence is admissible.

Question # 37 - Evidence

A defendant is charged with aggravated assault. The physical evidence at trial has shown that the victim was hit with a lead pipe in the back of the head and on the forearms and left in an alley. The medical examiner has testified that the injuries to the victim's forearms appear to have been defensive wounds. The victim has testified that he cannot remember who attacked him with the lead pipe. He would further testify that he remembers only that a passerby found him in the alley, and that he told the passerby that the defendant had hit him with the lead pipe; he then lost consciousness. The defendant objects to this proposed testimony, arguing that it is hearsay and that the victim had no personal knowledge of the identity of the perpetrator.

Is the victim's testimony concerning his previous statement to the passerby admissible?

(A) No, because the prosecutor has failed to show that it is more likely than not that the victim had personal knowledge of the perpetrator's identity.

Incorrect. The standard for personal knowledge under Rule 602 is whether a reasonable juror could find that the witness is speaking on the basis of personal knowledge. This standard is referred to as "prima facie" proof and is significantly easier to satisfy than "more likely than not."

(B) No, because the victim has no memory of the attack itself and therefore cannot be effectively cross-examined.

Incorrect. The U.S. Supreme Court held in *United States v. Owens* that a declarant-witness is subject to cross-examination within the meaning of the hearsay exception for prior identifications even if the witness lacks all memory of the prior identification.

(C) Yes, because the victim is subject to cross-examination, and there is sufficient showing of personal knowledge.

Correct. The U.S. Supreme Court held in *United States v. Owens* that a declarant-witness is subject to cross-examination within the meaning of the hearsay exception for prior identifications even if the witness lacks all memory of the prior identification. As to personal knowledge, the evidence of defensive wounds is more than sufficient to persuade a reasonable juror that the victim saw his attacker.

(D) Yes, because it is the victim's own out-of-court statement.

Incorrect. The rule against hearsay applies to any out-of-court statement admitted for its truth, including earlier statements of trial witnesses. In this case, however, there is a hearsay exception for prior identifications when the declarant is testifying and subject to cross-examination.

Question # 38 - Constitutional Law

Congress recently enacted a statute creating a program that made federal loans available to family farmers who had been unable to obtain loans from private lenders. Congress appropriated a fixed sum of money to fund loans made pursuant to the program and gave a designated federal agency discretion to decide which applicants were to receive the loans.

Two weeks after the program was established, a family farmer applied to the agency for a loan. Agency officials promptly reviewed her application and summarily denied it.

The farmer has sued the agency in federal district court, claiming only that the denial of her application without the opportunity for a hearing violated the due process clause of the Fifth Amendment. The farmer claims that she could have proved at such a hearing that without the federal loan it would be necessary for her to sell her farm.

Should the court uphold the agency's decision?

(A) No, because due process requires federal agencies to provide a hearing before making any factual determination that adversely affects an identified individual on the basis of his or her particular circumstances.

Incorrect. The due process clause obligates agencies to provide an individual with an opportunity for a hearing only when the agency makes an adjudicatory decision that deprives the individual of a property or liberty interest that is protected by the clause. The court should uphold the agency's decision, because the due process clause does not require the government to provide the farmer an opportunity for an administrative hearing on her loan application. The farmer had no legitimate claim of entitlement to a loan, because the statute gave the agency discretion to decide which applicants were to receive the loans. The agency's denial of the farmer's application therefore did not deprive her of a property or liberty interest protected by the due process clause.

(B) No, because the denial of a loan may deprive the farmer of an established liberty interest to pursue her chosen occupation.

Incorrect. The farmer's decision to pursue her chosen occupation does not qualify as a liberty interest protected by the due process clause. The court should uphold the agency's decision, because the due process clause does not require the government to provide the farmer an opportunity for an administrative hearing on her loan application. The farmer had no legitimate claim of entitlement to a loan, because the statute gave the agency discretion to decide which applicants were to receive the loans. The agency's denial of the farmer's loan application therefore did not deprive her of a property or liberty interest protected by the due process clause.

(C) Yes, because the applicable statute gives the farmer no legitimate claim of entitlement to receive a loan.

Correct. The court should uphold the agency's decision, because the due process clause does not require the government to provide the farmer an opportunity for an administrative hearing on her loan application. The farmer had no legitimate claim of entitlement to a loan, because the statute gave the agency discretion to decide which applicants were to receive the loans. The agency's denial of the farmer's application therefore did not deprive her of a property or liberty interest protected by the due process clause.

(D) Yes , because the spending clause of Article I, Section 8, gives Congress plenary power to control the distribution of appropriated funds in any manner it wishes.

Incorrect. Although Congress has broad authority to control the distribution of appropriated funds, that authority is subject to many constitutional limitations on the legislative power, including the due process clause of the Fifth Amendment. While the court should uphold the agency's decision, it should do so because the due process clause does not require the government to provide the farmer an opportunity for an administrative hearing on her loan application. The farmer had no legitimate claim of entitlement to a loan, because the statute gave the agency discretion to decide which applicants were to receive the loans. The agency's denial of the farmer's application therefore did not deprive her of a property or liberty interest protected by the due process clause.

Question # 39 - Torts

A woman signed up for a bowling class. Before allowing the woman to bowl, the instructor required her to sign a waiver explicitly stating that she assumed all risk of injuries that she might suffer in connection with the class, including injuries due to negligence or any other fault. After she signed the waiver, the woman was injured when the instructor negligently dropped a bowling ball on the woman's foot.

The woman brought a negligence action against the instructor. The instructor has filed a motion for summary judgment based on the waiver.

What is the woman's best argument in opposition to the instructor's motion?

(A) Bowling is an inherently dangerous activity.

Incorrect. Bowling is not inherently dangerous; virtually no one is seriously injured while bowling. Even if bowling were inherently dangerous, that characterization would support an argument for permitting recreational participants who appreciate the risks of the activity to assume the risks by signing a waiver rather than constituting a reason for ignoring the waiver.

(B) In circumstances like these, it is against public policy to enforce agreements that insulate people from the consequences of their own negligence.

Correct. Waivers are most easily justified when an activity poses inherent risks that are familiar to the participants and cannot be entirely eliminated without removing the pleasure from the activity. The risk that materialized here is not inherent to bowling but could arise whenever someone is careless while holding a heavy object. A court might find that it is against public policy to permit individuals or businesses to insulate themselves from the deterrent incentives provided by the threat of negligence liability. For that reason, the court might find that the waiver did not present the woman with a fair choice and could hold the waiver ineffective.

(C) It was unreasonable to require the woman to sign the waiver before she was allowed to bowl.

Incorrect. Although the court might find that the waiver did not present the woman with a fair choice and therefore hold the waiver to be no bar when the harm was due to the instructor's negligence, asking the woman to sign the waiver was not in itself negligent or unreasonable. For example, the waiver might have barred recovery against the instructor if the woman were injured by the negligence of another class participant, or the court might have decided that the waiver was not inconsistent with public policy given the recreational nature of the activity.

(D) When she signed the form, the woman could not foresee that the instructor would drop a bowling ball on her foot.

Incorrect. Pre-injury waivers are often enforced despite the fact that the precise injury that materializes is virtually never foreseen with a high level of specificity at the time of the signing of the waiver. The problem here is that the risk that materialized was not inherent to the enjoyment of bowling.

Question # 40 - Constitutional Law

A state law provides that only U.S. citizens may serve as jurors in the state courts of that state. A woman who is a lawful resident alien and who has resided in the state for many years was summoned for jury duty in a state court. The woman's name was selected from a list of potential jurors that was compiled from a comprehensive list of local residents. She was disqualified from service solely because she is not a U.S. citizen.

The woman has filed an action for a declaratory judgment that the state law is unconstitutional. Who should prevail in this action?

(A) The state, because a state may limit to U.S. citizens functions that are an integral part of the process of self-government.

Correct. The state should prevail, because the law excluding aliens from jury service is rationally related to the state's legitimate interest in ensuring that only citizens perform functions that are central to self-government. Although strict scrutiny generally applies to state laws that discriminate against aliens, rational basis scrutiny is appropriate when alienage classifications restrict the right to participate in functions that are central to self-government, such as voting, running for office, or serving on a jury.

(B) The state, because jury service is a privilege, not a right, and therefore it is not a liberty interest protected by the due process clause of the Fourteenth Amendment.

Incorrect. Application of the due process clause no longer turns on whether the individual interest involved is a right or a privilege. In any event, the woman's constitutional challenge to the state law should be based on the equal protection clause rather than on the due process clause. While the state should prevail, it is because the law excluding aliens from jury service is rationally related to the state's legitimate interest in ensuring that only citizens perform functions that are central to self-government. Although strict scrutiny generally applies to state laws that discriminate against aliens, rational basis scrutiny is appropriate when alienage classifications restrict the right to participate in functions that are central to self-government, such as voting, running for office, or serving on a jury.

(C) The woman, because the Constitution gives Congress plenary power to make classifications with respect to aliens.

Incorrect. Although the Constitution gives Congress plenary power to control immigration, states may exercise their police powers to regulate the conduct of aliens within their borders unless the regulation is preempted by federal law or otherwise violates the Constitution. While strict scrutiny generally applies to state laws that discriminate against aliens, rational basis scrutiny is appropriate when alienage classifications restrict the right to participate in functions that are central to self-government, such as voting, running for office, or serving on a jury. The state should prevail here, because the law excluding aliens from jury service is rationally related to the state's legitimate interest in ensuring that only citizens perform functions that are central to self-government.

(D) The woman, because the state has not articulated a legitimate reason for prohibiting resident aliens from serving as jurors in the state's courts.

Incorrect. The state should prevail, because the law excluding aliens from jury service is rationally related to the state's legitimate interest in ensuring that only citizens perform functions that are central to self-government. Although strict scrutiny generally applies to state laws that discriminate against aliens, rational basis scrutiny is appropriate when alienage classifications restrict the right to participate in functions that are central to self-government, such as voting, running for office, or serving on a jury.

Question # 41 - Torts

A pedestrian was crossing a street in a crosswalk when a woman walking just ahead of him was hit by a truck. The pedestrian, who had jumped out of the way of the truck, administered CPR to the woman, who was a stranger. The woman bled profusely, and the pedestrian was covered in blood. The woman died in the ambulance on the way to the hospital. The pedestrian became very depressed immediately after the incident and developed physical symptoms as a result of his emotional distress.

The pedestrian has brought an action against the driver of the truck for negligent infliction of emotional distress. In her defense, the driver asserts that she should not be held liable, because the pedestrian's emotional distress and resulting physical symptoms are not compensable.

What is the strongest argument that the pedestrian can make in response to the driver's defense?

(A) The pedestrian saw the driver hit the woman.

Incorrect. Most states allow plaintiffs to recover damages for the emotional distress of seeing another person injured or killed by a negligent driver, but they usually require that there be a close relationship between the plaintiff and the injured person before recovery is allowed.

(B) The pedestrian was acting as a Good Samaritan.

Incorrect. Normally, the fact that someone chooses to come to the aid of another neither insulates that person from liability for his or her own negligence nor provides that person with a cause of action for the pure emotional distress suffered as a consequence of providing the aid.

(C) The pedestrian was covered in the woman's blood and developed physical symptoms as a result of his emotional distress.

Incorrect. The negligent driver did not herself touch or impact the pedestrian, so the fact that the pedestrian became covered in blood and ultimately suffered physical symptoms as a result of emotional distress is not alone sufficient to support a claim for damages.

(D) The pedestrian was in the zone of danger.

Correct. Because the pedestrian was in the path of the truck, he was under a direct physical threat from the driver's negligence. He could recover for the emotional distress that he suffered as a result of his fear for his own safety, and many courts would also allow him to recover for all other emotional distress that he suffered in connection with the event.

Question # 42 - Contracts

A buyer purchased a new car from a dealer under a written contract that provided that the price of the car was $20,000 and that the buyer would receive a "trade-in allowance of $7,000 for the buyer's old car." The old car had recently been damaged in an accident. The contract contained a merger clause stating: "This writing constitutes the entire agreement of the parties, and there are no other understandings or agreements not set forth herein." When the buyer took possession of the new car, she delivered the old car to the dealer. At that time, the dealer claimed that the trade-in allowance included an assignment of the buyer's claim against her insurance company for damage to the old car. The buyer refused to provide the assignment.

The dealer sued the buyer to recover the insurance payment. The dealer has offered evidence that the parties agreed during their negotiations for the new car that the dealer was entitled to the insurance payment.

Should the court admit this evidence?

(A) No, because the dealer's acceptance of the old car bars any additional claim by the dealer.

Incorrect. A buyer's mere acceptance of goods does not waive its potential claims against a seller. The dispositive issue here is whether the parol evidence rule will allow the proffered evidence. Under that rule, a merger clause does not conclusively determine that an agreement is completely integrated. Moreover, a finding that an agreement is completely integrated does not necessarily bar the admission of extrinsic evidence. Although extrinsic evidence is inadmissible to supplement or contradict the express terms of a completely integrated agreement, such evidence is admissible to explain the terms of an agreement. In this case, evidence of the parties' discussions during their negotiations is admissible to aid in explaining whether they intended "trade-in allowance" to include an assignment of the buyer's claim against her insurance company.

(B) No, because the merger clause bars any evidence of the parties' prior discussions concerning the trade-in allowance.

Incorrect. Under the UCC's parol evidence rule, a merger clause does not conclusively determine that an agreement is completely integrated. Moreover, a finding that an agreement is completely integrated does not necessarily bar the admission of extrinsic evidence. Although extrinsic evidence is inadmissible to supplement or contradict the express terms of a completely integrated agreement, such evidence is admissible to explain the terms of an agreement. In this case, evidence of the parties' discussions during their negotiations is admissible to aid in explaining whether they intended "trade-in allowance" to include an assignment of the buyer's claim against her insurance company.

(C) Yes, because a merger clause does not bar evidence of fraud.

Incorrect. The UCC's parol evidence rule allows the introduction of extrinsic evidence to establish fraud even if an agreement is completely integrated. Because there is no indication of fraud in this case, the fraud exception is irrelevant. The dispositive issue here is whether the parol evidence rule will allow the proffered evidence. Under that rule, a merger clause does not conclusively determine that an agreement is completely integrated. Moreover, a finding that an agreement is completely integrated does not necessarily bar the admission of extrinsic evidence. Although extrinsic evidence is inadmissible to supplement or contradict the express terms of a completely integrated agreement, such evidence is admissible to explain the terms of an agreement. In this case, evidence of the parties' discussions during their negotiations is admissible to aid in explaining whether they intended "trade-in allowance" to include an assignment of the buyer's claim against her insurance company.

(D) Yes, because the merger clause does not bar evidence to explain what the parties meant by "trade-in allowance." Correct. Under the UCC's parol evidence rule, a merger clause does not conclusively establish that an agreement

is completely integrated. Moreover, a finding that an agreement is completely integrated does not necessarily bar the admission of extrinsic evidence. Although extrinsic evidence is inadmissible to supplement or contradict the express terms of a completely integrated agreement, such evidence is admissible to explain the terms of an agreement. In this case, evidence of the parties' discussions during their negotiations is admissible to aid in explaining whether they intended "trade-in- allowance" to include an assignment of the buyer's claim against her insurance company.

Question # 43 - Real Property

A woman inherited a house from a distant relative. The woman had never visited the house, which was located in another state, and did not want to own it. Upon learning this, a man who lived next door to the house called the woman and asked to buy the house. The woman agreed, provided that the house was sold "as is." The man agreed, and the woman conveyed the house to the man by a warranty deed.

The man had purchased the house for investment purposes, intending to rent it out while continuing to live next door. After the sale, the man started to renovate the house and discovered serious termite damage. The man sued the woman for breach of contract.

There are no applicable statutes. How should the court rule?

(A) For the woman, because the man planned to change the use of the house for investment purposes.

Incorrect. The man's proposed change of use was not known to the woman, nor was it stated in the contract. His planned change to the use of the house is irrelevant to the outcome of the case. The woman should prevail, but it is because she sold the house "as is."

(B) For the woman, because she sold the house "as is."

Correct. A seller may disclaim any duty to disclose defects if the disclaimer is sufficiently clear and specific. In this case, the contract specifically noted that the house was being sold "as is." The woman made no misrepresentations regarding the condition of the house. There are no statutes that might require an owner-occupier to disclose known defects, and in any case the woman inherited the house and had never visited or lived in it. In addition, this is not the sale of a new house by a builder/seller, which may impose a warranty of habitability.

(C) For the man, because of the doctrine of caveat emptor.

Incorrect. The doctrine of caveat emptor states that the buyer accepts the property in its current condition. Therefore, the caveat emptor doctrine would not protect the man as the buyer. In fact, a seller may disclaim any duty to disclose defects if the disclaimer is sufficiently clear and specific. In this case, the contract specifically noted that the house was being sold "as is," and therefore the woman should prevail.

(D) For the man, because he received a warranty deed.

Incorrect. A warranty deed provides remedies for breaches of title matters. Termite damage affects the physical quality of the property, not title to the property. A seller may disclaim any duty to disclose physical defects if the disclaimer is sufficiently clear and specific. In this case, the contract specifically noted that the house was being sold "as is," and therefore the woman should prevail.

Question # 44 - Evidence

A man suffered a broken jaw in a fight with a neighbor that took place when they were both spectators at a soccer match.

If the man sues the neighbor for personal injury damages, which of the following actions must the trial court take if requested by the man?

(A) Prevent the neighbor's principal eyewitness from testifying, upon a showing that six years ago the witness was convicted of perjury and the conviction has not been the subject of a pardon or annulment.

Incorrect. A witness can never be excluded from testifying simply because there is impeachment evidence that could be used against that witness. Under Rule 601, all witnesses are presumed to be competent. The man can use this evidence to impeach the witness when the witness testifies.

(B) Refuse to let the neighbor cross-examine the man's medical expert on matters not covered on direct examination of the expert.

Incorrect. The trial court is not required to prohibit a cross-examiner from asking questions unrelated to the direct examination. Rule 611(b) states that the court "may allow inquiry into additional matters."

(C) Exclude nonparty eyewitnesses from the courtroom during the testimony of other witnesses.

Correct. Rule 615 provides that if a party moves to exclude prospective witnesses before they testify, "the court must order witnesses excluded so they cannot hear other witnesses' testimony."

(D) Require the production of a writing used before trial to refresh a witness's memory.

Incorrect. Under Rule 612, the trial court has discretion to order a party to produce for the adversary a writing used before trial to refresh the memory of a witness called by the party, but the court is not required to do so.

Question # 45 - Constitutional Law

Congress enacted a statute that made it illegal for "any employee, without the consent of his or her employer, to post on the Internet any information concerning the employer." The purpose of the statute was to prevent employees from revealing their employers' trade secrets.

Is the statute constitutional?

(A) No, because it is not narrowly tailored to further a compelling government interest.

Correct. The statute violates the freedom of speech protected by the First Amendment. The statute targets speech based on its content, because it prohibits employees from posting only "information concerning the employer" on the Internet. Because the statute is a content-based restriction on speech, it is subject to strict judicial scrutiny. Speech restrictions rarely survive strict scrutiny; the government must prove that the restriction is necessary to further a compelling government interest. Even if the government's interest in preventing employees from revealing trade secrets were deemed compelling, Congress could enact legislation utilizing less speech-restrictive means to protect trade secrets.

(B) No, because it targets a particular medium of communication for special regulation.

Incorrect. The statute does target one medium of communication--Internet postings--and this focus may cause a court to look more closely at the restriction when evaluating its constitutionality. However, a statute does not violate the First Amendment simply because it targets a particular medium. In this case, the statute violates the freedom of speech protected by the First Amendment because it targets speech based on its content; it prohibits employees from posting only "information concerning the employer" on the Internet. Because the statute is a content-based restriction on speech, it is subject to strict judicial scrutiny. Speech restrictions rarely survive strict scrutiny; the government must prove that the restriction is necessary to further a compelling government interest. Even if the government's interest in preventing employees from revealing trade secrets were deemed compelling, Congress could enact legislation utilizing less speech-restrictive means to protect trade secrets.

(C) Yes, because it leaves open ample alternative channels of communication.

Incorrect. The statute leaves open channels of communication other than the Internet, but this fact does not save the statute. The availability of ample alternative channels of communication is an element of the First Amendment test for evaluating speech restrictions that are content-neutral, but it is not as important with respect to content-based restrictions. In this case, the statute violates the freedom of speech protected by the First Amendment because it targets speech based on its content; it prohibits employees from posting only "information concerning the employer" on the Internet. Because the statute is a content-based restriction on speech, it is subject to strict judicial scrutiny. Speech restrictions rarely survive strict scrutiny; the government must prove that the restriction is necessary to further a compelling government interest. Even if the government's interest in preventing employees from revealing trade secrets were deemed compelling, Congress could enact legislation utilizing less speech-restrictive means to protect trade secrets.

(D) Yes, because it prevents employees from engaging in unethical conduct.

Incorrect. The statute may prevent employees from engaging in unethical conduct, but this fact does not save the statute. The statute violates the freedom of speech protected by the First Amendment because it targets speech based on its content; it prohibits employees from posting only "information concerning the employer" on the Internet. Because the statute is a content-based restriction on speech, it is subject to strict judicial scrutiny. Speech restrictions rarely survive strict scrutiny; the government must prove that the restriction is necessary to further a compelling government interest. Even if the government's interest in preventing employees from revealing trade secrets were deemed compelling, Congress could enact legislation utilizing less speech-restrictive means to protect trade secrets.

Question # 46 - Real Property

A man owned a large tract of land. The eastern portion of the land was undeveloped and unused. A farmer owned a farm, the western border of which was along the eastern border of the man's land. The two tracts of land had never been in common ownership.

Five years ago, the farmer asked the man for permission to use a designated two acres of the eastern portion of the man's land to enlarge her farm's irrigation facilities. The man orally gave his permission for such use. Since then, the farmer has invested substantial amounts of money and effort each year to develop and maintain the irrigation facilities within the two-acre parcel. The man has been fully aware of the farmer's actions. Nothing regarding this matter was ever reduced to writing.

Last year, the man gave the entire tract of land as a gift to his nephew. The deed of gift made no reference to the farmer or the two-acre parcel. When the nephew had the land surveyed and discovered the facts, he notified the farmer in writing, "Your license to use the two-acre parcel has been terminated." The notice instructed the farmer to remove her facilities from the two-acre parcel immediately. The farmer refused the nephew's demand.

In an appropriate action between the nephew and the farmer to determine whether the farmer had a right to continue to use the two-acre parcel, the court ruled in favor of the farmer.

What is the most likely reason for the court's ruling?

(A) The investments and efforts by the farmer in reliance on the license estop the man, and now the nephew as the man's donee, from terminating the license.

Correct. In most jurisdictions, the farmer may acquire the unconditional right to use the land following the oral license, provided that the farmer expended money and labor in reliance on the license. The farmer has acquired what is known as an irrevocable license or an equitable easement.

(B) The nephew is merely a donee.

Incorrect. It does not matter if the nephew acquired title to the property as a donee or as a purchaser. The farmer, by her expenditure of labor and money in reliance on the oral license, has acquired an irrevocable license (also known as an equitable easement).

(C) The farmer has acquired an easement based on prior use.

Incorrect. The two parcels of land have never been in common ownership and therefore an easement based on prior use cannot be implied. The farmer, by her expenditure of labor and money in reliance on the oral license, has acquired an irrevocable license (also known as an equitable easement).

(D) The farmer received a license coupled with an interest.

Incorrect. The license granted to the farmer was not a license coupled with an interest. A license coupled with an interest permits a person who owns personal property on the land of another to enter the land to retrieve the personal property. The farmer, by her expenditure of labor and money in reliance on the oral license, has acquired an irrevocable license (also known as an equitable easement).

Question # 47 - Torts

Upon the recommendation of her child's pediatrician, a mother purchased a vaporizer for her child, who had been suffering from respiratory congestion. The vaporizer consisted of a gallon-size glass jar, which held water to be heated until it became steam, and a metal heating unit into which the jar fit. The jar was covered by a plastic cap with an opening to allow the steam to escape. At the time the vaporizer was manufactured and sold, there was no safer alternative design.

The booklet that accompanied the vaporizer read: "This product is safe, spillproof, and practically foolproof. It shuts off automatically when the water is gone." The booklet had a picture of a vaporizer sending steam over a baby's crib.

The mother used the vaporizer whenever the child was suffering from congestion. She placed the vaporizer on the floor near the child's bed.

One night, the child got out of bed to get a drink of water and tripped over the cord of the vaporizer as she crossed the room. The top of the vaporizer separated from the base, and boiling water from the jar spilled on the child when the vaporizer tipped over. The child suffered serious burns as a consequence.

The child's representative brought an action for damages against the manufacturer of the vaporizer. The manufacturer moved to dismiss after the representative presented the evidence above.

Should the manufacturer's motion be granted?

(A) No, because a jury could find that the manufacturer expressly represented that the vaporizer was spillproof.

Correct. The vaporizer may not have been "defective," in that there was no reasonable alternative design, but the express promise by the manufacturer that it was "safe" and "spillproof," especially when combined with the manufacturer's picture suggesting that it was safe to place the vaporizer near a child's bed, could be the basis of recovery on the ground of misrepresentation.

(B) No, because the vaporizer caused a serious injury to the child.

Incorrect. The fact that a product poses a danger to a user or a bystander will not support the manufacturer's liability in the absence of negligence, defect, or misrepresentation. The manufacturer's motion should not be granted, but it is because the express promise by the manufacturer that the vaporizer was "safe" and "spillproof," especially when combined with the manufacturer's picture suggesting that it was safe to place the vaporizer near a child's bed, could be the basis of recovery on the ground of misrepresentation.

(C) Yes, because it should have been obvious to the mother that the water in the jar would become boiling hot.

Incorrect. The mother could be found to have reasonably relied upon the manufacturer's express promise that the vaporizer was "safe" and "spillproof," especially when those words were combined with the manufacturer's picture suggesting that it was safe to place the vaporizer near a child's bed. The mother could have believed that the boiling water posed no danger if it could not be spilled. She would have an action against the manufacturer for misrepresentation.

(D) Yes, because there was no safer alternative design.

Incorrect. The fact finder may conclude that the vaporizer could not be found to be "defective" because there was no reasonable alternative design, but the manufacturer's express promise that the vaporizer was "safe" and "spillproof," combined with the manufacturer's picture suggesting that it was safe to place the vaporizer near a child's bed, could still be the basis of recovery on the ground of misrepresentation.

Question # 48 - Contracts

A buyer agreed in writing to purchase a car from a seller for $15,000, with the price to be paid on a specified date at the seller's showroom. The contract provided, and both parties intended, that time was of the essence. Before the specified date, however, the seller sold the car to a third party for $20,000. On the specified date, the buyer arrived at the showroom but brought only $10,000. When the seller did not appear at the showroom, the buyer called the seller and asked whether the seller would accept $10,000 for the car immediately and the remaining $5,000 in six weeks. The seller told the buyer that he had sold the car to the third party.

If the buyer sues the seller for breach of contract, will the buyer be likely to prevail?

(A) No, because the contractual obligations were discharged on the ground of impossibility.

Incorrect. While the seller's sale of the car to a third party rendered it impossible for the seller to sell the car to the buyer, such conduct does not meet the standard to establish impossibility as a legal defense for nonperformance. Similarly, the buyer's tender of less than the full payment does not, without more, establish a legal basis for impossibility. The dispositive issue here relates to the effect of neither party tendering performance on the date specified in the contract. Under UCC Article 2, a seller's tender of delivery of goods and a buyer's tender of payment are concurrent conditions of exchange. Therefore, the buyer and the seller were obligated to simultaneously tender their respective performances. Because neither party was prepared to tender performance at the time or in the manner stipulated in the contract, each party's performance obligation was discharged. Accordingly, neither the buyer nor the seller has a claim for breach of contract.

(B) No, because the buyer was not prepared to tender her performance on the specified date.

Correct. Even though the facts demonstrate that the seller repudiated the contract by selling the car to a third party, the seller did not end up breaching the contract. Under UCC Article 2, a seller's tender of delivery of goods and a buyer's tender of payment are concurrent conditions of exchange. Therefore, the buyer and the seller were obligated to simultaneously tender their respective performances. Because neither party was prepared to tender performance at the time or in the manner stipulated in the contract, each party's performance obligation was discharged. Accordingly, neither the buyer nor the seller has a claim for breach of contract.

(C) Yes, because the buyer's breach was not material.

Incorrect. UCC Article 2 adopts the perfect tender rule, rather than the material breach rule, as the generally applicable standard. The dispositive issue here relates to the effect of neither party tendering performance on the date specified in the contract. Under Article 2, a seller's tender of delivery of goods and a buyer's tender of payment are concurrent conditions of exchange. Therefore, the buyer and the seller were obligated to simultaneously tender their respective performances. Because neither party was prepared to tender performance at the time or in the manner stipulated in the contract, each party's performance obligation was discharged. Accordingly, neither the buyer nor the seller has a claim for breach of contract.

(D) Yes, because the seller anticipatorily repudiated the contract when he sold the car to the third party.

Incorrect. While the seller's sale of the car to a third party would seem to constitute an anticipatory repudiation, as it turned out, neither party was prepared to tender performance at the time or in the manner specified in the contract. UCC Article 2 provides that a seller's tender of delivery of goods and a buyer's tender of payment are concurrent conditions of exchange. Therefore, the buyer and the seller were obligated to simultaneously tender their respective performances. Because neither party was prepared to tender performance at the time or in the manner stipulated in the contract, each party's performance obligation was discharged. Accordingly, neither the buyer nor the seller has a claim for breach of contract.

Question # 49 - Criminal Law and Procedure

A state statute divides murder into degrees and defines murder in the first degree as murder committed willfully with premeditation and deliberation. The statute defines murder in the second degree as all other murder at common law and defines voluntary manslaughter as at common law.

A man hated one of his coworkers. Upon learning that the coworker was at a neighbor's house, the man grabbed his gun and went to the neighbor's house hoping to provoke the coworker into attacking him so that he could then shoot the coworker. After arriving at the house, the man insulted the coworker and bragged that he had had sexual relations with the coworker's wife two weeks earlier. This statement was not true, but it enraged the coworker, who grabbed a knife from the kitchen table and ran toward the man. The man then shot and killed the coworker.

What is the most serious homicide offense of which the man could properly be convicted?

(A) Murder in the first degree.

Correct. The killing was committed willfully with premeditation and deliberation. The killing cannot be justified as having been in self-defense, because the man was the clear aggressor who intentionally provoked the coworker so that he could shoot and kill him.

(B) Murder in the second degree.

Incorrect. Murder in the second degree is not the most serious homicide offense of which the man could properly be convicted. The man is guilty of first-degree murder, because he committed the killing willfully with premeditation and deliberation. The killing cannot be justified as having been in self-defense, because the man intentionally provoked the coworker so that he could shoot and kill him.

(C) Voluntary manslaughter, because he provoked the coworker.

Incorrect. Voluntary manslaughter is not the most serious homicide offense of which the man could properly be convicted, because he was not acting in the heat of passion when he killed the coworker. The man is guilty of first-degree murder, because he committed the killing willfully with premeditation and deliberation, and the killing cannot be justified as having been in self-defense.

(D) No form of criminal homicide, because he acted in self-defense.

Incorrect. The killing cannot be justified as having been in self-defense, because the man intentionally provoked the coworker so that he could shoot and kill him. The man is guilty of first-degree murder, because he committed the killing willfully with premeditation and deliberation.

Question # 50 - Evidence

A defendant is charged with robbing a bank. The prosecutor has supplied the court with information from accurate sources establishing that the bank is a federally insured institution and that this fact is not subject to reasonable dispute. The prosecutor asks the court to take judicial notice of this fact. The defendant objects.

How should the court proceed?

(A) The court must take judicial notice and instruct the jury that it is required to accept the judicially noticed fact as conclusive.

Incorrect. In criminal cases, the trial judge may not instruct the jury to accept a judicially noticed fact as conclusive. To do so would impermissibly limit the defendant's right to a jury trial. The court must take judicial notice of a fact if the court is supplied with the necessary information to indicate that the fact is not subject to reasonable dispute. However, Rule 201(f) provides that in a criminal case, "the court must instruct the jury that it may or may not accept the noticed fact as conclusive."

(B) The court must take judicial notice and instruct the jury that it may, but is not required to, accept the judicially noticed fact as conclusive.

Correct. The court must take judicial notice of a fact if the court is supplied with the necessary information to indicate that the fact is not subject to reasonable dispute. Rule 201(f) provides that in a criminal case, "the court must instruct the jury that it may or may not accept the noticed fact as conclusive."

(C) The court may refuse to take judicial notice, because judicial notice may not be taken of essential facts in a criminal case.

Incorrect. The court must take judicial notice of a fact if the court is supplied with the necessary information to indicate that the fact is not subject to reasonable dispute. Here the facts indicate that the court has been supplied with the necessary information. However, Rule 201(f) provides that in a criminal case, "the court must instruct the jury that it may or may not accept the noticed fact as conclusive."

(D) The court must refuse to take judicial notice, because whether a bank is federally insured would not be generally known within the court's jurisdiction.

Incorrect. Whether a bank is federally insured is a fact that would be generally known within the jurisdiction. Even if it were not, however, under Rule 201(b) judicial notice must be taken if the indisputability of a fact "can be accurately and readily determined from sources whose accuracy cannot be questioned." The facts here so provide. However, Rule 201(f) provides that in a criminal case, "the court must instruct the jury that it may or may not accept the noticed fact as conclusive."

Question # 51 - Evidence

The beneficiary of a decedent's life insurance policy has sued the life insurance company for the proceeds of the policy. At issue is the date when the decedent first experienced the heart problems that led to his death. The decedent's primary care physician has testified at trial that the decedent had a routine checkup on February 15. The physician then identifies a photocopy of a questionnaire completed by the decedent on that date in which the decedent wrote: "Yesterday afternoon I broke into a big sweat and my chest hurt for a while." The beneficiary now offers the photocopy in evidence.

Should the court admit the photocopy?

(A) No, because the original questionnaire has not been shown to be unavailable.

Incorrect. This answer refers to the best evidence rule. Under the best evidence rule, a copy of a document is as admissible as the original unless a genuine question is raised about the authenticity of the original or the circumstances make it unfair to admit the copy. No such question or circumstances are present here. The photocopy should be admitted as a statement for the purpose of obtaining medical treatment.

(B) No, because the statement related to past rather than present symptoms.

Incorrect. Statements of medical history can be admitted under the hearsay exception in Rule 803(4) if they are pertinent to diagnosis or treatment, regardless of whether the statements relate to past or present symptoms. The decedent's statement clearly qualifies under this hearsay exception.

(C) Yes, as a business record.

Incorrect. For a recorded statement to be admissible as a business record under Rule 803(6), the business record must be kept in the course of a regularly conducted activity and it must be a regular practice of the business to make the record. Here, the record was made by the decedent, not by the physician, and there is no indication that the decedent regularly prepared such records. However, the photocopy should be admitted as a statement for the purpose of obtaining medical treatment.

(D) Yes, as a statement for the purpose of obtaining medical treatment.

Correct. The decedent's statement of his medical history was made for the purpose of diagnosis and treatment, and it is clearly pertinent to the physician's diagnosis and treatment. Therefore, it is admissible under Rule 803(4).

Question # 52 - Real Property

Two friends planned to incorporate a business together and agreed that they would own all of the corporation's stock in equal proportion.

A businesswoman conveyed land by a warranty deed to "the corporation and its successors and assigns." The deed was recorded.

Thereafter, the friends had a disagreement. No papers were ever filed to incorporate the business. There is no applicable statute.

Who owns the land?

(A) The businesswoman, because the deed was a warranty deed.

Incorrect. The businesswoman owns the land, but she does so because the deed was void. To be valid, a deed must be properly executed and delivered. A deed to a nonexistent grantee, such as a corporation that has not yet been legally formed, is void. It does not matter whether the deed is a warranty, quitclaim, or special warranty deed. At the time the businesswoman attempted to convey the land to the corporation, the corporation had not yet been legally formed, so the deed was void.

(B) The businesswoman, because the deed was void.

Correct. To be valid, a deed must be properly executed and delivered. A deed to a nonexistent grantee, such as a corporation that has not yet been legally formed, is void. At the time the businesswoman attempted to convey the land to the corporation, the corporation had not yet been legally formed, so the deed was void.

(C) The two friends as tenants in common, because they intended to own the corporation's stock in equal proportion.

Incorrect. To be valid, a deed must be properly executed and delivered. A deed to a nonexistent grantee, such as a corporation that has not yet been legally formed, is void and thus conveys no title. It is irrelevant that the two friends intended to own the corporation's stock in equal proportion.

(D) The two friends as tenants in common, because they were the intended sole shareholders.

Incorrect. To be valid, a deed must be properly executed and delivered. A deed to a nonexistent grantee, such as a corporation that has not yet been legally formed, is void and thus conveys no title. It is irrelevant that the two friends intended to be the sole shareholders. At the time the businesswoman attempted to convey the land to the corporation, the corporation had not yet been legally formed, so the deed was void.

Question # 53 - Constitutional Law

A state law imposed substantial regulations on insurance companies operating within the state with respect to their rates, cash reserves, and financial practices.

A privately owned insurance company operating within the state advertised that it wanted to hire a new data processor. After reviewing applications for that position, the company hired a woman who appeared to be well qualified. The company refused to consider the application of a man who was better qualified than the woman, because he was known to have radical political views.

The man sued the company, alleging only a violation of his federal constitutional right to freedom of expression. Is the man likely to prevail?

(A) No, because hiring decisions are wholly discretionary and thus are not governed by the First Amendment.

Incorrect. The First Amendment applies to discretionary decisions of governments and government officials. The man is unlikely to prevail, but it is because the First and Fourteenth Amendments generally apply only to the actions of governments and government officials, not to the actions of privately owned companies such as the insurance company.

(B) No, because the company is not subject to the provisions of the First and Fourteenth Amendments.

Correct. The man is unlikely to prevail, because the First and Fourteenth Amendments generally apply only to the actions of governments and government officials, not to the actions of privately owned companies such as the insurance company.

(C) Yes, because the company is affected with a public interest.

Incorrect. The question whether the First and Fourteenth Amendments apply to the actions of a privately owned company does not turn on whether the company is affected with a public interest. The man is unlikely to prevail, because the First and Fourteenth Amendments generally apply only to the actions of governments and government officials, not to the actions of privately owned companies such as the insurance company.

(D) Yes, because the company is substantially regulated by the state, and thus its employment decisions may fairly be attributed to the state.

Incorrect. The fact that the company is substantially regulated by the state does not make the company's actions subject to the First and Fourteenth Amendments. The man is unlikely to prevail, because the First and Fourteenth Amendments generally apply only to the actions of governments and government officials, not to the actions of privately owned companies such as the insurance company.

Question # 54 - Real Property

A landlord leased a building to a tenant for a term of six years. The lease complied with the statute of frauds and was not recorded. During the lease term, the tenant sent an email to the landlord that stated: "I hereby offer to purchase for $250,000 the building that I am now occupying under a six-year lease with you." The tenant's name was placed below the word "signed" on the message.

In response, the landlord emailed the tenant: "That's fine. We'll close in 60 days." The landlord's name was placed below the word "signed" on the reply message.

Sixty days later, the landlord refused to tender the deed to the building when the tenant tendered the $250,000 purchase price. The tenant has sued for specific performance.

Who is likely to prevail?

(A) The landlord, because formation of an enforceable contract to convey the building could not occur until after the lease term expired.

Incorrect. A contract to convey the building could be made during the lease term or thereafter. The email exchange satisfied the statute of frauds, the contract was valid, and the tenant is entitled to specific performance.

(B) The landlord, because the landlord's email response did not contain a sufficient signature under the statute of frauds.

Incorrect. The statute of frauds does require a signature by the party against whom enforcement is sought. However, courts are liberal regarding the nature of a signature; it need only reflect an intent to authenticate the writing. Both the tenant's and the landlord's names were placed below the word "signed," which adequately reflected their desire to be bound. The other requirements of the statute of frauds were also met: the writings identified the parties and the property, expressed an intent to buy and sell, and contained a price term.

(C) The tenant, because the email messages constitute an insufficient attornment of the lease.

Incorrect. Attornment is not an issue in this case, because it is the tenant who wants to purchase the property. The tenant is likely to prevail, but it is because there was a valid contract of sale. The exchange of emails satisfies the statute of frauds, because the writings identified the parties and the property, expressed an intent to buy and sell, and contained a price term and adequate signatures.

(D) The tenant, because the email messages constitute a sufficient memorandum under the statute of frauds.

Correct. The statute of frauds requires a contract for the sale of land to identify the parties, contain a description of the land, evidence an intent to buy and sell, recite (usually) a price term, and be signed by the party against whom enforcement is sought. The email messages here fulfill those requirements. Courts are liberal regarding the nature of a signature; it need only reflect an intent to authenticate the writing. Both the tenant's and the landlord's names were placed below the word "signed," which adequately reflected their desire to be bound.

Question # 55 - Torts

A man was admitted to a hospital after complaining of persistent severe headaches. While he was there, hospital staff failed to diagnose his condition, and he was discharged. Two days later, the man died of a massive brain hemorrhage due to a congenital defect in an artery.

The man's wife has brought a wrongful death action against the hospital. The wife offers expert testimony that the man would have had a "reasonable chance" (not greater than 50%) of surviving the hemorrhage if he had been given appropriate medical care at the hospital.

In what type of jurisdiction would the wife's suit most likely be successful?

(A) A jurisdiction that applies traditional common law rules concerning burden of proof.

Incorrect. If traditional common law rules concerning burden of proof were applied, the wife would be required to prove that reasonable action on the part of the hospital (presumably a correct diagnosis) would, more likely than not, have led to the man's survival. Here, however, the wife cannot establish that the chances of the man's survival would have been greater than 50% even if he had been given appropriate medical care. Therefore, the wife could not carry her burden of proof on the issue of cause in fact in such a jurisdiction.

(B) A jurisdiction that allows recovery based on strict liability.

Incorrect. Cause in fact is a necessary element of a plaintiff's case in strict liability as well as in negligence. Under either theory, the wife must establish that reasonable action on the part of the hospital (presumably a correct diagnosis) would, more likely than not, have led to the man's survival. Here, however, the wife cannot establish that the chances of the man's survival were greater than 50% even if he had been given appropriate medical care. Therefore, the wife could not carry her burden of proof on the issue of cause in fact in such a jurisdiction.

(C) A jurisdiction that allows recovery for the loss of the chance of survival.

Correct. Jurisdictions that allow recovery for the loss of the chance of survival have created an exception to the traditional common law rules for establishing cause in fact. Under the traditional rules, the wife would be required to prove that reasonable action on the part of the hospital (presumably a correct diagnosis) would, more likely than not, have led to the man's survival. Here, the wife cannot establish that the chances of the man's survival would have been greater than 50% even if he had been given appropriate medical care. A jurisdiction that allows recovery for loss of the chance of survival, however, would allow the wife to recover for the reduction in her husband's chance of surviving that was caused by the failure to properly diagnose.

(D) A jurisdiction that recognizes loss of spousal consortium.

Incorrect. Cause in fact is a necessary element of a plaintiff's case for loss of spousal consortium, as well as in cases in which a plaintiff is suing for personal injury. In a loss of consortium action, the wife must establish that the hospital's negligence was the cause of her husband's death. Traditional rules of proof regarding causation would require that the wife prove that reasonable action on the part of the hospital (presumably a correct diagnosis) would, more likely than not, have led to her husband's survival. Here, the wife cannot establish that the chances of her husband's survival would have been greater than 50% even if he had been given appropriate medical care. Therefore, the wife could not carry her burden of proof on the issue of cause in fact in such a jurisdiction and she could not recover for loss of spousal consortium.

Question # 56 - Criminal Law and Procedure

A wife decided to kill her husband because she was tired of his infidelity. She managed to obtain some cyanide, a deadly poison. One evening, she poured wine laced with the cyanide into a glass, handed it to her husband, and proposed a loving toast. The husband was so pleased with the toast that he set the glass of wine down on a table, grabbed his wife, and kissed her passionately. After the kiss, the wife changed her mind about killing the husband. She hid the glass of wine behind a lamp on the table, planning to leave it for the maid to clean up. The husband did not drink the wine.

The maid found the glass of wine while cleaning the next day. Rather than throw the wine away, the maid drank it. Shortly thereafter, she fell into a coma and died from cyanide poisoning.

In a common law jurisdiction, of what crime(s), if any, could the wife be found guilty?

(A) Attempted murder of the husband and murder or manslaughter of the maid.

Correct. As to the husband, the wife intended to murder him and took a substantial step to carry out that murder; the husband would have been killed had he drunk the wine. As to the maid, a trier of fact could view the wife's conduct as depraved-heart recklessness (which would make her guilty of murder) or at the very least as criminal negligence (which would make her guilty of manslaughter).

(B) Only attempted murder of the husband.

Incorrect. The woman could be found guilty of attempted murder of the husband, because she intended to murder him and took a substantial step to carry out that murder; the husband would have been killed had he drunk the wine. However, the wife could also be found guilty of murder or manslaughter of the maid. As to the maid, a trier of fact could view the wife's conduct as depraved-heart recklessness (which would make her guilty of murder) or at the very least as criminal negligence (which would make her guilty of manslaughter).

(C) Only murder or manslaughter of the maid.

Incorrect. The wife could be found guilty of murder or manslaughter of the maid, because a trier of fact could view the wife's conduct as depraved-heart recklessness (which would make her guilty of murder) or at the very least as criminal negligence (which would make her guilty of manslaughter). However, the wife could also be found guilty of attempted murder of the husband. As to the husband, she intended to murder him and took a substantial step to carry out that murder; the husband would have been killed had he drunk the wine.

(D) No crime.

Incorrect. The wife could be found guilty of attempted murder of the husband and murder or manslaughter of the maid. As to the husband, the wife intended to murder him and took a substantial step to carry out that murder; the husband would have been killed had he drunk the wine. As to the maid, a trier of fact could view the wife's conduct as depraved-heart recklessness (which would make her guilty of murder) or at the very least as criminal negligence (which would make her guilty of manslaughter).

Question # 57 - Contracts

A mill and a bakery entered into a written contract that obligated the mill to deliver to the bakery 1,000 pounds of flour every Monday for 26 weeks at a specified price per pound. The mill delivered the proper quantity of flour in a timely manner for the first 15 weeks. However, the 16th delivery was tendered on a Tuesday, and amounted to only 800 pounds. The mill told the bakery that the 200-pound shortage would be made up on the delivery due the following Monday. The late delivery and the 200-pound shortage will not significantly disrupt the bakery's operations.

How may the bakery legally respond to the nonconforming tender?

(A) Accept the 800 pounds tendered, but notify the mill that the bakery will cancel the contract if the exact amount is not delivered on the following Monday.

Incorrect. Because the contract authorizes the delivery of flour in separate lots to be separately accepted, the parties entered into an installment contract. UCC § 2-612 adopts a "substantial impairment" standard for determining whether a buyer can reject a particular installment or cancel the entire contract. A buyer can reject an installment if a nonconformity substantially impairs that installment and the nonconformity cannot be cured. A buyer can cancel the contract only when the nonconformity with respect to one or more installments substantially impairs the value of the whole contract. Here, the mill's tender of less than the contracted-for quantity did not amount to a nonconformity that substantially impaired the value of either the 16th installment or the whole contract. The mill's proposed cure, the delivery of the remaining 200 pounds on the following Monday, is sufficient given that the late delivery and the shortage will not significantly disrupt the bakery's business. Accordingly, not only must the bakery accept the delivery of the tendered 800 pounds of flour, it also must accept the remaining 200 pounds that the mill proposes to deliver on the following Monday.

(B) Accept the 800 pounds tendered, but notify the mill that the bakery will deduct from the price any damages for losses due to the nonconforming tender.

Correct. Because the contract authorizes the delivery of flour in separate lots to be separately accepted, the parties entered into an installment contract. UCC § 2-612 adopts a "substantial impairment" standard for determining whether a buyer can reject a particular installment or cancel the entire contract. A buyer can reject an installment if a nonconformity substantially impairs that installment and the nonconformity cannot be cured. Here the mill's tender of less than the contracted-for quantity did not amount to a nonconformity that substantially impaired either the value of the 16th installment or the whole contract. The mill's proposed cure, the delivery of the remaining 200 pounds on the following Monday, is sufficient given that the late delivery and the shortage will not significantly disrupt the bakery's business. Accordingly, the bakery must accept the delivery of the tendered 800 pounds of flour but may deduct from the price any damages for losses resulting from the late delivery.

(C) Reject the 800 pounds tendered, but notify the mill that the bakery will accept delivery the following Monday if it is conforming.

Incorrect. Because the contract authorizes the delivery of flour in separate lots to be separately accepted, the parties entered into an installment contract. UCC § 2-612 adopts a "substantial impairment" standard for determining whether a buyer can reject a particular installment or cancel the entire contract. A buyer can reject an installment if a nonconformity substantially impairs that installment and the nonconformity cannot be cured. Here the mill's tender of less than the contracted-for quantity did not amount to a nonconformity that substantially impaired either the value of the 16th installment or the whole contract. The mill's proposed cure, the delivery of the remaining 200 pounds on the following Monday, is sufficient given that the late delivery and the shortage will not significantly disrupt the bakery's business. Accordingly, not only must the bakery accept the delivery of the tendered 800 pounds of flour, it also must accept the remaining 200 pounds that the mill proposes to deliver on the following Monday.

(D) Reject the 800 pounds tendered, and notify the mill that the bakery is canceling the contract.

Incorrect. Because the contract authorizes the delivery of flour in separate lots to be separately accepted, the parties entered into an installment contract. UCC § 2-612 adopts a "substantial impairment" standard for determining whether a buyer can reject a particular installment or cancel the entire contract. A buyer can reject an installment if a nonconformity substantially impairs that installment and the nonconformity cannot be cured. Additionally, a buyer can cancel the contract only when the nonconformity with respect to one or more installments substantially impairs the value of the whole contract. Here, the mill's tender of less than the contracted-for quantity did not amount to a nonconformity that substantially impaired the value of the 16th installment or the whole contract. The mill's proposed cure, the delivery of the remaining 200 pounds on the following Monday, is sufficient given that the late delivery and the shortage will not significantly disrupt the bakery's business. Accordingly, the buyer has no right to reject the tender or to cancel the contract.

Question # 58 - Evidence

A defendant is charged with mail fraud. At trial, the defendant has not taken the witness stand, but he has called a witness who has testified that the defendant has a reputation for honesty. On cross-examination, the prosecutor seeks to ask the witness, "Didn't you hear that two years ago the defendant was arrested for embezzlement?"

Should the court permit the question?

(A) No, because the defendant has not testified and therefore has not put his character at issue.

Incorrect. When a defendant calls a character witness, the prosecutor is permitted to test the character witness's knowledge of the defendant. The fact that the defendant has not put his character at issue is irrelevant.

(B) No, because the incident was an arrest, not a conviction.

Incorrect. For purposes of testing the witness's knowledge of the defendant's reputation for honesty, the bad act need not have resulted in a conviction. An arrest is sufficient to have an impact on the community's view of the defendant's honesty.

(C) Yes, because it seeks to impeach the credibility of the witness.

Correct. The witness has testified that she knows about the defendant's reputation. The prosecutor has the right to test the basis and adequacy of that knowledge, as well as the nature of the community itself. If the witness answers that she had not heard about the arrest, that admission could indicate that she is not very knowledgeable about the defendant's reputation in the community, because such an arrest would likely have a negative effect on that reputation. If the witness says that she had heard about the arrest, a negative inference could be raised about the community itself and its view of what it is to be an honest person.

(D) Yes, because the earlier arrest for a crime of dishonesty makes the defendant's guilt of the mail fraud more likely.

Incorrect. The prosecutor is not allowed to use a bad act to show that the defendant has a propensity to commit a similar bad act. Rule 404 limits the use of character evidence to prove conduct in accordance with a character trait.

Question # 59 - Constitutional Law

In order to foster an environment conducive to learning, a school board enacted a dress code that prohibited all public high school students from wearing in school shorts cut above the knee. Because female students at the school considered it unfashionable to wear shorts cut at or below the knee, they no longer wore shorts to school. On the other hand, male students at the school regularly wore shorts cut at or below the knee because they considered such shorts to be fashionable.

Female students sued to challenge the constitutionality of the dress code on the ground that it denied them the equal protection of the laws.

Should the court uphold the dress code?

(A) No, because the dress code is not necessary to further a compelling state interest.

Incorrect. The court should uphold the dress code, because the code is rationally related to the state's legitimate interest in fostering a proper educational environment. The dress code should not trigger heightened judicial scrutiny, because there are no facts to suggest that the purpose of the code is to discriminate against female students.

(B) No, because the dress code is not substantially related to an important state interest.

Incorrect. The court should uphold the dress code, because the code is rationally related to the state's legitimate interest in fostering a proper educational environment. The dress code should not trigger heightened judicial scrutiny, because there are no facts to suggest that the purpose of the code is to discriminate against female students.

(C) Yes, because the dress code is narrowly tailored to further an important state interest.

Incorrect. While the court should uphold the dress code, it should do so because the code is rationally related to the state's legitimate interest in fostering a proper educational environment. The dress code should not trigger heightened judicial scrutiny, because there are no facts to suggest that the purpose of the code is to discriminate against female students.

(D) Yes, because the dress code is rationally related to a legitimate state interest.

Correct. The court should uphold the dress code, because the code is rationally related to the state's legitimate interest in fostering a proper educational environment. The dress code should not trigger heightened judicial scrutiny, because there are no facts to suggest that the purpose of the code is to discriminate against female students.

Question # 60 - Torts

A mother purchased an expensive television from an appliance store for her adult son. Two years after the purchase, a fire started in the son's living room in the middle of the night. The fire department concluded that the fire had started in the television. No other facts are known.

The son sued the appliance store for negligence. The store has moved for summary judgment. Should the court grant the store's motion?

(A) No, because televisions do not catch fire in the absence of negligence.

Incorrect. Even if it were true that televisions do not catch fire in the absence of negligence, the fact that this television did is insufficient to establish that the store acted negligently. This is not an appropriate case for res ipsa loquitur, because the manufacturer, rather than the store, may have been negligent or the negligence may have occurred after the sale (for example, during a repair or while the television was being used by the son). Because the son cannot establish the store's negligence, the court should grant the store's motion.

(B) No, because the store sold the television.

Incorrect. The son sued the store for negligence, not for strict liability. To recover on a negligence claim, the son must establish that the store itself was negligent. If the son had sued under strict liability, he would have had to establish that the television was defective at the time it was sold to his mother. Because the son cannot establish the store's negligence, the court should grant the store's motion.

(C) Yes, because the son is not in privity with the store.

Incorrect. A lack of privity is not a barrier to negligence claims based on malfunctioning products. Anyone foreseeably put at risk by a defective product and actually injured by the product's defective condition can sue for negligence. The court should grant the store's motion, but it is because the son cannot establish that the store was the negligent actor.

(D) Yes, because there is no evidence of negligence on the part of the store.

Correct. The son is suing in negligence, not in strict liability. To make out a prima facie case in negligence, the son must introduce evidence that the store was negligent. However, the son has not pointed to any negligent action or omission by the store. This is not an appropriate case for res ipsa loquitur, because the manufacturer, rather than the store, may have been negligent or the negligence may have occurred after the sale (for example, during a repair or while the television was being used by the son).

Question # 61 - Contracts

A buyer agreed to purchase a seller's house for $250,000 "on condition that the buyer obtain mortgage financing within 30 days." Thirty days later, the buyer told the seller that the buyer would not purchase the house because the buyer had not obtained mortgage financing. The seller asked the buyer where the buyer had tried to obtain mortgage financing, and the buyer responded, "I was busy and didn't have time to seek mortgage financing."

If the seller sues the buyer for breach of contract, is the court likely to find the buyer in breach?

(A) No, because the buyer's performance was subject to a condition that did not occur.

Incorrect. A performance that is subject to an express condition cannot become due unless the condition occurs or its non-occurrence is excused. However, the duty of good faith, which is implied in every contract, imposed an obligation on the buyer to make reasonable efforts to secure mortgage financing. Because the buyer made no such efforts, the non-occurrence of the condition to the buyer's obligation to purchase the house--the buyer's securing financing--was excused. Accordingly, the court is likely to find that the buyer is in breach.

(B) No, because the promise was illusory since the buyer was not obligated to do anything.

Incorrect. The duty of good faith, which is implied in every contract, imposed an obligation on the buyer to make reasonable efforts to secure mortgage financing. Accordingly, the buyer's promise to secure financing was not illusory. A performance that is subject to an express condition cannot become due unless the condition occurs or its non-occurrence is excused. In this case, the non-occurrence of the condition to the buyer's obligation to perform was excused, because the buyer failed to make reasonable efforts to secure mortgage financing. Therefore, the court is likely to find that the buyer is in breach.

(C) Yes, because a promise was implied that the buyer had to make reasonable efforts to obtain mortgage financing.

Correct. A performance that is subject to an express condition cannot become due unless the condition occurs or its non-occurrence is excused. However, the duty of good faith, which is implied in every contract, imposed an obligation on the buyer to make reasonable efforts to secure mortgage financing. Because the buyer made no such efforts, the non-occurrence of the condition to the buyer's obligation to purchase the house--the buyer's securing financing--was excused. Accordingly, the court is likely to find that the buyer is in breach.

(D) Yes, because a reasonable interpretation of the agreement is that the buyer had an obligation to purchase the house for $250,000 in 30 days.

Incorrect. The contract explicitly stated that the buyer's obligation to perform was expressly conditioned on the buyer obtaining mortgage financing. A performance that is subject to an express condition cannot become due unless the condition occurs or its non-occurrence is excused. However, the duty of good faith, which is implied in every contract, imposed an obligation on the buyer to make reasonable efforts to secure mortgage financing. Because the buyer made no such efforts, the non-occurrence of the condition to the buyer's obligation to purchase the house--the buyer's securing financing--was excused. Accordingly, the court is likely to find that the buyer is in breach.

Question # 62 - Criminal Law and Procedure

In a crowded football stadium, a man saw a wallet fall out of a spectator's purse. The man picked up the wallet and found that it contained $100 in cash. Thinking that he could use the money and seeing no one watching, the man put the wallet in the pocket of his coat. Just then, the spectator approached the man and asked if he had seen a missing wallet. The man said no and went home with the wallet.

Of what crime, if any, is the man guilty?

(A) Embezzlement.

Incorrect. The initial taking of the wallet was a trespass, because the man knew that the wallet belonged to the spectator and he intended to convert the wallet to his own use in permanent deprivation of the spectator's right. Accordingly, and because the spectator never entrusted the man with the wallet, the man is guilty of larceny rather than embezzlement.

(B) False pretenses.

Incorrect. The initial taking of the wallet was a trespass, because the man knew that the wallet belonged to the spectator and he intended to convert the wallet to his own use in permanent deprivation of the spectator's right. Accordingly, and because the man never obtained title to the wallet, he is guilty of larceny rather than false pretenses.

(C) Larceny.

Correct. The initial taking of the wallet was a trespass, because the man knew that the wallet belonged to the spectator and he intended to convert the wallet to his own use in permanent deprivation of the spectator's right. Accordingly, the man is guilty of larceny.

(D) No crime.

Incorrect. The initial taking of the wallet was a trespass, because the man knew that the wallet belonged to the spectator and he intended to convert the wallet to his own use in permanent deprivation of the spectator's right. Accordingly, the man is guilty of larceny.

Question # 63 - Constitutional Law

A company owned a large tract of land that contained coal deposits that the company intended to mine. The company acquired mining equipment and began to plan its mining operations. Just as the company was about to begin mining, Congress enacted a statute that imposed a number of new environmental regulations and land-reclamation requirements on all mining operations within the United States. The statute made the company's planned mining operations economically infeasible. As a result, the company sold the tract of land to a farmer. While the sale price allowed the company to recover its original investment in the land, it did not cover the additional cost of the mining equipment the company had purchased or the profits it had expected to earn from its mining operations on the land.

In an action filed against the appropriate federal official, the company claims that the statute effected a taking of its property for which it is entitled to just compensation in an amount equal to the cost of the mining equipment it purchased and the profits it expected to earn from its mining operations on the land.

Which of the following is the most appropriate result in the action?

(A) The company should prevail on its claims for the cost of the mining equipment and for its lost profits.

Incorrect. The company should not prevail on any aspect of its claim for just compensation. The statute did not effect a taking of the company's land or of the mining equipment, because the new regulations did not deny all economically viable use of the land. The company recovered its original investment in the land by selling it to the farmer, and the land is economically viable as farmland. The company may sell the mining equipment or use it for mining on other land. Finally, the profits the company expected to earn from its mining operations do not constitute a property interest subject to the takings clause.

(B) The company should prevail on its claim for the cost of the mining equipment, but not for its lost profits.

Incorrect. The company should not prevail on any aspect of its claim for just compensation. The statute did not effect a taking of the company's land or of the mining equipment, because the new regulations did not deny all economically viable use of the land. The company recovered its original investment in the land by selling it to the farmer, and the land is economically viable as farmland. The company may sell the mining equipment or use it for mining on other land. Finally, the profits the company expected to earn from its mining operations do not constitute a property interest subject to the takings clause.

(C) The company should prevail on its claim for lost profits, but not for the cost of the mining equipment.

Incorrect. The company should not prevail on any aspect of its claim for just compensation. The statute did not effect a taking of the company's land or of the mining equipment, because the new regulations did not deny all economically viable use of the land. The company recovered its original investment in the land by selling it to the farmer, and the land is economically viable as farmland. The company may sell the mining equipment or use it for mining on other land. Finally, the profits the company expected to earn from its mining operations do not constitute a property interest subject to the takings clause.

(D) The company should not prevail on its claim for the cost of the mining equipment or for its lost profits.

Correct. The company should not prevail on any aspect of its claim for just compensation. The statute did not effect a taking of the company's land or of the mining equipment, because the new regulations did not deny all economically viable use of the land. The company recovered its original investment in the land by selling it to the farmer, and the land is economically viable as farmland. The company may sell the mining equipment or use it for mining on other land. Finally, the profits the company expected to earn from its mining operations do not constitute a property interest subject to the takings clause.

Question # 64 - Real Property

A tenant leased a commercial property from a landlord for a 12-year term. The property included a large store and a parking lot. At the start of the lease period, the tenant took possession and with the landlord's oral consent installed counters, display cases, shelving, and special lighting. Both parties complied with all lease terms.

The lease is set to expire next month. Two weeks ago, when the landlord contacted the tenant about a possible lease renewal, she learned that the tenant had decided not to renew the lease, and that the tenant planned to remove all of the above-listed items on or before the lease termination date. The landlord claimed that all the items had become part of the real estate and had to remain on the premises. The tenant asserted his right and intention to remove all the items.

Both the lease and the statutes of the jurisdiction are silent on the matter in dispute. At the time the landlord consented and the tenant installed the items, nothing was said about the tenant's right to retain or remove the items.

The landlord has sued the tenant to enjoin his removal of the items. How is the court likely to rule?

(A) For the landlord, because the items have become part of the landlord's real estate.

Incorrect. This is a commercial lease, and the tenant has been using the items in his business. Therefore, even if the items have become fixtures, they are trade fixtures, which may be removed by the tenant before the end of the lease term unless very substantial damage would be done by the removal. It is unlikely that the removal of these items will cause substantial damage; if so, however, the tenant must either restore the premises or pay the cost of restoration.

(B) For the landlord as to items bolted or otherwise attached to the premises, and for the tenant as to items not attached to the premises other than by weight.

Incorrect. This is a commercial lease, and the tenant has been using the items in his business. Therefore, even if the items have become fixtures, they are trade fixtures, which may be removed by the tenant before the end of the lease term unless very substantial damage would be done by the removal. It is unlikely that the removal of these items will cause substantial damage; if so, however, the tenant must either restore the premises or pay the cost of restoration. Whether an item is bolted or otherwise attached to the premises is only a factor in determining if it is a fixture.

(C) For the tenant, provided that the tenant reasonably restores the premises to the prior condition or pays for the cost of restoration.

Correct. This is a commercial lease, and the tenant has been using the items in his business. Therefore, the items are trade fixtures, and the tenant may remove them before the end of the lease term unless very substantial damage would be done by the removal. It is unlikely that the removal of these items will cause substantial damage; if so, however, the tenant must either restore the premises or pay the cost of restoration.

(D) For the tenant, because all of the items may be removed as trade fixtures without any obligation to restore the premises.

Incorrect. The tenant may be obligated to restore the premises. This is a commercial lease, and the tenant has been using the items in his business. Therefore, the items are trade fixtures, and the tenant may remove them before the end of the lease term unless very substantial damage would be done by the removal. It is unlikely that the removal of these items will cause substantial damage; if so, however, the tenant must either restore the premises or pay the cost of restoration.

Question # 65 - Evidence

At a woman's trial for bank robbery, the prosecutor has called a private security guard for the bank who has testified, without objection, that while he was on a coffee break, the woman's brother rushed up to him and said, "Come quickly! My sister is robbing the bank!" The woman now seeks to call a witness to testify that the brother later told the witness, "I got my sister into trouble by telling a security guard that she was robbing the bank, but now I realize I was mistaken." The brother is unavailable to testify.

Is the witness's testimony admissible?

(A) No, because the brother will be afforded no opportunity to explain or deny the later statement.

Incorrect. What is being offered here is an inconsistent statement of a hearsay declarant. The goal is to impeach that declarant's credibility. The brother's original statement would have been admitted as an excited utterance under the Rule 803(2) hearsay exception. While it is ordinarily true that a witness impeached with a prior inconsistent statement must be given an opportunity to explain or deny the statement, that opportunity is not available when a hearsay declarant is not produced at trial. Rule 806 provides that the ordinary requirement of a "fair opportunity to explain or deny" is not applicable to hearsay declarants who are being impeached with prior inconsistent statements.

(B) No, because the prosecutor will be afforded no opportunity to confront the brother.

Incorrect. A prosecutor has no right to confrontation; only a criminal defendant has that right. In any case, here it is the prosecutor who offered the statement that the brother made at the time of the crime, so the prosecutor cannot argue a lack of opportunity to confront the brother.

(C) Yes, because it is substantive proof that the woman did not rob the bank.

Incorrect. The statement later made by the brother was an out-of-court statement, and if offered for its truth, it is hearsay. There is no applicable hearsay exception.

(D) Yes, but only as an inconsistent statement to impeach the brother's credibility.

Correct. It is ordinarily true that a witness impeached with a prior inconsistent statement must be given an opportunity to explain or deny the statement. That is not possible, however, when a hearsay declarant is not produced at trial. Therefore Rule 806 provides that the ordinary requirement of a "fair opportunity to explain or deny" is not applicable to hearsay declarants who are being impeached with prior inconsistent statements. The inconsistent statement is probative of the brother's credibility, and Rule 806 permits such impeachment.

Question # 66 - Contracts

A producer contracted to pay an inexperienced performer a specified salary to act in a small role in a play the producer was taking on a six-week road tour. The contract was for the duration of the tour. On the third day of the tour, the performer was hospitalized with a stomach disorder. The producer replaced her in the cast with an experienced actor. One week later, the performer recovered, but the producer refused to allow her to resume her original role for the remainder of the tour.

In an action by the performer against the producer for breach of contract, which of the following, if proved, would be the producer's best defense?

(A) The actor, by general acclaim, was much better in the role than the performer had been.

Incorrect. After the performer became ill, the temporary impracticability doctrine excused the performer's contractual obligation and also gave the producer the right to suspend his performance obligation during the period that the performer's illness prevented her from acting. The critical issue here is whether the producer also had the right to cancel the contract. Circumstances that would give the producer the right to cancel include the degree of uncertainty relating to the nature and duration of the performer's illness and the extent to which a delay in making substitute arrangements would have prevented the producer from continuing the tour. The relative quality of the actor's performance is not a circumstance that would give the producer the right to cancel the performer's contract.

(B) The actor was the only replacement the producer could find, and the actor would accept nothing less than a contract for the remainder of the six-week tour.

Correct. After the performer became ill, the temporary impracticability doctrine excused the performer's contractual obligation and also gave the producer the right to suspend his performance obligation during the period that the performer's illness prevented her from acting. The critical issue here is whether the producer also had the right to cancel the contract. Circumstances that would give the producer the right to cancel the contract include the degree of uncertainty relating to the nature and duration of the performer's illness and the extent to which a delay in making substitute arrangements would have prevented the producer from continuing the tour. The unwillingness of the actor, the only replacement available, to take a contract for less than the remainder of the six-week tour and the uncertainty surrounding when the performer might return to work would have discharged the producer's performance obligations and justified his cancellation of the contract with the performer.

(C) The producer offered to employ the performer as the actor's understudy for the remainder of the six-week tour at the performer's original salary, but the performer declined.

Incorrect. After the performer became ill, the temporary impracticability doctrine excused the performer's contractual obligation and also gave the producer the right to suspend his performance obligation during the period that the performer's illness prevented her from acting. The critical issue here is whether the producer also had the right to cancel the contract. Circumstances that would give the producer the right to cancel include the degree of uncertainty relating to the nature and duration of the performer's illness and the extent to which a delay in making substitute arrangements would have prevented the producer from continuing the tour. Because the producer had the right to cancel the contract, his action in offering the performer a job as understudy is irrelevant.

(D) Both the producer and the performer knew that a year earlier the performer had been incapacitated for a short period of time by the same kind of stomach disorder.

Incorrect. After the performer became ill, the temporary impracticability doctrine excused the performer's contractual obligation and also gave the producer the right to suspend his performance obligation during the period that the performer's illness prevented her from acting. The critical issue here is whether the producer also had the right to cancel the contract. Circumstances that would give the producer the right to cancel include the degree of uncertainty relating to the nature and duration of the performer's illness and the extent to which a delay in making substitute arrangements would have prevented the producer from continuing the tour. A history of having been ill for a short time would not justify the producer's cancellation of the contract. In fact, the short period of time that the performer had been incapacitated a year earlier from the same illness would weaken the producer's defense.

Question # 67 - Constitutional Law

A number of psychotherapists routinely send mailings to victims of car accidents informing the victims of the possibility of developing post-traumatic stress disorder (PTSD) as the result of the accidents, and offering psychotherapy services. Although PTSD is a possible result of a car accident, it is not common.

Many accident victims in a particular state who received the mailings complained that the mailings were disturbing and were an invasion of their privacy. These victims also reported that as a result of the mailings, their regard for psychotherapists and for psychotherapy as a form of treatment had diminished. In response, the state enacted a law prohibiting any licensed psychotherapist from sending mailings that raised the concern of PTSD to any car accident victim in the state until 30 days after the accident. The state justified the law as an effort to address the victims' complaints as well as to protect the reputation of psychotherapy as a form of treatment.

Is this law constitutional?

(A) No, because the law singles out one type of message for prohibition while allowing others.

Incorrect. It is true that the law singles out one type of message for prohibition while allowing other types. Such content-based restrictions on speech typically are subjected to strict judicial scrutiny and are invalidated. This law, however, is subject to a less exacting form of judicial scrutiny because it restricts commercial speech.

The law is constitutional, because it satisfies the First Amendment standards for government restrictions on commercial speech. The mailings qualify as commercial speech, because they advertise services provided by the psychotherapists. A restriction on commercial speech is subject to a form of intermediate judicial scrutiny, requiring the government to show that the restriction directly advances an important government interest and that the restriction is not substantially more extensive than necessary to protect that interest. The law here satisfies that standard; the 30-day waiting period for the psychotherapists' mailings narrowly serves the government's substantial interests in protecting both the privacy of accident victims and the public regard for psychotherapy.

(B) No, because the mailings provide information to consumers.

Incorrect. The fact that the mailings provide information to consumers entitles the mailings to First Amendment protection. However, because the mailings advertise the services of psychotherapists, they contain commercial speech and therefore are entitled to less constitutional protection than other forms of speech.

The law is constitutional, because it satisfies the First Amendment standards for government restrictions on commercial speech. A restriction on commercial speech is subject to a form of intermediate judicial scrutiny, requiring the government to show that the restriction directly advances an important government interest and that the restriction is not substantially more extensive than necessary to protect that interest. The law here satisfies that standard; the 30-day waiting period for the psychotherapists' mailings narrowly serves the government's substantial interests in protecting both the privacy of accident victims and the public regard for psychotherapy.

(C) Yes, because mailings suggesting the possibility of developing PTSD as the result of an accident are misleading.

Incorrect. Misleading commercial speech is not protected by the First Amendment, and governments therefore are free to restrict such speech. The mailings in this case are not misleading, however, because the facts state that "PTSD is a possible result" of car accidents.

The law is constitutional, because it satisfies the First Amendment standards for government restrictions on commercial speech. The mailings qualify as commercial speech because they advertise services provided by the psychotherapists. A restriction on commercial speech is subject to a form of intermediate judicial scrutiny, requiring the government to show that the restriction directly advances an important government interest and that the restriction is not substantially more extensive than necessary to protect that interest. The law here satisfies that standard; the 30-day waiting period for the psychotherapists' mailings narrowly serves the government's substantial interests in protecting both the privacy of accident victims and the public regard for psychotherapy.

(D) Yes, because the law protects the privacy of accident victims and the public regard for psychotherapy without being substantially more restrictive than necessary.

Correct. The law is constitutional, because it satisfies the First Amendment standards for government restrictions on commercial speech. The mailings contain commercial speech, because they advertise services provided by the psychotherapists. A restriction on commercial speech is subject to a form of intermediate judicial scrutiny, requiring the government to show that the restriction directly advances an important government interest and that the restriction is not substantially more extensive than necessary to protect that interest. The law here satisfies that standard; the 30-day waiting period for the psychotherapists' mailings narrowly serves the government's substantial interests in protecting both the privacy of accident victims and the public regard for psychotherapy.

Question # 68 - Torts

A shopper was riding on an up escalator in a department store when the escalator stopped abruptly. The shopper lost her balance and fell down the escalator steps, sustaining injuries. Although the escalator had been regularly maintained by an independent contractor, the store's obligation to provide safe conditions for its invitees was nondelegable. The shopper has brought an action against the store for damages, and the above facts are the only facts in evidence.

The store has moved for a directed verdict. Should the court grant the motion?

(A) No, because the finder of fact could infer that the escalator malfunction was due to negligence.

Correct. There is enough evidence here to support an inference of negligence on the part of the store. A jury could find that the malfunction was due to the negligent installation, maintenance, or operation of the escalator; the store would be responsible for all these possible causes under the nondelegable duty doctrine.

(B) No, because the store is strictly liable for the shopper's injuries.

Incorrect. Landowners and occupiers are not strictly liable even for injuries to their business invitees. The court should not grant the motion, but it is because the fact finder could infer negligence on the part of the store.

(C) Yes, because an independent contractor maintained the escalator.

Incorrect. Even if the malfunction were due to the negligence of the independent contractor, the store would also be responsible under the nondelegable duty doctrine. These facts illustrate a common situation in which that doctrine is applied: the defendant owns a building and invites the public to enter the building for the defendant's financial benefit. There is enough evidence here to support an inference of negligence on the part of the store. A jury could find that the malfunction was due to the negligent installation, maintenance, or operation of the escalator; the store would be responsible for all these possible causes under the nondelegable duty doctrine.

(D) Yes, because the shopper has not produced evidence of negligence.

Incorrect. There is enough evidence here to support an inference of negligence on the part of the store. A jury could find that the malfunction was due to the negligent installation, maintenance, or operation of the escalator; the store would be responsible for all these possible causes under the nondelegable duty doctrine.

Question # 69 - Criminal Law and Procedure

A woman went to an art gallery and falsely represented that she was an agent for a museum and wanted to purchase a painting that was hanging in the gallery. The woman and the gallery owner then agreed on a price for the painting to be paid 10 days later, and the woman took the painting. When the gallery failed to receive the payment when due, the owner called the museum and discovered that the woman did not work there. The owner then notified the police.

When interviewed by the police, the woman admitted making the false representation and acquiring the painting, but she said she believed that the painting had been stolen from her by someone who worked in the gallery.

Is the woman guilty of obtaining property by false pretenses?

(A) No, because she believed that the painting belonged to her.

Correct. The crime of false pretenses, like other theft crimes, requires the intent to steal. The woman cannot properly be found guilty of obtaining property by false pretenses, because she made the false statements to obtain property that she subjectively believed belonged to her.

(B) No, because the gallery owner would have sold the painting to anyone who agreed to pay the price.

Incorrect. This fact does not excuse the woman for knowingly making false statements to obtain property that she would not otherwise have been able to obtain. The reason the woman cannot properly be found guilty of obtaining property by false pretenses is that she lacked the requisite intent to steal; she made the false statements to obtain property that she subjectively believed belonged to her.

(C) Yes, because even if her representation was not material, she never intended to pay for the painting.

Incorrect. In some jurisdictions, a false pretenses conviction can be based on a promise to make payment in the future if the promisor had no present intent to make the future payment. But the promisor must have the intent to steal the property. The woman cannot properly be found guilty of obtaining property by false pretenses, because she lacked the requisite intent to steal; she made the false statements to obtain property that she subjectively believed belonged to her.

(D) Yes, because she knowingly made a false representation on which the gallery owner relied.

Incorrect. Even assuming that the woman otherwise could be convicted of false pretenses, false pretenses requires the intent to steal required for other theft crimes. Accordingly, the woman cannot properly be found guilty of obtaining property by false pretenses, because she made the false statements to obtain property that she subjectively believed belonged to her.

Question # 70 - Real Property

For 22 years, the land records have shown a man as the owner of an 80-acre farm. The man has never physically occupied the land.

Nineteen years ago, a woman entered the farm. The character and duration of the woman's possession of the farm caused her to become the owner of the farm under the adverse possession law of the jurisdiction.

Three years ago, when the woman was not present, a neighbor took over possession of the farm. The neighbor repaired fences, put up "no trespassing" signs, and did some plowing. When the woman returned, she found the neighbor in possession of the farm. The neighbor vigorously rejected the woman's claimed right to possession and threatened force. The woman withdrew.

The woman then went to the man and told him of the history of activity on the farm. The woman orally told the man that she had been wrong to try to take his farm. She expressly waived any claim she had to the land. The man thanked her.

Last month, unsure of the effect of her conversation with the man, the woman executed a deed purporting to convey the farm to her son. The son promptly recorded the deed.

The period of time to acquire title by adverse possession in the jurisdiction is 10 years. Who now owns the farm?

(A) The man, because the woman's later words and actions released title to the man.

Incorrect. The woman acquired her title to the farm by adverse possession. The woman's title was an original title and did not derive from the man's title. The statute of frauds requires that any conveyance of real property be in writing. Therefore, the woman's oral statement was insufficient to release the title to the man, and the woman validly conveyed the farm to her son.

(B) The neighbor, because the neighbor succeeded to the woman's adverse possession title by privity of possession.

Incorrect. The woman acquired title to the farm by adverse possession. The woman's title was an original title and did not derive from the man's title. The neighbor's actions may have started the statute of limitations running on his adverse possession of the farm, but he has been in possession of the farm for only three years. In addition, the neighbor was never in privity with the woman.

(C) The son, because he succeeded to the woman's adverse possession title by privity of conveyance.

Correct. The woman acquired title to the farm by adverse possession. The woman's title was an original title and did not derive from the man's title. The statute of frauds requires that the conveyance of the farm be in writing. Therefore, the woman's oral statement was insufficient to release the title to the man, and the woman validly conveyed the farm to her son.

(D) The woman, because she must bring a quiet title action to establish her title to the farm before she can convey the farm to her son.

Incorrect. The woman acquired title to the farm by adverse possession. The woman's title was an original title and did not derive from the man's title. The statute of frauds requires that any conveyance of real property be in writing. Therefore, the woman's oral statement was insufficient to release the title to the man. Having established title to the farm by adverse possession, there is no requirement that the woman sue to establish title. Therefore, she could convey the farm to her son.

Question # 71 - Contracts

An art collector paid a gallery $1,000 to purchase a framed drawing from the gallery's collection. The price included shipping by the gallery to the collector's home. The gallery's owner used inadequate materials to wrap the drawing. The frame broke during shipment and scratched the drawing, reducing the drawing's value to $300. The collector complained to the gallery owner, who told the collector to take the drawing to a specific art restorer to have the drawing repaired. The collector paid the restorer $400 to repair the drawing, but not all of the scratches could be fixed. The drawing, after being repaired, was worth $700. The gallery owner subsequently refused to pay either for the repairs or for the damage to the drawing.

In an action by the collector against the gallery owner for damages, which of the following awards is most likely?

(A) Nothing.

Incorrect. The gallery's use of inadequate materials to wrap the drawing constituted a breach of warranty. Therefore, the collector is entitled to be placed in the position he would have been in but for the gallery's breach. Awarding the collector nothing would violate the expectation damages principle. Under UCC § 2-714(2), the generally applicable standard for measuring the collector's resulting damages would be the difference between the value of the drawing as accepted and the value of the drawing if it had been as warranted. Repair costs often are used to determine this difference in value, but when repairs fail to restore the goods to their value as warranted, an adjustment is required. The collector is entitled to recover the repair costs ($400) plus the difference between the value of the drawing if it had been as warranted and its value after the repairs ($1,000 -$700 = $300). Accordingly, the collector should recover $700.

(B) $300.

Incorrect. The gallery's use of inadequate materials to wrap the drawing constituted a breach of warranty. Therefore, the collector is entitled to be placed in the position he would have been in but for the gallery's breach. Awarding the collector $300 would violate the expectation damages principle. Under UCC § 2-714(2), the generally applicable standard for measuring the collector's resulting damages would be the difference between the value of the drawing as accepted and the value of the drawing if it had been as warranted. Repair costs often are used to determine this difference in value, but when repairs fail to restore the goods to their value as warranted, an adjustment is required. The collector is entitled to recover the repair costs ($400) plus the difference between the value of the drawing if it had been as warranted and its value after the repairs ($1,000-$700 = $300). Accordingly, the collector should recover $700.

(C) $400.

Incorrect. The gallery's use of inadequate materials to wrap the drawing constituted a breach of warranty. Therefore, the collector is entitled to be placed in the position he would have been in but for the gallery's breach. Awarding the collector $400 would violate the expectation damages principle. Under UCC § 2-714(2), the generally applicable standard for measuring the collector's resulting damages would be the difference between the value of the drawing as accepted and the value of the drawing if it had been as warranted. Repair costs often are used to determine this difference in value, but when repairs fail to restore the goods to their value as warranted, an adjustment is required. The collector is entitled to recover the repair costs ($400) plus the difference between the value of the drawing if it had been as warranted and its value after the repairs ($1,000 -$700 = $300). Accordingly, the collector should recover $700.

(D) $700.

Correct. The gallery's use of inadequate materials to wrap the drawing constituted a breach of warranty. Therefore, the collector is entitled to be placed in the position he would have been in but for the gallery's breach. Under UCC § 2-714(2), the generally applicable standard for measuring the collector's resulting damages would be the difference between the value of the drawing as accepted and the value of the drawing if it had been as warranted. Repair costs often are used to determine this difference in value, but when repairs fail to restore the goods to their value as warranted, a further adjustment is required. Here the repairs failed to restore the drawing to its value as warranted. Therefore, the collector is entitled to recover the repair costs ($400) plus the difference between the value of the drawing if it had been as warranted and its value after the repairs ($1,000 - $700 = $300). Accordingly, the collector should recover $700.

Question # 72 - Evidence

A woman's car was set on fire by vandals. When she submitted a claim of loss for the car to her insurance company, the insurance company refused to pay, asserting that the woman's policy had lapsed due to the nonpayment of her premium. The woman sued the insurance company for breach of contract.

At trial, the woman testified that she had, in a timely manner, placed a stamped, properly addressed envelope containing the premium payment in the outgoing mail bin at her office. The woman's secretary then testified that every afternoon at closing time he takes all outgoing mail in the bin to the post office. The insurance company later called its mail clerk to testify that he opens all incoming mail and that he did not receive the woman's premium payment.

The woman and the insurance company have both moved for a directed verdict. For which party, if either, should the court direct a verdict?

(A) For the insurance company, because neither the woman nor her secretary has any personal knowledge that the envelope was mailed.

Incorrect. Under Rule 301, the rule on presumptions, the woman has presented sufficient evidence that the envelope containing the premium payment was mailed. The rule does not require that the woman have personal knowledge that the envelope reached the post office. The insurance company then has the burden of producing evidence to rebut the presumption that the envelope was received. Because the insurance company has produced such evidence, the presumption is taken out of the case and it is up to the fact finder to determine whether the insurance company received the payment.

(B) For the insurance company, because the mail clerk's direct testimony negates the woman's circumstantial evidence.

Incorrect. Under Rule 301, once the woman provides evidence that the envelope containing the premium payment was mailed, the insurance company has the burden of producing evidence sufficient to rebut the presumption that the envelope was received. That does not mean, however, that if the insurance company does provide such evidence it is entitled to a directed verdict. Instead, the presumption is taken out of the case and it is up to the fact finder to determine whether the insurance company received the payment.

(C) For the woman, because there is a presumption that an envelope properly addressed and stamped was received by the addressee.

Incorrect. It is true that the woman's evidence has triggered the presumption that the envelope containing the premium payment was received. But under Rule 301, the insurance company then has the burden of producing enough evidence to rebut the presumption. Here the insurance company has done so. Consequently, the presumption is taken out of the case and it is up to the fact finder to determine whether the insurance company received the payment. Therefore, it would be error to grant a directed verdict for the woman.

(D) For neither the woman nor the insurance company, because under these circumstances the jury is responsible for determining whether the insurance company received the payment.

Correct. The woman has presented sufficient evidence to trigger the presumption that her payment was received. The insurance company has presented sufficient evidence to rebut that presumption. Consequently, the presumption is taken out of the case and it is up to the fact finder to determine whether the insurance company received the payment. Therefore, it would be error to grant a directed verdict for either the woman or the insurance company.

Question # 73 - Torts

A 14-year-old teenager of low intelligence received her parents' permission to drive their car. She had had very little experience driving a car and did not have a driver's license. Although she did the best she could, she lost control of the car and hit a pedestrian.

The pedestrian has brought a negligence action against the teenager. Is the pedestrian likely to prevail?

(A) No, because only the teenager's parents are subject to liability.

Incorrect. The parents and the teenager may both be liable. The teenager was engaging in a dangerous adult activity, so she will be held to the adult standard of care and can be sued for the injuries caused by her negligent driving.

(B) No, because the teenager was acting reasonably for a 14-year-old of low intelligence and little driving experience.

Incorrect. The teenager was engaging in a dangerous adult activity, so she will be held to the adult standard of care. No adjustment will be made to that standard to reflect her low intelligence and lack of experience. Her lack of intelligence and her inexperience put others at risk, and she will be held to the standard of a reasonably prudent driver even if she is not capable of reasonable prudence.

(C) Yes, because the teenager was engaging in an adult activity.

Correct. The teenager was engaging in a dangerous adult activity, so she will be held to the adult standard of care. No adjustment will be made to that standard to reflect her low intelligence and lack of experience. Her lack of intelligence and her inexperience put others at risk, and she will be held to the standard of a reasonably prudent driver even if she is not capable of reasonable prudence.

(D) Yes, because the teenager was not old enough to obtain a driver's license.

Incorrect. In the absence of a statute setting a different standard, the teenager's failure to obtain a license ordinarily would not be evidence that she was actually negligent at the time of the accident. The plaintiff would have to prove actual negligence, which should be easy given that the teenager lost control of the car and given the fact that the teenager will be held to an adult standard of care because she was engaging in an adult activity.

Question # 74 - Constitutional Law

A clerical employee of a city water department was responsible for sending out water bills to customers. His work in this respect had always been satisfactory.

The employee's sister ran in a recent election against the incumbent mayor, but she lost. The employee had supported his sister in the election campaign. After the mayor found out about this, she fired the employee solely because his support for the sister indicated that he was "disloyal" to the mayor. The city's charter provides that "all employees of the city work at the pleasure of the mayor."

Is the mayor's action constitutional?

(A) No, because public employees have a property interest in their employment, which gives them a right to a hearing prior to discharge.

Incorrect. A public employee has a property interest in his or her employment if the employee can be fired only for cause. Because the city's charter provides that "all employees of the city work at the pleasure of the mayor," the clerical employee does not have a property interest in his employment.

Nevertheless, the mayor's action is unconstitutional, because it violates the employee's right to freedom of expression and association protected by the First Amendment. The U.S. Supreme Court has held that the government may not fire an employee because of the employee's political views or affiliations unless certain political views or affiliations are required for the effective performance of the employee's job. The political views or affiliations of a clerical employee of a city water department are not relevant to the employee's job, and thus the employee may not be fired because of them.

(B) No, because the mayor's action violates the employee's right to freedom of expression and association.

Correct. The mayor's action is unconstitutional, because it violates the employee's right to freedom of expression and association protected by the First Amendment. The U.S. Supreme Court has held that the government may not fire an employee because of the employee's political views or affiliations unless certain political views or affiliations are required for the effective performance of the employee's job. The political views or affiliations of a clerical employee of a city water department are not relevant to the employee's job, and thus the employee may not be fired because of them.

(C) Yes, because the employee has no property interest in his job since the city charter provides that he holds the job "at the pleasure of the mayor."

Incorrect. It is true that the employee has no property interest in his job, and therefore he is not entitled to the constitutional protections of procedural due process. Nevertheless, the mayor's action is unconstitutional, because it violates the employee's right to freedom of expression and association protected by the First Amendment. The U.S. Supreme Court has held that the government may not fire an employee because of the employee's political views or affiliations unless certain political views or affiliations are required for the effective performance of the employee's job. The political views or affiliations of a clerical employee of a city water department are not relevant to the employee's job, and thus the employee may not be fired because of them.

(D) Yes, because the mayor may require members of her administration to be politically loyal to her.

Incorrect. The mayor may require members of her administration to be politically loyal to her only if political loyalty is required for the effective performance of the job in question. The U.S. Supreme Court has held that the government may not fire an employee because of the employee's political views or affiliations unless certain political views or affiliations are required for the effective performance of the employee's job. The political views or affiliations of a clerical employee of a city water department are not relevant to the employee's job, and thus the employee may not be fired because of them. The mayor's action is unconstitutional, because it violates the employee's right to freedom of expression and association protected by the First Amendment.

Question # 75 - Real Property

In the most recent deed in the chain of title to a tract of land, a man conveyed the land as follows: "To my niece and her heirs and assigns in fee simple until my niece's daughter marries, and then to my niece's daughter and her heirs and assigns in fee simple."

There is no applicable statute, and the common law Rule Against Perpetuities has not been modified in the jurisdiction. Which of the following is the most accurate statement concerning the title to the land?

(A) The niece has a life estate and the daughter has a contingent remainder.

Incorrect. The gift to the niece was to the niece "and her heirs and assigns," thereby creating a fee estate rather than a life estate. The fee simple estate was made defeasible by the addition of the words of limitation "until my niece's daughter marries." A remainder interest may follow a life estate; however, a remainder does not follow a fee simple estate. A future interest created in a grantee following a defeasible estate is an executory interest. The executory interest in this case does not violate the Rule Against Perpetuities, because it will be known within the lifetime of the validating lives--the niece and the niece's daughter--whether the condition of marriage has occurred.

(B) The niece has a fee simple and the daughter has no interest, because after the grant of a fee simple there can be no gift over.

Incorrect. The niece was given a defeasible fee simple. A limitation may be expressly attached to a fee simple estate. The express limitation attached to the grant was "until my niece's daughter marries." A future interest held by a grantee following a defeasible estate is an executory interest. The executory interest in this case does not violate the common law Rule Against Perpetuities, because it will be known within the lifetime of the validating lives--the niece and the niece's daughter--whether the condition of marriage has occurred.

(C) The niece has a fee simple and the daughter has no interest, because she might not marry within 21 years after the date of the deed.

Incorrect. The niece was granted a defeasible fee simple. The express limitation was the marriage of the niece's daughter. If the limitation occurs, the estate transfers automatically to the niece's daughter. The future interest held by a grantee following a defeasible estate is an executory interest. Executory interests are subject to the common law Rule Against Perpetuities; however, the niece and the niece's daughter are both validating lives and the condition of the marriage either will or will not occur during their lifetimes. The additional 21 years after the death of all validating lives is not needed, and the rule is not violated.

(D) The niece has a defeasible fee simple determinable and the daughter has an executory interest.

Correct. The niece has a defeasible fee simple because of the limitation placed on the estate by the words "until my niece's daughter marries." If the niece's daughter marries, the estate in the niece will end automatically and will pass to the holder of the future interest (the niece's daughter). The future interest given to the daughter, a grantee, is an executory interest. The executory interest in this case does not violate the common law Rule Against Perpetuities, because it will be known within the lifetime of the validating lives--the niece and the niece's daughter--whether the condition of marriage has occurred.

Question # 76 - Evidence

At a defendant's trial for mail fraud, the defendant calls his wife to testify that she committed the fraud herself without the defendant's knowledge. On cross-examination, the prosecutor asks the wife, "Isn't it true that you have fled your home several times in fear of your husband?"

Is this question proper?

(A) No, because it is leading a witness not shown to be hostile.

Incorrect. Leading questions are generally permitted on cross-examination, and the question is proper because it explores the wife's possible motive for testifying falsely.

(B) No, because its probative value is outweighed by the danger of unfair prejudice to the defendant.

Incorrect. This answer applies the wrong balancing test. Under Rule 403, evidence that is probative is admissible unless its probative value is substantially outweighed by the risk of unfair prejudice. That test favors admitting probative evidence. It is not the case, therefore, that the probative value must outweigh the prejudicial effect for the evidence to be admissible. The question is proper because it explores the wife's possible motive for testifying falsely.

(C) Yes, because by calling his wife, the defendant has waived his privilege to prevent her from testifying against him.

Incorrect. The defendant does not have a privilege to prevent his wife from testifying against him. The privilege against adverse spousal testimony is held by the wife, as the witness, not by the defendant. The question is proper, however, because it explores the wife's possible motive for testifying falsely.

(D) Yes, because it explores the wife's possible motive for testifying falsely.

Correct. A cross-examiner is entitled to question in such a way as to raise inferences about the motive of a witness to testify falsely. Here, the question raises an inference that the wife is in fear of her husband and is therefore taking the blame for her husband's crime.

Question # 77 - Criminal Law and Procedure

A woman broke off her engagement to a man but refused to return the engagement ring the man had given her. One night, the man entered the woman's house after midnight to retrieve the ring. Although the woman was not at home, a neighbor saw the man enter the house and called the police. The man unsuccessfully searched for the ring for 10 minutes. As he was walking out the front door, the police arrived and immediately arrested him.

The man has been charged with burglary in a jurisdiction that follows the common law. Which of the following, if proved, would serve as the man's best defense to the charge?

(A) The man knew that the woman kept a key under the doormat and he used the key to enter the house.

Incorrect. This fact does not provide a defense to burglary, because the man still broke into and entered the house without the woman's consent. Instead, the man's subjective belief that he was entitled to the ring (even if that belief was incorrect and unreasonable) negates the intent required for the underlying felony of larceny.

(B) The man incorrectly and unreasonably believed that he was legally entitled to the ring.

Correct. The crime of burglary requires that the breaking and entering of the dwelling have been done with the intent to commit an underlying felony (in most cases, larceny). The man's subjective belief that he was entitled to the ring (even if that belief was incorrect and unreasonable) negates the intent required for the underlying felony of larceny.

(C) The man knew that no one was at home when he entered the house.

Incorrect. This fact does not provide a defense, because the crime of burglary does not require that the dwelling be occupied at the time of the breaking and entering. Instead, the man's subjective belief that he was entitled to the ring (even if that belief was incorrect and unreasonable) negates the intent required for the underlying felony of larceny.

(D) The man took nothing of value from the house.

Incorrect. This fact does not provide a defense, because burglary requires that the person breaking and entering intend to commit a felony, not that the person be successful in committing the felony. Instead, the man's subjective belief that he was entitled to the ring (even if that belief was incorrect and unreasonable) negates the intent required for the underlying felony of larceny.

Question # 78 - Contracts

A businesswoman sold her business to a company for $25 million in cash pursuant to a written contract that was signed by both parties. Under the contract, the company agreed to employ the businesswoman for two years as a vice president at a salary of $150,000 per year. After six months, the company, without cause, fired the businesswoman.

Which of the following statements best describes the businesswoman's rights after the discharge?

(A) She can recover the promised salary for the remainder of the two years if she remains ready to work.

Incorrect. The company's unjustified termination of the businesswoman's employment constituted a breach of contract entitling the businesswoman to recover monetary damages. However, a wrongfully discharged employee is expected to mitigate damages by making reasonable efforts to seek comparable employment. In this case, to avoid a reduction in her damages, the businesswoman is required to do more than remain ready to work. Her recovery will be reduced by the compensation she earned or could have earned if she had made reasonable efforts to secure comparable employment.

(B) She can recover the promised salary for the remainder of the two years if no comparable job is reasonably available and she does not take another job.

Correct. The company's unjustified termination of the businesswoman's employment constituted a breach of contract entitling the businesswoman to recover monetary damages. A wrongfully discharged employee is expected to mitigate damages by making reasonable efforts to seek comparable employment. However, if no comparable employment is reasonably available and the businesswoman does not take another job, the businesswoman is entitled to recover the promised salary for the remainder of the two years.

(C) She can rescind the contract of sale and get back her business upon tender to the company of $25 million.

Incorrect. The company's unjustified termination of the businesswoman's employment constituted a material breach of contract. Nevertheless, a court would likely employ the concept of divisibility to preclude the businesswoman from rescinding the contract of sale. As stated in Restatement (Second) of Contracts § 240, a contract is divisible where "the performances to be exchanged under an exchange of promises can be apportioned into corresponding pairs of part performances so that the parts of each pair are properly regarded as agreed equivalents." Here, the agreed equivalents would be the sale of the business and the corresponding $25 million purchase price, and the businesswoman's promise to work for the company and the corresponding yearly salary of $150,000. Applying this concept, the businesswoman would be able to recover damages for the company's breach of its promise to employ her, but she would not be permitted to rescind the contract of sale.

(D) She can get specific performance of her right to serve as a vice president of the company for two years.

Incorrect. The company's unjustified termination of the businesswoman's employment constituted a breach of contract entitling the businesswoman to recover monetary damages. The general rule is that employers cannot obtain specific performance requiring an employee who has breached a personal services contract to work for the employer. It is also true generally that courts refuse to grant specific performance of an employment contract against a breaching employer. Consequently, the businesswoman's recovery will consist of the unpaid salary under the contract, reduced by the compensation she earned or could have earned if she had made reasonable efforts to secure comparable employment.

Question # 79 - Torts

A firstborn child was examined as an infant by a doctor who was a specialist in the diagnosis of speech and hearing impairments. Although the doctor should have concluded that the infant was totally deaf due to a hereditary condition, the doctor negligently concluded that the infant's hearing was normal. After the diagnosis, but before they learned that the infant was in fact deaf, the parents conceived a second child who also suffered total deafness due to the hereditary condition.

The parents claim that they would not have conceived the second child had they known of the high probability of the hereditary condition. They have sought the advice of their attorney regarding which negligence action against the doctor is most likely to succeed.

What sort of action against the doctor should the attorney recommend?

(A) A medical malpractice action seeking damages on the second child's behalf for expenses due to his deafness, on the ground that the doctor's negligence caused him to be born deaf.

Incorrect. The parents assert that they would not have conceived a second child had the doctor properly diagnosed the first child's deafness. Under that theory, the second child would never have been born had the doctor acted properly. Most courts are unwilling to say that it is worse to be born deaf than to never be born at all. Where that approach is taken, the second child has suffered no injury under this theory.

(B) A wrongful birth action by the parents for expenses they have incurred due to the second child's deafness, on the ground that but for the doctor's negligence, they would not have conceived the second child.

Correct. This cause of action will be permitted in many states. The parents sought an accurate assessment of their first child, which the doctor failed to provide. Unaware of the hereditary condition, the parents conceived a second child and incurred unexpected expenses that could have been avoided had the doctor acted properly.

(C) A wrongful life action by the parents for expenses for the entire period of the second child's life, on the ground that but for the doctor's negligence, the second child would not have been born.

Incorrect. A wrongful life action would be brought by a child who would not have been born. An action by the parents based on advice that would have avoided a conception of a child is a wrongful birth action. Also, most courts would not permit the parents to recover all of the expenses for the second child's life even in a proper action, but only those additional expenses attributable to the child's disability.

(D) A wrongful life action on the second child's behalf for expenses for the entire period of his life, on the ground that but for the doctor's negligence, he would not have been born.

Incorrect. Most states reject this claim, and of the few states that do permit it, some would limit recovery to the special damages attributable to the disability. The parents' wrongful birth action is more likely to be successful in almost all jurisdictions.

Question # 80 - Constitutional Law

An environmental organization's stated mission is to support environmental causes. The organization's membership is generally open to the public, but its bylaws permit its officers to refuse to admit anyone to membership who does not adhere to the organization's mission statement.

In a recent state administrative proceeding, the organization opposed plans to begin mining operations in the mountains surrounding a small town. Its opposition prevented the mine from being opened on schedule. In an effort to force the organization to withdraw its opposition, certain residents of the town attended a meeting of the organization and tried to become members, but the officers refused to admit them. The residents sued the organization, claiming that the refusal to admit them was discriminatory and violated a local ordinance that prohibits any organization from discriminating on the basis of an individual's political views. The organization responded that the ordinance is unconstitutional as applied to its membership decisions.

Are the residents likely to prevail in their claim?

(A) No, because the membership policies of a private organization are not state action.

Incorrect. It is true that the membership policies of a private organization are not state action. The local ordinance on which the residents base their suit is state action, however, and it is subject to the requirements of the First Amendment.

The residents are not likely to prevail in their claim, because it would violate the environmental organization's First Amendment right to freedom of association if the state were to force the organization to accept the residents as members. The U.S. Supreme Court has held that the forced inclusion of an unwanted person in a group violates the group's freedom of association if including that person would significantly affect the group's ability to express its viewpoints. The freedom of association entitles the environmental organization to refuse membership to the residents, because admitting them would effect a change in the organization's viewpoint on the mining operations.

(B) No, because the organization's right to freedom of association allows it to refuse to admit potential members who do not adhere to its mission statement.

Correct. The residents are not likely to prevail in their claim, because it would violate the environmental organization's First Amendment right to freedom of association if the state were to force the organization to accept the residents as members. The U.S. Supreme Court has held that the forced inclusion of an unwanted person in a group violates the group's freedom of association if including that person would significantly affect the group's ability to express its viewpoints. The freedom of association entitles the environmental organization to refuse membership to the residents, because admitting them would effect a change in the organization's viewpoint on the mining operations.

(C) Yes, because the action of the officers in refusing to admit the residents as members violates equal protection of the laws.

Incorrect. The action of the officers in refusing to admit the residents as members is not subject to the equal protection clause, because the environmental organization is a private entity, and therefore the conduct of the organization's officers does not constitute state action.

The residents are not likely to prevail in their claim, because it would violate the environmental organization's First Amendment right to freedom of association if the state were to force the organization to accept the residents as members. The U.S. Supreme Court has held that the forced inclusion of an unwanted person in a group violates the group's freedom of association if including that person would significantly affect the group's ability to express its viewpoints. The freedom of association entitles the environmental organization to refuse membership to the residents, because admitting them would effect a change in the organization's viewpoint on the mining operations.

(D) Yes, because the ordinance serves the compelling interest of protecting the residents' free speech rights.

Incorrect. The U.S. Supreme Court has held that even statutes that support compelling interests do not justify the severe burden on an organization's freedom of association that would result from forcing an organization to accept members who would significantly affect the organization's ability to express its viewpoints.

The residents are not likely to prevail in their claim, because it would violate the environmental organization's First Amendment right to freedom of association if the state were to force the organization to accept the residents as members. The U.S. Supreme Court has held that the forced inclusion of an unwanted person in a group violates the group's freedom of association if including that person would significantly affect the group's ability to express its viewpoints. The freedom of association entitles the environmental organization to refuse membership to the residents, because admitting them would effect a change in the organization's viewpoint on the mining operations.

Question # 81 - Contracts

On June 15, a teacher accepted a contract for a one-year position teaching math at a public high school at a salary of $50,000, starting in September. On June 22, the school informed the teacher that, due to a change in its planned math curriculum, it no longer needed a full-time math teacher. The school offered instead to employ the teacher as a part-time academic counselor at a salary of $20,000, starting in September. The teacher refused the school's offer. On June 29, the teacher was offered a one-year position to teach math at a nearby private academy for $47,000, starting in September. The teacher, however, decided to spend the year completing work on a graduate degree in mathematics and declined the academy's offer.

If the teacher sues the school for breach of contract, what is her most likely recovery?

(A) $50,000, the full contract amount.

Incorrect. The teacher is entitled to recover damages that will place her in the position she would have been in but for the school's breach. However, an injured party is expected to make reasonable efforts to mitigate the loss resulting from the other party's breach. In the case of a wrongfully discharged employee, the employee is expected to accept an offer of comparable employment. If the employee fails or refuses to do so, the employee's recovery is reduced by the amount of the loss that the employee could have avoided by accepting comparable employment. Here, the teacher's damages of $50,000 should be reduced by the $47,000 she would have earned if she had accepted the comparable teaching position at the private academy. Therefore, the teacher is entitled to recover $3,000 from the school.

(B) $30,000, the full contract amount less the amount the teacher could have earned in the counselor position offered by the school.

Incorrect. The teacher is entitled to recover damages that will place her in the position she would have been in but for the school's breach. However, an injured party is expected to make reasonable efforts to mitigate the loss resulting from the other party's breach. In the case of a wrongfully discharged employee, the employee is expected to accept an offer of comparable employment. If the employee fails or refuses to do so, the employee's recovery is reduced by the amount of the loss that the employee could have avoided by accepting comparable employment. Because it is unlikely that a court would consider the counseling position to be comparable employment, the teacher's damages should not be reduced by the $20,000 she would have earned if she had accepted that position. On the other hand, her damages of $50,000 should be reduced by the $47,000 she would have earned if she had accepted the comparable teaching position at the private academy. Therefore, the teacher is entitled to recover $3,000 from the school.

(C) $3,000, the full contract amount less the amount the teacher could have earned in the teaching position at the academy.

Correct. The teacher is entitled to recover damages that will place her in the position she would have been in but for the school's breach. However, an injured party is expected to make reasonable efforts to mitigate the loss resulting from the other party's breach. In the case of a wrongfully discharged employee, the employee is expected to accept an offer of comparable employment. If the employee fails or refuses to do so, the employee's recovery is reduced by the amount of the loss that the employee could have avoided by accepting comparable employment. Here, the teacher's damages of $50,000 should be reduced by the $47,000 she would have earned if she had accepted the comparable teaching position at the private academy. Therefore, the teacher is entitled to recover $3,000 from the school.

(D) Nothing, because the school notified the teacher of its decision before the teacher had acted in substantial reliance on the contract.

Incorrect. The teacher and the school entered into an enforceable contract, and the school's unjustified nonperformance constituted a breach of contract. The teacher is therefore entitled to recover damages that will place her in the position she would have been in but for the breach and need not show reliance in order to recover. However, while she is entitled to damages from the breach, an injured party is expected to make reasonable efforts to mitigate the loss resulting from the other party's breach. In the case of a wrongfully discharged employee, the employee is expected to accept an offer of comparable employment. If the employee fails or refuses to do so, the employee's recovery is reduced by the amount of the loss that the employee could have avoided by accepting comparable employment. Here, the teacher's damages of $50,000 should be reduced by the $47,000 she would have earned if she had accepted the comparable teaching position at the private academy. Therefore, the teacher is entitled to recover $3,000 from the school.

Question # 82 - Torts

A boater, caught in a sudden storm and reasonably fearing that her boat would capsize, drove the boat up to a pier, exited the boat, and tied the boat to the pier. The pier was clearly marked with "NO TRESPASSING" signs. The owner of the pier ran up to the boater and told her that the boat could not remain tied to the pier. The boater offered to pay the owner for the use of the pier. Regardless, over the boater's protest, the owner untied the boat and pushed it away from the pier. The boat was lost at sea.

Is the boater likely to prevail in an action against the owner to recover the value of the boat?

(A) No, because the owner told the boater that she could not tie the boat to the pier.

Incorrect. The boater was privileged to trespass on the owner's property under the doctrine of private necessity, because the boater's property was at risk. Because the boater's intrusion onto the pier was privileged, the owner had no right to exclude her or her boat from the pier. In telling the boater that she could not tie the boat to the pier, the owner was asserting a right that he did not possess. When the owner untied the boat, he committed an unprivileged trespass upon the boater's property, so the owner must pay for the loss of the boat.

(B) No, because there was a possibility that the boat would not be damaged by the storm.

Incorrect. The boater was privileged to trespass on the owner's property under the doctrine of private necessity, because her property was at risk. In order to establish that privilege, the boater need not establish that harm to the boat was inevitable, but only that her actions were reasonable given the circumstances. Because the boater's intrusion onto the pier was privileged, the owner had no right to exclude her or her boat from the pier. When the owner untied the boat, he committed an unprivileged trespass upon the boater's property, so the owner must pay for the loss of the boat.

(C) Yes, because the boater offered to pay the owner for the use of the pier.

Incorrect. The boater is likely to prevail, but it is because the boater was privileged to trespass on the owner's property under the doctrine of private necessity. Because the boater's property was at risk, her intrusion onto the pier was privileged, and the owner had no right to exclude her or her boat from the pier. Whether or not the boater offered to pay the owner is irrelevant to the privilege of private necessity. When the owner untied the boat, he committed an unprivileged trespass upon the boater's property, so the owner must pay for the loss of the boat.

(D) Yes, because the boater was privileged to enter the owner's property to save her boat.

Correct. The boater was privileged to trespass on the owner's property under the doctrine of private necessity, because the boater's property was at risk. Because the boater's intrusion onto the pier was privileged, the owner had no right to exclude her or her boat from the pier. When the owner untied the boat, he committed an unprivileged trespass upon the boater's property, so the owner must pay for the loss of the boat.

Question # 83 - Evidence

A driver sued her insurance company on an accident insurance policy covering personal injuries to the driver. The insurance company defended on the ground that the driver's injuries were intentionally self-inflicted and therefore excluded from the policy's coverage.

The driver testified at trial that she had inflicted the injuries, as her negligence had caused the crash in which she was injured, but that she had not done so intentionally. She then called as a witness her treating psychiatrist to give his opinion that the driver had been mentally unbalanced, but not self-destructive, at the time of the crash.

Should the court admit the witness's opinion?

(A) No, because it is a statement about the driver's credibility.

Incorrect. The witness is not offering to testify that the driver is telling the truth. (If the witness were to do so, the testimony would be inadmissible, because credibility is a question for the jury to assess.) The witness is offering to testify only to the driver's pertinent mental state, which is permissible in a civil case such as this.

(B) No, because it is an opinion about a mental state that constitutes an element of the defense.

Incorrect. Rule 704(b), which prohibits an expert from testifying that a criminal defendant had or did not have the requisite mental state to commit the crime charged, is applicable to criminal cases only. There is no absolute bar to such testimony in a civil case such as this.

(C) No, because the witness did not first state the basis for his opinion.

Incorrect. Under Rule 705, an expert may state an opinion "without first testifying to the underlying facts or data."

(D) Yes, because it is a helpful opinion by a qualified expert.

Correct. The witness's opinion helps the jury understand a relevant mental state. The standard for qualification of an expert is not high; a psychiatrist is qualified to testify to a person's mental state.

Question # 84 - Criminal Law and Procedure

A woman wanted to kill a business competitor. She contacted a man who she believed was willing to commit murder for hire and offered him $50,000 to kill the competitor. The man agreed to do so and accepted $25,000 as a down payment. Unbeknownst to the woman, the man was an undercover police officer.

In a jurisdiction that has adopted the unilateral theory of conspiracy, is the woman guilty of conspiracy to murder the business competitor?

(A) No, because the man did not intend to kill the competitor.

Incorrect. In jurisdictions that recognize unilateral conspiracies, it is enough that one person agree with another person to commit a crime (and in some jurisdictions, that an overt act in furtherance of that agreement be committed). It is no defense to unilateral conspiracy that the other person was feigning agreement or acting in an undercover capacity. Therefore, the man's lack of intent does not make the woman any less guilty.

(B) No, because it would have been impossible for the woman to kill the competitor by this method.

Incorrect. In jurisdictions that recognize unilateral conspiracies, it is enough that one person agree with another person to commit a crime (and in some jurisdictions, that an overt act in furtherance of that agreement be committed). It is no defense to unilateral conspiracy that the other person was feigning agreement or acting in an undercover capacity. Therefore, the woman cannot prevail on any impossibility defense.

(C) Yes, because the woman believed that she had an agreement with the man that would bring about the competitor's death.

Correct. In jurisdictions that recognize unilateral conspiracies, it is enough that one person agree with another person to commit a crime (and in some jurisdictions, that an overt act in furtherance of that agreement be committed). It is no defense to unilateral conspiracy that the other person was feigning agreement or acting in an undercover capacity. Here, the woman agreed to commit a crime and she committed an overt act in furtherance of that agreement when she paid the man $25,000. She therefore is guilty of conspiracy in a jurisdiction that recognizes unilateral conspiracies.

(D) Yes, because the woman took a substantial step toward bringing about the competitor's death by paying the man $25,000.

Incorrect. The woman is guilty, but not because she took a substantial step, which is a concept relevant under the Model Penal Code to attempt rather than conspiracy. The woman is guilty of conspiracy because in jurisdictions that recognize unilateral conspiracies, it is enough that one person agree with another person to commit a crime (and in some jurisdictions, that an overt act in furtherance of that agreement be committed). It is no defense to unilateral conspiracy that the other person was feigning agreement or acting in an undercover capacity.

Question # 85 - Real Property

A businessman executed a promissory note for $200,000 to a bank, secured by a mortgage on commercial real estate owned by the businessman. The promissory note stated that the businessman was not personally liable for the mortgage debt.

One week later, a finance company obtained a judgment against the businessman for $50,000 and filed the judgment in the county where the real estate was located. At the time the judgment was filed, the finance company had no actual notice of the bank's mortgage.

Two weeks after that filing, the bank recorded its mortgage on the businessman's real estate.

The recording act of the jurisdiction provides: "Unless the same be recorded according to law, no conveyance or mortgage of real property shall be good against subsequent purchasers for value and without notice or against judgment creditors without notice."

The finance company sued to enforce its judgment lien against the businessman's real estate. The bank intervened in the action, contending that the judgment lien was a second lien on the real estate and that its mortgage was a first lien.

Is the bank's contention correct?

(A) No, because the judgment lien was recorded before the mortgage, and the finance company had no actual notice of the mortgage.

Correct. The judgment lien was recorded first in a jurisdiction that expressly protects judgment creditors without notice. The finance company had no actual notice of the mortgage and had no constructive notice because the mortgage was not recorded until two weeks after the judgment was filed. The bank's mortgage was not a purchase-money mortgage, which would have given it priority.

(B) No, because the businessman was not personally liable for the mortgage debt, and the mortgage was therefore void.

Incorrect. The fact that the businessman was not personally liable for the mortgage debt is irrelevant and does not make the mortgage void. The judgment was recorded first in a jurisdiction that expressly protects judgment creditors without notice. The finance company had no actual notice of the mortgage and had no constructive notice because the mortgage was not recorded until two weeks after the judgment was filed. The bank's mortgage was not a purchase-money mortgage, which would have given it priority.

(C) Yes, because a mortgage prior in time has priority over a subsequent judgment lien.

Incorrect. The judgment was recorded first in a jurisdiction that expressly protects judgment creditors without notice. The finance company had no actual notice of the mortgage and had no constructive notice because the mortgage was not recorded until two weeks after the judgment was filed. The bank's mortgage was not a purchase-money mortgage, which would have given it priority. Priority is determined under these facts by the order of filing.

(D) Yes, because the recording of a mortgage relates back to the date of execution of the mortgage note.

Incorrect. The recording of a mortgage does not relate back to the date of execution of the mortgage note. The mortgage gives constructive notice as of the date of its recording. Therefore, at the time the judgment was recorded, the finance company had neither actual nor constructive notice of the mortgage and is protected under the jurisdiction's recording act. The bank's mortgage was not a purchase-money mortgage, which would have given it priority.

Question # 86 - Contracts

A produce distributor contracted to provide a grocer with eight crates of lettuce at the distributor's listed price. The distributor's shipping clerk mistakenly shipped only seven crates to the grocer. The grocer accepted delivery of the seven crates but immediately notified the distributor that the delivery did not conform to the contract. The distributor's listed price for seven crates of lettuce was 7/8 of its listed price for eight crates. The distributor shipped no more lettuce to the grocer, and the grocer has not yet paid for any of the lettuce.

How much, if anything, is the distributor entitled to collect from the grocer?

(A) Nothing, because the tender of all eight crates was a condition precedent to the grocer's duty to pay.

Incorrect. The distributor's nonconforming shipment constituted both an acceptance of the grocer's offer to purchase and a breach of the parties' contract. With respect to a nonconforming tender, UCC § 2-601 allows a buyer to accept the whole, reject the whole, or partially accept or reject commercial units. A buyer who accepts a tender of goods, whether conforming or nonconforming, becomes obligated to pay the seller the contract price of the goods. Accordingly, the grocer's acceptance of the nonconforming shipment obligated it to pay the distributor's listed price for the seven crates, reduced by any damages for losses resulting from the nonconforming shipment.

(B) The reasonable value of the seven crates of lettuce, minus the grocer's damages, if any, for the distributor's failure to deliver the full order.

Incorrect. The distributor's nonconforming shipment constituted both an acceptance of the grocer's offer to purchase and a breach of the parties' contract. With respect to a nonconforming tender, UCC § 2-601 allows a buyer to accept the whole, reject the whole, or partially accept or reject commercial units. A buyer who accepts a tender of goods, whether conforming or nonconforming, becomes obligated to pay the seller the contract price of the goods. Accordingly, the grocer's acceptance of the nonconforming shipment obligated it to pay the distributor's listed price for, rather than the reasonable value of, the seven crates of lettuce. The price paid by the grocer will be reduced by any damages for losses resulting from the nonconforming shipment.

(C) The listed price for the seven crates of lettuce, minus the grocer's damages, if any, for the distributor's failure to deliver the full order.

Correct. The distributor's nonconforming shipment constituted both an acceptance of the grocer's offer to purchase and a breach of the parties' contract. With respect to a nonconforming tender, UCC § 2-601 allows a buyer to accept the whole, reject the whole, or partially accept or reject commercial units. A buyer who accepts a tender of goods, whether conforming or nonconforming, becomes obligated to pay the seller the contract price of the goods. Accordingly, the grocer's acceptance of the nonconforming shipment obligated it to pay the distributor's listed price for the seven crates, reduced by any damages for losses resulting from the nonconforming shipment.

(D) The listed price for the seven crates of lettuce.

Incorrect. The distributor's nonconforming shipment constituted both an acceptance of the grocer's offer to purchase and a breach of the parties' contract. With respect to a nonconforming tender, UCC § 2-601 allows a buyer to accept the whole, reject the whole, or partially accept or reject commercial units. A buyer who accepts a tender of goods, whether conforming or nonconforming, becomes obligated to pay the seller the contract price of the goods. Accordingly, the grocer's acceptance of the nonconforming shipment obligated it to pay the distributor's listed price for the seven crates. However, that price should be reduced by any damages for losses resulting from the nonconforming shipment.

Question # 87 - Contracts

A seller borrowed $5,000 from a bank. Soon thereafter the seller filed for bankruptcy, having paid nothing on his debt to the bank.

Five years after the debt had been discharged in bankruptcy, the seller contracted to sell certain goods to a buyer for $5,000. The contract provided that the buyer would pay the $5,000 to the bank "as payment of the $5,000 the seller owes the bank." The only debt that the seller ever owed the bank is the $5,000 debt that was discharged in bankruptcy. The seller delivered the goods to the buyer, who accepted them.

If the bank becomes aware of the contract between the seller and the buyer, and the buyer refuses to pay anything to the bank, is the bank likely to succeed in an action against the buyer for $5,000?

(A) No, because the buyer's promise to pay the bank was not supported by consideration.

Incorrect. The buyer and the seller entered into a bargained-for exchange for the sale and purchase of goods. Thus their agreement was supported by consideration. Moreover, a promisee (the seller) can intend that a third party be the beneficiary of the performance the promisee expects to receive from a promisor (the buyer). Because the parties' agreement provided that the buyer would pay to the bank the $5,000 that the buyer had promised to pay for the goods, the bank was an intended beneficiary of the enforceable agreement between the seller and the buyer, and the buyer is obligated to pay the bank.

(B) No, because the seller's debt was discharged in bankruptcy.

Incorrect. The bank was an intended beneficiary of the contract between the buyer and the seller, and the fact of discharge is irrelevant. The seller and the buyer entered into a bargained-for exchange for the sale and purchase of goods. Because their agreement provided that the buyer would pay to the bank the $5,000 that the buyer had promised to pay for the goods, the bank was an intended beneficiary of the enforceable agreement between the seller and the buyer, and the buyer is obligated to pay the bank.

(C) Yes, because the bank was an intended beneficiary of the contract between the buyer and the seller.

Correct. The buyer and the seller entered into a bargained-for exchange for the sale and purchase of goods. Because their agreement provided that the buyer would pay to the bank the $5,000 that the buyer had promised to pay for the goods, the bank was an intended beneficiary of the enforceable agreement between the seller and the buyer, and the buyer is obligated to pay the bank.

(D) Yes, because no consideration is required to support a promise to pay a debt that has been discharged in bankruptcy.

Incorrect. It is true that a promise by a debtor to pay a debt that has been discharged in bankruptcy requires no consideration to be enforceable. In this case, however, the discharge of the seller's debt is irrelevant. Here, the seller and the buyer entered into a bargained-for exchange for the sale and purchase of goods. Because their agreement provided that the buyer would pay to the bank the $5,000 that the buyer had promised to pay for the goods, the bank was an intended beneficiary of the enforceable agreement between the seller and the buyer, and the buyer is obligated to pay the bank.

Question # 88 - Constitutional Law

A fatal virus recently infected poultry in several nations. Some scientific evidence indicates that the virus can be transmitted from poultry to humans.

Poultry farming is a major industry in several U.S. states. In one such state, the legislature has enacted a law imposing a fee of two cents per bird on all poultry farming and processing operations in the state. The purpose of the fee is to pay for a state inspection system to ensure that no poultry raised or processed in the state is infected with the virus.

A company that has poultry processing plants both in the state and in other states has sued to challenge the fee. Is the fee constitutional?

(A) No, because although it attaches only to intrastate activity, in the aggregate, the fee substantially affects interstate commerce.

Incorrect. Having a substantial effect on interstate commerce does not make the fee unconstitutional. The fee in this case is constitutional, because it does not violate the negative implications of the commerce clause: it does not discriminate against interstate commerce, and its burden on interstate commerce is not clearly excessive in relation to the legitimate public health benefit the inspection system will bring to the state.

(B) No, because it places an undue burden on interstate commerce in violation of the negative implications of the commerce clause.

Incorrect. The fee does not violate the negative implications of the commerce clause, because it does not discriminate against interstate commerce, and its burden on interstate commerce is not clearly excessive in relation to the legitimate public health benefit the inspection system will bring to the state. The fee is therefore constitutional.

(C) Yes, because it applies only to activities that take place wholly within the state, and it does not unduly burden interstate commerce.

Correct. The fee does not violate the negative implications of the commerce clause, because it does not discriminate against interstate commerce, and its burden on interstate commerce is not clearly excessive in relation to the legitimate public health benefit the inspection system will bring to the state.

(D) Yes, because it was enacted pursuant to the state's police power, which takes precedence over the negative implications of the commerce clause.

Incorrect. The fee was enacted pursuant to the state's police power, but the supremacy clause of the Constitution prohibits state laws that violate federal constitutional limits on state authority. The fee is constitutional, nonetheless, because it does not violate the negative implications of the commerce clause: it does not discriminate against interstate commerce, and its burden on interstate commerce is not clearly excessive in relation to the legitimate public health benefit the inspection system will bring to the state.

Question # 89 - Criminal Law and Procedure

A state statute provides as follows: "The maintenance of any ongoing enterprise in the nature of a betting parlor or bookmaking organization is a felony."

A prosecutor has evidence that a woman has been renting an office to a man, that the man has been using the office as a betting parlor within the meaning of the statute, and that the woman is aware of this use.

Which of the following additional pieces of evidence would be most useful to the prosecutor's effort to convict the woman as an accomplice to the man's violation of the statute?

(A) The woman was previously convicted of running a betting parlor herself on the same premises.

Incorrect. The woman's prior conviction would not necessarily show that she has a personal stake in the continuing success of the man's criminal venture (and thus an intent to aid in that venture).

(B) The woman charges the man considerably more in rent than she charged the preceding tenant, who used the office for legitimate activities.

Correct. Showing that the woman benefits from the gambling would indicate her personal stake in the continuing success of the man's criminal venture (and thus her intent to aid in that venture).

(C) The woman has personally placed bets with the man at the office location.

Incorrect. Showing that the woman has placed bets would confirm that she knows that the premises are being used for gambling. However, it would not necessarily show that she has a personal stake in the continuing success of the man's criminal venture (and thus an intent to aid in that venture).

(D) The man has paid the woman the rent in bills that are traceable as the proceeds of gambling activity.

Incorrect. The source of the rent payments, assuming that the rent is not above the market price for the premises, would not necessarily show that the woman has a personal stake in the continuing success of the man's criminal venture (and thus an intent to aid in that venture).

Question # 90 - Real Property

A seller conveyed residential land to a buyer by a warranty deed that contained no exceptions and recited that the full consideration had been paid. To finance the purchase, the buyer borrowed 80% of the necessary funds from a bank. The seller agreed to finance 15% of the purchase price, and the buyer agreed to provide cash for the remaining 5%.

At the closing, the buyer signed a promissory note to the seller for 15% of the purchase price but did not execute a mortgage. The bank knew of the loan made by the seller and of the promissory note executed by the buyer to the seller. The buyer also signed a note to the bank, secured by a mortgage, for the 80% advanced by the bank.

The buyer has now defaulted on both loans. There are no applicable statutes.

Which loan has priority?

(A) The bank's loan, because the seller can finance a part of the purchase price only by use of an installment land contract.

Incorrect. A seller may finance the purchase of property in a number of ways, including by an installment land contract, by securing the note with a purchase-money mortgage, or by an equitable vendor's lien. However, the seller did not secure the note with a mortgage, nor was an installment land contract used. The seller may have had an equitable vendor's lien for the unpaid purchase price, but the deed recites that the full consideration was paid. Therefore, the bank's purchase-money mortgage takes priority over the seller's unsecured loan and any implied equitable vendor's lien even if the bank knew of the vendor's lien.

(B) The bank's loan, because it was secured by a purchase-money mortgage.

Correct. The bank has a purchase-money mortgage, because the loan proceeds were used to help purchase the land. A purchase-money mortgage, executed at the same time as the deed to the land, takes precedence over any other lien that attaches to the property. The seller's loan could also have been secured by a purchase-money mortgage, but it was not; the buyer signed an unsecured note to the seller. The seller also may have had an equitable vendor's lien for the unpaid purchase price, but the deed recites that the full consideration was paid. Therefore, the bank's purchase-money mortgage takes priority over the seller's unsecured loan and any implied equitable vendor's lien even if the bank knew of the vendor's lien.

(C) The seller's loan, because a promissory note to a seller has priority over a bank loan for residential property.

Incorrect. The seller's promissory note could have been secured by a mortgage, but it was not. The seller may have had an equitable vendor's lien for the unpaid purchase price, but the deed recites that the full consideration was paid. Therefore, the bank's purchase-money mortgage takes priority over the seller's unsecured loan and any implied equitable vendor's lien even if the bank knew of the vendor's lien.

(D) The seller's loan, because the bank knew that the seller had an equitable vendor's lien.

Incorrect. The seller may have had an equitable vendor's lien for the unpaid purchase price, but the deed recites that the full consideration was paid. Therefore, the bank's purchase-money mortgage takes precedence over the seller's unsecured loan as well as any implied equitable vendor's lien, and it is irrelevant that the bank knew of the vendor's lien.

Question # 91 - Torts

Unaware that a lawyer was in the county courthouse library late on a Friday afternoon, when it was unusual for anyone to be using the library, a clerk locked the library door and left. The lawyer found herself locked in when she tried to leave the library at 7 p.m. It was midnight before the lawyer's family could find out where she was and get her out. The lawyer was very annoyed by her detention but was not otherwise harmed by it.

Does the lawyer have a viable claim for false imprisonment against the clerk?

(A) No, because it was unusual for anyone to be using the library late on a Friday afternoon.

Incorrect. The fact that it was unusual for anyone to be using the library at the time the clerk locked the door might lead a fact finder to conclude that the clerk was not negligent in failing to detect the lawyer. However, because false imprisonment is an intentional tort, the reasonableness of the clerk's conduct is irrelevant. If the clerk had intended to lock the lawyer in the library, the lawyer would have a claim for false imprisonment even if it was unusual for anyone to be using the library at the time. Under these facts, however, the clerk did not intend to lock the lawyer in the library, so the lawyer does not have a viable claim for false imprisonment.

(B) No, because the clerk did not intend to confine the lawyer.

Correct. Intent to confine the claimant (or to commit some other intentional tort) is essential to establishing liability for false imprisonment. There is no evidence that the clerk had such an intent.

(C) Yes, because the clerk should have checked to make sure no one was in the library before the clerk locked the door.

Incorrect. Whether a reasonable person in the clerk's position would have checked before locking the door is irrelevant to a claim for false imprisonment. False imprisonment is an intentional tort requiring intent to confine the claimant (or to commit some other intentional tort). What a reasonable person would have done is relevant to a negligence claim, but not to a false imprisonment claim.

(D) Yes, because the lawyer was aware of being confined.

Incorrect. In cases involving false imprisonment, courts often hold that the plaintiff must have been aware of the confinement at the time of the imprisonment or else must have sustained actual harm. It is also essential, however, that the defendant have had an intent to confine the plaintiff (or to commit some other intentional tort). If the clerk had had such an intent, the lawyer's awareness that she was confined might have completed the prima facie case, but the clerk had no such intent.

Question # 92 - Evidence

A plaintiff has brought a products liability action against a defendant, the manufacturer of a sport-utility vehicle that the plaintiff's decedent was driving when she was fatally injured in a rollover accident. The plaintiff claims that a design defect in the vehicle caused it to roll over. The defendant claims that the cause of the accident was the decedent's driving at excessive speed during an ice storm. Eyewitnesses to the accident have given contradictory estimates about the vehicle's speed just before the rollover. It is also disputed whether the decedent was killed instantly.

Which of the following items of offered evidence is the court most likely to admit?

(A) A videotape offered by the defendant of a test conducted by the defendant showing that a sport-utility vehicle of the same model the decedent was driving did not roll over when driven by a professional driver on a dry test track at the top speed testified to by the eyewitnesses.

Incorrect. In order for product demonstrations to be admissible under Rule 403 to prove how an accident happened, the conditions must be substantially similar to the conditions at the time in question. This test was conducted on a dry track with a professional driver. Even if the court admits this evidence in its discretion, the question calls for the evidence that the court is most likely to admit. This evidence is not it.

(B) A videotape offered by the plaintiff of a television news program about sport-utility vehicles that includes footage of accident scenes in which the vehicles had rolled over.

Incorrect. This evidence is not very probative, because it shows sport-utility vehicles in general, not necessarily the model used by the decedent, and there is no indication that the conditions in the accident scenes were in any way similar to the conditions in question. Under Rule 403, the probative value of this evidence is likely to be substantially outweighed by its prejudicial effect and risk of jury confusion. Even if the court admits this evidence in its discretion, the question calls for the evidence that the court is most likely to admit. This evidence is not it.

(C) Evidence offered by the defendant that the decedent had received two citations for speeding in the previous three years.

Incorrect. This evidence would not be admissible, because it is attempting to show that the decedent had a propensity to drive too fast, to create the inference that the decedent was driving too fast at the time in question. Under Rule 404, proof of character in order to show conduct consistent with that character is inadmissible in civil cases.

(D) Photographs taken at the accident scene and during the autopsy that would help the plaintiff's medical expert explain to the jury why she concluded that the decedent did not die instantly.

Correct. This evidence is most likely to be admitted. If these photographs are offered to illustrate the expert's testimony, the jury can be instructed to use the evidence only for that purpose. Moreover, this evidence is not as prejudicial or potentially confusing to the jury as the evidence in options (A) and (B), while the evidence in option (C) is inadmissible.

Question # 93 - Contracts

A builder borrowed $10,000 from a lender to finance a small construction job under a contract with a homeowner. The builder gave the lender a writing that stated, "Any money I receive from the homeowner will be paid immediately to the lender, regardless of any demands from other creditors." The builder died after completing the job but before the homeowner paid. The lender demanded that the homeowner pay the $10,000 due to the builder directly to the lender. The homeowner refused, saying that he would pay directly to the builder's estate everything that he owed the builder.

Is the lender likely to succeed in an action against the homeowner for $10,000?

(A) No, because the builder's death terminated the lender's right to receive payment directly from the homeowner.

Incorrect. The builder never gave the lender a valid assignment. An assignment arises when the holder of a right, an obligee, manifests the intent to make a present transfer of that right to another, the assignee. An assignment is to be distinguished from a promise to do something in the future, such as the payment of money. Here, the writing in which the builder promised to pay the lender the $10,000 he received from the homeowner did not transfer to the lender the right to receive payment directly from the homeowner, and thus it did not create an assignment.

(B) No, because the writing the builder gave to the lender did not transfer to the lender the right to receive payment from the homeowner.

Correct. An assignment arises when the holder of a right, an obligee, manifests the intent to make a present transfer of that right to another, the assignee. Upon an assignment, the assignor's rights are extinguished and transferred to the assignee. An assignment is to be distinguished from a promise to do something in the future, such as the payment of money. Here, the writing in which the builder promised to pay the lender the $10,000 he received from the homeowner did not transfer to the lender the right to receive payment directly from the homeowner, and thus it did not create an assignment.

(C) Yes, because the builder had manifested an intent that the homeowner pay the $10,000 directly to the lender.

Incorrect. It may have been the builder's subjective intent to have the homeowner pay the $10,000 directly to the lender if the builder died, but more was required in order for the lender to have the right to receive that direct payment. The dispositive issue here is whether the builder gave the lender a valid assignment. An assignment arises when the holder of a right, an obligee, manifests the intent to make a present transfer of that right to another, the assignee. An assignment is to be distinguished from a promise to do something in the future, such as the payment of money. Here, the writing in which the builder promised to pay to the lender the $10,000 he received from the homeowner did not transfer to the lender the right to receive payment directly from the homeowner, and thus it did not create an assignment.

(D) Yes, because the lender is an intended beneficiary of the builder-homeowner contract.

Incorrect. Because any rights that may have been granted to the lender were not created by the contract between the builder and the homeowner, the lender did not acquire third-party beneficiary status. The dispositive issue here is whether the builder gave the lender a valid assignment. An assignment arises when the holder of a right, an obligee, manifests the intent to make a present transfer of that right to another, the assignee. An assignment is to be distinguished from a promise to do something in the future, such as the payment of money. Here, the writing in which the builder promised to pay to the lender the $10,000 he received from the homeowner did not transfer to the lender the right to receive payment directly from the homeowner, and thus it did not create an assignment.

Question # 94 - Criminal Law and Procedure

After a defendant was indicted on federal bank fraud charges and released on bail, his attorney filed notice of the defendant's intent to offer an insanity defense. The prosecutor then enlisted the help of a forensic psychologist who was willing to participate in an "undercover" mental examination of the defendant. The psychologist contacted the defendant and pretended to represent an executive personnel agency. She told the defendant about an attractive employment opportunity and invited him to a "preliminary screening interview" to determine his qualifications for the job. As part of the purported screening process, the psychologist gave the defendant psychological tests that enabled her to form a reliable opinion about his mental state at the time of the alleged offense.

What is the strongest basis for a defense objection to the psychologist's testimony regarding the defendant's mental state?

(A) The Fourth Amendment prohibition against unreasonable searches and seizures.

Incorrect. The Fourth Amendment does not prevent the government from using deception to obtain incriminating admissions.

(B) The Fifth Amendment privilege against compelled self-incrimination.

Incorrect. The Fifth Amendment privilege protects against compelled self-incrimination, not against the use of deception to obtain a suspect's voluntary admissions.

(C) The Sixth Amendment right to the assistance of counsel.

Correct. After a defendant is indicted, the right to counsel attaches, and authorities may not use deception to deliberately elicit statements related to the crime from the defendant without the representation of counsel.

(D) The federal common law privilege for confidential communications between psychotherapist and patient.

Incorrect. While there is such a federal common law privilege for communications intended to be kept confidential for the purpose of obtaining psychiatric services, the facts in this case do not support the privilege.

Question # 95 - Torts

A man tied his dog to a bike rack in front of a store and left the dog there while he went inside to shop. The dog was usually friendly and placid.

A five-year-old child started to tease the dog by pulling gently on its ears and tail. When the man emerged from the store and saw what the child was doing to the dog, he became extremely upset.

Does the man have a viable claim against the child for trespass to chattels?

(A) No, because the child did not injure the dog.

Correct. Trespass to chattels requires that the plaintiff show actual harm to or deprivation of the use of the chattel for a substantial time. Here the child's acts caused emotional distress to the man, but the acts did not result in harm to the man's material interest in the dog.

(B) No, because the child was too young to form the requisite intent.

Incorrect. Even a small child can commit an intentional tort, such as trespass to chattels, so long as the child is old enough to form an intent to touch. But trespass to chattels requires that the plaintiff show actual harm to or deprivation of the use of the chattel for a substantial time. Here the child's acts caused emotional distress to the man, but the acts did not result in harm to the man's material interest in the dog.

(C) Yes, because the child touched the dog without the man's consent.

Incorrect. Trespass to chattels requires that the plaintiff show actual harm to or deprivation of the use of the chattel for a substantial time. Here the child's acts caused emotional distress to the man (because they were without his consent), but the acts did not result in harm to the man's material interest in the dog.

(D) Yes, because the child's acts caused the man extreme distress.

Incorrect. Trespass to chattels requires that the plaintiff show actual harm to or deprivation of the use of the chattel for a substantial time. Here the child's acts caused emotional distress to the man, but the acts did not result in harm to the man's material interest in the dog.

Question # 96 - Evidence

At the start of the trial of a defendant and a codefendant for robbery, the codefendant and her attorney offered to give the prosecutor information about facts that would strengthen the prosecutor's case against the defendant in exchange for leniency toward the codefendant. The prosecutor refused the offer. Shortly thereafter, the codefendant committed suicide.

During the defendant's trial, the prosecutor called the codefendant's attorney and asked him to relate the information that the codefendant had revealed to the attorney.

Is the attorney's testimony admissible?

(A) No, because the codefendant's communications are protected by the attorney-client privilege.

Correct. The prosecutor is asking for confidential communications between the codefendant and her attorney, which is privileged information. If the codefendant had actually provided information to the prosecutor, the privilege would have been waived as to any communications previously made to her attorney. However, the codefendant did not disclose any confidential communications.

(B) No, because the plea discussion was initiated by the codefendant rather than by the prosecutor.

Incorrect. The prosecutor is asking for confidential communications between the codefendant and her attorney, which is privileged information, and it makes no difference who initiated the plea discussion. The question is whether the codefendant waived the privilege by offering information to the prosecutor, which she did not. Because the codefendant did not actually disclose any confidential communications to the prosecutor, there was no waiver.

(C) Yes, because the codefendant intended to disclose the information.

Incorrect. The prosecutor is asking for confidential communications between the codefendant and her attorney, which is privileged information. If the codefendant had actually provided information to the prosecutor, the privilege would have been waived as to any communications previously made to her attorney. However, the codefendant did not disclose any confidential communications, and whether she intended to disclose the information is irrelevant.

(D) Yes, because the information the codefendant gave to her attorney revealing her knowledge of the crime would be a statement against the codefendant's penal interest.

Incorrect. A declaration against interest is one that tends to expose the declarant to criminal liability. Any statement to the attorney could not have subjected the codefendant to a risk of criminal liability, because the statement was privileged.

Question # 97 - Torts

A mother and her six-year-old child were on a walk when the mother stopped to talk with an elderly neighbor. Because the child resented having his mother's attention diverted by the neighbor, the child angrily threw himself against the neighbor and knocked her to the ground. The neighbor suffered a broken wrist as a result of the fall.

In an action for battery by the neighbor against the child, what is the strongest argument for liability?

(A) The child intended to throw himself against the neighbor.

Correct. To recover on a claim for battery, it is sufficient for the neighbor to show that the child intended to touch the neighbor in a way that would be considered harmful or offensive, even though the child may have been too young to understand that what he was doing was wrong or to appreciate that the neighbor might be unusually vulnerable to injury.

(B) The child was old enough to appreciate that causing a fall could inflict serious injury.

Incorrect. Proof of intent to cause injury or knowledge that injury may result is not necessary to recover on a claim of battery. Instead, it is sufficient that the child intended to touch the neighbor in a way that would be considered harmful or offensive, even though the child may have been too young to understand that what he was doing was wrong or to appreciate that the neighbor might be unusually vulnerable to injury.

(C) The child was old enough to appreciate the riskiness of his conduct.

Incorrect. Whether the child was old enough to appreciate the riskiness of his conduct is irrelevant to the neighbor's battery claim. It is sufficient that the child intended to touch the neighbor in a way that would be considered harmful or offensive, even though the child may have been too young to understand that what he was doing was wrong. Whether a child is old enough to appreciate a given risk would be relevant in a negligence action, but not in an action for battery.

(D) The child was not justified in his anger.

Incorrect. It is sufficient that the child intended to touch the neighbor in a way that would be considered harmful or offensive, whether or not the child was justifiably angry. The motive for a defendant's actions may be relevant to an affirmative defense in some situations, but even justified anger is not a defense to an intentional tort.

Question # 98 - Criminal Law and Procedure

A defendant is charged with an offense under a statute that provides as follows: "Any person who, while intoxicated, appears in any public place and manifests a drunken condition by obstreperous or indecent conduct is guilty of a misdemeanor."

At trial, the evidence shows that the defendant was intoxicated when police officers burst into his house and arrested him pursuant to a valid warrant. It was a cold night, and the officers hustled the defendant out of his house without giving him time to get his coat. The defendant became angry and obstreperous when the officers refused to let him go back into the house to retrieve his coat. The officers left him handcuffed outside in the street, waiting for a special squad car to arrive. The arrest warrant was later vacated.

Can the defendant properly be convicted of violating the statute?

(A) No, because the defendant's claim of mistreatment is valid.

Incorrect. The defendant cannot properly be convicted, regardless of whether his claim is valid, because of the general legal rule that a person is not guilty of a crime unless the act constituting the crime was committed voluntarily. This rule precludes the defendant's conviction, because he did not voluntarily appear in a public place.

(B) No, because the statute requires proof of a voluntary appearance in a public place.

Correct. The general legal rule is that a person is not guilty of a crime unless the act constituting the crime was committed voluntarily. This rule precludes the defendant's conviction, because he did not voluntarily appear in a public place.

(C) Yes, because the defendant voluntarily became intoxicated.

Incorrect. The general legal rule is that a person is not guilty of a crime unless the act constituting the crime was committed voluntarily. This rule precludes the defendant's conviction because, while the defendant voluntarily became intoxicated, he did not voluntarily appear in a public place.

(D) Yes, because the defendant voluntarily behaved in an obstreperous manner.

Incorrect. The general legal rule is that a person is not guilty of a crime unless the act constituting the crime was committed voluntarily. This rule precludes the defendant's conviction because, while the defendant voluntarily behaved obstreperously, he did not voluntarily appear in a public place.

Question # 99 - Real Property

A seller and a buyer signed a contract for the sale of vacant land. The contract was silent concerning the quality of title, but the seller agreed in the contract to convey the land to the buyer by a warranty deed without any exceptions. When the buyer conducted a title search for the land, she learned that the applicable zoning did not allow for her planned commercial use. She also discovered that there was a recorded restrictive covenant limiting the use of the land to residential use.

The buyer no longer wants to purchase the land. Must the buyer purchase the land?

(A) No, because the restrictive covenant renders the title unmarketable.

Correct. Unless the contract provides to the contrary, the law will imply that the seller will provide the buyer with a marketable title on the date of closing. A marketable title is not a perfect title but is a title a court will force an unwilling buyer to purchase. A right held in the land by a third party, such as the right to enforce a restrictive covenant, renders the title unmarketable, and the buyer need not purchase the land.

(B) No, because the zoning places a cloud on the title.

Incorrect. Although in some cases an existing violation of a zoning code may render title unmarketable, the mere existence of a zoning code does not render the title unmarketable or place a cloud on the title. Unless the contract provides to the contrary, the law will imply that the seller will provide the buyer with a marketable title on the date of closing. A right held in the land by a third party, such as the right to enforce a restrictive covenant, renders the title unmarketable, and the buyer need not purchase the land.

(C) Yes, because the buyer would receive a warranty deed without any exceptions.

Incorrect. Unless the contract provides to the contrary, the law will imply that the seller will provide the buyer with a marketable title on the date of closing. However, after a buyer accepts the deed, the doctrine of merger prevents the buyer from raising the issue of marketability of title, and the buyer's remedy regarding title issues, if any, will be based on the deed.

(D) Yes, because the contract was silent regarding the quality of the title.

Incorrect. Unless the contract provides to the contrary, the law will imply that the seller will provide the buyer with a marketable title on the date of closing. This contract was silent on the quality of title and therefore a marketable title will be implied. A marketable title is not a perfect title but is a title a court will require an unwilling buyer to purchase. A right held in the land b a third party, such as the right to enforce a restrictive covenant, renders the title unmarketable, and the buyer need not purchase the land.

Question # 100 - Criminal Law and Procedure

A police officer had a hunch, not amounting to probable cause or reasonable suspicion, that a man was a drug dealer. One day while the officer was on highway patrol, her radar gun clocked the man's car at 68 mph in an area where the maximum posted speed limit was 65 mph. The officer's usual practice was not to stop a car unless it was going at least 5 mph over the posted limit, but contrary to her usual practice, she decided to stop the man's car in the hope that she might discover evidence of drug dealing. After she stopped the car and announced that she would be writing a speeding ticket, the officer ordered the man and his passenger to step out of the car. When the passenger stepped out, the officer saw that the passenger had been sitting on a clear bag of what the officer immediately recognized as marijuana. The officer arrested both the man and the passenger for possession of marijuana.

At their joint trial, the man and the passenger claim that their Fourth Amendment rights were violated because the officer improperly (1) stopped the car for speeding as a pretext for investigating a hunch rather than for the stated purpose of issuing a traffic ticket and (2) ordered the passenger to step out of the car even though there was no reason to believe that the passenger was a criminal or dangerous.

Are the man and the passenger correct?

(A) No, as to both the stop of the car and the officer's order that the passenger step out of the car.

Correct. The stop of the car was constitutional, because it was objectively justifiable (regardless of the officer's subjective motivation), and both the driver and any passengers may be ordered to step out of a car during a lawful traffic stop.

(B) No as to the stop of the car, but yes as to the officer's order that the passenger step out of the car.

Incorrect. It is correct that the stop of the car was constitutional, because it was objectively justifiable (regardless of the officer's subjective motivation). However, it is also correct that both the driver and any passengers may be ordered to step out of a car during a lawful traffic stop.

(C) Yes as to the stop of the car, but no as to the officer's order that the passenger step out of the car.

Incorrect. It is correct that both the driver and any passengers may be ordered to step out of a car during a lawful traffic stop. However, it is also correct that the stop of the car here was constitutional, because it was objectively justifiable (regardless of the officer's subjective motivation).

(D) Yes, as to both the stop of the car and the officer's order that the passenger step out of the car.

Incorrect. The stop of the car was constitutional, because it was objectively justifiable (regardless of the officer's subjective motivation), and both the driver and any passengers may be ordered to step out of the car during a lawful traffic stop.